PUBLIC LAW

PUBLIC LAW

Text, Cases, and Materials

SECOND EDITION

Andrew Le Sueur

LLB (Lond), Barrister, of the Middle Temple
Professor of Public Law, Queen Mary, University of London

Maurice Sunkin

LLB (Lond), LLM (Lond), PhD (Essex), Barrister, of the Middle Temple
Professor of Public Law and Socio-Legal Studies
School of Law, University of Essex

Jo Eric Khushal Murkens

LLB (Lond), PhD (EUI), Barrister, of the Inner Temple
Senior Lecturer, Department of Law, London School of Economics and Political Science

OXFORD
UNIVERSITY PRESS

OXFORD

UNIVERSITY PRESS

Great Clarendon Street, Oxford, ox2 6dp,
United Kingdom

Oxford University Press is a department of the University of Oxford.
It furthers the University's objective of excellence in research, scholarship,
and education by publishing worldwide. Oxford is a registered trade mark of
Oxford University Press in the UK and in certain other countries

First edition 2010

Impression: 1

British Library Cataloguing in Publication Data

Data available

ISBN 978-0-19-964418-6

Printed in Italy by
L.E.G.O. S.p.A.—Lavis TN

To our families, partners, and friends

PREFACE

Public law is amongst the most fast-moving, contentious, and exciting areas of law to study. There is much written on the subject and an ever-growing range of key texts for university courses on public law or constitutional and administrative law, as it is often referred to: the big textbooks, shorter works, and a number of 'text, cases, and materials' books. For us, it is this latter type which provides an ideal medium for an account of the legal aspects of the British constitution. There are three main reasons. First, it gives students a chance to read at first hand the analysis and arguments of academics and participants in the constitution, most aspects of which are contested: the extracts convey the debates and disagreements most effectively. In selecting the materials for use in this book and adding our commentaries we have attempted to focus on subjects that are in the mainstream of the majority of public law or constitutional and administrative law courses in the United Kingdom. We have focused on *legal* aspects of the constitution, not least because most users of the book will be studying public law as a core area of their undergraduate *law* studies, but we hope that non-lawyers will also find the book of value.

A second reason for a text, cases, and materials approach is that it is good for presenting case studies that breathe life into the law. In this book, we look at a variety of constitutional issues and episodes, including troop deployment powers (Chapter 9); the making and implementation of the EU race directive (Chapter 12); relations between the House of Commons and House of Lords (Chapter 13); and in relation to the Human Rights Act 1998, the interaction of school uniform policies and rights to manifest religion, and recent anti-terrorism legislation in the United Kingdom (both in Chapter 17). The case studies are designed to encourage readers to 'drill down' into specific constitutional goings-on to see how general principles and processes operate in a particular context and to gain an understanding of the law that is difficult to achieve when using other types of book.

A third reason is that the text, cases, and materials approach provides students with access to key sources of law and other materials. This book, for example, provides readers with a carefully selected range of extracts from important statutes and leading judgments, as well as from materials drawn from a wide range of official reports. In our commentary we explain these extracts and seek to place them in their context.

The best way to learn about constitutional law is to become engaged in the issues. Recognizing that this cannot be done passively, throughout the book we pose questions that are intended to prompt readers to check their understanding and to critically reflect on what they are reading. In this way we hope that the book will be a valuable resource that will complement the work of lecturers and teachers.

Any book of the length of this one requires an organized structure, though we do not assume that all readers will use the chapters in the order in which they are presented. In Part I, the chapters examine the fundamental constitutional arrangements and principles. In this second edition, we have taken the opportunity to reorganize these chapters. Chapter 1 has been substantially rewritten. Material previously in the second chapter is now presented as two discrete chapters: Chapter 2 on parliamentary supremacy and Chapter 3 on the rule of law (including aspects of the case study on the office of Lord Chancellor which in the first edition was Chapter 5). The former third chapter is also now presented as two stand-alone chapters: Chapter 3 on separating and balancing powers; and Chapter 4 on multilevel governance. We hope that this new structure will assist readers navigate through the topics more easily.

Part II looks at executive functions. Part III considers issues to do with legislation and the legislative processes. Part IV is concerned with the judiciary and some of the main ways in which grievances between citizens and the state are handled.

The book was finalized in October 2012, although we have done our best to include mention of some developments in November and December of that year. The Online Resource Centre that accompanies the book will enable us to provide regular updates for students studying our changing constitution.

Andrew Le Sueur
Maurice Sunkin
Jo Eric Khushal Murkens

November 2012

ACKNOWLEDGEMENTS

A book of this sort is a team effort in several senses. We thank those whose words we have extracted in our efforts to paint a picture of the British constitution as a dynamic and contested system. The OUP team have been superb. The first and second editions of this book would not have been completed more or less on schedule had it not been for Kate Whetter's encouragement and support during her time at OUP and for Thomas Young's continuing support and encouragement since taking over the management of the project. Pamela Skipwith provided copy-editing expertise.

Several colleagues have taken time to provide comments and criticisms on draft chapters in the first or second editions, or both, and our particular thanks are given to: Professor Brigid Hadfield; Dr Mario Mendez; VardaBondy; and to the anonymous reviewers commissioned by OUP. Several students using the first edition contacted us with helpful comments and suggestions. We are also grateful to Chris Luff for assisting with research. We also gratefully acknowledge the support of our families, partners, and friends, to whom this book is dedicated. We are, of course, responsible for any errors and omissions.

SOURCE ACKNOWLEDGEMENTS

Grateful acknowledgement is made to all the authors and publishers of copyright material which appears in this book, and in particular to the following for permission to reprint material from the sources indicated:

Crown copyright material is reproduced under Class Licence Number C2006010631 with the permission of the Controller of HMSO and the Queen's Printer for Scotland. Parliamentary copyright material is reproduced with the permission of the Controller of Her Majesty's Stationary Office on behalf of Parliament.

Audiovisual Library of the European Commission: © European Union, 2010: Figure 11.1 Heads of state and government sign the Treaty of Lisbon, 13 December 2007—photo; Figure 17.1 Brussels—22 January 1972 Accession Treaty signed by Prime Minister Edward Heath on behalf of the United Kingdom—photo. Cambridge University and the authors: extracts from NW Barber, 'Prelude to the Separation of Powers' [2001] Cambridge Law Journal 59, 71–72; Christopher Forsyth, 'Of fig leaves and fairy tales: The ultra vires doctrine, the sovereignty of Parliament and judicial review' [1996] Cambridge Law Journal 122, 134–40; Paul Craig, 'Ultra Vires and the Foundations of Judicial Review' [1999] Cambridge Law Journal 63, 86-89; H.W.R. Wade, 'The Basis of Legal Sovereignty' [1955] Cambridge Law Journal 172, 174, 187–188.

Cambridge University Press: extracts from C.J.S. Knight, 'Bi-polar sovereignty restated' [2009] Cambridge Law Journal 361, 362, 365–6.

European Parliament: Figure 11.2 Turnout in European Parliamentary elections; Box 11.7 Percentage of registered UK voters who actually voted at European Parliament elections from 1979–2009; Figure 11.5 Presentation of the co-decision procedure.

Frankfurter Allgemeine Zeitung: Figure 7.1 EU Chart, redrawn from an original first published in *Frankfurter Allgemeine Zeitung*, 1 December 2009.

John Harper Publishing: extract from David Spence, 'The President, the College, and the cabinets' in D. Spence (ed) *The European Commission* (2006, London: John Harper Publishing), pp. 46–48

Hart Publishing: extracts from Martin Loughlin, 'Constitutional Law: the Third Order of the Political' in N. Bamforth and P. Leyland (eds), *Public Law in a Multi-layered Constitution* (2003, Oxford: Hart Publishing), ch. 3; Edward C. Page, *Governing by Numbers* (2001, Oxford: Hart Publishing), pp. 20–21.

House of Lords Reports: extracts are Parliamentary copyright and are reproduced by permission of the Controller of HMSO on behalf of Parliament.

David Howarth MP: Extract from 'Who wants the Abolition of Parliament Bill?' *The Times* 21 February 2006.

ICLR: extracts from *R v Secretary of State for the Home Department, ex parte Pierson* [1998] AC 539, 587-8, Lord Steyn; *Cheney v Conn* (Inspector of Taxes) [1968] 1 WLR 242, Ungoed-Thomas J; *Thoburn v Sunderland City Council* [2002] EWHC 195 (Admin), Laws LJ, Laws J; *R v Lord Chancellor ex parte Witham* [1998] QB 575, Lord Reid; *Burmah*

Oil Company v Lord Advocate [1965] AC 75, 99-100; *R v Secretary of State for the Home Department, ex parte Northumbria Police Authority* [1989] 1 QB 26, 42–43, Lord Browne-Wilkinson; *R v Secretary of State for the Home Department, ex parte the Fire Brigades Union* [1995] 2 AC 513, 551–552; *R v Secretary of State for the Home Department ex parte Fire Brigades Union and others* [1995] 2 AC 513, 546, 550, Lord Reid; *Padfield v Ministry of Agriculture, Fisheries and Food* [1968] AC 997, 1030–1033; *Blackburn v Attorney General* [1971] 1 WLR 1037, 1039–1040, Lord Denning; *R (on the application of Jackson and ors) v Her Majesty's Attorney General* [2005] EWCA Civ 126; *Anisminic v Foreign Compensation Commission* [1969] 2 AC 147.

United Kingdom Independence Party: Box 11.1 European Union treaties and the legislative process, number of Statutory Instruments laid down under ECA 1972.

MIT Press Journals: extract from Andrew Moravcsik, 'The Origins of Human Rights Regimes: Democratic Delegation in Postwar Europe' (2000) 54 International Organisation 217 at 238.

Oxford University Press: extracts from Andrew Le Sueur, 'Accountability' in P. Cane and J. Conaghan (eds) *The New Oxford Companion to Law* (2008, Oxford: OUP), pp. 7–8; Evelyn Ellis, 'Sources of Law and the Hierarchy of Norms' ch 1B in D Feldman (ed), *English Public Law*, 2nd edn (2009, Oxford: OUP), paras 1.173–1.175; Cheryl Saunders, 'Entrenchment of constitutions and legislation' in P. Cane and J. Conaghan, *The New Oxford Companion to Law* (2008, Oxford: OUP), pp. 382–383; Ronald Dworkin, 'Political Judges and the Rule of Law' in *A Matter of Principle* (1985, Oxford: OUP), ch. 1, pp. 11–12; Adam Tomkins, *Public Law* (2003, Oxford: OUP), pp. 46–7; Gary Marks and Liesbet Hooghe, 'Contrasting Visions of Multi-level Governance' in Ian Bache and Matthew Flinders (eds), *Multilevel Governance* (2004, Oxford: OUP), ch. 2, pp. 15–16; Andrew Le Sueur, 'Fundamental Principles' in D Feldman (ed) *English Public Law*, 2nd edn (2009, Oxford: OUP), ch. 1A, paras 1-74–1-76; Anthony King, *The British Constitution* (2007, Oxford: OUP), pp. 208–209, 129–130; A. Le Sueur, 'The Nature, Powers, and Accountability of Central Government', in D. Feldman (ed), English Public Law, 2nd edn (2009, Oxford: OUP), paras 3.12–3.14; Mark Janis, Richard Kay and Anthony Bradley, *European Human Rights Law* (2007, Oxford: OUP), pp. 5–8; Anthony Lester QC and Kate Beattie, 'Human Rights and the British Constitution', in J Jowell and D Oliver (eds) *The Changing Constitution*, 6th edn (2007, Oxford: OUP), ch. 3, pp. 62–63; Richard Clayton and Hugh Tomlinson, *The Law of Human Rights*, (2000, Oxford: OUP), pp. 59–61; Maurice Sunkin, 'Crown' in P. Cane and J. Conaghan (eds), *The New Oxford Companion to Law* (2008, Oxford: OUP), pp. 286–287; I. Bache and S. George, *The Politics in the European Union*, 2nd edn (2006, Oxford: OUP), pp. 265–266; J. Peterson and M. Shackleton, 'Conclusion', in J. Peterson and M. Shackleton (eds) *The Institutions of the European Union*, 3rd edn (2012, Oxford: OUP), p. 384; Terrance Daintith and Alan Page, *The Executive in the Constitution: Structure, Autonomy and Internal Control* (1999, Oxford: OUP), pp. 259–260; Renaud Dehousse and Paul Magnette 'Institutional Change in the EU', in J. Peterson and M. Shackleton (eds) *The Institutions of the European Union*, 3rd edn (2012, Oxford: OUP), ch. 2, p. 23; N. Nic Shiubhne, 'The Court of Justice of the European Union', in J. Peterson and M. Shackleton, *The Institutions of the European Union* 3rd edn (Oxford: Oxford University Press, 2012) 163-164; Genevra Richardson, 'Existing Approaches to Process in Administrative Law, The Legal Regulation of Process' in Genevra Richardson and Hazel Genn (eds) *Administrative Law and Government Action* (1994, Oxford: Clarendon Press), ch. 5, pp. 111–114.

Oxford University Press Journals: extracts from Jo Murkens, 'The Quest for Constitutionalism in UK Public Law Discourse' (2009) 29 OJLS 3, 430–2, 454–5; Mark Elliott, 'Parliamentary sovereignty under pressure' [2004] International Journal of Constitutional Law 545; Aileen Kavanagh, 'The Role of Parliamentary Intention in Adjudication under the Human Rights Act 1998' [2006] Oxford Journal of Legal Studies 26(1): 179; P. P. Craig, 'Sovereignty of the United Kingdom Parliament after Factortame' (1991) 11 Yearbook of European Law 221, 250–251.

Palgrave Macmillan: extracts from; Mark Glover and Robert Hazell, 'Introduction: Forecasting Constitutional Futures' in R Hazell (ed), *Constitutional Futures Revisited: Britain's Constitution to 2020*, ch. 1, pp 14–16 inclusive of table.

H.J. Papier: extract from 'Europe's New Realism: The Treaty of Lisbon' (2008) 4 European Constitutional Law Review 421–428, 421–422.

Parliamentary & Health Service Ombudsman: extracts from some of the main investigations undertaken by the Parliamentary ombudsman and reproduced from a timeline published to mark the Parliamentary and Health Service Ombudsman's 40th anniversary in 2007: Ann Abraham, The Parliamentary Ombudsman: withstanding the test of time HC 421 Parliamentary and Health Service Ombudsman 4th report, Session 2006–2007 (March 2007), Foreword.

Pearson: extracts from Sir Maurice Amos, *The English Constitution* (1930, London: Longmans, Green & Co.), pp. 65–6.

Reed Elsevier (UK) Limited trading as LexisNexis: extracts from *R (on the application of National Association of Health Stores) v Secretary of State for Health* [2005] EWCA Civ 154, Sedley LJ, Laws LJ.

Scotland Office: extract from *Commission on Scottish Devolution, Serving Scotland Better: Scotland and the United Kingdom in the 21st Century* (2009).

Scottish Council of Law Reporting: extracts from *Whaley v Lord Watson Of Invergowrie* [2000] SC 340, Lord President.

Sweet & Maxwell: extracts from N.W. Barber, 'Laws and constitutional conventions' (2009) 125 Law Quarterly Review 294, 294; Richard Rawlings, 'Concordats of the Constitution' (2000) 116 Law Quarterly Review 257, 258, 279; Jeffrey Jowell, 'Parliamentary sovereignty under the new constitutional hypothesis' [2006] Public Law 562, 578; Eric Barendt, 'Separation of powers and constitutional government' [1995] Public Law 599, 603–604, 605–607; Elizabeth Wicks, 'A new constitution for a new state? The 1707 Union of England and Scotland' (2001) 117 Law Quarterly Review 109, 117–20; Harry Woolf, Jeffery Jowell and Andrew Le Sueur, *de Smith's Judicial Review* (2007, London: Sweet & Maxwell), paras 5-044–5-045; Francesca Klug, 'A Bill of Rights: Do We Need One or Do We Already Have One?' [2007] Public Law 701, 717–719; Mark Elliott, 'After Brighton: between a rock and a hard place' [2012] *Public Law* XX; Rodney Brazier, '"Monarchy and the Personal Prerogatives": a personal response to Professor Blackburn' [2005] Public Law 45, 45–46; Mark Elliott and Amanda Perreau-Saussine, 'Pyrrhic Public Law: Bancoult and the Sources, status and content of common law limitations on Prerogative Power' [2009] Public Law 697–722, 705–706; Robert Hazell, 'Time for a new convention: parliamentary scrutiny of constitutional bills 1997–2005' [2006] Public Law 247, 247, 276; D Oliver 'Improving the Scrutiny of Bills:

The Case for Standards and Checklists' [2006] Public Law 219, 219–220, 226–227; David Feldman, 'Parliamentary Scrutiny of Legislation and Human Rights' [2002] Public Law 323, 324–327; Alison L. Young, 'Hunting sovereignty: Jackson v Her Majesty's Attorney-General' [2006] Public Law 187, 194–5; Jeffrey Jowell, 'Parliamentary sovereignty under the new constitutional hypothesis' [2006] Public Law 562, 577–9; Genevra Richardson and Hazel Genn, 'Tribunals in Transition: resolution or adjudication?' [2007] Public Law 116, 128–132 (footnote numbering has been changed and some footnotes in the original are omitted); Ann Abraham, 'The ombudsman and "paths to justice": a just alternative or just an alternative?'[2008] Public Law 1, 2–3; Nick O'Brien, 'Ombudsmen and social rights adjudication' [2009] Public Law 466, 468–469; Richard Kirkham, Brian Thompson and Trevor Buck, 'When Putting Things Right Goes Wrong: Enforcing the Recommendations of the Ombudsman' [2008] Public Law 510, 521–530; Andrew Le Sueur, 'Three strikes and it's out? The UK Government's strategy to oust judicial review from immigration and asylum decision making', (2004) Public Law 225–233; Sir Jack Beatson, 'Should judges conduct public inquiries?' (2005) 121 Law Quarterly Review, 221; Lord Steyn, 'Deference; a tangled story [2005] Public Law 346–359.

University of London Press: extracts from Sir Ivor Jennings, *The Law and the Constitution*, 5th edn (1959, London: University of London Press), pp. 134-135.

John Wiley & Sons: extracts from Gavin Little, 'Scotland and parliamentary sovereignty' (2004) 24 Legal Studies 540, 543-4; Diana Woodhouse, 'The Constitutional and political implications of a United Kingdom Supreme Court', (2004) 24 Legal Studies 134–155, 143–154.

Every effort has been made to trace and contact copyright holders prior to publication. If notified, the publisher will undertake to rectify any errors or omissions at the earliest opportunity.

RECENT DEVELOPMENTS

A British Bill of Rights?

See Chapter 6, pages 203-206.

On 18 December 2012 The Commission on a Bill of Rights published its final report, *A UK Bill of Rights? - The Choice Before Us* (<http://www.justice.gov.uk/news/press-releases/cbr/the-commission-on-a-bill-of-rights-report-a-uk-bill-of-rights-the-choice-before-us>).

In the press release accompanying publication of this report the Commission noted that:

'On the key central issue of a UK Bill of Rights, seven of the Commission's nine members believe that, on balance, there is a strong argument in favour of a UK Bill of Rights on the basis that such a Bill would incorporate and build on all of the UK's obligations under the European Convention on Human Rights, and that it would provide no less protection than is contained in the current Human Rights Act and the devolution settlements – although some of the majority believe that it could usefully define more clearly the scope of some rights and adjust the balance between different rights. For the majority as a whole the most powerful arguments for a new constitutional instrument are the lack of ownership by the public of the existing Human Rights Act and the European Convention on Human Rights, and the opportunity which a UK Bill of Rights would offer to provide greater protection against possible abuses of power.

The two members opposed to this conclusion – Helena Kennedy and Philippe Sands – believe that the moment is not ripe for the conclusion that a future process should be focussed on a new UK Bill of Rights. They believe that the majority has failed to identify or declare any shortcomings in the Human Rights Act or its application by our courts. While they remain open to the idea of a UK Bill of Rights were they to be satisfied that it carried no risk of decoupling the UK from the European Convention on Human Rights, they fear that one of the principal arguments relied upon by the majority – the issue of public ownership of rights – will be used to promote other aims, including the diminution of rights available to all people in our community, and a decoupling of the UK from the European Convention on Human Rights.'

GUIDE TO THE
ONLINE RESOURCE CENTRE

www.oxfordtextbooks.co.uk/orc/lesueur2e/

Oxford University Press's Online Resource Centres are developed to provide lecturers and students with ready-to-use teaching and learning resources. They are free of charge, designed specifically to complement the textbook, and offer additional materials which are suited to electronic delivery.

Using an Online Resource Centre saves you time by providing you with ready-made teaching and testing materials, while facilitating blended learning and enhancing the student experience. Use these resources to complement your own teaching notes or as a platform to update and restructure your course.

While the student resources are open-access, the lecturer resources are only available to lecturers who are adopting the book, so that lecturers can control access to these resources.

If you would like advice or help at any point, do not hesitate to contact our ORC helpdesk at: orc.help@oup.com.

FOR STUDENTS

The following resources are accessible to all, with no registration or password required.

More detail on the devolved governments

To look in more detail at the work of the devolved governments in Ireland, and Wales click on the following links:

- Scottish Government
- Northern Ireland Executive
- Welsh Assembly Government.

Page 289

Examples of ministers being called to account for their wor

To get a deeper understanding of how Parliament operates to ca is a good idea to look at some examples.

Prime Minister's Question Time takes place once a week when t

Error of law

In R (Cart) v Upper Tribunal [2011] UKSC 28 [2011] 3 WLR 107, the considered the circumstances in which decisions of the Upper Tribu judicial review. The lower courts had taken the view that the Upper T unusually broad jurisdiction, such that—unlike administrative decisio determinations on questions of law would not normally be susceptib judicial review. Although the Supreme Court decided that the Upper would be reviewable only quite rarely, it rejected the lower courts' re the Supreme Court's decision in Cart (in contrast to the lower court limited general relevance to the circumstances in which judicial revi ground of error of law.

Le Sueur, Sunkin & Murkens: Public Law: Text, Cases, and Mat

Web links

Chapter 1: Getting started in public law

http://www.statutelaw.gov.uk/
http://www.archive.official-documents.co.uk/document/parliment/nola
http://www.nationalarchives.gov.uk/pathways/citizenship/struggle_de
http://www.parliament.uk/parliamentary_committees/reform_committ
http://www.number10.gov.uk/Page13008 .

Additional Material

Additional material is provided to supplement each chapter and offer additional information about reforms and acts referenced in the book. The latest legislation and changes to acts and reforms passed are detailed, while further reading and contextual information offer a background to the study of public law, developing an understanding of the law in practice.

Updates

The Online Resource Centre provides each student with up-to-date information and details of the latest legislation following publication to ensure that they gain an awareness of the newest developments in a constantly changing and dynamic area of law.

Web links

A selection of annotated web links, chosen by the authors and organized by chapter, allowing you to research those topics that are of particular interest to you. Links are provided to all the websites referred to in the book to allow for easy access and reference.

FOR LECTURERS

Password protected to ensure only lecturers can access these resources. If you are thinking of adopting this book, or if you already adopt it, then please follow the simple steps outlined on the website in order to gain access.

Which of the following is the principal characteristic of the British

- The Monarch acts only on the advice of ministers.
- The Monarch can only act independently of government whe
- The monarch has absolutely no role in government.
- The Monarch can decide to take executive decisions whene

1 out of 1
Correct. The practice was settled at the end of Queen Victoria's simply agrees to whatever ministers decide. The role is purely f
Page reference: 270-271

Test bank

A fully customizable resource containing ready-made assessments with which to test your students and aid their learning. Offering versatile testing tailored to the content of this book, each answer is accompanied by feedback to explain to the student why their answer is correct or incorrect and where in this book they can find further information. The test bank is downloadable into Questionmark Perception, Blackboard, WebCT, and most other virtual learning environments capable of importing QTI XML.

OUTLINE TABLE OF CONTENTS

DETAILED CONTENTS

PART I   CONSTITUTIONAL FUNDAMENTALS   1

1 CONSTITUTIONAL FUNDAMENTALS   3

2 LEGITIMACY IN THE CONSTITUTION AND PARLIAMENTARY SUPREMACY   39

TABLE OF CASES

References are to page numbers. The abbreviation n indicates a footnote.

TABLE OF UK STATUTES

References are to page numbers. The abbreviation n indicates a footnote.

TABLE OF UK STATUTORY INSTRUMENTS

References are to page numbers. The abbreviation n indicates a footnote.

TABLE OF EUROPEAN
UNION LEGISLATION

References are to page numbers. The abbreviation n indicates a footnote.

TABLE OF INTERNATIONAL AND FOREIGN INSTRUMENTS

References are to page numbers. The abbreviation n indicates a footnote.

PART I

CONSTITUTIONAL FUNDAMENTALS

1

CONSTITUTIONAL FUNDAMENTALS

CENTRAL ISSUES

1. In the United Kingdom, the important rules setting out the structure and powers of government and people's freedoms and rights are found in several different sources, including Acts of Parliament, judicial decisions, conventions, European Union law, and international law.

2. So many rules, from various sources, are in written form that it is a misnomer to describe the UK constitution as 'unwritten'; it is however 'uncodified'.

3. For the first time, in October 2011 the government published a brief account of the principal constitutional rules as *The Cabinet Manual*. There is disagreement about the significance and status of this document.

4. Looking at the constitution as creating a whole system for government, the UK constitutional arrangements have often been described as 'the Westminster model'. This refers to ministers (the government) being drawn from members of Parliament; the UK Parliament as the pinnacle of the system; and effective procedures for ministers to be accountable to Parliament. Many changes to the constitutional system call into question the Westminster model.

1 INTRODUCTION

'Coalition set to drop elected peers plan' (*Financial Times*, 3 August 2012 reporting on government proposals for reform of the upper House of Parliament). 'Judicial review bid granted over North Somerset youth cuts' (BBC News, 17 May 2012 on a legal challenge to a local authority's decision to reduce spending on youth services). 'Defiant Bob Diamond [former chief executive of a major bank] gets grilled by MPs' (*The Sun*, 5 July 2012 reporting a House of Commons select committee inquiry into interest rate rigging). 'Even if Euro-judges were minimally competent, there would be no reason to accept their jurisdiction' (*The Telegraph*, 22 May 2012 on views of a Member of the European Parliament). 'England and Wales want Scots to stay in the union, poll reveals' (*The Independent*, 7 June 2012 on public reaction to proposals for Scotland to become an independent country). Questions about the constitution of the United Kingdom are never out of the news, as these headlines show. Constitutional arrangements—how we are governed and what our rights and freedoms are—are often controversial.

In this opening chapter, we look at constitutions in general and the constitution of the United Kingdom in particular from two angles. The first is the idea that a constitution is a *rulebook*: for constitutional arrangements to work well, people need to know what the rules are and there also needs to be broad consensus that the rules are right. The second is the idea that constitutions create *systems of government*. This perspective involves standing back from the rulebook and trying to see the patterns, traditions, underlying ideals, and principles expressed or implied by the rules; it also requires an understanding of what happens in practice (which may be different from the rules). Many epithets have been used to try to encapsulate the UK constitution: it is a parliamentary democracy; a constitutional monarchy; and academics have often described it as 'the Westminster model' or 'Westminster-style constitutionalism',[1] though it is open to question how much of this model has survived the significant constitutional developments of the past 40 years.

This is a book written by and for lawyers. The law-related aspects of the rulebook and of the system of government are therefore of particular interest. Public lawyers need, however, to be broad-minded: many of the most important rules are not found in legislation or case law but in other sources; and the legal aspects of the constitutional system need to be understood in their political context.

2 THE CONSTITUTION AS A RULEBOOK

A workaday definition of 'a constitution' of a country is: a set of the most important rules about the structure and powers of government and of people's most basic freedoms and rights. In almost all countries around the world, it is possible to go into a bookshop or download from the Internet a copy of a document called 'the Constitution' or 'Basic Law', which methodically states the rules.[2] Every nation state has its own particular mix of rules leading to their own distinctive constitutions. At a very general level, most constitutional frameworks share similar characteristics. There is an institution or set of public office holders that is the government, responsible for carrying out the many executive actions needed in a well-ordered society.[3] There is an institution described as a legislature, which is responsible for producing laws in accordance with its powers; these days most legislatures consist of elected representatives chosen in periodic elections.[4] Additionally, constitutional frameworks generally create a role for judges, though judicial functions vary quite strikingly between systems.[5] Constitutions also typically contain statements of people's basic rights and freedoms, reflecting the declarations in international human law on these subjects that have been agreed (if not always respected) since the 1950s.

---

[1] The Palace of Westminster is the building in London that accommodates the Houses of Parliament (the House of Commons and House of Lords).

[2] For an online collection of every constitution, see www.oup.com/online/us/law/ocw/. Most are relatively new.

[3] See Part II of this book.

[4] See Part III of this book.

[5] See Part IV of this book.

The United Kingdom of Great Britain and Northern Ireland (to give the country its full but rarely used name) is well known for not having one legal document setting out the basic structures of government and people's freedoms and rights. In an official publication, senior civil servants recently described the position as follows.

Cabinet Office, *The Cabinet Manual*, 1st edn (2011, London: Cabinet Office) p. 2

The UK does not have a codified constitution. There is no single document that describes, establishes or regulates the structures of the state and the way in which these relate to the people. Instead, the constitutional order has evolved over time and continues to do so. It consists of various institutions, statutes, judicial decisions, principles and practices that are commonly understood as 'constitutional'. The UK does not have a constitutional court to rule on the implications of a codified constitution, and the sovereignty of Parliament is therefore unrestrained by such a court...

We label this state of affairs as 'the dispersed constitutional rulebook'. The expression 'unwritten constitution' is often used but it is apt to be misleading: certainly it is true to say that the important constitutional rules of the United Kingdom are not written down in one legal instrument but almost all rules are written down somewhere. Most rules are reasonably clear—though there are some rules about which there is controversy, either because people disagree about what the rule actually is or because there are disagreements about what the rule *should* be. Despite not having a codified document, plainly the United Kingdom has a sophisticated and reasonably well-organized system of government, broadly speaking people's fundamental freedoms and rights are respected, and politicians, journalists, and academics discuss the 'British constitution'. So the term 'constitution' is capable of being used in different ways, as Dr Geoffrey Marshall (1929–2003) explains.

Geoffrey Marshall, 'The Constitution: Its Theory and Interpretation', in V. Bogdanor (ed.) *The British Constitution in the Twentieth Century* (2004, Oxford: OUP for the British Academy), ch. 2, p. 31

Four distinguishable senses of 'constitution' [...] would be:

(a) the combination of legal and non-legal (or conventional) rules that currently provide the framework of government and regulate the behaviour of the major political actors;

(b) a single instrument promulgated at a particular point in time and adopted by some generally agreed authorisation procedure under the title 'constitution' (or equivalent rubric such as 'basic law');

(c) the totality of legal rules, whether contained in statutes, secondary legislation, domestic judicial decisions or binding international instruments or judicial decisions, that affect the working of government;

(d) a list of statutes or instruments that have an entrenched status and can be amended or repealed only by a special procedure.

These are not mutually exclusive definitions: a country may have a constitution in some or all of these senses. The United Kingdom has a constitution in meanings (a) and (c), but not (b) and (d). Some scholars are sceptical whether it makes much difference whether or not there is a 'single instrument' (or 'capital C' constitution), as Professor Anthony King argues:

Anthony King, *Does the United Kingdom Still Have a Constitution?* (2001, London: Sweet & Maxwell) p. 3

Constitutions…are never—to repeat, *never*—written down. They might possibly in principle be written down, but in practice they never are. There are, of course, written documents called Constitutions—with a capital 'C'—but they are never, ever coextensive with all of a country's most important rules regulating the relations between different parts of government and those between the government and the people. Constitutions as defined here ['*A constitution is the set of important rules that regulate the relations among the different parts of the government of a given country and also the relations between the different parts of the government and the people of the country*'] and the written documents called Constitutions overlap to a greater or lesser degree. Of course they do: all capital-C Constitutions have at least *some* bearing on how the countries that have them are actually governed. But capital-C Constitutions and small-c constitutions are never the same thing, and sometimes the relationship between the two is quite tenuous (even if, in a given country, the capital-C Constitution is taken seriously).

In the United Kingdom, with its dispersed constitutional rulebook, where should one look for '*the set of important rules*' that form the constitutional framework?

(a) THE CABINET MANUAL 2011

One option is a publication already referred to, namely *The Cabinet Manual*, which is subtitled 'A guide to laws, conventions and rules on the operation of government'. It was written in 2010–11 by the Cabinet Secretary (the United Kingdom's most senior civil servant) and has the endorsement of two Prime Ministers—Gordon Brown (in 2010 when a draft was circulated for comment) and David Cameron (who wrote a foreword to the first edition in October 2011).[6] The Cabinet Secretary's preface explains that '*It is primarily a guide for those working in government, recording the current position rather than driving change. It is not intended to be legally binding or to set issues in stone. The Cabinet Manual records rules and practices, but is not intended to be a source of any rule*'.[7] It has eleven chapters covering the main institutions and relationships in the British constitution and runs to 106 pages.

The draft *Manual* generated a great deal of interest among those who care about these things and was considered by three parliamentary select committees.[8] The reaction of two of the committees was less than enthusiastic. The House of Lords Constitution Committee concluded as follows.

---

[6] Available online at www.cabinetoffice.gov.uk/resource-library/cabinet-manual.

[7] p. iv.

[8] On select committees, see Chapter 7. Consisting of a dozen or so MPs (in the Commons) or peers (in the House of Lords), their role is to scrutinize government and inquire into matters of public concern.

House of Lords Constitution Committee, *The Cabinet Manual*, Twelfth Report of 2010–12, HL 107

95. In our view the Cabinet Manual has limited value and relevance. We acknowledge that it provides greater transparency on certain aspects of the operation of government and it is to be welcomed in that context. However, this value has been given undue prominence by the helpful publication of Chapter Two in draft prior to the May 2010 general election;[9] the benefits of the publication of that chapter do not, on the whole, extend to the rest of the Manual.

96. In summary we conclude that the Cabinet Manual is not the first step towards a written constitution; it should be renamed the Cabinet Office Manual and its greater relevance to officials than to politicians emphasised; it should only seek to describe existing rules and practices; it should not be endorsed by the Cabinet nor formally approved by Parliament; and it must be entirely accurate and properly sourced and referenced.

The House of Commons Public Administration Committee was slightly more positive (*'We welcome the intention behind the compilation and publication of the draft Cabinet Manual'*) but echoed the Constitution Committee's conclusions: *'It should not be construed as the start of a written constitution'* and *'It follows that we do not consider that the Cabinet Manual should be endorsed by either the Cabinet or Parliament. It is strictly a guidance document for ministers and civil servants'*.[10] In contrast, a third committee was rather more upbeat in its assessment:

House of Commons Political and Constitutional Reform Committee, *Constitutional implications of the Cabinet Manual*, Sixth Report of 2010–12, HC 734, 'Conclusions and recommendations'

7. The foreword to the draft suggests that the Cabinet Manual is a document of limited ambition, which is not intended to 'set issues in stone' or to 'resolve or move forward' matters of public debate. Despite these intentions, there is scope for the constitutional impact of the Cabinet Manual to be greater than this. This becomes particularly true where the Cabinet Manual's content extends beyond matters that are purely for the Executive. (Paragraph 36)

8. Whether or not the Cabinet Manual should be open to amendment and decision by Parliament depends in our view on what the Cabinet Manual is or might become. If it is simply a document by the Executive, about the Executive and for the Executive, then for Parliament to decide on its content would give it a status it should not have. (Paragraph 40)

9. The Manual, however, seems in part to be intended as—or might become, whatever the intention—the basis for a shared understanding beyond the Executive of important parts of the United Kingdom's previously uncodified constitution. Parliamentary intervention would be entirely appropriate in such circumstances. An official document, approved by the Cabinet, will have a status unlike that of existing academic texts on the same subject. We intend to

---

9 This deals with 'Elections and government formation'. At the time the draft was written, opinion polls correctly suggested that in the general election no single party would have an overall majority of MPs—until 2010, an unusual state of affairs in recent decades in the United Kingdom.

10 House of Commons Public Administration Select Committee, *Cabinet Manual*, Eight Report of 2010–11, HC 900, paras 55, 57.

monitor closely how the Cabinet Manual develops, and how it is used both within and beyond Government during the life of this Parliament. (Paragraph 41)

10. Whatever the status of the Cabinet Manual as a document, it covers ground which is significant enough to merit regular debate in the House. We therefore propose that, soon after the Cabinet Manual is finalised, the House should have the opportunity to debate it as a whole and should seek the Government's assurance that such a debate should become an annual fixture in the parliamentary calendar. Alternatively, the debate could occur twice during the course of a five-year Parliament [...]. The Government should publish a list of changes made to the Manual during the preceding year to inform this debate. As the Manual is largely about the conduct of the Executive, we would expect this debate to take place in Government time. (Paragraph 42)

Relationship to a written constitution

11. The Cabinet Manual is not a written constitution. It has, however, considerable overlap in content with what might be expected of a constitution. The Cabinet Secretary has suggested to us that it would be likely to be a starting point for any attempt to produce such a constitution. By bringing together and publishing the Government's interpretation of existing constitutional rules and conventions, the Government has already begun to spark debate about both the nature of these rules and conventions, and if and how they should be written down. This is a debate in which Parliament needs to play a full part. (Paragraph 54)

By December 2012, no debate of the *Manual* had taken place. The one thing everybody seems to agree on is that the *Manual* is not, itself, a source of constitutional rules.

(b) THE STATUTE BOOK

Apart from *The Cabinet Manual*, where else might we look for the contents of the dispersed rulebook? Another option would be 'the statute book', which is a general (rather than legal or technical) term for all the Acts of Parliament that have received Royal Assent—the final stage of the legislation-making process in Parliament—and which are in force or waiting to be brought into force.[11] No single volume could accommodate this vast body of legislation; in any event, it is now much more conveniently found on an official website.[12]

A quick browse through the legislation will reveal several Acts of Parliament that can be described as 'constitutional' in the sense used by King: they include '*important rules that regulate the relations among the different parts of the government of a given country and also the relations between the different parts of the government and the people of the country*'. In 2003, the Joint Committee on the Draft Civil Contingencies Bill drew up a list of statutes set out in Table 1.1 that could be taken to be 'fundamental parts of constitutional law' (with our own brief outline next to each one and where, if at all, it is discussed in this book):[13]

---

[11] See Chapter 10.

[12] See http://www.legislation.gov.uk/uk.

[13] Joint Committee on the draft Civil Contingencies Bill, First Report of 2002-03, HL Paper 184/HC Paper 1074, para. 183.

Table 1.1 Constitutional statutes

Magna Carta 1297	Proclamation of liberties, including that no freeman may be punished except by lawful judgment of his peers or by the law of the land; and that the Crown 'will sell to no man, we will not deny or defer to any man either Justice or Right'.
Bill of Rights 1688	Requires parliamentary approval for the Crown to levy tax and keep a standing army; prohibits excessive bail, fines and 'illegall and cruell Punishments inflicted'; affirms the right of trial by jury; and in Art. 9 provides 'That the Freedome of Speech and Debates or Proceedings in Parlyament ought not to be impeached or questioned in any Court or Place out of Parlyament'—a significant element of 'parliamentary privilege': see Chapter 4.
Crown and Parliament Recognition Act 1689	Confirms William and Mary as the lawful king and queen following the 'Glorious Revolution' (see Chapter 7) and the validity of law passed in previous parliaments.
Act of Settlement 1700	Requires the monarch to be a member of the Church of England: see Chapter 7.
Union with Scotland Act 1707	Formation of Great Britain, as a union between the kingdoms of England and Wales, and Scotland: see Chapter 5.
Union with Ireland Act 1800	Formation of the United Kingdom of Great Britain and Ireland, with the addition of Ireland to the realm: Chapter 5.
Parliament Acts 1911–49	Rules ensuring the primacy of the House of Commons over the House of Lords by enabling the Commons to present a bill for Royal Assent even if the Lords disagree: see Chapters 10 and 13.
Life Peerages Act 1958	Creates a new type of peerage, based on appointment rather than the hereditary principle; these peers are members of the House of Lords for life.
Emergency Powers Act 1964	Largely repealed and replaced by the Civil Contingencies Act 2004.
European Communities Act 1972	Gives legal effect to the UK's membership of the European Union and all that entails: see Chapters 8, 12, and 18.
House of Commons Disqualification Act 1975	Limits number of ministers who may sit in the House of Commons and excludes full-time professional judges from being MPs or members of the House of Lords: see Chapters 4 and 7.
Ministerial and Other Salaries Act 1975	Rules about payment of salaries to ministers: see Chapter 7.
British Nationality Act 1981	Main piece of legislation on citizenship.

Supreme Court Act 1981 (now renamed Senior Courts Act 1981)	Sets out structure for courts of England and Wales; protects judicial independence by making senior judges removable from office only by 'Her Majesty on an address presented to her by both Houses of Parliament': see Chapter 14.
Representation of the People Act 1983	Rules about elections to the UK Parliament and local authorities in England.
Government of Wales Act 1998 (now superseded by the Government of Wales Act 2006)	The devolution framework for Wales: see Chapter 5.
Human Rights Act 1998	'Brings home' provisions from the European Convention of Human Rights and Fundamental Rights: see Chapters 6 and 17.
Northern Ireland Act 1998	The devolution framework for Northern Ireland: see Chapter 5.
Scotland Act 1998 (now amended by the Scotland Act 2012)	The devolution framework for Scotland: see Chapter 5.
House of Lords Act 1999	Ended the rights of hereditary peers to have an automatic seat in the House of Lords; created rules enabling 92 to be elected by the hereditary peers: see Chapter 13.
Civil Contingencies Act 2004	The framework for government during a time of emergency.

Several of these Acts have been amended or repealed and, in 2012, some are under discussion for reform (the Human Rights Act 1998 and the House of Lords Act 1999): so it would be wrong to see these Acts as set in stone. Moreover, most of these Acts contain relatively trivial rules as well as important ones, so it would be wrong to think of them as containing constitutional rules and nothing but constitutional rules. The list is also incomplete, as, since 2003, Acts have been put into the statute book that are obviously or arguably of constitutional importance:

Constitutional Reform Act 2005	Reformed office of Lord Chancellor, created the UK Supreme Court (replacing the Appellate Committee of the House of Lords), and introduced new system of judicial appointments for England and Wales: see Chapters 3, 4 and 14.
Tribunals, Courts and Enforcement Act 2007	Created a simplified tribunal system based on the First-tier Tribunal and the Upper Tribunal: see Chapter 14.
Parliamentary Standards Act 2009	Following a scandal about expenses, created the Independent Parliamentary Standards Authority (IPSA) to manage expenses and records of MPs' outside interests.
Constitutional Reform and Governance Act 2010	Reformed prerogative powers by putting the civil service on a statutory footing and putting in place a statutory framework for parliamentary approval of treaties: see Chapter 9.

Localism Act 2011	Radical changes to local government in England, including referendums, directly elected mayors, and a 'general power of competence': see Chapter 4.
European Union Act 2011	Creates framework for referendums on proposals to amend the EU treaties; section 18 includes a declaration about the relationship between national and EU law: see Chapter 12.
Scotland Act 2012	Amends the framework of devolution to Scotland giving greater powers to the Scottish Government and Scottish Parliament, following recommendations by the Calman Commission: see Chapter 4.

Acts do not come neatly labelled as 'constitutional' so it is a question of judgement as to which ones should be included on a list and there is room for disagreement: for example, in 2004 the committee's list does not include the Freedom of Information Act 2000 (giving people in the United Kingdom a legal right to official information for the first time), which some people would regard as of constitutional significance. The most basic problem with looking at the statute book is that it does not provide a complete set of rules: it contains only rules that have been enacted by Parliament and will show little or nothing of rules in other forms, such as conventions, or general principles.[14]

In Chapter 2 we will return to the idea of 'constitutional statutes'. In orthodox legal thinking, Acts dealing with constitutional matters are no different from Acts of Parliament on any other subject: an Act regulating the dentistry profession has the same status as one dealing with the constitutional union between England and Scotland, according to the most influential nineteenth-century public lawyer.[15] This is no longer a tenable view.

(c) JUDICIAL DECISIONS

Another part of the United Kingdom's dispersed constitutional rulebook is to be found in the law reports. Despite the lack of a designated constitutional court in the United Court, judges in the three separate jurisdictions within the United Kingdom (England and Wales, Scotland, and Northern Ireland) have contributed to the development of constitutional principles. The judgments of the highest court in civil matters are of obvious importance: until October 2009, this was the Appellate Committee of the House of Lords; after then, under the framework created by the Constitutional Reform Act 2005, it is the new UK Supreme Court. In Chapter 3 we examine in more detail the role of the judiciary in the practical protection of the rule of law, and the controversies that exist about this: in brief, views are strongly divided as to how much influence UK judges, and judges sitting in the two European Courts—the Court of Justice of the European Union (in Luxembourg) and the European Court of Human Rights (in Strasbourg)—should have in controlling the policy

---

[14] There have been occasional references in Acts of Parliament to constitutional conventions, e.g. s. 1 of the Health and Social Care Act 2012 alludes to individual ministerial responsibility ('The Secretary of State retains ministerial responsibility to Parliament for the provision of the health service in England') and to broad constitutional principles, e.g. s. 1 of the Constitutional Reform Act 2005 refers to the principle of the rule of law.

[15] A.V. Dicey, *Introduction to the Study of the Law of the Constitution*, 10th edn (1959, London: Macmillan), p. 145; the first edition was published in 1885; the last edition substantially revised by Dicey himself was the seventh edition in 1908. Professor Dicey lived between 1835 and 1922. See further, Mark D. Walters, 'Dicey on Writing the *Law of the Constitution*' (2012) 32 Oxford Journal of Legal Studies 21.

options open to the UK Parliament and the UK government. The areas of counter-terrorism measures, immigration and asylum, and prisoners' rights have proved to be particularly contentious but underlying these are deeper questions about the role of judges in a constitutional democracy. For the purposes of this chapter, it is enough to introduce the two main ways in which judges contribute to developing and applying the constitutional rulebook.

The first is by statutory interpretation: making definitive rulings on the meaning of provisions in Acts of Parliament and other legislation. The orthodox starting point is that judges are seeking to find and give effect to 'the intention of Parliament' as expressed in the words of the Act in question.[16] This may seem to imply a rather limited, subordinate role for judges but courts have developed principles that in some cases suggest a far more expansive function. For example, judges have been extremely reluctant to take at face value statutory provisions that oust the jurisdiction of the courts to review the legality of government decisions.[17] They have developed the 'principle of legality', which means that an Act of Parliament will not be interpreted as depriving people of common law rights except by the clearest words.[18] Parliament has also changed the way in which judges are expected to carry out the task of interpreting statutes. Section 3 of the Human Rights Act 1998 places a new obligation on the courts: '*So far as it is possible to do so, primary legislation and subordinate legislation must be read and given effect in a way which is compatible with the Convention rights*'. Exactly what this requires or permits a judge to do has been the subject of much debate in court and in academic circles.[19] Moreover, where rights or interests protected by European Union law are in issue, all courts and tribunals in the UK must strive to read UK Acts of Parliament to achieve consistency with EU law (which always has priority over national law).[20]

A second way in which judges contribute to the development and application of the rulebook is through common law methods. As this is the first point in the book at which we discuss 'the common law', some words of explanation are called for. The common law is a term used to refer to the legal tradition that developed in England after the Norman Conquest in 1066. It was subsequently transplanted to many other countries during the era of the British Empire and is the root of legal systems in, for example, Australia, Bangladesh, Canada, India, New Zealand, and the United States of America.[21] Distinctions can be drawn between common law jurisdictions and those based on 'civilian' or Roman law traditions (in continental Europe and Latin America, for instance). Scotland is a 'mixed' or 'pluralistic' jurisdiction, drawing on both traditions—but its public law is based on common law. For our purposes, the following are the most significant features of the common law tradition:

i)   there is no designated constitutional court separate from the main court system—as is typical in civilian jurisdictions;

ii) in several important and broad fields of law, judges not only apply rules but generate them independently of Parliament through the application of precedent—instead of being confined to the interpretation and application of a codified set of rules for a field of law as in civilian jurisdictions;

---

[16] In the landmark case *Pepper (HM Inspector of Taxes) v Hart* [1993] AC 593, it was held that courts may, in interpreting an ambiguous statutory provision, allow a party to refer to a minister's statement during the passage of the bill through Parliament, reported in *Hansard*.

[17] *Anisminic v Foreign Compensation Commission* [1969] 2 AC 147, discussed further in Chapter 16.

[18] *Pierson v Secretary of State for the Home Department* [1988] AC 539, discussed in Chapter 3.

[19] See Chapter 17.

[20] See Chapter 18.

[21] For a much fuller account than is possible here, see W. Morrison, A. Geary, and R. Jago, *The Politics of the Common Law: Perspectives, Rights, Processes, Institutions* (2008, Abingdon: Routledge-Cavendish).

iii) the style of judgments in common law systems tend to be longer and contain more justification for the rulings based on detailed discussion of previous judgments;

iv) judges may make obiter statements in judgments: these are discussions of propositions of law that are not strictly speaking necessary to decide the particular case before the court but are a way of judges floating ideas and setting an intellectual agenda. Judges have used obiter dicta to discuss important constitutional principles, including parliamentary supremacy, the rules of law, and the separation of powers.

v) judges are appointed from mid-career lawyers in private practice—rather than at a relatively young age immediately after completing their legal studies as occurs in many civilian jurisdictions for the ordinary courts or from academia for constitutional courts.[22]

Chapters 2, 3, and 16 will explore in more detail how and with what effect judges in the UK have added to the constitutional rulebook. They have done so through different branches of tort law, including trespass, negligence and misfeasance in public office. For example, in the celebrated case of *Entick v Carrington*, Lord Camden held that officials have no general power to enter and search property unless authorised by statute or common law.[23] The other field of common law rule-making of constitutional significance is judicial review. Over the years, and especially over the past 40 years, the courts have enunciated grounds of review that may be used to question the legality of decisions by public bodies and delegated legislation.[24] The courts have also extended their common law jurisdiction to review different types of decision (including those made by ministers under authority of prerogative powers[25] and non-statutory bodies)[26] to hold ministers in contempt of court in the (admittedly very rare) situation where a minister or an official acting in the minister's name ignored undertakings given to a court or a court order.[27]

Going against the grain of mainstream thinking, a number of senior judges supported by sympathetic academics look to the common law broadly and argue that the body of case law embodies fundamental values of the constitution: they suggest that, in extreme situations, judges would have the constitutional duty to set aside an Act of Parliament that undermined democracy or people's basic rights in some profound way. Consider, for example, the following academic writing by Sir John Laws, when he was a judge of the High Court in England and Wales.

Sir John Laws, 'Law and democracy' [1995] Public Law 72, 84

Now it is only by means of compulsory law that effective rights can be accorded, so that the medium of rights is not persuasion, but the power of rule: the very power which, if misused, could be deployed to subvert rights. We therefore arrive at this position: the constitution must guarantee by positive law such rights as that of freedom of expression, since otherwise its credentials as a medium of honest rule are fatally undermined. But this requires for its achievement what I may call a higher-order law: a law which cannot be abrogated as other laws can, by the passage of a statute promoted by a government with the necessary majority in Parliament. Otherwise the right is not in the keeping of the constitution at all; it is not a

---

[22] See Chapter 14.
[23] (1765) 19 St Tr 1030, discussed in Chapter 3.
[24] See Chapter 11 (delegated legislation) and Chapter 16 (on judicial review).
[25] *Council of Civil Service Unions v Minister for the Civil Service* [1985] AC 374.
[26] *R v Panel on Takeovers and Mergers, ex parte Datafin* [1987] QB 815.
[27] *M v Home Office* [1994] 1 AC 277.

> guaranteed right; it exists, in point of law at least, only because the government chooses to let it exist, whereas in truth no such choice should be open to any government.
>
> The democratic credentials of an elected government cannot justify its enjoyment of a right to abolish fundamental freedoms. If its power in the state is in the last resort absolute, such fundamental rights as free expression are only privileges; no less so if the absolute power rests in an elected body. The byword of every tyrant is 'My word is law'; a democratic assembly having sovereign power beyond the reach of curtailment or review may make just such an assertion, and its elective base cannot immunise it from playing the tyrant's role.

To be clear: this is controversial stuff and runs counter to orthodox thinking on the principle of parliamentary supremacy (under which courts are said to be bound to recognize as valid law any Act of Parliament). We return to these issues in Chapter 2.

(d) CONSTITUTIONAL CONVENTIONS

The Cabinet Manual's description of the UK constitution makes plain the importance of 'constitutional conventions' as a source of rules. It defines conventions as *'rules of constitutional practice that are regarded as binding in operation but not in law'*. Among the particular conventions discussed in the *Manual* are:

i) *'By convention, the Sovereign does not become publicly involved in party politics of government.'*

ii) *'The roles of the Prime Minister and Cabinet are governed largely by convention.'*

iii) *'By modern convention, the Prime Minister always sits in the House of Commons.'*

iv) *'There is a convention that an individual will be a minister only if they are a Member of the House of Commons or the House of Lords.'*

v) *'By convention, Cabinet and Cabinet committees take decisions which are binding on members of the Government.'*

vi) *'The two Houses of Parliament acknowledge various conventions governing the relationship between them, including in relation to primacy of the House of Commons, financial privilege and the operation of the Salisbury-Addison convention.'*

vii) *'In 2011, the Government acknowledged that a convention had developed in Parliament that before troops were committed the House of Commons should have an opportunity to debate the matter and said that it proposed to observe that convention except when there was an emergency and such action would not be appropriate.'*

It is easy enough to identify rules set out in the form of legislation, because they have been made according to a defined process and a published in a prescribed format,[28] but how do we identify rules in the form of conventions? Professor Sir Ivor Jennings (1903–65) suggested a three-part test.

Sir Ivor Jennings, *The Law and the Constitution*, 5th edn (1959, London: University of London Press), pp. 134–5

> It is clear, in the first place, that mere practice is insufficient. The fact that an authority has always behaved in a certain way is not warrant for saying that it ought to behave in that way.

---

[28] See Chapter 10.

But if the authority itself and those connected with it believe that they ought to do so, then the convention does exist. This is the ordinary rule applied to customary law. Practice alone is not enough. It must be normative. For example, the fact that the monarch has refused a dissolution [of Parliament, for a general election to be held] for over a century when advised by his Cabinet does not in itself create a convention that the monarch must always accept the advice tendered. [. . .] Similarly, the fact that the Sovereign has once behaved in a certain way does not bind him to act in that way. [. . .] Something more must be added. As in the creation of law, the creation of a convention must be due to the reason of the thing because it accords with the prevailing political philosophy. It helps to make the democratic system operate; it enables the machinery of the State to run more smoothly; and if it were not there, friction would result. Thus, if a convention continues because it is desirable in the circumstances of the constitution, it must have been created for the same reason. We have to ask ourselves three questions: first, what are the precedents; secondly, did the actors in the precedents believe that they were bound by the rule; and thirdly, is there a good reason for the rule? A single precedent with a good reason may be enough to establish the rule. A whole string of precedents without such a reason will be of no avail, unless it is perfectly certain that the persons concerned regarded them as bound by it.

The second element in the Jennings' test is helpful in distinguishing conventions from mere practices that, although routinely followed, do not really serve any 'good reason' relevant to the functioning of the constitution and which could be changed without being thought to breach a constitutional rule. Examples of practices that should not be regarded as constitutional conventions are: the Prime Minister spends the Christmas holidays at Chequers (the Prime Minister's official country residence); that ministers' official papers are transported in red leather-covered boxes; and that Prime Minister's Question Time takes place for 30 minutes at 12 noon on Wednesdays when the House of Commons is sitting.[29]

Are conventions different from laws? Dicey drew a sharp distinction between laws 'in the strictest sense' and constitutional conventions. The difference between the two categories lay, he stressed, in the role of the courts in relation to enforcement of failures to comply with the rules.

A.V. Dicey, Introduction to the Study of the Law of the Constitution (1885; 10th edn 1959, London: Macmillan & Co), pp. 23–4

[. . .] the rules which make up constitutional law, as the term is used in England, include two sets of principles or maxims of a totally distinct character.

The one set of rules are in the strictest sense 'laws', since they are rules which (whether written or unwritten, whether enacted by statute or derived from the mass of custom, tradition, or judge-made maxims known to common law) are enforced by the courts; these rules constitute 'constitutional law' in the proper sense of that term, and may for the sake of distinction be called collectively 'the law of the constitution'.

The other set of rules consist of conventions, understandings, habits, or practices which, though they may regulate the conduct of several members of the sovereign powers, of the Ministry, of the officials, are not in reality laws at all since they are not enforced by the courts. This proportion of constitutional law may, for the sake of the distinction, be termed the 'conventions of the constitution', or constitutional morality.

---

[29] In 1997, Tony Blair changed the previous arrangement, which was to have two 15-minute sessions during the week.

He also made clear that the distinction was not related to whether the rules were 'written' or 'unwritten', because many constitutional conventions are expressed in 'printed rules'. He included in the category of conventions '*the whole of our parliamentary procedure*', which he said '*is nothing but a mass of conventional law*'.

The idea that it is possible, or helpful, to draw a clear dividing line between rules in the form of laws and those in the form of convention has long been questioned. Jennings argued that '*there is not distinction of substance or nature*' between laws and conventions, although he went on to say that it is '*important from the technical angle*' to know into which category a rule falls. More recently, N.W. Barber argues that we should view laws and conventions not as separate categories of rules, but as a spectrum.

N.W. Barber, 'Laws and constitutional conventions' (2009) 125 Law Quarterly Review 294, 294

The difference between law and convention is one of degree: laws and conventions should be placed upon a spectrum of types of social rules, a spectrum gradated in terms of the formalisation of rules. Laws lie at the most formalised end of this spectrum, but there is no single, definable, point at which rules shift from being conventions into being laws. Alongside this argument, it will be contended that conventions can become laws through judicial intervention, and that conventions can 'crystallise' into laws over time by becoming increasingly formalised.

[By way of an example, Barber considers the Ministerial Code—the set of rules governing the conduct of ministers issued by the Prime Minister.[30]]

Since its publication in 1992, the Code has grown in political strength. In recent years those alleging ministerial misconduct have frequently argued that the Code has been violated. When, for instance, it was discovered that Tessa Jowell's husband had received a substantial sum from Silvio Berlusconi, the challenge to her integrity was framed within the Code. [At the time, she was Secretary of State for Culture, Media and Sport.] Her critics argued that this was a gift, and should, under the Code, have been reported to her Permanent Secretary [the senior civil service in her department]. The Prime Minister [Tony Blair] concluded, after an investigation by the Cabinet Secretary, that by the time Jowell knew of the money the Inland Revenue had classed it as earnings, and it consequently did not need to be declared under the Code. On both sides of the controversy the Code was accepted as the source of the relevant constitutional obligation. The Code has been invoked in a similar fashion in other recent political battles. Controversies surrounding Lord Sainsbury's loans to the Labour Party [he was a minister in the Department for Trade and Industry], David Blunkett's intervention in an application for a visa [he was Home Secretary], and John Prescott's stay at a ranch and receipt of a "cowboy outfit" [he was Deputy Prime Minister], have all been fought out within the context of the Code.

The focus of political attention on the Code suggests the emergence of a new convention: one of the rules of ministerial responsibility now places a duty on Ministers to follow the rules set out in the Code. Failure to do so will lead to political censure and may end with the Minister leaving office. This new convention does not fit into our traditional model of constitutional conventions. It is a rule which identifies a formalised set of rules, and which, by recognising them, renders them constitutionally obligatory. The convention tells Ministers—and those who wish to criticise them for falling short of their duties—that they should look to the Code for an authoritative statement of at least part of ministerial responsibility.

---

[30] See Chapter 7.

[. . .] Even if constitutional scholars baulk at the claim that the Ministerial Code is a legal system, the Code has become steadily more law-like over recent years. It is not a clear, or central, instance of a legal system, but it now possesses many of the characteristic features of a legal system. There may come a point, indeed, we may even have reached this point, when the Code joins the pack of normative systems that roam in the penumbra of law. Along with religious law, international law, lex mercatoria and other such entities, the Code provides an example of the softness of the line between law and other formalised normative systems.

Enforcing constitutional conventions

What happens if a political actor breaches a constitutional convention? Dicey's answer is that, in case of a breach, the courts would not enforce compliance directly, but that violation of conventions leads inexorably to breach of the law (which the courts can enforce).

A.V. Dicey, *Introduction to the Study of the Law of the Constitution* (1885; 10th edn 1959, London: Macmillan & Co), p. 440

Suppose [. . .] that on the passing by both Houses of an important bill, the Queen should refuse her assent to the measure, or (in popular language) put her 'veto' on it. Here there would be a gross violation of usage, but the matter could not by any proceeding known to English law be brought before judges. [. . .] The puzzle is to see what is the force which habitually compels obedience to rules which have not behind them the coercive power of the courts.

He considered three possibilities. The first was impeachment, an ancient procedure by which any person can be prosecuted and tried not in the courts, but by Parliament. Dicey dismissed this (in 1908) as an obsolete practice. Second, he said '*a current answer is, that obedience to the conventional precepts of the constitution is ensured by the force of public opinion*'. He thought that this was an unsatisfactory answer because '*if taken without further explanation, it amounts to little else than a re-statement of the very problem that which it is meant to solve*'. Dicey's third and preferred explanation is as follows.

A.V. Dicey, *Introduction to the Study of the Law of the Constitution* (1885; 10th edn 1959, London: Macmillan & Co), pp. 445–6

[. . .] the sanction which constrains the boldest political adventurer to obey the fundamental principles of the constitution and the conventions in which these principles are expressed, is the fact that the breach of these principles and of these conventions will almost immediately bring the offender into conflict with the courts and the law of the land.

Dicey gave several illustrations of how this worked. If Parliament were not to meet for two years (contrary to the convention that Parliament assembles annually), no law would be broken, but this breach of convention would have several consequences: '[al]*though most taxes would still come into the Exchequer, large proportions of the revenue would cease to be legally* due and could not be legally collected, whilst every official, who acted as collector, would expose himself to actions or prosecutions'. Further, what would happen if the government were to lose a vote of confidence in the House of Commons, but refuse to resign? Dicey's answer is that the House of Commons would refuse to pass the annual Appropriation Act (by which legal authority is given to ministers to spend money from the Consolidated Fund, into which tax revenues are paid), meaning that government expenditure would cease to be legal and could be challenged in the courts.

Jennings was critical of this analysis. He pointed to many instances in which a breach of a convention would not lead to a breach of law—for example, 'all the conventions relating to the conduct of business in the House of Commons' and a departure from the convention of collective ministerial responsibility.[31] More recently, some scholars have begun to argue—against constitutional orthodoxy—that there are circumstances in which the courts can, and should, be prepared to enforce constitutional rules directly. The following extract is the conclusion drawn by Professor Trevor Allan at the end of a discussion of the Supreme Court of Canada's judgment in *Re: Resolution to amend the Constitution*.[32] The Federal Government of Canada wanted to repatriate the Canadian constitution. Up to that point, the statute law that formed the basis of Canada's constitution was an Act of the UK Parliament (the British North America Act 1867), reflecting Canada's history as a dominion of the United Kingdom. Some provinces in Canada were opposed to the repatriation proposals and challenged the planned resolution of the two Houses of Parliament in Canada (which was to be in the form of an address to the Queen, requesting this reform). The provinces opposed to the change argued that any amendment to the constitutional system could not occur without the consent of the provinces of Canada. The majority of the court accepted that there was a convention that provinces consent, but held that the powers of the two Canadian Houses of Parliament were unlimited as a matter of law. Allan disagreed with this approach.

T.R.S. Allan, 'Law, conventions, prerogative: Reflections prompted by the *Canadian Constitutional Case*' [1986] Cambridge Law Journal 305

The present argument envisages that the validity of a statute might properly give way, in an extreme case, to the force of convention. On one view, the fundamental nature of the convention threatened in the Canadian patriation case would justify that result. Such a result would obviously be rare. There is no reason, however, why legal remedies should not be granted in support of a convention, where that convention enjoys a firm foundation in principle. In substance, the Crossman Diaries case acknowledged that possibility.[33] As a source of law, a constitutional convention could rarely prevail over the explicit terms of an Act of Parliament: legislative supremacy is itself a major component of our conventional morality. [. . .] the authority of Parliament to legislate for Canada could not be constrained—as a matter of English law—by any convention requiring dominion consent. It does not follow, however, that convention may not be an important source of law governing the interpretation of statute, or influencing the development of the common law. As a practical matter, the enforcement of any particular convention must normally involve the application of existing

---

[31] See Chapter 7.
[32] [1981] 1 SCR 753.
[33] In *Attorney-General v Jonathan Cape Ltd* [1976] QB 752, the government attempted to suppress the publication of *Diaries of a Cabinet Minister*, an account of life as a government minister by Richard Crossman MP, on the grounds that it breached the constitutional conventions that Cabinet proceedings are confidential and of collective ministerial responsibility.

legal doctrine in order to provide a suitable remedy. The equitable doctrine protecting matters of confidence, in Crossman, and the rules of natural justice, in GCHQ, were harnessed to supply a legal remedy for breach of convention.[34] The sharp law/convention dichotomy, however, neglects the sense in which recognition of convention by the courts has a normative aspect. It imports an application of political principle. The traditional orthodoxy is worth contesting because it obscures the important sense in which constitutional morality is a legitimate source of law. It rests on a separation of legal from political principle which, in the last analysis, cannot be sustained.

Concordats, codes, etc.

Most—perhaps almost all—conventions now exist in written form of various kinds. Different parts of the government system have, from time to time, set down in writing the principles and key aspects of practice governing their relationship, called 'memoranda of understanding' or 'concordats'. These are in essence agreements to create a convention or set of conventions to regulate a particular relationship. The driving force for the creation of a concordat has often been constitutional reform—devolution, changes to the office of Lord Chancellor, and alterations in the role of local authorities. Examples include:

i) In October 1999, the UK government and governments of Scotland, Wales, and Northern Ireland signed a memorandum of understanding (latest version in March 2010), agreements on the working of the Joint Ministerial Committee, and concordats on issues such as coordination of EU policy and financial assistance to industry.[35]

ii) In January 2004, Lord Woolf (Lord Chief Justice) and Lord Falconer of Thoroton (Lord Chancellor) negotiated arrangements on the principles that should govern the future relationship between the judiciary of England and Wales, and the minister responsible for judiciary-related matters.[36]

iii) In December 2007, the UK government and Local Government Association agreed the 'Central–Local Concordat' to establish '*a framework of principles for how central and local government work together to serve the public*' in England and Wales.[37]

These concordats are regarded as political in character and were not envisaged by those who made them to be enforceable by the courts. For example, the devolution memorandum of understanding states that it '*is a statement of political intent, and should not be interpreted as a binding agreement. It does not create legal obligations between the parties. It is intended to be binding in honour only*'. Whether concordats turn out to be a no-go area for courts may be open to question: the courts might view as unattractive an argument that one party to a carefully negotiated agreement should be able to breach it with impunity. What is the constitutional status of concordats? In the following extract, Professor Richard Rawlings considers the use of concordats in the context of devolution.

---

[34] In the *GCHQ* case (*Council of Civil Service Unions v Minister for the Civil Service* [1985] AC 374), trade unions—which had, in the past, always been consulted on changes to terms and conditions of employment—sought judicial review of a unilateral decision by Mrs Thatcher to ban workers at an intelligence-gathering agency from belonging to an independent trade union. See Chapter 9 and Chapter 16.

[35] http://www.scotland.gov.uk/About/Government/concordats

[36] http://webarchive.nationalarchives.gov.uk/+/http:/www.dca.gov.uk/consult/lcoffice/judiciary.htm

[37] http://www.communities.gov.uk/documents/localgovernment/pdf/601000.pdf

Richard Rawlings, 'Concordats of the constitution' (2000) 116 Law Quarterly Review 257, 258, 279

There is currently evolving another species of pseudo-contract, which is of major constitutional significance. Devolution to Scotland, Wales and Northern Ireland spawns a raft of inter-institutional administrative agreements between the U.K. Government and the devolved administrations. In fact 'concordatry', to adopt the Whitehall term, constitutes one of the main pillars of the novel devolutionary architecture of the United Kingdom. It is soft law or 'administrative quasi-legislation' par excellence.

The new style pseudo-contract is not the old style constitutional convention. Far more specific and detailed, the concordats represent a further step down the road of juridification in the form of 'bureaucratic law'. They involve establishing the ground rules for administrative co-operation and exchanges of information: in lawyer's parlance, a form of 'codification' of the (previously internal) processes of government. The purpose, according to Ministers, is to preserve the good working relationships that existed under the old Whitehall model incorporating territorial departments. [. . .]

Concordatry involves a reworking of the informal character of the British Constitution. The use of pseudo-contract is thus a minimum response to the demand for intergovernmental structures and processes that is the inevitable consequence of devolution. The great stress on flexibility and scope for institutional learning is indicative of an evolutionary approach. The current development may in this way prove an embryonic form of intergovernmental relations. Different but related is the close fit with the administrative and constitutional values of co-operation, co-ordination and partnership typically associated with the general New Labour project of modernisation and newly textured democratic culture. The preference for soft law techniques represents a deliberate constitutional choice.

Viewed in comparative perspective, the United Kingdom is thus seen at the end of a spectrum of systems of intergovernmental relations. The classification is the standard legal one of formal structures and institutional processes by reference to the sources of authority. Constitutional status, statutory underpinning, judicial recognition, and pure soft law: the categories serve to illustrate the propensity of different systems to various combinations of mix and match. The blanket use in the United Kingdom of pseudo-contract is the more striking in view of the qualitative differences in the territorial models of devolution. At one and the same time, there is a formal symmetry and a real substantive asymmetry in the relationships with central government. To push home the point, the argument for statutory underpinning or flanking measures may be said to carry greater force in the case of Wales, precisely because of the strong dependency of the National Assembly under the scheme of executive devolution.

Waving a piece of paper is not always apt to inspire confidence. Concordats may be designed to foster co-operation and goodwill but are also by their very nature highly dependent for effective operations on there being concord. In evaluation, it is important to bear in mind the strong dynamics in the new modalities of intergovernmental relations, and, further, the different mixes in concordatry of political and administrative involvement. [. . .]

In July 2007, the House of Lords Constitution Committee considered the concordat relating to judiciary–government relations.

House of Lords Constitution Committee, Relations between the Executive, the Judiciary and Parliament, Sixth Report, Session 2006–07, HL 151

13. Soon after that announcement [in June 2003, that the government planned to abolish the office of Lord Chancellor, Lord Woolf (then Lord Chief Justice) and Lord Falconer (then Lord Chancellor) started negotiations over the key principles and principal arrangements that should govern the new situation in which the Lord Chief Justice rather than the Lord Chancellor would be head of the judiciary. The outcome of those talks was set out in January 2004 in an agreement known as "the Concordat" (formally entitled "The Lord Chancellor's judiciary-related functions: Proposals"). Many aspects of the Concordat were put on a statutory footing by the CRA [Constitutional Reform Act 2005], but it is clear to us that the Concordat continues to be of great constitutional importance.

14. Lord Falconer agreed with this: "it seems to me to be a document of constitutional significance because, although much of it was then enacted in the Constitutional Reform Act, it sets out the basic principles on which the judges and the executive will relate to each other in the future. I have never known any piece of legislation to be utterly comprehensive; there are bound to be issues that come up in the future where it is the principle that matters rather than precise detailed legislation and I believe the Concordat will be important for that" (Q 41). Similarly, the current Lord Chief Justice, Lord Phillips, told us: "I would like to think it has an entrenched quality about it. It has certainly been treated as if it were a constitutional document laying down the division of functions, now largely of course overtaken by the Act but not exclusively, and where the Act does not cover something one needs to go back to the Concordat" (Appendix 8, Q 6).

15. On the question of whether the Concordat might be amended in the future, Professor Robert Hazell of the UCL Constitution Unit suggested that "it has the status of a constitutional convention, and all constitutional conventions are liable to evolve over time in the light of experience and new circumstances, and I would be very surprised if the Concordat did not itself evolve partly in its interpretation, as other conventions have evolved, but partly it could be revisited, and I hope at some point it will be revisited, and possibly this inquiry could provide the trigger for that. I do not think myself it is written in tablets of stone" (Q 473).

Another way in which conventions may be written down is as a 'code'. These differ from concordats in that they are not the subject of negotiation between different institutions or office-holders, but published by one part of government. Examples include: *The Ministerial Code*, governing the conduct of ministers, issued by the Prime Minister[38] and *The Code of Practice on Consultation*, setting out how the UK government will consult the public and interested organizations about proposals to change policy.[39]

(e) EUROPEAN UNION LAW

The United Kingdom has been a member state of what is now the European Union since January 1973. A consequence of membership of the European Union is that executive,

---

[38] http://www.cabinetoffice.gov.uk/sites/default/files/resources/ministerial-code-may-2010.pdf discussed in Chapter 7.

[39] http://www.bis.gov.uk/files/file47158.pdf discussed in Chapter 10.

legislative, and judicial decisions on many fields of policy are now made through or influenced by EU institutions. We examine this in Chapter 8 (executive power), Chapter 12 (legislation), and Chapter 18 (EU law in the courts of the United Kingdom).

For the purposes of the present discussion of the United Kingdom's dispersed constitutional rulebook, it is sufficient to note that EU membership has changed what is arguably *the* most basic rule of the UK constitution. Prior to 1973, it was clear that Acts of the UK Parliament were the highest form of law recognised in the constitutional system.[40] Almost a decade before the United Kingdom's accession to the European Economic Community (the forerunner of the EU), the court of the EEC had ruled in a landmark judgment that European Community (now EU) law has supremacy over national law, where there is a conflict between the two.[41] From the word go, membership has therefore qualified orthodox ideas of parliamentary supremacy.[42] The UK court system faced up to the practical consequence of this new rule in the 1990s, when for the first time British judges were asked by a party (Spanish owners of fishing vessels, arguing that they were being discriminated against on grounds of their nationality) to suspend the operation of an Act of Parliament (the Merchant Shipping Act 1988).[43]

(f) INTERNATIONAL LAW

A final place to try to locate rules relevant to the United Kingdom's dispersed constitutional rulebook is in international law. Until the 1950s, the subject matter of international law was largely confined to high-level agreements between the governments of nation states that had little impact on either internal constitutional arrangements or the rights of individual citizens. In the past fifty years, this has changed dramatically. What happens *within* national constitutional systems is becoming increasingly influenced and constrained by transnational institutions and agreements between countries.

The term 'globalization' is used to describe the momentous and complex changes in the way in which we live and do business. One strand in the phenomena is technology: electronic communications and air travel have transformed the ability of people and business enterprises to reach each other. A second strand is the development of a single global market. Goods and services are increasingly traded across national frontiers. The World Trade Organization (WTO) was established in 1993 to enforce a system of free trade agreed between the majority of the world's countries.[44] A third thread is the rise and acceptance of the notion of universal human rights and the establishment of international judicial bodies to protect them. The treatment of people by national governments is no longer regarded as a purely domestic matter; instead, people are viewed as universally having 'rights' by virtue of being human and these rights cannot be withdrawn by the national laws of any state.[45]

Globalization also describes the fact that multinational organizations are increasingly determining the collective policies to be followed within nation states, especially in defence and security matters through bodies such as the United Nations (UN), the North Atlantic Treaty Organization (NATO), and the Western European Union (WEU). This is a recognition that,

---

[40] See Chapter 2.

[41] Case 6/64 *Falminio Costa v ENEL* [1964] ECR 585; discussed in Chapter 18.

[42] Discussed further in Chapter 2.

[43] *R v Secretary of State for Transport, ex parte Factortame Ltd. and ors (No. 1)* [1990] 2 AC 85, discussed in Chapter 18.

[44] http://www.wto.org for a critique, see John Gray, *False Dawn: Delusions of Global Capitalism* (1998, London: Granta).

[45] See Chapter 6.

in a world in which nuclear and biological weapons exist, no single nation state is any longer capable of fulfilling the most fundamental need of its citizens for physical protection. Policing citizens too, is becoming a matter for international cooperation and collective decision-making through bodies such as Interpol: no nation state in isolation is now capable of dealing with drug smuggling, money laundering, terrorism, or international fraud. Our constitutional system—and the citizens within it—are not hermetically sealed off from the rest of the world.

There are two main forms of international law: customary international law and treaties.

Customary international law

Shaheed Fatima, *Using International Law in Domestic Courts* (2005, Oxford: Hart Publishing), pp. 38–43

2.13 Customary international law [...] has two constituent elements: the actually widespread and consistent conduct of states ('state practice') and the belief that such conduct is required because a rule of law renders it obligatory ('*opinio juris*').

2.14 To constitute state practice for the purpose of creating a rule of customary international law, the rule must have endured over time and achieved a wide level of consistency and acceptance. There is no specific time limit for which the practice must exist before it can be elevated into a rule of customary international law. Instead, this will depend on, for example, the subject matter of the rule, the nature of the state practice and the extent of its observance. [...]

2.15 *Opinio juris* is the belief, by states, that the relevant conduct is required because a rule of law renders it obligatory.

2.16 Within rules of customary international law, certain principles have the status of *jus cogens*. *Jus cogens*, or peremptory norms of customary international law, are principles of an acknowledged superiority: those which refer to the obligations of a state to the international community in general, rather than one to a group of states, also known as obligations *erga omnes*. Examples of *jus cogens* include the prohibition of genocide, the prohibition of torture and the right to self-determination. Before a rule can become a peremptory norm it must be established as a principle of international law and also accepted as part of *jus cogens*.

Customary international law is a source of English common law and may be relied on in the UK courts.

Evelyn Ellis, 'Sources of Law and the Hierarchy of Norms', in D. Feldman (ed.) *English Public Law*, 2nd edn (2009, Oxford: OUP), ch. 1B, paras 1.173–1.175 (footnotes omitted)

1.173 The remaining part of international law, 'customary international law', derives like the common law from long usage and judicial decisions. There has been, and still is, some debate about the precise way in which such customary international law influences the content of English law. The original view was that customary international law was automatically incorporated into English law. This theory owed much to the notion of 'natural law' which was considered in medieval times to be the ultimate source of both the common law and the law governing relations between one sovereign and another; each was a manifestation in its own sphere of the law of nature. However, during the 19th and 20th centuries, this approach gave way to a more reluctant admission of customary international law by the English courts. International law was by that date regarded as requiring transformation into English law, which meant that it required an act of positive acceptance by the courts or by Parliament. Lord Atkin encapsulated this view in *Chung Chi Cheung v R* [1939] AC 167–168:

'[S]o far, at any rate, as the Courts of this country are concerned, international law has no validity save in so far as its principles are accepted and adopted by our own domestic law. There is no external power that imposes its rules upon our own code of substantive law or procedure. The Courts acknowledge the existence of a body of rules which nations accept amongst themselves. On any judicial issue they seek to ascertain what the relevant rule is, and, having found it, they will treat it as incorporated into the domestic law, so far as it is not inconsistent with rules enacted by statutes or finally declared by their tribunals.'

1.174 The problem presented by this second view is that, if followed slavishly, it could embed in English law an outdated version of an international rule. The approach therefore taken today appears to be that adopted by the majority of the Court of Appeal in *Trendtex Trading v Bank of Nigeria* [[1977] 1 QB 529], namely to acknowledge that the rules of customary international law change with the times and that it is the modern manifestation of an old rule which is to be applied by the courts. In the words of Lord Denning MR:

'Seeing that the rules of international law have changed—and do change—and that the courts have given effect to the changes without any Act of Parliament, it follows to my mind inexorably that the rules of international law, as existing from time to time, do form part of our English law.'

1.175 Whatever the mechanism by which international law, whether customary or treaty-based, finds its way into the substantive content of English law, as Lord Atkin pointed out it is certain that it can always be ousted by an Act of Parliament.

Treaties

James Crawford, 'Treaties', in P. Cane and J. Conaghan (eds) *The New Oxford Companion to Law* (2007, Oxford: OUP), p. 1193

A treaty is an agreement under international law, usually between states but also between other subjects of international law, in particularly international organizations. There is no specific requirements of form, though the Vienna Convention on the law of Treaties of 1969—the accepted statement of the law—says that a treaty should be in writing. Exchanges of notes may constitute a treaty and the name of the document is not decisive. How parties conclude treaties is also left for them to agree. Treaties may be binding on signature or provide for subsequent ratification. It is normal for multinational treaties to require ratification or, for non-signatories, accession. [. . .]

Treaties address a vast range of topics, from bilateral interstate relations to the regulation of the world political and economic order. Most subjects of international concern are now regulated by multilateral treaty and the number of multilateral treaties has increased correspondingly. The Consolidated Treaty Series contains some 466 multilateral treaties from 1864 to 1919; the League of Nations Treaty Series and the United Nations Treaty Series include 3,462 multilateral treaties in force. [. . .] Sometimes the major instruments are regional, as with economic integration agreements (the treaties covering the European Union, the North American Free Trade Agreement, and so on). In the field of human rights much standard setting is done by universal agreements, but the most important implementing mechanisms are regional (Europe (1950), the Americas (1969), Africa (1981)).

Note use of the term 'regional'. International lawyers use the term to refer to parts of the world (such as Europe); constitutional lawyers use the term for parts of a nation state (such as 'north-east England').

Constitutional systems vary in terms of how they recognize treaties. Broadly, there are two possible arrangements. In 'monist' systems, a treaty entered into by the government of the state is self-executing in the national legal system and becomes a source of law that may be applied by the national courts.

In 'dualist' systems (such as the United Kingdom), treaties become a source of law recognized by the national courts only if, and to the extent that, they are expressly incorporated into domestic law by national legislation. The constitutional rationale for this is that the government, exercising the prerogative power of signing and ratifying treaties, should not be able to create laws that have not been agreed to by the UK Parliament. Some treaties are never incorporated (because there is no need to create any domestic law to support their implementation); and there may also be a gap in time between the government ratifying a treaty and the UK Parliament enacting legislation (for example, the ECHR was ratified in 1951, but was not given legal effect in national law until October 2000, when the Human Rights Act 1998 was brought into force).

Harry Woolf, Jeffery Jowell, and Andrew Le Sueur, *de Smith's Judicial Review* (2007, London: Sweet & Maxwell), paras 5.044–5.045

It is wrong to think of incorporation as a single phenomenon; a treaty may be received into and given effect in the law of England and Wales in more than one way. The most straightforward situation is where an Act of Parliament is enacted to bring a treaty into English law, but even here there are various drafting techniques. In some Acts, the text or part of the text, of a treaty has been "copied out"; in others parliamentary counsel have used English statutory language to give general effect to the treaty (but which may, upon proper interpretation, confer rights that are narrower or broader than those contained in the treaty). There are other ways of bringing about incorporation—including what may variously be called "indirect" or "for practical purposes" or an "informal mode" of incorporation. Thus, s. 2 of the Asylum and Immigration Act 1993 provides, under the heading "Primacy of the Convention" that "Nothing in the immigration rules [made under the Immigration Act 1971] shall lay down any practice which would be contrary to the Convention"—a reference to the Convention and Protocol relating to the Status of Refugees.

If a treaty has been incorporated (by whatever technique) into domestic law, the question then is how should the courts approach the task of interpreting the treaty. The language of treaties is often broader and more open-textured than the precise wording that is the earmark of English statutory drafting. The Vienna Convention on the Law of Treaties 1969, especially Arts 31–33, provides the basic guidelines. Generally, it can be said that: 151 the starting point is the language and structure of the text in question; words should be given the natural and ordinary meaning, avoiding over-sophisticated analysis and "prolonged debate about the niceties of language"; treaties may contain implied as well as express provisions; where a provision is ambiguous, "the interpretation which is less onerous to the State owing the Treaty obligation is to be preferred" and regard may be had to the *traveaux préparatoires*; good faith is required in the interpretation and performance of a treaty; the provisions "must be read together as part and parcel of the scheme" of the treaty; relevant reservations and derogations must be considered; and, above all, a broad, purposive interpretation is required.

> The court must not lose sight of the fact that it is an international legal instrument that is being interpreted, and that its concepts have a meaning that is autonomous of the particularities of a domestic legal system. Interpretations reached by courts in other national systems is of persuasive authority; inevitably, however, courts in different legal systems may reach interpretations that are difficult to reconcile.

Unincorporated treaties—those that have not been expressly enacted into national legislation—are not entirely ignored by the courts in the United Kingdom. If a court is interpreting an ambiguous word or concept in legislation and there is a treaty—whether incorporated or unincorporated—covering the same area of policy, it will be assumed that the legislation was intended by Parliament to conform to the United Kingdom's international law obligations.[46] An unincorporated treaty may also create a ground of review called 'legitimate expectation' in which a claimant may argue that a public body (here, a minister) is bound by an assurance (here, any assurances set out in the unincorporated treaty).[47]

QUESTIONS

1. In terms of their importance, how would you rank the various sources of the United Kingdom's 'dispersed constitutional rulebook'?

2. How significant is *The Cabinet Manual*? What is its status? Should it be regularly debated in Parliament? What are the implications of its publication for the future development of the UK constitution?

3. A Martian lands in the United Kingdom and, wanting to know about the country's constitution, reads the statute book. (Martians are fast and accurate readers.) What will the Martian learn about the constitution? What gaps will there be in the Martian's understanding if this is all it reads?

4. What are the similarities and differences between constitutional conventions and laws dealing with important constitutional rules?

5. In what ways are norms of international law part of the United Kingdom's constitutional rulebook?

6. On the basis of the evidence you have read so far in this chapter, in what senses (if any) is it correct to say that the United Kingdom has an 'unwritten constitution'.

---

3 THE CONSTITUITON AS A SYSTEM

The preceding section focused on the constitution as providing a rulebook. We now need to stand back from the rulebook to see what patterns, traditions, and values can be discerned—explicitly or implicitly—from the rules. The starting point for many accounts of the UK constitution is the 'Westminster model' or 'Westminster constitutionalism'. This refers to a set of arrangements in which:

---

[46] *R v Secretary of State for the Home Department, ex parte Brind* [1991] 1 AC 696, 747, 760. For an example, see *Cheney v Conn (Inspector of Taxes)* [1968] 1 WLR 242, discussed in Chapter 2.

[47] *R v Secretary of State for the Home Department, ex parte Ahmed* [1999] Imm AR 22 (CA); see Chapter 16.

i) the government of the country[48] is drawn from the House of Commons (so, not a presidential system, as in many other countries);

ii) the UK Parliament is at the pinnacle of the constitutional system, with unlimited legislative competence (so, no constitutional or supreme court with powers to strike down Acts of Parliament); and

iii) there are effective systems for ensuring that ministers are politically accountable to Parliament between elections.

(a) THE WESTMINISTER MODEL

The following explanation of the Westminster system was set out in a government White Paper[49] on reform of the House of Lords, issued by the government during Tony Blair's premiership. You will see that reference is made to 'the Crown': we will examine the meaning of 'the Crown' in more detail later,[50] but here it is sufficient to note that, up to the seventeenth century, in relation to executive functions,[51] it generally meant the king or queen; in modern times, most powers of the Crown are exercised by the Prime Minister and other senior ministers. In relation to the making of Acts of Parliament ('the Crown in Parliament'), the Crown's role is to give royal assent to Bills passed by Parliament; this is done formally in the name of the monarch.[52]

The House of Lords: Completing the Reform, A Government White Paper
Presented to Parliament by the Prime Minister by Command of Her Majesty,
Cm 5291 (November 2001)

13. The United Kingdom is a Parliamentary democracy. Sovereignty rests with the Crown in Parliament. Law making rests with the tripartite sovereignty of Crown in both Houses of Parliament.

14. In practice, the powers of the three parts are uneven. The history of the development of our democracy has been the history of the gradual growth of the power of the Commons compared to the other two elements. The Crown, or Executive, has over the centuries become increasingly accountable to Parliament for its exercise of its powers. Within Parliament, power has transferred from the Lords to the Commons. The Commons has from as far back as the 15th century asserted the sole right to grant or withhold supply.[53] The changes to the public finances since the 17th century, with the end of the practice of granting the yield of certain taxes for life, coupled with the increasing need of the Government for money as the demands on it rose, enabled the Commons to turn that right into a formidable weapon to demand accountability. Since 1678, when the Commons formally resolved that "all aids and supplies, and aids to His Majesty in Parliament, are the sole gift of the Commons", the Lords

---

[48] In other words, 'the executive' or 'ministers': see Part II Introduction of this book.

[49] A 'White Paper' is a document written by civil servants in the name of a minister and formally published as a 'Command Paper' under the authority of Parliament; typically they are used to set out policy plans. More recent ones are at http://www.official-documents.gov.uk

[50] See Chapter 7.

[51] On executive functions, see the Part II Introduction.

[52] See Chapter 10.

[53] In other words, to give legal permission to the government to spend money from funds collected through taxation or borrowing.

has rarely even attempted to challenge that position. On the most famous occasion when it did so, in 1909, this led directly to reductions in its powers.

15. The basis on which the Commons asserted its right was always its position as the representative body of the people, even in the days when the people who elected it comprised a small minority of even the adult male population. Beginning with the 1832 Reform Act, the gradual extension of the franchise increased the authority of the Commons. It is now elected on a universal franchise and enables the people to give a clear and unequivocal answer to the question "Whom do you choose to govern you?" The UK's political system is built around that principle.

16. The House of Commons has thus long since been established as the pre-eminent constitutional authority within the UK. The Government is formed by the Party which can command the support of the House of Commons. A Government which loses the support of the people's elected representatives in the Commons cannot remain in office. General Elections return individual MPs who are expected to look to the interests of their constituents irrespective of Party affiliation. They are also contests between political parties vying for supremacy in the House of Commons. The Party which secures a majority has the right to form a Government and, subject to sustaining its Parliamentary majority, to carry through the programme set out in its election Manifesto. Ministers are continuously accountable to the House of Commons through debates and votes; a process formalised and fortified by the role of the non-Government Parties in forming an Opposition, with the largest non-Government Party occupying the position of Official Opposition. Governed largely by convention, Britain's constitutional practice is flexible enough to accommodate alternative arrangements, including coalition Governments formed by the major political parties; but these have occurred only in exceptional circumstances (including the two World Wars),[54] and even then the House of Commons has continued to perform its functions of legitimising the Government, enacting legislation and holding Ministers to account.

17. This constitutional framework, founded on the pre-eminence of the House of Commons, has provided Britain with effective democratic Government and accountability for more than a century, and few would wish to change it. [...]

A key principle in the Westminster model is the idea and practice of 'accountability'. We return to explore this in Chapter 7 and for now the following explanation will suffice.

Andrew Le Sueur, 'Accountability', in P. Cane and J Conaghan (eds) *The New Oxford Companion to Law* (2008, Oxford: OUP), pp. 7–8

Accountability is a principle which requires public authorities to explain their actions and be subject to scrutiny. It may also entail sanctions, such as resignation from office or censure. Effective accountability depends on a commitment to open government and rights to freedom of information. The news media and pressure groups also play vital roles in ensuring that accountability is achieved.

---

54 This was written before the formation in May 2010 of the Conservative–Liberal Democrat coalition government.

In a democracy, the ultimate form of public accountability is through elections. In the UK, for example, MPs sit in the House of Commons and councillors serve on local authorities. However, elections can only provide periodic and partial opportunities for calling those in power to account because much public sector activity is carried out by unelected officials and appointees.

Political accountability between elections is therefore important. In systems of parliamentary government, ministers are members of parliament and hold office individually and collectively for only so long as they enjoy the confidence of their fellow members of the legislature. Ministers are held to account on a day-to-day basis through parliamentary questions (written and oral), in debates on the floor of the chambers of parliament, and through the work of policy scrutiny committees (called 'select committees' in the UK Parliament).

Courts too may be regarded as mechanisms for securing accountability. Individuals, groups and businesses may use judicial review procedures to challenge the lawfulness of action taken by public authorities. Especially where human rights are at stake, there is a growing 'culture of justification' in which government must present cogent explanations for its actions to the courts. Yet, *quis custodiet ipsos custodes?*—'who will watch the watchmen?' It is sometimes said that the principle of judicial independence prevents judges from being held to account for their decisions. Certainly it would be constitutionally wrong for government to impose sanctions on courts which made politically unpalatable decisions. However, judges and courts are subject to accountability insofar as they must explain and justify their decisions (for example, by giving reasoned judgments in public). [. . .]

Some commentators complain that the 'accountability revolution' has gone too far. Rather than promoting the legitimacy of public institutions, it now risks undermining public confidence in them. Others express different concerns, for example, that changes in the way we are governed has created an accountability deficit. Globalization has shifted decision-making in some spheres to international institutions—such as the European Union, World Trade Organisation, and the United Nations. Privatization has resulted in some public functions being carried out by non-governmental bodies (including businesses and charities). On both these contexts, it is open to question whether adequate accountability arrangements have been established.

(b) PROBLEMS WITH THE WESTMINSTER MODEL

Many constitutional scholars, commentators, and active participants would dismiss an account of the constitution based on the Westminster model in the terms set out in the White Paper *The House of Lords: Completing the Reform*, on pp. 27–8. as a fiction (not, as the government presumably intended, a factual account). There are certainly grounds for criticizing the Westminster model as a realistic explanation of how the modern British constitution operates in practice.

Government control of the House of Commons

First, the Westminster model presents a picture of the government being held in check by Parliament. The reality is more that Parliament (especially the House of Commons) is controlled by the government, not the other way around. Except for the occasional private member's Bill, the government has exclusive use of the legislative procedures to steer through the legislation that it has drafted. The government controls the agenda and timetable followed by the House of Commons, with inadequate opportunities for MPs outside government to initiate debates and call ministers to account. It is questionable how well the procedures for asking ministers questions work.[55]

From Cabinet to prime ministerial government?

Peering inside government, it is also possible to detect changes in the role of the Prime Minister and the Cabinet (the committee of twenty or so senior ministers selected by the Prime Minister to give political leadership to government departments). The experiences of government during the tenure of Margaret Thatcher (1979–90) and Tony Blair (1997–2007) are interpreted by many commentators as periods of prime ministerial, rather than collective Cabinet government. John Major (1990–97) and Gordon Brown (2007–2010) are often seen as administrations in which the Cabinet had more influence over government decision-making. The Conservative–Liberal Democrat coalition government formed after the 2010 election has required a more collaborative approach by David Cameron.

The rise and rise of delegated legislation

As we shall see in Chapter 11, the vast bulk of legislation is now made in the form of delegated legislation by ministers (on the advice of civil servants) rather than by Acts of Parliament. The role of the UK Parliament in scrutinizing the making of delegated legislation is far more limited than it is in relation to primary legislation, calling into question the idea that elected representatives are the heart of the legislative process.

Multilevel governing: European integration and devolution

Another challenge to the idea of the Westminster model is multilevel governing.[56] In recent decades, the UK Parliament and the UK government have ceased to be the sole legislative and executive body. In 1973, the United Kingdom became a member of the European Economic Community (EEC), which, in the ensuing years, has transmogrified into the European Union. Decision-making, legislation, and court rulings in many fields of policy are now strongly influenced by EU law.[57]

Within the United Kingdom, in 1998, a programme of decentralizing executive and legislative powers to new institutions in Scotland, Wales, and Northern Ireland was started. As has often been remarked, devolution is a 'process not an event' and there have been almost constant debates about the transfer of greater powers to the government systems in these three parts of the United Kingdom.[58] Against this background, the Westminster model can no longer provide a satisfactorily comprehensive account of the main features of the modern British constitutional set-up.

The rise of the judges?

A further development that calls into question the traditional account of the Westminster model is the dramatic rise of the powers of judges in the constitutional system. As a result of

---

[55] See Chapter 7.
[56] See Chapter 5.
[57] See Chapter 8 and Chapter 12.
[58] See Chapter 5.

European integration, judges in two international courts—the European Court of Human Rights (based in Strasbourg, France) and the Court of Justice of the European Union (based in Luxembourg)—have influence over the development of public policy in those fields of law over which they have jurisdiction. The Human Rights Act 1998 and the European Communities Act 1972 require domestic courts to look to the case law of the two European courts. Leaving the influence of the two branches of European law to one side, British judges have, in the past 40 years, used their powers to develop the common law to create a modern system of judicial review of executive action and delegated legislation.

An institutional crisis?

A final difficulty for the Westminster model is the crisis of public confidence that has enveloped the UK Parliament. Turnouts of voters at elections have declined and there are very low levels of trust in politicians. This came to a head during 2009, after revelations in the news media about the expenses that MPs and peers were claiming. Some claims were dishonest and broke the criminal law; some were clearly contrary to the rules in place at the time; others were excessive or unnecessary. By international standards, this was not major corruption. Nonetheless, a 2009 Ipsos/Mori opinion poll found that 71 per cent of the public were dissatisfied with how Parliament was doing its job.[59] After much feet-dragging, and then an unseemly rush, the Parliamentary Standards Act 2009 was enacted to create an independent body to deal with future expenses claims by MPs—a major constitutional innovation because, until that time, it had been regarded as important that the UK Parliament should be self-regulating. Further, in May 2009, the House of Lords took action, unprecedented in modern times, to suspend two peers from membership for six months after they were found to have offered to use their influence in return for financial payment. Against this background, the idea of placing the UK Parliament at the centre of the constitution may not be as attractive as it was in the past.

(c) WHAT IS THE FUTURE OF THE WESTMINSTER MODEL?

If it is true to say that the old Westminster model of the British constitution is ill, dying, or dead, what should be done? The answer is controversial, and politicians, commentators, and scholars disagree. In this section, we outline five sets of proposals that have, in recent times, been placed on the political agenda, aimed at:

   i) attempting to reinvigorate the Westminster system;
   ii) creating opportunities for people to participate more directly in government decision-making;
   iii) embracing a more 'legal' constitution in which judges would have a greater role;
   iv) the disintegration of the United Kingdom as a single nation state; and
   v) disengagement from the processes of European integration.

Reinvigorating the Westminster system

Parliament's roles include sustaining the government and holding the government to account. In recent years, there have been a series of reforms of the ways in which the work

---

[59] House of Commons Reform Committee, *Rebuilding the House*, First Report, Session 2008–09, HC 1117.

of the Commons is organized (and to an extent, also the Lords), designed to give Parliament more opportunities to call government to account. These reforms include:

i) the creation of a 'parallel chamber' in Westminster Hall to allow more time for debates on issues raised by select committees (which scrutinize the policies and performance of central government departments);

ii) 'topical debates' on the floor of the Commons to enable MPs to call ministers to account for matters of current concern;

iii) reforms to the legislative process, such as allowing committees of MPs to take expert evidence on the subject matter of Bills being scrutinized;

iv) the government publishing some Bills in draft form some months ahead of the start of the formal start of the legislative process, to enable better consultation and scrutiny;

v) election of chairs of select committees by secret ballot of all members (rather than being chosen behind closed doors by 'the usual channels'—the term used for the business managers in the main political parties);

vi) the creation of a Backbench Business Committee in the House of Commons to consider representations from MPs on topics for debate in the parliamentary time set aside for non-government business; and

vii) the Constitutional Reform and Governance Act 2010 gives the UK Parliament a more formal role in relation to scrutiny of treaty-making.

It remains to be seen to what extent reform of the UK Parliament can rebuild public confidence in the national political system.

Greater emphasis on popular participation?

A second debate over the future of the British constitution concerns ways in which the general public could be better engaged in the process of governing the country. One of the themes in the Labour government's July 2007 Green Paper *Governance of Britain*, published soon after Gordon Brown became Prime Minister, was the need to 'to invigorate our democracy, with people proud to participate in decision-making at every level'.[60] Citizens' juries were formed to discuss issues such as children, crime, and communities, and the future of the National Health Service.

Gordon Brown, 'Speech to the National Council of Voluntary Organizations on Politics' (3 September 2007)[61]

The members of these juries will be chosen independently. Participants will be given facts and figures that are independently verified, they can look at real issues and solutions, just as a jury examines a case. And where these citizens juries are held the intention is to bring people together to explore where common ground exists.

The Coalition government formed in May 2010 has also pursued policies aimed at empowering people and local communities to have greater influence on policy. The slogans 'the Big Society' and 'Localism' are used to encapsulate these initiatives. The Localism Act 2011 aims

---

[60] Secretary of State for Justice and Lord Chancellor, *Governance of Britain*, Cm 7170, para. 10.
[61] http://news.bbc.co.uk/1/hi/uk_politics/6976445.stm.

to renew local democracy. This is achieved by conferring a 'general power of competence': no longer do local authorities have to point to a specific power in an Act of Parliament authorizing them to take action; s. 1 provides that 'A local authority has power to do anything that individuals generally may do'.[62] Part 5 of the 2011 Act, entitled 'Community empowerment' creates a duty to hold local referendums on council tax increases if the Secretary of State believes the increase is 'excessive'. Eleven cities were required to hold referendums on whether there should be directly elected mayors (nine voted 'No') and in a separate initiative, since November 2012 there are elected Police and Crime Commissioners with oversight duties over police constabularies in England and Wales.

In his 2009 book, *The New British Constitution*, Professor Vernon Bogdanor places particular emphasis on the need for the public to participate in government. He argues that the changes in the constitution in recent decades—such as devolution, the Human Rights Act 1998, and the Freedom of Information Act 2000—'*have done little to counteract the widespread disenchantment with politics that characterizes modern Britain, as well as other advanced democracies*'.[63] There are declining turnouts at elections—at local, national, and European levels, especially among younger people—coupled with a steady decline in membership of political parties: Bogdanor alleges that, some 50 years ago, one in eleven of the electorate belonged to a political party, whereas now it is one in eighty-eight.

Vernon Bogdanor, *The New British Constitution* (2009, Oxford: Hart Publishing), p. 297

The real achievement of constitutional reform is to have redistributed power, but it has redistributed power between elites, not between elites and the people. It has redistributed power 'downwards' to politicians in Edinburgh, Cardiff, Belfast and London, 'sideways' to the life peers in the House of Lords and 'sideways' to the judges interpreting the Human Rights Act. The value of this dispersal of power should not be underestimated. It has made it easier for the power of government to be made subject to constitutional control so that twenty-first century Britain is much less of an elective dictatorship than it was in the 1970s when Lord Hailsham first produced his famous characterisation. But constitutional reform has not redistributed power to the voter. It has not shifted power from the politicians to the people. That is the crucial weakness in the constitutional reform programme, as it has so far been implemented. That is the central reason it has made so little impact on entrenched attitudes towards the political system.

So what is Bogdanor's solution? He wants to see a new style of participative democracy in which '*the people are able both to make more decisions for themselves and also more effectively control decisions made by those in government*'.[64] He favours 'open primary elections', run by political parties—a step preceding the official election contest for seats in the House of Commons and other elected bodies. Such a process would move decisions on candidates away from the political party in question (often, in reality, a small committee of died-in-the-wool activists) to include interested members of the general public. A further proposal is greater use of referendums (see Box 1.1).

---

[62] See Chapter 5.
[63] V. Bogdanor, *The New British Constitution* (2009, Oxford: Hart Publishing), p. 291.
[64] Op. cit., p. 300.

Vernon Bogdanor, *The New British Constitution* (2009, Oxford: Hart Publishing), p. 304

So far its use has been strictly limited to those questions defined as 'constitutional' by governments, which have often used it as a tactical weapon. A referendum in Britain remains a weapon under the control of the political class, not, as in countries with codified constitutions, an instrument whose use is determined by the constitution. But the referendum can, in principle, yield legislative power to the people.

BOX 1.1 REFERENDUMS HELD IN THE UNITED KINGDOM

1973 *(Northern Ireland only)* 'Do you want Northern Ireland to remain part of the United Kingdom?' (98.9 per cent 'yes' majority) or 'Do you want Northern Ireland to be joined with the Republic of Ireland outside the United Kingdom?' (1.1 per cent 'yes' minority).

1975 *(Whole UK)* 'Do you think the UK should stay in the European Community (Common Market)?' (67 per cent 'yes' majority).

1978 On devolution in Scotland and Wales.

1998 Three relating to devolution (all with a 'yes' majority): on whether there should be a Scottish Parliament and whether that Parliament should have tax-varying powers *(Scotland only)*; on whether there should be a National Assembly for Wales *(Wales only)*; and on the Belfast Agreement reached by the parties to the peace process *(Northern Ireland only)*.

1998 *(London only)* On the creation of a Mayor for London and the Greater London Assembly (with a 'yes' majority).

2004 *(North-east England region)* On an elected regional assembly (with a 'no' majority).

2011 *(Whole UK)* 'At present, the UK uses the "first past the post" system to elect MPs to the House of Commons. Should the "alternative vote" system be used instead?' (68 per cent voted 'no').

The European Union Act 2011 creates a requirement for a referendum to be held in the United Kingdom if the governments of EU member states decide to amend or replace the basic treaty framework of the European Union.

Direct democracy is not without its drawbacks, as the Labour government recognized in the following extract.

Ministry of Justice, *A National Framework for Greater Citizen Engagement: A Discussion Paper* (July 2008), p. 11

Direct democracy, at the national level, in which the public makes the decision rather than their elected representative has some advantages, but it is not a panacea. It can reduce complex national policy decisions to simple choices which can result in serious public policy problems in the future. National direct democracy can be vulnerable to being manipulated by the wealthy and the powerful who can dominate single-issue campaigns more easily than the complex layers of political activity that characterise the operation of parliamentary democracy. A balance must be struck between increasing the public's participation in decision-making and maintaining the Government's accountability for its actions to the people, their representatives in Parliament and their will expressed in elections.

A more legal constitution?

A different kind of response to the failures of the Westminster model is to argue for a greater role for law, legal processes, and the judiciary in the constitution. This would build on developments that have already occurred with the rise of judicial review,[65] the Human Rights Act 1998,[66] and the court's role in relation to enforcing EU law.[67] It is certainly easy to find examples of cases in which the courts have had a major impact of choices made by politicians (see Box 1.2).

BOX 1.2 EXAMPLE OF IMPACTS BY THE COURTS ON GOVERNMENT POLICYMAKING

2001 The Court of Appeal quashed delegated legislation, which had been debated and approved in the Commons and Lords, on the grounds that it was unreasonable (in a legal sense) because in proposing new rules for the expedited return of failed asylum seekers to Pakistan, the government had failed to think carefully about the treatment of women and members of the Ahmadi religious minority.

2002 A major consultation exercise over airport capacity in south-east England was halted when the High Court held that it was unreasonable (in a legal sense) to exclude the possibility of expanding Gatwick Airport from the proposals (see *R (Medway Council and ors) v Secretary of State for Transport* [2002] EWHC 2516 Admin).

2004 The House of Lords held that the scheme for detention without trial under the Anti-terrorism, Crime and Security Act 2001 of foreign nationals who were suspected of involvement in terrorism, but who could not be removed to their home countries, was incompatible with the ECHR. Ministers responded by bringing forward a new scheme of 'control orders', which, in turn, was subjected to judicial scrutiny and the imposition of procedural standards that ministers considered seriously undermined the scheme.[68]

In the following extract, Sir Christopher Foster, a former adviser to both Labour and Conservative governments, sketches out what this might entail (making clear in his book that he views this as an unattractive way forward).

Sir Christopher Foster, *British Government in Crisis* (2005, Oxford: Hart Publishing), pp. 263, 274–5

By a more legal constitution I mean one where some constitutional conventions are replaced by laws—as well as some poor constitutional laws by better laws—so that our constitutional arrangements are clearer and, when necessary, legally enforceable.

---

[65] See Chapter 16.
[66] See Chapter 17.
[67] See Chapter 18.
[68] See Chapter 17.

Broadly there are two variants. The more pragmatic argument is that more law is needed to sort out particular muddles and shortcomings. [. . .] A more extreme position [. . .] is based on such disillusionment with the present political system that—certainly in its more thorough going forms—it wants it largely replaced by legal process. In its less extreme forms it foresees a future in which extended human rights legislation and the courts would transform our political system. But it would be the end of democracy and, if really preferable, a tremendous indictment of our ability to reconstruct our political system to acceptable standards.
[Sir Christopher goes on to speculate about the future.]
The minister's lawmaking role then might become that they have the ideas which germinate into law. As the recipients of grievances, concerns and policy ideas from a mass of sources, their job is then somehow to outline new policies and introduce new bills, which may well continue confused and otherwise bad. Thereafter judges knock them into shape, making them compliant with previous law and pre-determined norms or 'rights'. [. . .]

Some of what permeates the thinking of lawyers—quite the most energetic we have— about our constitution future sees that as that of a participatory democracy, in which Parliament slides into the shadows, and where public opinion is consulted in surveys and focus groups before being reflected in new laws, which are then tested by the courts to ensure that they are consistent with other law and do not infringe rights. If they are inconsistent or infringe primary rights, then the courts adjust them accordingly.

We return in Chapter 2 to the idea that there is a shift from a political, or Westminster model, constitution to a more legal one in the context of debates about the future of parliamentary supremacy and the rule of law.

The disintegration of the United Kingdom?

Political parties exist in the three smaller parts of the United Kingdom—Scotland (the Scottish National Party), Wales (Plaid Cymru), and Northern Ireland (Sinn Fein)—the policies of which include independence or, in the case of Northern Ireland, reunification with the Republic of Ireland. During the first decade of the twenty-first century, ministers from the separatist parties were members of the devolved governments in all three parts of the United Kingdom. The Scottish Government is proposing a referendum on independence in 2014.[69]

Britain out of Europe?

Another response to the changing nature of the Westminster model is campaigns for the United Kingdom's participation in the processes of European integration to end. In recent years, the United Kingdom Independence Party (UKIP) has won some support in elections, becoming the second largest party in the 2009 UK elections for the European Parliament. In the past, important steps towards further integration were taken by Conservative governments—Prime Minister Edward Heath signed the treaty by which the United Kingdom became a member state of the then EEC in 1972 and Prime Minister John Major signed the Maastricht Treaty, which created the European Union. The current Conservative Party leadership has adopted anti-integrationist positions but remains committed to the United Kingdom remaining a member state.

[69] See Chapter 5.

QUESTIONS

1. Does the Westminster model provide a convincing explanation of the modern UK constitution?

2. In order of importance, what do you regard as the five most notable constitutional reforms in the UK since 1997? To what extent have they either challenged or reinforced the Westminster model?

3. What does it mean to say that something is 'constitutional' or 'unconstitutional' in the United Kingdom?

4. A government agency is setting up a website to help to explain the UK constitutional system to members of the general public. An introductory page of no more than 200 words is needed. What would you write?

5. In what sense(s) can the outcome of the following scenario be said to be democratic? In *Chahal v United Kingdom* (1997) 23 EHRR 413, the European Court of Human Rights (the international court which adjudicates on the ECHR) held that a person may not be deported to a country where he or she will face a real risk of torture or inhuman or degrading treatment. This ruling is binding on the UK government in international law. In 2001, the government proposed legislation to enable ministers to order that foreign nationals suspected of involvement in terrorism be detained in prison without charge or trial in cases in which it was not possible (because of the *Chahal* ruling) to remove them from the United Kingdom. That legislation was passed by Parliament as the Anti-terrorism, Crime and Security Act 2001 (although many MPs were opposed to the proposals). In 2004, judges of the United Kingdom's highest court held that those provisions were incompatible with the ECHR on the grounds that they were disproportionate and discriminatory: see *A v Secretary of State for the Home Department* [2004] UKHL 56. The government responded to this ruling by introducing legislation to repeal the relevant parts of the 2001 Act and create a different way of monitoring suspects (through 'control orders'). In October 2005, 79 per cent of people questioned in a survey in London said that deporting or excluding non-UK citizens who encourage terrorism is acceptable.

4 CONCLUDING COMMENTS

As a first step, this chapter has introduced the UK constitution from the perspectives of a rulebook and a system of governing. We saw that the United Kingdom has what may be called an uncodified or 'dispersed' rulebook: most rules are written down, but not in a single document with legal authority. We will return in Chapter 19 to consider the advantages and disadvantages of adopting a codified constitution.

The chapter moved on to consider the Westminster model and how this has provided the dominant explanation of how the whole system meshes together, but points out that this model now faces several challenges.

The remaining chapters in Part I examine in more detail some of the functions of and principles underpinning the constitutional system: parliamentary supremacy (Chapter 2), the rule of law (Chapter 3), separating and balancing powers (Chapter 4), multilevel governing (Chapter 5) and protecting rights (Chapter 6).

5 FURTHER READING

Bogdanor, V., *The New British Constitution* (2009, Oxford and Portland: Hart Publishing)

Cabinet Office, *The Cabinet Manual: A guide to the laws, conventions and rules on the operation of government* (2011, London: Cabinet Office)

Gordon, R., *Repairing British Politics: A Blueprint for Constitutional Change* (2010, Oxford: Hart Publishing)

Judge, D., 'Whatever happened to parliamentary democracy in the United Kingdom?' (2004) 57 Parliamentary Affairs 682

King, A., *The British Constitution* (2007, Oxford: Oxford University Press)

ONLINE RESOURCE CENTRE

Further information about the themes discussed in this chapter can be found on the Online Resource Centre at www.oxfordtextbooks.co.uk/orc/lesueurt2e/

2

LEGITIMACY IN THE CONSTITUTION AND PARLIAMENTARY SUPREMACY

CENTRAL ISSUES

1. The concept of parliamentary supremacy has a central place in the UK constitution. It asserts that Acts of the UK Parliament are the highest form of law and prevents the judiciary adjudicating on the validity of primary legislation.

2. There is a battle between two broad schools of thought regarding what should provide legitimacy in the UK constitution. For 'political constitutionalists', it is the political process, Parliament, and the principle of parliamentary supremacy that should be central. 'Legal constitutionalists' contend that the judiciary should have a greater role, with power to strike down Acts of Parliament that are contrary to fundamental rights or constitutional principles.

3. There is a debate about whether constitutionally important Acts of Parliament may be 'entrenched', making it more difficult than normal to repeal or amend.

4. The rule of implied repeal states that where a later Act is inconsistent with an earlier Act that remains in force, the courts should recognize the later Act as valid law. Current legal thinking suggests that this rule should not apply where the earlier Act is constitutionally important.

1 INTRODUCTION

There are some despotic governments around the world that try to rule by fear and oppression. (Which ones would be at the top of your list?) But if we accept the idea that constitutional systems embrace the idea of *legitimacy*, we should not regard those tyrannical regimes as being 'constitutional'. Consider carefully the explanation given by Professor Wheare (1907–79).

K.C. Wheare, *Modern Constitutions*, 2nd edn (1966, Oxford: OUP), p. 137

Constitutional government means something more than government according to the terms of a Constitution. It means government according to rule as opposed to arbitrary government; it means government limited by the terms of a Constitution, not government limited only by the desires and capacities of those who exercise power. It might happen, therefore, that although government in a particular country was conducted according to the terms of the Constitution, that Constitution did no more than establish the institutions of government and leave them free to act as they wished. In such a case we would hardly call the government constitutional government. The real justification of Constitutions, the original idea behind them, is that of limiting government and of requiring those who govern to conform to law and rules. Most Constitutions [...] do purport to limit the government. Before we can conclude, however, that a country which has a Constitution limiting the government, has also constitutional government, we must see how the Constitution works in practice, and see in particular whether usage and convention operate to strengthen or to weaken constitutional limitations. In the same way we cannot conclude that a country lacks constitutional government simply because its Constitution appears to impose no limitations on the government; it may well be that further study will show that the ordinary law of the land combined with usage and convention supply those checks which the law of the Constitution did not.

Wheare goes on to say that various forces may '*operate against constitutional government, to weaken and destroy it*'. These include: war; a state of crisis or emergency; and economic distress or difficulty.

Systems of constitutional governance rely on various guiding principles to confer legitimacy on their actions. In relation to the UK constitution, two principles have attracted special attention:

- parliamentary supremacy (the subject matter of this chapter) and
- the rule of law (examined in Chapter 3).

As we shall see, people disagree about these principles, their interrelationships, and their application in the modern British constitution.

2 LEGITIMACY

It is possible to take the view that 'the law is the law is the law'—in other words, that if a law has been made according to a stipulated process and in the prescribed format, then it should in all circumstances be regarded as legitimate. (The stipulated process and prescribed format are, in most countries, laid down in a codified constitutional document.)[1] But what if the process and format are grossly unfair? For example, a constitutional system *could* exclude a proportion of the population from standing for election to the legislature on account of their race and laws might be secret in the sense that the constitution places no obligation on the legislature to publish them. In these circumstances, should the law be treated as legitimate?

---

[1] In the United Kingdom, without a codified constitution, the procedures for making primary legislation are contained in a variety of sources, including Acts of Parliament, the standing orders of each House of Parliament, and conventions: see Chapter 7.

To answer that question, we need to define what is meant by 'legitimacy'. Although this term of political science is not clear-cut, scholars often emphasize the two-sidedness of the concept of legitimacy: it is people's *belief* that they *ought* to comply with a law or decision, and it is a *claim* by institutions of the State that their determinations *ought* to be complied with. For the purposes of this chapter, we can say that conditions of legitimacy exist if, for good reason, people are generally prepared to accept the laws and decisions of public authorities, even though they may disagree with some individual determinations.

QUESTIONS

Think about the following statements that might be made about a controversial policy (for example, banning hunting—a topic at which we look in Chapter 13). What can you infer from each statement about the speaker's view of legitimacy?

1. 'It's the law, so I should comply with it.'

2. 'It may be the law, but this particular law is wrong, so I won't comply with it.'

3. 'Parliament doesn't represent people like me; the judges are out of touch. I don't care what they say about anything.'

Legitimacy is therefore closely related to, but extends beyond, the idea of public compliance or consent.

To understand properly the significance of parliamentary supremacy and the rule of law, we need to place these principles in the context of a vitally important debate about what makes the exercise of government power in modern Britain *legitimate*. There are, broadly speaking, two main competing views held by scholars, politicians, and judges (see Box 2.1 for some of the protagonists). These views can be labelled 'political constitutionalism' and 'legal constitutionalism'.

BOX 2.1 SOME OF THE PROTAGONISTS IN THE POLITICAL VS LEGAL CONSTITUTIONALISM DEBATE

Political constitutionalists	Legal constitutionalists
J.A.G. (John) Griffith (LSE)	Sir Jeffrey Jowell (Bingham Centre for the Rule of Law)
Adam Tomkins (University of Glasgow)	T.R.S. (Trevor) Allan (University of Cambridge)
Keith Ewing (King's College, London)	Lord Steyn (former Law Lord)
Thomas Poole (LSE)	

(a) POLITICAL CONSTITUTIONALISM

In one view, power and the making of law *is and should be legitimized through Parliament*. General elections every four to five years result in the leaders of the largest political party in the House of Commons having authority to form the government and govern the nation. A Prime Minister can say: 'We legitimately rule because we won the election.' In Chapter 7, we see that the government of the UK, and its individual ministers, are able to remain in office for up to five years between elections, but only if they enjoy 'the confidence' of the House of Commons; if this confidence is lost, the Prime Minister must ask the Queen for a dissolution of Parliament, giving rise to a general election. We will examine how, between elections, ministers are held accountable to Parliament through the requirement that they answer questions and explain government policy to Parliament, and are regulated by the constitutional conventions of individual and collective ministerial responsibility. Ministers are thus able to say 'we legitimately have power to develop and implement policies, because we are called to account for them by Parliament'.[2]

In this chapter, we consider another strand in the idea that power is legitimized through Parliament: that is, the principle of 'parliamentary supremacy' (also called 'parliamentary sovereignty'). In a nutshell, this is the idea that Acts of Parliament are the highest form of law in the United Kingdom. The consequence is that courts have no constitutional power to set aside provisions of Acts of Parliament as incompatible with constitutional principles. It is sometimes said that the British constitution can be encapsulated in only eight words: '*What the Queen in Parliament enacts is law*.'[3]

Politicians are, and should be, the top dogs. Major decisions affecting the life of the nation should be debated and decided in Parliament (not in courtrooms). The notion of democracy that underpins all of this is *majoritarianism*. The views of the majority, as reflected in the composition of the House of Commons, should be decisive. Parliament should therefore be, by its procedures and composition, well-equipped to hold good quality debates and inquiries.

A deep vein of scepticism about the constitutional role of the judiciary runs through the political constitutionalists' thinking. In some writing in previous years, judges were seen as having an agenda of their own that risked undermining policies pursued by elected government and approved by Parliament. Aneurin ('Nye') Bevan, the health minister in the 1945–51 Labour government and responsible for the creation of the National Health Service, bluntly expressed concerns about the prospect of 'judicial sabotage' of 'socialist legislation'. Adjudication on many entitlements to welfare benefits and public services were allocated to specialist tribunals—which included lay people and experts—rather than to the courts.[4]

In his controversial book *The Politics of the Judiciary* (1977), J.A.G. Griffith (1918–2010) used a selection of cases (on areas such as race relations, trade union law, police powers, and students) to advance an argument that judges in Britain, by reason of their upper-class background—private schools and Oxbridge degrees—and their institutional position in society, *necessarily* had a strong ideological bias towards 'established authority' and views associated with the Conservative Party at that time. In other words, they routinely ruled against trade unionists (in an age when trade unions were more influential in public life than they are now), demonstrators, students, and so on. In Griffith's view, judges could not be seen as politically neutral and they were not effective guardians of individual liberty against the State. This was not a criticism of individual judges, but an analysis of the institutional role played by the judiciary.

Graham Gee, '*The political constitutionalism of J.A.G. Griffith*' (2008) 28 Legal Studies 20, 28 (footnotes omitted)

[. . .] Griffith is not troubled by limiting government per se, but rather by limiting government through judicially imposed constraints, and even then he is troubled only by certain judicially

[2] See further Graham Gee and Grégoire C.N. Webber, 'What is a Political Constitution?' (2010) 30 Oxford Journal of Legal Studies 273.

[3] For an explanation of the term 'Queen in Parliament', see Chapter 10.

[4] On tribunals, see Chapter 15.

imposed constraints. On my reading, Griffith's political constitutionalism is just that: a *political* model of *constitutionalism*. And any model of constitutionalism must include an account of the norms creating, structuring and defining the authority of the governing institutions, including an explanation as to how those norms *constrain* the power of those institutions. For Griffith, politics, and in particular the parliamentary process, should create, structure and define the authority of the governing institutions, including imposing constraints on those institutions. That is to say, politics, and to some extent law, should (and do in fact) constrain the governing institutions.

From what has been said so far, it might seem as if all adherents of political constitutionalism belong to the political left—but this is certainly not the case; rather, it is a view of the world that has cross-party appeal. Conservatives and others on the Right in British politics have attached great weight to the principle of parliamentary supremacy and the central place of Parliament in the constitutional set-up. The ability of the national Parliament to legislate free from unnecessary constraints from the European Union (EU) is a defining view of many on the right. Politicians in both Labour and Conservative governments have vented frustration at what they see as judicial 'activism', and have, in the past fifteen years or so, breached convention by being outspokenly critical of court judgments and occasionally of judges in general. For example, David Blunkett MP (Home Secretary in Tony Blair's Labour government) made an angry statement following a court ruling in 2003: '*Frankly, I'm fed up with having to deal with a situation where Parliament debates issues and the judges overturn them.*'[5]

In the following extract, Professor Tomkins—a leading exponent of political constitutionalism—praises Parliament and warns against trusting the courts.

Adam Tomkins, *Our Republican Constitution* (2005, Oxford: Hart Publishing), p. 3

What is beautiful about the British constitution is that it [...] uses politics as the vehicle through which the purpose of the constitution (that is, to check the government) may be accomplished. This is beautiful for at least two reasons: first, because it is democratic; and secondly, because it can actually work. Politics really can stop governments from abusing their authority.

Turning instead to the courts to provide ways of holding the government to account endangers both democracy and effectiveness. No matter how democracy is defined, judges can never hope to match the democratic legitimacy of elected politicians. Whether you conceive of democracy in terms of the representativeness of the personnel or in terms of the openness and accessibility of the institution, Parliaments will always enjoy greater democratic legitimacy than courts.

And Professor Loughlin warns against the idea that the text(s) of a constitution can provide all of the answers needed to resolve conflicts.

[5] http://www.news.bbc.co.uk/2/hi/uk_news/2779343.stm

Martin Loughlin, 'Constitutional Law: The Third Order of the Political', in N. Bamforth and P. Leyland (eds) *Public Law in a Multi-layered Constitution* (2003, Oxford: Hart Publishing), ch. 2, pp.48–9

Although advocating a more formal separation of powers, Montesquieu also recognised the political character of the exercise, believing that, provided each of these roles is properly acknowledged, the three branches of government 'are constrained to move by the necessary motion of things'. With the emergence of constitutional legalism, however, came the belief that solutions to these intrinsically political matters are to be found in, or through, the text. Consequently, whenever—as has been the case in all modern states—the executive has acted to fill those spaces which exist within all constitutional documents, this has been the occasion for disapprobation.

The error of constitutional legalism is of a most basic kind, that of mistaking the part for the whole. Such legalism fails properly to acknowledge the provisional character of constitutional arrangements and that 'the development and acceptance of a constitutional framework can occur only as the contingent result of irresolvable conflict'. Indeed, this must be so, because its object—the activity of governing—is interminable. The arrangements of governing are in a permanent state of disequilibrium, since 'the system has never been designed as a whole, and such coherence as it possesses is the product of constant readjustment of its parts to one another'. What Michael Oakeshott [1901–90, a philosopher] calls 'the system of superficial order' is, of course, always 'capable of being made more coherent'. And while this can often be a useful and positive exercise, 'the barbarism of order appears when order is pursued for its own sake and when the preservation of order involves the destruction of that without which order is only the orderliness of the ant-heap or the graveyard'.

(b) LEGAL CONSTITUTIONALISM

There is a different view. This sees the courts and legally enforceable rights as the keys to creating conditions under which government power is limited. Parliamentary control of government is regarded as ineffective—the reality, it is said, is that government controls Parliament (rather than the other way around). The principle of parliamentary supremacy is therefore too weak to be an effective restraint on government. It provides no guarantee for fundamental rights or the rights of minorities. Those who advocate legal constitutionalism are concerned that a majority of members of Parliament (MPs) could pass legislation restricting rights, such as freedom of speech and association, on which the idea of democracy rests. People in some minority groups (such as people in prison and people seeking political asylum in the United Kingdom) may not have any 'voice' in Parliament: they have no vote and MPs are reluctant to take up their cause. So instead of parliamentary supremacy being the dominant rule in the UK constitution, legal constitutionalists argue that we should rely on other principles—notably the rule of law.[6]

Legal constitutionalists (like the political constitutionalists) claim that democracy underpins their views—but they reject the notion of majoritarianism. Democracy, for them, is not only about counting votes at general elections or in the House of Commons, but also involves insisting on the protection of the rights that protect individual liberty. It would not be 'democratic' for legislation to be passed that restricts freedom of expression ahead of an

[6] See Chapter 3.

election, even if a majority of MPs were to favour this. The courts are regarded as having an essential role in protecting rights.

Terence Daintith, 'Constitutionalism', in P. Cane and J. Conaghan (eds), *The New Oxford Companion to Law* (2008, Oxford: OUP), pp. 209–10

Constitutionalism, as political theory and practice, posits that the powers of government must be structured and limited by a binding constitution incorporating certain basic principles if the protection of values like human liberty and dignity is to be assured. This is a vision expressed in the first 'modern' constitutions, those of the United States (1789), and of France (1789, 1791), in contradistinction to the notion of the constitution—previously dominant, but still commanding some support in the United Kingdom—as merely describing how the state's functions are allocated and organized at any given time.

Today, the great majority of states are 'constitutionalist' in that they have codified constitutions which proclaim themselves as supreme law; are based on popular sovereignty; incorporate the principles of limited, representative and accountable government, and the separation of powers; guarantee judicial independence; protect human rights; and require special procedures for amendment. Many also accept the principle that the constitution, as a binding legal document, can be authoritatively interpreted only by the courts, or by a specialist constitutional court. Constitutionalism so enhanced appeals to lawyers, since it places law above politics and makes judges, not legislators or governments, the custodians of the fundamental values of society.

The fact that the United Kingdom constitution, though departing in important respects from the precepts of constitutionalism, nonetheless secures its values, while many 'constitutionalist' states fail in this, is attributed by constitutionalists not to any weakness of their theory but to unusual features of our national character and political development.

And consider the following from Lord Steyn, writing at a time when he was a serving Law Lord.

Lord Steyn, 'The weakest and least dangerous department of government' [1997] Public Law 84, 87–8

Constitutionalism is a political theory as to the type of institutional arrangements that are necessary in order to support the democratic ideal. It holds that the exercise of government power must be controlled in order that it should not be destructive of the very values which it was intended to promote. It requires of the executive more than loyalty to the existing constitution. It is concerned with the merits and quality of constitutional arrangements.

But if (as legal constitutionalists believe) Acts of Parliament should not be the highest form of law, what should? The answer for many is a written constitution and an entrenched Bill of rights, enforced when necessary by the courts. For others, the answer is the common law, as developed by the judges. Either way, the courts should be democracy's referees. Professor Jowell, a leading exponent of legal constitutionalism, develops this idea in the following extract.

Jeffrey Jowell, 'Parliamentary sovereignty under the new constitutional hypothesis' [2006] Public Law 562, 578 (footnotes omitted)

It can no longer be doubted that one of the preconditions of any constitutional democracy, properly so-called, is respect for certain rights that neither the executive nor the legislature, representative as it may be, should be able to deny with impunity. But how convincing is the claim of the supporters of parliamentary sovereignty that its demise would have the effect of simply transferring unfettered power from the elected legislature to the unelected judiciary? That claim is misleading. It ignores the fact that the spheres of the judiciary and the legislature are distinct. For a start, even under the model of a rights-based democracy, legislative authority inevitably contains a wide area of discretion to make social and economic policy, over which the courts have no dominium. It is not for the judges to second-guess the legislature on utilitarian calculations of the social good. Their role is strictly confined to the limited issue of whether the various inherent elements of democracy have been infringed by other branches of government and therefore cannot be sustained. Even within the bounds of parliamentary sovereignty, as we have seen, the courts already exercise this role to some degree. The historic dialogue and process of iteration and self-correction between Parliament and the courts has allowed the development of public law rights and duties to which both the legislature and judiciary have contributed.

If parliamentary sovereignty were to be discarded as our prime constitutional principle, it is true that "the last word" would pass from the legislature to the courts—but only on the question whether the legislature has strayed beyond the line of its democratic confines. The assertion of this authority would require of the courts a boldness to interpret constitutional principles as they ought to be. However, it will also require a modest appreciation of their own limitations. There will be issues on the margins of legal principle and socio-economic policy which will inevitably invite the charge of judicial overreach. Parliament, however, is not in a position to judge these matters in its own cause. And there is much to be said for having these decisions made by those who are insulated from the necessity to respond to the perceived opinion of the moment.

If a future Parliament were to pass a law which infringed the rule of law or other constitutional fundamentals, it may be that our judges will feel that they still lack sufficient authority to strike it down on the ground that it subverts the implied conditions—the essential features—of our constitutional democracy. However, some of those conditions, such as free and regular elections, underlie the legitimacy of the principle of parliamentary sovereignty itself. Others, such as access to justice, are necessary requirements of a modern hypothesis of constitutionalism.

(c) WHAT IS THE TRAJECTORY?

If there is a debate over the future direction of the British constitution, then we need to ask who's winning. The answer is that there is no straightforward answer. On the one hand, there continues to be a very strong attachment to the principle of parliamentary supremacy. This might be seen as evidence that political constitutionalism remains the dominant force. On the other hand, several of the reforms put in place during Tony Blair's premiership 1997–2007 can be seen as part of a trend towards a more 'legal', less 'political' constitutional set-up. In the following extract, Glover and Hazell refer to Griffith's work and postulate a spectrum, with elements of the 'political constitution' at one end and the 'legal constitution' at the other. They suggest that, up to the mid-1990s, the British constitution tended towards the 'political' end of the spectrum, whereas since then more and more characteristics of a 'legal constitution' have emerged.

Mark Glover and Robert Hazell, 'Introduction: Forecasting Constitutional Futures', in R. Hazell (ed.) *Constitutional Futures Revisited: Britain's Constitution to 2020* (2008, Basingstoke: Palgrave Macmillan), ch. 1, pp. 14–16 (references omitted)

One pole [that is, end of the spectrum] represents the political constitution. Parliamentary sovereignty is the dominant principle. Ministers have very wide discretion, including over how much or little information to disclose, but they are called to account and kept in check by Parliament. There are no recognised rights: it is up to Parliament to protect civil liberties. The judiciary are appointed by the executive and show deference to parliamentary sovereignty and executive necessity. There are few external checks on the executive apart from Parliament, and the system is based on a high degree of trust that the executive and Parliament are the best judges of the public interest.

The logic of this system is that solutions to political problems must be political themselves—'law is not and cannot be a substitute for politics' [a reference to Griffith]. Political constitutionalism, therefore, does not allow for the entrenchment of rights in the constitution because there is no consensus, for example, on what a Bill of Rights should contain. Rights are simply an expression of power relationships—'concealed political propaganda' [Griffith again] or 'little more than the view held by the hegemonic group or officials with the power to decide'. The process of judicial review is also not democratically satisfactory: judges 'resolve their disputes by the very democratic procedure they claim to supersede—majority vote'. Further, responsibility for problem solving would be passed from Parliament to the judiciary (and from an accountable body to an unaccountable one).

At the other pole, which represents the legal constitution and the principle of legal constitutionalism, power is passed in this direction. Legal constitutionalism is a theory of limited government which constrains the supremacy of Parliament, subjecting it to a range of legal checks and balances and relocating the final authority to interpret and enforce fundamental law in the judiciary. Here the logic is that Parliament cannot be trusted always to uphold democratic values and human rights. This is not a particularly new idea in itself but has gained relevance recently for a number of reasons: first, the perceived inability of the legislature to hold the executive to account; second, globalisation and the increasing importance of international law; third, the perception that judges are apolitical and as a result able to make objective decisions as opposed to partisan or politically motivated decisions. The basis of governance is no longer parliamentary sovereignty but the rights of the individual, and it is judges that interpret whether or not the rights of the individual are being upheld.

In practice this involves the creation of statutes which entrench certain rights of individuals and organisations in the law beyond the reach of Parliament. There is greater separation of powers and the judiciary constrains legislative and executive freedom by means of interpreting the statutes. Specialist constitutional watchdogs are also set up (such as the office of the Information Commissioner) to regulate the executive.

[Glover and Hazell go on to set out two lists, showing the characteristics of a political and of a legal constitution.]

Political constitution	Legal constitution
Parliamentary Sovereignty	Constitutionalism
Fusion of powers	Separation of powers
Elected politicians	Unelected guardians

Ministerial discretion	Tighter rule of law
Political accountability	Legal checks and balances
Unfettered executive	Constrained executive
Weak judiciary	Activist judiciary
Weak human rights regime	Enforcement of human rights
Few external checks	Strong constitutional watchdogs
Based on trust	Based on mistrust

QUESTIONS

1. Explain in your own words how (a) the political constitutionalists and (b) the legal constitutionalists would tend to view the following:

   - the process by which Acts of Parliament are made (we look at this in detail in Chapter 10); and
   - the constitutional role of judges in the United Kingdom.

2. Think about the following issues that have to be decided. Who, generally speaking, do you think should make such decisions: politicians (MPs and ministers), or judges, or some other body?

   (a) The maximum time for which people suspected of involvement in terrorism may be detained by the police before a decision is made to charge them or release them.

   (b) Whether children should be allowed to wear religious dress that obscures their faces when at school.

   (c) The site of a new airport.

   (d) Whether the National Health Service should finance a new treatment for cancer.

3. At this stage, on which side of the debate do your sympathies lie: do you consider yourself a political or a legal constitutionalist?

Is 'constitutionalism' a useful concept?

The use of the term 'constitutionalism' raises a number of difficulties.

Jo Eric Khushal Murkens, 'The quest for constitutionalism in UK public law discourse' (2009) 29 Oxford Journal of Legal Studies 427, 430–2, 454–5 (footnotes omitted)

In the United Kingdom, the lack of consensus amongst public law scholars as to the nature and scope of constitutionalism is even more pronounced, even though 'constitutionalism' appears comparatively rarely in the discourse. According to the British and Irish Legal Information Institute, since 1996 there has been only one substantive occurrence of the word 'constitutionalism' in an Opinion by the Lords of Appeal, and not a single occurrence in the Court of Appeal or the Administrative Court. However, a significant number of scholars do feel the need to make at least cursory reference to the concept in their textbooks and other publications. Of course, textbooks are introductory texts and their contents are unavoidably constrained in scope and by space, but they nonetheless indicate constitutionalism's (lack of) weight. [...]

Never does the discussion of constitutionalism in public law textbooks, if it is discussed at all, exceed one page. None of the scholars above attend to 'constitutionalism' with the same detail they reserve for, say, the 'rule of law' or the 'separation of powers'. The scope, meaning and role of constitutionalism are routinely overlooked in public law writings and, therefore, remain uncertain. So why has 'constitutionalism' been included in textbooks?

The short answer is that public law scholars have used constitutionalism for three different purposes. First, it fills the void left by the absence of a constitutional theory. Turpin and Tomkins note (derisively and ahistorically): 'although we lack a general theory of the constitution, there has come down to us the idea of constitutionalism—of a constitutional order which acknowledges the necessary power of government while placing conditions and limits upon its exercise'. Second, 'constitutionalism' steps into the shoes of an absent constitutional document. For Bradley and Ewing 'the absence of a written constitution makes all the more necessary the existence of a free political system in which official decisions are subject to discussion and scrutiny by Parliament'. Third, 'constitutionalism' is used as an umbrella term to cover either the new constitutional settlement between the judiciary, Parliament and Government, or distinct constitutional concepts such as democracy, Parliamentary sovereignty, the rule of law, separation of powers, accountability, and legality (constitutionality), fundamental rights (especially liberty) and the avoidance of arbitrary power.

The longer answer stems from recent efforts to create a constitutional counterweight to the absence of a constitutional theory and a constitutional document in the United Kingdom.

[Murkens draws the following conclusion.]

[...C]onstitutionalism is too big a concept for the small boots that public law scholars are prepared to give it. At present, the Orwellian 'belief in the law as something above the State' does not exist in the United Kingdom. At a formal level constitutionalism in the UK is an umbrella term that consists of the following limbs:

(i) it concentrates ultimate public power in one institution (the sovereignty of Parliament);

(ii) the government is organized by means of majority rule (representative government);

(iii) the granting and exercise of public power is determined and controlled by constitutional principles, such as the rule of law, separation of powers, and respect for individual rights (limited government);

(iv) the government is held to account by Parliament for its policies and its conduct (political accountability);

(v) the government is held to account by an independent judiciary through the principal mechanism of judicial review (legal accountability).

Constitutionalism is thus shorthand for the creation, carrying out, and control of public power. But removed from the constraints of UK public law discourse, however, constitutionalism is also a concept in its own right, with distinct yet malleable contours, and high-minded yet modest aspirations. Whereas the political constitution sets up public power, constitutionalism identifies its purpose. Whereas the rule of law concerns the law-based exercise of governmental power, constitutionalism creates a normative benchmark for the evaluation of government action. Whereas in other jurisdictions with a Supreme or Constitutional Court, constitutionalism is understood as the mechanism by which the ordinary political processes are disturbed or overridden, in the United Kingdom constitutionalism could only ever govern the legitimacy of government action.

A nuanced and normative discussion of constitutionalism does not take place in UK public law scholarship. Either entire new chapters expounding the concept of constitutionalism need to be written and inserted into public law textbooks, or its usage should be purged from the discussion. The meaning currently attributed to constitutionalism could easily be reduced to the doctrinal cornerstones of the existing and evolving constitution (limited government, political and legal accountability). Hinting at constitutionalism as a new but hollow vessel is constitutionally inaccurate, analytically fallacious, and explanatorily vacuous.

Constitutionalism could determine in a comprehensive and legally-binding manner the grounds of legitimacy and the proper exercise of political power. [. . . C]onstitutionalism is not a thesis for rights-foundationalism or a written constitution, especially not in the United Kingdom context. At its most compelling it is a normative thesis, a meta-legal doctrine and a political ideal that reconciles the 'virtues associated with the constitution of government authority and reasonable fears concerning the abuse of that authority'. Constitutionalism does not ask whether a proposal or decision is constitutional, but whether it should be constitutional. Such questions have for the past century fallen by the wayside in public law discourse. But the concerns of constitutionalism can, nay must, be addressed within the undocumented political or historical constitution of the United Kingdom.

QUESTIONS

1. How would you define 'constitutionalism'?

2. Is constitutionalism a useful concept? Do you agree with Murkens' thesis that constitutionalism is an umbrella term?

3. What, according to Daintith's summary (see Terence Daintith, 'Constitutionalism' on p. 45), are the main criteria against which constitutions should be evaluated? Is this a 'political' or a 'legal' conception of constitutionalism?

---

3 PARLIAMENTARY SUPREMACY

This section examines parliamentary supremacy in two main ways. Some of the extracts and commentary deal with the 'technical' aspects of the topic—that is, the concept and the legal authority relating to parliamentary supremacy.

As well as dealing with these, we also look at the 'normative' question: is parliamentary supremacy *a good idea*? For the political and legal constitutionalists,[7] parliamentary supremacy is the major battleground. The political constitutionalists believe that parliamentary supremacy is, and should continue to be, the centrepiece of the British constitution—that it enables our elected representatives to have the final say over the laws under which we live our lives. The legal constitutionalists disagree, seeing parliamentary supremacy as a dangerous arrangement that puts our liberties at risk—that it places no legal constraints on the politicians' ability to make law.

---

[7] See section 2, Legitimacy on p. 40.

(a) PARLIAMENTARY SUPREMACY AS A SET OF RULES

Parliamentary supremacy is a cluster of rules about the 'legislative competence' of the UK Parliament, how courts should deal with Acts of Parliament made at different times that inadvertently or intentionally say contradictory things, and the powers of courts to consider whether a particular Act of Parliament is a valid source of law.

Parliamentary supremacy applies only to the UK Parliament, not to the other legislatures in the United Kingdom. The Scottish Parliament, Northern Ireland Assembly, and National Assembly for Wales[8] are each created by an Act of the UK Parliament. They have only those legislative powers that are conferred on them.[9] Acts of the Scottish Parliament and of the Northern Ireland Assembly, and Measures of the National Assembly for Wales, may be held to be invalid by the courts—ultimately, the UK Supreme Court—if they are not within the legislative competence. Nor does parliamentary supremacy prevent courts from quashing delegated legislation.[10]

As we will see shortly, the rules on the supremacy of UK Acts of Parliament are to be found in case law, constitutional conventions, statute law, and elaborated in the writings of learned authors. Professor Dicey was enthusiastic to the point of extremism about the importance of parliamentary supremacy as a defining feature of the British constitution (in contrast to other constitutional systems, which he regarded as inferior).

A.V. Dicey, *Introduction to the Study of the Law of the Constitution* (1885; 10th edn 1959, London: Macmillan & Co), pp. 39–40

The principle of Parliamentary sovereignty means neither more nor less than this, namely, that Parliament [. . .] has, under the English constitution, the right to make or unmake any law whatever; and, further, that no person or body is recognised by the law of England as having a right to override or set aside the legislation of Parliament.

A law may, for our present purpose, be defined as "any rule which will be enforced by the Courts". The principle then of Parliamentary sovereignty may, looked at from its positive side, be thus described: Any Act of Parliament, or any part of an Act of Parliament, which makes a new law, or repeals or modifies an existing law, will be obeyed by the Courts. The same principle, looked at from its negative side, may be thus stated: There is no person or body of persons who can, under the English constitution, make rules which override or derogate from an Act of Parliament, or which (to express the same thing in other words) will be enforced by the Courts in contravention of an Act of Parliament.

There are rather more rules than the two suggested by this extract from Dicey. If the rules applying today were to be codified, they *might* look something like the following.

NOTE: This is the authors' unofficial attempt to summarize the rules in the drafting style of a statute.

---

1 Legislative competence of the Queen in Parliament (hereafter 'the UK Parliament')

(1) The UK Parliament may—

---

[8] See Part II Introduction.
[9] See *AXA General Insurance Ltd v HM Lord Advocate* [2011] UKSC 46, [2012] 1 AC 868.
[10] See Chapter 11.

(a) make laws, known as Acts of Parliament, and

(b) define what constitutes an Act of Parliament.[11]

(2) The UK Parliament may make laws on any matter whatsoever.

(3) In making an Act of Parliament, the UK Parliament may have regard to—

(a) the United Kingdom's agreement in international law to comply with European Union law, which includes a requirement that no provision in an Act of Parliament shall infringe European Union law,[12]

(b) the United Kingdom's agreement in international law to comply with the European Convention on Human Rights, which includes a requirement that no provision in an Act of Parliament shall infringe a Convention right,[13] and

(c) the constitutional convention that where legislative competence over a subject matter has been devolved to the Scottish Parliament, the UK Parliament will not legislate on that subject matter without the consent of the Scottish Parliament.[14]

2 Express repeal and entrenchment

(1) Any provision contained in an Act of Parliament ('Act A') may be repealed or amended by an Act of Parliament enacted at a later date ('Act B').

(2) Subsection (1) does not apply[15] to a provision in Act A that expressly states that the provision may be repealed or amended only—

(a) by a procedure in one or both Houses of Parliament other than the normal procedure for making Acts of Parliament, or

(b) if the repeal or amendment is approved in a referendum,

unless Act B conforms to the stated requirements.

3 Implied repeal

(1) Where there is a conflict between provisions contained in one Act of Parliament ('Act C') and an Act of Parliament enacted at a later date ('Act D'), the provision in Act D is to be enforced and applied by courts and tribunals.[16]

(2) Subsection (1) does not apply[17] where—

(a) Act C is a constitutional statute, and

(b) in making Act D, the UK Parliament did not intend to repeal or abrogate Act C.

(3) For the purposes of subsection (2), an Act of Parliament is a constitutional statute if it—

(a) relates to the legal relationship between citizen and state in some general, overarching manner, or

---

[11] 'Act of Parliament' was redefined, in certain circumstances, by the Parliament Act 1911 to include legislation given royal assent with the consent of the House of Lords: see Chapter 13.

[12] On the impact of the EU on parliamentary supremacy, see Chapter 18.

[13] We deal with the ECHR in Chapter 6.

[14] This is known as 'the Sewel convention': see Gavin Little, 'Scotland and parliamentary sovereignty' on p. 59.

[15] Many people would disagree with this formulation of the rule, as discussed on p. 63, Entrenchment: Can an Act of Parliament be made that binds future parliaments?.

[16] See p. 71, Implied repeal.

[17] See *Thoburn v Sunderland City Council* [2002] EWHC 195 (Admin), [60]–[67].

(b) enlarges or diminishes the scope of a fundamental constitutional right.

(4) A constitutional statute may be amended only by express words in a later Act of Parliament.

4 Jurisdiction of courts over Acts of Parliament

(1) No court or tribunal in the United Kingdom shall call into question the binding character of an Act of Parliament as a source of law except—

    (a) where, in accordance with the case law of the European Court of Justice, a court or tribunal is satisfied that a provision contained in an Act of Parliament is incompatible with European Union law, the court or tribunal must disapply that provision,[18] and

    (b) in relation to section 1(1)(b), the court may consider whether, where an Act of Parliament ('Act E') is given Royal Assent without the consent of the House of Lords, Act E is an Act of Parliament within the meaning of the Parliament Act 1911 (as amended by the Parliament Act 1949).[19]

(2) The European Court of Justice has jurisdiction[20] to find that, in the making of an Act of Parliament, the United Kingdom has failed to fulfil an obligation under the EU treaties and may—

    (a) require the United Kingdom to comply with the judgment of the Court, and

    (b) if the United Kingdom fails to take the necessary measures to comply with the Court's judgment, may impose a lump sum or penalty payment to be paid by the United Kingdom.

(3) The European Court of Human Rights has jurisdiction to find that, in the making of an Act of Parliament, the United Kingdom has violated a victim's right under the European Convention on Human Rights and may award 'just satisfaction' to the victim.[21]

(4) In accordance with section 4 of the Human Rights Act 1998, if a court is satisfied that a provision contained in an Act of Parliament is incompatible with a Convention right, the court may make a declaration of incompatibility (but a declaration of incompatibility does not affective the validity, continuing operation or enforcement of the provision in respect of which it is given).

What the courts have said about parliamentary supremacy

The law reports contain numerous statements supporting the rules of parliamentary supremacy. The following extracts provide a flavour of what the courts have said that they cannot do in relation to Acts of the UK Parliament.

The first extract concerns a legal challenge made by a Mr Pickin (a campaigner to keep a railway line open in Somerset), who failed to persuade the Law Lords that a private Act of Parliament[22] should be set aside because allegedly fraudulent statements had been made during the parliamentary proceedings.

---

[18] See Chapter 8.

[19] See discussion of *Jackson and ors v Her Majesty's Attorney General* [2005] UKHL 56 in Chapter 13.

[20] See the Treaty on European Union (the 'Maastricht Treaty'), Arts 226–8.

[21] See Chapter 17.

[22] On the distinction between private and public Acts, see Chapter 10.

British Railways Board v Pickin
[1974] AC 765, 782, 787–8

Lord Reid

In earlier times many learned lawyers seem to have believed that an Act of Parliament could be disregarded in so far as it was contrary to the law of God or the law of nature or natural justice but since the supremacy of Parliament was finally demonstrated by the Revolution of 1688 any such idea has become obsolete [...].

The function of the Court is to construe and apply the enactments of Parliament. The Court has no concern with the manner in which Parliament or its officers carrying out its Standing Orders perform these functions. Any attempt to prove that they were misled by fraud or otherwise would necessarily involve an enquiry into the manner in which they had performed their functions in dealing with the Bill which became the British Railways Act 1968. [...]

For a century or more both Parliament and the Courts have been careful not to act so as to cause conflict between them. Any such investigations as the Respondent seeks could easily lead to such a conflict, and I would only support it if compelled to do so by clear authority. But it appears to me that the whole trend of authority for over a century is clearly against permitting any such investigation.

The courts' refusal to look behind the text of a statute to consider allegations of procedural impropriety during the legislative process is sometimes referred to as 'the enrolled Bill rule'.

In the next extract, Mr Cheney (a peace campaigner) challenged a tax demand issued to him on various grounds. One was that the tax demand under statute was contrary to an international treaty against nuclear weapons and was thereby invalid.

Cheney v Conn (Inspector of Taxes)
[1968] 1 WLR 242, 244–5

Ungoed-Thomas J

The submission is that the assessments are invalid because it is to be taken that what is collected will be, in part, applied in expenditure on the armed forces and devoted to the construction of nuclear weapons with the intention of using those weapons if certain circumstances should arise. It is conceded for the purposes of this case that a substantial part of the taxes for the years that I have mentioned was allocated to the construction of nuclear weapons. The issue therefore becomes whether the use of [tax] for the construction of nuclear weapons, with the intention of using them should certain circumstances arise, invalidates the assessments.

[...] I shall deal first with the relationship of statute law to international law and international conventions.

First, international law is part of the law of the land, but it yields to statute. That is made clear by the case of *Collco Dealings Ltd v Inland Revenue Commissioners*, where Viscount Simonds, quoted with approval, and in accordance with the decision of the House of Lords in that case, *Maxwell on the Interpretation Of Statutes* (10th edn), p 148. I quote: "But if the statute is unambiguous, its provisions must be followed even if they are contrary to international law." It is therefore very understandable why the taxpayer in this case relies primarily, at any rate, not on a conflict between international law in general and the statute, but on the conflict between the [Geneva Convertions] Act of 1957, and its reference to ratification, and another statute, the Finance Act 1964. Secondly, conventions which are ratified by an Act of Parliament are part of the law of the land; and, thirdly, conventions which are ratified, but not by an Act of Parliament, which would thereby give them statutory force, cannot prevail against a statute in unambiguous terms. [...]

It is, I may add, the Queen in Parliament and not the Queen independently of Parliament, acting as the executive through the cabinet, who makes what is law in this land.

In the next extract—which is frequently quoted by courts—the question before the Law Lords was whether it was lawful for prison governors to refuse permission for prisoners to have oral interviews with journalists as part of a campaign to show that there has been a miscarriage of justice. The governors relied on the Prison Rules, which are *delegated legislation* made under the Prison Act 1952, so the case was not directly relevant to parliamentary supremacy; Lord Hoffmann's words were therefore *obiter dicta*.

R v Secretary of State for the Home Department, ex parte Simms and O'Brien
[1999] UKHL 33, [2000] 2 AC 115, 131

Lord Hoffmann

Parliamentary sovereignty means that Parliament can, if it chooses, legislate contrary to fundamental principles of human rights. The Human Rights Act 1998 will not detract from this power. The constraints upon its exercise by Parliament are ultimately political, not legal. But the principle of legality means that Parliament must squarely confront what it is doing and accept the political cost. Fundamental rights cannot be overridden by general or ambiguous words. This is because there is too great a risk that the full implications of their unqualified meaning may have passed unnoticed in the democratic process. In the absence of express language or necessary implication to the contrary, the courts therefore presume that even the most general words were intended to be subject to the basic rights of the individual. In this way the courts of the United Kingdom, though acknowledging the sovereignty of Parliament, apply principles of constitutionality little different from those which exist in countries where the power of the legislature is expressly limited by a constitutional document.

The Law Lords held that the 1952 Act did not permit the Prison Rules to restrict access to journalists in this way.[23] Note Lord Hoffmann's firm assertion that had it done so in clear words, Parliament has the power to make primary legislation contrary to basic rights—such as those recognized by international human rights treaties, including the European Convention, including on Human Rights (ECHR). But also important is what he says about 'the principle of legality'—a concept to which we return in Chapter 3, in discussing *R v Secretary of State for the Home Department, ex parte Pierson*.[24]

---

[23] Michael O'Brien served eleven years in prison; following a media campaign, his conviction for murder was eventually overturned by the Court of Appeal (and, following further legal proceedings, he was awarded compensation). Ian Simms has been in prison since 1989, serving a life sentence for murder; denied parole on several occasions, he maintains that he is innocent.

[24] [1998] AC 539.

The next illustration is taken from a test case[25] in which pro-hunting campaigners sought to argue that the Hunting Act 2004 was not an Act of Parliament. It had received Royal Assent without the consent of the House of Lords under the terms of the Parliament Acts 1911 and 1949.

Jackson v Her Majesty's Attorney General
[2005] UKHL 56, [159]

Baroness Hale of Richmond

The concept of Parliamentary sovereignty which has been fundamental to the constitution of England and Wales since the 17th century (I appreciate that Scotland may have taken a different view) means that Parliament can do anything. The courts will, of course, decline to hold that Parliament has interfered with fundamental rights unless it has made its intentions crystal clear. The courts will treat with particular suspicion (and might even reject) any attempt to subvert the rule of law by removing governmental action affecting the rights of the individual from all judicial scrutiny. Parliament has also, for the time being at least, limited its own powers by the European Communities Act 1972 and, in a different way, by the Human Rights Act 1998. It is possible that other qualifications may emerge in due course. In general, however, the constraints upon what Parliament can do are political and diplomatic rather than constitutional.

In the final extract, the UK Supreme Court had to decide whether the Scottish Parliament has exceeded its legislative competence in enacting the Damages (Asbestos-related Conditions) (Scotland) Act 2009.

AXA General Insurance Ltd v HM Advocate
[2011] UKSC 46, Lord Hope

50. The question whether the principle of the sovereignty of the United Kingdom Parliament is absolute or may be subject to limitation in exceptional circumstances is still under discussion. For Lord Bingham, writing extrajudicially, the principle is fundamental and in his opinion, as the judges did not by themselves establish the principle, it was not open to them to change it: *The Rule of Law*, p. 167. Lord Neuberger of Abbotsbury, in his Lord Alexander of Weedon lecture, *Who are the masters now?* (6 April 2011), said at para. 73 that, although the judges had a vital role to play in protecting individuals against the abuses and excess of an increasingly powerful executive, the judges could not go against the will of Parliament as expressed through a statute. Lord Steyn on the other hand recalled at the outset of his speech in *Jackson*, para. 71, the warning that Lord Hailsham of St Marylebone gave in *The Dilemma of Democracy* (1978), p 126 about the dominance of a government elected with a large majority over Parliament. This process, he said, had continued and strengthened inexorably since Lord Hailsham warned of its dangers. This was the context in which he said in para. 102 that the Supreme Court might have to consider whether judicial review or the ordinary role of the courts was a constitutional fundamental which even a sovereign Parliament acting at the behest of a complaisant House of Commons could not abolish.
51. We do not need, in this case, to resolve the question how these conflicting views about the relationship between the rule of law and the sovereignty of the United Kingdom Parliament may be reconciled. The fact that we are dealing here with a legislature that is not sovereign relieves us of that responsibility. It also makes our task that much easier.

---

[25] Examined in detail in Chapter 13.

Political criticism of legislation

Both Lord Hoffmann and Baroness Hale of Richmond, in these extracts, draw a distinction between the political constraints on Parliament and legal limitations. It is certainly the case that when government Bills progress through Parliament they are often criticized as offending constitutional principles or impinging on human rights. These are points made in debates by MPs and peers, and contained in reports issued by the House of Lords Constitution Committee and the Joint Committee on Human Rights. Some of these criticisms turn into major public campaigns (as was the case in 2008, when the government sought new powers to detain terrorist suspects without charge for up to forty-two days). Members of Parliament may also have the sense that a general election is around the corner. Jennings put it as follows.

Sir Ivor Jennings, *The Law and the Constitution*, 5th edn (1959, London: University of London Press), p. 148

[...I]f they wish for re-election, they may be called upon to give an account of their actions, they must consider in their actions what the general opinion of them may be. Parliament passes many laws that people do not want. But it never passes any laws which any substantial section of the population violently dislikes.

The judges recognize this practical reality: '*Parliamentary sovereignty is an empty principle if legislation is passed which is so absurd or so unacceptable that the populace at large refuses to recognize it as law.*'[26]

If political opposition is sufficiently strong, the government may back down and withdraw the legislative proposals (as it did with the 42-day detention scheme). Once enacted, an Act of Parliament may face continued political opposition including civil disobedience—in which people refuse to obey the law—or even violent demonstrations (as occurred against the 'poll tax' legislation in 1990). All of this criticism is *political*; there is a general consensus among ministers, parliamentarians, judges, and civil servants that whatever may be the merits of such political criticisms, Bills may be given royal assent to become Acts of Parliament, the *legality* of which cannot be challenged in the courts.

What governments say about parliamentary supremacy

Parliamentary supremacy continues to be regarded by most politicians and commentators as a central characteristic of the UK constitution. Constitutional reform proposals made by the Labour governments of 1997–2010 often sought to assure people that the change in question would not undermine the principle, as in this extract from the Green Paper on a British Bill of rights and responsibilities.

---

[26] *Jackson v Her Majesty's Attorney General* [2005] UKHL 56, [120], *per* Lord Hope of Craighead.

Ministry of Justice, *Rights and Responsibilities: Developing Our Constitutional Framework*, Cm 7577 (March 2009), para. xv

Parliamentary sovereignty resides at the heart of our constitutional arrangements. And Parliament, rightly, claims legitimacy to exercise power on behalf of the people who elect it, making laws for the courts to apply, and holding the executive to account—indeed, providing authority for the executive to govern.

Similar assurances were given (by the then Conservative government) in the run-up to the United Kingdom's accession to the European Communities in 1973. Although EU law overrides any inconsistent national law, the argument often advanced is that this is because Parliament, by the European Communities Act 1972, has agreed to this arrangement; it would be open to Parliament to repeal the 1972 Act if the United Kingdom were to decide to withdraw from (what is now) the EU.

Against the background of a campaign against a controversial 'ouster clause' contained in a Bill, a Liberal Democrat peer and prominent QC—a 'legal constitutionalist' who is no fan of parliamentary supremacy (he has called it an 'authoritarian doctrine')—asked the government for its views of parliamentary supremacy in 2004. The clause in the Immigration and Asylum Bill would, had the government not eventually agreed to modify it, have removed the jurisdiction of the courts to review judicially many decisions made by officials and ministers in relation to immigration and asylum applications.

House of Lords Hansard, 31 March 2004, col. WA160

Parliament: Legislative Powers

Lord Lester of Herne Hill asked Her Majesty's Government: Whether, in preparing legislative proposals to introduce into Parliament, they operate on the basis that the legislative powers of Parliament are, as a matter of British constitutional law, unlimited powers.

The Attorney-General (Lord Goldsmith): The Government consider that it is a fundamental principle of British constitutional law that the competence of Parliament to legislate on any matter is unlimited.

The Attorney General's answer accords with the generally accepted understanding of the status of parliamentary supremacy and the legislative powers of Parliament.

A different approach in Scotland?

There is a strand of writing in Scotland that advances the argument that parliamentary supremacy is a particularly English concept, with no equivalent in the law and constitution of Scotland prior to the 1707 union.[27] As you read the following extract, consider what the implications of this might be for the constitution of the whole United Kingdom.

---

[27] See Chapter 4.

Gavin Little, 'Scotland and parliamentary sovereignty' (2004) 24 Legal Studies 540, 540, 543–4

Parliamentary sovereignty has, both in political and legal terms, long been a matter of controversy in Scotland. In the context of Scottish constitutional reform, unionists have often viewed parliamentary sovereignty as an important symbol of Westminster's claim to political supremacy over Scotland. Importantly, however, the idea that an alternative concept of popular sovereignty operates in Scotland, whilst obviously of great significance to nationalists, also has a broad, non-party-political currency north of the border.' [. . .]

[. . .I]t should be noted that Dicey's arguments have attracted criticism in the Scottish courts. For Scottish constitutional lawyers, the issue of parliamentary sovereignty has historically and conceptually been associated with important questions regarding the legal status of the Treaty of Union of 1707 between Scotland and England. Can the Treaty of Union, which created a new entity, the Parliament of Great Britain, and, inter alia, purports to guarantee the continued existence of certain historic Scottish institutions, prevail over inconsistent Acts of Parliament as a form of fundamental or higher law? Was, in JDB Mitchell's phrase, the UK Parliament 'born unfree'? As is well known, the status of parliamentary sovereignty was considered in the Scottish courts by Lord Cooper of Culross in the 1953 case of *MacCormick v The Lord Advocate*. The pursuer in the action was John MacCormick, who was then a leading figure in Scottish politics and the campaign for Scottish Home Rule. He challenged the new Queen's title as 'Elizabeth the Second' on the basis that it was, inter alia, incorrect historically (there has never been an Elizabeth the First in Scotland), and in conflict with Article I of the Treaty of Union. In his decision, Lord Cooper stated:

> The principle of unlimited sovereignty of Parliament is a distinctly English principle which has no counterpart in Scottish constitutional law. It derives its origin from Coke and Blackstone, and was widely popularised during the nineteenth century by Bagehot and Dicey [. . .] Considering that the Union legislation extinguished the Parliaments of Scotland and England and replaced them by a new Parliament, I have difficulty in seeing why it should have been supposed that the new Parliament of Great Britain must inherit all the peculiar characteristics of the English Parliament but none of the Scottish Parliament, as if all that happened in 1707 was that Scottish representatives were admitted to the Parliament of England. That is not what was done.

Whatever may have motivated Lord Cooper's comments on sovereignty, it must be recognised that their legal significance is unclear and open to question on four main grounds. First, however much Lord Cooper may have wished it otherwise, it is a matter of political fact that, although both the Scottish and English Parliaments ceased to exist in 1707, the new Parliament of Great Britain was in reality the English Parliament with a small number of additional Scottish representatives. Secondly, a number of significant reforms which are contrary to the Treaty of Union have been made by statute over the centuries. Thirdly, his remarks were obiter dicta, and were qualified by the comment that there was no authority for the view that the domestic courts had the jurisdiction to determine the validity of statute by reference to Treaty provisions. Fourthly, although the Scottish courts have, since *MacCormick*, left open the question of whether legislation seeking to abolish important national institutions (such as the Court of Session or the Church of Scotland) could be invalid in terms of the Treaty of Union, they have been most unwilling to claim the power to review the legal validity of Acts of Parliament.

> QUESTIONS
> 1. What, if any, legal constraints are there on the legislative competence of the UK Parliament?
> 2. What political constraints are there?

(b) WHAT IS THE SOURCE OF PARLIAMENTARY SUPREMACY?

So far, we have spoken broadly about 'the rules' of parliamentary supremacy. Having now seen the general scope of these rules, more thought needs to be given to the source of these rules. As we have seen,[28] the elements of the rulebook of the UK constitution—in the absence of a codified constitution—are to be found in the following:

- statute law;
- common law; and
- constitutional conventions.

Into which, if any, of these do the parliamentary supremacy rules fall? Working out the right answer is important for practical, as well as academic, reasons. For example, if we say that they are common law rules, it would seem to follow that the judiciary could change the rules (as they can with common law rules in other fields of law such as contract and tort). If, however, the rules are of some other kind, then it is not clear that the judiciary would be able to introduce a change.

Statute law?

The basic rules of parliamentary supremacy are not, at present, set out in an Act of Parliament—but *could* they be? Some commentators take the view that this would be impossible.

Sir John Salmond, *Jurisprudence,* 12th edn (1966, London: Sweet & Maxwell), p. 111

All rules of law have historical sources. As a matter of fact and history they have their origin somewhere, though we may not know what it is. But not all of them have legal sources. Were this so, it would be necessary for the law to proceed *ad infinitum*, in tracing the descent of its principles. It is requisite that the law should postulate one or more first causes, whose operation is ultimate and whose authority is underived [...] The rule that a man may not ride a bicycle on the footpath may have its source in the by-laws of a municipal council; the rule that these by-laws have the force of law has its source in an Act of Parliament. But whence comes the rule that Acts of Parliament have the force of law? This is legally ultimate; its source is historical only, not legal [...]. It is the law because it is the law, and for no other reason that it is possible for the law itself to take notice of. *No statute can confer this power upon Parliament, for this would be to assume and act on the very power that is to be conferred.*

---

[28] See Chapter 1.

Eric Barendt, *An Introduction to Constitutional Law* (1998, Oxford: OUP), p. 87

Naturally, Parliament could declare by an Act of Parliament that it is legally sovereign and that it has unlimited entitlement to enact any legislation it likes. But such a declaratory statute would not add anything to its legislative capacity. Parliament can hardly confer constitutional authority on itself by its own enactment.

None of this, however, affects the power of Parliament to *acknowledge* in legislation that it retains its law-making power. So, for example, the following provision appears in the Scotland Act 1998 in s. 28, which confers legislative power on the Scottish Parliament: '*This section does not affect the power of the Parliament of the United Kingdom to make laws for Scotland.*'

Common law?

If the rules of parliamentary supremacy cannot be, and have not been, set out in statute, then does it make sense to say that they are rules of the common law?

Eric Barendt, *An Introduction to Constitutional Law* (1998, Oxford: OUP), pp. 86–7 (footnotes omitted)

What is the source of the United Kingdom Parliament's legislative authority and what is the scope of that power? The short answer is that the source of its legislative authority is the common law, the uncodified rules of law formulated by judges when they decide particular cases. Further, it is for the courts to determine the scope of that authority. They must decide, for instance, whether Parliamentary legislative authority prevails over or gives way to inconsistent rules of European Community law [. . .]. It is largely for this reason the United Kingdom constitution can be described, among other things, as a common law constitution. The law reports are full of statements to the effect that it is the duty of the courts to give effect to enactments of Parliament, or that they cannot be challenged for infringing some fundamental right or the rules of international law. For example, a court easily rejected the argument that it was unconstitutional for Parliament to introduce the offence of incitement to racial hatred, because the law limited the fundamental right to freedom of speech. Judges have emphasized that the United Kingdom Parliament has unlimited legislative supremacy, or that it is sovereign.

It is therefore the courts, rather than Parliament itself, which have formulated the principle which is the corner-stone of the uncodified constitution of the United Kingdom.

A constitutional convention?

The idea that parliamentary supremacy might be a convention can be rejected on the basis that one of the defining characteristics of conventions is that they are not justiciable and enforceable by the courts. Clearly, the courts apply the parliamentary supremacy rules.

Some other category of norm?

Several writers argue that parliamentary supremacy is in a class of its own. As we have seen, Sir John Salmond (1862–1924)[29] wrote that it '[...] *is legally ultimate; its source is historical only, not legal* [...]. *It is the law because it is the law.*' Professor William Wade (1918–2004)[30] suggested that it is the 'ultimate *political* fact' in the following extract.

H.W.R. Wade, 'The basis of legal sovereignty' [1955] Cambridge Law Journal 172, 174, 187–8 (footnotes omitted)

An orthodox English lawyer, brought up consciously or unconsciously on the doctrine of parliamentary sovereignty stated by Coke and Blackstone, and enlarged upon by Dicey, could explain it in simple terms. He would say that it meant merely that no Act of the sovereign legislature (composed of the Queen, Lords and Commons) could be invalid in the eyes of the courts; that it was always open to the legislature, so constituted, to repeal any previous legislation whatever; that therefore no Parliament could bind its successors; and that the legislature had only one process for enacting sovereign legislation, whereby it was declared to be the joint Act of the Crown, Lords and Commons in Parliament assembled. He would probably add that it is an invariable rule that in case of conflict between two Acts of Parliament, the later repeals the earlier. If he were then asked whether it would be possible for the United Kingdom to 'entrench' legislation—for example, if it should wish to adopt, a Bill of Rights which would be repealable only by some specially safeguarded process—he would answer that under English law this is a legal impossibility: it is easy enough to pass such legislation, but since that legislation, like all other legislation, would be repealable by any ordinary Act of Parliament the special safeguards would be legally futile. This is merely an illustration of the rule that one Parliament cannot bind its successors. It follows therefore that there is one, and only one, limit to Parliament's legal power: it cannot detract from its own continuing sovereignty. It is tempting to add that Parliament's power is therefore inalienable, but that is to anticipate a question which must be investigated later on. For, leaving that point aside, we have already entered the area of controversy. Even the proposition that English law knows no means of 'entrenching' sovereign legislation, which most English lawyers would accept as a self-evident truth, has been questioned or denied by leading authorities. [...]

[I]f no statute can establish the rule that the courts obey Acts of Parliament, similarly no statute can alter or abolish that rule. The rule is above and beyond the reach of statute [...] because it is itself the source of the authority of statute. This puts it into a class by itself among rules of common law, and the apparent paradox that it is unalterable by Parliament turns out to be a truism. The rule of judicial obedience is in one sense a rule of common law, but in another sense—which applies to no other rule of common law—it is the ultimate *political* fact upon which the whole system of legislation hangs. Legislation owes its authority to the rule: the rule does not owe its authority to legislation. To say that Parliament can change the rule, merely because it can change any other rule, is to put the cart before the horse. For the relationship between the courts of law and Parliament is first and foremost a political reality.

---

[29] After studying law at UCL, Salmond returned to New Zealand where he held posts as Solicitor General and as a judge.

[30] Wade's academic career was spent at the universities of Oxford and Cambridge. His biographer noted: '*The confidence and clarity of Wade's vision of the law could sometimes come across as cocksure. But it was always logical, principled, and practical.*'

Professor Goldsworthy—an Australian academic—argues that it is a mistake to think of the doctrine of parliamentary supremacy as a 'creature of common law'.

Jeffrey Goldsworthy, 'Abdicating and limiting Parliament's sovereignty'
(2006) 17 King's College Law Journal 255, 261

[...] the doctrine of parliamentary sovereignty is constituted by a consensus among the senior officials of all branches of government. It was not (as history confirms) made by the judges alone. Its content is fixed by official consensus, and it is unclear insofar as there is no consensus. It cannot be changed unilaterally by any one branch of government, unless it is part of the consensus that it can be so changed, and there is little evidence that it is. Of course, any change to a rule of recognition must start somewhere: someone has to initiate the requisite change in consensus. The courts can attempt to initiate change, but they can succeed only if the other branches of government are willing to accept it.

Goldsworthy suggests that it would be wrong for the courts to alter parliamentary supremacy because *'they could impose all kinds of limits on Parliament's authority without any democratic input'.*[31] But, equally, it would be wrong for Parliament to attempt to do so: '[I]*f Parliament had such authority, a political party with temporary control of both Houses could protect its partisan policies, enacted into law, from amendment or repeal by majorities in future Parliaments, which would also be undemocratic.'*[32]

QUESTIONS

1. Which of the following best describes the source of parliamentary supremacy?

   (a) A common law rule.

   (b) The ultimate political fact of the UK constitution.

   (c) Something else (please specify).

2. Could Parliament unilaterally alter or dispense with parliamentary supremacy (for example, by amending the Human Rights Act 1998 to give the courts power to quash Acts of Parliament that are held to contravene a Convention right)?

3. Could the courts unilaterally alter or dispense with parliamentary supremacy by deciding that henceforth they have power under the common law to quash Acts of Parliament that contravene fundamental rights recognized by the common law?

(c) ENTRENCHMENT: CAN AN ACT OF PARLIAMENT BE MADE THAT BINDS FUTURE PARLIAMENTS?

This section examines three questions, as follows.

(a) In what circumstances might it be desirable to 'entrench' an Act of Parliament—that is, make it more difficult than normal for that Act to be repealed or amended?

---

[31] Jeffrey Goldsworthy, 'Abdicating and limiting Parliament's sovereignty' (2006) 17 King's College Law Journal 255, 261.
[32] Ibid.

(b) What mechanisms might be used to do this?

(c) Is it *possible* to entrench legislation in the UK constitutional system?

It is a matter of legal controversy as to whether this can actually be achieved in the British constitutional system, because the practice of 'entrenchment' can be thought to be incompatible with parliamentary supremacy.

In the next extract, Professor Saunders, an Australian academic, explains what is meant by the term 'entrenchment'.

Cheryl Saunders, 'Entrenchment of Constitutions and Legislation', in P. Cane and J. Conaghan (eds) *The New Oxford Companion to Law* (2008, Oxford: OUP), pp. 382–3

Entrenchment subjects the constitution or legislation to which it applies to an alteration procedure that is more difficult than that for ordinary laws. In extreme cases, it may prevent alteration altogether. Mechanisms for entrenchment typically range from requirements for special parliamentary majorities to use of the referendum. Typically, the provision that prescribes the special alteration procedure is itself entrenched, to prevent it from being altered by ordinary law, thus circumventing the effect of entrenchment.

There is no constitutional obstacle to entrenchment in states in which prevailing political theory accepts that the people is sovereign and can confer a system of government on itself. Difficulty may arise, however, where, as in the United Kingdom, theory assigns legal sovereignty to the parliament. There are at least two possible understandings of what sovereignty involves in this context. First, it might mean that the legislative authority of the current parliament can never be constrained by legislation of an earlier parliament, making entrenchment impossible. Secondly, it might mean that the authority of a current parliament extends even to protecting its own legislation from future change, albeit at cost to the authority of later parliaments. In *The Concept of Law* (Oxford: Oxford University Press, 1961), HLA Hart described the distinction as being between 'continuing' and 'self-embracing' sovereignty.

The former remains the orthodox understanding in the United Kingdom, favoured by AV Dicey and some early twentieth century case law. The latter applies in most other countries in the British constitutional tradition. Comparison is complicated by the colonial origins of the constitutional arrangements in these states. Nevertheless, it is increasingly difficult to reconcile continuing sovereignty with actual practice in the United Kingdom, and the question should be regarded as unsettled.

Its resolution is affected by various factors. First, an entrenching provision that prescribes the manner or the form in which amending legislation must be passed can be understood as altering the composition or the procedures of a future parliament for this purpose, rather than limiting parliamentary authority. This line of thought reconciles the possibility of entrenchment with the continuing view of parliamentary sovereignty, although in a highly artificial way. Secondly, the Parliament Acts of 1911 and 1949 have already altered the composition of parliament for some purposes. While these Acts make legislation easier, rather than more difficult, it has been held that they create an additional primary legislation-making procedure, and some judicial comments offer further encouragement to the possibility of entrenchment. Thirdly, the manner in which the United Kingdom gives effect to its obligations under European law in the European Communities Act 1972 appears to have settled that one parliament can constrain a later parliament at least in relation to the form in which alterations to its legislation are made. Finally, acceptance of entrenchment would have implications for the rule that courts will not look behind an Act of Parliament to examine the procedure by which it was made.

The desirability (or otherwise) of entrenching legislation

Entrenchment might be thought to be desirable to prevent fundamental constitutional characteristics and rights being repealed or amended at a later date. At the turn of the seventeenth and eighteenth centuries, a central concern in the negotiations over the union of England and Scotland was the need to ensure, 'in all times coming', the status of the Protestant faith (in the wake of generations of conflict between the Protestant and Catholic branches of the Christian Church). Accordingly, the Union with Scotland Act 1706 sought to do this.[33] In recent years, calls for entrenched legislation have related to the possibility of a Bill of rights, which would provide stronger protection than is currently offered by the (unentrenched) Human Rights Act 1998. This is against a background in which senior politicians in the Labour and Conservative Parties have called into question the continued existence of the Human Rights Act—for example, it was reported that '*David Cameron* [...] *called for the Human Rights Act to be scrapped outright for the first time amid mounting anger that the controversial law had allowed the killer of the head teacher Philip Lawrence to escape deportation*'.[34]

The arguments against the desirability of entrenchment (in the context of a possible Bill of rights) were considered by a parliamentary committee in August 2008.

Joint Committee on Human Rights, *A Bill of Rights for the UK?* 29th Report, Session 2007–08, HL 165-I/HC 150-I

233. A number of witnesses to our inquiry addressed the question of whether a Bill of Rights should be entrenched. They expressed a range of views. Some favoured entrenchment in order to ensure the superiority of a Bill of Rights and protect it from easy amendment by Parliament. One witness suggested that entrenchment is required to protect the power of the UK courts to adjudicate upon claimed violations of human rights and ensure an effective remedy.

234. On the other hand, other witnesses suggested that entrenchment may not be desirable. Professor Harlow opposed entrenchment because in her view the common law combined with parliamentary sovereignty allows rights to be easily updated as society changes, although she recognised that this could also mean that rights may be swept away more easily.

235. We are not in favour of entrenching a UK Bill of Rights against future amendment or repeal by requiring that any such amendments or repeal must satisfy a special procedure, such as approval by a special parliamentary majority or by the people in a referendum. In our view such forms of entrenchment are not compatible with our tradition of parliamentary democracy which has carefully preserved the freedom of each Parliament to legislate according to its view of the public interest.

How might entrenchment be achieved?

Assuming for a moment that it *is* possible to entrench Acts of Parliament in the UK (and be clear, the jury is out on this), the following are some of the main ways in which this might be attempted.

First, there could be a simple statement that a whole Act or section in an Act shall continue in force for all time in the future. In the following provision, the limitation was substantive

---

[33] See Chapter 4.

[34] C. Hope and C. Gammell, 'David Cameron: Scrap the Human Rights Act', *Daily Telegraph*, 22 August 2007. The case turned on EU law as much as the HRA.

rather than procedural. The negotiators of the union between England and Scotland were intent on ensuring *for all time* the 'fundamental and essential' place of the Protestant religion in the new United Kingdom.

Union with Scotland Act 1706, art. XXV, s. V (emphasis added)

That the said Act passed in this present Session of Parliament intituled An Act for securing the Church of England as by Law established and all and every the matters and things therein contained And also the said Act of Parliament of Scotland intituled Act for securing the Protestant Religion and Presbyterian Church Government with the Establishment in the said Act contained *be and shall for ever* be held and adjudged to be and observed as Fundamental and Essential Conditions of the said Union And shall *in all times coming* be taken to be and are hereby declared to be essential and fundamental parts of the said Articles and Union And the said Articles of Union so as aforesaid ratified approved and confirmed by Act of Parliament of Scotland and by this present Act And the said Act passed in this present Session of Parliament intituled an Act for securing the Church of England as by Law established And also the said Act passed in the Parliament of Scotland intituled Act for securing the Protestant Religion and Presbyterian Church Government are hereby enacted and ordained to be and continue *in all times coming* the complete and intire Union of the two Kingdoms of England and Scotland.

Attempts in the Act of Union to entrench provisions have not been successful: several other articles, said to be unchangeable, have in fact been amended or repealed in subsequent centuries.

A second way would be to make future legislation dependent on a referendum. Consider the following provision, originally included in the Northern Ireland Constitution Act 1973.

Northern Ireland Act 1998, s. 1

Status of Northern Ireland

(1) It is hereby declared that Northern Ireland in its entirety remains part of the United Kingdom and shall not cease to be so without the consent of a majority of the people of Northern Ireland voting in a poll held for the purposes of this section in accordance with Schedule 1.

(2) But if the wish expressed by a majority in such a poll is that Northern Ireland should cease to be part of the United Kingdom and form part of a united Ireland, the Secretary of State shall lay before Parliament such proposals to give effect to that wish as may be agreed between Her Majesty's Government in the United Kingdom and the Government of Ireland.

In other words, s. 1 seeks to place a limitation on Parliament enacting legislation to cede Northern Ireland to the Republic of Ireland, which may be done, it seems, only after there is a positive vote in a referendum. Another possible procedural hurdle, used in some countries, is to require a 'super-majority' of MPs (for example, two-thirds) to pass an amendment to a piece of legislation regarded as being of constitutional importance.

A third way would be to require a special parliamentary procedure before amendment or repeal takes place. This could be in the form of a 'super-majority' in the House of Commons. Another procedural requirement could be to specify that both chambers of Parliament have to consent to the alteration in the law. This would involve changes to the arrangements under the Parliament Act 1911 (as amended in 1949), whereby it is possible for a Bill to be presented for royal assent after two years even if the House of Lords is opposed to it.[35] These possibilities were considered by a committee of JUSTICE, the all-party law reform group, in a report examining what form a possible British Bill of rights might take.[36]

JUSTICE, *A British Bill of Rights: Informing the Debate—The Report of the JUSTICE Constitution Committee* (2008, London: JUSTICE), pp. 55–6

Amending the Parliament Acts

Under present UK constitutional arrangements, by far the most effective of these procedures would be to establish a requirement that the second chamber (House of Lords) gives its approval to all proposed amendments to the bill of rights. This is because the Parliament Acts allow the House of Commons, in certain circumstances, to overrule the House of Lords. A requirement that both Houses of Parliament must approve all proposed amendments to a bill of rights might represent the closest to constitutional entrenchment possible under current British constitutional arrangements.

Such a move would enhance the constitutional authority of the House of Lords, which under the terms of the Parliament Acts only possesses a maximum power of one year's delay over legislation (with the exception of bills to suspend general elections and the approval of statutory instruments). The implementation of this amendment procedure would probably form part of a wider programme of parliamentary reform involving working out the basis for the future composition of a revised second chamber. This wider reform would also need to involve some modernising redefinition of the functions and powers of the UK second chamber generally. These might include, among others, the scrutiny and approval of emergency derogating measures from the bill of rights and the consideration of administrative and legislative compliance with human rights generally. Drafting the provision in the bill of rights that future amendments will require the consent of both Houses of Parliament should be straightforward. All that is needed is a reference to the 1911 Parliament Act, excepting amendments to the bill of rights from the terms of its provisions.

Requirement of special voting majorities

Special majority voting is more problematic. This is principally because it is not an established part of existing UK constitutional and political practice. In addition there is the problem of a sovereign Parliament which, in theory, can amend or repeal any legislative provision. There is no precedent for special majority voting in Parliament, though standing orders regulate voting practice by laying down various requirements, for example that no fewer than 100 MPs must vote in support of a motion to end a debate in the House of Commons. The British government has included special majority voting in the amendment process of many of the Commonwealth constitutions it has drafted or helped draft for its former colonies and dominions, including Australia and South Africa.

---

[35] See Chapter 10 and Chapter 13.
[36] Andrew Le Sueur was a member of the committee.

An appropriate requirement for amending a UK bill of rights might be that the votes in favour must exceed one half of the total membership of the House concerned, or a two-thirds majority among those present and voting. Different or similar voting requirements might apply in each House. A two-thirds majority in both legislative chambers is the option most usually found abroad. This is the case in Canada, Germany and South Africa (in addition to support in six out of nine of the provinces). The same was supported by IPPR and Liberty in their draft bills of rights in the 1990s. By contrast, a Parliamentary majority suffices in New Zealand and Australian jurisdictions, where the bills of rights are ordinary statutes. The recent enactment process in the state of Victoria for its Charter of Rights and Responsibilities explicitly envisages amendment by providing that there be a review of the Act four years from its enactment and again in eight years.

Is it possible to entrench legislation in the UK constitutional system?

One basic constitutional question to be addressed in relation to the United Kingdom is whether it would be *possible* for the UK Parliament to entrench legislation (substantively or procedurally). Views on this are divided. In addressing this question, there appears at first to be a paradox. If we say that Parliament *is able to limit* its powers to enact legislation in the future and if Parliament were to do this, then it would cease to have full legal supremacy: in Dicey's words, 'A sovereign power cannot, while retaining its sovereign character, restrict its own powers by any particular enactment'.[37] But equally, if we say that Parliament *lacks capacity* to enact legislation restricting its future powers, then Parliament appears to lack full legal supremacy.

As we saw in the Saunders extract, there are two main schools of thought. Be clear: the disagreement here is over entrenchment, not over a Bill of rights. One of the prominent 'no entrenchment is possible' theorists, Sir William Wade, was firmly on the side of incorporating the ECHR into the UK constitution.[38]

The 'no entrenchment' school of thought can be found in the writings of Dicey and Wade, among others. The UK Parliament cannot, they say, effectively restrict how future Parliaments will exercise their primary law-making powers. Of course, there might, in the future, be some dramatic change to the nature of the UK constitution—such as a revolution or a consensus that judges should have power to review the constitutionality of statutes—but until any such 'Big Bang', people who support the concept of continuing supremacy take the view that the UK Parliament has no limits on its power to enact primary legislation. Speaking about the argument that there should be an *entrenched* Bill of rights, Wade said as follows.

H.W.R. Wade, *Constitutional Fundamentals*, 32nd Hamlyn Lectures (1980, London: Stevens), pp. 24–5

I approach this [...] as a purely technical problem of legislation: how can our legislative machinery be made to deliver these particular goods? In any normal situation there is no need for any question, since Parliament is omnipotent. But the one inherent limit on its

---

[37] A.V. Dicey, *Introduction to the Study of the Law of the Constitution* (1885; 10th edn 1959, London: Macmillan & Co), p. 68.

[38] H.W.R. Wade, *Constitutional Fundamentals*, 32nd Hamlyn Lectures (1980, London: Stevens), p. 24.

omnipotence, which is the consequence of that omnipotence itself, is that the Parliament of today cannot fetter the Parliament of tomorrow with any sort of permanent restraints, so that entrenched provisions are impossible. That, at any rate, appears to be the view of the legal establishment.

The gist of the concept of continuing supremacy is that Parliament's ability to legislate on any matter by the normal procedures is therefore (in Wade's words) 'indestructible by legislation'. An Act may specify a special procedure, or a limit on the substance of the legislation, but if a later Act repeals or amends that provision, the judges will follow what is stipulated in the later Act (because that is Parliament's most recent word on the matter). Wade stated '*it is always for the courts, in the last resort, to say what is a valid Act of Parliament*',[39] but he was not by this suggesting that the courts could take unilateral action to *change* the rules for recognizing legislation; rather, it was the job of the judges to be guardians of parliamentary supremacy. On the fundamental point of parliamentary supremacy, the famously flexible British constitution is not flexible at all.

Those who hold the different and opposing view of parliamentary supremacy (the consequence of which is that entrenchment *is* possible without any sort of 'Big Bang' revolution in the legal system) have what is labelled as the 'self-embracing', 'manner and form', or 'new' approach to supremacy. Sir Ivor Jennings was a leading exponent of this view. He contended that Dicey and Dicey's supporters were muddled about the term 'sovereignty'. We should, Jennings argued, stop thinking about Parliament as having 'supreme power' and instead focus on the key principle in the British constitution—that is, that '*the courts accept as law that which is made in the proper legal form*'. Jennings argued that it was possible for Parliament to refine the way in which law-making power was exercised—the 'manner and form' of legislation—which would bind future Parliaments.

Sir Ivor Jennings, *The Law and the Constitution*, 5th edn (1959, London: University of London Press), pp. 152–4 (emphasis in original)

'A sovereign power cannot, while retaining its sovereign character, restrict its own powers by any particular enactment,' says Dicey [...]. This is a perfectly correct deduction from the nature of a supreme power. If a prince has supreme power, and continues to have supreme power, he can do anything, even to the extent of undoing the things which he had previously done. If he grants a constitution, binding himself not to make laws except with the consent of an elected legislature, he has power immediately afterwards to abolish the legislature without its consent and to continue legislating by his personal decree.

But if the prince has not supreme power, but the rule is that the courts accept as law that which is made in the proper legal form, the result is different. For when the prince enacts that henceforth no rule shall be law unless it is enacted by him with the consent of the legislature, the law has been altered, and the courts will not admit as law any rule which is not made in that form. Consequently a rule subsequently made by the prince alone abolishing the legislature is not law, for the legislature has not consented to it, and the rule has not been enacted according to the manner and form required by the law for the time being.

The difference is this. In the one case there is sovereignty. In the other, the courts have no concern with sovereignty, but only with the established law. 'Legal sovereignty' is merely a

---

[39] H.W.R. Wade, 'The basis of legal sovereignty' [1955] Cambridge Law Journal 172, 189.

name indicating that the legislature has for the time being power to make laws of any kind in the manner required by the law. That is, a rule expressed to be made by the Queen, 'with the advice and consent of the Lords spiritual and temporal, and Commons in this present Parliament assembled, and by the authority of the same,' will be recognised by the courts, *including a rule which alters this law itself*. If this is so, the 'legal sovereign' may impose legal limitations upon itself, because its power to change the law includes the power to change the law affecting itself.

Academics continue to pore over the arguments and make assessments as to which one is more coherent.[40]

QUESTION

Suppose the government is concerned that a political campaign to abolish the monarchy is attracting a support. The government wants to introduce a Bill to provide that Her Majesty the Queen (and her successors) shall not cease to be Head of State unless:

(a) three-quarters of all MPs vote in favour of a change;

(b) both Houses of Parliament vote in favour of a change;

(c) in a referendum, 70 per cent of voters support a change; and

(d) any amendments to the Bill are subject to the same restrictions.

Write a briefing note advising whether these conditions will be binding on future Parliaments.

An alternative to entrenchment: A new judicial oath?

When judges take office, they swear or make a solemn affirmations of allegiance and the judicial oath under the terms of the Promissory Oaths Act 1868 (see Box 4.2 in Chapter 4). Sir William Wade suggested that this could provide a different way of achieving a kind of entrenchment.

H.W.R. Wade, *Constitutional Fundamentals*, 32nd Hamlyn Lectures (1980, London: Stevens), pp. 37–8

[...M]y own suggestion will seem, I fear, very simply and obvious. But I believe it to be one to which logic inexorably leads. All that needs to be done in order to entrench any sort of fundamental law is to secure its recognition in the judicial oath of office. The only trouble at present is that the existing form of oath gives no assurance of obedience to statutes binding later Parliaments. But there is every assurance that if the judges undertake upon their oath to act in some particular way they will do so. If we should wish to adopt a new form of constitution, therefore, all that need be done is to put the judges under oath to enforce it. An Act of Parliament can be passed to discharge them from their former oaths, if it were thought necessary, and to require them to be resworn in the new terms.

---

[40] See, e.g., Michael Gordon, 'The conceptual foundations of parliamentary sovereignty: Reconsidering Jennings and Wade' [2009] Public Law 519 (Gordon is a supporter of Jennings).

> QUESTION
>
> Can you draft a new oath that would achieve this goal?

(d) IMPLIED REPEAL

There is a further set of technical rules relating to parliamentary supremacy that is under-pinned by views of the nature of sovereignty and the constitution—that is, the rules on 'implied repeal'. With tens of thousands of pages of statute law, it is perhaps not surprising that on occasion—however careful parliamentary counsel are[41]—a situation arises in which Parliament has inadvertently made two Acts of Parliament that do not sit comfortably with each other. If the courts cannot reconcile them by interpretation and it is accepted that this is an incompatibility between two provisions in different Acts, then the implied repeal rules have to be deployed.

At first sight, these are disarmingly straightforward. The basic rule is that the later pro-vision is regarded by the courts as the one that is binding. Parliament is treated as having impliedly repealed the first provision when it enacted the second one. In the words of Laws LJ, '*The rule is that if Parliament has enacted successive statutes which on the true construc-tion of each of them make irreducibly inconsistent provisions, the earlier statute is impliedly repealed by the later*'.[42]

That basic rule is not, however, obviously a good one in all situations. There are a number of Acts of Parliament that (in the absence of a codified constitution) set out the ground rules for the operation of the British constitutional system. In the next extract, Laws LJ lists some of them and suggests a formula for working out whether an Act should be regarded as a 'constitutional statute' of this sort. If the basic rule of implied repeal were to apply to consti-tutional statutes, Parliament might end up inadvertently chipping away at the ground rules if, unintentionally, provisions are included in Acts that are incompatible with a constitu-tional statute. Laws LJ put forward the proposition, now widely accepted, that the basic rule does not apply in relation to constitutional statutes; rather, the courts will treat these Acts as amended or repealed only if Parliament amends or repeals them expressly, in clear words. The constitutional statute in question was the European Communities Act 1972.

The legal issue that Laws LJ faced was whether local authority officers could lawfully insist that unpackaged fruit, vegetables, and fish be sold in metric units rather than impe-rial measures (pounds and ounces)—and whether they could confiscate scales from green-grocers and fishmongers who refused to comply, and bring criminal proceedings against them. Steven Thoburn was one of 'the metric martyrs' who campaigned against this requirement. In his judgment, Laws LJ refers to the *Factortame* litigation of the 1990s, in which the British courts accepted that EU laws had primacy over any inconsistent UK law; we look at *Factortame* in detail in Chapter 18, along with the EU-law aspects of *Thoburn*. For current purposes, our focus is on what Laws LJ says about the general idea of 'consti-tutional statutes'

---

[41] On parliamentary counsel, see Chapter 9.

[42] *Thoburn v Sunderland City Council* [2002] EWHC 195 (Admin) [37].

Thoburn v Sunderland City Council
[2002] EWHC 195 (Admin)

Laws LJ

[59] [. . .] Parliament cannot bind its successors by stipulating against repeal, wholly or partly, of the ECA [that is, the European Communities Act 1972]. It cannot stipulate as to the manner and form of any subsequent legislation. It cannot stipulate against implied repeal any more than it can stipulate against express repeal. Thus there is nothing in the ECA which allows the Court of Justice, or any other institutions of the EU, to touch or qualify the conditions of Parliament's legislative supremacy in the United Kingdom. Not because the legislature chose not to allow it; because by our law it could not allow it. That being so, the legislative and judicial institutions of the EU cannot intrude upon those conditions. The British Parliament has not the authority to authorise any such thing. Being sovereign, it cannot abandon its sovereignty. Accordingly there are no circumstances in which the jurisprudence of the Court of Justice can elevate Community law to a status within the corpus of English domestic law to which it could not aspire by any route of English law itself. This is, of course, the traditional doctrine of sovereignty. If is to be modified, it certainly cannot be done by the incorporation of external texts. The conditions of Parliament's legislative supremacy in the United Kingdom necessarily remain in the United Kingdom's hands. But the traditional doctrine has in my judgment been modified. It has been done by the common law, wholly consistently with constitutional principle.

[60] The common law has in recent years allowed, or rather created, exceptions to the doctrine of implied repeal: a doctrine which was always the common law's own creature. There are now classes or types of legislative provision which cannot be repealed by mere implication. These instances are given, and can only be given, by our own courts, to which the scope and nature of Parliamentary sovereignty are ultimately confided. The courts may say—have said—that there are certain circumstances in which the legislature may only enact what it desires to enact if it does so by express, or at any rate specific, provision.

[. . .] In the present state of its maturity the common law has come to recognise that there exist rights which should properly be classified as constitutional or fundamental: see for example such cases as *Simms* [2000] 2 AC 115 per Lord Hoffmann at 131, *Pierson v Secretary of State* [1998] AC 539, *Leech* [1994] QB 198, *Derbyshire County Council v Times Newspapers Ltd.* [1993] AC 534, and *Witham* [1998] QB 575. And from this a further insight follows. We should recognise a hierarchy of Acts of Parliament: as it were "ordinary" statutes and "constitutional" statutes. The two categories must be distinguished on a principled basis. In my opinion a constitutional statute is one which (a) conditions the legal relationship between citizen and State in some general, overarching manner, or (b) enlarges or diminishes the scope of what we would now regard as fundamental constitutional rights. (a) and (b) are of necessity closely related: it is difficult to think of an instance of (a) that is not also an instance of (b). The special status of constitutional statutes follows the special status of constitutional rights. Examples are the Magna Carta, the Bill of Rights 1689, the Act of Union, the Reform Acts which distributed and enlarged the franchise, the HRA, the Scotland Act 1998 and the Government of Wales Act 1998. The ECA clearly belongs in this family. It incorporated the whole corpus of substantive Community rights and obligations, and gave overriding domestic effect to the judicial and administrative machinery of Community law. It may be there has never been a statute having such profound effects on so many dimensions of our daily lives. The ECA is, by force of the common law, a constitutional statute.

[63] Ordinary statutes may be impliedly repealed. Constitutional statutes may not. For the repeal of a constitutional Act or the abrogation of a fundamental right to be effected by

statute, the court would apply this test: is it shown that the legislature's actual – not imputed, constructive or presumed – intention was to effect the repeal or abrogation? I think the test could only be met by express words in the later statute, or by words so specific that the inference of an actual determination to effect the result contended for was irresistible. The ordinary rule of implied repeal does not satisfy this test. Accordingly, it has no application to constitutional statutes. I should add that in my judgment general words could not be sup-plemented, so as to effect a repeal or significant amendment to a constitutional statute, by reference to what was said in Parliament by the minister promoting the Bill pursuant to *Pepper v Hart* [1993] AC 593. A constitutional statute can only be repealed, or amended in a way which significantly affects its provisions touching fundamental rights or otherwise the relation between citizen and State, by unambiguous words on the face of the later statute.

[64] This development of the common law regarding constitutional rights, and as I would say constitutional statutes, is highly beneficial. It gives us most of the benefits of a written constitution, in which fundamental rights are accorded special respect. But it preserves the sovereignty of the legislature and the flexibility of our uncodified constitution. It accepts the relation between legislative supremacy and fundamental rights is not fixed or brittle: rather the courts (in interpreting statutes, and now, applying the HRA) will pay more or less defer-ence to the legislature, or other public decision-maker, according to the subject in hand. Nothing is plainer than that this benign development involves, as I have said, the recognition of the ECA as a constitutional statute.

The approach taken by Laws LJ is not an orthodox one. In the past, commentators have often stressed that there are not different categories of statute in the United Kingdom—the Dentists Act 1984 or the Dangerous Dogs Act 1991 (statutes of no constitutional signifi-cance) are 'the same as' the Human Rights Act 1998 or the Parliament Acts (statutes that are very clearly of constitutional significance). But no judge has yet called into question Laws LJ's approach in *Thoburn*.

QUESTIONS

1. Laws LJ's rule in *Thoburn* requires a distinction to be made between constitutional and ordinary statutes. How easy or difficult is it to make such a distinction?

2. Analyse whether the following are 'constitutional' or 'ordinary' statutes, using the test proposed by Laws LJ:

 (a) a tax statute;

 (b) an Act making it compulsory for children to receive education;

 (c) an Act establishing the National Health Service; and

 (d) an Act creating a new criminal offence.

(e) EUROPE

As has already been noted, the United Kingdom's participation in the two European inte-gration projects—the Council of Europe and the EU—has had an impact on the concept and practice of parliamentary supremacy, as the next extract discusses. We return to these issues in Chapter 6 (in relation to the Human Rights Act 1998) and Chapter 18 (in relation to the EU).

Mark Elliott, 'Parliamentary sovereignty under pressure' [2004] International Journal of Constitutional Law 545, 552–4 (footnotes omitted)

The Human Rights Act gives effect in U.K. law to many of the provisions of the European Convention on Human Rights. None of the rights contained in the ECHR are placed beyond parliamentary interference by the HRA: indeed, when the government set out its proposals for legislation in this area, it emphasized its ongoing attachment to the traditional doctrine of parliamentary sovereignty. This, however, evidences a rather myopic view, which unhelpfully dislocates legislative power from the wider political environment within which it subsists, and which the HRA has changed radically. The attention of Parliament is now systematically drawn to the human rights implications of draft legislation: its enactments must, whenever possible, be read consistently with relevant provisions of the ECHR—an obligation that the courts have discharged with notable enthusiasm in some cases. Further, some national courts are empowered to issue declarations of incompatibility if legislation is found to fall short of ECHR norms, thereby triggering the possibility of fast-track amendment by means of administrative legislation. In the unlikely event that these national provisions prove insufficient to secure respect for human rights in a particular case, there remains the prospect of proceedings before the European Court of Human Rights. As Lord Borrie said in a House of Lords debate on the Human Rights Bill (as it then was known) 'the political reality will be that, while historically the courts have sought to carry out the will of Parliament, in the field of human rights Parliament will carry out the will of the courts [. . . T]he intention of the Bill surely is that government and Parliament will faithfully implement any declaratory judgment made by the High Court.'

Like its power to depart from EU law, Parliament's ability to derogate from the ECHR, although formally undisturbed by the HRA, begins to look increasingly notional. A new political environment is emerging in which a legal doctrine of legislative supremacy appears at least anomalous.

The same point can be made in relation to the program of asymmetric devolution by which varying amounts of legislative and administrative power have been transferred to Northern Ireland, Wales and Scotland, reflecting different levels of public support for self-government in the constituent nations of the United Kingdom. Notwithstanding substantial differences among the schemes, an important common factor is that the U.K. Parliament has not renounced legislative sovereignty in relation to the three nations concerned. For example, the Scottish Parliament is empowered to enact primary legislation on all matters, save those in relation to which competence is explicitly denied, but this power to legislate on what may be termed 'devolved matters' is concurrent with the Westminster Parliament's general power to legislate for Scotland on any matter at all, including devolved matters. In theory, therefore, Westminster may legislate on Scottish devolved matters whenever it chooses; in practice, however, it does not. A constitutional convention rapidly emerged to the effect that 'the U.K. Parliament would not normally legislate with regard to devolved matters except with the agreement of the devolved legislature.' The reason for this convention is self-evident: unilateral interference in devolved matters by the U.K. Parliament would fundamentally undermine the spirit of the devolution scheme. It would be politically unacceptable for the Westminster Parliament to ignore the wishes of the Scottish people as expressed by their elected representatives in the Scottish Parliament. As time passes, and as devolution is woven ever more closely into the constitutional fabric of the United Kingdom, the theoretical ability of the U.K. Parliament to interfere unilaterally with devolved matters will be seen increasingly as a vestige of an unreconstructed doctrine of absolute legislative authority.

In practice, the UK Parliament is bound by the terms of the treaties establishing the European Union; but politicians make the point that the European Communities Act 1972 is *not* entrenched. Consider, for example, the following answer from Denis MacShane, a Minister for Europe.

House of Commons Hansard, 15 December 2003, col. 732W

Mr MacShane

The ultimate guarantee of parliamentary sovereignty lies in the power of Parliament to repeal all or any of the Acts which give effect to the EU treaties in this country. It is within Parliament's power to legislate contrary to the UK's treaty obligations. [...] The result of so doing, however, would be to place the UK in breach of its treaty obligations.

(f) THE FUTURE OF PARLIAMENTARY SUPREMACY

We end this examination of parliamentary supremacy with speculation about its future. There seem to be three main possibilities. The first is that parliamentary supremacy remains the dominant principal in the British constitution—albeit modified to make possible UK membership of the EU and Council of Europe.

A second is that the United Kingdom adopts a codified constitution, which becomes the source of Parliament's law-making powers with the courts (or maybe a constitutional court separate from the main court system) responsible for enforcing the provisions of new constitution.

A third possible scenario is that the UK Supreme Court may, at some point in the future, decide that the British judiciary henceforth has power to adjudicate on the constitutional validity of Acts of Parliament, in order to protect rights recognized by the common law. Changes in apparently settled principles of common law relating to the constitution do occasionally occur. For example, in 1984, the Law Lords held that the exercise of prerogative powers was not immune from judicial review.[43] Among senior judges, there are some who appear to contemplate this at least as a theoretical option.

Jackson v Her Majesty's Attorney General
[2005] UKHL 56, [102]

Lord Steyn

We do not in the United Kingdom have an uncontrolled constitution as the Attorney General implausibly asserts [...] The classic account given by Dicey of the doctrine of the supremacy of Parliament, pure and absolute as it was, can now be seen to be out of place in the modem United Kingdom. Nevertheless, the supremacy of Parliament is still the general principle of our constitution. It is a construct of the common law. The judges created this principle. If that is so, it is not unthinkable that circumstances could arise where the courts may have to qualify a principle established on a different hypothesis of constitutionalism. In exceptional circumstances involving an attempt to abolish judicial review or the ordinary role of the

---

[43] *Council of Civil Service Unions v Minister for the Civil Service* [1985] AC 374 (the *GCHQ* case).

courts, the Appellate Committee of the House of Lords or a new Supreme Court may have to consider whether this is a constitutional fundamental which even a sovereign Parliament acting at the behest of a complaisant House of Commons cannot abolish.

Some have suggested that the whole concept of Parliament alone 'being sovereign' is no longer appropriate in a modern constitution for Britain, and there has been talk of 'bipolar sovereignty' in which the powers of both Parliament *and the judiciary* are recognized.

C.J.S. Knight, 'Bi-polar sovereignty restated' [2009] Cambridge Law Journal 361, 362, 365–6

[...B]i-polar sovereignty [...] can be theoretically justified by reference to the work of Sir Stephen Sedley [a judge of the Court of Appeal in England and Wales] and W.J. Rees [an academic]. What their work can provide is an understanding of the functional overlap between Parliament and the courts. The setting against which the overlap is conceived is the constitutional history of institutional pragmatism. One can consider the relationship between the two concepts in the following way: how the restated bi-polar sovereignty presented can work is explained theoretically here in the context of a constitution which has a long history of evolving practical answers to problems, anticipated or actual. Institutional pragmatism as used here is conceived as a readiness to use one institution to compensate for perceived or actual weaknesses in another, or to take on new functions as the institution develops. [...]

[...] Sir Stephen [...] wrote that there was emerging a new "constitutional paradigm" that was: '[...] no longer of Dicey's supreme parliament to whose will the rule of law must finally bend, but of a bi-polar sovereignty of the Crown in Parliament and the Crown in its courts, to each of which the Crown's ministers are answerable—politically to Parliament, legally to the courts.'

The suggestion is an extremely important one, not least because of the position of its author, and has attracted a good deal of attention. It is often grouped together with the classic suggestions of a higher-order law that might permit the courts to strike down legislation if it was thought to sufficiently breach the rule of law, and more particularly, exclude the role of the judiciary. Lord Irvine [Lord Chancellor 1997–2003] certainly treated all four extra-judicial articles as similar expressions of judicial supremacism and famously labelled them as "extra-judicial romanticism".

[...] While higher-order law relates to constitutional theory, it might be more accurately classified as part of a notion of a substantive rule of law with all the writings, legal and theoretical baggage that go along with that debate. In contrast, bipolar sovereignty is firmly located in constitutional theory. The theory provides a method of questioning the simplicity of the sovereign being the Crown-in-Parliament and seeks to supply a new understanding that better recognises the complexity of the relationship between the judicial and legislative/executive branches. A common law system means that, at least in reality, the courts make law just as the legislature does. Its pronouncements may be altered or overruled by the legislature, but that does not deny the force of the common law.

But for every judicial statement calling into question orthodox thinking about parliamentary supremacy, it is possible to find a hundred showing commitment to the notion that the judge's role is to uphold parliamentary supremacy. For one such statement, see Lord Millet's statement in a case relating to the protection in the Rent Act 1977 following the death of a tenant. Originally, the 1977 Act stated that where a tenancy was in the name of one party to a marriage (it was usually in that of the husband), the other could not be evicted. That was later extended to cover unmarried men and women (in situations in which the survivor had lived with the tenant '*as* his or her wife or husband'). In *Ghaidan*, the question arose whether that protection also covered gay couples if the phrase was interpreted so as to be compatible with Convention rights under the Human Rights Act 1998, s. 3.[44] Lord Millet, dissenting, thought that the words should not be stretched to extend to gay people.

Ghaidan v Godin-Mendoza
[2004] UKHL 30, [57]

I have given long and anxious consideration to the question whether, in the interests of una-nimity, I should suppress my dissent, but I have come to the conclusion that I should not. The question is of great constitutional importance, for it goes to the relationship between the legislature and the judiciary, and hence ultimately to the supremacy of Parliament. Sections 3 and 4 of the Human Rights Act were carefully crafted to preserve the existing constitutional doctrine, and any application of the ambit of s. 3 beyond its proper scope subverts it. This is not to say that the doctrine of Parliamentary supremacy is sacrosanct, but only that any change in a fundamental constitutional principle should be the consequence of deliberate legislative action and not judicial activism, however well meaning.

4 CONCLUDING COMMENTS

This chapter has examined the constitutional principles of parliamentary supremacy, setting them in the context of an ongoing debate between supporters of political and legal constitutionalism.

5 FURTHER READING

Bradley, A., 'The Sovereignty of Parliament: Form or Substance?' in J. Jowell and D. Oliver (eds) *The Changing Constitution*, 7th edn (2011, Oxford: OUP), ch. 1

Bellamy, R., 'Political constitutionalism and the Human Rights Act' (2011) 9 International Journal of Constitutional Law 86

ONLINE RESOURCE CENTRE

Further information about the themes discussed in this chapter can be found on the Online Resource Centre at www.oxfordtextbooks.co.uk/orc/lesueur2e/

---

[44] On s. 3, see Chapter 17.

3

THE RULE OF LAW

CENTRAL ISSUES

1. The 'rule of law' is widely acknowledged to be an essential component of a good constitution: it is a principle that is concerned with constraining governmental action. First articulated in the nineteenth century, it has become increasingly frequently used by academics, politicians and judges during the twentieth century.

2. Academics disagree about how to define the rule of law. Some argue it should be 'content-free', dealing only with the form of law and the procedures by which law is made. Others favour a 'content-rich' meaning, so that the substance of laws should have to comply with fundamental rights. Dicey's influential three-limb explanation of the rule of law continues to be a point of reference despite strong criticism. Some academics take a sceptical stance, doubting whether it is possible or desirable to have an agreed definition of the rule of law.

3. Judges have an important but not exclusive role in protecting the rule of law using a variety of 'tools': recognizing fundamental rights and freedoms integral to the common law; through the application of tort law; and by use of techniques of statutory interpretation such as the 'principle of legality'.

Various criticisms may be made of these approaches and it is open to question how effective they are.

4. Parliament has the power, through Acts of Parliament, both to safeguard the rule of law and to weaken it. In recent years, improved parliamentary procedures provide more systematic checks on government proposals that deliberately or inadvertently breach rule of law principles. But parliamentary supremacy (see Chapter 2) means that Parliament can, if it chooses, legislate contrary to fundamental principles of human rights and the rule of law.

5. Within government, various office holders are responsible for ensuring respect for the rule of law. Among these, the Lord Chancellor's role is regarded as being of particular importance. Radical reforms to the office of Lord Chancellor made in 2005 are thought by some to have weakened the ability of this office to protect the rule of law even though the Constitutional Reform Act 2005 s. 1 declares that the reforms do not adversely affect the existing constitutional principle of the rule of law or the Lord Chancellor's role in relation to that principle.

1 INTRODUCTION

The aim of this chapter is to explain 'the rule of law'. This idea developed in the British constitutional system during the nineteenth century; throughout the twentieth century, academics, judges, lawyers and politicians have referred to it with increasing frequency. Comparable though not identical ideas exist in other countries: in Germany, for example, the term used is *Rechtsstaat* ('recht' means 'law', 'staat' means 'state'); in France, *l'État de droit*.

To understand the rule of law, it is necessary to ask at least two basic questions. First: how is the rule of law defined? As we see in section 2, Defining the rule of law, the late Lord Bingham proposed a definition that has quickly become influential. Underlying his definition is a number of academic controversies, which need to be explored.

Second: how is the rule of law protected? If the rule of law is going to make a practical contribution to better government it has to be enforced. In the United Kingdom, we will see in section 3, Practical protection of the rule of law, that different constitutional actors are involved: the courts using a variety of techniques; Parliament; and government (especially the Lord Chancellor).

QUESTION

Imagine what sort of country you want to live in. Suppose your employer is posting you and your family abroad and gives you a choice between two countries. Which would you prefer?

In country A, the parliament sometimes sits in secret session to pass legislation that is never published. The police have broad powers to enter anybody's home without a search warrant. People suspected of having disrespectful thoughts about government ministers may be held in custody indefinitely, without being charged or brought to trial. There is a constitution setting out some basic rights, such as freedom of expression, but the government has an overriding power to order the courts to ignore those rights if there is deemed to be a national emergency. Politicians and officials have immunity from being sued in the civil courts or tried in the criminal courts. Only those who have demonstrated loyalty to the governing party are appointed to be judges; courts normally sit in private.

In country B, all legislation passed by the parliament is easily accessible on a website, along with well-written guides written for lay people. The powers of officials are strictly limited by the constitution and basic freedoms contained in all relevant international human rights treaties have been incorporated into national law. There is a generous system of legal aid, enabling anybody concerned by the legality of government action to bring legal proceedings even if they cannot afford to pay a lawyer; cases are determined in public with only minimal delays. There is a high degree of judicial independence. Politicians and officials are respectful of adverse court rulings and always implement them.

---

2 DEFINING THE RULE OF LAW

As a starting point, we need to work out what 'the rule of law' means. Throughout the twentieth century, it is a term that has become evermore widespread in academic legal writing, court judgments, parliamentary debates, and official documents. Section 1 of the

Constitutional Reform Act 2005 (the only statute expressly referring to the concept) seeks to reassure us that reforms to the office of Lord Chancellor introduced by the government of Tony Blair *'does not adversely affect— (a) the existing constitutional principle of the rule of law, or (b) the Lord Chancellor's existing constitutional role in relation to that principle'.* International treaties also use the concept. The preamble to the European Convention on Human Rights, written in the aftermath of the catastrophic breakdown of democracy in Europe, speaks of *'a common heritage of political traditions, ideals, freedom and the rule of law ...'* The preamble to the Treaty on European Union states the EU *'draws inspiration'* from *'the universal values of the inviolable and inalienable rights of the human person, freedom, democracy, quality and the rule of law'.* The World Bank (an international body that funds poverty reduction projects in developing countries) routinely seeks to measure and lay down compliance conditions relating to the rule of law, believing these aid democratization and economic progress.

But what do these references to the rule of law mean? One approach is to understand the rule of law as a list of essential characteristics relating to law and legal process that ought to exist in a good constitutional system. A recent attempt at this is by the late Lord Bingham (1933–2010) who was successively Master of the Rolls, Lord Chief Justice of England and Wales, and the Senior Law Lord. In a lecture subsequently elaborated on in a book, he argued that *'the core of the existing principle is ... that all persons and authorities within the state, whether public or private, should be bound by and entitled to the benefit of laws publicly and prospectively promulgated and publicly administered in the courts'.*[1] He then went on to identify and discuss eight 'sub-rules':

1. *'The law must be accessible and so far as possible intelligible, clear and predictable.'*
2. *'Questions of legal right and liability should ordinarily be resolved by application of the law and not the exercise of discretion.'*
3. *'The laws of the land should apply equally to all, save to the extent that objective differences require differentiation.'*
4. *'Ministers and public officers at all levels must exercise the powers conferred on them in good faith, fairly, for the purpose for which the powers were conferred, without exceeding the limits of such powers and not unreasonably.'*
5. *'The law must afford adequate protection of fundamental rights.'*
6. *'Means must be provided for resolving, without prohibitive cost or undue delay, bona fide civil disputes which the parties themselves are unable to resolve'.*
7. *'Adjudicative procedures provided by the state should be fair.'*
8. *'The rule of law requires compliance by the state with its obligations in international law as in national law.'*

Coming from the pen of one of our greatest and most humane judges, it is not surprising that this checklist quickly became influential. The European Commission on Democracy through Law ('the Venice Commission') adopted it in its 2011 report on the rule of law.[2] The Bingham Centre for the Rule of Law, based in London and named after Lord Bingham, is an organisation of lawyers, academics, and judges 'devoted to identifying rule of law issues in national, regional and international systems and seeking to analyse, establish and promote

---

[1] 'The Rule of Law' (2007) 66 CLJ 67, 69 (the published version of the lecture); *The Rule of Law* (2010, London: Allen Lane) p. 37.

[2] European Commission for Democracy through Law (Venice Commission), *Report on the Rule of Law* (Adopted by the Venice Commission at its 86th plenary session, Venice, 25–26 March 2011).

the rule of law's fundamental qualities'.[3] Against this background, it may seem tempting simply to agree that Lord Bingham's criteria form a definitive statement of what the rule of law is in the twenty-first century. To do so would, however, ignore several important disagreements.

> **QUESTION**
>
> Look back at scenarios in the first question and analyse carefully how well or badly countries A and B match up to Lord Bingham's eight sub-rules.

(a) CONTENT FREE OR CONTENT RICH?

The first academic and political controversy goes to the heart of what should be included within the notion of the rule of law.

On one view, the rule of law should only be about the form of law and the procedures by which law is made. These aspects of the rule of law map onto Lord Bingham's sub-rules 1, 2, 6, and 7. This view does not prescribe any particular content for legal rules. In his 1977 article advocating this understanding, the legal philosopher Professor Joseph Raz argued strongly against '*the promiscuous use made in recent years of the expression "the rule of law"*'.[4] He offered a 'very incomplete' list of the '*principles that can be derived from the basic idea of the rule of law*', which can be summarized as follows: all laws should be prospective, open, and clear; laws should be relatively stable; the making of particular laws (particular legal orders) should be guided by open, stable, clear, and general rules; the independence of the judiciary must be guaranteed; the principles of natural justice must be observed—meaning procedural fairness in decision-making by public officials; the courts should have review powers over the implementation of other principles; the courts should be easily accessible; and the discretion of the crime-preventing agencies should not be allowed to pervert the law. Raz draws the following conclusions.

Joseph Raz, 'The rule of law and its virtue' (1977) 93 Law Quarterly Review 195, 210–11

Conformity with the rule of law is a matter of degree, and though other things being equal, the greater the conformity the better—other things are rarely equal. A lesser degree of conformity is often to be preferred precisely because it helps realisation of other goals.

In considering the relations between the rule of law and the other values the law should serve it is of particular importance to remember that the rule of law is essentially a negative value. It is merely designed to minimise the harm to freedom and dignity which the law may cause in its pursuit of its goals however laudable these may be. Finally regarding the rule of law as the inherent excellence of the law means that it fulfils essentially a subservient role. Conformity to it makes the law a good instrument for achieving certain goals, but conformity to the rule of law is not itself an ultimate goal. This subservient role of the doctrine shows both its power and its limitations. On the one hand if the pursuit of certain goals is entirely incompatible with the rule of law then these goals should not be pursued by legal means. But

---

[3] http://www.biicl.org/binghamcentre/
[4] 'The Rule of Law and its Virtue' (1977) 93 LQR 195, 196.

on the other hand one should be wary of disqualifying the legal pursuit of major social goals in the name of the rule of law. After all the rule of law is meant to enable the law to promote social good, and should not be lightly used to show that it should not do so. Sacrificing too many social goals on the altar of the rule of law may make the law barren and empty.

So Raz argues for a negative, content-free, 'thin' version of the rule of law. If this is correct, then it is possible to say that an evil legal system (for example, one based on race or religious discrimination) could nonetheless be regarded as respectful of the rule of law if it conformed to required forms and processes. A law removing the right to vote from members of a religious minority could be described as 'undemocratic' and 'wrong' but if the law was passed according to normal parliamentary procedures, was published and accessible to all, and if there was adequate access to the courts for people who want to argue that they were not a member of that minority, then it could be rule of law compliant.

A content-free rule of law also takes little account of social and economic equality between people—what matters is formal equality. The French writer Anotole France captures this in his bon mot: *'The law, in its majestic equality, forbids the rich and the poor alike to sleep under bridges, to beg in the streets, and to steal bread'*. So the rule of law is not concerned with socio-economic rights, such as rights to food, housing, health, and education. Only if economic equality directly impinges on one of the basic elements of the content-free rule of law, such as access to the courts, does it become relevant. A judge's quip that *'In England, justice is open to all – like the Ritz hotel'* is frequently invoked a century after it was made whenever cuts to public funding of litigation (legal aid) is proposed.[5] In Lord Bingham's words, 'denial of legal protection to the poor litigant who cannot afford to pay is one enemy of the rule of law'.[6]

Why do some people believe that it is a good idea to confine the rule of law to formal matters and steer clear of the substance of the law? Professor Paul Craig (not himself a supporter of this content-free version of the rule of law) gave the following explanation to the House of Lords Constitution Committee.

Paul Craig, 'The Rule of Law' A paper for the House of Lords Constitution Committee, 6th Report 2006–07, HL 151 *Relations between the Executive, the Judiciary and Parliament* p. 101.

The rationale for restricting the rule of law in this manner is as follows. We may all agree that laws should be just, that their content should be morally sound and that rights should be protected within society. The problem is that if the rule of law is taken to encompass the necessity for 'good laws' in this sense then the concept ceases to have an independent function. There is a wealth of literature devoted to the discussion of the meaning of a just society, the nature of the rights which should subsist therein, and the appropriate boundaries of governmental action. Political theory has tackled questions such as these from time immemorial To bring these issues within the rubric of the rule of law would therefore rob this concept of an independent function. Laws would be condemned or upheld as being in conformity with, or contrary to, the rule of law when the condemnation or praise would simply be reflective of attachment to a particular conception of rights, democracy or the just society. The message

---

[5] The Ritz Hotel is one of the most luxurious and expensive in London.
[6] Tom Bingham, *The Rule of Law* (Allen Lane, 2010), p. 85.

is therefore that if you wish to argue about the justness of society do so by all means. If you wish to defend a particular type of individual right then present your argument. Draw upon the wealth of literature which addresses these matters directly. It is however on this view not necessary or desirable to cloak the conclusion in the mantle of the rule of law, since this will merely reflect the conclusion which has already been arrived at through reliance on a particular theory of rights or the just society.

In the following extract, Professor Ronald Dworkin challenges the idea of a content-free rule of law (which he derides as a 'rule book conception') and puts forward an alternative 'rights' conception.

Ronald Dworkin, 'Political Judges and the Rule of Law', in *A Matter of Principle* (1985, Oxford: OUP), ch. 1, pp. 11–12

What is the rule of law? Lawyers (and almost everyone else) think that there is a distinct and important political ideal called the rule of law. But they disagree about what that ideal is. There are, in fact, two very different conceptions of the rules of law, each of which has its partisans. The first I shall call the 'rule book' conception. This insists that, so far as is possible, the power of the state should never be exercised against individual citizens except in accordance with rules explicitly set out in a public rule book available to all. The government as well as ordinary citizens must play by these public rules until they are changed, in accordance with further rules about how they are to be changed, which are also set out in the rule book. The rule-book conception is, in one sense, very narrow, because it does not stipulate anything about the content of the rules that may be put in the rule book. It insists only that whatever rules that may be put in the rule book must be followed until changed. Those who have this conception of the rule of law do care about the content of the rules in the rule book, but they say that this is a matter of substantive justice, and that substantive justice in an independent ideal, in no sense part of the ideal of the rule of law.

I shall call the second conception of the rule of law the 'rights' conception. It is in several ways more ambitious than the rule-book conception. It assumes that citizens have moral rights and duties with respect to one another, and political rights against the state as a whole. It insists that these moral and political rights be recognized in positive law, so that they may be enforced *upon the demand of individual citizens* through the courts and other judicial institutions of the familiar types, so far as this is practicable. The rule of law on this conception is the ideal of rule by an accurate public conception of individual rights. It does not distinguish, as the rule-book conception does, between the rule of law and the substantive justice; on the contrary it requires, as part of the ideal of law, that the rules in the rule book capture and enforce moral rights.

That is a complex ideal. The rule-book conception of the rule of law has only one dimension along which a political community might fall short. It might use its police power over individual citizens otherwise than as the rule book specifies. But the rights conception has at least three dimensions of failure. A state might fail in the scope of the individual rights it purports to enforce. It might decline to enforce rights against itself, for example, though it concedes citizens have such rights. It might fail in the accuracy of the rights it recognizes: it might provide for rights against the state, hut through official mistake fail to recognize important rights. Or it might fail in the fairness of its enforcement of rights: it might adopt rules that put the poor or some disfavored race at a disadvantage in securing the rights the state acknowledges they have.

The rights conception is therefore more complex than the rule-book conception. There are other important contrasts between the two conceptions; some of these can be identified by considering the different places they occupy in a general theory of justice. Though the two conceptions compete as ideals of the legal process (because. as we shall see, they recommend different theories of adjudication), they are nevertheless compatible as more general ideals for a just society. Any political community is better, all else equal, if its courts take no action other than is specified in rules published in advance, and also better, all else equal, if its legal institutions enforce whatever rights individual citizens have. Even as general political ideals, however, the two conceptions differ in the following way. Some high degree of compliance with the rule-book conception seems necessary to a just society. Any government that acts contrary to its own rule book very often—at least in matters important to particular citizens cannot be just, no matter how wise or fair its institutions otherwise are. But compliance with the rule book is plainly not sufficient for justice; full compliance will achieve very great injustice if the rules are unjust. The opposite holds for the rights conception. A society that achieves a high rating an each of the dimensions of the rights conception is almost certainly a just society, even though it may be mismanaged or lack other qualities of a desirable society. But it is widely thought, at least, that the rights conception is not necessary to a just society, because it is not necessary, in order that the rights of citizens be protected, that citizens be able to demand adjudication and enforcement of these rights as individuals. A government of wise and just officers will protect rights (so the argument runs) on its own initiative, without procedure whereby citizens can dispute, as individuals, what these rights are. Indeed, the rights conception of the rule of law, which insists on the importance of that opportunity, is often dismissed as legalistic, as encouraging mean and selfish concern with individual property and title.

Going back to Lord Bingham's definition of the rule of law (discussed at the start of this section on p. 80), it clearly is not content-free. To comply with the rule of law as he defines it, there needs to be adherence to various formal and procedural aspects but additionally his sub-rules 5 and 8 require laws to comply with human rights. Human rights norms include requirements about the substance of the law, for example freedom of expression and freedom of association.

QUESTION

Which version of the rule of law do you prefer and why: content-free or content-rich?

(b) DICEY AND HIS CRITICS

So far our exploration of definitions has focused on a contemporary dispute between content-free and content-rich conceptions of the rule of law. Into the mix, we now need to introduce a definition of the rule of law that continues to carry significant authority (as well as generating opprobrium from critics)—that of Professor A.V. Dicey (1835–1922). A Canadian academic has argued that for us to continue to focus on Dicey's work '*is to belabour a horse which is thought to have died so long ago, after assaults so numerous and savage, that humane considerations might dictate another line of investigation*'.[7] This is an attractive suggestion but Dicey's enduring influence requires that we take his work on the rule of law seriously.

---

[7] H.W. Arthurs, 'Rethinking Administrative Law: a slightly Dicey business' (1979) 17 Osgoode Hall LJ 1, 4.

For Dicey, the rule of law was a particularly British achievement, marking out the United Kingdom as superior to other nations.

A.V. Dicey, *Introduction to the Study of the Law of the Constitution* (1885; 10th edn 1959, London: Macmillan & Co), pp. 187–95

When we say that the supremacy or the rule of law is a characteristic of the English constitution, we generally include under one expression at least three distinct though kindred conceptions.

We mean, in the first place, that no man is punishable or can be made to suffer in body or goods except for a distinct breach of law established in the ordinary legal manner before the ordinary courts of the land. [...]

We mean in the second place not only that [...] no man is above the law, but that [...] every man, whatever his rank or condition, is subject to the ordinary law of the realm [...that...] every official, from the Prime Minister down to a constable or a collector of taxes, is under the same responsibility for every act done without legal justification as any other citizen. [...]

We may say [thirdly] that the constitution is pervaded by the rule of law on the ground that the general principles of the constitution (as for example the right to personal liberty, or the right of public meeting) are [...] the result of judicial decisions determining the rights of private persons [...].

One early, influential riposte to Dicey came from Professor Sir Ivor Jennings (1903–65). Jennings was a Fabian socialist who welcomed the increasing government regulation of business, social security provision, and who shared none of Dicey's hostility to the interventionist state. Jennings' own book (*The Law and the Constitution*, 1st edn 1933, 5th edn 1958) criticized the whole scope of Dicey's analysis, arguing that Dicey failed to deal with the *powers* of government: Dicey *'seemed to think that the British constitution was concerned almost entirely with the rights of individuals'*.[8] In fact, even when Dicey was writing, central and local government had considerable discretionary legal powers to carry out all sorts of functions from the compulsory purchase of land to restricting overseas trade. Jennings' assessment was that Dicey *'honestly tried ... to analyse [the constitution], but, like most, he saw the constitution through his own spectacles, and his own vision was not exact'*.[9]

In Appendix II of his book, Jennings considers Dicey's theory of the rule of law. In relation to Dicey's first meaning (the absence of arbitrary and discretionary powers) Jennings explains that what Dicey really meant was that 'wide administrative or executive powers are likely to be abused *and therefore ought not to be conferred'*.[10] But the discretionary powers of ministers and local authorities were as much part of the 'regular' law of the land as any others. And while, of course, occasional abuse of power might occur, this was no reason for not conferring discretionary powers on officials. These powers were used to ensure socially progressive goals such as minimum standards of health and safety in work places and the clearing of slum housing. This, Jennings said, was of no interest to Dicey:

8 *The Law and the Constitution* (5th edn 1958) 55.
9 Ibid. 316.
10 Ibid. 307.

Sir Ivor Jennings, *The Law and the Constitution*, 5th edn (1958, London: University of London Press) pp. 310–11

> Dicey ... was much more concerned with the constitutional relations between Great Britain and Ireland than with the relations between poverty and disease on the one hand, and the new industrial system on the other. In internal politics, therefore, he was concerned not with the clearing up of the nasty industrial sections of towns, but with the liberty of the subject. In terms of powers, he was concerned with police powers, and not with other administrative powers.

In relation to Dicey's second definition of the rule of law (equality before the law), Jennings flatly denied that there was any equality between the rights and duties of an official and that of an ordinary person. Dicey surely realized this, but had chosen to ignore the public law position of officials, for example the duty of local authorities to provide education to children and the powers of the tax inspectors to demand information. Dicey was only writing about the position in tort law—not public law. While it was true that generally officials could be sued personally by an aggrieved citizen for a tortious act or omission in the course of their duty, Jennings' withering retort was that '*this is a small point upon which to base a doctrine called by the magnificent name of "rule of law", particularly when it is generally used in a very different sense*'.[11]

Lastly, Jennings questioned Dicey's proposition that the rule of law meant that 'the constitution is *the result* of the ordinary law of the land' rather than a constitutional code. Jennings could not see Dicey's point.

Sir Ivor Jennings, *The Law and the Constitution*, 5th edn (1958, London: University of London Press) p. 314

> I do not understand how it is correct to say that the rules are the consequence of the rights of individuals and not their source. The powers of the Crown and of other administrative authorities are limited by the rights of individuals; or the rights of individuals are limited by the powers of the administration. Both statements are correct; and both powers and rights come from the law—from the rules.

QUESTIONS

1. What assumptions are made by Dicey and Jennings, respectively?
2. Dicey's ideas about the rule of law continue to be quoted by academics, judges, and official bodies. Should they be, or do Jennings' arguments so dent Dicey's definition of the rule of law that we should stop referring to it?

(c) SCEPTICAL VIEWS

So far, we have considered two academic controversies about the rule of law: whether it is content-free or content-rich; and whether Dicey's ground-breaking writings on the subject

---

[11] *The Law and the Constitution*, p. 312.

withstand later criticisms. There is a third controversy. Some academics take the sceptical view that the rule of law is not a useful concept.

In the following extract, Professor John Griffith (1918-2010)—a leading political constitutionalist of his generation, based at the LSE—berates what he saw as the extravagant and politically partisan use of the idea of 'the Rule of Law' (note the capital letters) in the 1970s by campaigners for incorporation of the ECHR into English law and other developments of which he disapproved.

J.A.G. Griffith, 'The Political Constitution' (1979) 42 Modern Law Review 1, 15

[In recent years] 'the law' has been raised from its proper and useful function as a means towards ends (about which it is possible to have differing opinions) to the level of a general concept. On this view, individual rules of law may be good or bad but 'the law' is undeniably good and must be upheld or chaos will come again. There is more than a suspicion of slight of hand here. For nobody, except committed anarchists, suggests that 'the law' should be dispensed with.

The ground is then shifted slightly and what becomes sacred and untouchable is something called the Rule of Law. The Rule of Law is an invaluable concept for those who wish not to change the present set-up. A person may be said not to be in favour of the Rule of Law if he is critical of the Queen, the Commissioner of the Metropolitan Police, the Speaker of the House of Commons or Lord Denning. Statutes may be contrary to the Rule of Law [...] but the common law, it seems, can never be. Objection to the rules of international law in their application to the United Kingdom is wholly excusable on proper occasions. Defiance of regulations and directives emanating from Brussels may often be accounted as a positive virtue.

If the Rule of Law means that there should be proper and adequate machinery for dealing with criminal offences and for ensuing that public authorities do not exceed their legal powers, and for insisting that official penalties may not be inflicted save on those who have broken the law, then only an outlaw could dispute its desirability. And Bracton is a thirteenth-century authority in its support. But when it is extended to mean more than that, it is a fantasy invented by Liberals of the old school in the late nineteenth century and patented by the Tories to throw a protective sanctity around certain legal and political institutions and principles which they wish to preserve at any cost. Then it is become a new metaphysic, seeming to resolve the doubts of the faithful with an old dogma.

More recently, Professor Martin Loughlin (of the LSE) expresses doubts on different grounds. The European Commission for Democracy through Law (the Venice Commission) invited Loughlin to prepare a discussion paper for their deliberations on the meaning of the rule of law.

Martin Loughlin, 'The Rule of Law in European Jurisprudence', Study 512/2009 (Venice Commission, 2009)

There is every reason to accept that the rule of law must be a mere slogan and that, however laudable its underlying intentions, the goal of achieving a 'government of laws and not of men' is one that is incapable of realization. One reason is that since in the modern era law is universally acknowledged to be a human creation, it cannot be placed above human will:

law cannot therefore be placed above a 'government of men'. A second is that laws cannot be said to rule, for the obvious reason that ruling involves action and, in themselves, laws do not act. The rule of law, it would appear, is merely a rhetorical expression, and this conviction is reinforced by virtue of its intrinsic ambiguity: the ubiquity of usage of the expression, 'the rule of law', is matched only by the multiplicity of its meanings. [...]

... precision in public law might demand abandonment of these concepts altogether in favour of a less charged investigation into the nature of the relationship between state, constitution, governing and law. The difficulty is that the very ubiquity of the expression demands that it be examined, especially for the purposes of revealing its underlying values, determining whether any coherent account of the general concept can be assembled, and assessing the force of the claim that it is a foundational element of the discipline. In this paper [written for the Venice Commission], the origins of these expressions in English, German and French thought will be examined, and an argument made about the coherence of the directing idea. My argument will be that although a coherent formulation of the general concept can be devised, that this formulation is entirely unworkable in practice. Consequently, the rule of law cannot be conceived as amounting to a foundational concept in public law. So far as it has utility, it must be deployed with precision, especially because, precisely because it is unrealizable, it is susceptible to being used for ideological purposes. The main value of the concept, it would appear, concerns its aspirational quality. But acceptance of this quality must be tempered by recognition that the extent to which the directing idea can—and should—be realized remains an essentially political task.

QUESTIONS

1. Who do you think Griffith is having a dig at when he says that the rule of law is a fantasy 'invented by Liberals of the old school in the nineteenth century'?

2. Does Griffith approve of a content-free rule of law, or is he against the whole idea?

3. Do you agree with Loughlin's conclusion that 'the rule of law cannot be conceived as amounting to a foundational concept in public law'?

4. What would be the implications of adopting the standpoint that the rule of law is 'a mere slogan'?

---

3 PRACTICAL PROTECTION OF THE RULE OF LAW

Having considered various definitional disputes and problems, we now turn to a second major question: how is the rule of law protected? Each country has its own set of institutions and processes that play a role in this. In Britain, all three of the major branches of the state—the judiciary, Parliament, and government (especially through the office of Lord Chancellor)—have functions in the development and application of rule of law principles.

(a) THE JUDICIARY

The contribution of the judiciary to protecting rule of law principles can be seen in three areas, each considered here: articulating common law fundamental rights; applying the law of tort against public office-holders; and interpreting legislation in ways supportive of rule of law principles. In addition, since October 2000, British judges have applied the Human Rights Act 1998 in protection of the rule of law—a new area of activity considered in Chapter 6 and Chapter 17.

Common law rights and freedoms

In countries that have written constitutions, judicial responsibility for the rule of law is usually understood as their power to interpret and apply the express and implied terms of that codified constitution. In Britain, by contrast, judges have asserted the common law as the basis for their protective functions.

The development, through the common law, of grounds of judicial review by which people are able to challenge government decisions will be explored in Chapter 16. These are, in effect, a series of legal arguments that may be used to challenge the legality of government action, including 'illegality' (a public body has failed to understand properly the legal framework within which it operates), 'irrationality' (a decision is so unreasonable that no reasonable public body could lawfully have made it), and 'procedural impropriety' (in making a decision, a public body did not follow the requirements of fair procedures set out in legislation or common law rules). The existence of judicial review contributes to enforcing several of Lord Bingham's sub-rules (especially 2, 3, and 4).

In cases reaching back many years, the courts have recognized that the common law protects some basic rights. As we have already noted, Dicey emphasized, as the third limb of his definition of the rule of law, that in the British system rights flow from particular decisions of the courts rather than from general principles of the constitution. Laws J explained: *'In the present state of its maturity the common law has come to recognise that there exist rights which should properly be classified as constitutional or fundamental ... This development of the common law regarding constitutional rights, and as I would say constitutional statutes, is highly beneficial. It gives us most of the benefits of a written constitution, in which fundamental rights are accorded special respect. But it preserves the sovereignty of the legislature and the flexibility of our uncodified constitution'.*[12] Writing in 2007, Woolf, Jowell, and Le Sueur identified a list of such rights from the Law Reports, including the rights to: life; liberty of the person; the delivery of justice in public; a fair hearing; prohibition on the retrospective imposition of criminal penalties; freedom of expression; access to legal advice, including the right of a person to communicate with a lawyer confidentially; prohibition on the use of evidence obtained by torture; prohibition of the deprivation of property without compensation; privilege against self-incrimination; and freedom of movement within the United Kingdom.[13]

QUESTION

Why might problems arise if protection of fundamental rights is left to the judiciary, working case by case from precedent?

---

[12] *Thoburn v Sunderland City Council* [2002] EWHC 195, [62], [64].

[13] H. Woolf, J. Jowell, and A. Le Sueur, *De Smith's Judicial Review*, 6th edn (2007, London: Sweet & Maxwell), para. 5.039.

Tort law

The common law has typically worked by balancing two often competing ideas: one is the idea that people have freedom to act as they please; the other is the idea that people have certain rights and interests that should be protected from interference. The result is the principle that people are free to act unless their actions interfere with the rights of others. How, then, are rights protected and the rule of law upheld by this principle? One answer is that rights will be protected if the law of tort recognizes them. Rights to property and the person, for example, are protected by the tort of trespass; the right to personal liberty is protected by the tort of false imprisonment; the right to a reputation is protected by defamation. Where a person can rely on a cause of action in tort, he or she can seek the court's protection and will receive a remedy unless the defendant public office-holder can show that law justifies the action.

The celebrated decision in *Entick v Carrington*, 250 years ago, illustrates this.[14] John Entick was a printer and had printed pamphlets written by John Wilkes.[15] He was arrested under a general warrant (which identified the crime but not the name of the suspect) and his papers were seized by 'King's messengers' (led by Nathan Carrington) who were looking for copies of this allegedly seditious newssheet. Carrington and his men were acting on the orders of Lord Halifax, the Secretary of State to King George III.

Entick v Carrington
(1765) 19 St Tr 1030, Lord Camden

The messenger, under this warrant, is commanded to seize the person described, and to bring him with his papers to be examined before the secretary of state. In consequence of this, the house must be searched; the lock and doors of every room, box, or trunk must be broken open; all the papers and books without exception, if the warrant be executed according to its tenor, must be seized and carried away; for it is observable, that nothing is left either to the discretion or to the humanity of the officer. [...] This power, so claimed by the secretary of state, is not supported by one single citation from any law book extant [...].

If honestly exerted, it is a power to seize that man's papers, who is charged upon oath to be the author or publisher of a seditious libel; if oppressively, it acts against every man, who is so described in the warrant, though he be innocent. It is executed against the party, before he is heard or even summoned; and the information, as well as the informers, is unknown.

It is executed by messengers with or without a constable [...] in the presence or the absence of the party, as the messenger shall think fit, and without a witness to testify what passes at the time of the transaction; so that when the papers are gone, as the only witnesses are the trespassers, the party injured is left without proof.

If this injury falls upon an innocent person, he is as destitute of remedy as the guilty: and the whole transaction is so guarded against discovery, that if the officer should be disposed to carry off a bank bill he may do it with impunity, since there is no man capable of proving either the taker or the thing taken.

[...] Such is the power, and therefore one should naturally expect that the law to warrant it should be clear in proportion as the power is exorbitant. If it is law, it will be found in our books. If it is not to be found there, it is not law.

---

14 (1765) 19 St Tr 1030.
15 Wilkes (1725–97) was an MP and Lord Mayor of London, and an outspoken critic of the government of his day.

The great end, for which men entered into society, was to secure their property. That right is preserved sacred and incommunicable in all instances, where it has not been taken away or abridged by some public law for the good of the whole. The cases where this right of property is set aside by private law, are various. Distresses, executions, forfeitures, taxes etc are all of this description; wherein every man by common consent gives up that right, for the sake of justice and the general good. By the laws of England, every invasion of private property, be it ever so minute, is a trespass. [...] The justification is submitted to the judges, who are to look into the books; and if such a justification can be maintained by the text of the statute law, or by the principles of common law. If no excuse can be found or produced, the silence of the books is an authority against the defendant, and the plaintiff must have judgment. According to this reasoning, it is now incumbent upon the defendants to show the law by which this seizure is warranted. If that cannot be done, it is a trespass.

I can safely answer, there is none; and therefore it is too much for us without such authority to pronounce a practice legal, which would be subversive of all the comforts of society.

[Lord Camden finds that there is no law justifying the search and seizure. He moves on to deal with the argument that the search and seizure was justified by necessity.]

It is then said, that it is necessary for the ends of government to lodge such a power with a state officer [...] with respect to the argument of state necessity [...] the common law does not understand that kind of reasoning [...].

The corollary of using tort as a means of enforcing rights is that if no cause of action in tort exists, then the 'right' will not be protected. This is graphically illustrated by the decision from the 1970s in *Malone v Commissioner of Police*. James Malone, an antiques dealer, was prosecuted for handling stolen goods. During his trial, it emerged that the Metropolitan Police had, without entering his land, collected evidence by secretly monitoring his telephone conversations. The police had obtained a warrant from the Home Secretary that authorized the Post Office (which operated the telephone system) to make recordings. Malone unsuccessfully sought a declaration that the covert tapping of his telephone was unlawful. At the time, legislation did not authorize the tapping, nor did the police or the Home Secretary claim to have specific legal power under the prerogative to authorize the interception. It was held that Malone could not use the common law to seek redress when his telephone had been tapped, because there had been no trespass on his property. He claimed invasion of his right to privacy, but was told that the common law does not protect people's privacy. This decision provided an example of the haphazard and limited nature of common law rights' protection.

Malone v Metropolitan Police Commissioner (No. 2)
[1979] Ch 344, 367, Sir Robert Megarry V-C

There is the contention [argued by Malone] that as no power to tap telephones has been given either by statute or common law, the tapping is necessarily unlawful. The underlying assumption of this contention, of course, is that nothing is lawful that is not positively authorised by law. [...] England is not a country where everything is forbidden except what is expressly permitted. One possible illustration is smoking. I enquired what positive authority was given by the law to permit people to smoke. Counsel for the plaintiff accepted that there was none; but tapping, he said, was different. It was in general disfavour, and it offended against usual and proper standards of behaviour, in that it was an invasion of privacy and an interference with the liberty of the individual and his right to be let alone when lawfully engaged on his own affairs.

> I did not find this argument convincing. [...] The notion that some express authorisation of law is required for acts which meet with 'general disfavour' and 'offend the proper standards of behaviour', and so on, would make the state of the law dependent on subjective views on indefinite concepts, and would be likely to produce some remarkable and contentious results. Neither in principle nor in authority can I see any justification for this view, and I reject it. If the tapping of telephones by the Post Office at the request of the police can be carried out without any breach of the law, it does not require any statutory or common law power to justify it: it can lawfully be done simply because there is nothing to make it unlawful.

After losing in the High Court, Malone successfully applied to the European Court of Human Rights arguing that the interception had infringed his rights to privacy under Art. 8 of the ECHR.[16] The law on telephone tapping was subsequently altered in response to this decision by the Interception of Communications Act 1985. This gave the Home Secretary specific powers to authorize telephone tapping in defined circumstances.

QUESTION

It is often said that the decision in *Entick v Carrington* indicates that the common law recognizes a presumption in favour of rights, but that rights can be infringed. According to Lord Camden, in what circumstances can rights be infringed?

Criticisms of the common law

While the common law has long been associated with rights, several types of criticism are made of the ability of the common law to protect constitutional rights and the rule of law. First, some commentators, while recognizing their value, argue that common law rights are too weak. The common law is unable to deal with situations in which an Act of Parliament expressly limits or abolishes a right previously recognized by the courts to be of constitutional importance—as in the Criminal Evidence (Witness Anonymity) Act 2008 (discussed in *R v Davis* [2008] on p. 98).

A second criticism is that the common law can provide protection only in certain circumstances. There are great landmark cases, such as *Entick v Carrington*, which show the willingness of the judges to use the common law to protect rights. But even decisions such as these illustrate the limitations of the common law as a vehicle for securing protection for individuals against the powerful institutions of government. Note, for example, the following comment on *Entick v Carrington* made by Professors Keith Ewing and Connor Gearty.

K.D. Ewing and C.A. Gearty, *The Struggle for Civil Liberties: Political Freedom and the Rule of Law* 1914–1945 (2000, Oxford: OUP), p. 14

> [W]hat was under attack by the courts was not the exercise of arbitrary power but the coincidence that there had been a trespass, that is to say a violation of established property rights. As later cases relating to surveillance activities of the Special Branch and the secret service were to demonstrate, it did not always follow that unrestrained exercise of public power would coincide with the violation of any common law right of the individual.

---

[16] *Malone v UK* (1987) 7 EHRR 14.

A third type of criticism is more general, and rooted in the link between law and economic theory. It argues that the limits of the common law are rooted in the way in which the common law has evolved to protect individuals within a predominantly liberal economic system. The common law, it is argued, adopts a particular view of individual rights that is concerned with legal (or formal) rights rather than with actual rights. When judges talk, for example, about 'equality', they have traditionally been more concerned with equality in a legal sense than with whether people are actually equal in a real-world sense. In the following extract, Professor Ewing provides a critique of the common law's preoccupation with economic liberalism, with economic freedom, and with formal rather than actual equality.

K.D. Ewing, 'The Unbalanced Constitution', in T. Campbell, K.D. Ewing, and A. Tomkins (eds) *Sceptical Essays on Human Rights* (2003, Oxford: OUP), pp. 105–7 (footnotes omitted)

[The common law gives rise to several points of concern.] The first is the unequivocal commitment to liberty as a fundamental principle: not so much political liberty which has never been a robust principle of the common law, but economic liberty which enables parties to contract as equals, without regard to the relative differences in their position. So far as employment is concerned, parties are free to contract on whatever terms they like, and although there are implied terms which regulate the content of the contract, crucially there is no implied term that workers should be paid a fair wage. So while slavery is not permitted, there is no line drawn at wage slavery [...] It was a question of liberty and a matter of choice. People were free to work for subsistence wages if they chose to do so, and to do so in unhealthy and dangerous conditions if that was also their choice. The parties were also free to contract in a manner which violated what some would regard as human rights: free to discriminate between men and women; and free to discriminate on the grounds of race. Indeed, public authorities were constrained by common law principles—borrowed from equity—to contract on a basis which reflected a total disregard for human rights: discrimination against women was not only permitted by the law but in some circumstances actively required.

The second concern with the common law is the converse of the first: its lack of commitment to equality as a constitutional principle, except as a rhetorical fig leaf [...].

A fourth criticism is directed at the erratic nature of judgments. There are ground-breaking judgments that protect rights and it is true that even before the enactment of the Human Rights Act 1998, British judges were becoming attuned to human rights issues and were much readier to adopt a more dynamic approach to the common law. Nonetheless, the record of the judges has been very mixed. One of the cases that Ewing and Gearty had in mind when they were talking about surveillance was *Malone v Metropolitan Police Commissioner* (that we have just discussed). To this example may be added many other decisions that have failed to protect rights, including:

- *Liversidge v Anderson*,[17] in which the House of Lords failed to protect the right to liberty under defence regulations that permitted detention without trial;
- *Council for Civil Service Unions v Minister for the Civil Service*,[18] in which the House of Lords refused to apply the rules of natural justice when ministers claimed that national security was at stake;

[17] [1942] AC 2306.
[18] [1985] AC 374.

- *R v Deputy Governor of Parkhurst Prison, ex parte Hague*,[19] in which the House of Lords held that a prisoner could not rely on the tort of false imprisonment when complaining about his conditions of detention unless he could show that the conditions had resulted in actual injury; and

- *R v Secretary of State for the Home Department, ex parte Brind*,[20] in which the House of Lords held that where Parliament confers broad powers on ministers and public authorities, there is no presumption that Parliament intended those powers to be exercised in accordance with the ECHR.

Different explanations have been given for this erratic approach to rights issues. Some—notably, Professor J.A.G. Griffith—say that judges are typically temperamentally and institutionally conservative, and therefore disinclined to protect certain rights and certain groups in society. In his book *The Politics of the Judiciary*,[21] Griffith argues that judges, by virtue of their background and their position in the establishment, are '*necessarily conservative, not liberal*' and possess '*tenderness towards private property and dislike of trade unions, strong adherence to the maintenance of order, distaste for minority opinions, demonstrations and protests, support for government secrecy*'. Others simply argue that cases such as those listed illustrate what Anthony Lester QC has described as the 'ethical aimlessness' of the common law.[22]

Whatever the reasons, there is no doubt that the common law has been an uncertain vehicle for the protection of rights and that concern about the various weaknesses of the common law was one of the driving forces behind calls for the United Kingdom to incorporate Convention rights into national law (see Chapter 6).

QUESTION

Four reasons have been given for why the common law may be considered a weak and erratic vehicle for protecting rights. Can you think of any others?

Statutory interpretation

Parliamentary legislation can attempt to safeguard rule of law values. The safeguarding role is especially relevant where the state needs to take some positive action to respect the rule of law, such as by establishing a court system: for example, the Constitutional Reform Act 2005 (establishing the UK Supreme Court), the Tribunals, Courts and Enforcement Act 2007 (setting up a new system of tribunals), and in England and Wales, the Courts Act 2004, the County Courts Act 1998, and the Senior Courts Act 1998.

Legislation may also threaten the rule of law. One cause célèbre in 2004 was a proposal by the government to include an ouster clause in the Asylum and Immigration (Treatment of Claimants, etc.) Bill. This provision would have severely restricted access to the courts by failed asylum seekers seeking to challenge the lawfulness of decisions to remove them from the country. The government watered down its proposals in the face of widespread criticism inside and outside Parliament. Another example of legislation widely criticized as breaching rule of law principles is the Legal Aid, Sentencing and Punishment of Offenders Act 2012, which was designed to enable the government to cut the legal aid budget of £2.1 billion by

---

[19] [1991] 3 All ER 733.
[20] [1991] 1 AC 696.
[21] 5th edn (1997, London: Fontana), p. 336. See also Chapter 14.
[22] A. Lester, 'English judges as law makers' [1993] Public Law 267.

one sixth. The House of Lords Constitution Committee, in a report on the bill, drew attention to Lord Bingham's statement that '*denial of legal protection to the poor litigant who cannot afford to pay is one enemy of the rule of law*'.[23]

Once legislation is enacted, the courts seek to protect rule of law principles through techniques of statutory interpretation. Applying 'the principle of legality', the courts examine closely situations in which a public authority claims to have a right conferred by statute to interfere with a common law right.

John Pierson was convicted of murdering his parents in 1984. At the time, the Home Secretary had power to determine how many years of a murderer's mandatory life sentence had to be served for the purposes of retribution and deterrence before the prisoner would be allowed to apply to the Parole Board for release on licence (if he or she was no longer assessed as being a danger to the public). The Home Secretary consulted the trial judge and the Lord Chief Justice; they recommended the 'tariff' period should be fifteen years and the Home Secretary agreed. A later Home Secretary revised this decision, deciding that twenty years should be the tariff. The House of Lords considered whether the Home Secretary had legal power to increase the tariff retrospectively.

R v Secretary of State for the Home Department, ex parte Pierson
[1998] AC 539, 587–8,

Lord Steyn

Parliament has not expressly authorised the Home Secretary to increase tariffs retrospectively. If Parliament had done so that would have been the end of the matter. Instead Parliament has by s 35(2) of the Criminal Justice Act 1991 entrusted the power to take decisions about the release of mandatory life sentence prisoners to the Home Secretary. The statutory power is wide enough to authorise the fixing of a tariff. But it does not follow that it is wide enough to permit a power retrospectively to increase the level of punishment.

The wording of s 35(2) of the Act of 1991 is wide and general. It provides that "the Secretary of State may [...] release on licence a life prisoner who is not a discretionary life prisoner." There is no ambiguity in the statutory language. The presumption that in the event of ambiguity legislation is presumed not to invade common law rights is inapplicable. A broader principle applies. Parliament does not legislate in a vacuum. Parliament legislates for a European liberal democracy founded on the principles and traditions of the common law. And the courts may approach legislation on this initial assumption. But this assumption only has prima facie force. It can be displaced by a clear and specific provision to the contrary. These propositions require some explanation.

For at least a century it has been "thought to be in the highest degree improbable that Parliament would depart from the general system of law without expressing its intention with irresistible clearness [...]": see the 4th ed. of Maxwell on the Interpretation of Statutes, (1905) at 121, and the 12th ed. of the same book, (1969), at 116. The idea is even older. In 1855 Sir John Romilly observed that "[...] the general words of the Act are not to be so construed as to alter the previous policy of the law, unless no sense or meaning can be applied to those words consistently with the intention of preserving the existing policy untouched [...]": Minet v Leman (1855) 20 Beav. 269, at 278. This observation has been applied in decisions

---

[23] See House of Lords Constitution Committee, *Part 1 of the Legal Aid, Sentencing and Punishment of Offenders Bill* (HL 2010-12, 222), para. 7.

of high authority [...]. In his Introduction to the Study of the Law of the Constitution; 10th ed., London, (1968), Dicey explained the context in which Parliament legislates as follows (at 414):

> "By every path we come round to the same conclusion, that Parliamentary sovereignty has favoured the rule of law, and that the supremacy of the law of the land both calls forth the exertion of Parliamentary sovereignty, and leads to its being exercised in a spirit of legality."

But it is to Sir Rupert Cross that I turn for the best modern explanation of "the spirit of legality", or what has been called the principle of legality. (The phrase "the principle of legality" I have taken from Halsbury's Laws of England, 4th ed., reissue, vol. 8(2), para. 6.) The passage appears in Cross, Statutory Interpretation, 3rd ed., at 165-166, which has been edited by Professor John Bell and Sir George Engle, Q.C., formerly First Parliamentary Counsel, but it is worth noting that the passage is in all material aspects as drafted by the author: see Cross, Statutory Interpretation, (1976), 142-143. In the 3rd ed. the passage reads as follows:

> "Statutes often go into considerable detail, but even so allowance must be made for the fact that they are not enacted in a vacuum. A great deal inevitably remains unsaid. Legislators and drafters assume that the courts will continue to act in accordance with well-recognised rules [...] Long-standing principles of constitutional and administrative law are likewise taken for granted, or assumed by the courts to have been taken for granted, by Parliament. Examples are the principles that discretionary powers conferred in apparently absolute terms must be exercised reasonably, and that administrative tribunals and other such bodies must act in accordance with the principles of natural justice. One function of the word 'presumption' in the context of statutory interpretation is to state the result of this legislative reliance (real or assumed) on firmly established legal principles. There is a 'presumption' that mens rea is required in the case of statutory crimes, and a 'presumption' that statutory powers must be exercised reasonably. These presumptions apply although there is no question of linguistic ambiguity in the statutory wording under construction, and they may be described as 'presumptions of general application'. [...] These presumptions of general application not only supplement the text, they also operate at a higher level as expressions of fundamental principles governing both civil liberties and the relations between Parliament, the executive and the courts. They operate here as constitutional principles which are not easily displaced by a statutory text. [...]"

This explanation is the intellectual justification of the often quoted proposition of Byles J. in Cooper v Wandsworth Board of Works 1863 14 C.B.N.S. 180 that "[...] although there are no positive words in a statute requiring that a party shall be heard, yet the justice of the common law will supply the omission": see Ridge v Baldwin [1964] A.C. 40, at p. 69, per Lord Reid; and Bennion, Statutory Interpretation, 2nd ed., at 726-727.

[...] And our public law is, of course, replete with other instances of the common law so supplementing statutes on the basis of the principle of legality. A recent and pertinent example is provided by the speeches of the majority in the House of Lords in Regina v Secretary of State for the Home Department, Ex parte Venables [1997] 3 W.L.R. 23, so far as a majority decided that in fixing a tariff the Home Secretary may not take into account public protests in aggravation of a particular tariff. That ruling depended on the proposition that the Home Secretary was in substance engaged in a decision on punishment. He was "under a duty to act within the same constraints as a judge": per Lord Goff of Chieveley, 41G. The assumption was that the Home Secretary would act in conformity with fundamental principles of our law governing the imposition of criminal punishment.

Judges presume that Parliament does not intend to deprive people of their common law rights, such as access the courts.[24] It is also presumed that Parliament does not intend to enact legislation that would be inconsistent with the United Kingdom's international obligations, including its obligations under international human rights treaties to which it is a party.

(b) PARLIAMENT

We have stated that Parliament has the power, though legislation, both to protect and promote the rule of law and also to undermine it, consciously or inadvertently. The principle of parliamentary supremacy leads to Parliament, not the courts, having the final say on the validity of provisions in Acts of Parliament that offend the rule of law. Dicey thought it unlikely that Parliament would undermine the rule of law, as he explains:

A.V. Dicey, *Introduction to the Study of the Law of the Constitution* (1885; 10th edn 1959, London: Macmillan & Co), pp. 406–410 (Chapter XIII 'Relation between Parliamentary Sovereignty and the Rule of Law')

The sovereignty of Parliament and the supremacy of the law of the land — the two principles which pervade the whole of the English constitution — may appear to stand in opposition to each other, or to be at best only counterbalancing forces. But this appearance is delusive; the sovereignty of Parliament, as contrasted with other forms of sovereign power, favours the supremacy of the law, whilst the predominance of rigid legality throughout our institutions evokes the exercise, and thus increases the authority, of Parliamentary sovereignty.

The sovereignty of Parliament favours the supremacy of the law of the land.

That this should be so arises in the main from two characteristics or peculiarities which distinguish the English Parliament from other sovereign powers.

The first of these characteristics is that the commands of Parliament (consisting as it does of the Crown, the House of Lords, and the House of Commons) can be uttered only through the combined action of its three constituent parts, and must, therefore, always take the shape of formal and deliberate legislation. The will of Parliament can be expressed only through an Act of Parliament. [...]

The second of these characteristics is that the English Parliament as such has never, except at periods of revolution, exercised direct executive power or appointed the officials of the executive government.

No doubt in modern times the House of Commons has in substance obtained the right to designate for appointment the Prime Minister and the other members of the Cabinet. But this right is, historically speaking, of recent acquisition, and is exercised in a very roundabout manner; its existence does not affect the truth of the assertion that the Houses of Parliament do not directly appoint or dismiss the servants of the State; neither the House of Lords nor the House of Commons, nor both Houses combined, could even now issue a direct order to a military officer, a constable, or a tax-collector; the servants of the State are still in name what they once were in reality—'servants of the Crown'; and, what is worth careful notice, the attitude of Parliament towards government officials was determined originally, and is still regulated, by considerations and feelings belonging to a time when the 'servants of the

---

[24] *Chester v Bateson* [1920] 1 KB 829.

Crown' were dependent upon the King, that is, upon a power which naturally excited the jealousy and vigilance of Parliament.

Hence several results all indirectly tending to support the supremacy of the law. Parliament, though sovereign, unlike a sovereign monarch who is not only a legislator but a ruler, that is, head of the executive government, has never hitherto been able to use the powers of the government as a means of interfering with the regular course of law; and what is even more important, Parliament has looked with disfavour and jealousy on all exemptions of officials from the ordinary liabilities of citizens or from the jurisdiction of the ordinary Courts; Parliamentary sovereignty has been fatal to the growth of 'administrative law.' The action, lastly, of Parliament has tended as naturally to protect the independence of the judges, as that of other sovereigns to protect the conduct of officials. It is worth notice that Parliamentary care for judicial independence has, in fact, stopped just at that point where on a priori grounds it might be expected to end. The judges are not in strictness irremovable; they can be removed from office on an address of the two Houses; they have been made by Parliament independent of every power in the State except the Houses of Parliament.

In recent years, Parliament has put in place procedures that help ensure that Acts of Parliament comply with rule of law principles—or, at least, if they do not then Parliament legislates knowingly. In Chapter 10 we examine in particular the work of the House of Lords Constitution Committee (which reviews bills for compliance with all constitutional principles) and the Joint Committee on Human Rights (which, as its name suggests, focuses on compliance with human rights and in particular the ECHR).

There is no doubt, however, that if an Act of Parliament clearly enacts legislation in conflict with rule of law principles, the role of the courts is limited. Parliament may enact legislation to abolish or limit a 'fundamental' right that has been recognized by the common law.

This was demonstrated in 2008 when, shortly after the House of Lords reasserted a rule of the common law that defendants in criminal trials have a right to confront their accuser, Parliament abolished that rule. In *R v Davis*,[25] the accused stood trial for shooting two people dead at a New Year's Eve party in London. Witnesses were reluctant to come forward. The police assured them that their identities would be protected if they were to give evidence in court. The judge made an order allowing witnesses to use pseudonyms, to be hidden behind screens in court, to have their voices mechanically distorted, and to bar Davis' counsel from asking questions that might enable any of them to be identified. Davis was convicted. He appealed on the ground that he did not receive a fair trial because the anonymity arrangements prevented his counsel from cross-examining the witnesses.

R v Davis
[2008] UKHL 36, [5]

Lord Bingham of Cornhill

It is a long-established principle of the English common law that, subject to certain exceptions and statutory qualifications, the defendant in a criminal trial should be confronted by his accusers in order that he may cross-examine them and challenge their evidence. This principle originated in ancient Rome [...]. But in continental Europe the principle was greatly attenuated in early mediaeval times and the procedure of the Inquisition, directed

25 [2008] UKHL 36.

to the extirpation of heresy and the preservation of society, depended heavily on evidence given secretly by anonymous witnesses whom the suspect was denied the opportunity to confront. In England, where proof of crime depended on calling live evidence before a jury to convince it of a defendant's guilt, there was no room for such procedures. But concern as to national security and intimidation of witnesses did lead to reliance on secret, anonymous evidence and evidence not adduced in court, and thus to departures from the rule of confrontation, notably in the Court of Star Chamber and in common law trials for treason, as notoriously at the trial of Sir Walter Raleigh. The Court of Star Chamber, popular at first, came over time to attract the same popular loathing as the Inquisition, its procedures regarded as foreign, cruel, oppressive and unfair. It was promptly abolished by the Long Parliament in 1641, and steps were taken [...] to bring the procedure of treason trials into line with that required at common law. [...] The practice of confronting defendants with their accusers so that the latter may be cross-examined and the truth established was recognised by such authorities as Sir Matthew Hale [...] Blackstone [...] and Bentham [...]. The common law right to be confronted by one's accusers was included within the colonial constitutions of several North American colonies [...] and other states adopted similar declarations at the time of independence. By the sixth amendment to the United States constitution adopted in 1791 it was provided that "In all criminal prosecutions, the accused shall enjoy the right [...] to be confronted with the witnesses against him [...]". The rule has been strictly applied: in *Alford v United States* 282 US 687 (1931) a conviction was quashed where a government witness had been excused from answering a question about where he lived.

The House of Lords held that the trial judge had no power to make the anonymity order that he did: it infringed an important common law right. Reaction to this ruling in the some sections of the new media was unfavourable (and in the following example, ludicrously overblown).

The Sun, 'Anarchy is unleashed', 25 June 2008

Barmy Law Lords were last night accused of unleashing anarchy by barring anonymous witnesses in court trials. Worried police warned that dozens of terrorists and murderers will walk free unless the judges' ruling is swiftly overturned by the Government. They fear Britain could witness unrestrained violence like the slaughter in Zimbabwe.

Within a few weeks of the judgment, a Bill was rushed through Parliament designed to allow judges to make wide-ranging anonymity orders.

Criminal Evidence (Witness Anonymity) Act 2008, s. 1

New rules relating to anonymity of witnesses

(1) This Act provides for the making of witness anonymity orders in relation to witnesses in criminal proceedings.

(2) The common law rules relating to the power of a court to make an order for securing that the identity of a witness in criminal proceedings is withheld from the defendant (or, on a defence application, from other defendants) are abolished.

(3) Nothing in this Act affects the common law rules as to the withholding of information on the grounds of public interest immunity.

From a constitutional perspective, what happened following the *Davis* case was not particularly controversial. Although a common law right was abolished, the scheme set out in the 2008 Act required trial judges to exercise their new powers in such a way as to ensure that there would be a fair trial that complies with the requirements of Art. 6 of the ECHR (part of national law following the Human Rights Act 1998). The House of Lords, in their judgment, had indeed suggested that Parliament should consider the whole area. There was cross-party support for the new scheme replacing the common law right.

It is, however, possible to imagine different and more contentious circumstances in which a court seeks to protect a common law right and Parliament responds by seeking to overturn it. As we saw in Chapter 2, orthodox accounts of parliamentary supremacy state that Parliament may make and unmake any law. It has, however, been argued that Parliament's sovereign power is not absolute and that certain inherent constitutional limitations on its power exist. The thrust of the argument is that since Parliament derives its sovereignty from the constitution, the scope of its sovereignty is delineated by the constitution and by the basic principles of the constitutional system. This means that Parliament cannot claim sovereign power to subvert the basic principles upon which its very sovereignty is based. It cannot, for example, enact legislation that is contrary to essential notions of democracy or rights that are fundamental.

T.R.S. Allan, *Law, Liberty, and Justice* (1994, Oxford: OUP), p. 282

A parliamentary enactment whose effect would be the destruction of any recognizable form of democracy—for example, a measure purporting to deprive a substantial section of the population of the vote on the grounds of their hostility to government policies—could not consistently be applied by the courts as law. Judicial obedience to the statute...could not coherently be justified in terms of the doctrine of parliamentary sovereignty, since the statute would violate the political principle which the doctrine itself enshrines.

Allan argues that limitations on Parliament do not imply a conflict between the rule of law and democratic principle. On the contrary, since both ideas flow from a basic moral commitment to democracy, they are both necessary and each supports the other. Sir John Laws (a Court of Appeal judge) has taken a similar approach in his academic writing.

Sir John Laws, 'Law and Democracy' [1995] Public Law 72

[A]s a matter of fundamental principle [...] the survival and flourishing of a democracy in which basic rights (of which freedom of expression may be taken as a paradigm) are not only respected but enshrined requires that those who exercise democratic, political power must have limits set to what they may do: limits which they are not allowed to overstep. If this is right, it is a function of democratic power itself that it be not absolute.

The constitution, he goes on to argue, must guarantee such rights as freedom of expression *'since otherwise its credentials as a medium of honest rule are fatally undermined'*. This requires a 'higher-order law', which cannot be abrogated by a statute promoted by a government with the necessary majority in Parliament. It is, he argues, the constitution rather than Parliament that is sovereign. These are issues to which we shall return at various points in this book.

The power of Parliament to legislate contrary to fundamental rights and rule of law principles remains even after the enactment of the Human Rights Act 1998, which assumes that Parliament may pass legislation that is incompatible with Convention rights.[26] A minister introducing a bill may *'make a statement to the effect that although he is unable to make a statement of compatibility the government nevertheless wishes the House to proceed with the Bill'* (s. 19). A court which subsequently determines that a provision of an Act of Parliament is not compatible with a Convention right may make only a 'declaration of incompatibility' which 'does not affect the validity, continuing operation or enforcement of the provision in respect of which it is given' (s. 4).

QUESTION

What justifications are there for permitting Parliament to abolish rights regarded as 'constitutional' or 'fundamental' by the courts?

(c) GOVERNMENT: THE LORD CHANCELLOR

Within central government, the Lord Chancellor is regarded as having special responsibility for ensuring compliance with rule of law principles. Other public offices also contribute to this function, notably the Attorney General and the Solicitor General (the two 'law officers of the Crown'); but we focus on the Lord Chancellor.

Before the reforms, the Lord Chancellor was a senior lawyer affiliated to the governing party, appointed and dismissed like other ministers by the prime minister. He sat as a judge in the highest courts; he was speaker of the House of Lords; he was the ministerial head of a government department; he was a senior government minister with a place in the Cabinet; and he was also head of the judiciary, occasionally sitting as a judge. In 2003, the Prime Minister Tony Blair decided to abolish the post of Lord Chancellor, to create a new system for appointing judges, and to set up a supreme court of the United Kingdom. Modified plans were eventually and after much debate put on a statutory basis in the Constitutional Reform Act 2005 (CRA 2005). The Lord Chancellor would no longer be a judge, head of the judiciary, or the speaker of the House of Lords. We focus on three points. First, is a lawyer likely to be better at protecting the rule of law than a non-legally trained politician? Second, there was speculation that the reason Tony Blair dismissed Lord Irvine (Lord Chancellor 1997–2003) and replaced him with Lord Falconer (Lord Chancellor 2003–10) was because Lord Irvine had been too protective of rule of law principles inside government. Third, we examine the decision to include express reference to the rule of law in the CRA 2005.

Is a lawyer better at protecting the rule of law?

After the government had accepted, in the face of opposition within the House of Lords, that the office of Lord Chancellor should be retained in a reformed form, attention focused

---

[26] See further Chapter 16.

on whether the new-style Lord Chancellor should continue to be a lawyer. There was never any legal requirement that a Lord Chancellor should be a lawyer, but it was a strong convention.[27] It was suggested by some that only a lawyer could properly understand the meaning of 'the rule of law' and promote it in government. The Bill was eventually amended to reflect a compromise—although it is no longer essential for the Lord Chancellor to have a background in the law, in choosing a new Lord Chancellor, the Prime Minister needs 'to take into account' various factors.

Constitutional Reform Act 2005, ss. 1 and 2

The rule of law

1. This Act does not adversely affect—
   (a) the existing constitutional principle of the rule of law, or
   (b) the Lord Chancellor's existing constitutional role in relation to that principle.

Qualifications for office of Lord Chancellor

2. (1) A person may not be recommended for appointment as Lord Chancellor unless he appears to the Prime Minister to be qualified by experience.

   (2) The Prime Minister may take into account any of these—
   (a) experience as a Minister of the Crown;
   (b) experience as a member of either House of Parliament;
   (c) experience as a qualifying practitioner;
   (d) experience as a teacher of law in a university;
   (e) other experience that the Prime Minister considers relevant.

   (3) In this section 'qualifying practitioner' means any of these—
   (a) a person who has a Senior Courts qualification, within the meaning of section 71 of the Courts and Legal Services Act 1990;
   (b) an advocate in Scotland or a solicitor entitled to appear in the Court of Session and the High Court of Justiciary;
   (c) a member of the Bar of Northern Ireland or a solicitor of the Court of Judicature of Northern Ireland.

In what ways does—or did—the Lord Chancellor help to promote the rule of law inside government? Consider this extract from evidence given to a select committee by one former Lord Chancellor. Lord Mackay was Lord Chancellor 1987–97.

Oral Evidence to the House of Lords Select Committee on the Constitutional Reform Bill, QQ 277–8

Lord Mackay of Clashfern: [...] the Lord Chancellor is [...] in the Cabinet and in the Cabinet his job is to ensure that the Cabinet decides and takes executive action in accordance with the law, but he is not the legal adviser. I think there have been mistakes in the past when the Lord Chancellor has assumed the task of advising the Government about the law. That is not

---

[27] On constitutional conventions, see Chapter 1.

the Lord Chancellor's function; the Lord Chancellor is a judge and it would be improper for him, in fact, to act as legal adviser in that sense. The legal adviser is the Attorney General, but the Lord Chancellor's job is to see that if an issue arises which requires legal advice is taken, because often non-lawyers do not appreciate—naturally enough, because they are not lawyers—there is a legal question involved.

Q278 Lord Holme of Cheltenham [a Liberal Democrat peer]: It is the difference between generic advice that the Government is generally acting or not within the law, and specific advice on specific issues.

Lord Mackay of Clashfern: It is really a responsibility to see, if the law is unclear in an area, that it is clarified by advice before the Cabinet proceeds. If the law is clear then the Lord Chancellor will note that situation. He is the best qualified to realise whether or not there is a risk in what the Cabinet are proposing from the point of view of the law, and to see that the minister, whoever it is, that is making the proposal takes the appropriate legal advice.

The House of Lords Select Committee on the Constitutional Reform Bill considered the issues of including an express provision about the rule of law in the Bill, and whether the minister responsible for judiciary-related issues should have a background in the law. At the time of the committee's deliberations, there was doubt as to whether the minister responsible for courts and judiciary-related matters would be an ordinary Secretary of State (as the government wanted) or a reformed Lord Chancellor (as critics of the government demanded). The committee heard from Sir Tom Legg, a retired Permanent Secretary (the top senior civil servant) in the former Lord Chancellor's Department (which was transformed into the Department for Constitutional Affairs in 2003 and then as the Ministry of Justice in 2006) and his successor, Sir Hayden Phillips.

Oral Evidence to the House of Lords Select Committee on the Constitutional Reform Bill, Q 689

Sir Tom Legg: [...] Of course there has also been a fairly strong convention that the Lord Chancellor should either be a judge or a very senior lawyer. I think myself that if the Office of Lord Chancellor goes in selecting a Secretary of State for Constitutional Affairs the Prime Minister will want to take into account, as in every other case, the qualifications of candidates. All other things being equal for some parts of the job, yes, it probably will be an advantage to be a lawyer but all other things are unlikely to be equal and I would not regard that as a very important feature. The difficulty which I am sure is at the bottom of your question is the question of preserving the rule of law. It is a very tricky, slippery concept a lot of the time, at least in general terms. My own feeling is there would not be very much to be gained from the protection of the public by putting a requirement into statute that ministers, and so on, should uphold the rule of law because in any given case people can have disagreement about what that means. I have to say I doubt whether there would be anything very much to be gained by requiring the Secretary of State to be a lawyer because you might just exclude from the Government and from that post some other well qualified people.

Sir Hayden Phillips: I agree with what Tom said. I think most people would agree that it is the personality, temperament and clout of the individual who holds the job. I can think of many Secretaries of State over the years, and I will not name names, who were not lawyers who have been some of the best upholders of the rule of law and that goes with personality and understanding and it does not go with legal qualification. I reach for the Lord Chief Justice's comments the other day about his doubts about my suitability, not personally, but professionally to do the job and his realisation if you are really in touch and understand what this is all about then legal qualification is not a necessary condition to do the job.

The Select Committee also questioned Professor Robert Hazell, director of the UCL Constitution Unit.

Oral Evidence to the House of Lords Select Committee on the Constitutional Reform Bill, Q 182

Lord Kingsland [a Conservative peer, formerly a member of the European Parliament, barrister, and legal academic]: Professor Hazell, my question really flows from a series of questions that you have been asked about the role of the Lord Chancellor, in which House he should sit and as to whether or not he should be a lawyer. Setting aside those issues, you, in your opening remarks, said that the Lord Chancellor had an important role in defending the rule of law. Would you accept that that, from time to time, might bring him into conflict with a senior member of the Cabinet like the Home Secretary? If you would accept that, would you further accept that to stand up for rule of law in the Cabinet against a political figure who would be as authoritative as the Home Secretary, the Lord Chancellor, or the Secretary of State for Constitutional Affairs, would have to wield equivalent authority in Cabinet? He would have to be, in other words, fearless in protecting the rule of law against all comers. Would you agree with that proposition?

Professor Hazell: Yes, but, if I may, I would like to generalise it a bit rather than personalise it even between those offices because what you have described is a tension which is universal between the values of justice on the one hand and the values of order on the other. Post 11 September 2001, the conflict between those two values has become really acute and very difficult I think for all advanced democracies and all governments are wrestling with how to resolve the tension between those two values and coming down at different points on the spectrum. So, this tension is universal, all governments have to address it and generally in most governments there is one figure, call him the Minister of the Interior or whatever, who upholds the values of order and there is another figure, often called the Minister of Justice, who upholds the values of justice. They will always clash.

Q183 Lord Kingsland: I accept that. My question was rather to the relative strengths of the two figures in Cabinet. If there is to be a conflict between order and justice in the Cabinet, would you agree that the person representing justice ought, in principle at any rate, to be a political figure, whether or not a lawyer, of equivalent political weight to the Home Secretary?

Professor Hazell: Ideally, yes, and, in most governments, the Minister of the Interior is a relatively senior minister. Interestingly, in governments which have introduced an enforceable Bill of Rights, the Minister of Justice has become a much more important figure politically. In Canada, that has been strongly remarked upon. They have had an enforceable Bill of Rights for 20 years since the introduction of the Canadian Charter of Fundamental Rights and Freedoms in 1982. We did some research on that and one of the things I had not expected in interviewing both in provincial governments, which were affected by the legislation, as well as the federal government was that some of our interviewees, including civil servants, said, 'One of the unexpected effects has been that the Minister of Justice is now much more important in the Government' and some even went so far as to say that he was equivalent in weight to the Minister of Finance. Our own Human Rights Act is less than five years old in terms of its coming into force and I think we have yet to see the full knock-on effects of that very, very big constitutional change and I do think that our own Minister of Justice figure is going to be an increasingly important member of the Government.

Why did Tony Blair replace Lord Irvine?

The role of the Lord Chancellor in warning ministerial colleagues that proposed policies may be contrary to rule of law principles is relevant not only to questions of reform, but also to understanding the reasons why Lord Irvine (Lord Chancellor 1997–2003) was removed from office by the Prime Minister in June 2003. During parliamentary debates on the government's reform proposals, some members of the House of Lords speculated about what had happened behind the scenes. Lord Hoffmann, who, at the time, was a serving judge (but, as a Law Lord, entitled to sit and vote in general debates on the floor of the House of Lords), took part in a debate on a motion *'That this House takes note of Her Majesty's Government's proposals for a United Kingdom Supreme Court, an independent Judicial Appointments Commission and the abolition of the office of Lord Chancellor'.*

House of Lords Hansard, 12 February 2004, col. 1259

Lord Hoffmann: My Lords, on 2 April last year, the then Lord Chancellor [Lord Irvine] gave evidence in another place [the House of Commons] to the Select Committee on the Lord Chancellor's Department. It was a considered statement of government policy and I have no doubt that, in accordance with the usual practice, it had been cleared with the Prime Minister's office in advance. He was asked about the constitutional position of the Lord Chancellor, and he replied by quoting with approval what my noble and learned friend Lord Bingham of Cornhill [a former Lord Chief Justice of England and Wales; the Senior Law Lord] had written on behalf of the Judges' Council when he said: 'We have no doubt that the Lord Chancellor's dual role [i.e. as a politician and a judge] has historically proved invaluable in maintaining the independence of the judiciary in England and Wales and we have considerable anxiety that any other arrangement would result in time in the encroachment of executive government into the proper sphere of judicial independence essential in a democratic society'.

When he was asked about the principle of the separation of powers, my noble and learned friend Lord Irvine of Lairg said: 'We are a nation of pragmatists, not theorists and we go quite frankly for what works'. When he was asked about creating a Supreme Court, the then Lord Chancellor said: 'The question is whether the present system is a good system'. He said that in his opinion it was. Furthermore, he said that a new Supreme Court would require a suitable building. There was in his opinion a prior need for other court buildings up and down the country.

Less than 10 weeks later, on 12 June, the Prime Minister announced that the office of the Lord Chancellor had been abolished. Someone must have pointed out that he had no power to abolish that office; because the press office at No. 10 Downing Street then issued a clarification saying that it was the Government's intention to abolish the office. Meanwhile, my noble and learned friend Lord Irvine of Lairg was removed and replaced.

It was a remarkable change of policy; made in such haste that, as the first announcement showed, it did not allow time even for private consultation with someone who understood the constitutional position of the Lord Chancellor. And the reason given for the Government's volte face was a sudden realisation that the position of the Lord Chancellor infringed the principle of the separation of powers. Well, that may be, but I doubt whether many juries would believe it. The circumstantial evidence—the secrecy, the haste, the misfired announcement, the public knowledge of personality clashes between my noble and learned friend Lord Irvine of Lairg and other members of the Cabinet—all points to a different explanation. Perhaps my noble and learned friend Lord Hutton ought to be asked to investigate.

One possible answer is that the Prime Minister decided that the then Lord Chancellor had to go, and for some reason his removal had to be dressed in the robes of high constitutional principle. And as the Government were representing that the principle of the separation of powers was the reason for the abolition of the office of Lord Chancellor, it was necessary for the sake of consistency to abolish the judicial functions of your Lordships' House.

It is sad that a great constitutional change should be adopted as a quick fix for personal squabbles in the Cabinet. One of the glories of this country's constitution, unique in the world, has been its continuity. Institutions such as the Lord Chancellor have adapted themselves over centuries to new constitutional roles without having to make a new start. We have never had a year zero in this country. But that has been achieved not by statutes, and not as is said by the particular personalities of those who held the office, but by the acceptance of constitutional conventions about how the holder of the office ought to behave. It is those conventions, accepted and handed on by successive Lord Chancellors, which have given us an independent judiciary of a quality which is the envy of many other countries.

It is no use crying over spilt milk. My noble and learned friend the Lord Chancellor [Lord Falconer, appointed by Tony Blair to replace Lord Irvine] has renounced the powers of his office [by saying that he would not sit as a judge] and the conventions that went with it. He has broken the mechanism which served us so well in the past. Its effectiveness depended on the willingness of people to make it work. Once it is gone, I doubt whether it can be put together again. So my noble and learned friend the Lord Chief Justice and the Judges' Council were doing the best they could to try to ensure that these new and untested proposals for securing the independence of the judiciary are the best that can be devised.

Lord Ackner, a retired Law Lord, spoke in the same debate.

House of Lords Hansard, 2 February 2004, col. 1278

Lord Ackner: [...] If one goes back and asks, 'What is the genesis out of which these proposals have arisen?' we do not have the clearest evidence but we can probably start with the unconstitutional and inexcusable behaviour of the Home Secretary in attacking the decision of the Appellate Committee of this House for holding that under the human rights legislation—the Government had embraced it enthusiastically as part of the law—a politician was not entitled to play any part in the decision of how long a person convicted of murder should stay in prison [R (Anderson) v Secretary of State for the Home Department [2002] UKHL 46]. That gave rise to a strong attack by the Home Secretary [David Blunkett MP] on the judiciary. It was followed by an even more direct attack on a High Court judge's decision of the legality of the Home Secretary's action under the then current immigration legislation.

I have no doubt that the then Lord Chancellor acted with enormous energy behind the scenes to try to sort this out. He was unsuccessful. He appeared before a Select Committee and, in the course of giving his evidence, said in substance that it is wrong for the Government to cheer when they get a decision in their favour but when the decision is adverse then to attack the judiciary. That was said in public and no one had any doubt that he was directing his criticism towards the Home Secretary.

There then followed a pause and to most of us it was apparent that it would be very difficult to see both remaining in office—the Lord Chancellor and the Home Secretary. To those who knew the personalities, and those who supported them, the bets were that the Home Secretary would survive; and survive he did.

Baroness Kennedy of the Shaws (Helena Kennedy)—a Labour peer and a Queen's Counsel (QC)—amplified matters.

House of Lords Hansard, 12 February 2004, col. 1278

Baroness Kennedy of the Shaws: [...] My Lords, it is interesting to hear noble Lords puzzle over the events of 13 June. There we were, expecting simply a reshuffle, and yet we were plunged into this extraordinary constitutional drama. It was described by the noble and learned Lord, Lord Hoffmann, as an issue of personalities in the Cabinet. Was it simply a drama of loyalty? I am sure, as the noble and learned Lord, Lord Hoffmann, suggested, that the removal of the Lord Chancellor in that reshuffle must have caused considerable anguish. It must have been a source of great distress to a Prime Minister who had known that Lord Chancellor so intimately and who had him as a mentor and pupil master. It must have felt like an act of patricide. It may be that, like many an employer, one would want to say that the person was now redundant because their post was abolished, rather than that one was sacking them.

We were seeing more than a drama of loyalty. It was a drama of loyalty not such as is simply part and parcel of the soap opera of politics, but a drama of loyalty of much greater proportion. At the heart of this is the issue of loyalty—to whom does the Lord Chancellor owe his loyalty? When someone becomes a Lord Chancellor, no doubt because of political connections, first and foremost they may feel themselves to be there for political reasons. I am sure that our last Lord Chancellor felt that his long connection with the Prime Minister created loyalty. I am sure that his long-established membership of the Labour Party since he was a teenager created loyalty.

Of course, what a Lord Chancellor learns in our constitution is a greater loyalty—a loyalty to the constitution. The weight of that loyalty is probably not there in the beginning. It comes as you feel the weight of the role; you are more than a member of the Cabinet, you are the guardian of the Great Seal, the protector of the judiciary, the protector of an independent legal profession, careful of access to justice and mindful of the special role that you play. Because of your life in the law, you know about those checks and balances. Because of your life in the law, you know why law matters. Because of your life in the law, you have come to understand that you cannot only consider the short term in policy-making when it comes to law.

The role of the Lord Chancellor creates for that person a great conflict of loyalty. That was the drama that unfolded in the prologue to 13 June. The prologue, as has been described, involved a conflict of loyalty. What we saw unfolding was the drama that is crucial in any Cabinet, where on the one hand there is a Home Secretary who argues about law and order, and on the other there is a Lord Chancellor who is to be the voice of justice and who speaks about what is right and just. We saw that conflict of loyalty played out. The noble and learned Lord, Lord Ackner, described very powerfully the subject matter over which those battles ensued, where it became necessary for the Lord Chancellor to say to the Home Secretary, 'Take your tanks off the Middle Temple's lawns. Take your tanks away from the front of the Royal Courts of Justice'. The Home Secretary did not receive that message too kindly.

The Prime Minister had to decide where his loyalty lay—did it lie with authoritarianism or liberalism? Did it lie with the protection of justice or with the short-term politics of satisfying the hunger of a media that are often not too concerned about justice? That drama of the constitution was played out, and inevitably, I am afraid, a decision was made that meant that not just the Lord Chancellor himself was removed, but his role was abolished. It may well be that as the noble and learned Lord, Lord Hoffmann, described it, we saw that event dressed in the robes of high constitutional principle.

That saddens me, because I am a constitutional reformer. I chaired Charter 88 [a campaign organization] for five years prior to the 1997 election. I strongly believe that an evolving process of reform should take place. The role of the Lord Chancellor, in the form that existed, was becoming untenable. In the new world that we live in it was, and is, unacceptable for a Lord Chancellor to sit in the Cabinet and also to sit as a judge. Politics has changed, and the interface of law and politics is much more complex than ever before.

Therefore, this suggestion that the Lord Chancellor's role had to be reformed did not come out of the side-field. It had been discussed and debated since 1988, when the constitutional reform organisation, Charter 88, was established, and debates had taken place about our constitution. The Lord Chancellor should no longer be sitting and making appointments in the way in which he has done.

The statutory reference to the rule of law

As the Constitutional Reform Bill went through Parliament in 2004–05, the idea emerged that the bill should contain an express reference to the rule of law. Finding the right form of words proved difficult. Ministers and others were concerned that if too much was said in a clause about the rule of law, the Lord Chancellor might become subject to judicial review if he or she were to fail in the duty. Some ministers would have preferred for the Bill to say nothing about the rule of law. But in December 2004, as the Bill neared the end of its passage in the House of Lords, the government put forward an amendment, which was enacted as follows.

Constitutional Reform Act 2005, s. 1

The rule of law

This Act does not adversely affect—

(a) the existing constitutional principle of the rule of law, or

(b) the Lord Chancellor's existing constitutional role in relation to that principle.

Lord Falconer, the new Lord Chancellor, explained the government's thinking.

House of Lords Hansard, 20 December 2004, cols 1538–9

Lord Falconer of Thoroton: My Lords, we have had several useful debates on the rule of law. Perhaps I may summarise the position which I think we reached. We all agreed that we do not want to change the Lord Chancellor's existing role in relation to the rule of law. That role goes further than simply respecting the rule of law in discharging his ministerial functions. It includes being obliged to speak up in Cabinet or as a Cabinet Minister against proposals that he believes offend the rule of law. That role does not require him proactively to police every act of government. The role is not one that is enforceable in courts.

In the debate on this issue at Report stage, the noble Lord, Lord Kingsland [the Conservative frontbench spokesman], supported by the noble Lord, Lord Goodhart [the Liberal Democrat front-bench spokesman], sought reassurance that the Government's previous amendment covered the Lord Chancellor's "constitutional duty to speak up in Cabinet". I think that that was the only issue between us. Amendment No. 1 [set out above] provides such clarity.

The new draft also avoids any possibility of inadvertently infringing on the Lord Chancellor's existing statutory duty regarding the rule of law. Perhaps I can draw attention particularly to the speech on Report of the noble and learned Lord, Lord Mackay of Clashfern, in which he referred specifically to the *Witham* case.[28] I think that the new wording puts this issue beyond any doubt whatever. I have discussed it fully with the noble Lords, Lord Kingsland and Lord Goodhart, and I think that they are content.

The legality of the Government's conduct is no less crucial to the rule of law than the matters within the Lord Chancellor's remit. The ministerial code requires all Ministers to consult the Attorney-General on issues involving legal considerations.[29] The Attorney-General is the authoritative source of legal advice within the Government.

The Government have listened very carefully to all the concerns raised in previous stages and shown their willingness to meet those concerns and to engage in constructive debate. I think that we can now be satisfied that not only do we now share the same objectives, but that the draft before us successfully achieves those objectives. I beg to move.

Lord Goodhart: My Lords, during the tripartite discussions between the noble Lord, Lord Kingsland, the noble and learned Lord the Lord Chancellor and myself it became apparent that we were agreed on the principle that we should continue with the existing standard of the rule of law and with the existing constitutional responsibility of the Lord Chancellor to uphold it. We had some difficulty in finding a form of words acceptable to us all, but I am satisfied with the form of words in the amendment. Therefore, I am happy to support the amendment.

Lord Tebbit [a former minister in Margaret Thatcher's Cabinet]: My Lords, the adverb "adversely" clearly qualifies the verb "affect". Is it intended to strengthen or to weaken the impact of that verb?

Lord Falconer of Thoroton: My Lords, the words "does not adversely affect" make it clear that the Bill does not affect, one jot, the duty of the Lord Chancellor in relation to the rule of law.

Lord Tebbit: My Lords, I understand that that is the intention, but would it not be clearer—-or less clear—if the adverb "adversely" was left out?

Lord Falconer of Thoroton: My Lords, we humbly thought it made it clearer.

Lord Tebbit: My Lords, I apologise for being more dense than usual.

A year after the CRA 2005 came into force, a parliamentary select committee considered how the rule of law should be defined.

---

28 In the judicial review case *R v Lord Chancellor, ex parte Witham* [1998] QB 575, the High Court held that there was a common law constitutional right of access to a court, which the Lord Chancellor had breached when he made secondary legislation removing exemption from court fees for people on low incomes.

29 On the Ministerial Code, see Chapter 7. This express requirement was removed when Gordon Brown (prime minister 2007–10) revised the Code in 2007.

House of Lords Select Committee on the Constitution, *Relations between the Executive, the Judiciary and Parliament,* Sixth Report, Session 2006–07, HL Paper 151

23. Section 1 of the CRA states that "This Act does not adversely affect (a) the existing constitutional principle of the rule of law, or (b) the Lord Chancellor's existing constitutional role in relation to that principle". This provision begs several questions, the first of which is what the "rule of law" actually means. To assist our understanding of this term, we commissioned a paper from Professor Paul Craig, Professor of English Law at the University of Oxford (Appendix 5).

24. Although Professor Craig shed much light on the matter, it is apparent that despite its inclusion in the statute book, the rule of law remains a complex and in some respects uncertain concept. Professor Craig drew our attention to three different meanings. First, "a core idea of the rule of law [...] is that the government must be able to point to some basis for its actions that is regarded as valid by the relevant legal system". This is, however, too limited so, secondly, the rule of law requires that legal rules "should be capable of guiding one's conduct in order that one can plan one's life". In other words, legal rules should meet a variety of criteria, including that they should be prospective, not retrospective; that they should be relatively stable; and that there should be an independent judiciary. Professor Craig told us that some commentators regard these "formal" attributes of law to be necessary but not sufficient. So a third meaning of the rule of law held by some is that it encompasses substantive rights, thought to be fundamental, which can be "used to evaluate the quality of the laws produced by the legislature and the courts".

25. Lord Falconer [Lord Chancellor 2003–07] told us that "the rule of law includes both national and international law as far as I am concerned, therefore if we remained in breach of the European Convention then we would be in breach of international law. I think the rule of law also goes beyond issues such as specific black letter law. I think there are certain constitutional principles which if Parliament sought to offend would be contrary to the rule of law as well. To take an extreme example simply to demonstrate the point, if Parliament sought to abolish all elections that would be so contrary to our constitutional principles that that would seem to me to be contrary to the rule of law. The rule of law goes beyond specific black letter law; it includes international law and it includes, in my view, settled constitutional principles. I think there might be a debate as to precisely what are settled constitutional principles but it goes beyond, as it were, black letter law" (Q 8).

26. On the question of who is responsible for upholding the rule of law, the Lord Chief Justice [Lord Phillips of Worth Matravers 2005–07] told us that "it is the role of the judiciary, in practice, to uphold the rule of law, to apply the rule of law, to enforce the rule of law, and to do that they have to be independent of outside influence. Insofar as it is the Lord Chancellor's job to uphold the rule of law, this must be very largely a job of ensuring that our independence is observed. Equally, there must be occasions in government where a question may arise as to whether the conduct that the Government is contemplating is or is not in accordance with the rule of law, and there, I would imagine, the Lord Chancellor would have a role to play in his capacity as a minister" (Appendix 8, Q 7). In relation to the rule of law and the HRA, the Lord Chief Justice explained that if a court made a declaration of incompatibility "it would be open to the Government to say, 'the court has ruled that this is contrary to the Human Rights Act. Notwithstanding that, we do not intend to comply with the Human Rights Act on this point' and that would be contrary to what I would call rule of law". That would, however, be the end of the argument "because Parliament is in that field supreme" (Appendix 8, QQ 9, 10).

QUESTIONS

1. Using the information and evidence set out in this chapter, explain and assess the effectiveness of (i) the judiciary using the common law, (ii) Parliament, and (iii) the Lord Chancellor in defending the rule of law.

2. What is the significance of s. 1 of the Constitutional Reform Act 2005? What assumptions does it make?

3. Suppose that the Ministry of Justice is writing a guide to the UK constitution, to help people in Britain to understand their rights and responsibilities. The Ministry asks you to provide a definition of the rule of law in no more than 150 words.

4. In the wake of a major terrorist attack in the United Kingdom, in which 10,000 people were killed and many thousands more injured, and in the face of credible threats of more to follow, the UK Parliament enacts the Authorization to Torture (Exceptional Circumstances) Act, which provides as follows.

   (1) It shall not be unlawful for a police officer to torture an individual if he—

      (a) has reasonable grounds for suspecting that the individual is or has been involved in terrorism-related activity; and

      (b) considers it necessary to attempt to obtain information by means of torture for the purpose of protecting the members of the public from an imminent risk of terrorism; and

      (c) the Secretary of State has made a declaration of emergency for the purposes of this section which has been approved by the House of Commons.

   (2) This Act shall be interpreted, applied and enforced by the court notwithstanding any incompatibility with the international human rights law, customary international law, the laws of the European Union, or the common law.

   (3) The Human Rights Act 1998 does not apply to this Act.

   Suppose that a state of emergency is invoked and suspect X is being held by the police and is being subjected to torture. X's lawyer seeks an injunction from the court to stop this. The matter comes before a judge. You are the judge's judicial assistant and she asks you to prepare a note setting out what options the court has in relation to its approach to the Authorization to Torture (Exceptional Circumstances) Act.

4 CONCLUDING COMMENTS

This chapter has examined the rule of law, in particular its definition and some of the main ways in which the institutions of the British constitution seek to protect it. While there continues to be academic debate about the best definition of the rule of law, or whether the rule of law is a valuable concept, there is no doubt that a broad idea of the rule of law has become implanted in British constitutional thinking and practice.

We will return to look at further aspects of the rule of law in later chapters; in particular, Chapter 6 the international human rights movement, and how this has been 'brought home' to Britain by the Human Rights Act 1998 and the continuing political debates as to whether socio-economic rights should be included in a British bill of rights.

5 FURTHER READING

Bingham, T., *The Rule of Law* (2010, London: Allen Lane)

Craig, P., 'Constitutional foundations, the rule of law and supremacy' [2003] Public Law 92

European Commission for Democracy through Law (Venice Commission), *Report on the Rule of Law* (Adopted by the Venice Commission at its 86th plenary session, Venice, 25–26 March 2011)

Jowell, J., 'The Rule of Law and its Underlying Values', in J. Jowell and D. Oliver (eds) *The Changing Constitution*, 7th edn (2011, Oxford: OUP), ch. 1

ONLINE RESOURCE CENTRE

Further information about the themes discussed in this chapter can be found on the Online Resource Centre at www.oxfordtextbooks.co.uk/orc/lesueur2e/

4

SEPARATING AND BALANCING POWERS

CENTRAL ISSUES

1. An important task for a constitutional system is to determine how power is to be distributed across different institutions and public office-holders.

2. The main roles within the constitutional system are usually referred to as the 'executive', 'legislative', and 'judicial' roles. The relationships between these roles, and the institutions and processes through which they are carried out, are informed by the principle that powers should be separated. The content of this principle and its practical application are contentious in the United Kingdom in several ways.

3. The concept of separation of powers has various functions. It is a template for designing constitutions and constitutional reform. It may protect individual liberty by ensuring that too much power is not concentrated into the hands of one person or institution. It may promote efficiency, by ensuring that appropriate institutions make decisions.

4. There is an academic argument that, historically, the more important division of powers within Britain was between the Crown and Parliament (rather than the executive/legislative/judicial distinction that emerged first in other constitutional systems).

5. The concept of separation of powers is implicit in court judgments that have to adjudicate on questions about the relative powers of government, Parliament and the judiciary.

6. In the UK system, separation of powers is a justification for basic constitutional arrangements. MPs and peers cannot serve as senior judges. Judges cannot serve as MPs or in the House of Lords. 'Parliamentary privilege' prevents courts scrutinizing parliamentary matters. 'Sub judice' rules generally prevent MPs and peers discussing cases before the courts.

7. As the UK system is a parliamentary democracy, not a presidential one, there is no separation between Parliament and government. Indeed, ministers are required to be in Parliament to ensure they are held to account.

1 INTRODUCTION

One of the main tasks of a constitutional system is to determine which institutions and office-holders have power and responsibility for carrying out public functions. This chapter looks at the traditional division between 'executive', 'legislative', and 'judicial' roles—a three-part distinction that is central to much thinking about the constitutional principle of separation of powers. As we will see, there is debate as to whether, why, and how separation of powers should occur in the United Kingdom's constitutional system.

At the heart of the idea of separation of powers is the proposition that there are different *kinds* of public function that:

(a) ought to be distinguished from each other, and
(b) ought either to be exercised by different institutions or personnel, or somehow 'balanced' to prevent an overconcentration of power in the hands of a single person or institution.

Some commentators are, however, sceptical about stressing *separation*, preferring instead to highlight the need for institutions to work together.

Ralf Dahrendorf, 'A confusion of powers: Politics and the rule of law' (1977) 40 Modern Law Review 1, 11–12 (footnotes omitted)

Like the division of labour, the separation of powers is a very theoretical concept indeed. It is above all a concept, and not a fact; what we see is not the division of labour, but its combination in the co-operative structure of organisations; it is not the separation of powers, but their co-ordination and sometimes their confusion. It is useful to think of government, parliament and the judiciary as separate functions; it may to some extent be important to institutionalise this separateness, for example by safeguarding the independence of the judiciary; but the theoretical separation of powers is merely the preface to the main volume of practical problems of how the different and possibly separate powers should be co-ordinated.

James Madison [1751–1836, one of the founding fathers of the USA] saw this even more clearly than Montesquieu[1] himself, who of course realised that the powers of legislature and executive in Britain were anything but separate. Like Montesquieu, Madison preferred the term 'distribution of power' and proceeded to look for 'the sense in which the preservation of liberty requires that the three great departments of power should be separate and distinct.' And this seems quite clear to Madison, as it does to common sense, that it does not make sense to assume 'that the legislative, executive and judiciary departments should be wholly unconnected with each other'; on the contrary, the real question is how they are 'connected and blended.'

2 PRACTICAL SCENARIOS

If this all sounds rather abstract, consider the following practical scenarios. These are situations in which disagreements have erupted over whether the 'wrong person' or 'wrong institution' was carrying out the public function in question.

---

[1] See extract, Charles de Secondat (Baron de Montesquieu), *L'Esprit des Lois* on p. 120.

Politicians and murderers

When a court passes a life sentence on a person convicted of murder, who should have power to order for how long the person must remain in prison for the purposes of punishment before being eligible for release 'on licence' (if he or she is no longer a danger the public)? Should a government minister—a politician accountable to Parliament and influenced by public opinion—have this function, or should it be exercised by the judiciary? Section 61(1) of the Criminal Justice Act 1967, passed when the death penalty for murder was abolished in the United Kingdom, gave the function to the Home Secretary. The power was re-enacted, in slightly modified form, in s. 29 of the Crime (Sentences) Act 1997. Anderson, a life prisoner brought a judicial review challenge.

R v Secretary of State for the Home Department, ex parte Anderson
[2002] UKHL 46

Lord Steyn

39. In a series of decisions since *Doody* in 1993 [...], the House of Lords has described the Home Secretary's role in determining the tariff period to be served by a convicted murderer as punishment akin to a sentencing exercise. In our system of law the sentencing of persons convicted of crimes is classically regarded as a judicial rather than executive task. Our constitution has, however, never embraced a rigid doctrine of separation of powers. The relationship between the legislature and the executive is close. On the other hand, the separation of powers between the judiciary and the legislative and executive branches of government is a strong principle of our system of government. The House of Lords and the Privy Council have so stated: *Attorney-General for Australia v The Queen and the Boilermakers' Society of Australia* [1957] AC 288, 315; *Liyanage v The Queen* [1967] 1 AC 259, 291; *Hinds v The Queen* [1977] AC 195; *Duport Steels Ltd v Sirs* [1980] 1 WLR 142, 157B. It is reinforced by constitutional principles of judicial independence, access to justice, and the rule of law. But the supremacy of Parliament is the paramount principle of our constitution. Whatever arguments there were about the precise nature of the Home Secretary's role in controlling the release of convicted murderers, Parliament had the power to entrust this particular role to the Home Secretary. It did so unambiguously by enacting section 29 of the 1997 Act and its precursors. While a series of House of Lords' decisions have revealed concerns about the compatibility of the operation of the system with the rule of law, the lawfulness in principle of the Home Secretary's role was not in doubt.

40. The question is now whether the Home Secretary's decision-making power over the terms to be served by mandatory life sentence prisoners is compatible with a later statute enacted by Parliament, namely the Human Rights Act 1998 by which Parliament incorporated the European Convention on Human Rights into the law of the United Kingdom. Article 6(1) of the Convention, so far as it is material, provides: 'In the determination of his civil rights and obligations or of any criminal charge against him, everyone is entitled to a fair and public hearing within a reasonable time by an independent and impartial tribunal established by law.' [...]

51. The power of the Home Secretary in England and Wales to decide on the tariff to be served by mandatory life sentence prisoners is a striking anomaly in our legal system. It is true that Parliament has the power to punish contemnors by imprisonment. This power derives

from the medieval concept of Parliament being, amongst other things, a court of justice: see *Erskine May: Treatise On The Law, Privileges, Proceedings and Usages of Parliament*, 22nd edn (1997), p. 131 et seq. Subject to this qualification, there is in our system of law no exception to the proposition that a decision to punish an offender by ordering him to serve a period of imprisonment may only be made by a court of law: *Blackstone's Commentaries on the Laws of England*, 2001, vol. 1, [...] para. 137. It is a decision which may only be made by the courts. Historically, this has been the position in our legal system since at least 1688. And this idea is a principal feature of the rule of law on which our unwritten constitution is based. It was overridden by Parliament by virtue of section 29 of the 1997 Act. Now the duty to decide on the compatibility of that statutory provision with article 6(1) has been placed by Parliament on the courts under the Human Rights Act. [...]

The House of Lords made a declaration of incompatibility under the Human Rights Act 1998 that s. 29 of the Crime (Sentences) Act 1997 was incompatible with Art. 6 of the European Convention on Human Rights (ECHR).

The ultimate court of appeal as a parliamentary committee

A second scenario is the background to the creation of the UK Supreme Court. Until 30 September 2009, the United Kingdom's highest court—the Appellate Committee of the House of Lords—operated as a committee of one of the Houses of Parliament. The court's professional judges—the Lords of Appeal in Ordinary—were peers and took part in some aspects of the House of Lord's legislative and scrutiny work when not sitting as judges—including chairing a select committee on scrutiny of EU legal proposals; hearings were held in committee rooms in Parliament; judgments were delivered in the chamber of the Lords (before legislative and scrutiny business started). In 2003, Tony Blair's government adopted a policy, eventually put into law by the Constitutional Reform Act 2005, that there should be an institutional separation of the 'judicial business' from the legislative and scrutiny work of the House of Lords, with judicial functions transferred to a newly created Supreme Court of the United Kingdom.

The government's thinking is set out in the following extract from a consultation paper issued by the department responsible for the reforms.

Department for Constitutional Affairs, *Constitutional Reform: A Supreme Court for the United Kingdom* (July 2003), para. 3

It is not always understood that the decisions of the 'House of Lords' are in practice decisions of the Appellate Committee and that non-judicial members of the House never take part in the judgments. Nor is the extent to which the Law Lords themselves have decided to refrain from getting involved in political issues in relation to legislation on which they might later have to adjudicate always appreciated. The fact that the Lord Chancellor, as the Head of the Judiciary, was entitled to sit in the Appellate and Judicial Committees and did so as Chairman, added to the perception that their independence might be compromised by the arrangements. The Human Rights Act, specifically in relation to Article 6 of the European Convention on Human Rights, now requires a stricter view to be taken not only of anything which might undermine the independence or impartiality of a judicial tribunal, but even of anything which might appear to do so. So the fact that the Law Lords are a Committee of the House of Lords can raise issues about the appearance of independence from the legislature. Looking at it from the other way round, the requirement for the appearance of impartiality and independence also increasingly limits the ability of the Law Lords to contribute to the work of the House of Lords, thus reducing the value to both them and the House of their membership.

The need to separate judges from Parliament was not accepted by everyone. Giving evidence to the House of Commons Constitutional Affairs Committee after the government announced their reform plans, Lord Lloyd of Berwick, a retired Law Lord, made the following statement to members of Parliament (MPs).

House of Commons Constitutional Affairs Committee, *Judicial Appointments and a Supreme Court (Court of Final Appeal)*, First Report, Session 2003–04 (HC 48-I), para. 20

Since it is the judges who have to decide whether ministers are breaking the law or exceeding their powers or whatever it may be, it is obviously vital that the judiciary and the executive should be separate and distinct. But there has never been a reason—not one that I can see— why the judges and the legislature should be distinct and separate.

Civil servants imposing penalties on irresponsible fathers

This third scenario is about designing a system for applying pressure on non-resident parents (usually fathers) to pay child maintenance. The government decided on a policy of confiscating non-payers' passports. Who, in such a scheme, was to make decisions about imposing this sanction? Was it objectionable on constitutional grounds for a civil servant (civil servants are responsible for the administration of central government and work within the executive) working in the Child Maintenance Enforcement Commission (CMEC) to have these powers? The government and the House of Lords Constitution Committee disagreed about this.

House of Lords Constitution Committee, *Welfare Reform Bill*, Ninth Report, Session 2008–09, HL 79

8. We remain of the view, expressed in our December 2007 report [which criticized previous proposals], that it is constitutionally unsatisfactory for CMEC and its contractors—rather than the courts—to have a sanction power to withdraw a person's right to hold a passport. The freedom to travel to and from one's country is a constitutional right of such significance that restricting this right as a punishment demands rigorous examination by an independent and impartial judge.

9. In recent years, there has been a notable transfer of sanction powers from the courts to the executive. In recent reports and correspondence with ministers, we have sought to ensure that where the executive is conferred with coercive sanction powers there are

safeguards for ensuring fair procedures are followed and that there is an effective appeal to the courts to ensure judicial oversight. In relation to the present bill, we acknowledge that a person who is disqualified by CMEC from holding a passport would have a right of appeal to a court and that if such a right of appeal is exercised, the disqualification will be suspended until the appeal is determined. The possibility of an appeal does not, however, answer the prior question: is the sanction power one which the executive, rather than the courts, should be allowed to exercise.

10. In the present bill, the Government seek to transfer sanction powers from the courts to civil servants in relation to passports and driving licences. It should be noted that the Child Maintenance and Other Payments Act 2008 created other sanction powers, including the imposition of curfew orders and an associated power to search premises and confiscate any money found. Curfew orders and search powers are, under current arrangements, made and authorised by the courts following an application by CMEC. While the Government have not proposed that the executive should have power to impose curfew orders or search premises without reference to the courts, we are concerned that an unintended change in the constitution is occurring in which the executive is acquiring ever more powers to impose sanctions and punish people that a generation ago would have been regarded as falling within the remit of the courts. A line needs to be drawn around the type of power that civil servants can appropriately exercise and those for which judges should be responsible. In our view, suspending a person's right to hold a passport, because of its impact on a constitutional right, should fall into the latter category (along with powers to impose curfew orders and order searches of premises).

The conclusion that can be drawn from these three scenarios is that far from being dry, abstract, textbook topics, debates about what kind of institution or person exercises different public functions take place regularly. These examples also show that the way in which powers are allocated and separated is often a contentious matter.

3 LEGISLATIVE, EXECUTIVE, AND JUDICIAL FUNCTIONS

The three-part distinction between legislative, executive, and judicial powers has its origins in the eighteenth century. This model is, however, open to criticism, as we shall see. Some commentators doubt whether the complex range of governmental functions in modern constitutional systems can be reduced to only three types of power. It is also argued by some scholars that this tripartite division is not grounded in the historical development of the British constitution, which, as we have noted, did not undergo the revolutionary transformations experienced towards the end of eighteenth century in France and the USA (see Box 4.1).

BOX 4.1 TYPES OF FUNCTION AT A GLANCE	
Legislative	Making legally binding sets of rules that apply to people generally
Executive	Foreign relations; military action; administration; developing national policy on a wide range of subjects
Judicial	Applying the law to resolve civil disputes; conduct of criminal trials

In its *institutional* form (applied in few, if any, constitutional systems), the concept of separation of powers suggests that these three functions must be exercised by completely different institutions: legislation should only be made by legislative bodies (parliaments); executive functions should only be carried out by governments (ministers and civil servants); and courts alone should be responsible for judicial functions. In practice, in many constitutional systems, institutions exercise functions from more than one of the categories: for example, the government may have rule-making powers (a legislative function).

In its *personnel* form, the idea of separation of powers stresses that a single person should not exercise more than one of the functions. For example:

- a person who is a member of the executive branch (a minister or an official) should not also be a member of the judiciary or of the legislature;
- a person who is a member of the judiciary should not simultaneously be a member of the legislature (Parliament) or the government (as a minister or official); and
- a person who is a member of the legislature (an MP) should not be a judge or a member of the executive (as a minister or civil servant).

We will see shortly that the UK constitutional system does not match up to all of these requirements (which leads some commentators to suggest that the separation of powers is not particularly important in the United Kingdom).

There is one very obvious way in which the United Kingdom—along with many other major constitutional systems around the world—does not fit the 'personnel separation' model: ministers (who exercise executive functions) are *required* to be members of the legislature (Parliament), in which they have a dominant role in the legislative process.[2] There is therefore an important distinction to be made between presidential systems (in which executive and legislature are separate—as in the USA, Mexico, and Brazil) and parliamentary systems (in which they are not—as in the United Kingdom, Ireland, Australia, Canada, and the Netherlands).

It is often stressed that the separation of powers does not aim only, or mainly, to separate different functions, but to ensure that there are 'checks and balances' within the constitution so that power is not overly concentrated in one institution. For example, if the legislature were to delegate some law-making powers to ministers, the courts (exercising their judicial function) should have powers to review whether those powers are lawfully exercised in accordance with the intention of the legislature.

In Chapter 2, the debate between the 'political' and 'legal' constitutionalists was introduced in the context of the principles of parliamentary supremacy and the rule of law. It should be no surprise that the tensions surface again in relation to debates over the meaning and application of the doctrine of separation of powers. Political constitutionalists tend to downplay the role of courts: as we see shortly, Tomkins, for example, argues that it is wrong in the English constitutional set-up to view the judiciary as a 'third branch'.[3] Legal constitutionalists, on the other hand, tend to be keen on using the idea of separation of powers to bolster the importance of the courts as a major 'check and balance' on the institutions that carry out the other two functions (legislative and executive).

[2] See extract, Walter Bagehot, *The English Constitution* on p. 121.
[3] See extract, Adam Tomkins, *Public Law* on p. 125.

What is the point of separating powers?

There are three main reasons why theorists and more practically minded people have been interested in the idea of separation of powers.

(a) First, it may be thought of as a template for the design of a constitutional system. If a country is starting from scratch (after a revolution of some kind, for example), the idea of separation of powers offers guiding principles on allocating legislative, executive, and judicial functions to various kinds of institution.

(b) Second—and this is a view taken in different centuries by Baron Montesquieu (1689–1755) and Professor Eric Barendt, in the extracts that follow—the point of separation of powers may be to protect liberty. The gist of the idea is that if too much of one kind of power is concentrated in the hands of one person or institution, there is more of a risk of that power being abused to curtail freedom than if the powers are kept distinct or if there is a system of 'checks and balances'.

(c) Third, we will see that N.W. Barber argues that '*it is efficiency, not liberty, which is at the heart of separation of powers*'. If the various types of power are allocated sensibly to the right kind of institution, it is more likely to be exercised efficiently.

Montesquieu (Charles-Louis de Secondat) was a French aristocrat who travelled widely in Europe, who lived in England for two years in 1729–31, and who had great knowledge of the ancient Roman and Greek civilizations. The overarching theme of his book *The Spirit of Laws*, on which he worked for twenty years, was to examine how judgments should be made about the qualities of laws and systems of government (which he classified as 'republican', 'aristocratic', and 'despotic'). In that part of his book entitled 'Of the laws that form political liberty, with regard to the constitution', he describes a picture under the heading 'Of the constitution of England' that bore no resemblance to the *actual* arrangements then (or now), so presumably his aim was to outline an idealized system.

Charles de Secondat (Baron de Montesquieu), *L'Esprit des Lois [The Spirit of the Laws]* (1748), Book XI, ch. VI, p. 181

Of the constitution of England

In every government there are three sorts of power; the legislative; the executive, in respect of things dependent on the law of nations; and the judicial, in regard to things that depend on the civil law.

By virtue of the first, the prince or magistrate enacts temporary or perpetual laws, and amends or abrogates those that have been already enacted. By the second, he makes peace or war, sends or receives embassies, establishes the public security, and provides against invasions. By the third, he punishes criminals, or determines the disputes that arise between individuals. The latter we shall call the judicial power, and the other simply the executive power of the state.

The political liberty of the subject is a tranquillity of mind, arising from the opinion each person has of his safety. In order to have this liberty, it is requisite the government be so constituted as one man need not be afraid of another.

When the legislative and executive powers are united in the same person, or in the same body of magistrates, there can be no liberty; because apprehensions may arise, lest the same monarch or senate should enact tyrannical laws, to executive them in a tyrannical manner.

Again, there is no liberty, if the power of judging be not separated from the legislative and executive powers.

Were it joined with the legislative, the life and liberty of the subject would be exposed to arbitrary control; for the judge would then be the legislator. Were it joined to the executive power, the judge might behave with all the violence of an oppressor.

There would be an end of every thing, were the same man, or the same body, whether of nobles or of the people to exercise those three powers, that of enacting the laws, that of executing public resolutions, and that of judging the crimes and differences of individuals.

Compare this with Bagehot's analysis 120 years later. Walter Bagehot (1826–77) qualified as a lawyer, but went into business as a journalist and founded *The Economist* magazine. In his view, the nineteenth-century British constitution was characterized by the fusion, not the separation, of powers—with the Cabinet at the epicentre.[4]

Walter Bagehot, *The English Constitution* (1867; 1963, London: Fontana/Collins), pp. 68–9

A Cabinet is a combining committee—a *hyphen* which joins, a *buckle* which fastens, the legislative part of the State to the executive part of the State. In its origins it belongs to one, in its functions it belongs to the other. [...]

The fusion of the legislative and executive functions may, to those who have not much considered it, seem but a dry and small matter to be the latent essence and effectual secret of the English constitution; but we can only judge of its real importance by looking at a few of its principal effects, and contrasting it very shortly with its great competitor, which seems likely, unless care be taken, to outstrip it in the progress of the world. That competitor is the Presidential system. The characteristic of it is that the President is elected from the people by one process, and the House of Representatives by another. The independence of the legislative and executive powers is the specific quality of Presidential government, just as the fusion and combination is the precise principle of Cabinet government.

Having noted that Dicey says almost nothing about separation of powers, in the next extract, Professor Barendt takes issue with Sir Ivor Jennings' analysis in *The Law and the Constitution* (1959).

Eric Barendt, 'Separation of powers and constitutional government' [1995]
Public Law 599, 603–4 (footnotes omitted)

Journal

The principal criticism made by Sir Ivor Jennings was that there are no material differences between the three functions, so the separation principle fails to explain why certain tasks

---

4 See Chapter 6.

should be given to one body rather than another. For instance, the differences between judicial and administrative decisions are in his view not really ones of substance, but are only formal or procedural. It is better that some decisions are taken by persons or bodies which observe formal legal procedures—impartial tribunals considering a case in public and on the evidence—rather than by administrators who are concerned to execute policies which they have developed. But we cannot say that some decisions are inherently judicial rather than administrative.

Jennings did admit that the legislative function may be identified as that of making 'general rules of law' , but it did not much matter that in practice in the U.K. (as in other countries) ministers issue a lot of general rules under delegated legislative authority. There would only be tyranny if all laws were made in this way, or, he might have added, if they were made by the executive without any legislative authority at all. Moreover, he concluded that the separation principle was irrelevant as a safeguard against bureaucracy or tyranny; what prevented that was democratic control through the House of Commons and the party system.

Geoffrey Marshall shares Jennings' view that it is impossible to define with precision the separate functions of government and consequently determine to whom their performance should be allocated. Moreover, it is the universal practice for governments to enjoy massive delegated legislative authority. Another of his points is that while most jurisdictions regard the independence of the judicial branch as sacrosanct, there is frequently (as in the U.K.) at least partial fusion of the legislative and executive branches. Finally, on some versions of the separation principle, e.g. the partial separation of powers found in the United States, constitutional judicial review is appropriate to check the legislative and executive branches, while it would be an unwarrantable violation of it according to the pure theory. The judiciary would then be interfering with the discharge by the legislature or executive of its functions. Marshall's conclusion is that the doctrine is far too imprecise and incoherent to be of any use in the analysis or critique of constitutions: '[i]t may be counted little more than a jumbled portmanteau of arguments for policies which ought to be supported or rejected on other grounds'. But he does not explain what these other arguments might be.

Finally, the separation of powers principle arguably amounts to a constraint on legislative supremacy. For that reason alone English commentators are generally reluctant to take the principle too seriously. It would require, for example, the courts to strike down criminal law statutes which retrospectively amended the law to deal with a particular incident. For such legislation would be viewed as a usurpation of the judicial function or an interference with the independence of the judiciary, whose role is to apply general rules and principles framed for all contingencies. [...]

[Having set out criticisms of the separation of powers principle, Barendt then turns to defend the doctrine.]

A number of points can be made in reply to the argument deployed by Sir Ivor Jennings. First, he was too sceptical about the possibility of a coherent allocation of functions. It is possible to define in general terms the legislative, executive and judicial functions, which are allocated by a constitution to particular bodies or institutions. What is crucial is that this distribution is enforceable by the courts. They are entitled to take the final decision whether in practice a function is to be regarded as legislative, executive or judicial. Of course, Jennings was right to point out that the theoretical criteria for determining, say, whether a decision is properly to be characterised as 'administrative' or 'judicial' are unclear and that there are many borderline cases. But it is perfectly coherent to claim, for instance, that decisions on personal rights and liberties are inherently suitable for judicial resolution, and so must be made by a court, while the distribution of other goods and benefits may be regarded as a matter for administrative decision. This particular distinction is captured by Article 66 of the Constitution of the Fifth French Republic: '[t]he judicial authority, guardian of the liberty of the individual, ensures respect for this principle in conditions determined by the law'. As a consequence a statute giving the police wide powers to inspect vehicles on the public streets was declared unconstitutional—in the absence of either adequate standards to guide the exercise of these powers or provision for judicial control. Similarly, English courts have held that a statute should not be interpreted to allow a final decision on a matter of legal liability, for example, to pay taxes, to be taken by an administrative authority. These decisions show that even within the context of an unwritten, or uncodified, constitution, courts are able to draw a clear line between administrative and judicial functions.

Equally, courts are able to draw lines between legislative functions on the one hand, and judicial and executive functions on the other. The legislative function is broadly the function of framing general rules applicable to a potentially unlimited range of circumstances. [...]

But perhaps a more significant point to make in reply to the critique of Jennings and Marshall is that the separation of powers is not in essence concerned with the allocation of functions as such. Its primary purpose [...] is the prevention of the arbitrary government, or tyranny, which may arise from the concentration of power. The allocation of functions between three, or perhaps more, branches of government is only a means to achieve that end. It does not matter, therefore, whether powers are always allocated precisely to the most appropriate institution—although an insensitive allocation would probably produce incompetent government and run counter to Locke's efficiency rationale.

This point is perhaps most clearly appreciated if we consider what has become one of the most complex areas for separation of powers analysis: the organization, and control, of administrative authorities and agencies. These range from bodies which allocate social security and welfare benefits (such as public housing), to regulatory bodies, for example, the Independent Television Commission and the Monopolies and Mergers Commission, and finally to supervisory or investigatory officers, such as the Comptroller and Auditor-General and the Parliamentary Commissioner for Administration (PCA). Now it can be asked whether these bodies perform legislative (or rule-making, to use the American term), administrative, or judicial functions. But these are impossible questions to answer. For in truth many agencies perform at least two, and perhaps all three, functions. This is apparent in the United States, where it is common for an independent regulatory agency to engage in rule-making, to formulate and apply policies, and to take individual decisions, often after a formal hearing. Perhaps in the United Kingdom the only authorities which consistently discharge all three functions are local authorities, which may make by-laws, formulate planning, highways and housing policies, and decide applications for planning permission which might be characterised as judicial, or at least quasi-judicial decisions. But certainly many agencies, including government ministers, exercise a variety of functions, some of which can be characterised as executive and some as judicial.

Does this phenomenon mean that separation of powers analysis should be abandoned as hopeless? It would seem so, if the pure theory is adopted, with its rigid insistence that each function of government is discharged by a separate institution. But the answer may be quite different if we see the principle as essentially concerned with the avoidance of concentrations of power. For then questions may be asked about the relationship of the agency to the three traditional branches of government. Does Parliament or the government have sole right to hire and fire members of the authority and its staff? Does the government have exclusive power to issue directions or guidance to the agency? If the agency takes judicial or quasi-judicial decisions, how far is it subject to review by the ordinary courts? On this approach there would be a violation of the principle if the executive were entitled, without assent of the legislature, to give detailed directions to an agency, and appoint its members, when that agency takes decisions affecting individual rights and judicial review is (virtually) excluded. That would not be because an executive agency carried out judicial functions, but because it was so structured as to create or reinforce a concentration of power in the hands of the government.

N.W. Barber disagrees with Eric Barendt's thesis that the main rationale for separation of powers is to protect liberty. He argues instead that the purpose of the doctrine is efficiency.

N.W. Barber, 'Prelude to the separation of powers' [2001] Cambridge Law Journal 59, 71–2 (footnotes omitted)

Separation of powers is a distinctively constitutional tool. It addresses itself to the authors of the constitution; it enjoins them to match function to form in such a way as to realise the goals set for the state by political theory. Having decided that a particular goal ought to be striven after in a society, the doctrine then focuses our attention on the manner by which it may be achieved. At this stage in the article the political assumptions that lie behind the broad understanding of the separation of powers must be thickened up. Whereas in the earlier part of the article all that was assumed was the thin assumption that powers should be allocated to the institution which was best placed to execute them, further assumptions must now be made about what factors may make an institution good at undertaking certain tasks. Again, though, these assumptions are weak ones. They merely indicate issues of significance, they do not necessarily require the prioritisation of one factor over the others. Separation of powers encourages us to consider various interconnected structural factors that affect the competency of institutions in the performance of their tasks. First, the composition and skills of an institution must be examined: the knowledge and experience of the actors within it. Secondly, the scope of the institution's information-gathering powers may be of interest; some bodies are better than others at gathering different types of information. Thirdly, the manner of the institution's decision-making process may be significant; some issues may lend themselves well to expert decision-making, others will be better allocated to amateur processes which have the virtues of openness and inclusivity. This point leads on to a fourth consideration: the vulnerability of the institution to outside pressures. Whether this is considered an advantage or a danger will depend both on the particular issue before the decision-maker and on our understanding of the nature and importance of citizens' participation in decision-making. As this fourth consideration shows, this thin understanding of separation of powers rests on a slippery slope. These structural concerns obviously relate to deeper issues of legitimacy, and drag us towards richer, thicker, normative theories involving rights and democracy. These issues are as relevant to a full vision of the separation of powers as the structural issues that have just been raised, and elide into them. However, there is profit in holding back from descending into a full normative theory. By focusing on these relatively uncontroversial factors we can outline reasons for and against the attribution of functions that will exist within all understandings of the separation of powers, but it must not be forgotten that these reasons are not strong enough in themselves to provide a conclusive answer to the question of attribution of function.

4 'CROWN VS PARLIAMENT' SEPARATION

So far, we have been examining the idea of a separation of powers between executive, legislative, and judicial powers. Professor Tomkins takes issue with this approach in two respects and, in its place, puts forward a 'Crown versus Parliament' thesis. His main objection is that this tripartite division does not reflect the historical development of the English constitution. The executive–legislative–judicial model emerged from the writings of Montesquieu (as we saw previously) and was influential in the planning of the US Constitution—but is not a good fit for England. He also prefers the term separation 'of power' rather than 'of powers', because '*it is not so much that discrete functions of powers are allocated to separate bodies, but that constitutional authority—power—is divided between the Crown and Parliament*'.[5]

In the following extract, Tomkins refers to the English Civil War (1641–51). This was a series of bitter armed conflicts between supporters of Charles I (an adherent to the notion of the 'divine right of kings') and the parliamentary forces led by Oliver Cromwell. Charles I attempted to rule without convening Parliament, resorting to a variety of means to raise revenue (such as 'ship money') to run the country without parliamentary approval for general taxation. In 1649, Charles I was executed for treason. For eleven years, the country was ruled without a king; monarchy was restored in 1660 when Charles II became king.

Adam Tomkins, *Public Law* (2003, Oxford: OUP), pp. 46–7 (footnotes omitted)

The Civil War, of course, was fought not between three powers separate but equal, but between two. On the one side there was the Crown, and on the other stood Parliament. Just as the war was fought between parliamentarians and royalists, so too were the peace settlements of 1660–1662 and 1689–1700 negotiations between the forces of Parliament on the one hand and of the Crown on the other. Now, it is one thing to sketch an historical argument to the effect that seventeenth century constitutionalism was based on a separation of power between the Crown and Parliament; it is quite another to take the argument further and to suggest that contemporary public law continues to reflect this historical division. But such is precisely the issue that we will now explore: in what sense may it be argued that contemporary English public law is based on a separation of power between the Crown and Parliament, a separation derived from England's political history?

The argument presented here will be that the separation of power in today's English public law does indeed continue to reflect its seventeenth century heritage. The separation of power English-style, it will be argued, is and remains a confrontational, bi-partisan, bi-polar separation, between the only two powers the constitution has ever recognized as enjoying

---

5 Tomkins, *Public Law* (2003, Oxford: OUP), p. 46, fn 24.

any degree of sovereign authority, namely the Crown, and Parliament. Every constitutional actor falls on one side or the other of this great divide, in that all constitutional actors ultimately draw their power from either the Crown or from Parliament. This is a separation of power which is designed to facilitate accountability [...]. As with Magna Carta so too with the Bill of Rights and the Act of Settlement: the purpose of these instruments is to find ways of holding the power of the Crown to some form of constitutional or parliamentary account. This stands in some contrast to the classical, eighteenth century understanding of the separation of powers, which, as Madison made clear, was designed not to facilitate constitutional accountability, but to safeguard liberty.

In short, the key to understanding power in England is not the separation of power between legislature, executive, and judiciary, but that between the Crown and Parliament. Tomkins presents the following evidence to support his thesis.

(a) First, he cites parliamentary supremacy—that is, Acts of Parliament *'represent the legal moment when the two sovereign authorities of England come together and agree: Parliament on the one hand, the Crown on the other'.*[6] 'The Crown' here refers to royal assent.[7]

(b) Second, there is the constitutional convention that ministers—Tomkins stresses that they are *ministers of the Crown*—are accountable to Parliament.[8] Ministers are 'the monarch's advisers' and their *'oath of allegiance is to the Crown, and they may exercise considerable royal prerogative power on behalf of the Crown'.*[9] In order for ministers to be accountable to Parliament, *'the English version of the separation of powers requires that ministers simultaneously be parliamentarians'.*[10]

(c) Third, Tomkins points to what he calls *'the tortuous relationship of the law to the Crown'* and deals at some length with the case of *M v Home Office*.[11] The question in that case was whether a minister (the Home Secretary) could be held to be in contempt of court for failing to respect undertakings given to a court that an asylum seeker would not be removed from the United Kingdom until the court had time to consider a judicial review challenge to the lawfulness of the rejection of his asylum application. Eventually, the House of Lords held that English law permitted the Home Secretary to be found liable for this contempt in his official capacity. Tomkins concludes: *'What this case shows [...] is that even as recently as the 1990s the courts in England have found it exceptionally difficult to subject the Crown and its sovereign authority to the rule of law.'*

Where, in Tomkins' 'Crown versus Parliament' thesis, are the courts? He says (acknowledging that this is a controversial proposition) that *'the courts are in some sense part of, or dependent upon, the Crown, and are not independent of it'.*[12]

---

[6] Ibid., p. 48.

[7] On royal assent, see Chapter 10.

[8] On ministerial accountability, see Chapter 7.

[9] Tomkins, op. cit., pp. 49–50.

[10] Ibid., p. 50.

[11] [1994] 1 AC 377.

[12] Tomkins, op. cit., pp. 54–5.

Adam Tomkins, *Public Law* (2003, Oxford: OUP), p. 55 (footnotes omitted)

A few words of clarification on this important point are called for here. First, it should be made clear what the argument is not saying. It is no part of the present argument to claim that individual judges can be removed from office by mere royal whim, as James I and Charles I thought 400 years ago. The Act of Settlement put a stop to that in 1701. Neither is it being argued here that in disputes involving the Crown the courts will always or necessarily hold for the Crown. Such a thesis would be bound to fail [...]. What the argument here is suggesting, however, is that the judiciary derives its constitutional power ultimately from that of the Crown. Unlike the position under Article III of the US Constitution, or under Article 220 (formerly Article 164) of the EC Treaty, for example, in English law there is no independent source of judicial authority. The English judiciary is not the third branch of the State, separate yet equal, as is the case in the United States. In England the judiciary is, properly conceived, neither entirely separate nor entirely equal: it is not fully separated (even now) from the Crown, and it remains subservient to it as a source of authority.

What does Tomkins mean when he says that the judiciary 'remains subservient' to the Crown? Chapter 14 examines the various ways in which the British constitution seeks to ensure the constitutional principle of the independence of the judiciary—including making it hugely difficult for a senior judge to be removed from office (a vote in the Commons and the Lords is required), the new judicial appointments commissions working at arm's length from ministers, and the statutory duties of ministers to respect judicial independence. While there may be practical restraints on *ministers* of the Crown interfering with the judiciary, there are, however, strong formal and symbolic ties between the judicial system and the Crown (meaning, in this context, not ministers, but an abstract idea of constitutional authority). The royal heraldic symbols hang behind the judges in most courts.[13] The judicial oath (or for non-religious people, affirmation) of office also reflects this intimate link (see Box 4.2).

BOX 4.2 JUDICIAL OATHS/AFFIRMATIONS

Under the Promissory Oaths Act 1868, judges take two oaths or affirmations—one of allegiance and a specifically judicial one. The following are the words used by those who choose to affirm.

I, _____, do solemnly sincerely and truly declare and affirm that I will be faithful and bear true allegiance to Her Majesty Queen Elizabeth the Second, Her Heirs and Successors, according to Law.

I, _____, do solemnly sincerely and truly declare and affirm that I will well and truly serve our Sovereign Lady Queen Elizabeth the Second in the office of _____, and I will do right to all manner of people after the laws and usages of this Realm without fear or favour affection or ill will.

---

[13] Not, however, in the UK Supreme Court, which uses its own badge.

5 JUDICIAL ANALYSIS OF SEPARATION OF POWERS

In this and the next subsections, we move on from the academic controversy over the separation of powers (or power) to consider practical institutional arrangements in the British constitution. Consider first the following three extracts from judgments in which senior members of the judiciary set out their understanding of the separation of powers principle.

In the first case, the issue was whether a minister had acted unlawfully when he decided not to exercise a power (by making delegated legislation) to bring into force provisions in an Act of Parliament that set out a scheme for compensating victims of violent crime.[14] The government planned instead to put in place a new non-statutory scheme (because this was cheaper). The Fire Brigades Union and other trade unions were involved because they were concerned that their members would lose out. The Law Lords were split three to two, the majority holding that the minister had acted unlawfully by deciding that he would never bring into force a provision that had been passed by Parliament.[15] Lord Mustill was in the minority, taking the view that it would be constitutionally inappropriate for the courts to intervene in this situation. His speech concluded with some general reflections on the nature of separation of powers, to which we shall return in Chapter 14.

R v Secretary of State for the Home Department, ex parte Fire Brigades Union
[1995] 2 AC 513, 567

Lord Mustill

It is a feature of the peculiarly British conception of the separation of powers that Parliament, the executive and the courts have each their distinct and largely exclusive domain. Parliament has a legally unchallengeable right to make whatever laws it thinks right. The executive carries on the administration of the country in accordance with the powers conferred on it by law. The courts interpret the laws, and see that they are obeyed. This requires the courts on occasion to step into the territory which belongs to the executive, to verify not only that the powers asserted accord with the substantive law created by Parliament but also that the manner in which they are exercised conforms with the standards of fairness which Parliament must have intended. Concurrently with this judicial function Parliament has its own special means of ensuring that the executive, in the exercise of delegated functions, performs in a way which Parliament finds appropriate. Ideally, it is these latter methods which should be used to check executive errors and excesses; for it is the task of Parliament and the executive in tandem, not of the courts, to govern the country. In recent years, however, the employment in practice of these specifically Parliamentary remedies has on occasion been perceived as falling short, and sometimes well short, of what was needed to bring the performance of the executive into line with the law, and with the minimum standards of fairness implicit in every Parliamentary delegation of a decision-making function. To avoid a vacuum in which the citizen would be left without protection against a misuse of executive powers the courts have had no option but to occupy the dead ground in a manner, and in areas of public life, which could not have been foreseen 30 years ago. For myself, I am quite satisfied that this unprecedented judicial role has been greatly to the public benefit. Nevertheless, it has its risks, of which the courts are well aware. As the judges themselves constantly remark, it is not they who are appointed to administer the country.

---

[14] On 'commencement provisions', see Chapter 11.
[15] See also Chapter 9.

Absent a written constitution much sensitivity is required of the parliamentarian, administrator and judge if the delicate balance of the unwritten rules evolved (I believe successfully) in recent years is not to be disturbed, and all the recent advances undone.

QUESTIONS

1. What do you think Lord Mustill had in mind when he stated that 'Parliament has its own special means of ensuring that the executive, in the exercise of delegated functions, performs in a way which Parliament finds appropriate'? (See Chapter 6 for some ideas.)

2. What are the 'risks' referred to by Lord Mustill?

In the second case, the issue was whether the legal powers contained in the Anti-Terrorism, Crime and Security Act 2001 to detain foreign nationals suspected of terrorism—indefinitely and without charge or trial—breached Convention rights.[16] These powers were enacted in response to the 9/11 attacks in the USA. The Law Lords held that the powers in the 2001 Act were incompatible with Convention rights, leading the government to abandon its policy of imprisonment without trial (and to replace it, under the Terrorism Act 2005, with a system of 'control orders'). The 'question' referred to in the first sentence was whether there was a 'public emergency threatening the life of the nation'. Only if there were such a situation would there be a legal basis under the ECHR for the UK government to 'derogate' from its obligations to respect the right to liberty protected by Art. 5.

A v Secretary of State for the Home Department
[2004] UKHL 56

Lord Bingham

[29] [...] I would accept that great weight should be given to the judgment of the Home Secretary, his colleagues and Parliament on this question, because they were called on to exercise a pre-eminently political judgment. It involved making a factual prediction of what various people around the world might or might not do, and when (if at all) they might do it, and what the consequences might be if they did. Any prediction about the future behaviour of human beings (as opposed to the phases of the moon or high water at London Bridge) is necessarily problematical. Reasonable and informed minds may differ, and a judgment is not shown to be wrong or unreasonable because that which is thought likely to happen does not happen. It would have been irresponsible not to err, if at all, on the side of safety. As will become apparent, I do not accept the full breadth of the Attorney General's argument on what is generally called the deference owed by the courts to the political authorities. It is perhaps preferable to approach this question as one of demarcation of functions or what Liberty in its written case called 'relative institutional competence'. The more purely political (in a broad or narrow sense) a question is, the more appropriate it will be for political resolution and the less likely it is to be an appropriate matter for judicial decision. The smaller, therefore, will be the potential role of the court. It is the function of political and not judicial bodies to resolve political questions. Conversely, the greater the legal content of any issue, the greater the potential role of the court, because under our constitution and subject to the

---

[16] See Chapter 17.

> sovereign power of Parliament it is the function of the courts and not of political bodies to resolve legal questions. The present question seems to me to be very much at the political end of the spectrum (see *Secretary of State for the Home Dept v Rehman* [2001] UKHL 47 at [62], [2002] 1 All ER 122 at [62], [2003] 1 AC 153, per Lord Hoffmann).

In the last case, the question before the UK Supreme Court was whether the legality of decisions of the Special Immigration Appeals Commission and the Upper Tribunal could be challenged in claims for judicial review.[17] Both of these statutory bodies were described in the legislation setting them up as '*superior courts of record*' and, on behalf of the bodies, it was contended that this status exempted them from judicial review challenges (in the same way as the High Court, Court of Appeal, and UK Supreme Court are not subject to judicial review).

R (on the application of Cart) v Upper Tribunal; R (on the application of U and XC) v Special Immigration Appeals Commission
[2011] UKSC 28

Lord Phillips

[89] ... The administration of justice and upholding of the rule of law involves a partnership between Parliament and the judges. Parliament has to provide the resources needed for the administration of justice. The size and the jurisdiction of the judiciary is determined by statute. Parliament has not sought to oust or fetter the common law powers of judicial review of the judges of the High Court and I hope that Parliament will never do so. It should be for the judges to decide whether the statutory provisions for the administration of justice adequately protect the rule of law and, by judicial review, to supplement these should it be necessary. But, in exercising the power of judicial review, the judges must pay due regard to the fact that, even where the due administration of justice is at stake, resources are limited. Where statute provides a structure under which a superior court or tribunal reviews decisions of an inferior court or tribunal, common law judicial review should be restricted so as to ensure, in the interest of making the best use of judicial resources, that this does not result in a duplication of judicial process that cannot be justified by the demands of the rule of law.

The UK Supreme Court held that SIAC and the Upper Tribunal were amenable to judicial review. The courts would, however, exercise their discretion to grant permission for a judicial review challenge to the tribunals to go ahead only if there was an important point of principle in question or some other compelling reason to review the case.[18]

QUESTION

Analyse the three extracts from the judgments set out here and list the matters that are said to be (a) within and (b) beyond the judicial function of the courts.

---

[17] See Chapter 15.
[18] On the judicial review procedure, see Chapter 16.

6 INTERACTIONS BETWEEN PARLIAMENT, THE EXECUTIVE, AND JUDGES

There are many constitutional rules—some of which are contained in legislation, others of which are set out in the form of constitutional conventions or practices—governing the interactions between those who exercise legislative, executive, and judicial power.

Can members of Parliament be judges?

Statutory rules state that MPs and peers are not eligible to serve as full-time members of the judiciary, and vice versa.[19] There is, however, no prohibition on MPs or peers holding part-time judicial appointments (for example, as a recorder or a deputy High Court judge in England and Wales), and several legally qualified MPs and peers have done so. In England and Wales, and Northern Ireland, a very large proportion of less serious criminal cases are heard by benches of non-legally qualified volunteers known as 'lay magistrates', or 'Justices of the Peace' (JPs). In Northern Ireland, members of the House of Commons, House of Lords, European Parliament, or one of the devolved parliamentary assemblies may not be appointed or sit as a lay magistrate. There are no similar restrictions in England and Wales, and several MPs sit as magistrates.

Can judges participate in the legislative process?

Until 2009, senior judges who had been conferred with a peerage—the twelve Lords of Appeal in Ordinary and some other senior judges—were entitled to sit and vote during the House of Lords' legislative work, although few did so. Eyebrows were raised when two Law Lords (Lords Scott of Foscote[20] and Hoffmann[21]) voted against proposals contained in the Hunting Bill—a piece of legislation on which the Law Lords were later to rule.[22] Because they had expressed pro-hunting views through voting during the passage of the Bill through Parliament, Lords Scott and Hoffmann were unable to be members of the nine-judge panel of Law Lords in *Jackson v Attorney General*.[23] Taking part in the appeal would have breached Art. 6 ECHR (on fair trails), which prohibits a person who has participated in the legislative process from subsequently adjudicating on issues under that legislation.[24] The European Court of Human Rights takes the view that an accumulation of functions—in the legislative and then judicial roles—gives rise to doubts regarding the impartiality of the judge (viewed from an objective point of view). Up to October 2009, Law Lords also took part in the political scrutiny work of the House of Lords, such as chairing the European Union (EU) Select Committee Subcommittee E, which examines proposals in the area of EU law and institutions. All of these roles came to an end with the transfer of the House of Lords' 'judicial business' to the UK Supreme Court and the consequential statutory disqualification of the judges of the Supreme Court from participating in the work of Parliament.[25]

Although serving judges cannot now participate *directly* in the legislative process for making Acts of Parliament,[26] they nonetheless may have an interest in commenting on legislative proposals, as a senior judge explains to MPs in the following extract.

---

[19] House of Commons Disqualification Act 1975, Sch. 1; Constitutional Reform Act 2005, s. 137.
[20] 12 March 2001.
[21] 19 March 2002, 21 October 2003, and 26 October 2004.
[22] Chapter 13.
[23] [2005] UKHL 56.
[24] *McGonnell v United Kingdom* (2000) 30 EHRR 289 (a case concerning the Bailiff of Guernsey, an ancient office that combined the role of presiding officer of the island's legislature with being chief justice).
[25] Constitutional Reform Act 2005, s. 137.
[26] See Chapter 10.

House of Commons Justice Committee, Oral Evidence, 2 July 2008

Q42 Alun Michael [a Labour MP]: Obviously there is an interplay between the role of the judiciary and the role of Parliament in legislation. How do you think that relationship or the connection between those roles can and should be developed, especially if we are looking at a more structured sentencing framework in the future?

Lord Phillips Of Worth Matravers [the then Lord Chief Justice of England and Wales]: The relationship between judges and Parliament in relation to legislation is a tricky area. It first arises when legislation is being proposed where my view is that judges have a valid advisory role in relation to the implications on running the justice system of the legislation that is proposed and we frequently comment, 'If you introduce that, it is going to impose a substantial demand on judicial resources because it is going to lead to appeals in this area or that area', that is a perfectly legitimate area in which judges should be advising. We should not be involved in advising in relation to policy which is a matter ultimately for Government and Parliament. If you then ask what interrelationship should there be between judges and Parliament in relation to the act of sentencing and the implications sentencing has, I think the answer must be it is for Parliament to legislate and for judges to do their best to apply the legislation in accordance with its provisions and that is what is happening.

From time to time, judges do, however, make suggestions for legislative reform. For example, interviewed on BBC Radio 4, Lord Justice Sedley suggested that the whole population of the United Kingdom and all visitors should have their DNA recorded on a national database—prompting a government spokesman to say that this would create '*huge logistical and bureaucratic issues*' and civil liberty concerns.[27]

Judges also have a formal role in the making of delegated legislation[28] about court procedures. For example, the Constitutional Reform Act 2005, s. 45, provides that '*The President of the Supreme Court may make rules (to be known as "Supreme Court Rules") governing the practice and procedure to be followed in the Court.*' While these rules are drafted by the President (no doubt in close collaboration with civil servants in the Ministry of Justice), it is not possible for the President (who is not a member of Parliament) to initiate the formal legislative process, so under s. 46 this is a role carried out by the Lord Chancellor (a minister and member of Parliament).

Can judges scrutinize parliamentary matters?

A principle of great importance in many constitutions is parliamentary privilege, as the following extract outlines.

House of Lords Constitution Committee, *Parliamentary Standards Bill: Implications for Parliament and the Courts*, 18th Report, Session 2008–09, HL 135

14. As many others have noted, the term 'parliamentary privilege' risks being misunderstood in modern times insofar as it may suggest that Parliament and its members seek advantages that other institutions and people do not enjoy. The reality is that parliamentary privilege is a set of principles that underpin democracy. It is 'the rights and immunities which the two Houses of Parliament and their members and officers possess to enable them to carry out their parliamentary functions effectively'. Article IX of the Bill of Rights states 'That the Freedome of Speech and Debates or Proceedings in Parlyament ought not to be impeached or questioned

---

[27] BBC News, 'All UK "must be on DNA database"', 5 September 2007.
[28] Chapter 11.

in any Court or Place out of Parlyament'. This embodies a fundamental feature of the British Constitution (common to many other legislatures around the world) that there needs to be a clear borderline between the functions and powers of Parliament and those of the courts.

15. For sound constitutional reasons, the courts have historically respected the right of Parliament to govern itself and have refused to be drawn into any disputes that may arise about things said or done in Parliament. This ensures the freedom of members and witnesses giving evidence to parliamentary committees to speak openly without concern that what they say or do during "proceedings in Parliament" may subsequently be used in court proceedings.

Article 9 of the Bill of Rights 1689 continues to be respected and enforced by the courts, often following interventions from the parliamentary authorities. Subject to one major exception, courts should not allow parties to litigation to put in as evidence statements that were made in Parliament, whether by MPs and peers on the floor of each House, and reported in *Hansard* or evidence given to or reports made by parliamentary committees.[29] The justification for this prohibition is that it could have a chilling effect on free speech and debate in Parliament, which, in a democracy, ought to be sacrosanct.

The major exception to the bar on referring to parliamentary proceedings in court is contained in the controversial ruling of the House of Lords in *Pepper (Inspector of Taxes) v Hart*,[30] a case about the interpretation of a tax statute. This permits a judge to receive evidence in the form of extracts from *Hansard* in which a minister responsible for introducing a Bill to Parliament explains what a provision is intended to achieve—but regard can be had to such ministerial statements only if:

(a) the statutory provision that the court is trying to interpret is ambiguous; and
(b) the minister's statement is itself clear.

The House of Lords reasoned in *Pepper v Hart* that using *Hansard* in this way would not breach Art. 9 of the Bill of Rights because the court was not questioning what was said in Parliament, but on the contrary was seeking to give effect to the intention of Parliament. The reasoning of *Pepper v Hart* has been subject to criticism on a number of grounds, not least that it confuses the intention of a minister (that is, a member of the executive) with the intention of Parliament.[31]

In subsequent cases, the courts have sought to limit the circumstances in which *Hansard* may be referred to in legal proceedings. For example, when a judge is ruling on whether legislation is 'proportionate' for the purposes of assessing whether a provision is compatible with the Human Rights Act 1998, reference should not be made to explanations given to Parliament by ministers as to the various policy options that the government had explored before introducing the Bill.

Wilson v Secretary of State for Trade and Industry [2003] UKHL 4, [67]

Lord Nicholls of Birkenhead

[...] the content of parliamentary debates has no direct relevance to the issues the court is called upon to decide in compatibility cases and, hence, these debates are not a proper matter for investigation or consideration by the courts. In particular, it is a cardinal constitutional principle that the will of Parliament is expressed in the language used by it in its enactments. The pro

---

[29] See Chapter 7.
[30] [1993] AC 593.
[31] See, e.g., Lord Steyn, '*Pepper v Hart*: A re-examination' (2001) 21 OJLS 66.

portionality of legislation is to be judged on that basis. The courts are to have due regard to the legislation as an expression of the will of Parliament. The proportionality of a statutory measure is not to be judged by the quality of the reasons advanced in support of it in the course of parliamentary debate, or by the subjective state of mind of individual ministers or other members. Different members may well have different reasons, not expressed in debates, for approving particular statutory provisions. They may have different perceptions of the desirability or likely effect of the legislation. Ministerial statements, especially if made ex tempore in response to questions, may sometimes lack clarity or be misdirected. Lack of cogent justification in the course of parliamentary debate is not a matter which 'counts against' the legislation on issues of proportionality. The court is called upon to evaluate the proportionality of the legislation, not the adequacy of the minister's exploration of the policy options or of his explanations to Parliament. The latter would contravene article 9 of the Bill of Rights. The court would then be presuming to evaluate the sufficiency of the legislative process leading up to the enactment of the statute.

Can members of Parliament discuss judges and judgments?

Just as the courts are careful not to intrude into parliamentary proceedings, so too does Parliament try to steer away from undue interference with courts and judges. The *sub judice* rule requires that MPs should not seek to bring up in debates, questions, and motions cases that are pending or being heard by a court. The House of Commons Standing Order 42A provides that '*The Speaker, or the chairman, may direct any Member who breaches the terms of the sub judice resolution of the House to resume his seat.*' The rationale for this rule is that discussion of a case may have a prejudicial effect and may prevent the parties to the civil or criminal case from having a fair trial. There is, however, a discretion for the Speaker and Lord Speaker to allow discussion if it is in the national interest.

More broadly, parliamentarians are expected to be careful in any criticisms that they make of judges or judgments, as the following extract explains.

Joint Committee on Parliamentary Privilege, First Report, Session 1998–99, HL 43-I/HC 214-I

Parliament and the judiciary

226. Much of this report is necessarily concerned with the relationship between Parliament and the courts. The effective working of the constitution depends on the courts being ever sensitive to the need to refrain from trespassing upon the province of Parliament or even appearing to do so, and on Parliament being similarly sensitive to the need to refrain from trespassing upon the province of the courts. This is generally recognised by both institutions. This relationship would not be helped if judges were to make unnecessary or exaggerated critical comments on the actions of politicians, or if politicians use parliamentary privilege to attack particular judicial decisions or the character of individual judges.

227. So far as Parliament is concerned, both Houses consider opprobrious reflections on members of the judiciary to be out of order unless made on motion. In the Commons 36 motions critical of judges or seeking their removal have been tabled since 1961. None has been debated.

228. Occasionally statements or actions by members of Parliament may merit judicial criticism. Likewise, judicial decision or comment may merit criticism by members of Parliament. It is important for both institutions that such criticism is made in measured terms. In all cases members should pause to consider before tabling motions which often receive

> wide publicity. We agree with the Lord Chief Justice of England that a tradition of mutual reticence serves the country best.

This is not to say that parliamentarians cannot inquire into how courts interpret and apply legislation. In an interesting development, the Joint Committee on Human Rights reported twice on what it saw as the wrong approach adopted by the courts in deciding that private care homes were not covered by the Human Rights Act 1998.[32] These reports were influential in encouraging Parliament to reverse the effect of a House of Lords' decision that had maintained a narrow approach to the meaning of '*function of a public nature*'.[33] Parliamentary investigations into how courts are handling legislation may become more frequent in the future as procedures for post-legislative scrutiny are put in place.[34]

What is the relationship between ministers and judges?

We discuss in Chapter 14 the statutory duties of ministers to uphold the independence of the judiciary and the role of the Lord Chancellor (a minister) in defending that independence. As we will see, ministers have, on occasion, been outspokenly critical of individual judges, the judiciary as a whole, and particular judgments.

What is the role of the executive in Parliament?

In a system of parliamentary government, there is no separation between 'the legislature' and 'the executive'; on the contrary, ministers are *required* to be members of Parliament. As we discuss elsewhere, while this arrangement can be justified as enabling Parliament to hold ministers to account on a regular basis, the danger is that those parliamentarians who are ministers dominate the work of Parliament. This is especially so in relation to the legislative process. As we see in Chapters 9 and 10, the executive (ministers and civil servants) have dominant roles in the making of both primary and delegated legislation. Whereas some legislatures take the lead in developing policy and drafting legislation, the role of the UK Parliament is largely reactive: its role is to scrutinize and then approve (or reject) proposals from the government. There are few opportunities for members of the legislature—whether MPs or peers—who are not members of the government to initiate legislation and see it through to enactment: few private member's Bills reach the statute book.

There are, however, some limited legal constraints on the executive. A cap is placed on the total number of MPs who can serve as ministers.[35] Civil servants, members of the armed forces, police officers, and a long list of holders of public offices are disqualified from being MPs by the House of Commons Disqualification Act 1975, s. 1. Except for ministers (who receive a salary on top of their MPs' salary), there is also a general prohibition on an MP '*holding an office or place of profit under the Crown*' (s. 1(4)). This provides a procedural device for an MP's resignation: he or she is appointed, temporarily, to an office of the Crown and is thereby disqualified from sitting in the Commons.[36]

---

[32] Joint Committee on Human Rights, *The Meaning of Public Authority under the Human Rights Act*, Seventh Report, Session 2003–04 (HL 39/HC 382); Ninth Report, Session 2006–07 (HL 77/HC 410).

[33] See Chapter 17.

[34] See Chapter 10.

[35] See Chapter 7.

[36] The offices to which MPs are appointed are 'Crown Steward and Bailiff of the three Chiltern Hundreds of Stoke, Desborough and Burnham' or 'Steward of the Manor of Northstead'.

QUESTIONS

1. What are the rival explanations of the purpose of separation of powers? Which do you find most convincing?

2. In relation to each of the following rules, explain the constitutional rationale and whether it is contained in legislation or a constitutional convention.

   (a) Ministers must be members of one of the Houses of Parliament.

   (b) Judges cannot sit or vote as a member of either House of Parliament.

   (c) In relation to legislation, judges *'should not be involved in advising in relation to policy which is a matter ultimately for Government and Parliament'*.

   (d) Civil servants cannot be members of either House of Parliament.

3. The Child Maintenance Enforcement Commission (CMEC) is a public body run by civil servants responsible for getting absent parents (usually fathers) to pay child maintenance to the parent living with a child (usually mothers) in accordance with the Child Support Act 1991. In 2009, the law was changed to give civil servants power to require fathers who have not paid to surrender their passports and driving licences. Do you think that it is right for civil servants to have this power? Does it make any difference to your answer that fathers may appeal against a CMEC order to a court, and that the order will then be suspended until the court hears the appeal?[37]

4. To what extent can it be said that separation of powers is an important principle in the UK constitution?

7 CONCLUDING COMMENTS

This chapter has examined the separation of powers between executive, legislative, and judicial functions. Chapter 5 now turns to look at another function of the constitution—distributing power between different levels of government.

8 FURTHER READING

Vile, M.C.J., *Constitutionalism and the Separation of Powers*, 2nd edn (1998, Indianapolis, IN: Liberty Fund)

ONLINE RESOURCE CENTRE

Further information about the themes discussed in this chapter can be found on the Online Resource Centre at www.oxfordtextbooks.co.uk/orc/lesueur2e/

---

[37] For background, see the House of Lords Constitution Committee, *Welfare Reform Bill*, Ninth Report, Session 2008–09, HL 79.

5

MULTILEVEL GOVERNING

CENTRAL ISSUES

1. An important task for a constitutional system is to determine how, if at all, executive and legislative power is distributed within a nation state. There are a variety of ways in which this could be achieved: a unitary state distributes little or no power away from national level; federalism creates distinct sovereign entities within a nation; devolution (the method chosen in the United Kingdom) is the delegation of power by the national level, which nonetheless reserves ultimate sovereign power to itself.

2. The United Kingdom of Great Britain and Northern Ireland, as the country's name suggests, was formed as a union of separate nations. Until 1998, the United Kingdom was a highly centralized state, with important decisions taken at national level by the UK government and UK Parliament.

3. Since 1998, a process of devolution is transferring executive and legislative powers to three parts of the United Kingdom: Northern Ireland, Scotland, and Wales. The Acts of Parliament creating devolution have all been amended since first enacted. They create a detailed technical framework and questions have arisen about how the courts should approach interpreting them.

4. England, by far the largest part of the United Kingdom, has been left out of the devolution process. This has given rise to the 'English Question', with calls for changes to the way the UK Parliament enacts legislation that applies only to England.

5. Governing activity also takes place at local level. In the United Kingdom, this tier of government has been subject to almost constant reform for many years. The latest development, introduced by the Localism Act 2011, is a 'general power of competence' for local authorities in England.

1 INTRODUCTION

(a) STARTING FROM SCRATCH

Let's start with a blank piece of paper and an imaginary a country in Europe. It has a population of about 62 million people and a landmass of about 240,000 km^2. What system would you design for the concentration or distribution of executive and legislative power within this country? For example, the task of setting standards for the control of atmospheric pollution is better decided by a large unit rather than left to very small areas, as it is inevitable that wind will blow contamination for a long way. On the other hand, decisions about the provision, location, and maintenance of publicly funded playgrounds for children may be better decided at quite a local level, to be responsive to the needs of local residents. A method is needed for deciding where decisions are made.

One option would be to have little or no distribution: a single national government and a single national parliament could be responsible for almost everything. Examples of unitary states in Europe are the Republic of Ireland and Greece. A possible advantage of a unitary system is that it promotes uniformity across the whole country. It might, for example, be thought right for people to have the same entitlement to government-provided health care, regardless of where in the country they live. In other respects, uniformity may be less desirable: different legal frameworks on social housing may be better if some parts of the country are sparsely populated and rural and other parts urban.

Another option would be to adopt a federal system. Countries based on federal principles in Europe include Germany and Belgium.

Andrew Scott, 'Federalism', in P. Cane and J. Conaghan (eds) *The New Oxford Companion to Law* (2007, Oxford: OUP), p. 450

Federalism is an organization of government in which the authority to govern is divided between a central (national) government on the one hand, and a number of constituent regions, provinces, states, or other territorially distinct political authorities on the other hand. Federal systems are therefore characterized by a division of policy competences between the different levels of government that comprise the federation, some of which are exercised at central—federal—level and others at the sub-central level. While no two federations will have an identical division of competences between the central and sub-central governments, a feature common to all federations is that the assignment of competences will be set out in relevant articles of a written constitution and may only be changed in accordance with the provisions of that constitution.

So this is a division of sovereign powers to govern and legislate. Each level of government is autonomous within its demarcated powers. The constitutional instrument could either list the competences reserved to national government or, alternatively, list the competences for which the sub-national units are responsible. In our imaginary country, the 'competences' (areas of government activity) that national government could be responsible for might include: national defence and security; border control; citizenship; a common currency; some aspects of environmental protection; and responsibility for the constitutional system.

A further option would be devolution. Like federalism, this allocates power to different levels of government but does so in a constitutionally different way. The Royal Commission on the Constitution defined devolution as '*the delegation of central government powers without the relinquishment of sovereignty*'.[1] The national government and parliament retain a unilateral power to transfer the relevant powers back to themselves, should this be thought to be necessary or desirable in the national interest, and to legislate for policy areas that have been devolved. Whereas federalism systems must be based on a settled constitutional framework, devolution may be achieved by ordinary legislation made by the national parliament. Examples of European countries with regional government based on devolution principles include Italy, Spain, and the United Kingdom.

Whether a unitary, federal or devolved system is chosen, a further decision to be made is whether our imaginary country should become part of the European integration project. As we have seen in previous chapters, this is taking place in two ways. Focusing on human rights, the Council of Europe and its judicial organ the European Court of Human Rights promote uniform respect for basic freedoms and rights across 47 European countries. The European Union, with 28 member states, provides an institutional framework for making policy and law across a wide range of subjects. A quid pro quo for the benefits of joining either or both international organizations is the acceptance of constraints on policy and law-making by national and any sub-national governments.

In designing how, if at all, public power is to be distributed within the country, thought should also be given to a tier of local government (below the national and any sub-national tiers). A range of interconnected questions would need to be considered. How 'local': neighbourhoods or much larger units? How will local government be financed—will units have powers to raise taxation or will they rely on allocations of funds from national government? Is local government going to be an agent of national government or do we envisage that they will be elected political bodies able to pursue their own policy choices?

(b) THE UNITED KINGDOM APPROACH

The size and location of the imaginary country is, of course, similar to the United Kingdom. The possibility of starting with a blank sheet does not exist. The United Kingdom is a product of its historical development rather than a one-off planning exercise. Clues to its constitutional evolution are in the country's name: the United Kingdom of Great Britain and Northern Ireland. It may be described as a 'union' state, as its historical roots are in the joining together of previously separate territories in the eighteenth and nineteenth centuries. It has therefore never been a 'unitary' state in the sense described here: Scotland (part of the union since 1707) and Northern Ireland (since 1922 or 1801: as we shall see) retained legal systems and other institutions of government that were distinct and separate from those of England and Wales. Nonetheless, the United Kingdom was a highly centralized state—run by the UK government from 'Whitehall' and the UK Parliament at Westminster for much of the twentieth century.[2] At the same time, there remained strong cultural differences between the parts of the United Kingdom.

---

[1] *Royal Commission on the Constitution 1967–73*, vol.1 (Cm 5460), para. 543 (often called 'the Kilbrandon report' after the commission's chairman).

[2] See Chapter 7.

[3] This ultimately may need to be decided in the courts: see Part III Introduction.

Table 5.1 Distribution of executive and legislative power

Level	Powers defined by	Main government and legislative institutions	Examples of areas of competence	Types of legislation made
Local	Localism Act 2011; Local Government Act 1972 and numerous subject-specific Acts	Local authorities	Social services; planning; refuse; libraries; social housing	By-laws
Devolved (also in some contexts known as 'regional', 'sub-national')	(a) Northern Ireland Act 1998 (b) Scotland Act 1998 as amended by the Scotland Act 2012 (c) Government of Wales Act 2006	Northern Ireland Executive, Northern Ireland Assembly Scottish Government, Scottish Parliament Welsh Government, National Assembly for Wales	See pp. 155–157.	(a) Acts of the Northern Ireland Assembly plus delegated legislation (b) Acts of the Scottish Parliament plus delegated legislation (c) Acts of the Assembly [Wales], plus delegated legislation
National (also known as 'central') See further Chapter 7, Chapter 9, Chapter 10 and Chapter 11	In theory, the UK Parliament has unlimited legislative competence (and may confer competence on any matter to ministers)	HM Government (ministers, departments, executive agencies, etc) UK Parliament	UK tax; defence; national security; citizenship; border control; currency; international relations; the Crown; the UK Parliament	Acts of the UK Parliament Delegated legislation
European Union (also known as supra-national) See further Chapter 8 and Chapter 12	Treaty on European Union (TEU) and Treaty on the Functioning of the European Union (TFEU)	Commission Council European Parliament	See Box 12.7 in Chapter 12	Directives Regulations

One of the main tasks of a constitutional system is to provide a framework specifying where public power lies, and then ensuring that this is respected.[3] This chapter explores, from the perspective of constitutional law, how the current division has come about and some of the technicalities as to how the allocation of power is defined. For the United Kingdom, the practical process of governing and legislating now takes place at four main levels (see Table 5.1). The momentous decision to join the European Economic Community (the forerunner of the European Union) in 1973 added a new tier. Within the United Kingdom, centralization was alleviated in 1998 by the introduction of regional devolved government for three parts of the country: Northern Ireland, Scotland, and Wales. With the passing of the Localism Act 2011 and national government committed to promoting 'localism', a new era seems to be opening up for local government, with greater powers to act independently of national government.

Parliamentary supremacy

The UK framework for distribution of powers is anything but settled. Indeed, it is no exaggeration to say that the allocation of public power to take executive action and legislate is one of the most contentious aspects of the UK constitution; because of this there have been many profound changes (and possibly more on the horizon). In the absence of any codified constitution with special amendment procedures, politicians have found it possible to introduce sweeping changes, thanks to parliamentary supremacy.

Orthodox constitutional thinking (the Westminster model)[4] places the national level—the whole United Kingdom—at the centre of the picture. The principle of parliamentary supremacy[5] asserts that the UK Parliament has unlimited legislative competence (it can pass laws on whatever it wants to) and the UK government, accountable to the UK Parliament, is the directing force. Certainly, it is possible to tell the story of the development of distribution of power from this standpoint. In the late 1960s, the UK government (led at the time by Prime Minister Edward Heath) decided that it would be in the national interest for the country to become a member of the European Economic Community (the forerunner of the European Union), and the UK Parliament in enacting the European Communities Act 1972 agreed. In the late 1990s, the UK government (led at the time by Prime Minister Tony Blair) decided that it would be in the national interest for there to be decentralization of executive and legislative power to Northern Ireland, Scotland and Wales and the UK Parliament agreed in enacting the Northern Ireland Act 1998, Scotland Act 1998, and the Government of Wales Act 1998 (known collectively as 'the devolution Acts'). Citywide government was reintroduced to London in 1998, with the creation of a directly elected mayor and Greater London Assembly. A new era for local government began under the Localism Act 2011, which promises far greater freedom of action than existed previously.

Evidence of the continued control of parliamentary sovereignty can be found in the statute book. Each of the devolution Acts expressly preserves parliamentary sovereignty: so s. 28(1) of the Scotland Act 1998 provides that the Scottish Parliament '*may make laws, to be known as Acts of the Scottish Parliament*' but s. 28(9) states '*This section does not affect the power of the Parliament of the United Kingdom to make laws for Scotland*'. In relation to

---

[4] See Chapter 1.
[5] See Chapter 2.

EU law, the European Union Act 2011 contained what the government calls 'a declaratory provision':

European Union Act 2011, s. 18: Status of EU law dependent on continuing statutory basis

Directly applicable or directly effective EU law (that is, the rights, powers, liabilities, obligations, restrictions, remedies and procedures referred to in section 2(1) of the European Communities Act 1972) falls to be recognised and available in law in the United Kingdom only by virtue of that Act or where it is required to be recognised and available in law by virtue of any other Act.

The Explanatory Notes accompanying the 2011 Act, written by government lawyers, stated:

120. This declaratory provision was included in the Act in order to address concerns that the doctrine of parliamentary sovereignty may in the future be eroded by decisions of the courts. By providing in statute that directly effective and directly applicable EU law only takes effect in the UK legal order through the will of Parliament and by virtue of the European Communities Act 1972 or where it is required to be recognised and available in law by virtue of any other Act, this will provide clear authority which can be relied upon to counter arguments that EU law constitutes a new higher autonomous legal order derived from the EU Treaties or international law and principles which has become an integral part of the UK's legal system independent of statute.

Power of the people: consent through referendums

An account based only on the UK government and UK Parliament as controlling strategic decisions about the allocation of power would, however, miss a vital part of the picture: the views of the electorate, expressed in referendums. *Almost all* the referendums held in the United Kingdom have been about the territorial division of powers.[6] 'No' votes have the capacity to stop national government pursuing its aims. In 1978, an insufficient number of people voted for devolution proposals. UK government proposals to decentralize power to nine regions of England failed in 2004, when voters in a referendum in one region decisively rejected the idea. Most recently, the European Union Act 2011 has created legal obligations for referendums to take place before the UK government may agree to various changes to the foundational treaties of the European Union.[7] In June 2012, Prime Minister David Cameron said he would consider a referendum on the United Kingdom's relationship with the European Union when the time was right.[8] There is broad agreement of the principle that the Scottish people, having elected in a pro-independence government in 2007, should have the opportunity to vote on a referendum about Scotland's constitutional future within or separate from the United Kingdom.

Some commentators suggest that the consistent use of referendums in relation to questions about distribution of powers requires new thinking about orthodox ideas about parliamentary supremacy.

---

[6] See Box 1.1 in Chapter 1. For further discussion, see House of Lords Constitution Committee, *Referendums in the United Kingdom*, Twelfth Report of 2009–10, HL Paper 99.

[7] See Chapter 12.

[8] David Cameron, 'We need to be clear about the best way of getting what is best for Britain', *The Telegraph*, 30 June 2012.

Timothy H. Jones, 'Wales, Devolution and Sovereignty'
(2012) 33 Statute Law Review 1, 3 (footnotes omitted)

From the viewpoint of the Westminster Parliament, nothing in the 2006 [Government of Wales] Act affects the continuing sovereignty of that body. All the legislative powers conferred on the National Assembly depend upon the Act for their legal effect. They derive from the will of Parliament expressed in the Act. Thus, the 2006 Act provides that the legislative competence of the National Assembly 'does not affect the power of the Parliament of the United Kingdom to make laws for Wales'. The National Assembly is a devolved legislature with limited powers. It may legislate only to the extent that it has been given power by Westminster to do so under the 2006 Act (or any future legislation). From its own perspective, of course, there is no restriction upon the Westminster Parliament amending or even repealing the 2006 Act: it would not be bound by the Act of its predecessors and could, in theory, withdraw any or all the National Assembly's devolved powers. (And of course devolution was suspended in Northern Ireland for some years following a breakdown in the peace process, until being restored in 2007.) However, what is legally possible may not be constitutionally or practically achievable. And if Parliament did legislate for Wales in a devolved area, such as health or education, the legitimacy of its doing so would be questioned.

The paradox, however, is that the traditional approach reflected in the 2006 Act is undermined by the Act's own reliance upon the constitutional referendum to secure the endorsement of the Welsh electorate. The use of the referendum emphasizes the sovereignty of the people in determining the legislative powers of the National Assembly. In fact, there have been three such referendums in Wales. The first, in 1979, sought approval for the scheme of devolution contained in the Wales Act 1978. It was rejected overwhelmingly. Latterly, the Government of Wales Act 1998 followed the referendum of September 1997, where there was narrow approval of the idea to establish a National Assembly. And in March 2011, there was overwhelming approval of a move to 'full' legislative devolution, under Part 4 of the Government of Wales Act 2006.

In the following extract, Marks and Hooghe show that decentralization and internationalization of governance are a worldwide phenomenon. The trends seen in the United Kingdom are therefore part of a general change in the way in which people are governed.

Gary Marks and Liesbet Hooghe, 'Contrasting Visions of Multi-level Governance', in I. Bache and M. Flinders (eds) *Multilevel Governance* (2004, Oxford: OUP), ch. 2, pp. 15–16 (footnotes omitted)

Centralized authority has given way to new forms of governing. Formal authority has been dispersed from central states both up to supranational institutions and down to regional and local governments. A recent survey finds that sixty-three of seventy-five developing countries have undergone some decentralization of authority. [. . . N]o EU country has become more centralized since 1980, while half have decentralized authority to a regional tier of -government. The 1980s and 1990s have also seen the creation of a large number of transnational regimes, some of which exercise real supranational authority. At the same time, public/private networks of diverse kinds have multiplied from the local to the international level.

The diffusion of authority in new political forms has led to a profusion of new terms: multi-level governance, multi-tiered governance, polycentric governance, multi-perspectival governance, functional, overlapping, competing jurisdictions (FOCJ), fragmegration (or spheres of authority), and consortio and condominio, to name but a few. The evolution of similar ideas in different fields can be explained partly as diffusion from two literatures—federalism and public policy. But we suspect that this conceptual invention has independent sources. In this chapter, we do not summarize the particularities of the concepts that have been put forward, nor do we do justice to the intellectual history of the field. Instead we mine the relevant literatures for some conceptual benchmarks in order to facilitate empirical analysis.

These literatures agree that the dispersion of governance across multiple jurisdictions is both more efficient than, and normatively superior to, central state monopoly. They claim that governance must operate at multiple scales in order to capture variations in the territorial reach of policy externalities. Because externalities arising from the provision of public goods vary immensely—from planet-wide in the case of global warming to local in the case of most city services—so should the scale of governance. To internalize externalities, governance must be multi-level. This is the core argument for multi-level governance, but there are several other perceived benefits. For example, more decentralized jurisdictions can better reflect heterogeneity of preferences among citizens. Multiple jurisdictions can facilitate credible policy commitments. Multiple jurisdictions allow for jurisdictional competition. And they facilitate innovation and experimentation.

However, beyond the presumption that governance has become (and should be) multi-jurisdictional, there is no agreement about how multi-level governance should be organized. [...]

[One vision] conceives of dispersion of authority to jurisdictions at a limited number of levels. These jurisdictions—international, national, regional, meso, local—are general-purpose. That is to say, they bundle together multiple functions, including a range of policy responsibilities, and in many instances, a court system and representative institutions. The membership boundaries of such jurisdictions do not intersect. This is the case for jurisdictions at any one level, and it is the case for jurisdictions across levels. In this form of governance, every citizen is located in a Russian Doll set of nested jurisdictions, where there is one and only one relevant jurisdiction at any particular territorial scale. Territorial jurisdictions are intended to be, and usually are, stable for several decades or more, though the allocation of policy competencies across levels is flexible.

QUESTIONS

If this all sounds rather technical or abstract, consider the following scenarios.

1. Jo is a keen surfer. He particularly enjoys surfing off the coast of Wales, but is concerned that toxic waste is being discharged into the sea. Who should be responsible for setting standards for pollution and enforcing the rules? The local authority in whose area the beach in situated? The Welsh Government? The Department for Environment, Food and Rural Affairs (DEFRA, a central government department)? The Environment Agency? The European Union?

2. Maurice is a businessman who wants to import components for electric vehicles into the United Kingdom, make cars, and sell them all over the world. He wants to employ specialist staff from several different countries and to build a new state-of-the-art factory. Who should be responsible for setting the rules on importation of goods into the United Kingdom? Who should decide whether Maurice's staff can have work permits? Who should decide whether to grant him planning permission for his factory?

> 3. Andrew is an animal rights campaigner who wants the law changed to ban a particular sort of experiment on animals that he claims is now unnecessary. Which level of government should he lobby?

The remainder of this chapter is organized around three levels of governing—national (part 2), regional (part 3), and local (part 4). The focus is therefore on multilevel governing within the United Kingdom. The European Union is dealt with separately in Chapter 8 (executive power) and Chapter 12 (treaties and legislative processes). Part IV Introduction considers the distinct question of the United Kingdom's separate legal jurisdictions, the origins of which pre-date devolution by centuries.

2 GOVERNING NATIONALLY

(a) ENGLAND AND WALES

England (a single territorial entity by 927AD) and Wales (a principality) were created into a single realm in law by the Laws in Wales Acts 1535–42. For some purposes, England and Wales are treated as a single entity. There is a single court and judicial system covering both of these parts of the United Kingdom—although even here there is some differentiation, because there are statutory rights about the use of the Welsh language in court proceedings that apply only to proceedings in Wales.[9] For other purposes, England and Wales are constitutionally distinct. Since 1998, there has been a directly elected National Assembly for Wales, with law-making and executive powers in relation to Wales only.

'England' has a prosaic statutory definition as an aggregate of the units of local government defined by the Local Government Act 1972. The extent of the 'English' territorial sea is normally assumed to be that part of the territorial sea that has not been assigned to another part of the United Kingdom.

Wales is similarly defined in terms of *'the combined area of the counties which were created by section 20 of the Local Government Act 1972, as originally enacted, but subject to any alteration made under s 73 of that Act (consequential alteration of boundary following alteration of watercourse)'*. Wales *'includes the sea adjacent to Wales out as far as the seaward boundary of the territorial sea'*. For the purposes of devolution, there is also the concept of *'an English border area'*, which is a part of England adjoining Wales *'but not the whole of England'*.

(b) GREAT BRITAIN

A formal political union between two independent nations—England and Wales, and Scotland which had been ruled by the same monarchs since 1603—was forged by the Treaty of Union and the Acts of Union 1706–07 passed by the Scottish and English Parliaments, which created a Parliament of Great Britain, the Crown of Great Britain, and thus a government of Great Britain. The union produced a new flag, common coinage, uniform taxation, and a common market. Distinctive Scottish institutions were intended to be preserved—some 'in all perpetuity', according to the Treaty of Union—including the Presbyterian

---

[9] Welsh Language Act 1993.

Church, educational institutions, and the system of local government. The new Parliament of Great Britain's power to legislate for Scotland was limited in that no alteration can be made in laws '*which concern private right, except for the evident utility of the subjects within Scotland*'. The Treaty also protected the jurisdiction of the High Court of Justiciary (so explaining why, in modern times, the UK Supreme Court has no jurisdiction over criminal appeals from Scotland). For some Scottish scholars, lawyers, and politicians—even judges—the Treaty and Act of Union, along with the Claim of Right Act 1689[10] (an Act of the Scottish Parliament prior to the union), are to be regarded as foundational to the British constitution.[11] The different and dominant view, from a largely English perspective and embodied most strenuously in the work of A.V. Dicey, is the principle of parliamentary supremacy, which means that the UK Parliament cannot be constrained by any such supposed 'superior law'.[12]

Act of Union with Scotland 1707[13] (extracts)

ARTICLE I The Kingdoms United; Ensigns Armorial

That the two Kingdoms of England and Scotland shall upon the First day of May which shall be in the year One thousand seven hundred and seven and for ever after be united into one Kingdom by the name of Great Britain And that the Ensigns Armorial of the said United Kingdom be such as Her Majesty shall appoint and the Crosses of St. George and St. Andrew be conjoyned in such manner as Her Majesty shall think fit and used in all Flags Banners Standards and Ensigns both at Sea and Land.

ARTICLE II Succession to the Monarchy

That the Succession to the Monarchy of the United Kingdom of Great Britain and of the Dominions thereto belonging after Her most Sacred Majesty and in default of Issue of Her Majesty be remain and continue to the most Excellent Princess Sophia Electoress and Duchess Dowager of Hanover and the Heirs of her body being Protestants upon whom the Crown of England is settled by an Act of Parliament made in England in the Twelfth year of the reign of His late Majesty King William the Third intituled an Act for the further Limitation of the Crown and better securing the rights and Liberites of the Subject And that all Papists and persons marrying Papists shall be excluded from and for ever incapable to inherit possess or enjoy the Imperial Crown of Great Britain and the Dominions thereunto belonging or any part thereof and in every such Case the Crown and Government shall from time to time descend to and be enjoyed by such person being a Protestant as should have inherited and enjoyed the same in case such Papist or person marrying a Papist was naturally dead according to the Provision for the descent of the Crown of England made by another Act of

---

[10] A 'deeply sectarian document': see A. O'Neill, 'Constitutional reform and the UK Supreme Court: A view from Scotland' [2004] JR 216, 229–30.

[11] For discussion, see N. MacCormick, 'The English constitution, the British State, and the Scottish anomaly' (1999) 101 *Proceedings of the British Academy* 289.

[12] A.V. Dicey, *Introduction to the Study of the Law of the Constitution* (1885; 10th edn 1959, London: Macmillan & Co). He quipped that '*neither the Act of Union with Scotland nor the Dentists Act 1878, has more claim than the other to be considered a supreme law*' (p. 145). He sought to demonstrate his point empirically by listing the occasions on which the 1707 Act had been amended, notwithstanding its assertion that it was legislating in perpetuity. The Scotland Act 1998, s.37, expressly provides that '*The Union with Scotland Act 1706 and the Union with England Act 1707 have effect subject to this Act*'.

[13] Taken from the UK Statute Law Database.

Parliament in England in the first year of the reign of Their late Majesties King William and Queen Mary intituled an Act declaring the Rights and Liberites of the Subject and settling the Succession of the Crown.

ARTICLE III Parliament

That the United Kingdom of Great Britain be represented by one and the same Parliament to be stiled The Parliament of Great Britain.

ARTICLE IIII Trade and Navigation and other Rights.

That all the Subjects of the United Kingdom of Great Britain shall from and after the Union have full freedom and Intercourse of Trade and Navigation to and from any port or place within the said United Kingdom and the Dominions and Plantations thereunto belonging And that there be a Communication of all other Rights Privileges and Advantages which do or may belong to the Subjects of either Kingdom except where it is otherwise expressly agreed in these Articles.

ARTICLE VI Regulations of Trade, Duties, &c.

That all parts of the United Kingdom for ever from and after the Union shall have the same Allowances Encouragements and Drawbacks and be under the same prohibitions restrictions and regulations of Trade and liable to the same Customs and Duties on Import and Export And that the Allowances Encouragements and Drawbacks prohibitions restrictions and regulations of Trade and the Customs and Duties on Import and Export settled in England when the Union commences shall from and after the Union take place throughout the whole United Kingdom. [...]

ARTICLE XIX Court of Session. Writers to the Signet admitted Lords of Session. Court of Justiciary. Other Courts. Causes in Scotland not cognizable in Courts in Westminster Hall.

That the Court of Session or Colledge of Justice do after the Union and notwithstanding thereof remain in all time coming within Scotland as it is now constituted by the Laws of that Kingdom and with the same authority and privileges as before the Union Subject nevertheless to such regulations for the better Administration of Justice as shall be made by the Parliament of Great Britain and that hereafter none shall be named by Her Majesty or Her Royal Successors to be ordinary Lords of Session but such who have served in the Colledge of Justice as Advocates or Principal Clerks of Session for the Space of Five years or as Writers to the Signet for the Space of ten years with this provision that no Writer to the Signet be capable to be admitted a Lord of the Session unless he undergo a private and publick Tryal on the Civil Law before the Faculty of Advocates and be found by them qualified for the said Office two years before he be named to be a Lord of the Session yet so as the Qualifications made or to be made for capacitating persons to be named ordinary Lords of Session may be altered by the Parliament of Great Britain And that the Court of Justiciary do also after the Union and notwithstanding thereof remain in all time coming within Scotland as it is now constituted by the Laws of that Kingdom and with the same authority and privileges as before the Union Subject nevertheless to such regulations as shall be made by the Parliament of Great Britain and without prejudice of other rights of Justiciary [...] And that the heretable rights of Admiralty and Vice Admiralties in Scotland be reserved to the respective proprietors as rights of property Subject nevertheless as to the manner of exercising such heretable rights to such regulations and alterations as shall be thought proper to be made by the Parliament of Great Britain And that all other Courts now in being within the Kingdom of Scotland do remain but Subject to alterations by the Parliament of Great Britain And that all inferior Courts within the said limits do remain Subordinate as they are now to the supreme Courts of Justice within the same in all time coming And that no Causes in Scotland be cognoscible by the Courts of Chancery Queen's Bench Common Pleas or any other Court in Westminster Hall and that the said Courts or any other of the like nature after the Union shall have no Power to cognosce review or alter the Acts or Sentences of the Judicatures within Scotland or stop the Execution of the same [. . .]

In the next extract, Dr Elizabeth Wicks considers the constitutional status of the Treaty and Acts of Union.

Elizabeth Wicks, 'A new constitution for a new state? The 1707 Union of England and Scotland' (2001) 117 Law Quarterly Review 109, 117–20 (footnotes omitted)

"Constituent" and "constitutional"—is there a difference?

The Acts and Articles of Union are clearly constituent documents. [. . .] they have an important role to play in constituting, or creating, a new state. They are also constituent in the sense of constituting a new legal order for that new state. This new legal order includes at its apex a new Parliament—the supreme law-making body within the new state. The consequences of the creation of a new Parliament is probably the issue which has provoked most debate in respect of the Acts of Union [. . .] However, the significance of the creation of a new Parliament should not be permitted to obscure the much greater significance of the creation of an entirely new legal order.

Allott has written that a constitution "describes the way in which the political power of the society is concentrated and places the source of that concentration somewhere other than in the mere fact of power". The idea behind this statement is that the power of government derives not from the use of force but from the state's constitution. There is a legitimacy of government which would otherwise be lacking if political power were seized unilaterally, and may also be lacking in the future if the constitutional government were illegally overthrown. A constitution therefore not only constitutes a new legal order (although it will by definition do this), but it also legitimises that order and the rules according to which it operates.

MacCormick asked the question: "If a State has at some time been set up, 'constituted' by some deliberate act or acts, can these constituent acts be other than constitutions?" The answer is, undoubtedly, yes. In part this is due to the legitimising role of a constitution described above, but there is also a further distinction. A constituent document constitutes something. It establishes a state and/or a legal order. As such it is a singular act. A "constitution", however, must have continuing significance. It will include elements of a constituent nature, and these elements will be traceable back to a singular moment in time, but their incorporation into a constitution enables contemporary light to be cast upon them. A constitution reflects the present reality of a state and legal order which were constituted in the past. A constitution goes beyond constituting a legal order and also determines how that legal order will function today, tomorrow and into the future. It does this by binding the organs of government. The Acts of Union are constituent. An entirely separate question is whether they amount to a "constitution".

The Acts of Union as higher law

There seems little doubt that the Union legislation was intended by its drafters to be a higher law, binding upon the legislature which it created. This is indicated by the language used. The union between England and Scotland, for example, was expressed to be 'for ever after'. However, such language was not unusual in the seventeenth and eighteenth centuries and, although the Scottish Union legislation has been described as "not so obviously in tatters" as the Irish Union legislation, there have been breaches of provisions which were intended in 1707 to remain in force for ever.

There is much disagreement over the extent of the breaches. Munro claims "almost all of the articles and sections of the legislation have been repealed in whole or in part" and by contrast Mitchell argues that it is "doubtful if there has as yet been any breach". The truth, as usual, probably lies somewhere between the two extremes. Some commentators who accept that provisions of the Union have been breached continue to claim that it remains a binding "constitution". Two arguments are used to support this inconsistency and both are unconvincing. Firstly, it has been argued that there is evidence in legislative practice that the Union imposes limits on the legislature. The "evidence" usually quoted is the abandonment of proposals to abolish the appellate jurisdiction of the House of Lords and Privy Council in 1872. Lord Chancellor Selborne, however, when withdrawing the proposals due to "constitutional objections", emphasised the dangers in transferring Scots appeals to a new court "without first ascertaining that such a transfer would be approved by the people of Scotland". This suggests that Parliament was influenced more by public opinion than by the provisions in the Acts of Union.

The issue of consent in a wider context is the second argument used to support the inconsistent view outlined above. For unexplained reasons a breach of a Union provision which has the consent of the Scottish people is generally regarded by commentators as not being a genuine "breach". Mitchell, Smith and Upton all refer in passing to the distinguishing factor of Scottish consent without expanding on why this should be relevant in a legal, as opposed to a political, sense. The only circumstances under which consent to a breach would have legal relevance would be with regard to a treaty under international law. A material breach by one party to a bilateral treaty enables the other party to terminate or suspend the treaty. Consent to the breach will therefore enable the treaty to remain in force. This rule of international law cannot be applied to the Treaty of Union, however, because neither party to the Treaty remains in existence. The issue of consent therefore seems to be merely an attempt to bolster an argument which has no legal basis. Upton even claims that a "parliamentary convention" requires "that alterations of the fundamental terms expressed in England's favour must be allowed if favoured by England, and similarly for Scotland". This view cannot be correct. If the Union legislation is no more binding on Parliament than any other statute, consent is irrelevant except to the extent that Parliament will always have regard to public opinion. If, however, as Upton, Mitchell and Smith themselves believe, the Union legislation is a "constitution", their argument amounts to saying that a fundamental law may be breached if the public support such a breach. This is a dangerous proposition which would render a fundamental law worthless.

To conclude on the question of whether the Acts of Union may be regarded as a "constitution", it must be stated that it would not be realistic to regard them as such. It is clear that not all of the Union provisions have the status of higher law. Despite their constituent role, the Acts of Union are not in their entirety binding on Parliament today, not least because the U.K. Constitution has been subject to many changes since 1707. This does not mean, however, that the Acts of Union are of no constitutional significance today. Certain provisions, such as the existence of a joint Parliament and the protection of the Scottish legal system, continue to bind the organs of government. They do so, however, as a result of their inclusion in a complex, diverse and adaptable modern Constitution of the United Kingdom.

(c) UNITED KINGDOM

In 1801, there was a formal political union of Great Britain and Ireland (which had been under the rule of English, and later British, monarchs since 1155). The new state was named the 'United Kingdom of Great Britain and Ireland'. During later decades of the nineteenth century and early years of the twentieth century, there were increasingly strong demands for 'home rule' for Ireland. Several attempts to create autonomous government, under the UK Crown, for the whole of Ireland failed. In the last of these attempts, the Government of Ireland Act 1920 divided the island of Ireland into Southern Ireland and Northern Ireland. Further negotiations led to the Anglo–Irish Treaty of 1921, creating the Irish Free State as a Dominion within the British Empire and Northern Ireland (consisting of six counties). In 1922, after civil war, the Irish Free State constituted itself an independent state, separate from the United Kingdom. Until an amendment in 1999, the Constitution of Ireland claimed the whole of the island of Ireland (thus including Northern Ireland) to be part of its national territory. This history is reflected in the first section of the Northern Ireland Act 1998.

Northern Ireland Act 1998

1 Status of Northern Ireland
  (1) It is hereby declared that Northern Ireland in its entirety remains part of the United Kingdom and shall not cease to be so without the consent of a majority of the people of Northern Ireland voting in a poll held for the purposes of this section in accordance with Schedule 1.

  (2) But if the wish expressed by a majority in such a poll is that Northern Ireland should cease to be part of the United Kingdom and form part of a united Ireland, the Secretary of State shall lay before Parliament such proposals to give effect to that wish as may be agreed between Her Majesty's Government in the United Kingdom and the Government of Ireland.

The United Kingdom has existed with its current boundaries for fewer than a hundred years. Its future as a nation state is uncertain. The devolved Scottish Government created in 1999 (as we shall see) has since the 2007 elections been formed by members of the Scottish National Party. The SNP is committed to Scotland becoming an independent state, separate from the United Kingdom. The SNP government proposed holding a referendum on the constitutional future of Scotland in 2014. The Conservative–Liberal Democrat coalition national government formed after the May 2011 general election is unionist in its outlook—as is the official opposition in the UK Parliament, the Labour Party. One of the first disputes is whether the Scottish Government has the necessary legal power to organize a referendum under the powers devolved to it by the Scotland Act 1998. Schedule 5 reserves to the United Kingdom the power to legislate on 'the Union of the Kingdoms of Scotland and England'. The UK government argued that this prohibits the Scottish Parliament from passing legislation for a referendum on independence. One counter-argument is that legislation enabling an advisory referendum falls outside the scope of this restriction because a non-binding referendum would not in and of itself affect the legal status of the union.[14] Another dispute

---

[14] See House of Lords Constitution Committee, *Referendum on Scottish Independence*, 24th Report, Session 2010–12 (HL 263).

is over the wording of the referendum. The Scottish Government has indicated that it would like a referendum offering three choices: independence; 'devo max' or 'devolution plus' (more devolved powers); and the status quo. The UK Government wants there to be a single question.

QUESTIONS

1. Wicks refers to the legislation that formed the union between England and Wales and Scotland as a 'constituent document'. Why does she prefer this term to that of a 'constitution'?

2. Could the status of Scotland, Northern Ireland as Wales as part of the United Kingdom be altered without a referendum, if the majority of members of the UK Parliament were to support such a change? (Review the discussion in Chapter 2.)

---

3   GOVERNING REGIONALLY

For most of the twentieth century, Great Britain (England, Wales, and Scotland) formed a centralized political unit, with policymaking and law-making being led by the UK government and the UK Parliament. There was devolved government in Northern Ireland from 1922, but this was brought to an end by the UK government in 1972 amid mounting civil unrest and paramilitary violence. The eighteen years of Conservative UK government (1979–97) is often characterized as a time of a high degree of political centralization. Conservative policy was opposed to the devolution of executive and legislative powers to elected bodies in Wales and Scotland.[15]

(a)   DEVOLUTION: A PROCESS NOT AN EVENT

Devolution was on the political agenda for most of the twentieth century in the United Kingdom.

The failure of Northern Irish devolution 1922–72

Between 1922 and 1972, devolved government operated in Northern Ireland under the Government of Ireland Act 1922. There was a Northern Ireland Parliament, a Prime Minister, and a Northern Ireland government (formally, the 'Executive Committee of the Privy Council of Northern Ireland'). The UK government suspended this system of government in 1972 and the institutions were formally abolished by the Northern Ireland Constitution Act 1973. From 1972 to 1998, 'direct rule' was in place. The Northern Ireland Office (a UK government department) and the Secretary of State for Northern Ireland (a minister in the UK government) were responsible for executive action in the province; the UK Parliament made laws for Northern Ireland. The failure of devolved government was due to mounting paramilitary violence between the minority nationalist communities (which favoured reunification with the Republic of Ireland) and the majority unionist communities (who

---

[15] There has always been a high degree of decentralization of *judicial* powers, with three separate legal systems: see Part IV Introduction.

wished to see Northern Ireland continue as part of the United Kingdom). There was widespread systematic discrimination against nationalists.

The rejection of Welsh and Scottish devolution 1978

An attempt to put in place devolved governments in Scotland and Wales was made in 1978. The Labour government, led by Prime Minister James Callaghan, pushed the Scotland Act 1978 and the Wales Act 1978 through the UK Parliament. Although there was no constitutional *requirement* for them do so, it was recognized that such a significant change should take place only with the consent of the people in those parts of the United Kingdom. Both Acts therefore stated that referendums should be held; moreover, they stipulated that at least 40 per cent of the registered electorate had to approve. In Scotland, 51.6 per cent of those who voted supported devolution, but these 1.2 million 'yes' votes represented only 32.9 per cent of the electorate. In Wales, a large majority voted 'no' in answer to the question: 'Do you want the provisions of the Wales Act 1978 to be put into effect?' Both Acts were repealed and no further steps towards devolution were contemplated by the Conservative government in office for the next eighteen years.

The 1997 proposals

Devolution returned to the political agenda at the 1997 general election, which Labour won.

Labour Party General Election Manifesto, *New Labour Because Britain Deserves Better* (1997)

Devolution: Strengthening the Union

The United Kingdom is a partnership enriched by distinct national identities and traditions. Scotland has its own systems of education, law and local government. Wales has its language and cultural traditions. We will meet the demand for decentralization of power to Scotland and Wales, once established in referendums.

Subsidiarity is as sound a principle in Britain as it is in Europe. Our proposal is for devolution not federation. A sovereign Westminster Parliament will devolve power to Scotland and Wales. The Union will be strengthened and the threat of separatism removed.

As soon as possible after the election, we will enact legislation to allow the people of Scotland and Wales to vote in separate referendums on our proposals, which will be set out in white papers. These referendums will take place not later than the autumn of 1997. A simple majority of those voting in each referendum will be the majority required. Popular endorsement will strengthen the legitimacy of our proposals and speed their passage through Parliament.

For Scotland we propose the creation of a parliament with law-making powers, firmly based on the agreement reached in the Scottish Constitutional Convention,[16] including defined

---

[16] The Scottish Constitutional Convention was an unofficial body that carried out work to prepare for devolution during the 1990s.

and limited financial powers to vary revenue and elected by an additional member system. In the Scottish referendum we will seek separate endorsement of the proposal to create a parliament, and of the proposal to give it defined and limited financial powers to vary revenue. The Scottish parliament will extend democratic control over the responsibilities currently exercised administratively by the Scottish Office. The responsibilities of the UK Parliament will remain unchanged over UK policy, for example economic, defence and foreign policy.

The Welsh assembly will provide democratic control of the existing Welsh Office functions. It will have secondary legislative powers and will be specifically empowered to reform and democratise the quango state. It will be elected by an additional member system.

Following majorities in the referendums, we will introduce in the first year of the Parliament legislation on the substantive devolution proposals outlined in our white papers.

The Conservatives were opposed to devolution.[17]

Within months of the Labour government taking office in 1997, White Papers setting out the government plans for devolution in Scotland and Wales were published and referendums held—this time *before* Bills setting out the details of devolution were introduced to the UK Parliament—and following 'yes' votes in both Wales (50.3 per cent indicating 'I agree that there should be a Welsh Assembly') and Scotland (74.3 per cent indicating 'I agree that there should be a Scottish Parliament' and 63.5 per cent indicating 'I agree that a Scottish Parliament should have tax-varying powers'). Faced with the political reality of popular support for devolution, the Conservatives accepted the principle of decentralization. Elections for the Scottish Parliament and the National Assembly for Wales were held in May 1999, and devolved powers were transferred shortly afterwards. The phrase 'devolution is a process, not an event' is often quoted, because it reflects the reality that the 1998 devolution Acts were not a once-and-for-all-time settlement, but rather the first stage of a developing set of arrangements.

The devolution process for Northern Ireland

The protracted peace process in Northern Ireland was slowly leading to all-party agreement during 1998. The Belfast (or 'Good Friday') Agreement was signed in April 1998, and received majority support in referendums held in Ireland and Northern Ireland. A central strand in the negotiations was a plan for devolved government. Elections for the Northern Ireland Assembly were held in 1998, 2003, and 2007. Devolution has been suspended periodically, as parties in the Assembly were unable to cooperate. Devolved government was restored after the 2007 elections. A further milestone in the devolution process was achieved with the transfer of police and judicial powers in 2010.

The devolution process for Wales

Within months of devolution in Wales starting, there was cross-party dissatisfaction with one central feature of the governing arrangements set out in the Government of Wales Act 1998—namely, that the National Assembly was a corporate body without a formal separation between its legislative and scrutiny activities, on the one hand, and executive functions, on the other. In other words, there was no 'government' separate from the Assembly as a whole. In 2002, the First Minister (as the First Secretary was by then styled) set up a ten-person Commission on the Powers and Electoral Arrangements of the Assembly to look into

---

[17] Conservative Party General Election Manifesto, *You Can Only Be Sure with the Conservatives* (1997).

this and other aspects of the operation of devolution. The Commission reported in 2004, concluding: '*We do not think the status quo is a sustainable basis for future development.*' The UK government accepted some, but rejected others, of the Commission's proposals. The Government of Wales Act 2006 replaced the 1998 Act.

The devolution process for Scotland

In 2008, the UK government (*not* the Scottish government) set up a commission chaired by Sir Kenneth Calman (a medic and university leader) to review the experience of devolution. It concluded that devolution in Scotland had been 'a real success'.

Commission on Scottish Devolution, *Serving Scotland Better: Scotland and the United Kingdom in the 21st Century* (2009)

Devolution inside a political Union

15. In thinking about how devolution should develop further, we have looked very carefully at how it fits into the wider Union that is the United Kingdom. This is first of all a political Union, with a Parliament at Westminster where every part of the country is represented. Some things like defence and foreign relations can only be dealt with there if we are to have a Union at all. There should be no change in those. But we have considered what impact they have on matters that are now quite properly dealt with by the Scottish Parliament. For instance, working with the other members of the European Union critically affects agriculture and fisheries. This is an example of a recurring theme in our report—the different levels of government in the United Kingdom have to work more closely together.

16. The United Kingdom is an asymmetrical Union. Not only are the four nations very different in size, but devolution in Wales and Northern Ireland is different from devolution in Scotland, and there is no devolution for England. It is not our job to say whether this should change, or to make recommendations about how England is governed, but we cannot ignore the fact that the Parliament at Westminster is England's parliament as well as the Parliament for the whole of the UK. We can learn lessons from federal countries about how to help different levels of government to cooperate, but the tidy solutions that work where every part of a larger country can be governed in the same way cannot simply be applied here.

17. The UK Parliament still has, as a matter of law, the power to legislate for Scotland on devolved as well as reserved matters. But there is an important convention according to which it does not do so unless it has the agreement of the Scottish Parliament. This works very well in practice and is probably the best example of where Scottish and UK institutions already cooperate well together. [...]

[The Commission made several reform recommendations. It advocated an explicit declaration of a UK-wide 'social union'.]

20. We think that there are certain social rights which should also be substantially the same, even when it is best that they are separately run in Scotland. The most important of these are that access to health care and education should be, as now, essentially free and provided at the point of need. And when taxes are shared across the UK they should take account of that need. Our first recommendation is therefore that the Scottish and UK Parliaments should confirm their common understanding of what those rights are, and the responsibilities that go with them.

The Commission wanted to see more active engagement between the UK Parliament and the Scottish Parliament, for example through a standing committee of the two legislatures. Some fine-tuning of the allocation of policy areas between Scotland and the UK were suggested. The Commission argued that the Scottish Parliament should have greater tax-raising powers. The Scotland Act 2012 gives legal effect to many of the Calman Commission's recommendations. Among the more significant enlargements of devolved powers is that the Scottish Parliament may set a rate of income tax for Scottish taxpayers and restrictions on the Scottish Government borrowing money are relaxed. Debate continues about still further devolution, particularly of tax and spending powers, sometimes called 'devo max' or 'devo plus'.

(b) THE TECHNICAL FRAMEWORK FOR DEVOLUTION

The definitions of what is and is not 'devolved' (a colloquial, rather than a legal, term) are detailed and sometimes complex. Our aim is not to explore these in depth, but instead to focus on the main features. As we have already noted, devolution is asymmetrical. This is not only because England has been left out of the picture, but also because the powers devolved, and the way in which they are defined, vary between Scotland, Wales, and Northern Ireland. Any system of allocating powers between two levels of government has two main choices—it may either:

(a) define the powers that are exercised at national level and say that the subnational unit has all other powers; or

(b) define the powers of the subnational unit, saying that all other powers are exercised nationally.

The devolved settlements use both methods. The three devolution settlements impose similar general restrictions on the devolved governments and legislatures. They may not legislate or take executive action that is contrary to European Union law or Convention rights.

One consequence of devolution is that different policies, authorized by different laws, are being implemented in different parts of the United Kingdom. One might say that this is the *purpose* of the constitutional process of devolution. Examples include: in Scotland there is free long-term care for the elderly whereas England and Wales have rejected that policy; university tuition fees were increased in England and Wales, but not in Scotland; and school 'league tables' are not published in Wales as they are in England.

Scotland

The Scottish Parliament and Scottish Government have powers over 'matters' that are not expressly 'reserved' to the United Kingdom. In Sch. 5 to the Scotland Act 1998, 'general reservations' are: the constitution; regulation of political parties; foreign affairs, etc.; the civil service; defence; and treason. The schedule goes on to list 'specific reservations' under various 'heads' in some detail. The 'heads' are: financial and economic matters; home affairs; trade and industry; energy; transport; social security; regulation of the professions; employment; health and medicines; media and culture; and miscellaneous (covering judicial remuneration and equal opportunities among other topics).

Northern Ireland

The Northern Ireland Act 1998, s. 4 creates three categories: 'excepted matters' (which are intended never to be devolved); 'reserved matters' (which may be devolved but have not yet been); and 'transferred matters'.

Schedule 2 excepted matters are: the Crown; the UK Parliament; international relations; defence; control of nuclear, biological, and chemical weapons and other weapons of mass destruction; dignities and titles of honour; treason; nationality, immigration and asylum; UK tax; national insurance; various tax credits and benefits; 'The Supreme Court, but not rights of appeal to the Supreme Court or legal aid for appeals to the Supreme Court'; elections in respect of the Northern Ireland Assembly, the European Parliament and district councils; political parties; coinage, legal tender and bank notes; the National Savings Bank; national security; nuclear energy; regulation of sea fishing outside the Northern Ireland zone; regulation of activities in outer space; the Northern Ireland Constitution Act 1973; and the office and functions of the Advocate General for Northern Ireland (the principal legal adviser, to the UK government on Northern Ireland law).

Schedule 3 sets out reserved matters, which include: navigation, civil aviation, domicile; postal services; disqualification for membership of the Assembly; civil defence; Pt 2 of the Civil Contingencies Act 2004; minimum wages; financial services; telecommunications; human genetics; and consumer safety in relation to goods.

'Transferred matters' are devolved under s. 4. Ministerial departments within the Northern Ireland Executive include: education; enterprise, trade and investment; health, social services and public safety; social development; employment and learning; justice; environment; culture, arts and leisure; regional development; and agriculture and rural development.

Wales

Between 2006 and May 2011, under Pt 3 of the Government of Wales Act 2006, the National Assembly had power to make laws in the form of 'Assembly Measures'. Following a referendum in favour of further devolution, Pt 4 of the 2006 Act came into force in May 2011, giving the National Assembly legislative powers in the form of 'Acts of the Assembly' within the 'subjects' set out in Sch. 7. These subjects are: agriculture, forestry, animals, plants, and rural development; ancient monuments and historic buildings; culture; economic development; education and training; environment; fire and rescue services and fire safety; food; health and health services; highways and transport; housing; local government; National Assembly for Wales; public administration; social welfare; sport and recreation; tourism; town and country planning; water and flood defence; and the Welsh language. Legislation is drafted in both the English and the Welsh languages.

The powers under Pt 4 are subject to 'general restrictions'. Acts of the Assembly may not remove or modify any function of a minister of the Crown that was in place before the 2006 Act came into force. Four Acts of the UK Parliament cannot be modified: European Communities Act 1972; Data Protection Act 1998 (along with The Re-use of Public Sector Information Regulations 2005); Human Rights Act 1998; and Civil Contingencies Act 2004. Nor may provisions in the 2006 Act relating to the Auditor General and Welsh public records be altered.

Why the differences?

The different ways in which devolved powers are defined were discussed in the following report.

House of Commons Welsh Affairs Committee, *Government White Paper: Better Governance for Wales,* First Report of 2005–06, HC 839

139. Whilst the White Paper does not include any detail about the way in which the limits of the National Assembly's powers are to be defined, the Government's written evidence outlined two potential options

* to specify the subjects on which the National Assembly could legislate (this was the model adopted in relation to Scotland in the Scotland Act 1978, which never came into force); or

* to provide that the National Assembly could legislate on anything unless it was specifically reserved to the UK Parliament and then to specify those reserved matters (which was the model adopted in relation to Scotland by the Scotland Act 1998).

140. The Government has opted for the first option. It coming to its decision it cited four main reasons. First, that Wales unlike Scotland does not have its own legal system and institutions. Second, that Wales shared a common legal jurisdiction with England, so a definition along the Scotland 1998 lines would be more complicated in Wales, and could have far reaching consequences in terms of the common legal jurisdiction. Third, that the list of reserved powers would be substantially longer and more complex in Wales compared to Scotland. Fourth, that the Scotland 1978 model built on the executive function already devolved to the National Assembly, and therefore could develop out of the existing pattern of Welsh devolution.

141. In his evidence to us, Professor Rawlings, highlighted the problems with the Scotland 1978 model. He argued that, 'the Assembly only having power to legislate where it is expressly authorised to do so carries strong potential for time-consuming and complicated problems of legal competence, and, in turn, for intergovernmental wrangling and even substantial forms of litigation'. Furthermore he reminded us that the 1978 model was rejected for Scotland in 1998 on grounds of 'complexity from the need to spell out the devolved areas in considerable detail'. He concluded that 'Lord Richard was well aware of the England and Wales jurisdiction point, so his response was to take out the most obvious things relating to the England and Wales jurisdiction...Lord Richard took the view that this was a manageable position'.

(C) ARE THE DEVOLUTION ACTS 'CONSTITUTIONS'?

Some commentators predicted that litigation about the scope of devolved powers would be frequent and controversial. This has not proved to be the case, though in a number of cases courts have been called on to interpret the devolution Acts.

In an early case, Mr Peter Robinson, a Democratic Unionist member of the Northern Ireland Assembly, took legal action seeking to quash the appointment of First Minister and Deputy First Minister in November 2001.[18] The majority of the Assembly had, after lengthy negotiations, agreed to these appointments—but two days after the six-week period prescribed by s. 16(8) of the Northern Ireland Act 1998 for such an election. The two ministers, supported by the UK government, argued that the expiry of the time limit did not affect the Assembly's powers to make lawful appointments. The Law Lords agreed.

[18] Mr Robinson himself became First Minister in 2008.

Robinson v Secretary of State for Northern Ireland
[2002] UKHL 32, Lord Bingham of Cornhill

10. The 1998 Act, as already noted, was passed to implement the Belfast Agreement, which was itself reached, after much travail, in an attempt to end decades of bloodshed and centuries of antagonism. The solution was seen to lie in participation by the unionist and nationalist communities in shared political institutions, without precluding (see s 1 of the Act) a popular decision at some time in the future on the ultimate political status of Northern Ireland. If these shared institutions were to deliver the benefits which their progenitors intended, they had to have time to operate and take root.

11. The 1998 Act does not set out all the constitutional provisions applicable to Northern Ireland, but it is in effect a constitution. So to categorise the Act is not to relieve the courts of their duty to interpret the constitutional provisions in issue. But the provisions should, consistently with the language used, be interpreted generously and purposively, bearing in mind the values which the constitutional provisions are intended to embody. Mr Larkin [counsel for Mr Robinson] submitted that the resolution of political problems by resort to the vote of the people in a free election lies at the heart of any democracy and that this democratic principle is one embodied in this constitution. He is of course correct. Sections 32(1) and (3) expressly contemplate such elections as a means of resolving political impasses. But elections held with undue frequency are not necessarily productive. While elections may produce solutions they can also deepen divisions. Nor is the democratic ideal the only constitutional ideal which this constitution should be understood to embody. It is in general desirable that the government should be carried on, that there be no governmental vacuum. And this constitution is also seeking to promote the values referred to in the preceding paragraph.

12. It would no doubt be possible, in theory at least, to devise a constitution in which all political contingencies would be the subject of predetermined mechanistic rules to be applied as and when the particular contingency arose. But such an approach would not be consistent with ordinary constitutional practice in Britain. There are of course certain fixed rules, such as those governing the maximum duration of parliaments or the period for which the House of Lords may delay the passage of legislation. But matters of potentially great importance are left to the judgment either of political leaders (whether and when to seek a dissolution, for instance) or, even if to a diminished extent, of the crown (whether to grant a dissolution). Where constitutional arrangements retain scope for the exercise of political judgment they permit a flexible response to differing and unpredictable events in a way which the application of strict rules would preclude.

In the next case, the Scottish courts considered the status of the Scottish Parliament, which was created by the Scotland Act 1998. Lord Watson of Invergowrie,[19] a member of the Scottish Parliament (MSP), proposed to introduce a private member's Bill to the Scottish Parliament, seeking to ban hunting with dogs. Three pro-hunt campaigners sought an injunction to prevent Lord Watson from doing so; they said that Lord Watson received administrative and legal assistance from an anti-hunt organization, which they argued amounted to 'remuneration' contrary to the Scottish Parliament rule prohibiting MSPs from engaging in paid

---

[19] Lord Watson (Mike Watson) went on to serve as a minister in the Scottish Government. In 2004, however, he was convicted of criminal offences relating to starting a fire in a hotel and sentenced to a term of imprisonment.

advocacy.[20] The Lord President (Lord Rodger of Earlsferry) sitting in the First Division, Inner House, Court of Session made the following statement.

Whaley v Lord Watson Of Invergowrie
2000 SC 340, Lord President

The Lord Ordinary [the first-instance judge] gives insufficient weight to the fundamental character of the Parliament as a body which—however important its role—has been created by statute and derives its powers from statute. As such, it is a body which, like any other statutory body, must work within the scope of those powers. If it does not do so, then in an appropriate case the court may be asked to intervene and will require to do so, in a manner permitted by the legislation. In principle, therefore, the Parliament like any other body set up by law is subject to the law and to the courts which exist to uphold that law. In the 1998 Act Parliament did, however, put one important limitation on the powers of the court in proceedings involving the Scottish Parliament. In s 40(3) and (4) [. . .] it provided that in such proceedings the court should not grant an order for suspension, interdict, reduction or specific performance but might instead grant a declarator; nor should it grant any order against an individual which would have equivalent effect. [. . .]

Some of the arguments of counsel for [Lord Watson] appeared to suggest that it was somehow inconsistent with the very idea of a parliament that it should be subject in this way to the law of the land and to the jurisdiction of the courts which uphold the law. I do not share that view. On the contrary, if anything, it is the Westminster Parliament which is unusual in being respected as sovereign by the courts. And, now, of course, certain inroads have been made into even that sovereignty by the European Communities Act 1972. By contrast, in many democracies throughout the Commonwealth, for example, even where the parliaments have been modelled in some respects on Westminster, they owe their existence and powers to statute and are in various ways subject to the law and to the courts which act to uphold the law. The Scottish Parliament has simply joined that wider family of parliaments. Indeed I find it almost paradoxical that counsel for a member of a body which exists to create laws and to impose them on others should contend that a legally enforceable framework is somehow less than appropriate for that body itself.

Members of the Scottish Parliament hold office by virtue of the 1998 Act and, again, their rights and duties derive ultimately from the Act. Qua[21] members of the Parliament, just as in all the other aspects of their lives, they are in general subject to the law and to the -decisions of the courts. Of course, in ss 41 and 42 the Act makes certain specific provisions to ensure freedom of speech for members of the Parliament and to permit proper reporting of its proceedings. In addition s 40(4) recognises one particular respect in which the position of members vis à vis the courts is different from the position of other people: in certain situations the courts cannot grant an order for suspension, interdict, reduction or specific performance (or other like order) against them. But the immunity thus granted to the members of the Parliament is not granted in order to afford protection to the members themselves but simply to buttress the immunity of the Parliament from orders of that kind. In other respects the law applies to members in the usual way. In particular—to come to the specific issue in

---

[20] The Scottish Parliament went on to enact the Protection of Wild Mammals (Scotland) Act 2002. Mr Whaley and others unsuccessfully sought judicial review of that Act: *Whaley and anor v Lord Advocate* [2007] UKHL 53.

[21] *Qua* is Latin meaning 'in the capacity of'.

> this case—[Lord Watson] is legally bound by the terms of Article 6 of the transitional order on members' interests [[22]]. If he breaches that Article, then he contravenes the law of the land and indeed commits an offence. The breach may have other consequences which make it proper for the civil courts to notice it.

The majority of the Court of Session (including the Lord President) nonetheless held that the temporary rules regulating MSPs' interests did not give rise to rights that could be enforced by members of the public in civil proceedings; sanctions might, however, lie in retrospective criminal prosecutions.

In another case, a tobacco multinational challenged the lawfulness of legislation made by the Scottish Parliament. The Tobacco and Primary Medical Services (Scotland) Act 2010 banned open display of cigarettes in shops. Under the Scotland Act 1998, Sch. 5, Head C Trade and Industry, various aspects of 'consumer protection' were reserved to the UK Parliament. The question for the court was whether the 2010 Act trespassed into those matters. On appeal, the Court of Session was unanimously held that the 2010 Act was within the Scottish Parliament's competence.

Imperial Tobacco Ltd v HM Lord Advocate as Representing The Scottish Ministers
[2012] ScotCS CSIH 9, [14], Lord President (Lord Hamilton)

> … Parties before us were in agreement that the court should favour constructions which render the constitutional settlement coherent, stable and workable. I agree. Mr Mure further argued that the statutory provisions should be read in a "generous and purposive manner". Reference was made to *Robinson v Secretary of State for Northern Ireland* [2002] UKHL 32 —in particular to the speech of Lord Bingham of Cornhill at paras 10–11. But in that case a clear background purpose (implementation of the Belfast Agreement) could be discerned. Here the purpose (discernible from the statute itself) is the division of functions between the Scottish Parliament and the United Kingdom Parliament. There is nothing in the statute or in its background which suggests that one should read the provisions of Schedule 5, or of any of the other provisions of the statute, expansively or restrictively. One must simply interpret them having regard to any relevant legislative background—such as the Consumer Protection Act 1987.

In *AXA General Insurance Ltd and others v HM Advocate and others*,[23] the UK Supreme Court heard a challenge from insurance companies challenging the lawfulness of provisions in the Damages (Asbestos-related Conditions) (Scotland) Act 2009, legislation passed by the Scottish Parliament that sought to reverse in Scotland case law that has held that people who developed asymptomatic pleural plaques in their lungs as a result of exposure to asbestos did not have an injury in respect of which an employer could have tortious liability. Lord Hope noted that *'The question whether the principle of the sovereignty of the United Kingdom Parliament is absolute or may be subject to limitation in exceptional circumstances is still under discussion'* and continued:

---

[22] A piece of legislation was temporarily in place until the Scottish Parliament had an opportunity in 2000 to devise standing orders of its own dealing with members' interests.

[23] [2011] UKSC 46, [2012] 1 AC 868.

AXA General Insurance Ltd and others v HM Advocate and others
[2011] UKSC 46

[51] We do not need, in this case, to resolve the question how these conflicting views about the relationship between the rule of law and the sovereignty of the United Kingdom Parliament may be reconciled. The fact that we are dealing here with a legislature that is not sovereign relieves us of that responsibility. It also makes our task that much easier. In our case the rule of law does not have to compete with the principle of sovereignty. As I said in *Jackson* [2005] UKHL 56], para 107, the rule of law enforced by the courts is the ultimate controlling factor on which our constitution is based. I would take that to be, for the purposes of this case, the guiding principle. Can it be said, then, that Lord Steyn's endorsement of Lord Hailsham's warning about the dominance over Parliament of a government elected with a large majority has no bearing because such a thing could never happen in the devolved legislatures? I am not prepared to make that assumption. We now have in Scotland a government which enjoys a large majority in the Scottish Parliament. Its party dominates the only chamber in that Parliament and the committees by which bills that are in progress are scrutinised. It is not entirely unthinkable that a government which has that power may seek to use it to abolish judicial review or to diminish the role of the courts in protecting the interests of the individual. Whether this is likely to happen is not the point. It is enough that it might conceivably do so. The rule of law requires that the judges must retain the power to insist that legislation of that extreme kind is not law which the courts will recognise.

[52] As for the appellants' common law case, I would hold, in agreement with the judges in the Inner House (2011 SLT 439, para 88), that Acts of the Scottish Parliament are not subject to judicial review at common law on the grounds of irrationality, unreasonableness or arbitrariness. This is not needed, as there is already a statutory limit on the Parliament's legislative competence if a provision is incompatible with any of the Convention rights: section 29(2)(d) of the Scotland Act 1998. But it would also be quite wrong for the judges to substitute their views on these issues for the considered judgment of a democratically elected legislature unless authorised to do so, as in the case of the Convention rights, by the constitutional framework laid down by the United Kingdom Parliament.

QUESTIONS

1. In general constitutional terms, what are the main differences between the devolution arrangements for Northern Ireland, Wales, and Scotland?

2. Civil servants in Northern Ireland, Wales, and Scotland seek your advice as to whether their respective legislatures may make legislation on the following areas of policy. You will need to consult the relevant parts of the devolution Acts: (i) same-sex marriage; (ii) nuclear power; and (iii) the minimum hourly wage that employers must pay.

3. How have the courts approached the task of interpreting the devolution Acts?

(d) ROLE OF SECRETARY OF STATES FOR SCOTLAND, WALES, AND NORTHERN IRELAND

Prior to devolution in 1998, three members of the UK government's Cabinet were the Secretary of State for Scotland (the political head of the Scotland Office), the Secretary of State for Wales (the Wales Office), and the Secretary of State for Northern Ireland (the Northern Ireland Office). The posts in relation to Wales and Scotland are now held by ministers who also have other ministerial posts (reflecting the lessening of the UK government's day-to-day work in relation to those parts of the United Kingdom). The fragility of the Northern Ireland devolution settlement continued to require a full-time minister in the UK government.

The Scotland Office, *Devolution Guidance Note 3: The Role of the Secretary of State for Scotland* [24]

3. The Secretary of State for Scotland holds the post jointly with another post in the Cabinet. In addition to his other ministerial duties, he continues to represent the interests of Scotland in Cabinet as Secretary of State for Scotland, particularly in those matters reserved to the Government by the Scotland Act. He is responsible for the smooth -running of the Scotland's devolution settlement and acts as guardian of the Scotland Act, especially in relation to orders made under its authority. The Secretary of State is supported on ministerial matters by the Parliamentary Under Secretary of State for Scotland. Both ministers are advised on their work in relation to Scottish devolution by the Scotland Office, a distinct entity within the Department for Constitutional Affairs. Scotland Office officials report to the Secretary of State and the Parliamentary Under Secretary of State for policy purposes.

4. The Secretary of State and the Parliamentary Under Secretary of State are members of most Cabinet Committees and Sub-Committees touching their duties in relation to Scotland independently of the Secretary of State's other ministerial duties. The Secretary of State should therefore be copied in at the Scotland Office for all relevant ministerial correspondence. He expects to be consulted by colleagues on the impact their proposals will have on Scotland and how they fit in with the terms of the Scottish devolution settlement.

5. The Secretary of State for Scotland promotes the devolution settlement provided for by the Scotland Act 1998 by encouraging close working relations between the UK Departments and the Scottish Executive, and between the UK and Scottish Parliaments. This does not mean acting as a conduit for the necessary communication between the Government and the Scottish Ministers. Normally Departments should deal with the Scottish Executive direct. But the Secretary of State should be kept closely informed about issues which involve both reserved and devolved matters, and more generally about relations with the Scottish Executive. Departments should therefore copy to the Secretary of State or the Scotland Office all correspondence between UK Ministers and Scottish Ministers.

6. Scotland Office ministers and officials can provide advice in relation to Government policy in Scotland. In particular, where colleagues agree, Scotland Office ministers may be able to help with presentation when major announcements are made on non-devolved matters that

---

[24] https://update.cabinetoffice.gov.uk/resource-library/devolution-guidance-notes in which the roles of the other two territorial Secretaries of State are also set out.

will have a major effect in Scotland. They should inform Scotland Office ministers when such announcements are to be made.

7. The Secretary of State for Scotland is the custodian of the Scotland Act 1998, and secondary legislation under the Act ("Scotland Act Orders") should be made only with the agreement of the Secretary of State. Scotland Act Orders are used both to implement and (occasionally) to amend Scotland's devolution settlement. Scotland Office ministers usually lead on Parliamentary proceedings on these orders and the process of agreeing policy for and laying such orders is managed by the Constitutional Branch of the Scotland Office, who also ensure that the order is consistent with the Scottish devolution settlement. Such Orders often cover wide policy areas and involve lengthy discussion between the Scotland Office, UK Departments and the Scottish Executive before they can be made.

8. In addition, the Secretary of State retains responsibility for certain limited executive functions, notably in relation to the financial transactions between the UK Government and the Scottish Executive, in elections in Scotland and undertakes certain residual functions for Scotland in reserved areas.

It has been suggested that the three separate territorial Secretaries of State should be combined into a single ministerial office (perhaps called the 'Secretary of State for Devolution'), with responsibility for the maintenance and development of devolution.[25]

(e) INTERGOVERNMENTAL RELATIONS

Any system of decentralized governance—whether federal or devolved—requires some institutions and procedures for managing the relationships between the national level and the other political units, and for enabling dialogue between the political units.

A. Le Sueur, 'The Nature of Central Government in the United Kingdom',
in D. Feldman (ed.) *English Public Law,* 2nd edn (2009, Oxford: OUP),
ch. 1, paras 1.71–1.73 (footnotes omitted)

(e) Intergovernmental relations

There are areas of policy over which jurisdiction is shared between devolved institutions and central government. Joint powers are those where it is a legal requirement for ministers from a devolved administration and UK ministers to act in agreement and together, or for UK Ministers to act only after consultation with the devolved administration ministers (or vice versa). Concurrent powers are those which either UK or devolved administration ministers or both are able to exercise in Scotland, Northern Ireland or Wales. A Memorandum of Understanding and a series of supplementary agreements (often referred to as 'concordats') provide a framework for intergovernmental relations within the United Kingdom. Concordats cover such topics as how executive bodies in Scotland, Northern Ireland, and Wales participate in deciding the United Kingdom's stance on agenda items before the EU Council, regulation of regional incentives promoting inward investment, and UK ministerial meetings with the fishing industry in Scotland.

---

[25] R. Hazell, *Three into One Won't Go: The Future of the Territorial Secretaries of State* (2001, London: UCL Constitution Unit).

Relations between the UK government, Northern Ireland, Scotland, and Wales are on the face of it coordinated through the Joint Ministerial Committee (JMC), established under the Memorandum of Understanding supplemented by a number of 'concordats' governing cooperation and coordination between UK departments and the devolved administrations on particular areas of policy. In practice, more reliance has been placed on informal working relationships between officials and ministers than on the formal machinery of intergovernmental relations. The JMC did not meet in plenary session between 2002 and 2008. The JMC on Europe, effectively a subcommittee, has been the most active, meeting three or four times a year to discuss European Union affairs. Commentators and parliamentary committees have expressed concern at the apparent lack of formality in the conduct of inter-governmental relations and the lack of transparency in work of the JMC.

The only formal process for resolving any disputes that may arise between the UK and the devolved administrations are the provisions in the devolution Acts for 'devolution issues' about legislative competence to be decided by the UK Supreme Court.

Alan Trench, 'Devolution: The withering-away of the Joint Ministerial Committee' [2004] Public Law 513

The [JMC] lies at the centre of the structure of intergovernmental relations established in the United Kingdom for devolution. In its plenary form, this high-level forum for the leaders of the UK Government, the Scottish Executive, the National Assembly for Wales and (when devolution is not suspended) the Northern Ireland Executive is supposed to meet every 12 months. But as of June 2004, it had not met for over 20 months, since October 2002. What does this lack of meeting signify? Is the JMC being allowed to wither away, and, if it is, does that matter?

In its origins, the JMC—like much of the framework for intergovernmental relations—seems something of an afterthought. The suggestion that it be established emerged during the Lords Committee stage of debate on the Scotland Bill in July 1998, and was elaborated subsequently in the Memorandum of Understanding published in July 1999, after the first devolved elections. The requirement was that the plenary JMC should meet at least annually, to review the working of the arrangements for intergovernmental relations, discuss the impact of non-devolved matters on devolved ones and vice versa, share experiences regarding devolved functions, and to "consider" (not resolve) disputes between administrations. As the JMC's membership comprises the UK Prime Minister, Deputy Prime Minister, Secretaries of State for Scotland, Wales and Northern Ireland, and the First Ministers and Deputy First Ministers from Scotland, Wales and Northern Ireland, it is a gathering of the politicians most directly involved in the working of devolution and its implications. While any of the governments may call for a meeting or refer matters to the JMC, the initiative for doing so clearly lies with the UK Government, and UK Ministers chair all JMC meetings. Of the various elements of the Committee's remit, dealing with disputes is clearly the most important, and closely linked to reviewing the arrangements for liaison between governments.

As political differences between the political units have become more pronounced, there have been calls for a more formal and transparent process. In 2006 and 2007, the House of Lords Constitution Committee added to the criticisms that the Joint Ministerial Committee (JMC) was at risk of falling into disuse.[26] The UK government started calling JMC meetings again in 2008—a fact that was welcomed by the Calman Commission.

[26] *Government of Wales Bill*, Eighth Report, Session 2005–06 (HL 142); *European Union (Amendment) Bill and the Lisbon Treaty: Implications for the UK Constitution*, Sixth Report, Session 2007–08 (HL 84), para. 96.

Alan Trench, 'The Calman Commission and Scotland's disjointed constitutional debates' [2009] Public Law 686, 694

The Calman Commission [...] recommended beefed-up forms of intergovernmental liaison and co-ordination (discussed in Part 4 of the report, especially paras.4.160–4.205).

Whether this will in fact be sufficient has to be questioned. The formal machinery of intergovernmental relations was always limited, and the UK Government allowed even that to fall into disuse after 2002. The SNP government in Scotland has sought to revive more formal mechanisms of intergovernmental coordination since it took office in 2007, with a limited degree of success—the plenary JMC met again in June 2008 for the first time in five and a half years, and a new format for discussing policy issues, the JMC (Domestic) met for the first time in March 2009 and again in May 2009. But the second plenary JMC due in June 2009 was postponed indefinitely, and some officials suggest that it is proving difficult to find business to transact at the JMC (Domestic) given the different powers devolved and policy interests of the three devolved administrations. If a more formal and structured set of meetings encourage the UK Government to take devolution seriously, that is a useful contribution, but the inherent value of such meetings is limited. Meetings that the UK Government uses simply to tell the devolved what it is going to do are unlikely to change matters much, especially if the root cause of the difficulties is where the boundary lies between devolved and non-devolved matters.

(f) THE ENGLISH QUESTION

While there has been decentralization of executive and legislative powers to new bodies in Wales, Scotland, and Northern Ireland, this has not occurred in relation to England (by far the largest part of the United Kingdom, with over 80 per cent of the total population).

Robert Hazell, 'Introduction: What is the English Question?' in R. Hazell (ed.) The English Question (2006, Manchester: Manchester University Press), p. 1

England is the gaping hole in the devolution settlement: some believe that devolution will not be complete, and the settlement will not stabilise, until the English Question has been solved; others believe that England can be left out indefinitely and devolution confined to the Celtic fringe. Opinions vary not only about the answers, but about the nature of the question.

Andrew Le Sueur, 'Fundamental Principles', in D. Feldman (ed.) English Public Law, 2nd edn (2009, Oxford: OUP), ch. 1A, paras 1.74–1.76 (footnotes omitted)

The Government of England

[...] England is not a political unit; it has no executive body or legislature separate from the UK Government and the UK Parliament. Consideration of the government of England has two aspects. First, there are questions about the place of England within the United Kingdom, in particular the handling of English legislation by the UK Parliament. A second aspect is the prospect of regional government within England and whether a programme of decentralisation of government power within England is desirable. The term 'the English Question' has been coined as an overarching term for the debates.

(a) England and the UK Parliament

The practical problem (according to some), is that since 1998, MPs representing Welsh, Northern Irish and Scottish constituencies in the UK Parliament have continued to be able to vote on legislation that applies only to England. It is said that this is unfair in general and in particular on those occasions where a majority of MPs from England oppose an initiative but it is nonetheless passed because of votes from MPs in other parts of the UK who were prepared to support the Government, even though their constituents will not be affected by what is proposed. The Conservative Party, among others, advocate 'English votes for English laws' in which only MPs from constituencies in England would vote on provisions in bills which apply only to England. Critics argue that such a reform would undermine the United Kingdom, in whose Parliament all MPs should be free to vote equally on any issue.

(b) Regional government within England

For a number of purposes, England is divided into nine regions. Of these, only London at present has a democratically elected and accountable unit of regional government in England, in the form of the Greater London Authority (the GLA, consisting of a directly elected Mayor and the Greater London Assembly), a tier of government above local authorities (the 32 London Boroughs).Though lacking directly elected bodies, each of the nine English regions has a number of bodies which provide strategic planning and oversight. First, there are nine Government Offices for the regions, the remit of which is both to 'join up' the work of various central departments within the regions and, through local knowledge, to have input into the development of government policy for the area. Secondly, each region also has a statutory body known as a Regional Development Agency (RDA), which has specific statutory powers related to economic performance. The RDAs consist of a board whose members are appointed by a central government minister (or in the case of London, by the Mayor of London) from people drawn from business, local authorities, trade unions and voluntary organisations; RDAs have significant budgets but no clear democratic mandate. Thirdly, outside London, there are regional assemblies (-originally called 'regional chambers'), which consist of representatives of local authorities in the region plus appointed representatives drawn from the regions' social, economic, and environmental sectors. Regional assemblies are not statutory bodies but they have been conferred with a number of statutory duties and powers: they must be consulted by RDAs; they prepare 'draft regional spatial strategies'; and they provide advice to central government on strategies for using in their region. Regional assemblies have few resources, no significant executive powers, and little democratic legitimacy. Fourth, in 2007, as part of the 'Governance of Britain' reform programme, the Prime Minister appointed a minister for each of the regions (from among existing ministerial posts). There are also a range of other bodies operating at regional level, including Strategic Health Authorities and Learning and Skills Councils.

It is widely accepted that more needs to be done to improve accountability for regional level governance in England. In 2004, the Government proposed referendums in three of the English regions (North West, North East, and Yorkshire and the Humber) on the creation of directly-elected regional assemblies. By a very large majority, voters in the North East (often thought to be the part of England with the strongest regional identity) rejected the proposals and the other referendums did not take place. Since then, focus has turned to how local authorities and the UK Parliament could provide better accountability, including proposals for a House of Commons select committee for each region.

The absence of an executive body for the whole of England means that UK government departments are sometimes concerned with 'whole-UK' matters and sometimes with England-only issues (see Box 5.1). The remit of some departments focuses almost exclusively on UK matters: for example, HM Treasury, the Ministry of Defence, the Department for International Development, and the Foreign and Commonwealth Office. In others—such as the Department for the Environment, Rural Affairs and Food (DEFRA), the Department of Health, and the Department for Children, Schools, and Families—England-only work dominates (because the comparable policy areas are devolved to Wales, Scotland, and Northern Ireland).

In February 2012, an expert committee ('the McKay Commission') began work 'to consider how the House of Commons might deal with legislation which affects only part of the United Kingdom, following the devolution of certain legislative powers to the Scottish Parliament, the Northern Ireland Assembly and the National Assembly for Wales'.[27]

BOX 5.1 WHOLE-UK AND ENGLAND-ONLY POLICY AREAS

'Central government' relating to whole UK*	'Central government' relating to England only
Defence	Education
Foreign and Commonwealth relations	Rural affairs, fishing, and food
Tax and economic policies	Housing
Immigration and nationality	Health
Constitutional reform	Tourism
Human rights and equality issues	Aspects of trade and industry
Energy	Town and country planning
Aviation	Highways
Regulation of political parties	

*These are some of the main areas of policy that are 'reserved matters' under the Scotland Act, 'exempted' or (currently) reserved under the Northern Ireland Act, and which are not enumerated as functions of the Welsh Assembly Government under the Government of Wales Act 2006.

QUESTIONS

1. What is the best answer to the English Question?
2. How significant is the process of devolution in the United Kingdom?

---

4 GOVERNING LOCALLY

A great deal of the activity of governing takes place at a local level, below those of national and devolved government. The main institutions through which this occurs are the more than 400 local authorities throughout the United Kingdom. These vary considerably in size, both in terms of their territorial area that they cover and their populations. These have a range of executive functions and also limited powers to make legislation.

---

[27] http://tmc.independent.gov.uk/

(a) EXECUTIVE POWERS

Legislation confers responsibility on local authorities for carrying out executive functions over a range of policy areas. Examples include: planning and building control; local authorities have a duty to secure accommodation for people who are homeless, and to provide or fund care homes for elderly and other vulnerable people; registering births, deaths, marriages, and civil partnerships; parking control; collecting and recycling waste; running parks and other recreational facilities; and managing town centres and promoting business. Often, these functions are shared with the UK government (in relation to England) or the devolved governments (in Scotland, Wales, and Northern Ireland). Executive action is carried out both by elected politicians and politically neutral officials (called 'local government officers', rather than 'civil servants'). Some decisions are made by the whole council, some by an executive committee of councillors (in effect, a 'cabinet'), some by subject committees (such as a planning applications committee), and some decisions are delegated to local government officers. Local authorities have 'schemes of delegation' that set out where within their structure decision-making power resides.[28] Some cities have directly elected mayors with executive powers.

Local authorities are required to have in place a system for seeking competitive tenders from firms to carry out delivery of many of their services, such as the collection of refuse, provision of school meals, and IT. The extent to which public services are now delivered by the private sector has led commentators to describe local authorities as 'enablers', rather than 'providers'.

A recent innovation that has the capacity dramatically to change the scope of local authority activity is the 'general power of competence' created by s. 1 of the Localism Act 2011.

Localism Act 2011, s. 1

Local authority's general power of competence

(1) A local authority has power to do anything that individuals generally may do.

(2) Subsection (1) applies to things that an individual may do even though they are in nature, extent or otherwise—

   (a) unlike anything the authority may do apart from subsection (1), or

   (b) unlike anything that other public bodies may do.

(3) In this section "individual" means an individual with full capacity.

(4) Where subsection (1) confers power on the authority to do something, it confers power (subject to sections 2 to 4) to do it in any way whatever, including—

   (a) power to do it anywhere in the United Kingdom or elsewhere,

   (b) power to do it for a commercial purpose or otherwise for a charge, or without charge, and

   (c) power to do it for, or otherwise than for, the benefit of the authority, its area or persons resident or present in its area.

---

[28] See Chapter 15.

(5) The generality of the power conferred by subsection (1) ("the general power") is not limited by the existence of any other power of the authority which (to any extent) overlaps the general power.

(6) Any such other power is not limited by the existence of the general power (but see section 5(2)).

At second reading of the Bill that became the 2011 Act, Eric Pickles MP (Con), Secretary of State for Communities and Local Government, said:

HC Deb, 17 January 2011, c. 561

The reason why the general power of competence is so important is that it turns the determination requirements on their head. All those fun-loving guys who are involved in offering legal advice to local authorities, who are basically conservative, will now have to err on the side of permissiveness. That is a substantial change …

The government believes that the formula used is judge-proof. Junior minister Andrew Stunell MP (Lib Dem) assured colleagues on the public bill committee 'just how broad that power is' and, thanks to subsections (5) and (6), the 'courts will find it difficult—we have been advised that they will find it impossible—to unpick that'. Later he said, clarifying the intended reach of the new general power:

Public Bill Committee, 1 February 2011, c. 193

In the past, local authorities could only do things that were permitted to them by legislation. We are now inverting that and saying, "You can do anything that isn't forbidden by legislation." That does not mean that we are taking away the current forbidden territory and saying to authorities that they can go into the forbidden territory. It is not saying that they can abandon their statutory and legal duties that are imposed by existing legislation.

(b) LEGISLATIVE POWERS

Local authorities have legislative power. Acts of Parliament may confer powers on local authorities to make delegated legislation in the form of by-laws.[29] To take just two examples, Wandsworth Borough Council in London has made a by-law controlling the number of dogs walked by a person in parks and open spaces. The Seashore By-laws made by West Mercia Town Council state that '*No person shall sell or advertise tout or importune either verbally or by the distribution of handbills or adverts*' and '*No person shall break in a horse or other animal or negligently drive a horse or other animal in a race so as to cause danger or annoyance*'.

These are not subject to parliamentary scrutiny, but, in many situations, a process of confirmation is required under which approval must be sought from the UK government minister responsible for local government—which, in England and Wales, is the Secretary of State

---

[29] See Chapter 11.

for Communities and Local Government. The Local Government Act 1972 sets out various procedures that a local authority may have to follow, which can include a requirement to place advertisements in local newspapers giving notice of its intention to make a by-law. Many by-laws empower local government officials to impose fixed penalty notices (typically £50–£80) for breaches of by-laws.

Local Government Act 1972, s. 235

Power of councils to make byelaws for good rule and government and suppression of nuisances.

(1) The council of a district or the council of a principal area in Wales and the council of a London borough may make byelaws for the good rule and government of the whole or any part of the district, principal area or borough, as the case may be, and for the -prevention and suppression of nuisances therein.

(2) The confirming authority in relation to byelaws made under this section shall be the Secretary of State.

(3) Byelaws shall not be made under this section for any purpose as respects any area if provision for that purpose as respects that area is made by, or is or may be made under, any other enactment.

Local authorities may also seek powers through private Bills in the UK Parliament.[30]

(c) THE LOCALISM AGENDA

Current government policy is to promote 'localism'. In 2011, a House of Commons select committee looked at this critically.

House of Commons Communities and Local Government Committee, *Localism*, Third Report of 2010–12, HC 547, Conclusions and recommendations

Defining localism and its aims

1. We welcome the Government's commitment to localism and decentralisation. We agree with the Government that power in England is currently too centralised, that each community should be able to influence what happens in its locality to a much greater extent, that there has been in the past too much central government interference in the affairs of local authorities, and that public services have been insufficiently accountable to their local populations. (Paragraph 15)

[30] See Chapter 9.

The Government's definition of localism

2. The explanations of localism and decentralisation that the Government has thus far provided invoke very diffuse aims from which it is difficult to construct a coherent picture of the end goal. There is little clarity about who will ultimately be responsible for what. Increasing the influence of local decision-making is bound to result in some unpredictable outcomes, but we recommend that the Government undertake to provide a more detailed explanation of the framework within which it envisages such changes taking place and the limits that will be set to central intervention. A constitutional settlement, overseen by a joint committee, could provide such a framework, at least insofar as it relates to the role of local government. (Paragraph 24) [...]

Central government in a localist system

8. Ministers must rein in their interventionist instincts if the Government's localism agenda is to be credible. Central government cannot have it both ways—on the one hand giving local authorities the freedom to make their own choices, and on the other maintaining that only one of those choices is the 'sensible' one. The Government must make its own choice: does it wish local authorities to exercise local discretion, or does it want to continue to prescribe and recommend courses of action centrally? The litmus test of localism will be the Government's reaction to local decisions with which it disagrees. The concept of 'guided localism' is an unhappy compromise which is neither helpful to local authorities nor as radical as the Government seems content to believe. (Paragraph 57)

9. Ministers are not alone in needing to curb their appetite for intervention. Changing the cultures of the civil service and of Parliament to support a more localist system will be crucial. The former will be decisive in ensuring that Ministers' intentions are put into practice, and the latter in altering the parameters of debate to reflect the distribution of powers to local agencies. Opposition spokesmen, too, bear some responsibility for ensuring that central government is not tempted to interfere beyond its proper remit. (Paragraph 58)

Setting limits to localism

10. Localism has its critics, and they have legitimate concerns: about fairness, about the need to safeguard vulnerable people, and about services underperforming. Some stakeholders and sections of the community evidently do not trust the present forms of local democratic accountability to look after their interests when the apparatus of centralised, bureaucratic accountability.is dismantled. We recommend that the Government consider how best to help these groups use the available means for holding their local service providers to account, beyond the ballot box. In particular, the Government must address the contribution to accountability that can be made by robust—and if necessary enhanced—local authority scrutiny functions. (Paragraph 74)

11. We accept the case for some form of minimum national standards in services such as adult social care and child protection, where the needs of the most vulnerable must be protected. We recommend that where such standards are adopted they are formulated in consultation with local government, in order to ensure that they reflect the level of central government oversight appropriate to a localist system and do not simply recreate an overly-interventionist performance regime. (Paragraph 75)

12. We recommend that the Government make clear the principles on which it will determine at what level different decisions will be made, and the grounds on which intervention in

local services will be deemed necessary. These questions should not be decided purely on a case-by-case basis. Communities need clarity about which decision-makers they should be seeking to influence, and an explicit statement of the Government's intent would help to fore-stall campaigning groups' reliance on national government to enforce acceptable standards of service. A constitutional commitment to decentralisation would be one way of achieving this clarity; in the shorter term, we will expect the forthcoming progress report on localism in each department to be an opportunity to flesh out the principles on which the departments are expected to act. (Paragraph 76)

QUESTIONS

1. Why is there a tier of elected local government throughout the United Kingdom?

2. What is the significance of the new 'general power of competence' conferred on local authorities? How does this relate to their existing powers and duties under numerous Acts?

5 CONCLUDING COMMENTS

The focus of this chapter has been on multilevel governing within the United Kingdom. To continue exploring the European Union as a tier of government, turn to Chapter 8 (executive power) and Chapter 12 (treaties and legislative processes).

The chapter has said relatively little about the distribution of judicial power within the United Kingdom. For discussion of the distinct legal systems that exist in England and Wales, Scotland, and Northern Ireland turn to Part IV Introduction, which considers the United Kingdom's separate legal jurisdictions, the origins of which pre-date devolution by centuries.

6 FURTHER READING

Hadfield, B., 'Devolution: a national conversation?', ch. 8 in J. Jowell and D. Oliver (eds), *The Changing Constitution*, 7th edn (2011, Oxford: Oxford University Press)

Leigh, I., 'The changing nature of local and regional democracy', ch.9 in J. Jowell and D. Oliver (eds), *The Changing Constitution*, 7th edn (2011, Oxford: Oxford University Press)

ONLINE RESOURCE CENTRE

Further information about the themes discussed in this chapter can be found on the Online Resource Centre at www.oxfordtextbooks.co.uk/orc/lesueur2e/

6

PROTECTING RIGHTS

CENTRAL ISSUES

1. One of the key tasks of a constitutional system is to protect basic or fundamental rights.

2. As we have seen in Chapter 3, the judges, in developing the common law have often claimed a role in protecting constitutional rights, although there is a lively debate between those scholars who see great value in the common law, and those who doubt the courts' commitment to liberty and equality.

3. Since World War II, many treaties seeking to protect human rights have been agreed by states. There is now an 'International Bill of Rights' comprising the Universal Declaration of Human Rights 1948, the International Covenant on Civil and Political Rights 1966 and its two Optional Protocols, and the International Covenant on Economic, Social and Cultural Rights 1966. The United Nations Human Rights Council monitors compliance. In this chapter we introduce the ways these international treaties have influenced the British public law.

4. Within Europe, the European Convention for the Protection of Human Rights and Fundamental Freedoms (the ECHR) is of particular importance. It creates a powerful enforcement mechanism through the European Court of Human Rights (ECtHR). Since 1966, people under the jurisdiction of the United Kingdom have had a right of 'individual petition' to the court, after they have exhausted domestic remedies.

5. Although the United Kingdom has been bound by the ECHR in international law since 1953, it was not until the Human Rights Act 1998 that Convention rights could be directly relied upon before British courts. The 1998 Act is one of the most significant pieces of legislation enacted. In this chapter we examine its impact on the British constitution, and how it is affecting the relationships between the judiciary and Parliament, and the judiciary and the executive. These issues are explored in relation to the case law in Chapter 17.

6. Politicians are now discussing whether new legislation on human rights is needed in the United Kingdom, perhaps a new 'British Bill of Rights'. The chapter looks at the arguments for and against such a development and at the ways in which new legislation might

change the arrangements set out in the Human Rights Act 1998.

7. The European Union and those member states implementing EU law may, from time to time, infringe fundamental rights. What protection is offered by the EU Court of Justice? What is the significance of the EU Charter of Fundamental Rights? These questions are discussed in the final section of the chapter.

1 CONSTITUTIONAL RIGHTS

In constitutional systems around the world, a great deal of attention is given to identifying and protecting important human rights—variously referred to as rights which are 'basic', 'inviolable', 'fundamental', or 'constitutional'. A great deal has been written about the nature of constitutional and human rights, and they have been surrounded by much controversy for centuries.[1]

It has long been argued that states are formed and constitutions established because individuals recognize that their rights are better protected when they come together to achieve the benefits of mutual protection. John Locke, writing in the seventeenth century, famously asked the following question.

J. Locke, *Two Treatises of Government*, 3rd edn (1698), p. 368

If Man in the State of Nature be so free [. . .] If he be absolute Lord over his own Person and Possessions, equal to the greatest, and subject to no Body, why will he part with his Freedom?

[The answer that Locke proposed was as follows.]

[. . .] the enjoyment of the property that he has in this state is very unsafe, very unsecure. This makes him willing to quit a Condition, which however free, is full of fears and continual dangers: And 'tis not without reason, that he seeks out, and is willing to join in Society with others who are already united [. . .] for the mutual Preservation of their lives, Liberties and Estates [. . .].

The claim that the *raison d'être* of societies, of constitutional systems, and of government was the protection of peoples' lives, liberties, and estates formed the backdrop to the revolutions that occurred in the USA and in France in the eighteenth century, which, in turn, laid the foundations upon which modern constitutional and international human rights law has been built.

---

[1] For an excellent discussion from a political science perspective see: Peter Jones, *Rights*, (1995, Palgrave).

Mark Janis, Richard Kay, and Anthony Bradley, *European Human Rights Law*
(2008, Oxford: OUP), pp. 5–8 (footnotes omitted)

Locke's prose celebrated the rights of the English under the limited government won by the Glorious Revolution of 1688. The particular advantages of England's unwritten constitution, especially the separation and balance of powers among the executive, legislative and judicial branches of government, were elaborated and popularized by the French political philosopher, Montesquieu, in the *Spirit of the Laws* in 1748. In 1762, the revolutionary potential of human rights – 'Man is born free; and everywhere he is in chains' – was proclaimed by Jean Jacques Rousseau. Democratic revolutions were soon to follow in America and throughout Europe.

On 4 July 1776, the American Declaration of Independence issued from Philadelphia. [. . .] In a ringing affirmation of human rights and the duty of governments to protect them, the delegates of the thirteen United States of America proclaimed:

We hold these truths to be self-evident, that all men are created equal, that they are endowed by their Creator with certain unalienable Rights, that among these are Life, Liberty and the pursuit of Happiness. That to secure these rights, Governments are instituted among Men, deriving their just powers from the consent of the governed. That whenever any Form of Government becomes destructive of these ends, it is the Right of the People to alter or to abolish it, and to institute new Government, laying its foundation on such principles and organizing its powers in such form, as to them shall seem most likely to effect their Safety and Happiness.

Politically, the last decades of the eighteenth century were a good time for affirmations of human rights. As the constitutions of the newly independent American states were drafted in 1776, bills of rights enumerating specific rights were directly incorporated therein [. . .] The fashion of bills of rights spread to Europe. [. . .]

The French Declaration (27 August 1789) recognized and proclaimed 'in the presence and under the auspices of the Supreme Being, the following rights of man and citizen':

1. Men are born and remain free and equal in rights; social distinctions may be based only upon general usefulness.

2. The aim of every political association is the preservation of the natural and inalienable rights of man; these rights are liberty, property, security, and resistance to oppression.

3. The source of all sovereignty resides essentially in the nation; no group, no individual may exercise authority not emanating expressly therefrom.

4. Liberty consists of the power to do whatever is not injurious to others; thus the enjoyment of the natural rights of every man has for its limits only those that assure other members of society the enjoyment of those same rights; such limits may be determined only by law.

5. The law has the right to forbid only actions which are injurious to society. Whatever is not forbidden by law may not be prevented, and no one may be constrained to do what it does not prescribe.

[. . .]

On 25 September 1789, less than a month after the promulgation of the French Declaration, the first Congress of the new Federal Government of the United States of America proposed the first ten amendments to the United States Constitution [. . .] they make up the United States Bill of Rights. [. . .]

> Close in kinship and in substance, the American Declaration of Independence, the French Declaration of the Rights of Man and Citizen, and the United States Bill of Rights make up the eighteenth century intellectual and documentary foundation on which two centuries of legal protection of human rights have come to be built. Constitutional guarantees of human rights are now widespread. One study showed that 82 per cent of the national constitutions drafted between 1788 and 1948, and 93 per cent of the constitutions drafted between 1949 and 1975, provided some sort of human rights and fundamental freedoms. Nowadays, more than 100 national constitutions explicitly protect human rights.

From this short account, we gain some insight into the historical and constitutional importance of rights, particularly to Western liberal democracies. We can see how rights have driven revolutionary change, how rights are widely considered to form the core of constitutional systems, how rights help to define the limits of governmental power, and how rights may be used to protect people and to provide them with redress against the state.

While this book concentrates on law in the United Kingdom, rights have a long history and rights issues are widely debated around the world. These are often controversial issues and it would be wrong to see rights only from a Western perspective. Not all systems and cultures understand free speech, for example, in the way in which it is usually understood in the West. Nor are rights such as free speech or privacy necessarily accorded the high priority that may be placed on them in rich, well-resourced countries. To some, such rights are luxuries that are far less important than more basic rights, such as rights to water and to basic health care. Suffice to say, we can only touch on issues such as these here. Nonetheless for these and other reasons it is necessary to consider the international dimension.

2   THE INTERNATIONAL DIMENSION

Since the late 1940s, the constitutional rights present—or missing—in many national constitutions have been buttressed by international law and the development of systems to provide international protection of human rights. The result is that we now have a situation in which rights of broadly similar scope may be protected at international, regional (for example, within Europe), and national levels.

Consider, as an example, the right to freedom of expression. At the global level, this right is recognized by the parties to the International Covenant on Civil and Political Rights 1966 (Art. 19); at the regional level, within Europe, it is recognized by the parties to the ECHR (Art. 10) and by EU members, as expressed by the Charter of Fundamental Rights of the European Union (Art. 11).

International Covenant on Civil and Political Rights 1966, Art. 19

(1) Everyone shall have the right to hold opinions without interference.

(2) Everyone shall have the right to freedom of expression; this right shall include freedom to seek, receive and impart information and ideas of all kinds, regardless of frontiers, either orally, in writing or in print, in the form of art, or through any other media of his choice.

(3) The exercise of the rights provided for in paragraph 2 [. . .] carries with it special duties and responsibilities. It may therefore be subject to certain restrictions, but these shall only be such as are provided by law and are necessary:

(a) for respect of the rights or reputations of others;

(b) for the protection of national security or of public order (*ordre public*), or of public health or morals.

ECHR, Art. 10

(1) Everyone has the right to freedom of expression. This right shall include freedom to hold opinions and to receive and impart information and ideas without interference by public authority and regardless of frontiers. This article shall not prevent States from requiring the licensing of broadcasting, television or cinema enterprises.

(2) The exercise of these freedoms, since it carries with it duties and responsibilities, may be subject to such formalities, conditions, restrictions or penalties as are prescribed by law and are necessary in a democratic society, in the interests of national security, territorial integrity or public safety, for the prevention of disorder or crime, for the protection of health or morals, for the protection of the reputation or the rights of others, for preventing the disclosure of information received in confidence, or for maintaining the authority and impartiality of the judiciary.

Charter of Fundamental Rights of the European Union, Art. 11

(1) Everyone has the right to freedom of expression. This right shall include freedom to hold opinions and to receive and impart information and ideas without interference by public authority and regardless of frontiers.

(2) The freedom and pluralism of the media shall be respected.

Freedom of expression is also recognized in English common law. This is illustrated by a case arising from the publication by *The Times* of articles criticizing the way in which a local authority was managing a pensions fund for its employees. The local authority subject to the criticism began legal proceedings for defamation. Lord Keith of Kinkel, with whom the other Law Lords agreed, held that a local authority had no right to commence such a legal action: '*It is contrary to the public interest because to admit such actions would place an undesirable fetter on freedom of speech.*'

Derbyshire County Council v Times Newspapers Ltd
[1993] AC 534, 551

Lord Keith of Kinkel

My Lords, I have reached my conclusion upon the common law of England without finding any need to rely upon the European Convention. My noble and learned friend, Lord Goff of Chieveley, in *Attorney-General v Guardian Newspapers Ltd. (No. 2)* [1990] 1 A.C. 109, at p. 283–284 [a case about the *Spycatcher* book], expressed the opinion that in the field of freedom of speech there was no difference in principle between English law on the subject and Article 10 of the Convention. I agree, and can only add that I find it satisfactory to be able to conclude that the common law of England is consistent with the obligations assumed by the Crown under the treaty in this particular field.

(a) THE INTERNATIONAL BILL OF RIGHTS

In the wake of the horrors of the Second World War, one of the priorities of the newly formed United Nations (UN) was to *'reaffirm faith in fundamental human rights, in the dignity and worth of the human person, in the equal rights of men and women and of nations large and small'*.[2] To achieve this end, the UN resolved to combine the efforts of the international community to set human rights standards and to establish international machinery that would provide concrete protection of rights. This project was considered to be central to the fundamental goal of saving (in the words of the UN Charter) *'succeeding generations from the scourge of war, which twice in our lifetime has brought untold sorrow to mankind'*.

The key challenge was to change the way in which international law viewed individuals and states. Experience showed that the greatest threats to individuals came from states. A system therefore had to be devised that would prevent states from infringing rights, and give individuals and groups within states ways of challenging their treatment by states.

International law was, however, based on the notion of state sovereignty. This implied two ideas that had to be fundamentally rethought if international human rights protection was to become a reality: the first was the idea that states were free to act within their jurisdiction as they thought fit; the second was the idea that since international law was concerned only with the rights and obligations of states, individuals and groups had no legal status in international law. These ideas, however, could only change, and international human rights law develop, with consent among the states themselves.

As a first step, on the 10 December 1948, the UN General Assembly adopted the Universal Declaration of Human Rights. As a *'common standard of achievement for all people and all nations'*, the Declaration defined, for the first time in the history of international law, the basic human entitlements. This was a groundbreaking document, but it was not enforceable. The establishment of enforcement mechanisms took rather longer and was more contentious.

Eventually, after much debate within the UN over the nature of the rights to be protected and the ways in which they should be enforced, in 1966, two International Covenants were opened for signature. One was the Covenant on Civil and Political Rights, and the other was a Covenant on Economic, Social and Cultural Rights. The two Covenants came into force in 1976. Together with the 1948 Declaration, these instruments form what is now widely referred to as the 'International Bill of Rights'. These instruments are reinforced by several other UN human rights conventions, including the Conventions on the Elimination of All Forms of Discrimination Against Women (1979), against Torture and Cruel, Inhuman or Degrading Treatment or Punishment (1984), and on the Rights of the Child (1989).

International law potentially provides two essential features of human rights protection that are lacking in domestic law. The first is that international law imposes obligations on states to protect the rights of people in their jurisdictions. These rights and obligations are most clearly expressed in treaties to which states are free to agree or not, but they may also be contained in customary international law, which is binding on states even without their express agreement. The fact that law imposes obligations on states to protect human rights means that states cannot claim that the way in which they treat the people under their control is no one else's business (or, as the UN Charter 1945 puts it, is essentially within their domestic jurisdiction—Art. 2(7)). If states fail to provide the protection that international law demands, they will be answerable before international bodies such as the Committee on

---

2 Preamble to the Charter of the United Nations 1945.

Human Rights [3](which is established under the UN Covenant on Civil and Political Rights 1966 and is responsible for seeing that parties to this Covenant comply with its obligations) and the UN Council on Human Rights (which has more general responsibility for overseeing compliance with human rights on behalf of the UN).[4]

The second essential feature of international human rights law is that it gives victims of violations perpetrated by states methods of bringing their situation to the notice of international bodies and the international community. Certain human rights treaties (but not all), therefore, establish procedures that enable individuals to complain about their treatment to an international body. Under the Optional Protocol to the UN Covenant on Civil and Political Rights 1966, for example, states may allow people to complain about their treatment to the Committee on Human Rights. This procedure is set out in an Optional Protocol because states can be party to the treaty even though they do not agree to allow rights of individual complaint. Similarly, in the context of the ECHR, although the United Kingdom agreed to be bound by the Convention in 1953, it was only in 1966 that it accepted the right of individuals to bring complaints against it to the European Commission on Human Rights (now the European Court on Human Rights). That right is now a vital part of the machinery for protecting human rights in Europe and in the United Kingdom.

3 THE EUROPEAN CONVENTION ON HUMAN RIGHTS[5]

For people in the United Kingdom, the most directly and immediately important international treaty dealing with human rights is the European Convention for the Protection of Human Rights and Fundamental Freedoms (ECHR).

Henry J. Steiner, Philip Alston, and Ryan Goodman, *International Human Rights in Context*, 3rd edn (2008, Oxford: OUP), p. 933

The ECHR is of particular importance within the context of international human rights for several reasons: it was the first comprehensive treaty in the world in this field; it established the first international complaints procedure and the first international court for the determination of human rights matters; it remains the most judicially developed of all the human rights systems; it has generated a more extensive jurisprudence than any other part of the international system; and it now applies to some 30% of the nations in the world.

Although the United Kingdom has been bound by international law to respect the rights set out in the ECHR since 1953, the Convention became particularly significant when the Human Rights Act 1998 (HRA) incorporated 'Convention rights' into domestic law so that they became directly enforceable before domestic courts.[6] Remember that while the United Kingdom is bound by international treaties to which it is a party, treaties in general only alter internal UK law and can only be relied on in domestic courts if they have been incor-

---

[3] See the Committee's homepage at: http://www2.ohchr.org/english/bodies/hrc/
[4] See the Council's homepage at: http://www.ohchr.org/EN/HRBodies/HRC/Pages/HRCIndex.aspx
[5] http://www.echr.coe.int/echr/
[6] See Chapter 17.

porated into UK law by an Act of Parliament.[7] We will look at the HRA more closely later, but we must first learn more about the ECHR.

In the following extract, Anthony Lester QC and Kate Beattie summarize the initial impetus for establishing the ECHR.

Anthony Lester QC 'Human Rights and the British Constitution', in J. Jowell and D. Oliver (eds) *The Changing Constitution,* 7th edn (2011, Oxford: OUP), ch. 3, p. 74 (footnotes omitted)

[. . . I]n Western Europe, a second terrible war in half a century and the barbarous atrocities of the Nazi Holocaust convinced European politicians and jurists of the need to forge a new Europe. The need to guard against the rise of new dictatorships, to avoid the risk of relapse into another disastrous European war, and to provide a beacon of hope for the peoples of Central and Eastern Europe living under Soviet totalitarian regimes, inspired the foundation, in 1949, of the Council of Europe. Members of the Council of Europe are obliged to accept the principles of the European rule of law and the enjoyment by everyone within their jurisdiction of human rights and fundamental freedoms.

One of the Council of Europe's first tasks was to draft a human rights convention for Europe, conferring enforceable rights upon individuals against sovereign states. The inventors of the Convention were determined never again to permit state sovereignty to shield from international liability the perpetrators of crimes against humanity, never again to allow governments to shelter behind the traditional argument that what a state does to its own citizens or to the stateless is within its exclusive jurisdiction and beyond the reach of the international community. So they resolved create a binding international code of human rights with effective legal safeguards for victims of violations by contracting states.

For the first time, individuals would be able to exercise personally enforceable rights under international law, before an independent and impartial tribunal—the European Court of Human Rights—against the public authorities of their own states.

Some sense of how revolutionary the enterprise was considered to be may be gleaned from the UK government's reaction to it. The United Kingdom was one of the greatest supporters of improving human rights protection and, indeed, was the first state to sign the ECHR. While it approved of human rights in the abstract, however, the government, like most others, was extremely uneasy about accepting enforcement mechanisms that enabled individuals to take their cases to an independent international court. In fact, only three of the original ten signatory states initially signed up to the right of individual petition. The UK government insisted that it would sign up to the Convention only if it could opt out of the procedure (that is, only if the procedure were optional). This was agreed and it was not until 1966 that the government agreed to allow the right of individual petition—and even then it did so only on a temporary basis. Things have now moved on, and the right of individual petition is now a compulsory and very heavily used element of the ECHR.

The government's early concerns are explained by Andrew Moravcsik.

---

[7] See Chapter 3.

Andrew Moravcsik, 'The origins of human rights regimes: Democratic delegation in postwar Europe' (2000) 54 International Organization 217, 238

The British [. . .] supported international declaratory norms but firmly opposed any attempt to establish binding legal obligations, centralized institutions, individual petition, or compulsory jurisdiction. As W. E. Beckett, legal advisor to the Foreign Office and the initiator of the British government's participation [in the drafting of the ECHR], put it, "We attach the greatest importance to a well-drafted Convention of Human Rights but we are dead against anything like an international court to which individuals who think they are aggrieved in this way could go" [. . .].

The defence of British institutional idiosyncrasy elicited the most violent rhetoric from British politicians and officials. Lord Chancellor Jowitt's official paper criticized the draft convention [. . .] as:

"so vague and woolly that it may mean almost anything. Our unhappy legal experts [. . .] have had to take their share in drawing up a code compared to which [. . .] the Ten Commandments [. . .] are comparatively insignificant. [. . .] It completely passes the wit of man to guess what results would be arrived at by a tribunal composed of elected persons who need not even be lawyers, drawn from various European states possessing completely different systems of law, and whose deliberations take place behind closed doors. [. . .] Any student of our legal institutions must recoil from this document with a feeling of horror."

A common complaint was that judicial review would undermine parliamentary sovereignty. Beckett wrote: "It seems inconceivable that any Government, when faced with the realities of this proposal, would take the risk of entrusting these unprecedented powers to an international court, legislative powers which Parliament would never agree to entrust to the courts of this country which are known and which command the confidence and admiration of the world." "Our whole constitution," a government document intoned, "is based on the principle that it is for the Parliament to enact the laws and for the judges to interpret the laws." [. . .]

The specific issue cited most often by the government's legal authorities was the British policy toward political extremists. A ministerial brief referred to a "blank cheque" that would "allow the Governments to become the object of such potentially vague charges by individuals as to invite Communists, crooks, and cranks of every type to bring actions." [. . .] Lord Chancellor Jowitt's complaint was that "the Convention would prevent a future British government from detaining people without trial during a period of emergency [. . .] or judges sending litigants to prison for throwing eggs at them; or the Home Secretary from banning Communist or Fascist demonstrations."

What blunted British opposition [. . .] was, above all, the fear of resurgent totalitarianism abroad that might pose an eventual military threat to the United Kingdom [. . .]. The West, the government argued, needed not only to maintain the military balance but also to strengthen continental democracies.

In the minds of British officials, however, the primacy of domestic sovereignty over collective defence of the democratic peace remained unchallenged. The cabinet mandated efforts to water down the force of any agreement [. . .]. Acting on Prime Minister Clement Atlee's direct instruction, the British delegation successfully pressed to place the right of individual petition and the jurisdiction of the court into optional clauses [. . .].

BOX 6.1 THE ECHR RIGHTS

- Article 2 Right to life
- Article 3 Prohibition of torture
- Article 4 Prohibition of forced labour
- Article 5 Right to liberty and security
- Article 6 Right to a fair trial
- Article 7 No punishment without law
- Article 8 Right to respect for private and family life
- Article 9 Freedom of thought, conscience and religion
- Article 10 Freedom of expression
- Article 11 Freedom of assembly and association
- Article 12 Right to marry
- Article 13 Right to an effective remedy
- Article 14 Prohibition of discrimination in the enjoyment of rights and freedoms

First Protocol

- Article 1 Protection of property
- Article 2 Right to education
- Article 3 Right to free elections

Sixth Protocol

- Article 1 Abolition of the death penalty
- Article 2 Death penalty in time of war

Other Protocols set out further rights, including the Fourth Protocol (rights in relation to civil imprisonment, freedom of movement, and expulsion) and the Twelfth Protocol, which establishes a free-standing right against discrimination. The United Kingdom has yet to agree to these rights.

QUESTIONS

1. The list of rights and freedoms protected by the ECHR extends to the main civil and political rights. Are there other rights or freedoms that you would expect to see listed? For example, should the ECHR also expressly mention rights such as the right to work, to health, to an adequate standard of living, and to take part in cultural life? Should it expressly protect environmental rights, or group rights, such as the right of peoples to self-determination?

2. If you think that all, or any, of these should be included, can you suggest reasons why they have been omitted?

(a) ENFORCING RIGHTS IN THE EUROPEAN COURT OF HUMAN RIGHTS[8]

The European Court of Human Rights (ECtHR) at Strasbourg is the judicial institution of the ECHR.[9] This court is not to be confused with the Court of Justice of the European Union, which sits in Luxembourg and which is responsible for adjudicating on European Union law.[10] Although the jurisprudence of the ECtHR may be relevant to the human rights dimensions of EU law, these two courts are very different, have very different jurisdictions, and operate under different treaty provisions.

Matters are taken to the ECtHR in two ways. The first involves states bringing cases against other states claiming that they have failed to comply with the ECHR (Art. 33). This interstate procedure is rarely used, although there have been some notable cases. Between 1956 and 1999, there were sixteen such cases, including:

- two brought by Greece against the United Kingdom (1956 and 1957) concerning Cyprus (then a British colony);
- cases brought by Denmark, the Netherlands, Norway, and Sweden against Greece (1967 and 1970) relating to the *coup d'état* carried out by the Greek colonels in 1967;
- cases brought by Ireland against the United Kingdom (1971 and 1972) relating to the state of emergency in Northern Ireland;
- cases brought by Cyprus against Turkey relating to the Turkish armed occupation of northern Cyprus (1974, 1975, 1977, and 1996); and
- cases brought by Denmark, France, the Netherlands, Norway, and Sweden against Turkey (1982) alleging violations, including torture, by the Turkish military government.

Two cases lodged by Georgia against Russia in 2007 and 2008 are currently pending before the ECtHR.

Since 1959, only three interstate cases have led to ECtHR judgments: *Ireland v UK* (1978); *Denmark v Turkey* (2000); and *Cyprus v Turkey* (2001).

The second method is the individual petition procedure, which we have already mentioned (Art. 34). This enables individuals, legal persons (companies), groups, or non-governmental organizations (NGOs) that claim to be victims of violations by states to bring claims before the Court.

There are now thousands of individual petitions each year. By the end of 2011, more than 151,600 applications were pending before the Court. As in previous years, over half of these concerned four states: Russia (26.6%); Turkey (10.5%); Italy (9.1%); and Romania (8.1%). If cases against Ukraine and Serbia were added, almost two-thirds of the cases pending concerned six states. The number of cases pending against the United Kingdom was relatively low compared with these figures (3,650 or 2.4%).[11]

In order to be accepted as admissible, complainants must show that they have exhausted their domestic remedies, that the complaint is not manifestly ill-founded, that it has been brought

---

[8] See further Ed Bates, *The Evolution of the European Convention on Human Rights From Its Inception to the Creation of a Permanent Court of Human Rights* (2010, Oxford: OUP).

[9] See Chapter 17 for further discussion on how courts in the United Kingdom use the ECHR.

[10] See Chapter 18 for further discussion on the Court of Justice.

[11] *2011 Annual Report of the European Court of Human Rights* (2012, Registry of the European Court of Human Rights), paras 9–12, and p. 135. For reform of the Court see p. 206.

within six months of the final decision in the domestic system, and that it does not concern a matter that is substantially the same as one that has already been examined by the Court.

The current constitution of the ECtHR stems from November 1998 when the procedures for dealing with complaints were radically reformed in an attempt to improve their efficiency.[12] The Court is now composed of a number of judges equal to that of the contracting parties. The judges are elected by the Parliamentary Assembly of the Council of Europe from a list of candidates put forward by the governments. They sit in their individual capacity and do not represent any state, and they are forbidden from engaging in any activity that is incompatible with their independence or impartiality.

(b) UK CASES BEFORE THE EUROPEAN COURT OF HUMAN RIGHTS

The following extract provides a summary of the wide range of UK cases that has been handled by the ECtHR. In it, Anthony Lester QC emphasizes that judgments of this Court may involve findings against any of the three branches of government within the United Kingdom. It is not only the executive that may be held to have breached the ECHR, but also the legislature and the judiciary.

Anthony Lester QC 'Human Rights and the British Constitution', in J. Jowell and D. Oliver (eds) *The Changing Constitution*, 7th edn (2011, Oxford: OUP), ch. 3, pp. 75–6

Acceptance of the right of petition gave British lawyers an important opportunity to obtain effective redress for their clients under the ECHR, for want of effective remedies within the UK. In the *East African Asians' case*, the Commission decided that Parliament itself had breached the ECHR in enacting the Commonwealth Immigrants Act 1968, which subjected British Asian passport-holders to inherently degrading treatment by excluding them on racial grounds from their country of citizenship [*Commission's admissibility decision of 14 December 1973* (1981) 3 EHRR 76].

The first case where the European Court found a breach by the UK was [*Golder v UK* (1975) 1 EHRR 524] which held that the Home Secretary had infringed a prisoner's right of access to the English courts and his right to respect for his correspondence. The first case in which the Court held that the House of Lords had breached the ECHR arose from an injunction restraining *The Sunday Times* from publishing an article about the 'thalidomide' tragedy because it was prejudicial to pending civil proceedings. By a narrow majority, the Court held the Law Lords' decision to have interfered unnecessarily with the right to free expression [*Sunday Times v UK* (1979) 2 EHRR 245].

There have been more than 270 judgments of the [. . .] Court finding breaches by the UK, many of them politically controversial and far-reaching. They include: the inhuman treatment of suspected terrorists in Northern Ireland; inadequate safeguards against telephone tapping by the police; unfair discrimination against British wives of foreign husbands under immigration rules; unjust administrative restrictions upon prisoners' correspondence and visits; corporal punishment in schools; excessive corporal punishment by a parent; the criminalisation of private homosexual conduct; the exclusion of homosexuals from the armed services; the

---

[12] The European Commission on Human Rights was abolished. The Court normally sits in chambers of up to nine judges. It also sits as a Grand Chamber with up to 17 judges.

lack of legal recognition of transsexuals; ineffective judicial protection for detained mental patients, or would-be immigrants, or individuals facing extradition to countries where they risk being exposed to torture or inhuman treatment, or homosexuals whose private life is infringed; the dismissal of workers because of the oppressive operation of the closed shop; interference with free speech by unnecessarily maintaining injunctions restraining breaches of confidence, or because of a jury's award of excessive damages for libel, or by punishing a journalist for refusing to disclose his confidential source; the absence of a right to have a detention order under the Mental Health Act judicially reviewed; denial of parental access to children; access to child care records; inadequate review of the continuing detention of those serving discretionary and mandatory life sentences; the blanket exclusion of the right of prisoners to vote in elections; lack of effective remedy for violations of personal privacy; lack of access to legal advice for fine and debt defaulters; unfair court martial procedures; lack of availability of legal aid in some criminal cases; the unnecessary retention of DNA samples in violation of the right to personal privacy; and lack of access to civil justice.

4 CAMPAIGN TO INCORPORATE CONVENTION RIGHTS

The growing use of the Convention and the decisions that were being taken by the ECtHR had both indirect and direct effects for UK law. Elsewhere we note that during the 1980s and 1990s the judges were becoming more attuned to human rights or constitutional rights issues, even if attitudes and judgments remained somewhat erratic in this regard.[13] Certainly, more use was being made of the ECHR as a source of argument in courts (although the provisions could not be relied on directly). Moreover, people were aware that if claimants lost their cases in UK courts, they could pursue them at the ECtHR level. There were also a growing number of situations in which the Strasbourg Court had held the United Kingdom to be in breach of the Convention, which led to the government having to reconsider and change UK law. The *Malone* case was one such example.[14] Having unsuccessfully challenged the legality of the surveillance before the High Court, Mr Malone successfully took the United Kingdom to the ECtHR, where it was held that his Art. 8 rights had been infringed. This decision led to the enactment of the Interception of Telecommunications Act 1985, which placed the imposition of telephone taps on a statutory basis. As we will see in the mini-case study on the right of prisoners to vote (see later), the United Kingdom has not always been ready to implement decisions of the Strasbourg court.

Despite these developments, as Professor Anthony King explains in the following extract, there was a mounting campaign to improve the situation further by drafting a tailor-made modern Bill of Rights, or at least by incorporating the ECHR into UK law.

Anthony King, *The British Constitution* (2007, Oxford: OUP), pp. 129–30 (footnotes omitted)

[. . .]In the eyes of many of those most concerned with human rights in the UK, all this, although a great deal, was still not enough. Anthony Lester published a Fabian pamphlet to this effect as early as 1968, and Sir Leslie Scarman [. . .] used his Hamlyn Lectures in 1974 to

---

[13] See further Chapter 3, Chapter 16, and Chapter 17.
[14] See Chapter 3.

propound the case for Britain's having its own bill of rights. 'It is the helplessness of the law in face of the legislative sovereignty of Parliament', he wrote, 'which makes it difficult for the legal system to accommodate the concept of fundamental and inviolable human rights'. He argued that means must therefore be found for incorporating into English law a declaration of such rights and then for protecting them against all possible encroachments, including encroachments by parliament. As time passed, and despite the fact that the courts were gradually adapting British law to meet the requirements of the European convention, the list of those in favour of some kind of British bill of rights grew longer and longer. By the 1990s, it included an array of the country's most eminent judges [. . .] Crucially, John Smith, the then leader of the Labour Party, used the occasion of a 1993 lecture to Charter 88 to commit Labour to the cause. By this time, most of the advocates of a UK bill of rights had come round to the view that the best way of achieving their object would be to find some means of incorporating the terms of the European Convention on Human Rights into United Kingdom domestic law.

There were a number of reasons why so many in the field felt that the situation as it stood, although better than in the past, was still not good enough. One was the lack of entrenchment. Successive governments over the years had ratified the European convention and its various protocols, but a government at some time in the future could always un-ratify them. Another was that British judges, although increasingly disposed to interpret British law in the light of the European convention and the associated rulings of the European Court of Human Rights, were still reluctant to construe British law in its entirety as though it were subject to or conformed to the European convention's terms and the European court's rulings. They would do that if but only if parliament said explicitly that that was what they were supposed to do. For example, in a 1991 case, *Regina v Secretary of State for the Home Department, ex parte Brind*, Lord Donaldson, the Master of the Rolls, emphatically refused to impute to parliament 'an intention to import the Convention into domestic law by the back door, when it has quite clearly refrained from doing so by the front door. Rulings like the one in the *Brind* case made the advocates of a UK Human Rights Act even more determined to persuade parliament to import the convention through the front door.

But perhaps the main reason the human rights campaigners found the existing state of affairs so unsatisfactory—and certainly the part of their argument that they found easiest to deploy in public—was the seeming absurdity of people, whether British citizens or not, having to go to a court hundreds of miles away in Strasbourg to obtain rights under the European convention that were, or should have been, theirs already. It was expensive going to Strasbourg. It could be immensely time-consuming (it often took the commission and court years to settle cases). The European judges were often not familiar with local circumstances. If the court found against the UK government or one of its agencies, the UK government then had to change the law. Not least, the sight of UK citizens having to trek all the way to Strasbourg to obtain justice was just embarrassing. Sir Thomas Bingham readily -acknowledged in a lecture, given in 1993, that incorporating the European convention into British law would not usher in the New Jerusalem:

But the change would over time stifle the insidious and damaging belief that it is necessary to go abroad to obtain justice. It would restore this country to its former place as an international standard-bearer of liberty and justice. It would help to reinvigorate the faith, which our eighteenth and nineteenth century forbears would not for an instant have doubted, that these were fields in which Britain was the world's teacher, not its pupil.

QUESTIONS

1. Which of the reasons given for reform do you consider to be the most important from:

   (a) a constitutional law perspective?

   (b) a practical perspective?

   (c) the perspective of the reputation of the United Kingdom's legal systems?

2. Which of these perspectives do you consider to be the most important?

As Anthony King goes on to point out, not everyone agreed that reform was needed. In particular, there was strong opposition, especially from those on the Left and from political constitutionalists, to any proposal that would give more power to the judges—especially if this enabled judges to strike down or otherwise frustrate legislation. There were also those who argued that the common law was satisfactory and provided a better way forward than would incorporation of the vague and uncertain provisions of the ECHR.

In the event, the Labour Party fought the 1997 general election with the promise to enact human rights legislation in its manifesto. And soon after it was elected, in May 1997, Tony Blair's government published a White Paper, *Rights Brought Home: The Human Rights Bill*, together with the Bill itself. The Human Rights Act 1998 received royal assent on 9 November 1998 and was brought fully into force on 2 October 2000.

The case for incorporating the rights set out in the ECHR into UK law was summarized in the Labour government's *Rights Brought Home* in the following way.

Secretary of State for the Home Department, *Rights Brought Home: the Human Rights Bill* (Cm 3782, October 1997)

Bringing Rights Home

1.18 We [. . .] believe that the time has come to enable people to enforce their Convention rights against the State in the British courts, rather than having to incur the delays and expense which are involved in taking a case to the European Human Rights Commission and Court in Strasbourg and which may altogether deter some people from pursuing their rights. Enabling courts in the United Kingdom to rule on the application of the Convention will also help to influence the development of case law on the Convention by the European Court of Human Rights on the basis of familiarity with our laws and customs and of sensitivity to practices and procedures in the United Kingdom. Our courts' decisions will provide the European Court with a useful source of information and reasoning for its own decisions. United Kingdom judges have a very high reputation internationally, but the fact that they do not deal in the same concepts as the European Court of Human Rights limits the extent to which their judgments can be drawn upon and followed. Enabling the Convention rights to be judged by British courts will also lead to closer scrutiny of the human rights implications of new legislation and new policies. If legislation is enacted which is incompatible with the Convention, a ruling by the domestic courts to that effect will be much more direct and immediate than a ruling from the European Court of Human Rights. The Government of the day, and Parliament, will want to minimise the risk of that happening.

1.19 Our aim is a straightforward one. It is to make more directly accessible the rights which the British people already enjoy under the Convention. In other words, to bring those rights home.

> **QUESTIONS**
>
> 1. How many reasons can you find in the extract for 'bringing Convention rights home'? Had you been involved, would you have added any others?
>
> 2. The proposal was to 'bring rights home': why do you think this phrase was used?
>
> 3. What differences might there have been between bringing rights in the ECHR home and establishing a new Bill of Rights?

5 HUMAN RIGHTS ACT 1998

In Chapter 17, we look more closely at how the Human Rights Act 1998 (HRA) is used in the courts. For now, our concern is to understand the basic structure and design of the HRA, and to examine its principal constitutional impacts.

(a) AIMS

In the words of its long title, the purpose of the HRA is '*to give further effect to the rights and freedoms guaranteed under the European Convention on Human Rights*'. As was explained in *Rights Brought Home*, the HRA makes the rights in the ECHR accessible to people in Britain so that they can be directly relied on in domestic courts. Note that despite the phrasing used in *Rights Brought Home*, the rights extend to everyone within the jurisdiction of the United Kingdom and not only to British people. The Act may apply in a limited range of circumstances outside the United Kingdom[15] Of course, if the domestic courts do not provide the protection sought, claims can still be taken to the ECtHR.

The HRA improves the ability of the people to assert their rights in court. But it also has the wider aim of helping to inculcate a culture of human rights within all public authorities, independently of whether litigation is threatened or pursued. This means that public authorities, and those who work in them, must be aware of relevant human rights requirements and comply with them on a day-to-day basis in whatever they do.

The HRA can therefore be said to have two basic aims:

(a) to improve rights enforcement; and

(b) to encourage public authorities to adopt a human rights culture in all of their decision-making.

Bodies such as the Equality and Human Rights Commission may be more important than the courts in relation to achieving a human rights culture. [16]

---

[15] The clearest examples are when acts occur within embassies, consulates, or British registered vessels and aircraft. *R (Al-Skeini) v Secretary of State for Defence* [2007] UKHL 26 held that the Act applies in British military prisons abroad, and therefore extended to circumstances surrounding the death of Mr Mousa, an Iraqi civilian, while in custody at a British military prison in Iraq. In *R (Smith) v Oxfordshire Assistant Deputy Coroner* [2010] UKSC 29 the majority of the UK Supreme Court held that the Act did not extend to circumstances surrounding the death of a serving soldier outside his army base in Iraq. The ECtHR takes a broader approach to the application of the ECHR: see *Al-Skeini v UK* App NO 55721/07, 7 July 2011.

[16] http://www.equalityhumanrights.com/

(b) CONSTITUTIONAL STATUS

The HRA was designed to achieve its aims without expressly altering the constitutional principle of parliamentary sovereignty. This means that Parliament ultimately retains the ability to enact legislation that conflicts with Convention rights.[17] It also means that Parliament is free to amend, or even repeal, the HRA in the same way as it might amend or repeal any other Act of Parliament. In other words, the HRA has not 'entrenched' Convention rights into our constitutional system by limiting Parliament's ability to remove the rights.

In order to understand this point a little better, it is useful to consider the various ways in which human rights instruments have been implemented into domestic systems, as summarized by Richard Clayton QC and Hugh Tomlinson QC.

Richard Clayton and Hugh Tomlinson, *The Law of Human Rights* (2000, Oxford: OUP), pp. 59–61 (footnotes omitted)

Methods of entrenchment

There are a number of different ways of implementing human rights instruments into domestic law: by full entrenchment, by limited entrenchment and by a rule of construction. The approach taken in the Human Rights Act was to introduce a strong rule of construction under section 3; and the various alternatives that the Government rejected need only be summarised.

Where a human rights instrument is fully entrenched, the courts have the ultimate power to strike down legislation which violates human rights. The strongest means of achieving this status is where judicial powers are derived from a constitutional instrument which has superior status over ordinary legislation. Thus, in the famous [US] case of *Marbury v Madison* ((1803) 5 US 137 at 177) Marshall CJ held that 'it is emphatically the province and duty of the judicial department to say what the law is' with the result that the United States Supreme Court had the ultimate responsibility to interpret the constitution. Germany also exemplifies the judicial entrenchment of constitutional rights. The constitutions in numerous new Commonwealth countries contain a statutory provision which states that its constitution is the supreme law and that any other law, to the extent it is inconsistent, is void. These constitutions also include Bills of Rights enabling the courts to strike down legislation and they have done so, notably in India and Zimbabwe.

A form of limited entrenchment which provides scope for legislative supremacy is the 'notwithstanding' provision of the Canadian Charter of Rights and Freedoms. Under section 33 of the Canadian Charter the federal or provincial Parliament can expressly declare that a statutory provision is operative notwithstanding that it contravenes the Charter. [. . .]

A different way of achieving limited entrenchment was used in the Hong Kong Bill of Rights Ordinance 1990 which sharply distinguished between legislation passed before or after the Bill of Rights. If legislation had been enacted earlier, legislation had to be interpreted consistently with the Bill of Rights; if no such interpretation was possible, the courts could declare that the legislation was of no effect. On the other hand, where legislation was passed after the Bill of Rights came into force, the court remained under a duty to interpret it consistently with the Bill of Rights; however, if no such interpretation was possible, then the court had no power to declare the legislation ineffective but was obliged to apply it.

---

[17] See the principle of legality discussed in Chapter 3.

The use of a human rights instrument as a rule of construction is exemplified by the New Zealand Bill of Rights. The Bill of Rights was originally drafted along the lines of the Canadian Charter of Rights but opposition to judicial review of the validity of legislation meant that it became enacted as ordinary legislation. Under section 6 the court is obliged wherever an enactment can be given a meaning that is consistent with the rights and freedoms contained in the Bill of Rights, to prefer that meaning to any other meaning. Although a bill of rights instrument which has the status of ordinary legislation could be viewed as no more than a symbolic gesture, this ultimately depends on the attitude taken by the judiciary; and the approach of the judiciary to the New Zealand Bill of Rights shows that, even as an interpretative aid, it can have a considerable impact on the general law.

(c) MAIN ELEMENTS OF THE ACT[18]

The HRA brings 'Convention rights' into the domestic law of the United Kingdom. Note, however, that not all of the rights that are set out in the Convention and the Protocols are 'Convention rights'. For example, the Art. 13 right to a remedy is not a Convention right, nor are those rights to which the United Kingdom has yet to agree, including the free-standing right against discrimination in the Twelfth Protocol.

All legislation (both primary and secondary) *'must be read and given effect in a way which is compatible with Convention rights in so far as it is possible to do so'* (s. 3). This interpretative obligation is imposed on everyone who has to apply legislation. It is most important for judges, who are ultimately responsible for determining what legislation means.

If legislation cannot be interpreted in a way that is compatible with Convention rights, the higher courts, can issue *'a declaration of incompatibility'* (s. 4). If such a declaration is made, it makes it clear that the legislation conflicts with Convention rights, but this does not affect the validity of the legislation. This reflects Parliament's right to legislate contrary to human rights.

Where legislation has been declared to be incompatible with Convention rights, ministers are given powers to take steps to amend the legislation so as to remove the incompatibility (ss 10(2) and (3)).

It is unlawful for public authorities to act in a way that is incompatible with Convention rights (s. 6).

Public authorities may have a defence if primary legislation forces them to act incompatibly with Convention rights (s. 6(2)). This provision therefore also recognizes Parliament's sovereignty.

The duty in s. 6 is imposed on public authorities. The term 'public authority' is, however, not defined in the HRA. The Act says only that it includes the courts, but not the two Houses of Parliament (s. 6(3)). It includes central government, local authorities, and the police.

Private bodies, such as charities or private companies, may also be treated as public authorities for the purposes of the HRA when they exercise *'functions of a public nature'* (s. 6(3)(b)). As we see in Chapter 17, the meaning of this expression has been considered in several judicial decisions.

Those claiming to be 'victims' of actions (or threatened actions) of public authorities that are unlawful under s. 6 can rely on Convention rights arguments in legal proceedings. If

---

[18] The points mentioned here are dealt with more fully in Chapter 17.

they are successful, the court has a wide range of remedies available, including the ability to award damages (ss 7 and 8).

(d) THE CONSTITUTIONAL IMPACTS

The HRA may have potentially far-reaching—even revolutionary—implications for the United Kingdom's constitutional system, although it is still too early to know what its long-term effects are going to be. It is clear that the HRA is significantly enhancing the role of the judiciary, and that this is generating important questions about 'legal constitutionalism', the separation and balance of powers, and the appropriate scope of the courts' jurisdiction. These issues are discussed at various points throughout this book.

The HRA, the judiciary, and Parliament

The impact of the HRA on the relationships between the judiciary and Parliament, and the judiciary and the executive, has been considered by the House of Lords Constitution Committee. The following is an extract from the evidence submitted to the Committee by Professor Anthony Bradley, summarizing what he considers to be the major constitutional impacts of the HRA—including, in particular, its effect on parliamentary sovereignty. You will see that Professor Bradley refers to the *Belmarsh* case. This case is considered in detail in Chapter 17.

Anthony Bradley, *Paper to the House of Lords Constitution Committee: Relations Between the Executive, the Judiciary and Parliament*, Sixth Report, Session 2006–07, Appendix 4

27. [. . .A] statement that the sovereignty of Parliament is not affected tells only part of the story, since the HRA extended the jurisdiction of the courts to deal with matters that previously were not arguable before a judge. The duty under the HRA to interpret all legislation where it is possible to do so consistently with the Convention is a much stronger duty than that which previously stemmed from the principle that certain common law rights could not be taken away except by express enactment. The new interpretative duty, together with the possibility of a declaration of incompatibility if an interpretative outcome is not possible, takes the courts into the examination of questions that, apart from the HRA, would have been regarded as political questions. In respect of delegated legislation, the HRA empowers the courts to quash delegated legislation on Convention grounds; this power is similar to, but goes beyond, the long-established power of the courts to quash delegated legislation that is *ultra vires*.

28. Moreover, for a superior court to decide to make a declaration of incompatibility, the court must first have reached a view on the substance [of the meaning of the legislation] [. . .] The fact that the HRA does not give power to the courts to quash primary legislation on Convention grounds is a limitation on the *remedy* that the courts provide, not on the *substance* of what may be argued in court and if necessary decided.

29. This is not to suggest that the new powers entrusted to the courts by the HRA are unsuitable for judicial decision-making. A power to review primary legislation on Convention grounds may indeed be new in the United Kingdom, but such a power is similar to the position in many countries where a court can go further and may set aside legislation that conflicts with the constitution. Under the HRA, a claimant that obtains a declaration of incompatibility

will have secured a considerable victory on the substance of the case. He or she will be well placed to go to Strasbourg if the offending legislation continues in being. Indeed, in practical terms the statutory provision can probably no longer be relied on by the Government, unless either the national law is changed (as happened after the *Belmarsh* case) or the Government is prepared to derogate from the Convention obligation in question.

30. The implications of entrusting the judiciary with greater powers of protecting Convention rights were probably not understood by the public at large when the HRA was enacted, despite the clarity with which the White Paper in 1997 explained the scheme. Given the intentions behind the HRA, and the fact that the jurisdiction of the courts was thereby enlarged to include matters akin to the constitutional enforcement of fundamental rights, it is not surprising that appellate judges have given much time to questions arising under the Act. But I do not consider that the record of these decisions establish a case for either re-considering the scheme of the Act, or supporting allegations that the judges are usurping the authority of the executive or Parliament. In his judgment in the Belmarsh case, Lord Bingham set out the great weight that should be given to decisions of Ministers and of Parliament in matters that involve a pre-eminently political judgment, and said:

> Conversely, the greater the legal content of any issue, the greater the potential role of the court, because under our constitution and subject to the sovereign power of Parliament it is the function of the courts and not of political bodies to resolve legal questions.

He drew attention to the Convention regime for the international protection of human rights, which "requires national authorities, including national courts, to exercise their authority to afford effective protection". On the proportionality of the scheme for detaining foreigners suspected of terrorist involvement indefinitely without trial, Lord Bingham did not accept a submission by the Attorney-General that distinguished between democratic institutions and the courts, saying:

> The Attorney-General is fully entitled to insist on the proper limits of judicial authority, but he is wrong to stigmatise judicial decision-making as in some way undemocratic—[particularly when the court was performing functions assigned to it under the HRA]. [. . .] The 1998 Act gives the courts a very specific, wholly democratic mandate. As Professor Jowell has put it: 'The courts are charged by Parliament with delineating the boundaries of a rights-based democracy'.

31. The review of case-law by the Department for Constitutional Affairs in July 2006 concluded that decisions of the courts had had no significant impact on criminal law or on the Government's ability to fight crime. The HRA had had an impact on the Government's counter-terrorism legislation, but the main difficulties had arisen from decisions of the Strasbourg Court. The Act had had a significant but beneficial effect on the development of policy by central Government. But it had been widely misunderstood by the public and sometimes misapplied, and some 'damaging myths about human rights' had taken root. The Government remained fully committed to the ECHR and HRA, but would take steps to give new guidance to departments on human rights, would take a proactive approach to human rights litigation, and would make efforts to inform the public about the benefits of the HRA and to debunk myths that had grown up around Convention rights.

32. This appraisal of the HRA has not, however, always been reflected in the reaction of some Ministers to decisions by the courts. A later section will examine some difficulties that have arisen from the response of Ministers to judicial decisions.

33. The question discussed in this section has been: 'In what ways has the HRA affected the constitutional balance between Parliament, the executive and the Judiciary?' In summary, my answer is that, so far as the protection of rights guaranteed by the ECHR is concerned, the HRA has vested new powers in the courts to determine the limits of those rights and to decide whether those rights have been respected by public authorities (including the executive) and whether legislation by Parliament (whenever enacted) is compatible with those rights. The HRA has created a new form of judicial review of legislation, and new grounds for the review of executive decisions, thus enabling judicial decisions to be made on human rights claims. However, when primary legislation is concerned, ultimate legislative authority remains with Parliament, acting on the proposal of the executive. This new form of protection for human rights is exactly that envisaged by the framers of the HRA. The effects of the Act have often been misunderstood both in some political quarters, in the media, and by the public at large. Some recent criticisms of the judiciary may have come about because of a failure to understand the constitutional implications of the HRA.

Professor Bradley looks more closely at the sovereignty of Parliament in his chapter in *The Changing Constitution*. In this, he explains why he believes the principle to be more a matter of form than substance when human rights issues are involved.

Anthony Bradley, 'The Sovereignty of Parliament: Form or Substance?',
in J. Jowell and D. Oliver (eds) *The Changing Constitution*, 7th edn (2011, Oxford: OUP), p. 65

Although a declaration of incompatibility 'does not affect the validity, continuing operation or enforcement of the provision in respect of which it is given', a court that makes such a statement will have scrutinized the legislation closely against the Convention jurisprudence, and will explain the reasons for incompatibility. The court will in effect have found that someone's Convention rights have been infringed because of the statutory provision in question. It would be surprising if that person did not immediately consider having recourse to the European Court of Human Rights. Even if the Human Rights Act 1998 states that the offending legislation continues in force, in practice it may become inoperative, for the reason that every time it is applied, others affected by it may wish to have recourse to Strasbourg. As the Home Secretary stated in the House of Commons,

> One of the questions that will always be before Government, in practice, will be, 'Is it sensible to wait for a further challenge to Strasbourg, when the British courts have declared the provision to be out with the Convention?'

While therefore the courts have not acquired the power to strike down an Act of Parliament, the courts may under the Human Rights Act 1998 deliver a wound to Parliament's handiwork that is likely to prove fatal, even though life support for it must be switched off by the government or by Parliament, not by the courts.

Against this background, it is difficult to accept without qualification the many statements that judges and ministers have made asserting that the sovereignty of Parliament is not affected. [. . .]

> QUESTION
>
> While Professor Bradley may be right to say that the HRA empowers the courts to deliver potentially fatal wounds to legislation, it does not follow that Parliament's sovereign power lacks substance. After all, Parliament can withdraw the power that it has conferred at any time. It can repeal or amend the HRA—and it may have a good deal of public and political support were it to do so. Discuss.

The HRA, the judiciary, and the executive

Turning to the impact of the HRA on the relationship between the judiciary and the government, we now draw on the report of the House of Lords Constitution Committee, *Relations Between the Executive, the Judiciary and Parliament*. In this extract, the Committee notes how the HRA has contributed to increasing tension between the judiciary and the executive. While some believe this to be damaging and unwelcome, others consider it to be both inevitable and potentially beneficial.

House of Lord's Constitution Committee, *Relations Between the Executive, the Judiciary and Parliament*, Sixth Report, Session 2006–07, ch. 2 (footnotes omitted)

31. [. . .T]he nature of the relationship between the executive and the judiciary has changed substantially since the Constitutional Reform Act (CRA) and the Human Rights Act (HRA) were passed. The CRA was intended to represent a move away from the traditional "fusion" model of the British constitution and towards [. . .] a more explicit separation of powers [model . . .] it would not be unreasonable to expect that such profound structural changes, with the judiciary assuming a more distinct identity, would lead to increased tensions between these two branches of the state.

32. The impact of the HRA upon the relationship between the executive and the judiciary has been equally significant. As Professor Anthony Bradley argued in his paper, "the HRA extended the jurisdiction of the courts to deal with matters that previously were not arguable before a judge [. . . and] takes the courts into the examination of questions that, apart from the HRA, would have been regarded as political questions" (Appendix 4). Similarly, Professor Vernon Bogdanor has predicted that "issues which, in the past, were decided by ministers accountable to Parliament will now come to be decided by the courts". Charles Clarke MP, the former Home Secretary, agreed that the HRA had "shifted the balance of power towards the judiciary" The possible ways of resolving the tensions that this change has created, particularly with regard to anti-terrorism legislation, are discussed later [. . .].

33. Summing up the way in which the role of the judiciary has changed in recent years, Professor Kate Malleson wrote, "the senior judges are now required to police constitutional boundaries and determine sensitive human rights issues in a way which would have been unthinkable forty years ago. This new judicial role is still developing, but [. . .] the effect of this trend will be to reshape the relationship between the judiciary and the other branches of government" (Appendix 3).

Strained Relationships?

34. None of the witnesses doubted that there had been periods of strain in the relationship between the executive and judiciary in recent years. Opinion was however divided on whether these tensions should so far as possible be avoided, or whether they should be accepted as part of the new checks and balances of modern constitutional life. Charles Clarke told us that "there is a constitutional tension which is not properly resolved and which it would be beneficial to resolve" and Paul Dacre, editor of the *Daily Mail*, believed that "the relationship between the executive and the judiciary has become a story and it is possibly creating a gladiatorial sense about some of the reporting that might be causing anxieties on the judicial side".

35. By contrast, Sir Igor Judge, [then] President of the Queen's Bench Division, thought that "a degree of tension is healthy". The former Lord Chancellor, Lord Mackay of Clashfern, agreed with this: "a certain degree of tension between the judiciary and the executive is inevitable and healthy because from time to time the judiciary are called upon to adjudicate under the judicial review procedure and in other ways on actions of the executive, and there are not many people who completely welcome their activities being judged, particularly if they are found to have failed". Indeed, he felt that "the present situation between the judiciary and the executive is in fact quite a good relationship; I do not think that, generally speaking, the relationship is in crisis or anything of that sort".

36. Lord Bingham of Cornhill, the senior Law Lord, took a similar approach in a recent speech, stating that "there is an inevitable, and in my view entirely proper, tension between the two [branches]". He also explained that the tension "is greater at times of perceived threats to national security, since governments understandably go to the very limit of what they believe to be their lawful powers to protect the public, and the duty of the judges to require that they go no further must be performed if the rule of law is to be observed".

Managing the Tensions

37. Whether or not the current levels of tension in this relationship are predictable and in general acceptable, they nevertheless have to be managed and kept in proportion if public confidence is to be maintained in the independence of the judiciary and the integrity of government. The Lord Chancellor, with his traditional position as a "bridge" between the executive and the judiciary, has a particular responsibility to ensure that neither the government as a whole nor individual ministers exacerbate these tensions inappropriately [. . .].

QUESTIONS

1. Over what issues might the HRA have generated tension between the judiciary and the executive?

2. What are the positive and negative aspects of tension between the judiciary and the executive?

3. Would you expect politicians or judges to be more anxious to resolve tension in the relationship? Why do you think this?

(e) TENSION OR DIALOGUE[19]

Interestingly, while the extract focuses on the way in which the HRA may have increased tensions between judges and government, many commentators argue that the HRA—and, indeed, similar rights instruments in other jurisdictions—far from increasing tension, have led to greater constitutional dialogue between the courts, the legislature, and the executive.

It has been claimed that the HRA has encouraged the legislature and the executive to learn from judgments on rights issues so that judges have been able to play a greater role in the constitutional system. Francesca Klug, for example, has commented that the HRA's great innovation is that it enables courts to participate in and generate debate about rights. Courts, she argues, can raise arguments of fundamental principle that are relevant to wider debates in society, although they cannot resolve these debates. One of the main opportunities provided by the HRA for the judges to participate in this way is by the use of declarations of incompatibility. These declarations enable judges to tell the executive that, having heard its arguments, they consider the legislation to conflict with rights. This, in turn, may trigger a fast-track procedure by which the executive can amend the Act of Parliament by passing delegated legislation if it wants to do so; or a bill may be introduced if primary legislation is thought more appropriate. This, it may be argued, encourages a form of conversation—or even partnership—between the three branches of government.[20]

QUESTION

At various points in the book we assess whether it is more accurate to view the relationship between the judiciary and the other institutions of the state (Parliament and government) as one of tension or of partnership. Which of these possibilities do you currently consider to be a) the more appropriate, or b) the more beneficial?

At this point in the chapter you may want to read a short case study on how the UK government responded to the decision of the ECtHR in the prisoner voting case, *Hirst (No. 2) v UK*. The study illustrates some of the issues that have been explored in the chapter and provides a backdrop for our later discussion of a possible UK Bill of Rights and reform of the ECtHR.

6 CASE STUDY: PRISONER VOTING: *HIRST V UK (NO. 2)* AND ITS AFTERMATH

In this case study we summarize the aftermath of *Hirst v UK (No. 2)*.[21] In this case the Grand Chamber of the ECtHR held that UK legislation preventing all convicted prisoners from voting in elections is contrary to the ECHR. This decision was unwelcome by the UK government and was unpopular across a broad cross-section of MPs. So much so that over many

---

[19] See further Chapter 17.

[20] See F. Klug, 'The Human Rights Act: A "third way" or a "third wave Bill of Rights"' [2001] EHRLR 361, discussed by Tom R. Hickman, 'Constitutional dialogue, constitutional theories and the Human Rights Act 1998' [2005] Public Law 306, 308–9. See also Kavanagh, A. *Constitutional Review under the UK Human Rights Act*, (2009, Cambridge University Press) Tom Hickman, *Public Law after the Human Rights Act* (2010, Hart Publishing) and further literature referred to in Chapter 17.

[21] Application no. 74025/01.

years the UK government failed to introduce legislation implementing the decision, despite severe criticism from the Joint Committee on Human Rights (a body of the UK Parliament) and the Council of Europe's Committee of Ministers (the body responsible for ensuring that States implement decisions of the ECtHR).

From the perspective of the ECHR a failure to implement a decision of the ECtHR is a breach of the Convention and flouts the rule of law.[22] Others involved in the saga will see things rather differently. From the point of view of many in Parliament, the saga reflects the democratic power of a national legislature not to be forced to adopt law (especially, some would say, 'European law') that is considered to be wrong and unacceptable.

However the issues are viewed, the saga provides graphic insight into why the relationship between the United Kingdom and the ECtHR matters and is so contentious; and helps to explain why so much attention has been placed in recent years on the power of that Court. The episode also helps to explain some of the attitudes to reform of the HRA and the possible introduction of a Bill of Rights. More broadly, it also raises important questions about the relationship between courts and politicians. [23]

The existing UK law is contained in s. 3 of the Representation of the People Act 1983, which provides: '(1) A convicted person during the time that he is detained in a penal institution in pursuance of his sentence ... is legally incapable of voting at any parliamentary or local election.' The disqualification does not apply to persons imprisoned for contempt of court (s. 3(2)(a)) or to those imprisoned only for default in, for example, paying a fine (s. 3(2)(c)).

Section 3 re-enacted the provisions of s. 4 of the Representation of the People Act 1969. These dated back to the Forfeiture Act 1870, which in turn reflected earlier laws relating to the forfeiture of certain rights by a convicted 'felon' dating back to the time of King Edward III. The Representation of the People Act 2000 permitted remand prisoners and unconvicted people detained under the mental health legislation to vote.

Successive governments have taken the view that prisoners convicted of crimes warranting a sentence of imprisonment have lost the moral authority to vote. This view has been supported by many politicians, across a broad political spectrum.

In *Hirst v UK (No. 2)*[24] the Grand Chamber of the ECtHR held (by a majority of 12 to 5) that s. 3 breached the right to vote in Art. 3 of the First Protocol to the ECHR: It said that: '*Such a general, automatic and indiscriminate restriction on a vitally important Convention right had to be seen as falling outside any acceptable margin of appreciation*'.

The decision of the Grand Chamber was delivered on 30 March 2004. Note that the Court did not decide that prisoners could not be prevented from voting. What is unlawful is the imposition of a ban that is applied automatically to all prisoners irrespective of their crime or their circumstances. While the Court indicated that States have a 'margin of appreciation', imposing an automatic and indiscriminate ban on the right to vote could not fall within that margin. This was an aspect of the decision that the UK government found particularly difficult to accept.

The decision clearly meant that s. 3 was incompatible with the ECHR and had to be amended or repealed.

[22] On the rule of law, see Chapter 3.

[23] There are some excellent blogs commenting on the issues in this saga: e.g. the UK Constitutional Law Group's blog by: Colm O'Cinneide: Prisoners' Votes (Again) and the 'Constitutional Illegitimacy' of the ECHR http://ukconstitutionallaw.org/2012/06/03/colm-ocinneide-prisoners-votes-again-and-the-constitutional-illegitimacy-of-the-echr/; Jeff King: Should prisoners have the right to vote? http://ukconstitutionallaw.org/2011/05/18/jeff-king-should-prisoners-have-the-right-to-vote/

[24] Application no. 74025/01.

The UK government responded by commencing a public consultation on prisoner voting. That consultation initially ended in March 2007. Possibly because the consultation revealed significant support for reform, rather than using the results of the consultation to formulate a legislative response to the *Hirst (No. 2)*, the government instead embarked on a second more detailed consultation, the outcome of which was not published until April 2009.[25] By this point the Labour Government had accepted that: '*to meet the terms of the [ECtHR] judgment a limited enfranchisement of convicted prisoners in custody should take place, with eligibility determined on the basis of sentence length*', although it acknowledged that the final decision on the extension of the franchise to convicted prisoners must rest with Parliament.[26]

During the long period of consultation the Joint Committee on Human Rights had asked the government to explain how it was intending to implement the *Hirst No. 2*. In its 31st report of 2007–08 the Committee noted the Government's delay and reiterated the need for urgent action to resolve the issue:

> 62. [. . .] the Government's [. . .] failure to set a concrete timetable for its response raises serious questions about its reluctance to deal with this issue. In our previous reports, we have drawn attention to a number of cases where significant delay in implementation has tarnished the otherwise good record of the United Kingdom in responding to the judgments of the European Court of Human Rights. For the most part, these cases have been legally straightforward, but politically difficult. This case appears destined to join a list of long standing breaches of individual rights that the current Government, and its predecessors, have been unable or unwilling to address effectively within a reasonable time frame. The Government should rethink its approach.
>
> 63. [. . .] If the Government fails to meet this timetable, there is a significant risk that the next general election will take place in a way that fails to comply with the Convention and at least part of the prison population will be unlawfully disenfranchised.[27]

On 3 December 2009 the Council of Europe Committee of Ministers adopted a resolution calling for the UK Government to lift the blanket ban on prisoners voting. In the resolution the Committee of Ministers expressed 'serious concern':

> [. . .] that the substantial delay in implementing the judgment has given rise to a signifi cant risk that the next United Kingdom general election, which must take place by June 2010, will be performed in a way that fails to comply with the Convention; [. . .]

At their meeting on 2–4 March 2010 the Committee of Ministers issued a warning to the UK Government to 'rapidly adopt' measures to enable prisoners to vote in the forthcoming general election.

Despite continuing pressure from the Joint Committee and the Committee of Ministers the legal position remained unchanged and no convicted prisoners were able to vote in the May 2010 election, over six years after the decision of the Grand Chamber.

---

[25] *Voting rights of convicted prisoners detained within the United Kingdom: second stage consultation.* Consultation Paper CP6/09, Ministry of Justice, 8 April 2009. Available at http://www.justice.gov.uk/downloads/consultations/prisoner-voting-rights.pdf/

[26] Ibid. p. 21.

[27] The concerns of the Committee were repeated in its fourth report of 2008–09.

In November 2010 the European Court of Human Rights, in *Greens and MT v UK*,[28] reiterated its decision in *Hirst (No. 2)* and gave the UK six months from the final decision in the case to introduce appropriate legislative proposals. Attempting to appeal against this deadline, the UK government asked for the case to be referred to the Court's Grand Chamber. This request was refused on 11 April 2011 and the six months time limit for new legislation was triggered from that date.

However, we need to go back to 20 December 2010 when the Minister for Political and Constitutional Reform, Mark Harper, told the Commons that the government was finally to propose legislation. This would give offenders sentenced to a custodial sentence of less than four years the right to vote in UK Westminster Parliamentary and European Parliament elections, unless the judge considered this inappropriate when making the sentence.

Following that announcement the Commons debated prisoner voting on two occasions. The first was on 11 January 2011[29] and the second was on 10 February 2011, when an all-day debate took place on the floor of the House of Commons on a motion put forward jointly by Jack Straw (former Labour Party Minister) and David Davis (a Conservative and former Minister for Europe). The motion was:

> That this House, noting that the [ECtHR] commented in *Hirst v. the United Kingdom* that 'it cannot be said that there was any substantive debate by members of the legislature on the continued justification in light of modern day penal policy and of current human rights standards for maintaining such a general restriction on the right of prisoners to vote', and conscious of the treaty obligations of the UK, is of the opinion that (a) legislative decisions of this nature should be a matter for democratically elected lawmakers and (b) that on the merits of the issue, the current policy by which no sentenced prisoner is able to vote except those imprisoned for contempt, default or on remand, is confirmed.

The motion was carried by 234 votes to 22.[30]

The following is an extract from the Standard Note on prisoner voting prepared by Isobel White in the House of Commons Library; the extract summarizes what was said in the debate by the Attorney General and the Shadow Minister for Justice about the nature of the UK's legal obligations. The note also refers to the issue of compensation to prisoners, which was clearly becoming a factor of importance to the government.

Standard Note on Prisoners' voting rights, by Isobel White, House of Commons Library, SN/PC01764 pp 22–23 (footnotes omitted) 26–27.

> The Attorney-General, Dominic Grieve, said the Government would reflect on the views expressed by the House and bring forward proposals in the light of the debate. However, Mr Grieve reminded the House of the United Kingdom's obligations under international law:

---

[28] Applications nos. 60041/08 and 60054/08.

[29] On 17 January 2011 the Court of Appeal decided in *Regina (Chester) v Secretary of State for Justice and Another* (*The Times* 17 January). It was not for the courts to construe existing statutes so as give prisoners a right to vote. This is a task for Parliament. In this instant the legislation patently did not give this right and the judges would have been acting as a legislator. In November 2010 the ECtHR decided *Frodl v Austria* (Application no. 20201/04), holding that prisoners could only be deprived of their right to vote in very limited circumstances.

[30] Government ministers and their official Opposition counterparts abstained from voting.

We are dealing with an international treaty. That international treaty was signed by the United Kingdom Government under the royal prerogative and was laid before both Houses of Parliament for their consideration. The rule that has been long established in this country is that once a treaty has been ratified by the United Kingdom Government through that process, the Government and their Ministers consider themselves to be bound by its terms.

Mr Grieve described the dilemma faced by the Government: 'how can we find a way to persuade the Court to respect the views that the legislature may express without having to withdraw from the Convention or the Council of Europe entirely, which...would not come without cost or consequence for this country.'

Chris Bryant (Shadow Minister for Justice) said the Labour Party supported the European Court of Human Rights but 'as a critical friend.' He argued that 'for the UK to leave the court would be fatally to undermine its authority. It would be to abandon much of Europe to precisely the same disregard of human rights as was evident when the Court was founded', instead the UK 'could seek to reform the Court, steering it away from trying to be a form of supra-national supreme court and quasi-legislature.' Mr Bryant asked the Attorney-General about the compensation that might be awarded to prisoners. Dominic Grieve replied:

All I will say on the issue of compensation is that it is very difficult to know how much compensation might or might not have to be paid. Let us suppose that there were two elections in which the entirety of the sentenced population in the prison system were deprived of the right to vote and they were all to bring a claim. On the basis of there being about 73,000 people in the prison system in that category and on the basis that about £1,000 to £1,500 of compensation and costs might have to be paid, the hon. Gentleman will be able to start to work out what sort of total cost might be involved. Of course, lots of prisoners might decide not to bring a claim, so I must accept that all the Government can do is provide a reasonable guide of the potential for the matter to be very costly.

QUESTION

From this extract how would you summarize the Opposition's attitude to the ECtHR? (on the question of Reform of the ECtHR, see p. 206)

While the vote in the House of Commons was not binding, the government considered it provided a clear indication of the nature and strength of feeling in the House. The vote may have vindicated the government's general approach, but it also indicated that the government could not rely on the House to support its proposed amendment of the law: an issue that was becoming increasingly pressing given the timetable imposed in *Greens and MT.*

In the event, a further case on prisoner voting, *Scoppola v Italy (No. 3)*[31] was referred to the Grand Chamber of the ECtHR and the Court agreed to an extension to the deadline of six months from the date of the judgment in the case. This was delivered by the Grand Chamber on 22 May 2012.

In *Scoppola No. 3* the Grand Chamber confirmed its decision in *Hirst (No. 2)* and reiterated that general, automatic, and indiscriminate restrictions on voting are contrary to the ECHR.[32] However, the Court accepted the UK's argument on the breadth of the margin of

---

[31] Application No. 126/05.
[32] Para. 102 of the judgment.

appreciation: States should have a wide discretion as to how they regulate a ban on prisoners voting 'both as regards the types of offence that should result in the loss of the vote and as to whether disenfranchisement should be ordered by a judge in an individual case or should result from general application of a law'. [33]

Although the decision, predictably, attracted the ire of some sections of the media (the *Daily Mail*, for example saw it as showing 'Contempt for Democracy'), it has been said that the judgment effectively extends an olive branch to the UK government which it would be wise to accept.[34] Not everyone is in favour of a peaceful outcome and on 24 May 2012, David Davis and Jack Straw wrote in the *Daily Telegraph* arguing that the UK must continue to defy Strasbourg on prisoners' votes.

In Parliament Mr Nigel Dodds (Belfast North) (DUP) asked the Prime Minister whether he would: 'give an undertaking that he will not succumb to the diktat from the European Court of Human Rights in relation to prisoners voting, that he will stand up for the resolution that was agreed in this House by an overwhelming majority and that he will stand up for the sovereignty of this House and the British people?'

The Prime Minister replied[35]:

> The short answer to that is yes. I have always believed that when someone is sent to prison they lose certain rights, and one of those rights is the right to vote. Crucially, I believe that it should be a matter for Parliament to decide, not a foreign court. Parliament has made its decision, and I completely agree with it.[36]

Note that on 27 June 2012, when the House of Lords Reform Bill was introduced in the House of Commons, the Deputy Prime Minister made the following statement:

> I am unable to make a statement of compatibility under section 19(1)(a) of the Human Rights Act 1998 in respect of the House of Lords Reform Bill. This is only because of clause 6, which applies to House of Lords elections the laws on entitlement to vote at House of Commons elections, including the rules which prevent prisoners serving sentences from voting. The Government nevertheless wishes the House to proceed with the Bill.

On 22 November 2012, just before the deadline, the government published the Voting Eligibility (Prisoners) Draft Bill setting out three options: a ban for prisoners sentenced to four years or more; a ban for prisoners sentenced to more than six months; a ban for all convicted prisoners. The Bill was to be considered by a joint Committee of both Houses. The Council of Europe's Committee of Ministers welcomed the Bill but noted that the third option, 'cannot be considered compatible with the European Convention on Human Rights'. (Decision of the Committee of Ministers, 4-6 December 2012.) It decided to resume consideration of the matter, at the latest, at its September 2013 meeting.

[33] European Court of Human Rights Press release, 22 May 2012.

[34] Joshua Rozenberg, Law Society Gazette, opinion, Thursday 31 May 2012. Cited by Colm O'Cinneide: Prisoners Votes (Again) and the 'Constitutional Illegitimacy' of the ECHR. UK Constitutional Law Blog

[35] The Prime Minister had earlier commented that the prospect of implementing a decision of the Strasbourg Court enabling prisoners to vote made him 'physically ill': HC Deb., vol. 517, col. 921 (3 November 2010).

[36] 23 May 2012: HC Deb., col. 1127.

QUESTIONS

1. How would you respond to those who say that this saga displays the ECtHR's contempt for democracy?

2. What, if anything, does this saga tell us about the UK's attitude to the rule of law?

3. Who should have the final say on whether there should be a blanket ban on prisoner voting—a court or Parliament? Does it matter that the court is an international rather than a domestic court?

4. Does the saga suggest that the relationship between courts and government is one of conflict or dialogue?

5. What would be the outcome should the UK continue to defy the ECtHR and the Committee of Ministers?

7 THE HUMAN RIGHTS ACT UNDER CHALLENGE

The HRA has always been controversial. From the outset, there were some who considered it too weak and the rights protected too limited; others considered it unnecessary or undesirable. These controversies have continued at various levels. Among academic commentators, as we have seen, there has been on-going debate between legal constitutionalists and political constitutionalists over whether the HRA is moving too much power to legal mechanisms and away from political processes. Among politicians much critical discussion of the HRA continues to be influenced by a Euro-sceptic view that sees the HRA as a vehicle for imposing European law on the UK. As we have seen, the Prime Minister, perhaps responding to those in his own party who take such a view, famously commented that the prospect of implementing judicial decisions that would give some prisoners the right to vote at elections makes him feel 'physically ill'.[37] The decision of the UK Supreme Court in *R(F) v Secretary of State for the Home Department*[38] (to the effect that sex offenders must be given the right to challenge their entry on the sex offenders register) is unlikely to have pleased him or many backbench MPs either. Criticisms of the HRA have been reinforced by the way individual cases have been reported in the media and especially in newspapers that have been hostile to the HRA, claiming that the HRA is a charter for the undeserving.

As we saw earlier, similar fears about the misuse of rights have existed since the earliest days of the ECHR.

In the next extract, the Parliamentary Joint Committee on Human Rights summarizes some of the criticisms made of the Act and its response to them.

Parliamentary Joint Committee on Human Rights, Sixth Report, Session 2007–08

3. The Human Rights Act reached the statute book ten years ago, with the support of all the main political parties. Today it is under threat. It is frequently and inaccurately derided in the tabloid press as a charter for terrorists, criminals and illegal immigrants. The Leader of the Opposition [David Cameron, now the Prime Minister] has even called on a number of

---

[37] HC Deb., vol. 517, col. 921 (3 November 2010).
[38] [2010] UKSC 17.

occasions for the Act to be repealed. Calls from a high level for the Human Rights Act to be repealed or substantially modified first gained momentum in the wake of the infamous Anthony Rice case, in which the Government followed the media in asserting that the Human Rights Act had been responsible for the tragic death of Naomi Bryant because it had required her killer to be released. We inquired carefully into the matter to ascertain if this was true and established that there was no evidence that Naomi Bryant had been killed as a result of officials misinterpreting the Human Rights Act. Despite our clear finding, however, both the Government and the media have continued to repeat the unfounded assertion that the Human Rights Act caused the death of an innocent woman. Similarly, before that, the Human Rights Act had not been responsible for the provision of a takeaway meal to a prisoner making a rooftop protest or the provision of pornography to a serial killer in prison (an application which, in any case, failed): unfortunately the catalogue of mythology continues to grow.

4. [. . .] All politicians have a duty to act responsibly in relation to the protection of human rights and should not use the Human Rights Act as a convenient scapegoat for unpopular decisions, when they are usually nothing to do with human rights or the Human Rights Act. It is essential that Ministers refrain in future from misleading the public by continuing the practice of blaming the Human Rights Act for judicial or other decisions with which they disagree or which embarrass them. [. . .]

8. In our judgment the Government has done nowhere near enough over the past decade to use the Human Rights Act as a tool to improve the delivery of public services. This failure has contributed to the poor public image of the Act and 'human rights' in general. We challenge the Government to improve this situation. [. . .]

10. Human rights apply to everyone, from the elderly in the health care system, adults with learning disabilities and the victims of trafficking, to groups which attract less public support. Prisoners and asylum seekers also have rights which, though sometimes limited, must be respected. We repeat human rights are universal. They help protect us all from abuses of state power as well as violent crime, such as terrorism; they provide a powerful vehicle to improve public services; and they ensure that the most vulnerable people in society are not overlooked. Police suspects, prisoners and migrants are highly vulnerable and their human rights—the rights to a fair trial, or not to be subjected to inhuman treatment for example—assume a greater importance as a result. A democratic society must respect the human rights of all, if it is to be worthy of the description.

QUESTIONS

1. Are you convinced by what the Committee has to say?
2. What more could the government do to improve the image of the HRA?

8 A BRITISH BILL OF RIGHTS?

By the general election in May 2010 each of the three main UK political parties had proposed the introduction of a UK Bill of Rights. The Labour government had said that while it was proud to have introduced the HRA[39] there is need for a new Bill that would reflect both

[39] Ministry of Justice, *Governance of Britain*, Cm 7170, July 2007.

rights and responsibilities. This could include the rights that are protected by the HRA and the common law or it could sit alongside these, possibly with a wider range of rights such as social and economic rights.[40] Before the election the Conservative Party was in favour of replacing the HRA with a new Bill of Rights, but not one adding a further level of rights.[41] The Liberal Democrats said that they would introduce a Bill of Rights as part of a written constitution.[42]

Following the election the Coalition government indicated its intention to review the need for a British Bill of Rights. Unsurprisingly the Coalition does not speak with a single voice on this issue. While the Liberal Democrats have tended to favour extending human rights protection in the UK, the Conservatives are much more divided over both the HRA and the prospect of a Bill of Rights. Given such divisions, reform is likely to be highly contentious. With that in mind, the government decided to establish a commission to consider the matter and in March 2011 the Commission on a Bill of Rights was set up. Its terms of reference are to:

> investigate the creation of a UK Bill of Rights that incorporates and builds on all our obligations under the European Convention on Human Rights, ensures that these rights continue to be enshrined in UK law, and protects and extend our liberties. It will examine the operation and implementation of these obligations, and consider ways to promote a better understanding of the true scope of these obligations and liberties.

The Commission is also charged with providing advice on reform of the ECtHR. The Commission is to report by the end of 2012.[43]

The Commission published a discussion paper in August 2011 which asked some key questions, including: 'Do we need a UK Bill of Rights? If so, what should it contain? How should it apply to the UK as a whole, including to England, Northern Ireland, Scotland and Wales?' The paper attracted over 900 responses. [44] The Commission embarked on a second consultation in July 2012. In this it summarized the findings of the first consultation as follows:

Commission on a Bill of Rights, *A Second Consultation*, July 2012

> 10. Of the respondents to our first consultation paper approximately a quarter advocated a UK Bill of Rights; just under half opposed such a Bill; with the remainder being neither clearly for nor against such a Bill.

---

[40] Ministry of Justice, *Rights and Responsibilities: Developing Our Constitutional Framework*, Cm 7577, March 2009.

[41] Nick Herbert MP, 'Rights without responsibilities: A decade of the Human Rights Act', Lecture to the British Institute of Human Rights, 28 November 2008.

[42] Liberal Democrat Party Policy Paper, *For the People, By the People*, September 2007.

[43] The Commission is chaired by Sir Leigh Lewis, a former Permanent Secretary to the Department of Works and Pensions and is made up of 'human rights experts'. Initially there were eight members; seven lawyers, and one non-lawyer, four of whom were nominated by the Conservatives and four nominated by the Liberal Democrats. They were: Martin Howe QC (principally a commercial lawyer); Anthony Lester QC (a leading human rights lawyer); Jonathan Fisher QC (tax and criminal fraud); Helena Kennedy QC (a leading human rights lawyer); Anthony Speaight QC (commercial lawyer); Phillipe Sands QC (international lawyer); Sir David Edward (former judge of the ECJ). Michael Pinto-Duschinsky, the only non-lawyer member (a political scientist) resigned from the Commission in March 2012 and was replaced by Lord Faulks QC.

[44] These can be found on the Commission's website: http://www.justice.co.uk/about/cbr/consultation-prog.

11. A variety of models for a UK Bill of Rights were envisaged both by those advocating, and by those opposing, such a Bill. In particular, a section of those who were against a Bill of Rights opposed it because they considered that a UK Bill of Rights would be "HRA (Human Rights Act) minus", whilst a proportion of those supporting such a Bill did so because they envisaged it as building on the Human Rights Act by the inclusion of additional rights.

12. Views were expressed by opponents of a UK Bill of Rights in particular that the Human Rights Act 1998 was already a legally enforceable bill of rights and that it was working well, and that, even if it had flaws, a UK Bill of Rights was not the answer because it would pose risks to rights protections in the UK. These risks, in the view of some, stemmed from a political motivation to dilute human rights protections and to reduce the powers of the European Court of Human Rights.

13. Some respondents, in particular in Northern Ireland, Scotland and Wales, were also concerned that any attempt to introduce a UK Bill of Rights at this time could have adverse constitutional and political consequences for the UK, particularly if it were undertaken to the exclusion of a Bill of Rights for Northern Ireland or if it were undertaken without regard to the implications of the independence debate in Scotland. It was also argued by many of these respondents that there was little or no call for a UK Bill of Rights from people in Northern Ireland, Scotland or Wales. It was also argued by some that the protection of rights was now a matter for the devolved legislatures rather than for the UK Parliament. We discuss these issues later in this paper.

14. Finally, some respondents thought that, even if there were problems or perceived problems with the Human Rights Act, or its adjudication by the courts, there were other ways to address these, such as improved public education, and through amendments to the Human Rights Act or to other existing statutory or regulatory provisions.

15. Views were expressed by those who favoured a UK Bill of Rights that the Human Rights Act was negatively perceived, that it often resulted in decisions that were unpopular, and that a UK Bill of Rights would increase public confidence in the legal protection of their civil rights and liberties against the misuse of public powers.

16. Others who favoured a UK Bill of Rights thought that such a Bill would provide an opportunity to distance our fundamental rights from the European label which they have under the European Convention on Human Rights. Some believed that such rights should be called fundamental or constitutional rights and could be written in language that better reflected their UK heritage. Some thought such rights should be entrenched as part of a written constitution while others thought that it would be sufficient for such a bill of rights to be declaratory.

17. Either way, it was viewed by many of these respondents that a UK Bill of Rights would have an important symbolic and emotional appeal to the public that they believed that the Human Rights Act has lacked. Some also thought that a UK Bill of Rights would provide an opportunity to create or enshrine other constitutional rights and give them the same status as Convention rights.

18. [. . .] we have reached no decisions on what we might recommend on the issue of a UK Bill of Rights. But through this consultation paper we want to provide a further opportunity to hear your views on the issue of whether changes to the existing arrangements are needed and whether a UK Bill of Rights might be desirable, in particular by seeking views on the main arguments that have been put to us opposing or supporting a UK Bill of Rights. [. . .]

Amongst the questions posed in the second consultation were these:

Q1:   What do you think would be the advantages or disadvantages of a UK Bill of Rights? Do you think that there are alternatives to either our existing arrangements or to a

UK Bill of Rights that would achieve the same benefits? If you think that there are disadvantages to a UK Bill of Rights, do you think that the benefits outweigh them? Whether or not you favour a UK Bill of Rights, do you think that the Human Rights Act ought to be retained or repealed?

Q2: In considering the arguments for and against a UK Bill of Rights, to what extent do you believe that the European Convention on Human Rights should or should not remain incorporated into our domestic law?

Q3: If there were to be a UK Bill of Rights, should it replace or sit alongside the Human Rights Act 1998?

Q4: Should the rights and freedoms in any UK Bill of Rights be expressed in the same or different language from that currently used in the Human Rights Act and the European Convention on Human Rights? If different, in what ways should the rights and freedoms be differently expressed?

Q5: What advantages or disadvantages do you think there would be, if any, if the rights and freedoms in any UK Bill of Rights were expressed in different language from that used in the European Convention on Human Rights and the Human Rights Act 1998?

Q6: Do you think any UK Bill of Rights should include additional rights and, if so, which? Do you have views on the possible wording of such additional rights as you believe should be included in any UK Bill of Rights?

Q7: What in your view would be the advantages, disadvantages or challenges of the inclusion of such additional rights?

Q8: Should any UK Bill of Rights seek to give guidance to our courts on the balance to be struck between qualified and competing Convention rights? If so, in what way?

Q10: Should there be a role for responsibilities in any UK Bill of Rights? If so, in which of the ways set out above might it be included?

QUESTIONS

1. Were you to have responded to these questions, what answers would you have given?

2. The Commission has given its answers to these questions. (*A UK Bill of Rights? - The Choice Before Us*, 18 December 2012, see further: Recent Developments, page xv.) What are these answers? Do you agree with them?

Reform of the ECtHR

One of the tasks of the Commission on a Bill of Rights is to advise on reform of the ECtHR. A number of issues arise. The most obvious are concerned with the immediate need to improve the ability of the Court to handle its massive caseload. There are also issues to do with the authority and power of the Court. Partly as a consequence of prisoner voting issue, high on the government's agenda has been the desire to reduce the influence of the Court.

Opportunity to reform the ECtHR arose at the high-level Conference on the Future of the European Court of Human Rights in Brighton in April 2012, which was the culmination of the United Kingdom's chairmanship of the Council of Europe's Committee of Ministers (a role that is shared by members of the Council of Europe in rotation). Prior to the conference the government had prepared a draft of what was to become the Brighton Declaration. That draft aimed to reduce the influence of the court. For instance it proposed that the Court should not deal with cases that are the 'same in substance' as those already dealt with by a national court, unless the national court has 'seriously erred' or the case raises a 'serious question'. The draft also stressed the 'margin of appreciation' enjoyed by states to depart from decisions of the Court (remember the importance of this issue in the prisoner voting saga). These proposals, however, were not ultimately accepted and the Brighton conference did not substantially weaken the Court.

In the following extract Mark Elliott explains why the standing of the ECtHR is important in relation to the HRA within the UK. He also links the outcome of the Brighton conference with proposals to introduce a Bill of Rights. His concluding comments point to the need to think holistically about the interrelationships between the formal and actual role of the HRA within domestic law and influence of the ECtHR.

Mark Elliott, After Brighton: between a rock and a hard place [2012] Public Law 691, 621–628 (footnotes omitted)

By exercising an interpretative function that results in (at least [some]) definitional precision, and by applying the Convention rights in a way that yields legally binding judgments, the ECtHR confers upon those rights a degree of concrete prescriptiveness that transcends the quasi-aspirational nature of some international human rights instruments. [. . .] from the perspective of the effectiveness of domestic human rights protection . . . the Strasbourg Court . . . occupies a pivotal position. Behind a British judicature lacking constitutional authority to invalidate rights-incompatible legislation stands an international tribunal willing and able to render judgments that are binding upon the UK as a matter of international law. Indeed the very possibility of recourse to the ECtHR invests domestic courts' judgments concerning the compatibility of primary legislation with a practical force that far outstrips their formally declaratory character. [. . .] The authority of [the ECtHR's judgments] is implicitly enhanced by the fact that they reflect a judicial conclusion that executive action fails to measure up against benchmarks that are, in an important sense, non-negotiable [. . .] In this way, the Convention rights assume the character (viewed from a UK perspective) of an unusually hard legal constraint upon both the administrative and legislative branches. [. . .] the existing institutional dimension of the ECHR regime confers upon the Convention rights a degree of binding force that is both unusual for an international human rights instrument, and which renders the HRA a stronger constraint than it would otherwise be. [. . .] reducing the practical extent of the European Court's role [. . .] might, [. . .] diminish the HRA as a real constraining force. Equally, it might carve out scope for a Bill of Rights constituting a looser restraint upon the political branches, while formally honouring the commitment, recorded in the Bill of Rights Commission's terms of reference, to continue to enshrine the Convention rights in domestic law. [. . .] The Declaration that emerged from the Brighton Process [. . .] incorporates measures that are intended to address the Court's serious caseload problem: for instance, the window of opportunity for applying to the Court will be reduced from six months to four. But the final version of the Declaration leaves undisturbed the fundamental nature of the relationship between the Court and national authorities.[45] [. . .]

---

[45] E.g. The margin of appreciation is no longer said to be 'considerable'; it is merely something to which the Court must have 'due regard' (Brighton Declaration para. 11); the proposal to amend the admissibility criteria in Article 35 has been dropped and the ECtHR will not be so easily displaced if the matter has already been addressed by a domestic tribunal. (Brighton Declaration paras 14–15).

The upshot, then, is that the essential characteristics of the Convention regime, and of the Court's role within it, are preserved by the final version of the Brighton Declaration: and so, in turn, the potency of the HRA is maintained.

Before leaving the Bill of Rights, let us briefly consider why some who are committed to human rights protection might be sceptical about the benefits of a Bill of Rights, even one that potentially extends the scope for legal protection of rights. The following short extract by Professor Klug explains why she is sceptical about introducing a Bill of Rights in the present political climate.

Francesca Klug, 'A Bill of Rights: Do we need one or do we already have one?' [2007] Public Law 701, 717–19

[. . .] The really difficult challenge is not to seek perpetually for the promised land but to bed down what has already been achieved. That means liberating human rights from the law courts and lawyers and returning them to where they came from; the struggles of people in their every day lives from abuse of power and their quest for equality, dignity and fair treatment. It means rebutting false stories; promoting good ones and speaking about human rights in plain English. It means working with grass roots campaigns and sometimes for unpopular causes, building common ground through the values we can all share.

   Thomas Jefferson, the third president of the United States, once said "a bill of rights is what the people are entitled to against every government on earth". But it is worth remembering the words of another wise constitutionalist, Justice Learned Hand, who said: "Liberty lies in the hearts of men and women; when it dies there, no constitution, no law, no court can save it". Or as Alice might have said to the Mad Hatter: "Yes it *is* possible to have less". A bill of rights which is based-not on the principles of universal human rights-but on chauvinism and nationalism, would be *much* less than we have now.

ONLINE RESOURCE CENTRE

There is much speculation as to what the Commission will recommend and whether it will be able to reach a consensus. Whatever its recommendations, they will be subject to further consultation and reforms are unlikely before the next election. Please see Recent developments at the beginning of this book. To keep up to date with developments consult the Online Resource Centre.

9 THE EUROPEAN UNION AND HUMAN RIGHTS

When the European Community was established and the Treaty of Rome signed in 1957 the extent to which Community law would affect individuals was unclear. Initially, the Treaty was economic and inter-governmental, [46] and so fundamental rights were not included. But from the late 1960s, the European Economic Community generally, and the European

[46] See Chapter 7.

Court of Justice (ECJ) in particular, came under increased pressure from national courts (especially in Germany and Italy) to recognize fundamental rights. National courts found themselves in the difficult position of having to uphold fundamental rights protected by their national constitution and also give effect to the European Court of Justice's supremacy doctrine. This stipulates that Community law prevails over national law (even national constitutional law) when they conflict.[47]

The ECJ indicated that fundamental rights would be protected in the Community order in a case called *Stauder*.[48] The ECJ went on to secure fundamental rights in *Internationale Handelsgesellschaft*.[49] Although it did not allow national courts to judge Community law against principles of national constitutional law, the ECJ held that fundamental rights formed an integral part of Community law. In later cases, the ECJ recognized three legal sources for fundamental rights.[50] First, they were part of the 'general principles' of Community law which the ECJ had to guarantee. Second, they were drawn from the common constitutional traditions of the Member States, which would help guide the ECJ; finally, the ECJ would consider international human rights instruments, such as the ECHR. In short, the ECJ developed a jurisprudence of fundamental rights in order to ensure that national courts accepted the supremacy principle.

Paul Craig, *EU Administrative Law*, 2nd edn (2012, Oxford: OUP) 449

Prior to the Charter the protection of rights was nonetheless fragmented and piecemeal, thereby making it more difficult for the citizenry to understand the legal status quo.16 Moreover, the very fact that the scope of Community power had increased considerably made the promulgation of some form of Community bill of rights more pressing. It is a basic tenet of liberal democratic regimes that a quid pro quo for governmental power is the existence of rights-based constraints on the exercise of that power. This fundamental idea is just as applicable to the EU as to traditional nation states. Thus even if the ECJ had not been 'pressed' into recognizing fundamental rights by the threat of revolt from the German and Italian courts, it would, in all likelihood, have realized the necessity for such limits on governmental power of its own accord, more especially because it was at that time developing administrative law controls on Community action.

Even after several treaty revisions in the 1990s,[51] there were still few references to fundamental rights in the body of EU law. The following provisions were the most important.

BOX 6.2 GENERAL REFERENCES TO FUNDAMENTAL RIGHTS PRIOR TO THE LISBON TREATY

- Art. 6(2) TEU (Treaty of Maastricht 1992): 'The Union shall respect fundamental rights, as guaranteed by the European Convention on Human Rights and as they

---

[47] See Chapter 11.
[48] Case 26/69 *Stauder v City of Ulm* [1969] ECR 419.
[49] Case 11/70 *Internationale Handelsgesellschaft mbH v Einfuhr- und Vorratsstelle für Getreide und Futtermittel* [1970] ECR 1125.
[50] Case 4/73 *Nold v Commission* [1974] ECR 491.
[51] See Chapter 11.

> result from the constitutional traditions common to member states as general principles of Community law';[52]
>
> - Art. 6(1) TEU (Treaty of Amsterdam 1997): 'The Union is founded on the principles of liberty, democracy, respect for human rights and fundamental freedoms, and the rule of law, principles which are common to the Member States'.
>
> These provisions were backed up by a sanctions procedure in Art. 7 TEU, that was also introduced by the Treaty of Amsterdam, whereby a Member State's rights could be suspended if it engaged in 'serious and persistent breach . . . of principles mentioned in Art. 6(1)'.

Prior to the Lisbon Treaty, the European Union did not have legal personality, and so could not itself become a party to the ECHR. As the ECJ opined: 'No Treaty provision confers on the Community institutions any general power to enact rules on human rights or to conclude international conventions in this field'.[53] But the Lisbon Treaty allows the EU to do this. One result will be to ensure a parallel interpretation of human rights in the EU and ECHR contexts. Moreover, the EU Charter of Fundamental Rights, first proclaimed at the Nice Inter-Governmental Conference in December 2000, is given legal recognition by the Treaty of Lisbon (although note that the text of the Charter has not been incorporated into the Treaty). This means that for the first time, the EU has set out in one place the existing fundamental rights that can benefit every EU citizen.

Article 6 Treaty of European Union

1. The Union recognises the rights, freedoms and principles set out in the Charter of Fundamental Rights of the European Union . . . which shall have the same legal value as the Treaties.

The provisions of the Charter shall not extend in any way the competences of the Union as defined in the Treaties.

The rights, freedoms and principles in the Charter shall be interpreted in accordance with the general provisions in Title VII of the Charter governing its interpretation and application and with due regard to the explanations referred to in the Charter, that set out the sources of those provisions.

2. The Union shall accede to the European Convention for the Protection of Human Rights and Fundamental Freedoms. Such accession shall not affect the Union's competences as defined in the Treaties.

3. Fundamental rights, as guaranteed by the European Convention for the Protection of Human Rights and Fundamental Freedoms and as they result from the constitutional traditions common to the Member States, shall constitute general principles of the Union's law.

---

[52] The formulation of this provision is clearly drawn from the ECJ's case law.
[53] Recital 27, *Opinion 2/94 re Accession to the ECHR* [1996] ECR I-1759.

The EU Charter of Fundamental Rights (the Charter) has six sections and covers the whole range of civil, political, economic and social rights of European citizens and all persons resident in the EU. It is 'possibly the most wide-ranging human rights treaty in the world today'.[54] Those sections are: (i) dignity; (ii) freedoms; (iii) equality; (iv) solidarity; (v) citizens' rights; (vi) justice. Some of the rights and freedoms are traditional and familiar (right to life, prohibition of torture) and are borrowed from the ECHR; some (such as the right to a fair trial, the presumption of innocence, and the right not to be punished twice for the same offence) are important and necessary legal safeguards that the EU must protect as it moves towards greater co-operation in criminal justice.[55] The Charter also covers social and economic rights (e.g. the right to fair and just working conditions, and the right to a family and professional life), as well as modern safeguards for the twenty-first century (the right of access to information in relation to the EU institutions, and the protection of personal data).

Ian Ward, *A Critical Introduction to European Law*, 3rd edn (2009,Cambridge: Cambridge University Press), 47

It is all reasonably familiar, and so are all the attendant problems of interpretation and meaning. What, for example, does 'human dignity' mean? And what does the 'right to life' mean? In what jurists term 'hard cases', where there is no clear moral certitude, it is quite possible for such rights to be in direct contradiction. Does the 'right to life' forbid abortions? Does the right to 'human dignity' require that women have a right to abort? Charters of rights rarely provide answers, just lots of different interpretations and opinions. In the end the politicians lost their nerve, and so we do not need to immerse ourselves in the darker mists of moral philosophy in search of answers; at least not yet. Like Banquo's ghost, the anticipated guest of honour who was rudely despatched along the way, the Charter was, between the Friday evening and the Monday morning of the Nice IGC, demoted from grand vision to passing aside. It eventually emerged rather apologetically in the form of a Declaration.

Following Ward's comments, the Charter represents another autonomous source of human rights law that will generate its own cases, meanings, and interpretations. After all, it has been promoted from a political 'Declaration' to a legally binding 'Charter' by the Lisbon Treaty, which also gives it the same legal status as the EU Treaties. This suggests that it may be recognized or interpreted in new ways by the ECJ.

That said, Art. 6 TEU states that the Charter may not be used to extend the competences of the Union. Moreover, Art. 52(3) of the Charter requires the ECJ to interpret fundamental rights cases in conformity with ECHR (subject to the caveat that Union law can provide more extensive protection, although the ECJ has tended to follow the Strasbourg court's interpretation of the ECHR in its own case law). Finally, it must be noted that the rights under the Charter apply *only* in two situations: first, in relation to the activities of EU institutions (e.g. the European Commission, European Parliament, and the Council of the EU); and second, when EU law is implemented into national law by the Member States. In other words, the Charter does not create new and general fundamental rights for citizens to challenge legislative, executive, or private actions.

---

[54] Damian Chalmers, 'Viewpoint: EU Won't Rule by Charter', BBC *Inside Europe*, 21 November 2009.
[55] See Chapter 11.

The Charter thus upholds the rule of law idea by making the exercise of public power subject to fundamental rights. In that sense, the Charter is a document of *constraint* rather than a new and independent source of power. It is quite possible that the Charter's legal impact will be only minimal.[56] In any case, the interesting questions in future cases are likely to involve a clash of legal sources (national constitutional, or European Union, or ECHR) in the determination of individual rights. It is a real possibility that inconsistent decisions will emerge from the ECJ and the European Court of Human Rights.

The United Kingdom, Poland, and the Czech Republic negotiated interpretations of the Lisbon Treaty that are described in their Protocol (annexed to the Treaty). The UK is concerned about the ECJ's ability to force changes to its labour law and Poland is concerned about same-sex marriage and abortion. It is important to note that the Protocol is *not* an opt-out! The Charter will be applied by UK courts, although the Protocol limits the justiciability of the Charter and the way it may be interpreted. The President of the Czech Republic, Vaclav Klaus, also negotiated an opt-out from the Charter designed (to prevent property claims by Germans expelled from Czechoslovakia after World War II) as a condition for signing the Treaty late in 2009.

Protocol on the Application of the Charter of Fundamental Rights of the European Union to Poland and to the United Kingdom

Article 1

1. The Charter does not extend the ability of the Court of Justice of the European Union, or any court or tribunal of Poland or of the United Kingdom, to find that the laws, regulations or administrative provisions, practices or action of Poland or of the United Kingdom are inconsistent with the fundamental rights, freedoms and principles that it reaffirms.

2. In particular, and for the avoidance of doubt, nothing in Title IV of the Charter creates justiciable rights applicable to Poland or the United Kingdom except in so far as Poland or the United Kingdom has provided for such rights in its national law.

Article 2

To the extent that a provision of the Charter refers to national laws and practices, it shall only apply to Poland or the United Kingdom to the extent that the rights or principles that it contains are recognised in the law or practices of Poland or of the United Kingdom.

10 CONCLUDING COMMENTS

This chapter has examined the development and nature of constitutional rights. The issues covered are developed further in other chapters in this book—in particular, in Chapter 17 on using human rights in domestic courts.

---

[56] Lord Goldsmith, 'The Charter of Rights: A Brake Not an Accelerator' (2004) 5 European Human Rights Law Review 473–478.

11 FURTHER READING

Bates, E., *The Evolution of the European Convention on Human Rights From its Inception to the Creation of a Permanent Court of Human Rights* (2010, Oxford: OUP)

Bradley, A.W., 'Relations between executive, judiciary and Parliament: An evolving saga? [2008] Public Law 470

Clayton, R., and Tomlinson, H., *The Law of Human Rights* (2000, Oxford: OUP)

Hickman, T., Public Law after the Human Rights Act (2010, Oxford: Hart Publishing)

Janis, M., Kay, R., and Bradley, A., *European Human Rights Law, Text and Materials*, 3rd edn (2008, Oxford: OUP)

Kavanagh, A., *Constitutional Review under the UK Human Rights Act* (2009, Cambridge, Cambridge University Press)

Steiner, H.J., Alston, P., and Goodman, R., *International Human Rights in Context*, 3rd edn (2008, Oxford: OUP)

Wadham, J., Mountfield, H., Edmundson, A., and Gallagher, C., *Blackstone's Guide to the Human Rights Act 1998*, 5th edn (2009, Oxford: OUP)

Young, A.L., *Parliamentary Sovereignty and the Human Rights Act* (2009, Oxford: Hart Publishing)

WEBSITES

UN Human Rights Council	http://www2.ohchr.org/english/bodies/hrcouncil/
European Court of Human Rights	http://www.echr.coe.int/echr/
European Union and human rights	http://europa.eu/pol/rights/index_en.htm
	http://www.consilium.europa.eu
Ministry of Justice	http://www.justice.gov.uk/whatwedo/humanrights.htm
UK Parliamentary Joint Committee on Human Rights	http://www.parliament.uk/parliamentary_committees/joint_committee_on_human_rights.cfm
Equality and Human Rights Commission	http://www.equalityhumanrights.com/

ONLINE RESOURCE CENTRE

Further information about the themes discussed in this chapter can be found on the Online Resource Centre at www.oxfordtextbooks.co.uk/orc/lesueur2e/

PART II

EXECUTIVE FUNCTIONS

INTRODUCTION TO EXECUTIVE FUNCTIONS

CENTRAL ISSUES

1. The 'executive functions' carried out by various bodies will be examined in Chapter 7, Chapter 8 and Chapter 9. As we saw in Chapter 4 in relation to the concept of separation of powers, in very broad terms, the 'executive function' may be defined as the powers of government to decide issues of policy, to raise and spend public money, and to implement decisions. Our focus is on the institutional and legal frameworks that make these activities possible.

2. Constitutions have a twin role in relation to executive functions: they *enable* executive action (by providing institutional and procedural frameworks for decision-making) and they also *constrain* it (to ensure that it stays within what is permitted by law and to make governments accountable for their actions).

3. One persistent theme is that there is, in the United Kingdom, an imbalance of power. Critics say that UK central government controls Parliament too much. Reforms are being introduced to allow the UK Parliament to have better opportunities to call ministers to account.

4. Another theme is the fragmentation of executive functions. In recent decades, some aspects of executive power have moved from UK central government to the 'devolved administrations' in Scotland, Wales, and Northern Ireland (as we saw in Chapter 5). Executive power has also moved from UK central government to the institutions of the European Union (and we examine this in Chapter 8).

1 FACTS AND THEMES

This Introduction to Part II is an overview of the main ideas and facts that will be covered in Chapter 7 ('Government and accountability in the United Kingdom'), Chapter 8 ('Exercise and control of executive power in the European Union'), and Chapter 9 ('Prerogative powers').

(a) WHAT IS THE 'EXECUTIVE FUNCTION'?

An obvious starting point is to work out what is meant by the 'executive function'. Consider carefully what Professors Craig and Tomkins say in the following extract.

Paul Craig and Adam Tomkins, 'Introduction', in P. Craig and A. Tomkins (eds) *The Executive and Public Law* (2006, Oxford: OUP), p. 1

Executive power is the power of governments. It is the legal authority vested in, and exercised by, for example, prime ministers, presidents, cabinets, and councils. It is the political power that all those who embark on a career in politics dream of wielding. It is the power to set policy, to take action, and to implement the law. In the great theory of the separation of powers that has hovered over western constitutional thinking since the mid eighteenth century, the preserve of the executive is to *do*. While the role of the legislature is to speak and that of the judiciary is to judge, governments *act*.

Few would deny that, at the opening of the twenty-first century, governments have become the most powerful organs of nation states. They determine the direction, if not always the detail, of domestic policy. They decide how public money should, and should not, be spent. Foreign policy is made almost entirely by governments. And control of military power is likewise the preserve of the executive. Whatever the truth of the claim that, in this era of apparent globalization, states are no longer the only or even the most powerful units of political power, within nation states governments still retain very considerable power. This is not to say that their power can never be checked. Governments may rule, but they do not always rule supreme. In democracies the personnel of the executive is subject to the verdict of the electorate; the policies of the executive may be subject to political or parliamentary accountability; and the legality of executive action may be reviewed by the courts of law.

In relation to the United Kingdom, executive functions are not carried out by a single institution. We cannot point a finger at, say, the Prime Minister and say 'executive functions are vested in him'. We will see in Chapter 7 that a range of official bodies throughout the United Kingdom are, as a matter of law or constitutional convention, responsible for carrying out executive functions. The same is true of the European Union: we see in Chapter 8 that executive functions are dispersed, with the Council (consisting of members of the governments of member states) and the Commission (consisting of Commissioners—almost always politicians and politically neutral officials). In order to understand the significance of this dispersal of functions, it is helpful to go back to the idea of multilevel governing introduced in Chapter 5. There, we saw the debate over the future of the centralized nation state.

As we explore in some detail in Chapter 7, the United Kingdom can be said to have a system of 'parliamentary government' (meaning that ministers who give political leadership to 'the executive' *must* be members of one or the other of the Houses of Parliament). As Professor Munro explains in the following extract, this does not mean that Parliament *governs* in the sense of carrying out executive functions. The UK Parliament does, however, have a key role in *scrutinizing* the exercise of executive functions.

Colin R. Munro, *Studies in Constitutional Law*, 2nd edn (1999, London: Butterworths), pp. 324–5 (footnotes omitted)

As John Stuart Mill said, 'there is a radical distinction between controlling the business of government, and actually doing it'. England had unhappy experience of a Parliament's efforts to govern the country in 1648 and 1649 when the Long Parliament proved to be so inefficient, intolerant, and meddlesome, as to provoke Cromwell's further intervention. That experience was perhaps in Mill's mind when he expressed the view that a representative assembly was 'radically unfit' to govern. In practice, the parliamentary body is not organised in such a way as would enable it to execute foreign policy or implement domestic policies. When it is said that we have 'parliamentary government', this must be understood as referring not to government by Parliament, but by an executive drawn from and accountable to Parliament.

QUESTIONS

1. Look at a serious British newspaper. Identify five specific things that the UK government can be said to be 'doing', according to the journalists. What kind of legal powers authorize each of the actions that you have identified?

2. Look at the summaries of the various levels of government set out later—UK central government, the devolved administrations, and institutions of the EU—and look back at the discussion in Chapter 5. Which level, in your opinion, is the most powerful? What is your definition of 'power' in this context?

3. Look back at Chapter 5. Which level of government do you think is responsible for deciding what the policy should be on the following and then implementing that policy?

(a) The immigration rules that regulate entry to the United Kingdom.

(b) Setting income tax.

(c) What, if any, tuition fees can be charged to university students.

(d) The acceptable level of pollution on beaches.

(b) WHAT IS THE ROLE OF A CONSTITUTION IN RELATION TO EXECUTIVE FUNCTIONS?

As Craig and Tomkins explain in the first extract (Paul Craig and Adam Tomkins, 'Introduction' on p. 218), the executive function involves determining public policy (domestic and foreign), allocating public finance (raised by taxation or borrowed), and controlling military force. But what is the role of a constitution in this context? The answer is one that we have examined several times before—namely, that there is dual aspect to constitutions.

- They *enable* governments by providing a framework for policymaking and implementation—we want governments to be able to take action in the public interest.
- A constitution also seeks to *constrain* executive power—ensuring that executive functions are carried out in accordance with the rule of law and in an accountable way.

Looking at executive functions from this perspective, it is possible to identify several overlapping 'constitutions', as follows.

(i) There is, first, the uncodified constitution of the whole of the UK, in which both law and constitutional conventions are important. Critics suggest that the uncodified nature of the UK constitution and its heavy reliance on convention create an insufficiently robust set of constraints on the power of government. Looked at from the other side of the coin, we can say that the principle of parliamentary supremacy is strongly *enabling* of the UK government—because a government that has a majority in the House of Commons will often find it possible to develop and implement policies without rigid rules on how the process takes place or the content of the policies. (You may find it helpful to look back at the survey of the debate between 'political constitutionalists' and 'legal constitutionalists' at the start of Chapter 2.)

(ii) The treaties on which the European Union (EU) is founded—the Treaty on European Union (TEU) and the Treaty on the Functioning of the European Union (TFEU)—can be regarded as providing a constitutional framework for the operation of the EU institutions and their relationship to member states.

(iii) The 'devolution Acts'—the Scotland Act 1998, the Northern Ireland Act 1998, and the Government of Wales Act 2006—provide a framework for the operation of the devolved governments.

(c) ASYMMETRY IN THE UK CONSTITUTION

When thinking about executive functions in the United Kingdom, it is important to keep in mind that the policy of devolution has led to new executive bodies being created in Scotland, Wales, and Northern Ireland, *but not in England*. As we saw in Chapter 5, government proposals to create regional governments in different parts of England were abandoned when it became clear in a referendum that there was no public appetite for such a development. Only London has regional government, in the form of the Greater London Authority (GLA) and the Mayor of London.

2 GOVERNMENTS AT A GLANCE

This section contains a summary of the basic constitutional and legal aspects of the various executive bodies considered in Chapter 7, Chapter 8, and Chapter 9.

BOX II.1 THE GOVERNMENT OF THE UNITED KINGDOM

Figure II.1 No. 10 Downing Street   © Oversnap/istockphoto.com

Name: Her Majesty's Government (HMG) or 'central government'. The terminology of 'the Crown' may also be used in some contexts.

Main websites: http://www.number10.gov.uk/ and http://www.cabinetoffice.gov.uk/. Every department and executive agency has its own website.

Head of government: The Prime Minister (who also hold the title 'First Lord of the Treasury').

Other members of government:

- Chancellor of the Exchequer
- Secretaries of State (no fixed number; in recent years, approximately sixteen)
- Lord Chancellor
- Junior ministers

Collective meetings of the government: In the Cabinet, usually on Thursday mornings at No. 10 Downing Street, but may meet at other times and places. Numerous Cabinet committees meet at other times.

Source of legal powers: Acts of Parliament; prerogative powers (in relation to some executive functions); 'the third source'.

Sources of legal advice:

- The Attorney General and Solicitor General, collectively known as 'the Law Officers', in relation to whole-UK, and England and Wales legal matters (online at http://www.attorneygeneral.gov.uk/).
- The Advocate General for Scotland in relation to issues of Scottish Law (online at http://www.oag.gov.uk/oag).

- The Advocate General for Northern Ireland (same person as the Attorney General of England and Wales—see Justice (Northern Ireland) Act 2002) advises on issues of Northern Ireland law.
- The Government Legal Service (online at http://www.gls.gov.uk/), including the Treasury Solicitor's Department (online at http://www.tsol.gov.uk/).
- The First Treasury Counsel (colloquially known as 'the Treasury Devil'), a barrister in private practice who is instructed to represent the government in the most important litigation and to advise on matters of legality.

Principal government departments: These may be reorganized and renamed by the Prime Minister from time to time. In September 2012, the main departments were:

- Her Majesty's Treasury;
- the Department for Work and Pensions;
- the Department of Health;
- the Department of Education;
- the Ministry of Defence;
- the Department for Communities and Local Government;
- the Home Office;
- the Department for Transport;
- the Department for Business, Innovation and Skills;
- the Department for International Development;
- the Ministry of Justice;
- the Department for Environment, Food and Rural Affairs;
- the Foreign and Commonwealth Office;
- the Department for Culture, Media and Sport; and
- the Department for Energy and Climate Change.

Executive agencies: Most departments have several agencies that implement policy and deliver services—for example, the Department of Transport (based in London SW1, near to Parliament and No. 10 Downing Street) has six executive agencies:

- the Driving Standards Agency (headquarters in Nottingham);
- the Driver and Vehicle Licensing Agency (based in Swansea);
- the Vehicle Certification Agency (based in Bristol);
- the Vehicle and Operator Services Agency (Bristol);
- the Highways Agency (eight offices around England); and
- the Maritime and Coastguard Agency (Southampton).

Non-departmental public bodies (NDPBs): Bodies acting at 'arm's length' from ministers may have executive functions; ministers are accountable for their work to Parliament. For example, the Department of Transport sponsors the following NDPBs:

- the British Transport Police Authority;
- the Northern Lighthouse Board;
- the Rail Passengers Council;
- the Renewable Fuels Agency; and
- Trinity House.

Civil service: The Home Civil Service; the Diplomatic Service.

BOX II.2 THE SCOTTISH GOVERNMENT

Name: The Scotland Act 1998, s. 44, created 'the Scottish Executive', also referred to as 'the Scottish Ministers'; it was formally renamed 'the Scottish Government' by the Scotland Act 2012.

Figure II.2   Scottish Government Building, Victoria Quay, Leith, Edinburgh

Main website: http://www.scotland.gov.uk
Head of government: The First Minister (Scotland Act 1998, ss 45–47)
Other members of government:

- *'The First Minister may, with the approval of Her Majesty, appoint Ministers from among the members of the Parliament'*: Scotland Act 1998, s. 47

- Junior ministers: Scotland Act 1998, s. 49

- The Lord Advocate and the Solicitor General for Scotland: Scotland Act 1998, s. 44

Source of legal powers: The Scotland Act 1998, as amended by the Scotland Act 2012, provides a constitutional framework; other powers stem from Acts of the UK Parliament and Acts of the Scottish Parliament; some specific prerogative powers.

Sources of legal advice: The 'Scottish Law Officers'—the Lord Advocate and Solicitor General for Scotland (Scotland Act 1998, s. 48).

Principal government departments:

- Health and Well-being
- Finance and Sustainable Growth
- Education and Lifelong Learning
- Justice
- Rural Affairs and the Environment

Civil service: '*The Scottish Ministers may appoint persons to be members of the staff of the Scottish Administration*'; those staff '*shall be service in the Home Civil Service*' (Scotland Act 1998, s. 51).

BOX II.3 THE WELSH ASSEMBLY GOVERNMENT

Figure II.3 The Welsh Assembly Government Building at Cathays Park, Cardiff

Name: The Welsh Assembly Government (*Llywodraeth Cynulliad Cymru*), established by the Government of Wales Act 2006, s. 45.

Main websites: http://wales.gov.uk

Head of government: The First Minister (Government of Wales Act 2006, ss. 46–47).

Other members of government: (Limited to fourteen members in total)

- The Welsh Ministers (*Gweinidogion Cymru*): Government of Wales Act 2006, s. 48.
- The Deputy Welsh Ministers (*Dirprwy Weinidogion Cymru*): Government of Wales Act 2006, s. 50.
- The Counsel General to the Welsh Assembly Government (*Cwnsler Cyffredinol i Lywodraeth Cynulliad Cymru*): Government of Wales Act 2006, s. 49.

Source of legal powers: The Government of Wales Act 2006 provides a constitutional framework; various Acts of the UK Parliament; Assembly Measures.

Sources of legal advice: The Counsel General to the Welsh Assembly Government and lawyers in the Legal Services Department.

Principal government departments:

- Heritage
- Social Justice and Local Government
- Public Health and Health Professionals
- Environment, Sustainability and Housing
- Constitutional Affairs, Equality and Communication
- Rural Affairs
- Public Services and Performance
- Economy and Transport
- Health and Social Services
- Children, Education, Lifelong Learning and Skills

Civil service: '*The Welsh Ministers may appoint persons to be members of the staff of the Welsh Assembly Government*'; '*Service as a member of the staff of the Welsh Assembly Government is service in the Home Civil Service*' (Government of Wales Act 2006, s. 52).

BOX II.4 THE NORTHERN IRELAND EXECUTIVE

© Robert Mayne/istockphoto.com

Figure II.4 Stormont, Northern Ireland Executive and Assembly

Name: The Northern Ireland Executive—strictly speaking the 'Executive Committee' of the Northern Ireland Assembly (see Northern Ireland Act 1998, s. 20: '*There shall*

be an Executive Committee of each Assembly consisting of the First Minister, the deputy First Minister and the Northern Ireland Ministers').

Main websites: http://www.northernireland.gov.uk/

Heads of government: The First Minister and Deputy First Minister: Northern Ireland Act 1998, s. 16.

Other members of government: The First Minister and the Deputy First Minister acting jointly determine the number and the functions of 'ministerial offices' (Northern Ireland Act 1998, s. 18) and junior ministers (Northern Ireland Act 1998, s. 19).

Source of legal powers: The Northern Ireland Act 1998 provides a constitutional framework; Acts of the UK Parliament; Acts of the Assembly; *'the prerogative and other executive powers of Her Majesty in relation to Northern Ireland shall be exercisable on Her Majesty's behalf by any Minister or Northern Ireland department'* (Northern Ireland Act 1998, s. 23).

Sources of legal advice: The Attorney General for Northern Ireland (Justice (Northern Ireland) Act 2002) and staff.

Principal government departments:

- Office of the First Minister and Deputy First Minister
- Department of Agriculture and Rural Development
- Department of Culture, Arts and Leisure
- Department of Education
- Department for Employment and Learning
- Department of Enterprise, Trade and Investment
- Department of the Environment
- Department of Finance and Personnel
- Department of Health, Social Services and Public Safety
- Department for Regional Development
- Department for Social Development

Civil service: Northern Ireland Civil Service

7

GOVERNMENT AND ACCOUNTABILITY

CENTRAL ISSUES

1. Tony Benn MP famously asks five 'democratic questions' of people who have power: what power do you have? Where did you get it? In whose interests do you exercise it? To whom are you accountable? How can we get rid of you? These are pertinent questions for constitutional lawyers.

2. Government at national level in the United Kingdom includes: monarchy; ministers; civil servants; and people appointed to public office.

3. A constitutional assessment of government needs to consider both the legality of power and its legitimacy. The concept of accountability has become a central aspect of legitimacy. In a parliamentary system such as the United Kingdom, Parliament plays a central role in securing accountability.

4. Parliament itself does not exercise executive functions, but ministers are *required* to be members of either the Commons or the Lords in order to be held accountable for their policies and actions. A legal cap on the number of ministers is designed to prevent the government from dominating Parliament, but the government has considerable control through party 'whips' and its power to control what is debated.

5. Since the eighteenth century, executive power has moved from the monarch to ministers. The monarch's role is limited to one of being consulted, to encourage, and to warn ministers. 'The Crown' is a multi-faceted concept that is not easy to define.

6. 'The Secretary of State', the most senior type of minister, exercises most statutory powers. The Prime Minister and the Cabinet are 'creatures of convention' rather than established by an Act of Parliament.

7. The vast majority of executive actions are taken not by ministers but by politically neutral civil servants.

8. Constitutional conventions (rather than law) require ministers to be accountable to Parliament. These include the convention of individual ministerial responsibility (ministers are answerable to Parliament) and the convention of collective responsibility (ministers cannot publicly disagree with government policy). The precise scope of these conventions is not

settled; in particular, there are difficulties over the extent to which civil servants should be directly answerable for the exercise of executive powers.

9. Parliament has developed a variety of practical mechanisms for holding ministers to account, including: debates; select committees; and parliamentary questions.

1 INTRODUCTION

In Chapter 4, we examined the idea of executive power in a fairly abstract way (thinking about the concept of separation of powers and the extent to which that principle applies in the UK constitution). The present chapter returns to the idea of executive power, but now we look at it in a more concrete way, focusing on the people and processes that comprise government in the United Kingdom. At first sight, the array of office-holders and institutions can seem like a bewildering machine (see Figure 7.1).

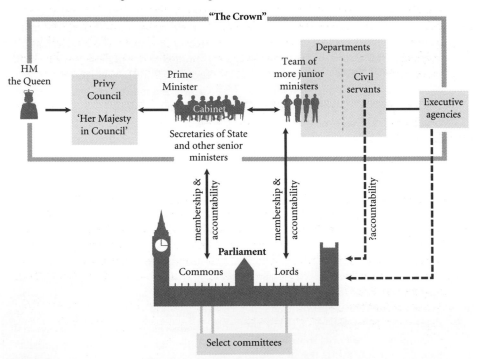

Figure 7.1 Institutions of UK government

To simplify matters, so that we can focus on key questions, the chapter considers (a) the monarchy, (b) ministers, and (c) civil servants, as well as (d) holders of appointed public offices.

Tony Benn was a Labour MP for fifty years[1] and served as a minister in Labour-led governments in the 1970s. During a debate on the controversial European Parliamentary Elections Bill, he referred to the 'five democratic questions' that he has often presented in his writing and oratory.

House of Commons Hansard, 16 November 1998, col. 319

The House will forgive me for quoting five democratic questions that I have developed during my life. If one meets a powerful person...one can ask five questions: (i) what power do you have; (ii) where did you get it; (iii) in whose interests do you exercise it; (iv) to whom are you accountable; and, (v) how can we get rid of you?

These are indeed pertinent constitutional questions. In thinking about government, constitutional lawyers need to address the 'what power?' and 'where did you get it?' questions. In most countries, the answers would start with 'those powers conferred by the Constitution'. In the absence of a codified constitution in the United Kingdom,[2] a longer answer is needed: in general terms, those who govern have such powers as are conferred by Acts of Parliament, prerogative powers (in the case of some ministers and the monarch), and the common law.[3] The chapters in Part II will continue to map these out in more detail.

The remaining questions—in whose interests, to whom accountable, and how removed from office—relate to the idea of legitimacy. In a good constitution, it is not enough for those who govern to say 'the law gives us power to govern' (*legality*); they must also implicitly or expressly make a claim as to why their powers to govern ought to be accepted, and that claim must be accepted by most of the people most of the time. This is the idea of *legitimacy*.

Andrew Le Sueur, 'People as "users" and "citizens": the quest for legitimacy in British public administration' ch.3 in Matthias Ruffert (ed), *Legitimacy in European Administrative Law* (2011, Groningen: Europa Law Publishing), p. 30 (footnotes omitted)

Many academic studies of legitimacy of public authority preface their analysis with a warning that the concept of legitimacy is 'problematic' or 'contested'. [...C]onditions of legitimacy may encompass normative and empirical perspectives. Normative perspectives seek to provide moral reasons for citizen's acceptance of, acquiescence in or engagement with government decision-making: what entitles a public authority to act? Empirical perspectives seek to measure people's sentiments—their opinions and beliefs—about governance: why people accept (if they do) that a public authority is entitled to act.

Conditions of legitimacy exist if, for good reason, people have confidence in administrative processes and respect and accept decisions of public authorities, even though they may

---

[1] Benn campaigned for the right of hereditary peers to renounce their titles. While an MP, on his father's death he inherited a peerage and therefore (at the time) the right to sit in the House of Lords and was automatically disqualified from the House of Commons for three years during the 1960s until the reform was introduced.

[2] See Chapter 1.

[3] On prerogative and common law powers, see Chapter 9.

disagree with some individual determinations. The notion of 'diffuse support' is important: people may be willing to comply with determinations even when they disagree with them; 'specific support' relates to particular determinations. If conditions of legitimacy exist, winners and losers—in individual decisions and in broader political debates—should accept the outcome. Legitimacy is therefore closely related to, but extends beyond, the idea of public compliance or consent. Compliance in a legitimate system is based on reason and principle not merely 'a matter of lingering habit, or expediency, or necessity'.

Accountability is an important aspect of legitimacy in modern constitutions. As we noted in Chapter 1, it *is a principle which requires public authorities to explain their actions and be subject to scrutiny. It may also entail sanctions, such as resignation from office or censure*.[4] Accountability may take place in the political arena (which is the focus of this chapter) and also in courts—a minister or other public body whose decision is challenged as unlawful in judicial review proceedings can be thought of as being 'legally accountable'.[5]

The legitimacy claims of each element of government rest on different footings.

(a) MONARCHY

Up to the seventeenth century, claims of a 'divine right' to rule as monarch were made and believed by many. In a secular and democratic society, the idea that God has ordained a particular person, or family, to exercise public power is untenable. The legitimacy claim for monarchy now relies on the established usage of the institution: hereditary monarchy enjoys continuity with the past and practical effectiveness. The idea of monarchy is unlikely to appeal to a person designing a new constitution for a new country from scratch, but for the United Kingdom it 'works' (or, at least, that is the normative claim).

Andrew Lansley and Richard Wilson, *Conservatives and the Constitution*
(1997, London: Conservative 2000 Foundation)

Conservatives contest the theory...that the application of reason would make the world intelligible to man and that institutions designed by man in accordance with theoretical principles were the only institutions which would have beneficial consequences...Conservatives reject the notion that it is a simple matter to design a constitution in accordance with abstract principles.

Opinion polls show that an overwhelming proportion of people in the United Kingdom support a constitutional monarchy rather than its main alternative—a directly elected president as head of state.

Routine accountability of the British monarchy is quite limited but does include publishing financial information.[6] As the monarch must act on the advice of ministers, it is ministers who are accountable (to the electorate and in Parliament) for the exercise of 'Crown' powers. As to Benn's final question ('how can we get rid of you?'), the answer is that a

---

[4] See extract Andrew Le Sueur, 'Accountability' in Chapter 1 on p. 28.
[5] See Chapter 16.
[6] Available on http://www.royal.gov.uk/

monarch remains in office so long as he or she has the confidence of ministers. Edward VIII had to abdicate in 1936, when the Prime Minister (Stanley Baldwin) made the government's view plain, that Edward should not marry Wallis Simpson.[7] This was however exceptional. Generally, the monarch cannot be removed from office without sparking a constitutional crisis.

(b) MINISTERS

The legitimacy claim of ministers rests on democratic foundations. The vast majority of ministers are elected to the House of Commons and, like all other MPs, must stand for re-election in their constituencies every five years.[8] They stand for election on the basis of their party's manifesto. The party with the largest number of MPs forms the government (in coalition with another party, if necessary).[9] Ministers remain in office only for as long as they command the 'confidence' of the House of Commons. If an individual minister loses the confidence of the Prime Minister, he or she must resign from ministerial office (and return to the backbenches); if ministers collectively lose the confidence of the House, the whole government must resign. Resignations are, however, rare. More important on a day-to-day basis is the requirement that ministers must be accountable to Parliament for their decisions—through answering oral and written parliamentary questions, justifying the government's stance in debates, and by appearing to be questioned by select committees.

(c) CIVIL SERVANTS

Ministers set the agenda and provide political leadership to government departments. They are assisted in that role by politically non-partisan senior civil servants who (unlike their counterparts in many other constitutional systems) remain in office when the government changes after a general election. Hundreds of thousands of civil servants are also involved in delivering public services and enforcing regulation; this is now usually done through 'executive agencies', which work at arm's length from the departments responsible for policy issues. Civil servants are appointed on merit on the basis of fair and open competition. *The Cabinet Manual* states:[10]

Cabinet Office, *The Cabinet Manual* (2011, London: Cabinet Office), para. 7.1

Civil servants are servants of the Crown. The Civil Service supports the government of the day in developing and implementing its policies, and in delivering public services. Civil Servants are accountable to ministers, who in turn are accountable to Parliament.

So civil servants' legitimacy rests *indirectly* on a democracy-based justification—they are working to implement the policies of the elected government using powers authorized by

---

 [7] See Declaration of Abdication Act 1936 on p. 234.
 [8] Some ministers are unelected members of the House of Lords: see later.
 [9] Rather than working to a single manifesto, a coalition government will publish an agreed programme for government.
 [10] On *The Cabinet Manual*, see Chapter 1.

Parliament (in Acts and other legislation). Very senior civil servants (chief of executive agencies) may also now answer written parliamentary questions posed by MPs, with their replies being printed in *Hansard*. Chief executives and senior civil servants may also be called on to appear before parliamentary select committees to explain policies, defend or apologise for failures, and as 'accounting officers' to answer for the financial stewardship of a department or agency—they do so under the direction and on behalf of ministers.[11] Like other employees, civil servants are also subject to internal reviews and appraisals as part of the normal human resources processes of running an organization. Recently, it has been suggested that ministers should be involved in appraisals for the most senior civil servants in their departments. Civil servants have been known to resign for serious failures and some senior ones have been dismissed.

(d) APPOINTEES TO PUBLIC OFFICE

Senior professional people who are appointed to some specific offices carry out a variety of governing functions. Examples include: the chair of the Competition Commission; the chair of the Commission for Equality and Human Rights; the chair of the Environment Agency; the chair of the Civil Aviation Authority; the Children's Commissioner; and the Governor of the Bank of England. These are high-profile roles that require the office-holder to work independently from ministers because their actions need to be, and seen to be, politically neutral (in the sense that they do not follow instructions from party-affiliated politicians).

For holders of public offices such as these, a legitimacy claim can rest on the fact that they have professional or technical expertise (for example in the fields of transport, energy, health, safety, the environment), which calls to be respected: '*Command and obedience are considered to be legitimate because the power-holder possesses some type of expertise which makes him the person best suited to exercise power.*'[12] Their work is subject to sporadic scrutiny from parliamentary select committees, and to that limited extent they are accountable to Parliament. They all produce annual reports and have informative websites, contributing to 'explanatory' accountability. A minister, advised by experts to ensure that the appointment decision is made on merit, appoints most public office-holders of this type. In an innovation proposed by the government in 2007, a further type of accountability was introduced. Candidates selected by minsters would appear before a relevant House of Commons select committee to be questioned before their appointment is confirmed.[13]

We know turn to look in more detail at these features of government.

2 MONARCH

The United Kingdom is one of several European countries to have a hereditary monarch as head of state: others include Denmark, the Netherlands, Norway, Spain, and Sweden. Queen Elizabeth II (the UK monarch since 1952) is also monarch of fifteen other countries around

---

[11] See extract Scott L. Greer, 'Whitehall' on p. 253.

[12] Craig Matheson, 'Weber and the classification of forms of legitimacy' (1987) 38, The British Journal of Sociology 199, 203. Max Weber (1864–1920) was a sociologist whose work explored how in modern states, legitimacy was increasingly based on 'rational-legal authority'.

[13] See extract House of Commons Liaison Committee, *Pre-appointment Hearings by Select Committees*, on p. 255.

the world, including Australia, Canada, Jamaica, and New Zealand as stipulated by their respective constitutions.

The United Kingdom is described as a 'constitutional monarchy' or having a 'constitutional sovereign', indicating that the monarch's role as head of state[14] is closely circumscribed by rules and practices and that the monarch is able to act only as advised by ministers.

Cabinet Office, _The Cabinet Manual_ 1st edn (2011, London: Cabinet Office) (footnotes omitted)

Ceremonial and constitutional duties

1.1 The Sovereign fulfils a number of ceremonial and constitutional duties relevant to the Government. The Sovereign appoints the Prime Minister and, on his or her advice, other ministers [...] The Sovereign opens each new session of Parliament, and brings the session to an end, proroguing Parliament if necessary by Order in Council. Under the Fixed-term Parliaments Act 2011, Parliament is dissolved automatically 17 working days before the fixed date for the election. Where in accordance with the Act there is to be an early election, the Sovereign fixes the date of the election by Proclamation on the recommendation of the Prime Minister. The Sovereign in all cases fixes by Proclamation the date for the next meeting of Parliament. A bill which has completed all of its prior Parliamentary stages becomes law when Royal Assent (the formal approval of the Sovereign) is given. The Sovereign also appoints the First Minister of Scotland and the First Minister for Wales, and has a role in relation to the Devolved Administrations, as set out in legislation.

1.2 The Sovereign is Head of the Armed Forces. Armed Forces recruits are required to swear an oath of allegiance to the Sovereign (or make a solemn affirmation to the same effect). All titles of honour (for example knighthoods) are conferred by the Sovereign, mostly on the advice of the government of the day, although there are some honours that the Sovereign confers at his or her own discretion. An example would be an Order of Merit. British honours are usually conferred by the Sovereign on the advice of the Cabinet Office, while the Foreign and Commonwealth Office (FCO) advises the Sovereign where honorary decorations and awards are granted to people from other countries.

1.3 As Head of State, the Sovereign undertakes and hosts a number of state visits, helping to build relations with other nations. In addition to the UK, the Sovereign is Head of State of a number of other Commonwealth realms. Her Majesty the Queen is also Head of the Commonwealth, a voluntary association of 54 countries.

(a) HISTORICAL DEVELOPMENT OF MONARCHY

Government based on hereditary monarchy stretches back into the mists of time, but events and ideas in the seventeenth century were particularly important in shaping British understandings of the role of kings and queens. James I (the first monarch of the separate kingdoms of England & Wales and Scotland from 1603) and Charles I (who reigned 1625–49) clashed with Parliament and the courts over the ambit of royal authority, in particular the

---

[14] The Prime Minister is 'head of government'.

power to impose taxation. Charles I attempted to rule without summoning regular meetings of Parliament. In 1642 a bloody civil war began between factions loyal to the king (Royalists) and those against (Parliamentarians). The Parliamentarians won and Charles I was executed in Whitehall as a traitor in 1649. For almost ten years, there was a 'Commonwealth' without a monarch, led by the military under Oliver Cromwell. The Commonwealth was at war with the Dutch and Spanish and spiralled out of control with renewed arguments about powers to levy tax as the Parliamentarian cause splintered. The propertied classes represented in the House of Commons, fearing anarchy, summoned Charles II (the previous king's son) from exile. The monarchy was restored in 1660 and men of influence attempted to forge a new constitutional settlement during Charles II's reign and that of his son, James II (1685–88). They failed: father and son had pretentions to rule as absolute monarchs and James II was a Roman Catholic. James II fled into exile in France amid anti-Catholic riots in London.

In the 'Glorious Revolution' of 1688, the men of influence characterized James II's departure as an abdication, and called on James II's son-in-law and daughter (William III and Mary II—both protestants) to become joint monarchs under conditions laid down by Act of Parliament as the Bill of Rights 1689. The analysis of these events by legal historian F.W. Maitland was, *'it was extremely difficult for any lawyer to make out that what had then been done was lawful'*,[15] but it was the start of a *constitutional* monarchy. The Act of Settlement 1700 provided further restrictions on royal power, including preventing the monarch from removing judges from office unless requested to do so by resolutions passed by both Houses of Parliament. The 1770 Act also specified the line of succession: after the death of Queen Anne (the child of James II and sister of Queen Mary) who became queen in 1702, the Crown would pass to the Electress Sophia of Hanover (in fact, she died before Anne) and her heirs. On Anne's death in 1714, Sophia's son (Anne's second cousin) became King George I.

For the next 222 years the Crown passed from parent to child and monarchs remained in office until their deaths.[16] In 1936, Edward VIII was forced to abdicate: his proposed marriage to Mrs Simpson, an American divorcée, was unacceptable to the government in an era when divorce was morally offensive in polite society. An Act of Parliament gave legal effect to this.

Declaration of Abdication Act 1936

(1) Immediately upon the Royal Assent being signified to this Act the Instrument of Abdication executed by His present Majesty on the tenth day of December, nineteen hundred and thirty-six, set out in the Schedule to this Act, shall have effect, and thereupon His Majesty shall cease to be King and there shall be a demise of the Crown, and accordingly the member of the Royal Family then next in succession to the Throne shall succeed thereto and to all the rights, privileges, and dignities thereunto belonging.

(2) His Majesty, His issue, if any, and the descendants of that issue, shall not after His Majesty's abdication have any right, title or interest in or to the succession to the Throne, and section one of the Act of Settlement shall be construed accordingly.

---

[15] F.W. Maitland, *The Constitutional History of England* (1908, Cambridge: Cambridge University Press) p. 283.

[16] Succession is dictated by common law and various statutory provisions, including the Coronation Oath Act 1689, the Act of Settlement 1700, the Royal Marriages Act 1772, the Accession Declaration Act 1910, the Declaration of Abdication Act 1936, and the Regency Act 1937 (as amended in 1943 and 1953).

The common law dictated, in relation to the descent of the Crown, that male heirs take precedence over females, with children representing their deceased ancestors. In 2011, the heads of government of the sixteen countries that have Queen Elizabeth II as their monarch agreed that order of succession would be determined by order of birth and that a member of the Royal family marrying a Roman Catholic would not be barred from succeeding to the throne. In the United Kingdom, this will be implemented by amending the Royal Marriages Act 1772. The monarch remains under the legal duty to be a protestant.

Accession Declaration Act 1910, *Schedule*

I [here insert the name of the Sovereign] do solemnly and sincerely in the presence of God profess, testify, and declare that I am a faithful Protestant, and that I will, according to the true intent of the enactments which secure the Protestant succession to the Throne of my Realm, uphold and maintain the said enactments to the best of my powers according to law.

(b) THE MONARCH AND MINISTERS

The main characteristic of a constitutional monarchy in the British sense, settled since the end of Queen Victoria's reign, is that the monarch acts only on the advice of ministers. The Prime Minister keeps the monarch closely informed about major political events at weekly 'audiences'. The monarch receives a selection of important government documents on a daily basis, including Cabinet papers and reports from British ambassadors abroad.

Rodney Brazier, 'The Monarchy' in V. Bogdanor (ed.) *The British Constitution in the Twentieth Century* (2003, Oxford: British Academy/OUP), ch. 3, p. 78

A sovereign exercises influence in governmental matters by using conventional attributes famously summarised by Bagehot as the right to be consulted, to encourage and to warn ministers. That formulation has occasionally been rendered as the rights to *advise*, to encourage and to warn, but a sovereign cannot offer advice nor support action, counsel against proposed action without knowing what ministers are doing. Perhaps, therefore, it is more accurate, albeit more prolix, to say that the sovereign has five conventional rights rather than three—to be informed, to be consulted, to advise, to encourage and to warn. A right of information would embrace even those cases where the sovereign is not expected to take any action, but is merely being made aware of what is happening. A right to be consulted, however, necessarily involves the notion that the sovereign may wish to express a view about the subject-matter, or indeed may have to exercise a prerogative power in order to give legal effect to it. Personalities and relationship affected the giving of information and of consultation to a degree.

In relation to matters relating to the Scottish government, the monarch is advised by the First Minister (whom she appoints, in accordance with the terms of the Scotland Act 1998).[17] In relation to matters relating to the Welsh government, the formal position is that the Queen is

---

[17] House of Lords Hansard, 1 July 1999, vol. 603, cols 50–51WA.

advised by ministers in the UK government, although the *'Queen holds audiences from time to time with the First Minister to keep abreast of business in Wales'*.[18]

When the monarch carries out an executive function, she therefore acts *formally*, to confer legal authority on a decision that, in reality, has been taken by someone else. This can be seen clearly in relation to her role in making public appointments. Have a look, for example, at the following statutory provision.[19]

Constitutional Reform Act 2005, Pt 3

The Supreme Court

23—(1) There is to be a Supreme Court of the United Kingdom.

(2) The Court consists of 12 judges appointed by Her Majesty by letters patent.

(3) Her Majesty may from time to time by Order in Council amend subsection (2) so as to increase or further increase the number of judges of the Court.

(4) No recommendation may be made to Her Majesty in Council to make an Order under subsection (3) unless a draft of the Order has been laid before and approved by resolution of each House of Parliament.

(5) Her Majesty may by letters patent appoint one of the judges to be President and one to be Deputy President of the Court. [. . .]

Selecting the Prime Minister

There is one vital act in respect of which the monarch may not be able to rely on ministers' advice: this is where a Prime Minister must be appointed (most commonly, after a general election). Where the result of a general election gives one political party a clear overall majority in the Commons, the convention is straightforward: the monarch invites the leader of that party to become Prime Minister and form the government. The position is more complicated where there is a 'hung' Parliament, in which no single party has an overall majority—as happened after the May 2010 general election. There is academic disagreement about the extent to which the monarch has discretion.

Robert Blackburn, 'Monarchy and the personal prerogatives'
[2004] Public Law 546, 553–4

The appointment of a Prime Minister

Generally of course, there is no issue of royal intervention in prime ministerial appointment. The leader of the party with an overall majority in the Commons is appointed (or remains) Prime Minister. It is 'hung' Parliament situations which have generated much academic speculation (and encouragement) of royal intervention.

In this matter, 'she [the Queen] need not accept advice as to the appointment of a Prime Minister', according to Sir Ivor Jennings. A constitutional authority of a similar view today is Rodney Brazier, Professor of Constitutional Law at Manchester University and the author of

---

[18] http://www.royal.gov.uk/MonarchUK/QueenandGovernment/QueenandWelshAssembly.aspx
[19] On judicial appointments generally, see Chapter 14.

several leading works on the constitution. In his book *Constitutional Practice*, Brazier says, 'there are no rules about government formation from a hung Parliament'. Elsewhere he maintains, echoing Jennings' theorising about the monarch as mediator, that 'the Queen is ideally placed to moderate between any competing wishes of party leaders in a hung Parliament'. As to the political setting in which such mediation/moderation would occur, Brazier's opinion is that, 'the Queen should hear the views in audience of each party leader in turn'.

But it is unreal politically and inappropriate constitutionally to acknowledge—and indeed advocate—a personal discretionary power for an hereditary monarch to operate as the means for determining the outcome of a general election. There needs to be, and is already in existence, an established procedure and basis for the resolution of who will be Prime Minister after a general election that produces a House of Commons with no overall majority for a single party. The true position is as follows:

There is really no problem in establishing the constitutional answer to the question of who is appointed Prime Minister under a hung Parliament. Yet reams of academic speculative theorising, and much hype about 'grey areas' has been generated on the subject, misleadingly suggesting that the Queen will/should/must somehow get involved to mediate/moderate competing claims from party leaders. This is removed from political actuality, and indeed convention.

Rodney Brazier, '"Monarchy and the personal prerogatives": A personal response to Professor Blackburn' [2005] Public Law 45, 45–6 (footnotes omitted)

Appointment of a Prime Minister

Professor Blackburn misrepresents my analysis of how a Prime Minister should be chosen on the return of a hung Parliament. Royal intervention in that event is literally the last thing that should happen in appointing a Prime Minister. The main thrust of my treatment of hung Parliaments, in Ch.3 of *Constitutional Practice*, is to suggest ways in which so far as possible the monarch could be kept out of the process of government-formation. Indeed, I say that '[...] the guiding light ought to be that the political crisis should if possible be resolved by politicians—in a phrase, that there should be political decisions, politically arrived at'. I argue that the monarch should stand back—as she did in February/March 1974—and let the elected politicians decide the shape of the Government in a hung Parliament. I go on to say that '[...] such a guiding light would help to refute any allegation that a non-elected head of state had imposed a particular solution on the elected House instead of allowing that House, through the party leaders, to arrive at a conclusion. It would also enhance the Queen's impartiality as between the political parties and between individuals, which would be crucially important if a political compromise were to prove impossible, when only the Queen could end the political crisis'. Far from encouraging royal intervention, I actually urge the opposite: that the Queen's undoubted legal power to choose a Prime Minister should be used to enhance the democratic process, rather than to pre-empt it. Only if politicians failed to produce a way forward in a hung Parliament—which might be highly unlikely—would any royal action be necessary. It would be then—and only then—that my idea (cited by Professor Blackburn) of the Queen receiving the party leaders in turn might possibly come into play. In that context I say that if a majority coalition Government was proposed, rather than the more usual outcome in a hung Parliament of a minority Government taking office, then such a coalition should be appointed only if the party leaders worked out the details and presented a copper-bottomed agreement to the Queen. Once more I stress the importance of the party leaderships deciding these things. Professor Blackburn represents what I say about royal audiences as being the norm at the start of a hung Parliament, when in fact I discuss them as a process for use if politicians cannot decide themselves what should be done.

Moreover, I advocate this guiding light in the separate case where a Prime Minister, like Wilson in 1976 or Thatcher in 1990, is to resign for personal reasons. The monarch formally does nothing until the Government party has elected a new leader, when the monarch will receive the outgoing Prime Minister's resignation and formally appoint the successor. That process can now surely be classified as a constitutional convention, one which would be followed if (for example) Tony Blair were to retire from No.10. The monarch's role in that sort of case should be as automatic and formal as in the case when the Prime Minister changes following a conclusive General Election.

All that is the opposite of the Queen '[…] operating free from democratic […] control […]', a state of affairs to which Professor Blackburn objects, and one which I actually argue that the monarch can largely avoid. While I am flattered to be grouped with Sir Ivor Jennings, I do not share all his views. What I certainly do say is that a monarch retains reserve powers, and rightly so, for no one can foresee every constitutional twist and turn. It is also true that I posit a number of other exceptional—perhaps even fanciful—situations in which royal intervention in the appointment of a Prime Minister might be unavoidable. But they are so far outside the bounds of probability that I am prepared to live with them.

In the run-up to the May 2010 general election, it seemed quite likely that no party would have a majority. Officials therefore took steps to clarify and state the conventions that would apply. This official statement is now in *The Cabinet Manual*.

Cabinet Office, *The Cabinet Manual*, 1st edn (2011, London: Cabinet Office) (footnotes omitted)

The principles of government formation

2.8 Prime Ministers hold office unless and until they resign. If the Prime Minister resigns on behalf of the Government, the Sovereign will invite the person who appears most likely to be able to command the confidence of the House to serve as Prime Minister and to form a government.

2.9 Historically, the Sovereign has made use of reserve powers to dismiss a Prime Minister or to make a personal choice of successor, although this was last used in 1834 and was regarded as having undermined the Sovereign. In modern times the convention has been that the Sovereign should not be drawn into party politics, and if there is doubt it is the responsibility of those involved in the political process, and in particular the parties represented in Parliament, to seek to determine and communicate clearly to the Sovereign who is best placed to be able to command the confidence of the House of Commons.

As the Crown's principal adviser this responsibility falls especially on the incumbent Prime Minister, who at the time of his or her resignation may also be asked by the Sovereign for a recommendation on who can best command the confidence of the House of Commons in his or her place.

2.10 The application of these principles depends on the specific circumstances and it remains a matter for the Prime Minister, as the Sovereign's principal adviser, to judge the appropriate time at which to resign, either from their individual position as Prime Minister or on behalf of the government. Recent examples suggest that previous Prime Ministers have not offered their resignations until there was a situation in which clear advice could be given to the Sovereign on who should be asked to form a government. It remains to be seen whether or not these examples will be regarded in future as having established a constitutional convention.

(c) THE CONCEPT OF 'THE CROWN'

So far, we have focused on the monarch in person. It is more difficult to define comprehensively the legal and constitutional concept of 'the Crown', as the next extract explains.

Maurice Sunkin, 'Crown', in P. Cane and J. Conaghan (eds) *The New Oxford Companion to Law* (2008, Oxford: OUP), pp. 286–7

The expression 'The Crown' has institutional and symbolic meanings. Institutionally it refers to both the monarch and the executive branch of government, and it symbolizes the formal location of authority within the UK's constitution. In both these senses the Crown presents difficulties for commentators and much disagreement exists as its precise meaning. These disagreements can have important practical constitutional implications, not least because the Crown (in its institutional sense) possesses significant privileges and immunities, including from judicial process.

First, then, the Crown in its institutional sense: Lord Diplock said that 'the Crown' means 'the government' and includes 'all of the ministers and parliamentary secretaries under whose direction the administrative work of government is carried on': *Town Investments Ltd v Department of the Environment* (1978). Professor Sir William Wade considered this 'extraordinary'. He wrote that '[I]n truth, "the Crown" means simply the Queen, though the term is usually confined to her political or constitutional capacity' (M. Sunkin and S. Payne (eds), *The Nature of the Crown* (Oxford: Oxford University Press, 1999), 24). There can be no doubt that 'the Crown' extends to the monarch in her official capacity, but it is impossible to confine the Crown to the Queen. In particular, this is because circumstances exist in which the Crown's powers are exercised by ministers as agents of the Crown, so that their decisions are decisions of the Crown. Examples include the exercise of the prerogative of mercy by the Home Secretary and the disposition of the armed forces by the Prime Minister and the Secretary of State for Defence.[20] However, such situations are comparatively rare and most powers exercised by ministers are not Crown powers but powers conferred upon ministers specifically, usually by statute. In such situations ministers are members of Her Majesty's Government and serve the Crown: but they do not act as the Crown itself. For this reason, while Lord Diplock's statement may be colloquially correct, it is almost certainly inaccurate from a strictly legal perspective.

Turning to the Crown in its symbolic sense: in their leading textbook on Constitutional Law, Professors Bradley and Ewing say that: 'It is still formally the case that executive power in the United Kingdom is vested in the Crown however little this may reflect the reality of modern government' (AW Bradley and KD Ewing, *Constitutional and Administrative Law* (London:

---

20 On prerogative powers over military deployment, see Chapter 9.

Pearson, 14th edn, 2007, 242). In reality executive power is vested not in the Crown but in the government by virtue of its ability to command the political support of Parliament that derives from electoral success. So what sense is there in saying that formally executive power vests in the Crown? The essential answer is rooted in the fact that the monarch is the longest established source of power in the UK. While over the centuries its powers to dispense justice, to legislate, and to govern have been transferred to other institutions, the Crown continues to symbolize the continuity of a system in which those who exercise power do so because they have constitutional authority to do so.

(d) THE PRIVY COUNCIL

Note the reference in s. 23 of the Constitutional Reform Act 2005 to '*Her Majesty in Council*' (see extract Constitutional Reform Act 2005 on p. 236). This is because some formal acts of the Queen—in that case, agreeing to legislation to change the number of judges in the Supreme Court—take place at one of the monthly meetings of the Privy Council, which typically involve four ministers and the Queen. The Privy Council as a whole consists of about 500 members; there is no limit on the number. They include senior politicians and retired politicians, senior judges, and senior members of the Church of England. The number of politician Privy Counsellors is much larger than the number of current ministers because appointment is for life. Appointments are, in some cases, honorific, but in the case of currently serving ministers, they are functional. At any given time, however, the executive functions of the Privy Council are carried out by the monarch and members of the current government. Privy Counsellors are referred to as 'Right Honourable'. In his diary entry for 22 October 1964, the Rt Hon. Richard Crossman MP describes rather irritably what happened after his appointment as Minister for Housing and Local Government when he was required to be sworn in as a member of the Privy Council.

Anthony Howard (ed.) *Diaries of a Cabinet Minister: Selections, 1964–70*
(1979, London: Hamish Hamilton), p. 31

[...L]ast Monday we new ministers were summoned to the Privy Council offices to rehearse the ceremony of becoming a Privy Councillor. I don't suppose anything more dull, pretentious, or plain silly has ever been invented. There we were, sixteen grown men. For over an hour we were taught how to stand up, how to kneel on one knee on a cushion, how to raise the right hand with the Bible in it, how to advance three paces towards the Queen, how to take the hand and kiss it, how to move back ten paces without falling over the stools—which had been carefully arranged so that you did fall over them. Oh dear! We did this from 11.10 to 12.15. At 12.15 all of us went out, each to his own car, and we drove to the Palace and there stood about until we entered a great drawing-room. At the other end was this little woman with a beautiful waist, and she had to stand with her hand on the table for forty minutes while we went through this rigmarole. We were uneasy, she was uneasy. Then at the end informality broke out and she said, 'You all moved backwards very nicely,' and we all laughed. And then she pressed a bell and we all left her. We were Privy Councillors: we had kissed hands.

At its monthly meetings, the Privy Council no longer has any deliberative or consultative function. Its regular formal meetings are mainly to confer validity on documents and decisions that have already been agreed upon in Cabinet or by a government department. They are accordingly short; nobody sits down.

The Lord President of Council is the government minister who is head of the Privy Council Office (a department that deals with administrative matters relating to the Privy Council). The Lord President may be either a member of the House of Commons or the House of Lords. In the following extract, taken from a House of Lords debate, the government sets out its view of the role of the Privy Council in rather glowing terms.[21]

House of Lords Hansard, 12 May 2009, col. 1009

The Lord President of the Council (Baroness Royall of Blaisdon): [...] I take huge pride in the fact that I am a privy counsellor, and indeed that I am Lord President of the Council.

The Privy Council dates back to at least the 13th century. It formerly ran the whole Government, along with the Exchequer. The Cabinet is a committee of the Privy Council, which is why all Cabinet Ministers have to be privy counsellors too. Some modern departments were originally boards of the Privy Council, such as the Board of Trade and the Board of Education.

These days the Privy Council is simply another way of saying "Ministers collectively". It is a thoroughly modern example of joined-up government which provides a highly effective means of dispatching a great deal of public business. The Privy Council approves amendments to the byelaws and statutes of chartered institutions. It also approves rules made by the statutory registration councils responsible for the medical and certain other professions, and it makes instruments of government for higher education corporations. In addition, it makes certain appointments to statutory bodies. [...]

On prerogative business, where there is no legislation allocating the responsibility to a particular Minister, the council provides a mechanism for giving ministerial advice to the Queen, as constitutionally the Queen acts only on such advice. On statutory business, where the use of "the Privy Council" rather than "the Secretary of State" in an Act enables more than one government department to be involved, it allows joined-up government. It also enables the devolved Administrations to be involved, as the First Ministers are all privy counsellors.

There are only small areas of government business which Ministers deal with as privy counsellors. The fact is that almost all the prerogative powers formerly exercised by the Privy Council have been taken over by Parliament. The vast majority of the prerogative business done by the Privy Council is not significant enough for Parliament to want to take it over—for example, the affairs of chartered bodies.

The role of privy counsellors, and indeed of the Privy Council, is often misunderstood. The main misconception relates to the name and the council's historical role. "Privy Council" suggests secrecy and a body acting as a counterpart to the elected Government. As I have said, the Privy Council simply means "Ministers collectively". There can be no difference between Privy Council policy and government policy, and Ministers are accountable to Parliament for all matters conducted through the Privy Council.

---

[21] For a more critical assessment, see P. O'Connor, *A Justice Report: The Constitutional Role of the Privy Council and the Prerogative* (2009, London: Justice).

(e) AN ALTERNATIVE TO MONARCHY?

In 2012, opinion polls suggested an overwhelming proportion (80 per cent) of British adults favour the United Kingdom remaining a monarchy. The main political parties support the continuation of monarchy. Republic, a campaign organization, takes a different view, arguing '*the monarchy is the heart of the British constitution and as such it denies us the best democracy we could have. It keeps from us the power to rule ourselves, it crushes the democratic spirit in order to justify its own existence*'.[22]

---

http://www.republic.org.uk (accessed 7 August 2012)

The monarchy is a 'broke' institution. Constitutionally it has abdicated all responsibility. For most of the time the Queen is both powerless and pointless.

There is a cosy arrangement in place which allows the government of the day to exercise the Queen's power in return for political support for the monarchy. Officials use euphemisms to hide the true nature of this deal—they say the Queen acts "on the advice of the prime minister", meaning she does what she is told. We hear debate about the "royal prerogative", which can be more accurately described as "prime ministerial powers". They talk about the Queen owning land, palaces and priceless art "in trust for the nation", which simply means we pay for them and she keeps them.

Politically the monarch serves little purpose. There are some powers she can and has used, but on these occasions we are reminded why the monarchy is unacceptable in a modern democracy. The Queen can, for example, play a role in choosing our prime minister. It's a job an elected president could do if we had a hung parliament, but an unelected, unaccountable monarch has no right to play any part in our political process.

QUESTIONS

1. What constitutional functions does the monarch perform?

2. On the monarch's role in appointing a Prime Minister where there is a hung parliament, does the statement of conventions set out in *The Cabinet Manual* (2011) support the views of Blackburn or Brazier?

3. What does the term 'the Crown' mean?

4. What, if any, constitutional purpose is served by behind closed doors ceremonies, such as those in the Privy Council described by Richard Crossman MP?

5. From a constitutional standpoint, what are the advantages and disadvantages of the United Kingdom having a constitutional monarchy?

6. Do you think that it is constitutionally acceptable in the twenty-first century for the United Kingdom to have a head of state who:

   (a) inherits the role,

   (b) is required to be a protestant Christian?

---

[22] http://www.republic.org.uk/

3 MINISTERS

Ministers exercise political power in the UK constitution.

Cabinet Office, *The Cabinet Manual*, 1st edn (2011, London: Cabinet Office) (footnotes omitted) p. 2

Constitutional convention is that executive power is exercised by the Sovereign's government, which has a democratic mandate to govern. Members of the Government are normally Members of the House of Commons or the House of Lords and the Government is directly accountable to Parliament. The government of the day holds office by virtue of its ability to command the confidence of the House of Commons. Elections are held at least every five years to ensure broad and continued accountability to the people. Election candidates can stand independently but they usually represent political parties, and party numbers in the House of Commons determine the composition of the Government.

(a) MINISTERIAL OFFICE

The most senior ministers in the UK system are mostly called 'Secretary of State'. In law, there is a single office of 'Secretary of State', which is shared by some fifteen senior politicians chosen by the Prime Minister. Senior ministers other than Secretaries of State are: the Prime Minister' (formally 'First Lord of the Treasury' and 'Minister for the Civil Service'); the Chancellor of the Exchequer, who is the ministerial head of HM Treasury, in which a junior minister is the Chief Secretary to the Treasury (who is a member of the Cabinet); the President of the Council is the ministerial head of the Privy Council Office; and the Lord Chancellor (a post currently combined with that of Secretary of State for Justice). The Prime Minister may designate a senior minister as 'First Secretary of State' to emphasize his or her status in the government (a title that Tony Blair gave to John Prescott, and Gordon Brown to Lord Mandelson) and may create the post of deputy Prime Minister.

Each senior minister has a small team of other politicians, selected by the Prime Minister, working with him or her to provide political leadership to a department. These junior ministers normally hold the title 'Ministers of State' and 'Parliamentary Under-Secretaries of State'.

Many ministers have a 'parliamentary private secretary' (PPS). PPSs are other MPs who act as the minsters' 'eyes and ears' in the Commons and who assist ministers with parliamentary work (for example, arranging meetings with MPs). Being a PPS, which carries no salary on top of that of an MP, is regarded as being a stepping-stone to appointment as a junior minister. PPSs are not part of the government, but they are expected to be active supporters of government policy.

There is a long-standing debate as to whether the UK system is moving, or has moved, from a situation in which the Prime Minister is 'first among equals' in relation to other ministers, to one in which he or she has a more 'presidential role'. There is also a more recent debate as to whether the 'centre of government'—meaning the Prime Minister, the Cabinet Office, and HM Treasury—have assumed too much power in relation to other departments (for example, by imposing targets of various kinds).[23] From a constitutional perspective, a

---

[23] House of Lords Constitution Committee, *The Cabinet Office and the Centre of Government*, Fourth Report, Session 2009–10 (HL Paper 30).

concern that grows out of these developments is that the Prime Minister is insufficiently accountable to Parliament.

From a strictly legal point of view, however, it is ministers as individual office-holders that matter. The standard statutory drafting technique is nowadays to confer legal powers on 'the Secretary of State', as in the following example.

National Health Service Act 2006

1.—(1) The Secretary of State must continue the promotion in England of a comprehensive health service designed to secure improvement—(a) in the physical and mental health of the people of England, and (b) in the prevention, diagnosis and treatment of illness. [...]

(3) The Secretary of State retains ministerial responsibility to Parliament for the provision of the health service in England.

(b) WHAT DO MINISTERS DO?

A House of Commons inquiry into the implications of the Coalition government's aim at reducing significantly the cost of government suggested there were three areas of work for ministers.

House of Commons Select Committee on Public Administration, *Smaller Government*, Seventh Report, Session 2010-12, HC 530

...we have formulated our own account of what we believe the proper role of a minister is. These functions can be grouped in terms of the bodies with which ministers have a relationship: Government, Parliament, and the public.

Within Government

21. Within Government, a minister—especially a Minister of the Crown—fulfils three key tasks. The first is to set policy priorities. This is their primary function. Ministers are responsible for setting the policy and providing leadership to their department to ensure their objectives are met. Once policy is set it is the job of civil servants to ensure that the outcomes are delivered. This function of ministers has been made particularly clear by the existence of a Coalition Government. The two parties agreed a programme for government and then ministers, within their own departments, created business plans which set out how they would be delivered.

22. This does not mean that when policy has been set the minister will have no further involvement with it; the implementation of policies can be as politically sensitive as the policy decision itself. It is not possible to draw a line through the policy process after which no more ministerial involvement is required. The process of designing and implementing a scheme can raise issues that require a minister to make further political judgements. In such a situation, civil servants should present ministers with a range of options about how the policy could be implemented, the minister should make a decision and then the civil servants act on that instruction.

23. The second function that a minister must perform within government is to negotiate on behalf of their department, in cabinet committees, in bilateral meetings and in formal

meetings of the Cabinet, as well as with the Treasury about their spending programmes. The classic study of British Cabinet Ministers by Bruce Headey found that these two tasks —being able to take a view and to fight departmental battles within government—were those that civil servants looked to ministers to fulfil. Ministers must also represent the UK at inter-Governmental meetings, such as the EU Council of Ministers.

24. Thirdly, ministers must also ensure those charged with running the department, their senior civil servants, are able to do so, but they should not personally manage the department. We welcome recent decisions to have Secretaries of State chair their departmental boards and to have junior ministers as members. Setting strategic direction at board level, thereby setting the overall objective of an organisation, is the right focus for ministerial effort, rather than attempting to micromanage the department. Once policies are decided and priorities are set it should be possible to delegate implementation to civil servants and agencies. The guidance and strategy that ministers have provided should be sufficient to enable civil servants to make these decisions.

Answering to Parliament

Ministers must also discharge certain duties in Parliament. They must be accountable to the legislature through answering oral and urgent questions, opening and responding to debates and appearing before select committees. Ministers must also explain and justify their legislative proposals as they go through Parliament.

The public face of Government

Acting as the public face of Government is an important ministerial function. Ministers need to get outside their departments and meet a wide range of stakeholders to ensure that their policy decisions reflect the reality on the ground; and to guard against them getting captured by their department's own agenda. Attending public events, while essential to ensure that ministers keep in touch with the issues affecting the people they serve, will necessarily compete with other demands on their time. Ministers must prioritise the numerous demands on their time to ensure that their energy is directed to where it is best spent.

(c) REQUIREMENT FOR MINISTERS TO BE IN PARLIAMENT

The United Kingdom has a system of *parliamentary government*. So whereas some constitutional systems (such as that of the USA) insist that members of the executive are barred from membership of the legislature, in the United Kingdom, all ministers are *required* to be members of either the House of Commons or the House of Lords. This firm rule is a constitutional convention rather than a legal requirement. A Prime Minister is therefore constrained in the choice of ministers to MPs and members of the House of Lords, though occasionally a person has been appointed as a minister shortly before they become a member of the Lords. The rationale for the requirement that all ministers are in Parliament is that Parliament is thereby able to exert accountability over the executive.

Things *might* have turned out differently. As Sir Maurice Amos (1872–1940) explains, there was a moment of opportunity in the early eighteenth century that might, had it been taken, have established a constitutional system in which the ministers were not excluded from Parliament, giving Britain a system of separation of powers.

Sir Maurice Amos, *The English Constitution* (1930, London: Longmans, Green & Co.), pp. 65–6 (footnotes omitted)

[...] Ministers are Members of Parliament and generally, in modern times, of the House of Commons; and [...] Ministers are chosen from that party which has a majority in that House. These two facts, taken together, are of primary importance. It is only because Ministers are Members of Parliament, entitled to vote and speak, sharing the corporate life and the traditional feelings of the House to which they belong, taking a continuous and prominent part in all its business, familiarly known by daily association to friends and foes alike, and, last but not least, both leading and depending on the votes and cheers of the party which is in the ascendancy, that it is possible to bring about that intimate union between the management of Parliament and the management of the executive administration which is the essence of Cabinet government. It is a striking fact that it was almost by chance that at a critical moment in the development of the Constitution, Ministers of the Crown were not excluded from the House of Commons. When the Act of Settlement was passed in 1701, to take effect when the anticipated change of dynasty should be realised, so great was the fear of the corrupting influence of the Crown, that it was provided that 'after the said limitation (of the Crown to the House of Hanover) shall take effect, no person who has an office or place of profit under the King or receives a pension from the Crown shall be capable of serving as a Member of the House of Commons.' This drastic provision was so amended in 1706, before it came into force, as to permit of Ministers becoming Members of the House of Commons if they had been elected, or re-elected, after appointment. If the original plan had been carried into effect and had remained law, it is impossible to calculate what our Government would have become: it certainly could not have developed as it has done. Either the Parliament and the Crown must have remained in a relationship of perpetual loggerheads—which it is impossible to conceive; or Parliament must have dwindled to impotent subserviency; or possibly, again, some awkward arrangement, difficult to picture, would have been worked out by which the Departments of State became the secretariats of standing committees composed of unofficial Members of Parliament—some such arrangement as would exist in America if the President were eliminated. From this choice of uninviting paths we were delivered by 'that remarkable system which combines unity, steadfastness, and initiative in the executive, with the possession of supreme authority alike over men and measures in the House of Commons'.

(d) CAP ON THE NUMBER OF MINISTERS

The House of Commons Disqualification Act 1975 caps the number of ministers who may sit in the House of Commons at ninety-five. The Ministerial and Other Salaries Act 1975 limits the number of ministers (across both Houses) who may receive a salary to 109, including twenty-one Cabinet ministers plus the Lord Chancellor. In 2010, a select committee called for reforms to reduce the number of ministers.[24] The constitutional rationale for restricting the number of ministers is to restrict the government's control over the Commons.

From time to time, 'them and us' tensions bubble up between MPs who hold ministerial office and those who do not. Consider the following exchange between two Conservative MPs during debates on the Parliamentary Standards Bill (which proposed to require MPs to keep records and disclose any non-parliamentary work).

---

[24] House of Commons Public Administration Select Committee, *Too Many Ministers?* Ninth Report, Session 2009-10, HC 457.

House of Commons Hansard, 29 June 2009, col. 67

Mr. Gerald Howarth (Aldershot) (Con): I notice that my hon. Friend has not mentioned clause 5, which is of concern to a number of us. Will he share with us his view on a point made by our right hon. Friend the Member for Wokingham (Mr. Redwood), who challenged the Lord Chancellor on his unpaid post,[25] and sought to establish from him why Ministers were excluded? After all, the Prime Minister, like us, is a right hon. Member of the House, but he also moonlights as Prime Minister, for a fairly substantial fee. Ministers do not have to go through the rigmarole of having to account for their every hour and minute spent on that outside interest, whereas those who have other outside interests that enable them to bring some serious experience to the House will be subject to that process.

Alan Duncan [Conservative front-bench spokesman]: My hon. Friend has made that point in the House a number of times. The loose use of the phrase "full-time MP" is increasingly vacuous. It does not mean much. The Prime Minister and other Ministers are Members of Parliament, working for their constituencies, and have very busy jobs as Ministers. Members who are paid as Chairmen of Select Committees also have that as an extra job. So the notion that we are either full-time MPs or not requires us to help inform people about how this place works. If ever there was a time when educating people and helping them understand this place were needed, now is such a time. [...]

(e) GOVERNMENT INFLUENCE OVER THE HOUSE OF COMMONS

A cap on the number of ministers in the Commons has not, according to many critics, been sufficient to curb the influence of the government on the operation of Parliament. Political parties are an important part of the picture. Each of the major parties takes steps to ensure that their members in Parliament are well organized—turning up at significant debates and voting in 'divisions'. The governing party is no exception. If the government is to thrive, it is essential that it ensures that the members of its party in the Commons and the Lords support its policies and are not unduly critical (at least in public). This means instructing party members when and where to vote. A 'three-line whip' is the strongest requirement, a failure to comply leading to disciplinary action that, in serious cases, can lead to suspension or expulsion from the party (making re-election at the next general election unlikely). Twenty or so MPs and peers are appointed as 'whips' by the Prime Minister to organize turnout at key votes. They differ from the whip of the other parties in that they are appointed to salaried posts and are thus members of the government. The government chief whip—whose official title is Parliamentary Secretary to the Treasury—is a member of the Cabinet.

The one area in which party discipline is not strongly enforced is in relation to the work of the select committees in the Commons.[26] Here, MPs try to work on a consensual, cross-party basis in scrutinizing the executive. The findings and recommendations of select

---

[25] Since 2003, the ministerial office of Lord Chancellor has been combined with that of a Secretary of State—first, the Secretary of State for Constitutional Affairs, and when that was abolished, the Secretary of State for Justice. A minister holding two ministerial posts is paid for only one of them. In 2012, a Secretary of State's salary was paid just under £68,827 on top of an MP's salary of £65, 738. The Prime Minister receives £76,762 on top of his MP's salary.

[26] On select committees, see extract House of Commons Liaison Committee, *Pre-appointment Hearings by Select Committees* on p. 255.

committees are, however, not binding on the government (unlike the outcomes of many other types of government parliamentary business).

Law academics disagree over whether it would be feasible or desirable to reduce party influence in Parliament.

Danny Nicol, 'Professor Tomkins' House of Mavericks' [2006] Public Law 467

In his book *Our Republican Constitution* Professor Adam Tomkins identifies "the problem of party" as chief obstacle to deliberative, contestatory democracy in Britain. Party and party loyalty, he insists, must be removed from Parliament, whips and whipping must be banned, and MPs must be free to vote in the interests of the public good. This analysis argues, *contra* Tomkins, that in fact the party system is the indispensable foundation of British political democracy.

The argument will be in three parts: first, MPs do not "unthinkingly" toe the party line: in fact the *status quo* strikes an appropriate balance between backbench influence and the ability of democratically-accountable governments to govern. Secondly, Tomkins' depoliticised notion of the "public good" glosses over the way in which different conceptions of public good depend overwhelmingly on ideological considerations. This leads him to pay insufficient regard to the importance of party for electoral choice. Thirdly, whatever his intentions, the effect of Tomkins' anti-party stance would be permanently to relegate those outside the hallowed portals of Westminster to the role of ineffectual onlookers. The article concludes by dwelling on the merits of a polity of democratised parties as a normative ideal.

It is not only party politics that enables the government to exert control over Parliament; the government also effectively controls the timetabling of business in the House of Commons, as specified in the House of Commons Standing Orders.

House of Commons Standing Orders

Arrangement and Timing of Public and Private Business

14.—(1) Save as provided in this order, government business shall have precedence at every sitting.

(2) Twenty days shall be allotted in each session for proceedings on opposition business, seventeen of which shall be at the disposal of the Leader of the Opposition and three of which shall be at the disposal of the leader of the second largest opposition party; and matters selected on those days shall have precedence over government business [. . .].

While allowing opposition parties some opportunities to choose the subjects of debate on the floor of the chamber and enabling backbench MPs of all parties opportunities to initiate short debates, Standing Order 14 gives government the upper hand. There have been calls for reform, including making a House of Commons business committee—which would feature representatives of all the main political parties—responsible for deciding what is debated and on what votes are taken.[27]

---

[27] See, e.g., Hansard Society, *Representative Democracy Briefing Paper 1: House of Commons Reform* (June 2009), available online at http://www.hansardsociety.org.uk; Select Committee on Reform of the House of Commons, *Report: Rebuilding the House*, First Report, Session 2009–10 (HC 111).

(e) THE PRIME MINISTER

The Prime Minister has surprisingly few *statutory* powers or duties. The Prime Minister's main legal capacity to take action stems from *prerogative* powers, which are examined in more detail in Chapter 9.

A. Le Sueur, 'The Nature, Powers, and Accountability of Central Government',
in D. Feldman (ed.) *English Public Law*, 2nd edn (2009, Oxford: OUP), para. 3.09 (footnotes omitted)

The office of Prime Minister is not a 'creature of law' but rather of convention. From a strictly legal point of view, the Prime Minister has very few statutory powers compared to those in the hands of other ministers. In 2008, the Prime Minister is referred to in only 75 Acts of Parliament. Few of these references confer any important power: we learn that the Prime Minister appoints and receives reports from the Chief Surveillance Commissioner; that the Prime Minister must take into account specified factors in deciding who to appoint as the Lord Chancellor, and has an entirely formal role in communicating the name of a recommended appointee to the UK Supreme Court to the Queen; that the Prime Minister has power to appoint people to various posts; and has a country residence. This rag-bag of relatively minor provisions tells us little about the real nature of the Prime Minister's constitutional functions.

BOX 7.1 PRIME MINISTERS SINCE THE 1970S AND CONSTITUTIONAL AFFAIRS

1964–70	Harold Wilson	Labour	A range of liberal laws making divorce more widely available; decriminalizing gay sex; abolishing capital punishment; ending theatre censorship; legalizing abortion
1970–74	Edward Heath	Conservative	Accession to the European Community
1974–76	Harold Wilson	Labour	1975 referendum on remaining in the EC
1976–79	James Callaghan	Labour	Proposals for devolution to Wales and Scotland rejected in referendums
1979–90	Margaret Thatcher	Conservative	Programme of privatization of state-owned enterprises
1990–97	John Major	Conservative	Start of negotiations for peace settlement in Northern Ireland; 'Citizen's Charter' reforms of public service; creation of the European Union by the Maastricht Treaty
1997–2007	Tony Blair	Labour	Devolution; Human Rights Act 1998; Freedom of Information Act 2000; creation of UK Supreme Court; reform of office of Lord Chancellor; new judicial appointments process for England and Wales
2007–2010	Gordon Brown	Labour	'Governance of Britain' reform agenda focusing on prerogative powers; MPs' expenses scandal
2010–	David Cameron	Conservative	Localism; fixed-term Parliaments; system for referendums on EU treaty changes

(f) CABINET

Taking a narrow legal point of view, there is little to say about the Cabinet: it has no legal personality; it has no legal powers. Like the Prime Minister, it can be described as 'a creature of convention'. From a broader constitutional perspective, it is, however, of considerable importance.

A. Le Sueur, 'The Nature, Powers, and Accountability of Central Government', in D. Feldman (ed), *English Public Law*, 2nd edn (2009, Oxford: OUP), paras 3.12–3.14 (footnotes omitted)

It is the gathering of senior ministers, typically 20 or so in number, normally once a week at 10 Downing Street, though it may meet at any time and location. Much work is done through a plethora of committees and subcommittees, some of which include officials as well as ministers. The Cabinet Secretariat, part of the department called the Cabinet Office, supports the work of the Cabinet. Ministers often meet each other outside the formal structures of Cabinet. Although the Cabinet is composed entirely of members of the House of Commons and House of Lords, more particularly the leading members of the majority party in the Commons, it is not a committee of Parliament. Decisions taken in Cabinet and its committees nevertheless exert significant control over Parliament, as it is a Cabinet committee that decides upon and manages the legislative agenda in each annual session of Parliament. The organization of the forthcoming week's business in Parliament is discussed at the preceding Thursday's Cabinet meeting.

The relative powers of the Prime Minister and the Cabinet have been the subject of much analysis and debate. For some, the 'central directing instrument of government, in legislation as well as in administration, is the Cabinet [...] It is the Cabinet which controls Parliament and governs the country.' For another, the 'post-war epoch has seen the final transformation of Cabinet Government into Prime Ministerial Government'. Still others relate the role and importance of the Cabinet to the leadership styles of particular Prime Ministers. What is indisputable is that the Prime Minister has considerable control over the agenda of the Cabinet itself and the number, membership and terms of reference of Cabinet committees. The Prime Minister presides over the Cabinet and any Cabinet committees of which he is a member. The Prime Minister may also exercise prerogative powers without prior reference to Cabinet. It is equally clear, however, that the Cabinet is the source of a Prime Minister's political authority: without the support of Cabinet colleagues, a Prime Minister cannot continue in power for long.

Decisions made or ratified by Cabinet and its committees are given legal effect through the statutory or prerogative powers of individual ministers, or if no legal basis exists, the relevant minister will introduce a Bill in Parliament.

QUESTIONS

1. What roles do ministers have in the constitutional system?

2. From a constitutional perspective, what are the pros and cons of the convention that requires all ministers to be members of one or other House of Parliament?

3. Are there too many ministers?

4. Does the government have too much influence over the House of Commons?

4 THE CIVIL SERVICE

Clearly, ministers cannot personally make all of the hundreds of thousands of individual determinations that have to be made every day in the exercise of executive functions. Politically neutral, professional civil servants are therefore an important element of the government system. Some decision-making is also thought better kept at arm's length from political partisan ministers and are instead taken by people appointed to senior public offices. We look at these in turn.

During the nineteenth century, ideas about the organization of government changed, and new techniques and structures of public administration were introduced. In 1853, two senior civil servants, Sir Stafford Northcote and Sir Charles Trevelyan, conducted a wide-ranging review of administration. Their admirably short twenty-page report was the impetus for transforming the British civil service.

Stafford H. Northcote and C.E. Trevelyan, *Report on the Organization of the Permanent Civil Service*, Presented to both Houses of Parliament by Command of Her Majesty (1854, London)

That the Permanent Civil Service, with all its defects, essentially contributes to the proper discharge of the functions of Government, has been repeatedly admitted by those who have successively been responsible for the conduct of our affairs. All however, who have had occasion to examine its constitution with care, have felt that its organisation is far from perfect, and that its amendment is deserving the most careful attention.

It would be natural to expect that so important a profession would attract into its ranks the ablest and the most ambitious of the youth of the country; that the keenest emulation would prevail among those who had entered it; and that such as were endowed with superior qualifications would rapidly rise to distinction and public eminence. Such, however, is by no means the case. Admission into the Civil Service is indeed eagerly sought after, but it is for the unambitious, and the indolent or incapable that it is chiefly desired. [...]

It may be noticed in particular that the comparative lightness of work, and the certainty of provision in case of retirement owing to bodily incapacity, furnish strong inducements to the parents and friends of sickly youths to endeavour to obtain for them employment in the service of Government [...]

The general principle [...] which we advocate is, that the public service should be carried on by the admission into its lower ranks of a carefully selected body of young men [...]

Upon a review of the recommendations contained in this paper, it will be seen that the objects we have principally in view are these:—

1. To provide, by a proper system of examination, for the supply of the public service with a thoroughly efficient class of men.

2. To encourage industry and foster merit, by teaching all public servants to look forward to promotion according to their deserts, and to expect the highest prizes in the service if they can qualify themselves for them.

3. To mitigate the evils which result from the fragmentary character of the Service, and to introduce elements of unity, by placing the first appointments upon an uniform footing, opening the way to the promotion of public officers to staff appointments in other departments than their own, and introducing into the lower ranks a body of men (the supplementary clerks) whose services may be made available at any time in any office whatever.

It remains for us to express our conviction that if any change of the importance of those which we have recommended is to be carried into effect, it can only be successfully done through the medium of an Act of Parliament. The existing system is supported by long usage and powerful interests; and were any Government to introduce material alterations into it, in consequence of their own convictions, without taking the precaution to give those alterations the force of law, it is almost certain that they would be imperceptibly, or perhaps avowedly, abandoned by their successors, if they were not even allowed to fall into disuse by the very Government which had originated them. A few clauses would accomplish all that is proposed in this paper, and it is our firm belief that a candid statement of the grounds of the measure would insure its success and popularity in the country, and would remove many misconceptions which are now prejudicial to the public service.

Traditionalists viewed these proposals with hostility when they were first published—some even seeing in them 'the seeds of republicanism', because objective examinations (rather than Crown discretion) were to determine who was appointed to the civil service. But public outrage over the lives lost in the Crimean War due to administrative inefficiencies helped to prepare the ground for the adoption of the proposals. In 1870, when Gladstone was Prime Minister, a new civil service Order in Council (a piece of primary legislation made under the royal prerogative)[28] was made implementing most of the proposals in the Northcote–Trevelyan report.

There are two main bodies of civil servants: some 435,000 who serve in the Home Civil Service and some 16,000 in Diplomatic Service. Home Civil Servants work in departments of the UK government, executive agencies, various 'non-departmental public bodies' (NDPBs), and for the Scottish Government and Welsh Assembly Government. There is a separate Northern Ireland Civil Service. The term 'Whitehall' is often used to refer collectively to government departments (after the London street on which several departments have their headquarters).

Cabinet Office, *The Cabinet Manual*, 1st edn (2011, London: Cabinet Office) (footnotes omitted)

The Civil Service

7.1 Civil servants are servants of the Crown. The Civil Service supports the government of the day in developing and implementing its policies, and in delivering public services. Civil servants are accountable to ministers, who in turn are accountable to Parliament.

---

[28] See Chapter 9.

The role of ministers and officials

7.2 Ministers are required to uphold the political impartiality of the Civil Service and not ask civil servants to act in any way that would conflict with the Civil Service Code or the requirements of the Constitutional Reform and Governance Act 2010. Ministers also have a duty to give fair consideration and due weight to informed and impartial advice from civil servants, as well as to other considerations and advice in reaching policy decisions.

7.3 In addition, civil servants should not be asked to engage in activities likely to call into question their political impartiality or give rise to the criticism that resources paid from public funds are being used for party political purposes.

The following extract summarizes some of the key features of the British civil service.

Scott L. Greer, 'Whitehall', in R. Hazell (ed.) *Constitutional Futures Revisited: Britain's Constitution to 2020* (2008, Basingstoke: Palgrave Macmillan), ch. 8, p. 125

Nonpartisanship

What is distinctive about [...] Whitehall is the importance of nonpartisanship at the top. There are many civil services [in other countries] that have strict nonpartisanship rules for average employees but a high degree of formal or informal political engagement at the top. In Whitehall systems, by contrast, the entire civil service hierarchy, up to its apex where it meets the politician in the private office and the top officials, is traditionally nonpartisan. This nonpartisanship makes it possible to think of the civil service as a check on government and consequently part of the constitution.

Meritocracy

Meritocracy means principally admission and promotion by ability. This was originally born as a response to the pressures of patronage, and meant the insulation of jobs from political preference. It meant examination-based entrance followed by promotion through performance evaluations carried out within the civil service. The UK is distinctive because of the extent to which it is applied at the top.

Ministerial responsibility

Ministerial responsibility is a third major component of the Whitehall model. Ministerial responsibility means that ministers are responsible for the decisions of their departments. In theory, this means that officials canvass all reasonable options and put them to the minister for a decision. It makes accountability clear and eases nonpartisanship in the civil service by detaching them from ultimate responsibility for decisions. But it means politicians are held responsible for maladministration in giant organizations they cannot always control. Viewed in most countries as a problem or necessary evil of public administration, in Whitehall systems this accountability mismatch is elevated to the status of a constitutional principle.

Secrecy

Secrecy logically comes with this desire to clarify accountability for decisions and obscure accountability for advice, on the grounds that elections are accountability enough [...].

Unity

Unity means that civil servants are defined by their membership in the UK civil service rather than their departmental or territorial affiliations. The unified civil service grew principally as a response to the challenges of enacting policy amidst recalcitrant islands of bad administration and the challenges of weeding out corruption—both in the name of good public administration and because the pressures for patronage overloaded MPs and governments. With unification comes generalist: only if we believe that there are general civil service skills (policy and management) can we believe that it is appropriate to have one career ladder span education, prisons, and EU infrastructure fund in Cornwall. Unity has a relatively simple indicator: the strength of internal labour markets. We know that the Navy or the Catholic Church—or McKinsey Consultants—are unified because they promote internally. The civil service is unified to the extent that its jobs are filled from within by generalists.

The most senior civil servant in each department is the Permanent Secretary. As well as providing managerial leadership for the department, the Permanent Secretary is also the 'accounting officer' for the department, appointed by HM Treasury under s. 22 of the Exchequer and Audit Department Act 1866. In this role, a Permanent Secretary is directly accountable to the House of Commons (through the Public Accounts Committee) for the financial management of the department. Chief executives are the accounting officers for executive agencies.

The Constitutional Reform and Governance Act 2010 placed the regulation of the civil service on a statutory footing for the first time (rather than it being based on prerogative powers). There is broad consensus that this is a good idea—indeed, one that is long overdue. Previously, the terms and conditions under which civil servants work were regulated under prerogative powers by the Minister for the Civil Service (a post that, in modern times, is held by the Prime Minister)—in the form of the Civil Service Order in Council (a highly unusual piece of *primary* legislation made by ministers rather than by Parliament) and a Civil Service Code.

QUESTION

Do you think that the function of the civil service should be a 'check on government', or should its role simply be to work out how best to implement the policies decided on by ministers?

---

5 APPOINTEES TO PUBLIC OFFICE

As we noted earlier, appointed public office-holders exercise public power of importance in the governing of the country, with the holders of the offices having a high degree of personal independence from political pressures. One of the purposes of having these public offices is to ensure that ministers cannot dictate to the holders how they should approach their roles and what decisions they should reach. In July 2003, the House of Commons Public Administration Select Committee published a report on appointed offices.

House of Commons Public Administration Select Committee, *Government By Appointment: Opening Up The Patronage State,*
Fourth Report, Session 2002–03, HC 165-I

This report is the first major Parliamentary examination of the new appointments procedures for public bodies. The system, established in the 1990s, sought to base appointments on merit and to subject them to independent scrutiny. The creation of the post of Commissioner for Public Appointments, combined with independent assessment in every department, has brought greater integrity to these processes. Overall, there has been considerable improvement in the public appointments system in recent years. [. . .]

The general public still believes that appointments are the preserve of the privileged few, even if not always a 'fix', or the product of 'cronyism' as often alleged by the media. We are satisfied that the Government is genuinely committed to opening up appointments to a wider range of people, and especially to increasing the proportions of women, members of ethnic minorities and people with disabilities on the boards of public bodies. There has been real progress in doing so since 1997, but appointed members of these boards are still overwhelmingly (in the Commissioner's phrase) 'male, pale and stale'.

Diversity on public bodies must be increased. In our view, more representative bodies would assist the Government's goal of increasing public confidence in the integrity of the appointments process.

We do not believe that merit and diversity are incompatible. We are satisfied that attempts to achieve greater diversity have not led either to unlawful positive discrimination or a dilution in standards. Greater diversity on public bodies is not simply a desirable goal. It is a significant component of the basic human right to equal regard and treatment, regardless of difference. The Government should bring forward a Single Equality Bill to promote equality and end discrimination for all minorities. This would provide a statutory framework for equality and more diverse appointment as well as satisfying international and EU commitments to equal treatment for all. [. . .]

Socio-economic background is a major barrier to increasing diversity on public bodies, not only inhibiting the recruitment of women, people from ethnic minorities and people with disabilities, but also a wider range of white men. Age and regional background are also likely to create barriers.

In 2009, a new process was put in place by which House of Commons committees hold public session 'pre-appointment hearings' with people recommended by the government for appointment to major offices. Responding to a report by the House of Commons Liaison Select Committee (which comprises the chairs of all of the select committees), the government explained its thinking in encouraging this constitutional innovation.

House of Commons Liaison Committee, *Pre-appointment Hearings by Select Committees: Government Response to the Committee's First Report of Session 2007–08,* First Special Report, Session 2007–08, HC 594

The Government is committed to increasing democratic scrutiny of public appointments. The Governance of Britain: Constitutional Renewal White Paper, published on 25 March 2008, re-affirms this commitment and sets out the process by which Parliamentary and public scrutiny of key public appointments will be enhanced: Parliamentary select committees will be given the opportunity to hold pre-appointment hearings to scrutinise and take evidence from candidates for key public appointments before they are appointed. The hearings will be non-binding but the Government will consider committees' conclusions and recommendations before deciding whether to proceed with the appointments.

The Government welcomes the Committee's report and their support for pre-appointment hearings. It also wishes to acknowledge the contribution of the Public Administration Select Committee for their work on this issue. The Government recognises that it will be for individual select committees to decide whether or not to hold pre-appointment hearings on the particular posts put forward by Government. However, the Government believes that the introduction of pre-appointment hearings will help ensure that the Executive is properly accountable to Parliament and will provide greater public reassurance that those appointed to key public offices are appointed on merit. Following the introduction of hearings on a pilot basis, the Government will want to work with Parliament to assess the success of this new approach and consider what lessons can be learned.

In October 2009, the Select Committee on Children Schools and Families became the first committee not to endorse a government-preferred candidate for a post (that of the Children's Commissioner for England). The Committee reported that while it was satisfied that the candidate '*demonstrated a high degree of professional competence* [...] *we would like to have seen more sign of determination to assert the independence of the role, to challenge the status quo on children's behalf, and to stretch the remit of the post, in particular by championing children's rights*'.[29] The minister nonetheless went ahead and confirmed the appointment.

6 ACCOUNTABILITY OF GOVERNMENT

So far in this chapter we have looked at the constitutional and legal status and role of the monarch, ministers, the civil service, and holders of appointed public office. We saw that in the United Kingdom it is *ministerial* and *parliamentary*. We now move on to consider one of the central features of a good constitution, namely that it provides opportunities for those who exercise public power to be 'held to account' or 'accountable' for their decisions and conduct. Accountability is a key aspect of legitimacy.

(a) THE MEANING OF 'ACCOUNTABILITY'

Look back at the definition of accountability in Chapter 1.[30] 'Accountability' can be *explanatory* (that is, a person is called on to explain their conduct or proposals) and it may also entail the imposition of *sanctions*. In relation to ministers, the ultimate political sanction is to be sacked—or to be forced to tender their resignation—by the Prime Minister. This is a rare occurrence. The focus of this section is therefore on the ways in which ministers are called on to explain and justify their, and their departments', work. Remember that the constitutional justification for insisting that ministers are members of either the House of Commons or the House of Lords is that this enables Parliament to call the government to account. Two constitutional conventions operate to encourage accountability:

- individual ministerial responsibility; and
- collective ministerial responsibility.

---

[29] Eighth Report for 2008–09 (HL 998), para. 18.
[30] See extract A. Le Sueur, 'The Nature, Powers, and Accountability of Central Government' on p. 250.

(b) INDIVIDUAL MINISTERIAL RESPONSIBILITY

The starting point in understanding the rules and practices by which ministers are held accountable is to consider the convention of 'individual ministerial responsibility'.[31] Much ink has been used trying to pin down the exact scope of the constitutional convention of individual ministerial responsibility, as Dawn Oliver explains in the following extract.

Dawn Oliver, 'Reforming the United Kingdom Parliament', in D. Oliver and J. Jowell (eds) *The Changing Constitution*, 7th edn (2011, Oxford: OUP), ch. 7, p. 172 (footnotes omitted)

Individual ministerial responsibility: government's duty to parliament

A major challenge has been, and remains, to give teeth to the convention of individual ministerial responsibility to Parliament. The classic version of the doctrine is that ministers are responsible to Parliament for all that happens in their departments, though they will only be regarded as culpable in respect of their own decisions or failures. They must give an account to Parliament, and they are expected to make amends if something has gone wrong. The effectiveness, and content, of this convention had become a high-profile issue over a number of decades but it crystallized in the Arms to Iraq Affair in the early 1990s. Certain defendants had been prosecuted for breach of the rules relating to the export of arms to Iraq, but it emerged during the trial that members of the government had known about the exports and had, in effect, allowed the prosecution to proceed in the knowledge that the defendants were at risk of wrongful convictions. The trial judge stopped the trial. Sir Richard Scott, then Vice Chancellor (Head of the Chancery Division of the High Court), was asked to report on the matter. His Report made severe criticisms of ministers. These were debated in Parliament, ministers rejected the criticisms, and no ministers resigned. However, concerns about the basis and weaknesses of the conventions of ministerial responsibility that emerged from that affair were accepted as valid by the John Major government, and the requirement that ministers be accountable to Parliament was reaffirmed by both Houses and formalized through the resolutions on ministerial accountability passed by each House just before the 1997 general election.

The resolution passed by the Commons is as follows.

House of Commons Hansard, 19 March 1997, col. 1046

Motion made, and Question put forthwith, pursuant to Order [19 March], 'That, in the opinion of this House, the following principles should govern the conduct of Ministers of the Crown in relation to Parliament:'

(1) Ministers have a duty to Parliament to account, and be held to account, for the policies, decisions and actions of their Departments and Next Steps Agencies;

(2) It is of paramount importance that Ministers give accurate and truthful information to Parliament, correcting any inadvertent error at the earliest opportunity. Ministers who knowingly mislead Parliament will be expected to offer their resignation to the Prime Minister;

[31] Look back at Chapter 1 for a general discussion of conventions.

> (3) Ministers should be as open as possible with Parliament, refusing to provide information only when disclosure would not be in the public interest, which should be decided in accordance with relevant statute and the Government's Code of Practice on Access to Government Information (Second Edition, January 1997);
>
> (4) Similarly, Ministers should require civil servants who give evidence before Parliamentary Committees on their behalf and under their directions to be as helpful as possible in providing accurate, truthful and full information in accordance with the duties and responsibilities of civil servants as set out in the Civil Service Code (January 1996).

The reference in para. (3) to the Code of Practice on Access to Government Information has now been superseded by the Freedom of Information Act 2000, which provides a *statutory* right of access to official information (subject to a number of significant exceptions).

The House of Lords passed a similar resolution on 20 March 1997 and, unlike the Commons, debated it. Lord Renton made the following speech.[32]

House of Lords Hansard, 20 March 1997, cols 1057–8

Lord Renton

My Lords, this is a matter of great constitutional importance. I am grateful to my noble friend the Leader of the House[33] for his lucid explanation of it. It is a matter of great satisfaction that this is agreed between the parties. For centuries ministerial responsibility has been a matter of convention. Now we have it clearly laid down. I believe that sometimes in the past it went too far. Ministers were held responsible for the actions of all their civil servants, sometimes several thousands of them, with an ever-widening scope of activity. It was impossible for Ministers to know about everything that was happening in their departments, even within the scope of the policies that they had declared and laid down. With that in mind, I invite your Lordships' attention to paragraph (1), which says: 'Ministers have a duty to Parliament to account, and be held to account, for the policies, decisions and actions of their Departments and Next Steps agencies'.

Let us briefly consider that proposition in the light of what I have said about the vast number of civil servants and the scope of their activities. It is quite clear that Ministers should be responsible for policies and decisions of a major kind, but not all of the minor decisions that must be taken from time to time to implement those policies. It is right that they should be responsible for the actions of the government departments so long as Ministers know in advance what those actions are required to be.

For Ministers to be responsible for every minor incident, which has sometimes led to parliamentary embarrassment and even the resignation of Ministers in unjust circumstances, would be absurd. Therefore I hope that that important paragraph will, in future, always be interpreted in the light of reason.

[Viscount Cranborne (Leader of the House) responded for the government.]

---

32 Lord Renton was an MP for thirty-four years and a member of the Lords for twenty-eight years. A barrister, he was a member of the legal team that drafted the European Convention on Human Rights in 1950. He served as a minister for six years.

33 The member of the government responsible for organizing the government's business in the House of Lords.

Viscount Cranborne

My noble friend Lord Renton, almost predictably, puts his finger on an extremely important point. It has become almost a truism that, in the days of highly complex government and administration, often involving many civil servants, it is impossible for a Minister to know everything that happens in his department. Nevertheless, those of us who have had the privilege to be departmental Ministers—in my case an extremely junior one—will know that any hard working, conscientious Minister will make it his or her business to know the essentials of what is going on in the department and to be able to make a judgment. [. . .]

Nevertheless it means that Ministers have an extraordinarily difficult judgment to make, but also—dare I say it?—Parliament has a difficult judgment to make, particularly when Parliament inevitably will have its judgment coloured—I make no complaint about this—by considerations of party politics. There have been, as the House will know perhaps better than any other body, attempts, particularly by my right honourable friends, to try to define, as is only right, where that difficult decision should lie. There have been attempts to differentiate between operational responsibility and ministerial accountability.

In the end, it is a matter of careful judgment. Ministers are only human; they can get things wrong. I dare say that we all do, and that if in a decade or so the party opposite found itself in office it would be faced with similar decisions. [. . .]

If, like me, your Lordships are fans of that extraordinarily perspicacious programme, 'Yes, Minister',[34] you will remember that often both civil servants and Ministers are depicted by Mr. Anthony Jay and his co-writers as saying that the object of Answers to Parliamentary Questions is to reveal as little as possible. It might be for the edification of your Lordships if you allowed me to take a trip down memory lane to when I made what was clearly a joke in very poor taste to the first civil servant who came to brief me on a Parliamentary Question, implying that perhaps that was the object of all civil servants. I shall never forget the chastening look that I received from the individual concerned; it made it very clear that one does not joke about such matters.

For many decades, every Prime Minister would publish a relatively short document entitled *Questions of Procedure for Ministers*. Until 1992, it was a secret document; Prime Minister John Major then decided that it should be published by the Cabinet Office. Today, it is called *The Ministerial Code*. The following is an extract from the version of the Code issued by David Cameron when he became Prime Minister in May 2010. Notice para. 1.2, which incorporates much of the March 2007 parliamentary resolution.

Cabinet Office, *Ministerial Code* (May 2010)

1 MINISTERS OF THE CROWN

General principle

1.1 Ministers of the Crown are expected to behave in a way that upholds the highest standards of propriety.

1.2 The *Ministerial Code* should be read alongside the Coalition agreement and against the background of the overarching duty on Ministers to comply with the law including international law and treaty obligations and to uphold the administration of justice and to protect

---

34 A satirical comedy first broadcast on British television during the 1980s.

the integrity of public life. They are expected to observe the Seven Principles of Public Life set out at annex A, and the following principles of Ministerial conduct:

a. The principle of collective responsibility, save where it is explicitly set aside, applies to all Government Ministers;

b. Ministers have a duty to Parliament to account, and be held to account, for the policies, decisions and actions of their departments and agencies;

c. It is of paramount importance that Ministers give accurate and truthful information to Parliament, correcting any inadvertent error at the earliest opportunity. Ministers who knowingly mislead Parliament will be expected to offer their resignation to the Prime Minister;

d. Ministers should be as open as possible with Parliament and the public, refusing to provide information only when disclosure would not be in the public interest which should be decided in accordance with the relevant statutes and the Freedom of Information Act 2000;

e. Ministers should similarly require civil servants who give evidence before Parliamentary Committees on their behalf and under their direction to be as helpful as possible in providing accurate, truthful and full information in accordance with the duties and responsibilities of civil servants as set out in the *Civil Service Code*;

f. Ministers must ensure that no conflict arises, or appears to arise, between their public duties and their private interests;

g. Ministers should not accept any gift or hospitality which might, or might reasonably appear to, compromise their judgement or place them under an improper obligation;

h. Ministers in the House of Commons must keep separate their roles as Minister and constituency Member;

i. Ministers must not use government resources for Party political purposes;

j. Ministers must uphold the political impartiality of the civil service and not ask civil servants to act in any way which would conflict with the *Civil Service Code* as set out in the Constitutional Reform and Governance Act 2010.

1.3 It is not the role of the Cabinet Secretary or other officials to enforce the Code. If there is an allegation about a breach of the Code, and the Prime Minister, having consulted the Cabinet Secretary feels that it warrants further investigation, he will refer the matter to the independent adviser on Ministers' interests.

1.4 The Code provides guidance to Ministers on how they should act and arrange their affairs in order to uphold these standards. It lists the principles which may apply in particular situations. It applies to all members of the Government and covers Parliamentary Private Secretaries [...] .

1.5 Ministers are personally responsible for deciding how to act and conduct themselves in the light of the Code and for justifying their actions and conduct to Parliament and the public. However, Ministers only remain in office for so long as they retain the confidence of the Prime Minister. He is the ultimate judge of the standards of behaviour expected of a Minister and the appropriate consequences of a breach of those standards.

1.6 Ministers must also comply at all times with the requirements which Parliament itself has laid down in relation to the accountability and responsibility of Ministers. For Ministers in the Commons, these are set by the Resolution carried on 19 March 1997 (*Official Report* columns 1046–47), the terms of which are repeated at b. to e. above. For Ministers in the Lords, the Resolution can be found in the *Official Report* of 20, March 1997 column 1057. Ministers must also comply with the Codes of Conduct for their respective Houses and also any requirements placed on them by the Independent Parliamentary Standards Authority.

There is some debate as to the status of the Code and the rules contained within it. On one view, it is only a statement by the Prime Minister of his or her expectations of ministerial colleagues. On this basis, nothing said in the Code is in and of itself a constitutional convention—although it may provide evidence of the Prime Minister's view as to what the convention entails. On another view, the Code has acquired a more important status. A House of Commons select committee conducted an inquiry into the *Ministerial Code* and, in the following extract, reports some of its findings.

Public Administration Select Committee, *The Ministerial Code: Improving the Rule Book*, Third Report, Session 2000–01, HC 235

15. [...] We believe that the development of such codes of conduct across public life reinforces the need for the constitutional status of the Ministerial Code to be properly recognised. It is not a legal document but a set of guidelines. It does not necessarily cover all aspects of what should be considered acceptable Ministerial practice or behaviour and should not substitute for the Prime Minister's judgement, for which he must account to Parliament. It is unsatisfactory for its status still to be in doubt. It is the rule book for ministerial conduct, including the responsibilities of Ministers to Parliament, and its status should reflect its importance. It may have developed in a private and ad hoc way, but it is now an integral part of the new constitutional architecture. It is time for it to be recognised as such. [...]

Publication

38. Whatever the structure and presentation of the Code, we believe that its status and importance requires a formal basis for its publication. At present there is no requirement for the Ministerial Code to be published: only convention dictates that it is issued by each new administration. Furthermore, its contents may be added to or amended during the lifetime of a Government without such changes having to be published or consulted upon. If, as John Major and Lord Butler agreed, it would be unwise for a Prime Minister to seek to dispense with the Code, then it is appropriate that it should be published on a formal basis. **We therefore recommend that the proposed Ministerial Code is presented to Parliament within three months of a new administration taking office.** Although the Code contains issues of prime importance for Parliament, no debate on its contents is held in the House and there is no public or parliamentary consultation on its contents prior to publication. As we argue above, this is unsatisfactory with respect to its provisions on the responsibilities of Ministers to Parliament. **We therefore recommend that a debate be held on the Ministerial Code immediately following its publication, prior to the approval process we recommend above, that any subsequent revisions to it are also published, and that any revisions relating to parliamentary accountability should be considered and approved by Parliament.**

Conclusion

39. In our view the Ministerial Code has an important contribution to make to good Government. It is not merely an arcane subject of esoteric interest. Rules of conduct for Ministers, and their responsibilities to Parliament, are fundamental to sound public administration and effective accountability. Indeed, the Prime Minister's personal foreword to the Code endorses this view. Beginning as private guidance to Ministers on assorted matters, the Code has now become a public document of constitutional significance.

The government in 2000 was unimpressed by the select committee's recommendations. It said the following in a formal response.

HC 439, Session 2001–02

The Ministerial Code is the Prime Minister's guidance to his Ministers on how he expects them to undertake their official duties. It is for the Prime Minister to determine the terms of the Code. The Government notes the Committee's concern that there is no requirement for the Ministerial Code to be published. It is, however, normal practice for the Ministerial Code to be updated after an Election, and since 1992, each revision has been published. The Prime Minister undertakes that he will continue to publish the Code and any revisions to it on this basis.

What happens if an allegation is made that a rule contained in the Code has been breached? Until about 2006, Prime Ministers adopted an approach of appointing an ad hoc investigator to look into serious allegations. Since 2006, Prime Ministers have appointed a single adviser to provide advice and handle any investigations that may be required.

Notable resignations due to criticism of ministerial conduct were:

i) **1982** Lord Carrington (Foreign Secretary) and two junior ministers resigned following the invasion of the Falkland Islands by Argentina. It was said that the Foreign and Commonwealth Office ought to have anticipated the attack.

ii) **1986** Leon Brittan (Secretary of State for Trade and Industry) resigned when it emerged that he authorized the leak of confidential advice from the Solicitor General about government financial support for Westland, a helicopter manufacturer.

iii) **2004** Beverley Hughes (Minister of State for Immigration, Citizenship and Counterterrorism) resigned when it emerged that she had known that visas had been granted on the basis of false documents, but had earlier told the House of Commons that, had she known about this, she would have done something.

Ministers have resigned somewhat more often due to personal misconduct or misjudgement.

QUESTIONS

1. Explain why the resolutions adopted by each House of Parliament in March 1997 and the *Ministerial Code* are not 'law'. (Tip: Look back at the general discussion about constitutional conventions in Chapter 1.)

2. What might it mean to say that the Code should have 'constitutional status'?

(c) ACCOUNTABILITY OF CIVIL SERVANTS

The *Cabinet Manual* asserts that *'Civil servants are accountable to ministers, who in turn are accountable to Parliament'*. This does not paint a full picture and, increasingly, civil servants can be seen giving evidence to parliamentary select committees.[35] The

---

[35] On Select committees, see p. 273.

following extract from what are sometimes called 'the Osmotherly rules' (after the civil servant who first drafted them) explains the basis on which they do so (according to the government).

Cabinet Office, *Departmental Evidence and Response to Select Committees* (July 2005)

SECTION 1: INTRODUCTION

Status of the Guidance

1. This memorandum gives guidance to officials from Departments and their Agencies who may be called upon to give evidence before, or prepare memoranda for submission to, Parliamentary Select Committees. [...]

3. In providing guidance, the memorandum attempts to summarise a number of longstanding conventions that have developed in the relationship between Parliament, in the form of its Select Committees, and successive Governments. As a matter of practice, Parliament has generally recognised these conventions. It is important to note, however, that this memorandum is a Government document. Although Select Committees will be familiar with its contents, it has no formal Parliamentary standing or approval, nor does it claim to have. [...]

Central Principles

9. Select Committees have a crucial role in ensuring the full and proper accountability of the Executive to Parliament. Ministers have emphasised that, when officials represent them before Select Committees, they should be as forthcoming and helpful as they can in providing information relevant to Committee inquiries. In giving evidence to Select Committees, officials should take care to ensure that no information is withheld which would not be exempted if a parallel request were made under the Freedom of Information Act.

SECTION 3: ROLE OF OFFICIALS GIVING EVIDENCE TO SELECT COMMITTEES

General

40. Civil servants who give evidence to Select Committees do so on behalf of their Ministers and under their directions.

41. This is in accordance with the principle that it is Ministers who are accountable to Parliament for the policies and actions of their Departments. Civil servants are accountable to Ministers and are subject to their instruction; but they are not directly accountable to Parliament in the same way. It is for this reason that when civil servants appear before Select Committees they do so, on behalf of their Ministers and under their directions because it is the Minister, not the civil servant, who is accountable to Parliament for the evidence given to the Committee. This does not mean, of course, that officials may not be called upon to give a full account of Government policies, or indeed of their own actions or recollections of particular events, but their purpose in doing so is to contribute to the central process of Ministerial accountability, not to offer personal views or judgements on matters of political controversy [...], or to become involved in what would amount to disciplinary investigations which are for Departments to undertake [...].

42. This Guidance should therefore be seen as representing standing instructions to officials appearing before Select Committees. These instructions may be supplemented by specific Ministerial instructions on specific matters.

Summoning of Named Officials

43. The line of ministerial accountability means that it is for Ministers to decide which official or officials should represent them. [. . .]

Agency Chief Executives

50. Where a Select Committee wishes to take evidence on matters assigned to an Agency in its Framework Document, Ministers will, normally, wish to nominate the Chief Executive as being the official best placed to represent them. While Agency Chief Executives have managerial authority to the extent set out in their Framework Documents, like other officials they give evidence on behalf of the Minister to whom they are accountable and are subject to that Minister's instruction. [. . .]

Parliamentary Privilege

52. Parliamentary proceedings are subject to absolute privilege, to ensure that those participating in them, including witnesses before select committees, can do so without fear of external consequences. This protection, enshrined in the Bill of Rights, is an essential element in ensuring that Parliament can exercise its powers freely on behalf of its electors. There must be no disciplinary action taken against civil servants or members of NDPBs (or anyone else) as a consequence of them giving evidence to a Select Committee. Any such action might be regarded as contempt of the House, with potentially serious consequences for those involved. [. . .]

Discussion of Government Policy

55. Officials should as far as possible confine their evidence to questions of fact and explanation relating to government policies and actions. They should be ready to explain what those policies are; the justification and objectives of those policies as the Government sees them; the extent to which those objectives have been met; and also to explain how administrative factors may have affected both the choice of policy measures and the manner of their implementation. Any comment by officials on government policies and actions should always be consistent with the principle of civil service political impartiality. Officials should as far as possible avoid being drawn into discussion of the merits of alternative policies where this is politically contentious. If official witnesses are pressed by the Committee to go beyond these limits, they should suggest that the questioning should be referred to Ministers.

Conduct of Individual Officials

73. Occasionally questions from a Select Committee may appear to be directed to the conduct of individual officials, not just in the sense of establishing the facts about what occurred in making decisions or implementing Government policies, but with the implication of allocating individual criticism or blame.

74. In such circumstances, and in accordance with the principles of Ministerial accountability, it is for the Minister to look into the matter and if necessary to institute a formal inquiry.

Such an inquiry into the conduct and behaviour of individual officials and consideration of disciplinary action is properly carried out within the Department according to established procedures designed and agreed for the purpose, and with appropriate safeguards for the individual. It is then the Minister's responsibility to inform the Committee of what has happened, and of what has been done to put the matter right and to prevent a recurrence. Evidence to a Select Committee on this should be given not by the official or officials concerned, but by the Minister or by a senior official designated by the Minister to give such evidence on the Minister's behalf.

QUESTIONS

1. How would you describe the status of this Cabinet Office publication?

2. It claims to 'summarize a number of longstanding conventions'. Identify what these are and list them.

3. To what extent can it be said that civil servants are accountable to select committees? How does this differ from the position of ministers?

4. Some people claim that the Widget Agency (an executive agency of the Department for Contraptions) has been unacceptably slow in dealing with applications for widget export licences. Who should a select committee question about this: the Secretary of State for Contraptions, the Permanent Secretary in the Department for Contraptions (i.e. the most senor civil servant in the department), or the chief executive of the Widget Agency?

In the next extract, a select committee reports on its findings following an inquiry into the possible trend towards the politicization of the public service (and whether this is a good or bad thing). This involved examining the respective roles of ministers and civil servants. It is a long extract, but you should read it carefully.

House of Commons Public Administration Select Committee, *Politics and Administration: Ministers and Civil Servants*, Third Report, 2006–07, HC 122–I (footnotes omitted)

2 The Accountability Gap

23. There is no consensus about the respective responsibilities of ministers and civil servants. Indeed, Janet Paraskeva, the First Civil Service Commissioner[36] told us "I believe that the doctrine of ministerial responsibility needs to be reviewed. [. . .] We no longer understand what it means [. . .]". It has been possible to reconcile a doctrine of ministerial accountability which holds that ministers are ultimately accountable for everything done on their behalf (whether by civil servants or other public employees) with the doctrine of civil service independence for over a century. Why has it now become more problematic? There are many reasons for this, but it is likely that the new attention to transparency, accountability and performance has played a major part. Indeed, the development of scrutiny by Parliamentary Committees has exposed the difficulties of assigning responsibilities. Senior civil servants have been made more visible by their regular appearances before Committees, supposedly

---

[36] Head of the public body that seeks to ensure that the civil service is effective and impartial, and that appointments are made on merit.

on ministers' behalf. At the same time, Permanent Secretaries [the top civil servants in each department] continue to appear before the Public Accounts Committee in their role as Accounting Officers, where they are individually responsible.

24. If ideas about ministerial and civil service responsibilities are varied and inconsistent, it is no wonder that the public service bargain[37] is no longer as straightforward as once it seemed. We try here to tease out some of the theory and reality of civil service and ministerial responsibility. This is a complex area, where different kinds of responsibility and accountability are closely interrelated, and where assumptions about the proper roles of ministers and civil servants are contested. We look at:

- the doctrine of ministerial accountability to Parliament;
- the extent to which civil servants are responsible to ministers and to what extent they have wider responsibilities;
- the effect of civil service independence on ministers' ability to run their departments;
- where authority and accountability should lie;
- the extent to which clear division between political and administrative responsibilities is possible; and
- the benefits of impartiality and the extent to which they are effectively secured.

This brief survey will give some idea of the muddle that is reality. We then consider whether there are ways in which the muddle could at least be tidied up.

Ministerial accountability to Parliament

25. The last Parliamentary examination of ministerial accountability was our predecessor Public Service Committee's report on Ministerial Accountability and Responsibility, which gives a detailed historical analysis. As that Report says, government has attempted to draw a distinction between actions for which ministers are responsible, where their acts and omissions have contributed to a policy or operational failure; and those for which they are accountable where, although they are not directly culpable, they have a duty to explain to Parliament what happened. That formulation has influenced debate on the issue, but has not been entirely accepted.

26. The Public Service Committee recommended the following as a working definition of Ministerial Accountability:

Ministers owe a fundamental duty to account to Parliament. This has, essentially, two meanings. First, that the executive is obliged to give an account—to provide full information about and explain its actions in Parliament so that they are subject to proper democratic scrutiny [. . .].

Second, a Minister's duty to account to Parliament means that the executive is liable to be held to account: it must respond to concerns and criticisms raised in Parliament about its actions because Members of Parliament are democratically-elected representatives of the people. A Minister's effective performance of his functions depends on his having the confidence of the House of Commons. [. . .]

---

37 The report explains this term at para. 5: '*That bargain held that officials were expected to trade political activity and high salaries for "relative anonymity, a trusted role at the heart of government and job security with generous pensions and honours", and politicians were expected to give up the right to hire and fire in return for "a lifetime of loyal service from the best and brightest the top universities could produce, with the highest ability to work the state machine and offer better informed and more politically acute advice than anyone else could provide". This bargain no longer appears to be universally accepted.*'

27. The Committee also considered that, as part of ministers' obligation to explain their actions to Parliament, they should make civil servants available to committees. The Government accepted the broad principles set out by the Select Committee, but was concerned that giving civil servants the responsibility to give information to Parliament on their own behalf would muddle their accountability.

[...]

29. The Public Service Committee did a great deal to clarify the nature of ministerial responsibility, and the Resolution of 1997 set out the best compromise which could be reached on the matter. Nonetheless, the Committee did not wholly accept the Government's attempts to distinguish between matters for which ministers were directly responsible and those for which they were merely accountable. As the Committee concluded "it is not possible absolutely to distinguish an area in which a minister is personally responsible, and liable to take blame, from one in which he is constitutionally accountable. Ministerial responsibility is not composed of two elements which have a clear break between the two". We agree that under our current constitutional arrangements there will never be precise clarity about the boundaries of ministerial accountability. That in itself suggests that we should be wary of constitutional changes which reduce ministerial responsibility without clearly transferring responsibility and accountability elsewhere. The question is, whether it is possible to clarify matters further in a way that would improve the effectiveness and accountability of our governing arrangements.

Civil service accountability to ministers

30. Just as it is impossible to be definitive about the boundaries of ministerial accountability, so civil service accountability is far from clear. The doctrine enunciated at the time of the Crichel Down affair[38] was that civil servants were accountable to ministers. Sir David Maxwell Fyfe[39] asserted confidently that:

The position of the civil servant is that he is wholly and directly responsible to his minister. It is worth stating again that he holds his office "at pleasure" and can be dismissed at any time by the Minister; and that power is nonetheless real because it is seldom used. The only exception relates to a small number of senior posts, like a permanent secretary, deputy secretary or principal finance officer, where since 1920, it has been necessary for the Minister to consult the Prime Minister, as he does on appointment.

It is clear from more recent cases, including the attempt by a former Home Secretary to dismiss the Director of the Prison Service, that matters are much less straightforward than that.[40] In 1996 the Employment Rights Act extended many employment rights to civil servants. When we pressed on the current constitutional position, we were told that employment law "applies to civil servants in the same way as it does to employees" and that the "Civil Service Management Code assumes that it is civil servants who take the actual decision to dismiss". Yet successive governments have stressed that civil servants are responsible to ministers, not Parliament.

31. Some of our witnesses felt that civil service independence had a political function, in balancing the strong executive power of British governments. This concern with the wider

[38] A scandal erupted in 1954 when it became known that a government department had broken a promise to a farmer that his land, requisitioned for use for bombing practice during the Second World War, would be returned to him when no longer needed.

[39] The Home Secretary at the time; as Lord Kilmuir, he was later appointed as Lord Chancellor.

[40] In 1997, there was an inquiry into a series of escapes from prisons. The Home Secretary of the time (Michael Howard) sought to pin the blame on the Prison Service (an executive agency of the Home Office) and refused to accept that he, as minister, was responsible.

responsibility of the civil service is not new. When the Armstrong Memorandum famously asserted that "civil servants are servants of the Crown [...] for all practical purposes the Crown in this context is represented by the government of the day", the FDA[41] expressed concern that this approach ignored the wider responsibilities civil servants had to Parliament.
[...]

Accounting to Parliament

54. The doctrine of accountability described above by Michael Howard [a Home Secretary in John Major's Conservative government in the 1990s], in which "Ministers should be responsible for decisions which they have taken; civil servants should be responsible for decisions which they have taken", can only work if there is transparency about what decisions were taken, and who took them. The current conventions about civil service relationship to Parliament prevent that transparency, and therefore inhibit accountability. The one exception is in the extremely rare cases when an Accounting Officer has formally advised against expenditure [...].

55. In the past Committees have called for civil servants to have some direct accountability to Parliament. This has been resisted, on the grounds that it would produce a division of loyalties for civil servants. Yet it is clear that in other jurisdictions civil servants have far more freedom to account for themselves, while ministers remain accountable for policy.

56. The doctrine of ministerial accountability means that when civil servants appear before Parliament it is as ministers' proxies. They get neither credit nor blame. By contrast, in both Finland and Sweden, civil servants operate under legal frameworks which give them a considerable degree of autonomy and accountability. As we have already noted, political and constitutional systems are complex, and must be considered in their entirety. In the United Kingdom, the legal assumption is that civil servants act on ministers' behalf, and exercise ministers' powers. In contrast, in Sweden and Finland civil servants are legally accountable themselves for the decisions they take, and will personally be held to account for those decisions. We have argued against the feasibility or desirability of a formal separation of accountability of this kind. Nonetheless, we believe that civil servants could be considerably more open with Parliament without threatening the doctrine of ministerial responsibility.

57. Times are changing. We now have a Freedom of Information Act. Recent major inquiries have illuminated the inner workings of government. The Leader of the House has undertaken that select committees will have access to the civil servants they consider best able to help them. Witnesses before this committee have been remarkably frank about the policy making process. These are welcome changes, but the formal position has not altered since the 1997 Resolution on ministerial responsibility. We consider it is time for it to do so. We consider that increasing the expectation that civil servants will account honestly to Parliament does not undermine the principle of ministerial responsibility, but strengthens accountability as a whole.

QUESTIONS

1. Summarize what the select committee says about the accountability of civil servants to Parliament.

2. Drawing on the material in this section, draft a statement about what the constitutional convention of individual ministerial responsibility entails.

---

41 The First Division Association is the professional association and union for the United Kingdom's senior public servants and professionals.

3. Does the constitutional convention of individual ministerial responsibility distinguish between accountability (that is, explaining what went wrong) and direct responsibility (that is, accepting blame for mistakes that a minister made)?

(d) CONSTITUTIONAL CONVENTION OF COLLECTIVE RESPONSIBILITY

Having looked at the constitutional convention of *individual* ministerial responsibility, we need now to consider (more briefly) the convention of *collective* ministerial responsibility. A statement of what this entails, in the view of the government, is set out in the *Ministerial Code*.

Cabinet Office, *Ministerial Code* (May 2010)

Collective responsibility

2.3 The internal process through which a decision has been made, or the level of Committee by which it was taken should not be disclosed. Decisions reached by the Cabinet or Ministerial Committees are binding on all members of the Government. They are, however, normally announced and explained as the decision of the Minister concerned. On occasion, it may be desirable to emphasise the importance of a decision by stating specifically that it is the decision of Her Majesty's Government. This, however, is the exception rather than the rule.

2.4 Matters wholly within the responsibility of a single Minister and which do not significantly engage collective responsibility need not be brought to the Cabinet or to a Ministerial Committee unless the Minister wishes to inform his colleagues or to have their advice. No definitive criteria can be given for issues which engage collective responsibility. The Cabinet Secretariats can advise where departments are unsure. When there is a difference between departments, it should not be referred to the Cabinet until other means of resolving it have been exhausted. It is the responsibility of the initiating department to ensure that proposals have been discussed with other interested departments and the outcome of these discussions should be reflected in the memorandum or letter submitted to Cabinet or a Cabinet Committee.

A minister who feels unable to support government policy is expected to resign from office. It is not possible for ministers simultaneously to remain in office and to seek to disagree or disassociate themselves from the collective view of the government. Ministers who resign in these circumstances may make a personal statement on the floor of the Commons.

Examples of ministerial resignations over disagreements with collective decisions include:

  i) **Robin Cook** (Tony Blair's Labour government), a former Foreign Secretary, resigned as Leader of the House of Commons in March 2003 in protest over government policy on Iraq. John Denham, a junior minister in the Ministry of Defence, also resigned.
  ii) **Sir Geoffrey Howe** (Margaret Thatcher's Conservative government) resigned as Deputy Prime Minister in November 1990 over government policy on the European single currency and the general approach to the European Union.

This rule applies even if the minister in question was not involved in actually making the decision (for example, if it was made in another department or a Cabinet committee of which the minister was not a member). There are, however, some matters of public interest on which the government does not have a collective view; if such a matter comes before Parliament, there is a 'free vote', meaning that the whips do not seek to instruct members of the governing party on how to vote. One example of this was in 2008 in relation to the Human Fertilization and Embryology Bill, and whether *in vitro* fertilization (IVF) treatment should be provided for single women and gay couples.

Departures from the practice of collective ministerial responsibility

On a couple of occasions during the 1970s, the Prime Ministers of the day were obliged to suspend the full operation of collective responsibility because of intractable internal disagreements within the government. Harold Wilson permitted ministers, subject to conditions, to take different views in the 1975 referendum on whether the United Kingdom should remain a member of the European Community. In 1977, James Callaghan allowed ministers to take different views on direct elections to the European Parliament.[42]

Vernon Bogdanor, *The New British Constitution* (2009, Oxford: Hart Publishing), p. 136

In [...] cases when collective responsibility was suspended, the Cabinet agreed to it in order to hold a warring government together. The implication would seem to be that collective responsibility is as much a maxim of political prudence as it is a convention of the constitution. It is in general sensible for a government to observe it, just as it is sensible for any collective executive, such as, for example, the board of a company, to maintain a united front, so as not to weaken its position by publicly displaying differences of opinion. On certain occasions, however, when there are deep-seated differences of opinion which cannot easily be reconciled, it maybe the lesser evil to suspend the principle.

Such occasions, when it seems the path of prudence to suspend collective responsibility, are likely to occur with increasing frequency in Scotland and Wales. But they could occur also at Westminster whether or not the electoral system is changed. For the principle of collective responsibility is more appropriate to an era of collective duopoly and tribal politics than to a period of multi-party politics, when governments are less likely to be unified ideologically than they once were.

Coalition government and collective responsibility since 2010

The formation of a coalition government after the May 2010 general election required negotiation between the Conservatives and Liberal Democrats to create a joint programme of government to be implemented over the following five years.[43] The agreement that emerged recognized that collective responsibility would generally apply to agreed government policy—so ministers, whether Conservative or Liberal Democrat, are expected to defend policy in Parliament and in public. On some areas of policy, however, the coalition agreement allows ministers to speak against government policy, or for MPs of one party to be given

---

[42] On the European Parliament, see Chapter 12.
[43] HM Government, *The Coalition: our programme for government* (2010, London: Cabinet Office).

permission to abstain from key votes in Parliament. The programme expressly recognized five areas on which there was agreement to disagree:

i) the Liberal Democrats would not have to vote for a policy of 'transferable tax allowances for married couples' (a Conservative manifesto commitment designed to use the tax system to promote marriage);

ii) the two parties, having acted jointly to secure legislation for a referendum on an alternative vote electoral system for the House of Commons were free to campaign on different sides in the actual referendum campaign—the Parliamentary Voting System and Constituencies Act 2011 was enacted and in a subsequent referendum people voted decisively against adopting AV;

iii) 'Liberal Democrats will continue to make the case for alternatives' to Trident, Britain's nuclear weapons programme—a final decision on this will not be made until 2016;

iv) the Liberal Democrats will be able to abstain in parliamentary votes on higher education funding for England and Wales, if they disagree with recommendations to be made by Lord Browne—in December 2010 all members of the government supported legislation to increase tuition fees, but twenty-one backbench Liberal Democrat MPs voted against;

v) and the agreement also allows the parties to agree to disagree about nuclear power policy—though in fact the two parties were subsequently able to agree a policy.

Confidence in government

Collective ministerial responsibility is important in terms of ensuring that there is effective accountability to Parliament. The government as a whole needs to defend its policies—and if the House of Commons were to lose confidence in the government as a whole, then the Prime Minister would, under a constitutional convention, be obliged to ask the monarch to exercise her prerogative power to dissolve Parliament, triggering a general election.

Writing in 1967, Marshall and Moodie said that '*The defeat of any substantial bill is nowadays regarded as a loss of confidence* [...] *governments now regard it as politically incumbent upon them to avoid defeat in the Commons on any issue whatsoever*'.[44] They were critical of the rigidity of this practice—and rightly so. Current practice is far more relaxed, and there have been occasions on which the government's proposed policy contained in a Bill has been defeated on a vote and withdrawn, and it has not been suggested that the government as a whole should resign. For example, in November 2005, a proposal to allow terrorist suspects to be detained without charge or trial for ninety days was voted down by the Commons.

Occasionally, the House of Commons is called on to debate a motion expressing 'no confidence' (or, if the government is moving the motion, 'confidence'). The last time that a government was defeated on a confidence motion was in March 1979. After the debate, the Prime Minister made the following statement.

House of Commons Hansard, 28 March 1979, cols 589–90

Mr James Callaghan: Mr Speaker, now that the House has declared itself, we shall take our case to the country. Tomorrow I shall propose to Her Majesty that Parliament be dissolved

---

[44] G. Marshall and G. Moodie, *Some Problems of the Constitution*, 4th edn (1967, London: Hutchinson University Library), p. 62.

> as soon as essential business can be cleared up, and then I shall announce as soon as may be—and that will be as soon as possible—the date of Dissolution, the date of the election and the date of meeting of the new Parliament.
>
> Mrs Margaret Thatcher: As the Government no longer have authority to carry on business without the agreement of the Opposition, I make it quite clear that we shall facilitate any business which requires the agreement of the Opposition so that the Dissolution can take place at the very earliest opportunity and the uncertainty ended.

A vote of this sort will succeed in dislodging a government from power if the government has a small (or no overall) majority.

QUESTIONS

1. Can collective responsibility really be regarded as a convention if governments are able to choose to suspend it?

2. Tricia Trout, the Secretary of State for Animal Welfare, announces during a radio interview that her department will be publishing a consultation document on making angling unlawful. Peter Pike MP, a junior minister in the Foreign Office (who, in his private life, is a keen angler) is shocked about this and tells a journalist 'this is a bonkers initiative from a department that is out of touch with reality'. This quote features prominently on the front page of a national newspaper. Has Ms Trout breached the *Ministerial Code*? Has Pike?

(e) THE MECHANICS OF ACCOUNTABILITY

Having now looked at the key *concepts* about how ministers and to some extent senior civil servants are accountable to Parliament (individual responsibility, collective responsibility, 'confidence in government'), we can now examine the *practical ways* in which this accountability is achieved (through select committees; answers to written and oral questions; and in debates on the floor of each House). There is a broad political consensus about the need for government to be subject to effective scrutiny, although there is considerable disagreement about how this should be achieved. In 1979, the then Conservative government (led by Margaret Thatcher) encouraged the House of Commons to establish the system of departmental select committees that we shall go on to examine. As we have seen, a resolution on ministerial responsibility was passed in the dying days of John Major's premiership in 1997.[45] Under the Labour governments of 1997–2010, further attempts were made to strengthen parliamentary accountability, including the introduction of 'pre-appointment hearings' (at which select committees question a minister's nominee for certain major public offices such as the ombudsmen and regulators),[46] introducing formal requirements for some government decisions taken under prerogative powers (including treaty-making and ordering British troops into armed combat) to be approved by Parliament,[47] and a Backbench Business Committee, which decides what is debated in the House of Commons on a few days each month.

---

[45] See extract House of Commons Hansard, 19 March 1997 on p. 257.

[46] See House of Commons Liaison Committee, *Pre-appointment Hearings by Select Committees: Government Response to the Committee's First Report of Session 2007–08* on p. 255.

[47] See Chapter 9.

Select committees

Before the 1980s, there was a rather ramshackle collection of House of Commons committees of backbench MPs responsible for scrutinizing the work of some government departments and various areas of policy. A new, far more comprehensive system of 'select' committees—a better name would be 'scrutiny' committees—was introduced in 1979. Now, every major department has a corresponding select committee, typically comprising between twelve and fifteen MPs reflecting the party-political composition of the House of Commons as a whole. Distinct from these 'departmental' select committees is the influential Public Accounts Committee, which scrutinizes public expenditure rather than policy.

Figure 7.2 A House of Commons select committee

The role of select committees is advisory and their methods of work inquisitorial. The relevant department is obliged to respond to committee reports, but there is no obligation to accept their findings. Committees devise a programme of topics on which they wish to conduct inquiries. Some inquiries have a much wider focus than what happened within government: for example, the 2011 inquiry by the Culture, Media and Sport Committee into phone hacking took evidence from Rupert Murdoch and the police.

Each committee is assisted by a clerk (who will normally take a lead in drafting a report for MPs to consider) and a small number of other staff. Specialist advisers, often academics, may be appointed to help the committee to identify suitable witnesses and to draft questions for MPs to ask. The questioning to which ministers may be subjected at an appearance before a select committee is far more rigorous and sustained than is the case when ministers appear 'at the despatch box' to answer oral questions on the floor of the chamber. The role of chairman can be a demanding one and the MPs appointed to this role receive a payment on top of their MPs' salary. The methods of working will vary according to the requirements of the particular inquiry, but usually include a public call for written evidence and several oral evidence sessions with key witnesses—including the relevant minister and senior civil servants. The questioning to which ministers may be subjected at an appearance before a select committee is far more rigorous and sustained than is the case when ministers appear 'at the despatch box' to answer oral questions on the floor of the chamber.

Most of the time, select committees are able to work in a consensual, cross-party manner rather than dividing along party lines. They provide an oasis of non-party activity in an institution that is otherwise dominated by the cut and thrust of party politics. Party whips do not overtly issue instructions to committee members on how to vote; and in 2010, changes were made to the system of selection of chairs, with most now being elected by fellow MPs rather than agreed behind the scenes through private negotiations between political parties.

A 2011 study by UCL Constitution Unit sought to measure the impact select committees have on government policy. The report concluded that *'we almost invariably end up with a mixed picture. The select committees are influential, but not all of the time'.* Data analysed in the study showed that *'roughly 40% of committee recommendations were accepted and implemented by government, though two thirds of recommendations calling for a medium or large policy change ultimately failed'.*[48]

There are also select committees in the House of Lords. Unlike most of the House of Commons' select committees, they do not shadow the work of particular government departments, but instead have remits to cover general topics. The House of Lords' Constitution Committee scrutinizes all government Bills[49] and also conducts thematic inquiries into broader constitutional issues. In Chapter 9, we examine the Committee's report on the reform of war-making powers; other inquiries have looked at the constitutional implications of the 'surveillance society', the relationship between the executive, judiciary, and Parliament, the operation of the Cabinet Office, and referendums. Other select committees include the European Union Committee (which operates through a system of subcommittees),[50] the Economic Affairs Committee, and the Science and Technology Committee.

Time—too little, critics say—is allowed for committee reports to be debated on the floor of the respective House.

Parliamentary questions

Parliamentary questions (PQs) to ministers may be asked orally and in written form by MPs and peers. All questions must conform to certain guidelines, and MPs and peers may seek advice from parliamentary officials to ensure that they comply with these guidelines.

House of Commons Information Office, *Parliamentary Questions*, Factsheet P1 (December 2008)

A parliamentary question must:

- either (a) seek information ('what, how many, when...') or (b) press for action ('if he will ...');
- not offer or seek expressions of opinion;
- not convey information nor advance a proposition, an argument or debate;

---

[48] Meg Russell and Meghan Benton, *Selective Influence: the policy impact of House of Commons select committees* (2011, London: UCL Constitution Unit,) p. 96.
[49] See Chapter 10.
[50] See Chapter 8.

- have a factual basis for which the tabling Member is responsible (it may not, for example, seek confirmation or denial of rumours or media reports);

- relate to a matter for which the Minister addressed is responsible as a Minister (it may not, for example ask about: activities in a Minister's capacity as party leader or member; reports or research by independent organisations, no matter how pertinent; or matters which are the statutory responsibility of the devolved administrations);

- not seek an expression of opinion on, or an interpretation of, a question of law, since this is for the courts to decide;

- not refer to a matter active before a UK court or court martial (including a coroner's court), as this is prohibited by the House's sub judice rule;

- not ask for information: readily available elsewhere (including in Hansard); or provided or blocked / otherwise denied by the same Minister in the same session;

- not be hypothetical or obviously about opposition policy.

In the Commons, the first hour of business in the chamber on weekdays is devoted to ministers answering oral questions from MPs. There is a rota, so that the ministerial team from each department has to appear before the chamber every few weeks. There are always more MPs wanting to ask questions than can be accommodated in the time available, so MPs have to enter a ballot and are able to ask their question—followed by one or more 'supplementary' questions—only if they win a slot. Ministers have advance notice of some questions, but time is also set aside for 'topical' questions on any relevant subject.

Since 1961, there has been a practice of the Prime Minister answering oral questions on a weekly basis—known as the Prime Minister's Questions (PMQs). Initially, this happened twice weekly for 15 minutes, but since 2003, the practice has been for the Prime Minister to appear before the Commons for 30 minutes at noon on Wednesdays (when Parliament is sitting). This gladiatorial contest between the Prime Minister, the leaders of the Opposition parties, and other MPs is widely reported, and is an important opportunity for the Commons to call the government to account publicly.

Many thousands of written PQs are tabled in Parliament each year and ministers' responses (drafted on behalf of ministers by civil servants) are published in *Hansard*. Concerns have been expressed as to how effective written PQs are in calling the government to account. Criticisms include that there are delays in providing answers, that answers are sometimes incomplete and irrelevant, and that answers are not given on the grounds that the cost of researching the answer would be disproportionate (currently, the threshold is £750).

Barry Hough, 'Ministerial responses to parliamentary questions: Some recent concerns' [2003] Public Law 211 (footnotes omitted)

[...] Whilst it will always be a characteristic of parliamentary government that the relationship between the House of Commons and the government involves a continuing political struggle on the part of MPs to gain more information than ministers are willing to provide, there have recently been sustained allegations that something more sinister than the adversarial dynamic is at work; namely, that government is unduly secretive, and that ministers are both disregarding the Ministerial Code and the parliamentary resolutions enshrined within it. Members have made claims that the convention of individual ministerial responsibility is "frequently" breached. It has also been alleged that PQs "repeatedly" put to ministers fail to receive answers. Such was the concern that the Speaker was persuaded to provide a ruling on the matter. Indeed, the criticisms were judged to be sufficiently serious to justify the attention of the Procedure and the Public Administration Select Committees. The Parliamentary Ombudsman has also become involved, and he has expressed his disappointment that departments are refusing access to information in order to avoid political embarrassment.

The fundamental purpose of the convention of individual ministerial responsibility is that it provides an important means of drawing information into the public domain. The obtaining of information, by MPs on behalf of their constituents, lies at the heart of the scrutiny process: the public accountability of government is a necessary and basic characteristic of any democratic system and ill-informed debate will not be effective. More generally, the openness and accountability of government is required by the fourth and fifth principles of public life set out by the Committee on Standards in Public Life, which have been incorporated into the Ministerial Code. However, where ministers refuse to provide information, the complaints of Westminster MPs that there are no sanctions recall Hobbes' axiom that, 'Covenants without the sword are but words'. The Speaker has advised members who do not receive satisfactory responses that their only present recourse is either to press the minister concerned, or to raise the matter with the chair of the Public Administration Select Committee.

Debates on the floor of the House

Debates on the floor of the Commons and the Lords are a further way in which the government is called to account for its policies and alleged failings, and for Parliament to discuss matters of public interest. In Chapter 10, we will see that much debating time is taken up with discussion of Bills—the government's proposals for legislation—but debates also focus on how the government is conducting its executive functions. During 2012, Opposition day debates included 'Banking (responsibilities and reform'), adult social care, and the National Heath Service. In 'adjournment debates', the House is not called on to come to any specific conclusion and there is no vote at the end of deliberations. Debates may be initiated by the government, by leaders of the Opposition parties (twenty days are allocated for this purpose every year), or by backbench MPs (for the final 30 minutes of every day).

Since 1999, in order to make more time for debates initiated by backbench MPs and select committees, there has been a 'parallel chamber' in which the House of Commons may sit simultaneously in the main chamber and another debating room known as 'Westminster Hall'.

QUESTIONS

1. If you were an MP, would you rather be a junior minster or the chairman of a select committee? Which of these roles do you think has more influence?

2. Have a look through the archive of PMQs on the No. 10 Downing Street website. How effective is this practice in calling the government to account? Or do you think that it is only theatre?

3. Joe Bloggs is a new MP. Imagine that you are a clerk in the Table Office. Advise Mr Bloggs on his draft PQ: 'Will the minister confirm that she has read the reports in *The Ambridge Times* [a newspaper] about the utterly deplorable and unlawful way in which people in my constituency have been treated by the local council deciding to evict them from their allotments and will she do something about it?'

7 CONCLUDING COMMENTS

This chapter has considered some of the main institutions of government—monarchy, ministers, civil servants, and appointed public office-holders—and has considered how they are called to account, focusing on the work of the UK Parliament. To continue reading about government, turn to Chapter 8 (which looks at executive power in the United Kingdom) or Chapter 9 (which considers how UK government ministers and the Crown exercise prerogative powers). To explore how government is structured at devolved level, turn back to Chapter 5 (multilevel governing).

8 FURTHER READING

Kaufman, G., *How to Be a Minister* (1997, London: Faber and Faber)

Stanley, M., *Politico's Guide to How to Be a Civil Servant*, 2nd edn (2004, London: Methuen)

ONLINE RESOURCE CENTRE
Further information about the themes discussed in this chapter can be found on the Online Resource Centre at www.oxfordtextbooks.co.uk/orc/lesueur2e/

8

EXERCISE AND CONTROL OF EXECUTIVE POWER IN THE EUROPEAN UNION

CENTRAL ISSUES

1. Who or what is the government of the European Union? The principal institutions are listed in Art. 13 TEU. This chapter will consider the role of those institutions that exercise executive power—namely, the European Council, the Council of the European Union, and the Commission.

2. What are the functions of the main executive institutions? In the EU context, it is impossible to identify one institution as the sole executive. Whereas, traditionally, governmental functions were divided along legislative, executive, and judicial lines, many of the functions are shared between the EU institutions. The European Union has replaced the doctrine of the separation of powers with the doctrine of 'institutional balance'.

3. What are the controls on the exercise of executive power? Although the European Union has been successful in shifting policymaking away from national governments by developing so-called governance structures, it is often criticized for having neglected political accountability. To whom are the EU policymakers accountable? Should national parliaments have a greater role to play in holding national ministers (who make policy in the Council) to account?

4. The chapter will also examine whether, and if so by what standards, the European Union has democratic legitimacy. The EU institutions with executive powers are not directly elected by the people. Does that mean that those institutions are undemocratic and that the entire European Union lacks legitimacy? Or are there alternative ways of generating legitimacy that need to be explored?

1 INTRODUCTION

This chapter introduces the European Union (EU), explains the role and functions of those EU institutions that wield executive powers, and touches upon their different rationales ('supranationalism' versus 'intergovernmentalism'). It then relates the institutional discussion to key concepts within constitutional law (democracy, legitimacy, accountability, and transparency). The chapter concludes with a discussion of the UK Parliament's role in the European policymaking process.

We encourage readers to study the EU institutions critically, but with an open mind. When viewed from the nation state's perspective, the way in which the EU exercises power, and the purposes for which it does so, are easily and often dismissed as autocratic, obscure, unaccountable, and out-of-touch with the popular will. In light of this perception, it is important to consider whether the EU ensures that the general constitutional and administrative law principles of good government, and the fundamental standards of accessibility, transparency, and reasoned and rational decision-making, are, in fact, met.

2 UNDERSTANDING THE TREATY STRUCTURE

Before going any further, an introduction to the legal foundations of the European Union is needed. The EU and its forerunners were created by treaties agreed between the member states (see Chapter 12). The United Kingdom joined on 1 January 1973. In broad terms, the treaties can be thought of as falling into three main phases.

BOX 8.1 THE EU TREATY FRAMEWORK

1950s–1993	1993–2009**	Since December 2009***
Treaty Establishing the European Coal and Steel Community	Treaty on European Union (TEU, or 'Maastricht Treaty')	Treaty on European Union (TEU) (revised)
Treaty Establishing the European Atomic Energy Community	Treaty Establishing the European Communities (TEC)	Treaty on the Functioning of the European Union (TFEU)
Treaty Establishing the European Economic Community*	*Expansion from fifteen to twenty-five, and then to twenty-seven, members*	*Twenty-eight members (from July 2013)[1]*
Membership grows from six, to nine, to twelve		

* Reformed by the Single European Act (a treaty) in 1987
** Reforms made by the Treaty of Amsterdam (1999) and the Treaty of Nice (2003)
*** Reforms introduced by the Treaty of Lisbon 2009

The various reforms to the treaties have periodically required Articles to be renumbered and some Articles have moved between treaties. When reading older material, it is therefore necessary to bear in mind that an Article referred to by number may be different from the Article of that same number in the treaties now in force. In this book, we use the treaty numbering introduced when the Lisbon Treaty came into force on 1 December 2009.

---

[1] Croatia signed the EU accession treaty in December 2011 and will formally accede to the European Union as the 28th member state in July 2013.

3 THE ORIGINS OF THE EUROPEAN UNION (1945–57)

In Chapter 7, we looked at the role of government—'the executive'—in the modern British constitutional system. There is, we saw, a twofold aspect to constitutional processes and institutions. Constitutional law *empowers* governments by providing a framework for policymaking and implementation, but it also seeks to *constrain* governmental power, ensuring that executive functions are carried out in accordance with the rule of law and in an accountable way.

This tension between empowerment and constraint is also a dominant theme in relation to the operation of the European Union, with which this chapter is concerned. But before we examine the exercise of executive power in the EU, we need to remind ourselves that the story of the EU is a remarkable political project, with humble origins and ambitious plans.

D. Dinan, *Europe Recast: A History of European Union* (2004, Boulder, CO: Lynne Rienner), pp. 1–2

The idea of a united Europe is a recurring theme in the long and often violent history of the continent. The Holy Roman Emperors, Napoleon, Hitler, and others all sought, in sometimes horrifying ways, to achieve a continental unity based variously on princely alliances, ethnic cohesion, ideology, or raw power. Ever since the emergence of the modern state, philosophers and political thinkers have also imagined a united Europe triumphing over narrow national interests and allegiances. Today's European Union (EU) is unique among these competing visions. Tempering the nationalist ethos that had become the ruling principle of European political development, the countries that formed the European Communities, the basis of the European Union, chose to limit (but not eliminate) their own sovereignty, the hallmark of a modern nation-state, in favour of collective peace, economic integration, and supranational governance.

Their reasons for doing so were rooted in the disastrous decades of the early twentieth century. The miserable legacy of heroic European nationalism—two world wars, countless millions dead, and economic ruin—was not lost on the people of Europe, who generally supported economic and political integration after World War II. Eurofederalism was popular. European politicians wanted above all to end international strife, foster social harmony, and promote economic well-being. They sought to build a better world, free of the hatreds and rivalries that had destroyed their countries in recent years. For their generation, European integration became synonymous with peace and prosperity.

Yet, there was nothing inevitable about the emergence of European integration in the form with which we are now familiar. European politicians were (and still are) instinctively averse to sharing national sovereignty, despite rhetorical flourishes to the contrary. National leaders decided to share sovereignty in supranational organizations primarily because they perceived that it was in their countries' (and therefore their own) interests to do so. Ideas, intellectual fashion, opportunity, chance, conviction, calculation, personal predilection, and ambition all played a part. Ultimately, however, European integration emerged as it did because of a rational response by politicians, businesspeople, and other key actors to changing economic, political, and strategic circumstances, ranging from Germany's postwar recovery, to the fall of the Berlin Wall, to the acceleration of globalization. Despite growing public concern about the process and politics of European integration, Europeans generally acquiesced because the outcome seemed worthwhile and the alternatives less attractive.

The lessons of the Second World War, and of the burgeoning Cold War between the West and Stalin's Soviet Union, brought home the need for Western Europe to unite. Externally, the USA supported the process of integration from 1947—most notably in the form of the Marshall Plan. It was administered by the Organisation for European Economic Co-operation (OEEC), and was designed to build a stronger foundation for the countries of Western Europe and to act as a bulwark against communism. The US ideal of a single European plan modelled on the USA in its political (federal) and economic (free trade, free market) structure was echoed by Winston Churchill in his famous speech in 1946 to the Academic Youth in Zurich: '*The cannons have ceased firing. The fighting has stopped; but the dangers have not stopped. If we are to form the United States of Europe, or whatever name it may take, we must begin now.*' Ultimately, the plan to federalize did not work, and could never have worked, for a number of reasons: because the geopolitical situation in Europe did not lend itself to becoming the 'USA Mark II'; because the United Kingdom, still a world power in its own eyes, would not have taken part; and because France was hoping to resurrect its central European role in the future.

Internally, too, some early European federalists wanted to create a new European order as a counterweight to the excesses and the flaws of nationhood and sovereignty that had brought about totalitarian regimes. Altiero Spinelli was a former member of the Italian Communist Party who had been interned by Mussolini on the island of Ventotene. The manifesto that he co-wrote during captivity in 1941, calling for a united Europe to replace the old one of competing nation states, had to be smuggled off the island. Later, Spinelli's European federalist movement played a central role in the creation of the European Defence Community (EDC)—a pan-European defence force that was to act as a military counterweight to the Soviet Bloc, as well as an alternative to Germany's rearmament and accession to the North Atlantic Treaty Organization (NATO). The EDC failed (and the federalist movement lost its momentum) when France refused to ratify the Treaty in 1954. Today, one of the European Parliament's buildings in Brussels is named after Spinelli.

Jean Monnet, the head of France's General Planning Commission, reacted to the collapse of the EDC by relaunching the process of uniting Europe in steps and stages. Contrary to US plans of immediate federalization, the monumental process of achieving a 'United States of Europe' began with a series of strategic and pragmatic planning decisions. Monnet drafted a government proposal for the then-French Foreign Minister Robert Schuman with the ambitious goal of making a future war between France and Germany '*not only unthinkable but materially impossible*' by entangling West German and French affairs.[2] Monnet's aspiration was to create '*the first concrete foundations of the European Federation which is indispensable to the maintenance of peace*'.[3] The Treaty of Paris (1951)—which was also signed by Italy, Belgium, Luxembourg, and the Netherlands—made two important innovations. First, it created a common market for coal, iron, and steel (the key resources of the war industries), within which market prices were freely set, and import/export duties, subsidies, and other restrictions and discriminatory practices were gradually removed. Second, it placed these industries under a supranational authority, the European Coal and Steel Community (ECSC), which was governed by a 'High Authority' (of which Jean Monnet became President), checked politically by bodies representing governments and members of Parliament (MPs), and legally by an independent judiciary.

---

[2] Robert Schuman's proposal of 9 May 1950.
[3] J. Monnet, *Memoirs* (1978, New York: Doubleday and Company), p. 298.

But Monnet was not merely concerned with creating a federation of states. He famously remarked that Europe's circumstances required '*that we unite Europeans and that we do not keep them separated. We are not joining states, we are unifying men*'.[4] The next step was the proposal of an economic union, which was finally agreed in March 1957 and incorporated in the Treaty of Rome. The aims of the European Economic Community (EEC) were to create a common market, to approximate the economic policies of the six member states, to promote a harmonious development of their economic activities, to create the framework for gradual economic expansion and stability, and to improve the living standards of the citizens of the member states. The Treaty also provided for the free movement of the factors of production (labour, goods, services, and capital) within the Community, common agricultural and transport policies, and the coordination of economic policies of the member states.

The ultimate goal of European integration and unity may not be immediately apparent with respect to the EEC, which focused firmly on economic and trade development. After all, human rights, democracy, and the rule of law were conspicuous only by their absence from the Treaty of Rome. (These constitutional principles, it should be noted, were already covered by the slightly older and separate Council of Europe, established in 1949, which adopted the European Convention for the Protection of Human Rights and Fundamental Freedoms—known as the European Convention on Human Rights, or ECHR—in 1950.) But more to the point, the themes of European integration, peace, and prosperity were gradually being put into operation through the immediate and progressive opening, widening, and internationalizing of the economic market, and by the long-term possibility of political unity.

J. Peterson and M. Shackleton, 'Conclusion', in J. Peterson and M. Shackleton (eds) *The Institutions of the European Union*, 3rd edn (2012, Oxford: OUP), p. 384

[...] European integration as a project began with what, in retrospect, were strikingly narrow and overwhelmingly economic objectives: first, to manage jointly the production of coal and steel; then, to develop a common market. Yet the earliest moves to institutionalize European cooperation were never seen as final. They represented something new and unspecified, but which definitely went beyond the intergovernmental cooperation of, for example, the Council of Europe, with its limited agenda and resources and nonbinding decision-making. From the beginning, EU institution-building had a decidedly political purpose: to make European states ever more mutually dependent on one another. Then, as now, this aim generates tensions between those who wish to reinforce the central institutions in a federalist direction and those who see them as instrumental vehicles for maximizing state interests.

The creation of the EEC and Schuman's idea of European integration can be seen as imaginative and pragmatic responses to the project of uniting Europe, and creating peace and prosperity,[5] and as an *alternative* to the US Plan for European Integration.[6] The EEC

---

[4] Speech of 30 April 1952, see J. Monnet, *Les États-Unis d'Europe ont Commencé: La Communauté Européene du Charbon et de l'Acier, Discours et Allocutions 1952–1954* (1955, Paris: Robert Laffont), p. 132.

[5] See now Art. 3(1) TEU: '*The Union's aim is to promote peace, its values and the well-being of its peoples*'.

[6] E. Hobsbawm, *Age of Extremes: The Short Twentieth Century 1914–1991* (1994, London: Michael Joseph), pp. 239–41.

immediately had to deal with economic challenges (such as Germany's rapid economic recovery, the worsening East–West conflict, and differing US, French, and German needs and objectives), and also with real changes in political structures. In October 2012, the EU was awarded the Nobel Peace Prize for its efforts in advancing peace in Europe over six decades. In an important book, the historian Alan Milward argued that the model of the nation state—that is, the dominant form of political, economic, and social organization in Western Europe from the sixteenth century—had gradually been weakening since the eighteenth century. The experience of most European states in the late 1930s and early 1940s was that they were incapable of fulfilling their primary duty—namely, the defence of the national territory and the protection of their citizens. After the Second World War, European states (as well as the model of the nation state) were on the brink of collapse. Milward argued that the new political consensus among leading French, German, UK, and US politicians was built on the coalescence of European and national interests, and the sharing of sovereignty. The development of the European Community was, therefore, designed to rescue the European nation state. At the same time, it set in train a lengthy, unpredictable, ambitious, and controversial process of economic and political European integration.

Alan S. Milward, *The European Rescue of the Nation State*, 2nd edn (2000, London: Routledge), pp. 2–3

That these nation-states, some of them of the most ancient lineage, with their distinctive histories and cherished myths, on which have been nurtured generations of citizens, should declare their intention of voluntarily achieving political unification is a political and historical change of the first magnitude. Yet it remains one of the most ill-understood aspects of recent history and present political life. For this lack of understanding much blame must lie with the absorption into popular discussion of an assumption which underlies most of the theoretical and scholarly writing about the European Community, the assumption that it is in antithesis to the nation-state.

The word which is commonly used to describe the evolution of the European Community, 'integration', is itself a reflection of that assumption. It implies that the economies, societies and administrations of these national entities become gradually merged into a larger identity. Defenders of the nation-state, those for whom it remains an indispensable form of organization, politically, economically, culturally or even psychologically, therefore clamour for a halt to the process of integration. The most ardent supporters of the European Community in return denounce the nation-state as an anachronistic barrier to the final achievement of a more advanced stage of government and society, the supranation. This antithesis between the concepts of nation-state and Community has frequently been emphasized by the European Community's interpretation of its own history. Homage has always been required to the idea that the Community represented the birth of a new historical epoch, in which the nation-state would wither away. Lord Cockfield, rumoured to have been originally appointed as a European Commissioner by the British government because of his alleged scepticism about the Community, summed up his views after his replacement by saying "The gradual limitation of national sovereignty is part of a slow and painful forward march of humanity."[7] Against such an argument only a similarly categorical statement is likely to serve. Thus opponents of the European Community demand that a finite limit be drawn now to the process of integration in order to save the nation.

[7] *The Guardian*, 11 November 1988.

> But is there in fact an antithesis between the European Community and the nation-state? Does the evolution of the Community imply the replacement of the nation-state as an organizational framework and its eventual supersession? It is the argument of this book that there is no such antithesis and that the evolution of the European Community since 1945 has been an integral part of the reassertion of the nation-state as an organizational concept. The argument goes, however, beyond this, because the historical evidence points to the further conclusion that without the process of integration the west European nation-state might well not have retained the allegiance and support of its citizens in the way that it has. The European Community has been its buttress, an indispensable part of the nation-state's post-war construction. Without it, the nation-state could not have offered to its citizens the same measure of security and prosperity which it has provided and which has justified its survival. After 1945 the European nation-state rescued itself from collapse, created a new political consensus as the basis of its legitimacy, and through changes in its response to its citizens which meant a sweeping extension of its functions and ambitions reasserted itself as the fundamental unit of political organization. The European Community only evolved as an aspect of that national reassertion and without it the reassertion might well have proved impossible. To supersede the nation-state would be to destroy the Community. To put a finite limit to the process of integration would be to weaken the nation-state, to limit its scope and to curb its power.

Since integration has always been carefully tailored to European national needs and sensitivities, and deliberately did not follow the US model of federalism, US commentators sometimes look down on, and misunderstand, the European project. The geopolitical need for cooperation on the crowded westernmost peninsula of Eurasia is often compared unfavourably with the USA's military ability to act unilaterally. In relation to strategic and foreign policy issues, Robert Kagan famously argued that '*Americans are from Mars, and Europeans are from Venus*'.[8] This suggests that European states are emasculated, shorn of their own distinct national identity, and unable to form individual judgement or to reach tough political decisions. Francis Fukuyama refers derisively to '*those flabby, prosperous, self-satisfied, inward-looking, weak-willed states whose grandest project was nothing more heroic than the creation of the Common Market*'.[9] Such statements reinforce the view that European states have capitulated to a new form of (weak) European governance and surrendered their political sovereignty.

By way of contrast, Milward argues that the post-war evolution of the EEC was designed purposively by the European states themselves. Contrary to the comments given, European integration constitutes precisely an act of national will—that is, an expression of political sovereignty. The aspiration to reassert the nation state as the fundamental organizational unit of political, economic, and social existence, and to transfer sovereign power to the EEC is all the more impressive if one bears in mind the political, economic, and psychological obstacles that first needed to be overcome.

---

[8] R. Kagan, *Of Paradise and Power: America and Europe in the New World Order* (2003, New York: Knopf), p. 3.

[9] Francis Fukuyama, 'The end of history?', *The National Interest*, Summer 1989, p. 8.

D. Dinan, *Europe Recast: A History of European Union* (2004, Boulder, CO: Lynne Rienner), p. 6

The six countries that launched the European Community in the 1950s were far from flabby, prosperous, self-satisfied, or inward looking. Nor were they weak willed. Despite Fukuyama's disgust for a vision devoid of colour and heroic derring-do, it took a leap of faith and rare political courage for most of those countries to turn their backs on traditional nation-state aspirations and agree to exercise some of their powers in common. For France, in particular, accepting the EC meant abandoning decades of protectionism, overcoming deep distrust of Germany, and embracing economic modernization—a drastic revision of the country's long-standing self-image as a great power. For Germany, utterly destroyed at the end of the war, European integration offered salvation and international rehabilitation. Britain stayed outside the Communities because its national interests, or at least the government's perception of its national interests, pointed in a different direction.

The United Kingdom's momentous decision in 1973 to join what is now the European Union has had the consequence that considerable policymaking and law-making power has been transferred from institutions in the United Kingdom to those in the EU. To take only one example: in 1970, governmental decisions about agriculture were exclusively matters for UK ministers and the UK Parliament; now, most aspects of policy and law regulating agriculture is made by the EU institutions. We therefore need to examine the main EU institutions that have executive functions—notably, the European Council, the Council of the European Union, and the Commission—and discuss issues of legitimacy and accountability.

A major criticism levelled at the European Union is that it suffers from a 'democracy deficit'. In the political system of the European Union, executive power is generated through two separate, but related, processes. First, policy powers and responsibilities are transferred from national political systems to the European level, and now cover most areas of public policy. Second, the European Union has its own institutions and decision-making processes. In other words, executive power is divided vertically (between the member states and the European Union) and horizontally (between the EU institutions). There is also a national dimension. Public accountability is the other side of executive power. As we saw in Chapter 7, the UK Parliament holds the executive to account by scrutinizing the decisions of ministers. We need to examine how UK ministers participate in the work of the EU institutions and, importantly, how they can be held to account in the UK Parliament for their decisions on EU matters. In so far as there is a democracy deficit in the EU, can this be filled—from the British perspective—by good systems of accountability within UK institutions?

4 WHERE DOES EXECUTIVE POWER IN THE EUROPEAN UNION LIE?

Generally, we can say that 'executive power' refers to the power of politicians to develop new policy initiatives and to take action in what they see as the national interest. Their decisions and actions are implemented by politically neutral civil servants and other officials. The locus of executive or administrative power in the European Union cannot be easily identified. Decision-making takes place on different levels and involves at least three types of actor.

In the first instance, the European Union has its own institutions, three of which lay claim to executive or administrative authority within the EU:

- the European Council brings together the heads of state or government of the member states and the President of the Commission;

- the Council of the European Union (colloquially referred to as the 'Council of Ministers', or simply as the 'Council') provides a decision-making forum for the ministers of the member states who share the same or similar portfolio (for example, health ministers or agriculture ministers); and

- the Commission is headed by a 28-member College of Commissioners.

The second group of actors are the governments of the member states, which want to protect their own interests and preferences, and have their own internal organizational arrangements for dealing with EU day-to-day business. From time to time, the national governments also exercise the most fundamental of executive powers when they negotiate over reforms of the international treaties that create the EU institutions and confer power on them.

The final group of active participants in the EU policy process involves a host of other actors, such as non-member state governments, subnational levels of government (in the United Kingdom, the Scottish Government, Northern Ireland Executive, and the Welsh Assembly Government), business corporations, and interest groups (such as trade unions and environmental groups) that seek to organize and represent their interests at national or European level.

The European Union was designed with its own multilevel set of actors and institutions, which highlights not only their own specific characteristics (as we shall see), but also the limitations of the powers of the nation-state. International organizations such as the European Union (but also the Council of Europe) were created because (as we saw in the extract by Milward) the political form of the nation-state was no longer considered adequate to guarantee the full implementation of the democracy principle. The questions for the project of European integration were, first, whether, and to what extent, the known 'models' of *government* could transcend state borders and be translated to the supranational level; and second, whether the European Union envisaged, and was based on, a different kind of *governance*.

V. Bogdanor, *Legitimacy, Accountability and Democracy in the European Union,* A Federal Trust Report (2007), p. 19

The institutions of the European Union were set up in the 1950s, and they were based very much on the ethos, although not the specific institutions, of the Fourth Republic in France, where important political decisions were often made by unelected civil servants. The legacy of Jean Monnet was that of an apparently depoliticised and functionalist bureaucracy which could somehow lead the way towards a united Europe.

The truth is, however, that the European Union was founded in the 1950s on a conception of government that is outdated in the modern world of participatory and assertive democracy. The ethos of Fourth Republic France insulated technocratic leadership from effective parliamentary scrutiny. The ethos of consensual democracy legitimises decision-making by elites, with the role of the electors being confined to that of ratifying these decisions. This method did not work too badly in the early years of the European Community, when the leaders led and the followers followed. But the reaction in many Member States to the Maastricht Treaty in 1992 and to the Constitutional Treaty in 2005 showed that, while the leaders continued to try to lead, the followers were no longer willing to follow. Thus, the institutional forms of the European Union have become increasingly incongruent with the popular forces behind modern democratic government. The central task for those concerned to make Europe more effective and more democratic is to bring the institutional forms into line with the democratic forces.

The depoliticized, functionalist, technocratic, leading-from-above nature of the European Union informs its unique institutional structure, which serves to distinguish the European Union from existing parliamentary democracies, as well as from other international organizations. It reflects the *intergovernmental* interests of the member states—that is, areas in which the member states have retained their autonomous (or sovereign) powers and are simply working together. This traditional method of intergovernmental cooperation must be contrasted with the *supranational* interests of the European Union—that is, areas of action in which the member states have decided to pool their sovereignty and delegate decision-making powers to the EU institutions (see Chapter 12).

N. Nugent, *The Government and Politics of the European Union* (2010, Basingstoke: Macmillan), 428

Sovereignty is an emotive word, associated as it is with notions of power, authority, independence, and the exercise of will. Because of its emotiveness and its associations, it is a word to which several meanings are attached. The most common meaning, and the one which will be employed here, refers to the legal capacity of national decision-makers to take decisions without being subject to external restraints. This is usually called national, or sometimes state, sovereignty.

Intergovernmentalism refers to arrangements whereby nation-states, in situations and conditions they can control, cooperate with one another on matters of common interest. The existence of control, which allows all participating states to decide the extent and nature of this cooperation, means that national sovereignty is not directly undermined.

Supranationalism involves states working with one another in a manner that does not allow them to retain complete control over developments. That is, states may be obliged to do things against their preferences and their will because they do not have the power to stop decisions. Supranationalism thus takes inter-state relations beyond cooperation into integration, and involves some loss of national sovereignty.

The European Union's institutional structure is also necessitated by the twenty-four official languages, the distribution of power along vertical (between the European Union, the member states, and their regions) and horizontal (between the different EU institutions) lines, the wide functional reach of executive and legislative power, the evolving nature of the European Union, and its shifting geographical boundaries. The institutions and procedures were not designed for a 'super-state', but for a major international organization, the later impact of which on national politics and constitutions was not initially foreseen or appreciated. By the twenty-first century, the tasks for the European Union included not merely an internal agenda (internal market, social justice and protection, solidarity among member states), but also responses to the financial crises after 2008, monitoring the budgetary situation in Greece, carbon emissions and climate change, and (under Art. 3(5) TEU) global contributions to '*peace, security, the sustainable development of the Earth, solidarity and mutual respect among peoples, free and fair trade, eradication of poverty and the protection of human rights, in particular the rights of the child, as well as to the strict observance and the development of international law, including respect for the principles of the United Nations Charter*'. In a nutshell, the European Union had, within the space of fifty years, evolved from a regional strategic planning authority to '*the first non-imperial empire*'.[10] It is not surprising that the institutions and procedures do not conform to established standards of democracy and accountability (or what Bogdanor refers to as 'participatory and assertive democracy' and 'effective parliamentary scrutiny').

The twofold tension between intergovernmentalism and supranationalism should be borne in mind when examining the institutions. First, there is a difficulty, which is incorporated in the European Union's governing structure, in striking a fair balance between the supranational (EU) element and the member states' interest in maintaining control over the European policy process through intergovernmental cooperation. Second, there is the need to give the European Union a unique institutional structure (precisely because it is *not* an ordinary international organization and because it is *not* a state), and the need to resort to old and new ways in which to hold EU institutions and actors to account.

5 THE EU INSTITUTIONS

Whatever the political and legal pitfalls have been, the governments of the member states have, on several occasions, agreed to create and amend the treaties governing the EU institutions. In this section, we turn to examine the institutions that exercise executive power. Chapter 12 will focus on the legislative functions of the European Union—especially those of the European Parliament.

BOX 8.2 CONSTITUTIONAL FOUNDATIONS OF THE EUROPEAN UNION

The European Union's institutions, procedures, and objectives are set out in two treaties.

- The **Treaty on the Functioning of the European Union (TFEU)**, formerly the Treaty Establishing the European Community (TEC), means the Treaty establishing (what was then called) the European Economic Community, signed at Rome on 25 March 1957 (as amended and renamed by the Treaty of Lisbon).

- The **Treaty on European Union (TEU)** means the Treaty on European Union, signed at Maastricht on 7 February 1992 (as amended by the Treaty of Lisbon).

---

[10] EU Commission President José Manuel Barroso, quoted in the *Daily Telegraph*, 'Barroso hails the European "empire"', 11 July 2007.

Article 13 TEU

1. The Union shall have an institutional framework which shall aim to promote its values, advance its objectives, serve its interests, those of its citizens and those of the Member States, and ensure the consistency, effectiveness and continuity of its policies and actions.
   The Union's institutions shall be:

- the European Parliament,
- the European Council,
- the Council,
- the European Commission (hereinafter referred to as "the Commission"),
- the Court of Justice of the European Union,
- the European Central Bank,
- the Court of Auditors.

2. Each institution shall act within the limits of the powers conferred on it in the Treaties, and in conformity with the procedures, conditions and objectives set out in them. The institutions shall practice mutual sincere cooperation.

3. The provisions relating to the European Central Bank and the Court of Auditors and detailed provisions on the other institutions are set out in the Treaty on the Functioning of the European Union.

4. The European Parliament, the Council and the Commission shall be assisted by an Economic and Social Committee and a Committee of the Regions acting in an advisory capacity.

(a) THE EUROPEAN COUNCIL

The European Council was not listed as a formal institution of the European Union in the previous Treaty regime and so the European Union institutions were not legally bound by its decisions. The Lisbon Treaty boosts the powers of the European Council by allowing it to define the Union's directions and priorities (rather than merely setting out guidelines).

Article 15 TEU

1. The European Council shall provide the Union with the necessary impetus for its development and shall define the general political directions and priorities thereof. It shall not exercise legislative functions.

From an EU perspective, the European Council:

- provides a general political impetus to the construction of Europe;
- sets out approaches and issues general political guidelines for the European Union;
- deliberates on EU matters;
- initiates cooperation in new areas of activity;
- expresses a common position in questions of external relations; and
- amends and simplifies the Treaties.

The European Council consists of the twenty-eight heads of state or government, its President, and the President of the Commission. It is a summit meeting that used to be chaired by the leader of the member state that held the presidency of the Council of the European Union at the time (the presidency rotated between EU member states every six months). Those meetings were also attended by the ministers for foreign affairs, a member of the Commission, and a small number of civil servants.[11] European Council meetings were held *in camera*: no one else was allowed to be present and no formal minutes were kept. In sum, the European Council was headed by the chief executives of all member states, who were assisted by a limited number of public officials, who met in a closed room with no assistants.

Summit meetings have taken place sporadically since 1961. But it was not until 1975 (when the European Council was established) that it became a formal part of the EC's decision-making process; it was not until 1987 that its existence and importance was formally recognized in the Single European Act. Since 1999, the European Council has met at least four times a year—in the middle and at the end of each presidency of the Council (see Figure 8.1).

In order to make the European Council more proactive, the Lisbon Treaty created the post of a President of the European Council, who is elected by qualified majority for a term of two-and-a-half years (renewable once). The President, who may not hold a national office, is elected by the European Council under qualified majority voting (QMV). According to Art. 15(6) TEU, the role of the President is to guide the European Council (by chairing it), to coordinate its workload (by ensuring the preparation and continuity of the work of the European Council in cooperation with the President of the Commission), and to ensure that the European Council's decisions are implemented (for example, by presenting a report to the European Parliament after each of the meetings of the European Council). In November 2009, Belgian Prime Minister Herman van Rompuy was chosen as the first President of the European Council during a summit meeting in Brussels for a period of two and a half years, renewable once. On 1 March 2012 van Rompuy was re-elected by the heads of state or government, and the period of his second term is from 1 June 2012 to 30 November 2014.

The introduction of a President of the European Council is likely to clash with existing senior positions in the European Union, such as the President of the European Commission (as we shall see) and the High Representative of the Union for Foreign Affairs and Security Policy. The post of High Representative was introduced by the Treaty of Amsterdam (1999) and expanded under the Treaty of Lisbon (the High Representative is also Vice-President of the Commission and thus can directly influence legislative proposals in the European Union). In November 2009, Baroness Catherine Ashton took over from Javier Solana as the EU's High Representative (a position that the media understands as the EU foreign minister, foreign policy supremo, or the EU's chief diplomat). The two Presidents and the High Representative have roles in the European Union's external representation. This new 'foreign affairs triangle' will therefore require coordination to avoid significant overlap and sharing of responsibilities.

---

[11] Article 15(2) and (3) TEU.

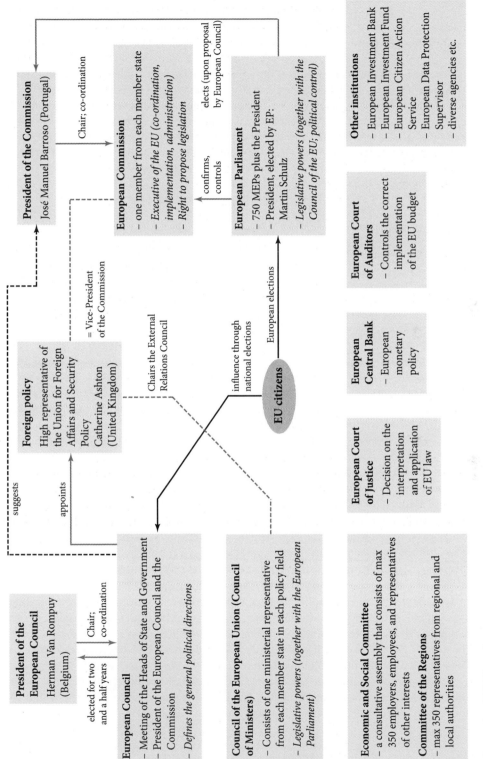

President of the European Council
Herman Van Rompuy (Belgium)

elected for two and a half years

European Council
- Meeting of the Heads of State and Government
- President of the European Council and the Commission
- *Defines the general political directions*

Chair; co-ordination

suggests

appoints

Foreign policy
High representative of the Union for Foreign Affairs and Security Policy
Catherine Ashton (United Kingdom)

= Vice-President of the Commission

Chairs the External Relations Council

President of the Commission
José Manuel Barroso (Portugal)

Chair; co-ordination

European Commission
- one member from each member state
- *Executive of the EU (co-ordination, implementation, administration*
- *Right to propose legislation*

confirms, controls

elects (upon proposal by European Council)

European Parliament
- 750 MEPs plus the President
- President, elected by EP: Martin Schulz
- *Legislative powers (together with the Council of the EU; political control)*

Council of the European Union (Council of Ministers)
- Consists of one ministerial representative from each member state in each policy field
- *Legislative powers (together with the European Parliament)*

influence through national elections

European elections

EU citizens

Economic and Social Committee
- a consultative assembly that consists of max 350 employers, employees, and representatives of other interests

Committee of the Regions
- max 350 representatives from regional and local authorities

European Court of Justice
- Decision on the interpretation and application of EU law

European Central Bank
- European monetary policy

European Court of Auditors
- Controls the correct implementation of the EU budget

Other institutions
- European Investment Bank
- European Investment Fund
- European Citizen Action Service
- European Data Protection Supervisor
- diverse agencies etc.

Figure 8.1 EU Flowchart
Source: Redrawn from an original first published in *Frankfurter Allgemeine Zeitung*, 1 December 2009

R. Corbett, J. Peterson, and E. Bomberg, 'The EU's Institutions', in E.Bomberg, J. Peterson, and R. Corbett, *The European Union: How does it work?* 3rd edn (2012, Oxford: OUP) p. 61

A number of factors led to creation of a 'permanent' and full-time President. Previously, the six-month term of office meant a new President every second or third meeting, making continuity and consistency impossible. The preparation of European Council meetings, involving consultation of all Heads of Government, was, with successive enlargements of the Union, becoming increasingly onerous for any President or Prime Minister with their own national government to run. Also, the task of representing the EU externally at summit meetings on foreign policy issues, whilst at the same time representing their own country, was felt to be inappropriate.

Member states with an intergovernmentalist view of the EU saw the European Council President as a useful counterweight to the President of the Commission. Many French observers, given their domestic institutional system, see the President of the European Council as a sort of *Président* of Europe, with the Commission President demoted to the status of a French Prime Minister, devoted largely to internal affairs and even then deferring on major decisions to the President. That view is not shared by all. The first European Council President, Van Rompuy described himself as being less than a *Président* but more than a chairman: a facilitator, not a dictator.

Formally, the main executive tasks of the European Council are described in Art. 15 TEU; in reality, the European Council provides overall strategic direction for the Commission, executes policies under the second and third pillars, puts pressure on the Council to adopt new policy competences for the European Union under Art. 352 TFEU (the so-called 'flexibility clause' which enables the Council to take appropriate measures when the Treaty does not provide the necessary powers), and reaches political agreements on contentious legislative proposals. In other words, the European Council is a decision-making heavyweight that Jean Monnet described as the 'Provisional European Government'.[12]

European Council meetings are characterized by private and informal 'fireside chats', which have advantages for political discussions (the President of the European Council and the High Representative of the Union for Foreign Affairs and Security Policy were elected by the heads of state and government over dinner in Brussels in November 2009) and for extraordinary meetings (such as the meeting on 21 September 2001 in the wake of the terrorist attacks in the USA). But the European Council can act only by reaching consensus. This process is less efficient than, say, QMV (in which member states have votes that are weighted roughly according to the size of their populations) and those issues on which agreement is not reached are postponed. The absence of more sophisticated procedural rules and written records of its meetings puts a question mark over the legitimacy of its decision-making powers. The existence of such a high-level body, while necessary for the functioning of the European Union, is at odds with the delicate balance between the need to share sovereignty and the desire to retain national control that underlies the institutional architecture of the European Union.

The Treaty justification for the European Council is to provide leadership: it guides the other EU institutions and facilitates major decisions in every area of policy. But the European Council has also—informally and over time—acquired the status of a final arbiter

---

[12] J. Monnet, *Memoirs*, ch. 21 and here fn 3. See also Pascal Fontaine, 'Le rôle de Jean Monnet dans la genèse du Conseil européen' (1979) 229 Revue du Marché Commun 357–65.

for problems that the Council of the European Union is unable to resolve.[13] It has no formal power to make binding decisions—but it fills a gap as the ultimate decision-making authority. This is an essential role within a federal structure, because the different layers of power can result in bottlenecks and blockages. As the engine behind European integration, the European Council has effectively spearheaded Treaty reforms and prevented gridlock.

Note that the Lisbon Treaty still falls short of giving the European Council the power to propose legislation, which (as will be seen) has always been the central role of the European Commission. Member states are allowed to refer issues to the European Council if they consider their national interests to be at stake. The European Council is then entitled to pull the 'emergency brake'.

With a new focus on accountability and transparency (see (b) The Council of the European Union), the European Council will also find it more difficult in the future to make decisions in secret.

(b) THE COUNCIL OF THE EUROPEAN UNION

The Council of the European Union is also informally known as the 'Council of Ministers', and the Treaties refer to it simply as the 'Council'. It is the EU's primary decision-making institution, and its Treaty basis is as follows.

Article 16 TEU

1. The Council shall, jointly with the European Parliament, exercise legislative and budgetary functions. It shall carry out policy-making and coordinating functions as laid down in the Treaties.

2. The Council shall consist of a representative of each Member State at ministerial level, who may commit the government of the Member State in question and cast its vote.

3. The Council shall act by a qualified majority except where the Treaties provide otherwise.

4. As from 1 November 2014, a qualified majority shall be defined as at least 55% of the members of the Council, comprising at least fifteen of them and representing Member States comprising at least 65% of the population of the Union.

A blocking minority must include at least four Council members, failing which the qualified majority shall be deemed attained.

The other arrangements governing the qualified majority are laid down in Article 238(2) of the Treaty on the Functioning of the European Union.

5. The transitional provisions relating to the definition of the qualified majority which shall be applicable until 31 October 2014 and those which shall be applicable from 1 November 2014 to 31 March 2017 are laid down in the Protocol on transitional provisions.

6. The Council shall meet in different configurations, the list of which shall be adopted in accordance with Article 236 of the Treaty on the Functioning of the European Union

The General Affairs Council shall ensure consistency in the work of the different Council configurations. It shall prepare and ensure the follow-up to meetings of the European Council, in liaison with the President of the European Council and the Commission.

---

[13] This practice has received formal recognition in relation to Common Foreign and Security Policy: see Art. 31(2) TEU.

The Council is part of the European Union's executive (with the European Council and the Commission) and part of the European Union's legislature (with the European Parliament). At first sight, it is an intergovernmental institution that comprises one minister from each of the twenty-eight governments, and provides a venue in which politicians and bureaucrats from the national and EU levels can negotiate and legislate. The composition, organization, and powers of the Council are designed to accumulate and articulate national interests. Although the Council is a permanent institution, it does not have a constant membership. Its composition is determined by the particular issues under consideration. Each Minister represents, and is thus empowered to commit, his or her government. The Minister is then accountable before the national Parliament, which ensures the (indirect) democratic legitimacy of the decisions of the Council.

Functions

When it comes to decision-making and law-making within the Council, the Council wears different 'hats' depending on which procedure is used to make a particular policy.

Under the TFEU, the Council is responsible for enacting European legislation (often in unison with the European Parliament using the ordinary legislative procedure),[14] coordinating the economic policies of the member states, the external relations of the European Union (for example, signing international agreements with third countries or other international organizations), and (together with the European Parliament) approving the EU's budget. In these areas, the character of the Council is mainly *supranational*, meaning that the member states have decided to delegate (or 'pool') their decision-making powers to the European Union.

In relation to the TEU (common foreign and security policy), the character of the Council is *intergovernmental*, meaning that member states have retained their sovereign powers over these policy areas, but have decided to work together. So, the Council is responsible for setting the EU's agenda based on guidelines set by the member states (meeting in the European Council). Council decisions—in these more nationally sensitive areas—have to be unanimous, which in practice means that each member state has a right to veto these decisions.

The Council is assisted by the Committee of Permanent Representatives (COREPER), or 'ambassadors' to the European Union from member states, which is responsible for preparing the work of the Council and carrying out tasks assigned to it. The United Kingdom's official delegation is known as 'UKREP'.

N. Nugent, *The Government and Politics of the European Union* (2010, Basingstoke: Macmillan), p. 140

The extent to which the Council must work with, and is dependent upon the cooperation of, the Commission and the EP in respect of policy and decision-making varies between policy areas and according to what type of decisions are being made. In broad terms, the Council has most room for independent manoeuvre when it is not acting within 'the Community method', for then the roles and powers of the Commission and the EP are normally restricted. Amongst policy issues where the Community method does not apply are foreign and defence policy, both of which have increased enormously in importance in recent years as the EU has come to issue numerous declarations on foreign policy matters and has come to engage in an array of foreign policy actions.

[14] See Chapter 12.

In sum, the Council has formal decision-making powers across all policy areas that make up the European Union. The TEU especially provides for direct Council executive authority. But even under the TFEU, Art. 241 gives the Council the power to '*request the Commission to undertake any studies the Council considers desirable for the attainment of the common objectives, and to submit to it any appropriate proposals*'. The Council has used this provision to issue clear instructions to the Commission. Because the ministers are democratically elected, the Council enjoys political weight that the Commission (consisting of appointees) cannot easily ignore.

The Council, therefore, has the following functions.

- **Legislative**—It develops and makes laws jointly with the European Parliament under co-decision (see Chapter 12).

- **Executive**—It has direct responsibility in policy areas such as Common Foreign and Security Policy, and (currently) Police and Judicial Cooperation in Criminal Matters, for exercising executive powers.

- **Steering**—It concludes international agreements for the European Union with third states or international organizations.

- **Forum**—It coordinates the broad macroeconomic policies of the member states.

The following commentator compares the Council to 'a club of member governments' which the national ministers use to compete for influence.

F. Hayes-Renshaw, 'The Council of Ministers', in J. Peterson and M. Shackleton (eds) *The Institutions of the European Union*, 3rd edn (2012, Oxford: OUP), pp. 91–3

The Council is regarded as the central body by those who stress the importance of national interests as the factor explaining outcomes in the EU. Indeed, the Council as it exists and operates today may be viewed as one of the living symbols of the continuing power of the member states in the EU, and of the desire of the national governments to remain at the centre of the process of European integration. Since it is also representative of the member governments who constitute the intergovernmental conferences (IGCs) that initiate constitutional reform in the EU, we can expect the Council to endure and to continue to play a central role in the larger EU.

Despite being the EU's intergovernmental institution par excellence, however, [. . .] in reality, the Council is a unique blend of the intergovernmental and the supranational. It represents member state interests that are aggregated under conditions frequently owing more to supranationality than to intergovernmentalism, and it is not necessarily the interests of the larger member states that determine the final outcomes. In addition, the Council as an institution works closely with the Commission and the EP, the views of both of which inform its work and impinge in important ways on its output.

[. . .] Two opposing suggestions for the Council linger in the debate over EU institutional reform. One advocates that it should become an explicitly representative and legislative rather than an executive institution. The other asserts that the Council should be made even more explicitly dominant, as the core of executive power within the EU. The Lisbon Treaty has neither resolved this argument nor clarified the situation. It is likely that the Council will have to continue to serve both camps, with all of the constitutional and operational ambiguities that this implies.

Composition and structure

The Council consists of many levels. At the top level, the Council '*consists of a representative of each Member State at ministerial level*'.[15] The members of the Council are not directly elected, but are dispatched to the Council in their capacity as ministers of their respective national government (or occasionally, in the case of Belgium and Germany, ministers from the regional level). They meet in Brussels or Luxembourg, and meetings last a day or two. As an institution, there is only one Council, but it currently meets in ten different configurations, depending on the subjects under discussion.[16]

   (i)   General Affairs (GAC)
   (ii)   Foreign Affairs (FAC)
   (iii)   Economic and Financial Affairs (Ecofin)
   (iv)   Agriculture and Fisheries (Agrifish)
   (v)   Justice and Home Affairs Council (JHA)
   (vi)   Employment, Social Policy, Health and Consumer Affairs Council (EPSCO)
   (vii)   Competitiveness (COCOM)
   (viii)   Transport, Telecommunications and Energy (TTE)
   (ix)   Environment (ENVI)
   (x)   Education, Youth, Culture and Sport (EYC).

Thus agriculture ministers from the member states meet to discuss and make decisions about farming, transport ministers about transport, and so on. Each Council has the power to discuss issues, enact legislation within its area of competence, and '*to commit the government of the Member State*'.[17] Ministers are usually appointed or nominated to that position by their Prime Minister, and thus enjoy indirect legitimacy when they meet in the Council. When gathered together in the Council, however, they inevitably take on collective responsibilities, and it is no longer clear whom they represent and to whom they are accountable.

Depending on the issue in question, which is governed by rules laid down in the Treaties, ministers in the Council vote on the basis of simple majority, QMV, or unanimity.

- Under the Treaty of Nice, simple majority voting was usually used for procedural or other non-controversial matters. Accordingly, each member state has a single vote and fourteen votes in favour are required to adopt a measure in the European Union of twenty-five plus.

- Nationally sensitive areas, such as foreign policy and defence, EU enlargement, taxation, and social security still have to be agreed unanimously by all member states. An aggrieved member state can exercise its power of veto, or abstain from voting (which, like a 'yes' vote, allows agreement by the others to go ahead).

- Most decisions (ca. 80%) in the Council are taken by QMV. Each member state is allocated a certain number of votes to reflect as closely as possible its size and population.

---

[15] Article 16(2) TEU.

[16] In the 1990s there were 22 configurations; this was reduced to 16 in June 2000 and then to nine in June 2002. Since the entry into force of the Treaty of Lisbon on 1 December 2009, there are ten configurations.

[17] Article 16(2) TEU.

BOX 8.3 DISTRIBUTION OF QUALIFIED MAJORITY VOTES FOR EACH MEMBER STATE

Germany, France, Italy, and the United Kingdom	29
Spain and Poland	27
Romania	14
The Netherlands	13
Belgium, Czech Republic, Greece, Hungary, and Portugal	12
Austria, Bulgaria, and Sweden	10
Denmark, Ireland, Lithuania, Slovakia, Finland, and Croatia	7
Cyprus, Estonia, Latvia, Luxembourg, and Slovenia	4
Malta	3
TOTAL	352

The Lisbon Treaty makes significant changes to the rules for calculating a qualified majority. The current rules will, however, continue to operate exclusively until 31 October 2014; between 1 November 2014 and 31 March 2017, any member state can request that a vote revert to these rules. That means that the new rules only take full effect from 1 April 2017.

Under the Lisbon Treaty, QMV becomes the default voting method in the Council (Art. 16(3) TEU), and includes areas previously subject to unanimity (these include justice and home affairs, and a number of matters relating to foreign and defence policy). Sensitive areas, such as tax and social security, however, remain to be decided by unanimity.

BOX 8.4 THE CHANGES TO QMV UNDER THE LISBON TREATY[18]

Treaty of Nice—used exclusively until 31 October 2014	The double majority QMV system—used from 1 November 2014 and exclusively from 1 April 2017
For a proposal from the Commission to pass: • there must be at least 260 votes (out of 352, meaning 73.9%); • representing a majority of Council members (one member, one vote) (that is, at least fourteen member states, currently); and • representing at least 62% of the Union population.	For a proposal from the Commission or High Representative to pass: • there must be votes from at least 55% of Council members (one member, one vote) (that is, at least fifteen member states, currently); and • representing at least 65% of the Union population.
For other proposals to pass: • there must be at least 255 votes (out of 345, meaning 73.9%); • representing two-thirds of Council members (one member, one vote) (that is, at least eighteen member states, currently); and • representing at least 62% of the Union population.	For other proposals to pass: • there must be votes from at least 72% of Council members (one member, one vote) (that is, at least twenty member states, currently); and • representing at least 65% of the Union population.

[18] See: Art. 205 TEC; Art. 16 LTEU; Art. 238 TFEU; Protocol on transitional provisions.

<table>
<tr>
<td>

Where not all members take part, for a proposal to pass, it needs:

- the same proportion of weighted votes (73.9%);

- the same proportion of the number of Council members (a majority or two-thirds); and

- the same percentage of the population of the member states concerned (62%) of the members taking part.

</td>
<td>

Where not all members take part, for a proposal to pass, it needs:

- the same proportion of votes (55% or 72%); and

- the same percentage of the population of the member states concerned (65%) of the members taking part.

</td>
</tr>
</table>

Source: House of Lords European Union Committee, *The Treaty of Lisbon: An Impact Assessment*, Tenth Report, Session 2007–08 (HL Paper 62-I).

For present purposes, it is important to note that under the current allocation—also called 'weighting'—of votes in the Nice Treaty, a qualified majority will be reached if:

- a majority of member states approve (in some cases, a two-thirds majority); and

- a minimum of 260 votes is cast in favour of the proposal, out of a total of 352 votes (roughly 73.9 per cent of the votes).

A member state may ask for confirmation that the votes in favour represent at least 62 per cent of the total population of the European Union. If this is found not to be the case, the decision will not be adopted. The most significant change to be made by the Lisbon Treaty is the percentage reduction from 73.9 per cent to 55 per cent required for QMV on a Commission proposal, because it makes EU law-making easier and more efficient.

The Lisbon Treaty formalizes the rules regarding the formation of a blocking minority. At least four countries are now needed to form a blocking minority. This system places countries with a smaller population on a fairer footing with the larger member states. The new rule is specifically designed to prevent any three of the large states (the United Kingdom, Germany, France, and Italy) from being able to block a proposal (any three of these states would represent more than 35 per cent of the Union's population). If the population requirement (65 per cent) were not met, a fourth state would be needed. The requirement for at least four member states would remain, regardless of future demographic shifts in member states.

So who wields the most influence in the Council? It is important to note that the Council, in the words of the German Federal Constitutional Court, is '*the representative body of masters of the Treaties; correspondingly, it is not constituted according to proportional representation, but according to the image of the equality of states*'.[19] But equality of states does not tell the whole story.

F. Hayes-Renshaw, 'The Council of Ministers', in J. Peterson and M. Shackleton (eds) *The Institutions of the European Union*, 3rd edn (2012, Oxford: OUP), ch. 4, pp. 84–5

In the small number of cases in which unanimity is the rule, influence is shared equally among the Council members. Since any national representative can block agreement, the interests

---

[19] The *Lisbon Treaty* decision in BVerfG, 2 BvE 2/08, 30 June 2009, at para. 271.

of all have to be taken into account. Under QMV, numbers matter, and those member governments with the largest number of votes (or biggest populations) could be expected to wield the largest amount of influence. However, safeguards have been built into the system to ensure that the smaller member states, working together, have as much chance as the larger ones to exert influence over the final outcome. Indeed, the big Member States are frequently out-voted in the Council [...]

Influence can also be exerted by large and small member states alike in more informal (and less easily quantifiable) ways, such as by putting forward compromise proposals acceptable to a majority of the member governments, forming coalitions with like-minded states, and making their point of view known to the Commission, the presidency, and the Council Secretariat. The formation of coalitions within the Council is an intrinsic part of the decision-making process under QMV, in which qualified majorities and blocking minorities matter, if only for the purposes of calculating which member states need to be won over in order to achieve a consensus.

The expansion of the European Union in territory, and in the scope of its competences, has naturally led to an increased number of specialized Council configurations and fragmentation of its activity. The Council is aided in its work by various bodies from above and from below. The General Affairs Council is responsible for coordinating the work of the Council as a whole. It also acts as final arbiter when the other Councils cannot agree on a legislative proposal. If the General Affairs Council fails to break the deadlock, the matter gets sent up to the European Council for a political decision.

At the lower (national) level, the Council consists of the Committee of Permanent Representatives (COREPER),[20] and around 250 committees and working groups. Working groups will discuss the technicalities of implementing a legislative proposal (from the Commission) that naturally arise in a union of twenty-eight member states. Their work paves the way for COREPER, the most important committee, which checks every proposal and deals with matters unresolved in the working groups. The senior national officials who comprise the Permanent Representatives have ambassadorial rank and reside in Brussels. They prepare and coordinate the agenda for the Council. Agreement among the Permanent Representatives will often be endorsed by the Council. Alternatively, the areas of disagreement will be kept as narrow as possible before sending the file up to the Council for decision. Only highly political issues have to be renegotiated by the national ministers. For these reasons, COREPER is sometimes viewed as the most powerful body in the EU's decision-making process. Since it is the national authorities that ultimately implement EU law, the early involvement of high-calibre national officials is key to the smooth administration of policy. The Council, therefore, needs to facilitate executive responsibilities.

Transparency and accountability

The Council meets almost every week in order to adopt new legislation, but until the Lisbon Treaty came into force, it had refused to meet publicly whenever it acted in its legislative capacity, nor would it hold press conferences or release transcripts (minutes) of its meetings. From a citizens' perspective, the Council's decision-making process has been described as

---

[20] Art. 240 TFEU.

'*a secretive and specialized affair*'.[21] The Council's working parties have negotiated a number of laws behind closed doors, which were then simply rubber-stamped by the ministers. The Council is the least transparent EU institution and the extent to which ministers are responsible to their own Parliament will be also be discussed.

This situation is, however, gradually changing. In December 2005, the Council decided to hold meetings in public should the issues fall under the co-decision procedure. This, it claims, has increased its openness by 20 per cent. Citizens and journalists are now able to follow positions taken by the ministers in the Council.

The Lisbon Treaty includes a transparency clause in Art. 16 TEU: '*The Council shall meet in public when it deliberates and votes on a draft legislative act.*' Each meeting will be divided into two parts, dealing separately with legislative and non-legislative activities. Only the first half will be public. Under Art. 7(3) of the Council's Rules of Procedure:[22]

> The opening to the public of Council meetings relating to the 'Legislative deliberations' part of its agenda shall be made through public transmission by audiovisual means, notably in an overflow room and through broadcasting in all official languages of the institutions of the European Union using video-streaming. A recorded version shall remain available for at least one month on the Council's Internet site. The outcome of voting shall be indicated by visual means.

The Council can be credited for having become a more transparent institution. For example, most documents are now directly available from its website (http://www.consilium.eu.int). And the Council Secretariat is working on a database containing all the voting records in a user-friendly form. But the problems of accountability are linked to the structure of the Council, as well as to the standard of legitimacy used to assess the Council.

Structurally, the Council has executive and legislative powers, and is therefore not captured by the traditional doctrine of separation of powers. The Council also enjoys plenary legislative power within the European Union, and it is composed of ministers who were elected in *national* elections and on *national* issues. The Council therefore enjoys indirect legitimacy. Crucially, the Council as an institution has permanent tenure (it cannot be voted out of office by the European Parliament) and it is not accountable to national parliaments.

V. Bogdanor, *Legitimacy, Accountability and Democracy in the European Union*
A Federal Trust Report (2007), pp. 8–9

> The Council of Ministers is frequently accused of giving too much discretion to the governments of the Member States and limiting their accountability to the parliaments and voters of the Member States. Many critics believe that European activities are given insufficient scrutiny by national legislatures and that parliaments do not have sufficient opportunities to examine new directives and regulations and give their opinion on them. Decisions in the European Union are often the result of a negotiated compromise between different points of view expressed by the various governments of the Member States. In consequence, national lines of accountability can become blurred, and a national government can claim that it was

---

[21] Robert Thomson, Frans N. Stokman, Christopher H. Achen, and Thomas König (eds) *The European Union Decides* (2006, Cambridge: Cambridge University Press), p. 329.

[22] Council Decision 2009/937/EU of 1 December 2009 adopting the Council's Rules of Procedure.

outvoted or outmanoeuvred in Brussels, even when that is not the case. It is sometimes highly convenient for national governments to blame 'Brussels' for reform, the necessity of which they themselves recognise but for which they are reluctant to accept responsibility. National governments are thus able to exploit the lack of accountability for their own short-term political aims. But this works to the long-term disadvantage of the public standing of the European Union.

Many argue also that unclarity and a lack of transparency characterise the working of the Council. Its day-to-day activities are conducted mainly by civil servants, and its meetings and decisions sometimes seem to be shrouded in secrecy until the announcement of the final political compromise between ministers which then forms part of European law. Thus, compared to national legislatures which debate in public and attract regular media attention, law-making in the Council does not seem to be characterised by a public exchange of views and it attracts little media coverage. Admittedly, the actions of the Council may not, in reality, be as opaque as is sometimes claimed, and major interested parties in Brussels and Strasbourg have gained access to papers and information which enables them to follow and sometimes influence the course of private debate within the Council. Nevertheless, the perception of the Council as inaccessible and secretive is an undoubted barrier to the confidence which European electors ought to have in the Union's legislative system.

In terms of assessing the Council, it is tempting to conceive the European Parliament and Council as the first and second chamber of a European legislature, but such an analogy is also fraught with difficulty. First, it would be an artificial attempt to shoehorn the evolving European institutions into a state-based model of government. Second, it does not address the problems of accountability. There are various ways in which the European Parliament can be bypassed in the name of intergovernmental cooperation. As a result, the democratically elected body (the European Parliament) is not able to hold the executive decision-maker (the Council) properly to account. This 'accountability gap', or 'democracy deficit', will be addressed in more detail.

QUESTIONS

1. In what context is the Council's role best described as 'supranational'? When is it 'intergovernmental'?

2. Was voting in the Council made easier or harder after the Lisbon Treaty? Explain your answer.

3. Former EU Commissioner Lord Brittan regrets the Council's move towards transparency. He claims that *'the position in which there was haggling and negotiation rather than the necessity to take up public positions was on the whole a good arrangement'.*[23] Is there any merit to this consideration?

4. Using the Council's webpage (http://www.consilium.europa.eu), what can you learn about the Council's recent activities? Do any of them strike you as controversial, unusual, or surprising?

---

[23] House of Lords European Union Committee, *The Treaty of Lisbon: An Impact Assessment*, Tenth Report, Session 2007–08 (HL Paper 62-I), para. 4.68.

(c) THE COMMISSION

Every political system needs an institution that sets the policy agenda, and offers guidance and leadership. We have already seen that the European Council fulfils that role. The other institution of the European Union that exercises executive power is the Commission.

The Commission is often understood as the civil service of the European Union. The civil service in most states, or state-like entities, is a part of public administration that is formally non-political. In that context, the Commission houses the Directorates-General (DGs)—a permanent bureaucracy that manages the administrative and policy affairs of the European Union. The Commission is also assisted by national agencies, which are responsible for the day-to-day implementation of administrative tasks. But more importantly, the College of Commissioners is also a source of (European) political power and direction. The Commissioners are not elected, however, and—at least formally—are independent of the member states whom they represent. The two-sided nature of the Commission makes it arguably 'the strangest administration ever created'.[24]

The Commission is a supranational institution—that is, it is independent of national governments. It is, according to its Secretary General, 'the only organization that is paid to think European'.[25] As such, it safeguards and promotes the common interest of the European Union as a whole. It is the executive branch of the EU that is—at least in theory—responsible for initiating and drafting legislation, as well as for implementing the decisions taken by the Council of the European Union and Parliament under the co-decision procedure, and for ensuring that member states comply with the law.[26]

The Commission is sometimes portrayed in the media as a distant, overbearing, and expensive bureaucracy. In fact, in 2009–10, the United Kingdom's payments to EU institutions amounted to £3.8bn and its contribution to the EU's budget to £4.7bn (these are typical figures)—which amounts to 0.8 per cent and 0.9 per cent respectively of a budget of £496bn for the same year. (The United Kingdom's 2011–12 contribution is forecast to rise to £7.7 (or 1.3 per cent) and 8.7bn (or 1.4 per cent of the UK budget) respectively due to planned increases in the EU Budget.) The European Union has an agreed budget for the period 2007–13 of €976bn, which is equal to 1.12 per cent of the gross national income (GNI) of the member states. The size of the Commission (30,000 civil servants) is roughly equal to the number of staff employed by a large city council in Europe,[27] and the total staff in all EU institutions, bodies and agencies all over the world is 55,000. The relatively small size of the Commission means that it relies for legislative proposals on the Council or the member states (approximately 80 per cent of proposals stem from the Council or the member states) and for the detailed implementation of EU law on the member states.

The Commission is appointed every five years, within six months of the European Parliament elections. The Commission's current term of office will run until 31 October 2014.

---

[24] J. Peterson, 'The College of Commissioners', in J. Peterson and M. Shackleton, *The Institutions of the European Union* (2012, Oxford: OUP), p. 97.

[25] Interview with European Commission Secretary-General Catherine Day, *EurActiv*, 25 September 2006.

[26] On the Commission's role in the law-making process, see further Chapter 12.

[27] In July 2012, Birmingham City Council employed 20,000 staff members, Edinburgh City Council had 23,000 employees and the 33 councils in London employed around 123,000 staff members.

BOX 8.5 RECENT COMMISSIONERS FROM THE UNITED KINGDOM

- Baroness (Catherine) Ashton of Upholland (2008–present), former Leader of the House of Lords
- Peter (now Lord) Mandelson (2004–October 2008), formerly Minister for Trade and Industry, and then Secretary of State for Northern Ireland in Tony Blair's Cabinet
- Neil Kinnock (1995–2004), formerly leader of the Labour Party
- Chris (now Lord) Patten (2000–04), formerly Governor of Hong Kong and a minister in Margaret Thatcher and John Major's Cabinets
- Leon (now Lord) Brittan QC (1989–99), formerly a minister in Margaret Thatcher's Cabinet

---

How does the Commission exercise power?

The Commission's responsibilities and powers are both formally prescribed, and have evolved (informally) through a necessity to respond to the requirements of the European Union.

Article 17 TEU

1. The Commission shall promote the general interest of the Union and take appropriate initiatives to that end. It shall ensure the application of the Treaties, and of measures adopted by the institutions pursuant to them. It shall oversee the application of Union law under the control of the Court of Justice of the European Union. It shall execute the budget and manage programmes. It shall exercise coordinating, executive and management functions, as laid down in the Treaties. With the exception of the common foreign and security policy, and other cases provided for in the Treaties, it shall ensure the Union's external representation. It shall initiate the Union's annual and multiannual programming with a view to achieving interinstitutional agreements.

2. Union legislative acts may only be adopted on the basis of a Commission proposal, except where the Treaties provide otherwise. Other acts shall be adopted on the basis of a Commission proposal where the Treaties so provide.

3. The Commission's term of office shall be five years.

    The members of the Commission shall be chosen on the ground of their general competence and European commitment from persons whose independence is beyond doubt.

    In carrying out its responsibilities, the Commission shall be completely independent. Without prejudice to Article 18(2), the members of the Commission shall neither seek nor take instructions from any Government or other institution, body, office or entity. They shall refrain from any action incompatible with their duties or the performance of their tasks.

4. The Commission appointed between the date of entry into force of the Treaty of Lisbon and 31 October 2014, shall consist of one national of each Member State, including its President and the High Representative of the Union for Foreign Affairs and Security Policy who shall be one of its Vice-Presidents.

5. As from 1 November 2014, the Commission shall consist of a number of members, including its President and the High Representative of the Union for Foreign Affairs and Security Policy, corresponding to two-thirds of the number of Member States, unless the European Council, acting unanimously, decides to alter this number.

The members of the Commission shall be chosen from among the nationals of the Member States on the basis of a system of strictly equal rotation between the Member States, reflecting the demographic and geographical range of all the Member States. This system shall be established unanimously by the European Council in accordance with Article 244 of the Treaty on the Functioning of the European Union.

6. The President of the Commission shall:

(a) lay down guidelines within which the Commission is to work;

(b) decide on the internal organisation of the Commission, ensuring that it acts consistently, efficiently and as a collegiate body;

(c) appoint Vice-Presidents, other than the High Representative of the Union for Foreign Affairs and Security Policy, from among the members of the Commission.

A member of the Commission shall resign if the President so requests. The High Representative of the Union for Foreign Affairs and Security Policy shall resign, in accordance with the procedure set out in Article 18(1), if the President so requests.

7. Taking into account the elections to the European Parliament and after having held the appropriate consultations, the European Council, acting by a qualified majority, shall propose to the European Parliament a candidate for President of the Commission. This candidate shall be elected by the European Parliament by a majority of its component members. If he does not obtain the required majority, the European Council, acting by a qualified majority, shall within one month propose a new candidate who shall be elected by the European Parliament following the same procedure.

The Council, by common accord with the President-elect, shall adopt the list of the other persons whom it proposes for appointment as members of the Commission. They shall be selected, on the basis of the suggestions made by Member States, in accordance with the criteria set out in paragraph 3, second subparagraph, and paragraph 5, second subparagraph.

The President, the High Representative of the Union for Foreign Affairs and Security Policy and the other members of the Commission shall be subject as a body to a vote of consent by the European Parliament. On the basis of this consent the Commission shall be appointed by the European Council, acting by a qualified majority.

8. The Commission, as a body, shall be responsible to the European Parliament. In accordance with Article 234 of the Treaty on the Functioning of the European Union, the European Parliament may vote on a motion of censure of the Commission. If such a motion is carried, the members of the Commission shall resign as a body and the High Representative of the Union for Foreign Affairs and Security Policy shall resign from the duties that he carries out in the Commission.

The Commission was initially designed as a depoliticized functionalist bureaucracy, the task of which was to advance the common interests of Europe's citizens. Its members were to act independently of national governments and were not accountable to the member states. We have already seen that Jean Monnet, the chief architect of the forerunner of the Common Market, endorsed a technocratic approach and the idea of elite-led gradualism, whereby action was to be initiated by experts rather than by elected politicians. The first task was to secure the economic basis; then, provided that the fruits of European integration were beneficial, it was thought that popular consent would develop as a *consequence* of those functional agreements. Interestingly, popular consent was initially not seen as a *requirement* of the functional organization of Europe.

As the process of European integration has taken shape—with more national competences being transferred to the European level—so the powers of the Commission have
grown. It now has a say in almost every function of EU governance. The following give only
a sample of the Commission's multiple identities.

- **Agenda setting**—The Commission's principal power has always been the exclusive
  right of initiative in the law-making process. The European Council and the European
  Parliament may request the Commission to submit proposals, but the ultimate decision
  is the Commission's own: Arts 241 and 225 TFEU.

- **'Honest broker' and mediator**—The Commission acts in the *general interest of the
  Union*: Art. 17(1) TEU. It increasingly uses its political neutrality and independence as a
  manager (rather than initiator) of policies that are made by other institutions. As a bro-
  ker and mediator, the Commission acts as a go-between for the member states and other
  EU institutions. To illustrate, when, between 2010 and 2012, the euro-area Member
  States and the International Monetary Fund agreed to provide financial support to
  Greece in the context of the deterioration of its financing conditions, the European
  Commission was entrusted with the coordination and administration of the pooled
  bilateral loans and the disbursement to Greece.

- **Voice of common interest**—The Commission acts as the guardian of EU law by ensuring that the Treaties are applied by the other institutions: Art. 17(1) TEU. If necessary, it will do so by bringing an action in the ECJ for failure to act: Arts 263 and 265
  TFEU.

The Commission has influence (rather than power) in two key areas: it may deliver opinions
on any EU matter and it must publish an annual report on the activities of the European
Union. It can influence policy debates and guide the European Union—but it is currently
not clear which of its functions the Commission performs best.

J. Peterson, 'The College of Commissioners', in J. Peterson and M. Shackleton
(eds) *The Institutions of the European Union*, 3rd edn (2012, Oxford: OUP), ch. 5,
pp. 119–120

Any analysis of the Commission must consider the normative question of what kind of organization the College should be. A policy entrepreneur? An honest broker? A manager of decisions taken by others? Or an 'engine of integration'? [. . .]

In an enlarged EU, the Commission may be even better placed than in the past to act as a
truly honest broker. It may rarely exercise control over new cooperative networks or reclaim
its old function as an engine of integration, but it will logically remain at the centre of many
EU policy networks. In any event, it will often find itself in a unique position to steer debates
in ways that serve collective European interests, as difficult as they may be to identify clearly
in the new EU.

To what extent can the Commission actually determine the direction in which the European
Union moves? This question has been subject to considerable academic debate. As we will
see in Chapter 12, successive increases in the European Parliament's power have been at the
expense of the Commission's power. Does the Commission face extinction as an independent political body?

I. Bache, S. George, and S. Bulmer *The Politics in the European Union,* 3rd edn (2011, Oxford: OUP), pp. 262–3

The Commission as an Agent of the Member States

The intergovernmentalist view of the Commission is that it is only an agent of the member states. Its function is to make it easier for governments to find agreement on the details of co-operation with each other. Where there is agreement on the broad agenda for co-operation, it is convenient for member states to delegate some control over the detailed agenda to the Commission. They see it as a reliable source of independent proposals because it has technical information, and is a neutral arbiter between conflicting national interests. Delegating the making of proposals to the Commission in this way reduces the costs of co-operation by reducing the risk that 'decisions will be delayed by an inconclusive struggle among competing proposals, or that the final decision will be grossly unfair'.[28] Where there are alternative proposals that might win majority support, the choice is often decided by which proposal is backed by the Commission. Although this delegation of the right to make detailed proposals gives the Commission a certain formal power to set the agenda, in the intergovernmentalist view the Commission does not determine the direction in which the EU moves. It is only helping the member states to agree on the details of what they have decided that they want to do anyway. [...]

The Commission as an Autonomous Actor

The alternative to the view that the Commission is no more than an agent of the Member States is that it can and does act autonomously to provide policy leadership to the EU. Defenders of this view point to key resources that allow it to do so: its sole right of initiative in the legislative process of the EC; its ability to locate allies among influential interest groups; and its powers under the competition clauses of the Treaties to act against monopolies.

The Commission does not have to wait passively for the Member States to ask it to bring forward proposals. It can identify a problem that has already started to concern governments, and propose a European solution. It can use its sole right of initiative to package issues in the form least likely to engender opposition in the Council of Ministers or the EP. Where there is opposition from member states to the full-blown development of a policy, the Commission may propose instead a limited small-scale programme; where there is resistance to a directive or regulation, the Commission may propose a less threatening recommendation or Opinion. In each case, the limited step establishes a precedent for action in the policy sector and can be followed up later with further steps if and when the environment in the Council of Ministers is more conducive.

In some ways, the executive rule-making power of the Commission can be compared to the executive powers of a government. For example, the Commission has the sole power to initiate policy and legislation under Art. 17(2) TEU, which is a power reminiscent of the UK government's near-monopoly on policymaking. The Commission also has several executive responsibilities that blur the distinction between political and administrative powers. The Commission consists of:

---

[28] A. Moravcsik, 'Preferences and power in the European Community: A liberal intergovernmentalist approach' (1993) 31(4) Journal of Common Market Studies 473–524, 512.

- a core executive (the College of Commissioners), with political responsibilities (proposing policies, initiating legislation, arbitration, and negotiating international trade and cooperation agreements);

- a bureaucracy (the DGs), which is responsible for legislative drafting, administrative work (such as managing the budget of €976bn for the period 2007–13 and running its Structural Funds, the main purpose of which is to even out economic disparities between the richer and poorer parts of the Union), and the regulation of competition, agriculture, and trade policy; and

- a network of committees and agencies that scrutinize, monitor, and regulate the implementation of primary and secondary EU law.

BOX 8.6 POLITICAL AND ADMINISTRATIVE POWER IN THE EUROPEAN UNION

	Executive power	
	Political	Administrative
Tasks	Agenda-setting	Policy implementation
	Policy initiative	Policy application
	Policy decision	Distribution of public funds
	External representation	Policy supervision

Source: Deirdre Curtin, *Executive Power of the European Union: Law, Practices, and the Living Constitution* (2009, OUP), 39.

The executive powers of the Commission are also different from those of a national government. In that sense, the Commission might be viewed as a new type of 'regulatory agency'. Although the Commission is equipped with rule-making, policymaking, and other executive powers, it does not have the same power to tax and spend as do national governments, nor does it have powers of coercion (the European Union has no police force or its own military). In the words of a former ECJ judge, '*the Community is only able to exist as a Community of law. It has no weapons or armies, it is held together by the authority of law*'.[29]

The differences between the Commission and national governments have important implications for accountability: in the eyes of the German Federal Constitutional Court, the Commission '*need not extensively fulfil the conditions of a government that is fully accountable either to Parliament or to the majority decision of the electorate because the Commission itself is not obliged to the will of the electorate in a comparable manner*'.[30]

A further illustration also highlights the dissimilarity. Whereas the Commission has competence over certain 'regulatory policies' (for example, competition, agriculture, trade), it does not have competence over 'non-regulatory policies' (for example, income redistribution). This is due to its financial dependence on the member states. We saw earlier that the EU's budget and levels of staff are small even when compared to the budgets of medium-sized municipal councils in the United Kingdom. Moreover, unlike a state, the European

---

[29] U. Everling, 'The *Maastricht* judgment of the Federal Constitutional Court and its significance for the development of the European Union' (1994) 14 Yearbook of European Law 1, 18. See also Sir Francis G. Jacobs, *The Sovereignty of Law: The European Way* (2007, Cambridge: Cambridge University Press), Ch. 4.

[30] The *Lisbon Treaty* decision in BVerfG, 2 BvE 2/08, 30 June 2009, at para. 271.

Union has no independent tax-raising power. As a result of these budgetary restrictions and in sharp contrast with national governments, the Commission is mainly engaged with regulatory activity rather than with non-regulatory activity.

C. Harlow, *Accountability in the European Union* (2002, Oxford: OUP), pp. 62–3

Because it is not in the business of service delivery nor, except in certain limited areas such as competition policy, of 'direct administration', most of the Commission's energies are devoted to policy-making and regulation, a sharp contrast with both national and regional administrations. The Commission does not, in New Public Management (NPM) jargon, have a direct relationship with 'customers' to hear their reactions. Again atypically, the EU administration is not conducted through executive agencies [...] The Commission is consequently heavily dependent on the administrations of Member States and their regions in respect of service delivery and enforcement [...] To paraphrase the famous aphorism of Osborne and Gaebler,[31] the Commission is a body which 'steers' and does not 'row'.

What are the legal and institutional restraints on that power?

Under the 'Westminster model' of executive power (at which we looked in Chapter 1 and Chapter 7), the UK government consists of the party (or parties) able to command a majority in Parliament. The ministers are affiliated to one party (or to a coalition of parties) and are led by the Prime Minister. This system of executive power is geared towards two characteristics: a shared political agenda and hierarchical organization.

The current Commission is structured very differently. Every member state (of which there are twenty-eight) is currently represented by one Commissioner. The Commissioners are not selected in order to ensure coherence of political ideas and beliefs within the Commission; rather, they are chosen '*on the ground of their general competence and European commitment from persons whose independence is beyond doubt*' (Art. 17(3) TEU). They are also representatives of their country based on the simple principle of 'one country, one Commissioner'.

The Treaty of Lisbon was supposed to provide for a reduction in the number of Commissioners from 2014 and their selection on the basis of an equal rotation system.[32] However, after the Irish voters rejected the Lisbon Treaty in a referendum, the Irish government ensured additional legal guarantees and assurances from the heads of state and government.[33] French President Nicolas Sarkozy confirmed that, under the new deal, '*every member state will have a commissioner*'—which represents a significant concession to Ireland (as well as to small states generally, which were unhappy with the reduction). This will require some form of Treaty at some point in the future. The European Council needs to act unanimously to alter the composition of the Commission.

---

[31] D. Osborne and T. Gaebler, *Reinventing Government* (1992, New York: Addison Wesley).

[32] Article 17(5) TEU.

[33] See Presidency Conclusions of 11–12 December 2008 (Document 17271/1/08 Rev 1), para. 2: 'On the composition of the Commission, the European Council recalls that the Treaties currently in force require that the number of Commissioners be reduced in 2009. The European Council agrees that provided that the Treaty of Lisbon enters into force, a decision will be taken, in accordance with the necessary legal procedures, to the effect that the Commission shall continue to include one national of each Member State.'

The Commission has some features of the Westminster system in relation to its internal structure. The Commission works 'under the political guidance of its President', who decides on its internal organization and on the allocation of responsibilities of the Commissioners.[34] Its President can (with the approval of the other Commissioners) dismiss a Commissioner.[35] Internally at least, the functions of the President are similar to the function of the UK Prime Minister as the head of government.

But in contrast to the Westminster model (in which the government is elected independently by Parliament), the Commission is appointed by the European Council (which nominates the President and the Commissioners) and by the European Parliament (which has to confirm the nominations)—in other words, by a unitary and a federal body acting in tandem. The European Council has, however, no power to dismiss the Commission. The European Parliament is empowered, in an extreme case, to retire the Commission by motion of censure and with a two-thirds majority.[36] Such a majority is difficult to organize at the best of times—and nigh on impossible, given the diversity of parties in the European Parliament. On a smaller scale, in 2004, the threat of a 'no' vote led Italy to withdraw Rocco Buttiglione, opposed by members of the European Parliament (MEPs) for his conservative views on homosexuality; in January 2010, it led Bulgaria's Rumiana Jeleva to withdraw her candidacy, following allegations that the declaration of her financial interests did not conform to the Code of Conduct for members of the European Commission.

On a more regular basis, the European Parliament is confronted with a bewildering array of reports, debates, and questions that are designed to hold the executive—particularly the Commission—to account. It exercises monitoring powers by scrutinizing Commission reports that are regularly submitted—for example, the Annual Commission Report on the Functioning of the Communities and the Annual Report on the Implementation of the Budget. The European Parliament has twenty policy-specific committees in which its detailed work is carried out. Like the select committees in the House of Commons and House of Lords, the European Parliament committees reflect the political composition of the European Parliament, they enjoy a high level of autonomy, and meetings have, since 1999, been held in public.

Committees scrutinize all legislative proposals before returning them to the plenary for a vote. Under Arts 24 TFEU and 228 TFEU, the European Ombudsman (who is elected by Parliament) is empowered to receive complaints from any citizen of the Union concerning instances of maladministration in the activities of the Union institutions. The Ombudsman submits an annual report to the European Parliament on the outcome of her inquiries. Finally, the European Parliament has consistently pressed for scrutiny rights equivalent to those of the Council over the implementing bodies—known as 'comitology committees'— that are chaired by the Commission and which bring together representatives of all of the member states. After the introduction of the co-decision legislative procedure, new comitology Decisions were introduced in 1999 and 2006. As a result, the European Parliament now receives more information and has the right to request re-examination of measures adopted under co-decision if the committee was suspected of acting *ultra vires*. (For more on comitology, see Chapter 12.)

[34] Article 248 TFEU.
[35] Article 17(6) TEU.
[36] Article 234 TFEU.

N. Nugent, *The Government and Politics of the European Union* (2010, Basingstoke: Macmillan), p. 130

...comitology committees can be seen as a means by which the governments of the member states, and to a lesser extent the EP, seek to ensure the Commission does not become too independent of them. In conceptual terms, the committees are one of a number of mechanisms and devices found throughout the EU system used by the EU's principals—mainly the national governments, but increasingly also the EP—to maintain control over their agents, especially the Commission, where control is desired. This is achieved in a number of ways. For example, although some of the committees do exercise important powers, for the most part they tend to work within fairly narrowly defined limits. Anything very controversial can be referred to a Council meeting, and increasingly also the EP. There is also the fact that the Council, and again increasingly the EP, are jealous of their powers and would move quickly against the Commission if it was thought comitology committees were being used to undermine those powers. And then there is the key point that the Council and EP know that it is just not in the Commission's long-term interests to abuse its powers by forcing unwelcome or unpopular measures through a committee. The Commission wants and needs the cooperation of the Council and EP.

(d) CASE STUDY: THE RESIGNATION OF THE COMMISSION IN 1999[37]

The European Commission resigned as a body on 15 March 1999 following the publication of a report by a Committee of Independent Experts entitled *Allegations Regarding Fraud, Mismanagement and Nepotism in the European Union*. Concern over the Commission's management of the EU budget had been growing for several years. From 1994 to 1996, for example, between 4 per cent and 5 per cent of the EU's budget could not be accounted for. The European Court Auditors (ECA) concluded that there had been an unacceptable incidence of error in operational expenditure payments (85 per cent of which had taken place in the member states). Stories of fraud and waste went through all of the European media and the public outcry was enormous. As a result of the ECA's annual report, the European Parliament, in 1999, refused to 'discharge' (that is, approve) the budget. To top it all, a Commission employee, Paul van Buitenen, blew the whistle on the Commission by passing to the European Parliament and ECA a dossier in which he detailed efforts by senior Commission officials to suppress investigations into fraud; he also made other allegations of mismanagement and nepotism. The most famous example concerned Commissioner Edith Cresson, who employed her personal dentist and close friend as a highly paid scientific adviser on HIV/Aids—a position for which he was unsuited and unqualified.

Using Art. 234 TFEU, the European Parliament might have been able to sack the Commission collectively in January 1998. The two main political groups in the European Parliament—the Socialist Party and the European People's Party—were, however, unable to manage the crisis and agree on a successful vote of censure. They did establish the Committee of Independent Experts to investigate the allegations. After two months, the Committee delivered its highly critical report on 15 March 1999, drawing the following conclusion.

---

[37] See generally House of Commons Research Paper, *The Resignation of the European Commission*, 99/32, 16 March 1999; A. Macmullen, 'Political responsibility for the administration of Europe: The Commission's resignation in March 1999' (1999) 52(4) Parliamentary Affairs 703–18.

European Committee of Independent Experts, *First Report on Allegations Regarding Fraud, Mismanagement and Nepotism in the European Commission,* 15 March 1999, para. 1.6.2

[The] reprehensible conduct of the Commission as a body, or of Commissioners individually, and more particularly [...] mismanagement in detecting or dealing with fraud, mismanagement or nepotism perpetrated by the administrative services of the Commission and by third parties working for the Commission, obviously involves the responsibility of the Commission as a whole, or of individual Commissioners.

The subsequent collective resignation of the College of Commissioners was unprecedented and briefly left the EU without its 'executive'. (In fact, the same Commission returned almost immediately to stay in office until the new one was sworn in six months later.)

Interestingly, the Committee of Independent Experts also said that the Commission had an 'ethical responsibility' to act in accordance with proper standards in public life (para. 1.6.2), in addition to its legal and political responsibility under the Treaty. Was the Committee tapping into underlying principles of constitutional responsibility at EU level? Tomkins identifies two problems with this view.

A. Tomkins, 'Responsibility and resignation in the European Commission' (1999) 62 Modern Law Review 744, 759–60

The first concerns the way in which collective responsibility is emphasised over individual responsibility. The Commission appears to have taken the view that collective responsibility means that Commissioners must not rock the boat: they must remain loyal, and speak with one voice, remembering at all times not to criticise fellow Commissioners. The constitutional vision of collective responsibility, however, is quite the reverse of this. Collective Commission responsibility should require that each and every member of the Commission has a constitutional obligation to keep watch over each and every other Commissioner. Collective responsibility should mean that no Commissioner is able to evade or avoid responsibility by passing the buck to another Commissioner, at least with regard to decisions which have been arrived at, and policies which have been developed by the Commission as a College—whether nominally or really. Once a policy has been announced, and once a decision has been reached, all Commissioners are responsible for it, whether the issue was actually discussed by the Commissioners themselves or not, and whether or not any individual Commissioner was or was not paying attention at the time. This must be what collective responsibility means, otherwise there is no means of preventing one Commissioner from evading questions on an issue merely by saying that this has nothing to do with her, and is the responsibility of some other Commissioner, who, when in his turn is questioned, might then also deny responsibility and blame someone else, and so on. As the European Parliament has expressed it, 'the principle of collegiality remains important but should not exempt individual Commissioners from the consequences, not only of any personal wrongdoing, but also of any incompetent or negligent management of their own areas of responsibility'.

The final problem with the way in which constitutional responsibility presently operates is connected to this privileging of collective responsibility over individual...As we have seen, unless the ECJ compulsorily retires an individual Commissioner under [Art. 247 TFEU], the Commission stands or falls together. In particular, the European Parliament has no power to require individual Commissioners to resign [...] Similarly, an individual Commissioner can be forced to resign only after court action, rather than as a result of parliamentary pressure. Not only is this a rather unsophisticated approach: it can also act as a protective shield allowing Commissioners more easily to escape facing up to the consequences of their actions. Forcing the entire Commission to resign is a draconian sanction—'nuclear option' was the phrase used to describe it in the European Parliament—and is likely therefore to be employed only in the most serious cases. That the Commission stands or falls together in this way may dissuade the European Parliament from calling for heads to roll where it is the resignation of an individual Commissioner which is really appropriate, rather than the premature nemesis of the Commission as a whole. The inability of the Parliament to require the resignation of an individual Commissioner is made more serious by virtue of the fact that resignation appears to be the only sanction available when things go wrong. This is a somewhat rudimentary approach. Ideally, a range of possible sanctions would be available to whichever person or body enforces or supervises the observation of the principles of responsibility. Commissioners should not be expected necessarily to resign in all cases where a mistake has occurred for which s/he is responsible. Resignation should be the ultimate sanction, but not the only one.

The Commission crisis of 1999 should not be exaggerated. It would appear that the collective resignation, as well as the political and the media reaction, were disproportionate to the evidence produced. True, the Committee found the Commission's behaviour to have been 'reprehensible', but the overall level of such behaviour within the Commission was not high. Also, the Committee only dealt with the details of allegations which had already been made—it did not conduct its own detective work to uncover new cases of mismanagement. In fact, most of the allegations originated in the period before 1995 (and were the responsibility of the Delors Commission rather than the Santer Commission) and had already been taken up internally and by the Commission's anti-fraud unit.

Had these allegations arisen in a Member State such as the UK, a normal response would have been to sacrifice controversial political figures, such as Ms Cresson, in a reshuffle. However, the Commission is a multinational institution, and appointments at senior level have to consider questions of national balance as well as merit. Transferring staff between posts is also much more complicated at EU than at national level. At the time of the crisis, neither the European Parliament nor the President of the Commission had the power to dismiss an individual Commissioner, and with Ms Cresson refusing to resign (she claimed she had the support of the French government), the Commission had no alternative but to pledge its collective responsibility and submit itself to a vote of no confidence before the European Parliament. As we saw, the Commission survived the vote (at the expense of splits within the two largest party groups along national lines) but had to accept scrutiny by, and the conclusion of, an independent committee. The Committee in turn stressed the concept of collective responsibility, and drew out implications which the Commission had never before been on the Commission's radar.

Today, the Commission is both collectively and individually accountable to the European Parliament. The European Parliament has a right to hear and interrogate commissioners, both orally and in writing, can establish *ad hoc* committees of inquiry, and it can still resign the entire Commission in case of gross misconduct. Since the Nice Treaty, the President of the Commission has the power to demand the resignation of individual commissioners.[38]

---

[38] Article 17(6) TEU.

The powers of the President of the European Commission—described by Hix as the most powerful office in the European Union[39]—are increased by the Lisbon Treaty. This saga shows that, under the existing Treaty regime, the President requires the consent of the College to dismiss an individual Commissioner. Under Art. 17(6) TEU ('*A member of the Commission shall resign if the President so requests*'), the President is given the formal power to 'hire and fire' Commissioners. This development clearly boosts the President's standing in relation to his or her colleagues, making him or her *primus inter pares* (that is, first among equals).

The additional (and existing) roles of the President are to shape the Commission's policies as a whole and to determine the future direction of the EU. The President also decides on the internal organization of the College: by allocating responsibilities to individual Commissioners; by ensuring that the Commission works efficiently and consistently; and by reshuffling the portfolios if necessary.

BOX 8.7 PRESIDENTS OF THE COMMISSION

- José Manuel Barroso (2004–present), a former Prime Minister of Portugal, was backed unanimously for a second term as President by EU leaders in June 2009 and confirmed by the European Parliament in September 2009.

- Romano Prodi (1999–2004) served as Prime Minister of Italy before and after his term as President of the Commission.

- Manuel Marín (1999), a Spanish politician, was President on an interim basis.

- Jacques Santer (1995–99), a former Prime Minister of Luxembourg, was—along with fellow commissioners—forced to resign over corruption allegations.

- Jacques Delors (1985–94) was a former French politician.

QUESTIONS

1. '*The Commission has not undergone any fundamental structural change since its inception. Its role is largely unchanged.*' Do you agree?

2. Was the Commission right to resign collectively over allegations of fraud, mismanagement, and nepotism?

3. Are the powers of the President of the European Commission too vast? To which office in the domestic (UK) context can the President's powers be likened?

4. '*The European Parliament already has sufficient powers and mechanisms to hold the Commission to account.*' Do you agree with this statement?

Does the Commission exercise power efficiently?

Arguably, the Commission does exercise its power efficiently—although not in the traditional way in which governments issue rules and regulations. The Commission leads through dialogue, through its powers of initiation and influence. The powers of the Commission

---

[39] Simon Hix, *What's Wrong with the EU and How to Fix It* (2008, Cambridge: Polity Press), p. 155.

(like the powers of the US president) are designed to identify new directions of European integration.

The multifarious nature of the Commission's tasks does, however, carry with it an inherent lack of efficiency. It has a choice between leading and mediating, and all too often tries to do both. It initiates sometimes sweeping policy proposals, which it then has to sell as being in the common interest. The Commission is thus easily caught between the rock of striking political bargains and the hard place of ensuring favourable reception—and the bigger the EU becomes, the more difficult it is for the Commission to put forward single policy proposals.

N. Nugent, *The Government and Politics of the European Union* (2010, Basingstoke: Macmillan), p. 137

Amongst practitioners, debate has tended to be focused mainly on the extent to which an institution that is unelected should be exercising significant powers. For those who take a broadly intergovernmentalist position on what the nature of the EU should be, the powers of the Commission need to be restricted and the exercise of what powers it has need to be firmly controlled. But, for those who are more integrationist in spirit, a strong and not over-shackled Commission is vital if the EU is to have policies that are sufficiently creative and ambitious to tackle the many policy problems the EU faces.

But whatever position is taken in these and related debates, it is indisputable that the Commission is a core institutional presence in the EU. When the EU is 'in operation', the Commission is almost invariably involved in some significant way. The frequent appearance on the EU agenda of politically sensitive matters, coupled with the desire of politicians not to cede too much power to others if they can avoid it, may have resulted in at least some member states being reluctant in recent years to grant too much further autonomy to the Commission, but the Commission nonetheless remains central and vital to the whole EU system.

QUESTIONS

1. Using the Commission's website, identify the Commissioner for Environment. What are the key policies that fall within his or her remit?

2. In comparison with the United Kingdom, does the Commission most resemble the UK Cabinet[40] or the UK Civil Service,[41] or both, or neither?

6 A DUAL EXECUTIVE

We have seen that the three main institutions perform different functions and that each institution makes an independent claim of legitimacy. The Council claims to be the guardian of national autonomy; the Commission (together with the Court of Justice) claims to be

---

[40] See Chapter 7.
[41] See Chapter 7.

the guardian of effective integration; and the European Parliament claims to be the guardian of democratic governance.[42]

But where does executive power in the EU lie? Simon Hix provides the most innovative answer by introducing the concept of a 'dual executive', within which the Council and Commission share the responsibilities of government. The Council is responsible for setting the medium- to long-term agenda, by reforming the EU Treaty, and delegating political and administrative tasks to the Commission. In the areas in which executive powers have been delegated, the Commission is responsible for distributing the EU budget, monitoring policy implementation by the member states, and making rules and regulations. We have seen that the member states have limited the Commission to certain regulatory matters, such as competition and agriculture, while they have retained control of key executive powers, such as Treaty reform, policymaking in relation to Common Foreign and Security Policy, the former third pillar (Police and Judicial Cooperation in Criminal Matters), long-term agenda setting, and the coordination of national macroeconomic policies in the European Council.

We have, however, also seen that the Commission has developed some of the attributes of a supranational 'government'. The College of Commissioners resembles Cabinet government and the Commission crisis of 1999 raised issues relating to collective responsibility. The Commissioners are career politicians who bring their own ideological objectives to the EU's policymaking process. Administratively, the Commission is supported by its own 'ministries' in the form of the DGs. In short, the Commission has the incentives, the resources, and the power to pursue its own agenda, independently from those of the member state governments.

S. Hix and B. Høyland, *The Political System of the European Union*, 3rd edn (2011, Basingstoke: Macmillan), pp. 47–8

The result is a system with strengths and weaknesses. The main strength is that the dual character of the EU executive facilitates extensive deliberation and compromise in the adoption and implementation of EU policies. This is a significant achievement for a continental-scale and multi-national political system, and it reduces the likelihood of system breakdown. However there are two important weaknesses. First, the flip side of compromise is a lack of overall political leadership and dual-executive systems tend to be characterized by policy stability. Second, and linked to this issue, there is the problem of democratic accountability. There is no single chief executive, whom the European public can 'throw out'.

Constitutional law, whether at national or at supranational level, consists of two sides. On the one hand, it maps out the executive powers and functions of political institutions (it *empowers*). We have seen that the EU has a dual—maybe even a triple—executive that consists of the Council of Ministers and the Commission, and behind the scenes, but more prominently after the Lisbon Treaty created a figurehead, the European Council. This chapter has so far tried to set out and analyse the roles and authority of these key European institutions—but political power, once created, needs to be controlled and *constrained*, and it is to this all-important second issue that we now turn.

---

[42] See Chapter 12.

7 DEMOCRACY, LEGITIMACY, ACCOUNTABILITY, AND TRANSPARENCY

As the powers of the European Union have grown, so have the problems of public mistrust and the legitimacy of the EU's central institutions. Contrary to Jean Monnet's functionalist assumption, the benefits of European integration are no longer taken for granted by citizens of the EU member states. The ratification of the Maastricht Treaty suffered a setback in 1992 when it was rejected by the Danes in a referendum. The Nice and Lisbon ratification crises in Ireland, and the French and Dutch rejections of the Constitutional Treaty highlight the citizens' perceived problems with the European Union.

(a) LEGITIMACY

Legitimacy is an important concept in political science, which asks whether the existing political institutions receive adequate support from the members of society—this they may do, for example, by being sufficiently representative and democratically accountable. A ruler may have the *power* to make laws by virtue of his or her office, but without the consent of a large proportion of the population, the ruler's edicts may lack *legitimacy*. Legitimacy is, therefore, a basic condition for rule and EU governance (like the government of any state) would not be legitimate unless it was carried out with the consent of the governed.

It is useful to distinguish 'formal' legitimacy from 'social' legitimacy. The European Union is legitimate in a formal sense because it was established, and has been extended, on the basis of treaties ratified by the member states. The European Union claims to respect the principle of the rule of law[43] and the Treaties impose strict limits on EU activities. On a day-to-day basis, the European Union even has a 'double democratic mandate', because it derives its legitimacy from two sources: the national governments (which are represented in the Council) and the directly elected European Parliament. In relation to accountability, even in the policy areas in which the European Union is competent to act alone, it is constrained by decision-making procedures that require either supermajorities (QMV) or even unanimity, as well as concurrent majorities among the three main EU organs. Far from being distant and detached, there are, in fact, multiple channels of political accountability, both directly via the European Parliament (as we have seen) and indirectly via elected national officials (see Accountability).

If we shift the focus away from formal procedures and turn to questions of broader social acceptance of the European Union by the people, then the problem becomes one of democratic control and, therefore, of social legitimacy in the operation of the institutions.[44] Thus, policymaking at EU level has not only branched out into new areas that are nationally sensitive, but it is also dominated by executive actors (national ministers in the Council and government appointees in the Commission). Executive dominance, by itself, is not problematic—provided that the actions can be scrutinized by national parliaments. The national ministers in the Council *are* ultimately accountable to their national parliaments, but only in a weak manner in relation to EU matters and the making of EU legislation. In other

---

[43] Article 19 TEU; see also Case 294/83 *Les Verts v European Parliament* [1986] ECR 1339, [23]; *Opinion 1/91* [1991] ECR I-6079, [35]; Joined Cases C-402/05 P and C-415/05 P, *Kadi and Al Barakaat International Foundation v Council of the European Union* [2009] 3 WLR 872 [281]–[284], [316].

[44] See, e.g., J.H.H. Weiler, *The Constitution of Europe: Do the New Clothes Have an Emperor? and Other Essays on European Integration* (1999, Cambridge: Cambridge University Press), pp. 83–6.

words, national ministers working at EU level enjoy a much higher degree of isolation from national parliamentary scrutiny and control than they do in the domestic policymaking process. As a consequence, one effect of European integration has been an increase in the power of executives and a decrease in the power of national parliaments.

The increased use of QMV in the Council since the mid-1980s and the comparative weakness of the European Parliament (in relation to the governments in the Council) have also helped to strengthen the executive and to highlight the legitimacy problem. It raises the question under what circumstances, and in what areas, are citizens of the EU member states prepared to accept majority rule? At national level, majority rule is accepted by the people precisely because there is 'a people'—in other words, a *Staatsvolk*, nation, or *demos*, which unites the existing political, economic, social, and cultural interests into a kind of sociopsychological glue that supports majority decisions through tolerance and solidarity.[45] In contrast, the European Union consists of numerous member states, the peoples of which do not share the same substantive cultural values, such as religion and language; in that sense, they clearly lack the same foundations as a nation state.

A. Moravcsik, 'Despotism in Brussels? Misreading the European Union' (2001)
Foreign Affairs 80(3): 114–23, 118

> Like most modern polities, the EU rests instead on pragmatic political practices consensually accepted by overlapping cultural and political groups. The true pillars of the EU—economic welfare, human rights, liberal democracy, and the rule of law—appeal to Europeans regardless of national or political identity. The resulting institution is stable not because it is culturally coherent, but because it serves the complex, increasingly interwoven interests of citizens in interdependent, advanced industrial democracies. No significant group in any member state favours withdrawal from this arrangement [...T]he EU's success and durability prove that alternative conceptions are possible.

One such alternative conception is Joseph Weiler's 'principle of constitutional tolerance', which captures the European citizens' acceptance of EU law as binding, even though their own government may have disapproved of the legal measure.[46] Member states with the smallest number of votes could be expected to feel particularly vulnerable in light of the influence and voting power wielded by the larger member states. So in order to protect the smaller member states from being bulldozed by the larger member states, safeguards have been built into the existing system of weighted voting in the Council. It is even possible for a coalition of smaller countries to outvote their larger (population-wise) counterparts, even though they represent less than one half of the EU's total population. The intrinsic absence of social glue among European citizens necessitates complex voting mechanisms and diffuses executive power—but it also highlights the importance of social legitimacy and the need to bring the European Union 'closer to the people'.

---

[45] See, e.g., Dieter Grimm, 'Does Europe need a constitution?' (1995) 1 European Law Journal 282.
[46] See J.H.H. Weiler, 'In Defence of the Status Quo: Europe's Constitutional *Sonderweg*', in J.H.H. Weiler and M. Wind (eds) *European Constitutionalism Beyond the State* (2003, Cambridge: Cambridge University Press), pp. 18–23.

(b) ACCOUNTABILITY

Accountability is increasingly viewed as a necessary condition for legitimacy and is connected to the idea of representation. In Western democracies, accountability is the counterpart of delegation and usually occurs along vertical lines—that is, the voters delegate fiduciary power to their popular representatives in elections, who delegate power to a cabinet of ministers, who delegate power to their civil servants or to other administrative bodies. This delegation of power does, however, come with strings attached: if the representatives abuse their power, they can be called to account. Political accountability operates in the opposite direction to that of delegation. Politicians routinely apologize, resign, and even lose elections, if they have lost the trust of their voters.

J.H.H. Weiler, 'The political and legal culture of European integration: an exploratory essay' (2011) 9(3/4) International Journal of Constitutional Law 678, 679–80

As regards accountability, even the basic condition of representative democracy, namely, that at election time the citizens "can throw the scoundrels out"—that is, replace the government—does not operate in Europe. The form of European governance, governance without government, is and will remain for considerable time, perhaps forever, such that there is no "government" to throw out. Dismissal of the Commission by Parliament (or approving the appointment of the Commission president) is not quite the same, not even remotely so. Startlingly, the political accountability of Europe is surprisingly weak. There have been some spectacular political failures of European governance. The embarrassing Copenhagen climate fiasco; the weak (at best) realization of the much-touted Lisbon agenda (a.k.a. Lisbon strategy or Lisbon process); the very story of the defunct "Constitution", to mention but three. It is hard to point, in these instances, to any measure of political accountability, of someone paying a political price, as would be the case in national politics. In fact, it is difficult to point to a single instance of accountability for political failure as distinct from personal accountability for misconduct in the annals of European integration. This is not, decidedly not, a story of corruption or malfeasance. My argument is that this failure is rooted in the very structure of European governance. It is not designed for political accountability.

Accountability is one of the hallmarks of democratic governance. The shift from policymaking by national *governments* to transnational EU *governance* has not only highlighted the absence of a social basis, or demos, but also accountability deficits, which in turn impact on the perceived legitimacy of the European Union. The key question is whether the European Union, as a new, transnational, and multilevel form of governance, requires new and different forms of accountability.

As we saw in Chapter 2 and Chapter 7, according to the 'Westminster model', political accountability is exercised hierarchically, or *vertically*, through ministerial responsibility to the UK Parliament. The system of hierarchical political accountability (by convention, ministers are accountable to Parliament for all of the actions of government, including those of civil servants) has, however, come under pressure from *horizontal* forms of accountability, which include accountability to administrative forums, citizens, and civil society, as well as more individual forms of accountability.[47] This is not only political rhetoric: the new Art. 11

---

[47] See Chapter 2.

TEU creates a requirement in general terms for dialogue between the EU institutions and civil society. The Lisbon Treaty also provides for a European Citizens Initiative (ECI), an experimental form of direct democracy that enables 1 million citizens to put an issue on the Commission's agenda (Art. 11(4) TEU; Art. 24(1) TFEU).[48] The establishment of ombudsmen, auditors, and quasi-autonomous or independent agencies challenge the traditional system of political control through the minister and offer alternatives to traditional vertical forms of accountability. Although these administrative forums may report to Parliament or to the minister, they do not stand in a hierarchical relationship to the actors. Nor do they replace the traditional forms of popular control: European governance requires both traditional and new forms of accountability.

Finally, as Peterson and Shackleton point out, accountability is not just a technical problem that can be fixed by tinkering with the national and/or European institutions. It is also a political problem that is exacerbated by the absence of politicians who are committed to the European cause, willing to take political risks to drive forward the project of integration, and draw inspiration from the 'heroic' epoch of European integration in the 1980s.

J. Peterson and M. Shackleton, 'Conclusion', in J. Peterson and M. Shackleton (eds) *The Institutions of the European Union*, 3rd edn (2012, Oxford: OUP), p. 399

If there is one single, burning question that arises from studying the EU's institutions, it is the vexed accountability question: how can the Union's institutions, in the absence of a truly European polity, become more accountable to European citizens and thus a more legitimate level of governance? In our view, it is difficult to imagine that the problem can be solved simply with a dose of direct democracy, such as by instituting the direct election of the President of the Commission, empowering national parliaments in EU decision-making, or spending more to foster truly pan-European political parties. It might be rather easier to envisage the future election of governments able and willing to do a better job of selling the EU's institutions to average citizens as both necessary and competent agents in the tasks of governing Europe, and defending its interests in a new, modern, and increasingly globalized world.

(c) TRANSPARENCY

Finally, the Lisbon Treaty also increases the transparency of the institutions and their decision-making processes. You will recall that meetings of the European Council and of the Council of the European Union were often held in secret. That will no longer be possible in the future.

Article 15 TFEU

1. In order to promote good governance and ensure the participation of civil society, the Union institutions, bodies, offices and agencies shall conduct their work as openly as possible.

---

[48] Regulation (EU) No. 211/2011 of the European Parliament and of the Council of 16 February 2011, on the citizens' initiative, took effect on 1 April 2012.

2. The European Parliament shall meet in public, as shall the Council when considering and voting on a draft legislative act.

3. Any citizen of the Union, and any natural or legal person residing or having its registered office in a Member State, shall have a right of access to documents of the Union institutions, bodies, offices and agencies, whatever their medium, subject to the principles and the conditions to be defined in accordance with this paragraph.

General principles and limits on grounds of public or private interest governing this right of access to documents shall be determined by the European Parliament and the Council, by means of regulations, acting in accordance with the ordinary legislative procedure.

Each institution, body, office or agency shall ensure that its proceedings are transparent and shall elaborate in its own Rules of Procedure specific provisions regarding access to its documents, in accordance with the regulations referred to in the second subparagraph.

The Court of Justice of the European Union, the European Central Bank and the European Investment Bank shall be subject to this paragraph only when exercising their administrative tasks.

The European Parliament and the Council shall ensure publication of the documents relating to the legislative procedures under the terms laid down by the regulations referred to in the second subparagraph.

8 NATIONAL PARLIAMENTARY SCRUTINY OF THE EUROPEAN UNION

Do European executive institutions exercise too much power? Do national parliaments merely rubber-stamp EU legislation that is placed before them? Do they have sufficient powers of scrutiny? We have already hinted that there is a role to play for national parliaments in the policymaking process—and it is one of the explicit aims of the Lisbon Treaty to enhance the '*democratic legitimacy of the Union*' (see Preamble). The following section will examine the role of the UK Parliament in that process.

It is up to each member state to devise its own mechanisms for scrutinizing proposed EU legislation, and for monitoring and challenging the European Union. The key issue is that, in the purely domestic context, a minister will succeed in steering a Bill into an Act of Parliament only if the UK Parliament accepts the legislative proposal; at the EU level, however, the same minister may agree to legislation without being subject to the same stringent procedural safeguards of a parliamentary democracy. Because Council proceedings are not transparent and because, in any case, Council members act collectively (so a UK minister may have been out-voted), it is virtually impossible to establish how an individual minister voted in the Council. This section will examine the limited ways in which national parliaments can scrutinize ministers and whether their role in the EU's institutional system should be enhanced.

Very soon after the UK's accession to the European Community in 1973, the Houses of both Commons and the Lords set up committees to scrutinize proposed EC directives and regulations.[49] Today, the House of Commons has two committees dealing with EU matters: the European Scrutiny Committee (ESC) and the Foreign Affairs Committee (FAC).

---

[49] See generally E. Denza, 'Parliamentary scrutiny of Community legislation' [1993] Statute Law Review 56; S. Bulmer and C. Lequesne, *The Member States of the European Union* (2005, Oxford: OUP), pp. 297–303.

(a) HOUSE OF COMMONS EUROPEAN SCRUTINY COMMITTEE

The European Scrutiny Committee (ESC) in the House of Commons examined the ability of national parliaments to scrutinize proposed EU legislation and to influence it before decisions are made in a June 2002 report entitled *Democracy and Accountability in the EU and the Role of National Parliaments.*[50] It recognized that legislative proposals are often put forward for agreement before national parliaments have had time to consider them, sometimes on the basis of last-minute negotiation.

A. Cygan, 'Democracy and accountability in the EU: The view from the House of Commons' (2003) 66 Modern Law Review 384, 387

The key issues for the House of Commons when scrutinising EU legislative proposals are time and the prompt provision of the necessary information. The primary objective of the scrutiny process is to influence the minister *prior* to the Council adopting its definitive common position. In this Report, the European Scrutiny Committee identified no less than nine occasions between April 2000 and June 2001 when a lack of time and information prevented adequate, or in some cases *any*, scrutiny from taking place. In all these instances the cause of the problem was either a failure by the relevant government department to provide an Explanatory Memorandum about the proposal, or a failure by the Commission to provide the text within the guidelines contained in the Amsterdam Protocol on National Parliaments.

The European Scrutiny Committee in the House of Commons has set out a definition of the purpose of the scrutiny system in the House of Commons.

House of Commons European Scrutiny Committee, *European Scrutiny in the Commons,* 30th Report, Session 2001–02, HC 152, para. 25

To ensure that members are informed of EU proposals likely to affect the United Kingdom, to provide a source of information and analysis for the public, and to ensure that the House and the European Scrutiny Committee, and through them other organisations and individuals, have opportunities to make Ministers aware of their views on EU proposals, seek to influence Ministers and hold Ministers to account.

It consists of sixteen MPs, with a party-political composition reflecting party representation in the House of Commons generally (so, in 2012, eight Conservative, six Labour, two Liberal Democrat, representatives). The ESC receives copies of EU documents (such as Commission proposals), together with an Explanatory Memorandum from the UK government department responsible for that area of policy. The ESC's task is to assess the 'legal and political importance' of each of the EU documents received—over 1,100 a year. It also determines which measure is to be discussed. Debates will more commonly take place in the ESC, rather than on the floor of the House of Commons. The ESC also scrutinizes the works of the

---

[50] 33rd Report, Session 2001–02, HC 152.

Council of the EU (through parliamentary questions and sometimes by questioning ministers in person), and may occasionally conduct general inquiries into legal, procedural, or institutional developments in the European Union.

A former ESC chairman, Jimmy Hood MP, described the method of work of the select committee as follows.

Select Committee on Modernization of the House of Commons, *Minutes of Evidence*, 5 May 2004

When we come to our weekly meeting on a Wednesday, you are right, we can have a pile about this high, 30 or 40 documents to look at. What we have with each document is an A4 paper from our adviser telling us the treaty base, whether it is legally or politically important or not, what it seeks to do, maybe some brief history on it and then there is a recommendation on whether it has been looked at and can be cleared or whether it is politically or legally important and it has to be further scrutinised, whether to hold it back and get fuller information (that is sending it to departments for further information, the Cabinet Office, etc.). With the other information it will then come back to us and the recommendation will either be to go to debate because it is legally or politically important, or even then we get some recommendations that the information is not satisfactory and we should despatch a request for a bit more information and then we will make a decision to hold it back again to get the information, and then eventually we make the recommendation. It may go to debate and when it goes to debate then it is cleared from our scrutiny process. It is then in the hands of Parliament, for the Standing Committees or on the Floor of the House.

(b) HOUSE OF COMMONS FOREIGN AFFAIRS COMMITTEE

The House of Commons Foreign Affairs Committee (FAC) is one of the departmental select committees,[51] and is made up of fourteen MPs from the government and Opposition political parties. It is charged with monitoring the work of the Foreign and Commonwealth Office, so its remit extends much wider than the European Union, although EU matters are an important aspect of its work. The FAC can call for both written and oral submissions from interested parties. The Foreign Secretary and his or her ministers often appear before it to give oral evidence. The FAC can launch inquiries, publish a report when the inquiry has finished, and reports to the House of Commons. These reports are sometimes debated by MPs. By convention, the government responds to an FAC report within two months of its publication.

(c) PARLIAMENTARY DEBATES ON EU MATTERS

The UK Parliament is able to call the government to account for its policies relating to the European Union through debates on the floor of both Houses of Parliament.

Legislative debates will deal with EU laws both requiring primary legislation (which are debated like other Bills) and implemented by delegated legislation[52] (which may be debated in standing committee).

---

[51] See Chapter 7.
[52] Under European Communities Act 1972, s. 2(2).

Non-legislative debates will deal with EU policies (for example, the Common Agricultural Policy), and will be initiated either by the government or the Opposition. Parliament has the chance to debate government White Papers. The six-monthly retrospective White Papers called *Developments in the European Union* have now been replaced by forward-looking White Papers called *Prospects for the EU in [year]*.

(d) PARLIAMENTARY QUESTIONS

A second mechanism through which the government can be called to account in relation to EU policies is through parliamentary questions (PQs).[53] Either the Foreign Secretary or the Minister for Europe will make statements and answer (written and oral) PQs on the European Union. Until 1985, there was a special (20-minute) slot for oral EU questions, but since then, they have been answered together with other foreign affairs questions for about an hour, once a month on average. Written questions are answered more frequently.

(e) THE HOUSE OF LORDS SCRUTINY

The House of Lords European Union Select Committee also scrutinizes EU legislative proposals and the government's response to them. Its formal terms of reference are '*To consider European Union documents and other matters relating to the European Union*'. It conducts regular and detailed inquiries into specific proposals (for example, fraud, third-pillar matters, the draft Constitutional Treaty), and reports either for information or with recommendation for debate in the Lords.

The EU Committee carries out much of its work through seven subcommittees (identified as A–G), each of which specializes in a particular subject area. The subcommittees prepare reports, which must be agreed by the Select Committee as a whole before publication. The Committees in the Commons and the Lords complement each other, and cooperate closely with one another.

BOX 8.8 POLICY AREAS OF THE HOUSE OF LORDS EU SUBCOMMITTEES

A	Economic and Financial Affairs, Trade and International Relations, including the EC Budget
B	Internal Market, including communications, energy, transport, research, and space
C	Foreign Affairs, Defence, and Development Policy
D	Environment and Agriculture
E	Law and Institutions
F	Home Affairs
G	Social Policy and Consumer Affairs, including health, worker protection, and education

Source: http://www.parliament.uk/documents/upload/hoflbpeuleg.pdf
Additional one-off subcommittees may be set up to examine specific proposals.

---

[53] On PQs generally, see Chapter 7.

(f) THE ROLE OF THE SCOTTISH PARLIAMENT

The Scotland Act 1998 gives the Scottish Parliament authority to implement EU law for Scotland in cases in which the subject matter of the new piece of legislation falls within or affects a devolved policy area.[54] The Scottish Parliament has its own European and External Relations Committee, the remit of which is to consider and report on:

(a) proposals for European Communities legislation;
(b) the implementation of European Communities legislation;
(c) any European Communities or European Union issue;
(d) the development and implementation of the Scottish Administration's links with countries and territories outside Scotland, the European Communities (and their institutions), and other international organizations; and
(e) coordination of the international activities of the Scottish Administration.

Like its Westminster counterpart, the Scottish committee monitors proposals for EU legislation and scrutinizes the manner in which the Scottish Government implements EU legislation, or the way in which it examines EU issues.

The Scottish Government has an EU Office in Brussels. It supports the EU-related work of the government and helps to increase Scotland's influence in the decision-making process. It also works closely with the United Kingdom's Permanent Representation to the EU, UKREP, which remains responsible for representing the views of the United Kingdom as a whole to the EU institutions.

(g) SHOULD NATIONAL PARLIAMENTS PLAY A GREATER ROLE IN THE EUROPEAN UNION?

What role should national parliaments play in the EU institutional system? On the one hand, the parliaments of the member states were given no formal functions under TEC and TEU (but note the obligations in the Lisbon Treaty), although they are responsible for implementing EU legislation. Therefore, involving national parliaments in the EU's law-making process may upset the balance between national parliaments and the EU institutions. In particular, the 'nationalizing' law-making process may produce 'selfish State-centric outcomes', which pay insufficient attention to European economic and social policies. Moreover, while qualified majority voting in the Council has made decision-making more efficient (member states do not have a veto and can be outvoted by the majority), it has also further marginalized national parliaments within the integration process: does scrutiny by national parliaments matter when national governments may be outvoted in the Council?

On the other hand, national parliaments have lost out in the process of European integration and so, arguably, national parliaments ought to have a much greater role than at present. National parliaments are an important source of legitimacy for the Union, and a direct and established link between the Union and the peoples of the member states, and the Treaty of Nice (2001) renewed interest in giving national parliaments a more formal role in the EU's legislative process—especially in relation to subsidiarity control.

[54] See Chapter 5.

The subsidiarity principle

Subsidiarity is a nebulous doctrine that is frequently politicized and misunderstood. The principle was introduced (although not by name) in the Single European Act 1986,[55] which authorized Community action regarding the environment to the extent that its objectives *can be attained better at the Community level*. Subsidiarity was elevated to a 'general principle' of Community law by the Maastricht Treaty in 1992. It is currently enshrined in the following provision.

Article 5 TEU

1. The limits of Union competences are governed by the principle of conferral. The use of Union competences is governed by the principle of subsidiarity and proportionality.

2. Under the principle of conferral, the Union shall act only within the limits of the competences conferred upon it by the Member States in the Treaties to attain the objectives set out therein. Competences not conferred upon the Union in the Treaties remain with the Member States.

3. Under the principle of subsidiarity, in areas which do not fall within its exclusive competence, the Union shall act only if and in so far as the objectives of the proposed action cannot be sufficiently achieved by the Member States, either at central level or at regional and local level, but can rather, by reason of the scale or effects of the proposed action, be better achieved at Union level.

   The institutions of the Union shall apply the principle of subsidiarity as laid down in the Protocol on the application of the principles of subsidiarity and proportionality. National Parliaments ensure compliance with the principle of subsidiarity in accordance with the procedure set out in that Protocol.

4. Under the principle of proportionality, the content and form of Union action shall not exceed what is necessary to achieve the objectives of the Treaties.

The institutions of the Union shall apply the principle of proportionality as laid down in the Protocol on the application of the principles of subsidiarity and proportionality.

In its procedural form, subsidiarity is a cautious device to determine the division of policymaking responsibilities between the European Union and the Member States. The principle does not threaten the sovereign powers of the Member States: Art. 4 TEU clarifies for the first time and in express terms that 'competences not conferred upon the Union in the Treaties remain with the Member States', and that the EU 'shall respect their essential State functions, including ensuring the territorial integrity of the State, maintaining law and order and safeguarding national security. In particular, national security remains the sole responsibility of each Member State.' Subsidiarity also does not apply in the few policy areas where the EU has exclusive competences (such as the common commercial policy, fisheries conservation, or monetary policy for the Euro-states).

Instead, it applies in areas of shared competences where there is a choice between using collective action through the EU institutions, or using individual national power. The principle of subsidiarity in Art. 5(3) TEU requires that legislative action be taken at the appropriate level, which means that the EU should act only if it can achieve the objectives of the

---

[55] This is a treaty, not an Act of the UK Parliament.

proposed EU action better than the Member States, and vice versa. Moreover, the principle of proportionality in Art. 5(4) TEU stipulates that 'Union action shall not exceed what is necessary to achieve the objectives of the Treaties'.

Subsidiarity also, however, has a substantive form, because it suggests that political decisions should be taken *as closely as possible to the citizen* (Art. 1 TEU), implying, where possible, a preference for devolved decision-making even within the member state. This was the form that was relied upon by the British government to reconcile the electorate to the federalizing implications of the Maastricht Treaty. Subsidiarity tends to be misunderstood in the United Kingdom, because it is not federally structured. In federal states, 'subsidiarity', or 'federalism', are ways in which to define and limit central powers and competencies. As Ruud Lubbers, a former Prime Minister of the Netherlands once remarked: '*I respect subsidiarity. As you know, for the Germans, the word for this is federalism.*'

The general view is that the Treaty of Lisbon and the Protocol on the Role of National Parliaments in the European Union (which will be annexed to the Treaty) will enhance the role of national parliaments in EU decision-making. The Lisbon Treaty makes numerous references to national parliaments and introduces the following new provision.

Article 12 TEU

National Parliaments contribute actively to the good functioning of the Union:

(a) through being informed by the institutions of the Union and having draft legislative acts of the Union forwarded to them in accordance with the Protocol on the role of national Parliaments in the European Union;

(b) by seeing to it that the principle of subsidiarity is respected in accordance with the procedures provided for in the Protocol on the application of the principles of subsidiarity and proportionality;

(c) by taking part, within the framework of the area of freedom, security and justice, in the evaluation mechanisms for the implementation of the Union policies in that area [...];

(d) by taking part in the revision procedures of the Treaties [...];

(e) by being notified of applications for accession to the Union [...];

(f) by taking part in the inter-parliamentary cooperation between national Parliaments and with the European Parliament, in accordance with the Protocol on the role of national Parliaments in the European Union.

Moreover, Art. 5 TEU and Art. 69 TFEU deal with national parliaments, ensuring compliance with subsidiarity (as we shall see). These provisions formalize the right of national parliaments to be involved in EU law-making.

The Protocol seeks to encourage '*greater involvement of national Parliaments in the activities of the European Union and to enhance their ability to express their views on draft legislative acts of the European Union as well as on other matters which may be of particular interest to them*'. It provides that all Commission consultation documents must be forwarded directly to national parliaments upon publication and it empowers national parliaments, for the first time, to enforce subsidiarity according to the following process.

The Lisbon Treaty introduces new procedures known as the 'yellow and orange cards'. National parliaments have eight weeks (rather than six, as under the Constitutional Treaty) to study draft EU legislative acts. Any national parliament may then decide to flag a proposal (that is, to express concerns) directly to the institution that initiated the proposal for not complying with the principle of subsidiarity. This 'early-warning mechanism' (or 'yellow card') consists of a two-step process. If one third of national parliaments (one quarter in the field of freedom, security, and justice) consider that the proposal is not in line with subsidiarity, the Commission will have to re-examine it and decide whether to maintain, adjust, or withdraw it. The Commission can decide to maintain its proposal against the objections by the national parliaments. In that case, it will have to explain its reasons, and it will be up to the European Parliament and the Council to decide whether or not to continue the legislative procedure.

The 'orange card' mechanism is a stronger subsidiarity control mechanism that applies only to the ordinary legislative procedure. Again, it involves a two-step process—but this time national parliaments require a higher threshold (a simple majority) before the Commission can be obliged to re-examine the proposal. The Commission may maintain it, but must give reasons. If the proposal is maintained, the Council and European Parliament must, in a second step, consider the proposal in light of the subsidiarity principle before the end of the first reading. This step leads to the definitive dismissal of the proposal if the Council (by a majority of 55 per cent) or the European Parliament (by a majority of votes cast) finds against the proposal.

House of Commons European Scrutiny Committee, *Subsidiarity, National Parliaments and the Lisbon Treaty,* 33rd Report, Session 2007–08 (HL 563)

Ev 38: Memorandum submitted by Andrew Duff MEP, Spokesman on Constitutional Affairs, Alliance of Liberals and Democrats for Europe (ALDE)

2. [...T]here is a danger that, in assessing the Treaty of Lisbon, national parliaments become obsessed by the early warning mechanism on subsidiarity. It was understood by those of us involved in its drafting and, then, re-drafting that the mechanism, although a necessary addition to the system of governance of the Union, was not really intended to be used. It is, in Bagehot's terms, more a dignified part of the European constitutional settlement than an efficient one. Or, in other words, if it were ever necessary actually to deploy the mechanism to block a legislative proposal, that deployment would signal a critical failure of the normal procedures. We would, in short, be facing a crisis of confidence in which a majority of member state governments had lost the support of their national parliaments on an important European issue, and in which the European Commission had not listened to warning signals from national parliaments at the earlier stage of proceedings.

3. The principle of subsidiarity has a respectable part to play in EU decision making but its importance should not be exaggerated. Instead, law making at the EU level would profit from more regular dialogue with national parliaments not on the problematic issue of subsidiarity but on the quality or direction of the actual measure. MEPs hear many views about our legislative work from trade, business and professional bodies, NGOs, social partners and member state and other governments: we hear little at the appropriate early phase of legislation from the relevant committees of national parliaments.

Aside from performing the task of institutional checks, promoting effectiveness, and adding substantive value to European legislation, monitoring the application of the subsidiarity principle has the additional side-effect of fostering a cooperative relationship between national parliaments and EU institutions, and among national parliaments themselves. The process is best understood as an institutional dialogue: the Commission may affirm, amend, or annul its proposal (while giving reasons), and the national parliaments may challenge the reasons before the ECJ if they consider them inadequate. But ultimately, the EU institutions have the final say on the fate of the original proposal.

In sum, the Lisbon Treaty and the Protocol clearly enhance the visible role of national parliaments in the decision-making process. National parliaments can torpedo proposed EU legislation on subsidiarity grounds—but the voting thresholds are high, and the final decision lies with the Council and the European Parliament. National parliaments, therefore, still rank below the European institutions in the EU's institutional pecking order.

V. Bogdanor, *Legitimacy, Accountability and Democracy in the European Union*, A Federal Trust Report (2007), p. 16

These new institutional changes mark the first time that national parliaments are being directly associated with the European policy process. Nevertheless, their impact may remain limited. It needs, above all, to be asked whether national parliaments are in fact being granted a new and significant power through the 'early warning mechanism'. The power is not wholly new since national parliaments were already able to object informally to EU legislation through their scrutiny procedures if they wished to do so. Nor is this power as significant as it might seem, since it is a purely negative power. Parliaments are only able to express a dissenting view, which does not even amount to a veto. But national parliaments cannot be constructive actors by, for example, placing new legislation on the agenda. Furthermore, as we have seen, parliaments can object to legislation only on the specific ground of subsidiarity. Yet this seems to be a comparatively minor problem in EU policy-making, since current evidence indicates that only a small proportion of legislative proposals gives rise to genuine issues of subsidiarity.

The principal argument for an increased role for the national parliaments in EU matters is that it would bring the EU closer to the citizens by making them part of the EU process. After all, citizens are more familiar with their national parliament and the issues discussed there. At the same time, national parliaments may not be ready for their new responsibilities. Although they have adapted their structures and procedures to keep up with the pace and scope of European integration, these steps have not been sufficient, which diminishes their legitimating capacity. Some national parliaments do not have the resources to scrutinize in depth and at short notice the complicated legislative proposals made by the Commission. Draft European proposals are often highly technical, and such detailed and meticulous inspection is often not the strong point of a national MP (note that, in the United Kingdom, it is the non-elected chamber, the House of Lords, which has been more effective at scrutiny than the democratically elected House of Commons). Also, the national parliaments of member states vary greatly, and they have their own understanding of their roles and priorities. As a result, their contribution to the legitimating process may differ greatly. In other words, while the EU has recognized that national parliaments must play a more important role in the future, the extent of that importance will depend considerably on the internal political and constitutional situation of the member states themselves.

The role that national parliaments play in EU affairs depends essentially on three considerations: the constitutional balance of power inside the national system between parliament and government; the nature of party government and the related issues of the nature of the party system, and particularly internal party relationships; and the extent to which EU affairs are regarded as domestic as opposed to foreign affairs.

QUESTIONS

1. Where does executive power in the EU lie? What is meant by 'dual executive'? Do you think executive power in the EU is comparatively strong or weak? What makes it strong? What makes it weak?

2. Does the European Council have executive power?

3. The Council of the European Union is the main decision-making body of the EU. In what areas is it dependent upon a Commission proposal? In what areas can it act alone?

4. 'The EU policy process is dominated by unelected officials from the European Commission and member governments, negotiating in a process that is closed and distant from European electorates. The result is undemocratic structure of European institutions and an illegitimate political system.' Do you agree with this statement?

5. Does the constitution of the EU ensure that those in positions of power will exercise that power responsibly? What does the resignation of the Commission in 1999 tell us about the principles of constitutional responsibility?

6. Does the EU require new forms of accountability that are different from the traditional accountability arrangements of the nation state?

7. Do you agree that the Council is not accountable to anybody? Is the performance of national scrutiny sufficiently rigorous to ensure accountability?

8. How effective is the UK Parliament in scrutinizing proposed EU regulations and directives? What reforms can you suggest?

9. Do you think that national parliaments have sufficient powers to scrutinize law-making at EU level? Is the 'yellow and orange card' mechanism satisfactory? Should national parliaments be given a veto (a 'red card') on European legislation?

---

9 CONCLUDING COMMENTS

This chapter has examined the constitutional frameworks through which executive functions of the European Union are exercised and how it is held to account. To carry on exploring the European Union, turn to Chapter 12, which considers legislative functions relating to EU matters. To carry on exploring executive functions related to the UK government, turn to Chapter 9, which looks at the use of prerogative powers.

10 FURTHER READING

Anderson, P., *The New Old World* (2009, London: Verso)

Bovens, M., 'New forms of accountability and EU governance' (2007) 5 Comparative European Politics 104–20

Burgess, M., *Federalism and European Union: The Building of Europe, 1950–2000* (2000, London: Routledge)

Hix, S., and Høyland, B., *The Political System of the European Union,* 3rd edn (2011, Basingstoke: Macmillan)

Jacobs, Sir F.G., *The Sovereignty of Law: The European Way* (2007, Cambridge: Cambridge University Press)

Majone, G., *Regulating Europe* (1996, London: Routledge)

Nugent, N., *The Government and Politics of the European Union,* 7th edn (2010, Basingstoke: Macmillan)

Peterson, J., and Shackleton, M., *The Institutions of the European Union*, 3rd edn (2012, Oxford: OUP)

Weiler, J.H.H., *The Constitution of Europe: Do the New Clothes Have an Emperor? and Other Essays on European Integration* (1999, Cambridge: Cambridge University Press)

ONLINE RESOURCE CENTRE

Further information about the themes discussed in this chapter can be found on the Online Resource Centre at www.oxfordtextbooks.co.uk/orc/lesueur2e/

9

PREROGATIVE POWERS AND CASE STUDY ON THE DEPLOYMENT OF ARMED FORCES ABROAD

CENTRAL ISSUES

1. A fundamental principle of the constitution is that executive action must be based on legal foundations.

2. Most public bodies are 'creatures of statute' established by an Act of Parliament. Statute provides their legal powers. Ministers in the UK government are in a different position, because the legal foundation for some of their specific actions is 'prerogative power'. Some actions of the monarch central to the running of the constitutional system also have their source in prerogative powers.

3. UK government ministers and some other public bodies that are not 'creatures of statute' may also claim to be able to carry out some kinds of action because there is no legal prohibition on them doing so. This is called the 'third source' of authority under the 'Ram doctrine'. The existence of this freedom of action is controversial and has not yet been settled by the courts.

4. There are fewer opportunities to hold ministers to account when government uses its prerogative powers than when

it exercises powers conferred by statute. Prerogative powers may therefore be thought to be out of step with modern constitutional requirements.

5. Judicial control over the legality of the exercise of prerogative powers has increased in recent years, but some important types of action are regarded by the courts as 'non-justiciable' and are effectively immune from judicial oversight.

6. In this chapter we use a case study on the power to deploy armed forces abroad to illustrate these issues. Decisions to deploy British armed forces abroad have a prerogative power as their source. In the past, such decisions were taken with minimal parliamentary oversight. A constitutional convention may have developed that Parliament should debate and approve deployments, but the scope of this convention is not settled. Committees in the Houses of Commons and the Lords have pressed for different reforms designed to ensure that Parliament has a greater influence.

1 INTRODUCTION

Section 2 of this chapter, Sources of legal authority, considers the various legal foundations on which public bodies may base their executive actions. Section 3, Prerogative
powers, examines prerogative power—a source of power possessed only by ministers
in UK government and the monarch—in more detail. Here we will see that the continued existence of prerogative powers in the UK constitution has been a source of debate
for several years. Many view the existence of these powers as being inconsistent with
modern notions of the rule of law, parliamentary democracy, and effective accountability over government action. A long-running campaign by backbench members of
Parliament (MPs) and peers saw several unsuccessful attempts to introduce Private
Member's Bills to reform prerogative powers. The highly respected House of Commons
Public Administration Select Committee (PASC) carried out several inquiries into various aspects of the prerogative.

While Tony Blair was Prime Minister (1997–2007), little progress was made. The government agreed in principle that the civil service ought to be placed on a statutory footing rather than continue to be regulated by prerogative powers, but was slow to introduce
legislation to implement this. Things changed dramatically during 2007. The government accepted for the first time that reforms ought to be introduced to give Parliament
greater control over ministers' decisions to deploy British armed forces abroad. The
pace of change quickened further when Gordon Brown took over as Prime Minister in
June 2007. A large part of his 'Governance of Britain' reform agenda was designed to
modernize prerogative powers. While the prerogative relating to treaties and the civil
service has now been reformed, some of the most important prerogative powers remain
unreformed. The story of progress towards reform is examined in section 4, Reforming
ministerial prerogatives. Section 5 contains a Case study: deployment of British armed
forces abroad. This issue has attracted much attention in recent years, especially following the war in Iraq and the deployment of forces to Afghanistan and more recently
in Libya. The controversy surrounding these operations has reinforced calls for reform
that would increase Parliament's involvement in these profoundly important decisions.
The case study shows, however, that arriving at reforms which are acceptable to all those
concerned is not proving easy.

2 SOURCES OF LEGAL AUTHORITY

Before considering prerogative powers in more detail, we need to understand the legal context in which they exist. As we have already seen, it is a fundamental principle of the constitution that public bodies must have legal authority for their actions. This requirement, basic
to the rule of law,[1] is laid down in cases such as *Entick v Carrington*[2] (in which searches under
a 'general warrant' were held to be unlawful).

What is the *source* of the legal authority on which a public body may rely as the legal
foundation for its executive action? In countries with written constitutions, the text of the
codified constitution may provide a direct legal foundation for functions of public bodies.

---

[1] See Chapter 3.
[2] (1765) 19 St Tr 1030, discussed in Chapter 3.

Without such a foundation in the United Kingdom, there are three main sources of legal authority on which a public body may seek to rely:

(a) **Statute law**—The vast majority of public bodies trace their legal powers to statutes or delegated legislation made under statutes.[3] All local authority powers stem from legislation,[4] as do the powers of the Scottish Government, Welsh Assembly Government, and Northern Ireland Executive.[5] These bodies are therefore sometimes described as 'creatures of statute', because they have only those powers that are expressly or implicitly conferred on them by statute law.

(b) **Prerogative powers**—We will examine the controversy over how these powers should be defined later in this chapter. For now, we can say that prerogative powers are a set of specific legal powers that are accepted by the courts as part of the common law. They may be exercised only by the monarch and UK government ministers acting in the name of 'the Crown'.

(c) **'Third source' power**—Public bodies that are not 'creatures of statute'. United Kingdom government ministers, for example, may also claim to be able to take action because there is no law preventing them from doing so. In other words, the action in question is not authorized by statute or a specific prerogative power, but it is said that the body has a freedom of action similar to that of a private individual. If this 'third source' is confined to activities such as entering into contracts for the supply of goods, then there may be no objection to them. If, however, these 'third source' powers are used for governmental activities, then they are a cause for concern.

Controversies and problems surround the creation and exercise of each of these sources of power. For example in relation to statute law, we will see that critics argue that the UK Parliament provides insufficient control over the passing of Bills and delegated legislation, the objects of which are often to confer executive powers on ministers and other public bodies.[6] The powers that are conferred are often very broadly drafted to give the public body in question a great deal of discretion as to if, when, and how they are exercised.

The use and continued existence of prerogative powers has been a matter of deep controversy for many years. Because prerogative powers are not conferred by Parliament and have not been subject to the same level of parliamentary discussion as have statutory provisions (and because government need not obtain the formal approval of Parliament before using them), many question whether it is appropriate for government to have prerogative powers. They argue that these powers should either be abolished or placed on a statutory footing.

(a) PREROGATIVE AND STATUTORY POWERS COMPARED

Before going any further, consider the main differences between executive power that is authorized by statute and that which is authorized by prerogative powers (see Box 9.1).[78]

---

[3] On primary and delegated legislation, see Chapter 10 and Chapter 11.
[4] See Chapter 5.
[5] See Chapter 5.
[6] See Chapter 10 and Chapter 11.
[7] See Chapter 1.
[8] See Chapter 16.

BOX 9.1 SUMMARY OF DIFFERENCES BETWEEN STATUTORY AND PREROGATIVE POWERS

	Statutory powers	Prerogative powers
Source	Created by Parliament	Residual executive powers, pre-dating the development of Parliament in its modern form
Parliament's role	Parliament debates, scrutinizes, and approves legislation conferring statutory powers	Parliament's role is reactive, calling ministers to account for the way prerogative power has been exercised.
Method of creating new powers	New statutory powers are created in every session of Parliament, as and when Bills containing executive powers receive royal assent	No new prerogative powers can be created—it is '350 years and a Civil War too late' for that (*per* Diplock LJ, *BBC v Johns* [1965] Ch 32, 79)
Place in hierarchy of legal rules9	Subject to them being consistent with EU law, Acts of Parliament are the highest form of law, although they may be repealed or amended by later Acts of Parliament	Prerogative powers are part of the common law and so may be abolished or restricted by Act of Parliament
Judicial review	Legality of exercise of executive powers conferred by statute may be subject to judicial review, unless the subject matter is 'non-justiciable'	Since 1984, exercise of prerogative powers may be subject to judicial review, unless the subject matter is 'non-justiciable'9

QUESTION

Drawing on the given points (and others that you can think of), list the main constitutional advantages and disadvantages of prerogative powers as compared with statutory powers from the points of view of (a) government and (b) Parliament.

(b) A 'THIRD SOURCE' OF AUTHORITY?

There is a school of thought (advanced by government, and accepted by some scholars and judges) that, in addition to specific statutory or prerogative powers, UK government ministers and some other public bodies (but only those that are not 'creatures of statute') also possess general common law powers. B.V. Harris refers to these as the 'third source' of legal authority for government action (the other two being statute and the prerogative).[10] The idea that there

---

9 See Chapter 16
10 B.V. Harris, 'The "third source" of authority for government' (1992) 108 Law Quarterly Review 626; B.V. Harris, 'The "third source" of authority for government revisited' (2007) 123 Law Quarterly Review 225.

are such powers is also called the 'Ram doctrine', after the government lawyer who set out an explanation for their existence in a memorandum in 1945.[11] Under this doctrine, it is said that the government's common law powers allow ministers residual freedom to do things, without statutory or prerogative authority, which have no legal consequences for others.[12]

Let us consider three cases in which this argument has been put forward.

Telephone tapping

In Chapter 6, we looked at the decision of Sir Robert Megarry VC in *Malone v Metropolitan Police Commissioner.*[13] We saw that, during Mr Malone's trial for handling stolen goods, it emerged that the police had, with a warrant obtained from the Home Secretary, secretly monitored and recorded his telephone conversations. Malone unsuccessfully sought a declaration that this covert tapping was unlawful. At the time, no statute expressly authorized telephone tapping, nor, in this case, did the police or Home Secretary claim to have any specific legal power under the prerogative to authorize the interception.

Malone v Metropolitan Police Commissioner
[1979] Ch. 344, 367

Megarry VC

If the tapping of telephones by the Post Office at the request of the police can be carried out without any breach of the law, it does not require any statutory or common law power to justify it: it can lawfully be done simply because there is nothing to make it unlawful.

Following a successful application to the European Court of Human Rights by Mr Malone, the law on telephone tapping was altered by the Interception of Telecommunications Act 1985, which gave the Home Secretary specific statutory powers to authorize tapping in defined circumstances. *Malone* no longer regulates what is lawful in this particular context, but the more general question remains whether the government does, indeed, have freedom to act in some situations without specific legal authority?

Making discretionary benefits payments to widowers

Harris accepts that the third source of authority has not been universally recognized by the UK courts, although he says that its existence *'appears to have been given implicit support'* by the majority of the House of Lords in *R (on the application of Hooper) v Secretary of State for Work and Pensions.*[14] Under the Social Security Contributions and Benefits Act 1992, women whose husbands die are eligible for a welfare benefit; until recently, however, there was no corresponding benefit for men whose wives die. The government accepted that this inequality was wrong and agreed to change the law.

---

[11] Sir Granville Ram was First Parliamentary Counsel between 1937 and 1947. See further A. Lester and M. Weaitt, 'The use of ministerial powers without parliamentary authority: The Ram doctrine' [2003] Public Law 415.

[12] M. Elliott, *The Constitutional Foundations of Judicial Review* (2001, Oxford: Hart), pp. 170–1.

[13] [1979] Ch 344, Sir Robert Megarry V-C.

[14] [2005] UKHL 29.

While plans were being made to do so, a group of widowers campaigned for discretionary payments to be made to them equivalent to those paid to women. One of the issues was whether the government had power to make the payments. Although there is no specific *prerogative* power to make such payments, it accepted that there was a common law power to make *ex gratia* payments. However it successfully argued that the failure to make the payments was not unlawful because it was justified by the legislation.[15]

While the case may offer implicit support for the existence of 'third source' powers, none of the judges expressly indicated that the government could use these 'common law' powers to make payments to widowers. Indeed, the Court of Appeal rejected this; in the House of Lords, Lord Nicholls was very cautious saying only that *'Whether the Crown, in exercise of its common law powers, could lawfully have made [...] payments to widowers is a difficult question with far-reaching constitutional implications'*.[16]

Reorganizing local government

The scope of the Ram doctrine was considered more fully by the Court of Appeal in *R (on the application of Shrewsbury and Atcham BC) v Secretary of State for Communities and Local Government*.[17] The UK minister responsible for local government in England and Wales decided that she wanted to look into reorganizing councils in Shropshire, a scheme that would involve abolishing some smaller councils. A statutory framework for consulting about proposals like this existed under the Local Government Act 1992. The minister decided not to use the statutory consultation scheme, because she already had plans to introduce a Bill to Parliament to replace that framework. Her department went ahead and published a White Paper setting out the government's proposals for Shropshire. A local authority that was under threat of abolition challenged the legality of this way of proceeding. All three Lords Justice agreed that the claimant's appeal should be dismissed (for reasons not relevant here), but they expressed differing views on the scope and significance of the concept of a 'third source' of power, beyond statutory and prerogative powers.

R (on the application of Shrewsbury and Atcham BC) v Secretary of State for Communities and Local Government
[2008] EWCA Civ 148, [48]

Carnwath LJ

Unlike a local authority, the Crown is not a creature of statute. As a matter of capacity, no doubt, it has power to do whatever a private person can do. But as an organ of government, it can only exercise those powers for the public benefit, and for identifiably 'governmental' purposes within limits set by the law. Apart from authority, I would be inclined respectfully to share the view of the editors of de Smith that 'The extension of the Ram doctrine beyond its modest initial purpose of achieving incidental powers should be resisted in the interest of the rule of law' (*de Smith's Judicial Review* (6th edn) para 5-025).

---

[15] And that a defence existed under s. 6(2) of the Human Rights Act 1998: see Chapter 17.
[16] At [6].
[17] [2008] EWCA Civ 148.

It was however unnecessary to invoke the concept of a 'third source' of power to explain the Secretary of State's powers to prepare and publish a White Paper: that was *simply a necessary and incidental part of the ordinary business of central government*', according to Carnwath LJ.[18] Dismissing the appeal, Carnwath LJ held that it was *'a constitutional principle of some importance that local authorities should be able to rely on the safeguards of a statutory framework for the processes leading to decisions of this importance'*; it was, however, *'impossible to avoid the conclusion that Parliament has (if only retrospectively) given its stamp of approval to the procedure in this case'*,[19] because by the time the judicial review had been heard, a new statutory scheme for consulting on local government reorganization had been enacted.

Richards LJ did not share Carnwath LJ's *'reservations about the extent of the common law powers of the* Crown'.

R (on the application of Shrewsbury and Atcham BC) v Secretary of State for Communities and Local Government
[2008] EWCA Civ 148, [76]

Richards LJ

It is still necessary to explain the basis on which ordinary business of government is conducted, and the simple and satisfactory explanation is that it depends heavily on the "third source" of powers, i.e. powers that have not been conferred by statute and are not prerogative powers in the narrow sense but are the normal powers (or capacities and freedoms) of a corporation with legal personality.

He held that it would be wrong to introduce qualifications to their exercise such as that the powers are only 'for the public benefit' or for 'identifiably "governmental" purposes'; *'any limiting principle would have to be so wide as to be of no practical utility or would risk imposing an artificial and inappropriate restriction upon the work of government'*.[20] Waller LJ said that he instinctively favoured *'some constraint on the powers by reference to the duty to act only for the public benefit'*.[21]

Uncertainty and the rule of law

The argument that, in addition to statute or prerogative ministers of the Crown have further common law powers to do things that have no legal consequences recognizes that government may need incidental powers to enable it to perform its functions, but a general freedom to do things that will not affect peoples' rights is inherently uncertain. As Lord Nicholls indicated in *Hooper*, when decisions are taken, it may be impossible to know whether the decision will or will not affect peoples' rights. For example, the use of common law powers to confer benefits may generate legitimate expectations that must later be

---

[18] *R (on the application of Shrewsbury and Atcham BC) v Secretary of State for Communities and Local Government* [2008] EWCA Civ 148, [49].
[19] Ibid., [70].
[20] Ibid., [74].
[21] Ibid., [81].

respected.[22] It may be possible to know whether actions have had legal consequences with the benefit of hindsight, but officials will not necessarily be able to predict these consequences in advance and they will therefore be unable to know that legal authority exists. As well as practical difficulties, this clashes with the principle of legal certainty that is an important element of the rule of law.

QUESTION

What objections are there to the idea that a public body has a 'freedom to act' that is not authorized by a specific legal source?

---

3 PREROGATIVE POWERS

Ministry of Justice, *The Governance of Britain*,
July 2007 (Cm 7170), para. 20

In most modern democracies, the government's only powers are those granted to it by a written constitution or by the legislature. A distinguishing feature of the British constitution is the extent to which government continues to exercise a number of powers which were not granted to it by a written constitution, nor by Parliament, but are, rather, ancient prerogatives of the Crown. These powers derive from arrangements which preceded the 1689 Declaration of Rights and have been accumulated by the government without Parliament or the people having a say.

(a) THE MAIN PREROGATIVE POWERS

In March 2004, the House of Commons PASC produced an influential report, *Taming the Prerogative*. This surveyed the use of the prerogative powers and strongly argued the case for reform. We shall turn to the question of reform later, but for the moment it is valuable to see what the PASC had to say about the scope and nature of prerogative powers. The following extract from *Taming the Prerogative* identifies three groups of prerogative powers, of which the third—prerogative powers of government ministers—is the one on which the Committee focused its attention.

House of Commons Public Administration Select Committee, *Taming the Prerogative: Strengthening Ministerial Accountability to Parliament*,
Fourth Report, Session 2003–04, HC 422 (footnotes omitted)

Defining the Ministerial prerogative

4. In preparing for our inquiry we identified three main groups of prerogative powers. This informal division allowed us to concentrate mainly on those prerogative powers which give executive authority to Ministers [...] The three areas are described in the following paragraphs.

---

[22] See Chapter 16 (on legitimate expectation).

5. **The Queen's constitutional prerogatives** are the personal discretionary powers which remain in the Sovereign's hands. They include the rights to advise, encourage and warn Ministers in private; to appoint the Prime Minister and other Ministers; to assent to legislation; to prorogue or to dissolve Parliament; and (in grave constitutional crisis) to act contrary to or without Ministerial advice. In ordinary circumstances The Queen, as a constitutional monarch, accepts Ministerial advice about the use of these powers if it is available, whether she personally agrees with that advice or not. That constitutional position ensures that Ministers take responsibility for the use of the powers.

6. Although we received some evidence about the merits or demerits of these prerogatives, they are not the subject of our inquiry, which is solely concerned with the powers of Ministers. We are not considering any change in the constitutional position of The Queen.

7. **The legal prerogatives of the Crown,** which The Queen possesses as the embodiment of the Crown. There are many such prerogatives which are legal (rather than constitutional) in character. Several are historical remnants, such as the Crown's rights to sturgeon, certain swans, and whales, and the right to impress men into the Royal Navy. But two legal prerogatives have more modern legal significance, namely, the principle that the Crown (or the state) can do no wrong, and that the Crown is not bound by statute save by express words or necessary implication. Many of these legal prerogatives have been amended by parliamentary legislation; others are in need of reform; some others may be obsolete. [. . .]

8. **Prerogative executive powers** form the category of prerogatives which has been the main subject-matter of the Committee's inquiry. Historically, the Sovereign by constitutional convention came to act on Ministerial advice, so that prerogative powers came to be used by Ministers on the Sovereign's behalf. As Ministers took responsibility for actions done in the name of the Crown, so these prerogative powers were, in effect, delegated to responsible Ministers. But Parliament was not directly involved in that transfer of power. This constitutional position means that these prerogative powers are, in effect though not in strict law, in the hands of Ministers. Without these ancient powers Governments would have to take equivalent authority through primary legislation. As with the legal prerogatives just outlined, the connection between these powers and the Crown, or The Queen, is now tenuous and technical, and the label 'royal prerogative' is apt to mislead. [. . .] It makes more sense to refer to these powers not as 'royal prerogative' but as 'Ministerial executive'.

[. . .]

10. We recognise that Parliament is not powerless in the face of these weighty prerogatives. In the past, it has limited or abolished individual prerogative powers, and has also put some prerogatives on a statutory footing, as with the Interception of Communications Act 1985, the Security Service Act 1989, and the Intelligence Services Act 1994. [the Civil Service and ratification of treaties was placed on a statutory footing by the Constitutional Reform and Governance Act 2010] [. . .] Many public appointments, too, are now subject to regulation and monitoring by a Commissioner and are made in accordance with the Nolan rules. The courts can also review the legality of the use of some prerogatives, although they do not have a remit over all of them, and the courts can only help the aggrieved citizen after the event. [. . .]

Ministers' uncertain powers

12. But these restrictions on Ministers' prerogative powers are inevitably limited. Ministers still have very wide scope to act without Parliamentary approval. Perhaps more surprisingly in an era of increasing freedom of information, Parliament does not even have the right to know

what these powers are. Ministers have repeatedly answered parliamentary questions about Ministers' prerogative powers by saying that records are not kept of the individual occasions on which those powers are used, and that it would not be practicable to do so. Ministers have also said that it would be impossible to produce a precise list of these powers, and have asserted that, as Rt Hon John Major put it when he was Prime Minister 'It is for individual Ministers to decide on a particular occasion whether and how to report to Parliament on the exercise of prerogative powers'. Further uncertainty over the scope of Ministerial power is caused by the Ram doctrine, which asserts that Governments have the power to do anything which is not prohibited by statute or the common law.

13. Ministers are certainly accountable to Parliament for the use of prerogative powers just as for things done under statutory or common law authority. But they are only accountable after the event. The United Kingdom is typical of states which permit Ministers to use certain powers without parliamentary approval, but it is highly unusual among democracies in having neither a codified constitution nor having made such express grants of power by the legislature.

Responding to concern about the uncertain scope and extent of prerogative powers, the government undertook a survey of central government departments and agencies with a view to obtaining an overview of areas in which prerogative powers are exercised '*in order to set out in one place an illustration of the contemporary prerogative*'. This was the first time such an exercise had been undertaken and its results are to be found in the Ministry of Justice's *Review of the Executive Royal Prerogative Powers: Final Report* (October 2009).

Ministry of Justice, *The Governance of Britain, Review of the Executive Royal Prerogative Powers:* Final Report, October 2009

17. The extent of prerogative powers has never before been explored or codified on a systematic basis within Government. In order to determine the scope of such powers the Government conducted a survey across all central Government departments and agencies between November 2007 and May 2008. Sixty-four departments and agencies were asked to identify prerogative powers used to perform executive functions, the exercise of which had effectively been delegated to Ministers. The results of this survey are set out in the Annex to this report [see below].

18. Although the survey involved wide internal consultation, the nature, range and complexity of the prerogative powers meant that the survey did not attempt to provide an exhaustive list of all those that may exist. [...] The intention was to provide an overview of areas where prerogative powers are exercised, or have been exercised recently, in order to set out in one place an illustration of the contemporary prerogative.

19. The scoping exercise was intended to identify extant prerogative powers, whether or not they had fallen into disuse [...] The resulting list of prerogative powers, appended as the Annex to this report, is divided into the following main categories:

   a) prerogative powers exercised by Ministers;

   b) executive constitutional / personal prerogative powers exercised by the Sovereign;

   c) legal prerogatives of the Crown, such as Crown immunity (to the extent that it continues to exist in view of the Crown Proceedings Act 1947) and

   d) archaic prerogative powers, most of which are either marginal (relating to small, specific issues or largely superseded by legislation), or no longer needed.

20. The inclusion of the fourth category has led the Government to classify some prerogative powers differently from PASC. It has, however, followed PASC's example in excluding from consideration the legal prerogatives of the Crown since these powers are in no way exercised or influenced by Ministers.

21. PASC also excluded The Queen's constitutional prerogatives from its consideration, in order to focus solely on the powers of Ministers. Albeit with the same intention, the Government has taken a different line, in view of the constitutional obligation on The Queen to exercise almost all of her constitutional prerogatives in strict adherence to Ministerial advice and/or established constitutional law.

The following extract from the Annex lists the ministerial prerogative powers that were identified in the survey; it does not list the constitutional or personal prerogatives of the monarch, the powers exercised by the Attorney General, the legal prerogatives of the Crown, and other archaic prerogative powers.

Ministry of Justice, *The Governance of Britain, Review of the Executive Royal Prerogative Powers:* Final Report, October 2009, Annex ('Ministerial prerogative powers')

Government and the Civil Service

Powers concerning the machinery of Government including the power to set up a department or a non-departmental public body

Powers concerning the civil service, including the power to appoint and regulate most civil servants

Power to prohibit civil servants and certain other crown servants from issuing election addresses or announcing themselves, or being announced as, a Parliamentary candidate or a Prospective Parliamentary candidate

Power to set nationality rules for 'non-aliens'—British, Irish and Commonwealth citizens—concerning eligibility for employment in the civil service

Power to require security vetting of contractors working alongside civil servants on sensitive projects

Powers concerning the Office of the Civil Service Commissioners, the Security Vetting Appeals Panel, the Office of the Commissioner for Public Appointments, the Advisory Committee on Business, the Civil Service Appeal Board and the House of Lords Appointments Commission, including the power to establish those bodies, to appoint members of those bodies and the powers of those bodies

Justice system and law and order

Powers to appoint Queen's Counsel

The power to make provisional and full order extradition requests to countries not covered by Part 1 of the Extradition Act 2003

The prerogative of Mercy

Power to keep the peace

Powers relating to foreign affairs

Power to send ambassadors abroad and receive and accredit ambassadors from foreign states

Recognition of states
Governance of British Overseas Territories
Power to make and ratify treaties
Power to conduct diplomacy
Power to acquire and cede territory
Power to issue, refuse or withdraw passport facilities
Responsibility for the Channel Islands and Isle of Man
Granting diplomatic protection to British citizens abroad

Powers relating to armed forces, war and times of emergency

Right to make war or peace or institute hostilities falling short of war
Deployment and use of armed forces overseas
Maintenance of the Royal Navy
Use of the armed forces within the UK to maintain the peace in support of the police or otherwise in support of civilian authorities (eg to maintain essential services during a strike)
The government and command of the armed forces is vested in Her Majesty
Control, organisation and disposition of armed forces
Requisition of British ships in times of urgent national necessity
Commissioning of officers in all three armed forces
Armed forces pay
Certain armed forces pensions which are now closed to new members
War pensions for death or disablement due to service before 6 April 2005 (section 12 of the Social Security (Miscellaneous Provisions) Act 1977 provides that the prerogative may be exercised by Order in Council
Crown's right to claim Prize (enemy ships or goods captured at sea)
Regulation of trade with the enemy
Crown's right of angary, in time of war, to appropriate the property of a neutral which is within the realm, where necessity requires
Powers in the event of a grave national emergency, including those to enter upon, take and destroy private property

The Annex goes on to list various other miscellaneous ministerial prerogatives, such as the power to establish corporations by royal charter and to amend existing charters (for example, that of the British Broadcasting Corporation, or BBC, was laid before Parliament in July 2006 and amended in March 2010), the right of the Crown to ownership of treasure trove (replaced for finds made on or after 24 September 1997 by a statutory scheme for treasure under the Treasure Act 1996), the power to hold public inquiries (where not covered by the Inquiries Act 2005); and powers in relation to the visitorial function of the Crown.

QUESTIONS

1. Go through the list of ministerial prerogative powers and place them into three categories: extremely important; important; unimportant. Explain why you have classified them as you have.

2. According to the PASC, in what ways are ministers accountable for the exercise of their discretionary powers? What are the main limitations on accountability?

(b) THE MONARCH'S CONSTITUTIONAL PREROGATIVES

The ministerial prerogative powers are the most important group of prerogative powers in terms of the day-to-day work of government and it is upon this group of prerogatives that this chapter focuses. While the monarch is not involved in making day-to-day executive decisions, as head of state she continues to exercise constitutional prerogatives that are of considerable importance to the smooth running of the system as a whole. In Chapter 7, we examined the constitutional status of the monarch and the meaning of the term 'the Crown'.[23] Several examples of the monarch's prerogative powers are considered in other chapters:

- formally appointing government ministers, including the Prime Minister (see Chapter 7);
- making 'prerogative legislation' in the form of Orders in Council (see Chapter 11, section 2 Orders in Council on p. 447); and
- giving royal assent to Bills (see Chapter 10).

In exercising these powers, the monarch will act in accordance with convention and on the advice of her ministers.

(c) CROWN IMMUNITY

'The Crown' enjoys immunities and exemptions from the law. An Act of Parliament is presumed not to bind the Crown unless it expressly or by clear implication provides that it does so (for example, the Planning Act 2008, s. 226, states that '*This Act binds the Crown* [...]', then lists some ways in which the application of the Act is modified). It is for this reason that the Queen, in her private capacity, is not liable to pay tax—although she has done so on a voluntary basis, following some public pressure, since 1992.

Moreover, the rule of common law that the Crown and 'emanations of the Crown' are immune from prosecutions for criminal offences (whether statutory or at common law) has significant practical consequences. This is reflected in the legal maxim 'The Crown can do no wrong'. For example, until the immunity was expressly removed, the National Health Service (NHS) could not be prosecuted for serious breaches of health and safety law; the NHS and Community Care Act 1990 removed Crown immunity from NHS premises. In 2001, an employee of the Royal Mint (at the time, an executive agency of HM Treasury) was killed at work. In a subsequent inquiry, a parliamentary select committee report stated that '*it is unacceptable that the Mint should hide behind Crown immunity*'. The following extract from evidence published with the report explains the legal background in more detail.

House of Commons Select Committee on Public Accounts, *Royal Mint Trading Fund 2001–02 Accounts,* 14th Report, Session 2002–03, Minutes of Evidence, Appendix 2: Supplementary memorandum submitted by HM Treasury (HC 588)

CROWN IMMUNITY FROM PROSECUTION

The Public Accounts Committee asked HM Treasury for a note on the Government's policy towards the Crown's immunity from prosecution in the context of the tragic fatality at the Royal Mint. [...]

---

[23] See extract Maurice Sunkin, 'Crown' in Chapter 7 on p. 239.

What is "Crown immunity"?

Crown immunity means that emanations of the Crown are not susceptible to prosecution for offences either created by statute or of the common law. It is more difficult to define precisely what is meant by an "emanation of the Crown", but it is clear that ministers and their departments are included. Crown immunity is today primarily an issue of the criminal law. The Crown Proceedings Act 1947 substantially reduced the Crown's immunity from civil proceedings.

It is important to be clear about what Crown immunity does not protect the executive from. It does not afford any protection from investigation, for example by the Health and Safety Executive in the Royal Mint context. In the case of legislation relating to food and health and safety, the law applies to the Crown, but the Crown cannot be prosecuted under it. Instead a system of Crown censure and Crown notices is used, publicising the inspectors' findings. The HSE investigation into the Mint resulted in Crown censure. Crown immunity also does not grant protection to individuals from prosecution. In the Mint case, a thorough investigation by Police and HSE concluded that no Director or Manager could be prosecuted. Crown immunity also does not give protection from a civil claim. In this particular case the Mint has already written to the representatives of the deceased to confirm admission of liability and asking them to provide details of the quantum of their claim (a schedule of dependency).

[...]

HM Treasury
December 2002

(d) DEFINING PREROGATIVE POWERS

Having looked at the given extracts, you might feel that you would be able to define the prerogative if you were asked to do so—but a word of caution is needed. There has been much debate among commentators about the true definition of 'prerogative powers'. And while prerogative powers are centuries old, it is perhaps somewhat surprising (or perhaps not) that legal experts still say that the meaning of the 'royal prerogative' remains 'far from clear-cut'.[24] Certainly, there is no clear, single, accepted definition of the royal prerogative and the various definitions that are offered appear to conflict with each other. One reason for the uncertainty is that the prerogative has been changing as it has evolved over the years and definitions that might have been appropriate in the past might not be appropriate today. Two main definitions of the royal prerogative are widely used (see Box 9.2).

BOX 9.2 DEFINITIONS OF THE ROYAL PREROGATIVE

- **Dicey**: *'The residue of discretionary or arbitrary authority, which at any given time is legally left in the hands of the Crown'*: A.V. Dicey, *Introduction to the Study of the Law of the Constitution* (1885; 10th edn 1959, London: Macmillan & Co), p. 424

- **Blackstone**: When referring to the royal prerogative, *'We usually understand that special pre-eminence which the King hath, over and above all other persons, and out of the ordinary course of the common law, in right of his regal dignity. [...It] must be in its nature singular and eccentrical; that it can only be applied to those rights and capacities which the King enjoys alone, in contradistinction to others, and not to those he enjoys in common with any of his subjects'*: William Blackstone, *Commentaries on the Laws of England*, 1765–69.

---

[24] Sebastian Payne, 'The Royal Prerogative', in M. Sunkin and S. Payne (eds) *The Nature of the Crown* (1999, Oxford: OUP), p. 78.

Dicey's definition tells us that royal prerogative powers are those discretionary powers that the Crown retains because they have not been abolished by Parliament or replaced by statutory powers—hence the reference to *residual* powers. The problem with this definition is that while it tells us that prerogative powers are discretionary and residual, it tells us nothing about the nature of the powers themselves. For example, it tells us nothing about how, if at all, they differ to powers conferred on the executive by statute.

Blackstone's definition, by contrast, does say something about the nature of the powers themselves. His view is that prerogative powers are special in that (in his eighteenth-century language) they are 'singular and eccentrical'. By this, Blackstone means that these are powers that only the monarch or the Crown can possess. Powers that ordinary people have, such as the power to make contracts, to employ people, or to establish trust funds to distribute money, are, according to this definition, not prerogative powers. By contrast, no one apart from the Crown has the legal authority to dissolve Parliament or to deploy the United Kingdom's armed forces abroad. Since Parliament can abolish prerogative powers or place them on a statutory footing, we can summarize Blackstone's definition by saying that prerogative powers are those powers of the Crown that:

(a) have not abolished by Parliament or placed on a statutory footing; and
(b) are exclusive to the Crown.

Professor Wade accepts Blackstone's definition, but argues that a further condition must be added—that is, the requirement that prerogative powers must have legal consequences in UK domestic law: '[T]*he prerogative consists of legal power—that is to say, the ability to alter people's rights, duties or status under the laws of this country.*'[25] If action does not affect legal rights under UK law, it should not, according to Professor Wade, be considered to have been taken by virtue of the prerogative.

It seems then that, according to Wade, certain decisions that are generally assumed to be based on the prerogative are actually 'spurious prerogatives' and not really exercises of prerogative power at all. Decisions by a minister of the Crown, such as that challenged in *Council for Civil Service Unions v Minister for Civil Service* (the *GCHQ* case)[26] to alter the terms and conditions on which civil servants work should not be considered to be prerogative decisions, because similar decisions could be made by any employer. Interestingly, for the same reason, Wade also argues that the power of the Crown to appoint and dismiss government ministers is not a prerogative power. It is '*nothing else than the power which all legal persons have at common law to employ servants or agents*'.[27]

Moreover, since Wade says that prerogative decisions must affect rights, he argues that a decision by the UK government to commit the United Kingdom to an international treaty would not be an exercise of prerogative power: entry into treaties cannot, by itself, alter rights in domestic UK law. Similarly, according to Wade, the granting of passports is not a prerogative power, because '[a] *passport has no status or legal effect at common law at common law whatever*'.[28]

Sebastian Payne criticizes this aspect of Wade's approach as follows.

---

[25] Sir William Wade, *Constitutional Fundamentals*, revised edn (1989, London: Stevens and Sons), p. 58.
[26] [1985] AC 374, discussed later in this chapter and also in Chapter 16.
[27] Ibid., p. 60
[28] Ibid., p. 63

Sebastian Payne, 'The Royal Prerogative', in M. Sunkin and S. Payne (eds)
The Nature of the Crown (1999, Oxford: OUP), pp. 84–5

[E]very act will have a legal effect somewhere along the line, for instance the giving away of money by the Crown will, [...] have the legal effect of entitling 'the recipient to retain the money'. The granting of a passport will have the legal effect of entitling that person to use the passport [...]. Even a treaty that has not been incorporated into domestic law may lead to a particular interpretation of a statute on the presumption that legislation would not be passed in contravention of our treaty obligations unless expressly stated.

Payne is surely correct, but it is nonetheless important to understand that one implication of Wade's approach is to narrow the range of decisions that fall within the prerogative discretion of the executive and potentially beyond the reach of the judicial review. This was important before the House of Lords held in the *GCHQ* case that prerogative powers can be reviewed in the same way as statutory powers.

This brief discussion illustrates some of the problems involved in defining the royal prerogative and in identifying which powers of the executive properly fall within its scope. At the risk of adding further confusion, we must also be aware of the historical context. The importance of this is evident from Lord Reid's judgment in *Burmah Oil v Lord Advocate*,[29] which provides one of the most sustained judicial discussions of the royal prerogative.

The *Burmah Oil* case

In March 1942, the British army blew up the installations and oil stocks owned by the Burmah Oil Company at Rangoon in order to prevent them from falling into the hands of the advancing Japanese forces. The Burmah Oil Company later sought compensation from the Crown for its losses. In the House of Lords, it was accepted that the actions were done under the royal prerogative and the question was whether compensation had to be paid. The House held by a three-to-two majority that, in the circumstances, compensation was payable. Controversially, the effect of the decision was subsequently retrospectively reversed by the War Damages Act 1965. For now, our interest focuses on Lord Reid's judgment.

Burmah Oil Company v Lord Advocate
[1965] AC 75, 99–100

Lord Reid

It is not easy to discover and decide the law regarding the royal prerogative and the consequences of its exercise. Apart from *In re a Petition of Right* [[1915] 3 KB 649] and Attorney-General v De Keyser's Royal Hotel Ltd. [[1920] AC 508] there have been no cases directly raising the matter for some centuries, and obiter dicta and the views of institutional writers and text writers are not always very helpful. The definition of Dicey [...] always quoted with approval [...] does not take us very far. It is extremely difficult to be precise because in former times there was seldom a clear-cut view of the constitutional position. I think we should beware of looking at older authorities through modern spectacles. We ought not to ignore the many changes in constitutional law and theory which culminated in the Revolution

---

[29] [1965] AC 75.

Settlement of 1688-89, and there is practically no authority between that date and 1915. I am no historian but I would suppose that Maitland is as good a guide as any. In his Constitutional History he says: 'I do not wish you to think that a definite theory to the effect that while legislative power resides in king and parliament, the so-called executive power is in the king alone, was a guiding theory of mediaeval politics. On the contrary, the line between what the king could do without a parliament, and what he could only do with the aid of parliament, was only drawn very gradually, and it fluctuated from time to time.' (p. 196.) [...] So it appears to me that we must try to see what the position was after it had become clear that sovereignty resided in the King in Parliament. Any rights thereafter exercised by the King (or the executive) alone must be regarded as a part of sovereignty which Parliament chose to leave in his hands. There is no doubt that control of the armed forces has been left to the prerogative (see *Chandler v Director of Public Prosecutions* [below] subject to the power of Parliament to withhold supply and to refuse to continue legislation essential for the maintenance of a standing army: and so also has the waging of war. But it may be interesting to note in passing the Scottish Act, 1703, c. 5, which provided that 'no person being King or Queen of Scotland and England shall have the sole power of making war with any prince, potentate or state whatsoever without consent of Parliament [...]'

The reason for leaving the waging of war to the King (or now the executive) is obvious. [...although...t]here is difficulty in relating the prerogative to modern conditions. In fact no war which has put this country in real peril has been waged in modern times without statutory powers of an emergency character. [...]

QUESTIONS

1. Why does Lord Reid say that '*we should beware of looking at older authorities through modern spectacles*'?

2. '*The prerogative is really a relic of a past age, not lost by disuse, but only available for a case not covered by statute*' (Lord Reid). Does this mean that the prerogative is now constitutionally unimportant?

3. From what Lord Reid says, could the courts review a decision to go to war?

(e) PREROGATIVE AND STATUTE

New prerogatives cannot be created

Earlier in the chapter, we identified some differences between prerogative and statutory powers (see Box 9.1). One point made was that while Parliament regularly confers new statutory powers on government and other public bodies, new prerogative powers cannot be acquired by the executive. The executive can only claim to possess prerogative powers if these powers are already recognized by the common law.[30] The principle was summarized by Diplock LJ (as he then was) in *BBC v Johns*, a case in which the Court of Appeal rejected the BBC's claim to be an 'emanation of the Crown' and thus entitled to be immune from paying income tax.

---

[30] See also *Malone v Commissioner of Police* [1979] Ch 344.

BBC v Johns
[1965] Ch 32, 79

Diplock LJ

Mr Bucher has submitted that because wireless telegraphy and telephony were new inventions the Crown had a prerogative right to a monopoly of their use and has chosen to exercise this monopoly as respects broadcasting [...] through the instrumentality of the BBC. This contention involves adopting what he describes as a modern [...] view of the scope of the prerogative. But it is 350 years and a civil war too late for the Queen's courts to broaden the prerogative. The limits within which the executive government may impose obligations or restraints upon citizens of the United Kingdom without any statutory authority are now well settled and incapable of extension.

Relationship between prerogative and statutory powers

Parliament can limit or abolish prerogative powers. It may also decide that the power should be retained, but placed on a statutory footing. Occasionally, situations arise in which Parliament has not abolished a prerogative power, but has enacted legislation that conflicts with the prerogative in some way. Where this happens, can government choose to use the prerogative rather than the statutory provisions?

The situation is illustrated by the decision in *Attorney General v De Keyser's Royal Hotel*.[31] This case concerned the requisitioning of a hotel in London during the First World War. The government had two ways in which it could requisition the hotel: by using a prerogative power and by exercising powers conferred by a statute. The difference was that, under the prerogative, compensation did not have to be paid to the owner, whereas under statute, it did. Could the government choose to use its prerogative powers and save money? Both the Court of Appeal and the House of Lords held that the government had to use the statutory powers.

Attorney General v De Keyser's Royal Hotel
[1920] AC 508, 526

Lord Dunedin

[...I]t is certain that if the whole ground of something which could be done by the prerogative is covered by the statute it is the statute that rules. On this point I think the observation of the learned Master of the Rolls[32] is unanswerable. He says: 'What use would there be in imposing limitations if the Crown could, at its pleasure, disregard them and fall back on prerogative?'

Another situation is that in which a statute deals with the same general subject matter as a prerogative power, but, unlike in *De Keyser's Royal Hotel*, it is not clear that the use of the prerogative would be incompatible with the statute. The issue arose in the controversial decision in *R v Secretary of State for the Home Department, ex parte Northumbria Police*

---

[31] [1920] AC 508.
[32] Swinfen Eady MR, in the Court of Appeal: [1919] 2 Ch 197, 216.

Authority.[33] In 1986, the Home Secretary sent a circular to all chief constables in England explaining that a central store for plastic bullets and CS gas would be set up, and that chief constables could buy this crowd-control equipment without having to obtain the permission of their local police authority (statutory bodies established to subject police forces to local accountability). Many police authorities were dismayed that this equipment could be purchased without their involvement and the Northumbria Police Authority unsuccessfully challenged the legality of the government's scheme. The Court of Appeal held that the Police Act 1964 permitted the establishment of a central store and the direct supply of this equipment to chief constables. It also said that the Home Secretary has prerogative power to '*maintain peace in the realm*', which included power to take precautionary steps to ensure that chief constables have access to a supply of crowd-control equipment. This power had not been removed by statutory provisions.

R v Secretary of State for the Home Department, ex parte Northumbria Police Authority
[1989] 1 QB 26, 42–3

Croom-Johnson LJ

Although there has always been what is called the war prerogative, which is the Crown's right to make war and peace, Mr. Keene submitted that there is no corresponding prerogative to enforce the keeping of what is popularly called the 'Queen's peace within the realm.' Mr. Keene based his submission by reference to *Chitty's Prerogatives of the Crown* (1820) and pointed out that there is no power referred to in it for keeping the peace. It does, however, contain an extensive section on 'The King as the Fountain of Justice' and courts and gaols. The argument is that if there was no prerogative power to keep the peace in 1820, at which date no organised police force existed, then all police forces exist and are controlled only by the later statutes by which they were created, and there is no residual prerogative power to draw on in cases of necessity.

In contrast to this submission, *O. Hood Phillips' Constitutional and Administrative Law*, 6th ed. (1978), ch. 21, p. 399 states unequivocally: "Although the preservation of the peace, which is a Royal prerogative, is one of the primary functions of any state, the administration of the police has always been on a local basis in this country."

It may be that the King's power to establish courts and gaols and to administer justice was no more than the larger power to see that the peace was kept. There were constables long before the establishment of Peel's Metropolitan Police in 1829. At all events, the assumption was early made that keeping the peace was part of the prerogative. [...] By its very nature the subject of maintaining the Queen's peace and keeping law and order has over the years inevitably been dealt with by statute much more than the war prerogative has been. Instances of the way in which such a prerogative may be used are more readily provided by example than by being placed in categories, but I have no doubt that the Crown does have a prerogative power to keep the peace, which is bound up with its undoubted right to see that crime is prevented and justice administered. This is subject to Mr. Keene's next submission, which was that any prerogative power may be lost by being overtaken by statute law[...]. *Attorney-General v De Keyser's Royal Hotel Ltd.* [1920] A.C. 508 was the decision which establishes that in the exercise of the war prerogative the Crown's power to requisition property had been limited by the Defence Act 1842 so as to require compensation to be paid to

---

[33] [1989] 1 QB 26.

the subject [...] It is clear that the Crown cannot act under the prerogative if to do so would be incompatible with statute. What was said here is that the Secretary of State's proposal under the circular would be inconsistent with the powers expressly or impliedly conferred on the police authority by section 4 of the Police Act 1964. The Divisional Court rejected that submission for reasons with which I wholly agree; namely that section 4 does not expressly grant a monopoly, and that granted the possibility of an authority which declines to provide equipment required by the chief constable there is every reason not to imply a Parliamentary intent to create one.

The House of Lords also had to consider the relationship between prerogative and statutory powers in *R v Secretary of State for the Home Department, ex parte the Fire Brigades Union*.[34] In this case, the central question was whether the executive can use prerogative powers in a manner that effectively means that an Act of Parliament will not be brought into force. The Criminal Injuries Compensation Scheme was introduced in 1964 using what were claimed to be prerogative powers.[35] In 1988, Parliament enacted the Criminal Justice Act 1988 in order to place the scheme on a statutory footing. Although the statute received the royal assent, the enacted provisions were only to come into effect 'on such day as the Secretary of State may [...] appoint'.[36] No such day was appointed and the provisions therefore did not come into effect.

Eventually, in March 1994, the Home Secretary told Parliament that the non-statutory scheme would be modified in a way that would introduce a lower level of compensation payments than the Act envisaged. He also said that, in due course, the provisions of the Criminal Justice Act 1988 would be repealed. The Home Secretary's decision to reduce compensation was challenged by several trade unions, which believed that their members would be disadvantaged by the failure to implement the legislation. In a majority decision, the House of Lords held that it was an abuse of power for the Home Secretary to exercise his purported prerogative powers to introduce a system that would conflict with his continuing duty to bring the statutory scheme into force.

R v Secretary of State for the Home Department, ex parte the Fire Brigades Union
[1995] 2 AC 513, 551–2

Lord Browne-Wilkinson

It does not follow that, because the Secretary of State is not under any duty to bring the section into effect, he has an absolute and unfettered discretion whether or not to do so. So to hold would lead to the conclusion that both Houses of Parliament had passed the Bill through all its stages and the Act received the Royal Assent merely to confer an enabling power on the executive to decide at will whether or not to make the parliamentary provisions a part of the law. Such a conclusion, drawn from a section to which the sidenote is "Commencement," is not only constitutionally dangerous but flies in the face of common sense. [...] Surely, it cannot have been the intention of Parliament to leave it in the entire discretion of the Secretary

---

[34] [1995] 2 AC 513.

[35] As we have seen, it is unclear whether creation of a compensation scheme would fall under the royal prerogative.

[36] Section 171(1) of the Criminal Justice Act 1988.

of State whether or not to effect such important changes to the criminal law. In the absence of express provisions to the contrary in the Act, the plain intention of Parliament in conferring on the Secretary of State the power to bring certain sections into force is that such power is to be exercised so as to bring those sections into force when it is appropriate and unless there is a subsequent change of circumstances which would render it inappropriate to do so.

If, as I think, that is the clear purpose for which the power in section 171(1) was conferred on the Secretary of State, two things follow. First, the Secretary of State comes under a clear duty to keep under consideration from time to time the question whether or not to bring the sections (and therefore the statutory scheme) into force. In my judgment he cannot lawfully surrender or release the power contained in section 171(1) so as to purport to exclude its future exercise either by himself or by his successors. [...] It follows that the decision of the Secretary of State to give effect to the statement in paragraph 38 of the White Paper (Cm. 2434) that "the provisions in the Act of 1988 will not now be implemented" was unlawful. [...]

My Lords, it would be most surprising if, at the present day, prerogative powers could be validly exercised by the executive so as to frustrate the will of Parliament expressed in a statute and, to an extent, to pre-empt the decision of Parliament whether or not to continue with the statutory scheme even though the old scheme has been abandoned. It is not for the executive, as the Lord Advocate accepted, to state as it did in the White Paper (paragraph 38) that the provisions in the Act of 1988 "will accordingly be repealed when a suitable legislative opportunity occurs." It is for Parliament, not the executive, to repeal legislation. The constitutional history of this country is the history of the prerogative powers of the Crown being made subject to the overriding powers of the democratically elected legislature as the sovereign body. The prerogative powers of the Crown remain in existence to the extent that Parliament has not expressly or by implication extinguished them. But under the principle in *Attorney-General v De Keyser's Royal Hotel Ltd.* [...] if Parliament has conferred on the executive statutory powers to do a particular act, that act can only thereafter be done under the statutory powers so conferred: any pre-existing prerogative power to do the same act is pro tanto excluded.

(f) JUDICIAL REVIEW OF PREROGATIVE POWERS[37]

If the government claims to exercise a prerogative power and its action is challenged in judicial review proceedings, the courts will examine whether the claimed prerogative power exists and, if it is found not to exist will invalidate any action taken under the purported power.[38] Until 1984, if the courts were satisfied that the prerogative power existed, they would not review the way in which the power was used. There is now no doubt that, in principle, courts can review prerogative powers on the same grounds as they can review the way in which statutory powers are used. As in the case of statutory powers, however, there may be occasions on which courts will not intervene because the subject matter of the power is regarded by the courts as 'non-justiciable' (in other words, the issues are not suitable for judicial determination). These occasions are now becoming increasingly rare.[39] These propositions have been established by two decisions of the House of Lords.

[37] See further Brigid Hadfield, 'Judicial Review and the Prerogative Powers', in M. Sunkin and S. Payne (eds) *The Nature of the Crown* (1999, Oxford: OUP), ch. 8.

[38] See, e.g., Lord Bingham in *Bancoult (No. 2)* [2008] UKHL 61.

[39] See further Chapter 16 and Chapter 17, especially in relation to deference.

The *GCHQ* case

The first was the decision in *Council for Civil Service Unions v Minister for the Civil Service* (the *GCHQ* case).[40] In this case, the civil service unions challenged a decision taken by the Minister for the Civil Service (a ministerial post normally held by the Prime Minister, at that time Mrs Thatcher) that workers at the Government Communications Headquarters (GCHQ, the government's electronic eavesdropping organization responsible for collecting intelligence) could no longer belong to a trade union. The decision was taken under powers conferred on the minister by the Civil Service Order in Council 1982, which was a legislative instrument enacted by the Queen in Council by virtue of prerogative powers.[41]

The unions claimed that the courts could review the decision even though it had been taken under prerogative powers. They submitted that the decision had been unlawful because the government's failure to consult before the decision breached the workers' legitimate expectation to consultation and was therefore procedurally unfair. The government argued that prerogative powers could not be judicially reviewed, but that even if they could in other situations, in this case, the decision had been taken in the interests of national security; therefore, the courts could not intervene. The government also denied that there had been a breach of any legitimate expectation or unfairness. To the government's dismay, in July 1984, Glidewell J granted the application for judicial review.

Council for Civil Service Unions v Minister for the Civil Service (the GCHQ case)
[1984] IRLR 309, 310

Glidewell J

I can see no reason in logic or principle why an exercise by a Minister of a power conferred by an Order in Council should not be subject to the same scrutiny and control by the courts as would be appropriate for the exercise of the same power if it had been granted by statute.

Having established that he could intervene, Glidewell J went on to emphasize the need for government to follow the correct and fair procedure required by the common law. In the circumstances, he held that the failure to consult prior to deciding to ban union membership was procedurally unfair. He therefore held that the Minister had acted unlawfully.

The government immediately appealed and, before the Court of Appeal, presented an argument that had not been explicitly put to Glidewell J—namely, that the failure to consult was justified by the interests of national security. The Court of Appeal accepted this argument and reversed Glidewell J's decision. In November 1984, the House of Lords upheld the Court of Appeal. Their Lordships held that although the failure to consult was contrary to the principles of natural justice, the courts should not interfere with it because the decision had been taken on grounds of national security, something into which the courts could not inquire.

---

[40] [1985] AC 374; see further A. Le Sueur and M. Sunkin, *Public Law* (1997, London: Longman) ch. 2, which provides more background to the litigation and its implications. See also Hugh Lanning and Richard Norton-Taylor, *A Conflict of Loyalties: GCHQ 1984–1991* (1992, London: New Clarion); G. Drewry (1985) Parliamentary Affairs 371; K. Ewing [1985] Cambridge Law Journal 1: J.A.G. Griffith [1985] Public Law 564; H.W.R. Wade (1985) 101 Law Quarterly Review 180.

[41] See Chapter 11, section 2 Orders in Council on p. 447.

In many ways, the actual decision of the House of Lords is a typical example of the courts being anxious to defer to the executive when national security is said to be involved. The judgment is a landmark, however, not because of the actual outcome, but because of what their Lordships said about the potential scope of judicial review in relation to prerogative powers. Lords Scarman, Diplock, and Roskill indicated that the courts can, in principle, review the exercise of any prerogative powers, provided that the matter is suitable for judicial determination (that is, justiciable). Lords Fraser and Brightman were more cautious: while they would have been willing to review the decision to ban unions taken under powers delegated by the Order in Council, they were not willing, on this occasion at least, to say that courts could also review the legality of an Order in Council itself.

Bancoult (No. 2)

The second case is the more recent decision in *R (on the application of Bancoult) v Secretary of State for Foreign and Commonwealth Affairs (No. 2)*.[42] This case concerned the Chagos Islands in the Indian Ocean, which, until 1965, were part of the British colony of Mauritius. In that year, the islands were made a separate colony, known as the 'British Indian Ocean Territory' (BIOT). During the 1960s, the UK government entered into negotiations with the USA over the establishment of a US military base on Diego Garcia, the main island in the BIOT. This required the removal of the population of the territory and, in 1971, the UK government, through the Queen in Council, made a piece of prerogative legislation known as the Immigration Ordnance 1971, which gave power to exile the population. In 2000 (*Bancoult No. 1*),[43] the Administrative Court allowed the challenge of Mr Bancoult (one of the islanders affected) to the legality of the relevant provisions of the Immigration Order 1971. After that decision, the government stated that it accepted the Court's ruling and would not appeal.

The government later decided, however, that resettlement of the islands was not feasible and that the territory was still wanted for defence purposes. Two further Orders in Council were therefore made by the Queen in Council on advice of the government.[44] These had the effect of preventing the islanders from returning to the islands. Mr Bancoult once again claimed judicial review, this time challenging the two Orders in Council. Note that, in this case, Mr Bancoult was challenging Orders in Council themselves rather than executive actions taken under the Orders in Council, as in the *GCHQ* case. Mr Bancoult argued that the right of abode was so fundamental that it could not be removed by the Crown in any circumstances; that the powers of the Crown were limited to enacting legislation for the 'peace, order and good government' of the territory, that the law had to be for the benefit of the inhabitants, and that the government's statement following *Bancoult (No. 1)* gave rise to a legitimate expectation on the part of the Chagossians that they would be allowed to return to the islands. He was successful in both the Divisional Court[45] and the Court of Appeal.[46]

On appeal to the House of Lords, the government argued, among other things, that the courts had no power to review the validity of an Order in Council legislating for a colony, because it was primary legislation comparable to an Act of Parliament, that, in any case,

---

[42] [2008] UKHL 61.

[43] *R (on the application of Bancoult) v Secretary of State for Foreign and Commonwealth Affairs* [2001] QB 1067.

[44] British Indian Ocean Territory (Constitution) Order 2004 and the British Indian Ocean Territory (Immigration) Order 2004.

[45] [2006] EWHC 1038 (Admin).

[46] [2007] EWCA Civ 498, [2008] QB 365.

the islanders did not have the fundamental rights that they claimed, and that there was no breach of a legitimate expectation that they would be allowed to return. The House of Lords accepted that courts can review the legality of Orders in Council and, to this extent, it developed the law beyond the *GCHQ* case. The following statement made by Lord Hoffmann represents the overall view of the House on this point.

R (on the application of Bancoult) v Secretary of State for Foreign and Commonwealth Affairs (No. 2)
[2008] UKHL 61

Lord Hoffmann

34 It is true that a prerogative Order in Council is primary legislation [. . .]

35 But the fact that such Orders in Council in certain important respects resemble Acts of Parliament does not mean that they share all their characteristics. The principle of the sovereignty of Parliament, as it has been developed by the courts over the past 350 years, is founded upon the unique authority Parliament derives from its representative character. An exercise of the prerogative lacks this quality; although it may be legislative in character, it is still an exercise of power by the executive alone. Until the decision of this House in *Council of Civil Service Unions v Minister for the Civil Service* [1985] AC 374, it may have been assumed that the exercise of prerogative powers was, as such, immune from judicial review. That objection being removed, I see no reason why prerogative legislation should not be subject to review on ordinary principles of legality, rationality and procedural impropriety in the same way as any other executive action.

The majority (Lords Bingham and Mance dissenting) nonetheless refused to accept that the Orders in Council were unlawful. The main elements of the majority decision on the legality of the Orders in Council may be summarized as follows. The Orders in Council were not repugnant to the Chagossians' fundamental right of abode and to return to the islands. The right of abode was a creature of the law, not a constitutional right, and there was no basis for saying that the right of abode was so fundamental that the Crown's legislative powers simply could not touch it. Nor was there support for the proposition that, in legislating for a colony, either Parliament or Her Majesty in Council had to have regard only, or even predominantly, to the immediate interests of the inhabitants. In essence, the Chagossians' right of abode was purely symbolic, because there was no prospect of them being able to live on the islands in the foreseeable future. Having regard to the practical interests of the Chagossians, the decision to reimpose immigration control on the islands could not be described as unreasonable or an abuse of power. Moreover, there had been no clear and unambiguous promise to the effect that the Chagossians would be free to return to the islands even if they could not be resettled there and therefore no legitimate expectation had been created.[47]

The argument that prerogative legislation must respect fundamental rights was clearly an important element in *Bancoult (No. 2)*. It was an argument that attracted a range of responses from the judges, helpfully summarized by Mark Elliott and Amanda Perreau-Saussine in the following extract.[48]

---

[47] On the legitimate expectation point, see further Chapter 16.

[48] See also M. Cohn, 'Judicial review of non-statutory executive powers after *Bancoult*: A unified anxious model' [2009] Public Law 260.

Mark Elliott and Amanda Perreau-Saussine, 'Pyrrhic public law: *Bancoult* and the sources, status and content of common law limitations on prerogative power' [2009] Public Law 697–722, 705–6 (footnotes omitted)

According to Lords Hoffmann, Bingham and Mance, British subjects do enjoy basic or con-stitutional rights that cannot lawfully be overridden or abrogated by the Crown without par-liamentary approval: these rights act as legally enforceable constraints on prerogative power. These three of the five judges in Bancoult recognise effectively "constitutional" common law rights which can only be abrogated (if at all) with clear and explicit parliamentary approval: they recognise certain basic common law rights which cannot be overridden or abrogated by the Crown, rights which act as legally enforceable constraints on prerogative powers

Lords Bingham and Mance include a constitutional right of abode among those rights and hold, both dissenting, that this right limits the scope of prerogative powers to legislate for colonies, Lord Mance terming the right of abode "fundamental and, in the informal sense in which that term is necessarily used in a United Kingdom context, constitutional". Lord Hoffmann recognises a right not to be tortured as a limit on the scope of prerogative powers of colonial governance, holding that an Order in Council could not lawfully sanction torture, but, crucially for the result in this case, denied that there was a right of abode.

Lord Carswell is opaque on the existence of constitutional or fundamental rights, doubting the existence of "fundamental principles" of English law yet also treating the case as raising the question of "how near" a right of abode is to "being an inalienable constitutional right", a characterisation that is senseless if there exist no such things. [...]

Lord Rodger concludes that it is "certainly arguable that there is a 'fundamental principle' of English law that no citizen should be exiled or banished from a British colony", but he also holds that those British subjects residing in colonial territory do not enjoy any rights immune from abrogation by the Crown. Torture in a colony, he holds, could be sanctioned by an Order in Council...

[The authors open their conclusion with the following statement.]

Importantly, the House of Lords' decision in Bancoult is the first English decision to establish clearly that the prerogative itself-as distinct from secondary powers derived from exercises of the prerogative-exists in the shadow of the rule of law. That is why, for example, the major-ity in Bancoult would have been willing to hold s.9 of the Constitution Order unlawful if it had offended the rule-of-law principle of legal certainty by having been enacted in breach of the Chagossians' legitimate expectations.

Yet Bancoult is a pyrrhic victory for those who regard executive power as constrained by the rule of law. This is unsurprising: recent history is replete with such victories in this area. The proposition in GCHQ itself that delegated exercises of prerogative power are reviewable had to be spelt out of obiter dicta, the Appellate Committee having held that the actual deci-sion in question was non-justiciable on account of its national security implications.

QUESTIONS

1. In relation to judicial review of prerogative powers, what is the significance of the decisions of the House of Lords in *GCHQ* and *Bancoult*?

2. '*Bancoult establishes the principle that courts can review primary legislation on the ground that the legislation conflicts with fundamental rights, although it also illus-trates the uncertain nature of these rights.*' Do you agree?

4 REFORMING MINISTERIAL PREROGATIVES

Vociferous calls for reform of prerogative powers have been made since at least the 1980s and 1990s. In 1994, Jack Straw MP, for example, wrote that the *'royal prerogative has no place in a modern western democracy* [...the prerogative] *has been used as a smoke-screen by Ministers to obfuscate the use of power for which they are insufficiently accountable'*. During the Blair governments of 1997–2007, however, the government showed no interest in placing prerogative powers on the constitutional reform agenda. It was left to backbenchers and the PASC to press for the need for change, with Liberal Democrat peer Lord Lester of Herne Hill leading the calls for his party. It was only when Gordon Brown became Prime Minister in 2007 that progress began to be made. As we shall see since the election of the Coalition government that progress appears to have ended.

As the following comments from William Hague MP (then a frontbench Conservative spokesman, now the Foreign Secretary) show, there has been widespread consensus across the political parties that the use of prerogative powers fits uneasily in a modern democratic constitution.

House of Commons Hansard, 15 May 2007, col. 485–93

Mr. Hague: In April 2003 the right hon. Tony Benn [a veteran Labour MP who retired in 2001] and I, in what some regarded as a highly unusual alliance, made a joint presentation to the Public Administration Committee, calling for the whole of the royal prerogative now exercised by Ministers, including the power to conclude treaties, the right to reorganise Government Departments, and the administration of the honours system, as well as the power to enter armed conflict, to be brought under parliamentary scrutiny and control. [...] The Public Administration Committee came to a clear conclusion in 2004. [...] that "the prerogative has allowed powers to move from monarch to Ministers without Parliament having a say in how they are exercised. This should no longer be acceptable to Parliament or the people. [...] It is now time for this unfinished business to be completed."

Given the breadth of support for reform, including from those who became senior ministers, it might be thought that reformers would be pushing at an open door. But, of course, the situation is not that straightforward. It is one thing to call for reforms when in Opposition, but quite another to make changes when in government (later in the chapter we see the position taken by William Hague now that he is the Foreign Secretary). Reforming the use of prerogative powers has proved to be an extremely complex matter—not least because the prerogative is used across a broad and diverse range of situations including decisions to go to war, the making of public appointments, decisions relating to passports, and the granting of honours. In *Taming the Prerogative*,[49] the PASC considered the case for reform to be 'unanswerable', but each of these areas raises distinct and difficult questions.

Here, we are at the heart of the constitutional system, where the imperatives of executive power, on the one hand, and the principles of democratic accountability, on the other, are inevitably in a state of tension. In this section, we see how these tensions have affected the process of reform and nature of the solutions reached.

---

[49] Public Administration Select Committee, *Taming the Prerogative: Strengthening Ministerial Accountability to Parliament*, HC 422, 2003–04.

(a) APPROACHES TO REFORM: PRAGMATISM OR PRINCIPLE?

Given these tensions, a basic question is how should reform be approached? In its 2004 report *Taming the Prerogative*, the PASC identified two broad options: one based on pragmatism and the other on principle. The pragmatic approach continues the long-standing practice of subjecting individual prerogative powers to parliamentary control on a case-by-case basis. Reform based on principle calls for comprehensive legislation to subject prerogative powers in general to parliamentary control.

The following extract is from the PASC's discussion of the virtues of each of these approaches. Assuming that some broad legislative approach is to be taken, the PASC also consider what form the legislation should take, as well as the question of whether special treatment should be given to particular powers and, if so, which.

House of Commons Public Administration Select Committee, *Taming the Prerogative, Strengthening Ministerial Accountability to Parliament,* Fourth Report, Session 2003–04 HC 422 (footnotes omitted)

The case for pragmatism

37. Lord Hurd[50] put to us the case for continued piecemeal and pragmatic extension of Parliamentary control: "I was brought up on a full diet of Edmund Burke and on the whole I believe the constitution evolves and is best looked at in the light of particular criticisms, particular mischiefs, that can be identified and then change made, rather than examining it on a philosophical basis, which rapidly turns artificial". [...]

39. He cited a number of individual examples in his own Ministerial experience where powerful practical and political considerations led government to subject the prerogative to much greater Parliamentary scrutiny: "every now and then a reform, a change, becomes clearly necessary. [...] two Acts of Parliament which put under statutory power or identity the three intelligence services: the Security Services Act 1989 and the Intelligence Services Act 1994. There were, if anyone is interested, very practical, cogent reasons which persuaded even the prime Ministers of the day, and certainly the heads of the services, that this was a good and necessary move".

40. Lord Hurd said that similar arguments now applied to the proposal for a Civil Service Act and war powers. He summarised his view by saying that: "there are issues all the time but in my view they are essentially practical rather than philosophical".

41. Those opposed to comprehensive legislation also make the practical point that Parliament could become overwhelmed by the task of overseeing such a wide range of actions and decisions.

42. Lord Hurd told us: "I think that Lord Lester's sketch of his 50 clauses—which, as I understand it, would only be a preliminary act—would occupy both Houses of Parliament for a very long time and would be followed by a whole series of discussions. I just wonder who in this country, outside of a fairly narrow but very talented and conscientious range, would feel better off as a result of that; who would sleep more safely in their beds; and who would think the country was better governed". [...]

---

50 Lord Douglas Hurd served in the Conservative government as a Secretary of State for Northern Ireland from 1984 to 1985, as Home Secretary from 1985 to 1989, and as Foreign Secretary from 1989 to 1995.

Putting democratic structures in place

[...]

45. Lord Lester set the argument in a broad constitutional context:"We were all brought up in our unwritten constitution to believe that there were two great principles to our constitution: one was parliamentary supremacy, that the executive was accountable to Parliament rather than to the king or queen; and, secondly, the principle of the rule of law, that public powers should be exercised according to the law. The difficulty about our unwritten, flexible, permeable, part monarchical and part parliamentary constitution is to make sure that those principles apply in practice".

46. Mr Hague also put the general case for a formal framework, telling us that "there is still a vast scope for extending parliamentary control of the royal prerogative". He cast doubt on the notion that a piecemeal approach to legislation was the most effective one, expressing his impatience "one problem with gradualism [...] it may not actually be sufficient. The other problem with gradualism is that it is not moving at all in some areas". [...]

48. [...] Mr Allen made an important distinction between "a democratic culture" which he called "our greatest strength in the UK", and "democratic structures" which were not, in his view, so firmly established. He urged the Committee to be "greedy and have the democratic culture and the democratic structures as well". [...]

49. Most of our witnesses, therefore, felt that serious consideration should be given to legislation on the prerogative. This is new constitutional territory, but it is being explored with increasing and welcome vigour.

The options for legislation

50. We do not underestimate the size and delicacy of the task. The prerogative offers much-needed flexibility to government and is a well-established part of the constitution. Ministers need executive powers. [...] and some of those things have to be done quickly in a complex and dangerous world. It would, therefore, be absurd to suggest that the prerogative should be abolished as an historical anachronism and not be replaced. Parliamentary scrutiny of prerogative powers must not unduly hamper the operation of government, and indeed of Parliament itself.

51. But in the last year or so there have been a number of practical proposals for reform, which have taken the debate on from the generalised 1990s expressions of concern. [...]

52. The debate has now reached the Upper House in the practical form of a Bill promoted by Lord Lester [the Executive Powers and Civil Service Bill]. Professor Rodney Brazier, the specialist adviser to this inquiry, has also put forward proposals for comprehensive legislation. His paper containing a draft Bill (which owes much to the Bill produced by Lord Lester) is at Appendix 1. It is a major contribution to the debate on the prerogative.

53. Professor Brazier outlines two possible approaches to legislation. [...] he describes an Act that would contain a 'sunset clause' for outmoded powers. It would state that "any prerogative powers which were not expressly confirmed by subsequent primary legislation by a date specified in the act would be abolished".

54. Like Professor Brazier, we are not attracted to this extreme option, because it runs the risk of leaving Ministers without important powers at times when urgent action is required. [...] Because there would be a deadline for enacting the legislation, mistakes could be made which could have far-reaching consequences for the workings of government.

55. The alternative option for prerogative reform, set out in Professor Brazier's draft Bill, is both more modest and more practical. It would require government to list the prerogative powers exercised by Ministers within six months of the Act's passing. The list would then be considered by a committee (probably a joint committee of both Houses) and appropriate legislation would be framed to put in place statutory safeguards where these are required. It does not envisage that such safeguards will be needed in every area where the prerogative is used.

56. In a number of areas, and without prejudice to the case for a general act which would ensure that Ministers gave Parliament information about their prerogative powers, some specific early legislative action needs to be taken. Professor Brazier's draft Bill makes provision for this, in three specific areas—the decisions on military conflict, treaties and passports. There are strong arguments in favour of making special provision for all three.

57. In particular, we believe that any decision to engage in armed conflict should be approved by Parliament, if not before military action then as soon as possible afterwards. In these most serious of cases, the decision whether or not to consult Parliament should never be dependent on the generosity or good will of government. A mere convention is not enough when lives are at stake. The increasing frequency of conflict in recent years is proof of the importance of ensuring that, when the country takes military action, Parliament supports the government in its decision. Professor Brazier also makes a powerful case for similar special requirements for early action on decisions on treaties and passports, and we commend it to the government.

[...]

Parliament's right to know

59. A major argument in favour of the approach suggested by Professor Brazier is that Parliament should have a right to know what powers are being exercised by Ministers. As Professor Brazier says, in setting out an important principle, "Ministers should not have imprecise powers". Although we have received from the Government a paper which contains a list of the prerogative powers (which deliberately does not attempt to be exhaustive) this is no substitute for full reporting to Parliament. Above all, we believe that there can be no effective accountability without full information. Because Parliament does not know what Ministers are empowered to do until they have done it, Parliament cannot properly hold government to account.

Recommendation

60. [...T]he Government should initiate before the end of the current session a public consultation exercise on Ministerial prerogative powers. This should contain proposals for legislation to provide greater parliamentary control over all the executive powers enjoyed by Ministers under the royal prerogative. This exercise should also include specific proposals for ensuring full parliamentary scrutiny of the following Ministerial prerogative actions: decisions on armed conflict; the conclusion and ratification of treaties; the issue and revocation of passports.

61. This is unfinished constitutional business. The prerogative has allowed powers to move from Monarch to Ministers without Parliament having a say in how they are exercised. This should no longer be acceptable to Parliament or the people. We have shown how these powers can begin to be constitutionalised, and in particular how certain key powers can be anchored in the consent of Parliament for their exercise. It is now time for this unfinished business to be completed.

QUESTIONS

1. Can you summarize the main arguments for and against adopting a pragmatic and a principled approach to reform? Which of these two approaches would you advocate and why?

2. We are about to look more closely at the prerogative power to deploy British armed forces abroad. Why does the PASC consider the prerogative powers relating to war to be a special case? What other situations are considered to be special?

The PASC's *Taming the Prerogative* report helped to frame the reform agenda. First, it strengthened the case for a move away from the pragmatism that has typified the approach to reform in the past. Second, it presented a cogent case for drawing a distinction between executive prerogatives in general (which might be reformed by using generalized legislation of the type suggested by Lord Lester and Professor Brazier) and special situations that give rise to particular difficulties, such as the decision to deploy armed forces abroad (often referred to as 'war power decisions').

ONLINE RESOURCE CENTRE

Keep up to date on reform of the prerogative powers on the Online Resource Centre at www.oxfordtextbooks.co.uk/orc/lesueur2e/

---

5 CASE STUDY: DEPLOYMENT OF BRITISH ARMED FORCES ABROAD

(a) INTRODUCTION

This section of the chapter is concerned with one of the most important, and potentially controversial, decisions that government can make. As well as potentially resulting in death and injury to soldiers and civilians, deployments carry a huge financial cost and risks to national security. In answer to inquiries from the House of Lords Constitution Committee, the Ministry of Defence stated that, between 1991 and 2005, there had been over ninety deployments of British armed forces abroad—the major ones relating to Iraq (in 1991 and 2003), Kosovo, Sierra Leone, and Afghanistan.[51]

When deploying armed forces, the United Kingdom does not exercise a prerogative power 'to declare war'.

House of Lords Constitution Committee, *Waging War: Parliament's Role and Responsibility*, 15th Report, Session 2005–06 (HL Paper 236), para. 10

The United Kingdom has made no declaration of war since that against Siam (modern Thailand) in 1942, and it is unlikely that there will ever be another. Developments in international law since 1945, notably the United Nations (UN) Charter, including its prohibition on

---

[51] House of Lords Constitution Committee, *Waging War: Parliament's Role and Responsibility*, 15th Report, Session 2005–06 (HL Paper 236), para. 27.

the threat or use of force in international relations, may well have made the declaration of war redundant as a formal international legal instrument [...]

The debates over this prerogative power raise a number of general and specific questions about the nature of reform. Regarding the best approach to reform two questions recur, as follows.

(a) In the context of deployment decisions, what are the advantages and disadvantages of parliamentary involvement?
(b) What are the merits and drawbacks of basing reform on statute as opposed to convention?

In this context, these are not arcane questions of technical detail. They matter not only to lawyers and legal theorists, but also to those performing practical tasks, including to the armed forces on the front line. From a legal perspective, the following, more basic, questions about the nature of this prerogative power may be asked.

(c) From where does the government derive legal authority to send armed forces abroad?
(d) Does the law specify the circumstances in which this decision can be taken?
(e) Does the law require a certain procedure to be followed by government before sending armed forces abroad?
(f) Must Parliament agree to the decision?
(g) Can those who are affected question the decision in the courts?

For now, a short answer may be given to each of these questions (the answers will be developed later in the chapter). The power of the executive to send armed forces abroad is a prerogative power—once exercised by the monarch personally, but now exercised by ministers. Ministers must exercise prerogative powers lawfully, although, as we shall see, the courts are likely to hold that the exercise of executive discretion in this context is non-justiciable.

Decisions of the United Kingdom and other states to go to war must be lawful in international law. International law permits the use of force in only three situations: for self-defence; if authorized by the Security Council acting under Chapter VII of the UN Charter exceptionally; or (arguably) to avert an overwhelming humanitarian catastrophe. Domestic courts will not determine whether actions are lawful as a matter of international law: they are concerned only with what UK domestic law requires. Nonetheless, arguments that UK law must reflect international law are increasingly made in domestic courts (see, for example, the arguments employed in *R v Jones and ors*, on p. 363).[52]

There is no set legal procedure that must be followed by ministers when deciding to deploy armed forces abroad. The government is under no *legal* obligation to obtain Parliament's consent. Nonetheless, the government says that, by convention, Parliament may debate these decisions and indicate its agreement or disagreement: as we shall see, whether in fact this convention exists—and if it does, what its precise scope is—remains somewhat contentious.

Strengthening Parliament's involvement has been a central concern of reformers. As we shall see, however, deciding on what basis, when, and how Parliament should be involved raises a number of difficult issues. For example, should Parliament be able to debate a decision to send armed forces abroad before they are sent or only afterwards? If Parliament is to be involved before armed forces are sent, should Parliament have a veto? What if the situation on the ground requires urgent or secret action? If Parliament is involved only after

---

[52] [2006] UKHL 16; see also *R (on the application of Gentle) v Prime Minister* [2008] UKHL 20.

armed forces have been committed, what substantive role can it play if it is limited to discussing decisions that have already been made?

(b) THE ROLE OF THE COURTS

Concern about the possible involvement of the courts has been one of the most important considerations in the debates about reform of the war powers prerogative. Ministers and some senior members of the armed forces argue that if reform further opens the way to litigation, this will undermine morale among service personnel and impinge upon operational effectiveness.

Can people affected by decisions to deploy armed forces overseas question the legality of those decisions? The short answer seems to be that even were the courts to accept that claimants have 'standing' to make a judicial review claim,[53] the decisions themselves are likely to be considered non-justiciable (see Lord Hoffmann in *R v Jones and ors*, considered on p. 363). Having said this, given the recent expansion in the scope of judicial review, developments in human rights law, and the growing influence of international law on domestic law, it cannot be assumed that this immunity from legal challenge is, or will remain, total.

It is generally said that decisions relating to the deployment of armed forces cannot be reviewed by the courts because they are solely for the executive. *Chandler v Director of Public Prosecutions*[54] is a leading case. Members of the Committee of 100 supported the aims of the Campaign for Nuclear Disarmament (CND) by non-violent demonstrations of civil disobedience. The Committee organized a demonstration at an airfield used by the US air force. It was planned that some demonstrators would sit outside the entrance to the base, while others would get into the airfield and sit in front of aircraft so as to prevent them from taking off. In the event, many demonstrators arrived, but they were stopped from entering the airfield. They were prosecuted and found guilty of conspiracy to commit a breach of s. 1 of the Official Secrets Act 1911, and were sentenced to terms of imprisonment.

They appealed to the Court of Appeal and the House of Lords, essentially arguing that they had not acted in a manner that was '*prejudicial to the safety or interests of the State in section 1 of the Official Secrets Act 1911*'. On the contrary, they contended, their campaign against nuclear weapons benefited the interests of the state. Unsurprisingly this argument did not succeed. The judges said that it was for government and not courts or juries to decide what is in the best interest of the state. Lord Devlin's observations in *Chandler* are referred to in the extract from the more recent decision of the House of Lords in *R v Jones and ors*, on p. 363. The following extract is from Lord Reid's judgment; he notes that the term 'state' does not mean 'the government' or 'the executive'.

Chandler v The Director of Public Prosecutions
[1964] AC 763, 791

Lord Reid

Who, then is to determine what is and what is not prejudicial to the safety and interests of the State? The question more frequently arises as to what is or is not in the public interest. I do not subscribe to the view that the Government or a Minister must always or even as a general rule have the last word about that.

---

[53] See Chapter 16.
[54] [1964] AC 763.

> But here we are dealing with a very special matter [...] It is in my opinion clear that the disposition and armament of the armed forces are and for centuries have been within the exclusive discretion of the Crown and that no one can seek a legal remedy on the ground that such discretion has been wrongly exercised. [...] Anyone is entitled, in or out of Parliament, to urge that policy regarding the armed forces should be changed; but until it is changed, on a change of Government or otherwise, no one is entitled to challenge it in court.

In this case, the Court was interpreting the words used by Parliament in the Official Secrets Act 1911. Parliament had used the expression '*prejudicial to the interests of the safety or interests of the state*'. Judges will normally determine whether legislative provisions have been properly interpreted and applied by ministers. Nonetheless, in this case, the House of Lords held that it was for government and not for judges or juries to decide what was prejudicial to these interests. That the House took this hands-off approach, even though it was dealing with statutory powers, should be borne in mind when, later in the chapter, we consider fears that removing or diminishing prerogative powers and rooting them in statute will lead to undesirable litigation.

R v Jones and ors is a more recent decision of the House of Lords. The facts were similar to those in *Chandler v The Director of Public Prosecutions*. Demonstrators who opposed the Iraq war broke into air force and other military establishments, and tried to stop planes, tanks, and other items of military equipment being sent to Iraq. When prosecuted, they argued in their defence that their actions were legally justified because they were attempting to impede, obstruct, or disrupt the commission by the UK and US governments of the crime of aggression, which they said was established as a crime in customary international law, and which forms part of domestic criminal law in England and Wales. Their appeals against conviction were dismissed by the Court of Appeal and by a unanimous decision of the House of Lords.

In the following extract, Lord Hoffmann considers the problems facing a domestic court in determining whether the UK government was committing the crime of aggression in conducting the war in Iraq. The first difficulty is the theoretical one of how to determine whether the state itself, of which the courts form a part, has acted unlawfully. In the extract, he considers the second practical difficulty.

R v Jones and ors
[2006] UKHL 16

Lord Hoffmann

[65] [...] Secondly, there is the practical difficulty that the making of war and peace and the disposition of the armed forces has always been regarded as a discretionary power of the Crown into the exercise of which the courts will not enquire. I say that it is a practical difficulty because, as Lord Devlin pointed out in *Chandler v DPP* [1964] AC 763, 806-812, the reason why the courts cannot enquire is not the technicality that the powers form part of the royal prerogative. Lord Devlin's view that the prerogative origin of the powers did not in itself exclude judicial control was affirmed by the House in *Council of Civil Service Unions v Minister for the Civil Service* [1985] AC 374. It is because of the discretionary nature of the power itself. As Lord Devlin said (at pp 809–810): 'When Lord Parker of Waddington in *The Zamora* [1916] 2 AC 77, 107 said that 'Those who are responsible for the national security must be the sole judges of what the national security requires,' he was not, I think, laying down any special constitutional doctrine about the powers of the Crown in relation to national security. He was simply stating the reason why the court should declare those powers to be discretionary.'

[66] It is of course open to the court to say that the act in question falls wholly outside the ambit of the discretionary power. But that is not the case here. The decision to go to war, whether one thinks it was right or wrong, fell squarely within the discretionary powers of the Crown to defend the realm and conduct its foreign affairs.

QUESTIONS

1. *'It is not their source which determines whether the courts will review discretionary powers but their nature.'* Consider this in the light of the decisions in *Chandler v The Director of Public Prosecutions* and *R v Jones and ors*.

2. What precisely is the practical difficulty to which Lords Devlin and Hoffmann refer?

3. Would a decision to send armed forces to fight in breach of international law be reviewable?

4. Lord Reid, it will be remembered, in *Burmah Oil Company v Lord Advocate*, emphasized that the meaning of the prerogative has changed over time (see p. 346). Does this suggest that even if the discretion to send armed forces abroad is not reviewable today, it may be reviewable in the future? If so, why might this be the case?

5. *'It is of course open to the court to say that the act in question falls wholly outside the ambit of the discretionary power.'* How would the courts determine whether an exercise of discretion falls 'wholly outside the ambit' of a prerogative power?

(c) THE CONVENTION THAT PARLIAMENT BE INVOLVED

In Chapter 1, we examined the characteristics of constitutional conventions as a source of rule governing the behaviour of public bodies, noting that they are especially important in regulating how prerogative powers are exercised. In the following extract, Jack Straw, then Leader of the House, explained to the Commons the government's view of what constitutional conventions govern decisions to deploy armed forces, given that in each of the war situations prior to Iraq, the government had reported regularly to the House of Commons in the form of statements and the issues were often debated.

House of Commons Hansard, 15 May 2007, col. 492–7

Mr Jack Straw MP

There is no question but that Ministers at that time recognised the need to gain—in one way or another—the consent of Parliament. [...] When, in 2002, military action against Iraq loomed as a possibility, many inside and outside this House demanded that any decision be subject to a substantive resolution by this place. I pay tribute to my late and much-missed friend Robin Cook for the way in which, as the then Leader of the House, he faithfully represented in government this House's views. I am glad to have worked with him on this, and the Cabinet unanimously agreed his propositions. In the event, alongside many statements, four full-length debates on Iraq were held in this place between September 2002 and March 2003. Three debates were on substantive motions: in November 2002; in February 2003;

and then, of course, in the crucial determining debate in March 2003, which confirmed the decision for military action by a majority of 263.[55]

That set of debates on substantive motions established a clear precedent for the future from which I do not believe there will be, or could ever be, a departure. Indeed, as my right hon. Friend the Prime Minister put it: 'The fact of the matter is that I cannot conceive of a situation in which a Government [. . .] is going to go to war—except in circumstances where militarily for the security of the country it needs to act immediately—without a full Parliamentary debate'.

QUESTIONS

1. Jack Straw says that the set of debates on substantive motions on the Iraqi war '*establish a clear precedent for the future*' from which there could be no departure. In other words, he says that they establish a clear convention. But what precisely does the convention appear to require? In particular, does it seem to require the executive to obtain Parliament's consent before sending armed forces to fight, or only that Parliament be permitted to debate the matter?

2. What do you think would have been be the legal position had the House of Commons not supported military action on 18 March 2003? Would it still have been lawful under UK law for the government to have sent armed forces to Iraq?

(d) PROS AND CONS OF PARLIAMENTARY INVOLVEMENT

While the main thrust of the reform agenda has been to strengthen Parliament's role in relation to the prerogative in general, and war powers decisions in particular, not everyone has enthusiastically supported the idea of greater parliamentary involvement. Some within government and the armed forces, in particular, have argued against it.

The case for ensuring 'full parliamentary scrutiny' of decisions on armed conflict was considered by the House of Lords Constitution Committee during its inquiry into the use of the prerogative. The following extract from the Committee's report summarizes what the Committee was told by witnesses. As we might expect, views varied, with some witnesses stressing the benefits and others stressing the drawbacks. The views are summarized in Box 9.3 and the extract from the report explains the points in more detail.

BOX 9.3 BENEFITS AND DRAWBACKS OF PARLIAMENTARY INVOLVEMENT IN DECISIONS ON ARMED CONFLICT

Benefits	Drawbacks
Increase legitimacy	Undermine operational effectiveness
Increase accountability	Shift responsibility from the executive
Improve decision-making	Lead to litigation
Improve morale	Undermine morale

---

55 The House of Commons gave its approval for the use of all necessary means, including force, to ensure the disarmament of Iraqi's weapons of mass destruction (HC Deb Vol. 401, Col. 760, 18 March 2003).

House of Lords Constitution Committee, *Waging War: Parliament's Role and Responsibility,* 15th Report, Session 2005–06, HL Paper 236-I (footnotes omitted)

THE BENEFITS OF INCREASING PARLIAMENTARY INVOLVEMENT

Legitimacy: source and exercise of the deployment power

37. A key concern over the current deployment power is one of constitutional principle: that Parliament should be the source of the Government's power and not the Crown. Lord Lester regarded the key question about the deployment power to be: "should it be Parliament that is Sovereign, to whom the executive is constitutionally account-able, or should it be the Monarch?" He considered it anomalous for the Crown to be able to exercise public powers without parliamentary authority, on the basis of medi-aeval notions of kingship and through Crown Ministers. Mr Sebastian Payne agreed: "Parliament should be the source of Government's power," a position also taken by Professor McEldowney. In oral evidence, Professor Bell noted that the principle of the rule of law, on which governments exercise power in most constitutions in Europe, means that there has to be a specific authorisation to exercise powers. Therefore, "having a rule about authorising the exercise of powers is just a natural consequence of that principle".

38. A number of witnesses considered that the extremely serious nature of the decision to deploy armed forces—involving possible loss of life and national consequences—meant that it should necessarily be undertaken, or approved, by Parliament [. . .]

Increased accountability of decision-making

40. Several witnesses advocated greater parliamentary involvement on the grounds that the current deployment power lacks sufficient accountability or restraint. [. . .] it could be said that the ability of United Kingdom governments to use the royal prerogative power to engage in conflict is paradoxically less democratic than when the Monarch exercised the power personally. In the past, the Monarch's power to make war and deploy armed forces was checked by Parliament's control of the resources necessary for the exercise of the power. Now, the Government of the day not only exercises the royal prerogative but also generally controls the House of Commons and therefore its power over finance—through parliamentary majorities, use of the Whips and control over the parliamentary timetable—thereby undermining this historical brake on executive power.

41. By contrast, the Government insists [. . .] that the current process is sufficient: "In the United Kingdom, ministers are accountable to Parliament for all their actions. Therefore Parliament is always in a position to hold the executive to account in any way it sees fit". [. . .]

42. However, some witnesses questioned the effectiveness of these accountability meas-ures in practice. The Rt Hon Kenneth Clarke MP considered that parliamentary discussion preceding both the Falklands and Kosovo engagements curtailed real accountability:"I think on both occasions the Government, when it had parliamentary debates, put down motions on the adjournment precisely to make sure that there was no substantive vote taking place at any stage. The whole thing was used more as a process of explanation and persuasion than it was of giving Parliament a real way to challenge the decision and to be accountable fully, which I think means throwing down before Parliament the opportunity to reject this policy if it wants to before any military action takes place." [. . .]

43. This view was echoed in other evidence. Professor John McEldowney, for example, told us that Parliament relies on the Government to provide sufficient information and allow debate. He thought the lessons of the Iraq war were that the Government could set the agenda, identify the issues and provide its own publicity on the need for military action and its subsequent outcome, leaving Parliament relatively weakened. Democratic Audit considered the current system of Ministerial accountability to Parliament to be too broad, retrospective and vulnerable to executive power to be an effective check on the Prime Minister's use of the prerogative. Accountability was also described as problematic because, in line with all prerogative power, it is "dependent on the goodwill of the executive or the existence of a convention that Parliament should be informed". Dr Ziegler told us that parliaments could be marginalised by lack of information (at any rate in time to influence their decisions) or by being confronted by *faits accomplis*: "this is known as the de-parliamentarisation of decision-making".

"Better" decision-making

44. Other witnesses proposed that a change to the current deployment power was necessary because the highly personalised nature of the royal prerogative power leads to poor processes of decision-making. Clare Short told us that because the royal prerogative power is exercised by the Prime Minister alone—without any formal requirement for scrutiny or discussion—this can lead to decisions being taken in a "vacuum". A requirement for scrutiny by Parliament, she argued, might lead to better considered and prepared decisions: "If any Prime Minister knew that he had to bring before the House of Commons—and maybe both Houses [...] a full statement of why and the analysis, I think that means the whole issue would have to be better scrutinised, better thought through, better prepared and the decision would be better made". [...]

The impact on military morale

45. Several witnesses suggested that more legitimate decision-making would result in greater support for deployment decisions among the public, senior military figures and serving troops. This opinion was evinced by a number of retired leaders of the Armed Forces. General Sir Michael Rose told us: "It would be enormously advantageous to members of the armed forces for such a formal and legal justification to be made by the government before entering into armed conflict. There can be no more debilitating effect on the morale of members of the armed forces for them to know that their country does not support the mission or that the case for war is based on doubtful moral or legal arguments. A proper justification should always be a sine qua non for engaging in conflict. A formal requirement for prior parliamentary authorisation for entering into conflict situations can therefore only be of benefit to members of the armed forces."

46. Lord King also believed "very strongly indeed" that it was important to the morale of the Armed Forces to know that the country is really behind them. Field Marshal Lord Bramall considered that the Armed Forces would like to know three things before being committed to a large scale military operation; that they had the support of the country; that they had the support of Parliament and that what they had been asked to do was legal. [...]

ARGUMENTS AGAINST INCREASING PARLIAMENTARY INVOLVEMENT

48. A range of arguments against increasing parliamentary involvement in the decision to deploy armed forces was outlined to us. In summary, they related to concerns about the

possible detrimental effect on operational effectiveness and coalition-working; the importance of maintaining executive authority over the decision; the difficulties Parliament might have in reaching an informed decision; the legal impact if legislation were put in place and the detrimental effect this may have on Armed Forces morale.

Undermining effectiveness of operations

49. Several witnesses regarded operational efficiency to be the key benefit of the present deployment arrangements, and one which could be undermined by greater parliamentary involvement in the process. Field Marshal Lord Vincent of Coleshill said that the success of many military operations relies on the need to maintain "secrecy, security and surprise". Admiral Lord Boyce summarised his concern:

> "[...] all my experience over conducting or being involved with the conduct of several wars over the last five or six years or so is that those allies who go through the parliamentary process are frankly in my view not as operationally effective as those who do not [...]"

Lord Boyce told us that an open debate in Parliament on deployments could undermine six key aspects of Armed Forces operations:

- escalating the conflict through rhetoric;
- skewing decisions through access to only limited information (since a great deal of intelligence cannot be revealed in public);
- compromising operational security by publicly discussing too much detail prior to action;
- impairing flexibility of operational response if parliamentary approval is required for every change of the situation on the ground;
- undermining clarity about the timetable for preparation, if it is contingent on a parliamentary debate or vote;
- removing the ability of United Kingdom Forces to have "strategic poise" by giving the opponent early notice of intent.

Coalition-working

51. Mr Ingram told us that in his experience coalition partners liked to work with British units because the current process gave the Government the capacity to make quick decisions about deployments and to provide wide mandates for British forces.

Maintaining executive responsibility for action

52. We have heard evidence to suggest that the responsibility for taking the decision to deploy armed forces should very clearly rest with the executive and not be dictated by the immediate views and reactions of Parliament or of the people. The Government has clearly stated that "the power to deploy troops is an executive power. Such decisions are by their nature most suitable for the executive to take". Professor Denza also considered the decision to be essentially an executive one: "While the government which has taken it should be required to explain and justify its decision to Parliament and to the people, the decision itself should not be dictated by the immediate views and reactions of Parliament or of the people".

53. There was also concern that any increase in the involvement of Parliament might lead to attempts to pre-empt operational decisions. [...]

Difficulties of informed decision-making

55. There was broad agreement that it is necessary to restrict some information in a potential deployment situation and an acknowledgement that this could compromise the ability of Parliament to make informed decisions about a given situation. Clare Short considered that a demand to put security information in the public domain could not be agreed to, because it might put people's lives in danger, but this could also be "used as a smokescreen". The Government told us that:

> "The provision of information to Parliament on any deployment will always be constrained by the need not to reveal sensitive information on the way the armed forces propose to act or the extent or nature of intelligence on the forces they will act against." [...]

Legal impact of legislation

57. We have heard that if parliamentary involvement in the deployment decision was enshrined in legislation that required, for instance, prior parliamentary approval, this would require language tantamount to definitions of what is lawful and might lead to the legality of any deployment being challenged in the United Kingdom courts. Some witnesses raised concerns that this could lead to individual servicemen facing criminal prosecution for actions in an "unlawful" deployment. In written evidence, Professor Rowe raised the issue of whether such legislation would have legal implications for members of the armed forces (the possibility of involving the courts in action against a particular soldier) and whether national obligations might differ from those they already have under international law. [...]

58. Others wondered whether a requirement for parliamentary approval might lead to troops refusing to obey orders to implement a deployment that they perceived to be unlawful. [...]

Undermining morale

59. While we have heard evidence to suggest that greater parliamentary involvement in the deployment power would improve morale (paragraphs 45–47), we also heard contrasting evidence to suggest that it might actually undermine it. The Lord Chancellor and Secretary of State for Constitutional Affairs told us that any restriction on deployment might introduce an "unpredictable and damaging level of uncertainty" as to the legality of the actions of Armed Forces on the ground. Lord Boyce told us that the uncertainty that resulted from relying on Parliament's approval would be bad for morale. Other concerns hinge on whether Parliament is shown to be unanimously in favour of action, or whether divisions are exposed [...]

Weighing the arguments

Had you been a member of the House of Lords Constitution Committee, you would have needed to assess and weigh these arguments, and form a view on whether it was desirable to increase Parliament's role and, if so, how. Looking over the arguments, some are based on constitutional principle and others are more practical in nature. How are arguments on principle and practice to be weighed against each other? Increasing the democratic legitimacy of decision-making is clearly important as a matter of principle, but does it outweigh risks to the operational effectiveness of military campaigns? Another problem that you would have faced is that of weighing conflicting opinions of experts. For example, we can see that senior military figures differed on whether parliamentary involvement would enhance or damage morale within the armed forces. How would you and your fellow committee members know which of these views is the more likely to be accurate? Without clear evidence, this is a question of judgement and approach. A cautious person might take a precautionary approach, whereby any risk to morale should be avoided; others might be inclined to press ahead with reform despite some risks.

It is significant in this context that the Lord Chancellor and Secretary of State for Constitutional Affairs argued that *'any restriction on deployment might introduce an "unpredictable and damaging level of uncertainty" as to the legality of the actions of Armed Forces on the ground'*. It is perhaps not surprising to find senior members of the executive arguing in favour of government retaining its discretion, nor perhaps is it surprising to see government taking a precautionary approach to operational concerns—but it is interesting to see how these positions shift as the reform process evolves.

From our perspective as lawyers, another issue of interest concerns what is said about litigation and its effects. Several witnesses argue that if Parliament were to become involved—especially if that involvement were secured by legislation—this would lead to possible arguments in courts on whether deployments were lawful and within the terms of the legislation. This, in turn, it is feared, would have adverse effects on morale within the armed forces and reduce operational freedom. The implication is that reform of this nature would have a 'double whammy' effect: government would now be accountable both to Parliament and the courts, and the latter might be more significant than the former. As we will see, this concern has been extremely influential in shaping the reforms.

QUESTIONS

1. If you were a member of the House of Lords Constitution Committee, would you favour greater parliamentary involvement in decisions to deploy armed forces or would you be against it?

2. Assuming, for the moment, that the Committee agrees that Parliament should be more involved and that discussion now moves on to consider the nature of that involvement. Let us alter our role. Now, instead of being a member of the Committee, you are an adviser to the Committee. The Committee has asked you to summarize the main options for reform in order to help it with its discussion. What do you think are the main options?

3. It is suggested to you that the main options for reform are as follows.

   • Things continue as now, but that it should be recognized that the power to deploy armed forces derives from Parliament, rather than from the prerogative.

   • Government remains responsible for the decision, but must provide Parliament with a justification for its action. Parliament should be able to debate this justification and be critical, but Parliament should not be able to veto a decision of the government.

   • Subject to specific exceptions, government should send military forces abroad to fight only with the prior agreement of Parliament.

   Do you agree that these are the main options? If not, what other options should be considered?

(e) RECOMMENDATIONS OF THE CONSTITUTION COMMITTEE

The Constitution Committee went on to emphasize the dynamic nature of the UK's constitution, which it likened to '*a living organism adapting to change as evolutionary circumstances require*'. The constitution, it said, '*is almost infinitely flexible: landmark judgments or pragmatic political deals can materially amend the constitution as comprehensively as primary legislation*' (para. 97). The prerogative, rooted as it is in the common law and governed by convention, it said, reflects the ability of the constitution to develop organically. For example, the Committee noted the change in the approach taken by governments when making military decisions.

House of Lords Constitution Committee, *Waging War: Parliament's Role and Responsibility*, 15th Report, Session 2005–06, HL Paper 236-I, para. 98

> In the nineteenth century governments could—and on occasion did—engage in military adventures with little or no reference to Parliament. Today, as the Prime Minister himself has said, there are unlikely to be any circumstances in which a government could go to war without the support of Parliament.

Having said this, the Committee noted that the precise meaning of the term 'support' is unclear in this context. It can either refer to the assumed support of Parliament (as when Parliament does not actually disapprove of government action) or it can mean the express support of Parliament as when parliamentary support is formally given.

Significantly, the Committee made two central recommendations: one substantive, and the other relating to method or process. Its substantive recommendation was that Parliament should be involved as a matter of right and not only as a matter of executive largesse. Obviously influenced by those who feared the adverse consequences of using legislation to achieve this change, it nonetheless recommended that the change should be achieved by using convention rather than by using legislation.

House of Lords Constitution Committee, *Waging War: Parliament's Role and Responsibility*, 15th Report, Session 2005–06, HL Paper 236-I (footnotes omitted)

> 100. The majority of our witnesses agreed that it is anachronistic, in a parliamentary democracy, to deny Parliament the right to pass judgement on proposals to use military force in pursuit of policy, although there was no consensus on the best means to bring that about. [. . .]
>
> 101. Although there have been exceptions, such as emergencies, recent history shows that the processes leading up to deployments are generally protracted, allowing plenty of time not only to evaluate and plan for the action but to obtain parliamentary support. The fact that it might be inconvenient for the Government to seek this support is hardly a justification for denying it. The Government's preparations have also been conducted under full media coverage, rendering the arguments about security and secrecy more theoretical than real. The Government also argues that it is in any case accountable to Parliament; but it seems to us that if substance is to be given to the glib cliché that "Parliament can decide" then significant adjustment needs to be made to the processes that are employed to enable it to do so.

102. As for the potential problem of politicisation of military decision making, we do not believe that constraints on the deployment power will affect the freedoms which military commanders have and should continue to enjoy. We fully acknowledge that controversy at home could have a deleterious effect on the morale of the troops in the field and agree the importance of guarding against it, but note that that would be so whatever process was followed. More to the point, we believe strongly that the balance of the argument falls in favour of ensuring that those troops know that Parliament is behind them rather than be left to speculate. [...]

103. [...] Our conclusion is that the exercise of the Royal prerogative by the Government to deploy armed force overseas is outdated and should not be allowed to continue as the basis for legitimate war-making in our 21st century democracy. Parliament's ability to challenge the executive must be protected and strengthened. There is a need to set out more precisely the extent of the Government's deployment powers, and the role Parliament can—and should—play in their exercise.

[The Committee then went on to explain why it rejected the use of legislation to secure Parliamentís involvement.]

104. [...] For us, the least persuasive argument is the one for a statutory solution on the lines of the Private Members bills that have been introduced in recent years in both Houses. We have not been persuaded that the difficulties of putting the deployment power on a statutory basis could easily be overcome, and consider that the problems of the uncertainty generated outweigh any constitutional merits. In our view, the possibility—however remote—of, for example, subjecting forces of the Crown to criminal prosecution for actions taken in good faith in protecting the national interest is unacceptable. We also see no merit in legislative architecture which creates the possibility of judicial review of Government decisions over matters of democratic executive responsibility. In addition, the need to provide for "emergency" exceptions would create loopholes that could be readily exploited by a future administration with ambitions less benign than those to which we are accustomed.

105. Nor are we persuaded by the proposal simply to transfer the prerogative from the Crown to Parliament, but otherwise leave its exercise to precisely the same discretions as currently prevail. For the constitutional purist, it has the attraction of resolving a historical anomaly and eroding the prerogative still further. But it would substitute a historical anomaly with a political one, and signally fail to address the fundamental constitutional issue of parliamentary oversight of the decision-making process.

[Rather than adopting a statutory solution, the Committee favoured continuing to use an approach based on convention that draws on cross-party support and consensus.]

108. [...] In that spirit, we recommend that there should be a parliamentary convention determining the role Parliament should play in making decisions to deploy force or forces outside the United Kingdom to war, intervention in an existing conflict or to environments where there is a risk that the forces will be engaged in conflict. [...]

110. While not seeking to be prescriptive, we recommend that the convention should encompass the following characteristics:

(1) Government should seek Parliamentary approval [...] if it is proposing the deployment of British forces outside the United Kingdom into actual or potential armed conflict;

(2) In seeking approval, the Government should indicate the deployment's objectives, its legal basis, likely duration and, in general terms, an estimate of its size;

(3) If, for reasons of emergency and security, such prior application is impossible, the Government should provide retrospective information within 7 days of its commencement or as soon as it is feasible, at which point the process in (1) should be followed;

(4) The Government, as a matter of course, should keep Parliament informed of the progress of such deployments and, if their nature or objectives alter significantly should seek a renewal of the approval.

111. These are matters of significant constitutional interest which we publish for the information and consideration of the House. We look forward to receiving the Government's response, and the opportunity to debate the issues, at the earliest possible date.

QUESTIONS

1. Summarize the reasons why the Committee was against putting the decision to deploy armed forces abroad on a statutory footing.

2. What appear to be the main practical differences between putting the decision on a statutory footing and establishing 'a parliamentary convention determining the role Parliament should play in making decisions to deploy force or forces outside the United Kingdom'?

(f) GOVERNMENT'S RESPONSE TO THESE RECOMMENDATIONS

This report was published on 27 July 2006. The government assured the Committee that it would respond by the end of the parliamentary summer recess on 9 October 2006. In fact, the government's response was not published until 7 November 2006. Even then, it was very brief.

Government Response to the House of Lords Constitution Committee's Report Waging War: Parliament's Role and Responsibility (Cm 6923), 7 November 2006

4. [We are] not presently persuaded of the case for [...] establishing a new convention determining the role of Parliament in the deployment of the armed forces. The existing legal and constitutional convention is that it must be the Government which takes the decision in accordance with its own assessment of the position. That is one of the key responsibilities for which it has been elected. But the matter needs to be kept under review.

The Constitution Committee was unimpressed by this response,[56] which it said was 'inadequate' and 'cursory', and 'fails genuinely to address the arguments or the recommendations which had been made' or 'to provide a comprehensive or stand-alone outline of the Government's position in reply to our final carefully deliberated report'.[57] In relation to the

---

[56] House of Lords Constitution Committee, *Waging War: Parliament's Role and Responsibility—Follow-up*, Third Report, Session 2006–07, HL Paper 51.

[57] Ibid., para. 5.

government's argument that it is elected and must remain responsible for decisions, the House of Lords select committee made the following statement.

House of Lords Constitution Committee, *Waging War: Parliament's Role and Responsibility—Follow-up,* Third Report, Session 2006–07 (HL Paper 51), para. 6

This underplays the fact that Parliament was also elected—indeed, the executive draws its strength and legitimacy from a democratic Parliament—and does not address our conclusion that "Parliament's ability to challenge the executive must be protected and strengthened". It is not sufficient simply to assert, as the Government do, that "adequate mechanisms for intense parliamentary scrutiny of executive actions are already in place'.

The Committee added that *'there is more than a suspicion of disagreement on this matter at the highest levels of government'.* It drew particular attention to conflicting statements made, on the one hand, by the Prime Minister and the Lord Chancellor (favouring the status quo), and on the other, statements made by the Chancellor of the Exchequer (Gordon Brown) and the Leader of the House of Commons (Jack Straw) favouring reform to increase Parliament's role. It concluded as follows.

House of Lords Select Committee, *Waging War: Parliament's Role and Responsibility—Follow-up,* Third Report, Session 2006–07 (HL Paper 51), para. 9

Irrespective of the response we received, we consider that a cross-party political consensus appears to be emerging that the current arrangements are unsustainable. Accordingly, we are optimistic that our recommendations will be revisited in the very near future. We hope that this vitally important constitutional issue will then be addressed in a more satisfactory manner and we look forward to playing our part in that debate.

(g) OVER TO THE HOUSE OF COMMONS

The House of Lords Constitution Committee was right—the matter did not rest there. There must have been important behind-the-scenes discussion among senior government ministers, because, by 15 May 2007, when an important debate took place on the issue in the House of Commons, the government had changed its mind. The following is a short extract from a long and interesting debate. In it, Jack Straw explains why the government had been hesitant and how it proposed to push the matter forward.

House of Commons Hansard, 15 May 2007, col. 492

The Leader of the House of Commons (Mr. Jack Straw):

For Parliament and any Government, no issue is of greater gravity and consequence than war: whether to put our servicemen and women in harm's way, in the certain knowledge that some will be injured and some may be killed; and whether to entertain the other two certainties of war—innocent civilian casualties and considerable financial cost—along with the uncertainty of war, of unintended consequences.

Precisely because of the seriousness of such decisions, Parliament, especially this House, has long played a role in holding the Prime Minister and Cabinet of the day fully to account for their decisions. Indeed, there has not been a significant armed conflict overseas since the beginning of the 20th century in which the United Kingdom has been involved where, in one way or another, at the time of decision or in retrospect, this House has not indicated whether, and in what way, it has consented to the Executive decision taken.

The very qualifications in the language that I have just used, however, tell their own story about the question that lies at the heart of today's debate—that the power to make war, and to enter into armed conflict, is currently based on the exercise of the royal prerogative. That, in turn, has meant that Parliament's role, though substantial, is imprecise and less than well defined. [...]

Let me now deal [...] with why there has been some hesitation in government on this issue. Hesitation to make more explicit our procedure has not arisen because of any nostalgia for our system of government before the 1689 Bill of Rights. It has done so because of concern about the adverse impact of any new process on the operational discretion of those in command and on the linked ability to respond to emergency situations and other instances requiring secrecy; and, above all, because of concern about the need not in any way to compromise the security and well-being of our troops or damage their morale. Each of those concerns is very serious and none should be dismissed. Many of them were raised by those who gave evidence to the Constitution Committee inquiry [...]

There are two models for making Parliament's role more explicit: one is by statute, the other by resolution of this House, including Standing Orders and convention. [...]

As we proceed with the consultation, we will look at the various ways to achieve the objective that I believe the whole House shares. As it happens, the Constitution Committee came down firmly against the statutory route, and raised a number of objections to it. [...]

Aside from creating legal problems and potentially drawing the courts into the decision-making process, a legislative framework would have to ensure explicitly that it did not have a negative impact on an ability to react to emergencies. Examples of such emergencies might be the hostage rescue mission in Sierra Leone or, more recently, the UK evacuation of civilians from the Lebanon, where secrecy and speed, respectively, were essential.

The deployment of our forces in the modern world will almost always be part of a coalition. Timetables are not necessarily under our control, and flexibility is needed. Our military involvement could be less timely, and therefore less effective, if an inflexible statutory process and legal challenges to a deployment further delayed commitment. [...]

The alternatives to statute could be a resolution of both Houses, Standing Orders or conventions. [...] that inevitably raises the question of differences between the two Houses and their respective roles. Of course, both Houses have an absolute right to discuss decisions relating to military action, and to be consulted and kept informed by Government. However, in the final analysis, the primacy of the Commons must be upheld—and I believe that that must apply even after the other place has been reformed.

[Following the debate, the House of Commons agreed the following resolution, calling upon the government to consult and come back to Parliament with detailed proposals for reform.]

The House of Commons Resolution

The House of Commons: welcomes the precedents set by the Government in 2002 and 2003 in seeking and obtaining the approval of the House for its decisions in respect of military action against Iraq; is of the view that it is inconceivable that any Government would in practice depart from this precedent; taking note of the reports of the Public Administration Select Committee, HC 422 of Session 2003–04, and of the Lords Committee on the Constitution, HL 236 of Session 2005–06, believes that the time has come for Parliament's role to be made more explicit in approving, or otherwise, decisions of the Government relating to the major, or substantial, deployment of British forces overseas into actual, or potential, armed conflict; recognises the imperative to take full account of the paramount need not to compromise the security of British forces nor the operational discretion of those in command, including in respect of emergencies and regrets that insufficient weight has been given to this in some quarters; and calls upon the Government, after consultation, to come forward with more detailed proposals for Parliament to consider.

(h) GOVERNMENT CONSULTATION

Reform of the prerogative relating to deployment of the armed forces became one part of a broader agenda for constitutional reform being pursued by the Labour government under the title 'Constitutional Renewal'. As we have noted, in July 2007, the government—by then led by Gordon Brown—published a Green Paper, *Governance of Britain* (Cm 7170), which set out for consultation various proposals for modernizing the role of the executive that were designed to *'make the executive and Parliament more accountable to the people and* [...] *reinvigorate our democracy'*. The government proposed *'immediate and specific changes'* to strengthen democracy and *'restrict the power of the Prime Minister and the executive'*. Its thinking is summarized in the following extract. As you will see, government now accepted that decisions to send armed forces to fight abroad ought to be taken with Parliament's approval.

Ministry of Justice, *Limiting the Power of the Executive: The Governance of Britain* (Cm 7170), July 2007

14. For centuries the executive has, in certain areas, been able to exercise authority in the name of the Monarch without the people and their elected representatives in their Parliament being consulted. This is no longer appropriate in a modern democracy. The Government believes that the executive should draw its powers from the people, through Parliament.

15. The flow of power from the people to government should be balanced by the ability of Parliament to hold government to account. However, when the executive relies on the powers of the royal prerogative—powers where government acts upon the Monarch's authority—it is difficult for Parliament to scrutinise and challenge government's actions. If voters do not believe that government wields its power appropriately or that it is properly accountable then public confidence in the accountability of decision-making risks being lost.

16. That is why the Government is proposing immediate and specific changes to strengthen our democracy—changes that will restrict the power of the Prime Minister and the executive.

17. It is important that the key decisions that affect the whole country—such as the decision to send troops into armed conflict—are made in the right way, and with Parliament's consent.

The same is true of treaties that the UK makes with its partners in Europe and across the world. Government's power to deploy troops and ratify treaties stems from the royal prerogative. In a modern 21st century parliamentary democracy, the Government considers that basing these powers on the prerogative is out of date. It will therefore seek to limit its own power by placing the most important of these prerogative powers onto a more formal footing, conferring power on Parliament to determine how they are exercised in future. And where archaic powers are no longer in use—for example the right to impress people into the Royal Navy—the Government will consider options for ending them. [...]

The government went on to say that, in general, prerogative powers should be put onto a statutory basis in order to ensure that *government is more clearly subject to the mandate of the people's representatives*. In relation to the deployment of armed forces, the government's views at the time are set out in the following extract.

Ministry of Justice, *The Governance of Britain* (Cm 7170), July 2007

Deploying the Armed Forces abroad:

25. There are few political decisions more important than the deployment of the Armed Forces into armed conflict. The Government can currently exercise the prerogative power to deploy the Armed Forces for armed conflict overseas without requiring any formal parliamentary agreement.

26. The Government believes that this is now an outdated state of affairs in a modern democracy. On an issue of such fundamental importance to the nation, the Government should seek the approval of the representatives of the people in the House of Commons for significant, non-routine deployments of the Armed Forces into armed conflict, to the greatest extent possible. This needs to be done without prejudicing the Government's ability to take swift action to protect our national security, or undermining operational security or effectiveness. The Government will therefore consult Parliament and the public on how best to achieve this. [...]

The Governance of Britain referred to the different recommendations that had been made by the PASC (in its *Taming the Prerogative* report) and the House of Lords Constitution Committee. As we have seen, the first of these said that reform should be based on legislation, whereas the second said that the legislative route was not the best way forward and instead recommended the establishment of a new convention to ensure that government acts with the approval of the House of Commons. The government said that it preferred this latter approach and proposed the following.

Ministry of Justice, *The Governance of Britain* (Cm 7170), July 2007

29. and 30. "[...] that the House of Commons develop a parliamentary convention that could be formalised by a resolution." In accordance with the motion approved by the House of Commons on 15 May 2007, the Government promised to "undertake further consultation on this issue before bringing forward more detailed proposals for Parliament to consider".

(i) DISCUSSION SHIFTS FROM SUBSTANCE TO METHOD: TOWARDS A WAR POWERS RESOLUTION

Between November 2006 and Spring 2007, the government had changed its position. Whereas, a few months earlier, the government was emphasizing its responsibility for decisions on military deployments, it was now arguing the case for limiting its powers and for parliamentary involvement. It had now accepted the substance of the case for reform of this prerogative. Attention shifted to the best means by which the reform could be achieved. But here, too, the government had shifted. In November 2006, it had responded to the House of Lords Constitution Committee's report by saying that it was not 'persuaded' of the case for *'establishing a new convention determining the role of Parliament in the deployment of the armed forces'*; by the spring of 2007, it was proposing just that. Given the fears expressed about the effect of legislation, it is not difficult to see why, once the case for reform has been accepted on grounds of democratic principle, government would prefer to achieve reform by using convention rather than legislation. It is not surprising, for example, that government would take a precautionary approach to fears that legislative-based reform could carry risks to morale and other adverse operational consequences.

The *Governance of Britain* Green Paper was followed by a consultation paper that focused specifically on war powers and treaties.[58] In relation to war powers, this summarized the history of parliamentary involvement in deployments abroad and reviewed the various considerations relevant to deployment decisions, including the need for operational flexibility and the need to maintain the morale of the armed forces. It also looked at the definition of 'armed conflict' and the problems associated with securing parliamentary involvement in emergencies or in relation to covert or secret operations: at what stage should Parliament be involved? And how much information should Parliament be given? It also raised the relative standing of the two Houses of Parliament.

The following extract returns to the vexed issue of whether parliamentary involvement should be secured by statute or by convention (or by some mix), and summarizes the advantages and disadvantages of the two main options. The paper noted that the House of Lords Constitution Committee came out firmly against putting the deployment power on a statutory basis and instead preferred to use a resolution of the House of Commons to create a new convention that would set out how Parliament's involvement would be secured.

Ministry of Justice, *Governance of Britain: War Powers and Treaties*, Cm 7239, October 2007

Should the new arrangements be contained in a freestanding convention, or in a resolution of the House, or in Legislation?

90. Conventions can take a number of forms. Some of the most fundamental of the UK's constitutional conventions are not formally set down anywhere outside the textbooks, for example that which says that a Prime Minister defeated on a motion of confidence must resign. In the Governance of Britain, the Government said that it would propose that the House of Commons develop a Parliamentary convention that could be formalised by a resolu-

---

[58] *The Governance of Britain War Powers and Treaties: Limiting Executive Powers*, 25 October 2007, CM 7239.

tion.' This is one of the more formal ways of establishing a convention. Nonetheless, there clearly is a difference between a resolution, however prescriptive, and legislation.

91. The advantages of a resolution are that:

- It can be created with less formality and more easily amended;

- Failure to comply with it is not automatically unlawful;

- Its interpretation (including the meaning of any exceptions) is primarily a matter for Parliament rather than the courts through judicial review; and

- It may be less likely to inspire speculative legal proceedings against individuals.

92. As opposed to that, there are the disadvantages that a resolution:

- Might appear to provide a weaker assurance of compliance by the government of the day;

- Does not formally constrain the exercise of the prerogative; and

- Would be silent as to its legal effect on the decisions to commit to armed conflict and would not ensure the complete protection of the armed forces from any possible consequential legal liability.

The consultation closed in January 2008 with only fifteen responses having been submitted. In summary, fourteen of the respondents were in favour of the principle of providing Parliament with a role in approving the deployment of armed forces into armed conflict, but expressed varying degrees of concern about the practical difficulties that would be involved.

In March 2008, the government said that *'while not ruling out legislation [...] a detailed resolution is the best way forward'*.[59] A draft Constitutional Renewal Bill was laid before Parliament on 25 March 2008.[60] While dealing with aspects of the prerogative in connection with the ratification of treaties and the civil service, this made no mention of the prerogative relating to the deployment of the armed forces. A Joint Committee of the House of Commons and the House of Lords reported on the Bill on 22 July 2008, reiterating the need to strengthen parliamentary involvement in armed-conflict situations and agreeing that a *'detailed resolution approach is a well balanced and effective way of proceeding'* (para. 318).

(j) THE CONTINUING NEED FOR REFORM

The Constitutional Reform and Governance Act 2010 placed the civil service and the process for making treaties on a statutory footing. However, as expected, no changes were made to prerogative powers in relation to the armed forces. Although in its 'wider review' of prerogative powers, published in October 2009, the Labour government had stated that it was preparing a draft of a detailed House of Commons resolution setting out the processes that the House of Commons should follow in order to approve any deployment of the armed forces in conflicts overseas, no draft appeared before the general election in May 2010.

The Conservative Party's manifesto promised to make decisions to send troops abroad to fight "subject to greater democratic control" and to ensure that Parliament is properly

---

[59] *The Governance of Britain: Constitutional Renewal*, Cm 7342.
[60] On draft Bills, see Chapter 10.

involved. The Liberal Democrats were also in favour of reform. However, no pledge on this was contained in the Coalition Agreement.

In March 2011 the issue once again became prominent when the government decided to embark on air strikes in Libya without seeking Parliament's prior agreement or approval, although Parliament was asked after the intervention had begun. In the House of Commons William Hague, now Foreign Secretary, said that the government would "enshrine in law for the future the necessity of consulting Parliament on military action"[61] Since then the House of Commons Select Committee on Political and Constitutional Reform has continued to press the government on the need for reform and has called for this to be undertaken before the end of the current Parliament in 2015. The minister responsible for constitutional reform, Mark Harper, has responded by saying that "a number of important questions of detail" need to be addressed and these must be considered properly and could not be "driven by an artificial deadline".[62]

Graham Allen MP, chair of the House of Commons Political and Constitutional Reform Committee, has summarized the current situation in the following way:"To all intents and purposes, a Prime Minister has the same power over our forces as Henry V, although without the same obligation to lead them in person. Nearly six centuries after Agincourt, Parliament still has no formal or agreed role in the decision to war or the conduct and purposes of a war"[63]

QUESTIONS

1. 'The approach to reform of the prerogative power in relation to deployment of armed forces abroad has been significantly affected by the fear that placing this prerogative on a statutory footing would lead to litigation. The case law indicates that this fear is unwarranted. The courts are no more likely to review deployment decisions if rooted in statute than they have been to review such decisions in the past.' Discuss.

2. 'The process of reform of prerogative war powers, once again highlights the extent to which the UK constitution is based on convenience and convention rather than principle and law.' Assess the accuracy of this statement.

3. 'Another lesson to be drawn from the government's approach to reform in this area is that government will only move forward with constitutional reform in an area as sensitive as war powers if it can secure consensus. Here at least government follows but will not lead. This is as it should be.' Discuss.

4. On more than one occasion during this saga, the importance of parliamentary committees has been evident. How did parliamentary committees contribute to the reform process?

5. In 1973, despite a presidential veto, the US Congress resolved that the President can send US armed forces into action abroad only with the authority of Congress, unless the US is already under attack or under serious threat. The constitutional status of this resolution has remained controversial and presidents have consistently treated it as being unconstitutional. Are there any lessons here for the United Kingdom?

---

[61] Hansard HC 21 March 2011 Col 722

[62] Graham Allen MP, the chair of the Political and Constitutional Reform Committee LSE Policy and Politics Blog 6 December 2011. 'Parliament "war powers" must be law by 2015, say MPs', BBC 6 December 2011.

[63] Ibid.

6 CONCLUDING COMMENTS

This chapter has examined the meaning and the continuing significance of prerogative powers. It has seen how courts have extended their ability to review the exercise of prerogative powers. While many prerogatives have now been placed on a statutory footing there is broad consensus that further reforms in this area are needed to modernise the system and improve legal and political accountability. The case study on the prerogative relating to the deployment of the armed forces, however, has shown that reform can be very difficult to achieve. To keep abreast of further developments, you should visit the Online Resource Centre.

7 FURTHER READING

Hadfield, B., 'Judicial Review and the Prerogative Powers', in M. Sunkin and S. Payne (eds) *The Nature of the Crown* (1999, Oxford: OUP), ch. 8

Maer, L., and Gay, O., *The Royal Prerogative*, House of Commons Standard Note 30 December 2009 SN/PC03861 (available online at http://www.parliament.uk)

Ministry of Justice, *The Governance of Britain, Review of the Executive Royal Prerogative Powers: Final Report* (October 2009)

ONLINE RESOURCE CENTRE

Further information about the themes discussed in this chapter can be found on the Online Resource Centre at www.oxfordtextbooks.co.uk/orc/lesueur2e/

PART III

LEGISLATIVE
FUNCTIONS

INTRODUCTION TO LEGISLATIVE FUNCTIONS

CENTRAL ISSUES

1. Chapter 10, Chapter 11, Chapter 12 and Chapter 13 examine the legislative process and legislation.

2. A distinction is made between primary and delegated legislation.

3. Legislation is constitutionally important. It affects everyday life and it is not surprising that the power to legislate is a prized commodity.

4. Governments dominate the process of making legislation.

5. Judges have a role in interpreting and enforcing legislation. Even in the United Kingdom, they have a role in monitoring the validity of legislation.

1 INTRODUCTION

(a) STRUCTURE OF PART III OF THIS BOOK

This Introduction is an overview of the facts, skills, concepts, and themes that will be covered in Chapter 10 (Primary legislation),[1] Chapter 11 (Delegated legislation), Chapter 12 (European Union legislation), and Chapter 13 (a case study).

In Chapter 10, we examine the processes involved in making Acts of the UK Parliament. This includes: policymaking; consultation; drafting Bills; the work of the House of Commons and House of Lords in scrutinizing Bills; bringing legislation into force; and 'post-legislative scrutiny' (a relatively new initiative).

Chapter 11 looks at 'delegated legislation'—that is, rules that have the binding force of law made by ministers and other authorities, in which Parliament has a limited scrutiny role.

---

[1] A note on grammar: 'legislation' is a mass noun; it therefore has no plural form (so never write 'legislations').

In a typical year, around forty Acts of Parliament are enacted, whereas over 3,000 pieces of delegated legislation are made. From the perspective of constitutional systems that have a stronger adherence to the principle of separation of powers,[2] it may appear surprising that, in the United Kingdom, the government has such extensive legislative powers.

Chapter 12 examines the legislative process of the European Union. The United Kingdom's membership of the EU brought with it a new layer of law-making, which produces 'regulations' and 'directives' within the framework of powers created by the EU Treaties. This legislation takes precedence over inconsistent national legislation.[3] As we shall see, critics argue that there is a 'democracy deficit' in this law-making process—a deficit that might be addressed if further reforms to the Treaties are implemented to give national parliaments a more formal role.

Chapter 13 is a case study designed to bring together and develop several key themes—notably, the relationship between the House of Commons and House of Lords in the legislative process. Hunting (especially of foxes) with dogs is, depending on your perspective, either a traditional country pursuit or an unspeakably cruel activity. The Hunting Act 2004 banned it, but only after protracted legislative battles in which the House of Lords (the Upper Chamber) refused on several occasions to pass government Bills seeking to outlaw it. Eventually, the Parliament Act 1911 (as amended in 1949) was used to enable the Bill to become law despite the Lords' continuing opposition. The Law Lords were called on to adjudicate on whether this was constitutional.

(b) LEGISLATION AND DEVOLUTION

Since 1998, devolution has resulted in three new legislative bodies: the Scottish Parliament; the Northern Ireland Assembly; and the National Assembly for Wales (see Box III.2 for overviews of these institutions). The asymmetric character of devolution[4] has the consequence that England has no legislature separate from that of the whole United Kingdom—that is, the UK Parliament. As we will see, this has given rise to the 'English question': in a nutshell, whether only members of Parliament (MPs) representing constituencies in England should vote on Bills that apply only to England.[5]

2 DEFINITIONS

Chapter 10, Chapter 11, Chapter 12, and Chapter 13 are concerned with *processes* (the legislative process) and *a source of law* (legislation), which is the outcome of the legislative process. What exactly are these?

---

[2] On separation of powers, see Chapter 4.
[3] See Chapter 18.
[4] See Chapter 5.
[5] See Chapter 5 and Chapter 10.

David Feldman, 'The impact of human rights on the UK legislative process' (2004) 24 Statute Law Review 91, 92

[The legislative process] signifies the complex series of events by which the legal implications of a policy or objective are identified, changes to legal rules are drafted in a form intended to be understood by lawyers, officials and (perhaps) ordinary people, and both the policy and the proposed new legal norms are subjected to parliamentary scrutiny and amendment before being accepted or rejected. It does not include the processes of implementing and interpreting the law once made, but the demands of those processes are (or should be) in the minds of everyone who is involved in the legislative process.

In examining the legislative process, it is salutary to bear in mind a saying, often misattributed to Otto von Bismarck: '*Laws, like sausages, cease to inspire respect in proportion as we know how they are made.*' The legislative process provides opportunities for democratic debate, but, as we shall see, critics often express concern that the making of legislation is a rushed affair in which the public and parliamentarians have too little time and influence.

And what, exactly, do we mean by 'legislation'?

T. St J. Bates, 'Legislation', in P. Cane and J. Conaghan (eds) *New Oxford Companion to Law* (2008, Oxford: OUP), p. 726

Legislation consists of written rules of law which are authoritatively ratified; it is an ancient form of law and examples are found in early Sumeria. In the modern state, legislation is commonly enacted or authorized by the Parliament, and takes precedence over conflicting rules or principles developed by the courts, but not over the written constitution of the state nor, in certain circumstances, certain of its international legal obligations.

The United Kingdom does not have a 'written constitution' in the sense referred to by Bates, so Acts of the UK Parliament are the highest form of law. This is the central feature of the principle of parliamentary supremacy, as we noted in Chapter 2.

(a) PUBLIC AND PRIVATE LEGISLATION DISTINGUISHED

The rules contained in public legislation should be of a general character, not aimed at a specific person. So it would not be constitutionally acceptable in the modern era for Parliament to enact legislation to impose a specific punishment on a particular person (as it did in 1531 when Henry VIII procured legislation declaring the Bishop of Rochester's cook guilty of treason by poisoning and ordering that he be put to death by boiling alive).

That said, sometimes legislation is passed that is specific to an organization (for example, a university, local authority, or company). These are 'private Acts of Parliament'[6] rather than the normal 'public Acts'. A Bill that contains both public and private provisions is called a 'hybrid Bill'. Special procedures exist for dealing with such legislation, involving hearings before a special committee, at which individuals and organizations directly affected by the

---

[6] Not to be confused with private member's Bills (on which, see Chapter 10).

private aspects may petition Parliament to oppose the Bill and may make representations (usually through counsel) to special committees.

BOX III.1 EXAMPLES OF PRIVATE AND HYBRID BILLS

- The Crossrail Bill 2007 (hybrid)—to secure the powers necessary to build a new railway line across London, including compulsory purchase powers.
- Kent County Council (Filming on Highways) Act 2010 (private) to give the local authority powers to close roads.

(b) PRIMARY AND SECONDARY LEGISLATION DISTINGUISHED

The terminology of 'primary' and 'secondary' (also called 'delegated', or 'subordinate') legislation will be used frequently, so it is worth starting by clarifying the distinctions between these two types (see Box III.2). In broad terms, 'primary legislation' is made by the legislative bodies of the United Kingdom: the UK Parliament; the Scottish Parliament; the Northern Ireland Assembly; and the National Assembly for Wales. 'Delegated legislation' is that legislation which is made by ministers (and sometimes other bodies) using powers that are delegated by the legislative bodies of the UK.

BOX III.2 MAIN TYPES OF LEGISLATION

	United Kingdom	Scotland	Wales	Northern Ireland	European Union
Government responsible for initiating the making of most legislation	UK Government	Scottish Government	National Assembly Government (Wales)	Northern Ireland Executive	EU institutions
Primary legislation	'Bills' introduced to UK Parliament, which, on royal assent, become 'Acts of Parliament'	'Bills' introduced to Scottish Parliament under Scotland Act 1998, s. 28, which, on royal assent, become 'Acts of the Scottish Parliament'	'Acts of the Assembly' made under Pt 4 of the Government of Wales Act 2006	'Acts' may be made by the Northern Ireland Assembly under Pt II of the Northern Ireland Act 1998	Treaty on European Union (TEU) and the Treaty on the Functioning of the EU (TFEU)

	United Kingdom	Scotland	Wales	Northern Ireland	European Union
Secondary legislation	UK statutory instruments (SIs) UK ministers given powers to make SIs by numerous Acts of Parliament	Scottish statutory instruments (SIs) Scotland Act 1998, Pt VI, gives Scottish ministers power to make 'subordinate legislation'	Welsh statutory instruments (SIs) Welsh ministers given powers to make orders and directions in the form of SIs	Northern Ireland statutory instruments (SIs)	Article 46 TFEU enables EU institutions to make 'regulations' and 'directives'

BOX III.3 PRIMARY AND SECONDARY LEGISLATION COMPARED

UK primary legislation	UK secondary legislation
'Bills' contain the text of proposed legislation. They are made up of numbered 'clauses'.	Also known as 'delegated' or 'subordinate' legislation, 'regulations', 'orders', and 'rules'.
A Bill is debated in each House of Parliament in turn, in a process involving a First Reading, Second Reading, Committee State, Report, and Third Reading.	Can only be made if an Act of Parliament provides ministers with a power to legislate on a given topic.
Once a Bill is approved by both Houses of Parliament, in practice, it automatically receives royal assent.	Most are made in the form of a 'statutory instrument' under general processes laid down by the Statutory Instruments Act 1949.
Thereafter, the legislation is known as an 'Act of Parliament' (or, more generically, 'a statute'). Clauses are known as 'sections'.	Delegated legislation is scrutinized by several parliamentary committees, but most are not subject to any debate and (unlike Bills) cannot be amended as they progress through Parliament

The terminology of 'primary' and 'secondary' legislation is also used in the context of the European Union (EU).[7] The treaties on which the EU is founded are 'primary legislation'; legislation made by the EU institutions in the form of regulations and directives is 'secondary'.

[7] See Chapter 12.

3 THE IMPORTANCE OF LEGISLATION

(a) IMPACT ON EVERYDAY LIFE

Although only a few obsessive lawyer types would see the world in this way, almost everything that we do in our daily lives is in some way regulated or facilitated by legislation. Consider the first hour in a typical day. The radio alarm clock goes off. The radio station is regulated by s. 67 of the Broadcasting Act 1996 and s. 314 of the Communications Act 2003. The electricity on which the clock runs it is regulated by the Office of Gas and Electricity Markets (Ofgem) and the Gas and Electricity Markets Authority (GEMA), which operate under legal frameworks established by the Electricity Act 1989, the Competition Act 1998, the Utilities Act 2000, the Enterprise Act 2002, and the Energy Act 2004. You have cornflakes and milk for breakfast: the information on the packets will be determined by a vast array of legislation, including the Food Safety Act 1990, the Food Labelling Regulations 1996 (SI 1996/1499), and the Food for Particular Nutritional Uses (Addition of Substances for Specific Nutritional Purposes) (England) Regulations 2002 (SI 2004/649)—much of which legislation is made to 'transpose' into national law EU legislation, such as Commission Directive 2004/5/EC,[8] amending Directive 2001/15/EC. We could go on ...

It would be madness to wake up every day and worry about our highly regulated lives. But when campaigns have to be waged or disputes resolved, it will be necessary for lawyers advising pressure groups, businesses, and individuals to know how to find relevant legislation, and to understand its legal significance.

Consider, for example, the following scenario. A lawyer is approached by a group of local farmers who want to start selling unpasteurized milk in their farm shops. Can they do so? Do they need a licence, and if so, from whom? What hygiene requirements would they have to follow? If they cannot sell unpasteurized milk in the way in which they want to, who would they lobby to get the law changed? Without knowledge of how legislation is made and where it can be found, giving advice would be impossible.

(b) THE USES OF LEGISLATION

For what purposes is legislation used? As we have seen, one of the main activities of government is to formulate and implement policy. In the case of the UK government, sometimes implementation can be achieved without new legislation (in cases in which there are sufficient powers authorizing executive action already on the 'statute book')[9] or without any legislative backing (in which cases prerogative or 'third source' powers are used).[10] But the pressure for new legislation is constant. Ministers and their departments view it as an important activity, and there is competition within government to secure time for a department's Bills in the crowded annual legislative programme. Outside government, pressure groups are constantly calling for new legislation in order to achieve the goals that they espouse (for example, better environmental protection and an end to cruelty to animals).

---

8 OJ No L14, 21 January 2004, p. 19.
9 Shorthand for all legislation; see http://www.legislation.gov.uk/.
10 See Chapter 9.

If you leaf through the statute book, you will see that legislation is in place for a wide range of purposes, including:

- **to set out public law rights**—for example, the Human Rights Act 1998, the Freedom of Information Act 2000, the Disability Discrimination Act 1995, and the Equality Act 2006;

- **to impose taxation**—the government cannot perform executive functions without access to funds, and tax can be levied only through legislation;

- **to create powers for public bodies to take action**—almost all public bodies created in recent years are 'creatures of statute', meaning that they have those powers (and only those powers) conferred on them by legislation;

- **the regulation of commercial activity**—one school of thought holds that there is simply too much legislation. In relation to the regulation of businesses, a cross-party consensus has emerged that 'red tape' (that is, legislation) should be minimized. A programme of 'regulatory reform' has been in operation for several years to review the regulatory requirements with which we could dispense;[11] and

- **social control**—traditionally, this has been through the creation of criminal offences; in more recent years, the courts have been empowered to make a wide range of preventative injunctions (such as antisocial behaviour orders).

QUESTIONS

1. Identify a piece of legislation that you would like to see repealed or amended. How would you set about achieving this?

2. Look at the output of Acts of Parliament over the last year or two at http://www.opsi. gov.uk/acts.htm. What other reasons for making legislation can you suggest in addition to those we have listed?

(c) STRUGGLES OVER LEGISLATIVE POWER

Because legislation provides legal authority for action by public bodies, politicians and pressure groups are keen to control or influence the process by which legislation is made. It should therefore be no surprise that there are power struggles. Some of the main constitutional debates can be understood as arguments about who has power to legislate.

Power within the UK Parliament

In the UK Parliament, there are two main battles over who controls the legislative process. First, critics say that the parliamentarians who form the government (that is, the ministers) have too much power compared to other parliamentarians (that is, backbench MPs and peers from all parties). It is government (not Parliament) that develops policy and drafts the text of proposed legislation. Government also controls the timetable by which Bills are scrutinized in the House of Commons—as a result of which, Bills are rushed through without proper scrutiny.

---

[11] See Chapter 11, on the Legislative and Regulatory Reform Act 2006.

Second, there are tensions between the two chambers, which we explore in Chapter 13. There is broad consensus that the Commons, as the elected part of Parliament, should have primacy—but the limited reforms that have taken place to the membership of the Lords (fewer Conservative hereditary peers and a more robust appointments system) has seen the Lords growing in confidence and in its ability to scrutinize government Bills. A government with a majority of MPs in the Commons may effectively control that chamber (because MPs from the governing party can be expected to support ministers), but there is no automatic government majority in the Lords when voting on Bills. The House of Commons can insist that a Bill receives royal assent even though the House of Lords disagrees with it—although it remains uncertain whether there are some limits to this power.[12]

The UK Parliament and the devolved legislatures

Legislative powers (of varying degrees) have been conferred by the UK Parliament on the Scottish Parliament, the Northern Ireland Assembly, and the National Assembly for Wales. Since 1998, greater powers to legislate have been given to Wales now under Pt 4 of the Government of Wales Act 2006.[13] Meanwhile, in the north of the United Kingdom, the legislative powers of the Scottish Parliament were extended by the Scotland Act 2012 and further powers remain high on the political agenda. In Northern Ireland, the transfer of law-making powers has been of crucial significance since 1998. Despite, or perhaps because of, all of these relatively recent innovations, the devolution Acts carefully spell out that the grant of legislative powers *does not affect the power of the Parliament of the United Kingdom to make laws* for those parts of the United Kingdom.[14]

The European Union and the United Kingdom

Over those fields of policy and law for which it has 'competence',[15] legislation made by the European Union has primacy over any inconsistent national law—and, in the event of a dispute, all national courts are required to adjudicate on the matter and, if necessary, 'disapply' the offending provision in national law. Moreover, member states are required to legislate to 'transpose' EU directives into national law. As we will see, this constitutional arrangement has sparked a range of responses.

(a) This may be seen as no more than a necessary consequence of a welcome political process of economic and political integration between the member states. The European Court of Justice (ECJ) had the following to say on the matter.

Case 6/64 *Falminio Costa v ENEL*
[1964] ECR 585, 593[16]

[... T]he law stemming from the treaty [establishing the European Community], an independent source of law, could not, because of its special and original nature, be overridden by domestic legal provisions, however framed, without being deprived of its character as community law and without the legal basis of the community itself being called into question.

---

[12] See Chapter 12.   [13] See Chapter 5.   [14] See Chapter 2 and Chapter 5.   [15] See Chapter 12.
[16] See further Chapter 18.

(b) The legal supremacy of EU law over national law may not be constitutionally objectionable in itself, but what is of concern is the 'democracy deficit' that makes the EU policy and law-making processes insufficiently responsive to public opinion, and at the same time has reduced the influence of elected representatives within national parliaments.

(c) It is wholly unacceptable that the UK Parliament has become subservient to the EU institutions. UKIP makes the following claim.

United Kingdom Independence Party, How We Are Governed: A Constitutional And Governmental Policy for an Independent Britain—A Policy Statement (July 2008)

Under both Labour and the Conservatives, Britain has surrendered so many powers to the UK that Westminster only generates around 20% of its own laws now. In Germany, the 84% of its laws originating from the EU there caused President Herzog to conclude: "The question has to be raised of whether Germany can still unreservedly be called a parliamentary democracy.' The same question can be asked of Britain—do we still have a working Parliamentary democracy? Or is Westminster well on the road to becoming a waxworks museum within a new European Superstate?"

QUESTION
Which, if any, of the propositions in the extract given most closely fits your own view?

---

4 SKILLS

Lawyers may need to find out several things about a piece of legislation. The development of the Internet has helped to make practical research easier, but some advanced skills are needed to find and understand the significance of legislative information.

(a) FINDING THE TEXT

The first task is to find the text of the piece of legislation in which you are interested.

- The National Archives manages the UK Statute Law Database (available online at http://www.legislation.gov.uk/), which is an official edition of the primary and secondary legislation.
- The British and Irish Legal Information Institute (BAILII), a charity, also makes texts of legislation available online at http://www.bailii.org
- For EU legislation, EUR-Lex provides free access online at http://eur-lex.europa.eu/en/index.htm.

(b) WORKING OUT WHETHER THE LEGISLATION IS IN FORCE

A second task is to work out whether the legislation is 'in force'—in other words, legally operative. An Act comes into force (a) immediately after royal assent, or (b) on a specific date set out in the Act, or (c) the Act may leave the decision as to when a piece of legislation is to be given binding force to the government—in other words, while *Parliament* enacts legislation, *government* often decides whether it is legally binding in practice. When scenario (c) applies, government brings primary legislation into force by making a piece of delegated legislation often known as a 'commencement order'.[17]

In principle, http://www.legislation.gov.uk/ should show whether a provision is in force, and if so, on what date; commercial law databases such as LexisNexis and Westlaw also do so. But a competent lawyer needs to know how to work out for him or herself whether legislation is in force, which requires that he or she:

(a) looks at the Act in question to find the 'commencement' provisions, which will be among the last sections;

(b) understands what the commencement provisions say; and

(c) if the commencement provisions allow discretion to the government to decide when sections come into force, finds the relevant commencement order. If there is no commencement order, it is not in force.

(c) RESEARCHING WHAT WAS SAID AND DONE DURING THE LEGISLATIVE PROCESS

You may think that once the sausage pops out of the machine (that is, once the legislation is made), there is little need to go back over what was said and done. As we will see, the 'enrolled Act rule' means that the courts never adjudicate on allegations of procedural irregularities in the legislative process for primary legislation,[18] although they do so in relation to delegated legislation.[19]

From time to time, however, there may be a practical or academic need to do this. A third necessary task may therefore be to find out what was said about the piece of legislation as it progressed through the legislative process. There may be a specific and practical need to do this as an aid to statutory interpretation. As we will see, the general approach of the courts is to give legislation a 'purposive construction'.[20] This can involve looking at Green Papers and White Papers. It may require reference to be made to the 'explanatory notes' that government lawyers write to accompany Bills.

Controversially, reference may also be made in some situations to statements made by minsters in Parliament, under the rule in *Pepper (Her Majesty's Inspector of Taxes) v Hart*,[21] in which a schoolteacher challenged the interpretation adopted by the Inland Revenue of provisions relating to how subsidized school places were valued for tax purposes. One of the most convenient ways of tracking down what was said during a Bill's passage through

---

[17] See Chapter 11.   18 See Chapter 2.   19 See Chapter 11.   20 See Chapter 16.   21 [1993] AC 593.

Parliament—at least for Bills in recent years—is the 'Bills before Parliament' page, available online at http://services.parliament.uk/bills.

(d) UNDERSTANDING AND EXPLAINING COMPLEX SYSTEMS

Studying public law requires a wider range of skills than does the study of many other legal subjects. As you tackle the chapters in Part III, you should be aware of the types of skill that you are being asked to deploy and develop, including:

(a) understanding how a complex network of institutions and processes operates (in this part of the book, the legislative process), and being able to communicate this to others succinctly;

(b) having an awareness of the historical and political contexts of the institutions and processes; and

(c) handling rules that are constitutional conventions by defining and applying them.

5 LEGISLATURES

Much of the focus of Chapter 10, Chapter 11, Chapter 12, and Chapter 13 will be on the operation of the legislatures. These institutions comprise elected representatives of the people, with the exception of the House of Lords. As Philip Norton—an academic and Conservative member of the House of Lords—says, 'Parliament matters'.

Philip Norton 'Reforming Parliament in the United Kingdom: The Report of the Commission to Strengthen Parliament' (2000) 6 Journal of Legislative Studies 1, 2

Our starting point was to establish that Parliament matters. It matters to the citizen and it matters to government. It matters to the citizen because it is the key, and authoritative, link between the citizen and government. It ensures that government is questioned and forced to justify itself. It makes sure that the voices of citizens are heard. It matters to government because government is elected through Parliament and its political authority rests on that very fact. Undermine Parliament and, in the long term, you undermine the authority of government, making it more difficult for it to mobilise support for its measures. Government may also benefit from critical scrutiny afforded its measures, ensuring that measures are enacted only after being subjected to informed and rigorous scrutiny. Good government needs an effective Parliament.

Our focus in these coming chapters is on the *legislative function* of parliaments—the scrutiny of proposed legislation and its formal 'enactment'. But it is important to recognize that they have several other constitutional roles beyond the making of legislation.

- **Representative function**—Parliaments are constituted to represent the interests of constituencies and the will of the people as a whole (the nation). They ensure that the voices of citizens, individually and collectively, are heard and that, where necessary, a redress of grievance is achieved.
- **Elective function**—The House of Commons and the devolved legislatures are elected by the people. In turn, they create and sustain a government and, if necessary, they may withdraw their support through votes of confidence. In a parliamentary constitution, all ministers must be MPs.
- **Scrutinizing government**—The parliaments scrutinize proposals from, and the conduct of, government on behalf of citizens and hold the government to account for its actions. Many of these proposals are in the form of proposed legislation, but as we have seen, governments have a great deal of scope to carry out executive functions under already existing legislation (and, in the case of the UK central government, the prerogative).[22]

Chapter 10, Chapter 11, Chapter 12, and Chapter 13 will examine the work of five legislative institutions. This section introduces some basic facts about each of them. Refer back to these mini-descriptions as you use the chapters that follow. You may also find it helpful to complete a 'compare and contrast' exercise by answering the questions at the end of this introduction.

BOX III.4 THE UK PARLIAMENT

Figure III.1 The House of Commons

---

[22] See Chapter 9.

Figure III.2 The House of Lords

Figure III.3 The Palace of Westminster ©Dhuss/istocksphoto.com

Location: Palace of Westminster, London

Website: http://www.parliament.uk/

House of Commons

Membership: 650 MPs are elected to represent geographical constituencies of some 68,000 electors (the boundaries of which are revised from time to time by the Boundary Commissions—independent bodies in England, Wales, Scotland, and Northern Ireland).

Electoral cycle: The Fixed-term Parliament Act 2011 requires a general election to be held every five years. The next scheduled election will be on 7 May 2015.

Electoral system: A 'first past the post' system dictates that, in each constituency, the candidate with the most votes (even if not a majority) is elected.

Franchise: Those aged 18 and over are entitled to vote provided that they are British citizens, Irish citizens, or 'qualifying Commonwealth citizens' resident in the United Kingdom. Overseas British nationals can vote for up to fifteen years after the date of their moving and a 'declaration of local connection' to the constituency can be made by those who are homeless. The electoral franchise is governed by the Representation of the People Act 1983, as amended.

Party-political composition at recent elections:

	Labour	Conservative	Lib Dems	Others	Total	Government
1997	418	165	46	30	659	Labour (majority 179)
2001	413	166	52	28	659	Labour (majority 167)
2005	356	198	62	30	646	Labour (majority 66)
2010	258	306	57	28	649	Conservative–Lib Dem coalition

House of Lords

Membership: Approximately 760 peers (there is no fixed number), of whom around 600 are appointed under the Life Peerages Act 1958; ninety-two hold life peerages under the terms of the House of Lords Act 1999 (from among those people who hold hereditary peerages, which no longer in itself entitles a person to sit in the Lords) and twenty-six are bishops in the Church of England. Members of the judiciary who hold peerages (for example, members of the UK Supreme Court) are disqualified from sitting in the Lords while they are serving judges.

Electoral cycle: None

Electoral system: None

Franchise: Not applicable.

Party-political composition:

	Labour	Conservative	Lib Dems	Cross-benchers	Others	Bishops	Total
Snapshot in December 1998	176	475	69	322	124		1,166 (includes 759 hereditaries)
Snapshot in December 2012	224	212	90	175	32	26	759 (includes 92 hereditaries)

BOX III.5 THE SCOTTISH PARLIAMENT

©David Hills/istockphoto.com

Figure III.4 The Scottish Parliament Building, Edinburgh

Location: Holyrood House, Edinburgh

Website: http://www.scottish.parliament.uk/

Membership: 129 members of the Scottish Parliament (MSPs), comprising seventy-three constituency members and fifty-six regional members.

Electoral cycle: Four-year fixed terms unless at least eighty-six of the MSPs agree that the Parliament should be dissolved, or the post of First Minister is vacant for more than twenty-eight days.

Electoral system: There is an 'additional member' proportional representation system, in which electors have two votes. One vote is for an MSP for a geographical constituency (of which there are seventy-three) on a 'first past the post' basis; the other vote is for MSPs for a larger region (of which there are eight) on a party list quota basis. In other words, seats are allocating according to the share of the vote in the region.

Franchise: Those aged 18 and over are entitled to vote provided that they are British, Irish, Commonwealth, or EU citizens resident at an address in Scotland.

Source of power to legislate: It may legislate on all matters except the (extensive and important) 'reserved matters' listed in Sch. 5 to the Scotland Act 1998.

Party-political composition at recent elections:

	SNP	Labour	Con	Lib Dems	Others	Government
1999	35	56	18	17	0	Labour–Lib Dem coalition
2003	27	50	18	17	2	Labour–Lib Dem coalition
2007	47	46	17	16	2	SNP minority
2011	53	15	3	2	0	SNP majority

BOX III.6 THE NORTHERN IRELAND ASSEMBLY

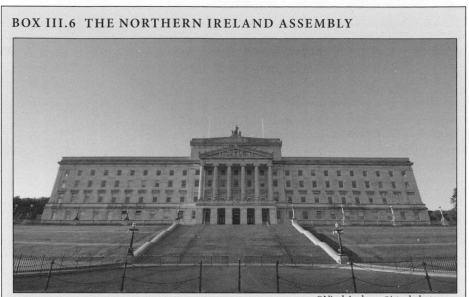

©Nigel Andrews@istockphoto.com

Figure III.5 The Northern Ireland Assembly

Location: Parliament Buildings, Stormont, Belfast

Website: http://www.niassembly.gov.uk

Membership: 108 members of the Legislative Assembly (MLAs)

Electoral cycle: Four-year fixed terms

Electoral system: It is a single transferable vote system, within which MLAs are elected from eighteen six-member constituencies. A voter ranks the candidates in order of preference. Seats are allocated according to a quota system.

Franchise: Those aged 18 and over are entitled to vote provided that they are British, Irish, Commonwealth, or EU citizens resident in Northern Ireland.

Source of power to legislate: Under the Northern Ireland Act 1998, there are three categories of policy: 'transferred matters' (on which the NIA may legislate); 'reserved matters' (the NIA may legislate on those that have been transferred); and 'excepted matters' (on which only the UK Parliament may legislate).

Party-political composition at recent elections:

	UU	SDLP	DUP	SF	A	Others	Executive
1998	28	24	20	18	6	12	Coalition of four largest parties
Devolution suspended on four occasions, the last in October 2002							
2003	27	18	30	24	6	0	Not formed
Devolution remained suspended until May 2007							
2007	19	16	36	24	7	0	Coalition of four largest parties
2011	16	14	38	29	8	3	Five parties represented

A = Alliance

DUP = Democratic Unionist Party

SDLP = Social Democratic and Labour Party

SF = Sinn Féin

UU = Ulster Unionist

BOX III.7 THE NATIONAL ASSEMBLY FOR WALES

© Ian Jeffrey/istockphoto.com

© Daiphoto/istockphoto.com

Figure III.6 National Assembly for Wales

Location: Parliament Buildings, Cardiff Bay, Cardiff

Website: http://www.assemblywales.org/

Membership: 60 Assembly members (AMs), comprising forty constituency AMs and twenty regional members

Electoral cycle: First Thursday in May every four years; next election due in 2011.

Electoral system: An 'additional member' proportional representation system applies, in which electors have two votes. One vote is for an AM for a geographical constituency (of which there are forty) on a 'first past the post' basis; the other vote is for an AM for a larger region (of which there are five) on a party list quota basis. In other words, seats are allocating according to the share of the vote in the region.

Franchise: Those aged 18 and over are entitled to vote provided that they are British, Irish, Commonwealth, or EU citizens resident at an address in Wales.

Source of power to legislate: Government of Wales Act 2006, Pt 4. The National Assembly for Wales may enact Acts of the Assembly in those areas of policy that are listed in Sch. 7:

Party-political composition at recent elections:

	Labour	Plaid Cymru	Conservative	Lib Dem	Other	Government
1999	27	17	9	6	0	Labour–Lib Dem coalition
2003	30	5	1	3	1	Labour
2007	26	15	12	6	1	Labour–Plaid Cymru coalition
2011	30	11	14	5	0	Labour minority

BOX III.8 THE EUROPEAN PARLIAMENT (FROM A UK PERSPECTIVE)

© LUke1138/istockphoto.com

Figure III.7 The European Parliament, Strasbourg

Location: Louise Weiss Building, Strasbourg, France, and Espace Léopold/Leopoldruimte, Brussels, Belgium

Website: http://www.europarl.europa.eu/

Membership: The United Kingdom elects seventy-two members of the European Parliament (MEPs) out of the total 736. Under Art. 14 of the Lisbon Treaty, the total number of seats is capped at 750.

Electoral cycle: Every five years; the next election is due in 2014.

Electoral system: The United Kingdom is divided into regions comprising: Northern Ireland (one region); Scotland (one region); Wales (one region); and England (nine regions). The number of MEPs representing each region varies between three and ten according to population. In England, Wales, and Scotland, MEPs are elected under a 'closed list' system of proportional representation, with people placing a cross next to the party that they support. In Northern Ireland, the proportional representation system used is the single transferable vote, within which votes rank candidates in order of preference.

Franchise: In the currently twenty-seven member states, there are approximately 375 million eligible voters (2009).

Source of power to legislate: Treaty on European Union (TEU) and Treaty Establishing the European Community (TEC), incorporated into UK law by the European Communities Act 1972.

Party-political composition: MEPs sit in party groupings rather than in national blocks. After the 2009 election, the groups were as follows. A small number of MEPs do not belong to any group.

Block	Politics[23]	Total MEPs	UK MEPs
European People's Party	'[...] committed to a federal Europe, based on the principle of subsidiarity—a democratic, transparent and efficient Europe'	265	No UK members
Progressive Alliance of Socialists and Democrats	'Campaigning for social justice, leading the economic recovery, reforming financial markets, fighting climate change, championing equality and creating a stronger and more democratic Europe [...]'	184	Thirteen Labour
Alliance of Liberals and Democrats for Europe	'We stand for individual liberty, a free and dynamic business culture, economic and social solidarity, sustainability in taking actions, protection of the environment and tolerance for cultural, religious and linguistic diversity'	84	Four Liberal Democrats
The Greens–European Free Alliance	'A European parliamentary group made up of Greens and representatives of stateless nations and disadvantaged minorities'	55	Two Greens Two SNP One Plaid Cymru
European Conservatives and Reformists	Conservative, Eurosceptic: 'The sovereign integrity of the nation state, opposition to EU federalism and a renewed respect for true subsidiarity'	54	Twenty-five Conservatives
European United Left–Nordic Green Left	Eco-socialist: 'firmly committed to European integration, although in a different form from the existing model'	34	One Sinn Féin
Europe of Freedom and Democracy	Conservative, Eurosceptic, 'rejects the bureaucratization of Europe and the creation of a single centralized European superstate'	32	Eleven UKIP

QUESTION

Advise the following four adults, none of whom are British, but all of whom are permanently resident in the United Kingdom, on the parliamentary elections in which they can vote:

- Virginie is a French national resident in Glasgow, Scotland;
- Wen is an Australian national living in Swansea, Wales;
- Franz is a Norwegian national living in Derry, Northern Ireland; and
- Adrian is an Irish citizen living in Birmingham, England.

23 Sourced from the website of each block.

6 THE EXECUTIVE AND LEGISLATION

The overwhelming proportion of Bills that reach the UK statute book are *government Bills*—in other words, they are designed to implement government policy. In the United Kingdom, legislative drafting is an executive function. Bills are produced by a team of around fifty highly specialist government lawyers based in Whitehall, called 'parliamentary counsel'. (We note in Chapter 11 that most delegated legislation is drafted by government lawyers within departments.) Bills are *not* drafted by lawyers employed by Parliament. Government ministers—one in the Commons, one in the Lords—steer the Bill through the various stages that it must navigate. Most of the amendments made to Bills during this process are actually proposed by ministers, not by other MPs and peers. And the government has a great deal of control of the speed at which a Bill proceeds.[24] Especially in the Commons—but less so in the Lords—the government is able to call a halt to debate and scrutiny of a Bill, and call on the MPs of its party to vote for the Bill to progress to the next stage. As a result, Bills quite often receive inadequate scrutiny.[25]

BOX III.9 COMPARISON WITH ANOTHER SYSTEM

Some constitutional systems have different arrangements. For example, in the USA, no member of the executive may sit in Congress, so there is no possibility of the executive branch of government introducing and steering a Bill through the US legislative process. In the USA, committees of the House of Representatives and of the Senate play a dominant role in both drafting and scrutinizing legislative proposals—but that is not the British way.

One key theme of Chapter 10, Chapter 11, Chapter 12, and Chapter 13 is that *governments* have a decisive role in the legislative process. To say in relation to the United Kingdom that 'Parliament is the legislature' may be formally true,[26] but significantly underplays the role of the UK government in policymaking, drafting legislation, controlling the timetable by which proposed legislation is scrutinized, deciding when Acts of Parliament actually come into force, and making 'delegated legislation'. Government is intimately involved in all of the aspects of legislation. Many critics—even, on occasion, the government itself—argue that this is a problem and that reforms are needed to help the UK Parliament operate more effectively at arm's length from government in scrutinizing and approving or rejecting the government's legislative proposals.

7 THE JUDICIARY AND LEGISLATION

The *judiciary* also has a role in relation to legislation. Most obviously, it is involved in interpreting legislation, and enforcing rights and duties contained in legislation.[27] As we have already seen, in designing a constitutional system, decisions have to be made as to when (if at all) the judiciary should have power to limit the law-making powers of

---

[24] See Chapter 10.
[25] Strictly speaking, it is 'the Queen in Parliament'.
[26] See Chapter 17.
[27] See Chapter 2.

legislatures. In the past in the United Kingdom, it was said that the principle of parliamentary supremacy meant that judges in Britain could not adjudicate on the validity of legislation—in contrast to many other constitutional systems, in which one of the roles of courts is to decide whether legislation is valid. We have seen that the kernel of the principle of parliamentary supremacy is still adhered to in the United Kingdom and that judges have no *general* power to decide that legislation is invalid.[28] If, however, we think about legislation generally, we can see that courts can be called on to adjudicate in several different situations, as follows.

(a) Any court in the United Kingdom—from the highest to the lowest—has a legal duty to deal with submissions that national law is inconsistent with EU law covering the same subject; if the court agrees with the submission, it *must* 'disapply' the offending provision in national law, even if that is a section of an Act of Parliament.

(b) Senior courts in the United Kingdom have power to hear arguments that a section in an Act of Parliament is incompatible with a Convention right under the Human Rights Act 1998; if the court agrees, it *may* make a declaration to that effect (although the offending provision remains legally valid).

(c) Courts may be called on to consider whether an Act of Parliament that received royal assent under the terms of the Parliament Acts (that is, without the consent of the House of Lords) is a valid statute.[29]

(d) Acts of the Scottish Parliament, Acts of the Northern Ireland Assembly, and Assembly Measures in Wales (the legislation made by the devolved legislatures) will be *quashed* by the senior courts in those parts of the United Kingdom or the UK Supreme Court if they are incompatible with Convention rights or EU law, or otherwise outside the powers conferred by the Scotland Act 1998, the Northern Ireland Act 1998, or the Government of Wales Act 2006.

(e) The principle of parliamentary supremacy does not stop the courts from considering whether delegated legislation—made by ministers, usually with minimal parliamentary oversight—is lawful. The normal grounds of judicial review apply (that is, illegality, procedural impropriety, irrationality, and the Human Rights Act 1998) and the court may make a quashing order if it finds a legal flaw.

Outside the United Kingdom, other courts have influence on the legislative process. The ECJ (the EU court) has power to consider whether legislation made by the EU in the form of directives and regulations conforms with the terms of the foundational treaties (principally, the TEU and the TEC). The ECJ will not rule directly on the question of whether national legislation is contrary to EU law, but it does make 'preliminary rulings' to guide national courts in their task of determining this question—see (a).

The European Court of Human Rights (the Council of Europe's court) may also be called on to consider whether national legislation breaches Convention rights.

[28] See Chapter 2.
[29] See Chapter 13.

8 WHERE TO GO FROM HERE

- If you want to read about primary legislation in the United Kingdom, turn to Chapter 10.
- For delegated legislation in the United Kingdom, turn to Chapter 11.
- Chapter 12 examines the EU legislative process.
- In Chapter 13, we examine the relationship between the House of Commons and the House of Lords.

10

PRIMARY LEGISLATION

CENTRAL ISSUES

1. Primary legislation—in the form of Acts of the UK Parliament—is one of the main ways in which government policy is put on a legal footing, enabling it to be implemented by public bodies.

2. Studying the legislative process sheds light on the practical application of the principles of parliamentary supremacy, the rule of law, and the separation of powers.

3. In formal terms, the legislature is 'the Queen in Parliament'. Almost all Bills are drafted by government; government controls the legislative process and government decides when Acts are brought into force. The role of Parliament is to scrutinize and occasionally to veto government proposals.

4. The consultation process enables the government to seek views on its proposals. The code governing consultation is not, however, legally binding and research reveals a degree of cynicism about what is achieved by consultation.

5. Bills are drafted by specialist government lawyers (parliamentary counsel). Some Bills are criticized for including unnecessary detail; others are criticized for being merely frameworks to be filled in later by ministers using powers to make delegated legislation.

6. Pre-legislative scrutiny, in which *draft* Bills are scrutinized by Parliament, is widely accepted to be a good idea—but government willingness to publish Bills in draft has varied in recent years.

7. The legislative process involves the House of Commons and House of Lords, in turn, debating and scrutinizing a Bill.

8. Doubts have been raised over the effectiveness of the scrutiny of Bills dealing with constitutional issues. Commentators suggest that a more systematic approach is needed.

9. Devolution has implications for the operation of the UK Parliament. The Scottish Parliament may (and does) give consent for the UK Parliament to legislate on matters that have been devolved to Scotland. Some politicians are concerned about the 'English question', asking why MPs from constituencies in Wales, Scotland, and Northern Ireland should be able to vote on Bills that will apply only to England.

1 INTRODUCTION

This chapter examines 'primary legislation', in the form of UK Acts of Parliament, and how they are made.

Studying legislation and the legislative process provides a good opportunity to think further about three of the key constitutional principles examined in Part I: parliamentary supremacy; the rule of law; and the separation of powers. By seeing how these principles operate in a particular context, it should be possible to achieve a deeper understanding of them.

(a) PARLIAMENTARY SUPREMACY

As we saw, the United Kingdom's constitutional set-up gives politicians, rather than the judiciary, the final say on whether an Act of Parliament is valid and should be recognized as binding law. The justification for this is generally said to be twofold.

First, the elections and the political process of making legislation are likely to lead to legislation that accords with the wishes of the electorate.

A.V. Dicey, *Introduction to the Study of the Law of the Constitution* (1885; 10th edn 1959, London: Macmillan & Co), p. 59

[... A]ny expressions which attribute to Parliamentary electors a legal part in the process of law-making are quite inconsistent with the view taken by the law of the position of the elector. The sole legal right of the electors under the English constitution is to elect members of Parliament. Electors have no legal means of initiating, of sanctioning, or of repealing the legislation of Parliament. No court will consider for a moment the argument that a law is invalid as being opposed to the opinion of the electorate; their opinion can be legally expressed through Parliament, and through Parliament alone.

[But Dicey goes on, however, to make the following assertion.]

[... W]e may assert that the arrangements of the constitution are now [he was writing in 1908] such as to ensure that the will of the electors shall by regular and constitutional means always in the end assert itself as the predominant influence in the country. But this is a political, not a legal fact. The electors can in the long run always enforce their will.

Dicey explains that, as a matter of politics (although not of law), members of Parliament (MPs) are subject to an 'external' limit on Parliament's legal power to legislate—that is, '*the possibility or certainty that* [...] *subjects, or a large number of them, will disobey or resist* [...] *laws*'.[30] There is also, he argued, an 'internal limit': each MP is '*moulded by the circumstances under which he lives, including under that head the moral feelings of the time and the society in which he belongs*'.

A second justification is that the legislative process is superior to the adjudicative processes of the courts for deliberating on and determining questions of public interest (which underpin every piece of legislation).

---

[30] See Dicey, pp. 76–7.

In assessing the extent to which there is an effective transmission mechanism between public views and what is enacted on the statute book, it needs to be recognized that *government* has a dominant role in the legislative process. Parliament may formally be the legislature for the whole United Kingdom, but it is the government that initiates policy, drafts Bills, steers Bills through the process, and often decides when (if at all) legislation is brought into force. To say that 'Parliament legislates' is, at best, a half-truth: formally, it is so—but in reality, it is the government that determines the content and timing of legislation.

A further factor that needs to be recognized is that the electoral system used for Commons' elections—that is, 'first past the post'—does not result in that House having a composition proportionate to the number of votes cast nationally for each of the political parties. Moreover, only one of the two Houses of Parliament (the Commons) is elected; the other (the Lords) is not. There may be good arguments in favour of first-past-the-post elections and an unelected second chamber, but ensuring that public opinion is reflected in the legislation that is passed is not one of them.

(b) RULE OF LAW

Ideas about the rule of law are relevant to legislation and the legislative process. As we saw,[31] there is a debate over the extent to which British judges *should* have power to adjudicate on the validity of Acts of Parliament. Since 1973, UK courts and tribunals have had powers to 'disapply' provisions in legislation that are not in accordance with European Community (now European Union) law.[32] Since the Human Rights Act 1998 came into force, the senior courts have also had powers to make 'declarations of incompatibility' in relation to provisions that are held to be contrary to Convention rights.[33] The 'legal constitutionalists' would like the courts to have *greater powers* to review legislation—including power to quash (rather than merely to 'declare incompatible') sections contrary to Convention rights and powers to strike down legislation that breaches other fundamental rights or principles.

There is another sense in which the rule of law comes into play and this relates to the way in which legislation confers power on *government*. Acts of Parliament often give ministers very broad discretionary powers to carry out executive action and to make rules in the form of delegated legislation.

(c) SEPARATION OF POWERS

Studying legislation and the legislative process also throws a searchlight on the principle of separation of powers. It should be clear from previous chapters that the United Kingdom does not adhere to any strict separation-of-powers arrangements (except for the associated principle of independence of the judiciary).[34] In fact, few countries do. Studying legislation and the legislative process is a good way of seeing just how muddy the waters are—in other words, the government is a dominant influence in the legislative process that leads to the enactment of an Act of Parliament; the government also has extensive power to make 'delegated legislation'. The following extract is written from a US perspective, but makes points that are relevant to the United Kingdom.

---

[31] See Chapter 2.   [32] See in more detail Chapter 18.   [33] See in more detail Chapter 5 and Chapter 17.
[34] See Chapter 4 and Chapter 14.

Jack Stark, 'The proper degree of generality for statutes' (2004) 25 Statute Law Review 77, 80

Looking from the perspective of political philosophy, counsel [the lawyers who draft legislation] will soon recognize the relevance to this problem of the concept of separation of powers, which has been cited in the discussion of always drafting generally and which, of course, is a bedrock of modern representative government. If the three branches of government ought to be distinctly separate, counsel should be wary of drafting very generally and thereby allocating to the judicial and executive branches considerable power to interpret the law. In effect granting that power, if the grant is broad enough, is indistinguishable from allocating legislative authority to the other branches of government. That chain of reasoning leads to the conclusion that, every other relevant consideration being set aside, counsel should ensure that they are drafting specifically enough. That is, they are well advised to move a little toward the specific end of the spectrum.

2 WHO OR WHAT IS THE 'LEGISLATURE'?

The process of making legislation is complex, although it is easy enough to state the basic elements of the system. We look at this in the next section. Before doing so, however, we should examine the main actors in the process.

The *government* takes a lead in many aspects of the process: ministers and civil servants develop policy initiatives; government lawyers draft Bills; ministers introduce Bills to Parliament and steer them through the House of Commons and the House of Lords, suggesting amendments along the way; often it is left to a Secretary of State to decide when an Act of Parliament should come into force.

The *Queen* has a formal involvement at two points. First, some Bills require 'Queen's consent' even to progress through Parliament. This situation arises in cases in which a Crown prerogative is involved. The Queen acts on the advice of ministers. Second, Bills require royal assent in order to become law; this is a formality. The requirement for royal assent makes the legislature, strictly speaking, 'the Queen in Parliament'—but the political reality is that Parliament (or, when the Parliament Act 1911 is invoked, the House of Commons) is the effective legislative body.

Sir Ivor Jennings, *The Law and the Constitution*, 5th edn (1959, London: University of London Press), pp. 137–8

The three parties to legislation

Technically speaking, laws are made by the Queen in Parliament, not by the Queen, the House of Lords and the House of Commons. In other words, laws are made at the curious ceremony which results when three noble lords, acting under a Commission from the Queen, seat themselves self consciously on the woolsack wearing their three-cornered hats. They send the Gentleman Usher of the Black Rod to request the attendance of the Commons [...].

> The Commons, as it happens, are discussing matters privately in their own Chamber; and, since they claim the right to do so, when Black Rod is seen approaching the door is shut in his face with studied discourtesy; for neither the Queen nor the Queen's messenger is allowed in except on the order of the House. Black Rod having tapped on the door three times, the Sergeant-at-Arms opens the wicket and asks, "Who's there ?" Having satisfied himself that it is not Her Majesty come with an armed guard to arrest the leaders of the Opposition, the Sergeant-at-Arms opens the door and allows Black Rod to do his bows and deliver his message; whereupon Mr. Speaker leads the Commons, or such of them as have not seen the show before, to attend the Lords Commissioners at the Bar of the House of Lords. The long title of the Bill being read, the Clerk of the Parliaments announces that "Le Reine le vault", and the Bill becomes an Act of Parliament.

Parliament's role is largely limited to scrutinizing the Bills introduced by ministers. MPs and peers may be involved in 'pre-legislative scrutiny' if a *draft* Bill is published, but in most cases, the first opportunity to examine a government Bill is at the point at which a minister formally introduces it to one of the Houses of Parliament (its 'First Reading'). Members of Parliament and peers also have limited opportunity to initiate legislation in the form of private member's Bills. The normal requirement is that a Bill is passed by both the House of Commons and the House of Lords before it may receive royal assent. A handful of Bills have, over the years, received royal assent under the terms of the Parliament Act 1911 (as amended in 1949), which permits royal assent to be given even though the Lords disagree with a Bill.[35]

These constitutional arrangements are reflected in the Preamble to each Act. The first applies to an Act passed in the normal way.

> Be it enacted by the Queen's most Excellent Majesty, by and with the advice and consent of the Lords Spiritual and Temporal, and Commons, in this present Parliament assembled, and by the authority of the same, as follows:—

A second type of Preamble is used if royal assent is received under the terms of the Parliament Acts.

> Be it enacted by The Queen's most Excellent Majesty, by and with the advice and consent of the Commons in this present Parliament assembled, in accordance with the provisions of the Parliament Acts 1911 and 1949, and by the authority of the same, as follows:—

3 POLICYMAKING

The main purpose of legislation is to give legal backing to government policies. Political scientists have spilt much ink over the definition and characteristics of 'policy'.[36] For the purposes of this chapter, we can say that government policy is an authoritative determination by ministers and civil servants of what will be done about something. Examples of that 'something' include: global warming; ensuring that British manufacturing industry survives the economic downturn; the challenge of ensuring financial support for older people in the context of an aging population; dealing with antisocial behaviour by young people; and so on.

---

[35] The operation of the Parliament Acts is examined in Chapter 13.
[36] A good starting point is H.K. Colebatch, *Policy* (1998, Buckingham: Open University Press).

S. James, *British Government: A Reader in Policy Making* (1997, London: Routledge), pp. 1–2

The policy making process

What is a policy? The working definition [. . .] is: a course of action which the government has taken a deliberate decision to adopt. This should be distinguished from a government's philosophy. A government comes into office with a certain set of ideas and values—its philosophy—and the government's policies are the practical plans through which that philosophy is translated into practice. So the Labour government came to power in 1974 with a philosophical intent of great social equality; increasing state pensions was one way of contributing to that aim. [. . .] A policy may be painstakingly constructed over years, or cobbled together in hours. And it is made in different ways on different subjects: the decisive way in which the government devised—and then scrapped—unit fines contrasts with the bumbling prevarication over the 1964 race relations bill. None the less, it is possible to chart a 'policy process', the various stages through which a policy will pass as it develops.

James suggests that there are six stages, as follows.

(a) A subject becomes an issue.
(b) The issue gets onto the policy agenda. (Other authors may group these two stages together as 'policy initiation'.)
(c) The government investigates an issue.
(d) The government takes a decision.
(e) There follow the stages of legislation and legitimization.
(f) The final stage is that of policy implementation and review.

For now, we are interested in stages (a)–(d)—in other words, the things that happen before a Bill is introduced to Parliament by the government. Of particular interest for us is what constitutional and legal constraints and incentives control these processes.

Policymaking takes place at many different speeds. Sometimes, the government feels the need to formulate a policy and seek to implement it very quickly. For example, on 18 June 2008, the Appellate Committee of the House of Lords (the forerunner of the UK Supreme Court) held that criminal courts did not have power to shield the identity of key prosecution witnesses from defendants and their lawyers, because this was contrary to a common law right for defendants to be able to face their accusers.[37] The government took the view that this was unacceptable, because there were serious problems with witness intimidation—particularly in gang-related crimes. A policy was rapidly decided; a Bill was drafted to reflect the government's policy; it was introduced to Parliament on 4 July 2008 and it received royal assent on 21 July 2008. A spate of 'fast tracked' Bills led the House of Lords Constitution Committee to conduct an inquiry into rapidly made legislation.[38] The Committee called for a requirement that ministers introducing Bills in these circumstances should make a statement explaining why fast-tracking was thought necessary, what consultation there has been with interested parties, and other matters. The Committee also recommended that there should be a presumption in favour of Bills that are being fast-tracked including a 'sunset

---

[37] See Chapter 3.
[38] House of Lords Constitution Committee, *Fast-track Legislation: Constitutional Implications and Safeguards*, Fifteenth Report of 2008–09, HL Paper 116.

clause', which would require the Act of Parliament to be debated and renewed after 18 months or some other specified period; it would continue in force only if that was approved by a positive vote. The Committee also recommended that Bills that had been fast-tracked through Parliament should be subject to post-legislative scrutiny ideally within one year.[39]

Normally, the development of policy and legislation takes much longer—sometimes years.

B. Jones, D. Kavanagh, M. Moran, and P. Norton, *Politics UK* (2004, Harlow: Pearson), p. 597

Each government decision has a long and complex provenance, but all must start somewhere. It is tempting to think that they originate, eureka-like, in the minds of single individuals, but they are more often the produce of debate or a general climate of opinion involving many minds. Policy initiatives, moreover, can originate in all parts of the political system. Setting the political agenda is a curiously elusive process. Items can be deliberately introduced by the government, and clearly it has many routes available to it, e.g. Tony Blair in the summer of 1999 announcing in an interview that fox hunting really would be banned. [...] The media too have enormous power to set the agenda: Michael Buerk's reports from Ethiopia detailing the scale of the family that touched the nation and initiated assistance. [...]

The public's role in policy making is usually limited to (the democratically vital function of) voting for a particular policy package at general elections. They do have other occasional opportunities, however, for example the referendums on the EC and Scottish and Welsh devolution [...], and pressures can be built up through lobbying MPs. Occasionally, events occur that create widespread public concern, and governments often take action in the wake of them. For example, legislation on dogs was enacted after a spate of attacks by dogs on children one summer in the 1980s, and after the Dunblane shootings of March 1996 handguns were banned. In many cases—as in the two just cited—such precipitate action, in reaction to the sudden rousing of public opinion, proves to be poorly framed and receives much criticism.

Consultation is a major aspect of the policymaking process (although it is easy to point to examples of situations in which the government has rushed ahead without proper consultation before announcing its final policy).[40]

For many years, the government has adopted various consultation practices. Typically, a Green Paper is published, outlining the government's initial views on a proposed policy, or setting out various policy options. A White Paper may follow some months later, in which the government lays out more firmly its policy plans on a given topic. Sometime later, a Bill will be introduced to Parliament (although bear in mind that not all policies will necessarily require new legislation to put them into practice).

---

[39] See Post-legislative scrutiny on p. 438.
[40] Such as its announcement to abolish the Lord Chancellor and create a UK Supreme Court: see Chapter 3 and Chapter 4.

C. Sandford, 'Open government: The use of Green Papers' (1980) British Tax Review 351

Green Papers were invented by the Labour Government in 1967. White Papers are of much earlier vintage. It is generally held that 'White Papers announce firm government policy for implementation. Green Papers announce tentative proposals for discussion.' Sir Harold Wilson wrote: 'A White Paper is essentially a statement of government policy in such terms that withdrawal or major amendment, following consultation or public debate, tends to be regarded as a humiliating withdrawal. A Green Paper represents the best that the government can propose on the given issue, but, remaining uncommitted, it is able without loss of face to leave its final decision open until it has been able to consider the public reaction to it'.

Consultation papers may be published in a variety of ways. Some are published informally on the relevant department's website; others are more formally published as 'Command Papers'.

Cabinet Office/Office of Public Sector Information, *How to Publish a Command Paper* (2006, London: HMSO)

1.1 Command Papers are Parliamentary Papers presented to the United Kingdom Parliament nominally by command of the Sovereign, but in practice by a Government Minister. The title derives from the formula originally carried on papers "Presented to Parliament by Command of Her (or His) Majesty". In recent years the approach has been to use the phrase: "Presented to Parliament by the Secretary of State for . . . . (or other title as appropriate) by Command of Her (or His) Majesty". Sometimes more than one Minister will present the Paper in which case all Ministers are listed, appearing in order of Cabinet precedence. In certain circumstances, e.g. reports produced by Royal Commissions, the original formula still applies.

1.2 Command Papers are papers of interest to Parliament where presentation to Parliament is not required by statute. The subjects may be, e.g.: major policy proposals and consultation documents (White and Green Papers), diplomatic documents such as treaties, Government responses to Select Committee reports (though these may be dealt with in correspondence with and subsequently published by the Committee), reports of major committees of inquiry or certain departmental reports or reviews and Draft Bills. There should, however, be a presumption that any Paper which will cause a statement to be made by a Minister or lead to a debate in Parliament should be published as a Command Paper.

In 2000, the government published for the first time a code on consultation. This extract is from the version issued in 2008.

HM Government, *Code of Practice on Consultation*, 3rd edn (2008, London: HMSO), pp. 4–6

Introduction

Ongoing dialogue between Government and stakeholders is an important part of policymaking. This dialogue will, at times, need to become more formal and more public. When developing a new policy or considering a change to existing policies, processes or practices, it will often be desirable to carry out a formal, time-bound, public, written consultation exercise. This kind of exercise should be open to anyone to respond but should be designed to seek views from those who would be affected by, or those who have a particular interest in, the new policy or change in policy. Formal consultation exercises can expose to scrutiny the Government's preliminary policy analysis and the policy or implementation options under consideration.

Status of the code

This Code sets out the approach the Government will take when it has decided to run a formal, written, public consultation exercise. It supersedes and replaces previous versions of the Code. The Code does not have legal force and cannot prevail over statutory or mandatory requirements. The Code sets out the Government's general policy on formal, public, written consultation exercises. A list of the UK departments and agencies adopting the Code is available on the Better Regulation Executive's website. Other public sector organisations are free to make use of this Code for their consultation purposes, but it does not apply to consultation exercises run by them unless they explicitly adopt it.

Ministers retain their existing discretion not to conduct formal consultation exercises under the terms of the Code. At times, a formal, written, public consultation will not be the most effective or proportionate way of seeking input from interested parties, e.g. when engaging with stakeholders very early in policy development (preceding formal consultation) or when the scope of an exercise is very narrow and the level of interest highly specialised. In such cases an exercise under this Code would not be appropriate. There is, moreover, a variety of other ways available to seek input from interested parties other than formal consultation. Such engagement work is not the subject of this Code. When departments decide only to carry out engagement with interested parties in ways other than formal, written consultation, they are encouraged to be clear about the reasons why the methods being used have been chosen.

Criterion 1 When to consult

Formal consultation should take place at a stage when there is scope to influence the policy outcome.

Criterion 2 Duration of consultation exercises

Consultations should normally last for at least 12 weeks with consideration given to longer timescales where feasible and sensible.

Criterion 3 Clarity of scope and impact

Consultation documents should be clear about the consultation process, what is being proposed, the scope to influence and the expected costs and benefits of the proposals.

Criterion 4 Accessibility of consultation exercises

Consultation exercises should be designed to be accessible to, and clearly targeted at, those people the exercise is intended to reach.

Criterion 5 The burden of consultation

Keeping the burden of consultation to a minimum is essential if consultations are to be effective and if consultees' buy-in to the process is to be obtained.

Criterion 6 Responsiveness of consultation exercises

Consultation responses should be analysed carefully and clear feedback should be provided to participants following the consultation.

Criterion 7 Capacity to consult

Officials running consultations should seek guidance in how to run an effective consultation exercise and share what they have learned from the experience.

Although the code says that it '*does not have legal force*', in a number of judicial review cases, attempts have been made to challenge the lawfulness of consultation exercises on the grounds that the terms of the code have not been followed. For example, in *R (on the application of Bhatt Murphy (a firm)) v The Independent Assessor*,[41] a firm of solicitors argued that the code had created a 'legitimate expectation' that there would be consultation by the government, according to the code, when it decided that it wanted to change the way in which victims of miscarriages of justice are compensated.[42]

R (on the application of Bhatt Murphy (a firm)) v The Independent Assessor
[2008] EWCA Civ 755

50. A very broad summary of the place of legitimate expectations in public law might be expressed as follows. The power of public authorities to change policy is constrained by the legal duty to be fair (and other constraints which the law imposes). A change of policy which would otherwise be legally unexceptionable may be held unfair by reason of prior action, or inaction, by the authority. If it has distinctly promised to consult those affected or potentially affected, then ordinarily it must consult (the paradigm case of procedural expectation). If it has distinctly promised to preserve existing policy for a specific person or group who would be substantially affected by the change, then ordinarily it must keep its promise (substantive expectation). If, without any promise, it has established a policy distinctly and substantially affecting a specific person or group who in the circumstances was in reason entitled to rely on its continuance and did so, then ordinarily it must consult before effecting any change (the secondary case of procedural expectation). To do otherwise, in any of these instances, would be to act so unfairly as to perpetrate an abuse of power.

---

[41] [2008] EWCA Civ. 755.
[42] On legitimate expectations, see further Chapter 16.

The Court of Appeal agreed with the judge at first instance (May LJ) and quoted his ruling with approval.

R (on the application of Bhatt Murphy (a firm)) v The Independent Assessor
[2007] EWCA Civ 1495, [23]–[24]

23 The Introduction states that the Code and the criteria apply to all public consultations by government departments and agencies. Mr Swift [counsel for the government, which had 'intervened' in the case] submits, correctly in my view, that this means that the Code is to apply whenever it is decided as a matter of policy to have a public consultation; not that public consultation is a required prelude to every policy change. The Code states that it does not have legal force but should generally be regarded as binding on United Kingdom departments and their agencies unless Ministers conclude that exceptional circumstances require a departure from it. Ministers retain their existing discretion not to conduct a formal written consultation exercise under the terms of the Code, for example where the issue is very specialised and where there is a very limited number of so-called stakeholders who have been directly involved in the policy development process.

24 For the reasons given by Mr Swift, I do not consider that it is possible to read this document as any form of governmental promise or undertaking that policy changes will never be made without consultation. It would be very surprising if it could be so read, not least because a decision in a particular case whether to consult is itself a policy decision. Rather the Code prescribes how generally public consultation should be conducted if there is to be public consultation.

In 2008, the Hansard Society (an educational charity seeking to strengthen parliamentary democracy and to encourage greater public involvement in politics) published the findings of a study on the legislative process. Its conclusions on the consultation phase are set out in the following extract.

Alex Brazier et al., *Law in the Making: Influence and Change in the Legislative Process* (2008, London: Hansard Society), p. 179

Growing cynicism

Although it can exert a noticeable influence on legislation, we found evidence of increasing evidence of cynicism about the consultation process. Many external groups questioned whether consultations are an effective means by which to influence policy, reporting that they vary considerably and do not always seem 'genuine'. While some departments have built up a reputation for regular and robust consultation, others are considered less effective or well-disposed toward gathering stakeholder input beyond 'trusted circles'; some make use of all the resources available, while others 'go through the motions'. One interviewee from a small charity criticised the predominant 'pro forma approach', which she feels at times 'seems designed with particular stakeholder groups in mind or to produce a particular set of responses'. These sentiments were echoed by many others. Even so, all of the stakeholders that we spoke to maintained that, at the very least, consultations enabled them to keep informed about the government's plans.

QUESTIONS

1. Explain how you would locate a Command Paper.

2. What is the status of the criteria in the government's Code of Practice on Consultation? Are they legally binding? Are they constitutional conventions? Or are they only non-binding assurances?

3. Suppose that your client is the Widget Manufactures Association, a group that campaigns for the interests of widget makers. It has only just noticed that a government department rushed out a consultation document on further regulation of widget making in the United Kingdom, giving only six weeks for responses to be received. That time has now passed. What advice would you give the Association?

4 DRAFTING BILLS

In the United Kingdom, there is a centralized system of drafting Bills. They are written by a team of just over sixty 'parliamentary counsel' (government lawyers) working from No. 36 Whitehall. They act on the basis of formal instructions sent by departments. Work is allocated to pairs or small teams of counsel. The first extract is from an article written by a senior and long-serving parliamentary counsel.

Geoffrey Bowman, 'Why is there a Parliamentary Counsel Office?' (2005) 26 Statute Law Review 69, 69, 81 (footnotes omitted)

Let me start with a homely insight into the drafter's mind. Some time ago a table in my room at work was sent away for french-polishing. When it came back it had a notice on it saying 'Nothing must be placed on this table.' I immediately thought that there were at least two things wrong. First, if nothing was to be placed on the table how did the notice get put onto it? And secondly, for how long was nothing to be put onto it? It defeats the object of a table if nothing can ever be put onto it. So I mentally redrafted the notice so that it read: 'Nothing (except this notice) must be placed on this table until such time as the french-polisher allows it.' But it does not stop there. What happens if the french-polisher dies or becomes ill or insane or goes out of business before he approves of the table's use? That may give you some idea of the slightly mad world that legislative drafters inhabit. [. . .]

The process of legislative drafting needs someone who will stand back; who will ruthlessly analyse the ideas; who will question everything with a view to producing something that stands up to scrutiny in Parliament and in the courts; who will break concepts down to their essential components; and who will then express them in easily digestible provisions and in language that is unambiguous, clear and simple. I think the Parliamentary Counsel Office achieves this by recruiting people with the right aptitude, and then by giving them a long and careful training. That is why we have a Parliamentary Counsel Office.

As for whether the job could be done by lawyers in private practice, it is interesting that there was an experiment in 1996 when part of the Finance Bill was drafted by private practitioners. It was not a success, and has not been repeated. As Daintith and Page say in their book *The Executive in the Constitution*: 'As well as being very expensive the contractors' work was thought to be opaque and "over-drafted".'

After researching the relevant field of law and analysing what it is the department seems to be seeking to achieve, drafting begins. Counsel hold meetings with department lawyers and officials as and when needed. Counsel see themselves as technicians rather than policy-makers. [...]

Edward C. Page, 'Their word is law: Parliamentary counsel and creative policy analysis' [2009] Public Law 790, 791 (footnotes omitted)

Earlier work on the officials in the UK charged with developing policy into legislation in bill teams, contained strong indications that parliamentary drafters of legislation had influenced the thinking of the policy officials responsible for its development. Moreover, in the UK system of government where few officials have any level of specialisation, the parliamentary drafter is a rare example of a specialist—a person with technical qualifications and experience who tends to make a career within the same small department. The drafting stage is likely to be the first at which the policy as a whole is subjected to a form of rigorous scrutiny, and a scrutiny with a high degree of legitimacy. If a drafter says that a policy cannot work it is taken extremely seriously. However, at present we can only hypothesise that the process of drafting shapes policy, and the central questions this paper addresses are: does it, and in what way? What sorts of policy issues get raised at this stage in the development of policy, how important are they and how are they resolved? [...]

Over the years, a drafting style has emerged in the United Kingdom that is markedly different from the 'continental' approach used in EU directives and in the legislation of most other member states. Generally, legislation in civil law jurisdictions tends to be simple, short, and concerned with setting down broad statements of principles and rules, whereas Acts of Parliament are inclined to be much more detailed and precise.

A criticism that has often been made of Acts of Parliament is that they are usually incomprehensible to non-lawyers, and sometimes even to lawyers, because of the complexity of their language, grammar, and structure. There may be several reasons for this. First, the statute may seek to give legal effect to a policy that itself is inherently highly complex.

Second, in some contexts, it may be important for people's rights and obligations to be spelt out with great precision so that they may plan their affairs accordingly. An aspect of the rule of law is that law needs to be certain and sometimes certainty may go hand in hand with complexity. This is particularly so where a statute imposes a tax (the right of government to require a transfer of wealth from a citizen or business) or penal sanctions.

A third reason for complexity is incremental change to policy, which is often given legal effect by several Acts amending earlier ones over a period of time. Until such time as these Acts are consolidated, people and their legal advisers may have to look at several different statutes to understand what the law requires.

Fourth, complexity may arise from a desire to control and restrict discretion in the implementation of policy. A government department may fear that unless contingencies are anticipated and details spelt out, other people may misunderstand exactly what the Act is intended to achieve: there may be 'misinterpretation' by the agency responsible for giving practical effect to a policy (such as a local authority) or, if litigation should arise, the courts. An illustration of this sort of drafting can be seen in the Local Government (Miscellaneous

Provisions) Act 1982. When the Home Office set up a system for the licensing of sex shops by local authorities, it was thought necessary to specify that, for the purpose of the Act, 'premises' include 'vessels', which means *any ship, boat, raft or other apparatus constructed or adapted for floating on water*'. A plethora of detail such as this can stand in the way of easy comprehension.

(a) COMPLEXITY OF BILLS

Legislation that is difficult to understand may create problems not only for the people whose rights and interests are affected by it, but also for Parliament. If MPs during the legislative process cannot understand what a Bill really means, they will not be able to probe and scrutinize the government's policy proposals effectively. Since 1999, all government Bills have been accompanied by 'explanatory notes', drafted by lawyers in the department sponsoring the Bill, which may go some way to addressing this problem.

On the one hand, there are calls for detailed legislation. As we have seen, Dicey argued that statutes ought to confer as little discretion as possible on ministers and other public bodies, and one way of restricting discretion is to spell out in statutes with considerable particularity what powers ministers and others have, and how they ought to set about making their decisions.[43] Today, some commentators continue to argue that the traditional British drafting style has the virtue of both prompting certainty and enabling democratic control. On the other hand, there are also calls for shorter, less detailed legislation. An editorial in *The Times* claimed: '*Because British laws are five times longer than comparable continental measures, Parliament faces a legislative workload that has become intolerable. There may be a case, therefore, for adopting some of the practices used in continental lawmaking to improve efficiency.*'[44]

(b) FRAMEWORK BILLS

Statutes often nowadays set out only the broad framework for the government's policy, leaving the detail to be filled in later by delegated legislation drafted in government departments. For example, the Policing and Crime Act 2010, s. 96, amended the Police and Criminal Evidence Act 1984 to give the Home Secretary very wide powers to make *delegated* legislation about the controversial topic of retention by the police of people's DNA samples. The House of Lords committee scrutinizing the Bill that became the 2010 Act were highly critical.

House of Lords Constitution Committee, *Policing and Crime Bill*, 16th Report, Session 2008–09, HL 128

15. Clause 96 of the bill seeks to amend the Police and Criminal Evidence Act 1984 by inserting new powers for the Secretary of State, by regulations, to "make provision as to the retention, use and destruction of material". It is in our view wholly unacceptable that the important

---

[43] See Chapter 2.
[44] *The Times*, 15 November 1993.

matter of retention of samples is to be dealt with by delegated legislation. The Government's proposals as to how they intend to implement the *Marper* judgment [of the European Court of Human Rights, holding that previous retention arrangements breached the ECHR] raise important and controversial questions, which the House will want to debate fully. Clause 96, if agreed to, will not allow that debate to happen. The principles governing samples should be set out on the face of primary legislation to enable Parliament to scrutinise them and, if needs be, to seek to amend them. Unamendable delegated legislation will not provide a sufficient opportunity for parliamentary oversight and control over the legal framework for the Government's policy.

16. We call on the Government to think again and bring forward proposals in a separate bill to regulate the National DNA Database.

The government did not heed that particular advice. Nor has criticism of this sort deterred government from using framework bills. The Coalition government formed in May 2010 adopted a policy of cutting public expenditure by reducing dramatically the number of public bodies by merging or abolishing several dozen of them. Rather than set out in detail what was to happen to each public body, the bill that became the Public Bodies Act 2011 conferred broad powers on ministers to implement the policy by delegated legislation. The House of Lords Constitution Committee report on the bill was caustic.

House of Lords Constitution Committee, *Public Bodies Bill*, Sixth Report of 2010–12, HL Paper 51

13. The Public Bodies Bill [HL] strikes at the very heart of our constitutional system, being a type of 'framework' or 'enabling' legislation that drains the lifeblood of legislative amendment and debate across a very broad range of public arrangements. In particular, it hits directly at the role of the House of Lords as a revising chamber.

14. The Public Bodies Bill [HL] is concerned with the design, powers and functions of a vast range of public bodies, the creation of many of which was the product of extensive parliamentary debate and deliberation. We fail to see why such parliamentary debate and deliberation should be denied to proposals now to abolish or to redesign such bodies.

As we will see later, delegated legislation is subject to significantly less parliamentary scrutiny than Bills and it cannot be amended; it can only be approved or rejected by Parliament, as drafted by a government department. So while skeleton-style Bills may give ministers maximum flexibility to alter and amend policy to suit changing circumstances, and while such Bills may appear to be clearer, there are fears that they confer too much unsupervised discretion on government. There is a risk that we are ending up with the worst of all worlds: Acts that are over-elaborate and so detailed as to prevent MPs and the public from understanding them, and which also confer too much regulation-making power on ministers. There is probably, however, no general cure-all for the ills that are diagnosed. The search for clearer, more easily scrutinized legislation needs to have regard to particular circumstances. Legislation likely to be read only by specialist practitioners (for example, accountants and lawyers advising companies) may well need to be phrased and structured differently from a statute dealing with the basic rights and entitlements of ordinary citizens.

5 PRE-LEGISLATIVE SCRUTINY OF DRAFT BILLS

A development in recent years is the practice of the government publishing a draft of a Bill some months (or even years) before it is finalized and ready to be formally introduced to Parliament. Draft Bills are published as Command Papers.

House of Commons Modernization Committee, *The Legislative Process*, First Report, Session 1997–98, HC 190, para. 20

There is almost universal agreement that pre-legislative scrutiny is right in principle, subject to the circumstances and nature of the legislation. It provides an opportunity for the House as a whole, for individual backbenchers, and for the Opposition to have a real input into the form of the actual legislation which subsequently emerges, not least because Ministers are likely to be far more receptive to suggestions for change before the Bill is actually published. It opens Parliament up to those outside affected by legislation. At the same time such pre-legislative scrutiny can be of real benefit to the Government. It could, and indeed should, lead to less time being needed at later stages of the legislative process; the use of the Chair's powers of selection would naturally reflect the extent and nature of previous scrutiny and debate. Above all, it should lead to better legislation and less likelihood of subsequent amending legislation.

While there is consensus about the desirability of the government publishing draft Bills, the reality is that there has been significant variation in how many Bills are published in draft each parliamentary year.

A. Kennon, 'Pre-legislative scrutiny of draft Bills' [2005] Public Law 477, 479–80

No Bill that is highly controversial between the political parties has been subject to pre-legislative scrutiny. [...]

Legislation starts in Whitehall. Within any department officials and Ministers have a list of subjects on which they would like to change the law. Ministers, with a weather eye on the vane above No.10 Downing Street, will have political priorities. Officials are also conscious of matters that need improving but which do not engage political attention. The Government's annual legislative programme needs to include high profile political measures. Limits on parliamentary time mean that the legislative programme of a couple of dozen Bills has to be split between the contentious and the non-contentious. Few departments would presume to claim more than one place in each category. [...]

It is against this background that the Government's tentative promise that "the presumption [is] that Bills will be published in draft for pre-legislative scrutiny unless there is good reason otherwise" needs to be considered. It is unrealistic to expect that a Minister who stands a good chance of securing a place in the legislative programme for a high profile Bill will want to delay its enactment by going through the longer process of pre-legislative scrutiny. By definition, this sort of Bill has a political impetus that may overwhelm detailed scrutiny. An evidence-taking committee might be carried away by the political avalanche behind the Bill and not have time to look at the minutiae. The understandable combat between Government and Opposition on a key issue might leave the details unexamined.

House of Lords Constitution Committee, *Pre-legislative Scrutiny in the 2007–08 Session*, Eighth Report, Session 2008–09, HL 66 (footnotes omitted)

Analysis of the trends in pre-legislative scrutiny

6. Parliamentary support for pre-legislative scrutiny, to which we referred in our previous report, has remained strong. A number of the Commons departmental committees that conducted pre-legislative scrutiny in 2007–08 affirmed its value. The Commons Liaison Committee stated that "Committees are keen to contribute their specialist knowledge to the legislative process through both the scrutiny of draft bills and of other legislation." The Joint Committee on the draft Constitutional Renewal Bill stated that the decision to present the draft Bill for pre-legislative scrutiny "is the right thing to do for a bill of this nature."

7. The Government, too, have continued to express their commitment to pre-legislative scrutiny. The Draft Legislative Programme stated that:

'The Government fully endorses the value of pre-legislative scrutiny of draft bills as a means of improving the quality of bills subsequently introduced to Parliament [. . .] for many [bills] it can be extremely valuable—where the subject matter is of particular interest to Parliament and where Committees can improve texts on the basis of expert evidence.'

8. At Second Reading of the Marine and Coastal Access Bill in the Lords, the Minister, Lord Hunt of King's Heath, told the House "how helpful the process of pre-legislative scrutiny has been in developing this Bill [. . .] As a result of this pre-legislative scrutiny process, a good draft bill has been improved—made stronger and more transparent." The Secretary of State for Justice and Lord Chancellor, Jack Straw MP, told us that, in terms of the legislative process, "on the whole it has certainly been working better than before we had pre-legislative scrutiny." However, he did add that "the main problem with pre-legislative scrutiny is getting people to give the same scrutiny to bills in draft as they do later on. There have been plenty of examples where there has been something in a bill which is potentially explosive but the dog does not bark until the last moment [. . .] The lesson is that you have to stir the dog." When asked if he thought this was happening at the moment, he said "to a degree it is, but I think that sometimes it is not."

9. In last session's report, we produced a table showing the number of draft bills that had been published in each session, comparing it with the number of Government bills introduced. This table was based upon statistics provided by the Government in answer to a written question from the Committee Chairman. We have reproduced the table below, adding the figures for 2007–08.

10. In our previous report, we noted with concern that both the number and proportion of draft bills had fallen between the 2003–04 session and the 2006–07 session, in spite of the Government's 2005 commitment "at least to maintain the proportion of bills published in draft." In their response, the Government stated that they had also "been disappointed at the lower numbers of draft bills published in recent sessions. But [. . .] it will not be possible to give a general undertaking to publish most bills in draft or regularly to achieve the figures reached in 2003–04. The main practical obstacle remains the need to have the freedom to bring forward much legislation on a timetable which does not allow for publication of the

proposed legislation in draft form." The Draft Legislative Programme stated that whilst the Government were "committed to publishing as many bills as possible in draft ... publication in draft is not suitable for every bill."

Government statistics			
Session	Number of Government bills introduced into at least one House	Number of draft bills published	Ratio of draft bills to Government bills
1997–98	53	3	1:18
1998–99	31	6	1:5
1999–2000	41	6	1:7
2000–01	28	2	1:14
2001–02	39	7	1:6
2002–03	36	9	1:4
2003–04	37	12	1:3
2004–05	34	5	1:7
2005–06	58	4	1:15
2006–07	36	4	1:9
2007–08	31	9	1:3

11. We therefore welcome the fact that in 2007–08, the number of draft bills, and the ratio of draft bills to Government bills, were at their healthiest since the high water mark of 2003–04. We are also pleased to see that a further seven draft bills are planned for the 2008–09 session (although only one of them had been published when we agreed this report). It is imperative that the progress made in the 2007–08 session is maintained.

12. We reaffirm our strong support for pre-legislative scrutiny and our desire to see it used more routinely. We welcome the increase in the number of draft bills published in 2007–08 from the low levels of previous sessions, and call on the Government to maintain this progress in 2008–09.

QUESTIONS

1. What is the added value (over and above 'normal' consultation) in a government department deciding to publish a Bill in draft?

2. What is the role of Parliament in relation to draft Bills?

3. What draft Bills have been published in the current parliamentary session? Explain how exactly you would find them.

6 THE PARLIAMENTARY YEAR

Parliament organizes its workload into annual sessions. Previously, sessions used to start in November or December and run for a little short of twelve months (with a long summer break). After the passing of the Fixed Term Parliament Act 2011, it is expected that each five-year Parliament will have five 12-month sessions, beginning and ending in the spring. In recent years, the government has adopted a practice of publishing a 'draft legislative programme' in which it sets out in outline the main Bills that it expects to introduce to Parliament in the following session.

The annual session starts with the State Opening of Parliament, one of the great ceremonial occasions. The monarch attends the House of Lords, to which MPs are summoned. From the throne, the monarch reads out a short speech ('the Queen's Speech') drafted by the government, which sets out the government's proposals for Bills.

7 PARLIAMENTARY STAGES OF A BILL

Political scientists surveying democracies have suggested that there are three kinds of legislature.[45]

(a) First, there are those that can be described as 'policymaking' or 'transformative' because they have the capacity to develop policy of their own. The US Congress is one of the few that falls into this category.

(b) Second (and this is the category into which the UK Parliament falls), there are 'policy-influencing', 'reactive', 'arena', or 'legitimizing' legislatures. They operate to modify or reject proposals from government, but they do not develop their own policies. The emphasis is on debate and ratifying decisions made elsewhere (that is, in government). One practical reason for these legislatures not being able to take a lead in policymaking is simply that they lack the resources to do so. Parliamentarians do not have a large body of advisory civil servants or much time.

(c) Third, there are legislatures that have 'little or no policy effect': their role is essentially to assent to whatever policy is made by government.

As you read the next two extracts, consider into which category the authors would fit the UK Parliament.

P. Norton, *Parliament in British Politics* (2005, Basingstoke: Palgrave Macmillan), pp. 61–2

In terms of their impact on public policy, three types of legislature can be identified: policy-making, policy-influencing, and those with little or no policy affect. Policy-making legislatures can involve themselves in the drawing up—the making—of policy. Policy-influencing legislatures have the formal capacity to amend, even to reject, measures of policy placed before them, but they are essentially dependent on government to put forward those measures. Even if they reject a measure, they look to government to formulate and bring forward a replacement. The legislature itself does not seek to generate—or make—policy. It lacks the political will, the institutional resources or even, in some cases, the constitutional power

---

[45] See, e.g., J.E. Schwarz 'Exploring a new role in policymaking: The British House of Commons in the 1970s' (1980) 74 American Political Science Review 23.

to do so. Legislatures with little or no policy effect exist mainly to give assent to measures laid before them.

Norton (a professor of government at Hull University who is also a Conservative peer) concludes that, for most of its history, the UK Parliament '*has not been a policy-making body*'. He explains that the UK Parliament has looked to the executive—first the monarch, then the king's government—to bring forward Bills for it to consider. The UK Parliament is, he argues, '*a policy-influencing legislature*'. It shares this characteristic with most legislatures around the world.

R. Blackburn and A. Kennon, with M. Wheeler-Booth, *Griffith & Ryle on Parliament: Functions, Practice and Procedures* (2003, London: Sweet & Maxwell), pp. 5–6

It is a central feature of Parliament, however, that it mainly performs a responsive rather than an initiating function within the constitution. The government—at different levels—initiates policy, formulates its policy on legislation and other proposals, exercises powers under the prerogative or granted by statute and, in all these aspects, performs the governing role in the State. Both Houses of Parliament spend most of their time responding, in a variety of ways, to these initiatives, proposals or executive actions.

The government, however, is not the only source of input of business for Parliament. Much business is originated by the opposition front-bench, and by back-benchers on either side of the two Houses. The inspiration for their input is largely found in general public opinion, outside pressures or interest groups, newspapers, radio and television, and in the minds and attitudes of millions of citizens represented in the Commons by Members.

Parliament, therefore, finds itself the recipient of a wide range of external pressures and proposals, broadly divided in origin between the government of the day on the one hand and the outside world the public on the other. Only in a limited context does either House have a policy of its own or initiate "parliamentary" proposals. For example, the House of Lords has a long standing concern with its own composition and powers. The Commons (and, to a lesser extent, the Lords) have jealously established, preserved and exercised "all their ancient and undoubted rights and privileges" (to quote the claim made to the sovereign on their behalf by the Speaker at the beginning of each Parliament). And both Houses adopt a "parliamentary" stance and concern themselves with their own interests when initiating or influencing policy on such matters as their own procedures and the pay, accommodation, facilities and conditions of service of Members or peers. But for most matters the initiative comes from outside Parliament.

Let us now move on to consider what happens from the point at which a Bill is 'introduced' to Parliament by the government. The basic rule is that a Bill needs to progress through various stages in the House of Commons and then the House of Lords—or vice versa. About half of the fifty or so government Bills start in the Commons and about half in the Lords. There is no real significance as to which House is chosen to start the Bill off, except that 'Money Bills' (Bills that deal only with taxation and government expenditure) always begin in the Commons.

You can follow the progress of Bills through Parliament online at http://services.parliament.uk/bills/ and see the various reprints of each Bill, updated to include amendments.

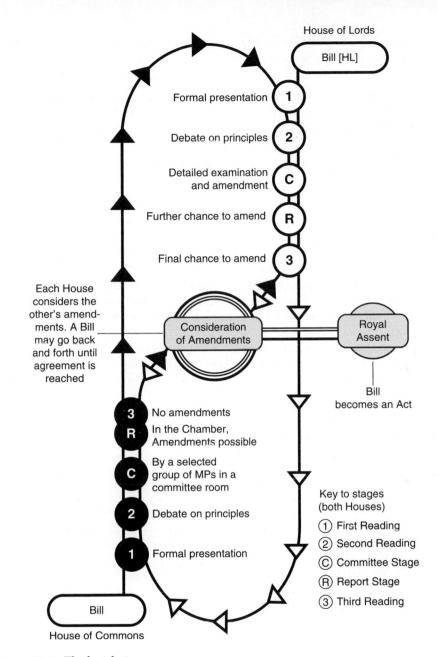

Figure 10.1 The legislative process

(a) FIRST READING

The First Reading is a formality (in effect, announcing that the Bill will be published and start its passage through the House). Since 1999, Bills are accompanied by 'explanatory notes', drafted by government lawyers, which seek to explain in some detail, but using non-technical language and avoiding 'advocacy', what the Bill is designed to achieve and how it will do this. Explanatory notes are not endorsed by Parliament.

(b) SECOND READING

The Second Reading typically takes place two to four weeks after the First Reading, and is an opportunity for MPs or peers to debate the general policy aims in the Bill. Debates are published in *Hansard*, the official record.

(c) COMMITTEE STAGE

The Committee Stage usually starts two weeks later, and is when detailed consideration of the policy and drafting of the Bill occurs.

In the Commons, this is normally in a public Bill committee of between fifteen and twenty MPs (in proportion, party-politically, to the composition of the House as a whole). For most Bills, the committee's work begins with oral evidence sessions in which MPs hear from experts, campaign groups, and finally the minister in charge of the Bill. There is then clause-by-clause debate, with Opposition MPs seeking to argue that amendments should be made; very few, if any, of these amendments are agreed to by the public Bill committee (on which the governing party has a majority of members), because the government instructs the MPs of its party, who will form a majority of the committee, to vote against them. It is normal also for the government to make amendments: often they will be 'technical', to tidy up drafting points; sometimes, they will alter the policy of the Bill slightly if the government has been convinced that it could be improved.

In the House of Lords, the Committee Stage normally takes place on the floor of the chamber, giving all peers interested in the Bill an opportunity to table amendments seeking (in their view) to improve it.

(d) REPORT AND THIRD READING

After the Committee Stage in the relevant house, there follow the Report and Third Reading stages. These stages often take place on the same day. They are further opportunities for MPs or peers (depending on in which House the Bill is in at that time) to press for acceptance of their amendments and for the government to make its own amendments.

(e) PING-PONG

Once the Bill has been through both Houses, agreement needs to be reached on the final text that will be presented for royal assent. Where there is disagreement, a 'ping-pong' process will arise, with proposed amendments and counter-amendments shuttling back and forth, until both Houses are willing to consent to the Bill.

(f) ROYAL ASSENT

Royal assent is the final stage of the legislative process. The grant of royal assent is a prerogative power of the Queen—although, by constitutional convention, it is always granted. The constitutional mechanics of royal assent are set out in the following statute.

Royal Assent Act 1967

1(1) An Act of Parliament is duly enacted if Her Majesty's assent thereto, being signified by Letters Patent under the Great Seal, signed with Her Majesty's own hand,—

(a) is pronounced in the presence of both Houses in the House of Lords in the form and manner customary before the passing of this Act; or

(b) is notified to each House of Parliament, sitting separately, by the Speaker of that House or in the case of his absence by the person acting as such Speaker.

1(2) Nothing in this section affects the power of Her Majesty to declare the Royal Assent in person in Parliament, or the manner in which an Act of Parliament is required to be endorsed in her Majesty's name.

The last time that a monarch signified royal assent in person was in 1854, when Queen Victoria attended Parliament. The normal practice is that the monarch has no personal involvement in the process. At the start of each annual parliamentary session, a small number of 'Lords Commissioner' are appointed at the start of the parliamentary year to carry out this formality. A short ceremony takes place in the House of Lords during a convenient break in other business, ending with a senior parliamentary official announcing '*La Reyne le veult*' (Norman French for 'The Queen wills it'). The grant of royal assent is then announced by Speaker in the House of Commons.

Printing and publication

After royal assent, the new Act of Parliament must be officially printed and published in three forms:

(a) a 'Queen's Printer's' version on paper, which will be found in good law libraries;

(b) on the www.legislation.gov.uk website managed by the National Archives);[46] and

(c) about six months later, one copy of the Act is printed on vellum parchment, and is signed by the Clerk of the Parliaments (the senior official in the House of Lords) and lodged in the House of Lords Record Office. Professor Jackson explains that '*This is the copy to which the courts would seek access, in case of any doubt regarding the authenticity or text of a statute*'.[47]

Acts are no longer put 'on the Parliamentary Roll'.

8 BILLS OF CONSTITUTIONAL IMPORTANCE

As we noted in Chapter 2, one of the apparent downsides of a constitutional system based on parliamentary supremacy is that this gives an awful lot of power to the governing party—because, as we have just seen, the reality is that the government controls Parliament rather than the other way around. The larger the governing party's majority in the House of

---

[46] http://www.legislation.gov.uk/ukpga.

[47] Bernard S. Jackson, 'Who enacts statutes?' (1997) 18 Statute Law Review 177, 182.

Commons, the more control it exerts. What, then, is there to prevent a government from introducing and steering through a Bill that seeks to undermine basic liberties or to change the constitutional set-up in a way that advantages the government? Previously, we examined Dicey's answers to this conundrum. Here, we look more practically at what happens in Parliament where there is a risk of this.

In the next extract, Professor Robert Hazell (director of the UCL Constitution Unit) considers the constitutional convention that Bills of 'first-class constitutional importance' have their Second Reading stage in the chamber of the House of Commons (a 'Committee of the Whole House', or CWH) rather than in a public Bill committee.

Robert Hazell, 'Time for a new convention: Parliamentary scrutiny of constitutional Bills 1997–2005' [2006] Public Law 247, 246 (footnotes omitted)

The origins of this convention go back to 1945, and the Attlee government's substantial post-war legislative programme. Anticipating that the task of post-war reconstruction would require a heavy legislative programme, the wartime coalition government's Machinery of Government Committee had recommended that in future all Bills should go to Standing Committee upstairs. But they recognised that: "An exception would have to be made if any Bill of first class constitutional importance were introduced, of the order, for instance, of the Parliament Act 1911 or the Statute of Westminster 1931". This sentence was repeated in the post-war Labour government's memorandum to the 1945–46 Procedure Committee, which also recognised that in addition to the "great measures of the Session", it had been the practice to retain on the floor of the House short Bills which were unlikely to require a detailed committee stage, and urgent Bills which needed to be passed in a few days. The Procedure Committee approved the proposal to refer substantially all Bills to Standing Committee, and approved the government's proposed exceptions of short Bills, urgent Bills and Bills of "first class constitutional importance". That is how the convention emerged that Bills of first class constitutional importance should take their committee stage on the floor. After 1997 the convention was challenged by the new Labour government, which attempted to split the committee stage (discussed further below).

From the outset it proved difficult to define exactly which Bills were of "first class constitutional importance", and which were not. The Leader of the House, Herbert Morrison, was pressed about the definition when he gave evidence to the Procedure Committee in 1945, and repeated the two examples of the Parliament Act 1911 and the Statute of Westminster 1931. [. . .]

[Hazell says that the main advantage of the convention is that it enables more MPs to take part in deliberations than would be the case if the Bill were to be considered in a committee room.]

Set against this are some significant disadvantages from taking the committee stage on the floor. First is the curtailment of time. Because time on the floor is prime parliamentary time, this is inevitably in more scarce supply than when the committee stage is taken upstairs. [. . .]. For constitutional Bills taken in CWH, the committee stage lasted on average 15 hours. For Bills referred to Standing Committee, the average committee stage lasted 25 hours.

Linked to the limited time is the limited number of amendments moved. For Bills taken in CWH, an average of 10 amendments were debated during the committee stage. In Standing Committee the number was five times higher, with an average of 51 amendments moved to each Bill. This supports the contention that debate in a CWH tends to be a continuation of the

Second Reading debate, staying with the general principles of the Bill rather than engaging in detailed scrutiny. Measured simply by number of amendments, the intensity of detailed scrutiny would appear to be a lot greater when a Bill is referred to Standing Committee.

It is hard to resist the conclusion that the CWH procedure has become a dignified part of the constitution, while the more efficient work of scrutiny is done in Standing Committee or in Select Committees of each House.

One possible reform that might improve the scrutiny of constitutional and other Bills is the use of 'checklists', as Professor Dawn Oliver explains.

D. Oliver 'Improving the scrutiny of Bills: The case for standards and checklists' [2006] Public Law 219, 219–20, 226–7 (footnotes omitted)

Scrutiny standards may be used either within government, at the stage when policy is under development and then the drafting process is undertaken, or in Parliament, when Bills and draft Bills are being scrutinised, for instance by select committees, or by independent bodies with responsibility for objective scrutiny, such as the New Zealand Legislation Advisory Committee or the French Conseil d'État. Scrutiny standards may be concerned with substantive, procedural or informational matters. Substantive matters include compliance with human rights requirements, EU law and constitutional principles, "fit" with the existing law, and compliance with "better legislation" standards such as those set out in the Hansard Society's 1992 report on the legislative process. Procedural ones include consultation with relevant bodies and compliance with departmental and Cabinet processes. Informational requirements could include the government's explanations of the policy objectives of the Bill, the government's views as to compatibility of a Bill with the ECHR and other international instruments, value for money, regulatory and other impact assessments, and the government's justifications for any non-compliance with normal substantive, procedural or informational requirements. [...]

There appears, however, to be a worrying lack of appreciation on the part of ministers and some parliamentarians of the existence and importance of the legal and constitutional values with which independent scrutineers concern themselves in the democracies referred to above. Examples are given in the case studies in this article and subsequent discussion. They include respect for the rule of law and for individual liberties and rights, rights of access to the courts, matters such as the burden of proof in criminal proceedings, the avoidance of certain retrospective legislation, certainty in relation to administrative powers, non-delegation of legislative power unless justified, and that there should be no taxation without the express consent of Parliament. In most democracies those values and principles would be taken into account explicitly and as matters of course at various stages in the legislative process: not so in the United Kingdom. There is, in other words, a noticeable divergence in the United Kingdom between two cultures, that of the lawyer and that of the politician. The case for scrutiny standards that would articulate legal and constitutional values here is, therefore, particularly strong. In an era when the courts are elaborating explicit constitutional principles, it is surely important that Parliament, parliamentarians and their select committees should not be left behind, or at least not without realising that this is happening and making a positive decision to participate in the articulation or development of constitutional principles or not to do so. Scrutiny standards or checklists could bring Parliament back into the constitutional arena. There are also good general public policy reasons for a checklist, given the real concern about the amount of badly thought out legislation brought forward by government in recent years, much of it amending earlier legislation.

Professor David Feldman, as well as being an academic, had practical experience of the parliamentary scrutiny during his time as legal adviser to the Joint Committee on Human Rights.

David Feldman, 'Parliamentary scrutiny of legislation and human rights' [2002] Public Law 323, 324–7

The first and essential point to bear in mind is that parliamentary scrutiny of legislation is a part-time activity for parliamentarians. In the House of Commons, M.P.s have a large number of other functions. They represent constituencies, and rely on their support in the constituency—both in the local party and among the electorate at large—to have a chance of retaining the seat at the next election. As constituency representatives, M.P.s spend a great deal of their time answering letters and telephone calls from constituents, holding "surgeries" in the constituency, and following up their grievances on their behalf by writing to ministers and other public authorities, asking parliamentary questions, or (more rarely) intervening on the floor of the House. They also open fêtes, visit hospitals, and so on. Much of their local reputation, and sometimes their prospects for re-election, will depend on how they deal with issues which are important to their constituencies. [...] Scrutinising legislation, by contrast, attracts little publicity (unless it is concerned with controversial issues such as sexuality or abortion). It requires a great deal of concentrated attention, and must take its place in the queue of activities vying for a member's time. Particularly if the member has little expertise in the field of policy and law with which the legislation is concerned, it is quite understandable that M.P.s tend to rely on the directions on voting given by the party's whips, rather than attempting to analyse all legislation in depth.

In the House of Lords, most peers, not being salaried politicians, have many non-political activities which take up much of their time. They have, perhaps, even less time than M.P.s to devote to scrutiny of legislation. There is a great deal of expertise among peers on which the House can rely to inform their debates. There is some support available to members of both Houses, but less than one might expect. Most M.P.s have some research assistance from their own, very limited staff; a few peers can call on similar resources, but the system relies to a significant extent on peers using their private resources to support their parliamentary duties. This applies as much to human rights as to any other subject. [...]

[...T]he prevailing atmosphere in both Houses gives one the feeling that people are doing important things at great speed, with remarkably little support, and in physical conditions which are improving gradually as more space is made available, but which for most members of both Houses are still cramped, uncomfortable, and inconvenient. Since both Houses normally sit after lunch, and continue late into the evening and night, many important legislative provisions are discussed at times when anyone with any sense would either be asleep or slumped in front of a television set. By the time business begins in earnest, many of the M.P.s will have spent a great deal of the morning and early afternoon in meetings, or dealing with constituency business, or travelling from their constituencies; peers (most of whom are unsalaried) will often have spent the early part of the day doing their proper jobs. We have a legislature which is run on the cheap, and depends on people doing shift work—usually several shifts a day, and often in different jobs. In short, we have part-time legislators.

In 2011, as part of a broader inquiry into the process of constitutional change, the House of Lords Constitution Committee considered scrutiny of constitutionally important

Bills.[48] The Committee was particularly critical of the way that some such Bills do not receive full scrutiny in Parliament due to pressure of time, especially at the end of an annual parliamentary session (the Bill that become the Constitutional Reform and Governance Act 2010 was cited as an example). The Committee was not in favour of creating new procedures, such as super-majorities, for significant constitutional Bills. The Committee did, however, recommend that a minister introducing such a Bill should make a detailed statement explaining, among other things: the impact of the proposal upon existing constitutional arrangements; what public engagement had taken place; and how the Bill had been scrutinized within government. A requirement for pre-legislative scrutiny of a draft Bill 'should be departed from only in exceptional circumstances'.

QUESTIONS

1. Should Bills dealing with constitutional matters be subject to different treatment during the legislative process?

2. How would you define 'constitutional' for this purpose?

---

9 BRINGING LEGISLATION INTO FORCE

After a Bill has completed its passage through Parliament and received royal assent, the next step is for it to be brought into force. Every Act contains a commencement provision towards its end. Some are very straightforward and say simply 'This Act comes into force on the day on which it is passed' (that is, the day on which it received royal assent) or may specify a date; most are more complex.

Children and Young Persons Act 2008

44 Commencement

(1) Section 7 and this Part come into force on the day on which this Act is passed.

(2) The reference in subsection (1) to this Part does not include—

    (a) paragraph 4 of Schedule 3 (which comes into force in accordance with subsection (9)); and

    (b) section 42 and Schedule 4 (which come into force in accordance with subsections (3) and (4)).

(3) In relation to Wales, the provisions specified in subsection (5) come into force on such day as the Welsh Ministers may by order appoint.

(4) Otherwise the provisions of this Act come into force on such day as the Secretary of State may by order appoint.

(5) The provisions are—

    (a) Parts 1 to 4 (except sections 7, 17, 18, 31 and 32);

    (b) section 42 and Schedule 4.

---

[48] House of Lords Constitution Committee, *The Process of Constitutional Change*, Fifth Report of 2010–12, HL Paper 177.

(6) An order under this section bringing subsection (2) of section 10 into force in relation to Wales requires the consent of the Secretary of State.

(7) An order under this section bringing section 17 or 18 into force requires the consent of the Welsh Ministers.

(8) Before making an order bringing section 31 or 32 into force, the Secretary of State must consult the Welsh Ministers.

(9) Paragraph 4 of Schedule 3 comes into force on the same day as section 7(1) of the Carers and Disabled Children Act 2000 (c. 16) comes into force for the purpose of inserting section 17B into the 1989 Act in relation to Wales.

(10) An order under this section may—

  (a) appoint different days for different purposes;

  (b) include transitional, saving or transitory provision.

Not knowing when new legislation is to be brought into force can be a major problem for businesses and citizens. Since 2008, a more coordinated approach has been taken, with the introduction of 'common commencement dates' twice a year.

A problem of a different sort arises if the government decides not to bring legislation into force. In 1993, the Home Secretary announced that he would not be bringing into force sections in the Criminal Justice Act 1988 that set out in statutory form the methods by which the Criminal Injuries Compensation Board calculates its payments to victims of crime. (The Board had, in fact, been operating on a non-statutory basis since 1964.) Instead, he said, the government would instruct the Board to make future payments according to a tariff system set by the Home Office (which was going to reduce the amounts of compensation payable in many cases). The Law Lords, by a majority, held that the Home Secretary's decision was unlawful: although he was entitled to decide when to bring a section into force, he was not able to declare he would never do this and make rules contrary to the will of Parliament expressed in the Act. The government subsequently introduced its tariff scheme in a new Act.

R v Secretary of State for the Home Department, ex parte Fire Brigades Union and ors
[1995] 2 AC 513, 546, 550

Lord Keith of Kinkel

[...] The applicants argue that to make payments under the proposed new tariff scheme would be unlawful because that would be inconsistent with the scheme embodied in sections 108 to 117, since that would make it impossible for all practical purposes ever to bring the statutory scheme into operation. The Secretary of State must at least be under a duty, so it is said, to keep under review from time to time whether to bring sections 108 to 117 into force. I would accept that the Secretary of State is under such a duty, but in my opinion it is one owed to Parliament and not to the public at large. On the other hand it does not seem to me that operating the proposed new tariff scheme would rule out any reasonable possibility of the statutory scheme ever being introduced. The decision not to introduce it at the present time is a political one and it is entirely predictable that political views might change, if not under the present administration then under a future one. If a political decision were made to bring in the statutory scheme then there is no reason to suppose that the political will would not be found, notwithstanding any difficulty there might be in dismantling the existing arrangements and setting up new ones. The extent to which it might be necessary to do so is in any event open to question.

Upon the whole matter I am clearly of opinion that the respondents' case fails upon a proper application of the rules of statutory construction and of the principles which govern the process of judicial review. To grant the respondents the relief which they seek, or any part of it, would represent an unwarrantable intrusion by the court into the political field and a usurpation of the function of Parliament.

Lord Browne-Wilkinson

[. . .] if the argument of the applicants is right, there must come a time when the Secretary of State comes under a duty to bring the statutory provisions into force and accordingly the court could grant mandamus against the Secretary of State requiring him to do so. Indeed, the applicants originally sought such an order in the present case. In my judgment it would be most undesirable that, in such circumstances, the court should intervene in the legislative process by requiring an Act of Parliament to be brought into effect.

That would be for the courts to tread dangerously close to the area over which Parliament enjoys exclusive jurisdiction, namely the making of legislation.

In the absence of clear statutory words imposing a clear statutory duty, in my judgment the court should hesitate long before holding that such a provision as section 171(1) imposes a legally enforceable statutory duty on the Secretary of State.

It does not follow that, because the Secretary of State is not under any duty to bring the section into effect, he has an absolute and unfettered discretion whether or not to do so. So to hold would lead to the conclusion that both Houses of Parliament had passed the Bill through all its stages and the Act received the Royal Assent merely to confer an enabling power on the executive to decide at will whether or not to make the parliamentary provisions a part of the law. Such a conclusion, drawn from a section to which the sidenote is "Commencement", is not only constitutionally dangerous but flies in the face of common sense. The provisions for bringing sections into force under section 171(1) apply not only to the statutory scheme but to many other provisions. For example, the provisions of Parts I, II and III relating to extradition, documentary evidence in criminal proceedings and other evidence in criminal proceedings are made subject to the same provisions. Surely, it cannot have been the intention of Parliament to leave it in the entire discretion of the Secretary of State whether or not to effect such important changes to the criminal law. In the absence of express provisions to the contrary in the Act, the plain intention of Parliament in conferring on the Secretary of State the power to bring certain sections into force is that such power is to be exercised so as to bring those sections into force when it is appropriate and unless there is a subsequent change of circumstances which would render it inappropriate to do so.

There is a second consequence of the power in section 171(1) being conferred for the purpose of bringing the sections into force. As I have said, in my view the Secretary of State is entitled to decide not to bring the sections into force if events subsequently occur which render it undesirable to do so.

But if the power is conferred on the Secretary of State with a view to bringing the sections into force, in my judgment the Secretary of State cannot himself procure events to take place and rely on the occurrence of those events as the ground for not bringing the statutory scheme into force. In claiming that the introduction of the new tariff scheme renders it undesirable now to bring the statutory scheme into force, the Secretary of State is, in effect, claiming that the purpose of the statutory power has been frustrated by his own act in choosing to introduce a scheme inconsistent with the statutory scheme approved by Parliament.

QUESTION

Is there any constitutional objection to the executive deciding when legislation should be brought into force?

10 POST-LEGISLATIVE SCRUTINY

A final step in the process is post-legislative scrutiny, introduced by the government in March 2008. This was prompted by recommendations of the Law Commission of England and Wales, which, in 2006, called for a more systematic approach.

The Law Commission, *Post-legislative Scrutiny* (2006, Law Com No 302)

[... W]e understand post-legislative scrutiny to refer to a broad form of review, the purpose of which is to address the effects of the legislation in terms of whether the intended policy objectives have been met by the legislation and, if so, how effectively. However, this does not preclude consideration of narrow questions of a purely legal or technical nature.

The government's response was positive.

Office of the Leader of the House of Commons, *Post-legislative Scrutiny: The Government's Approach* (2008, Cm 7320)

The Commission's proposed model seeks to combine in a complementary fashion internal departmental scrutiny with parliamentary scrutiny, with the central power of initiative for parliamentary scrutiny itself balanced between the Commons departmental committees and other elements within Parliament. The Government broadly endorses this approach but considers that greater clarity is necessary in the way the prime role of the Commons committees should be recognised. Much of the activity of Commons committees, even if not overtly labelled in that way, in practice involves examination of the effectiveness of existing primary legislation. It would be undesirable for that work to be subject to duplication or conflicting work from other committees.

11. The Government considers that its proposal will be a valuable and proportionate approach towards achieving the objective of better post-legislative scrutiny. This approach is set out in more detail in the Government's response to the individual Law Commission recommendations, as appended. In practice, given the lengths of time involved in the passage of new legislation and the lead times involved for the preparation of the Memoranda envisaged in these proposals, the operation of the proposed system and its effectiveness will have to be kept under continuous review. If the kind of Memorandum for parliamentary scrutiny which is proposed involves a disproportionate workload in their production, or if they do not prove to be the kind of document which Parliament finds helpful, then it would be appropriate to consider alternative approaches.

11 LEGISLATIVE FUNCTIONS AFTER DEVOLUTION

The Scottish Parliament, the Northern Ireland Assembly, and the National Assembly of Wales have power to enact primary legislation within the terms, respectively, of the Scotland Act 1998, the Northern Ireland Act 1998, and the Government of Wales Act 2006. Devolution has implications for *the UK Parliament* and it is this to which we now turn.

(a) THE SEWEL CONVENTION

During the passage of the bill that became the Scotland Act 1998, it was recognized that the UK Parliament would continue, in certain circumstances, to pass legislation on policy areas that were not 'reserved' to the UK Parliament (or, putting it the other way, areas that had been 'devolved'). The 1998 Act specifically preserves this power to legislate.[49] In 2002, the House of Lords Constitution Committee examined this.

House of Lords Constitution Committee, *Devolution: Inter-institutional Relations in the United Kingdom*, Second Report, Session 2002–03, HL 28

Legislating for Scotland after Devolution: The Sewel Convention

126. We also heard much evidence about the way Westminster continues to legislate for devolved matters in Scotland. As we have noted, the principles governing this were first stated by Lord Sewel in the Lords Second Reading debate on the Scotland Bill, and are now set out in the Memorandum of Understanding. Agreement to Westminster legislating for Scotland is given [by the Scottish Parliament . . .], in Sewel motions.

127. Professor Page's evidence to us emphasised that Westminster legislation on devolved matters was expected to be rare, but has in fact turned out to be common. To the end of June 2002, there had been 34 Sewel motions. Some bills have been the subject of more than one Sewel motion, while other motions have been passed for bills which have failed to complete their passage at Westminster. Professor Page's explanation for the frequency of legislation emphasised pulls toward uniformity across the UK despite the existence of a Scottish Parliament. These arose from a variety of factors, including electoral expectations, the administration of policies by UK bodies, avoiding 'regulatory arbitrage', applying EU or international law, or simply seeing no good reason why the law should differ between Scotland and other parts of the UK. Professor Page also highlighted reasons why such legislation may be attractive to the Scottish Executive, including the reliance on the UK Government to initiate reforms, avoiding disruption to the Executive's legislative programme for the Scottish Parliament, and avoiding any risk of legal uncertainty about the validity of Scottish legislation.

128. From the point of view of the Executive, we note that the convention offers significant benefits—in particular, enabling legislation to apply to Scotland without having to find legislative time for it.

[49] See Chapter 5.

129. A number of aspects of the operation of the Sewel convention cause us concern. One of these is the nature of the consent the Scottish Parliament gives when it assents to a Sewel motion put before it. It appears to us that this is very often in the nature of a blanket permission—'blank cheque'—for the Westminster legislation. If the matter were the subject of legislation before the Scottish Parliament, the Parliament would have several opportunities to consider the bill and propose amendments. When the matter is dealt with at Westminster, the Scottish Parliament receives only the one opportunity to consider the matter. It cannot propose amendments or, it appears, make its consent conditional on desired changes being made to the UK bill. It also gets no opportunity to consider the UK bill again, even if that has been the subject of extensive amendments. (The only circumstances in which the bill will return to the Parliament is if further amendments are made extending to Scotland provisions which did not apply there earlier, as with the Adoption and Children Bill.) From the point of view of the Scottish Parliament there appears to us to be a loss of control over legislation affecting devolved matters when that is made at Westminster, compared with the mechanisms that apply in the Scottish Parliament. The idea that amendments affecting devolved matters should be subject to a 'scrutiny reserve' in a way similar to EU measures, and so require further approval by the Scottish Parliament was put to us by Professor Page, and is one that interests us.

130. Second, we find it strange that an issue which is fundamentally about co-operation between legislatures has turned in practice into co-operation between executives. The convention itself states that it is for the UK Government to determine whether an approach should be made to the Scottish Executive, and for the Executive to signal whether that consent has been given. That appears to us to be inappropriate.

131. While the UK Government may have a view about whether a Bill affects devolved matters or not, and what action should be taken as a result, we recommend that such communication should be between the UK Parliament and Scottish Parliament, not mediated by the executives at each end.

132. Making such communication a parliamentary and not a government matter would involve considerable changes. Whether those changes should be made and what they should be are of course matters for the Scottish Parliament as well as the UK Parliament to determine. The Committee consider that these would include ensuring that the UK Parliament had access to advice so that it could determine whether a bill affected devolved matters or not. They would also include the establishment of a formal arrangement between the UK Parliament and Scottish Parliament to deal with procedural issues arising from such consent, and enabling the Scottish Parliament more routinely to express its views on amendments made during a bill's passage at Westminster. Such changes would of course also require the Scottish Parliament to make changes to its procedures as well, and improving procedures will require a shared will for the two parliaments to take control of this matter. However, in the interests of promoting a proper separation between the executive and the legislative functions, we think that should be undertaken.

133. Third, we note that the Sewel motion mechanism does not appear to operate in the Northern Ireland Assembly. There are have been only two votes on Westminster legislation affecting devolved matters. There is no formal exchange of information about Westminster legislation with the Northern Ireland Executive, and a flow of information that rests on the fact that the Speaker of the Assembly is a member of this House and receives Hansard as a matter of course.

134. While it is of course a matter for the Northern Ireland Assembly and Executive to deal with themselves, we consider it would be advantageous to the UK Parliament as well as the Assembly for there to be a proper procedure to deal with Sewel motions where a Westminster bill affects devolved matters in Northern Ireland.

(b) THE 'ENGLISH QUESTION'

A different concern that has emerged in the wake of devolution of devolved legislative powers to Scotland, Wales, and Northern Ireland is the role of the UK Parliament as the legislature for Bills that apply *only to England*.[50] The practical problem (according to some) is that, since 1998, MPs representing Welsh, Northern Irish, and Scottish constituencies in the UK Parliament have continued to be able to vote on legislation that applies only to England. It is said that this is unfair in general and in particular on those occasions on which a majority of MPs from England oppose an initiative, but it is nonetheless passed because of votes from MPs in other parts of the United Kingdom who are prepared to support the government, even though their constituents will not be affected by what is proposed. This is one aspect of what has been dubbed 'the English Question' (or 'the West Lothian Question', after the name of the Scottish constituency of the MP who first raised this issue during the devolution debates of the 1970s).

One possible solution would be to create an English Parliament, distinct from the UK Parliament. Another, supported by the Conservative Party, among others, is 'English votes for English laws', in which only MPs from constituencies in England would vote on provisions in Bills before the UK Parliament that apply only to England. Critics argue that such a reform would undermine the United Kingdom, in the Parliament of which all MPs should be free to vote equally on any issue.

Robert Hazell, 'The English Question' (2006) 36 Publius: The Journal of Federalism 37, 42–3 (citations omitted)

English Votes on English Laws: Westminster as a Proxy for an English Parliament

In contrast [to the idea of an English Parliament], English votes on English laws is a proposition that does command some elite support and considerable mass support. Polling data consistently show that between 50 and 60 percent of people in England agree that Scottish MPs should no longer be allowed to vote on English laws now that Scotland has its own parliament. It seems only logical and fair, since English MPs can no longer vote on matters devolved to Scotland. Even a majority of Scots support restricting the voting rights of Scottish MPs in this way. But the difficulties of implementing such a policy seem insuperable, at both a technical and a political level. The technical difficulty is identifying those English laws on which only English MPs would be allowed to vote. Strictly speaking there is no such thing as an English law, in the sense of a Westminster statute that applies only to England. The territorial extent clauses in Westminster statutes typically extend to the United Kingdom, Great Britain, or England and Wales. Many statutes vary in their territorial application in different parts of the act. In theory the Speaker could identify in advance those clauses or amendments that apply only to England and rule that only English MPs could take part in those divisions. But the complexity and confusion resulting from excluding non-English MPs from some votes but not others in the same bill would be immense. Only with the introduction of electronic voting at Westminster would it become feasible, because that would enable the voting terminals of non-English MPs to be disabled or discounted in divisions in which they were deemed ineligible to vote.

---

[50] See also Chapter 5.

If the technical difficulties are daunting, the political difficulties are even greater. Proponents of English votes on English laws tend to underestimate just what a huge change would be involved. It would create two classes of MP, ending the traditional reciprocity whereby all members can vote on all matters. It would effectively create a parliament within a parliament. And after close-fought elections, the U.K. government might not be able to command a majority for its English business, leading to great political instability. These political difficulties cast serious doubt on the likelihood of English votes on English laws ever becoming political reality.

In February 2012, an expert committee ('the McKay Commission') began work 'to consider how the House of Commons might deal with legislation which affects only part of the United Kingdom, following the devolution of certain legislative powers to the Scottish Parliament, the Northern Ireland Assembly and the National Assembly for Wales'.[51]

QUESTIONS

1. Critically assess the respective roles of the executive and Parliament in making primary legislation.

2. In your view, what, if any, reforms should be introduced to the legislative process?

---

12 CONCLUDING COMMENTS

This chapter has examined the legislative process for making primary legislation. To explore the process for making delegated legislation, turn now to Chapter 11.

13 FURTHER READING

Brazier, A. et al., *Law in the Making: Influence and Change in the Legislative Process* (2008, London: Hansard Society)

ONLINE RESOURCE CENTRE

Further information about the themes discussed in this chapter can be found on the Online Resource Centre at www.oxfordtextbooks.co.uk/orc/lesueur2e/

---

[51] http://tmc.independent.gov.uk/

11

DELEGATED LEGISLATION

CENTRAL ISSUES

1. To what extent are executive bodies, especially ministers, permitted to make legislation? In Chapter 4, we saw that some theories of 'separation of powers' suggest that legislation is a function that should be carried out by parliaments rather than governments. The British constitution has developed in ways that allow ministers considerable powers to make legislation.

2. Ministers use delegated legislation for a variety of purposes: to bring sections of Acts of Parliament into force; to fill in the detail of frameworks created by Acts of Parliament; to 'transpose' EU directives into national law (see Chapter 12); and, most controversially, to repeal and amend Acts of Parliament.

3. What are the respective roles of ministers (who formally sign delegated legislation) and civil servants (who advise on what delegated legislation is needed)?

4. How effectively does the UK Parliament control law-making by ministers? A range of parliamentary committees have been set up to examine both the merits of legislation proposed by ministers and its 'technical' correctness. Some commentators, however, question whether there is adequate scrutiny from the UK Parliament.

5. In a small number of cases, the courts have also had a role to play in ensuring that ministers do not act unlawfully in exercising their legislative powers. In relation to delegated legislation, the courts are not constrained by the principle of parliamentary supremacy and may quash legislation made by ministers.

6. There is a perplexing array of terminology relating to legislation made by ministers: 'delegated', 'subordinate', and 'secondary' legislation are all used as a general label; this may take the form of 'regulations', 'rules', and 'Orders in Council'. Most, but not all, take the form of 'statutory instruments'. This chapter will help you get to grips with this vocabulary.

1 INTRODUCTION

This chapter is about delegated legislation—also called 'subordinate' and 'secondary' legislation. We examine, first, why the constitution allows ministers (part of the *executive*) to make such legislation and the process by which it is made. In the final section of the chapter, we look at a case study on a controversial attempt by the government during the 2005–06 parliamentary session to acquire greater powers than it had held previously to bring about changes to Acts of Parliament (repealing or amending them) and the common law. Before we look at some of the specific problems raised by the Legislative and Regulatory Reform Act 2006, we need to set it in the broader context of the use of primary and secondary legislation in the British constitutional system.

As well as learning about delegated legislation, you can use the material in this chapter to shed light on two of the constitutional principles that we explored in Chapter 2 and Chapter 3. Through delegated legislation, the *government* makes legislation on a large scale with only minimal *parliamentary* involvement. To what extent can this fact of modern constitutional life be squared with the idea that 'Parliament legislates'—a core aspect of ideas about the sovereignty of Parliament? Another obvious question is how does the use of delegated legislation sit with the theory of separation of powers?

2 NATURE OF DELEGATED LEGISLATION

Let us start by looking at the general characteristics of delegated legislation. The following extract refers to 'statutory instruments' (SIs), which, as will be explained, are one of the main forms in which delegated legislation is made in the United Kingdom.

Edward C. Page, *Governing by Numbers* (2001, Oxford: Hart Publishing), pp. 20–1

What are statutory instruments?

Statutory Instruments are a form of law. Governments can make two broad types of domestic law—*primary* and *secondary* legislation. *Primary* legislation in Britain refers to laws which derive their authority directly from [...] the Crown in Parliament. According to the traditional principle of the sovereignty of Parliament [...], government is free to pass whatever Acts it chooses, as long as they pass through the formal stages of parliamentary approval and receive the Royal Assent. Acts of Parliament can, for example, limit or extend personal freedoms, create or abolish democratic institutions such as local governments and nationalise or privatise industries. Accordingly, Acts of Parliament are supreme laws which cannot be challenged in the courts. In practice the traditional notion of the sovereignty of Parliament no longer applies in the same way since the United Kingdom joined the European Union, but this does not detract from the fact that primary legislation is, in principle, a higher form of law which can be challenged through the courts only if it conflicts with an even higher form of law in the shape of European Union legislation.

Statutory Instruments are *secondary* (also termed *subordinate* or *delegated*) legislation. They are not the only type of secondary legislation, but rather the form most commonly associated with the term. Secondary legislation refers to laws which derive their legitimacy from powers given to a minister or a department in primary legislation—that is, in an Act of Parliament. The provisions of many Acts of Parliament contain clauses along the lines that a Secretary of State or a minister may make provisions by order to bring a particular clause into operation or to specify, amend or adjust how the clause is to be interpreted or applied. [...]

Secondary legislation can only be made where there is an explicit provision in primary legislation to do so; that is to say, where government has the legal powers or vires to issue delegated legislation. Consequently every Statutory Instrument must contain reference to specific clauses in Acts of Parliament that give governments vires to draw up subordinate legislation. All secondary legislation has 'parent' primary legislation. Moreover, provisions within delegated legislation can be declared invalid by the courts if, for example, they are judged not to be consistent with the powers granted in the parent legislation or if the procedures used to draw them up are invalid.

The focus in this chapter is on delegated legislation made by ministers on the advice of officials, departmental lawyers, and other government experts.

(a) DELEGATED AND PRIMARY LEGISLATION COMPARED

One of the main themes in the debates about the use (and alleged misuse) of delegated legislation by ministers is that, in some situations in which delegated legislation is used to give legal authority to a policy, it would be more constitutionally appropriate for primary legislation to be used. Box 11.1 sets out a summary of some of the main points of difference between the two categories of legislation. What should be obvious is that delegated legislation receives far less *political scrutiny* from Parliament than do Bills.

This is not to say that delegated legislation cannot be justified. A great deal of it is made every year—some 3,000 pieces compared to fifty or so Bills—so there must be something to be said for it.

BOX 11.1 DELEGATED AND PRIMARY LEGISLATION COMPARED

	Delegated legislation	Primary legislation (Acts of Parliament)
Who makes it?	Ministers, with the approval of Parliament	Parliament
By what procedure?	Varies All is subject to 'technical' scrutiny by the Joint Committee on Statutory Instruments The House of Lords Committee on the Merits of Statutory Instruments reports on significant legislation	Second Reading, Committee, Report, and Third Reading in Commons and Lords Scrutiny by Joint Committee on Human Rights and Constitution Committee
Is it amendable?	No: MPs and peers cannot suggest improvements	Yes: much of the debate is on amendments by MPs and peers

How long is the debate?	Most is not debated at all. If there is debate, it is strictly limited to 90 minutes	Varies according to importance and complexity—usually many days
Can the courts review it?	Yes: the courts may apply the normal grounds of judicial review and quash delegated legislation	Not generally: parliamentary sovereignty prevents this (but the courts may make a declaration of incompatibility under the Human Rights Act 1998 and 'disapply' a section of an Act that is contrary to EU law)

Consider Robert Baldwin's explanation.

R. Baldwin, 'Legislation, types of', in P. Cane and J. Conaghan (eds) *The New Oxford Companion to Law* (2009, Oxford: OUP), p. 721

The common justifications for secondary legislation are that delegations of rule-making are necessary and useful because Parliament does not have the time or the detailed knowledge to make specialist bodies of rules; that some subjects are too technical to justify parliamentary attention; that secondary rules are much more flexible and responsive than statutes; and that delegations of rule-making power allow adjustments and updating or amending exercises to be carried out efficiently.

Much modern legislation is carried out by means of 'framework' items of primary legislation, which do little more than confer on certain parties (usually ministers or agencies) powers to issue secondary legislation. This prompts the common criticism that parliamentary and democratic scrutiny is weakened by such heavy reliance on secondary legislation since such legislation does not involve the full parliamentary process and the debating stages that are associated with primary legislation. There is, indeed, widely seen to be some force in this point.

(b) GETTING TO GRIPS WITH THE TERMINOLOGY

What at first can seem like a baffling array of terms is used in discussion about the subject matter of this chapter. To get to grips with it, it can help to take things in two stages.

First, there is the vocabulary used for this *generic category* of law: the terms 'delegated', 'secondary', and 'subordinate' legislation are, in most contexts, interchangeable. Many constitutional systems make a distinction between 'primary' legislation (in the United Kingdom, this means Acts of Parliament) and delegated/secondary/subordinate legislation.[1] A piece of

---

[1] So see, e.g., Chapter 12, in which—in the context of the European Union—the foundational treaties are called 'primary legislation', and directives and regulations made under authority of the treaties, by the EU institutions, are termed 'secondary legislation'.

primary legislation (in the United Kingdom, 'the parent Act') 'delegates' or 'confers' power on a minister or other public authority to make rules (the delegated legislation). The specific section in the Act that confers this power is often called 'the enabling provision'.

Second, there are terms of a more technical nature that identify the various specific forms of delegated legislation *in the United Kingdom*. The vast majority of delegated legislation is made in the form of 'statutory instruments' (SIs), a form of law that is regulated by the Statutory Instruments Act 1946. The 1946 Act sets out the various types of parliamentary procedure that apply when a minister decides to make an SI—and here lies another confusing aspect of the terminology: the titles of particular SIs use the terms 'Order', 'Regulation', or sometimes 'Rules'. Generally speaking, there is no legal significance to the use of these titles—it is more to do with historical accident and drafting practices. Consider the following examples and note how to cite an SI using its number:

- the Disability Discrimination (Premises) **Regulations** 2006 (SI 2006/887);
- the Naval, Military and Air Forces Etc. (Disablement and Death) Service Pensions **Order** 2006 (SI 2006/606); and
- the Civil Procedure (Amendment) **Rules** 2006 (SI 2006/1689).

(c) ORDERS IN COUNCIL

A further word of clarification is needed about 'Orders in Council' (a term used in the extract from Edward C. Page, *Governing by Numbers*, on p. 444). There are two distinct meanings. One is that an Order in Council is a type of SI (like regulations, 'ordinary' orders, and rules, as we have explained): it differs from other SIs only in that as well as being signed by a minister before undergoing a parliamentary procedure, it also has the extra formality of being approved at one of the monthly meetings of the Privy Council (a very short meeting of the Queen and a handful of senior ministers at which legislation is nodded through without any debate).[2] An enabling provision in a parent Act will typically specify that the SI be in the form of an Order in Council when something of considerable importance is at stake.

The term 'Order in Council' is also used to refer a species of law that is *primary* legislation.[3] The Crown has retained prerogative power to make legislation dealing with a few matters, including, for example, regulation of the civil service. Thus the Civil Service Order in Council is primary legislation. The continued possibility of primary legislation made by the executive rather than Parliament is anomalous in a modern constitutional democracy.

3 WHY USE DELEGATED LEGISLATION?

In what circumstances does Parliament delegate law-making powers to ministers (and occasionally other public authorities, such as the National Assembly for Wales)? We can begin to answer this question by looking at a range of enabling provisions in Acts.

---

[2] See Chapter 7.
[3] See Chapter 9 and Chapter 10.

(a) COMMENCEMENTS

Identity Cards Act 2006

Short title, repeals, commencement, transitory provision and extent

44 —[...]

(3) This Act (apart from this section and sections 36 and 38) shall come into force on such day as the Secretary of State may by order appoint; and different days may be appointed for different purposes.

(4) The power to bring provisions of this Act into force on different days for different purposes includes power–

(a) to bring provisions into force on different days in relation to different areas or descriptions of persons;

(b) to bring provisions into force in relation to a specified area or a specified description of persons for the purpose of conducting a trial of the arrangements under which the provisions will have effect when brought into force in relation to other areas or descriptions of persons; and

(c) power to make transitional provision in connection with the bringing into force of any provision of this Act following the conduct of such a trial.

(5) Sections 36 and 38 come into force at the end of the period of two months beginning with the day on which this Act is passed.

This is an example of an *enabling provision* giving powers to ministers to allow them to decide when the time is right to bring into force sections of an Act of Parliament. What follows is an example of a commencement order made under this provision. Note that the enabling provision refers to 'the Secretary of State', but that the Order was, in fact, made by a junior minister on his behalf.

The Identity Cards Act 2006 (Commencement No. 2) Order 2006

Made 23rd September 2006

The Secretary of State, in exercise of the powers conferred by section 44(3) of the Identity Cards Act 2006, makes the following Order:

Citation

1. This Order may be cited as the Identity Cards Act 2006 (Commencement No.2) Order 2006.

Commencement

2. Section 37 of the Identity Cards Act 2006 (Report to Parliament about likely cost of ID cards scheme) shall come into force on 30th September 2006.

Joan Ryan
Parliamentary Under Secretary of State
Home Office 23rd September 2006

As a footnote to this example, it should be noted that the Coalition government formed in 2010 was opposed to compulsory identity cards for British and other EU nationals: the 2006 Act and delegated legislation made under it was repealed by the Identity Documents Act 2010.

The use of delegated legislation to bring into force primary legislation is generally regarded as a sensible practical arrangement. In relation to some provisions, it may be possible for the Act to specify a particular date for a section to come into force (or indeed the whole Act)—see s. 44(5) Identity Cards Act 2006 on p. 448. But where, for example, an Act sets up a large or complex administrative scheme, civil servants may have to be trained, computer equipment commissioned, and application forms printed and distributed. It is regarded as acceptable to delegate this decision about *timing* to the government and commencement orders are normally subject to no parliamentary scrutiny procedure. An enabling provision creates a *power*, not a *duty*, to bring sections of an Act of Parliament into force—but as long as an enabling provision has not been repealed, there is a continuing obligation on the Secretary of State to consider whether to bring a statutory scheme into force and he or she must avoid doing anything that would undermine that obligation (for example, announcing that he or she will *never* bring it into force).[4]

Delegating this discretion to ministers has the consequence that sections of Acts, although appearing on the face of the 'statute book', are in fact never brought into force and so are not binding law. There are no statistics as to what proportion of the statute book is not in force, but it may not be too far-fetched to suggest 10 per cent, including some apparently important provisions. Arguably, this creates a tension with the constitutional principle of parliamentary sovereignty: Parliament has decided that the law should be X, but that is never turned into binding law because the government decides otherwise (even if, following the *Fire Brigades Union* case, they keep an open mind). There may also be tensions with ideals of openness and accessibility of law, which are aspects of the rule of law: citizens and legal advisers must often struggle to work out whether a provision in an Act has actually been brought into force or not.

> **QUESTIONS**
>
> 1. Explain how you would set about working out whether a particular section of an Act of Parliament is or is not in force. What legislation would you need to consult? What databases would be helpful?
>
> 2. How easy or difficult is the task of tracking down commencement dates? Are the difficulties *practical* or *constitutional* (or both) in character?

(b) FRAMEWORK FILLING

Many Acts of Parliament set out only a general 'framework', or 'skeleton', for the policies sought to be achieved, delegating matters of detail to the government to be made by secondary legislation.

> **QUESTIONS**
>
> Consider the enabling provision in the following extract.
>
> 1. How much discretion does it confer on the government?

---

[4] *R v Secretary of State for the Home Department, ex parte Fire Brigades Union* [1995] 2 AC 513, discussed in Chapter 4 and Chapter 9.

2. How much do you think members of Parliament (MPs) and peers debating the Equality Bill would have known about how the government planned to exercise its discretion?

Equality Act 2006, Pt 3

DISCRIMINATION ON GROUNDS OF SEXUAL ORIENTATION

Regulations

81 (1) The Secretary of State may by regulations make provision about discrimination or harassment on grounds of sexual orientation.

(2) In subsection (1) "sexual orientation" has the meaning given by section 35.

(3) The regulations may, in particular:

(a) make provision of a kind similar to Part 2 of this Act;

(b) define discrimination;

(c) define harassment;

(d) make provision for enforcement (which may, in particular, include provision;

(i) creating a criminal offence of a kind similar to, and with the same maximum penalties as, an offence created by an enactment relating to discrimination or equality;

(ii) about validity and revision of contracts;

(iii) about discriminatory advertisements;

(iv) about instructing or causing discrimination or harassment);

(e) provide for exceptions (whether or not of a kind similar to those provided for by Part 2 of this Act or any other enactment relating to discrimination or equality);

(f) make provision which applies generally or only in specified cases or circumstances;

(g) make different provision for different cases or circumstances;

(h) include incidental or consequential provision (which may include provision amending an enactment);

(i) include transitional provision.

(4) The regulations

(a) shall be made by statutory instrument, and

(b) may not be made unless a draft has been laid before and approved by resolution of each House of Parliament.

(5) In subsection (3)(h) "enactment" includes an enactment in or under an Act of the Scottish Parliament.

There is a continuing debate about the pros and cons of including detailed rules in Acts of Parliament themselves or allowing the government to make detailed rules by secondary legislation on the basis of delegated powers. The Hansard Society, founded in 1944, is an independent and non-partisan educational charity working to stimulate knowledge of, and interest in, democracy. In the early 1990s, it carried out an inquiry into law-making, and received submissions from many organizations and individuals.

Hansard Society Commission on the Legislative Process, *Making the Law* (1992), pp. 64–5

254. Several people and bodies thought that the substantive provisions of statute law should be dealt with in Acts of Parliament, with only less important details being left to delegated legislation, or were unhappy about the extensive use of delegated legislation. Evidence to this effect was given in memoranda or orally by Lord Simon of Glaisdale, the Bar Council, Shelter, the CPAG, the Society of County Secretaries, the TUC, the CBI, the Law Society, the local authority associations, the Institute of Public Relations, the National Consumer Council, the Scottish Consumer Council, the Industry and Parliament Trust, the Institute of Directors, Dr John Cunningham, MP, Mr Andrew Bennett, MP, and Sir Peter Emery, MP.

255. The reasons for this critical view of the use of delegated legislation were numerous. They included objection to "skeleton bills"; the use of delegated powers to determine the principles rather than the detailed implementation of legislation (the local authority associations gave several examples of this); the increased power it gave to Ministers; the lack of parliamentary time for scrutiny of delegated legislation and inadequate parliamentary scrutiny; the difficulty of campaigning against bills that include extensive delegation of powers and against draft orders etc.; the fact that statutory instruments cannot be amended; the danger of the drafters of bills thinking they could rely on regulations to put matters right if there were a flaw in a bill (suggested to us by the Child Poverty Action Group); the fact that the drafting of statutory instruments was sometimes delayed till too near the time they had to be applied (noted by the FDA); the uncertainty of leaving things to regulations and waiting for them to be made; the difficulty of discovering the law on any matter if it is buried in a number of statutory instruments; and, as emphasised to us by many bodies, including the CBI and the Institute of Directors, the difficulty for Parliament and other bodies of appreciating the full effect of a bill before the relevant delegated legislation is available.

256. Others who gave evidence believed that only the policy elements and other major provisions of legislation need be included in bills, or saw some advantages in leaving more detail to delegated legislation. Supporters of these views in written or oral evidence included Lord Howe of Aberavon, Lord Renton, Lord Aberdare, the Association of British Insurers and Lloyd's, the BBC and the Institute of Chartered Accountants.

257. The main arguments advanced in favour of greater use of delegated legislation were also weighty. The included the advantage of keeping primary legislation uncluttered; the fact that delegated legislation is not subject to the same constraints of the parliamentary time-table as is primary legislation and that therefore there can be more time for consultation; the greater flexibility it permits (because it does not involve the passing of a bill through Parliament) in updating the law to match changed circumstances and in correcting or amending it in the light of experience; and its value for VAT and other fiscal legislation.

258. Others, including Mr Justice Paul Kennedy representing the Judges' Council, appeared to be content with the present balance between primary and delegated legislation.

259. The Renton Committee recommended that general principles should be set out in the body of an Act, with details of a permanent kind in its Schedules rather than its sections, and that only details liable to frequent modification should be dealt with by statutory instruments (para. 11.25).

260. Certain particular uses of delegated legislation were strongly criticised. Lord Renton, Lord Simon of Glaisdale, the Law Society and Mr Bob Cryer, MP, were strongly opposed to the increasing use of "Henry VIII clauses" which empower Ministers to amend primary legislation by statutory instrument.

Conclusions and recommendations

261. There has been a considerable increase in the volume of delegated legislation over the last thirty years, despite no great change in the annual number of statutory instruments. For example, in 1960 there were 2,496 instruments covering 2,820 pages; in 1988, 2,311 instruments required 6,342 pages; […] It is clear that more detail is being included in delegated legislation as well as in Acts. It may be that the use of delegated legislation for some purposes has decreased in some areas, which would explain the fairly stable number of statutory instruments each year, but it is still heavily used in some other areas. For example the Child Support Act 1991 contains over 100 regulation making powers.

262. As we have shown, there are strong differences of view on whether there should be more use of delegated legislation or less. There are good arguments each way. Opinion within our Commission was also divided. On balance however, we believe that the main advantages of making greater use of delegated legislation outweigh the very real disadvantages.

263. In particular we emphasise the merit of keeping bills as clear, simple and short as possible. This not only makes Acts easier for the user to follow, but it helps Parliament to focus on the essential points, and on policy and principle, in its debates on bills. Above all we find advantages - for the Government and for those affected by legislation - in keeping the legislative process flexible so that statute law can be kept as up-to-date as possible. If significant changes in the way the law is to work - in the light of experience of how it is operating, or following changed circumstances - can only be made through an Act of Parliament. then. given the pressures on the parliamentary time-table, such changes may have to wait several years before a bill can be introduced. It is much easier to bring in amending statutory instruments with less delay. Less rigidity in procedures and timing should also facilitate improved consultations.

264. We recognise the disadvantages of extensive use of delegated legislation, but many of them could be overcome. The scrutiny of statutory instruments in Parliament is inadequate and unsatisfactory, but it need not be. […] There are problems in debating bills before Members and those advising them know what is to be contained in the delegated legislation. […] Difficulty is undoubtedly experienced in accessing statute law when it is set out in a number of different documents - both Acts and statutory instruments. […]

265. A dividing line must be drawn somewhere; someone must decide what should be put in a bill and what left to delegated legislation. At present it appears rather haphazard, with Ministers, departmental officials and Parliamentary Counsel all having a say and differing solutions being adopted. Lord Renton has suggested various guidelines for what should be put in bills and what excluded.

266. We see great difficulty in laying down precise demarcation rules - the political needs, content, legal import and urgency of each bill differ - but we accept that some standard treatment, which does not appear to exist at present, would be desirable. We ourselves are not in a position to suggest what this might be. We welcome, however, the setting up by the House of Lords of the Delegated Powers Scrutiny Committee, which has been given, as its first task, the consideration of ground rules and criteria on what matters can appropriately be left to delegated legislation.

267. We emphasise that statutory delegation should never leave an Act bare of everything except a framework of ministerial powers, with all real substance being left to ministerial regulations etc. This has been done (see the legislation on student loans in the Education (Students Loans) Act 1990, for example); it should not be repeated. The main principles of the legislation and its central provisions should appear in the Act itself. Subject to that, and in the expectation that the new Lords Committee will be able to work out helpful ground rules,

on balance we recommend that the main provisions of statute law should be set out in Acts of Parliament, but that most detail should be left to delegated legislation, provided that much more satisfactory procedures are adopted by Parliament for scrutiny of delegated legislation and that improved arrangements are made for the publication of all statute law.

QUESTION

Which view do you find more attractive: the one that favours inclusion of detail in Acts, or the one that favours framework in Acts, later filled in by delegated legislation?

(c) IMPLEMENTATION OF EU LAW

As we will see in Chapter 12, the institutions of the European Union (the European Parliament, Commission, and Council) make various forms of legislation, including directives. Directives are addressed to member states and require them to be implemented within their national legal systems within a specified period (often twelve or eighteen months). Directives set out the general policy to be achieved. In the United Kingdom, if changes to national law are needed to achieve a directive's goals, the government may seek to do this either by primary legislation or by delegated legislation.[5]

(d) 'HENRY VIII' CLAUSES

So far, we have looked at the use of delegated legislation for the purposes of (a) bringing sections of Acts into force, (b) perhaps more significantly, filling in framework Acts, and (c) implementing European Union law. A fourth purpose may strike you as unusual: delegated legislation can be used *to amend or repeal Acts of Parliament*. Think about that for a moment: this is *secondary* legislation being used to change *primary* legislation. Enabling provisions that confer this surprising power on ministers have been dubbed 'Henry VIII' provisions, so-called because some critics argue that if abused, Henry VIII powers contained in Acts of Parliament risk giving ministers powers to suspend parliamentary legislation such as were enjoyed by the notoriously autocratic Tudor king.

Why would Parliament wish to give ministers these powers? One answer is that they are useful for relatively small-scale fine-tuning to the reforms being introduced by the Act without the need to trouble Parliament with a Bill. Often, minor problems come to light only after an Act has received royal assent. Many Acts contain an enabling clause similar to the following.

Consumer Credit Act 2006, s. 68

Consequential amendments

68 (1) The Secretary of State may by order made by statutory instrument make such modifications of—

[5] See Chapter 11.

(a) any Act or subordinate legislation (within the meaning of the Interpretation Act 1978 (c. 30)), or

(b) any Northern Ireland legislation or instrument made under such legislation,

as he thinks fit in consequence of any provision of this Act.

(2) An order under this section may include transitional or transitory provisions and savings.

(3) A statutory instrument containing an order under this section may not be made by the Secretary of State unless a draft has been laid before and approved by a resolution of each House of Parliament.

The use of Henry VIII clauses for reasons other than minor consequential amendments remains controversial. In 1997, the House of Lords established a select committee—now known as the Delegated Powers and Regulatory Reform Committee—to monitor the inclusion of Henry VIII powers in Bills. The Committee reports any concerns to the House of Lords, so that peers may, if they agree, seek to amend the Bill to remove or limit the power in question.

Consider the following example of a Henry VIII clause.

Animal Welfare Act 2006, s. 1

Animals to which the Act applies

1 (1) In this Act, except subsections (4) and (5), "animal" means a vertebrate other than man.

(2) Nothing in this Act applies to an animal while it is in its foetal or embryonic form.

(3) The appropriate national authority may by regulations for all or any of the purposes of this Act-

(a) extend the definition of "animal" so as to include invertebrates of any description;

(b) make provision in lieu of subsection (2) as respects any invertebrates included in the definition of "animal";

(c) amend subsection (2) to extend the application of this Act to an animal from such earlier stage of its development as may be specified in the regulations.

(4) The power under subsection (3)(a) or (c) may only be exercised if the appropriate national authority is satisfied, on the basis of scientific evidence, that animals of the kind concerned are capable of experiencing pain or suffering.

(5) In this section, "vertebrate" means any animal of the Sub-phylum Vertebrata of the Phylum Chordata and "invertebrate" means any animal not of that Sub-phylum.

QUESTIONS

1. How broad is the discretion conferred on ministers by this section?

2. Can you suggest any reasons why it was seen as impossible or undesirable to have a firm definition of 'animal' on the face of the Act?

(e) REGULATORY REFORM ORDERS

A final purpose for which SIs are used is to assist with government policy relating to regulation of business activity. Since the 1990s, both Conservative and Labour governments have recognized that, in some contexts, there is simply too much 'red tape'—unnecessary, overly complex, or disproportionately costly rules and procedures, set out in Acts of Parliament and SIs. Three Acts of Parliament have set out schemes for removing or amending regulatory requirements: the Deregulation and Contracting Out Act 1994; replaced by the Regulatory Reform Act 2001; and now the Legislative and Regulatory Reform Act 2006. These Acts all contained broad 'Henry VIII powers'. We will look at the issues that arise later in the chapter.

QUESTIONS

Any effective lawyer or law student should know how to track down SIs. To develop your skills, visit the Office for Public Sector Information (OPSI) website http://www.opsi.gov.uk and carry out the following exercises. You may not be able to answer some of the questions until you have read the rest of this chapter.

1. How many SIs were made in each of the past four years? How does this compare with the number of Acts of Parliament passed during the same periods?

2. How do you tell which 'enabling power' was used?

3. How do you cite an SI properly?

4. Look back at the work that you have done on parliamentary sovereignty. Does anything about SIs—their quantity, or the process by which they are made—cause you to doubt the proposition that 'Parliament is supreme'?

5. Make a random selection of ten SIs made during the past year and make an assessment of:

   (a) the range of subject matter with which they deal;

   (b) the importance of each one (perhaps you might create a scale from 'minor detail' to 'very important change of policy'); and

   (c) whether they are made under the 'negative' or 'affirmative' resolution procedure.

6. Find an SI made during the past twelve months that:

   (a) is a commencement order, bringing into force a section of an Act;

   (b) is being used for 'framework filling';

   (c) implements EC law; or

   (d) amends or repeals an Act of Parliament (using a 'Henry VIII power').

---

4 CIVIL SERVANTS AND MINISTERS MAKING DELEGATED LEGISLATION

Having surveyed the various types of delegated legislation that are routinely encountered in the British constitution system, we can now turn to look at the process by which the texts of SIs is created, which is significantly different from that relating to a Bill.

Terence Daintith and Alan Page, *The Executive in the Constitution: Structure, Autonomy, and Internal Control* (1999, Oxford: OUP), pp. 259–60

2.2 Departmental practice

It is in the nature of what is effectively a decentralized system of lawmaking that the procedures followed by any two departments in making subordinate legislation will not be exactly the same. The normal practice, however, 'is for the administrative division concerned with the subject matter of the enabling enactment to take the lead on the preparatory work, undertaking such consultation as necessary, obtaining Ministerial instructions, and co-operating with the legal staff on the drafting itself' (Joint Committee on Delegated Legislation 1972: Appendix 8, para. 8). Once a draft has been settled, a timetable is agreed for the printing, signature, laying, publication, and bringing into operation of the instrument. All but routine instruments are signed, or approved before signature, by ministers.

Departments which make extensive use of subordinate legislation usually have their own manuals setting out the procedures to be followed departmentally in the preparation and making of instruments. The Department of Health's *Preparation and Making of Statutory Instruments* (December 1995), which is addressed to administrators as well as lawyers, for example, provides a comprehensive statement of departmental procedures in relation to the making of instruments. HM Customs and Excise's Statutory Instruments: Practice and Procedure (1997), by contrast, is primarily intended for the use of lawyers in advisory teams who have little or no experience in the preparation and making of statutory instruments. Manuals intended for the use of lawyers usually address points of style as well as procedure.

In contrast to primary legislation, most secondary legislation is drafted by the legal branches of departments rather than by the PCO [Parliamentary Counsel Office]; the exceptions are those instruments, such as transfer of functions orders under the Ministers of Crown Act, which are drafted on behalf of the Cabinet Office by Parliamentary Counsel (or Scottish Parliamentary Counsel). Responsibility for ensuring legal effectiveness thus rests with departmental legal advisers. As a safeguard, instruments are usually subject to some form of scrutiny within departments, which may extend beyond strict questions of vires (on which the validity of instruments as law depends) to more general questions of structure and style. In the Home Office, the practice, which is said to be typical of practice across Whitehall, is for lawyers at former Grade 5 level to take responsibility for all instruments drafted in their teams. In the DTI another lawyer takes a 'second look' at instruments, while a senior lawyer acts as a source of advice on drafting issues. Instruments drafted by the Office of Solicitor to the Secretary of State for Scotland are scrutinized by a 'stylist' who is responsible for checking their vires and that they conform to the Solicitor's Office style. Where legal advisers are in doubt about the vires of proposed instruments, they are expected to consult the Law Officers (Cabinet Office 1997d: para. 22).

In the absence of centralized drafting arrangements, a measure of consistency in the structure and style of secondary legislation has been achieved through Statutory Instrument Practice, which provides a means of communicating best practice to departments, and through the work of the Joint Committee on Statutory Instruments and its predecessors.

This extract does not say anything about the role of ministers. This became a live issue in a judicial review challenge to an SI made under the Medicines Act 1968 prohibiting the sale for medicinal purposes of a drug called kava-kava, a widely used herbal tranquillizer, and another made under the Food Safety Act 1990 banning its use in foodstuffs. A minister in the relevant department must sign the text produced by civil servants and government lawyers; that minister may either be a junior minister or the Secretary of State (the most senior minister in that department, and a member of the Cabinet). But how much is the minister in question expected to know about the subject matter of the draft SI, or the reasons why it is being made? Is a ministerial signature just a rubber stamp for things done by officials?

R (on the application of National Association of Health Stores) v Secretary of State for Health
[2005] EWCA Civ 154, [1], [23]

Sedley LJ

In each case the measure was authorised by a minister in the name of the Secretary of State [...]

The principal ground of challenge is that in each instance the minister authorised the measure in ignorance of the relevant fact that prohibition was opposed by a leading psychopharmacological authority, Professor Ernst, on cogent grounds which he had spelt out in a published meta-analysis. [...]

What knowledge does the law impute to Ministers?

The next question is altogether more profound. It is not answered, only broached, by the historic decision of this court [the Court of Appeal] in *Carltona Ltd v Commissioners of Works* [1943] 2 All ER 560. There the court was presented with an attempt to transpose a familiar doctrine of the law of agency—the rule that one who is delegated cannot himself delegate—into the field of public administration, treating the minister as the Crown's delegate. Lord Greene MR, with his compendious knowledge of public administration, recognised the inappropriateness of the argument and answered it by holding that in law—as the Northcote-Trevelyan reforms had by then firmly established in practice—civil servants acted not on behalf of but in the name of their ministers.

Carltona, however, establishes only that the act of a duly authorised civil servant is in law the act of his or her minister. It does not decide or even suggest that what the civil servant knows is in law the minister's knowledge, regardless of whether the latter actually knows it. For the novel proposition that it is, Mr Cavanagh [counsel for the Department of Health] founds upon one sentence in Lord Diplock's speech in *Bushell v Secretary of State for the Environment* [1981] AC 75:

> "The collective knowledge, technical as well as factual, of the civil servants in the department and their collective expertise is to be treated as the minister's own knowledge, his own expertise."

It is Mr Cavanagh's submission that this affords a complete answer, without resort to evidence, to the accusation that Lord Hunt [the junior minister] was inadequately informed about Professor Ernst's views when he signed the Order. The departmental knowledge, which included everything that was material about Professor Ernst and his report, was the minister's, even if the minister did not in fact know it. This argument, advanced below by Mr Philip Sales [counsel for the Department of Health at first instance], was accepted by Crane J [the judge in the Administrative Court]. He held:

72. It follows that information available to officials involved in advising a minster is information that can properly be said to be information taken into account by the minister. It was submitted by Mr. Thompson QC that this would mean that information known to any official in the department can be said to be known to the minister taking a decision. I do not think that follows. If on a challenge to a decision, it were to be asserted that the Secretary of State took into account such information, when in fact no official involved in the matter knew of it, that would in my judgment be an inaccurate assertion. Nor, for example, would it be an accurate assertion if the relevant information was buried in a file but not in fact considered by any official in the matter. However, it does not follow that the court will in the ordinary way investigate whether such an assertion is accurate.

In my judgment, and with great respect to Crane J, this part of his decision is unfounded in authority and unsound in law. It is also, in my respectful view, antithetical to good government. It would be an embarrassment both for government and for the courts if we were to hold that a minister or a civil servant could lawfully take a decision on a matter he or she knew nothing about because one or more officials in the department knew all about it. The proposition becomes worse, not better, when it is qualified, as Crane J qualified it and as Mr Cavanagh now seeks to qualify it, by requiring that the civil servants with the relevant knowledge must have taken part in briefing or advising the minister. To do this is to substitute for the *Carltona* doctrine of ordered devolution to appropriate civil servants of decision-making authority (to adopt the lexicon used by Lord Griffiths in *Oladehinde* [1991] 1 AC 254) either a de facto abdication by the lawful decision-maker in favour of his or her adviser, or a division of labour in which the person with knowledge decides nothing and the decision is taken by a person without knowledge.

In contrast to *Carltona*, where this court gave legal authority to the practical reality of modern government in relation to the devolution of departmental functions, the doctrine for which Mr Cavanagh contends does not, certainly to my knowledge, reflect the reality of modern departmental government. The reality, subject no doubt to occasional lapses, is that ministers (or authorised civil servants) are properly briefed about the decisions they have to take; that in the briefings evidence is distinguished from advice; and that ministers take some trouble to understand the evidence before deciding whether to accept the advice. I will come later in this judgment to the critical question of how much of the evidence the minister needs to know; but I cannot believe that anybody, either in government or among the electorate, would thank this court for deciding that it was unnecessary for a decision-maker to know anything material before reaching a decision.

Four years after *Bushell* was decided, the High Court of Australia had before it an issue akin to the issue before us. A minister had made an order affecting land rights in ignorance of a potentially crucial fact. The fact was known, however, within his department. It is of interest that the minister's counsel, David Bennett QC (now S-G), one of Australia's leading constitutional lawyers, did not attempt to advance the argument which has been advanced by Mr Cavanagh. He contended only that the minister could lawfully delegate fact-finding to officials, and that there was no evidence that the material fact had been overlooked at official level: in other words, he sought to refine *Carltona* into a doctrine of split or partial delegation. The High Court rejected this endeavour. Gibbs CJ said:

"Of course the Minister cannot be expected to read for himself all the relevant papers that relate to the matter. It would not be unreasonable for him to rely on a summary of the relevant facts furnished by the officers of his Department. No complaint could be made if the departmental officers, in their summary, omitted to mention a fact which was insignificant or insubstantial. But if the Minister relies entirely on a departmental summary which fails to bring to his attention a material fact which he is bound to consider, and which cannot be dismissed as insignificant or insubstantial, the consequence will be that he will have failed to take that material fact into account and will not have formed his satisfaction in accordance with law."

Mason J (as he then was) pointed out that what was being proposed was that "the minister had power to delegate part of his decision-making function [...] to his department, and that he exercised this power by splitting the function, leaving his staff to decide what facts or matters would be taken into account." Any delegation, he went on to point out, must first be lawful and secondly be shown to have been made. He made it clear that in that case (as in this) the issue was whether the decision-maker had omitted a consideration which was in the obligatory class of relevance.

The High Court was unanimous in rejecting the argument, both on principle and from convenience, that the minister could decide without actually knowing something which bore the requisite degree of relevance to his decision. I will come below to the valuable remarks of Brennan J on the content of the ministerial obligation.

In the light of this significant Australian decision one comes back to what Lord Diplock said in *Bushell*. The full passage reads:

"What is fair procedure is to be judged not in the light of constitutional fictions as to the relationship between the minister and the other servants of the Crown who serve in the government department of which he is the head, but in the light of the practical realities as to the way in which administrative decisions involving forming judgments based on technical considerations are reached. To treat the minister in his decision-making capacity as someone separate and distinct from the department of government of which he is the political head and for whose actions he alone in constitutional theory is accountable to Parliament is to ignore not only practical realities but also Parliament's intention. Ministers come and go; departments, though their names may change from time to time, remain. Discretion in making administrative decisions is conferred upon a minister not as an individual but as the holder of an office in which he will have available to him in arriving at his decision the collective knowledge, experience and expertise of all those who serve the Crown in the department of which, for the time being, he is the political head. The collective knowledge, technical as well as factual, of the civil servants in the department and their collective expertise is to be treated as the minister's own knowledge, his own expertise."

[...] The serious practical implication of the argument [advanced by counsel for the Department of Health] is that, contrary to what the decided English cases take for granted, ministers need know nothing before reaching a decision so long as those advising them know the facts. This is the law according to Sir Humphrey Appleby. It would covertly transmute the adviser into the decision-maker. And by doing so it would incidentally deprive the adviser of an important shield against criticism where the decision turns out to have been a mistake.

The only authority Mr Cavanagh was able to produce which appeared to chime with his argument was a decision of Lord Clyde, sitting in the Outer House of the Court of Session, in *Air 2000 v Secretary of State for Transport (No 2)* [1990] SLT 335. Advice from the Civil Aviation Authority which by statute the Secretary of State was required to consider had been seen not by him but by an interdepartmental working party which advised him. Lord Clyde cited *Carltona* for the uncontroversial proposition that "what is done by his responsible official is done by [the minister]". However, while rejecting as "too extreme" a submission that the mere physical delivery of the advice to the department was sufficient, Lord Clyde accepted that "if it is given to an official who has responsibility for the matter in question, that should suffice". If by this Lord Clyde meant that such receipt would amount in law to consideration by the Secretary of State, I would respectfully disagree. For the reasons I have given, it would be incumbent on such an official to ensure that either the advice or a suitable précis of it was included in the submission to the minister whose decision it was to be.

Sedley LJ went on to consider the question 'Did the Minister leave relevant matter out of account in deciding to make the Order? Sedley LJ looked at the evidence to see what was included and what omitted from the briefing papers prepared for the Minister.

But what in the end I am unable to accept is that the minister had less information than the law required. The test is the familiar public law test: was something relevant left out of account by him in taking his decision? [...]

Given the constitutional position as this court now holds it to be, a minister who reserves a decision to himself—and equally a civil servant who is authorised by him to take a decision - must know or be told enough to ensure that nothing that it is necessary, because legally relevant, for him to know is left out of account. This is not the same as a requirement that he must know everything that is relevant. Here, for example, much that was highly relevant was appropriately sifted by the Commission in formulating its advice and then distilled within the department in order to make a submission to the minister which would tell him what it was relevant (not simply expedient or politic) for him to know. What it was relevant for the minister to know was enough to enable him to make an informed judgment. This centrally included the Commission's advice and the reasons for it. It also included the fact of Professor Ernst's opposition and the essential reasons for it. All this he had.

The Court of Appeal dismissed the National Association's appeal.

QUESTIONS

1. What differences are there between the way in which the text of a draft SI is created and the way in which the text of a Bill is produced?

2. Summarize in a few sentences what the Court of Appeal held in the *National Association of Health Stores* case about the constitutional role of (a) officials and (b) ministers in making delegated legislation.

3. What does Sedley LJ mean when he says '*This is the law according to Sir Humphrey Appleby*'?

---

5 PARLIAMENT'S ROLE IN DELEGATED LEGISLATION

One of the rationales for delegated legislation is that it relieves Parliament of some of the burden of legislating. It is therefore not surprising that draft SIs receive far less scrutiny than bills. Some SIs—those that make commencement orders bringing sections of an Act into force—are subject to no parliamentary procedures at all; other draft SIs are subject to a range of oversight mechanisms, depending on the importance of the subject matter.

To understand the following extract fully, you need to get to grips with some more technical terminology. An SI is said to be in 'draft' up until the point at which it is signed by a minister. An SI is 'made' when it is signed by the minister (look back at the example, The Identity Cards Act 2006 set out on p. 448). An SI is 'laid' when it is formally deposited in designated offices in the House of Commons and the House of Lords.

House of Commons Information Office, *Statutory Instruments*, Factsheet L7 (2008)

Many SIs are subject to parliamentary control; these SIs will follow one of the procedures laid down in the Statutory Instruments Act 1946. The type of parliamentary control will usually be prescribed in the parent Act. An instrument is laid before Parliament either in draft form or after the instrument has been made. According to the procedure applied to them, most SIs fall into one of the classes shown below:

[...]

Negative Procedure

Some SIs become law on the date stated on them but will be annulled if either House (or the Commons only, in the case of instruments dealing with financial matters) passes a motion calling for their annulment within a certain time. This time period is usually 40 days including the day on which it was laid. No account is taken of any time during which Parliament is dissolved or prorogued, or during which both Houses are adjourned for more than four days. A motion calling for annulment is known as a prayer, couched in such terms as: 'That an humble address be presented to Her Majesty praying that the Asylum Seekers (Interim Provisions) Regulations 1999 [...] be annulled'. In the House of Commons any Member may put down a motion to annul an SI subject to the Negative Procedure. In practice such motions are now generally put down as Early Day Motions (EDMs), which are motions for which no time has been fixed and, in the vast majority of cases, for which no time is likely to be available. A motion put down by the Official Opposition will often be accommodated although there is no absolute certainty of this. An annulment motion put down by a backbencher is unlikely to be dealt with but a debate may be arranged if there are a large number of signatories to the EDM. In the House of Lords prayers can be tabled by an individual Member and are usually debated, although rarely put to the vote. A recent example of a successful motion to annul occurred on 22 February 2000, when the House of Lords rejected the Greater London Authority Elections Rules (SI 2000/208). The House of Commons last annulled a Statutory Instrument on 24th October 1979 (the Paraffin (Maximum Retail Prices) (Revocation) Order 1979 (S.I. 1979, No. 797)).

Affirmative Procedure

This is less common than the negative procedure, currently representing about 10% of instruments subject to Parliamentary procedure, but provides more stringent parliamentary control since the instrument must receive Parliament's approval before it can come into force or to remain in force. Most SIs subject to the affirmative procedure are laid in the form of a draft Order, which is later printed and added to the numerical run of SIs when it has been approved by both Houses. Such orders cannot be made unless the draft order is approved by Parliament. To do this, a motion approving it has to be passed by both Houses (or by the Commons alone if deals with financial matters). The responsibility lies with the minister, having laid the Instrument, to move the motion for approval. Some Instruments are laid after making and will come into effect immediately but require subsequent approval within a statutory period, usually 28 days (or occasionally 40 days) to remain in force. This again excludes periods when Parliament is dissolved, prorogued or adjourned for more than four days. Again, the motion is generally prepared by the relevant minister, who is also responsible for ensuring that the motion is discussed within the necessary time limit. The last time a draft Statutory Instrument subject to affirmative procedure was not approved by Resolution of the House of Commons was on 12th November 1969 when House agreed to Motions that the draft Parliamentary Constituencies (England) Order 1969, the draft Parliamentary Constituencies (Wales) Order 1969, the Parliamentary Constituencies (Scotland) Order 1969 and the Parliamentary Constituencies (Northern Ireland) Order 'be not approved'. It is important to note that SIs cannot, except in extremely rare instances where the parent Act provides otherwise, be amended or adapted by either House. Each House simply expresses its wish for them to be annulled or passed into law, as the case may be. The parent Act (sometimes referred to as enabling Act) indicates which of the above procedures will apply to an SI. An appendix to the Votes and Proceedings of the House records the day on which an Instrument is laid.

Whether or not they are debated on the floor of the House of Commons or House of Lords (which is very rarely), SIs may be subject to scrutiny by select committees—committees of backbench MPs or Lords (or both). Most members of the committee have no legal expertise or training, but each committee carries out its work with the assistance of a lawyer on the parliamentary staff.

The Joint Committee on Statutory Instruments (a committee of both Houses) takes no view on the merits of the policy contained in the SIs, but instead considers whether each SI falls foul of a number of specified technical flaws, outlined in the Standing Orders of each House.

House of Commons Standing Order 151

[...]

(i) that it imposes a charge on the public revenues or contains provisions requiring payments to be made to the Exchequer or any government department or to any local or public authority in consideration of any licence or consent or of any services to be rendered, or prescribes the amount of any such charge or payment;

(ii) that it is made in pursuance of any enactment containing specific provisions excluding it from challenge in the courts, either at all times or after the expiration of a specific period;

(iii) that it purports to have retrospective effect where the parent statute confers no express authority so to provide;

(iv) that there appears to have been unjustifiable delay in the publication or in the laying of it before Parliament;

(v) that there appears to have been unjustifiable delay in sending a notification under the proviso to section 4(1) of the Statutory Instruments Act 1946, where an instrument has come into operation before it has been laid before Parliament;

(vi) that there appears to be a doubt whether it is intra vires or that it appears to make some unusual or unexpected use of the powers conferred by the statute under which it is made;

(vii) that for any special reason its form or purport calls for elucidation;

(viii) that its drafting appears to be defective;

or on any other ground which does not impinge on its merits or on the policy behind it; and to report its decision with the reasons thereof in any particular case.

In 2003, following concerns that most SIs were subject to insufficient scrutiny, the House of Lords established a Select Committee on the Merits of Statutory Instruments. Its terms of reference are to draw to the attention of the House of Lords to the following.

'House of Lords Select Committee on the Merits of Statutory Instruments'[6]

[...] any instrument laid in the previous week which it considers may be:

(a) politically or legally important or that gives rise to issues of public policy likely to be of interest to the House;

(b) inappropriate in view of the changed circumstances since the passage of the parent Act;

(c) inappropriately implementing European Union legislation; or

(d) imperfectly achieving its policy objectives.

QUESTIONS

Visit the home pages of these committees on the UK Parliament website (http://www.parliament.uk) and investigate what SIs they have drawn to the attention of the House in recent months.

1. Have you formed an impression as to how effective parliamentary scrutiny of draft SIs is?

2. Is it significant that, unlike Bills, draft SIs cannot be amended during their passage through the parliamentary process?

6 ROLE OF THE COURTS

As we have seen in relation to the *National Association of Health Stores* case, discussed in *R (on the application of National Association of Health Stores) v Secretary of State for Health* on p. 457, delegated legislation is amenable to judicial review. This is so even in those cases in which delegated legislation is subject to affirmative procedure in Parliament, where it has been debated and expressly approved. The principle of parliamentary supremacy has no application in relation to delegated legislation.[7] All of the grounds of judicial review[8] are potentially applicable: illegality (for example, the delegated legislation is outside the ambit of the enabling provision); procedural impropriety (for example, consultation was flawed or non-existent); irrationality

---

[6] http://www.parliament.uk/parliamentary_committees/merits/lords_merits_committee__terms_of_reference.cfm

[7] See Chapter 2.

[8] See Chapter 16.

(that is, the order defies logic or accepted moral standards); EU law; or that it is contrary to s. 6 of the Human Rights Act 1998. In cases in which the last of these grounds is held to apply, the court is not (as it is in relation to an Act of Parliament) confined to making a declaration of incompatibility; it may quash the order in question so that it has no legal effect.[9]

In *Javed*, that follows, the Court of Appeal had to consider whether the Asylum (Designated Countries of Destination and Designated Safe Third Countries) Order 1996 (SI 1996/2671) had been lawfully made by the Home Secretary; the Order had been debated and approved in both Houses of Parliament. The Order sought to give legal effect to a policy that certain countries should be designated as generally free from persecution, so enabling an expedited process to be used for returning failed asylum seekers who originally came from those designated countries (because the UK authorities could assume that people returned would not be subject to mistreatment). The claimants submitted that the Home Secretary had acted unlawfully in placing Pakistan on this 'white list'. One of the claimants was a member of the Ahmadi community, a religious minority in Pakistan.

R (on the application of Javed) v Secretary of State for the Home Department
[2001] EWCA Civ 789

57. [...] Whether there was *in general* a *serious* risk of persecution was a question which might give rise to a genuine difference of opinion on the part of two rational observers of the same evidence. A judicial review of the Secretary of State's conclusion needed to have regard to that considerable margin of appreciation. There was no question here of conducting a rigorous examination that required the Secretary of State to justify his conclusion. If the applicants were to succeed in showing that the designation of Pakistan was illegal, they had to demonstrate that the evidence clearly established that there was a serious risk of persecution in Pakistan and that this was a state of affairs that was a general feature in that country. For a risk to be serious it would have to affect a significant number of the populace.

58. It would not be right to conclude that, by approving the Order, each House of Parliament verified that Pakistan and the other countries named in that Order were countries in which there was, in general, no serious risk of persecution. The decision for each House was simply whether or not to approve the Order; the House was not required to rule on its legality. Neither House could amend the Order. It was for the Secretary of State, not for either House, to satisfy himself as to the legality of that Order. It cannot credibly be suggested that, in short debates in which no mention at all was made of the position of women, there was an evaluation which led to the conclusion that Pakistan was a country which the Secretary of State could legally include in the Order. The arguments advanced by the applicants and the conclusions of Turner J [the judge at first instance] did not, in the event, controvert the proceedings of either House of Parliament. Thus the Secretary of State's contention that Article 9 of the Bill of Rights,[[10]] was contravened fails both in law and on the facts.

Lord Phillips of Worth Matravers MR, giving the judgment of the Court, held that the Home Secretary could not have reasonably concluded, on the evidence, that women were not at risk from persecution in Pakistan. The same was true in relation to Ahmadis. Accordingly, the '*Secretary of State's inclusion of Pakistan in the White List was irrational*' and the Order, in relation to Pakistan, was quashed.

[9] See Chapter 17.
[10] On parliamentary privilege, see Chapter 4.

In one of its first cases, the new UK Supreme Court had to review the lawfulness of two pieces of delegated legislation that were designed to freeze the assets of suspected terrorists. The enabling provision relied on by the government was s. 1 of the United Nations Act 1946, which stated that if the UN Security Council called on the United Kingdom to implement measures, *'His Majesty may by Order in Council make such provision as appears to Him necessary or expedient for enabling those measures to be effectively applied, including (without prejudice to the generality of the preceding words) provision for the apprehension, trial and punishment of persons offending against the Order'.* The names of the three claimants appeared on a list drawn up by the UN as people being involved in terrorism. The UK government in turn designated them as people whose assets would be frozen under the orders. At no point was there any procedure for the claimants to challenge the UN or the government's determination, in clear contravention of basic principles of procedural fairness. The Supreme Court held that the orders were *ultra vires* as they fell outside the scope of s. 1 of the 1946 Act: the enabling provision was not sufficiently wide to permit ministers to interfere with fundamental rights to fair process.[11] Lord Phillips 'topped' and 'tailed' his judgment by reference to the constitutional framework in which the court was operating.

Ahmed and ors v HM Treasury (JUSTICE intervening) (Nos 1 and 2)
[2010] UKSC 2, [2010] 2 AC 544

85. It is particularly appropriate that these should be the first appeals to be heard in the Supreme Court of the United Kingdom, for they concern the separation of powers. At issue is the extent to which Parliament has, by the United Nations Act 1946 delegated to the executive the power to legislate. Resolution of this issue depends upon the approach properly to be adopted by the court in interpreting legislation which may affect fundamental rights at common law or under the European Convention on Human Rights. [...]

157. Nobody should conclude that the result of these appeals constitutes judicial interference with the will of Parliament. On the contrary it upholds the supremacy of Parliament in deciding whether or not measures should be imposed that affect the fundamental rights of those in this country.

In response to the ruling, the government fast-tracked a Bill through Parliament, which became the Terrorist Asset-Freezing (Temporary Provisions) Act 2010; this was subsequently replaced by the Terrorist Asset-Freezing etc. Act 2010. So, using primary legislation, the government now has power to implement UN Security Council measures on asset freezing. The primary legislation includes a right of appeal for the designated person.

QUESTIONS

1. The courts have considerable powers to review delegated legislation—but how *effective* are judicial review claims in monitoring the lawfulness of delegated legislation? Think about how easy or difficult it is for a person to launch a judicial review claim.

---

[11] On the principle of legality, see Chapter 3.

> 2. What constitutional justifications are there for the courts having a role in reviewing delegated legislation when the parliamentary supremacy denies them such a role in relation to *primary* legislation?

7 CASE STUDY: THE LEGISLATIVE AND REGULATORY REFORM BILL SAGA

As we have already noted, one particular use of SIs is to further the government's policy on 'better regulation' (cutting out unnecessary red tape from business and other activities). The SIs in this context are called 'regulatory reform orders' (RROs) made under the powers delegated to ministers by the Regulatory Reform Act 2001 and, more recently, its replacement, the Legislative and Regulatory Reform Act 2006.

In the final part of this chapter, we look at the background to the 2006 Act, which helps to shed light not only on issues about the use of delegated legislation, but also on some of the fundamental principles that underpin constitutional activity. The 2006 Act finally received royal assent in November 2006, but in a much revised form compared to the Bill first introduced by the government into the House of Commons in February 2006. Like its predecessor (the 2001 Act), the Legislative and Regulatory Reform Bill contained a broad Henry VIII power conferring power on ministers to change the statute book. But the Bill went much further.

Letter to *The Times*, 16 February 2006

Sir, Clause one of the Legislative and Regulatory Reform Bill (Comment, Feb 15) provides that: "A Minister of the Crown may by order make provision for either or both of the following purposes — a) reforming legislation; b) implementing recommendations of any one or more of the United Kingdom Law Commissions, with or without changes."

This has been presented as a simple measure "streamlining" the Regulatory Reform Act 2001, by which, to help industry, the Government can reduce red tape by amending the Acts of Parliament that wove it. But it goes much further: if passed, the Government could rewrite almost any Act and, in some cases, enact new laws that at present only Parliament can make.

The Bill subjects this drastic power to limits, but these are few and weak. If enacted as it stands, we believe the Bill would make it possible for the Government, by delegated legislation, to do (inter alia) the following:

- create a new offence of incitement to religious hatred, punishable with two years' imprisonment;
- curtail or abolish jury trial;
- permit the Home Secretary to place citizens under house arrest;
- allow the Prime Minister to sack judges;
- rewrite the law on nationality and immigration;
- "reform" Magna Carta (or what remains of it).

It would, in short, create a major shift of power within the state, which in other countries would require an amendment to the constitution; and one in which the winner would be the executive, and the loser Parliament.

David Howarth, MP for Cambridge, made this point at the Second Reading of the Bill last week. We hope that other MPs, on all sides of the House, will recognise the dangers of what is being proposed before it is too late.

PROFESSOR J. R. SPENCER, QC

PROFESSOR SIR JOHN BAKER, QC

PROFESSOR DAVID FELDMAN

PROFESSOR CHRISTOPHER FORSYTH

PROFESSOR DAVID IBBETSON

PROFESSOR SIR DAVID WILLIAMS, QC

Law Faculty,

University of Cambridge

David Howarth was Liberal Democrat MP for Cambridge and is Reader in Law at Cambridge University.

David Howarth, 'Who wants the Abolition of Parliament Bill?', *The Times*, 21 February 2006

Hardly anyone has noticed, but British democracy is sleepwalking into a sinister world of ministerial power. Least week all eyes were on the House of Commons as it debated identity cards, smoking and terrorism. The media reported both what MPs said and how they voted. For one week at least, the Commons mattered.

All the more peculiar then that the previous Thursday, in an almost deserted chamber, the Government proposed an extraordinary Bill that will drastically reduce parliamentary discussion of future laws, a Bill some constitutional experts are already calling "the Abolition of Parliament Bill".

A couple of journalists noticed, including Daniel Finkelstein of *The Times*, and a couple more pricked up their ears last week when I highlighted some biting academic criticism of the Bill on the letters page of this paper. But beyond those rarefied circles, that we are sleepwalking into a new and sinister world of ministerial power seems barely to have registered.

The boring title of the Legislative and Regulatory Reform Bill hides an astonishing proposal. It gives ministers power to alter any law passed by Parliament. The only limitations are that new crimes cannot be created if the penalty is greater than two years in prison and that it cannot increase taxation. But any other law can be changed, no matter how important. All ministers will have to do is propose an order, wait a few weeks and, voilà, the law is changed.

For ministers the advantages are obvious: no more tedious debates in which they have to answer awkward questions. Instead of a full day's debate on the principle of the proposal, detailed line-by-line examination in committee, a second chance at specific amendment in the Commons and a final debate and vote, ministers will have to face at most a short debate in a committee and a one-and-a-half hour debate on the floor. Frequently the Government will face less than that. No amendments will be allowed. The legislative process will be reduced to a game of take-it-or-leave-it.

The Bill replaces an existing law that allows ministers to relieve regulatory burdens. Business was enthusiastic about that principle and the Government seems to have convinced the business lobby that the latest Bill is just a new, improved version. What makes the new law different, however, is not only that it allows the Government to create extra regulation, including new crimes, but also that it allows ministers to change the structure of government itself. There might be business people so attached to the notion of efficiency and so ignorant or scornful of the principles of democracy that they find such a proposition attractive. Ordinary citizens should find it alarming.

Any body created by statute, including local authorities, the courts and even companies, might find themselves reorganised or even abolished. Since the powers of the House of Lords are defined in Acts of Parliament, even they are subject to the Bill.

Looking back at last week's business in the Commons, the Bill makes a mockery of the decisions MPs took. Carrying ID cards could be made compulsory, smoking in one's own home could be outlawed and the definition of terrorism altered to make ordinary political protest punishable by life imprisonment. Nor will the Human Rights Act save us since the Bill makes no exception for it.

The Bill, bizarrely, even applies to itself, so that ministers could propose orders to remove the limitations about two-year sentences and taxation. It also includes a few desultory questions (along the lines of "am I satisfied that I am doing the right thing?") that ministers have to ask themselves before proceeding, all drafted subjectively so that court challenges will fail, no matter how preposterous the minister's answer. Even these questions can be removed using the Bill's own procedure. Indeed, at its most extreme, in a manoeuvre akin to a legislative Indian rope trick, ministers could use it to transfer all legislative power permanently to themselves.

The Bill raises fundamental questions about the role of Parliament. Ministers, egged on, some suspect, by the Civil Service, treat Parliament as a voting machine. Its job, in their view, is merely to give legal cover to whatever ministers want to do. They treat debate and deliberation as mere chatter before the all-important vote. They see no great difference between full parliamentary procedure and a truncated procedure for statutory instruments because, for them, the result either way is the same, that ministers receive legal authority for their plans. Just as a perfect criminal statute for ministers appears to be one in which everything is illegal so that prosecutors have discretion to put anyone in front of a court, a perfect authorising statute is one that makes lawful any ministerial act or policy.

Some of us have a different view. We think that deliberation and debate matter, that they are part of what makes parliamentary democracy work and make the new laws we pass legitimate. Deliberation improves legislation but more importantly, it forces governments to give reasons for their proposals that go beyond their narrow self-interest. In private meetings of the governing party, or in the Cabinet, or above all in telephone calls between ministers and special advisers, purely partisan reasons can hold sway. But in public, especially where there is real debate, ministers have to offer reasons that might persuade others. If they cannot think of any such reasons, their embarrassment constrains them. As the political scientist Jon Elster says, even hypocrisy can have a civilising effect.

The Government claims that there is nothing to worry about. The powers in the Bill, it says, will not be used for "controversial" matters. But there is nothing in the Bill that restricts its use to "uncontroversial" issues. The minister is asking us to trust him, and, worse, to trust all his colleagues and all their successors. No one should be trusted with such power.

As James Madison gave warning in *The Federalist Papers*, we should remember when handing out political power that "enlightened statesmen will not always be at the helm". This Bill should make one doubt whether they are at the helm now.

By the time the Bill had passed through the House of Commons, the government had made several concessions in the face of opposition from MPs of all parties and a critical report from a House of Commons select committee. When the Bill was introduced to the House of Lords, it was scrutinized by the House of Lords Constitution Committee.

House of Lords Constitution Committee, *Legislative and Regulatory Reform Bill*, 11th Report, Session 2005–06, HL 194

2. [… T]he bill has been substantially amended in the House of Commons. The Government has conceded that the delegation by Parliament of widely drawn powers to Ministers to change the statute book for the broad purpose of "reforming legislation" is excessive for the avowed purposes of the bill. With cross-party support, that provision has been replaced with powers in Part 1 of the bill which are intended to be exercised only for purposes related to better regulation […]. The bill has also been amended to include an express power for committees of each House to recommend on certain specified grounds that a draft order be not proceeded with by the Minister (clauses 17(4), 18(3), and 19(5)). A further amendment prevents Part 1 powers to change the statute book being exercised in relation to Part 1 of the Legislative and Regulatory Reform Act itself or the Human Rights Act 1998 (clause 9).

3. Nonetheless, the bill continues to give rise to questions of principle about principal parts of the constitution. We concur with the statement of the Parliamentary Under-Secretary for the Cabinet Office (Mr Pat McFadden MP), made in the final stages of the bill's passage in the House of Commons: "Our subject matter is sensitive, because it [is] not just about what the Government of the day might want; it also takes us into the realm of the relationship between Government and Parliament, and Parliament's proper role in the scrutiny and approval of Government proposals in this sphere".

Delegation of law-making powers to ministers

30. The compromise that has been reached in the United Kingdom between effective legislative processes and parliamentary scrutiny is for Parliament to delegate some law-making powers to Ministers. In legal systems with different understandings from our own of the principle of separation of powers (such as the USA, Ireland and South Africa), such delegation is regarded as anathema and is constitutionally prohibited. Australia, Canada and India join the United Kingdom in permitting such delegation. So for many years it has been commonplace for Acts of Parliament to delegate powers to Ministers to make legislation in the form of orders (statutory instruments) to make detailed rules governing statutory schemes. More than 3,400 orders were made in 2004 alone.

31. Compared to the bill procedure, parliamentary procedures for scrutinising delegated legislation are less rigorous. The Joint Committee on Statutory Instruments considers whether a draft order needs to be drawn to the attention of Parliament as exceeding the limits of the authority delegated to the Minister. In this House, since December 2003, the Committee on the Merits of Statutory Instruments considers whether the policy implications of a draft order are such that it ought to be drawn to the attention of the House. Debates on orders are now rare. In the House of Commons, such debates are normally conducted in a standing committee. Debating time is limited to 90 minutes. No amendments can be moved. It is also of note that the text of delegated legislation is normally drafted by departmental lawyers rather than Parliamentary Counsel (who are responsible for bills).

32. Most legislative powers delegated to Ministers by Parliament are for the purpose of set-ting out in more detail the practical means to implement the policy enacted by the enabling Act of Parliament. But Ministers may also be conferred with "Henry VIII" powers to make orders that change the statute book. There are several good reasons for special caution about such powers. One is that they risk undermining the legislative supremacy of Parliament, a central principle of the United Kingdom's constitution, an aspect of which is that "no person or body is recognised by the law of England as having a right to override or set aside the legislation of Parliament". Another is that parliamentary scrutiny of ministerial orders is less rigorous than scrutiny meted out to legislative proposals that are contained in bills, yet in this case the Minister will be amending or repealing primary legislation.

33. A third and often overlooked reason for caution is that they make the statute book complex and uncertain. When a Minister exercises a Henry VIII power to amend a provision in an Act of Parliament, the order by which that is done is delegated legislation and the amended provision in the Act of Parliament retains the character of delegated legislation. The Parliamentary Roll con-clusively states what is and is not an Act of Parliament (subject to the principle of implied repeal). The fact that the Controller of HMSO, or a commercial publisher, may print an Act of Parliament with amendments to it made by order cannot, in and of itself, make those amendments part of the Act of Parliament. The fact that the order itself calls the amended provision part of an Act of Parliament cannot be conclusive of that status. The amended provision retains its status as delegated legislation. It would be open to a claimant to challenge the validity of an amended provision in judicial review proceedings on all the grounds available for challenging delegated legislation (illegality, irrationality and procedural impropriety). The constitutional principle of leg-islative supremacy of Acts of Parliament would not be an impediment to such a challenge.

34. The delegation to Ministers by Parliament of powers to change the statute book has nonetheless become a well-established feature of the law-making process in this country. Their routine use does not, however, diminish the constitutional oddity of allowing the execu-tive branch of government to set aside or amend primary legislation previously consented to by Parliament. The practical necessity for such an arrangement must be matched by clearly limited powers, to be exercised for specific purposes, and to be subject to adequate parlia-mentary oversight (including a veto) to guard against inappropriate use of such powers.

35. The general acceptability of delegating powers to Ministers to change the statute book is now accepted within the United Kingdom's constitutional system. The question in relation to the bill is therefore whether Ministers should have power to change the statute book for the specific purposes provided for in the bill and, if so, whether there are adequate procedural safeguards to ensure that Parliament has effective oversight and control over Ministers' leg-islative powers. The Government's original proposals for a power to be used for "reforming legislation" clearly failed this test. The bill as introduced to the House of Lords confers pow-ers for three specific purposes—two relating to better regulation and a third to implementa-tion of Law Commission proposals. [...]

Prohibit orders from changing constitutional fundamentals

52. From the outset, concerns have been expressed that orders made under Part 1 of the bill might enable important constitutional arrangements to be altered, deliberately or inadvert-ently. The new clauses, focused on regulation, reduce the opportunities for this to happen, though the powers related to Law Commission recommendations remain sufficiently wide to enable constitutional change. As we have noted, ministerial undertakings are no substitute for express legislative clarity.

53. There are two possible methods of excluding basic constitutional matters from the scope of the bill. One is to list enactments of a constitutional nature in respect of which ministerial orders may not be made. Such a list might include the following:

- Magna Carta 1297
- Bill of Rights 1689
- Crown and Parliament Recognition Act 1689
- Act of Settlement 1700
- Union with Scotland Act 1707
- Union with Ireland Act 1800
- Parliament Acts 1911-49
- Life Peerages Act 1958
- Emergency Powers Act 1964
- European Communities Act 1972
- House of Commons Disqualification Act 1975
- Ministerial and Other Salaries Act 1975
- British Nationality Act 1981
- Supreme Court Act 1981
- Representation of the People Act 1983
- Government of Wales Act 1998
- Northern Ireland Act 1998
- Scotland Act 1998
- House of Lords Act 1999.

54. Since that list was drawn up—by the Joint Committee on the draft Civil Contingencies Bill, as legislation in respect of which powers to modify or disapply legislation under the terms of that bill should not apply—further legislation of a constitutional nature has been enacted. One may therefore add:

- Constitutional Reform Act 2005
- Equality Act 2006
- Identity Cards Act 2006
- Racial and Religious Hatred Act 2006

55. There are a number of practical difficulties with this approach of simply listing Acts of Parliament. It may not be possible to agree on whether a particular Act is "constitutional". It is also something of a blunderbuss approach: there are provisions in some of these Acts which are not "constitutional" and it might be thought wrong to exclude such provisions from the general operation of the bill.

56. An alternative method of seeking to protect basic constitutional arrangements from amendment or abolition by order would be not to set out a list of statutory provisions but to enumerate those constitutional arrangements. A list of such arrangements might include:

- the powers of and succession to the Crown;
- the powers and composition of either House of Parliament;

- the basis of election or appointment of Members of either House of Parliament;
- the duration of Parliaments;
- the appointment, powers, duties and obligations of judges or magistrates of any court;
- the devolution settlements in Northern Ireland, Scotland and Wales;
- the establishment or disestablishment of any church or religion;
- the arrangements for local government;
- the fundamental rights and freedoms of those living in the United Kingdom, including rights under the European Convention on Human Rights, the right to jury trial, the right not to be detained without charge, rights concerning nationality or immigration status and the conditions under which any person may be extradited from the United Kingdom;
- the law relating to freedom of information, data protection, the regulation of investigatory powers, the powers and organisation of the police and the powers and organisation of the security services.

57. In our uncodified constitution, identifying constitutional legislation and constitutional arrangements is not entirely straightforward. Far from detracting from the point of principle that a ministerial order is not an appropriate method of bringing about constitutional reform, this reinforces the case for the committees to have a veto on orders of major importance.

The government rejected arguments that the Henry VIII power should be restricted, to exempt amendments to Acts of constitutional importance (although, as already noted, it conceded that the power should not apply to the 2006 Act itself or the Human Rights Act 1998). In many ways, the Legislative and Regulatory Reform Act 2006 shows Parliament at its most effective in scrutinizing government: there was a great deal of cross-party, non-partisan working, and debates on the floor of both Houses were made more effective by timely reports from select committees. All the more ironic, then, that what prompted this unusually strong parliamentary action was a Bill that (according to many critics) sought to deprive Parliament of much of its legislative power.

QUESTIONS

1. On the basis of the material set out in this chapter, do you have any concerns about the possible misuse of delegated legislative powers by the government?

2. Has anything you have learnt about delegated legislation given you cause to revise your views about the principles of parliamentary sovereignty, the rule of law, and the separation of powers?

8 CONCLUDING COMMENTS

This chapter has examined how delegated legislation is made, and the ways in which it is scrutinized by Parliament and the courts. Chapter 12 moves on to explore how legislation is made in the European Union.

9 FURTHER READING

Davis, P., 'The significance of parliamentary procedures in the control of the executive: The passage of Part 1 of the Legislative and Regulatory Reform Act 2006' [2007] Public Law 677

Page, E.C., *Governing by Numbers* (2001, Oxford: Hart Publishing)

ONLINE RESOURCE CENTRE

Further information about the themes discussed in this chapter can be found on the Online Resource Centre at www.oxfordtextbooks.co.uk/orc/lesueur2e/

12

EUROPEAN UNION TREATIES AND LEGISLATIVE PROCESSES

CENTRAL ISSUES

1. Chapter 8 focused on the nature, function, and scope of executive power in the European Union (EU); the present chapter will consider the process by which the EU enacts legislation. Although the law-making process looks complicated at first sight, it is actually transparent and rule-governed. We will focus only on the ordinary legislative procedure (OLP), which is set to become even more dominant in the future.

2. There are two very different types of 'legislation' in the EU. First, the treaties establishing the EU provide a legal (some would say 'constitutional') foundation for all of the EU's work. These treaties are revised every few years in a process that has always been politically and constitutionally difficult. Second, there is the 'day-to-day' legislation made through the EU legislative process, in the form of regulations and directives. This chapter examines the character of each type of legislation, the processes by which it is made, and the impact that it has on the UK constitution.

3. The Treaties of the European Union are made and amended at intergovernmental conferences (IGCs), at which governments from the soon to be twenty-eight member states come together from time to time to strike diplomatic bargains. The questions are whether the IGC process should be made more inclusive than it has been in the past, whether the transfer of powers to the European Union should be put before the national electorate in a referendum, and whether the courts should be entitled to intervene in what is essentially a political process.

4. We will examine closely the passage of a particular directive (the Race Directive) and look at its impact on UK legislation. The law-making process in general, and the enacting of specific regulations or directives, is the result of cooperation between EU institutions, interest groups, national parliaments, and national bureaucracies.

5. The European Parliament (EP) is directly elected to, and has over time emerged from the shadow of, the Council, with which it now has an equal role in the law-making process. It has a stronger democratic claim to participate in the law-making process than any other institution of the European Union. Yet turnout in EP elections has been steadily falling across the EU since 1979 and this has had repercussions for the legitimacy of the EP.

6. The chapter concludes with a case study of the Race Directive, which includes the United Kingdom's implementing measure. We will then look at the way in which the EU's law-making process operates and what happens in a situation in which the Directive has not been, or has been improperly, implemented into national law.

1 INTRODUCTION

So far, Part III of this book has considered the respective roles of the UK government and UK Parliament in making primary and secondary legislation. To complete our exploration of the constitutional significance of legislation in the modern British constitution, we need now to examine how legislation is made in the European Union (EU). The phenomenon of EU legislation is constitutionally important. We explore elsewhere in the book the rule that EU law 'trumps' any inconsistent national law.[1] Moreover, a significant proportion of policy that is given legal effect by the UK Parliament stems not from national initiatives, but from the EU.

A word of caution is needed: do not expect the material covered in this chapter to be simple. The EU is complex, opaque, and largely unintelligible to the average European citizen. To be an effective lawyer, there is, however, no alternative to getting to grips with some aspects of these intricacies. The aim of this chapter is not to go into every detail, but to help you to assess 'the bigger picture' of how EU legislation is made and what impact it has on the United Kingdom. Efforts were made from 2001 to draft a treaty to simplify matters and it took eight years to secure agreement on institutional reform.[2] The Lisbon Treaty is a classic example of a compromise between what was institutionally required, politically desired, and realistically possible.

(a) TYPES OF EU LEGISLATION: AN OVERVIEW

There are two very different kinds of EU legislation, emerging from very different kinds of legislative process. The aim of the chapter is to explain the constitutional implications of each type of legislation and legislative process for the UK constitution.

(i) In section 2, EU treaties and the treaty-creating process, we look at treaties and the 'once every few years' treaty-creating process. The two principal treaties are the Treaty on European Union (TEU) and the Treaty on the Functioning of the European Union (TFEU). Some would say that these treaties are analogous to the codified constitution of a nation state—although, be clear, the EU is not a state, but rather a souped-up international organization. The treaties, which can be described as 'primary legislation', underpin the EU in the sense that they create the institutions and set out the basic processes through which day-to-day decision-making takes place. Since the mid-1980s, the EU has reviewed and responded to changing political circumstances (such as the enlargement of the EU or a wish for there to be closer integration between member states) by amending and developing the treaty framework. This process is

---

[1] See the discussions of *Factortame* in Chapter 18.
[2] On the historical development of the EU and its precursors, see Chapter 8.

dominated by the governments of the member states. Box 12.1 and Box 12.2 outline how the treaty framework has developed. That 'semi-permanent treaty revision process'[3] may have come to a temporary end with the Lisbon Treaty, with EU leaders confessing that they were 'fed up' with negotiating European treaties.

(ii) Section 3 of this chapter, The everyday legislative process, deals with day-to-day legislation in the form of 'directives' and 'regulations'. This secondary legislation emerges from hugely complex legislative and political processes (set down in the TEU and TFEU). The elaborate institutional framework and legislative procedures seek to allow participation of a wide range of different interests (including governments of member states, directly elected representatives of the EU citizens sitting in the European Parliament, the EU itself through the Commission, and interest groups). Box 12.11 gives some illustrations of directives and regulations. The TFEU and the TEU are constituent treaties that empower EU institutions to enact legislation within the scope of the treaties. The EU system has legal power to make secondary legislation only on the subject matter and according to the procedures laid down in the treaties. This is an important rule of law issue: EU institutions are authorized to act only under the terms of the treaties—their powers are limited.

This is a book about the British constitution, so this chapter takes a special interest in how both kinds of EU legislation—the treaties and secondary legislation—fit into the UK constitution and law-making systems.

In relation to the treaties, we will examine two main features of the national process. First, there is now a legal requirement that the UK government hold a national referendum before formally agreeing to be bound by significant treaty changes. Second, EU treaties are formally incorporated into UK law by Acts of Parliament. In practice, this is done by amending the European Communities Act 1972, which was the statute that first brought the treaties into national law in preparation for the United Kingdom's accession on 1 January 1973. The UK Parliament therefore has an opportunity to debate treaty revisions agreed in principle by the UK government, although there is (as we shall see) relatively little scope for Parliament to do anything other than agree or—which has never happened—disagree.

Our examination of the national side of EU law-making also needs to consider the fact that the United Kingdom has devolved government and legislative functions to Scotland, Wales, and Northern Ireland. Relations between the United Kingdom and the EU is a matter for central government rather than the devolved governments, but the latter will often have views on proposed EU policy. These may not always coincide with those of the UK government (for example, the Scottish Government may have a different outlook on how EU policy on fishing should develop from that of the UK government).

(b) THEMES

In relation to the treaty-making process, we return to a dominant theme in Chapter 8—namely, *legitimacy*. You will remember that we raised the legitimacy question in relation to executive power and policymaking, and asked whether the political institutions were sufficiently representative and democratically accountable. Now, we will be asking whether the established process of revising the treaties is sufficiently legitimate and whether alternative processes (which appear to be more legitimate) are, in fact, radically different.

---

[3] Bruno de Witte, 'The Closest Thing to a Constitutional Conversation in Europe: The Semi-Permanent Treaty Revision Process', in P. Beaumont, C. Lyons, and N. Walker (eds) *Convergence and Divergence in European Public Law* (2002, Oxford: Hart), ch. 3.

Another recurring theme from Chapter 8 is the desire to *constrain executive power*. We will examine legal constraints on, and legal challenges to, the ratification of EU treaties. Think about the United Kingdom's constitutional culture, and the strengths and weaknesses of its institutions. From a domestic UK perspective, what is the best way in which to challenge the EU treaty-making process? Through a legal process (judicial review in the courts)? Or through political institutions (parliamentary debates, consultative referendums)?

The *democracy deficit* in Chapter 8 related to the unelected nature of technocratic institutions such as the Commission and the relative difficulty in holding national ministers to account for work done at EU level in the Council. In this chapter, the theme reappears in relation to the European Parliament (EP). To what extent does the directly elected EP represent a solidary European people (a *demos*) tied together in a pan-European democracy based on Europe-wide parties?

Does the Commission have too much *power* in the legislative process? The Commission has a powerful right to initiate legislative proposals; moreover, it operates behind closed doors and tends to make decision by simple majority vote (making it relatively easy for a Commissioner to be outvoted). But what are the internal and external *constraints* on the role of the Commission in the legislative process?

The EU's legislative process appears labyrinthine and convoluted, and it produces a variety of legal measures, which only adds to the confusion. You will remember from Chapter 3 that the rule of law prescribes that there be clear procedures for making laws and that law should be clear so as to be able to guide the individual's behaviour. Does the EU's legislative process undermine the *rule of law*? Or do the EU's procedures need to reflect other (more important) values? If so, how can the complexity of the law-making process, and the different legal measures, be justified?

2 EU TREATIES AND THE TREATY-CREATING PROCESS

Let us begin by examining the 'once every few years' activity of revising the EU treaties, which provide a legal (and, arguably, a 'constitutional') basis for all of the functions of the EU. The governments of the member states dominate the process. In formal terms, every member state is equal (whether it is Malta with a population of 400,000 or Germany with a population of 82 million). Any member state may say 'no' and effectively halt the process of agreeing a treaty revision—as happened when, following a referendum in 2008, the government of Ireland temporarily stopped the progress of ratification of the Lisbon Treaty.

BOX 12.1 TREATY DEVELOPMENT

1951	Treaty of Paris (ECSC)
1957	Treaty of Rome (EEC)
1986	Single European Act
1992	Treaty of Maastricht (EU)
1997	Treaty of Amsterdam
2001	Treaty of Nice
2004	Constitutional Treaty (failed)
2009	**Treaty of Lisbon**

BOX 12.2 DEVELOPMENT OF THE EU TREATY FRAMEWORK

There are currently two principal treaties under which the EU operates:

- the Treaty on the Functioning of the European Union (TFEU), which means the Treaty establishing (what was then called) the European Economic Community, signed at Rome on 25 March 1957 (as amended and renamed by the Treaty of Lisbon); and
- the Treaty on European Union (TEU), which means the Treaty on European Union signed at Maastricht on 7 February 1992 (as amended by the Treaty of Lisbon).

The TFEU establishes the institutional framework and powers of the EU, and some provisions also create rights and obligations that are enforceable in UK courts and tribunals,[4] but it has evolved into its current state from several earlier treaties.

- The original Treaty of Rome created the European Economic Community (EEC) in 1957 and was originally signed by the heads of six European states (West Germany, Italy, France, the Netherlands, Belgium, and Luxembourg). The United Kingdom joined the EEC in January 1973. The Treaty of Rome was not substantially amended (apart from the various Accession Treaties) for the next thirty years, but since then, its amendments have been frequent and far-reaching.

- The Single European Act (signed in 1986, entered into force on 1 July 1987), which is an international treaty and not—despite its name—a piece of domestic legislation, changed decision-making procedures in the Community institutions to speed up the completion of the single market within the existing Treaty of Rome.

- The Treaty on European Union (the 'Maastricht Treaty'; signed in 1992, entered into force on 1 November 1993) made a number of significant changes. For starters, it renamed the EEC as the 'European Community' (EC) and created a new body, the European Union (EU), that consists of three pillars. In addition to the first 'Community' pillar, the Treaty on European Union (TEU) added two further policies and forms of cooperation to the EC—namely, a 'Common Foreign and Security Policy'[5] and 'Police and Judicial Cooperation in Criminal Matters'.[6] A separate Protocol linked to the Maastricht Treaty led to the creation of a common currency, of which the United Kingdom decided to opt out.[7] The Maastricht Treaty also strengthened social and economic cohesion, introduced common citizenship,[8] and stated that the European Union would respect the fundamental rights as guaranteed by the European Convention on Human Rights (ECHR) and '*as they result from the constitutional traditions common to the member states, as general principles of Community law*'.

---

[4] The use to which the EU treaties are put in adjudication, including the concepts of direct effect and supremacy of some of their provisions in the national legal systems, is considered in Chapter 18.

[5] See Title V [V] TEU.

[6] See Title VI [VI] TEU.

[7] See Protocol on certain provisions relating to the United Kingdom of Great Britain and Northern Ireland. Denmark also decided not to adopt the euro, a decision that was confirmed in a referendum in September 2000. When Sweden acceded to the European Union in 1995, it also decided against joining the euro.

[8] See Art. 22 TFEU.

- The Amsterdam Treaty (signed in 1997, entered into force on 1 May 1999) incorporated the 'Social Chapter' into the TEC, but allowed the United Kingdom and the Republic of Ireland to opt out of the Schengen Agreement, which lifted the systematic internal border controls between the member states, as well as the single European currency, which was launched in 1999.

- The Treaty of Nice (signed in 2001, entered into force on 1 February 2003) was designed to reform the EU institutions in the run-up to enlargement of the European Union. The expansion from fifteen to twenty-five plus member states after 2004 necessitated a change in the relative voting weights in the Council of the European Union, a reduction in the size of the Commission, and an increase in the number of seats in the European Parliament.

(a) THE BEGINNINGS: THREE SEPARATE COMMUNITIES

From the 1950s until 1993, there were three separate 'communities' through which member states made collective decisions on specified areas of policy: coal and steel; nuclear power (EURATOM); and the broad European Economic Community (EEC). We examined the reasons for these first steps towards European integration in Chapter 8.

(b) MAASTRICHT: TREATY ON EUROPEAN UNION

A significant further step took place when the Treaty on European Union (TEU, or 'Maastricht Treaty') came into force in 1993. As well as introducing institutional reforms, the TEU created 'the European Union' as an umbrella term for the collective decision-making of the member states through the European institutional framework. The *character* of the decision-making varied across three broad fields of policymaking, which became known as 'pillars' (although this was not a term formally used in the TEU).

BOX 12.3 THE PILLAR STRUCTURE

Pillar I	The continuing broad scope of the European Community
Pillar II	A common foreign and security policy
Pillar III	From 1993–97, called 'Justice and home affairs'; from 1997, 'Police and judicial cooperation in criminal matters'

Pillar I, building on the European Economic Community (into which the Coal and Steel Community and EURATOM were merged), involved such close working between member states that it came to be described as a 'new legal order' and 'supranational'. The character of this decision-making has several features that marked it out from other international organizations.

(a) Member states agreed that, in relation to specified areas of policy, no member state should have a veto over decisions favoured by others.

(b) The institutions have power under the treaty framework to enact legislation (in the form of directives and regulations) that are binding on member states and their citizens.

(c) The European Court of Justice (ECJ) has power to interpret and enforce (Pillar I) Community law.

(d) Member states no longer have formal equality, because when voting in the Council (the institution representing the interests of the governments of the member states), larger countries have more votes than smaller ones—known as 'qualified majority' voting (QMV).

(e) A directly elected Parliament has gained greater powers of oversight and in the legislative process.

Pillars II and III differed from Pillar I in several respects, and the decision-making method process was therefore described as 'intergovernmental'. In many situations, member states could veto a policy that other members favoured.

BOX 12.4 EXAMPLES OF INITIATIVES TAKEN UNDER PILLARS II AND III

- Three anti-crime agencies have been established: Eurojust; Europol; and the European Police College (Cepol).
- An agreement on extradition between the European Union and the USA.

(c) THE CONSTITUTIONAL TREATY THAT FAILED

In 2001, member states agreed to start a process through which an EU 'constitution' would be drafted. One driving force for a constitution was the need to adapt the decision-making processes and institutions to ensure that they were effective for an enlarged membership of twenty-five plus. Another set of drivers was the need to make EU decision-making more transparent, democratic, and accountable. In 2004, the governments of member states agreed the text of a Constitutional Treaty, which was subsequently approved by the European Parliament. In order to become binding, it was also necessary for the Treaty to be 'ratified' by each member state, according to the requirements of its own national constitutional arrangements. In some, this was a parliamentary process; in others, there was the additional prerequisite of a referendum. It was at this point that the project to create a constitution came unstuck. By mid-2005, the Constitutional Treaty had been approved in thirteen member states, but voters in referendums held in France and the Netherlands voted 'no'.

(d) THE LISBON TREATY

In 2007, the governments of the member states agreed a 'plan B': accepting that the idea of a Constitutional Treaty was now dead, they gave their assent to the Lisbon Treaty, which reforms the existing TEU and Treaty Establishing the European Community (TEC), renaming the latter the 'Treaty on the Functioning of the European Union' (TFEU). Under EU law, the Treaty cannot enter into force unless and until all of the member states have ratified it.[9] According to an Irish Supreme Court ruling in 1987,[10] any major amendment to the EU Treaty entails an amendment to the Irish Constitution—and that, in turn, requires a referendum. The Lisbon Treaty was rejected by Irish voters in a referendum on 12 June 2008, but, following assurances from the European Union on various matters (for example, taxation powers, family policy, and guarantees for Ireland's political neutrality), endorsed by 67.1 per cent of Irish voters (on a turnout of 59 per cent) on 2 October 2009. The constitutional courts of Germany and the Czech Republic considered legal questions about the compatibility of the Lisbon Treaty with their national constitutions, and held that ratification could go ahead. The Lisbon Treaty came into force on 1 December 2009.

(e) UNITED KINGDOM 'OPT-OUTS'

At several points in the development of the European Union, the UK government has taken the view that it is not in the United Kingdom's national interest to take part in some aspects of the European Union's work. Opt-outs have therefore been negotiated at the various times at which the founding treaties are reviewed. These are set out as protocols to the treaties (the numbering here referring to where they appear at the end of the Lisbon Treaty).

(a) Protocol 18 states that the United Kingdom is not obliged to adopt, or committed to adopting, the euro without a separate decision to do so by its government and Parliament. A similar protocol was negotiated by Denmark.

(b) Protocol 20 is in relation to 'Schengen',[11] the term for the agreement now reached by twenty-five member states to the effect that they will not have routine border controls. Once people are within the 'Schengen area', they may move around freely without showing passports at fixed border posts. The United Kingdom and Ireland have never participated in this initiative.

(c) Under Protocol 22, the United Kingdom and Ireland do not always take part and are not bound by decision-making in relation to 'Title IV of Part 3' of the TFEU—that is, the 'Area of Freedom, Security and Justice' (formerly Pillar III under the Maastricht and Amsterdam Treaties). This includes policies on border checks, asylum, and immigration.

BOX 12.5 TREATY OF LISBON

The Treaty of Lisbon addresses the lack of efficiency, ineffectiveness, complexity, and problems of legitimacy not by replacing the two treaties after Maastricht with a single treaty (which would have been impossible to sell to an already sceptical public), but by amending the existing treaties (the Lisbon Treaty started life as the 'Reform Treaty'). It divides the content between the TEU (principles and objectives, provisions on the institutional framework, general provisions, and the Common Foreign and Security Policy) and TFEU (containing the details on how the EU is to function). The provisions of the two treaties are equal in weight and value. One of the novelties is that the first 'Community' and the third (Police and Judicial Cooperation in Criminal Matters)

---

[9] The process of 'ratification' is explained at p. 484, Signature, ratification, and enactment of treaties.
[10] *Crotty v Taoiseach*, Judgment of 9 April 1987, 1986 No.12036P.
[11] Schengen is a town in Luxembourg.

pillar are merged into one unitary supranational organization, with a unitary legal personality.

In addition, Art. 1 TEU declares that:

> The Union shall be founded on the present Treaty and on the Treaty on the Functioning of the European Union (hereinafter referred to as 'the Treaties'). Those two Treaties shall have the same legal value. The Union shall replace and succeed the European Community.

In other words, all references to the 'European Community' are replaced with references to the new 'European Union'.

In addition, there will be a President of the European Council (often casually referred to in the press as the 'President of Europe') and a High Representative of the Union for Foreign Affairs and Security Policy (see Chapter 8).

A handful of states had opt-outs prior to the Lisbon Treaty. Both Denmark and the United Kingdom secured an opt-out from the third stage of Economic and Monetary Union (that is, the common 'euro' currency), and the United Kingdom and Ireland are not a party to the Schengen border control arrangements, although they participate in certain provisions relating to judicial and police cooperation.

The second opt-out under the Lisbon Treaty relates to the change from unanimous decisions to qualified majority voting (QMV) in the sector of Police and Judicial Cooperation in Criminal Matters. The United Kingdom's 'red lines' approach to the 2007 IGC resulted in special provisions dealing with the integration of the former third pillar into the TFEU,[12] although both the United Kingdom (and Ireland) may opt in to the new policy in the future.

As discussed in Chapter 6, the Charter of Fundamental Rights of the European Union was a political document until the Lisbon Treaty came into force. It now has the same force as the treaties upon which the European Union is founded.

(b) THE TREATY-MAKING PROCESS

So far, we have considered the basic structure and content of the treaties. We now move on to examine the *process* by which these treaties are agreed.

Intergovernmental conferences (IGCs)

Ever since its founding, many of the EU's most important institutional changes were the result of protracted negotiations at intergovernmental conferences (IGCs), where governments of member states—in the form of ministers, diplomats, and civil servants—drafted the EU's governing treaties. IGCs are arranged periodically to review the treaty framework of the EU. IGCs have no regular schedule: they are called into being by the European Council, which, as we will see shortly, consists of senior political and official representatives from the member states, as well as the Commission and the European Parliament. Nor is their duration limited in time: negotiations leading to the signing of the Maastricht Treaty in 1992 took over two years.

---

[12] See Arts 10(4)–(5) of the Protocol on Transitional Provisions.

Figure 12.1 Heads of state and government sign the Treaty of Lisbon, 13 December 2007

Renaud Dehousse and Paul Magnette 'Institutional Change in the EU', in J. Peterson and M. Shackleton (eds) *The Institutions of the European Union*, 3rd edn (2012, Oxford: OUP), ch. 2, p. 23

The negotiations that gave rise to the Treaties of Paris and Rome were but the first in a long series of diplomatic bargains between the member states. They took the classic form of IGCs, rather than constitutional assemblies. Formally, the governments never departed from the canons of international practice. The outcome, arrived at through discrete and complex negotiations, was not a constitution, but a treaty agreed upon by 'the High contracting parties'. As such, it could only enter into force after being ratified by all the member states. In these conferences, in which each country was represented by a delegation of government officials, mixing diplomats and experts drawn from economic ministries, everything had to be decided by consensus. National experts gathered in working groups to examine the details of the arrangements, while the heads of delegation—usually senior diplomats — met regularly to assess the progress of the negotiations and settle the most sensitive issues in close consultation with foreign ministers. In addition, the heads of state and governments met bilaterally or multilaterally to provide the political impetus and address the most contentious issues.

The IGC 2007 was convened in order to draft the Treaty of Lisbon and it intended to push through treaty reform very quickly. The detailed version of the Lisbon Treaty, which appeared in October 2007, gave the member states only two weeks to debate the provisions and signal their consent. On the one hand, the speed with which the Lisbon Treaty was agreed is easily understood: after all, the key changes had already been debated in detail by the Convention and by the ICG 2004. On the other hand, the accelerated process exposed the member states to the charge that they were essentially trying to resell a package that had been rejected by voters in two member states.

It should be added that an alternative method of negotiation exists (first tried in 1999 to draft the Charter of Fundamental Rights). The convention method was used after 2001 with a view to drafting a constitution for the EU. Although the draft Constitution ultimately failed, the convention method has not disappeared entirely from view: under the Lisbon Treaty, Art. 48(3) TEU specifies the requirement to use it under the ordinary procedure for revising the treaties, although the Council may choose the simplified method.

QUESTIONS

1. Why did the member states in 2001 agree to prioritize reform the EU Treaties?

2. The UK government has been successful several times in negotiating opt-outs. What is so particular about those areas in which the UK does not wish to participate?

(c) SIGNATURE, RATIFICATION, AND ENACTMENT OF TREATIES

Once a text of a treaty has emerged from an IGC or convention, it is signed by each head of state or government (in the case of the United Kingdom, this is normally a role for the Prime Minister) to indicate a willingness to be bound by the treaty in international law.[13]

After signature, the next step is for there to be a process of 'ratification' in each member state. From the perspective of international law, ratification can take various forms, but often involves the lodging of a formal document. The constitutional and legal steps that a government must take within its own state before formal ratification is a matter for the constitution of each country. In the United Kingdom, the government's legal authority to ratify treaties was formerly a prerogative power, but is now regulated by the Constitutional Reform and Governance Act 2010, Pt 2.[14] The power to ratify EU treaties is subject to further (legal and conventional) constraints.

The process of preparing for ratification (an action in international law) and the process of giving effect to the treaty in domestic law (an action in national law) go hand in hand. This is partly for practical reasons: the UK government would not want to ratify a treaty and so become bound by it in international law if there were to be the slightest risk that the UK Parliament would refuse to pass a Bill incorporating the treaty into national law. So, by convention, a Bill needs to be passed *before* ratification (although it will not come into force until all member states have ratified the treaty). A further reason why preparing for ratification and incorporation happen at the same time is that, for the reasons about to be explained, the UK government is under a statutory duty to obtain the consent of the UK Parliament before ratification takes place. It is convenient for this approval to be signified in the Bill that will incorporate the treaty. So, for example, the European Union (Amendment) Act 2008, which incorporated the Lisbon Treaty into UK law, states in s. 4: '*The Treaty of Lisbon is approved for the purposes of section 12 of the European Parliamentary Elections*

---

[13] On the relationship between treats and national law in the United Kingdom generally, see Chapter 1.
[14] See Chapter 9.

Act 2002 (c. 24) (Parliamentary approval of treaties increasing the European Parliament's powers).'

The European Union Act 2011

The question of whether there should be a referendum emerged (not for the first time) in relation to the draft Constitutional Treaty in 2004. The UK government agreed that there should be one,[15] but in the event, there was no need to put the treaty to the vote, because it became clear that other member states were not going to ratify the treaty (following failures to obtain approval in referendums in their countries). A referendum had been held in 1975 in which sixty-seven per cent of people who voted supported continued membership in the (former) European Economic Community.

A number of constitutional locks (to be satisfied before the United Kingdom could approve EU treaties or sanction the transfer of sovereign powers to the EU) existed before the European Union Act 2011 entered into force (and continue to exist).

- The draft treaty must be approved by each House of Parliament: s. 1(3) of the European Communities Act 1972.
- Any treaty amending the founding 1957 Treaties (now TFEU) or the 1992 Treaty of European Union (Maastricht) (TEU) requires primary legislation: s. 5 of the European Union (Amendment) Act 2008.

In addition to these constitutional safeguards, the European Union Act (EUA) 2011 introduces a referendum requirement on any significant future transfer of power to the European Union (ss 2, 3, and 6 EUA). These provisions contain requirements for an Act of Parliament, majority support in a national post-legislative referendum, and a ministerial statement in the cases of ordinary treaty amendments in relation to TEU or TFEU (s.2 EUA).[16] They also address certain amendment procedures using the 'simplified revision procedure' (s. 3 EUA) that extend the objectives, competences, or powers of the EU, or facilitate the decision-making procedures by removing Britain's veto right in the Council or the European Council. The simplified revision procedure is set out in Art. 48(6) TEU and allows Member States acting unanimously by means of a Decision of the European Council to revise Part 3 TFEU ('Union Policies and Internal Actions') and to bypass the lengthy procedures of an ordinary revision of the Treaties (that would require an IGC which may or may not be preceded by a European Convention). There is an important rider: the proposed revision must 'not increase the competence conferred on the Union in the Treaties'.[17] This qualification is repeated by the 'significance condition' in s. 3(4) EUA: if the proposed revision and transfer of competences are insignificant, a referendum is not required.

A more detailed discussion of these provisions would quickly get too technical for present purposes, and would also disguise an important constitutional issue: to what extent are the referendum locks in the EUA legally binding on a future Parliament? Could the next Parliament decide to approve a significant transfer of power to the EU on the basis of an Act of Parliament alone, i.e. clearly disobeying the relevant provisions in the EUA?

---

[15] Labour Party Manifesto 2005: '*We will put* [the Draft Constitutional Treaty] *to the British people in a referendum and campaign wholeheartedly for a Yes vote.'*

[16] Provided that sovereign powers or competences are transferred from UK to EU.

[17] Article 48(6), third paragraph TEU.

M. Gordon and M. Dougan, 'The United Kingdom's European Union Act 2011: "Who won the bloody war anyway?"' (2012) 37(1) *European Law Review* 3–30, 23–24.

Whether the UK Parliament possesses the legislative authority to create binding "referendum locks", to which future governments will be bound to adhere, critically depends on our understanding of the doctrine of parliamentary sovereignty which, in the absence of a codified constitutional text, serves as the central organising principle of the UK constitution. In accordance with the orthodox conception of parliamentary sovereignty, as influentially explicated by A.V. Dicey, Parliament's authority "to make or unmake any law whatever" serves to preclude the legislature from binding its successors, either absolutely as to the substantive scope of its future lawmaking power, or as to the procedure by which this power is to be exercised. If this classical analysis of the sovereignty of Parliament remains applicable today, the referendum locks contained in ss 2, 3 and 6 of the EUA will be legally unenforceable, and could be entirely disregarded by a future government which sought to enact legislation securing an extension of the power or competence of the European Union.

The Diceyan orthodoxy has not, however, gone unchallenged. Of particular relevance to the present inquiry is the "manner and form" conception of the sovereignty of Parliament, which derives from the work of Sir Ivor Jennings. The manner and form theory is a reconfiguration of the notion of parliamentary sovereignty which postulates that Parliament's power to make or unmake any law whatever must include the power to legislate so as to modify the future lawmaking process. Parliament thus remains unable to bind its successors absolutely as to the substance of future legislation, but it is understood to be constitutionally capable of legislating to ensure that future statutes must be created in a particular way, in accordance with a specified "manner" and/or "form". As such, if the reinterpretation of the doctrine of parliamentary sovereignty offered by the manner and form theory is accepted, the referendum locks contained in the EUA could be viewed as legally valid alterations of the legislative process with which future parliaments would be bound to comply in order to enact legislation extending the power or competence of the European Union. Whether the manner and form theory of parliamentary sovereignty should now be seen to have displaced the traditional Diceyan orthodoxy is a matter which cannot be explored at length in this article. There may be conceptual, and indeed principled, reasons for preferring the position set out by Jennings to that of Dicey and Sir William Wade, Dicey's most influential defender. And it can further be argued that contemporary developments in UK constitutional practice can be viewed as providing significant evidence that a shift to the manner and form interpretation of legally unlimited legislative authority has occurred.

If this is the case, the EUA, while still an unprecedented constitutional experiment, can perhaps be seen to fit with the emerging recognition that the manner and form theory provides the best account of Parliament's contemporary legislative power. For in promulgating the EUA, the coalition government seems implicitly to have embraced the logic of the manner and form understanding of parliamentary sovereignty. And in enacting a statute which purports to modify the future legislative process, it seems that Parliament has accepted an interpretation of its sovereign authority which permits it to make statutory alterations to the manner and form which must be followed for the creation of valid legislation.

Professor Vernon Bogdanor goes a step further and asks whether the EUA has transformed 'Parliament' from a traditionally bicameral body (that was competent to legislate on all matters) to a tricameral body that includes the electorate in the law-making process. Obviously, Parliament is not a static institution: it was reformed in the past (think about the extension of the franchise in the nineteenth and early twentieth century or the Parliament Acts

1911 and 1949) and will be reformed in the future (think about a wholly or partially elected House of Lords or a House of Commons elected by proportional representation). To what extent, Bogdanor asks, is Parliament after such a reform identical (in constitutional terms) to Parliament before the reform?

Are there limits to Parliament's ability to redefine itself without becoming an entirely new body?

V. Bogdanor, 'Imprisoned by a Doctrine: The Modern Defence of Parliamentary Sovereignty' (2012) 32(1) *Oxford J Legal Studies* 179–195, 190.

Suppose that Parliament, to take an extreme and implausible example, were to pass a statute requiring the consent of the Institute of Directors before legislation relating to certain indus trial matters could be passed. Would Parliament then have been redefined so as to include the Institute of Directors? Would such a redefinition be accepted as valid by the courts? Could Parliament create as many extra chambers as it liked and at what point would such a multi-cameral legislature no longer be the 'same Parliament' as the one we have today? What indeed is the criterion for a parliament being the 'same Parliament'?

It is therefore difficult to escape the conclusion that the European Union Act imposes a substantive limitation upon the powers of Parliament by arguing that the Act yields merely manner and form entrenchment. The Act imposes a precondition over the area in which Parliament can legislate. It therefore reduces the area in which Parliament can legislate with-out securing the approval of voters in a referendum. If that is so, it has altered the rule of recognition. Parliament can now, on this interpretation, do anything it likes except amend a European Union treaty or transfer significant powers or competences to the Union without a referendum. It therefore seems reasonable to conclude that the referendum requirement in the European Union Act deprives the legislature of its sovereign power to legislate on cer-tain European Union matters by requiring, for these matters, the assent of a body external to the legislature. It amounts therefore to a partial renunciation of the legislative power, and so is a substantive restriction, rather than one involving merely the manner or form in which legislative power is exercised. But, if Parliament can successfully bind itself in this way, why not also in others? It is ironic that an Act purportedly designed to protect the sovereignty of Parliament raises such serious problems for the doctrine, which comes to resemble nothing more than the smile on the face of the Cheshire cat. In seeking to restore national sover-eignty, the European Union Act has, paradoxically, restricted parliamentary sovereignty.

Bogdanor's observations are powerful: the EUA does indeed inject a new stimulant (direct democracy) into the UK's traditional form of government (representative democracy). But is his analysis of the EUA accurate? It is true that the EUA purports to target future governments and Parliaments; however, they remain unequivocally able to repeal or amend the EUA with a simple majority in Parliament. Also, upon closer examination, the EUA is actually directed at Treaties amending or replacing TEU or TFEU (s. 2 EUA) and the amendment of TFEU under Art. 48(6) TEU (ss 3 and 4 EUA). In short, the EUA does not (and cannot) unilaterally change the rule of recognition; but it does seek to condition the exercise of ministerial power (s. 5, but also ss 3, 6, 7, 8, 9, 10 EUA). Finally, how different is the EUA from the devolution legislation for Scotland, Wales, and Northern Ireland, which also involved Acts of Parliament preceded by referendums?[18]

---

[18] See Chapter 5.

QUESTIONS

1. What are the steps a government must take for a treaty to come into effect?

2. If you could choose, how would you strengthen democratic scrutiny over the UK government's activities in relation to the European Union? By building on the existing, and maybe creating new, parliamentary control mechanisms? By introducing the far-reaching use of national referendums? Or through a mixture of both?

3. Which of the following statements is correct:

    a. Parliament remains sovereign, and the referendum locks in the EUA are legally unenforceable and could be entirely disregarded by a future government.

    b. Parliament has successfully modified the future law-making process and bound itself in *procedural* terms: future statutes seeking an extension of an EU competence must be created in accordance with the procedure (the 'manner' and 'form') set out in the EUA.

    c. Parliament has substantively limited its legislative authority (by depriving itself of its sovereign power to legislate on certain European Union matters without the need for a referendum), and thereby unilaterally altered the rule of recognition.

Legal challenges to UK government plans to ratify EU treaties

The draft treaties that have emerged from IGCs and the more recent 'convention' have been deeply politically contentious within the United Kingdom and most other member states. It is therefore not surprising that people have attempted to bring challenges in the UK courts to question the lawfulness of government's actions or proposed actions under its treaty-making powers (see Box 12.6). In the three most recent challenges, the grounds of review related to failure of the UK government to hold a referendum.

BOX 12.6 LEGAL CHALLENGES TO EU TREATIES IN THE UNITED KINGDOM

- In 1971, Raymond Blackburn, a litigant in person well known for bringing legal actions about constitutional matters, attempted to prevent the United Kingdom from acceding to the Community. He sought a declaration that the government would be acting unlawfully if it were to sign the Treaty of Accession to the EC. In essence, his argument was that the government would be surrendering '*the sovereignty of the Crown in Parliament*'. The Court of Appeal struck out his action.[19]

- Financed by the billionaire businessman Sir James Goldsmith, Lord Rees-Mogg, a cross-bench peer and former editor of *The Times*, applied for judicial review against the Foreign Secretary the day before the Bill incorporating the Maastricht Treaty was to receive royal assent in July 1993.[20] The application by Rees-Mogg was peremptorily dismissed by the High Court, so leaving the way clear for the Crown to proceed with ratification.

---

[19] *Blackburn v Attorney General* [1971] 1 WLR 1037.

[20] *R v Secretary of State of State for Foreign and Commonwealth Affairs, ex parte Rees-Mogg* [1994] QB 552. See further R. Rawlings, 'Legal politics: The United Kingdom and ratification of the Treaty on European Union (Part Two)' [1994] Public Law 367–91; G. Marshall, 'The Maastricht Treaty proceedings' [1993] Public Law 402.

- The draft Constitutional Treaty was also subject to legal challenge in the Court of Appeal in 2003. Like Blackburn, the applicants in this case sought to argue that the government would be acting unlawfully and/or contrary to convention were it to ratify the Constitutional Treaty without prior electoral approval. The Court of Appeal had no difficulty in finding that the applicants' case was not seriously arguable.[21]

- In February 2008, *a* UK Independence Party (UKIP) activist lost a legal challenge relating to the government's refusal to hold a referendum on the Lisbon Treaty. Stuart Bower accused ministers of a breach of contract. He said that the treaty was effectively the same as the European Constitution, on which the government promised a public vote at the 2005 general election. The judge in Brighton County Court said the effect of breaching a manifesto commitment was political, not legal.

- The last of the judicial review challenges to EU treaties was in June 2008. This time, it was by Mr Stuart Wheeler, a barrister turned investment banker who had made a fortune pioneering 'spread betting', and was once the Tories' biggest donor (he now backs UKIP). He sought a High Court order to force the government to hold a referendum on the Lisbon Treaty, agreed by member state governments in December 2007. As Prime Minister, Tony Blair had previously promised a UK referendum on the 2004 draft Constitutional Treaty (an *executive* decision). After the treaty was signed, a European Union Bill was introduced into Parliament in May 2005 and provided for the Constitutional Treaty to be given effect in domestic law subject to the outcome of a referendum (a *parliamentary* decision). Mr Wheeler claimed that the refusal to hold a referendum in relation to the Lisbon Treaty (which is ultimately a decision for Parliament) was unlawful because it was in breach of the claimant's 'legitimate expectation'.[22] Unsurprisingly, the Administrative Court rejected his claim.[23]

Although none of the legal challenges were high profile let alone successful, they do raise a broader question of constitutional significance: are the courts best placed institutionally to decide the question of whether or not a referendum on the Lisbon Treaty (or any other amending treaty) should be held? You will recall that the purpose of public law is to regulate actions by the government. This it does in two ways. The first way is political. Those who exercise political power (for example, government officials) are held to account through political institutions (for example, Parliament); we saw in Chapter 8 that government ministers and senior civil servants are regularly subjected to scrutiny (for example, debates, answering questions, and committees). The other way in which the government is to account is through the law and the courtroom. Chapter 16 will illustrate how individuals may seek judicial review of government action (instead of seeking political redress, for example by lobbying for parliamentary scrutiny).

The United Kingdom has historically favoured the first method of political accountability (although, as we saw in Chapter 2, we are seeing a move from a 'political' to a 'legal' constitution). It is therefore unsurprising that the repercussions of UK membership in the EU are largely political. One need only look at the Labour Party's attitude towards referendums in

---

[21] *R v Secretary of State for Foreign & Commonwealth Affairs, ex parte Southall* [2003] EWCA 1002; [2003] 3 Common Market Law Review 18.

[22] On the concept of legitimate expectations as a ground of judicial review, see Chapter 16.

[23] *R v Office of the Prime Minister, ex parte Wheeler* [2008] EWHC 1409 (Admin).

relation to the Lisbon Treaty or the lasting political divisions within the Conservative Party to get a sense of the political difficulties that the EU poses for party leaders.

Legal challenges, such as the one by Mr Wheeler, pale into insignificance when compared to the political ramifications of EU membership and also when compared to the constitutional challenges on the European continent—most famously in Germany, where the claimants argued (ultimately unsuccessfully) that the Maastricht Treaty[24] and the Lisbon Treaty[25] were incompatible with certain provisions of the Basic Law.

QUESTIONS

1. Do you think that the representation to hold a referendum in relation to the Constitutional Treaty created a 'legitimate expectation' that a referendum would be held in relation to the Lisbon Treaty?

2. Why have legal challenges to EU treaties always been unsuccessful? Can you imagine a situation in which a legal challenge might succeed?

In concluding the first part, the European Union has long struggled with the notion of 'legitimacy'. It began to give itself a 'human face'[26] by incorporating human rights, social justice, and proportionality in its case law (which were only later included in the body of the treaties). The symbolic choice of a convention method to draft a Constitutional Treaty, in addition to the formal requirement of an IGC, is another example of the EU's attempts to appear less elitist and formalist, and to improve its legitimacy rating. EU officials are constantly stressing the shared heritage and history of the member states (rather than, say, the need to make its executive institutions more democratic).

Has the EU been successful in convincing its citizens that it has a secure constitutional foundation (rather than mere cultural rhetoric)? Joseph Weiler, an important US scholar of European constitutionalism, emphasizes the need for social legitimacy.

J.H.H. Weiler, *The Constitution of Europe: Do the New Clothes Have an Emperor? and Other Essays on European Integration* (1999, Cambridge: Cambridge University Press), p. 83

What defines the boundary of the polity within which the majority principle should apply? There is no theoretical answer to this question. It is determined by long term, very long term, factors such as political continuity, social, cultural and linguistic affinity and a shared history. No one factor determines this but the interplay of some or all. People accept the majoritarian principle of democracy within a polity to which they see themselves as belonging.

The process of integration—even if decided upon democratically—brings about then, initially at least, a loss of direct democracy in its actual process of governance. What becomes crucial for the success of the integration process is the social legitimacy of the new integrated polity despite this loss of total control over the integrated areas by each polity.

[24] *Brunner v European Union Treaty* [1994] 1 CMLR 57.
[25] BVerfG, 2 BvE 2/08, 30 June 2009.
[26] George de Kerchove, *A Human Face for Europe*, European Documentation 4/1990, March 1990.

Social legitimacy is a major challenge for the EU (as well as a major theme of this chapter and Chapter 8). To what extent does the EU command popular support? This question is related to the referendum issue. Obviously, national governments could increase people's sense of belonging to the EU if it made them stakeholders of the future of the Union, for example by holding a referendum. But a referendum is a very crude mechanism for ascertaining people's preferences and not a very reliable compass either. Referendums are often influenced by national issues (and held for national purposes) as opposed to real European ones, and so a referendum could easily disintegrate into a poll on voters' (dis-)satisfaction with their own government. To illustrate, 80–90 per cent of negative votes in France, the Netherlands, and Ireland were motivated by protest voting against the national government, not by dissatisfaction with the EU. Ask yourself whether it is sensible to hold a referendum, say, on the *details* of the Lisbon Treaty? (Forty per cent of Irish 'No' voters admitted that they opposed the Treaty without knowing its content.) Would it not make more sense to ask a question on *principle*, such as whether the United Kingdom should continue to be a member of the EU? We saw that this question was asked in a referendum in 1975 and that over two-thirds supported continued membership. Should this 'political' question be asked at regular intervals in order to ensure continued legitimacy? Or was this 'constitutional' question decided in 1975, and the matter laid to rest once and for all?

The degree of the EU's democracy deficit depends on the benchmarks that are used to assess the EU's democratic quality and potential. The sociologist Fritz Scharpf, for example, distinguishes between two forms of legitimacy.[27] We are familiar with 'input-oriented' legitimacy, which focuses on *procedural* criteria (how we elect our law-makers and how we hold them to account in transparent institutions) for determining the popular will ('government *by the people*'). If this benchmark is used, the EU clearly falls short of the standards of democracy set by the member states. But if we focus on the EU's 'output-oriented' legitimacy, which is generated by achieving citizens' *substantive* common welfare and goals ('government *for the people*'), the EU has a much better track record. Twenty-eight states have joined the EU voluntarily (not one has requested to leave) and the EU has, through interinstitutional cooperation, improved the common welfare in various policy fields (we will be looking at the impact of the Race Directive later in this chapter). But is output-oriented legitimacy enough to raise the EU's democratic pedigree?

Beate Kohler-Koch and Berthold Rittberger, 'Charting Crowded Territory', in B. Kohler-Koch and B. Rittberger (eds) *Debating the Democratic Legitimacy of the European Union* (2007, Lanham, MD: Rowman & Littlefield), ch. 1, pp. 12–13

[…T]he distinctiveness of democratic legitimacy lies not (merely) in realizing a certain kind of combination of input, output, and social legitimacy, but in realizing the fundamental values of democracy. It is the principle of autonomy that stands at the centre stage of the democratic project. All modern traditions of democratic thought—from Liberalism to Republicanism to Social Democracy—share the underlying notion that for people to develop as free and equal they have to be autonomous […] Autonomy implies that people are free and equal in the determination of their own lives […] Democracy requires more than merely a commitment to popular sovereignty, majority rule, or effective problem solving: All these practices may well be related to the practice of democracy, but "they themselves do not define democracy".[28]

---

[27] Fritz Scharpf, *Governing in Europe: Effective and Democratic?* (1999, Oxford: OUP), ch. 1.
[28] Robert Dahl, *Democracy and Its Critics* (1989, New Haven, CT: Yale University Press), p. 105.

A political system is not democratic because particular decision-making procedures are in place which we commonly associate with democratic rule. What democracy requires is a commitment towards realizing a condition in which—negatively defined—people are not alienated from political decisions, and in which—positively defined—people are convinced that they are truly governing themselves [...] It is only when people are granted autonomy and the forms of participation that enable citizens to act autonomously that they will identify with the state, that is to say, regard the state as legitimate. Democracy thus requires that people not just enjoy the right to vote, but it also implies that citizens enjoy equal entitlements and rights to participate in communicative processes of debate and deliberation which "empower citizens to participate in public opinion in ways that will permit them to believe that public opinion will become potentially responsive to their views".[29]

The role of the citizen—civic society—as well as the responsiveness of EU laws to new social changes and demands are vital ingredients in the assessment of the legitimacy of the EU's legislative process (see further Chapter 8).

3 THE EVERYDAY LEGISLATIVE PROCESS: THE MAKING OF REGULATIONS AND DIRECTIVES

In this next section of the chapter, we move from the 'once in a while' processes of treaty revision to the more ordinary, everyday world of the making of regulations and directives by the EU. Examples of such legislation are set out in Box 12.11.

BOX 12.7 COMPETENCES AFTER THE LISBON TREATY

Exclusive competence	Shared competences	Supporting competence
The EU has six exclusive competences. In these areas, the EU is the sole legislator and decision-maker. The member states take no decisions and do not interfere with the competence in these matters transferred to the EU.	The vast majority of other policies come under this heading. In these areas, both member states and the EU have the power to make laws. If the EU has stopped taking initiatives in this area (or if it never did so), member states have the option of taking action themselves, using their own initiative and resources.	There are a number of areas in which the Commission has very little direct involvement. The EU can financially support the actions of the member states that have agreed to coordinate their domestic policies through the EU in the following areas.
Article 3 TFEU: 'The Union shall have exclusive competence in the following areas:'	Article 4 TFEU: 'The Union shall share competence with the Member States where the Treaties confer on it a	Article 6 TFEU: 'The Union shall have competence to carry out actions to support, coordinate or supplement

[29] R. Post, 'Democracy and equality' (2006) 603 Annals of the American Academy of Political and Social Sciences 24–36, 29.

- the customs union—that is, the internal free trade zone between member states who apply the same European customs duties (taxes) to goods coming into the EU zone;
- the economic and monetary policy of the EU, including sharing a single currency, the euro, overseen by the European Central Bank in Frankfurt;
- competition laws to ensure a level playing field between European businesses, controlling state aid from national governments (the European Commission has primary competence for enforcing EU competition law);
- a common position in international trade negotiations such as the World Trade Organization (WTO) trade rounds, as part of a common international trade policy;
- conservation of marine biological resources (part of the common fisheries policy between EU states); and
- the concluding of some international agreements.

competence which does not relate to the areas referred to in Arts 3 [exclusive competence] and 6 [supporting competence]'.
'Shared competence between the Union and the Member States applies in the following principal areas:'
- the internal market;
- social policy, for the aspects defined in this treaty;
- economic, social and territorial cohesion;
- agriculture and fisheries, excluding the conservation of marine biological resources;
- the environment;
- consumer protection;
- transport;
- trans-European networks;
- energy;
- the area of freedom, security and justice (this harbours the provisions on Police and Judicial Cooperation in Criminal Matters in Title IV TEC and Title VI TEU);
- common safety concerns in public health matters, for the aspects defined in this treaty; and
- other Union competences.

the actions of the Member States. The areas of such action shall, at European level, be:'
- the protection and improvement of human health;
- industry;
- culture;
- tourism;
- education, vocational training, youth and sport;
- civil protection; and
- administrative cooperation.

(a) SHARED, EXCLUSIVE, AND SUPPORTING COMPETENCES IN THE EU

As we saw in Chapter 8, the EU used to consist of three 'pillars', created by the TEU in 1992 and underpinned by the TEC, which set out the institutional framework that served all three pillars as well as detail on the scope of the European Community (Pillar 1). Serving all three pillars were common provisions on institutional and procedural arrangements, and the principles (maybe even 'constitutional principles') on which the EU operates. But the law adopted in the first 'Community' pillar (EC law), and the law adopted in the second and third pillars of the EU, had different legal effects.

The Lisbon Treaty merges the first and third pillars, and abolishes the European 'Community'—the distinction is no longer necessary, because the 'Community' is replaced and succeeded by one organization: the Union. After a five-year transition,[30] the old third pillar (Police and Judicial Cooperation in Criminal Matters) will move into the generally applicable mechanisms of the Union (which is based on those of the old first, or Community, pillar) set out in TFEU. EU policies enacted in the Area of Freedom, Security and Justice will be determined by the ordinary legislative procedure of QMV and the ordinary legislative procedure, and will eventually fall within the jurisdiction of the European Court of Justice (ECJ) and have 'primacy' over national law.[31] Legislation in this area can be initiated on a proposal from the Commission, or on the initiative of a quarter of the member states (Art. 76 TFEU). One commentator has said that converting the third pillar (Police and Judicial Cooperation in Criminal Matters) into a stronger Area of Freedom, Security and Justice is *the single most revolutionary achievement*[32] of the Lisbon Treaty.

The second pillar (Common Foreign and Security Policy) is outlined in TEU and remains subject to specific intergovernmental procedures. It remains outside the jurisdiction of the ECJ (Art. 275 TFEU). The principles of attributed power, subsidiarity, and proportionality are located in TEU, but it contains no legal bases for the adoption of Union legislation. According to Dougan, *the TEU has more the character of a mission statement coupled with some basic organizing principles on uses such as the institutional architecture*.[33] The decisions made pursuant to Common Foreign and Security Policy will remain distinct, as regards their effects within the national legal systems, from any other Union activity.

The Lisbon Treaty consists of areas of exclusive competence (Art. 3 TFEU), shared competence (Art. 4 TFEU), and other competences are listed in Arts 5 and 6 TFEU.

But the basic law-making process remains the same under Lisbon. The directly elected European Parliament can scupper plans pushed forward by governments.[34] The Commission is responsible (often controversially) for preparing policies and draft laws, and steering them through the legislative process—policies that some governments of member states may disagree with.[35] Moreover, the ECJ, comprising judges independent of governments of the member states, has the final say if disputes arise about the powers of the EU institutions to make law or take action.[36] The formal 'inputs' of member state governments in the EU law-making process is through the body known as the Council of the European Union.[37] Even here, a government may have to accept a law with which it disagrees because QMV (according to which each member state has a fixed number of votes that is roughly determined by its population, but is progressively weighted in favour of smaller countries) now applies in relation to most policy areas.[38] The EU's activities are here derived from TFEU, according to which the EU can make legislation—directives and regulations—which directly creates legally binding rights and obligations binding public authorities, businesses, and citizens in member states. The original focus was on economic policy, but the EU's competences have significantly expanded over the years.

The EU's legislative process, as in the United Kingdom, can be seen as a network of communication channels: some of which are given formal constitutional status; others of which

---

[30] Article 10 of the Protocol on Transitional Provisions.

[31] See Declaration No. 17 annexed to the Lisbon Treaty.

[32] C. Ladenburger, 'Police and criminal law in the Treaty of Lisbon' (2008) 4 European Constitutional Law Review 20–40, 40.

[33] M. Dougan, 'The Treaty of Lisbon 2007: Winning minds, not hearts' (2008) 45 Common Market Law Review 617, 623.

[34] On the European Parliament, see p. 496.

[35] On the Commission, see The centrality of the Commission in the legislative process on p. 503.

[36] On the European Court of Justice, see Part IV Introduction.

[37] On the Council, see Chapter 8.

[38] On qualified majority voting, see Chapter 8.

are quite informal (for example, the lobbying of the Commission by pressure groups). To formulate and agree on policy, and to give policy formal legal validity, dialogue is needed between people representing different interests. The best way in which to understand the EU is as a body to which the member states have decided to 'pool' their sovereignty. In other words, the member states have decided to delegate their decision-making powers to an additional institutional level in order to gain an amount of collective leverage, influence, and effectiveness that the states on their own would not otherwise have possessed. Each of the EU institutions involved in the legislative process has been designed to reflect different types of interest.

There is no single institution that is, by itself, the EU 'legislature'. Directives and regulations are made through the interactions of the Commission, the Council, and the European Parliament. Chapter 8 considered the various 'executive' functions of the European Council, the Council, and the Commission. The latter two bodies also play a role in the legislative process. The third institution in the process is the European Parliament.

QUESTIONS

1. The EU Commission believes that US computer giant Microsoft is engaging in anti-competitive behaviour by selling its own media player and browser together with its Windows operating system. By selling such a package, Microsoft is said to be abusing its virtual monopoly, because smaller rivals (who make media players and browsers) are unable to compete with Microsoft. Does the Commission have an exclusive, shared, or supporting power to challenge Microsoft's practices?

2. The EU manages access to fishing waters and determines how many fish a national fleet can catch (for example, through quotas), with the aim of conserving fish stocks. As you can see from Box 12.7, fisheries are both an exclusive and a shared competence. In 2002, Scotland landed 62 per cent of the total fish catch in the United Kingdom. There are three types of catching industry. Identify the competence that regulates:

   (a) fish living in the upper layers of the sea, such as herring and mackerel (the sector is profitable and stable);

   (b) shellfish, such as prawn, shrimps, lobster (the sector is profitable and stable); and

   (c) the whitefish industry, such as cod and haddock (stocks are depleted and in risk of collapse).

   Given the social, economic, and cultural significance of fishing for Scotland, do you think that the principle of subsidiarity (see Chapter 8) should apply to fisheries?

3. Margaret Thatcher once described monetary policy as the 'core of the core' of national sovereignty.[39] How is that policy controlled by the EU?

4. Switzerland is not a member of the EU. If it is to participate in EU education and training programmes (such as ERASMUS), a bilateral agreement must be concluded. What role will the Commission play in the process?

5. Should the EU be given the instruments and procedures that it needs to offer its citizens and residents security from terrorism and transnational crime? Or do you think that the role of protection rightly belongs to the member states?

---

[39] Cited in W. Wallace, 'Rescue or Retreat? The Nation State in Western Europe, 1945–1993', in P. Gowan and R. Anderson (eds) *The Question of Europe* (1997, London: Verso), p. 36.

(b) THE EUROPEAN PARLIAMENT

The European Parliament (in various guises) is one of the original institutions that dates back to the European Coal and Steel Community (ECSC). Back in 1952, it was called an 'assembly' and membership was drawn from the national parliaments of the member states. It has radically changed since then.

From 1979, members of the European Parliament (MEPs) have been directly elected. Before 1986, the European Parliament was 'consulted' by the Council only before enacting legislation. In other words, the European Parliament's opinion was not binding on the Council.

The European Parliament had always argued the case for it to be an effective co-legislator with the Council. This was gradually introduced, beginning with the cooperation procedure in the Single European Act. The TEU established, and the Amsterdam Treaty extended and made more effective, the 'co-decision procedure', which is now known as the 'ordinary legislative procedure' in Art. 289 TFEU. It acknowledges the parity of the European Parliament and the Council, meaning that assent from both institutions is required before legislation can be adopted. The EU now has a 'two-chamber legislature': ministers of the national governments represent the member states in the Council, and the political groups represent the European Union citizens in the European Parliament.

In the course of its lifetime, the European Parliament has transformed itself from a *consultant assembly* to a *working parliament*. It should not be compared with a traditional *debating parliament*: the European Parliament has fewer powers than, say, the Westminster Parliament to hold the government to account or to prescribe new legislation. But through its political independence and veto power, the European Parliament exercises more influence over the law-making process than most member states' legislatures, and is thus similar to the US Congress.

P. Dann, 'European Parliament and executive federalism' (2003) 9 European Law Journal 549, 556–7

The *debating parliament* is what in continental Europe is often perceived as the ideal parliament: it is centred around its plenary, which serves as the forum of the nation and draws its importance from mirroring different opinions in society within the parliament. This type is mostly found in parliamentary systems where the majority party in parliament forms the government, leading to, in the words of Walter Bagehot, a fusion of majority party and government. The political opposition uses the plenary to attack governmental measures as well as to lay out its own proposals. In short: debate is the centre of parliamentary life. The British House of Commons is the pre-eminent example.

The *working parliament*, on the other hand, receives its character and power from being fairly separated from the government and from operating as a counter-weight to it. Not the fusion of majority party and government, but the institutional combat between legislature and executive characterises the system and thereby the legislature. Moreover, an incompatibility rule which forbids members of the executive from sitting in the legislature, prevents public debates between government and opposition on the floor. It is more the strong and specialised committees and less the floor which functions as the main locus in working parliaments. These committees acquire expertise and power to control the bureaucracy, and heavily shape lawmaking. In sum: working committees are at the heart of parliamentary life. The US Congress is the classic example of this type of parliament. [...]

At first glance. it would seem that there are many similarities between the European Parliament and the working parliament model. Nevertheless, it should be mentioned that certain of its features are quite original to the European Parliament. These features justify the consideration of a third type, which can be seen as a sub-category of the working parliament. This type shall be more precisely named a *'controlling parliament'*. As such, it employs basically the same instruments as a working parliament (such as the US Congress), but its powers are generally more of a negative, and controlling nature than an autonomously creating one. In this respect the term 'controlling parliament' is more appropriate.

Elections are held every five years, and every citizen of a member state has the right to vote and to stand as a candidate in the member state of residence (rather than nationality) on the same conditions as those applying to nationals of that state.[40] The EP is elected by a variety of electoral systems (closed list, ordered list, open list, and single transferable vote). It was credited by the German Federal Constitutional Court as being *'an additional independent source'* of democratic legitimacy: it is the directly elected 'representative body' of more than 500 million EU citizens (over 375 million eligible voters in 2010), whose interests it represents in debates with the other EU institutions.[41] In Chapter 8, however, we said that legitimacy stems from support, and the EP continues to suffer from a lack of interest in its work and from a perception that it is an irrelevant institution that accommodates second-rate politicians.

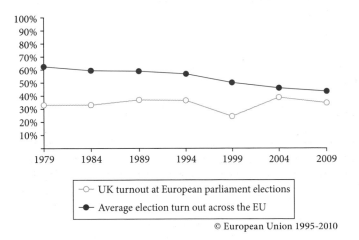

© European Union 1995-2010

Figure 12.2 UK turnout for European Parliament elections 1979–2009

Figure 12.2 shows the percentage of registered UK voters who actually voted at European Parliament elections from 1979 to 2009, and the average turnout across the European Union. Box 12.8 shows voter turnout for each EU country.

---

[40] See further Art. 19(2)TEC (Art. 22(2) TFEU), and Directive 93/109/EC (OJ No. L329, 30 December 1993, p. 34).

[41] See Art. 10(2) TEU; quotes from the *Lisbon Treaty* decision in BVerfG, 2 BvE 2/08, 30 June 2009, at [271].

BOX 12.8 TURNOUT FOR EUROPEAN PARLIAMENT ELECTIONS BY COUNTRY 1979–2009

Member state	1979	1984	1989	1994	1999	2004	2009
Belgium	91.36	92.09	90.73	90.66	91.05	90.81	90.39
Denmark	47.82	52.38	46.17	52.92	50.46	47.89	59.54
Germany	65.73	56.76	62.28	60.02	45.19	43.00	43.30
Ireland	63.61	47.56	68.28	43.98	50.21	58.58	58.64
France	60.71	56.72	48.80	52.71	46.76	42.76	40.63
Italy	85.65	82.47	81.07	73.60	69.76	71.72	65.05
Luxembourg	88.91	88.79	87.39	88.55	87.27	91.35	90.75
Netherlands	58.12	50.88	47.48	35.69	30.02	39.26	36.75
United Kingdom	**32.35**	**32.57**	**36.37**	**36.43**	**24.00**	**38.52**	**34.70**
Greece		80.59	80.03	73.18	70.25	63.22	52.61
Spain			54.71	59.14	63.05	45.14	44.90
Portugal			51.10	35.54	39.93	38.60	36.78
Sweden					38.84	37.85	45.53
Austria					49.40	42.43	45.97
Finland					30.14	39.43	40.30
Czech Republic						28.30	28.20
Estonia						26.83	43.90
Cyprus						72.50	59.40
Lithuania						48.38	20.98
Latvia						41.34	53.70
Hungary						38.50	36.31
Malta						82.39	78.79
Poland						20.87	24.53
Slovenia						28.35	28.33
Slovakia						16.97	19.64
Bulgaria							38.99
Romania							27.67
Ave. EU turnout	61.99	58.98	58.41	56.67	49.51	45.57	43.00

© *European Union, 1995–2010*

The average EU-wide turnout was 43 per cent, which was the lowest since the first direct elections to the European Parliament in 1979. Although turnout actually rose in seven countries, and was lower in Eastern than in Western Europe, almost everywhere turnout was far below levels in national elections. Moreover, voters in European elections tend to focus mainly on national issues, not European ones. A steady decline of turnout and interest over thirty years is a major concern not only for national and European politicians, but also for the legitimacy of the institution itself. In a barbed comment, the German Court added that the European Parliament *'cannot, and need not, [...] comply with the requirements that arise on the state level from the citizens' equal political right to vote'*.[42] This can mean either

---

[42] Ibid.

that the EP should be judged according to a different (that is, lower) standard of democratic legitimacy than national parliaments or that it is '*not up to the job*'.[43] What can be done to address the democracy and legitimacy deficits in the EP?

J. Blondel, R. Sinnott, and P. Svensson, *People and Parliament in the European Union: Participation, Democracy, and Legitimacy* (1998, Oxford: Clarendon Press), pp. 237–8

An often unquestioned assumption has been that the legitimacy problems of the European Union stem in large part from the 'democratic deficit' of its institutions and, therefore, that an increase in the democratic content of these institutions would automatically increase legitimacy. Low levels of participation in European Parliament elections are presumed to both reflect and accentuate the problems of democracy and legitimacy in the Union. Yet the connection between participation, democracy, and legitimacy is not simple. One, and not necessarily the most important, indication of this is that the election of the European Parliament by direct universal suffrage did not ostensibly increase, to say the least, the legitimacy of the Union. Cynics might indeed suggest, with some obvious exaggeration but with a grain of truth, that the direct elections to the European Parliament increased rather than diminished the visibility, if not necessarily the reality, of its lack of legitimacy. Secondly, and more importantly, legitimacy itself is not monolithic: on the contrary, it can be expected to go up and down, to be concerned with several and perhaps many bodies at the same time, as well as to relate to specific fields or to be bounded rather than universal. The extent and breadth of the legitimacy of the Union has therefore to be explored, not whether that level of governance is or is not legitimate. Thirdly, democracy is a complex concept and the attempt to apply it at the supranational level multiplies this complexity. [...] In short, it is not the case that more democracy would necessarily lead to more legitimacy; neither is it the case that more participation would necessarily mean more legitimacy. While low turnout may be a sign of a significant weakness in the process of democratic representation at the supranational level, the converse does not hold in all circumstances: more participation would not necessarily indicate a more representative political process at the European level; the effect would depend on the kind of participation involved.

The European Parliament has two meeting places. It conducts the bulk of its work in Brussels, Belgium. A growing number of plenary sessions are held in Brussels, which is also where committee meetings take place, political groups meet, and where the offices of the MEPs are based. However, for twelve four-day plenary sessions a year, it meets in Strasbourg, France, which is also its official seat. The General Secretariat of the European Parliament, the Parliament's administrative body, is based in Luxembourg.[44] This 'travelling circus' involves relocating MEPs, their staff, and a sizeable section of the EU's bureaucracy for one week every month at considerable cost to the taxpayer (an estimated annual cost of €200m) and the environment (it generates at least 20,000 extra tonnes of CO_2 emissions—equalling 13,000 return flights from London to New York). It gave rise to an online petition to establish one 'seat' for the EP, which attracted 1.2m signatures and was fiercely debated at the EP's petitions committee hearing.[45]

---

[43] As *The Economist* has repeatedly argued: 'The endless election round', *The Economist*, 11 June 2009; 'Constitutional concerns', *The Economist*, 23 July 2009.

[44] Protocol (No. 8) on the location of the seats of the institutions and of certain bodies and departments of the European Communities and of Europol (1997).

[45] L. Phillips, 'EU petitions committee debates Brussels–Strasbourg "travelling circus"', 26 February 2008, available online at http://euobserver.com/9/25722/?rk=1.

© LUke1138/istockphoto.com

© LUke1138/istockphoto.com

Figure 12.3 The European Parliament Building in Brussels (outside and interior)

©x-drew/istockphoto.com

Figure 12.4 The European Parliament Building in Strasbourg

N. Nugent, *The Government and Politics of the European Union* (2010, Basingstoke: Macmillan), p. 206

But notwithstanding the increased powers and influence it has secured, the EP is still widely viewed as not being quite a proper parliament. The main reasons for this are: it cannot overthrow a government; its formal legislative powers remain weaker than those of national parliaments; and in some important spheres of EU policy activity—notably EMU and foreign and defence policies—it is largely confined to information-receiving and consultative roles. However, the extent to which there is a 'formal powers gap' between the EP and national parliaments has greatly narrowed over the years, and in many important respects the Lisbon Treaty has narrowed it further. Indeed, the EP may be said to have been the principal institutional beneficiary of the Treaty, with gains for it including: significant extensions to its legislative powers; stronger budgetary powers; and EP approval becoming necessary for a number of important decisions that hitherto only required Council approval, such as the use of enhanced cooperation and a wide range of international agreements.

However, when assessing the importance of the EP attention should not be restricted to its formal capabilities. For when the comparison with national parliaments is extended to encompass what actually happens in practice, the powers exercised by the EP are, in several key respects, comparable to the powers exercised by many national parliaments. Indeed, it is not difficult to make out a case that in exercising some of its functions—most particularly scrutinising legislative proposals—the EP exerts a greater influence over affairs than do the more executive-dominated parliaments of many member states.

The Treaty of Lisbon changed the composition of the European Parliament. It ceased to be composed of representatives '*of the peoples of the States brought together in the Community*' (Art. 189(1) TEC), and instead is now composed of representatives of 'the Union's citizens' (Art. 14(2)(1) TEU). These representatives are elected '*by direct universal suffrage in a free and secret ballot*' (Art. 14 (3) TEU). The total number of representatives may not exceed 750, 'plus the President', and representation of the citizens of the Union is 'degressively proportional', with a minimum threshold of six members per member state and no member state being allocated more than ninety-six seats. In contrast, an MEP elected in the United Kingdom (which has seventy-two seats and a population of 60 million) represents 770,000 citizens, whereas an MEP from Luxembourg (which has six seats for 500,000 citizens) represents approximately only 83,000 Luxembourg citizens.[46]

MEPs tend to work and vote according to their political, rather than national, affiliations. There are seven Europe-wide political groups, the views of which cover the entire spectrum of European integration, from the federalists (who support the creation of European Federation based on the idea of unity in diversity) and the Eurosceptics (a group of nation-state sovereignists and anti-corruption fighters) at the margins, to the vast majority of integrationists in the middle, who favour an 'ever-closer union' for Europe.

[46] Data from *Europe in Figures: Eurostat Yearbook 2008*.

BOX 12.9 UK REPRESENTATION IN THE EUROPEAN PARLIAMENT

The United Kingdom is divided into twelve electoral regions made up of the nations and regions, as follows.

1. East Midlands

2. Eastern

3. London (comprises the seventy-four Westminster parliamentary constituencies in the Greater London area)

4. North East

5. North West

6. Northern Ireland

7. Scotland

8. South East

9. South West (which, since June 2004, includes residents of Gibraltar)

10. Wales

11. West Midlands

12. Yorkshire and the Humber

Each constituency has between three and ten MEPs, and each MEP in a region represents each person living there.

The United Kingdom has seventy-two representatives in the EP. The nine English regions elect fifty-nine MEPs , Scotland elects six, and Wales elects four MEPs. In Northern Ireland, three MEPs are elected under its own system of proportionate representation.

The MEPs sit in political groups: they are not organized by nationality, but by political affiliation. Groups are not parties, but looser coalitions. There are currently seven political groups in the European Parliament.

Twenty-five members are needed to form a political group and at least one quarter of the member states must be represented within the group. Members may not belong to more than one political group.

Some MEPs do not belong to any political group and are known as 'non-attached' MEPs.

The position adopted by the political group is arrived at by discussion within the group. MEPs exercise their mandate in an independent fashion and no MEP can be forced to vote in a particular way.

At present, 34 per cent of MEPs are women. The UK has 25 female (35 per cent of its total).

On 22 June 2009, the UK Conservative Party controversially withdrew from the European People's Party (the largest political group in the EP) and, with their European colleagues, launched the anti-federalist European Conservatives and Reformists Group, which includes fifty-three MEPs from across ten member states.

QUESTIONS

1. What is the job of the European Parliament? Do you agree that it is not up to it?

2. Do you agree with Blondel's claim that '*the connection between participation, democracy, and legitimacy is not simple*'?

3. What do you understand by the EP's 'degressively proportional' voting system? Is it a fair system?

(c) THE LEGISLATIVE PROCESS FOR REGULATIONS AND DIRECTIVES

The law-making process of the EU has a reputation for being endlessly complex. It is true that there were once no fewer than twenty-two different ways of enacting a piece of legislation. But the Lisbon Treaty has reduced the main legislative procedures that regulate the relationship between the European Parliament and the Council to three. The Commission, responsible for introducing draft directives and regulations, begins by identifying the Article in the TFEU that (in its view) provides a legal base for the proposed legislation. The Article in question will determine what role is played by the European Parliament. Under *consultation*, it merely has a consultative role, and the Council has the final word on whether to adopt, amend, or reject a proposal. Under *consent,* an absolute majority of all MEPs is required with respect to the admission of new member states and amendment of the procedural rules governing European Parliament elections. Under the *ordinary legislative procedure*, the European Parliament has the power to veto legislation even though the Commission and Council are in favour of it. In the Council, too, different procedures (unanimous voting and QMV) apply, depending upon the TFEU provision under which a regulation or directive is made. An overly complex decision-making process that was only understandable to the experts participating in the process would give rise to transparency and legitimacy concerns. As is we shall, however, after the Lisbon Treaty the ordinary legislative procedure (Art. 289 TFEU) applies to virtually all EU policy areas.

(d) THE CENTRALITY OF THE COMMISSION IN THE LEGISLATIVE PROCESS

Under the TEU, all legislation is adopted by the Council after consulting the Parliament. The proposal will typically be subject to a process of consideration and negotiation; if agreed, the legislation is eventually adopted and published.

Our focus here will instead be on legislating under the TFEU. Formal responsibility for initiating legislative proposals under this treaty lies with the Commission in all of the areas that are subject to the co-decision procedure. It is important to note that the Commission's right of initiative is a 'right to propose' legislation, not a 'right to legislate':[47] it does not

---

[47] On the Commission, see further Chapter 7.

prevent the Council[48] or the European Parliament[49] from asking the Commission to formulate and introduce any appropriate proposal—although the Commission is not bound to follow such requests. In practice, the Commission may be influenced by a range of interests. In short, the Commission's role in initiating legislative proposals is:

(a) exclusive;

(b) crucial in relation to its formulation and content; and

(c) political—legislation must be technically sound and politically feasible.

Although there is no single source of ideas that prompts a proposal, the Commission's right of initiative gives it real power in the legislative process. It publishes an annual work programme listing the initiatives it intends to take. In 2011, the programme included action in the financial services sector, the promotion of energy efficiency, and a legislative proposal on personal data protection. Under Art. 294(2) TFEU : 'The Commission shall submit a proposal to the European Parliament and the Council.' Once a legislative proposal has been submitted, it then becomes the property of the legislature (Council and EP acting under the ordinary legislative procedure).

Eurosceptic politicians and commentators like to express their aversion to the Commission's 'monopoly of initiative' for giving an unelected body such a central role in the policymaking process.

Christopher Booker and Richard North, *The Great Deception: Can the European Union Survive?* (2005, London: Continuum), pp. 358–9

The point about 'Brussels' was that it acted as a nexus. It had become the centre of an immense and complex network, linking institutions and organisations throughout the Community: not least the administrations of all the member states. On any given day in Brussels would be not only the officials of the Commission itself but also thousands of visiting national civil servants, all in one way or another engaged in 'the European construction.' Countless thousands more were at work back home in each country, all participating in what had become the most complex legislative machine ever known.[50]

This was reflected in the bewildering variety of ways by which proposals for Community laws came about in the first place. As Delors' study group on subsidiarity had reported in 1992, only 30 of 535 proposals made by the Commission in the previous year originated with the Commission itself. The rest came from other sources, ranging from the civil servants of national governments to an array of anonymous committees, which might include professional consultants, academics, environmental pressure groups, NGOs or even commercially funded lobbyists acting on behalf of a particular industry or company. It would later be estimated that there were 3000 such committees operating in Brussels, and beyond them 170,000 lobbyists of one kind or another across the EU, ranging from pan-European trade associations representing whole industries to the representatives of individual local authorities pleading for a share in regional funding.

---

[48] See Art. 241 TFEU.

[49] Article 225 TFEU.

[50] This point was latterly acknowledged by Thatcher in her book *Statecraft*, published in 2002. She notes that the figure given for the Commission staff—which by then had increased to 30,000—'*leaves out the much larger number of national officials whose tasks flow from European regulations*': (London: Harper Collins), p. 324.

From the 1980s onwards, the member states realized that policymaking by the Commission was not extraneous to national policymaking (and became anxious to ensure that their national interests were not excluded from the formation of Community interest). Over time, the Commission has enlarged the scope of its consultation processes to assist its analysis and to improve its processes. But this has opened the door still further for so-called 'stakeholders' who may be affected by particular legislation or the lack of it. These are interest groups that represent professional groups and trade associations, and, more generally, civil society. There are firms of consultants who 'lobby' on behalf of particular interests at the European, as well as the national, levels. Lobbying, which involves organizations 'pushing' forward their views to the Commission, is different from consultation, which involves the Commission 'pulling' views from others. The Commission is the object of much lobbying activity, at all stages from policy formation through the initiation of a legislative proposal and its development, to the adoption and implementation of legislation.

BOX 12.10 KEY CONCEPTS AND TERMS[51]

Civil society refers to the broad collection of associations and groups (including private firms, trades unions, community groups, and non-governmental organizations) active between the level of the individual and the state. These groups generally operate independently of direct government control.

Lobbying is an attempt to influence policymakers to adopt a course of action advantageous, or not detrimental, to a particular group or interest. A lobbyist is a person employed by a group, firm, organization, region, or country to carry out lobbying. Lobbyists in Brussels are increasingly referred to as interest representatives.

A **rapporteur** is the Member of the European Parliament responsible for preparing a report of one of the Parliament's committees.

Transparency refers to the process of making EU documents and decision-making processes more open and accessible to the public.

Consultation cannot be described as an internal Commission exercise. It allows for informal input from a range of voices and interests. The Commission's strategy for involving interest groups is twofold. In the early stages of the policy process, the Commission consults as widely as possible (via the Internet, open forums, seminars, and conferences). But during the policy formulation and implementation process, the Commission must consult the relevant expert committees (national officials and experts), who are there to offer detailed technical advice. The EU has a systemic dependence upon organized civil society, and the diffusion of power between and within its constituent parts results in an orientation towards 'consensus politics', as opposed to the more competitive politics that often characterizes the adversarial Westminster model.

The thirty-three Directorates-General (DGs), the 'departments' of the Commission, are each responsible for a particular area of policy. The text of proposed legislation that a DG produces has to serve two purposes: it must be drafted effectively to achieve the desired

[51] Table in R. Watson and R. Corbett, 'How Policies Are Made', in E. Bomberg, J. Peterson, and R. Corbett, *The European Union: How does it work?* 3rd edn (Oxford: OUP, 2012), 123.

policy goals; and it must also be politically acceptable—the Commission will not put forward a text unless it knows that it has broad support for a measure. Throughout the legislative process, the Commission remains 'master' of the text of any proposal for legislation: although, as we will see shortly, the European Parliament and the Economic and Social Committee (ECOSOC)—a consultative body to the Council, the Commission and the European Parliament—may propose amendments, it is up to the Commission to decide which, if any, of these amendments are ultimately put forward for adoption either by the Council alone or in conjunction with the European Parliament. The Council can make amendments to the proposal only if it acts unanimously.

The powers and resources of the DGs vary considerably and most policy proposals will be the result of coordination between several DGs (take, for instance, a proposal on energy which will attract input from DGs dealing with energy, but also industry, transport, consumers, and the environment). The Commission uses its power of initiative most clearly in areas in which it has exclusive or shared competences (for example, competition policy). In other areas, however, the nature of the policy and/or the limited capacity of the Commission will curb its central role in the policymaking process. The final decision as to proposed legislation still rests with the twenty-eight Commissioners. Naturally, there will be debates and disagreements among the individual Commissioners and their DGs. But, as with the Cabinet in the United Kingdom, the principle of collective responsibility applies, which means that a vote in favour of a policy will reflect the official position of the entire Commission. A tension can thus be identified between the Commission's formal power of initiative, and the need to consult and cooperate with other EU institutions and the national governments, which, arguably, has reduced the Commission's influence in the legislative process.

The Commission will, in the formulation and implementation of policy, liaise with different committees composed of external national officials and experts in a system called 'comitology'.

Comitology

You will recall from Chapter 8 that most EU law-making is not enacted as legislation by the Council and European Parliament, but as implementation measures under the executive duties of the Commission. Some legislative acts are necessarily incomplete and require further implementation and monitoring. A system of committees covering virtually all aspects of EU policymaking assists the Commission in line with a procedure known as 'comitology'. In 2009, there were 229 such comitology committees.[52]

The committees are forums for discussion and for problem-solving through scientific evidence. They consist of representatives from member states (for example, scientific experts) and are chaired by the Commission. It is difficult to conceive the institutional role of the committees. On the one hand, they support the Commission as a supranational entity with enforcing powers: the Commission can ensure that measures reflect the situation in every member state. But on the other hand, the members of the committee represent the interests of the member states ('intergovernmentalism'): committees enable the Commission to establish dialogue with national administrations before adopting implementing measures. They are best understood as 'gatekeepers', who can neither amend nor reject Commission

---

[52] Commission of the European Communities, *Commission Staff Working Document accompanying the Report from the Commission on the Working of Committees during 2007*, SEC (2008) 3018, Brussels.

proposals, but who may refer them to the Council if the proposal is not in accordance with the Committee's opinion.

The Lisbon Treaty draws a new distinction between legislative acts (Art. 289 TFEU), delegated acts (Art. 290 TFEU), and implementing acts (Art. 291 TFEU). It is possible for a legislative act itself to delegate the power. This empowers the EP in situations of co-decision. Alternatively, Article 291 provides that legislative acts can confer implementing powers on the Commission, subject to the supervision of 'comitology' committees of representatives of the member states.

M. Shackleton, 'The European Parliament', in J. Peterson and M. Shackleton (eds) *The Institutions of the European Union*, 3rd edn (2012, Oxford: OUP), ch. 6, p. 118

The debate about comitology may seem arcane but it raises essential questions about the openness and accountability of the EU system. The decisions involved are not simply technical: in the early 1990s, for example, the level of controls needed to stop the spread of bovine spongiform encephalopathy (BSE, or 'mad cow disease') was decided in a comitology committee, the Veterinary Committee. All such decisions are taken very far from the public gaze, remaining in the hands of the Commission and national experts. Advocating a more powerful role for the EP was designed therefore to improve the transparency of the system.

[...] Over a long period, member states did gradually agree to strengthen the Parliament's rights. These moves culminated in the Lisbon Treaty, which placed the EP on an equal footing with the Council for a new category of policy-implementing decisions, known as 'delegated acts' [under Art. 290 TFEU]. However, the decision did not cover all comitology activity and the dispute between the institutions continues. The differences of view show that the Parliament still exercises less-effective influence over policy-implementing decisions than it does over policy-making.

(e) INFLUENCE OF NATIONAL PARLIAMENTS ON POLICYMAKING

The ability of national parliaments in general, and the UK Parliament in particular, to scrutinize policymaking at EU level is analysed in detail in Chapter 8.

(f) THE DECISION-MAKING PROCESS IN THE ORDINARY LEGISLATIVE PROCEDURE

The *co-decision* legislative procedure was introduced by the Maastricht Treaty, and extended and revised by the Amsterdam Treaty in 1999. It is a framework for negotiations between the Council and the European Parliament, which is set out in Arts 293 and 294 TFEU. The procedure provides for a maximum of three parallel stages in the European Parliament and Council called 'first reading', 'second reading', and 'conciliation', or 'third reading'. Since the Amsterdam Treaty (1999), the procedure may be completed, and a proposal may be adopted, in fewer than three readings. So, unlike the UK system in which a Bill must complete all its stages to become an Act, if the Council and Parliament reach agreement earlier in the process, the legislation is adopted without recourse to the remaining stages. Interestingly, this can be done even after the first reading. The number of these so-called 'early agreements' has increased considerably over the last ten years.[53] The advantage of these early agreements is that they can be used to consolidate and streamline existing legislation. The disadvantage is that, especially in relation to new EU legislation (such as the EU's Climate Package 2009 on emissions cuts, renewables, and energy efficiency), the early agreements undermine the democratic process. As a newly elected EP President, Jerzy Buzek publicly declared that there should be 'as few first reading agreements as possible' in the future, as cutting short the legislative process does not provide for 'proper dialogue' on the issues.[54]

Co-decision was already established as by far the most important procedure when the Lisbon Treaty significantly added to the previous forty-three policy areas by including forty new areas, such as agriculture, fisheries, justice and home affairs, and the budget, and re-labelling it the *ordinary legislative procedure* (OLP). (Note that the OLP does not cover Common Foreign and Security Policy.) OLP is based on the principle of parity: the consent of both Council and European Parliament is required before legislation can be adopted. Unlike previous legislative procedures, OLP introduces the following innovations:

(a) the European Parliament is given a third reading of legislation;

(b) the European Parliament has a veto right (which can no longer be overturned by a unanimous Council);

(c) in the event of disagreement between the Council and the European Parliament, they will negotiate the final wording of the proposal together in the Conciliation Committee.

In essence, the law-making process in the EU mirrors that of the national systems.

R. Watson and R. Corbett, 'How Policies Are Made', in E. Bomberg, J. Peterson, and R. Corbett, *The European Union: How does it work?* 3rd edn (Oxford: OUP, 2012), 124

> In London, for instance, it is the civil service and the government that draft and table legislation. In Brussels, that task is performed by the Commission. In the UK, the text is then examined, amended, and (usually) approved by both the Houses of Commons and Lords. In the EU, that legislative role is given to the Council and the Parliament. If the proposal is relatively straightforward and these two co-legislators can agree on its contents, then the text may be approved after just one reading in each institution. If agreement between the two is harder to reach, then two or even three readings may be required.

In the following paragraphs, we will set out the formal steps of the OLP (Figure 12.5 sets them out in flowchart form.)

---

[53] A. Rasmussen, 'Early Conclusion in the Co-Decision Legislative Procedure', EUI Working Papers, MWP 2007/31.

[54] EU Observer, EU parliament 'has equal power' to member states, 09 July 2009.

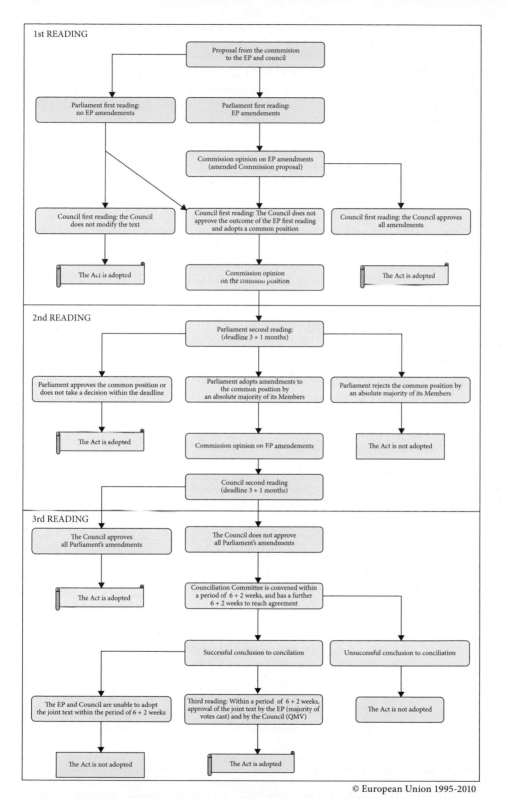

Figure 12.5 Presentation of the OLP

First reading

Under the OLP, the European Parliament considers the Commission's proposal—although the principle of parity means that the Commission passes its legislative proposal to both the Council and the European Parliament. Before the European Parliament, the proposal is considered first by one of twenty committees (each consisting of between twenty-eight and eighty-six MEPs) set up with responsibility for different subject areas. The committees discuss the substantive policy of the proposed measure, consider Commission and Council proposals, and, where necessary, appoint one of their members as 'rapporteur' to draw up the Committee's report (which includes amendments to the text), which is then presented to the European Parliament sitting in plenary session. At the first reading stage, the Council and European Parliament will agree their respective positions; Parliament adopts amendments at this stage by a simple majority vote.

If the Council approves the European Parliament's amendments, or if the European Parliament does not propose any, the act can be adopted. If the Council does not approve of the text as approved by the European Parliament, it concludes its first reading by adopting a common position, which it sends to the European Parliament.

The first reading is not subject to any time limits.

Second reading

The second reading is subject to strict time limits. As regards the common position (and within three months or four, if extended), the European Parliament may:

(a) adopt it (in which case, the act comes into effect);
(b) reject it (in which case, the proposed act will not come into effect if voted by an absolute majority of MEPs); or
(c) propose amendments (with an absolute majority of MEPs).

Essentially, the European Parliament is the only institution that has the opportunity to 'improve' the text—although it must, of course, stay within the limits of what is generally acceptable to the Commission and the Council. In theory, it could even suggest radical policy changes, making it a 'conditional agenda setter'.[55] In practice, the European Parliament's amendments are more likely to succeed if (similar to parliamentary committees in the domestic context) they are limited to procedural changes, clarifications, and scrutinizing the measure.[56] The new text is then sent to the Commission and Council for consideration. If the Council rejects the text, the OLP is exhausted and the proposal is withdrawn. If it approves the amendments, a qualified majority is needed to adopt the amended proposal. If the Commission rejects the amendments, the Council needs a unanimous vote to save the proposal.

In the OLP, the European Parliament has a real veto (as opposed to a conditional one in the other procedures); the Council cannot resurrect proposed legislation, even if ministers unanimously favour this, and it will fall. In that case, the matter may be referred to the Conciliation Committee. The power of the veto should not, however, be exaggerated: in practice, the European Parliament vetoes legislation very rarely. The reason for this is practical politics: EU legislation (like national legislation) tends to be the result of compromise;

[55] George Tsebelis, 'The power of the European Parliament as a conditional agenda-setter' (1994) 88 American Political Science Review 128–42.

[56] Amie Kreppel, 'Moving beyond procedure: An empirical analysis of European Parliament legislative influence' (2002) 35 Comparative Political Studies 784.

the power of the veto forces MEPs either to accept or to reject a piece of legislation—it does not recognize shades of grey. The European Parliament does not want to alienate other parties by frustrating their aims and objectives, and so the veto is used sparingly. It is through the threat of the veto, rather than through the exercise itself, that the European Parliament secures its influence.

Third reading: Conciliation

In the case of disagreement between the Council and the European Parliament, the Conciliation Committee must be convened within six weeks (or eight, if extended) of the Council's decision. The Conciliation Committee groups together twenty-eight ministerial members of the Council (or their official representatives) and an equal number of representatives from the European Parliament for the purpose of direct negotiations. The outcome of the conciliation is forwarded to the Council and the European Parliament for a third reading. In case of agreement, the Council and European Parliament must adopt the jointly established text within six weeks from approval. At this stage, the European Parliament can still reject the proposal with an absolute majority of the MEPs (this is sometimes described as the European Parliament's 'second veto'). In the absence of agreement, the proposal is automatically withdrawn.

From a public law perspective, the institutional consequences of the OLP have an impact on democracy. Although increasing the powers of the European Parliament goes some way towards improving the flagging democratic credentials of the EU, it does so at the expense of the powers of the member states (acting through the Council) and the Commission. The Commission's primary power to initiate legislation has to be weighed against the Council or European Parliament's power to amend the proposal. After the conciliation procedure, the Council may adopt a revised text by qualified majority (that is, member states' votes are weighted according the size of their populations) *even if* the Commission objects.

So does the loss of the Commission's influence and power correspond to a gain for the European Parliament? One school of thought suggests that the evolution of the EU's legislative regime from consultation to co-decision/OLP has substantially reduced the Commission's legislative powers, because it is not included in the final stages of decision-making. The Commission can be compared to a traditional bureaucracy that has the power to initiate legislation, but which lacks any power to determine its final content. The counter-argument is that so long as the Commission has the right to initiate legislation, it retains its central agenda-setting power, because it is much harder to shape legislation once it has been formally published.

N. Nugent, *The Government and Politics of the European Union* (2010, Basingstoke: Macmillan), 301–1

The ordinary legislative procedure illustrates in a specific way the growth in interinstitutional cooperation. Amongst its consequences it has: (1) encouraged the institutions to devise/accept a compromise text at an early legislative stage; (2) increased the need for the Council to be sensitive to the EP's views; (3) made trialogue meetings between representatives of the Commission, the Council and the EP a vital feature of much EU law-making; and (4) promoted (the already extensive) informal exchanges between representatives of the institutions to sound out positions, discover what may be possible, and identify areas where

> progress may be made. In short, the procedure has given a powerful stimulus to a 'cultural' change in the relations between the Commission, the Council and the EP that has been under way since the creation of the cooperation procedure by the SEA. At the heart of this cultural change is the notion that the three institutions must work closely with one another, and when legislation is being made they must operate on the basis of a genuinely triangular relationship.

As a result, in a relatively short space of time legislative politics in the EU has evolved into something that would be familiar to observers of two-chamber parliaments in other democratic political systems. The EU's law-making process is not only sophisticated, effective, and similar to national political systems, but it also satisfies key criteria of the rule of law. Although not as simple and straightforward as law-making in the United Kingdom (which is not always an asset if you think about the relative ease with which 'constitutional' statutes can be amended or repealed), co-decision is a *comprehensible* and *accessible* decision-making procedure. The law-making institutions and procedures are *identifiable* and *clear*. In short, law-making in the EU is a *slow, transparent,* and *rule-governed* process. Every law is *scrutinized* by the twenty-eight national governments, the directly elected European Parliament, and the technocratic Commission. Furthermore, as we saw in Chapter 8, EU legislation must pass by a high 60–70 per cent vote (slightly lower after 2014), and two of three law-making institutions (the exception is the Commission) are *accountable* either to the people or to their national representatives. Moreover, a member state may choose to have its national parliament approve all EU votes (like Denmark and Sweden).

R. Watson and R. Corbett, 'How Policies Are Made', in E. Bomberg, J. Peterson, and R. Corbett, *The European Union: How does it work?* 3rd edn (Oxford: OUP, 2012), 137

> Policy-making in the EU presents a paradox. On one hand, many of its core procedures are open, pluralistic, consensual and transparent. On the other hand, there is very little public knowledge of EU institutions and procedures which, for most citizens, remain distant and only occasionally feature on their radar screen. As a result, processes that are not necessarily (much) more elaborate than equivalent national procedures often appear to outsiders to be frightfully complex.
>
> EU procedures have also evolved tremendously over the last few decades. Of course, no procedure could be hallowed by centuries of tradition as might be found in some member states. But what is striking about the EU is that virtually no procedure has remained unchanged for more than two decades. That fluidity is likely to remain. As the Union has grown both in size and importance, the number of actors seeking to influence encourage, block, or simply report on its policies, has grown immensely.

As we discussed in this chapter, the EP's standing is further undermined by low turnouts at elections, which potentially threatens the legitimacy of the entire law-making process. The response to that charge is that concepts such as legitimacy (with its input, output, and social dimensions) and democracy (within and beyond the nation state) defy simple definition and call for more nuanced understandings, especially in the context of a supranational organization like the EU.

QUESTIONS

1. Has the OLP strengthened or weakened the role of the Commission in the legislative process?

2. How many vetoes does the European Parliament have in the OLP? Do you think that the EP should make frequent use of its veto powers?

3. Your boss in the law firm tells you about a proposal for a regulation on roaming on public mobile communications networks within the EU. Use Pre-Lex (http://ec.europa.eu/prelex/) to answer the following questions.

   i. Is the proposal in force? If so, what is the number of the regulation, and on what date did it enter into force?

   ii. How long did it take for the Directive to be implemented?

   iii. What is the legal basis of the Regulation?

   iv. What was the legal procedure used in the adoption process?

   v. Which DG was primarily responsible for the measure?

   vi. What is noteworthy about the decision-making process? How many institutions were involved? Did the European Parliament exercise its veto?

(g) INCORPORATING EU LEGISLATION INTO NATIONAL LAW

The legislative process results in one of the four principal types of EU legislation.

Article 288 TFEU

To exercise the Union's competences, the institutions shall adopt regulations, directives, decisions, recommendations and opinions.

A regulation shall have general application. It shall be binding in its entirety and directly applicable in all Member States.

A directive shall be binding, as to the result to be achieved, upon each Member State to which it is addressed, but shall leave to the national authorities the choice of form and methods.

A decision shall be binding in its entirety. A decision which specifies those to whom it is addressed shall be binding only on them.

Recommendations and opinions shall have no binding force.

These four types of legislation are referred to as 'secondary legislation', whereas the treaties are referred to as 'primary legislation'. We will be concerned only with the two main types of legislation: regulations and directives.

Once the text of a regulation or directive has finally been adopted by the Council of the EU, the next question is how this secondary legislation relates to the domestic legal system. The status of regulations and of directives is quite different.

Regulations

Regulations automatically become legally effective in domestic law once they have been approved by the EU institutions in accordance with the TEC. They are 'directly applicable', meaning that they require no further action to create legal effects. In other words, the UK Parliament plays no role in 'transposing' them into UK law. Indeed, it may be contrary to EU law for a national government to use domestic legislation to implement a regulation, even if it thinks that it might be desirable to do so.[57]

Directives

Directives are 'directed' at member states, not citizens or businesses, and give member states discretion to choose the method by which to implement the directive. A directive requires the United Kingdom and other member states to amend their laws so as to reach the result specified in the directive. The process by which this happens is known as 'implementing', or 'transposing', the directive. Member states have a specified time (usually twelve or eighteen months) in which to achieve this.

BOX 12.11 EXAMPLES OF REGULATIONS AND DIRECTIVES

- Council Regulation No. 834/2007 on Organic Production and Labelling of Organic Products (replaces Council Regulation (EEC) 2092/1991)

- Regulation (EC) No. 443/2009 of the European Parliament and of the Council of 23 April 2009 setting emission performance standards for new passenger cars as part of the EU's integrated approach to reduce CO_2 emissions from light-duty vehicles

- Commission Regulation (EC) No. 631/2009 of 13 July 2009 laying down detailed rules for the implementation of Annex I to Regulation (EC) No. 78/2009 of the European Parliament and of the Council on the type-approval of motor vehicles with regard to the protection of pedestrians and other vulnerable road users, amending Directive 2007/46/EC and repealing Directives 2003/102/EC and 2005/66/EC

- Council Directive 2000/78/EC of 27 November 2000 establishing a general framework for equal treatment in employment and occupation

- Council Directive 1999/31/EC of 26 April 1999 (the Landfill Directive) on the landfill of waste

- Directive 2009/60/EC of the European Parliament and of the Council of 13 July 2009 on the maximum design speed of and load platforms for wheeled agricultural or forestry tractors

---

Regulations and directives can make important constitutional changes (for example, equal treatment in employment) and have far-reaching political consequences (for example, setting emission performance standards for cars), but more commonly deal with highly technical matter (for example, the maximum design speed of forestry tractors).

In the United Kingdom, where there is a need to change the law, this can be done by an Act of Parliament. For example, the Anti-Terrorism Crime and Security Act 2001 implemented certain EU anti-terrorism measures, while the Crime (International Co-operation) Act 2003 implemented several outstanding EU commitments in the area of police and judicial cooperation.

More commonly, however, the government may choose to transpose a directive into English law by making delegated legislation.[58] Some directives are trickier than others.

---

[57] See Case 39/72 *Commission v Italy* [1973] ECR 101.
[58] On delegated legislation generally, see Chapter 11.

Council Directive EEC/89/654 '*on the approximation of the laws of the Member States relating to the permissible sound level and the exhaust system of motor vehicles*' required twenty-six separate statutory instruments (SIs) to implement it properly. Only two SIs were needed to transpose the EC Employment Directive (Directive 2000/78/EC) into national law, which made unlawful discrimination on the grounds of sexual orientation and religion or belief in employment and vocational training.[59]

Section 2(2) applies to measures of EU law that are neither directly applicable nor have direct effect. This provision gives ministers a power to give effect to such measures by delegated legislation (e.g. SIs). You will recall from Chapter 11 that the delegated legislative power includes the power to make such provision as might be made by Act of Parliament. As a result, such secondary legislation may amend an Act of Parliament (s. 2(4) ECA). In those cases where Schedule 2 ECA limits the scope of s. 2(2), an Act of Parliament is necessary to implement the measure.

European Communities Act 1972, s. 2

[...]

Subject to Schedule 2 to this Act, at any time after its passing Her Majesty may by Order in Council, and any designated Minister or department may by order, rules, regulations or scheme, make provision—

(a) for the purpose of implementing any EU obligation of the United Kingdom, or enabling any such obligation to be implemented, or of enabling any rights enjoyed or to be enjoyed by the United Kingdom under or by virtue of the Treaties to be exercised; or

(b) for the purpose of dealing with matters arising out of or related to any such obligation or rights or the coming into force, or the operation from time to time, of subsection (1) above;

and in the exercise of any statutory power or duty, including any power to give directions or to legislate by means of orders, rules, regulations or other subordinate instrument, the person entrusted with the power or duty may have regard to the objects of the EU and to any such obligation or rights as aforesaid.

Other statutes also confer more specific powers on ministers to use delegated legislation to transpose directives: for example, s. 47 of the Human Tissue Act 2004 and s. 156 of the Environmental Protection Act 1990.

QUESTION

From the point of view of the minister, what do you think are the advantages and disadvantages of implementing a Directive by (a) primary legislation and (b) delegated legislation? Think about both the UK parliamentary procedure and the role of the UK courts. (You may want to refer back to Chapter 10 and Chapter 11.)

---

[59] The Employment Equality (Sexual Orientation) Regulations 2003 (SI 2003/1661) and the Employment Equality (Religion or Belief) Regulations 2003 (SI 2003/1660).

4 CASE STUDY: THE RACE DIRECTIVE

In this section, we will examine the Race Directive. First, we will examine the stylistic and substantive differences between the Race Directive and the implementing legislation. The Directive states its broad purpose in Art. 1 before defining key concepts ('discrimination' and 'harassment') in Art. 2.

COUNCIL DIRECTIVE 2000/43/EC of 29 June 2000 implementing the principle of equal treatment between persons irrespective of racial or ethnic origin[60]

Article 1

Purpose

The purpose of this Directive is to lay down a framework for combating discrimination on the grounds of racial or ethnic origin, with a view to putting into effect in the Member States the principle of equal treatment.

Article 2

Concept of discrimination

1. For the purposes of this Directive, the principle of equal treatment shall mean that there shall be no direct or indirect discrimination based on racial or ethnic origin.

2. For the purposes of paragraph 1:
   (a) direct discrimination shall be taken to occur where one person is treated less favourably than another is, has been or would be treated in a comparable situation on grounds of racial or ethnic origin;
   (b) indirect discrimination shall be taken to occur where an apparently neutral provision, criterion or practice would put persons of a racial or ethnic origin at a particular disadvantage compared with other persons, unless that provision, criterion or practice is objectively justified by a legitimate aim and the means of achieving that aim are appropriate and necessary.

3. Harassment shall be deemed to be discrimination within the meaning of paragraph 1, when an unwanted conduct related to racial or ethnic origin takes place with the purpose or effect of violating the dignity of a person and of creating an intimidating, hostile, degrading, humiliating or offensive environment. In this context, the concept of harassment may be defined in accordance with the national laws and practice of the Member States.

4. An instruction to discriminate against persons on grounds of racial or ethnic origin shall be deemed to be discrimination within the meaning of paragraph 1.

As we have mentioned, implementing legislation is required for a directive. The member states were required to transpose the Race Directive into domestic law by 19 July 2003. Much of the necessary legislation was already available domestically in the form of the Race Relations Act 1976. But where additional changes to the law were needed to complete transposition of

---

[60] [2000] OJ L180/22.

the Race Directive, these were supplied by the Race Relations Act (Amendment) Regulations 2003 (SI 2003/1626) ('the 2003 Regulations').

Race Relations Act (Amendment) Regulations 2003 (SI 2003/1626), s. 3

Racial discrimination

3. In section 1 of the 1976 Act (racial discrimination), after subsection (1), insert –

"(1A) A person also discriminates against another if, in any circumstances relevant for the purposes of any provision referred to in subsection (1B), he applies to that other a provision, criterion or practice which he applies or would apply equally to persons not of the same race or ethnic or national origins as that other, but-

(a) which puts or would put persons of the same race or ethnic or national origins as that other at a particular disadvantage when compared with other persons,

(b) which puts that other at that disadvantage, and

(c) which he cannot show to be a proportionate means of achieving a legitimate aim."

Section 3(1A) translates the abstract concepts of direct and indirect discrimination in the Directive into a specific scenario. A discriminates against B on grounds of race if subsections (a) and (b) apply, and A cannot show that he or she is pursuing a legitimate aim using proportionate means.

The same process of transposition is visible in relation to 'harassment'. Directives typically contain an element of discretion. In this case, Art. 3 of the Directive allows for the concept of harassment to be defined '*in accordance with the national laws and practice of the Member States*'—but the same provision deems it to be a form of discrimination if certain conditions are met. These conditions are cited verbatim in s. 5(3A) of the 2003 Regulations.

Race Relations Act (Amendment) Regulations 2003 (SI 2003/1626), s. 5

Harassment

5. After section 3 of the 1976 Act insert -

Harassment

3A. (1) A person subjects another to harassment in any circumstances relevant for the purposes of any provision referred to in section 1(1B) where, on grounds of race or ethnic or national origins, he engages in unwanted conduct which has the purpose or effect of -

(a) violating that other person's dignity, or

(b) creating an intimidating, hostile, degrading, humiliating or offensive environment for him.

[...]"

European Union Committee on EU Proposals to Combat Discrimination, Ninth Report, HL Paper 68, 30 June 2000

Lord Lester of Herne Hill (col. 1193)

We are justly proud in this country of the fact that we were the first to introduce legislation to tackle racial discrimination in the areas covered by our Act, with the Commission for Racial Equality to be the strategic enforcement agency. But in some respects, the directive improves upon our own legislation. It is not a complete carbon copy. The concept of indirect discrimination in Section 1(1)(b) of our Act is expressed in narrowly technical language, more like an algebraic theorem of Euclid or an income tax Act than a human rights measure. In my view, the directive improves upon that with a more generous concept which tackles the real problems of discrimination.

As Lord Lester notes, the Race Directive modifies the categories of indirect racial discrimination. The first category was created by the Race Relations Act 1976 and is on grounds of colour or nationality. The second was introduced by the Race Relations Act (Amendment) Regulations 2003 to comply with the Race Directive and is on grounds of race, ethnic, or national origin. According to Art. 2(2)(b) of the Directive, indirect discrimination occurs *'where an apparently neutral provision, criterion or practice would put persons of a racial or ethnic origin at a particular disadvantage compared with other persons, unless that provision, criterion or practice is objectively justified by a legitimate aim and the means of achieving that aim are appropriate and necessary'*. For example, a department store that bans persons wearing headgear might be sued for race discrimination. Although the rule is neutral as to race on its face, it has the practical effect of excluding, for example, Sikh men and boys who wear a turban, or Jewish men or boys who wear a yarmulka, in accordance with practice within their ethnic or religious group. A claimant who can show that members of a particular ethnic group are 'put at a disadvantage' by such a rule makes a prima facie case of discrimination.

Using delegated legislation has obvious advantages for the government:[61] given the already overcrowded legislative timetable for Bills in Parliament, it would be impossible to use primary legislation to transpose all directives. The downside is that delegated legislation receives less parliamentary scrutiny than Bills. In particular, there is little opportunity to debate draft delegated legislation and members of Parliament (MPs) have no opportunity to make amendments—only to approve or reject it as it stands. Critics (including some MPs) argue that, in this respect, the UK Parliament is hardly more than a conveyor belt: it has little choice but to incorporate the contents of directives precisely. Although the UK government has the right to choose the 'forms and methods' of achieving the objectives of a directive, in practice, this may leave little room for manoeuvre.

QUESTIONS

1. A group of MPs believe that ethnic minorities should be treated 'differently' in employment situations. Is there anything that they can do to prevent the SI from transposing the Race Directive?

---

[61] See Chapter 11.

2. Would the situation change if a majority of MPs were to be against implementing the Directive?

3. Suppose that the UK government had voted against the adoption of the Directive in the Council of Ministers, but had been outvoted. Do you think that the adoption of the Directive would then be undemocratic? How can it be justified?

The Race Directive also provides an illustration of how the EU legislative process operates, including the role of the UK Parliament and what happens in cases in which the Directive has not, or has been improperly, transposed into national law. The first step is to consider the legal basis of the Race Directive.

Article 19 TFEU

[...T]he Council, acting unanimously on a proposal from the Commission and after consulting the European Parliament, may take appropriate action to combat discrimination based on sex, racial or ethnic origin, religion or belief, disability, age or sexual orientation.

Article 19 TFEU does not itself prohibit discrimination on these given grounds; instead, it is designed to enable the EU to adopt measures to combat discrimination on the grounds listed and within the overall framework of the Treaty. Using Art. 19 TFEU as the legal basis, the EU adopted in 2000 a package of anti-discrimination measures consisting of two directives— the Race Directive (2000/43/EC) and EC Equal Treatment Framework Directive (2000/78/EC)—and an anti-discrimination action programme to run from 2001 to 2006. The Treaty of Nice, which came into force on 1 February 2003, reinforced Art. 13 TEC, which now provides for the adoption of incentive measures countering discrimination to be adopted by the Council by QMV.

The Race Directive was adopted in June 2000 by the Council. Although Art. 19 TFEU is clearly groundbreaking in terms of policy development, the space that it gives to the three main EU institutions cannot be said to facilitate the adoption of new measures. The Commission is *permitted*, but not obliged, to act; measures require *unanimity* in the Council, which is extremely difficult to attain; and the European Parliament has only a *consultative* role in implementing Art. 19 TFEU, not the co-decision role that we have outlined. Given the normally slow process of EU law-making, it is surprising how quickly the Race Directive was adopted. One plausible reason is that the EU wanted to respond to the electoral success of the right-wing Freedom Party in Austria in February 2000 with a legislative gesture that committed itself to combating racism.

QUESTIONS

Use Pre-Lex (http://ec.europa.eu/prelex/) to search for the Proposal for a Council Directive implementing the principle of equal treatment between persons irrespective of racial or ethnic origin (COM (1999) 566).

1. How long did it take for the Directive to be implemented?

2. What was the legal procedure used in the adoption process?

3. Which DG was primarily responsible for the measure? How many DGs were associated?

4. What was the Commission's position to the European Parliament's amendments after the single reading?

5. Do you think it is right that such an important and far-reaching piece of legislation (some member states had to introduce new anti-discrimination legislation, create a body for the promotion of equal treatment of all persons, and redefine direct and indirect discrimination and harassment in their national law) was rushed through?

Why did the EU take legislative action in the 'first pillar', when most member states had ratified a number of international instruments under which they had obligations to combat racial discrimination? First, international instruments require implementation action by the states that are party to them and so do not provide a direct recourse to redress for individuals. Second, domestic measures to combat racial discrimination vary significantly in respect of the legal framework (scope, content, and enforceability), the demographic situation, the extent of public debate, and even the language with which discrimination issues are discussed. Third, in view of the impending enlargement of the EU and the increased diversity, the Commission deemed it essential to establish a common European framework in order to combat racism.

Why did the EU opt for a directive rather than a regulation? The advantage of a directive is that it provides a minimum level of harmonization, while also giving the member states a degree of discretion as regards the forms and methods of implementation. More so than regulations, directives respect the principle of subsidiarity and the cultural diversity of member states by allowing them to act in accordance with national traditions and practice.

The Directive:

- defines direct and indirect discrimination;

- gives victims of discrimination a right of redress through a judicial or administrative procedure, associated with appropriate sanctions for those who discriminate;

- shifts the burden of proof (in civil cases) once a prima facie case of discrimination has been made out by a complainant and accepted by the court or other instance;

- provides protection against harassment and victimization;

- covers discrimination in employment and training, education, social protection (including security and health care), social advantages, and the supply of and access to goods and services, including housing;

- requires the member states to provide information on their territory about the measures that they adopt to fight discrimination; and

- requires member states that have not already done so to establish bodies for the promotion of equal treatment that will provide independent assistance to the victims of discrimination, conduct surveys and studies, and publish reports and recommendations.

Every directive contains a deadline for the transposition of its objectives into national law. All member states were legally obliged to meet the deadline, unless an agreed alternative or exception was made. The deadline for the transposition of the Race Directive into national legislation expired on 19 July 2003, with member states obliged to report on their implementation of the Directive by 19 July 2005. The first deadline means that all member states must draft and bring into force new anti-discrimination laws and ethnic equality regulations, or alter their existing laws. The member states may request an additional period of up to three years to bring their legal systems into line with the provisions on disability and age.

If the Commission believes that a member state has breached EU law, it is entitled to initiate an 'infringement procedure' under Art. 258 TFEU. Once the deadline for meeting the transposition of a directive into national law has elapsed, one of two—or even both— preliminary processes will be launched by the European Commission that aim to resolve the issue as quickly as possible with the member state in question.

(a) Under 'non-communication', a member state will be notified that it has failed to communicate to the European Commission its national measures implementing the EC legislation by the required deadline for transposition. The member state will initially be given a two-month phase within which to communicate its reasons.

(b) Under 'non-conformity', a member state will be notified by the European Commission that its national measures do not conform with the Directive. The member state will be given a reasonable time by the European Commission to establish conformity in its legislation.

In July 2004, the Commission announced that it was taking legal action against Austria, Germany, Finland, Greece, and Luxembourg for failing to pass all of the necessary national measures to introduce, amend, or update their equality legislation. Either no legislation had been passed or communicated to the Commission, or gaps in the legislation had left the transposition incomplete. On 24 February 2005, Finland and Luxembourg were found by the ECJ to have failed in their obligations under the Directive.[62] Although all of the member states eventually transposed the Directive into national law, the Commission, as 'Guardian of the Treaties', studies the quality of the implementing national legislation in detail to see if it correctly reflects the requirements of the Directive.

If the Commission is unhappy with the way in which a member state has implemented a directive, it commences a two-step infringement procedure under Art. 258 TFEU. First, the Commission sends a 'letter of formal notice' explaining why it thinks the member state has incorrectly implemented the Directive into its national law. The member state then has two months within which to reply. If it does not reply, or if the Commission is not convinced by the reply, the Commission can go to the next step of the infringement procedure by sending a 'reasoned opinion'. This sets out in much more detail the legal arguments.

On 27 June 2007, the Commission followed the second step by announcing that it had sent formal requests to fourteen member states to implement the Race Directive fully. Again, the countries concerned—Spain, Sweden, the Czech Republic, Estonia, France, Ireland, the United Kingdom, Greece, Italy, Latvia, Poland, Portugal, Slovenia, and Slovakia—were given two months in which to respond. If, after two months, the Commission still thinks that the member state has incorrectly transposed the Directive, it can at this point refer the case to the ECJ in Luxembourg. If the ECJ upholds an infringement case, it may impose a financial penalty on the member state in question under Art. 260 TFEU, which can quickly run into millions of euros per day during which the member state fails to comply with the ECJ's ruling.

The Race Directive sets out minimum requirements. Member states may therefore provide for a higher level of protection against discrimination in national legislation. In the following case, the ECJ had to interpret the Race Directive in a reference from a Belgian labour court. The Centre for Equal Opportunities and Combating Racism (a body charged with the promotion of equal treatment in Belgium) brought proceedings against a company called

---

[62] Cases C-327/04 and C-320/04.

Firma Feryn, which specialized in the sale and installation of doors. One of its directors had stated publicly on national television that his company was not going to recruit 'immigrants' because their customers did not want Moroccans in their homes to install the doors. It should be noted that there was no evidence that the company had, in fact, rejected a job applicant on the basis of race or ethnicity. The question before the ECJ was whether the public statement amounted to direct discrimination and whether the company had infringed the Race Directive which had been implemented in Belgian Law against Discrimination 2003.

The UK and Irish governments intervened in the case, arguing that there could be no direct discrimination because (a) the company had not acted on its discriminatory statements, and (b) there was no identifiable victim of discrimination.

Case C-54/07 *Centrum voor gelijkheid van kansen en voor racismebestrijding v Firma Feryn NV*, Judgment of 10 July 2008

[21] With regard to the first and second questions, Ireland and the United Kingdom of Great Britain and Northern Ireland maintain that it is not possible for there to be direct discrimination within the meaning of Directive 2000/43, so that the directive is inapplicable where the alleged discrimination results from public statements made by an employer concerning its recruitment policy but there is no identifiable complainant contending that he has been the victim of that discrimination.

[24] The objective of fostering conditions for a socially inclusive labour market would be hard to achieve if the scope of Directive 2000/43 were to be limited to only those cases in which an unsuccessful candidate for a post, considering himself to be the victim of direct discrimination, brought legal proceedings against the employer.

[25] The fact that an employer declares publicly that it will not recruit employees of a certain ethnic or racial origin, something which is clearly likely to strongly dissuade certain candidates from submitting their candidature and, accordingly, to hinder their access to the labour market, constitutes direct discrimination in respect of recruitment within the meaning of Directive 2000/43. The existence of such direct discrimination is not dependant on the identification of a complainant who claims to have been the victim.

[28] In the light of the foregoing, the answer to the [question] must be that the fact that an employer states publicly that it will not recruit employees of a certain ethnic or racial origin constitutes direct discrimination in respect of recruitment within the meaning of Art 2(2)(a) of Directive 2000/43, such statements being likely strongly to dissuade certain candidates from submitting their candidature and, accordingly, to hinder their access to the labour market.

The ECJ accepts the definition of direct discrimination in the Race Directive as a situation in which '*one person is treated less favourably than another* [...] *in a comparable situation*'. There did not always have to be an identifiable complainant for a claim to come within the scope of the Directive. Such a requirement would be contrary to the objective of the Directive, which is '*to foster conditions for a socially inclusive labour market*'. As a result, the employer was guilty of direct discrimination in respect of recruitment, because such statements were likely strongly to dissuade certain candidates from submitting their candidature and, accordingly, to hinder their access to the labour market—even though no particular claimant could be identified.

The *Firma Feryn* case raises interesting issues about the scope of direct discrimination and the enforcement powers of equal treatment bodies, such as the Equality and Human Rights

Commission (EHRC). In the United Kingdom, it is already unlawful to publish advertisements that indicate an intention to discriminate, and the EHRC is equipped with various enforcement powers under the Race Relations Act 1976 and Equality Act 2006 in respect of discriminatory advertisements, discriminatory practices, and in circumstances in which it thinks that a person is likely to commit an unlawful act. But the EHRC does not have the legal standing to bring proceedings in cases in which there is no complainant. Individual complainants must therefore issue proceedings in response to an employer's public statements of its discriminatory recruitment policy.

(a) THE RACE DIRECTIVE IN THE UNITED KINGDOM

In the United Kingdom, the government drafted the Race Relations Regulations 2003, designed to amend the definitions of indirect discrimination and harassment contained in the Race Relations Act 1976. In April 2007, the UK Commission for Racial Equality presented a written memorandum to the Select Committee on European Union, in which it voiced support for the new policies of the EU.

UK Commission for Racial Equality, *Written Memorandum to the Select Committee on European Union* (April 2007)

5. Of most significance for the CRE (and most likely for the CEHR) is the EC proposal to extend and reinforce its equal opportunities policy. New initiatives designed to prevent and combat discrimination outside of the labour market are welcomed in particular, especially for those areas of equality which currently do not enjoy the same level of protection against discrimination provided in the EU Race Directive (2000/43/EC).

6. The CRE considers that religion, belief, disability, age and sexual orientation all merit similar level and scope of protection as provided for in the EU Race Directive. Indeed, the CRE has considerable experience of working on religious discrimination and therefore considers that a "leveling up" of other grounds, including religion, is important. In this regard, the UK has already gone further in the direction of 'leveling up' of all grounds of discrimination [...].

But other sections of the public were hostile to the new measure, because it was perceived to harm business interests and UK social policy. Eurosceptics argued that the Directive reversed the burden of proof in cases involving discrimination in the workplace and that employers would be 'forced to prove' their innocence in court. A spokesperson for the former EU Commissioner for Employment and Social Affairs, Anna Diamatopoulou, explained: '*It is a shift in the burden of evidence. The claimant still has to come up with a solid factual case to get the process going.*' But the Directive clearly puts the onus on the accused to prove his or her innocence '*once the complainant has established facts from which a court or tribunal can presume discrimination*'. The Conservative Party argued that the Directive would fuel a 'compensation culture' by tilting the balance in favour of third-party organizations and lobbies (for example, victim groups) to file race discrimination lawsuits on behalf of claimants. The *Daily Telegraph* claimed that the Directive was '*the most dramatic evidence to date of the EU's sweeping new powers to dictate social policy*'.[63]

---

[63] Ambrose Evans-Pritchard and George Jones, 'Firms forced to prove they are not racist', *Daily Telegraph*, 19 May 2000.

The European Union Committee on EU Proposals to Combat Discrimination was debated in the House of Lords on 30 June 2000, and offers a contrasting perspective.

European Union Committee on EU Proposals to Combat Discrimination, Ninth Report, HL Paper 68

Lord Wallace of Saltaire (cols 1179–80)

My Lords, some large issues of principle lie behind the directives: first, the expansion of EU jurisdiction versus the principle of subsidiarity; secondly, acceptable degrees of diversity of national cultures and practices, against the desirability of uniform standards across the single market and the wider European Community; thirdly, the acceptability and legitimacy of Europe-wide rules on such sensitive issues as discrimination, overriding national legislation and different national traditions; and fourthly, acceptable variations in the implementation and enforcement of common rules once agreed. I hope that in future Her Majesty's Government will ensure that the question of how those rules are to be implemented and enforced in all member states will be discussed as much as is the principle of the legislation. The fifth point is the desirability of sufficient flexibility in defining such very complex concepts as discrimination, disability, social advantage, or genuine occupational qualification, versus the dangers of legal uncertainty and 'fuzzy' law which threaten to condemn governments and companies to years of expensive litigation before national and European courts.

We approached the inquiry cautiously and, in some cases, even sceptically. Nevertheless, as a whole the committee welcomed both the race directive and, with a number of further qualifications, the intentions behind the framework directive. For me, the evidence received from the CBI was the most persuasive. The CBI stated in its written evidence:

> 'Our members believe that the directives meet the subsidiarity and proportionality tests and deserve support. The directives address genuinely transnational issues and will help complete the single market. Guaranteeing common levels of protection throughout Europe will help tackle unfair competition and make it easier for European citizens to work abroad and move freely between member states'.

The CBI, which is not exactly a Left-wing organisation, went on to say:

> 'The UK has one of the most comprehensive systems of discrimination law in Europe [...] Significant experience in this area means the UK is well placed to lead the debate in Europe and our priority should be to ensure that the directives create a clear and workable framework'.

[...] The race directive largely follows British legislation. We have been assured that its implementation will require only minor amendments to British legislation. The number of British citizens who work elsewhere in the EU, or who travel across the EU for study or leisure, continues to rise year by year. The extension of civil liberties protection across the EU is, therefore, clearly in Britain's interests and will ensure that other states bring their domestic law and practice up to the standard already in place in the United Kingdom and in particular in Ireland and the Netherlands.

Under the Race Directive, all member states must also have, or create, a specialized body for the promotion of equal treatment on grounds of race and ethnic origin. The Directive requires, as a minimum, that the body be able to give independent assistance to victims of discrimination, conduct independent surveys concerning discrimination, publish independent reports, and make recommendations on discrimination issues.

Three commissions existed in the United Kingdom at the time: the Equal Opportunities Commission (created under the Sex Discrimination Act 1975); the Commission for Racial Equality (established by the Race Relations Act 1976); and the Disability Rights Commission (set up by the *Disability Rights Commission* Act 1999). On 1 October 2007, the three equality commissions merged into the new Equality and Human Rights Commission (established under the Equality Act 2006). It is a non-departmental public body (NDPB), which means that it is accountable for its public funds, but independent of government. The new Commission has not only taken over the work of the three previous equality commissions, but has also taken on responsibility for the other aspects of equality: age; sexual orientation; and religion or belief; as well as human rights.

The EU is not solely responsible for the Commission's creation, but it did put the 'single equality body' on the political agenda. The second Equal Treatment Directive in 2000 required member states to enact legislation prohibiting discrimination in employment on grounds of age, disability, sexual orientation, and religion and belief. It had to be transposed by member states into their national law by 2 December 2003.

The Directive:

- prohibits discrimination in the labour market on grounds of religion and belief, disability, age, and sexual orientation;

- provides the same basic rights of protection as the Race Directive; and

- requires employers to make reasonable adjustments to cater for the needs of a person with a disability who is qualified to do the job in question. Such adjustments may, for example, be to workplaces, working patterns, or the distribution of tasks among employees.

The United Kingdom's Department of Trade and Industry (DTI) published a Green Paper on implementation of the Directive entitled *Towards Equality and Diversity* (2001). The Green Paper made the case for merging the existing equality commissions into a single equality body. The Equality Act 2006 created the Commission on Equality and Human Rights (CEHR), which has responsibility for all six equality grounds (age, disability, gender, proposed, commenced or completed gender reassignment, race, religion or belief, and sexual orientation).

S. Fredman, 'Equality: A new generation?' (2001) 30 Industrial Law Journal 145–68, 168

The EU assumption of responsibility for ensuring that Member States take measures to combat discrimination on grounds of race, ethnic origin, religion, age, disability and sexual orientation is a welcome if belated development. However, a closer look at the provisions has revealed that the substantive content has incorporated many of the limitations familiar to domestic law. In particular, the method of categorisation of groups and the definitions of discrimination remain problematic. Nevertheless, there is an explicit invitation within the directives for Member States to take the law further. One such step is being taken within UK legislation. The imposition of a positive duty within UK race discrimination legislation represents a significant reinforcement of existing attempts to create a new generation of equality laws. Although the details of this duty remain disturbingly vague, and its aims remain unformulated, this is certainly the direction of the future.

QUESTIONS

1. Why is the legislative process for making EU regulations and directives so complex?

2. What is the relative power of the European Commission, the Council of the European Union, and the European Parliament in the law-making process?

3. Does the Commission act at the behest and under the control of the member states, or is it an individual and autonomous actor in the policymaking process?

4. The Council embodies the recurrent tension in the construction of the European Union between the supranationalists and the intergovernmentalists. Why?

5. Why did the Commission choose the form of a directive rather than a regulation in its attempt to combat racism?

6. Is the Race Directive controversial? Find arguments both for and against.

7. Do you think that *Firma Feryn* was decided correctly? Why did the United Kingdom and Ireland intervene in this case?

5 FURTHER READING

Bache, I., George, S., and Bulmer, S., *The Politics in the European Union*, 3rd edn (2011, Oxford: OUP)

Bogdanor, V., 'Imprisoned by a Doctrine: The Modern Defence of Parliamentary Sovereignty' (2012) 32(1) Oxford J Legal Studies 179–195

Craig, P., *The Lisbon Treaty: Law, Politics, and Treaty Reform* (2010, Oxford: OUP)

Dougan, M., 'The Treaty of Lisbon 2007: Winning minds, not hearts' (2008) 45(3) Common Market Law Review 617–703

Maurer, A., and Wessels, W., *National Parliaments on Their Ways to Europe: Losers or Latecomers?* (2001, Baden-Baden: Nomos)

Piris, J.-C., *The Lisbon Treaty: A Legal and Political Analysis* (2010, Cambridge: Cambridge University Press)

Tsebelis, G., and Garrett, G., 'The institutional foundations of intergovernmentalism and supranationalism in the European Union' (2001) 55(2) International Organization 357

Wallace, H., Pollack, M.A., and Young, A.R., (eds), *Policy-Making in the European Union*, 6th edn (2010, Oxford: OUP).

ONLINE RESOURCE CENTRE

Further information about the themes discussed in this chapter can be found on the Online Resource Centre at www.oxfordtextbooks.co.uk/orc/lesueur2e/

13

CASE STUDY: WHAT HAPPENS WHEN THE COMMONS AND LORDS DISAGREE

CENTRAL ISSUES

1. In a bicameral parliamentary system, rules are needed about the relative powers of each chamber of the legislature. In some constitutions, each House has equal power and the consent of both is required for legislation. This is not so in the United Kingdom, where the Commons (dominated by the government) has power to disregard the views of the Lords and present a Bill for royal assent. What are the justifications for this arrangement? What are the limits on the Commons' ability to push through legislation?

2. In the United Kingdom, these rules are partly in the form of a constitutional convention (the 'Salisbury–Addison convention') and partly in legislation (the Parliament Act 1911 as amended by the Parliament Act 1949). This chapter explores the differences and similarities between these two different kinds of constitutional norm.

3. During the passage of a Bill, the Salisbury–Addison convention is that the Lords will give a Second Reading to a 'manifesto Bill' and avoid making 'wrecking amendments' that change the government's manifesto intention.

4. If, at the end of the legislative process, there is deadlock between the Commons and Lords, the Parliament Acts allow a Bill to receive royal assent without the agreement of the Lords. This mechanism has been used on only a handful of occasions since it was created in 1911—but always in highly contentious circumstances.

5. This chapter also examines the role of the courts in regulating disputes between the Commons and Lords. The courts have no remit to adjudicate on breaches of constitutional convention. In the *Attorney General v Jackson* litigation (2004–05), a pro-hunting pressure group sought to challenge the legal validity of the Hunting Act 2004 (banning hunting in England and Wales), which had received royal assent under the Parliament Acts. This provided the courts with an opportunity to consider the long-running debate over the nature of legislation enacted without the Lords' consent. Some commentators suggest that it opens the door to future courts modifying the principle of parliamentary supremacy.

1 INTRODUCTION

(a) USING THIS CHAPTER

This chapter looks at the circumstances surrounding two events. Section 2, Conventions regulating Commons–Lords relations, deals with the decision of the UK Parliament in 2005 to set up a committee to examine whether the constitutional conventions governing the relationship between the House of Lords and the House of Commons should be codified. The extracts and questions in Section 2 are designed to help you to understand:

- the nature of constitutional conventions;[1]
- the pros and cons of codifying constitutional conventions in the United Kingdom (and how this relates to the debate about adopting a written constitution); and
- how constitutional conventions operate to regulate the respective roles of the Lords and the Commons.

Section 3, the Parliament Acts, looks at the decision of the Commons (and the Labour government) to press ahead and present the Hunting Bill 2004 for royal assent despite the implacable opposition of the Lords to the policy of a total ban on hunting wild animals with dogs; the Lords preferred a policy of licensed hunting. To understand the significance of this episode, we will need to travel back in time to 1911 and 1949, when the Commons passed general statutory rules (the Parliament Acts) seeking to curb the powers of the Lords. The extracts and questions in Section 3 are designed to help you to understand:

- the nature of the Parliament Acts—did they 'delegate' power to pass Bills to the Commons, or did they 'redefine' the meaning of Parliament, in circumstances in which there is deadlock between the two Houses?
- the justifications for a system that allows one chamber of the UK Parliament (the Commons) to override the opposition of the other (the Lords) to a Bill; and
- the role of the courts in reviewing whether the Parliament Act 1949 (which sought to limit further the powers of the Lords) was a valid Act of Parliament. Representatives of the Countryside Alliance, a pro-hunting pressure group, pursued a judicial review claim arguing that the 1949 Act was invalid and therefore so was the Hunting Act 2004. This raises profound questions about the limits of the constitutional principle of parliamentary supremacy.[2]

You can use Sections 2 and 3 separately—but a common theme links both events.

(b) RELATIONS BETWEEN THE COMMONS AND THE LORDS

That common theme is the relationship between the respective roles and powers of the Commons and Lords. Almost all large democratic states have national legislatures consisting of two 'chambers' or 'houses'. The United Kingdom, of course, is no exception. The House of Commons, comprising 650 MPs elected on a 'first past the post' basis for geographical constituencies of about 68,000 people is referred to as the 'Lower Chamber', even

---

[1] On conventions generally, see Chapter 1.
[2] See Chapter 2.

though it has greater powers and democratic legitimacy. The House of Lords—the 'Upper Chamber'—comprises about 700 peers (there is no fixed number), none of whom are directly elected (until further reforms are introduced).

This arrangement is capable of leading to tensions and throws up two basic questions. First, what rules should govern how each of the two Houses approaches the scrutiny of government Bills? This is a matter of constitutional convention (rather than statute law), the main one being the Salisbury–Addison convention, named after the Lords who first agreed the rule in 1945. The convention seeks to prevent the Lords from voting down a policy contained in a government Bill supported by the Commons if the Bill seeks to fulfil a commitment contained in the manifesto on which the governing party was elected.[3]

Second, what rules apply if, when each House has finished scrutinizing a government Bill, they come to opposing views as to whether the Bill should be passed and presented for royal assent? Fortunately, this situation does not arise very often. As we saw in Chapter 10, there may be a process of 'ping-pong' between the two Houses, in which they debate differences of view on what the Bill to be presented for royal assent should contain. Behind the scenes, representatives of the main political parties try to hammer out a deal to which their supporters in each House can agree. It is also the case that the government may decide to withdraw controversial clauses from a Bill if it becomes clear that it will not gain the support of the Lords. Occasionally, however, there is deadlock: the Commons takes one view and the Lords another on what is desirable in the national interest.[4] The Parliament Act 1911, as amended by the Parliament Act 1949, provides statutory rules as to when a Bill approved by the Commons, but disagreed to by the Lords, may nonetheless be given royal assent.[5]

Fundamental questions of principle and politics lie within what can, at first sight, seem to be quite dry, technical issues of how two institutions—the Commons and the Lords—work together in the public interest. This was recognized by the Joint Committee on Conventions, the work of which we look at shortly.

Joint Committee on Conventions, *Report*, Session 2005–06, HL 265-I/HC 1212-I (footnotes omitted)

3. [...] This is a free country, and the Westminster Parliament is one of the things which make it so. Parliament is a complex mechanism, but at its heart is a simple balance: the balance between enabling the Government to do things, and holding them to account—asking questions, proposing alternatives, forcing them to reveal information and justify their actions. This report is about the most important aspects of how this crucial balance works.

4. Our remit refers to the relationship between the two Houses of Parliament. When a House of Parliament takes a position or exercises a power, it seldom does so because all the Members feel the same way; more often it is by negotiated agreement or by majority vote. In our parliamentary democracy the majority in the House of Commons is closely associated with the Government: it sustains it, and most Ministers are drawn from it. In the Lords, at present, the House's actions may at any time be dictated by a combination of opposition parties and Crossbenchers. Therefore, though "the relationship between the two Houses of Parliament" may sound rather abstract, in practical terms it usually means the relationships between Parliament and government, and between government and other members.

---

[3] See Section 2, Conventions regulating Commons–Lords relations, on p. 530.
[4] See Box 13.1.
[5] See Section 3, the Parliament Acts, on p. 538.

BOX 13.1 EXAMPLES OF SITUATIONS IN WHICH THE LORDS AND COMMONS HAVE DISAGREED ON KEY PROVISIONS IN A BILL

- **2007–08 Session**—The government's Counter-terrorism Bill sought to create police powers to detain terrorist suspects for forty-two days passed in the Commons (by a small majority of nine), but the Lords voted to remove the clause from the Bill. The Home Secretary, Jacqui Smith MP, announced that the government would reluctantly accept the Lords' view and not seek to use the Parliament Acts to insist on the power being created. Accordingly, the Counter-terrorism Act 2008 does not deal with detention without charge.

- **2005–05 Session**—The government's Constitutional Reform Bill proposed to abolish the office of Lord Chancellor (see Chapter 5). The Lords disagreed with this and voted for amendments that preserved the office in a modified form. The government was unhappy, but could not use the Parliament Acts, because the Bill had been introduced first to the Lords, rather than to the Commons.

- **2002–03 Session**—The government's Hunting Bill was amended in the Lords (by a large majority of 212) to change the proposed policy from an outright ban to one that permitted hunting under licence. The government, and consequently the Commons, refused to accept this and the Hunting Bill was not presented for royal assent. A new Bill was enacted in the following 2004–05 session without the Lords' agreement under the Parliament Acts. As we shall see later in the chapter, the courts were called on to adjudicate on whether this was lawful.

- **1999–2000 Session**—The government's Sexual Offences (Amendment) Bill sought to equalize the age of consent for straight and gay sex at 16 years old. The provision was passed in the Commons, but the Lords removed it from the Bill ('*Good parents do not want their sons to be encouraged to take up homosexual relationships at such an early age*', said one member of the Lords). The Salisbury–Addison convention was referred to in the Lords' debates, in which it was pointed out that the proposal was not included in Labour's 1997 general election manifesto. A new Bill in 2000–01 was enacted without the Lords' agreement under the Parliament Acts.

2 CONVENTIONS REGULATING COMMONS–LORDS RELATIONS

Let us start by considering what constraints are placed on the power of the Lords to vote down a government Bill, in cases in which that Bill is based on promises made in the general election manifesto of the governing party. The issue emerged starkly after the 1945 general election, which the Labour Party won. The Labour government embarked on a massive pro-gramme of social and political change, including the creation of the National Health Service (giving free medical care to all); the National Insurance Act 1946 laid the foundations for a welfare state and major industries were taken into public ownership. All of this required legislation.

(a) THE SCOPE OF THE SALISBURY–ADDISON CONVENTION

HM Government, *House of Lords: Reform* (Cm 7027), February 2007

3.7 The General Election of 1945 produced a Labour Government with a majority of 156 in the House of Commons. In the House of Lords, however, only a small number of peers took the Labour whip. Indeed, there were only 16 Labour peers out of a total of 831 voting peers. This imbalance posed a considerable strain on the relationship between the two Houses. During the Government of 1945–1951, the then Viscount Cranborne, Leader of the Opposition in the House of Lords ([who assumed the title of the] fifth Marquess of Salisbury from 1947) and Viscount Addison, the Labour Leader of the House of Lords, came to an agreement on the passage of major pieces of Government legislation through the House of Lords. Viscount Cranborne described his perspective on the agreement in the House of Lords debate on the King's Speech of 1945, in which the Government's legislative agenda was being considered:

> "Whatever our personal views, we should frankly recognise that these proposals were put before the country at the recent General Election and that the people of this country, with full knowledge of these proposals, returned the Labour Party to power. The Government may, therefore, I think, fairly claim that they have a mandate to introduce these proposals. I believe that it would be constitutionally wrong, when the country has so recently expressed its view, for this House to oppose proposals which have been definitely put before the electorate."

3.8 Since that time, the doctrine known as the "Salisbury-Addison Convention" has come to imply that the House of Lords should not reject at second or third reading an intention to legislate mentioned in the Government's election manifesto.

In the United Kingdom, there is a long-running debate about reform of the Lords. As part of this reform process, it was decided in 2006 that Parliament should set up a select committee of members from the Commons and the Lords (a 'joint committee') with the terms of reference '*to consider the practicality of codifying the key conventions on the relationship between the two Houses of Parliament which affect the consideration of legislation*'. The committee, which comprised eleven peers and eleven members of Parliament (MPs), interpreted its remit as being '*to seek consensus on the conventions applicable now, and to consider the practicality of codifying them*'.[6] The committee used the usual methods: it invited written evidence to be submitted; it drew up a list of people that it wished to question in oral evidence sessions; and having gathered all of the evidence, the committee agreed a report.

In this first extract from the committee's report, the focus is on how the convention has changed in recent years.

Joint Committee on Conventions, *Report*, Session 2005–06, HL 265-I/HC 1212-I (footnotes omitted)

66. The debate on the Salisbury-Addison Convention developed considerably in the 1990s. In 1993 the Crossbench peer, Lord Simon of Glaisdale [a retired Law Lord who, in his earlier

---

6 Joint Committee on Conventions, First Special Report, Session 2005–06, HL 189/HC 1151.

life, had been a Conservative MP], initiated a debate on the Convention and other practices which qualify the parliamentary role of the House of Lords. During that debate Lord Richard [a Labour life peer and QC], the Leader of the Opposition in the Lords, queried "whether the Salisbury doctrine, pure and simple, can any longer be wholly sufficient to cover the position [of the House of Lords] in this day and age [...]. There still seems to be a consensus in the House on the desirability of what, I suppose, I can call the general practice of self-restraint when it comes to legislative matters. But it is important to acknowledge that as the House has become busier, questions will increasingly be raised, and have been raised, about the viability of its former role [...]. The function of the House, though, has changed, as I see it, from being primarily a revising Chamber. One of the main functions the House now has in relation to the other place, is that it is effectively the only place in which the legislature can curb the power of the executive."

67. Lord Hesketh [a Conservative hereditary peer], the Government Chief Whip, said he was "an unashamed supporter of the doctrine" which he described as meaning "in practice that the House does not seek to vote down a manifesto Bill at second or third reading." In answer to the suggestion that the Convention should not be applicable in the case of framework Bills [that is, Bills that contain little detail—see Chapter 9] he said that he believed it would be difficult to distinguish categories of Bills to which the doctrine should not apply.

68. Viscount Cranborne [a Conservative hereditary peer, the grandson of the 'Lord Cranborne' referred to in para. 63, above], the Lord Privy Seal and Leader of the House of Lords, subsequently addressed the constitutional position of the House of Lords including the Salisbury-Addison Convention in a lecture to the think-tank Politeia in 1996. He commented "It is a doctrine that has become accepted in constitutional circles: so much so that it has come to be known as the Salisbury Convention: that is, it has been raised in the language of politics into a constitutional convention. That means it is definitely part of our constitution. I certainly regard it as such, and so does our party." Viscount Cranborne acknowledged, however, that were the Lords to be reformed, the House might choose to renounce the doctrine. Viscount Cranborne also referred to the convention that the committee stage of constitutional measures should be taken on the floor of the House of Commons which he saw as an important constitutional safeguard. He asked whether the Labour Party was planning "while insisting on the preservation of the Salisbury Convention in the House of Lords, to overturn this crucial convention [...] in the House of Commons?"

The Convention post-1999

69. In 1999, shortly after the enactment of the House of Lords Act [which removed most hereditary peers], the Leader of the Opposition in the House of Lords, Lord Strathclyde [a hereditary Conservative peer], gave a lecture to Politeia on Redefining the Boundaries between the Two Houses. He argued that most of the conditions that gave rise to the Salisbury doctrine had gone. "Some might therefore conclude that the doctrine itself, as originally conceived, has outlived its usefulness. I would be less dogmatic. Certainly it needs to be re-examined in the new conditions that arise." Lord Strathclyde then ventured some guesses about the Convention's new boundary. "The Salisbury-Addison agreement in essence held that the House of Lords would not vote against manifesto items at Second Reading, nor would it introduce wrecking amendments to such programme Bills. The House of Lords is not suddenly going to change all that. It will always accept the primacy of the elected House. It will always accept that the Queen's Government must be carried on. But, equally, it should always insist on its right to scrutinise, amend and improve legislation."

70. On 15 December 1999 Baroness Jay of Paddington [a Labour life peer, who coincidentally is the daughter of the Labour Prime Minister Jim Callaghan], Lord Privy Seal and Leader of the House of Lords [the Labour government's minister responsible for getting business through the Lords], said in reply to a starred (oral) question "[…] the Salisbury/Addison convention has nothing to do with the strength of the parties in either House of Parliament and everything to do with the relationship between the two Houses […] it must remain the case that it would be constitutionally wrong, when the country has expressed its view, for this House to oppose proposals that have been definitely put before the electorate."

71. The Wakeham report in January 2000 [this was the Royal Commission on reform of the House of Lords] described the Salisbury-Addison Convention as "an understanding that a 'manifesto' Bill, foreshadowed in the governing party's most recent election manifesto and passed by the House of Commons, should not be opposed by the second chamber on Second or Third Reading." The report further noted that the Convention has sometimes been extended to cover 'wrecking amendments' which 'destroy or alter beyond recognition' such a Bill.

72. The Wakeham report acknowledged that some people had argued that once the situation had been reached in which no one party could command a working majority in the second chamber there would be no need to maintain the Convention. It considered, however, that "there is a deeper philosophical underpinning of the Salisbury Convention which remains valid. This arises from the status of the House of Commons as the United Kingdom's pre-eminent political forum and from the fact that the general elections are the most significant expression of the political will of the electorate."

73. The Wakeham report recognised that "there are substantial theoretical and practical obstacles to putting any formal weight on manifesto commitments. Only a tiny minority of the electorate ever reads party manifestos; and as it is most unlikely that any voter will agree with every sentence of any manifesto, it is rarely possible to interpret a general election result as evidence of clear public support for any specific policy. […] Thinking on any given issue inevitably develops or changes over time and legislation introduced in the third or fourth session of a Parliament may differ significantly from the relevant manifesto commitment. To deny such legislation constitutional protection, while providing additional safeguards for other proposed legislation simply because it happened to be truer to the original commitment, would be unreasonable."

74. The report concluded that the principles underlying the Convention remain valid and should be maintained. "A version of the 'mandate' doctrine should continue to be observed: where the electorate has chosen a party to form a Government, the elements of that party's general election manifesto should be respected by the second chamber." Of particular interest in the context of our inquiry, the report continued, "It is not possible to reduce this to a simple formula, particularly one based on manifesto commitments. The second chamber should pragmatically work out a new convention reflecting these principles."

75. In 2001 Lord Simon of Glaisdale [a retired Law Lord] initiated another debate to call attention to the Parliament Acts and the Salisbury-Addison Convention. He noted that there was always something unreal about the Convention's reference to a manifesto "because a manifesto does not contain just a list of proposals which are committed for approval to the electorate […]. However, the great thing about the Salisbury convention is that it works. Generally, that is enough in this country […]. The last comment to make about it is that it is a constitutional convention and not constitutional law. In other words, it is binding only politically and morally but not legally, and only so long as it is convenient."

76. Viscount Cranborne [the hereditary Conservative peer] noted that the temporary agreement between his grandfather and Viscount Addison, had been transmogrified into a convention. "The convention says that the House will not vote at Second Reading against a manifesto Bill or pass a wrecking amendment during the remaining stages." He acknowledged that although he was sceptical about the doctrine of the manifesto he found it "difficult to see that it would be wise for this House, reformed or not, to oppose a specific commitment which formed part of the election platform of a new Government."

77. Lord Strathclyde considered that, given the new composition of the House, the Convention deserved to be reviewed, although he did not believe that even the new House had the right to challenge the Commons on Second Reading or by tabling wrecking amendments to core manifesto items. But he shared the concerns expressed by those Lords who had spoken about the status of manifestos. "Election promises can be vague and easily manipulated by governments, who reserve the right to jettison manifesto promises if things change. If governments can have the right, why cannot Parliaments too have a say on circumstances as they change? While the case for giving manifesto promises a relatively easy ride in the first few Sessions of a Government's life is largely unassailable, subject only to Parliament's overriding duty to safeguard the constitution, it does not mean that that should automatically extend to the whole five years."

78. The Attorney General, Lord Williams of Mostyn [a Labour life peer and QC], argued that "The basis of the Salisbury convention, therefore, does not change by virtue of any alteration in the composition of this House." He did not believe that it had fallen into disuse. [...]

Conclusions

The convention has evolved

97. We are persuaded by the strength of the argument that **the Salisbury-Addison Convention has changed since 1945, and particularly since 1999.** Indeed, this was tacitly admitted by the Government which said, in written evidence, "For a convention to work properly, however, there must be a shared understanding of what it means. A contested convention is not a convention at all." The continued validity of the original Salisbury-Addison Convention is clearly contested by the Liberal Democrats.

98. The Convention now differs from the original Salisbury-Addison Convention in two important respects. It applies to a manifesto Bill introduced in the House of Lords as well as one introduced in the House of Commons. It is now recognised by the whole House, unlike the original Salisbury-Addison Convention which existed only between two parties.

99. The Convention which has evolved is that:

In the House of Lords:

A manifesto Bill is accorded a Second Reading;

A manifesto Bill is not subject to 'wrecking amendments' which change the Government's manifesto intention as proposed in the Bill; and

A manifesto Bill is passed and sent (or returned) to the House of Commons, so that they have the opportunity, in reasonable time, to consider the Bill or any amendments the Lords may wish to propose.

QUESTIONS

1. In their first report, the committee said: *'We do not offer a definition of "convention". We believe we will know one when we see it.'* Do you agree with this approach?

2. What makes the rules about the Lords giving government manifesto Bills a Second Reading: (a) conventions rather than law, and (b) conventions rather than a mere political practice?

3. Rules in statutes are changed by being amended or repealed by later statutes. Rules contained in the common law are changed by judges re-evaluating them and handing down a judgment. Drawing as far as you can on evidence from the given extract, how would you describe the process by which conventions are changed?

4. What would be the (a) legal and (b) political consequences if the Lords were to breach the Salisbury–Addison convention?

5. Why should the Commons be regarded as having primacy over the Lords? Is this affected by the size of the government's majority (if any) in the Commons? Would this change if the composition of the Lords were to be changed to membership that is wholly or substantially elected?

6. In the 2005 UK general election, the Labour Party was the largest party and therefore, by convention, Labour MPs formed the government. But they gained only 35 per cent of the popular vote (that is, 22 per cent of the electorate on a 61 per cent turnout). Does this in any way call into question a convention that the Lords should defer to government Bills?

7. Suppose that, in a general election, the (fictitious) People's Action Party wins a large majority of seats in the Commons, having promised in its manifesto to curtail rights of various minority groups. Would the Lords be bound by the Salisbury–Addison convention in this extreme situation? Would it make any difference if it were clear that the People's Action Party's manifesto contravened the European Convention on Human Rights (ECHR)?

8. A political party about to start writing its general election manifesto seeks your advice about the constitutional implications of the Salisbury–Addison convention for what kinds of promises that it should make. What would you tell it?

(b) CODIFYING CONVENTIONS

As well as identifying the scope of conventions regulating relations between the Lords and Commons, the committee was asked to consider whether it was feasible to codify such conventions. 'Codifying' does not necessarily mean placing the conventions in legislation; it can also mean setting out rules or practices in a document (such as a committee report, rather than a 'Bill'), which is then debated and approved by a resolution of each House of Parliament, without that document becoming 'law'.

In order to set out rules or practices in such a document, it may be necessary first to define things. In Chapter 8, we saw that this was one of the issues that arose in debates about reforming the armed forced deployment prerogative powers. A similar issue arose in relation to the Salisbury–Addison convention.

Joint Committee on Conventions, *Report*, Session 2005–06, HL 265-I/HC 1212-I (footnotes omitted)

101. Each section of the Convention which has evolved over recent years refers to a manifesto Bill. One of the main problems to be addressed in deciding whether it would be practical to codify the Convention is how to define a manifesto Bill.

102. When agreeing the original Convention in 1945, Viscount Cranborne said that he believed "it would be constitutionally wrong, when the country has so recently expressed its view, for this House [of Lords] to oppose proposals which have been *definitely* put before the electorate" (emphasis added). Over 50 years later Baroness Jay of Paddington, the Leader of the House of Lords, restated that position: "it must remain the case that it would be constitutionally wrong, when the country has expressed its view, for this House to oppose proposals that have been *definitely* been put before the electorate." (emphasis added). How then can the question of whether a proposal has been *definitely* put to the electorate be decided?

103. The Leader of the House of Commons argued that the final decision on what a manifesto is "has to be a matter for the Commons as the body having primacy, it cannot lie in the role of the Lords for the Lords as an important but necessarily subordinate chamber to say, "Well, it may have said X but we think Y, or, to pick up your phrase on the 1945 manifesto, 'There is a difference between really important election commitments and those which are unimportant.' "Lord Falconer of Thoroton, Secretary of State for Constitutional Affairs and Lord Chancellor [a Labour life peer], considered that the Convention "would not be convincing if it depended on a very fine reading of each individual manifesto [...] it needs to be a general sensible reading both of what is in the manifesto and broadly what the government stands for in determining what is covered by it."

104. The Opposition [the Conservative Party] agree with the Wakeham report that " 'It is not possible to reduce this to a simple formula, particularly one based on Manifesto commitments.' The Convention was pragmatic in origin - and should continue to be addressed in pragmatic fashion from case to case."

105. The Liberal Democrats consider, however, that "manifestos are not - and, in our view, can never be - detailed enough to constitute a reliable, still less a justiciable basis on which to draft legislation." Manifestos are now much more complex and less precise than they were in 1945. This position has to be seen in the context of the Liberal Democrats' view that the Lords should not reject any government Bill at Second or Third Reading.

106. Lord Williamson of Horton, the Convenor of Crossbench Peers, thought it was reasonable "to consider what are the core elements on which a party goes to the electorate to have a mandate and you have to be careful, because every word in a manifesto may not necessarily be part of a core programme, that that does not tie too much the relations between the two Houses."

107. We agree that legislation often cannot easily be identified as a direct transportation from a manifesto. As several of our witnesses pointed out, the manifesto on which the Labour Party won the 1945 election contained 8 pages: that on which it won the 2005 election was 112 pages long and it would be unrealistic to expect that many, if any, voters agreed with every line of the manifesto.

108. Another potential difficulty relates to how the Convention would apply in the case of a minority government. The view of the Leader of the House of Commons "is that if any coalition or arrangement as in 1977 gains the support of the democratically elected House and endorsed by a motion of confidence then the programme for which they gain that endorsement should be respected by this House [of Lords]."

109. In the Liberal Democrats' view the "circumstances would be entirely different because the question of how the minority government managed to get its manifesto through would involve negotiation within the Commons."

110. Lord Strathclyde believed "If a government has a majority in the House of Commons, a government has a majority in the House of Commons and so the same conventions should apply. Equally where a government is trying to push through some very unpopular measure with a very, very small majority, with a substantial government rebellion, I think it is a clear signal for the House of Lords to take extra special care in examining that measure."

111. There is also the question of whether the Convention applies to matters included in regional manifestos. The Leader of the House of Commons confirmed that the specific issue on which he was questioned was in the UK manifesto but added "even if it had not been a reference in the Welsh manifesto would have been sufficient."

112. There are other obvious difficulties in deciding whether a Bill is a manifesto Bill. But those difficulties are not new. They have existed since the original Salisbury-Addison Convention was articulated in 1945 but have not prevented the Convention from operating effectively in the various political circumstances which have prevailed since then. The Government noted that the House of Lords had voted down a government Bill only three times since 1992. "Once was on the second introduction of the European Parliamentary Elections Bill in 1998, when the Bill had been reintroduced with a view to passing it under the Parliament Acts and killing the Bill on Second Reading was necessary for it to receive Royal Assent in time to allow the necessary secondary legislation to be made. A second occasion was on the Sexual Offences Amendment Bill in 1999, which was a Bill to which a free vote had been applied. Only the third, the Mode of Trial (No 2) Bill in 2000 which was voted down on Second Reading after its predecessor Bill (which had started in the Lords) had been subject to wrecking amendments in Committee, was a Government flagship policy Bill, but was not a Manifesto Bill."

113. **We do not recommend any attempt to define a manifesto Bill.** Nor do we consider that the difficulties in identifying a manifesto Bill are so substantial that they would prevent Parliament from articulating a convention concerning the House of Lords' practice in relation to manifesto Bills. Given the view of all our witnesses that the House of Lords has not breached the original Salisbury-Addison Convention, we think that there is little likelihood that it will breach the current convention in future. We also expect that it will be as possible to deal pragmatically with any problems which may arise in the future as it has been in the past.

Codification

114. In order to ensure that the convention now reflects an agreement between both Houses, and to give all parties and non-aligned Members in both Houses the opportunity to express their views, each House should have a chance to debate it. However, although both Houses have an interest in the convention, it concerns primarily the behaviour of the House of Lords. **We therefore propose that the Lords be given the opportunity to debate and agree a resolution setting out the terms of the convention, and that the resolution be then communicated by message to the Commons. The Commons could then hold a debate on a motion to take note of the message.**

A new name

115. In our view the Salisbury-Addison Convention has evolved sufficiently to require a new name which should also help to clarify its changed nature. We recommend that in future the Convention be described as the Government Bill Convention.

[In the concluding part of its report, the Committee made the following statement.]

279. In our view the word "codification" is unhelpful, since to most people it implies rule-making, with definitions and enforcement mechanisms. Conventions, by their very nature, are unenforceable. In this sense, therefore, codifying conventions is a contradiction in terms. It would raise issues of definition, reduce flexibility, and inhibit the capacity to evolve. It might create a need for adjudication, and the presence of an adjudicator, whether the courts or some new body, is incompatible with parliamentary sovereignty. Even if an adjudicator could be found, the possibility of adjudication would introduce uncertainty and delay into the business of Parliament. In these ways, far from reducing the risk of conflict, codification might actually damage the relationship between the two Houses, making it more confrontational and less capable of moderation through the usual channels. This would benefit neither the Government nor Parliament.

In December 2006, the government published a response to the committee's report, stating: '*We accept the Joint Committee's analysis of the effect of all the conventions, and the Joint Committee's recommendations and conclusions.*'[7] On 16 January 2007, the House of Lords debated the report. Peers praised the report and there was wide agreement with its proposals. Without a vote being called, the Lords approved the motion '*That this House takes note with approval of the report of the Joint Committee on Conventions of the UK Parliament (HL Paper 265, Session 2005–06)*'.

QUESTIONS

1. Why did the committee prefer not to define a 'manifesto Bill'?

2. What *precisely* will be achieved by codifying the convention and each House passing a resolution to approve or take note of it?

3. Do you agree that it is a 'contradiction in terms' to codify conventions?

3 THE PARLIAMENT ACTS

So far, we have focused on the main convention regulating relations between the Commons and the Lords while a Bill is under consideration. If, at the end of the legislative process for a particular Bill, there is stalemate between the Commons and the Lords, rules are set out in the Parliament Acts.

The following extract summarizes the background to the enactment of the Parliament Act 1911.

House of Lords Constitution Committee, *Constitutional aspects of the challenge to the Hunting Act 2004*, Seventh Report, Session 2005–06, Appendix 1: Professor Rodney Brazier, The Parliament Acts

3. [...] The House of Lords remained hereditary and permanently controlled by the Conservative Party. Yet the House of Commons had been made more representative of the electorate through extensions of the franchise. And in 1906 the Liberals won a landslide

---

[7] Government Response to the Joint Committee on Conventions' Report, Session 2005–06, *Conventions of the UK Parliament*, Cm 6997.

General Election victory on a programme which promised major social legislation, much of which was anathema to most peers. The House of Lords rejected some of the Liberal Government's reform bills, and in 1909, in its greatest act of defiance, the Lords rejected the Finance Bill which embodied Lloyd George's "People's Budget". In response the House of Commons passed a resolution which condemned that action as "[...] a breach of the Constitution and a usurpation of the rights of the Commons [...]" The Liberals won a General Election in January 1910, and as a result the House of Lords most reluctantly passed the Finance Bill. Asquith's Government had decided to settle the more general point about the relative legislative powers of the two Houses by changing the law, but could only persuade the House of Lords to accept the resulting Parliament Bill after a second General Election in 1910 (which the Government again won) and the subsequent publication of a guarantee from King George V that, if necessary, he would create enough Liberal peers to overcome the resistance of the House of Lords to the bill. Faced with the choice of the loss of its daily control of the upper House, or a reduction in its legislative powers, peers opted for the trimming of its power as the lesser of two evils. The Parliament Act 1911—passed, it should be noted, by both Houses before receiving Royal Assent—was the outcome of that long constitutional crisis.

4. The Parliament Act 1911 made no attempt to change the composition of the House of Lords, although the preamble stated the intention "to substitute for the House of Lords as it at present exists a Second Chamber constituted on a popular instead of a hereditary basis," but added (rather plaintively) that "such substitution cannot be immediately brought into operation." The 1911 Act changed the law in three main respects. It stripped the House of Lords of most of its power over money bills. It changed the absolute veto enjoyed by that House over most bills into a power to delay the passage of such bills for up to two years, spread over three parliamentary sessions, after which they would pass into law without the approval of the House of Lords. And the maximum life of Parliament was reduced from seven years to five.

The Parliament Act 1911 was used to present Bills for royal assent despite the Lords' disagreement three times, all in relation to constitutional change:

- the Welsh Church Act 1914 ('disestablishing' the Church of Wales);
- the Government of Ireland Act 1914 (setting up a framework for government in Ireland, the whole of which was then part of the United Kingdom); and
- the Parliament Act 1949 (amending the Parliament Act 1911 to restrict further the delaying powers of the Lords).

Vernon Bogdanor, *The New British Constitution* (2009, Oxford: Hart Publishing), p. 149 (footnotes omitted)

The 1911 Parliament Act thus marked a fundamental change in the British constitution. If Britain were to enjoy, for most practical purposes, single-chamber government, then the House of Commons which in practice means the governing party, could now unilaterally alter any part of the constitution, with the singe exception that it could not extend the five year maximum interval between general elections without the consent of the Lords. Under the post-1911 constitution, the governing party which controlled the House of Commons became the sole and supreme judge of the extent of its power. [...] It was for this reason that

Dicey declared in 1915 that the Parliament Act marked 'the last and greatest triumph of party government'. For it showed that party was 'not the accident or corruption, but so to speak, the very foundation of our constitutional system'. Dicey believed that the Act left a gap in the constitution, a gap which he believed should be filled by the referendum. Perhaps, however, the gap is now being filled by the judges.

The Parliament Act 1949—enacted under the Parliament Act 1911 without the Lords' consent—is of special interest to us. As with the emergence of the Salisbury–Addison convention, its political driver was the wish of the Attlee Labour government (1945–51) to have in place a constitutional assurance that the Bills approved by the Commons, needed to implement the social and economic revolution, would not be held back unreasonably by the Lords (which was dominated by Conservative hereditary peers). The government was particularly concerned that the Lords would delay the Iron and Steel Bill, which sought to nationalize those industries by setting up a government body to purchase compulsorily shares in all firms operating in that section in the United Kingdom. The 1911 Act, in effect, gave the Lords a veto over government Bills introduced in the last two years of a Parliament, because the government would not be able to reintroduce a Bill after two years' waiting and press for royal assent without the Lords' consent. The 1949 Act reduced the Lords' power of delay (see Box 13.2).

BOX 13.2 1911 AND 1949 ACTS COMPARED

1911 Act	1949 Act
Bill must be passed in three successive sessions by the Commons	Bill must have passed in two successive sessions by the Commons
Two years must have elapsed between Second Reading debate (first time round) and passing of the Bill for a third time	One year must have elapsed between the Second Reading debate (first time round) and the passing of the Bill for a second time

---

Introducing the Second Reading debate of the Parliament Bill in the Commons on 10 November 1947, Herbert Morrison MP (holding the ministerial office of The Lord President of the Council)[8] made the following statement.

House of Lords Hansard, 10 November 1947, col. 36

[... W]e are discussing an important constitutional issue, namely, the powers of the House of Lords in relation to the House of Commons—a progressive House of Commons and a progressive Government. [...] I mention that because it is part of the unfairness of the situation that a Conservative Government has no trouble with the Lords, whereas a progressive Government has.

---

[8] In one of those quirks of history, his grandson—another Labour politician—was appointed to the same ministerial post in 2009: Lord Mandelson.

Let us look more closely at s. 2(1) of the Parliament Act 1911, as amended by the 1949 Act.

Parliament Act 1911, as amended by the 1949 Act, s. 2

Restriction of the powers of the House of Lords as to Bills other than Money

(1) If any Public Bill (other than a Money Bill or a Bill containing any provision to extend the maximum duration of Parliament beyond five years) is passed by the House of Commons in two successive sessions (whether of the same Parliament or not), and, having been sent up to the House of Lords at least one month before the end of the session, is rejected by the House of Lords in each of those sessions, that Bill shall, on its rejection for the second time by the House of Lords, unless the House of Commons directs to the contrary, be presented to His Majesty and become an Act of Parliament on the Royal Assent being signified thereto, notwithstanding that the House of Lords have not consented to the Bill: Provided that this provision shall not take effect unless one year has elapsed between the date of the second reading in the first of those sessions of the Bill in the House of Commons and the date on which it passes the House of Commons in the second of those sessions.

In general terms, a 'money Bill' is one that deals only with taxation, the national debt, or 'supply' (legal permission for the government to spend public funds); such Bills cannot be amended by the Lords and automatically pass if the Lords have not passed them within a month, so s. 2(1) does not need to apply. The exclusion of Bills seeking to extend the duration of Parliament beyond five years means that the maximum life of any one Parliament can only be extended with the agreement of both Houses of Parliament. This reflects the constitutional importance of ensuring that general elections are held at least once every five years.

QUESTIONS

1. Why was the Parliament Act 1911 enacted? Why was the Parliament Act 1948 enacted?

2. Would you prefer to be living in a constructional system in which:

   (a) the will of democratically elected MPs can be implemented promptly without delays by the second chamber; or

   (b) there is a strong second chamber able to force the Commons to think again on legislative proposals?

(a) THE VALIDITY (OR OTHERWISE) OF THE PARLIAMENT ACT 1949

At first sight, the suggestion that an Act of Parliament is invalid appears rather implausible, given the principle of the supremacy of Parliament.[9] The Hunting Act litigation to which we

[9] See Chapter 2.

are about to turn, however, focused on a long-standing debate among constitutional lawyers over whether the Parliament Act 1949 was a valid Act of Parliament. Distinguished scholars were split on the point: see Box 13.3.

BOX 13.3 PROTAGONISTS IN DEBATE OVER THE PARLIAMENT ACT 1949

Arguing that the Parliament Act 1949 was invalid	Arguing that the 1949 Act was valid
Professor H.W.R. (later 'Sir William' Wade (1918–2004), Oxford and Cambridge	Professor Stanley de Smith (1922–74), LSE and Cambridge
Professor Owen Hood Phillips (1907–86), University of Birmingham	Professor Anthony Bradley, University of Edinburgh
Professor Graham Zellick, Queen Mary, University of London	Professor Rodney Brazier, University of Manchester

---

Wade's argument: Parliament Act 1911 delegates Parliament's power

In his book *Constitutional Fundamentals*[10] and his article 'The basis of legal sovereignty',[11] Wade said that Parliament has three constituent elements—the sovereign, the House of Commons, and the House of Lords—and that an Act of Parliament is legislation to which each of these three elements has assented. Legislation enacted under the provisions of the Parliament Act 1911 is only enacted by the sovereign and the House of Commons. It therefore has not been agreed to by Parliament. Wade argued that, in the Parliament Act 1911, Parliament *delegated* law-making capacity to the sovereign and the House of Commons, and that legislation enacted by virtue of the Parliament Act 1911 is therefore *delegated legislation* made under *delegated powers*. Moreover, he argued, an Act of the Queen and the Commons is only accepted by the courts as law because it has been passed in accordance with the Parliament Acts 1911 and 1949. The acid test for an Act of Parliament is whether it is valid on its face. Legislation passed in accordance with the Parliament Acts is not valid on its face; it is valid only because it has been passed in a manner that was set out in the Parliament Acts 1911–49.

As a general principle, a body that has been given delegated power cannot increase the power that has been given to it; only those delegating the power can do this. This means that the sovereign and the Commons could not use the Parliament Act 1911 to extend the power given to them by Parliament in that Act. The 1949 Act was enacted using the Parliament Act 1911. Without the consent of the House of Lords, it amended the 1911 Act by reducing the delaying power of the Lords. This had the effect of increasing the power of the Commons. Wade said that only Parliament could increase the power conferred on the Commons by the Parliament Act 1911.

The implication of these arguments is that the Parliament Act 1949 is not an Act of Parliament and therefore calls into question the validity of Acts of Parliament that have subsequently been made under its provisions, including the Hunting Act 2004.

---

[10] The Hamlin Lectures, 32nd Series (1980, London: Stevens & Son), esp. pp. 27–8.
[11] [1955] CLJ 172.

Counter-argument: It is redefinition, not delegation

Others disagreed with Wade and his supporters. In essence, their argument is that the Queen in Parliament can alter the procedure to be used for enacting legislation for particular purposes, so that, in effect, Parliament can redefine itself for these purposes. The Parliament Act 1911 enabled Parliament to redefine itself as the sovereign and Commons in relation to the Bills to which it applied. This being so, no question of delegation arises. This, they say, is reinforced by the actual wording of the Parliament Act 1911, which provides in s. 2(1) that a Bill made under its provisions will become an 'Act of Parliament'. This expression clearly indicates that provisions made using the Parliament Act procedure are Acts of Parliament and not items of delegated legislation.

QUESTION

Which of these two views are you inclined to agree with at this stage, and why?

---

4 THE HUNTING ACT 2004

In the 2002–03 session of Parliament, the Labour government introduced a Bill to ban hunting with dogs. It passed in the Commons (by 317 to 145 on a 'free vote'), but the Lords rejected the policy, amending the Bill to allow hunting under licence. The government found this proposal unacceptable and let the Bill lapse.

(a) THE PATH TO ROYAL ASSENT

In the following 2003–04 session, the government reintroduced the Bill to ban hunting. This was again passed by the Commons and again amended by the Lords in a way that was unacceptable to the government. On 18 November 2004—the final day of that parliamentary session—the government sought to bring an end to the 'ping-pong' process with the Lords and to invoke the Parliament Acts.

House of Commons Hansard, 18 November 2004, col. 1518

Hunting Bill

9.01 pm

Mr. Speaker: I have to inform the House that a message has been brought from the Lords as follows: "The Lords insist on their amendments to the Hunting Bill, to which the Commons have insisted on their disagreement, for which insistence they assign their reasons. They insist on their amendments to which the Commons have disagreed, for which insistence they assign their reasons, and they disagree to the amendment proposed by the Commons in lieu of the Lords amendments, for which disagreement they assign their reason."

Hon. Members: Explain.

Mr. Speaker: I read these messages; I don't understand them. It was not a Glasgow man who wrote that one, anyway.[12]

As the Minister made clear to the House in his remarks earlier today, a rejection on these lines has brought us to the end of the road. I am satisfied that all the provisions of the Parliament Acts have been met. [Hon. Members: "Hear, hear."] Accordingly, I have to tell the House that I have certified the Hunting Bill under section 2 of the Parliament Act 1911, as amended by the Parliament Act 1949. The Bill endorsed by me will be sent for Royal Assent at the time of prorogation in compliance with the provisions of the Parliament Acts.

At 9.02 p.m., the Speaker suspended the sitting of the Commons. An official walked to the Lords and handed to a Lords official the Hunting Bill, as approved by the Commons, tied up in pink tape. He bowed and left the Lords.

At 9.30 p.m., the Lords resumed their sitting and there followed a familiar ceremony whereby royal assent is given to Bills. Contrary to popular myth, royal assent does not actually involve the Queen personally.

House of Lords Hansard, 18 November 2004, cols 1658–9

Royal Commission

The Lord Chancellor (Lord Falconer of Thoroton): My Lords, it not being convenient for Her Majesty personally to be present here this day, she has been pleased to cause a Commission under the Great Seal to be prepared for proroguing this present Parliament.

Then the Lords Commissioners (being the Lord Chancellor, the Lord President of the Council (Baroness Amos), the Baroness Blatch, the Lord Donaldson of Lymington and the Baroness Williams of Crosby) being present and the Commons being at the Bar, the Lord Chancellor said: My Lords and Members of the House of Commons, Her Majesty, not thinking fit personally to be present here at this time, has been pleased to cause a Commission to be issued under the Great Seal, and thereby given Her Royal Assent to divers Acts, the Titles whereof are particularly mentioned, and by the said Commission has commanded us to declare and notify Her Royal Assent to the said several Acts, in the presence of you the Lords and Commons assembled for that purpose; and has also assigned to us and other Lords directed full power and authority in Her Majesty's name to prorogue this present Parliament. Which Commission you will now hear read. A Commission for Royal Assent and Prorogation was read.

The Lord Chancellor: In obedience to Her Majesty's Commands, and by virtue of the Commission which has been now read, We do declare and notify to you, the Lords Spiritual and Temporal and Commons in Parliament assembled, that Her Majesty has given Her Royal

---

[12] Mr Speaker Martin represented a Glasgow constituency.

Assent to the several Acts in the Commission mentioned; and the Clerks are required to pass the same in the usual Form and Words.

Royal Assent

The following Acts received Royal Assent:

- Armed Forces (Pensions and Compensation) Act,
- Civil Partnership Act,
- Housing Act,
- Pensions Act,
- Civil Contingencies Act.

The following Act, passed in accordance with the provisions of the Parliament Acts 1911 and 1949, received Royal Assent:

- Hunting Act.

An official then walked to the Commons and handed Mr Speaker a document. At 9.59 p.m., a minute before the House was due to rise for the end of the 2003–04 Session, Mr Speaker announced to the Commons that royal assent had been granted to those Acts.

The Hunting Act's words of enactment reflect the fact that the House of Lords did not assent to it being passed.

Hunting Act 2004, Preamble

Be it enacted by The Queen's most Excellent Majesty, by and with the advice and consent of the Commons in this present Parliament assembled, in accordance with the provisions of the Parliament Acts 1911 and 1949, and by the authority of the same, as follows [...]

(b) LEGAL CHALLENGE TO THE HUNTING ACT

The grant of royal assent can hardly have been a surprise to those who had long campaigned to keep hunting with dogs lawful. The Countryside Alliance, a pressure group formed in 1997 to lobby on rural issues, realized that it was time to move from demonstrations in the streets and to the courtroom. Their team of distinguished lawyers was led by the 83-year-old Sir Sydney Kentridge QC, who, while at the South African Bar, had defended Nelson Mandela and others in the infamous 1957 'Treason Trial' (see Box 13.4). Rather than bring the challenge in its own name, the Countryside Alliance identified three supporters who would act as the claimants. Mr Jackson was the chairman of the Countryside Alliance and owned land on which hunting took place. Mr Martin was a professional huntsman, whose income depended on the legality of hunting; he also lived in tied accommodation and this too depended on the legality of hunting. Mrs Hughes and her family had a business that was dependent on hunting; she also hunted.

BOX 13.4 LAWYERS INVOLVED IN THE JACKSON CASE

For claimants	For the defendant	For the interested party (League Against Cruel Sports)
Sir Sydney Kentridge QC Richard Lissack QC Martin Chamberlain Marcus Haywood (Instructed by Allen & Overy LLP)	Lord Goldsmith QC (the Attorney General himself) Clive Lewis (Instructed by the Treasury Solicitor)	David Pannick QC Gordon Nardell (Instructed by Collyer–Bristow)

The claimants asked for declarations that: (1) the Parliament Act 1949 is not an Act of Parliament and is consequently of no legal effect; and (2) accordingly, the Hunting Act 2004 is not an Act of Parliament and is of no legal effect.

The defendant in the case was to the Attorney General, the principal legal adviser to Parliament, the government, and Her Majesty.

(c) ADMINISTRATIVE COURT

The first court to hear the judicial review claim was the Administrative Court (Maurice Kay LJ and Collins J).

R (on the application of Jackson and ors) v Her Majesty's Attorney General
[2005] EWHC 94 (Admin) (28 January 2005)

Maurice Kay LJ

The Claimants' Arguments

[9] [...] The grounds of challenge mount the attack on the 1949 Act on three bases. *First*, it is said that, as a matter of construction, the 1911 Act cannot be used to achieve amendments to itself and that, accordingly, it was unlawful for the 1949 Act to reach the statute book without the approval of the House of Lords. *Secondly*, the Claimants seek to characterise the procedure prescribed by the 1911 Act as one of delegated legislation, such that it was unlawful for the delegated body, namely the Sovereign and the House of Commons, to enlarge the scope of its own authority without the approval of the parent body, which includes the House of Lords. *Thirdly*, even if legislation passed under the 1911 Act is not delegated legislation in the strict sense, it nevertheless emanates from a subordinate legislature which, in the absence of an express power, cannot modify or amend the conditions upon which its power to legislate was granted. There is an inevitable overlap between these three grounds.

[Maurice Kay LJ rejected the first argument on the ground that it conflicts with the 'clear language' of the 1911 Act.]

[17] [...] Section 2(1) expressly refers to *"any* Public Bill" (other than the specifically excluded Money Bill and a Bill to extend the maximum duration of Parliament). This has twofold significance. The word "any" is deliberately wide and the existence of express exclusions militates against the implication of additional excluded categories. In these circumstances, I accept the submission of the Attorney General that there is no scope for interpreting s 2 as containing an exclusion in relation to any Bill to amend the provisions of the 1911 Act. I also derive some assistance from a submission made by Mr David Pannick QC on behalf of the League Against Cruel Sports. He points to s 2(2) and the obligation placed on the Speaker to sign a certificate that "the provisions of this section have been duly complied with". It would be an unduly onerous obligation if there were considered to be such provisions which are not manifest from the words of s 2(1).

[You will notice that the second argument is that used by Wade and his supporters. Maurice Kay LJ acknowledged the *'very respectable academic pedigree'* of this argument, but concluded as follows.]

[23] [...] the label of delegated legislation is inapposite. I accept the submission of the Attorney General that the 1911 Act is a special case which arose in a specific context which bore little or no resemblance to delegated legislation as that concept is generally understood. The purpose of the 1911 Act was to change the relationship between the House of Commons and the House of Lords in the process of enacting legislation (save in the expressly excluded areas). To that extent, the language of "redefinition" or "remodelling" (the latter being the word used by Francis Bennion in his helpful article 'Is the New Hunting Act Valid?' Justice of the Peace, 27 November 2004, 928) is more appropriate than that of "delegation". Moreover, one only has to look at the product of the process for the position to become clear. What emerges when a Bill is enacted pursuant to s. 2 of the 1911 Act is itself an Act of Parliament—nothing less. Section 2(1) itself expressly provides that the Bill "shall [...] become an Act of Parliament on the Royal Assent being signified thereto". [...]

[24] In my judgment, the correct way to describe the 1911 Act is as a statute which redefined or remodelled the legislature in such a way that there were thenceforth two routes through which Acts of Parliament could be enacted — the traditional way involving the Sovereign, the House of Commons and the House of Lords and the 1911 Act way emanating from the Sovereign and the House of Commons, provided that the conditions imposed by the 1911 Act are met. [...]

[25] It has been a pleasure to engage with a debate which has divided constitutional experts for half a century. However, I have come to the conclusion that Professor Wade's theory—if I may so term it—does not fit the matrix of the 1911 Act. I reject the delegated legislation argument. [...]

Maurice Kay LJ also rejected the third argument, that a subordinate legislature cannot alter the conditions under which its power to legislate was given, unless it has been given express power to do so. This argument was also rejected because it was contrary to the wording of s. 2(1) of the Parliament Act 1911, which '*is wide enough to embrace a Bill which amends s. 2 itself*' (at [27]).

Collins J delivered a separate judgment agreeing that the claim should fail. The Administrative Court granted permission to appeal to the Court of Appeal.

R (on the application of Jackson and ors) v Her Majesty's Attorney General
[2005] EWHC 94 (Admin) (28 January 2005)

[51] We grant it not on the basis of a real prospect of success, but on the basis of other compelling reasons, those compelling reasons being obvious in the circumstances. This is an issue that has been around in the literature for many years. It has been raised at first instance on one previous occasion. It would be wrong if the matter were to end simply at first instance.

(d) COURT OF APPEAL

The Court of Appeal included both the Lord Chief Justice and the Master of the Rolls, indicating the great importance attached to the case. In a single judgment, the Court of Appeal dismissed the appeal—but, in doing so, explored two issues that are of considerable importance and interest. The first related to the jurisdiction of the courts to consider a challenge to the legality of Acts of Parliament. The second concerned the question of whether the Parliament Act 1911 procedure could be used to achieve fundamental constitutional change, such as to abolish the House of Lords. On this matter, the Court of Appeal disagreed with the view of the Administrative Court that the Parliament Act procedure could be used in relation to any public Bill except those specifically excluded, such as a Bill seeking to extend the life of a Parliament.

These two issues are considered in the following extracts from the Court of Appeal's judgment.

R (on the application of Jackson and ors) v Her Majesty's Attorney General
[2005] EWCA Civ 126 (16 February 2005)

[11] It is unusual, and in modern times probably unprecedented, for the courts to have to rule on the validity of legislation that has received the Royal Assent. (But as to earlier periods in our history see *The Prince's Case* 8 Co Rep 1A.) However, the Attorney General did not dispute that the courts could properly adjudicate on this issue and in the court below, Maurice Kay LJ remarked (paragraph 14) "the Attorney General wisely takes no point on justiciability". Despite these exchanges, we were concerned to satisfy ourselves that the issue before us was justiciable. We asked the Attorney General how this was. It was a question to which he gave us no convincing answer. He said that no point was taken on justiciability because it was recognised that it was desirable that the courts should decide the issue. When we suggested that this might not be a valid basis for assuming jurisdiction, he asserted that there was no absolute rule that the courts could not consider the validity of a statute. Here the courts had jurisdiction because the issue was one of statutory interpretation and because the Appellants were contending that the 1949 Act was not a statute at all.

[12] The reality is that the 1911 Act was a most unusual statute. By that statute the House of Lords, the House of Commons and the King used the machinery of legislation to make a fundamental constitutional change. Nearly 100 years after the event, the court has been invited to rule on the precise nature and extent of that change. We have decided that it was right for the Administrative Court to accept that invitation. The authority of the 1949 Act purported to be derived from the 1911 Act. The latter Act, by s. 3 [which provides the certificate of the Speaker that the provisions of the Parliament Act 1911 have been complied with, shall be *conclusive for all purposes and shall not be questioned in any court of law*'], expressly envisaged the possibility that the validity of subsequent Acts enacted pursuant to its provisions

might be subjected to judicial scrutiny. The effect of the 1911 Act was undoubtedly susceptible to judicial analysis. However, in considering that effect, the Administrative Court was acting as a constitutional court. There was no precise precedent for the jurisdiction that it was exercising.

[13] The conclusion to which we have come is that Lord Goldsmith was correct to make the concession that he did. The determination of questions of interpretation and ascertaining the effect of legislation is part of the normal diet of the courts. While we will refer to what has happened in debates in Parliament concerning the issue before us, we will not be adjudicating upon the propriety of what occurred in Parliament. The circumstances in which it will be appropriate for the courts to become involved in issues of this nature are limited, but in this case it is perfectly appropriate for the courts to be involved. If the courts did not adjudicate on the issue, there would be great uncertainty as to the legal situation, which could have most unfortunate consequences after 19 February 2005, when the Hunting Act is meant to come into force. In exercising this role, the Administrative Court and this court on appeal are seeking to assist Parliament and the public by clarifying the legal position when such clarification is obviously necessary.

QUESTIONS

1. If '[t]he determination of questions of interpretation and ascertaining the effect of legislation is part of the normal diet of the courts', why was the Court of Appeal so anxious to clarify on what basis the courts had jurisdiction in this case?

2. The Court of Appeal says that the Administrative Court had been 'acting as a constitutional court'. What difference does it make to say that the court was acting as a constitutional court?

3. The Court of Appeal says that, in this case:

   [I]t is perfectly appropriate for the courts to be involved. If the courts did not adjudicate on the issue, there would be great uncertainty as to the legal situation, which could have most unfortunate consequences after 19 February 2005, when the Hunting Act is meant to come into force. In exercising this role, the Administrative Court and this court on appeal are seeking to assist Parliament and the public by clarifying the legal position when such clarification is obviously necessary.

   Why would a decision that the legality of the Hunting Act cannot be adjudicated upon in the courts lead to uncertainty?

The Court of Appeal went on to consider whether the Parliament Act 1911 could be used to make fundamental constitutional changes.

R (on the application of Jackson and ors) v Her Majesty's Attorney General
[2005] EWCA Civ 126 (16 February 2005)

[39] The argument of the Attorney General, that once legislation has been created by the 1911 Act it is no different from legislation created in the traditional way with the consent of both Houses, is one which we question. [...]

[40] The main reason for our reservations as to this outcome is that it involves it being accepted that the 1911 Act could be used to extend the life of Parliament contrary to the express language of s. 2(1) of the 1911 Act for such period as the Commons determines. All that would be required would be for Parliament, in the shape of the Commons, to pass legislation deleting the words "Bill containing any provision to extend the maximum duration of Parliament beyond five years" and then to pass further legislation extending the life of Parliament. This would be quite contrary to the express limitation on extending the duration of Parliament contained in s. 2(1), and we are not prepared to accept that this is the position.

[41] We appreciate that it is most unlikely that the Commons would ever contemplate seeking to use the 1911 Act [...] to enact legislation to which the House of Lords had not consented, in order to extend the duration of Parliament or, for that matter, to abolish the House of Lords. However if [...] it did contemplate such action, we would regard this as being contrary to the intention of Parliament when enacting the 1911 Act. So, here we disagree with the views to the contrary expressed by the Administrative Court.

42] The purpose of the 1911 Act was to establish a new constitutional settlement that limited the period during which the Lords could delay the enactment of legislation first introduced to the Commons but which preserved the role of the Lords in the legislative processes. In our view it would be in conflict with the 1911 Act for it to be used as an instrument for abolishing the House of Lords. This would be so whether or not there was initially an attempt to use the 1911 Act process to amend the 1911 Act to provide an express power to abolish the Lords. We would view such an endeavour in the same way as an attempt to delete the prohibition on extending the life of Parliament. The preamble of the 1911 Act is inconsistent with the Attorney General's contention. The preamble indicates that the 1911 Act was to be a transitional provision pending further reform. It provides no support for an intention that the 1911 Act should be used, directly or indirectly, to enable more fundamental constitutional changes to be achieved than had been achieved already.

[43] Thus, it does not necessarily follow that because there is compliance with the requirements in the 1911 Act, the result is a valid Act of Parliament. Following the reasoning in the previous paragraph, if, without amending the 1911 Act further, the Commons attempted to extend the life of Parliament in excess of five years without the consent of the Lords, the attempt would be ineffective and, if necessary, the court's jurisdiction that we are now exercising could be invoked. The Attorney General in fact recognises this because, while he contends this could be done, he accepts it would be necessary for the 1911 Act to be amended first to remove the express exception to extending the life of Parliament.

[44] This concession recognises that there are differences between the traditional powers of Parliament when legislating, and its powers when legislating under the 1911 Act. With the consent of the Lords and Commons, Parliament could extend the life of Parliament for say two years without having to amend the 1911 Act. Indeed, it did so during the Second World War. (We deliberately confine the extension for a limited period because there could be different arguments if Parliament attempted to extend its life indefinitely.)

[45] Once it is accepted that the use to which the 1911 Act could be put is limited, the question arises as to the extent of the limitation. It is when we reach this stage that it becomes important to recognise that what could be suggested here is the power to make fundamental constitutional changes. If Parliament was intending to create such a power, surely it is right to expect that the power would be unambiguously stated in the legislation. This is not the case with s. 2 of the 1911 Act. [...]

QUESTIONS

1. What is a 'fundamental constitutional change'? Do you think that this can be defined sufficiently clearly for the purposes of making a workable qualification to the Parliament Acts?

2. Consider whether the following proposals should be regarded as fundamental constitutional changes.

   (a) Abolishing the right to jury trials in complex fraud cases.

   (b) Changes to the immigration laws that would make it more difficult for a certain category of person to enter the United Kingdom.

   (c) Reducing the voting age to 16 years.

As we shall see, this issue was taken up by the judges in the House of Lords.

(e) APPELLATE COMMITTEE OF THE HOUSE OF LORDS

In mid-June 2005, six months after the Court of Appeal delivered its judgment, a further appeal was heard by the Appellate Committee of the House of Lords at a two-day hearing. Nine Law Lords sat in the House of Lords, rather than the normal five—again reinforcing the importance of the case. The opinions that they delivered in October 2005 covered a broad range of issues. The House was unanimous in dismissing the appeal—but in statements that were largely obiter, the Law Lords dealt with a range of important issues.

BOX 13.5 WHAT THE LAW LORDS DECIDED

Proposition of law	Law Lords agreeing
The courts have jurisdiction to consider whether the Parliament Act 1949 is valid	Unanimous
The courts would not recognize as valid an 'Act' passed under the Parliament Act 1911 to extend the life of Parliament beyond five years	Seven out of nine
The courts would not recognize as valid an 'Act' passed under the Parliament Act 1911 that purported to amend s. 2(1) of the Parliament Act 1911 in order to permit the use of the Parliament Act procedure to extend the life of Parliament beyond five years	Five out of nine

---

Jurisdiction to consider the validity of an Act of Parliament

Lord Bingham said that, like the Court of Appeal, he felt a '*some sense of strangeness at the exercise which the courts have [...] been invited to undertake in these proceedings*'.[13] He noted, that '*the authority of* Pickin v British Railways Board[14] *is unquestioned, and it was there very clearly decided that "the courts in this country have no power to declare enacted law to be*

---

[13] *Jackson and ors v Her Majesty's Attorney General* [2005] UKHL 56, [27].
[14] [1974] AC 765, discussed in Chapter 2.

invalid" (Lord Simon of Glaisdale at 798)'. Lord Bingham was, however, persuaded that the court had jurisdiction in this case for two reasons.

Jackson and ors v Her Majesty's Attorney General
[2005] UKHL 56 (13 October 2005)

Lord Bingham

[27] [...] First, in *Pickin*, unlike the present case, it was sought to investigate the internal workings and procedures of Parliament to demonstrate that it had been misled and so had proceeded on a false basis. This was held to be illegitimate [...] Here [...] [t]he issue concerns no question of parliamentary procedure such as would, and could only, be the subject of parliamentary inquiry, but a question whether, in Lord Simon's language, these Acts are "enacted law". My second reason is more practical. The appellants have raised a question of law which cannot, as such, be resolved by Parliament. But it would not be satisfactory, or consistent with the rule of law, if it could not be resolved at all. So it seems to me necessary that the courts should resolve it, and that to do so involves no breach of constitutional propriety.

Lord Nicholls also thought the proceedings to be 'highly unusual'.

[49] At first sight a challenge in court to the validity of a statute seems to offend the fundamental constitutional principle that courts will not look behind an Act of Parliament and investigate the process by which it was enacted. Those are matters for Parliament, not the courts.

> [But he went on to say that the claimants '*do not dispute this constitutional principle*'; their challenge, he said, is based on '*the proper interpretation of s. 2(1) of the 1911 Act*'.]

[51] On this issue the court's jurisdiction cannot be doubted. This question of statutory interpretation is properly cognisable by a court of law even though it relates to the legislative process. Statutes create law. The proper interpretation of a statute is a matter for the courts, not Parliament. This principle is as fundamental in this country's constitution as the principle that Parliament has exclusive cognisance (jurisdiction) over its own affairs.

Lord Hope also accepted that there was '*no breach of constitutional propriety*'[15] in the courts entertaining the challenge. This was because, in the Parliament Act 1911, Parliament had itself '*appreciated that the question whether a Bill passed by the House of Commons alone was to receive effect as an Act of Parliament was in the final analysis one for the courts*'.[16] His point is that since s. 3 provides that a certificate of the speaker shall not be questioned in any court, Parliament must have assumed the possibility of legal proceedings.

Lord Carswell agreed that the case fell within the scope of the regular function of the courts.[17]

---

[15] *Jackson and ors v Her Majesty's Attorney General* [2005] UKHL 56, [110].
[16] Ibid.
[17] Ibid., [169].

QUESTIONS

1. If the Appellate Committee had jurisdiction to consider the challenge, did it also therefore have jurisdiction to decide that the Acts in question were invalid? If so, would this not be tantamount to undertaking a constitutional review of an Act of Parliament—something that has never been possible in the past?

2. Does it make any difference that, in this decision, the judges explain their jurisdiction as being a normal exercise of statutory interpretation? What is the difference between statutory interpretation and constitutional review, if the result is that legislation may be invalid?

Is legislation enacted under the Parliament Act 1911 delegated legislation?

The argument is that legislation enacted under the Parliament Act differs from normal Acts of Parliament in that '*it is delegated or subordinate in the sense that its validity is open to investigation in the courts*'.[18] Lord Bingham rejected this argument on two grounds: first, because he said that the wording of s. 2(1) of the 1911 Act is clear—that legislation made under the provisions of the Act shall '*become an Act of Parliament*', wording that is not '*doubtful, ambiguous or obscure*', and which can only '*denote primary legislation*'.[19]

Jackson and ors v Her Majesty's Attorney General
[2005] UKHL 56 (13 October 2005)

Lord Bingham

[24] [...] The 1911 Act did, of course, effect an important constitutional change, but the change lay not in authorising a new form of sub-primary parliamentary legislation but in creating a new way of enacting primary legislation.

[He also rejected the argument that the 1911 Act delegated legislative power or authority to the House of Commons.]

[25] [...] Section 1 [dealing with money Bills] of the 1911 Act involved no delegation of legislative power and authority to the Commons but a statutory recognition of where such power and authority in relation to supply had long been understood to lie. It would be hard to read the very similar language in s 2 as involving a delegation either, since the overall object of the Act was not to enlarge the powers of the Commons but to restrict those of the Lords.

Lord Nicholls,[20] Lord Steyn,[21] Lord Hope,[22] and Lord Brown[23] all agreed.

---

[18] Ibid., [22], *per* Lord Bingham.
[19] Ibid., [24].
[20] See ibid., [63].
[21] See ibid., [94].
[22] See ibid., [111].
[23] See ibid., [187].

Use of the Parliament Act 1911 to push through fundamental constitutional change

A second main plank in the appellants' case was their argument that the procedure in the Parliament Act 1911 could not be used to make substantial constitutional changes, including the further enlargement of the power of the House of Commons that was purported to be achieved by the Parliament Act 1949. In essence, they said that the express limits set out in the 1911 Act (providing that the Parliamentary Act procedure is not applicable to money Bills, Bills seeking to extend the life of a Parliament, or provisional conformation Bills) are not the only restrictions on its use. As well as these express restrictions, there are other implied restrictions. Here, they relied on the Court of Appeal's judgment to argue that the Parliament Act procedure cannot be used to make significant constitutional changes. Changes such as the abolition of the House of Lords (in this context, the second chamber of Parliament) could, they argued, be made only with the assent of the House of Lords.

The Law Lords were divided in their response to this. In the next extract, you will see Lord Bingham's analysis. It sets out why he disagreed with the Court of Appeal. In his view, the Parliament Act procedure can be used for *any* Bill except those falling within the specific exceptions.

Jackson and ors v Her Majesty's Attorney General
[2005] UKHL 56 (13 October 2005)

Lord Bingham

[28] Sir Sydney [Kentridge QC, counsel for Jackson] submits that, in accordance with long-established principles of statutory interpretation, the courts will often imply qualifications into the literal meaning of wide and general words in order to prevent them having some unreasonable consequence which Parliament could not have intended. [...] He relies on these authorities as establishing (as it is put in the appellants' printed case)

> "that general words such as section 2(1) should not be read as authorising the doing of acts which adversely affect the basic principles on which the law of the United Kingdom is based in the absence of clear words authorising such acts. There is no more fundamental principle of law in the UK than the identity of the sovereign body. Section 2(1) should not be read as modifying the identity of the sovereign body unless its language admits of no other interpretation."

[...]

[29] The Attorney General does not, I think, take issue with the general principles relied on by the appellants, which are indeed familiar and well-established. But he invites the House to focus on the language of the 1911 Act, and in this he is right, since a careful study of the statutory language, read in its statutory and historical context and with the benefit of permissible aids to interpretation, is the essential first step in any exercise of statutory interpretation. Here, s. 2(1) makes provision, subject to three exceptions, for any public bill which satisfies the specified conditions to become an Act of Parliament without the consent of the Lords. Subject to these exceptions, s. 2(1) applies to "any" public bill. I cannot think of any broader expression the draftsman could have used. [...]

[30] Sir Sydney is of course correct in submitting that the literal meaning of even a very familiar expression may have to be rejected if it leads to an interpretation or consequence which

Parliament could not have intended. But in this case it is clear from the historical background that Parliament did intend the word "any", subject to the noted exceptions, to mean exactly what it said. […] During the passage of the Bill through Parliament, there were […] repeated attempts to enlarge the classes of bill to which the new procedure would not apply, but save for the amendment related to bills extending the maximum duration of Parliament they were uniformly rejected […] The suggestion that Parliament intended the conditions laid down in s. 2(1) to be incapable of amendment by use of the Act is in my opinion contradicted both by the language of the section and by the historical record. This was certainly the understanding of Dicey, who was no friend of the 1911 Act. In the first edition of his Introduction after 1911 (the 8th edition, 1915), he wrote at p. xxiii:

"The simple truth is that the Parliament Act has given to the House of Commons, or, in plain language, to the majority thereof, the power of passing any Bill whatever, provided always that the conditions of the Parliament Act, section 2, are complied with."

[31] The Court of Appeal concluded […] that there was power under the 1911 Act to make a "relatively modest and straightforward amendment" of the Act, including the amendment made by the 1949 Act, but not to making "changes of a fundamentally different nature to the relationship between the House of Lords and the Commons from those which the 1911 Act had made". This was not, as I understand, a solution which any party advocated in the Court of Appeal, and none supported it in the House. I do not think, with respect, that it can be supported in principle. The known object of the Parliament Bill, strongly resisted by the Conservative party and the source of the bitterness and intransigence which characterised the struggle over the Bill, was to secure the grant of Home Rule to Ireland. This was, by any standards, a fundamental constitutional change. So was the disestablishment of the Anglican Church in Wales, also well known to be an objective of the government. Attempts to ensure that the 1911 Act could not be used to achieve these objects were repeatedly made and repeatedly defeated. […] Whatever its practical merits, the Court of Appeal solution finds no support in the language of the Act, in principle or in the historical record. Had the government been willing to exclude changes of major constitutional significance from the operation of the new legislative scheme, it may very well be that the constitutional Conference of 1910 would not have broken down and the 1911 Act would never have been enacted.

[32] It is unnecessary for resolution of the present case to decide whether the 1911 (and now the 1949) Act could be relied on to extend the maximum duration of Parliament beyond five years. It does not seem likely that such a proposal would command popular and parliamentary support (save in a national emergency such as led to extensions, by consent of both Houses, during both world wars), knowledge of parliamentary tyranny during the Long Parliament would weigh against such a proposal and art. 3 of the First Protocol to the European Convention on Human Rights now requires elections at reasonable intervals. The Attorney General, however, submits that the 1911, and now the 1949, Act could in principle be used to amend or delete the reference to the maximum duration of Parliament in the parenthesis to s. 2(1), and that a further measure could then be introduced to extend the maximum duration. Sir Sydney contends that this is a procedure which s. 2(1) very clearly does not permit, stressing that the timetable in s. 2(1) was very closely linked to the maximum duration of Parliament which the Act laid down. It is common ground that s. 2(1) in its unamended form cannot without more be relied on to extend the maximum duration of Parliament, because a public bill to do so is outside the express terms of s. 2(1). But there is nothing in the 1911 Act to provide that it cannot be amended, and even if there were such a provision it could not bind a successor Parliament. Once it is accepted, as I have accepted,

that an Act passed pursuant to the procedures in s. 2(1), as amended in 1949, is in every sense an Act of Parliament having effect and entitled to recognition as such, I see no basis in the language of s. 2(1) or in principle for holding that the parenthesis in that subsection, or for that matter s. 7, are unamendable save with the consent of the Lords. It cannot have been contemplated that if, however improbably, the Houses found themselves in irreconcilable deadlock on this point, the government should have to resort to the creation of peers. However academic the point may be, I think the Attorney General is right.

The other Law Lords agreed with Lord Bingham in relation to what he said about the Court of Appeal's approach. But the *majority did not agree* that the Parliament Act procedure could be used to introduce *any* Bill, save those expressly excluded.

In the next extract, Lord Nicholls considers it implicit that the Parliament Act could not be used in order to remove the exclusion relating to Bills extending the life of Parliament, because this would be clearly contrary to the intention of Parliament when enacting the Parliament Act 1911.

Jackson and ors v Her Majesty's Attorney General
[2005] UKHL 56 (13 October 2005)

Lord Nicholls

[57] [...] The wording of s. 2(1) of the 1911 Act makes clear beyond a peradventure that when enacting this statute Parliament intended the Commons should not be able, by use of the new s. 2 procedure, unilaterally to extend the duration of Parliament beyond this newly-reduced limit of five years. The political party currently in control of the House of Commons, whichever it might be, could not use its majority in that House as the means whereby to postpone accountability to the electorate. The government could not, of itself, prolong its period in office beyond a maximum of five years. Despite the 1911 Act, such an extension would still require the approval of the House of Lords.

[58] So much is apparent from the express language of the Act. But would it be open to the House of Commons to do indirectly by two stages what the House cannot do directly in one stage? In other words, could the s. 2 procedure be used to force through a Bill deleting from s. 2 the words 'or a Bill containing any provision to extend the maximum duration of Parliament beyond five years'? If this were possible, the Commons could then use the s. 2 procedure to pass a Bill extending the duration of Parliament.

[59] In my view the answer to these questions is a firm 'no'. The Act setting up the new procedure expressly excludes its use for legislation extending the duration of Parliament. That express exclusion carries with it, by necessary implication, a like exclusion in respect of legislation aimed at achieving the same result by two steps rather than one. If this were not so the express legislative intention could readily be defeated.

[60] Thus far, therefore, it is apparent that in one significant respect there is to be found in s. 2 an implied restriction on the type of legislation for which the new procedure may be employed. The crucial question for the purposes of this appeal is whether any other restriction is implicit in s. 2.

[61] I consider there is none. Section 2 specifically excludes from its scope legislation extending the duration of Parliament. The implied exclusion, or restriction, discussed above

is based on the existence of this express exclusion. This implied restriction is necessary in order to render the express restriction effectual. It is ancillary to the express exclusion. Section 2 contains no other significant express restriction on the types of legislation for which the new procedure may be employed. I can see no warrant for implying into s. 2 any further restriction in this regard.

The idea advanced by Lord Nicholls and supported by a majority—that s. 2 of the Parliament Act 1911 cannot be amended using the 1911 Act procedure to remove the restriction on its use to extend the life of Parliament—raises profound questions. Does it mean that s. 2 is 'entrenched'?[24]

Alison L. Young, 'Hunting sovereignty: *Jackson v Her Majesty's Attorney-General*' [2006] Public Law 187, 194–5 (footnotes omitted)

[…] Lords Hope, Nicholls and Carswell provide an […] explanation that does not challenge continuing parliamentary legislative supremacy. The 1911 Act modified the way in which valid legislation can be enacted. In doing so it claims to modify the rule of recognition, the rule used to define valid legal enactments. The rule of recognition is both a legal rule and a political fact. As a legal rule, courts are bound to apply the rule of recognition. However, as a political fact, it cannot be modified and changed by Parliament alone. When recognising a change in the rule of recognition, courts are acknowledging a change in political fact. The Parliament Act 1949, for example, is accepted as valid not merely because it satisfies the legal requirements of s. 2(1), but also because its validity is recognised as a political fact, implying that the change in the rule of recognition instigated by the Parliament Act 1911 is also recognised as a political fact. Parliament is bound by the provisions of the Parliament Act 1911. But it is so bound not merely because the Parliament Act 1911 is a valid Act of Parliament, but also because the change in the rule of recognition, derived from the constitutional crisis resolved by this Act, has been recognised as a political fact. Consequently the Parliament of 1911 was not able to bind future Parliaments in and of itself. If future Parliaments are bound, they are bound by the rule of recognition, which was changed due to the new provisions being accepted internally by at least a core of officials administering the legal system. Continuing parliamentary legislative supremacy is preserved. As Wade recognised, the definition of a valid law-making authority and the procedures required to make valid law are logically prior rules. Dicey affords parliamentary legislative supremacy to a particular definition of Parliament passing legislation according to a particular procedure. This particular definition and procedure cannot be made by Parliament alone if continuing parliamentary legislative supremacy is to be preserved.

It is possible to achieve the same practical effect as entrenchment whilst preserving continuing parliamentary legislative supremacy. Modifications of the definition of Parliament or the way in which legislation is passed occur through a change in the rule of recognition. A change in the rule of recognition cannot be enacted by Parliament alone; it needs to be internally accepted by officials of the UK constitution, which includes the courts. The desirability of entrenchment should not determine whether the United Kingdom adopts a self-embracing theory of parliamentary legislative supremacy. Nor should it depend upon whether one accepts the claims of common law constitutionalism that empower the courts to challenge legislation which overturns fundamental principles of the constitution. Our description of the

---

[24] See Chapter 2.

nature of parliamentary legislative supremacy depends upon our assessment of the fundamental constitutional rule that determines the identity of the sovereign law-making body
and the procedures used to enact valid legislation and, more precisely, the way in which this
can be modified. Continuing parliamentary legislative supremacy requires that modification
cannot be achieved by Parliament acting alone. If, for example, we identify this fundamental
provision as part of the rule of recognition, its modification requires internal acceptance by
at least some of the officials of the legal system. Self-embracing parliamentary legislative
supremacy regards the fundamental rule as one that can be modified by Parliament alone.
Jennings, for example, regarded this rule as part of the common law. As statutory provisions
could override the common law, Parliament could modify the common law provisions governing the identity of the sovereign and its functions.

Does *Jackson* open the door to constitutional review of other Acts of Parliament?

Lord Steyn accepted that, as a matter of 'strict legalism', the Attorney General may be right
that the wording of s. 2(1) allows use of the Parliament Act procedure for *any* Bill that is not
expressly excluded. But he said that if the Parliament Act were ever used to make fundamental changes to the constitutional system, this could test '*the relative merits of strict legalism
and fundamental constitutional legal principle in the courts at the most fundamental level*'.

Jackson and ors v Her Majesty's Attorney General
[2005] UKHL 56 (13 October 2005)

Lord Steyn

[101] The potential consequences of a decision in favour of the Attorney General are far-
reaching. The Attorney General said at the hearing that the government might wish to use the
1949 Act to bring about constitutional changes such as altering the composition of the House
of Lords. The logic of this proposition is that the procedure of the 1949 Act could be used
by the government to abolish the House of Lords. Strict legalism suggests that the Attorney
General may be right. But I am deeply troubled about assenting to the validity of such an
exorbitant assertion of government power in our bi-cameral system. It may be that such an
issue would test the relative merits of strict legalism and constitutional legal principle in the
courts at the most fundamental level.

[102] But the implications are much wider. If the Attorney General is right the 1949 Act could
also be used to introduce oppressive and wholly undemocratic legislation. For example, it
could theoretically be used to abolish judicial review of flagrant abuse of power by a government or even the role of the ordinary courts in standing between the executive and citizens.
This is where we may have to come back to the point about the supremacy of Parliament.
We do not in the United Kingdom have an uncontrolled constitution as the Attorney General
implausibly asserts. In the European context the second *Factortame* decision made that
clear: [1991] 1 AC 603. The settlement contained in the Scotland Act 1998 also point to a
divided sovereignty. Moreover, the European Convention on Human Rights as incorporated
into our law by the Human Rights Act, 1998, created a new legal order. One must not assimi-
late the ECHR with multilateral treaties of the traditional type. Instead it is a legal order in
which the United Kingdom assumes obligations to protect fundamental rights, not in relation

to other states, but towards all individuals within its jurisdiction. The classic account given by Dicey of the doctrine of the supremacy of Parliament, pure and absolute as it was, can now be seen to be out of place in the modern United Kingdom. Nevertheless, the supremacy of Parliament is still the general principle of our constitution. It is a construct of the common law. The judges created this principle. If that is so, it is not unthinkable that circumstances could arise where the courts may have to qualify a principle established on a different hypothesis of constitutionalism. In exceptional circumstances involving an attempt to abolish judicial review or the ordinary role of the courts, the Appellate Committee of the House of Lords or a new Supreme Court may have to consider whether this is a constitutional fundamental which even a sovereign Parliament acting at the behest of a complaisant House of Commons cannot abolish. It is not necessary to explore the ramifications of this question in this opinion. No such issues arise on the present appeal.

[Lord Hope also considered the issue of the supremacy of Parliament.]

[104] I start where my learned friend Lord Steyn has just ended. Our constitution is dominated by the sovereignty of Parliament. But Parliamentary sovereignty is no longer, if it ever was, absolute. It is not uncontrolled in the sense referred to by Lord Birkenhead LC in *McCawley v The King* [1920] AC 691, 720. It is no longer right to say that its freedom to legislate admits of no qualification whatever. Step by step, gradually but surely, the English principle of the absolute legislative sovereignty of Parliament which Dicey derived from Coke and Blackstone is being qualified. [...]

[107] Nor should we overlook the fact that one of the guiding principles that were identified by Dicey at p. 35 was the universal rule or supremacy throughout the constitution of ordinary law. [...] In its modern form, now reinforced by the European Convention on Human Rights and the enactment by Parliament of the Human Rights Act 1998, this principle protects the individual from arbitrary government. The rule of law enforced by the courts is the ultimate controlling factor on which our constitution is based. The fact that your Lordships have been willing to hear this appeal and to give judgment upon it is another indication that the courts have a part to play in defining the limits of Parliament's legislative sovereignty.

[Lord Hope concluded his judgment as follows.]

[126] [...] The principle of parliamentary sovereignty which in the absence of higher authority, has been created by the common law is built upon the assumption that Parliament represents the people whom it exists to serve.

[127] Like others of your Lordships I am unable to accept the distinction which the Court of Appeal drew between what it described [...] as relatively modest changes and changes [...] of a fundamentally different nature. The wording of s. 2(1) does not invite such a distinction. It raises questions of fact and degree about the effect of legislation which are quite unsuited for adjudication by a court. The argument that some provisions of the Acts of Union of 1707 are fundamental law as they were based on a treaty which preceded the creation of the United Kingdom Parliament is a different argument. Of course, as Dicey at p. 79 recognised, the sovereignty of Parliament is limited by the possibility of popular resistance to its exercise. Trust will be eroded if the s. 2(1) procedure is used to enact measures which are, as Lord Steyn puts it, exorbitant or are not proportionate. Nevertheless the final exercise of judgment on these matters must be left to the House of Commons as the elected chamber. It is for that chamber to decide where the balance lies when that procedure is being resorted to.

As we saw in Chapter 2, some constitutional experts hold the view that it is possible—indeed, desirable—for the British courts to reconsider their role in adjudicating on Acts of Parliament. For them, parliamentary supremacy is an outmoded concept that no longer reflects the 'true' meaning of democracy. Professor Jeffrey Jowell is one of them. Consider what he has to say about the *Jackson* case in the following extract.

Jeffrey Jowell, 'Parliamentary sovereignty under the new constitutional hypothesis' [2006] Public Law 562, 577–9 (footnotes omitted)

Who speaks for the constitution?

In the absence of any written constitutional order of a "logically prior" nature, by what authority could the courts prohibit fundamental violations of the rule of law and other rights inherent in this changed hypothesis of constitutional democracy? If we were looking for altered rules of recognition, we could draw support from the fact that in *Jackson* the House of Lords did indeed review Acts of Parliament (albeit without needing to impugn their validity). The review was justified under the guise of statutory interpretation. Yet the majority of the Law Lords engaged in exactly the kind of exercise that characterises review in countries with written constitutions, in particular when they considered whether any constitutional limits (such as prolonging the life of Parliament) stood in the way of an amendment to the 1911 Act. Most written constitutions contain generalised standards which do not supply cut-and-dried answers and need implications to be made about contemporary constitutional standards. The precedential force of *Jackson* was acknowledged by Lord Hope when he said: "The fact that your Lordships have been willing to hear this appeal and to give judgment upon it is another indication that the courts have a part to play in defining the limits of Parliament's legislative sovereignty."

Even Lord Bingham, who firmly endorsed parliamentary sovereignty, justified the judicial review on the ground that otherwise the points raised by the appellants could not be raised at all, which he considered " would not be […] consistent with the rule of law" !

One of the most important statements of constitutional principle was made right at the outset of the more intrusive judicial review of administrative action. In the famous *Padfield* case,[25] the House of Lords rejected the Minister's contention that the wide power conferred upon him amounted to "unfettered discretion". Lord Upjohn had no truck with the notion of any discretion being so broad. Even if the power were expressly defined by the term "unfettered", he said that: " [T]he use of that adjective, (' unfettered') even in an Act of Parliament, can do nothing to unfetter the control which the judiciary have over the executive, namely that in exercising their powers the latter must act lawfully and that is a matter to be determined by looking at the Act and its scope and object in conferring a discretion upon the Minister rather than by the use of adjectives […]".

If executive power may not be unfettered, or free from judicial review, what principle permits the legislature to be unbounded, or untroubled by any judicial oversight? The notion that no power may be unconstrained is compelling as a general democratic principle. Lord Steyn in *Jackson* drew support for the notion of a "new constitutional order" from the incorporation into our law of the European Convention on Human Rights by way of our Human Rights Act 1998. That Act does create new constitutional expectations, namely, that both Parliament and government will respect the rights designated in the European Convention on Human Rights. However, the great tyrannies of the 20th century had already demonstrated the

[25] See Chapter 16.

dangers of unconfined power, regardless of whether it was sanctioned by popular consent. As Lord Cooke has put it: "The truth is [...] that some rights are inherent and fundamental to democratic civilised society. Conventions, constitutions, bills of rights and the like respond by recognising rather than creating them."

It can no longer be doubted that one of the preconditions of any constitutional democracy, properly so-called, is respect for certain rights that neither the executive nor the legislature, representative as it may be, should be able to deny with impunity. But how convincing is the claim of the supporters of parliamentary sovereignty that its demise would have the effect of simply transferring unfettered power from the elected legislature to the unelected judiciary? That claim is misleading. It ignores the fact that the spheres of the judiciary and the legislature are distinct. For a start, even under the model of a rights-based democracy, legislative authority inevitably contains a wide area of discretion to make social and economic policy, over which the courts have no dominium. It is not for the judges to second-guess the legislature on utilitarian calculations of the social good. Their role is strictly confined to the limited issue of whether the various inherent elements of democracy have been infringed by other branches of government and therefore cannot be sustained. Even within the bounds of parliamentary sovereignty, as we have seen, the courts already exercise this role to some degree. The historic dialogue and process of iteration and self-correction between Parliament and the courts has allowed the development of public law rights and duties to which both the legislature and judiciary have contributed.

If parliamentary sovereignty were to be discarded as our prime constitutional principle, it is true that "the last word" would pass from the legislature to the courts—but only on the question whether the legislature has strayed beyond the line of its democratic confines. The assertion of this authority would require of the courts a boldness to interpret constitutional principles as they ought to be. However, it will also require a modest appreciation of their own limitations. There will be issues on the margins of legal principle and socio-economic policy which will inevitably invite the charge of judicial overreach. Parliament, however, is not in a position to judge these matters in its own cause. And there is much to be said for having these decisions made by those who are insulated from the necessity to respond to the perceived opinion of the moment.

If a future Parliament were to pass a law which infringed the rule of law or other constitutional fundamentals, it may be that our judges will feel that they still lack sufficient authority to strike it down on the ground that it subverts the implied conditions—the essential features—of our constitutional democracy. However, some of those conditions, such as free and regular elections, underlie the legitimacy of the principle of parliamentary sovereignty itself. Others, such as access to justice, are necessary requirements of a modern hypothesis of constitutionalism. Some of the dicta in *Jackson* confirm the real possibility that, in the words of Lord Hope: "The rule of law enforced by the courts is the ultimate controlling factor on which our constitution is based".

QUESTIONS

1. 'The bedrock of the British constitution is, and in 1911 was, the supremacy of the Crown in Parliament' (Lord Bingham, at [9]); 'The rule of law enforced by the courts is the ultimate controlling factor on which our constitution is based' (Lord Hope, at [107]). Can these two dicta be reconciled?

2. Discuss the following.

'The classic account given by Dicey of the doctrine of the supremacy of Parliament, pure and absolute as it was, can now be seen to be out of place in the modern United Kingdom. Nevertheless, the supremacy of Parliament is still the general principle of our constitution. It is a construct of the common law. The judges created this principle. If that is so, it is not unthinkable that circumstances could arise where the courts may have to qualify a principle established on a different hypothesis of constitutionalism.' (Lord Steyn, at [102])

3. Should final exercise of judgment in constitutional matters be left to the judges or to elected politicians?

'Trust will be eroded if the s. 2(1) procedure is used to enact measures which are, as Lord Steyn puts it, exorbitant or are not proportionate. Nevertheless the final exercise of judgment on these matters must be left to the House of Commons as the elected chamber. It is for that chamber to decide where the balance lies when that procedure is being resorted to.' (Lord Hope at [127])

Do you think that the Lords (that is, the upper House of Parliament) have too much, too little, or about the right amount of power in the legislative process? (Consider both the Salisbury–Addison convention and the Parliament Acts in answering this question.)

5 CONCLUDING COMMENTS

This chapter has examined the relationship between the House of Commons and the House of Lords. The composition and powers of the Lords continue to be debated. For the latest developments on reforms, visit the Online Resource Centre.

ONLINE RESOURCE CENTRE

Further information about the themes discussed in this chapter can be found on the Online Resource Centre at www.oxfordtextbooks.co.uk/orc/lesueur2e/

PART IV

JUDICIAL AND DISPUTE RESOLUTION FUNCTIONS

INTRODUCTION TO JUDICIAL AND DISPUTE RESOLUTION FUNCTIONS

CENTRAL ISSUES

1. One of the main tasks of a constitution is to provide a justice system for resolving disputes arising from the enforcement, application, and interpretation of the law.

2. The public must have confidence that judges possess the necessary intellectual and personal skills, and that the judiciary is independent.

3. Systems of redress must be fit for their purpose. They must cater for the sort of problems or wrongs that people suffer; their procedures should be suitable; and adequate remedies should be provided when wrongs are suffered.

4. Within the United Kingdom, there are three distinct territorial jurisdictions:

(a) England and Wales; (b) Scotland; and (c) Northern Ireland. Each has its own court system and head of judiciary.

5. The UK Supreme Court is the constitutional meeting point of the three jurisdictions and is the final court of appeal from most courts in the United Kingdom.

6. European integration has made the two main European courts—the European Court of Justice (ECJ) and European Court of Human Rights (ECtHR)—extremely important within the United Kingdom. These two courts are totally separate and should not be confused with each other.

1 THEMES AND ISSUES

This introduction to Part IV of the book is an overview of the main ideas, concepts, and facts that will be covered in Chapter 14 (The judiciary), Chapter 15 (Administrative justice: Tribunals and ombudsmen), Chapter 16 (Judicial review), Chapter 17 (Human rights in UK courts), and Chapter 18 ('EU law in UK courts').

So far, we have considered the executive function—to make and implement policy—and the legislative function, by which policies are enacted and become law. In this part of the book, we are concerned with the way disputes are resolved.

One of the main tasks of a constitutional system is to provide methods through which people can obtain definitive answers when they have disputes over the enforcement, application, and meaning of the law. It is the task of the various elements of the justice system to ensure that the law is interpreted and applied, and that these functions are performed in a manner that is fair, and is seen to be fair to all concerned. These tasks fall upon all who are involved in the justice system, whether as non-lawyer (lay) members of tribunals and magistrates, as professional judges sitting in trial courts, or as senior judges in appellate courts.

It is vital that the public is confident that justice will be delivered by people of integrity who possess the necessary intellectual and personal skills. The public must also be confident that judges approach their task impartially as between the parties and that the judiciary, as an institution, is independent from the other branches of government.[1] (This is particularly evident when they deal with disputes between individuals and the executive.)

Chapter 14 examines the constitutional position of judges within the United Kingdom, looking in particular at judicial independence and at the process by which judges are appointed. It also looks closely at the important matter of judicial diversity. Achieving a more diverse judiciary is now recognized to be an important goal: while there has been progress, this has been slow, and some argue that more radical steps are needed. As with many of the themes in this book, this is very much a live and controversial issue.

In Chapters 15–18, we are concerned with the main avenues of redress available for dealing with disputes involving public authorities. In Chapter 15, we look at redress mechanisms outside the court system—a terrain often referred to as the landscape of 'administrative justice'. This includes the work of ombudsmen and tribunals. Chapter 16 examines the grounds on which the courts will judicially review the legality of actions taken by public authorities; Chapter 17 examines the use of human rights arguments against these authorities; and Chapter 18 examines the reception of EU law into national law by the UK courts.

In these chapters, we return to some of the questions and controversies first discussed in Part I. The proper constitutional function of judges in a democracy continues to be the subject of academic and political debate. For supporters of the relatively recent changes, the greater role now played by the courts through the grounds of judicial review, enforcing EU law, and protecting human rights, is a welcome counterweight to the previously overly 'political constitution'. For critics, judicial power is problematic: the judicial process is too limited and the judges too unrepresentative to make it right to entrust them with powers to adjudicate about issues of social and political controversy.[2]

2 REDRESS MECHANISMS: ARE THEY FIT FOR PURPOSE?

As you read through this part of the book, ask yourself whether the systems of redress are fit for their purpose. Do they deal with the sort of problems or wrongs that people suffer? Are the procedures that they use suitable? Do they provide adequate remedies?

Broadly speaking, the systems deal with three types of claim against public bodies. The first and probably most common situation is that in which someone claims a benefit or a

---

[1] For discussion of separation of powers, see Chapter 4.
[2] See discussion of legal and political constitutionalism in Chapter 2.

service from a public authority and complains that the authority has made a mistake when dealing with their case: the complainant essentially says that the public authority has got it wrong and should make a more favourable decision. In practice, many complaints of this sort can be resolved quite quickly by the authority having another look at the case and checking to see whether a mistake has been made. If the claimed mistake is not rectified at this stage, there is often (although not always) a right to appeal against the authority's decision to a tribunal (or sometimes a court). We shall deal with such situations in Chapter 15.

Chapter 15 also deals with a second type of complaint, namely the situation in which someone claims to have been wronged by 'maladministration'—in other words, that the public body has behaved badly and has operated in a manner that falls below acceptable standards (for example, letters have been lost, questions are not answered, mistakes have been made, and so on). Such administrative failings can cause injustice, and leave people feeling frustrated and angry, but they may not give rise to legal claims that can be taken to the courts. Complaints that injustice has been caused by maladministration can be taken to an ombudsman, who may investigate and help to secure a remedy, as well as improvements in the way in which the public authority operates. There are now several ombudsmen in the public sector.

The third situation that we consider within the field of public law is that in which a claimant can establish that a public body has unlawfully infringed his or her Convention rights, or acted in a way that gives rise to grounds for seeking judicial review. (Note that public bodies must also comply with obligations arising from the law or contract or tort, but this book does not deal with these branches of the law.) It is at this point that the senior courts may become involved. Typically, the legal arguments will be that the public authority has committed one or more (or a combination) of the following errors.

(a) It has misinterpreted or misunderstood the applicable law.

(b) It has abused its discretionary powers by, for example, taking into account irrelevant factors or failing to take account of relevant factors.

(c) It has made a procedural error or acted unfairly.

(d) It has acted incompatibly with 'Convention rights' contrary to s. 6 of the Human Rights Act 1998.

(e) It has breached enforceable obligations imposed by EU law.

The first three of these arguments are considered in Chapter 16; the fourth is considered in Chapter 17; and the fifth is considered in Chapter 18.

(a) ARE THE PROCEDURES SUITABLE?

Procedures are important and getting procedures right is not easy. The achievement of proportionate dispute resolution (PDR) has been one of the goals of reform in recent years. Essentially, this means that public bodies should do all that they can to 'get it right' in the first place; if disputes do arise, then the procedures used should be suited to the dispute. Expensive court-like processes are not always necessary or desirable, and the drive for PDR has encouraged the development and use of alternatives to the courts, including mediation. In Chapter 15, we look more closely at the meaning and implications of PDR, and at some of the reasons why this concept is controversial.

The courts resolve disputes by using an adversarial process: the parties present their respective cases and show the weaknesses in the opposing case; an impartial judge then reaches a decision. This procedure has evolved over the centuries and has become the hallmark of the common law approach to adjudication in the courts. But this procedure is not suitable for resolving all disputes. As we shall see in Chapter 15, tribunals vary in terms of the procedures that they adopt: some are very similar to courts in the way they deal with disputes; others are more inquisitorial in approach, with the tribunal chair and members taking the lead by asking questions; others still are far less formal and resemble a meeting around a table. In principle, procedures should suit the nature of the issues. Adversarial procedures may be suitable when the parties are represented by lawyers and in cases in which the arguments are focused on issues of law—but they are less suitable, or necessary, where one side is an ordinary person who is not represented and in cases in which the main dispute concerns factual matters.

Ombudsmen do not use adversarial procedures, but are investigative in their approach. This means that they are in control of the matters to be examined, and they decide what evidence needs to be collected and what questions are to be asked. Inquisitorial approaches are considered much more suitable than adversarial procedures for investigating how public authorities have handled matters, not least because they are considered better suited for establishing trust and securing the cooperation of public bodies.

(b) ARE REMEDIES ADEQUATE?

A further matter concerns remedies. One of the main questions to be asked about a system of redress is whether it provides suitable remedies when grievances or claims are upheld. For example, we shall see that there has been discussion about the inability of the Parliamentary Ombudsman (the organization responsible for investigating central government departments and agencies) to award legally enforceable remedies when it has upheld complaints that injustice has been caused by the maladministration. Some see this as a fatal gap; others defend it on the grounds that this power would adversely affect the ombudsman's ability to work with departments. A related view is that the ombudsman should not be judged by its power to secure legally enforceable remedies for individuals, but rather by its broader role in achieving systemic changes. This dispute illustrates the basic point that different people will see redress procedures in different ways. Claimants and their advisers will understandably judge procedures according to the outcomes that can be achieved for them; others will be more concerned about the general impact that bodies such as ombudsmen have on the wider machinery of government.

Similar issues arise in relation to judicial review. Often, people use the judicial review procedure because they want to force a public body to make a more favourable decision in their case—but judicial review is not well suited to achieving this outcome. Judicial review provides a legal check on the process by which decisions are taken and on whether the body has acted within its legal powers; it does not determine whether decisions of public bodies are right or wrong and it does not lead to judges replacing a challenged decision with their own decision. A successful judicial review claim will often result in a public authority being required to retake its decision: provided that the body follows the correct process, it may be able to make the same decision again. Unless this is explained to claimants, it can cause confusion and feelings of frustration.

There is an important difference here between a judicial review claim based on the common law and a case in which a claimant relies on the Human Rights Act 1998 (HRA) to say that the public authority has infringed his or her Convention rights. Where the HRA is used, the court is concerned with whether the authority has infringed rights. If it has, this cannot be rectified by the authority simply looking at the decision again and then reaching the same decision. This is explained further in Chapter 17.

We shall see in Chapter 16 that a further weakness of judicial review, as it operates in England and Wales, is that successful claimants do not have a right to any remedy: all remedies are discretionary.

Moreover, successful claimants cannot obtain damages for any losses suffered (unless the public body is liable for a tort as well as acting unlawfully in a public law sense). Similarly, in Chapter 17, we will see that while damages may be awarded for breaches of the HRA, the awards are often very low and there has been much criticism of the principles applied by the courts.

(c) A SUMMARY

Box IV.1 summarizes some of the aspects of the discussion so far.

BOX IV.1 SUMMARY

	Independent	Binding decisions	Decision criteria	Method/procedure
Internal complaints/ reviews	No	Yes	Legality, merits, and maladministration	Inquisitorial; usually written
Ombudsmen	Yes	No	Maladministration	Inquisitorial; written
Tribunals	Yes	Yes	Legality and merits	Adversarial; inquisitorial; oral
Courts	Yes	Yes	Legality	Adversarial; oral

Source: Based on table supplied in Tom Mullen, *The Way Forward: Final Report of the Administrative Justice Steering Group* (2009, Glasgow: Administrative Justice in Scotland), p. 39

---

3 COURTS IN A MULTILEVEL SYSTEM

We need to say a word or two about the different jurisdictional 'systems' that are relevant to dispute resolution in the United Kingdom and the main courts that will be discussed in the following chapters.

As a result of the United Kingdom's development as a union between formerly independent countries in the seventeenth century (the union of England and Wales with Scotland to create Great Britain) and in the early nineteenth century (the union of Great Britain and Ireland, to form the United Kingdom)[3], within the United Kingdom, there are three distinct territorial jurisdictions: (a) England and Wales; (b) Scotland; and (c) Northern Ireland. Each has its own court system and head of judiciary (see Box IV.2).

BOX IV.2 HEADS OF THE JUDICIARY

England and Wales	Lord Chief Justice of England and Wales	Constitutional Reform Act 2005, s. 7
Scotland	The Lord President (of the Court of Session)	Judiciary and Courts (Scotland) Act 2008, s. 2
Northern Ireland	Lord Chief Justice of Northern Ireland	Justice (Northern Ireland) Act 2002, s. 12

---

[3] See Chapter 5.

The judges and heads of judiciary of the three jurisdictions carry out most of their work separately. Each head of the judiciary has their own channel of communication with the UK Parliament.

Constitutional Reform Act 2005, s. 5(1)

The chief justice of any part of the United Kingdom may lay before Parliament written representations on matters that appear to him to be matters of importance relating to the judiciary, or otherwise to the administration of justice, in that part of the United Kingdom.

Note that s. 5 is careful to make clear that 'matters' do not include those that are within the legislative competence of the Scottish Parliament or the Northern Ireland Assembly. In relation to devolved matters, the Lord President and the Lord Chief Justice of Northern Ireland have to look to their respective legislatures.

(a) THE COURTS IN SCOTLAND

The following account of the courts in Scotland is taken from the 2009 report of the Scottish Civil Courts Review.

Report of the Scottish Civil Courts Review (2009), ch. 3

The Court of Session

2. The Court of Session is the highest civil court in Scotland. It sits in Edinburgh and has jurisdiction throughout Scotland. It is divided into the Outer House, which hears cases at first instance, and the Inner House, which deals mainly with appeals.

3. The Court deals with a wide range of civil matters including commercial, personal injury, property, taxation, and family cases. It alone can hear applications for judicial review [...].

The Outer House

9. In the Outer House cases are heard by a judge (known as a Lord Ordinary) sitting alone or, in certain cases, with a jury. There are currently 24 judges in the Outer House, most of whom also sit in the High Court of Justiciary, the supreme criminal court.

The Inner House

26. The Inner House hears appeals from the Outer House, sheriff court and certain tribunals and other bodies. It is divided into two Divisions: the First Division, presided over by the Lord President, and the Second Division, presided over by the Lord Justice Clerk; both Divisions are of equal authority. [...] Appeals are generally heard by a bench of three judges. On occasion, if a case is of particular difficulty or importance or if the Court has to consider overruling a binding authority, a larger bench will be convened.

[...]

28. A further appeal lies from the Inner House to the [UK Supreme Court].

The Sheriff Court

29. Scotland is divided into six sheriffdoms, each presided over by a sheriff principal who amongst his other duties hears appeals in civil matters and is responsible for the management

of the sheriff courts in his sheriffdom. The sheriffdoms are sub-divided into a total of forty-nine sheriff court districts, each with a court presided over by one or more sheriffs. In the larger urban areas, particularly Edinburgh and Glasgow, a number of resident and floating sheriffs hear a large volume of cases every day; in rural areas one sheriff may cover a number of courts and sit only on particular weekdays. [...]

30. Sheriff courts deal with civil, criminal and commissary matters. A wide range of civil matters are heard, including personal injury, contractual disputes, housing and family cases. If the sum sued for is £5,000 or less the action must be raised in the sheriff court; there is no upper limit. Criminal cases dealt with are either solemn (more serious cases involving trial on indictment before a sheriff sitting with a jury) or summary (less serious cases involving a trial where there is no jury).

(b) THE COURTS IN ENGLAND AND WALES

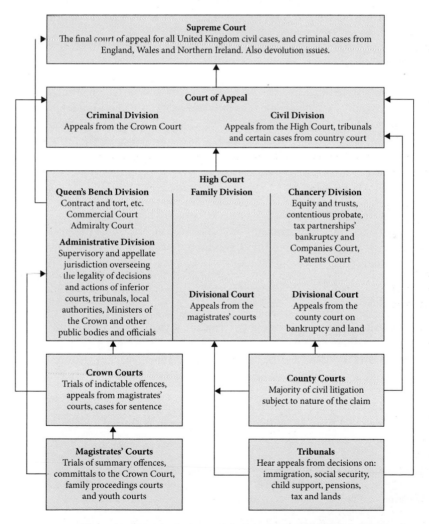

Supreme Court
The final court of appeal for all United Kingdom civil cases, and criminal cases from England, Wales and Northern Ireland. Also devolution issues.

Court of Appeal

Criminal Division
Appeals from the Crown Court

Civil Division
Appeals from the High Court, tribunals and certain cases from country court

High Court

Queen's Bench Division
Contract and tort, etc.
Commercial Court
Admiralty Court

Administrative Division
Supervisory and appellate jurisdiction overseeing the legality of decisions and actions of inferior courts, tribunals, local authorities, Ministers of the Crown and other public bodies and officials

Family Division

Divisional Court
Appeals from the magistrates' courts

Chancery Division
Equity and trusts, contentious probate, tax partnerships' bankruptcy and Companies Court, Patents Court

Divisional Court
Appeals from the county court on bankruptcy and land

Crown Courts
Trials of indictable offences, appeals from magistrates' courts, cases for sentence

County Courts
Majority of civil litigation subject to nature of the claim

Magistrates' Courts
Trials of summary offences, committals to the Crown Court, family proceedings courts and youth courts

Tribunals
Hear appeals from decisions on: immigration, social security, child support, pensions, tax and lands

Figure IV.1 The organizational chart of the courts in England and Wales

Source: Her majesty's court service http://www.hmcourts-service.gov.uk/aboutus/structure/index.htm

The magistrates' courts

Magistrates' courts deal with the less serious criminal cases and some civil matters.

The Crown Court

The Crown Court deals with more serious criminal cases, such as murder, rape, or robbery. It also handles cases on appeal and those referred to them by magistrates' courts. Trials are heard by a judge and a jury.

The County Court

The County Court sits in locations across England and Wales. It deals with civil matters, such as: claims for debt repayment, return of goods bought on credit, personal injury, and breach of contract; and family issues such as divorce or adoption; and housing disputes, including certain homelessness appeals from decisions of local housing authorities. Cases in the County Court are heard by a judge without a jury.

The High Court

The High Court sits in three divisions: the Chancery Division; the Queen's Bench Division; and the Family Division. Each Division has its own lead judge.[4] The most important for constitutional lawyers is the Queen's Bench Division, which includes the Administrative Court. This handles judicial review claims. Until April 2009, claims for judicial review had to be made in London; they can now be dealt with in centres at Cardiff, Manchester, Birmingham, and Leeds.

The Court of Appeal

The Court of Appeal sits in London. It has a civil section (headed by the Master of the Rolls) and a criminal section (headed by the Lord Chief Justice). The Court of Appeal is staffed by Lord Justices of Appeal. The Civil Division hears appeals from the High Court, the county court, and from certain tribunals.

(c) WALES

Although Wales has had a devolved government system since 1998, with the National Assembly for Wales producing distinctively Welsh legislation,[5] it does not have its own system of courts and is not yet regarded as an entirely distinct *legal* jurisdiction separate from that of England, although steps are being taken to establish a separate jurisdiction in Wales.

Tim H. Jones and Jane M. Williams, 'Wales as a jurisdiction' [2004] Public Law 78, 100 (footnotes omitted)

Taken together with the law-making powers of the National Assembly, and the growing tendency of Parliament to legislate separately for Wales, developments within the legal system have given rise to the phenomenon of 'Legal Wales'. It would be a mistake to dismiss the

---

[4] See Chapter 13.
[5] See Chapter 5.

significance of post-devolution changes on the basis that they do not amount to a jurisdiction that is more clearly separate from that of England, such as exists in Northern Ireland or Scotland. [...] Wales remains a jurisdiction that is emerging from the unified legal system of England and Wales. This is a process that deserves to be examined in its own terms. The trend towards greater differentiation in the public law area is likely to continue, whether or not the National Assembly gains primary legislative powers. Public bodies in Wales increasingly are going to be exercising powers that are different from their English counterparts.

In 2011, the National Assembly for Wales started an inquiry into the establishment of a separate Welsh jurisdiction.[6]

(d) THE COURTS IN NORTHERN IRELAND

The court system in Northern Ireland closely resembles that in England and Wales, although it has its own High Court judges and its own Northern Ireland Court of Appeal, which sits in Belfast.

(e) THE UK SUPREME COURT

The constitutional meeting point of the three separate legal jurisdictions is the UK Supreme Court. This court serves as a final court of appeal from most courts in the three territorial jurisdictions—the exception being the High Court of Justiciary in Scotland, which is the final court of appeal for Scottish criminal cases. The UK Supreme Court is also the final arbiter of 'division of powers' questions that may arise under the devolution system.[7] As s. 41 of the Constitutional Reform Act 2005 makes clear, the status of the Court differs according to whether it is acting as a final court of appeal from one of the territorial jurisdictions (when its judgments are formally binding only in the courts of the jurisdiction in question) or in relation to devolution adjudication (when the UK Supreme Court acts as a court of the whole United Kingdom).

Constitutional Reform Act 2005

41 Relation to other courts etc.

(1) Nothing in this Part is to affect the distinctions between the separate legal systems of the parts of the United Kingdom.

(2) A decision of the Supreme Court on appeal from a court of any part of the United Kingdom, other than a decision on a devolution matter, is to be regarded as the decision of a court of that part of the United Kingdom.

(3) A decision of the Supreme Court on a devolution matter—

(a) is not binding on that Court when making such a decision;

(b) otherwise, is binding in all legal proceedings.

---

[6] See http://www.senedd.assemblywales.org/mgIssueHistoryHome.aspx?IId=2594.
[7] See Chapter 5.

(4) In this section 'devolution matter' means—

　(a) a question referred to the Supreme Court under section 33 of the Scotland Act 1998 (c. 46) or section 11 of the Northern Ireland Act 1998 (c. 47);

　(b) a devolution issue as defined in Schedule 8 to the Government of Wales Act 1998 (c. 38), Schedule 6 to the Scotland Act 1998 or Schedule 10 to the Northern Ireland Act 1998.

Jack Straw, Lord Chancellor and Secretary of State for Justice, *Supreme Court Opening Is Major Milestone for Government's Constitutional Reform,* 16 October 2009

The opening of the UK Supreme Court marks the culmination of a long—and very British—process of separating out the branches of the state. The official opening today finally delivers an idea which was first proposed by Gladstone in 1873, that the UK's highest court should be separated from Parliament.

The creation of this new British institution is a significant step in the evolution of British tradition, culture and history—the very groundwork for our constitution which has developed organically over centuries—and provides greater clarity by further separating the judiciary from the legislature, underlining the independence of our judicial system.

Situated in Parliament Square—one of the most historic and recognisable public spaces in the world—the Supreme Court sits alongside other key British institutions—Houses of Parliament, Westminster Abbey and the Treasury, further emphasising the clear and physical separation of powers.

This new institution will be much more visible than the one it replaces, providing greater access to the public than ever before. No longer will our highest court in the land be hidden at the end of a corridor in the House of Lords, but instead members of the public will be able to walk in off the street to see for themselves the work of our senior judiciary.

The United Kingdom Supreme Court was set up under the Constitutional Reform Act 2005. The Law Lords of the Appellate Committee have now become the first Justices and the Senior Law Lord, the President. The Supreme Court began its business on 1 October 2009.

It will be the final court of appeal for all civil cases in the United Kingdom, all criminal cases in England, Wales and Northern Ireland and will also assume the devolution jurisdiction of the Judicial Committee of the Privy Council.

4 THE JUDICIAL ARCHITECTURE OF THE EU

We have already seen that European integration has made the two main European courts—the European Court of Justice (ECJ) and European Court of Human Rights (ECtHR)—extremely important within the United Kingdom. Before reading the chapters that follow, you may want to have another look at what was said about the ECtHR in Chapter 6. In the next sections, we look briefly at the judicial architecture of the European Union (EU) and the significance of the ECJ.

The European Union is part of a multilevel political system which is characterized by a number of institutions on each level competing for the available power resources. The relationship between the Court of Justice of the EU and the higher and lower national courts is both cooperative and competitive. The Court of Justice is named in Article 13 TEU as one of the institutions charged with ensuring 'the consistency, effectiveness and continuity of its policies and actions'.

Article 19 TEU states that the 'Court of Justice of the European Union' (which is the official title) and consists of three courts:

- the Court of Justice (still referred to as the ECJ),

- the General Court (which is the new name for the Court of First Instance, created in 1988)

- specialised courts, for which the Civil Service Tribunal (CST, created in 2004) is the only current example.

The seat of all three Courts is in Luxembourg. The ECJ's workload is reasonably steady: it receives between 500 and 600 new cases each year, completes between 500 and 600 cases each year, and has about 750 cases pending. The workload of the General Court is comparable, although it routinely has a higher number of cases pending (in excess of 1,000) each year.[8]

> The European Court of Justice in Luxembourg is frequently confused with the European Court of Human Rights, based in Strasbourg, or with the International Court of Justice in The Hague. The former was established by the Council of Europe to ensure observance of the European Convention on Human Rights and Fundamental Freedoms, while the latter is one of the principal organs of the United Nations and deals with disputes on questions of international law that are submitted to it by the States concerned. The Court of Justice of the EU should also be distinguished from the European Court of Auditors, whose headquarters are next door in Luxembourg, but which is not a judicial body.

House of Lords, European Union Committee, *The Future Role of the European Court of Justice* 6th Report of Session 2003–04

[10] International courts having jurisdiction over sovereign states are, compared to the proliferation of courts (civil, criminal and administrative) in most countries, relatively rare. Even more scarce are international courts to which the individual has a right of access. The Council of Europe's Convention for the Protection of Human Rights and Fundamental Freedoms (ECHR, drawn up in 1950) took the radical step of creating a Commission and a Court having jurisdiction to examine petitions from individuals claiming violation of their human rights. The ECHR regime also subjects States (members of the Council of Europe) to international legal scrutiny of their treatment of their own nationals on their own territory. But when establishing the European Communities the Member States went even further. They created institutions having the power in certain areas to make laws which were directly applicable in the Member States. They set up a European Court of Justice with ultimate authority in the Community legal order and the duty (under Article 220 of the EC Treaty) to ensure the observance of the law.

The inclusion of an independent judicial authority in the European Union's institutional structure was an integral part of the design of the organisation from its inception as the

---

[8] HL European Union Committee, Fourteenth Report, 'The Workload of the Court of Justice of the European Union', 6 April 2011, Ch. 3.

European Coal and Steel Community in 1951. From 1957 until 1989 the ECJ was the only court of the European Community. It has the following three functions:

- – to review the legality of the acts of the institutions of the European Union;
- – to ensure that the Member States comply with their obligations under EU law;
- – to interpret EU law at the request of the national courts and tribunals.

The composition of the ECJ expanded as the EU enlarged as it recruits one judge from every Member State. At present, it has 28 judges and eight Advocates General who both appointed by the governments of the Member States for a renewable term of six years. Under Art.253 TFEU, the judges and Advocates General are appointed 'by common accord of the governments of the member states' from candidates 'whose independence is beyond doubt and who possess the qualifications required for appointment to the highest judicial offices in their respective countries ...'. The number of Advocates-General may **rise to eleven if requested by ECJ. Such an increase would give Poland a permanent Advocate General (alongside Germany, France, Italy, Spain, and the UK), and two rotating posts** nominated by the smaller and medium-sized Member States.[9] Advocates General assist the ECJ in the form of a legal opinion. An Advocate General is assigned to a particular case in which she independently and impartially examines the legal issues and makes a recommendation. The AG's recommendation carries great weight and is usually followed, but it is not legally binding on the ECJ.

By the mid-1980s it became clear that the single-tier model could no longer manage the increasing workload of the ECJ. Whereas in 1975 the time necessary to respond to questions referred by national courts for preliminary rulings was six months on average, by 1988 it had increased to 17.5 months.

The General Court was established as the Court of First Instance in October 1989 with jurisdiction to decide, at first instance, certain categories of cases brought by natural or legal persons (such as private individuals or corporations, as opposed to national courts). Like the ECJ, the General Court is made up of at least one judge from each Member State (28 in 2013). Unlike the ECJ, the General Court does not have permanent Advocates General. Judgments and orders of the General Court may be appealed on a point of law and brought before the ECJ. Also unlike the ECJ, the workload of the General Court is more fact-intensive and labour-intensive as it is a court of fact and law.

The Treaty of Nice extended the EU's judicial architecture still further by providing for 'specialised judicial panels' in specific areas. The Council of the European Union in November 2004 agreed to establish the European Union Civil Service Tribunal, a specialised court that is composed of seven judges, which began work in December 2005. It has jurisdiction to adjudicate in disputes between the EU institutions in their capacity as employers and their respective staff members—a jurisdiction that had hitherto been exercised by the Court of First Instance.

House of Lords, European Union Committee, *The Future Role of the European Court of Justice* 6th Report of Session 2003-04

[11] The Court was provided with a wide and varied jurisdiction. It may act in different capacities:

- – as a constitutional or administrative court (determining whether [EU] institutions are acting within the scope of their powers, reviewing the legality of [EU] measures, such as Commission or Council acts);

---

[9] See Article 252 TFEU.

- as an international court (dealing with conflicts between Member States or between the Commission and Member States and with conformity of international agreements with the Treaties, and interpreting conventions such as the EUROPOL Convention and other Conventions made under or in the shadow of the Treaties);

- as a civil court (hearing disputes over contracts concluded by the [EU], usually on appeal from the [General Court]);

- as an appeal court (from the [General Court] in direct actions brought against Union institutions and other bodies).

Formerly the Court also acted as an employment tribunal (appeals by EU civil servants). Staff cases are now dealt with by the [General Court], the Court retaining an appellate jurisdiction.

[12] Finally, [Article 267 TFEU] enables the Court, on a reference from a national court, to give preliminary rulings on the interpretation of [EU] legislation (whether Treaty Articles or regulations or directives) and on the validity of acts of the institutions of the Union and of the European Central Bank. This jurisdiction provides a mechanism of judicial co-operation between the Court and national courts and is particularly important in maintaining certainty and consistency in the application of [EU] law.

Three main types of proceedings involving the ECJ will be briefly outlined.

First, Article 267 TFEU contains the preliminary reference procedure, which is the most significant power within the ECJ's jurisdiction. If in the course of hearing a case, a court or tribunal in the United Kingdom has to determine what rights or obligations flow from a piece of EU legislation, then it often decides to seek guidance on how to interpret it from the ECJ. This entails adjourning the proceedings, formulating a question for the ECJ, waiting 20 months or so for the ECJ to decide the issue, then resuming the proceedings in the national court or tribunal by applying the guidance given by the ECJ to the particular facts of the case. At first sight it would appear that the national court gives the final ruling on the cases it decided to refer to the ECJ. However, in practice the ECJ's interpretation of EU law is such that it accords little discretion to the national courts when applying the ECJ's ruling. Through its judgments under Article 267 TFEU, the ECJ has promoted legal integration and driven the gradual constitutionalization of the EU.

I. Bache, S. George, S. Bulmer, *Politics in the European Union* (Oxford: Oxford University Press, 2011) 329.

There is no doubt that the ECJ has the formal right to reach the decisions that it does. Whether those decisions are accepted as legitimate is another matter. Most decisions of the Court have not impinged on the consciousness of national politicians or members of the public. They have received legitimacy through being accepted by national courts, especially those lower down the legal hierarchy. When ECJ judgments have come to the attention of national politicians, there has sometimes been a strong negative reaction, suggesting that the legitimacy of the Court's doctrines does not extend beyond the national courts and professional judges. The strength of reaction in Britain to the *Factortame* judgment [see Ch. 17] is indicative of this. As Carrubba[10] noted, 'public perceptions of institutional legitimacy are critical to the EU legal system being able to act as an effective democratic check', but 'the ECJ remains woefully short on public legitimacy today'.

[10] C.J. Carrubba, 'The European Court of Justice, Democracy, and Enlargement' (2003) 4 European Union Politics 96–97.

Since national courts give effect to the ECJ's judgments, some commentators conclude that the ECJ 'can broadly be described as the supreme or constitutional court of the EU'.[11] According to this view, national courts make up the lower tier of an integrated EU court system.

Whereas aspects of the ECJ's functions can be so compared (for instance, when it scrutinizes the acts of the other EU institutions, or when it hears an appeal from the General Court), it is important to remember that in its relationship with national courts the ECJ hears references and not appeals. No individual has the right to appeal to the ECJ. Instead, the national court decides whether or not to refer the case to the ECJ.

Under Article 256(3) TFEU the General Court can also give preliminary rulings in specific areas. However, this power has not yet been used, and it is still the ECJ that hears all Article 267 TFEU cases.

Second, like UK courts, the Court of Justice of the EU has the power of judicial review (annulment proceedings) of EU legislative and executive acts. Under Article 263 TFEU any Member State, the Council, and the Commission are entitled to challenge the legality of EU legislation 'on grounds of lack of competence, infringement of an essential procedural requirement, infringement of this Treaty or of any rule of law relating to its application, or misuse of powers'. Individuals and businesses can also bring proceedings under Article 263 TFEU—in practice this can happen only in extremely limited circumstances.

Third, there are infringement proceedings under Article 258 TFEU. Where it is claimed that a Member State is failing to comply with EU law, either the Commission or another Member State may commence proceedings in the ECJ to ensure compliance. Since the Maastricht Treaty, the ECJ has had power to impose financial penalties for some breaches. In July 2000 Greece became the first Member State to be fined under procedure for its failure to comply with a judgment on the implementation of a directive on waste disposal. The ECJ imposed a penalty of €20,000 per day, which ran for six months when the Commission certified that the infringement had ceased. In July 2005 the ECJ imposed on France a lump sum payment of €20 million in addition to penalty payments of €57.8 million for each six-month period of future non-compliance.

N. Nic Shiubhne, 'The Court of Justice of the European Union', in J. Peterson and M. Shackleton, *The Institutions of the European Union* 3rd edn (Oxford: Oxford University Press, 2012) 163–4.

The reception of EU case law within national constitutional courts or other courts at the apex of national judicial hierarchies (such as the Supreme Court in the UK) is a more documented phenomenon. Taking the primacy of EU law as a case study, we can clearly see the continuing coexistence of parallel claims about the authority that underpins this fundamental legal principle. Lower courts, in general, are used to being lower: they can resolve the legal dispute before them, but they are still links in an appellate court chain. The highest courts within national systems have more to lose within the supranational EU legal order. They give up their more typical role of having the final say on legal questions, especially questions closely connected to national constitutional principles.

---

[11] HL European Union Committee, Fourteenth Report, 'The Workload of the Court of Justice of the European Union', 6 April 2011, Ch. 2.

The Court of justice attributes the principle of primacy to the nature of the EU itself. From this, the Court derived a 'new legal order' that the member states sought to create. It also placed itself and the tenets of EU law at the apex of supranational EU legal authority, so that only it could determine the outcome of any such cases of conflict. It is critical to remember, however, that the 'new legal order' is the Court's own description of things.[12] National constitutional courts tend to take a different stance. They allow rather than subjugate themselves to primacy. They permit the operation of primacy in practice so as to give effect to the temporary tolerant will of their national parliaments. [...] This perspective has been articulated most recently in the German Federal Constitutional Court's decision (in 2009) on ratification of the Lisbon Treaty. That judgment reaffirmed the sovereignty of the member states. It acknowledged the temporary transfer of limited sovereignty to the EU so that agreed political objectives can be achieved through the actions of the Union's institutions, where appropriate. It also understood the purpose of primacy in securing the effectiveness of progress towards realizing those objectives. But it located these decisions at the level of the states themselves—not the EU in general, and not the ECJ more specifically.

From the EU's perspective, the Lisbon Treaty will undoubtedly strengthen the authority of the Court of Justice in relation to the Member States. There will be a single preliminary ruling procedure under Article 267 TFEU (instead of the current three), which will make it easier for references to be made in the area of freedom, security, and justice. The changes are designed to make the institutional structure more efficient, and the procedural rules more streamlined. But the tensions regarding the proper relationship between the national courts (and especially the highest courts) and the ECJ are likely to continue for as long as there are several national constitutions under the aegis of the European Union.

QUESTIONS

1. In what respects does the ECJ resemble national constitutional courts? In what respects are they different?
2. Should national courts attempt to compete or cooperate with the ECJ?

5 FURTHER READING

Arnull, A., *The European Union and its Court of Justice*, 2nd edn (2006, Oxford: Oxford University Press)

Dehousse, R., *The European Court Of Justice: The Politics Of Judicial Integration* (1998, London: Palgrave Macmillan)

---

[12] The description comes from its landmark decisions in Case 26/62 *Van Gend En Loos* [1963] ECR 1 and Case 6/64 *Costa v ENEL* [1964] ECR 585.

WEBSITES

Council of Europe, including the European Court of Human Rights	http://www.coe.int/
European Court of Justice	http://europa.eu/institutions/inst/justice/index_en.htm
Judiciary in England and Wales	http://www.judiciary.gov.uk/about_judiciary
UK Supreme Court	http://www.supremecourt.gov.uk

ONLINE RESOURCE CENTRE

Further information about the themes discussed in this chapter can be found on the Online Resource Centre at www.oxfordtextbooks.co.uk/orc/lesueur2e/

14

THE JUDICIARY

CENTRAL ISSUES

1. The judiciary plays a vital role in the resolution of legal disputes, the interpretation and application of legislation, and the development of the common law. The public must be confident that judges possess the necessary intellectual and personal skills, and that they are impartial as between the parties who appear before them. The public must also have confidence that the judiciary has institutional independence.

2. The concept of judicial independence is therefore of central importance. It is protected by guarantees contained in s. 3 of the Constitutional Reform Act 2005.

3. The requirement of judicial independence does not mean that judges are unaccountable for their decisions, but rather that their accountability must be compatible with their judicial role.

4. The process by which judges are appointed is also of importance. It should satisfy the principles of independence, equality, and transparency. Public confidence in the judiciary also requires the judiciary to be diverse and to reflect society.

5. While the need for diversity is now acknowledged, progress towards its achievement has been slow and further steps are required.

6. As well as their judicial roles, judges are often called upon to chair public inquiries; since such tasks may draw judges into the political arena, there is much discussion as to whether they are compatible with judicial independence.

1 INTRODUCTION

(a) THE ROLE OF THE JUDICIARY IN THE UNITED KINGDOM

The primary role of the judiciary is to adjudicate upon legal disputes that are brought to courts and tribunals. This involves interpreting and applying legislation, and developing and applying the common law.

The expansion of the grounds on which judges may review the legality of governmental action and delegated legislation[13], the processes of European integration, and the development of human rights law, have placed new roles on the judiciary in the United Kingdom.

---

[13] See further Chapter 16.

Under the European Communities Act 1972, judges have been called on to 'disapply' Acts of Parliament;[14] under the Human Rights Act 1998, senior courts may declare legislation to be incompatible with rights contained in the European Convention on Human Rights (ECHR).[15] These tasks highlight that the judicial function is important both from the perspectives of litigants in particular cases and the broader constitution.

Judges are also required to perform other tasks that are considered to require a combination of high-level forensic skills and independence, such as chairing inquiries into matters of national concern. There is much debate as to whether such activities are compatible with maintaining a judiciary that is at arm's length from politics, especially when they draw judges into issues of political controversy. We shall consider this further later in the chapter.

(b) RELATIONSHIPS WITH OTHER INSTITUTIONS

The principle of the separation of powers was discussed in Chapter 4. There we considered in general terms the relationship between the judiciary and Parliament and the executive. In that chapter, we cited the judgment of Lord Mustill in the *Fire Brigades Union* case.[16] His comments are worth setting out once again.

R v Secretary for the Home Department, ex parte Fire Brigades Union
[1995] 2 AC 513, 567

Lord Mustill

It is a feature of the peculiarly British conception of the separation of powers that Parliament, the executive and the courts have each their distinct and largely exclusive domain. Parliament has a legally unchallengeable right to make whatever laws it thinks right. The executive carries on the administration of the country in accordance with the powers conferred on it by law. The courts interpret the laws, and see that they are obeyed. This requires the courts on occasion to step into the territory which belongs to the executive, not only to verify that the powers asserted accord with the substantive law created by Parliament, but also, that the manner in which they are exercised conforms with the standards of fairness which Parliament must have intended.

While Lord Mustill's statement explains that judges may be required to step into the executive domain, it says nothing about the ability of ministers or Parliament to step into the domain that is occupied by the judges. It may be implicit that this is something that cannot be done. The judicial domain is protected by the fundamental principle of judicial independence. Its importance has been stated and restated many times.

A and ors v Secretary of State for the Home Department; X and anor v Secretary of State for the Home Department
[2004] UKHL56, [42]

Lord Bingham

[...] the function of independent judges charged to interpret and apply the law is universally recognised as a cardinal feature of the modern democratic state, a cornerstone of the rule of law itself.

---

[14] See further Chapter 18.
[15] See further Chapter 17.
[16] Commencement of legislation, see Chapter 10.

The Judiciary of England and Wales, 'Judges and the constitution'[17]

[...] for hundreds of years the overriding principle of our legal system has been that judges are independent of government. That means they make their decisions without interference from the government or the executive. Judges also do not get involved with politics.

In this chapter we consider the constitutional position of the judiciary and of judges in more detail than in previous chapters. Of particular importance is the principle of judicial independence and its implications for:

(a) the judiciary as an institution in its relationship with the executive and Parliament; and

(b) individual judges responsible for the impartial application of the law to particular disputes.

We shall see that the concept of judicial independence continues to evolve as the key players in the constitutional system come to a better understanding of how to balance independence with other demands, such as the call for the judiciary to be responsive to changes in society. It is often said that judicial independence does not require judicial isolation. This is true—but is independence compatible with greater judicial accountability? Is judicial impartiality possible if the judiciary is expected to reflect the wider community?

(c) THE JUDICIARY: SOME FACTS AND FIGURES

In constitutional terms, the most important domestic judges sit in the UK's top court, the Supreme Court (until October 2009, the top court was the Appellate Committee of the House of Lords) and the 'higher', or 'senior', courts in each of the three territorial jurisdictions (see Box 14.1). The judges of these courts make the most significant contribution to the development and exposition of the law, and decide the cases that are likely to be the most difficult and to have the greatest impacts.

BOX 14.1 HIGHER OR SENIOR COURTS IN THE THREE TERRITORIAL JURISDICTIONS

England and Wales	Court of Appeal—Civil and Criminal Divisions
	High Court (including the Administrative Court)
Scotland	Court of Session—Inner House (first instance) and Outer House (appellate) civil cases
Northern Ireland	High Court of Justiciary—criminal jurisdiction Court of Appeal High Court

There are, however, many other judges handling the day-to-day work of the lower courts in each of the jurisdictions; tribunal judges (and lay members who serve on tribunals);[18] and the part-time lay magistrates (advised by legally qualified clerks) who, in England and

---

[17] Available online at http://www.judiciary.gov.uk. Lord Phillips of Worth Matravers, discusses judges, the constitution, and judicial independence in a video and podcast interview, available online at http://clients.westminster-digital.co.uk/judiciary/

[18] On tribunals, see Chapter 15.

Wales, deal with the bulk of criminal law matters. In this context, the term 'lay' refers to someone who is not a lawyer.

Box 14.2 lists the main types of judge in England and Wales, and their numbers in relation to England and Wales.

BOX 14.2 JUDICIAL POSTS IN ENGLAND AND WALES AS AT APRIL 2011

Position	Number of judges	Court
Supreme Court Justices	12	UK Supreme Court
Lord Justice of Appeal	38	Court of Appeal
High Court judges	108[19]	High Court
Circuit judges	665	Crown Court and County Court
Recorders	1,221	Crown Court and County Court (part-time)
District judges	581	County Court and Magistrates' Courts
Deputy District judges	931	County Court and Magistrates' Courts (part-time)
Lay magistrates	26,966	Magistrates' Courts
Tribunals judges	11,472	First-tier Tribunal and Upper-tier Tribunal

Source: based on Judicial Database 2011

Box 14.2 provides some idea of the variety of judicial positions and the number of people who perform full-time or part-time judicial roles in England and Wales. Surprisingly perhaps, it indicates that the vast majority of judges are non-lawyers and that, even among the legally qualified judges, the majority work on a part-time basis. From this perspective, the judiciary is a large and varied institution—but Box 14.3 shows that, in terms of gender and ethnic composition, diversity is not a hallmark of the judiciary.

BOX 14.3 WOMEN AND ETHNIC MINORITY JUDGES AS AT 1 APRIL 2011

	Total in post	Men	Women	White	Asian or Asian British	Black or Black British	Mixed	Other ethnic group	Not stated	% Black/ethnic minority	% Women
Supreme Court	12	11	1	12	0	0	0	0	1	0.0	8.3
Heads of Division	5	5	0	5	0	0	0	0	0	0.0	0.0
Lord Justice of Appeal	37	33	4	25	0	0	0	0	12	0.0	10.8
High Court	108	91	17	84	0	0	1	3	20	4.5	17.7
Circuit judge	665	559	106	583	3	2	3	7	67	2.5	15.9

Source: Compiled using data from Judicial Database 2011

---

[19] In addition a High Court judge is based at the International Criminal Court and another at the European Court of Human Rights.

We shall return to the issue of diversity. Suffice it to say here that these figures indicate that, despite developments over the past two decades or so, there has been no discernible change in either the gender or ethnic composition of the judiciary, and probably little, if any, change in its social composition either. Professor John Griffith's 1997 summary of the results of surveys that have been conducted on the gender and social background of the senior judiciary since the 1950s provides a picture that remains more or less accurate.

J.A.G. Griffith, The Politics of the Judiciary, 5th edn (1997, London: Fontana Press), p. 21

[...] 80 per cent of the senior judiciary are products of public schools and of Oxford or Cambridge, with an average age of about sixty; 5.1 per cent are women; 100 per cent are white. Some explanation of the gross disproportions in gender and colour can no doubt be found in the structure of the legal profession, in the financial and other difficulties facing those wishing to qualify as barristers, and then needing to support themselves in the early years of practice. Another part of the explanation is sexual and racial discrimination in the profession.

Professor Kate Malleson, a leading academic expert on the judiciary, observes that '*despite two decades of official activity, the pace of change has been far slower than anticipated by many in the judiciary, the government, and the legal profession and there remains little prospect of any significant shift in the composition of the bench in the near future*'.[20]

(d) QUALIFICATIONS FOR BEING A JUDGE

Later, we shall consider the range of qualities and abilities that judges are expected to possess. Here, we list the main statutory qualifications.[21, 22]

BOX 14.4 QUALIFICATIONS FOR JUDGES: CIRCUIT JUDGES AND ABOVE IN ENGLAND AND WALES

Position	Qualification
Justice of the UK Supreme Court	High judicial office for two years **OR** fifteen years as a 'qualifying practitioner'
Lord Justice of Appeal (mainly sits in the Court of Appeal)	High Court judge **or** ten years' right of audience in the High Court
High Court judge	Circuit judge for two years **or** ten years' right of audience in the High Court
Circuit judges (mainly sit in the Crown Court and County Court)	Recorder **or** ten years' right of audience in the Crown Court or County Court **or** other judicial office

---

[20] Kate Malleson, 'Diversity in the judiciary: The case for positive action' (2009) 36 Journal of Law and Society 376, 377.

[21] Courts and Legal Services Act 1990.

[22] Section 25(1) CRA 2005. The term 'qualifying practitioner' is defined in s. 25(2).

2 JUDICIAL INDEPENDENCE

Judicial independence is a fundamental constitutional principle, although, as we shall see, its meaning and its practical implications are still being worked out. Judges, as the ultimate arbiters of the law, must be able to decide cases impartially on the basis of the evidence and legal arguments put to them. The requirement of impartiality demands that judges be free from overt or subtle pressures exerted on them by others, including by the executive. Independence and judicial impartiality therefore go hand in hand, and are both fundamental to peoples' confidence in the judicial system.

Secretary of State for Justice and Lord Chancellor, *The Governance of Britain: Judicial Appointments,* Cm 7210 (October 2007), pp. 16–19

An independent judiciary

2.4 Judicial independence is vitally important to the rule of law, and in particular to public confidence in judges as a means of upholding the law. This in turn brings social and economic benefits. It enables people to be assured that when their rights are infringed, or when others' duties need to be enforced, the appropriate action will be taken. It assures people that justice will be done when a criminal allegation is made. It also helps to sustain international confidence in Britain as a stable country in which, and with which, it is safe to do business.

2.5 […] It is important to be clear about the meaning of judicial independence—from whom or from what judges need to be independent.

The Executive

2.6 In a country operating under the rule of law, judges need to be independent of the executive. It must not be possible for the executive to require or improperly influence judges to decide cases in a particular way. Otherwise, there is an inevitable danger that the law could be used (or would be perceived as being used) to service the interests of the executive. Just as important, it is essential that the public has confidence that judges will interpret the law impartially and, where appropriate, stand up for the rights of individuals irrespective of the wishes or interests of the state.

The Legislature

2.7 The judiciary also needs to be independent of Parliament. Parliament (in particular the House of Commons) is the national body where the interests and views of the public are represented and with the ultimate power to make law. It is the duty of judges to decide cases within the limits of the law Parliament lays down. However, within those limits, it is in the interests of justice that the judiciary should be left free to decide cases, protected from political pressure to reach particular decisions in individual cases.

Parties to a case

2.8 It is also vital that judges be independent of the parties in a case. Most obviously, it means that no party to a case—including the Government, directly as a party in civil cases, and indirectly through the Crown as prosecutor in criminal cases—should be able to procure a favourable result by means of exerting improper influence. Further, it is a fundamental feature of the justice system that judges should be free from bias, and from perceptions of bias.

Securing independence

2.9 One of the most important ways of securing judicial independence is to ensure that the appointments process does not result in politically biased judges, or judges who are, or feel, beholden to the appointing body or person, or to any individual or organisation. This in turn helps to ensure that the judges who are appointed are able to act independently, free from political or other improper pressure, in office.

2.10 There are a range of other factors—beyond the appointments process itself—that are vital to securing independence while a judge is in post. The first among these is security of tenure, ensuring that judges cannot be dismissed because they make unfavourable decisions against, or are unpopular with, Government. Judges are protected against threats of cuts to their salaries; against political pressure in relation to their judgments, for example by clear practices restricting what may be said publicly by the legislature or executive during ongoing legal proceedings; from intimidation; and may not generally be sued for the manner in which they discharge their responsibilities of office.

(a) JUDICIAL INDEPENDENCE: A HISTORICAL PERSPECTIVE

Judicial independence has not always been a feature of the constitutional system and some aspects have only been realized very recently. The basis of the modern system was laid by art. 7 of the Act of Settlement 1701, which provided that judges hold office during 'good behaviour' and can only be removed by an address to the Crown by both Houses of Parliament.[23] This provision, now contained in s. 11 of the Senior Courts Act 1981, continues to protect the independence of the most senior judges, although the Lord Chancellor, with the concurrence of the Chief Justice, can remove less senior judges, including High Court judges, on grounds of misbehaviour or inability to perform their duties.

Interestingly, while it was recognized that judges should be protected from the executive, there was no requirement that judges should be politically neutral, or that they should not be members of the legislature or the executive. Certainly, prior to Lord Haldane's time as Lord Chancellor (1912–15), it was common for judges to be appointed because of their politics and their party allegiance. Professor John Griffith, for example, quotes Lord Salisbury who, when Prime Minister in August 1895, wrote: '*That there is no clearer statute in* [the unwritten law of our party system] *than the rule that party claims should always weigh very heavily in the disposal of the highest* [judicial] *appointments.*'[24]

There have even been occasions on which judges have served in government. Lord Cave, for example, served as Home Secretary for a short time at the end of the First World War while being a Law Lord.[25] Although judges are not eligible to become members of the House of Commons,[26] until 2005 the Lord Chancellor combined judicial, executive, and legislative

---

[23] Only one judge has been removed under art. 7: Sir Jonah Barrington, in 1830 for embezzlement.
[24] J.A.G. Griffith, *The Politics of the Judiciary*, 5th edn (1997, London: Fontana Press), p. 15.
[25] http://www.judiciary.gov.uk.
[26] House of Commons Disqualification Act 1975, Sch. 1.

functions.[27] Neither do we need reminding that the highest court in the system until the establishment of the UK Supreme Court took the form of a committee of the legislature.

The modern relationships between the judiciary and the executive and Parliament must be understood against the backdrop of several key constitutional developments—particularly:

- the change in the status and role of the Lord Chancellor;
- the establishment of the Lord Chief Justice of England and Wales as the head of the judiciary in that part of the UK, and a formal recognition of a relationship between the other two chief justices and Parliament;
- the enactment of the Constitutional Reform Act 2005 (CRA);
- the creation of the UK Supreme Court; and
- the creation of the Ministry of Justice.

These events form the backdrop of this chapter. At this stage, we may note that these developments have led to:

(a) recognition that there are two facets of judicial independence—that is, the independence of individual judges and the independence of the judiciary as a whole;

(b) a clearer appreciation of the functions that fall within the province of the judiciary and the functions that fall within the province of the government; and

(c) a clearer view of the ways in which judges and the judiciary can be held to account.

They have also led to the first statutory recognition, in s. 3 of the Constitutional Reform Act 2005 (CRA), of judicial independence and of duties upon the executive to maintain it.

(b) STATUTORY GUARANTEES OF JUDICIAL INDEPENDENCE FROM THE EXECUTIVE

The reforms we have referred to were at least partly driven by a concern to create a greater separation between the judiciary and politicians (ministers and parliamentarians). An accompanying concern has been to achieve more explicit statements of the principle of judicial independence. These are now contained in three separate statutory provisions, as follows.

(a) **Constitutional Reform Act 2005, s. 3** (an Act of the UK Parliament)—In relation to the Lord Chancellor, other UK government ministers, and others involved in court administration, this applies to the UK Supreme Court, any *'other court established under the law of any part of the United Kingdom'*, and international courts.

(b) **Judiciary and Courts (Scotland) Act 2008, s. 1** (an Act of the Scottish Parliament)—In relation to the Scottish ministers, members of the Scottish Parliament (MSPs), and others involved in court administration, this applies to the UK Supreme Court, courts established under the law of Scotland, and international courts.

(c) **Justice (Northern Ireland) Act 2002, s. 1** (an Act of the UK Parliament)—This states that, in relation to that part of the United Kingdom, *'Those with responsibility for the administration of justice must uphold the continued independence of the judiciary'*.

---

[27] See Chapter 3, p. 101.

The three legislative provisions are an important step towards the codification of key constitutional principles, and a significant shift away from the traditional approach that left basic constitutional requirements to be protected by a rather loose combination of conventions, practices, and understandings (many of which, when tested, were found not to be very well understood).

We shall look more closely at the first and broadest of these provisions.

Constitutional Reform Act 2005 (CRA)

Continued judicial independence

3 Guarantee of continued judicial independence

(1) The Lord Chancellor, other Ministers of the Crown and all with responsibility for matters relating to the judiciary or otherwise to the administration of justice must uphold the continued independence of the judiciary.

[...]

(4) The following particular duties are imposed for the purpose of upholding that independence.

(5) The Lord Chancellor and other Ministers of the Crown must not seek to influence particular judicial decisions through any special access to the judiciary.

(6) The Lord Chancellor must have regard to—

(a) the need to defend that independence;

(b) the need for the judiciary to have the support necessary to enable them to exercise their functions;

(c) the need for the public interest in regard to matters relating to the judiciary or otherwise to the administration of justice to be properly represented in decisions affecting those matters.

[...]

The duties to maintain judicial independence

Section 3(1) of the CRA imposes a general duty on the Lord Chancellor, other government ministers, and *'all with responsibility for matters relating to the judiciary'* or *'the administration of justice'*, to *'uphold the continued independence of the judiciary'*. It also imposes the following particular duties.

- Government ministers have the duty *'not to seek to influence particular judicial decisions through any special access to the judiciary'*: s. 3(5) CRA.

- The Lord Chancellor has the duty 'to defend' judicial independence: s. 3(6)(a) CRA.

- The Lord Chancellor must ensure that the judiciary has *'the support necessary to enable them to exercise their functions'*: s. 3(6)(b) CRA.[28]

---

[28] The Lord Chancellor's duty to defend judicial independence is reflected in his oath: *'I [...], do swear that in the office of Lord High Chancellor of Great Britain I will respect the rule of law, defend the independence of the judiciary and discharge my duty to ensure the provision of resources for the efficient and effective support of the courts for which I am responsible. So help me God'* (Constitutional Reform Act 2005, s. 17).

The significance and implications of the duty upon the Lord Chancellor to defend judicial independence have been considered by the House of Lords Select Committee on the Constitution. In the following extract, the Committee emphasizes the link between the rule of law and the independence of the judiciary, noting that the CRA imposes duties upon the Lord Chancellor to defend both.

House of Lords Select Committee on the Constitution, *Relations between the Executive, the Judiciary and Parliament,* Sixth Report, Session 2006–07 (footnotes omitted)

39. [...] the Lord Chancellor must ensure that the principle of judicial independence is not violated. His duty to 'defend' the independence of the judiciary is stronger than the duty of all other ministers to 'uphold' that independence, giving him a special enforcement role in relation to the rest of the government. Lord Lloyd of Berwick, a former Law Lord, told us that there were two key aspects to defending judicial independence. The first is 'where there is an attempt [...] by Government [...] to restrict [...] the jurisdiction of the courts', for example the proposed 'ouster' clause in the Asylum and Immigration (Treatment of Claimants, etc.) Bill in 2004.[29] In such cases, 'the Lord Chancellor's duty is absolute; he must point out in Cabinet that this would undermine the independence of the judiciary'. Even though the Lord Chancellor is no longer head of the judiciary, it is essential that he should remain a jealous guardian of judicial independence in Cabinet.

40. The second aspect of defending the independence of the judiciary, Lord Lloyd said, was dealing with ministers who attack individual judges. [...]

The executive must not seek to influence particular decisions by special access

If the government is a party to a case, it can, will, and should seek to present arguments to the court that are intended to persuade the judge(s) that its view of the facts and/or the law is correct and should be adopted. This is a normal part of adjudication. What government cannot do is seek 'special access' to judges in order to influence particular decisions. This prohibition is intended to prevent attempts to influence judges beyond the transparency of the courtroom. But does it also prohibit government from seeking access to judges in order to obtain their opinion on the legality of government proposals, or other matters, before litigation arises? On one view, such access would be permissible and extremely useful. After all, if the government were able to obtain a judicial opinion on the legality of its proposals, this would enable government to amend its schemes in ways that may improve rights, and would save time and trouble later. It might even be argued that seeking the advice of judges at this stage would not offend the wording of s. 3, because it would not constitute an attempt to influence judges in relation to particular decisions.

That narrow interpretation, however, would not fully reflect the requirements of judicial independence. This can be illustrated by the following account given by Lord Phillips of Worth Matravers of the way in which senior judges reacted when the then Home Secretary,

---

[29] See Chapter 16 section 5(b), Excluding judicial review in asylum cases, on p. 739.

Charles Clarke, wanted to speak to the Law Lords about reforming the law relating to control orders under the counter-terrorism legislation.[30]

Lord Phillips of Worth Matravers, 'The Supreme Court and other constitutional changes in the UK', Address to the Members of the Royal Court, the Jersey Law Society, and the members of the States of Jersey, 2 May 2008 (footnotes omitted)

The public, and sometimes even politicians, do not always understand the importance of judicial independence. In 2006 Charles Clarke, the former Home Secretary gave evidence to the House of Lords Select Committee on the Constitution. The Prevention of Terrorism Act 2005 entitled the Home Secretary to make control orders for the restriction of the ambit of life of terrorist suspects. A series of Control Orders issued by Charles Clarke had been overturned by the court, and finally the House of Lords.

Charles Clarke vented his frustration at this before the Select Committee. He said—

'The judiciary bears not the slightest responsibility for protecting the public, and sometimes seems utterly unaware of the implications of their decisions for our security. I regard it as disgraceful that no Law Lord is prepared to discuss in any forum with the Home Secretary of the day the issues of principle involved in these matters. The idea that their independence would be corrupted by such discussions is risible [...] I strongly believe that the attitude of the Law Lords has to change. It fuels the dangerously confused and ill informed debate which challenges Britain's adherence to the European Convention on Human Rights. It is now time for the judiciary to engage in a serious and considered debate about how best to legally confront terrorism in modern circumstances.'

Charles Clarke wanted the Law Lords to meet with him to discuss broad issues of principle. I can understand the frustration that the former Home Secretary feels on this point. But judges must not risk collusion with the executive when they are likely to be required to adjudicate on challenges to the actions of the executive.

These sentiments were echoed by the Select Committee in its Report. It agreed that a meeting between the Home Secretary and the Law Lords *'risks an unacceptable breach of the principle of judicial independence.'* The Law Lords should not even be perceived to have prejudiced an issue as a result of communication with the Executive.

Improper criticism of the judiciary by the executive

As Lord Lloyd of Berwick (a retired Law Lord) explained to the House of Lords Constitution Committee, the duty to protect judicial independence requires judges to be protected from personal criticism by government ministers. The importance of this can be understood against the backdrop of criticism of judges following their decisions. In the mid-1990s, sections of the media launched attacks on the judges following several judicial review decisions that were unfavourable to the government. Andrew Le Sueur commented that these events suggested that it had become possible '*for ministers and their supporters to condemn unfavourable judicial review judgments in an unprecedentedly aggressive and confrontational manner*'. This, he said, upset the '*equilibrium in Britain's subtle uncodified constitution*'.[31]

---

[30] On which, see Chapter 17, section 5, Case study: Human rights and terrorism on p. 786.

[31] Andrew Le Sueur, 'The judicial review debate: From partnership to friction' (1996) 31 Government and Opposition 8, pp. 9, 24.

There have been similar attacks on judges more recently. Following a decision by Collins J (as he then was) concerning the rights of asylum seekers to seek financial support under s. 55 of the Nationality, Immigration and Asylum Act 2002 that was unfavourable to the government,[32] David Blunkett, then Home Secretary, said in a radio interview that he was '*fed up with having to deal with a situation where Parliament debates issues and the judges then overturn them. I don't want any mixed messages going out so I am making it absolutely clear that we don't accept what Mr Justice Collins has said*'.[33]

This criticism was followed by personal attacks in the media, possibly based on Whitehall briefings.[34] Professor Bradley, for example, tells us that the *Daily Telegraph* said: 'One man's rulings have thwarted all moves to stem the tide of refugees ... whenever the Government has been on the wrong end of an asylum ruling in recent years, Collins has often been the villain of the piece [...]. This particular judge is considered a serial offender in Whitehall.'[35]

The tabloids were more extreme in their comments. The *Daily Mail*, for example, referred to '*judges* [...] *who have it in for Britain* [...] *whose arrogance and perversity* [is] *setting the wishes of the people at nought and pursuing a liberal, politically correct agenda of their own*'.[36] Professor Bradley observes that '*it would be regrettable if similar recriminations were to occur whenever judges are exercising the functions that are entrusted to them by Parliament and which are essential in a democratic society that is committed to the rule of law*'.[37]

The *Craig Sweeney* case is a further example of a judicial decision that attracted direct criticism from a member of the government.

The *Craig Sweeney* case

Craig Sweeney was a convicted paedophile, having been convicted of indecently assaulting a 6-year-old girl. He had been released early from custody on a licence that was due to expire, but two days before it did he kidnapped a 3-year-old girl and committed serious sexual offences on her. He pleaded guilty to four offences of kidnap, three of sexual assault, and one of dangerous driving.

The appropriate sentence for a person who is convicted after being found guilty by a jury is eighteen years. This is set out in sentencing guidelines, issued by the Sentencing Guidelines Council, which is chaired by Lord Phillips of Worth Matravers under the authority of statute.

Lord Phillips of Worth Matravers, 'The Supreme Court and other constitutional changes in the UK', Address to the Members of the Royal Court, the Jersey Law Society, and the members of the States of Jersey, 2 May 2008

[In passing sentence, His Honour Judge Griffith Williams] explained that Sweeney's guilty plea reduced the tariff by one third to 12 years. In accordance with the Sentencing Guidelines Council's guidance he would normally be considered for parole after half his sentence had

---

[32] *R (on the application of Q) v Secretary of State for the Home Department* [2003] EWHC 195 Admin.

[33] *The Times*, 20 February 2003.

[34] Anthony Bradley, Judicial independence under attack' [2003] Public Law 397, 401.

[35] Bradley notes that the term 'serial offender' also appeared in the *Daily Mail* and *News of the World*: ibid., p. 401.

[36] Ibid., p. 401.

[37] Ibid., p. 405.

expired. Taking into account the time he had spent on remand meant that he would be sentenced to a sentence which would entitle him to consideration for parole after 5 years and 108 days.

The parents of the kidnapped girl declared that the sentence was an insult to their daughter. The Home Secretary, John Reid, said that the sentence was 'unduly lenient' and that the tariff did not 'reflect the seriousness of the crime.' He urged the Attorney General to refer it to the Court of Appeal for reassessment. Vera Baird, a junior constitutional affairs Minister publicly criticised the judge. She said that he had 'got the formula wrong' and deducted too much for the early guilty plea.

Areas of the media engaged in further personal criticism of the judge. The Daily Express wrote that judges were 'deluded, out-of-touch and frankly deranged' and that 'our legal system has not only lost touch with public opinion but with natural justice itself [...] sentencing now bears no relation at all to the seriousness of the crime.' The Sun Newspaper began a campaign on the day Mr. Sweeney was sentenced. The aim of the campaign was to pressurise the government to sack judges who it claimed were guilty of being soft on 'killers, child sex beasts and rapists'. It welcomed the comments of the Home Secretary, John Reid, as a success in its campaign to put the judges on trial.

House of Lords Select Committee on the Constitution, *Relations between the Executive, the Judiciary and Parliament*, Sixth Report, Session 2006–07 (footnotes omitted)

49. The Sweeney case was the first big test of whether the new relationship between the Lord Chancellor and the judiciary was working properly, and it is clear that there was a systemic failure. Ensuring that ministers do not impugn individual judges, and restraining and reprimanding those who do, is one of the most important duties of the Lord Chancellor. In this case, Lord Falconer did not fulfil this duty in a satisfactory manner. The senior judiciary could also have acted more quickly to head off the inflammatory and unfair press coverage which followed the sentencing decision.

The Committee recommended that when the Ministerial Code (the code of conduct and guidance on procedures for ministers, published by the Cabinet Office) is next revised, the Prime Minister should insert strongly worded guidelines setting out the principles governing public comment by ministers on individual judges.[38] The government has agreed that ministers should not make 'inaccurate or ill-considered' comments on the actions of any individual judge and to '*consider the committee's recommendations when the code is next revised*'.[39] To date the Ministerial Code has yet to be amended to include such a restriction on ministers.

Independence and court resources

The final duty referred to in s. 3 does not concern judicial independence directly, but is addressed at ensuring that the courts are properly resourced and supported. Like other

[38] On the Ministerial Code, see Chapter 7.
[39] Baroness Royall of Blaisdon, House of Lords Hansard, 18 November 2008, col. 1125.

public services, the court system depends on public money distributed by the government: it costs to have courts, and to have judges and the necessary personnel to run the courts. But the government has to balance many factors when deciding how much to spend on the court system and this provision arguably gives the court system some protection when resource allocation issues are being considered by government.

This provision came to the fore in the controversy that followed the government's announcement that it was to establish a Ministry of Justice, headed by the Lord Chancellor, with responsibility for both prisons and the court system. There was widespread concern, including among the judiciary, about the way in which the announcement had been made and criticism was especially levelled at the absence of consultation. But the judiciary was also concerned about the substance of the change. In particular, it was feared that, within the Ministry of Justice, there would be competition between the needs of HM Prison Service and the needs of the administration of justice, and that this would present the Lord Chancellor with a conflict of interest that would make it difficult for him to meet the s. 3 CRA duty to support the court system.

Lord Phillips of Worth Matravers, 'The Supreme Court and other constitutional changes in the UK', Address to the Members of the Royal Court, the Jersey Law Society, and the members of the States of Jersey, 2 May 2008

[The new Ministry of Justice] was to deal with constitutional affairs, civil and administrative justice, the judiciary, the courts, legal aid, the judiciary and the administration of justice. But there was also to be responsibility for prisons, offender management and criminal justice policy, which had been Home Office functions.

The judiciary were concerned that this was a constitutionally significant change to the machinery of government. One department was to uphold the rule of law and the independence of the judiciary and yet the same department would also have responsibility for criminal justice. That Department would have one pot of money from which to fund the court system, and the prisons. The judiciary was concerned that the Department would rob Peter to pay Paul. Peter being the judges and Paul being the prisons. Would the Department be able to prioritise the administration of justice whilst dealing with criminal justice policy?

The Constitutional Reform Act 2005 makes the Lord Chancellor the guardian of the independence of the judiciary. It was feared that this principle would be compromised by these, so called, machinery of government changes. It was intended that the role of Lord Chancellor would be performed by the Minister of Justice. Thus the Lord Chancellor would be required to lead on the government's criminal law policies.

The first I or the then Lord Chancellor, Lord Falconer, learnt of the creation of the Ministry of Justice was when we were reading our Sunday Telegraphs on the 21st of January 2007. Once again the government had not consulted on a key constitutional change. The handling of the abolition of the Lord Chancellor was brought to mind. No guarantees of the protection of the independence of the judiciary were given. There was no promise to protect the administration of justice within the new Department.

Once again we embarked on negotiations with the government. These negotiations remained on-going at the time the Ministry of Justice came into being on the 9th of May 2007. Lord Falconer and the Prime Minister refused to accept that the proposed changes were anything more than a machinery of government change.

I felt so strongly on these developments that I made a public statement highlighting my misgivings. This was unusual and came to the attention of the Constitutional Affairs Committee of the House of Commons. They concluded that the Ministry of Justice was indeed a major constitutional change. They criticised the Government for underestimating the concerns of the judiciary insofar as they related to the changes to the roles and responsibilities of the Lord Chancellor. The Committee concluded it was unfortunate that the creation of the new ministry seemed to have been a fait accompli as early as January 2007.

The negotiations were not getting very far when Lord Falconer was replaced by the Prime Minister with Jack Straw. Things started to progress. The negotiations were finally concluded on 1 April [2008], when the Lord Chancellor laid in Parliament a new Framework Document for the governance, resourcing and operation of Her Majesty's Court Service. [...]

The agreement referred to by Lord Phillips, originally contained in a document that was laid before Parliament in April 2008, is now set out in Her Majesty's Courts and Tribunals Service Framework Document, April 2011.[40] This recognizes that responsibility for the courts must be shared between judiciary and executive. The executive has overall responsibility for providing and maintaining the justice system, with the Lord Chancellor being responsible to Parliament for these matters. The judiciary is responsible for delivering justice, with the Lord Chief Justice, as head of the judiciary in England and Wales, being responsible for the deployment and training of judges. As we shall see, both the Lord Chancellor and the Lord Chief Justice of England and Wales are involved in decisions relating to appointment and discipline of judges. It has been said that this framework creates a partnership between judges and the executive that requires '*an open, equal and constructive dialogue between the Lord Chancellor and the Lord Chief Justice*'.[41]

QUESTIONS

1. Why is judicial independence considered to be important?

2. What are the main requirements for achieving and maintaining judicial independence?

3. Would it be appropriate for a member of the executive to ask judges to give their advice on the legality of a proposed change in the law? If not, why not? Is there anything that the government can do to obtain a judicial view of the legality of proposed action?

4. What are the main roles of the Lord Chancellor and the Lord Chief Justice in relation to the judicial system?

---

3 THE UK SUPREME COURT AND JUDICIAL INDEPENDENCE

A principal justification given for abolishing the Appellate Committee of the House of Lords and creating the Supreme Court of the United Kingdom was the desire to institutionalize judicial independence fully by drawing a clear line between the judicial functions carried out by the United Kingdom's top court and the UK Parliament and the executive.[42] This reflected the requirement for judicial independence in Art. 6 of the ECHR that was becoming

---

[40] Cm 8043

[41] Lord Justice Leveson, '*Dicey* revisited: Separation of powers for the 21st century', Lecture at University of Liverpool Law School, 28 November 2008, p. 10.

[42] See Chapter 5.

increasingly significant with the growth in human rights litigation and judicial review, as well as the growing number of situations in which judges are being called upon to determine whether Acts of Parliament conform to EU law or are compatible with Convention rights. Having a top court in the form of a parliamentary committee, senior judges who were members of the legislature, and a government minister (the Lord Chancellor) who sat occasionally as a judge was perceived to be irreconcilable with modern understanding of judicial independence. Leaving aside arguments about Art. 6 of the ECHR, many critics thought that this unusual set of institutional arrangements was confusing to the general public.

While the UK Supreme Court is both institutionally and physically separate from Parliament, some have argued that the desire for greater judicial independence was not the true motivation behind the creation of the Supreme Court. Professor Jeremy Webber, for example, argues that the real motivation was to move the United Kingdom towards a constitutionally limited political order.[43] Certainly the creation of the UK Supreme Court will not remove judges from the political arena; in the following extract, Professor Diana Woodhouse speculates on how the Supreme Court may act to increase the politicization of the judges without necessarily securing greater trust in the judiciary based on its independence. That extract is followed by Professor Kate Malleson's warning that we should not be complacent about the need to strengthen the legitimacy of the Supreme Court.

Diana Woodhouse, 'The constitutional and political implications of a United Kingdom Supreme Court' (2004) 24 Legal Studies 134–55, 143–54 (footnotes omitted)

While the establishment of a Supreme Court will confirm the independence of the individual judge in his or her own court and increase independence in the institutional or collective sense, it will not neutralise or depoliticise the judges. [...] there may be an expectation that the creation of a free-standing Supreme Court will, in some way, project senior judges into a vacuum in which they will make their decisions in isolation from, and without regard to, the political context and their own ideology. This will not happen. Indeed, there is the possibility that greater institutional independence may actually increase the extent to which senior judges are seen as political actors.

First, the status of the new court is likely to increase media exposure of opinions expressed by senior judges, through conference papers, interviews, journal articles and addresses to the profession. Their views on issues, such as sentencing and the reform of the legal system, are not value free, but confirm that judges, like everyone else, are political beings who operate in a political world. Secondly, the increased jurisdiction of the court and its more obvious constitutional role will affect the type and extent of media coverage the court receives. Controversial or sensitive decisions are likely to be scrutinised, with the political leanings and philosophical or moral positions of the various judges being subject to examination. This has already become a feature of press reporting of some cases. It was particularly notable in the *Pinochet case,* where both the *Telegraph* and *The Times* sought to position the members of the panel along a scale, ranging from 'liberal' to 'conservative'. *The Times* also provided brief pen portraits of the judges, in which Lord Browne- Wilkinson was described as 'humane, liberal and charming', Lord Hope as 'quiet [with a] meticulous style and middle of the road politics', Lord Hutton as the 'most right-leaning of the panel', Lord Saville as 'friendly, affable

[43] Jeremy Webber, 'Supreme Courts, independence and democratic agency' (2004) 24 Legal Studies 55–72.

and sporty', Lord Millett as 'the highest ranking Freemason in the judiciary', Lord Phillips as 'liberal' and Lord Goff as 'known for intelligence and moderation' .

[...] Thirdly, evidence from elsewhere suggests that institutional separation could result in the Supreme Court becoming a political institution in its own right, in the sense of being subject to increased use and lobbying by pressure and interest groups, many of which believe they are more likely to achieve their ends through the court than through elected representatives. In this way, the court is likely to be perceived as being more political than the [...] Appellate Committee of the House of Lords. Indeed, on occasions, it may seem to be in competition with the executive and the legislature. Much depends on how it reacts to those who seek to influence its thinking, but any idea that the establishment of a separate Supreme Court will in some way remove judges from the political arena is misplaced.

Similarly, to imply that the physical separation of the final court of appeal will in some way reduce, or limit, the relationship between law and politics is to misunderstand the nature of judicial decisions. This relationship may be more apparent during times of judicial activism, but a decision not to intervene is just as political as its counterpart and as likely to have political consequences. Jurisprudence cannot be considered in isolation or divorced from politics. [...] A new Supreme Court may [...] downplay its increase in status and jurisdiction in its early days. What will happen in the longer term will depend on a number of factors. There will, no doubt, be periods of activism and restraint, as there have been in the House of Lords and in other Supreme Courts.

[...]

The courts, in constitutional theory, are limited by parliamentary sovereignty but, in practice, this limitation has been significantly reduced by ... [recent developments] ... This trend is likely to continue, even to the extent that a United Kingdom Supreme Court, seeking to be more like its counterparts elsewhere, may, at some point in the future, claim an inherent power to strike down legislation or, at least, to render ineffective any Act of Parliament which it views as 'unconstitutional'. This may seem an extreme scenario but the embrace of comparative law by senior judges has, according to Lord Steyn, already 'come of age' and the new court's constitutional role may result in comparisons with the jurisdictions of other Supreme Courts and a move, consciously or otherwise, towards a matching, and hence increased, jurisdiction for the United Kingdom Court.

The outcome could be the further diminution of parliamentary sovereignty and the development of the United Kingdom into a constitutional democracy. [...] The increased constitutional role of the Supreme Court is likely to advance this development.

Kate Malleson, 'The evolving role of the UK Supreme Court' [2011] Public Law 754,771–772 (footnotes omitted)

The fact that the court has been given a new name is significant. The choice of the title 'Supreme Court' does not signify that the UK's top body will imitate any other particular supreme court. As Gavin Drewry notes, the great diversity in the role and functions of such top bodies is a reflection of the variety of local histories, cultures, traditions as well as different economic and political developments. But the cultural connotations of the title, particular given the long shadow of the US Supreme Court, is likely to impact psychologically in a way which affects both internal and external expectations of the role of the Court. While the UK Supreme Court may never be a full constitutional court, particularly if such a body is defined more narrowly as a body limited to a purely constitutional jurisdiction, it is likely to exhibit features shared by many other top courts bearing the name Supreme Court. Crucially, it may develop a general power of constitutional review, even if this is a power exercised very rarely to strike down legislation which conflicts with a small number of key constitutional statutes.

[...] This, in turn, raises some challenging questions about the legitimacy of the new Court and highlight the paradox that at a time of rapidly expanding judicial power the UK's top court can claim less political and institutional legitimacy than almost any other top court in a comparable liberal democracy. The high level of intellectual ability and integrity of the Justices will ensure that they occupy a place in the global community of judges but this should not be allowed to lead to complacency about the need for changes which will strengthen the legitimacy of an increasingly powerful and high-profile Supreme Court.

QUESTIONS

1. In what ways does the establishment of the UK Supreme Court help to further judicial independence?

2. 'Far from increasing public confidence in the independence of the judiciary the establishment of the UK Supreme Court could lead to an increase in the political role of the judges and undermine public confidence in its neutrality.' Discuss.

4 JUDICIAL ACCOUNTABILITY

House of Lords Select Committee on the Constitution, Relations between the Executive, *the Judiciary and Parliament*, Sixth Report, Session 2006–07, para. 27

Independence of the judiciary does not mean [...] and should not mean that the judiciary have to be isolated from the other branches of the State. Nor does it mean that the judiciary—individually and collectively—need to be insulated from scrutiny, general accountability for their role or properly made public criticisms of conduct inside or outside the courtroom.

There must be a balance between judicial independence and judicial accountability. We rightly expect those with power to be accountable for the way in which their power is exercised. The authority to decide cases, to determine the meaning of legislative provisions, to develop the common law, and to decide on the legality of government's actions clearly carries very real powers. We only have to consider the decisions of the courts on the legality of detention orders imposed under the Prevention of Terrorism Act 2005 and government's reaction to these to see that court decisions can matter.[44] But how are the requirements of judicial independence and judicial accountability to be reconciled? What forms of accountability are appropriate for judges and to whom should they account?

Professor Andrew Le Sueur has identified three schools of thought in relation to judicial accountability: the opponents to accountability; the reconceptualists; and the radicals. The opponents to judicial accountability, he has said, emphasize the need for judicial independence and argue that independence is not consistent with accountability. They say that the notion of an 'accountable judge' is an oxymoron. A judge cannot be both independent and

---

[44] See Chapter 7, section 5.

accountable—at least if this means that he or she is to be accountable to those who are outside the court system.

The reconceptualists, says Le Sueur, agree with this basic point, but say that, within the context of 'self-policing', judges are accountable and that certain forms of accountability are part and parcel of the normal processes of judging.

A. Le Sueur, 'Developing mechanisms for judicial accountability in the UK' (2004) 24 Legal Studies 73, 76

> Among the obvious activities that fall into this category are: the fact that most courts sit in public; the common practice of giving reasoned, written judgments; the possibility that judgments are appealable to a higher judicial body; and the scrutiny meted out to judgments (and judges) by a more-or-less well informed news media and scholarly work of academics.

Unsurprisingly, the radicals are not content with this. They call for more and new forms of accountability. Le Sueur, for example, quotes Professor Keith Ewing as arguing that the challenge is '*to ensure that the judges as political actors are more fully accountable to the people over whom they govern, in a manner which enhances rather than undermines their independence* [but this is] *a tall order'*.[45]

One way of achieving greater accountability for judges has been suggested by Professor Bogdanor, who distinguishes between 'sacrificial accountability' and 'explanatory accountability' to Parliament. The former, he accepts, is appropriate in relation to government ministers, but not judges. The latter, however, is appropriate in relation to judges and does not conflict with the needs of judicial independence.

Professor Vernon Bogdanor, 'Parliament and the judiciary: The problem of accountability', Sunningdale Lecture, 9 February 2006

> Must the judges be the single exception to the general rule of accountability? Let us distinguish between two different meanings of ministerial accountability to Parliament.
>
> The first meaning is one that we might call sacrificial accountability. This dictates that ministers take the credit for what goes right in their department, and the blame for what goes wrong, to the extent of resigning if something goes seriously wrong. Most ministers, of course, accept only the first part of this principle! Clearly, judges cannot be held accountable to Parliament in this sacrificial sense. They cannot be held to account for their decisions. If they were, this would make nonsense of the principle of the independence of the judiciary.
>
> [...]
>
> But it seems to me that there is no reason why judges should not regularly appear before Parliament, or rather before Select Committees of Parliament [...] to be cross-examined on their judicial philosophy. Indeed, in recent years, senior members of the judiciary, such as the Lord Chief Justice and the Master of the Rolls have appeared before Select Committees to answer questions on issues related to the machinery of Government, as it affects the judges. Judges cannot, of course, be expected to discuss particular judgements, nor matters which are likely to prove justiciable. Such matters would have to be explicitly excluded

---

[45] K. Ewing, 'The Unbalanced Constitution', in T. Campbell, K. Ewing, and A. Tomkins (eds) *Sceptical Essays in Human Rights* (2001, Oxford: OUP), p. 117.

from the terms of reference of the relevant Select Committee. But, if this proposal were to be accepted, judges would become accountable to Parliament not in the first sense, the sacrificial sense, but in another sense, a second sense, the explanatory sense.

[...] What I am proposing is that judges while not being answerable to Parliament, will nevertheless answer to Parliament. They would as it were be cross-examined on their lectures and articles in law journals, on their judicial philosophy, by a Select Committee. They would be cross examined by the representatives of the people in Parliament. Judges are in my opinion right to publicise their views, for senior judges are teachers in the field of human rights and civil liberties. But they should not object to discussing these views in a parliamentary forum, in the cause of greater public understanding.

Criticism of the judiciary in the media

Earlier in the chapter we discussed how improper criticism of judges by government ministers undermines judicial independence from the executive. To say that serving government ministers should refrain from criticizing judges does not mean that judges should be immune from being criticized by others, including by ex-ministers. Consider, for example, the decision in March 2012 taken by the Northern Ireland Attorney General to commence proceedings for contempt of court against Peter Hain MP, a former Northern Ireland Secretary, in relation to passages in his memoir, *Outside In*, criticising Judge Girvan's (now Lord Justice Girvan) decision in a 2006 judicial review case. The proceedings for contempt generated an all-party campaign to protect the freedom of MPs to comment on judgments, which led to the prosecution being dropped. The campaign also highlighted the more general question of whether there should be restrictions on free speech in order to prevent criticism of judges. In the House of Commons David Blunkett MP (a former Labour Home Secretary who, as we have seen, has been very critical of judges) asked the Prime Minister the following question: [46]

"Does the Prime Minister share my concern at the actions of the Northern Ireland Attorney-General in using an outdated and discredited law, of disrespecting the court, to invoke contempt proceedings against the former Northern Ireland Secretary, my right hon. Friend the Member for Neath (Mr Hain), for comments in his memoirs? Should not respect for the independence of the judiciary be balanced with the rights of individuals to fair comment on that judiciary?"

The Prime Minister replied:

"I do have a great deal of sympathy with what the right hon. Gentleman says. Parliamentary privilege, obviously and quite rightly, allows hon. Members to express their views in Parliament. In terms of what is said outside Parliament, let me just say this: there are occasions, as we all know, when judges make critical remarks about politicians; and there are occasions when politicians make critical remarks about judges. To me, that is part of life in a modern democracy, and we ought to keep these things, as far as possible, out of the courtroom."

[46] Oral Answers to Questions, House of Commons Hansard, 18 April 2012: Column 317.

It is perhaps significant that the Prime Minister refers to situations in which judges have been critical of politicians. Lord Neuberger (when MR), has also commented that *'[M]utual respect between the judges and the politicians is essential ... A judge can scarcely complain about ministers criticising him for the way he is doing his job if he criticises ministers for the way they are doing their jobs.'* [47] While some may see this to be a normal feature of democratic dialogue, Lord Neuberger considers there to be potentially serious consequences:

> "...if [judges and politicians] slang (sic) each other off in public, members of the judiciary and members of the other two branches of government will undermine each other, and, inevitably, the constitution of which they are all a fundamental part, and on which democracy, the rule of law, and our whole society rests" [48]

QUESTIONS

1. What advice would you give to the judiciary regarding the freedom of judges to criticize politicians? Would this advice apply to what they say in their judgments?

2. Do you agree with Lord Neuberger regarding the dangers that may flow when judges and politicians criticize each other?

---

5 IMPARTIALITY

Judges must be able to approach cases impartially on the basis of the evidence and legal arguments put to them. The requirement of impartiality demands that judges be free from overt or subtle pressures exerted on them by influences outside the courtroom. It also means that they cannot be connected with one or other of the parties in ways that could undermine the appearance of fairness. Independence and judicial impartiality therefore go hand in hand, and are both fundamental to peoples' confidence in the judicial system.[49]

While we expect our judges to be independent and impartial, we also expect them to be in contact with, and not isolated from, general trends in society. We expect judges to be aware of what is going on around them and capable of applying the law in a manner that strikes a chord with the rest of us. A balance must therefore be struck between the requirements of independence and the need for impartiality, on the one hand, and the desirability of judges to be in touch, on the other.

In the following extract, the House of Lords Select Committee on the Constitution considers the extent to which judges should be become embroiled in politically controversial issues. The Committee draws the distinction between the restraints that must be imposed on individual judges and the need for senior judges to speak on behalf of the judiciary as a whole in cases in which government policy may have an adverse impact upon the administration of justice.

---

[47] Lord Neuberger MR, 'Where Angels Fear to Tread' Holdsworth Club Presidential Address, 2 March 2012, para. 37.

[48] Ibid. para.

[49] See also Baroness Hale, *Gillies v Secretary of State for Work and Pensions (Scotland)* [2006] UKHL 2.

Select Committee on the Constitution, *Relations between the Executive, the Judiciary and Parliament,* Sixth Report, Session 2006–07 (footnotes omitted)

52. Just as ministers ought to demonstrate restraint in commenting on the judiciary, so judges should (and generally do) avoid becoming inappropriately involved in public debates about government policy, matters of political controversy or individual politicians. As the Lord Chief Justice told us, 'Essentially, you would not expect judges to comment on political policy'. Lord Falconer elaborated on this sentiment, suggesting that 'it is generally a bad idea for judges to be criticising the government on policy issues' because 'the public want judges to be unpolitical' and 'those very same judges then have to enforce laws about which it might be said they have expressed disagreement'. The Lord Chief Justice and Heads of Division have a responsibility to ensure that judges adhere to this principle.

53. However, the Lord Chief Justice, as head of the judiciary, and perhaps other senior judges with responsibility for specific parts of the justice system, are in a different position from that of other judges. On occasion, it is necessary for them to speak out publicly if a particular government policy is likely to have an adverse impact upon the administration of justice and ministers have failed to provide a satisfactory response during private consultations.

54. Effective channels of communication between the executive and the senior judiciary are vital to ensure that the impact of government legislation or policy proposals upon the administration of justice is fully understood at an early stage. Such communications are facilitated in a variety of ways. First, judges serve on a range of bodies with responsibility for the justice system, for example the National Criminal Justice Board. As Sir Igor Judge said, 'it is no longer [...] a concomitant of independence that judges should be isolated'.

55. Second, concerns amongst the judiciary about particular government proposals are conveyed through formal responses to consultations. For example, as was widely reported at the time, the Council of Her Majesty's Circuit Judges gave a largely negative response to the Home Office's paper *Convicting Rapists and Protecting Victims—Justice for Victims of Rape* in January 2007 [...]

56. Finally, there are private meetings which take place between ministers and judges (especially the Attorney General, the Home Secretary—probably now the Secretary of State for Justice—and the Lord Chief Justice) to discuss the practicality of particular government policies in terms of the administration of justice. As Sir Igor Judge explained, 'week after week these sorts of discussions are going on at ministerial level [and] at official level' [...] If these meetings do not lead to satisfactory mutual understandings, it should be noted that the Lord Chief Justice can also in appropriate circumstances ask to see the Prime Minister.

Constitutional Change

57. Effective two-way communication is of particular importance when a constitutional change is proposed which is likely to impact upon the judiciary or the administration of justice more broadly. As Lord Justice Thomas told us: 'Our constitution [...] is based both on statute law and on constitutional understandings and conventions. Those understandings and conventions include reliance upon full and appropriate respect for the different positions occupied by the three branches of government'. Therefore, he said, there should always be 'a proper [...] and detailed examination, so that you come to a solution that is acceptable across the board to the executive, to the legislature and to the judiciary'. [...]

QUESTION

'If government ministers are prevented from having "special access" to the judges surely judges should be prevented from having access to government ministers to discuss the impact of government policies on the administration of justice.' Do you agree with this statement, and if not, why not?

These discussions concern communications between judges and the executive in relation to proposals, and the underlying concern is to ensure that the judiciary is able to influence decisions to ensure that the court system operates justly without tarnishing the ability of judges to deal impartially with individual cases.

Judicial involvement in non-judicial activities can lead to problems in cases in which a judge's impartiality is questioned because of an association with a particular organization, or in which the judge has expressed views that indicate that he or she may have a preconceived attitude to an issue that is, or may be, brought to the courts. One well-known example of this occurred when the House of Lords had to rehear an appeal involving the extradition of the ex-President of Chile, General Pinochet: Lord Hoffmann, one of the Law Lords who had sat in the first hearing, was held to be too closely associated with Amnesty International, one of the parties in the case.[50] Similar issues may also arise if a judge has expressed views in a non-judicial capacity, such as in talks or interviews with the media. If we expect judges to be part of society, at what point does their involvement in activities that are normal for most of us undermine their ability to act impartially as between the parties in a particular case? These issues have been considered by the courts in a number of cases over the years.

An example is the decision of the House of Lords in *Helow v Secretary of State for the Home Department and anor* (on p. 604). The appellant was a Palestinian who claimed asylum in the United Kingdom, having been actively involved in the Palestinian Liberation Organization (PLO). Her claim was unsuccessful, as was her appeal to an adjudicator. Permission to appeal further was refused by the Immigration Appeal Tribunal. She filed a further application seeking review of that refusal by the Court of Session in Scotland. The judge refused this application. Her lawyers subsequently discovered that the judge was a member of the International Association of Jewish Lawyers and Jurists (the association) and was a founder member of its Scottish branch. The appellant appealed to the House of Lords, contending that the association had a '*strong commitment to causes and belief at odds with*' her own, and that the association was anti-Palestinian, anti-Muslim, and antipathetic to the PLO and supportive of Israel. She argued that the judge was therefore disqualified from dealing with her case.

As can be seen from the following extracts, the basic test is said to be whether a fair-minded and informed observer, having considered the relevant facts, would conclude that there existed a real possibility that the judge was biased, by reason (in this case) of the judge's membership of the Association. Applying this test, the House of Lords was unanimous in rejecting the argument and that judge was disqualified, although Lord Walker reached his conclusion on the issues, 'rather less readily' than did his colleagues.

---

[50] *R v Bow Street Metropolitan Stipendiary Magistrate and ors, ex parte Pinochet Ugarte (No. 2)* [1999] 1 LRC 1; *Helow v Secretary of State for the Home Department and anor* [2008] UKHL 62.

Helow v Secretary of State for the Home Department and anor
[2008] UKHL 62

Lord Mance

39. The basic legal test applicable is not in issue. The question is whether a fair-minded and informed observer, having considered the relevant facts, would conclude that there existed a real possibility that the judge was biased, by reason in this case of her membership of the Association: *Porter v Magill* [2001] UKHL 67; [2002] 2 AC 357. The question is one of law, to be answered in the light of the relevant facts, which may include a statement from the judge as to what he or she knew at the time, although the court is not necessarily bound to accept any such statement at face value, there can be no question of cross-examining the judge on it, and no attention will be paid to any statement by the judge as to the impact of any knowledge on his or her mind: *Locabail (UK) Ltd v Bayfield Properties Ltd* [2000] QB 451, para. 19 per Lord Bingham of Cornhill CJ, Lord Woolf MR and Sir Richard Scott V-C. The fair minded and informed observer is 'neither complacent nor unduly sensitive or suspicious', to adopt Kirby J's neat phrase in *Johnson v Johnson* (2000) 201 CLR 488, para 53, which was approved by my noble and learned friends Lord Hope of Craighead and Baroness Hale of Richmond in *Gillies v Secretary of State for Work and Pensions* [2006] UKHL 2; 2006 SC (HL) 71, paras 17 and 39.

40. The appellant also invokes or seeks assistance from the principle of automatic disquali-fication applied in *R v Bow Street Metropolitan Stipendiary Magistrate, Ex p Pinochet Ugarte (No 2)* [2000] 1 AC 119. It was there held that a judge was automatically disqualified not merely if he or she had a pecuniary interest in the outcome of the case, but also if his or her decision would lead to the promotion of a cause in which he or she was involved together with one of the parties. In that case the judge's involvement was as the chairman and a direc-tor of Amnesty International Charity Ltd, a charity wholly controlled by Amnesty International which had intervened in the case as a party to support the prosecution's application for the extradition of Senator Pinochet to Spain. However, in my opinion the present case is a long way away from *Ex p Pinochet*, since the Association was not a party to or in any way con-cerned with (or so far as appears even aware of) the proceedings involving Miss Helow.

Lord Hope of Craighead

[8] [...] The judge can be assumed, by virtue of the office for which she has been selected, to be intelligent and well able to form her own views about anything that she reads. She can be assumed to be capable of detaching her own mind from things that they contain which she does not agree with. This is why the complete absence of anything said or done by her to associate herself with the published material that the appellant complains of is so crucial to what the observer would make of this case. In the absence of anything of that kind there is no basis on which the observer would conclude that there was a reasonable possibility that the judge was biased.

Lord Rodger of Earlsferry

[23] [...] Even lay people acting as jurors are expected to be able to put aside any prejudices they may have. Judges have the advantage of years of relevant training and experience. Like jurors, they swear an oath to decide impartially. While these factors do not, of course,

> guarantee impartiality, they are undoubtedly relevant when considering whether there is a real possibility that the decision of a professional judge was biased. Taking all these matters into account, I am satisfied that the fair-minded observer would not consider that there had been any real possibility of bias in Lady Cosgrove's case.

As we have mentioned, Lord Walker of Gestingthorpe had more difficulty reaching his conclusion. He stressed that: *'Those who take on the responsibility of judicial office have to exercise a measure of restraint in associating themselves publicly with controversial causes'*[51] and warned that *'the fair-minded and informed observer would be tending towards complacency if he treated the fact of having taken the judicial oath as a panacea'.*[52]

QUESTIONS

1. Lord Mance says that there can be no question of subjecting a judge to cross-examination on her knowledge. Why do you think this is? Do you agree that judges should not be cross-examined when their impartiality is questioned?

2. Do you agree that the situation in this case was a long way off from that in *Pinochet Ugarte (No. 2)*? Suppose that the judge had been an active member of the Association, how would you answer then?

3. Should a judge who is a member of motoring organizations such as the RAC or AA be disqualified from hearing cases concerning road accidents?

---

6 APPOINTING JUDGES

The current system for making judicial appointments was created by the CRA. This established an independent Judicial Appointments Commission (JAC) for England and Wales with responsibility for recommending candidates when vacancies arise. Similar commissions exist in Scotland and Northern Ireland. A separate ad hoc selection commission is established to recommend candidates for appointment to the Supreme Court when vacancies arise. It is now accepted that the process by which judges are appointed should reflect the principles of judicial independence, transparency, effectiveness, diversity, and accountability. In the following extract from its recent report, *Judicial Appointments*, the House of Lords Constitution Committee explain the importance of these principles.

Select Committee on the Constitution, *Judicial Appointments*, 25th Report, Session 2010–12 (footnotes omitted)

Constitutional principles

14. [...] There was widespread agreement [amongst those who gave evidence to the committee] that the appointments process must be designed in such a way as to reinforce judicial independence. Judges in the United Kingdom should not be appointed through political patronage.

---

[51] *Helow v Secretary of State for the Home Department and anor* [2008] UKHL 62, [24].
[52] Ibid., [27].

15. It is important not only that the judiciary act independently, but that they are seen to do so. This principle also extends to the appointments process. Lord Justice Toulson, Vice-Chairman of the JAC, noted that prior to the enactment of the CRA "there was widespread public concern that judges were being appointed through cronyism and secret soundings. Nothing, really, could disabuse the public of that." The establishment of the JAC was intended to put an end to such concerns. By operating in an open and transparent manner—for example, by advertising vacancies, specifying the criteria for appointment and publishing diversity statistics—the existence of an independent appointments commission is aimed at helping to ensure that no suspicion of political patronage remains.

16. As well as upholding independence and being open and transparent, the judicial appointments process must be effective. Assessment of professional competence must be central to the selection of judges in order to ensure the efficient delivery of justice. The CRA uses the term "merit" to refer to these criteria, which have been set out in some detail by the JAC. We received different views as to how merit ought to be understood and applied in judicial selection. Given the importance of the merit principle, it is important that there is clarity over its basic meaning [...].

17. Another principle relevant to judicial appointments is diversity. At one level this means that the process must be fair and non-discriminatory: by that we mean that it must continue to result in the appointment of high quality judges, but without the imposition of barriers against talented legal practitioners from any section of society. However, the issue of diversity goes further than this: we received evidence, with which we concur, arguing that diverse courts are better equipped to carry out the role of adjudicating than courts that are not diverse and that the public will have greater trust and confidence in a more diverse judiciary. As we argue in Chapter 3, the primacy of the merit principle is not inconsistent with the appointment of a diverse judiciary which is more reflective of the society which it serves.

18. The principle of accountability is also important. Judicial independence does not require that no-one be held accountable for the operation of the appointments process or perhaps even, in exceptional cases, for individual appointments. Later in this Chapter we consider the practical mechanisms by which the JAC and the Lord Chancellor are held to account. Through annual reports, a detailed website and appearances before parliamentary committees, the JAC provides regular accounts of its work to Parliament, ministers and the public. The Lord Chancellor's role in the appointments process is justified as necessary to secure accountability to Parliament through the usual convention of individual ministerial responsibility. Some of the evidence we received questioned the effectiveness of the current accountability mechanisms, leading to calls for Parliament to have a greater role in the appointments process.

[...]

20. The principles which we believe should continue to underpin the judicial appointments process are judicial independence, appointment on merit, accountability and the promotion of diversity. The achievement of the correct balance between these principles is vital in maintaining public confidence in the judiciary and the legal system as a whole.

(a) THE APPOINTMENTS PROCESS PRIOR TO THE CRA

Prior to the CRA appointment of judges was exclusively in the hands of the executive. Judges were (and still are) formally appointed by the Queen, acting on the advice of Her Majesty's ministers, or by the Lord Chancellor on her behalf. In Scotland, the Lord Advocate would make recommendations to the Secretary of State for Scotland. In relation to the Law Lords and the most senior judges in the territorial jurisdictions, the Queen acted on the advice of the Prime Minister. Appointments to the High Court and to the Circuit Court were made by the Queen, on the advice of the Lord Chancellor. The Lord Chancellor appointed district judges, lay magistrates, and members of certain tribunals.

There were no open competitions for appointments to the High Court or to more senior positions. The Lord Chancellor—in those days, always a senior lawyer—decided whom to recommend for appointment after private consultations with the judiciary or senior members of the professions. This covert process was adopted by other Commonwealth countries, such as Australia, and was entirely different to the much more open approach used in the USA.[53] As Lord Justice Toulson told the House of Lords Select Committee on the Constitution, the process created 'widespread public concern that judges were being appointed through cronyism and secret soundings'. The process was also considered to enable the judiciary to be an essentially 'self-perpetuating' institution.[54] Some of its consequences are summarized by Kate Malleson.

Kate Malleson, 'Rethinking the merit principle in judicial selection' (2006) 33 Journal of Law and Society 126, 138 (footnotes omitted)

… [t]he senior judiciary has traditionally been recruited from an extremely narrow group consisting of white, male barristers drawn from a small number of commercial chambers in London. The structural relationship between the bench and Bar, whereby judges have maintained strong links with their chambers, combined with the key role judges play in the selection system through the consultations process has meant that barristers joining such elite chambers as pupils have found themselves on a 'golden road' to judicial office?[55] They have been, effectively, the beneficiaries of a particularly pervasive and entrenched form of reverse affirmative action.

The method of judicial appointment prior to the CRA patently failed to satisfy the fundamental principles to which we have referred.

(b) THE PROCESS FOR APPOINTING JUDGES UNDER THE CRA

Judicial Appointments Commissions now exist in each of the UK's jurisdictions. These operate at arm's length from government ministers. Their task is to carry out selection exercises when judicial vacancies arise and identify a single nominee whose name is put to the relevant government minister. The minister may accept the name, but has limited power to ask the commission in question to reconsider its selection or to reject it.

---

53 Lord Clarke of Stone-Cum-Ebony MR, 'Selecting judges: Merit, moral courage, judgment & diversity', 22 September 2009. Lecture available online at http://www.judiciary.gov.uk/docs/speeches/mr-selecting-judges-lecture-22092009.pdf.

54 J.A.G. Griffith, *The Politics of the Judiciary*, 5th edn (1997, London: Fontana Press), p. 22.

55 The term was used by a judge to describe his career path from an elite chambers to the bench: K. Malleson and F. Banda, *Factors Affecting the Decision to Apply for Silk and Judicial Office*, Lord Chancellors Dept Research Series No. 2/00 (2000), p. 29 (citation in original).

BOX 14.5 THE JUDICIAL APPOINTMENTS COMMISSIONS

Commission	Chair	Membership	To whom it makes recommendations	Legislative basis
Judicial Appointments Commission for England and Wales	Lay person	Fifteen—five judges, a barrister and solicitor, a legal tribunal member, a lay magistrate, and five lay people	Lord Chancellor	Constitutional Reform Act 2005, Pt 4
Judicial Appointments Board for Scotland	Lay person	Ten—five legal and five lay people	MSPs	Judiciary and Courts (Scotland) Act 2008
Northern Ireland Judicial Appointments Commission	Lord Chief Justice of Northern Ireland	Thirteen—five judges, a barrister and solicitor, and five lay people	Lord Chancellor (until such time as justice functions are devolved to the Northern Ireland Executive)	Justice (Northern Ireland) Acts 2002 and 2004
Ad hoc selection commission convened by the Lord Chancellor for vacancies on the UK Supreme Court	President of the UK Supreme Court	Five—two judges of the UK Supreme Court plus one member of each of the three territorial commissions (one of whom must be a lay person)	Lord Chancellor	Constitutional Reform Act 2005, ss 25–31

Judicial Appointments Commission for England and Wales

In this section, we take a closer look at the work of the largest of the commissions—that of England and Wales.

The Judicial Appointments Commission for England and Wales (JAC) is an independent body (not an executive agency of a government department) consisting of fifteen members. The chair must be a lay person; there are five judges, two practising lawyers, five lay members, a legal tribunal member, and a lay magistrate. The members of the JAC are appointed by the Crown on the advice of the Lord Chancellor.[56] Three of the judges are selected by the Judges Council, which is a body broadly representative of the judiciary as a whole that informs and advises the Lord Chief Justice on matters relating to the judiciary.

---

[56] The current membership can be found online at http://www.judicialappointments.gov.uk/

It plays a significant role in the self-governance of the judiciary and thereby contributes to its independence.[57]

The selection process for judges in England and Wales

When a judicial vacancy arises, the Lord Chancellor (having consulted with the Lord Chief Justice of England and Wales) requests the JAC to start a selection process. The JAC decides the most appropriate process to be followed. Vacancies are now routinely advertised in the press and always on the JAC website. The selection methods vary according to the seniority of the post to be filled; it may involve a combination of activities such as interviews, written tests, and role play. For posts in the High Court and courts below this level, selection decisions are taken by the JAC. For Court of Appeal and 'leadership' roles (such as heads of Division of the High Court), selection is not made by the JAC, but by a panel of four people appointed by the JAC: a justice of the UK Supreme Court; the Lord Chief Justice or his or her nominee; the head of the JAC or his or her nominee; and another lay member of the JAC. The process involves consultation with judges, and the JAC must consult with the Lord Chief Justice and another person who has held the office for which the selection relates, or has relevant experience. The judiciary therefore continues to have a significant degree of influence on the selection process undertaken by the JAC.

Once the JAC has arrived at a selection decision, it reports this to the Lord Chancellor who may accept the decision, reject it, or require the matter to be reconsidered. In practice almost all recommendations are accepted by the Lord Chancellor.[58]

Once selected, the person will be formally appointed.[59] The Lord Chancellor used to appoint members of the judiciary below the level of High Court judges, but the Crime and Courts Bill 2012 provides that these appointments will now be made by the Lord Chief Justice. The Queen formally appoints senior judges on the recommendation of the Lord Chancellor, or, in the case of the most senior judges, the Prime Minister.

Appointments to the UK Supreme Court

Justices of the Supreme Court, including the President and Deputy President of the Court, are appointed by the Queen following the process set out in ss 25–31 CRA. The minimum qualification for appointment is that the person has held judicial office for at least two years or has been a qualifying practitioner for at least fifteen years (s. 25(1)). Lord Sumption, who was appointed to the Supreme Court in January 2012, is the first Supreme Court Justice not to have served as a full-time judge in the UK.

When appointing justices of the Supreme Court, the Queen acts on the basis of a recommendation made by the Prime Minister (s. 26(1), although the Prime Minister will invariably recommend the person notified by the Lord Chancellor. The real decisions about who should be appointed to the Supreme Court are made by the Supreme Court Selection Commission and the Lord Chancellor.

---

[57] See J. Thomas, 'The Judges Council' [2005] Public Law 608.

[58] In the year 2011–12 only two recommendations for medical members of tribunals were rejected, because the Lord Chancellor considered that the candidates lacked the required experience for the particular post: see JAC, *Annual Report and Accounts*, HC 351, 11 July 2012, p. 9.

[59] Unless the person withdraws or medical reports indicate that the person cannot be appointed on health grounds.

The UK Supreme Court Selection Commission is not a permanent body with its own staff—the relatively light workload would not justify this, so a commission is convened as and when required. When convened, a Supreme Court Selection Commission consists of: the President and Deputy President of the Supreme Court; one member of the JAC; one member of the Judicial Appointments Board for Scotland; and one member of the Northern Ireland Judicial Appointments Commission.[60] At least one of the people from the territorial appointments commissions must be a non-lawyer.

The Commission's initial selection task is to compile a short list of candidates from among those who have applied. The Commission then conducts a confidential consultation exercise in accordance with s. 27 CRA to gather views about the possible appointees (see Box 14.6).

BOX 14.6 SHORTLIST CONSULTEES

Consultee	Rationale for consultation
The Lord Chancellor	This politician has overall ministerial responsibility for judiciary-related matters in the United Kingdom.
Very senior judges who are not themselves candidates	The UK Supreme Court hears appeals from the courts of appeal in the UK's three jurisdictions and it is important that the judges of those courts have confidence in anyone who is nominated to serve on the highest court.
First Minister of Scotland	The senior politician in the Scottish government
	Although relatively few Scottish appeals are heard by the UK Supreme Court (four or five civil appeals and no criminal appeals), the court is responsible for adjudicating on devolution issues that may raise politically sensitive issues.
First Minister for Wales	Wales is not a separate legal jurisdiction from England and there was no constitutional convention that one of the Law Lords was a Welsh judge (however that is defined). The rationale for consultation is therefore presumably because the UK Supreme Court may be called on to deal with devolution cases affecting Welsh affairs.
Secretary of State for Northern Ireland	Until such time as responsibility for policing and justice is transferred to the Northern Ireland Executive fully, it is the UK government minister responsible for Northern Ireland matters who is consulted.

Selection must be based on merit (s. 27(5) CRA). However, the merit principle is qualified to the extent that in making the selection, the Commission must ensure that '*between them the judges will have knowledge of, and experience in, the law of each part of the United Kingdom*' (CRA s. 27(8)). By *convention*, two of members of the UK's top court are from Scotland and—by a rather less well-established convention—one member has been from Northern Ireland. The Selection Commission must also have regard to any guidance given by the Lord Chancellor (s. 27(10) CRA).

---

[60] CRA 2005, Sch. 8.

Having identified its preferred nominee, the Commission reports the name of the person selected to the Lord Chancellor (s. 28). There is then a second round of consultation, with the Lord Chancellor seeking further views on the single name from very senior judges and from the consultees listed in Box 14.6. As with selections made by the JAC in relation to judicial appointments for the courts of England and Wales (as discussed), the Lord Chancellor has a statutory power to accept, reject, or ask the Commission to reconsider their nomination. Again, it is open to doubt whether a politician would be prepared to intervene to question the assessment of a candidate's suitability made by the Selection Commission. Once a selection is complete, the Lord Chancellor notifies the Prime Minister, who passes the recommendation to the Queen, who makes the formal appointment.[61]

The Government has indicated that these procedures are to be altered slightly in order to increase the role of non-lawyers in key appointments and to add a higher degree of political accountability. In particular, the Lord Chancellor is to be permitted to sit on the selection commissions for the Lord Chief Justice and the President of the UK Supreme Court. Also, in future, selection commissions for the Lord Chief Justice will be chaired by the lay chair of the JAC and the selection commission for the President of the UK Supreme Court will be chaired by a lay member from one of the territorial appointments commissions. These changes are designed to respond to criticism that the judiciary is able to appoint those in its own image. A further change in this context is that in future only one serving Supreme Court judge will be able to sit on selection commissions for new Supreme Court judges; and the President and Deputy of the court will not be able to sit on the selection commission for their successors.[62] Prior to the CRA, advertisements for vacancies to the UK's top court were never seen and there would certainly never have been an advert seeking applications to become the senior Lord of Appeal in Ordinary (equivalent to the President of the UK Supreme Court). Now when vacancies for these positions arise they are always advertised. The following, for example, is the notice inviting applications for the position of President of the Supreme Court on the retirement of Lord Phillips on 30 September 2012.

President of The Supreme Court of the United Kingdom

An Ad hoc selection commission has been established under section 27 and schedule 8 of the Constitutional Reform Act 2005 (the Act) to select a candidate to be recommended for appointment as President of the Supreme Court. The vacancy will be created by the retirement of Lord Phillips on 30 September 2012. The selection commission is anxious to attract applications from the widest field, including candidates who are not already Justices of the Supreme Court. The successful candidate must be able to demonstrate, in addition to the judicial qualities of a Supreme Court Justice, the ability to give outstanding leadership and to represent the Court in a wide range of circumstances.

The statutory minimum qualification for appointment is to have held high judicial office for a period of at least two years, or to have satisfied the judicial appointment eligibility condition on a 15-year basis or to have been a qualifying practitioner for a period of at least 15 years. In making its recommendation the selection commission will have regard to the requirements under section 27 of the Act that a selection must be on merit, and that the commission must "ensure that between them the Judges will have knowledge of, and experience of practice in, the law of each part of the United Kingdom."

---

[61] The Constitutional Reform and Governance Bill introduced to Parliament in the 2009–10 Session proposed to remove the Prime Minister's role altogether. This provision was removed from the Bill at the final stages.

[62] See Ministry of Justice, *Appointments and Diversity 'A Judiciary for the 21st Century' Response to public consultation* 11 May 2012, C

The selection commission invites applications from eligible candidates who fulfil one of the above statutory requirements and meet the criteria set out in the Information Pack. Additional information on the qualifications, the criteria, the selection process and how to apply can be found in the Information Pack which can be downloaded from the Supreme Court website (http://www.supremecourt.gov.uk) or requested from Grainne Hawkins [...]

The closing date for applications is 5pm on Thursday 19 April.

(c) JUDICIAL APPOINTMENTS AND CONDUCT OMBUDSMAN

The CRA also established the Judicial Appointments and Conduct Ombudsman (JACO) to provide redress for those dissatisfied with the way in which they were treated during a selection process in England and Wales, and to provide an element of independent oversight of the process.[63] The JACO is appointed by the Queen on the recommendation of the Lord Chancellor. The person appointed cannot have been a judge or practising lawyer. Previous service as a civil servant, a member of Parliament (MP), or with the JAC, or political activities may also make the person ineligible for appointment. Following an investigation, the JACO reports his or her findings, and any recommendations—including for the payment of compensation—to the Lord Chancellor, the JAC, and the complainant.[64] The Ombudsman may also investigate matters referred by the Lord Chancellor relating to the appointments process.

(d) The need to make appointments based on merit and the need for diversity

The JAC is under a statutory duty to select people of good character solely on merit.[65] In selecting on merit, the JAC must 'have regard to' the need to 'encourage diversity in the range of persons available for selection'.[66]

Constitutional Reform Act 2005

63 Merit and good character

[...]

(2) Selection must be solely on merit.

(3) A person must not be selected unless the selecting body is satisfied that he is of good character.

64 Encouragement of diversity

(1) The Commission, in performing its functions under this Part, must have regard to the need to encourage diversity in the range of persons available for selection for appointments.

(2) This section is subject to section 63.

---

[63] Section 62, Sch. 13. On ombudsmen generally, see Chapter 15.

[64] The JACO is also responsible for investigating the handling of matters relating to judicial conduct and discipline.

[65] Section 63 CRA 2005.

[66] Section 64 CRA 2005.

It is axiomatic that those appointed to become judges must have the qualities and abilities necessary for a judge. However, while s. 63 says that selection must be based solely on merit, the CRA does not define what constitutes 'merit'. One, perhaps surprising, reason is that there has been no single accepted understanding of what is meant by 'merit' in the context of judicial appointments. Professor Kate Malleson, for example, has pointed out that the qualities expected of candidates for judicial appointment have changed over the years, as the pool from which judges were selected altered.

Kate Malleson, 'Rethinking the merit principle in judicial selection' (2006) 33 Journal of Law and Society 126, 139

As the make-up and experiences of the recognized candidate pool changed over the years, so the construction of merit adapted accordingly. When once, for example, military service was common [...] successful service as an officer was taken to provide sound evidence of desirable judicial characteristics. As military service lost its popularity and upper-middle class education and career patterns changed, the link between military experience and judicial merit disappeared. [...] Had solicitors rather than barristers emerged from the Victorian period as the senior branch of the legal profession and therefore the natural recruitment pool for the judiciary [...] the requirement of many years of advocacy in the higher courts would not have been perceived as a prerequisite for appointment. Rather, the skills, experiences, and career patterns of elite groups of solicitors would instead have been taken as reflecting the desirable characteristics of a judge. Ability to negotiate with clients and management of an office, for example, might have been highly valued as evidence of judicial aptitude. Indeed, there is evidence that exactly this process of changing construction is taking place. In recent years, as the economic, political, and social influence of the solicitors' branch of the profession has grown, the 'junior' branch of the profession has lobbied successfully for changes to the appointments process which reorientate the definition and interpretation of merit towards them.

Against this background it has been important for the JAC to provide a transparent and objective statement of what it considers to constitute 'merit'. To this end, it has enunciated statements of the qualities that its selection process seeks to assess. Significantly, even in the relatively short period since its establishment, views on what are the necessary qualities and abilities for judicial office have developed and the JAC statements have been amended accordingly. The most recent statement, which follows, acknowledges that the abilities necessary for judicial office extend beyond those specifically associated with deciding disputes in accordance with the law to include an awareness of diversity issues. This factor was not explicitly mentioned previously and was included following recommendations of the Advisory Panel on Judicial Diversity, chaired by Baroness Rabbi Neuberger (as we shall see).

JAC Statement of the Qualities and Abilities Necessary for Judicial Office

1. Intellectual capacity

   High level of expertise in your chosen area or profession

   Ability quickly to absorb and analyse information

Appropriate knowledge of the law and its underlying principles, or the ability to acquire this knowledge where necessary

2. Personal qualities

Integrity and independence of mind

Sound judgement

Decisiveness

Objectivity

Ability and willingness to learn and develop professionally

Ability to work constructively with others

3. An ability to understand and deal fairly

An awareness of the diversity of the communities which the courts and tribunals serve and an understanding of differing needs

Commitment to justice, independence, public service and fair treatment

Willingness to listen with patience and courtesy

4. Authority and communication skills

Ability to explain the procedure and any decisions reached clearly and succinctly to all those involved

Ability to inspire respect and confidence

Ability to maintain authority when challenged

5. Efficiency

Ability to work at speed and under pressure

Ability to organise time effectively and produce clear reasoned judgments expeditiously (including leadership and managerial skills where appropriate)

Earlier in the chapter we noted that the senior judiciary is predominantly made up of white males. There is growing consensus that the need to diversify the judiciary is now urgent. The House of Lords Constitution Committee has explained that diversity 'means that the process [of judicial appointment] must be fair and non discriminatory', so that there are no 'barriers against talented legal practitioners from any section of society'. But, the committee said, 'the issue of diversity goes further than this ... diverse courts are better equipped to carry out the role of adjudicating than courts that are not diverse and that the public will have greater trust and confidence in a more diverse judiciary.' The following extract from *Judicial Appointments* expands upon the importance of diversity.

House of Lords Select Committee on the Constitution, *Judicial Appointments*,
25th Report, Session 2010–12 (footnotes omitted)

Chapter 3: Diversity

68. [...] The judge inhabiting a court room in England and Wales is stereotypically a white male from a narrow social background. Despite concerns raised over the last few decades,

the proportion of women judges, black, Asian and minority ethnic (BAME) judges and others from under-represented groups has increased too slowly. Many of the causes for this appear to stem from the structures of the legal professions (barristers and solicitors) and the pool of available mid-career legal professionals eligible and interested in putting themselves forward for selection. However, other barriers arise as a result of the appointments process itself or of the structures of the courts and tribunals in which judges work.

69. The slow rate of change is not only a problem for those whose careers are affected; it is a problem for society as a whole. We examine in this chapter why diversity is important and what changes to the constitutional and legal framework might help to bring about a truly diverse judiciary. [...]

The constitutional significance of a diverse judiciary

70. [...] the concept of merit should [not] be narrowly focused on intellectual rigour. Although the simple fact of being a member of an under-represented group will not in itself make someone a more meritorious candidate, our witnesses pointed to "limited empirical evidence that diverse judges can improve the decision-making process." Judging is a complex activity: it is necessary for judges to understand the wide array of concerns and experiences of those appearing before them. A more diverse judiciary can bring different perspectives to bear on the development of the law and to the concept of justice itself.

71. None of our witnesses argued that increasing diversity risks reducing the quality of the current judiciary. [...]

72. We consider it our responsibility to refute any notion that those from under-represented groups make less worthy candidates than the stereotypical white male. Indeed, we believe that increasing the pool of talent available will lead to an increased number of meritorious candidates from which to select. As Lord Neuberger MR argued:

> "if ... women are not less good judges than men, why are 80% or 90% of judges male? It suggests, purely on a statistical basis, that we do not have the best people because there must be some women out there who are better than the less good men who are judges."

73. Justice, fairness and equality are central values in the law which should be reflected in the composition of the judiciary itself. Judges are independent of Parliament and the executive, but they should not stand apart from the society in which they adjudicate: the public must have confidence in the judges who make the decisions which affect their day to day lives. This is less likely to be the case "if you have tribunal after tribunal with three members, all of whom are white men, particularly if that does not reflect the applicants coming through." People appearing before a court must trust the judges to make decisions based on fairness: levels of trust will be greater if the judiciary itself is seen to have been fairly appointed. As Lady Justice Arden argued: "People may well have more confidence that their concerns have been taken into account if the judiciary reflects more of a cross-section of society."

74. **A more diverse judiciary would not undermine the quality of our judges and would increase public trust and confidence in the judiciary.**

The argument that diversity should improve the quality of judicial decisions is not new. John Griffith, for example, argued that a diverse judiciary would be more open to arguments for change than a judiciary that was overwhelmingly male, white, and socially elite.

J.A.G. Griffith, *The Politics of the Judiciary,* 5th edn (1997, London: Fontana Press), pp. 7–8

When people like the members of the judiciary, broadly homogeneous in character, are faced with [political cases …] they act in broadly similar ways. It will be part of my argument to suggest that behind these actions lies a unifying attitude of mind, a political position, which is primarily concerned to protect and conserve certain values and institutions.

It has also been argued that having more female judges would make a difference. The following extract is taken from an article written by Madam Justice Bertha Wilson, who, in 1982, became the first woman judge on the Canadian Supreme Court.

Madam Justice Bertha Wilson, 'Will women judges really make a difference?' (1990) 28 Osgoode Hall Law Journal 507, 512–15

[…] studies show overwhelming evidence that gender-based myths, biases, and stereotypes are deeply embedded in the attitudes of many male judges, as well as in the law itself. Researchers have concluded that gender difference has been a significant factor in judicial decision-making, particularly in the area of tort law, criminal law and family law: Further many have concluded that sexism is the underlying premise of many judgments in these areas, and that that is not really surprising having regard to the nature of the society in which the judges themselves have been socialized.

[…] there are probably whole areas of the law on which there is no uniquely feminine perspective […] the principles and underlying premises are so firmly entrenched and so fundamentally sound that no good would be achieved by attempting to reinvent the wheel. In some other areas of the law, however, a distinctly male perspective is clearly discernible. It has resulted in principles that are not fundamentally sound and that should be revisited when the opportunity presents itself.

Baroness Hale has commented that '*it would be very surprising*' if these observations were not also applicable in the United Kingdom, '*given the restricted social, educational and professional background of most of our judges*'.[67] There is then some support for the view that diversity may affect the quality of decisions taken by judges, although Hale says that she is worried and sceptical about arguments based on the '*individual judges' ability or even willingness to make a difference*'.[68]

As we have seen, the House of Lords Select Committee on the Constitution argued that people are more likely to have confidence in a diverse judiciary. Baroness Hale relates this to democratic legitimacy.

Dame Brenda Hale, 'Equality and the Judiciary: Why should we want more women judges?' [2001] Public Law 489, 502–3 (footnotes omitted)

In a democratic society, in which we are all equal citizens, it is wrong in principle for that authority to be wielded by such a very unrepresentative section of the population. As

[67] Dane Brenda Hale, 'Equality and the Judiciary: why should we want more women judges' [2001] Public Law 489.

[68] Ibid., 501.

individuals, my colleagues are a remarkably diverse bunch, but I do not need to rehearse the facts about how unrepresentative they are: not only mainly male, overwhelmingly white, but also largely the product of a limited range of educational institutions and social backgrounds. [...] This matters because democracy matters. The judiciary may or should be independent of government and Parliament but ultimately we are the link between them both and the people. We are the instrument by which the will of Parliament and government is enforced upon the people. We are also the instrument which keeps the other organs of the state, the police and those who administer the laws, under control. [...]

How is judicial diversity to be achieved?

In April 2009 the Lord Chancellor established an Advisory Panel on Judicial Diversity, chaired by Baroness Rabbi Julia Neuberger. The Panel was charged with identifying the barriers to a more diverse judiciary, and making recommendations to achieve speedier and sustained progress to a judiciary that is more representative of the people it serves. The Panel reported in February 2010 making 53 recommendations.

Its key messages are summarized in the following extract.

Report of the Advisory Panel on Judicial Diversity, February 2010, pp. 4–6[69]

[After stressing the importance of having a diverse judiciary, the Panel's conclusions concluded as follows]

2. ... there is no quick fix to moving towards a more diverse judiciary. This will come as no surprise to those who have worked to promote diversity over recent years.

3. We pay tribute to those efforts [...] what has been lacking to date is a coherent and comprehensive strategy to promote diversity.

4. The message from our research and consultations is consistent with research and experience in other jurisdictions: we will achieve significant transformation if, and only if, diversity is addressed systematically—not only within the appointments process, but throughout a legal and judicial career, from first consideration of the possibility of joining the judiciary to promotion at the most senior level.

5. Delivering a more diverse judiciary is not just about recruiting talent wherever it may be found, important though that is, but about retaining talent and enabling capable individuals to reach the top.

[...]

7. Sustained progress on judicial diversity requires a fundamental shift in approach from a focus on selection processes towards a judicial career that addresses diversity at every stage.

8. This approach requires:

- ensuring that lawyers from all backgrounds recognise early on in their career that becoming a judge could be a possibility for them.

---

[69] http://www.justice.gov.uk/publications/docs/advisory-panel-judicial-diversity-2010.pdf.

- more effort by the legal professions to promote diversity at all levels and to support applications from talented candidates from all backgrounds.
- etter information on the career paths available. These career paths must promote opportunities across the courts and tribunals as one judiciary.
- providing a variety of means for potential applicants for judicial office to understand what the role involves and to gain practical experience and build confidence.
- open and transparent selection processes that promote diversity and recognise potential, not just at the entry points to the judiciary but also for progression within it to the most senior levels. [...]

9. To deliver the fundamental change that is needed will also require new ways of working together, from an approach that co-ordinates activity to one that actively drives change. In particular:

- Change must be implemented as a comprehensive package of reform.
- the existing tripartite judicial diversity strategy between the Lord Chancellor, the Lord Chief Justice and the Chairman of the Judicial Appointments Commission needs refocusing and extending to include the leaders of the legal profession (Bar Council, Law Society, and Institute of Legal Executives (ILEX)) and the Senior President of Tribunals. This Judicial Diversity Taskforce should oversee an agreed action plan for change as a result of this Panel's findings and publish an annual report that demonstrates where progress has been made and where it has not. It must measure its success, acting as a group that delivers change and holds its members to account.
- this group also needs to ensure that we learn from experience. That means systematic, consistent monitoring and evaluation of what works and what does not, so that resources can be allocated where they are most effective.
- there needs to be a proactive campaign of mythbusting to dispel the widespread misconceptions that are deterring good candidates from under-represented groups from coming forward.
- there must be a new form of engagement. The legal profession must actively promote judicial office among those who are currently not coming forward - the work of the Solicitors in Judicial Office Working Group outlined in this report represents a significant and welcome change. The Judicial Appointments Commission needs to be more responsive to the experience of its customers. The judiciary needs to support and encourage new entrants more actively.

10. We stand by the need to implement our recommendations as a package if we are to make significant progress. [...]

In November 2011 the then Lord Chancellor and Secretary of State for Justice, Kenneth Clarke, launched a consultation paper, *Appointments and Diversity: A Judiciary for the 21st Century*.[70] This indicated the Government's support for the Advisory Panel's recommendations and proposed changes to the judicial appointments process. The consultation closed in February 2012. Meanwhile, the House of Lords Select Committee on the Constitution also considered judicial appointments and in March 2012 it produced its report *Judicial Appointments*, to which references have already been made. The Committee reiterated the need to implement the recommendations of the Advisory Panel. Having

---

[70] 21 November 2011, CP 19/2011.

considered the responses to its consultation, in May 2012 the Government published its report, *Appointments and Diversity: A Judiciary for the 21st Century.*[71]

The Government accepted that more needs to be done to ensure greater judicial diversity, but stressed that 'there is no single or straightforward solution to the issue': as well as legislative changes 'there will be need to be strong and clear leadership at all levels, both within the judiciary and the legal professions.'[72]

In relation to legislative change, the Crime and Courts Bill 2012, currently before the House of Lords, includes two changes specifically designed to improve judicial diversity. The first is intended to make it easier for judges to work part time, thereby increasing opportunities for those, usually women, who have childcare and other family responsibilities. Thus, Schedule 12 seeks to replace the current statutory limits on the number of judges in the High Court, Court of Appeal, and Supreme Court with references to 'full-time equivalents'. This means, for example, that rather than having twelve Supreme Court Justices there will be the equivalent of twelve full-time judges.

The second legislative change relating to diversity concerns the merit criterion. The Bill proposes to introduce a new section 63(4) into the CRA so that section 159 of the Equality Act 2010 will be available in relation to judicial appointments. This will mean that where two candidates are of equal merit the selecting body may choose the one who will contribute to judicial diversity. Patrick O'Brien, from UCL's Constitution Unit, has commented on this as follows:

> "This is perhaps the most controversial issue in this area. The proposed use of section 159 reflects the conclusions of the Ministry of Justice's consultation ... and also those of the Lords Constitution Committee ... This is, however, about the most conservative implementation of a positive action policy that could be imagined. Given that many judges and lawyers are firmly of the opinion that it is logically impossible for two candidates to be of equal merit the tiebreaker provision could easily end up a dead letter. Section 63(4) preserves the principle of selection solely on merit ... and is not framed as a positive instrument to use diversity as a tiebreaker but rather as a negative statement that the act does not preclude it ..."[73]

QUESTIONS

1. Can you summarize the arguments for having a more diverse judiciary? Which of these do you consider to be the most compelling?

2. The Youth Justice and Criminal Evidence Act 1999 prevented the defendant in a rape trial from relying on evidence of the woman's sexual past to throw doubt on whether she consented to sex. In a case in 2001, it was argued that an all-male House of Lords could not impartially decide where the balance lies between the right of male defendants in a rape case to a fair trial and the rights of their female accusers to privacy and dignity. This argument failed—but, in your view, did it have any substance?

3. In your view, what further steps should be taken to achieve a more diverse judiciary? Would you, for example, be in favour of having a quota of judicial appointments of women, people who are Black or Asian, or members of other minority ethnic groups? For further discussion on this, see *Judicial Appointments*, paras 102–108.

---

[71] Ministry of Justice, 11 May 2012, response to consultation CP19/2011. This report also included the Government's reaction to the report of the House of Lords Select Committee on the Constitution.

[72] Ministry of Justice, *Appointments and Diversity A Judiciary for the 21st Century, response to public consultation*, CP19/2011, 11 May 2012, para. 6.

[73] Ibid. See also, Lord Sumption, 'Home Truths about Judicial Diversity', Bar Council Law Reform Lecture, 15 November 2012, http://www.supremecourt.gov.uk/docs/speech-121115-lord-sumption.pdf.

(e) EXECUTIVE INVOLVEMENT IN APPOINTING JUDGES

The appointments process must reflect the need for judicial independence from the executive and the legislature, but this does not necessarily mean that the executive should have no role in the appointment of judges. Arguments in favour of the executive being involved in the appointment of judges were set out by the then Secretary of State for Justice and Lord Chancellor in his 2007 report, *Governance of Britain*.

Secretary of State for Justice and Lord Chancellor, *The Governance of Britain: Judicial Appointments*, Cm 7210 (October 2007), pp. 32–3 (footnote numbers in original altered or omitted)

4.13 First and foremost, the Government has responsibility for the justice system overall, including the efficiency and effectiveness with which justice is delivered via the courts, and the level to which they are resourced. [...]

4.14 Some have argued that a role for the executive in the appointments process, at least in relation to senior appointments, is essential to maintaining the executive's confidence *in* the senior judiciary.[74] The Lord Chief Justice commented in a recent speech that: 'there is a case for a limited power of veto in relation to the most senior appointments. The senior judiciary today have, to some extent, to work in partnership with government. It would, I think, be unfortunate if a Chief Justice were appointed in whose integrity and abilities the Government had no confidence.'[75]

4.15 If the executive were completely removed from decisions on appointments, this would increase separation between the executive and judiciary. However, a side-effect of this might be that the Lord Chancellor would cease to operate so effectively as a bridge between the judiciary and Government. There would also be a risk that the Lord Chancellor would be seen as less inclined to defend the judiciary against criticism ...

4.16 Further, reducing or removing the executive's role would reduce or remove the 'long-stop' mechanism in the CRA, whereby the JAC's individual recommendations can be challenged. ... its existence means that the JAC's ability to recommend selections to individual vacancies is capable of being subject to some degree of scrutiny. [...]

4.17 The executive plays a wider constitutional role in appointments. In our constitution, The Queen directly appoints Ministers, the more senior judges and other public office-holders. It is a constitutional convention that The Queen does so on the advice of the Prime Minister or other Ministers, rather than by exercising her own discretion. This is so that Ministers can be held to account for those decisions. This fact provides a rationale for retaining a role for Ministers in the process. For their advice to be meaningful, it can be argued that a Minister should have at least some say in the recommendation.

4.18 Ministers are accountable to Parliament for the decisions they make and for the advice they give to The Queen. Therefore, they need to be able to defend it. To defend it, they must be confident in it, and therefore, arguably, they should be able to question the decision that was made, or at the very least to have some leverage over or ability to question the overall process. If the role of Ministers were further reduced or removed entirely, an alternative mechanism for providing that accountability would need to be found.

---

[74] For example, Professor Robert Hazell, UCL Constitution Unit, Evidence to the Select Committee on the Constitutional Reform Bill, 6 April 2004.
[75] Commonwealth Law Conference Speech, Nairobi, 12 September 2007.

The government went on to say that the executive's role in appointing judges could be reduced by limiting or removing the Lord Chancellor's ability to reject a candidate selected by the JAC or to require the JAC to reconsider a selection. Another possibility is that the Lord Chancellor's involvement could be made formal only. Likewise, the Prime Minister's role in appointing the most senior judges could be removed. However, reducing the role of the Lord Chancellor and the involvement, albeit normally only formal, of the Prime Minister has potential costs in terms of accountability. As we have indicated earlier, the current government has decided—despite the contrary views of the House of Lords Select Committee on the Constitution,[76] to enhance the role of the Lord Chancellor marginally in relation to appointments of senior judges but to remove the Lord Chancellor from the appointment of judges below the High Court.

(f) PARLIAMENT'S ROLE IN APPOINTING JUDGES

As we have seen, one of the motivations for setting up judicial appointments commissions in the United Kingdom was to demonstrate that individual appointments are not subject to political influences—but what about accountability? In the old systems of judicial appointments, the Lord Chancellor was, in principle, answerable to the UK Parliament for the appointments made (although, in practice, this rarely if ever happened). In some other constitutional systems, an element of accountability for appointments is secured by giving the legislature a say—even a veto—in the process.

The UK Parliament plays no direct role in the appointment of the judiciary, although MPs and peers may—through questions and debates—require the Lord Chancellor to account for judicial appointments. Parliamentary select committees can also question the members of the JAC and explore matters arising from its annual report or reports by the JACO. Compared with the mechanism for judicial appointments in other systems, parliamentary involvement is already 'minimal' and could hardly be reduced.[77] Moreover, while the Lord Chief Justice of England and Wales and other senior judges do now appear before parliamentary committees to answer questions relating to the judiciary, individual judges are not accountable to Parliament in the way that ministers are.[78]

The system in the UK contrasts with that of some other jurisdictions—most markedly, the USA, where appointments by the President to the Supreme Court are subject to the 'advice and consent' of the Senate, and where the views of appointees, including their political views, are openly examined at confirmation hearings that are widely reported in the media. The appointment of Judge Sonia Sotomayor to the US Supreme Court provides an example of the contrast between the US and UK systems.

Richard Cornes, 'Appointing Supreme Court Justices in the United States and United Kingdom: What role for the legislator?' [2009] Public Law 836–8 (footnotes omitted)

For Four days in the early summer of 2009, Judge Sonia Sotomayor [...] nominee for Associate Justice of the US Supreme Court, daughter of Puerto Rican immigrants, and graduate of Yale Law School, appeared before the Judiciary Committee of the US Senate.

---

[76] The committee feared that an increase in the Lord Chancellor's role would run the risk of politicizing the process: *Judicial Appointments*, para. 26.

[77] *Governance of Britain*, para. 4.33.

[78] See Chapter 7.

From July 13, to July 17, she answered questions from Senators concerning her approach to judging, her understanding of various constitutional rights, even her position on televising hearings of the Court (it was apparent she would be in favour). On the final day the Committee heard testimony from witnesses for and against her nomination, or simply offering neutral expert views (for example, the American Bar Association presented its assessment of the candidate) [...]

The proceedings were broadcast live to air and online. Numerous news outlets ran daily programmes, or published daily columns, analysing what the Senators had asked and how she had answered-all with a view to answering the questions dominating the week: what sort of Associate Justice would Judge Sotomayor make? What new dynamic would she bring to the Supreme Court? How would elevating her to that Bench influence the development of the law?

[...] While there were often areas into which the nominee declined to go (following a now well established formula for nominees to refuse to comment on any controversy conceivably likely to come before the Court), the people of the United States ended the week knowing rather more about Sotomayor than at the start of the week.

On July 20, the Committee voted to endorse her (13 to 6—with 1 Republican Senator joining the Democratic members in her favour). On August 6, the Senate voted 68 to 31 to confirm her as the 111th Associate Justice of the US Supreme Court. In the final vote 9 Republicans broke with their party to support her. While confirmation votes are becoming more partisan, Sotomayor goes to the Supreme Court as most successful nominees do, with support from both sides of the aisle.

The House of Lords Select Committee on the Constitution heard evidence on whether Parliament should have a greater role in relation to individual judicial appointments, either in the form of pre-appointment hearings of the sort described by Cornes, or in the form of post-appointment hearings of the sort now used to question new governors and deputy governors of the Bank of England, and other members of the Bank's Monetary Policy Committee.

House of Lords Select Committee on the Constitution, *Judicial Appointments*,
25th Report, Session 2010–12 (footnotes omitted)

38. It is the responsibility of Parliament to establish the statutory framework for the judicial appointments process. Parliament also has an accountability role to play in overseeing the process and reviewing the success or failure of its operation. To what extent should Parliament or parliamentarians be involved in individual appointments? And how best can Parliament hold the Lord Chancellor and the JAC to account for the operation of the process?

PRE- OR POST-APPOINTMENT HEARINGS

39. We received evidence arguing that candidates for some senior judicial posts should be subject to a pre-appointment hearing before a parliamentary committee. Professor Robert Hazell ... and Professor Kate Malleson ... set out the arguments in favour of such hearings as follows:

• hearings act as a check on political patronage, help to ensure that independent and robust candidates are appointed and add to the appointee's legitimacy;

- Parliament has the power to scrutinise all acts of the executive—appointments of senior judges are an important exercise of ministerial discretion and should be subject to parliamentary scrutiny which is a useful check against political bias;

- Parliament nowadays has little contact with the judges: the senior judges are largely unknown to MPs; Supreme Court Justices will be unknown to the Lords now that the law lords have departed—through dialogue, political and judicial actors can better understand the constraints under which the other operates; and

- the judges should meet the body vested with the constitutional power to dismiss them.

40. A number of witnesses focused the case for some form of pre-appointment hearing on the increasingly complex role of the senior judiciary and the legitimate role for Parliament to consider candidates' competing judicial philosophies. Individual decisions made by judges impact on policy and determine the interpretation of legislation enacted by Parliament. Some witnesses argued that in respect of legislation such as the Human Rights Act 1998, and in the development of judicial review, the judiciary has a wide margin in which to develop the law and that Parliament has a legitimate interest in the manner in which this is done. [...]

41. Jack Straw MP, a former Lord Chancellor, stressed the need to address the "lack of mutual confidence between the senior judiciary and this place [Parliament] in respect of the role of the senior judiciary and its broadening authority into areas that are inevitably political". Sir Thomas Legg, former Permanent Secretary in the Lord Chancellor's Department, considered it to be "more and more desirable that our most senior judges should be able to ground their mandate on the authority, not only of the executive, still less of the judges themselves and a few laymen alone, but of Parliament itself."

[...]

43. The weight of our evidence was against pre-appointment hearings for UK judges. Professor Brice Dickson ... stressed the ability of Parliament to overturn individual judicial decisions, whilst Lord Kerr, Justice of the Supreme Court, described such hearings as "the complete antithesis of the preservation of judicial independence". The benefits of pre-appointment hearings in respect of senior public appointments are many, but the relationship between Parliament and the judiciary is a unique one. Parliament is best placed to protect the independence of, for example, ombudsmen from the executive. Judges must be independent of both the executive and Parliament: it is imperative that they remain one step removed from the political process.

44. Our witnesses also raised more immediate concerns about pre-appointment hearings. It would be difficult to limit the questioning of candidates to matters of general judicial philosophy and approach. There is a real danger that questions might touch on specific issues that could come before the courts or on candidates' individual political positions. Even if parliamentarians did limit themselves, the answers would either be at a level of such generality as to be effectively meaningless or be sufficiently detailed as to risk politicising the process. Some witnesses were concerned that hearings would act as a disincentive to many potential candidates. There is a further question of what impact criticism of a candidate, explicit or implicit, might have on his or her future public standing.

45. Pre-appointment hearings "would also risk undermining the public's confidence that the senior judiciary is appointed strictly on merit and having regard to integrity and independence." Roger Smith, Director of JUSTICE, thus described the proposal as "a quagmire into which no one would want to go."

> 46. We are against any proposal to introduce pre-appointment hearings for senior members of the judiciary. However limited the questioning, such hearings could not have any meaningful impact without undermining the independence of those subsequently appointed or appearing to pre-judge their future decisions. In the United Kingdom, judges' legitimacy depends on their independent status and appointment on merit, not on any democratic mandate.

The Committee went on to discuss post-appointment hearings but found little support for these and concluded that they would serve no useful purpose, except in relation to the Lord Chief Justice and the President of the Supreme Court who undertake leadership roles for which they can properly be held to account.[79]

An alternative way of securing Parliamentary involvement in judicial appointments is to enable parliamentarians to sit as members of selection panels for senior judicial appointments. In their evidence to the House of Lord Select Committee on the Constitution, both Lord Justice Etherton and Baroness Hale argued for this on the grounds that *'politicians have the legitimacy of being elected'*,[80] and it would be a *'a small step towards increasing the democratic accountability of the process'*.[81] Baroness Hale also argued that it *'would reduce the potential for "cloning"'*.[82] Others, including Lord Phillips and Lord Neuberger, disagreed, essentially on the ground that it would be undesirable to allow political criteria to become part of the appointments process.[83] The committee agreed with this, concluding that *'[T]here is no useful role that parliamentarians can play that could not be played by lay members on selection panels.'*[84]

QUESTIONS

1. What are the main arguments for and against executive and parliamentary involvement in judicial appointments?

2. Would you be in favour of candidates having to appear at pre-appointment hearings before a select committee of MPs? If you were an MP, what would be the main questions that would you ask a candidate for senior judicial office?

3. What, if any, changes to the current system of judicial appointments would you like to see?

---

7 THE USE OF JUDGES TO CHAIR PUBLIC INQUIRIES

In the UK, as in some other countries, judges are sometimes called upon to undertake activities outside the courtroom, including chairing bodies such as the Law Commission, committees (for example, Lord Nolan's chairmanship of the Committee on Standards in Public Life), and public inquiries.

---

[79] *Judicial Appointments*, para. 48.
[80] *Judicial Appointments*, para. 49.
[81] Ibid.
[82] Ibid.
[83] Ibid., paras 50, 51.
[84] Ibid., para. 52.

Public inquiries may be held for a variety of purposes, including examining alleged failings by ministers and officials, and the causes and implications of accidents (see Box 14.7). The main legislation governing public inquiries set up by UK government ministers is the Inquiries Act 2005, although ministers and local authorities also have other powers to do so.

BOX 14.7 EXAMPLES OF PUBLIC INQUIRIES CHAIRED BY JUDGES

- Lord Denning's inquiry into the Profumo affair[85] focused on the relationship between John Profumo, a Conservative Secretary of State for War, and Christine Keeler, a prostitute who had slept with a Soviet naval attaché.

- Lord Scarman's 1981 inquiry focused on the riots in Brixton, South London.[86]

- Lord Taylor's inquiry into the Hillsborough disaster, in which ninety-five standing spectators at a football match were crushed to death and over 400 were seriously injured led to the requirement that all spectators should have seats.[87]

- Sir Richard Scott's inquiry into 'the arms for Iraq affair' led to a report that was highly critical of ministers and of the Attorney General, and generated considerable political and legal debate.[88]

- Sir William MacPherson chaired the inquiry into the death of Stephen Lawrence.[89]

- Lord Hutton chaired the inquiry into the circumstances surrounding the death of Dr Kelly.[90]

- Lord Saville's inquiry into the events surrounding the deaths that occurred in Londonderry on Sunday 30 January 1972, referred to as 'Bloody Sunday', took more than ten years and cost more than £200m.

- Lord Justice Leveson's inquiry into the role of the press and police in the phone-hacking scandal.

Sir Jack Beatson (a High Court judge) tells us that, during the twentieth century, around 30 per cent of departmental and statutory inquiries were chaired by a judge, and that, between 1990 and 2004, out of the thirty-one notable inquiries, 65.5 per cent were chaired by a serving or retired judge.

Sir Jack Beatson, 'Should judges conduct public inquiries?' (2005) 121 Law Quarterly Review 221 (footnotes omitted)

There was [...] a media frenzy after Lord Hutton published his report on 28 January 2004 into the circumstances surrounding the death of Dr David Kelly, the government arms expert caught up in the maelstrom between the British Government and the BBC that arose as the

---

[85] *The Security Service and Mr Profumo*, Cmnd 2152, September 1963.

[86] *The Scarman Report, The Brixton Disorders, 10–12 April* (1981, Manchester: Pelican Press).

[87] *The Hillsborough Stadium Disaster*, Interim Report Cm. 765 (December 1989); Final Report Cm. 962 (May 1990).

[88] *The Scott Report*, Cm 115 (February 1996).

[89] *Report of the Stephen Lawrence Inquiry*, Cm 4262-I (February 1999).

[90] *Report of the Inquiry into the Circumstances Surrounding the Death of Dr David Kelly*, HC 247 (January 2004).

result of an unscripted live news broadcast about the government's dossier on Iraqi weapons of mass destruction. Lord Hutton concluded that an allegation in the broadcast that Downing Street ordered what was then rather a bland document to be 'sexed up', and that the Government 'probably knew' that a statement in it that Iraq could deploy its biological and chemical weapons within 45 minutes, was unfounded. Politicians, lawyers and journalists opined not only on his conclusions, but also on the appropriateness of a judge chairing such an inquiry at all or without assessors.

[...]

On 13 May the Public Administration Committee questioned Lord Hutton about his report and its reception. This is, as far as I know, without precedent. The Committee agreed not to question him directly about his findings or to challenge his core judgment. He was asked how his terms of reference had been formulated, why he had construed them as he did, why he had not considered the reliability of the intelligence provided to the government, why he had not recalled the Prime Minister for further questioning, and many other probing questions. The Chairman of the Committee contrasted the press treatment before Lord Hutton reported with that afterwards. Before and during the inquiry he was seen as 'sainted, a fearless forensic investigator'; afterwards he was 'an Establishment lackey' unfamiliar with government or the media who had produced a 'whitewash'. Lord Hutton gave a robust defence to both the specific and the general criticisms.

Events such as these have generated serious debate as to whether judges should be employed in ways that draw them into political debate and controversy in a manner that risks damaging both the reputation of individual judges and the judiciary in general.

Should judges be called upon to chair inquiries?

Three reasons are given for using judges to chair inquiries:

(a) because they are considered to possess the skills necessary for running inquiries, such as handling the questioning of witnesses and conducting proceedings fairly;

(b) because of their independence and neutrality, especially from the government, they confer authority and legitimacy on the inquiry process and on its findings—a quality to which Professor Jowell has referred as 'symbolic reassurance';[91] and

(c) because they are available and it is relatively easy to transfer them from their normal judicial duties.

The Select Committee on Public Administration, however, which embarked on its own inquiry into 'Government by Inquiries' two weeks after the publication of Lord Hutton's report, said that it found none of these reasons to be totally compelling.

Select Committee on Public Administration, *Government by Inquiry*, First Report, Session 2004–05, HC 51-1 (footnotes omitted)

44. [...] Professor Jowell argues that judges operate in the context of 'guidance of principle derived from similar previous cases. Political controversies, however narrowly confined,

---

[91] Select Committee on Public Administration, *Government by Inquiry*, First Report, Session 2004–05 (HC 51 1), para. 42.

normally involve a wider set of relevant issues [...] and a different set of principles to those found in the law reports'. Mr Justice Beatson noted that the 'skills' argument is strongest where the task of the inquiry is solely to find facts. It is less compelling where issues of social or economic policy with political implications are involved'. Judges are also unlikely to have the professional expertise of someone like Lord Laming who told us:

'I would like to suggest that there are few judges who have managed a big workforce, managed a public agency, managed big budgets in competing priorities, dealt with the party political machine, both locally and nationally, dealt with trade unions going about their perfectly legitimate business and dealt with the media day by day'.

[...]

46. [...] Lord Woolf made [the] point [that], 'today, judges do not often have any insight into the workings of the public service'. Hence Mr Justice Beatson concludes: 'Given the political nature of the British constitution, judicial skills may not necessarily be the most appropriate where an inquiry concerns the relationship between the government and Parliament'. These reservations are reflected in the view of Lord Hutton's Report expressed by another of our witnesses, Sir Louis Blom-Cooper QC, who wrote: 'Perhaps it might be said that the Report reflected absolutely Lord Hutton's qualities as a judge, meticulous and superb in the analysis of details and evidence, but more evidently questionable on matters of wider judgment'.

47. The notion of judges as above the political process has also begun to be challenged. The growth of public law in recent years has made this more apparent as judges have come to play an increasing role in determining cases which raise political and constitutional issues. [...]

48. The authority of the judiciary, itself seen as a valuable import into an inquiry, risks being damaged by its aftermath. Those who do not agree with an inquiry's conclusions may not perceive it as independent and objective, regardless of whether the chair is a member of the judiciary. The authority that judges are said to lend to an inquiry may therefore not be sufficient for its conclusions to be accepted [...] and their authority can be undermined by attempts to discredit their findings. This is particularly true in politically sensitive inquiries. If their reports fail to conclude that ministers and senior officials are to blame, they may be heralded as a 'whitewash' by political opponents and the media and the judge criticised [...]

49. Such criticisms have the potential to damage the reputation of the individual judge, and Mr Justice Beatson considers that 'perceived deficiencies [...] whether procedural or substantive, will follow a judge back to the bench'. [...] As Professor Jowell suggested, this may have a 'corrosive effect on public trust in the judiciary'.

52. Nor is the use of judges cost free either from the House of Lords, as now, or from the Supreme Court in future. Extra judicial activities impact upon the workings of the courts. [...]

54. [...] the nature of judicial responsibilities and the requirements of judicial office have changed. The expansion of judicial review, the incorporation of the European Convention on Human Rights (ECHR) through the Human Rights Act 1998, and the devolution legislation [...] are likely to increase the number of constitutional issues that come before the courts. These could include such matters as alleged infringements of human rights by legislation or executive action and disputes about the division of power between the Scottish and Westminster Parliaments. Such cases give senior judges a larger constitutional, and hence political, role and make it even more important that they are not only independent and impartial but are seen as such. On its visit to the United States the Committee encountered the established view there that it was constitutionally and politically inappropriate for judges to undertake inquiries.

The Committee identified twenty-three questions that need to be addressed regarding inquiries, including whether it is appropriate for judges to chair them. Its view was that there is value in using senior judges to chair *fact-finding inquiries which are at a distance from government*', but it said that judges should not be required to chair inquiries into issues at the centre of government, which are, by their nature, politically contentious and require an understanding of how government works.[92]

The government responded by publishing its own consultation paper, *Effective Inquiries*,[93] in which it said that the most important criteria for a chair are independence and skills or experience appropriate for the task. In some cases, this will require a judge or senior lawyer, and in others, it may be more appropriate to appoint a non-judicial chairman.[94] This response is hardly surprising, but provides no answer to concerns about the standing and reputation of the judges. If judges are to be in politically controversial inquiries, it has been argued that there must be protections built into the system. Sir Jack Beatson, for example, has argued that it should not be for the government alone to choose the judge who is to chair an inquiry or to determine its terms of reference. In Israel, the head of the judiciary makes the appointment. Beatson argues that the appointment should at least be with the agreement of the Chief Justice. He also argues that the head of the judiciary and the individual judge should also have some input into agreeing the terms of reference. A further reform that would go some way towards protecting the judiciary would be a requirement that the government can reject a report only if reasons are given.[95]

When discussing the Scarman and MacPherson inquiries, Lord Morris of Aberavon, a former Attorney General, said that '[w]*hen a judge enters the market place of public affairs outside his court and throws coconuts he is likely to have the coconuts thrown back at him. If one values the standing of the judiciary [...] the less they are used the better it will be*'.[96] Having cited this comment, Sir Jack Beatson concludes as follows.

Sir Jack Beatson, 'Should judges conduct public inquiries?' (2005) 121 Law Quarterly Review 221 (footnotes omitted)

Judges should only be used to conduct inquiries where there is a vital public interest in them doing so and if they are given appropriate protective clothing against coconuts and other missiles. The protective clothing needed is not anything that would stifle wide debate about and close examination of a report by government, the media, and the public. It is provided by creating the institutional framework of an appropriate system for appointing the judicial members of inquiries, and a more structured and measured approach by government and other public bodies affected by an inquiry to its findings of fact and personal and policy recommendations.

In relation to the appointment of judges to chair inquiries, s. 10 of the Inquiries Act 2005 provides as follows.

---

[92] At para. 57.
[93] DCA Cp 12/04, May 2004.
[94] At para. 49.
[95] Sir Jack Beatson, 'Should judges conduct inquiries' (2005) 121 Law Quarterly Review 221.
[96] House of Lords Hansard, 21 May 2003, vol. 648, col. 883.

Inquiries Act 2005

10 Appointment of judge as panel member

(1) If the Minister proposes to appoint as a member of an inquiry panel a particular person who is a judge of a description specified in the first column of the following table, he must first consult the person specified in the second column.

Description of judge	Person to be consulted
Judge of the Supreme Court of England and Wales, or Circuit judge	The Lord Chief Justice of England and Wales
Judge of the Court of Session, sheriff principal or sheriff	The Lord President of the Court of Session
Judge of the Supreme Court of Northern Ireland, or county court judge in Northern Ireland	The Lord Chief Justice of Northern Ireland

QUESTIONS

1. '*Professor Robert Stevens has highlighted the irony of a government arguing, on the one hand, for the establishment of a Supreme Court and Judicial Appointments Commission and the abolition of the office of Lord Chancellor, on the grounds that "the judiciary and politics live in totally different systems and never the twain shall meet", while, on the other, continuing to "offer the judges on the sacrificial alter of public inquiries, which inevitably have a greater or lesser political content".'* (Select Committee on Public Administration, *Government by Inquiry*, First Report, Session 2004–05, HC 51 1, para. 56)

   In what circumstances, if at all, should judges be called upon to chair inquiries?

2. Commenting on the proposal to introduce s. 10 of the Inquiries Act 2005, Lord Woolf said that consultation with the senior judiciary is not sufficient: '[T]*he Chief Justice should be able to say no. In these days the Executive should not be able to tell a judge what he is going to do and select the judge who is going to do it. This is a retrograde step.*'[97] If you had been advising the executive, what arguments would you have advised ministers to make in response to Lord Woolf?

8 CONCLUDING COMMENTS

There are many indications that the constitutional reforms of the past decade or so have increased the constitutional importance of the judiciary. This has highlighted the need to provide a clearer articulation of what judicial independence means, and how it is to be achieved and maintained. Judges have been increasingly drawn into matters of controversy,

[97] Select Committee on Public Administration, *Government by Inquiry*, First Report, Session 2004–05 (HC 51 1), para. 56.

both in relation to their role as judges and when called upon to perform other activities, such as chairing inquiries. While few, if any, judges are household names (or celebrities), the profile of the judiciary and of individual judges is now much higher than it was a generation or so ago. But there is a need to ensure that judges maintain, and are seen to maintain, their impartiality and independence. Judges should not be disconnected from society, but they may need to be protected from personal criticisms—especially when that criticism comes from members of the government. As the judicial role has become more visible, the need to maintain public confidence in the judiciary has grown in importance. Public confidence will not be maintained if judges are perceived to be an out-of-touch, male-dominated elite; as we have seen, progress has been made towards achieving greater diversity, but progress has been slow and has only quickened in the past year or so.

9 FURTHER READING

Bradley, A.W., 'The Constitutional Position of the Judiciary', in D. Feldman (ed.) *English Public Law*, 2nd edn (2009, Oxford: OUP), ch. 6

Griffith, J.A.G., *The Politics of the Judiciary*, 5th edn (1997, London: Fontana Press)

Judiciary of England and Wales, *Lord Chief Justice's Review of the Administration of Justice in the Courts* (2010, London: HMSO)

Malleson, K., *The New Judiciary: The Effects of Expansion and Activism* (1999, London: Ashgate Press)

Malleson, K., and Russell, P., (eds) *Appointing Judges in an Age of Judicial Power: Critical Perspectives from Around the World* (2006, Toronto: University of Toronto Press)

Stevens, R., *The English Judges: Their Role in the Changing Constitution* (2002, Oxford: Hart Publishing)

WEBSITES

The Judicial Appointments Commission	http://www.judicialappointments.gov.uk/
The Judiciary of England and Wales	http://www.judiciary.gov.uk/

ONLINE RESOURCE CENTRE
Further information about the themes discussed in this chapter can be found on the Online Resource Centre at www.oxfordtextbooks.co.uk/orc/lesueur2e/

15

ADMINISTRATIVE JUSTICE: TRIBUNALS AND OMBUDSMEN

CENTRAL ISSUES

1. When public bodies make decisions about the rights and entitlements of individuals, these decisions must be correct and lawful. If people are dissatisfied, they should be able to have decisions reconsidered and have access to independent bodies that are able to ensure that the required standards have been met.

2. Access to the courts is a fundamental right, but the courts form only part of the 'landscape of administrative justice'. Only a small proportion of disputes between individuals and public bodies reach the courts; most are dealt with by the public bodies following complaints or requests to look at decisions again, by appeals to independent tribunals, or by complaints to ombudsmen.

3. It is important that disputes are resolved by the most appropriate procedures as quickly and as cheaply as possible. These requirements may be summarized by the requirement for 'proportionate dispute resolution' (PDR) and the need to get 'things right first time'. While recognizing the benefits of PDR, some fear that encouraging 'informal' resolution of disputes between individuals and public bodies, and discouraging involvement of the courts, may conflict with the underlying values of constitutionalism.

4. This chapter explores the main elements of the administrative justice system, including the importance of improving the quality of initial decision-making, the tribunal system, and the role and use of ombudsmen.

1 INTRODUCTION

Government ministers and officials make countless decisions that are directly concerned with the rights and interests of individuals in matters as diverse as claims for welfare benefits and pensions, the provision of services, rights to stay in the country, liability to pay taxes, and so on. A constitutional system should provide ways in which people can question such decisions and seek redress if errors and wrongs occur, and are not rectified. This requirement is basic, but what does it actually entail and what are the redress mechanisms available within the UK system?

Lawyers will tend to think in terms of access to courts and the availability of legal remedies—and in particular judicial review. This is of undoubted importance; judicial review and the main legal arguments that can be addressed to courts are examined in Chapter 16, Chapter 17, and Chapter 18. Using courts, however, is a last resort: the courts are only part of the picture—and some would say a very small part. Certainly, only a tiny proportion of disputes between individuals and public bodies ever reach the courts.

In this chapter, we consider the main ways in which disputes between individuals and public bodies are resolved outside the court system in what is widely referred to as the landscape of 'administrative justice'.

(a) THE LANDSCAPE OF 'ADMINISTRATIVE JUSTICE'

The expression 'administrative justice' indicates that the day-to-day administration of government must satisfy requirements of justice and that the delivery of justice is not the sole responsibility of civil or criminal courts. The use of the term 'justice' in this context also indicates that 'just' or 'good' administration is a matter of constitutional necessity rather than government largesse.[1] The following explanation of administrative justice was set out in the 2004 White Paper, *Transforming Public Services: Complaints, Redress and Tribunals*.

Secretary of State for Constitutional Affairs and Lord Chancellor, *Transforming Public Services: Complaints, Redress and Tribunals* (Cm 6243) July 2004

Administrative justice

1.3 In a democracy the framework within which we all live is set by democratic institutions acting in the public interest. But where State institutions do not just set a framework but make decisions about the rights and obligations of individuals, the state also has an important duty towards that individual. Central, devolved and local government make millions of such decisions every year. What if government gets it wrong? What if the individual feels aggrieved by the decision? What if the individual does not realise that government has got it wrong? Each of us has the right to expect that State institutions will make the right decisions about our individual circumstances.

1.4 The overwhelming majority of these decisions are taken by public officials, usually operating as part of a government department or State agency. Their job is to get those decisions about individuals right. [...]

1.5 No system will ever be perfect. There will always be errors and complaints. There will always be uncertainties about how the law should be applied to the circumstances of individuals. There will often be gaps in knowledge and understanding about an individual's circumstances. We are all entitled to receive correct decisions on our personal circumstances; where a mistake occurs we are entitled to complain and to have the mistake put right with the minimum of difficulty; where there is uncertainty we are entitled to expect a quick resolution of the issue; and we are entitled to expect that where things have gone wrong the system will learn from the problem and will do better in the future.

1.6 This is the sphere of administrative justice. It embraces not just courts and tribunals but the millions of decisions taken by thousands of civil servants and other officials.

---

[1] See, e.g., Lord Justice Laws, in *Niazi v Secretary of State* [2008] EWCA 755, discussed at p. 732.

Ann Abraham, Parliamentary and Health Services Ombudsman 2002–11, summarized the importance of administrative justice in the following way.

Ann Abraham, *The Parliamentary Ombudsman and Administrative Justice: Shaping the Next 50 Years*, JUSTICE, Tom Sargant Memorial Annual Lecture, October 2011

ADMINISTRATIVE JUSTICE: WHY IT MATTERS

[...] let me remind you why [Administrative Justice] matters. Administrative justice can sometimes seem the poor relation by comparison with the civil, criminal and family justice regimes. Yet citizens are just as likely, if not more likely, to come across administrative justice issues in their ordinary lives than civil or even family justice issues. The outcomes of decision making by a wide-range of public bodies on a daily basis affect family incomes, jobs, healthcare, housing, education and much, much more.

To illustrate the point—in 2010 in England and Wales:

- There were around 63,000 hearings/trials dealing with civil justice matters;

- There were over 200,000 criminal justice hearings/trials;

- There were over **650,000** administrative justice hearings—of which over 275,000 were about social security and child support.

Administrative justice, then, concerns the way in which public bodies deal with the rights and interests of individuals, and the provision of redress when things go wrong. The landscape of administrative justice can be considered from a point of view that focuses on the substance of the matters with which the bodies deal. From this angle, it is relevant across the broad spectrum of situations in which government public bodies make decisions that directly affect individuals, including social welfare, taxation, immigration, and housing, to name only a few.

The second point of view focuses on the institutions and processes by which administrative justice is delivered. Here, too, the spectrum is broad, extending from the millions of decisions taken daily by street-level or front-desk officials in, for example, housing or social service departments of local authorities, to decisions of independent tribunals and courts. This chapter focuses primarily on this procedural and institutional dimension of administrative justice.

(b) THE 'SYSTEM' OF ADMINISTRATIVE JUSTICE

A statutory definition of 'administrative justice system' is as follows.

Tribunals Courts and Enforcement Act 2007, Sch. 7, para. 13(4)

In this paragraph 'the administrative justice system' means the overall system by which decisions of an administrative or executive nature are made in relation to particular persons, including—

(a) the procedures for making such decisions,

(b) the law under which such decisions are made, and

(c) the systems for resolving disputes and airing grievances in relation to such decisions.

The purpose of this definition is to delineate the scope of the responsibilities to be undertaken by the Administrative Justice and Tribunals Council (AJTC).

Administrative Justice and Tribunals Council

The AJTC was established by the 2007 Act to replace the Council on Tribunals.[2] Its -purpose is to help make administrative justice and tribunals more accessible, fair, and -effective by:

(a) playing a pivotal role in the development of coherent principles and good practice;

(b) promoting understanding, learning, and continuous improvement; and

(c) ensuring that the needs of users are central.

The AJTC, and the Scottish and Welsh Committees, have been an important influence; their annual reports and publications provide a wealth of information on developments in administrative justice.

Nonetheless, one of the early initiatives of the Coalition Government was to propose the abolition of the AJTC as part of its 'bonfire of the QUANGOS' (a policy designed to cut public expenditure by reducing the number of public bodies). Unsurprisingly, there was widespread opposition, including that expressed by the House of Commons Public Administration Select Committee, which found that the Government's rationale for winding up the AJTC to be 'questionable'.[3] The Committee's chair Bernard Jenkin MP (a Conservative MP) said:

> "The AJTC should be part of the machinery to help government get decisions 'right first time'. Instead, over half a million decisions have to be reviewed each year, at great cost and considerable injustice and inconvenience to citizens. If the AJTC is abolished, what will take its place, and how will Government do better?"

Despite opposition, the Public Bodies Act 2011 opened the way for abolition of the AJTC and the government refused to back down. This decision represents a serious step backwards in the oversight of the administrative justice as it is unlikely that another body will have the expertise, resources, or independence needed to undertake this important work.

Such is the breadth and diversity of matters that fall within the statutory definition that the term 'system' cannot be taken literally. The truth is that there is no single coherent institutional structure of administrative justice equivalent to the systems of civil or criminal justice that are focused on the civil and criminal courts. On the contrary, the landscape of administrative justice is, in reality, populated by distinct institutions that have different access requirements, responsibilities, ways of operating, and powers. The following account gives an overview of the complex picture.

Administrative Justice Steering Group of the Scottish Consumer Council,
Administrative Justice in Scotland: The Way Forward—The Final Report (2009,
Glasgow: Consumer Focus Scotland)

3.21 The development of grievance machinery in the UK has been largely ad-hoc and resulted in the proliferation of bodies and procedures. At the end of the twentieth century,

---

[2] See http://www.ajtc.gov.uk/.

[3] House of Commons Public Administration Select Committee—Twenty-First Report, Session 2011–2012, _Future oversight of administrative justice: the proposed abolition of the Administrative Justice and Tribunals Council._

there was no overall system of administrative justice within either Scotland or the UK, and no serious attempt had ever been made to construct one. Tribunals in particular exhibited the effects of piece-meal evolution, there being a large number of specific tribunals each hearing appeals from different administrative agencies, and lacking a common approach on a range of important matters such as qualifications of members, rules of procedure, and whether there was a further right of appeal from the tribunal to a higher tribunal or to the courts. However, the tendency to proliferation of mechanisms was a general one exhibited also by ombudsmen and other complaints procedures. Like tribunals, these mechanisms for redress lacked a common approach to their function of providing redress of grievances. However, the last decade has been a period of great change in administrative justice and rationalisation and system design has been put firmly on the agenda. [. . .]

This report refers to tribunals, but precisely the same comments can be made in relation to the proliferation of ombudsmen (as we shall see). A result of the ad hoc proliferation has been to make the administrative justice system extremely difficult for users to navigate. It also means that while some aspects of a problem can be handled by one institution or process, other aspects must be handled by somebody else.

The resulting difficulties were clearly illustrated by the profoundly unsatisfactory way in which Mr and Mrs Balchin's complaints were handled. Mr and Mrs Balchin complained of maladministration by the Secretary of State for Transport when confirming road orders concerning the construction of a road in Norfolk. In the fourth report of the Parliamentary Ombudsman (PO) which dealt with their complaints, Ann Abraham (the then PO) noted that three previous reports of the PO had been successfully challenged in judicial review proceedings.[4] She also noted while she could investigate central government's involvement, aspects of the complaint concerned local government and these had to be separately investigated by the local government ombudsman.

In concluding her fourth report, Ann Abraham made the following comment.

Parliamentary Ombudsman Case No. C57/94, *Redress in the Round: Remedying Maladministration in Central and Local Government* (2005)

113. There is ... one final observation that I would like to make. Mr and Mrs Balchin's case has served to demonstrate very clearly to me the considerable complications which currently arise when cases cross more than one Ombudsman jurisdiction. Whilst the Local Government Ombudsman and I have collaborated closely throughout our respective investigations, the restrictions on our ability to work together have nevertheless meant that we have not been able to provide the sort of fully-joined up and coherent service for Mr and Mrs Balchin that we should be able to provide to all citizens who have such complaints. [. . .]

The particular problems identified here were largely addressed by a regulatory order made under the Regulatory Reform Act 2001, which amended provisions of primary legislation making it easier for the Parliamentary Ombudsman, the Health Service Ombudsman, and the Local Government Ombudsman for England to work together collaboratively on cases.[5]

---

[4] *R (Balchin and ors) v Parliamentary Commissioner for Administration (No. 1)* [1998] PLR 1; *R (Balchin and ors) v Parliamentary Commissioner for Administration (No. 2)* [2000] P&CR 157; *R (Balchin and ors) v Parliamentary Commissioner for Administration (No. 3)* [2002] EWHC 1876.

[5] The Regulatory Reform (Collaboration etc between Ombudsmen) Order 2007 (SI 2007/1889).

Nonetheless, the case highlights the more general problem of diversity and overlap that has remained one of the key issues that reformers have been trying to tackle in order to improve access to administrative justice.

(c) PERSPECTIVES ON ADMINISTRATIVE JUSTICE

Lawyers' dispute resolution work is focused on the courts. The typical legal view is that courts set precedents and establish legal standards that are intended to inform decision-making elsewhere in the system, so that decision-makers in public bodies, with the help of their lawyers, can learn from court judgments. In this way, it is expected that legal precedents will lead to improvement in the quality of decision-making.

Another way of viewing the system reflects how members of the general public experience administrative justice. In practice, people will come into contact with the administrative justice system whenever:

- decisions about their rights and interests are taken by officials;
- they want to have decisions looked at again by officials in the body concerned or to complain about the way in which their case has been handled;
- they want to appeal to an independent tribunal or complain to an ombudsman; or
- they seek further recourse to the courts.

This way of viewing things is now associated with the emphasis on 'proportionate dispute resolution' (PDR), to which we shall turn in a moment.

A third, and perhaps a more dynamic, way of viewing the system is one that reflects the idea that complaints can do more than lead to the resolution of an individual grievance; they can also alert the decision-makers to systemic problems within the organization and lead to overall improvements for the benefit of many others. Indeed, organizations are encouraged to view complaints in this positive light rather than to respond defensively to them.

This model is summarized in Figure 15.1, taken from the Administrative Justice and Tribunals Council's *Developing the Administrative Justice Landscape*.[6]

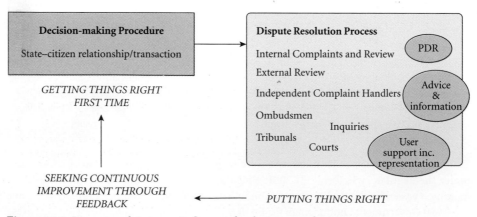

Figure 15.1 How complaints can influence the decision-making process

---

[6] http://www.ajtc.gov.uk/adjust/articles/landscape_paper.pdf.

(d) PROPORTIONATE DISPUTE RESOLUTION (PDR)

The UK government's stated strategy has been to help people to avoid problems and legal disputes in the first place. If problems arise, there must be tailored solutions to resolve the dispute as quickly and cost-effectively as possible without recourse to tribunals or courts. In cases in which tribunals and courts are used, they must also be cost-effective.

Secretary of State for Constitutional Affairs and Lord Chancellor,
Transforming Public Services: Complaints, Redress and Tribunals
(Cm 6243) July 2004

Proportionate Dispute Resolution

2.2 Our strategy turns on its head the [...] traditional emphasis first on courts, judges and court procedure, and second on legal aid to pay mainly for litigation lawyers. It starts instead with the real world problems people face. The aim is to develop a range of policies and services that, so far as possible, will help people to avoid problems and legal disputes in the first place; and where they cannot, provides tailored solutions to resolve the dispute as quickly and cost effectively as possible. It can be summed up as 'Proportionate Dispute Resolution'.

2.3 We want to:

- minimise the risk of people facing legal problems by ensuring that the framework of law defining people's rights and responsibilities is as fair, simple and clear as possible, and that State agencies, administering systems like tax and benefits, make better decisions and give clearer explanations;

- improve people's understanding of their rights and responsibilities, and the information available to them about what they can do and where they can go for help when problems do arise. This will help people to decide how to deal with the problem themselves if they can, and ensure they get the advice and other services they need if they cannot;

- ensure that people have ready access to early and appropriate advice and assistance when they need it, so that problems can be solved and potential disputes nipped in the bud long before they escalate into formal legal proceedings;

- promote the development of a range of tailored dispute resolution services, so that different types of dispute can be resolved fairly, quickly, efficiently and effectively, without recourse to the expense and formality of courts and tribunals where this is not necessary;

- but also deliver cost-effective court and tribunal services, that are better targeted on those cases where a hearing is the best option for resolving the dispute or enforcing the outcome.

2.4 [...] at the core of our vision is the idea that policies and services must be tailored to the particular needs of people in different contexts, moving away from the limited flexibility of the existing court and legal aid systems.

Genevra Richardson and Hazel Genn, 'Tribunals in transition: Resolution or adjudication?' [2007] Public Law 116, 122 (original footnote numbering altered)

[...] Although rather vague, the term PDR is intended to convey the principle that dispute resolution procedures should be appropriate and 'proportionate' to the nature of the dispute, meaning that issues capable of early and simple resolution should not be forced along the same, inflexible procedure, as issues that are more complex and perhaps intractable. It is the concept of 'fitting the forum to the fuss'[7] so that institutions are capable of offering a range of resolution procedures depending on the nature of the dispute.

(e) CLASHING VALUES: INFORMALITY AND CONSTITUTIONALISM

Few will object to the idea of improving the quality of decision-making and developing tailored solutions to problems, thereby reducing the need to use the courts. It has been argued, however, that this strategy is problematic—especially if it involves preventing people from using the courts and stops judges from developing standards that could improve the quality of administrative justice. Andrew Le Sueur, for example, argues that the trend towards greater 'constitutionalism', which is evident in the constitutional reform programme in general,[8] sits uneasily with the 'informality' that is implicit in the government's approach to administrative justice and represents a clash of values.

Andrew Le Sueur, 'Courts, Tribunals, Ombudsmen, ADR: Administrative Justice, Constitutionalism and Informality', in J. Jowell and D. Oliver (eds) *The Changing Constitution*, 6th edn (2007, Oxford: OUP), p. 333

What has been suggested [...] is that there are two currents – changes associated with the promotion of constitutionalism and changes designed to implement values associated with informality. It is paradoxical that just at a time when courts and tribunals, traditionally the arenas for adjudication by judges, are being put on new and firmer constitutional footings so – simultaneously – there are attempts to steer disputes away from them. If the 'informalization' project is as successful as its supporters hope, fewer cases will be decided by judges finding facts and applying the law, and more by civil servants and third-parties through negotiation, mediation, early neutral evaluation and so on.

We shall return to this clash of values.

2 INITIAL DECISION-MAKING

It is perhaps self-evident that justice is served when decisions are made correctly in the first place. This also has advantages for the public bodies in question. The 2004 *Transforming Public Services* White Paper introduced the phrase 'getting it right first time'.

---

[7] F. Sander and S. Goldberg, 'Fitting the forum to the fuss' (1994) 10 Negotiation Journal 49.
[8] See, e.g., the statutory frameworks for judicial independence and judicial appointments discussed in Chapter 14.

Secretary of State for Constitutional Affairs and Lord Chancellor, *Transforming Public Services: Complaints, Redress and Tribunals* (Cm 6243) July 2004

6.32 [...] 'Right First Time' means a better result for the individual, less work for appeal mechanisms and lower cost for departments.'

Getting 'it right first time' means that officials must:

- make decisions in a timely fashion;
- know the applicable law, procedure and policy;
- listen to what those affected by their decisions have to say;
- be able to assess and weigh the facts;
- provide clear and accurate reasons for decisions;

There must also be suitable mechanisms to review decisions within public bodies.

(a) WHY IS IT SO HARD TO GET IT RIGHT FIRST TIME?

It may seem elementary to say that public bodies should get things right first time—but experience indicates that large administrations, such as UK government departments, executive agencies, and local authorities, often find this difficult to do. There can be many reasons for this, including the complexity of the law and a failure to understand public law principles properly. Some of the additional problems are identified in the extract from the report of Robert Martin, President of Appeal Tribunals 2007–08, which follows.[9]

The President of Appeal Tribunals was responsible for tribunals that dealt with appeals from decisions taken by officials across a range of social security matters, such as Disability Living Allowance, Incapacity Benefit, Income Support, Child Support, and Jobseeker's Allowance. In strict law, these are decisions of the Secretary of State, although, of course, they are not taken by the Secretary of State, but by officials in his name.[10] In this extract, HHJ Robert Martin comments on the quality of initial decision-making and the ways in which this could be improved. Having surveyed case outcomes for the years 2000–01 to 2007–08, he notes that no significant changes occurred in the proportion of tribunal decisions that overturned initial decisions. This, he argues, indicates that no improvement occurred in the quality of initial decision-making during that period. He goes on to explain where the main errors were made and how the provision of effective feedback to the initial decision-makers might improve the situation.

President of Appeal Tribunals, *Report on the Standards of Decision-making by the Secretary of State 2007–2008* (2008, London: Tribunals Service) (footnotes omitted)

1.2 [...] Millions of decisions are made each year by the Secretary of State on entitlement to social security benefits. Only a small portion of those decisions—229,120 in

---

[9] Following the reform of the tribunal system (as we shall see shortly), the office of President of Appeal Tribunals was abolished and the jurisdiction of these tribunals transferred to the First-tier Tribunal. HHJ Robert Martin became President of the Social Entitlement Chamber of the First-tier Tribunal Chamber.

[10] See the *Carltona* doctrine, discussed in Chapter 16.

2007–2008—were challenged by way of appeal and referred to the Tribunals Service. It would be rash to extrapolate from that small portion when looking at overall standards of administrative decision making. While we cannot say definitively that the cases we see are more likely to be cases where the Secretary of State has reached the wrong conclusion, common sense suggests, subject to one proviso, that that is likely to be so. The proviso, of course, is that tribunals tend to see cases where claimants consider an adverse decision has been wrongly made: tribunals are less likely to see cases where a decision that is wrongly advantageous to the claimant has been made.

[The President reviewed the volumes of cases dealt with by his tribunals during the years 2000–08 and the percentage in which decisions of the Secretary of State were overturned.]

1.8 [...] one is left with the striking impression that there has been no significant improvement in the quality of administrative decisions coming before Appeal Tribunals. The proportion that is overturned by the tribunal is no less now than when the modernising reforms were introduced.

1.9 [...] Perhaps the most valuable source of feedback [that would help decision-makers] is to be gleaned from attending the hearing. Were the Secretary of State to be represented at the hearing, it would allow a direct flow of utilisable information channelled to the original decision-maker. It is not particularly helpful for a decision-maker merely to read from the decision notice issued by the tribunal that the appeal has been overturned (or, indeed, dismissed, since the tribunal might have dismissed it on completely different grounds from those underpinning the original decision). That bare statement is not sufficient because it does nothing to improve the decision-maker's understanding. [...] What, in my view, would be conducive to improved decision-making would be feedback from a Presenting Officer, drawn from observing what actually transpired at the hearing, directed to the original decision maker and tailored to such modifications to (or affirmations of) the decision-maker's approach as might be appropriate.

1.10 The importance of the Secretary of State being represented at the tribunal hearing has been stressed not only repeatedly in these reports, but also by the Social Security Commissioners [... the] Tribunals Service and by the Department's own Standards Committee. Yet [...] there has been a steady decline in the percentage of appeal hearings attended by a Presenting Officer. In the current year it is down from 27% to 23%.

[...]

Findings

1.13 Since the first report was published in 2001, the following key themes have regularly emerged:

- Decisions are most commonly overturned because the tribunal elicits additional information, usually by talking with the appellant at the hearing. The ready availability of this additional information suggests that there should be more engagement by the Department with the appellant, preferably face to face.

- There is no consistent evidence to show that cases are effectively reconsidered before coming to the tribunal. Often the appeal papers show an unwillingness on the part of the decision-maker to reconsider the decision in the absence of the appellant supplying fresh medical or other third party evidence.

- Some medical reports underestimate the severity of disability;

- There is confusion on the part of decision-makers about the appropriate evidential weight to be given to medical reports;
- People with particular disabilities, such as sensory impairment or mental health problems, may face additional difficulties in making benefit claims and using the process of appeal.

1.14 These have been fairly consistent findings from the annual reports over the past eight years. They are reinforced by the findings of other bodies, including the Department's own Standards Committee1, the National Audit Office (NAO) and the Committee of Public Accounts (PAC).

Problems with the quality of initial decisions are not limited to social security-type claims. Much criticism, for example, has also been levelled at the quality of decisions made by the UK Border Agency. For example, in its 2008–09 Annual Report, the AJTC noted that an estimated 70 per cent of asylum applicants appealed against initial decisions taken by the case owners. Of these, between 20 per cent and 25 per cent of appeals to the Asylum and Immigration Tribunal have been upheld annually since the end of 2005.[11]

Feedback from tribunals to the relevant departments is one way of identifying systemic failures and thereby improving the quality of initial decision-making. As the following comment indicates, however, feedback may be a controversial tool:

Genevra Richardson and Hazel Genn, 'Tribunals in transition: Resolution or adjudication?' [2007] Public Law 116, 121–5

[Some tribunals fear . . .] that too much regular exchange between themselves and the department could compromise their independence. By engaging in dialogue with only one party to the dispute some tribunals fear that they might be seen as assisting that party to succeed at the tribunal stage by helping it to make its decisions proof against appeal. Behind this fear, however, may lie some confusion as to the precise role of feedback. Ideally feedback should be designed to improve the substantive quality of the initial decision, not simply to render that decision immune from appeal. Dialogue aimed to achieve feedback in that sense should be of benefit to all potential parties and should not compromise a tribunal's independence.

QUESTIONS

1. If you were responsible for advising on how initial decision-making could be improved, what steps would you suggest are taken?
2. Why do you think problems with the quality of initial decision-making have persisted?

3 ACCESSING THE ADMINISTRATIVE JUSTICE 'SYSTEM'

It is considered good administrative practice (and it may be a legal requirement) for public bodies to provide complaints procedures; they should also be willing to look at decisions

---

[11] Annual Report of the Administrative Justice and Tribunals Council, 2008–09, p. 5.

again if those that they affect are dissatisfied.[12] Internal procedures of this sort do not have the independence of tribunals, ombudsmen, or the courts, but they may enable problems to be resolved relatively quickly, and with minimum expense and trouble.

National Health Service, 'Complaints about the National Health Service'[13]

What are my rights?

If you're not happy with the care or treatment you've received or you've been refused treatment for a condition, you have the right to complain, have your complaint investigated, and be given a full and prompt reply.

The NHS Constitution explains your rights when it comes to making a complaint.
You have the right to:

- have your complaint dealt with efficiently, and properly investigated,

- know the outcome of any investigation into your complaint,

- take your complaint to the independent Parliamentary and Health Service Ombudsman if you're not satisfied with the way the NHS has dealt with your complaint,

- make a claim for judicial review if you think you've been directly affected by an unlawful act or decision of an NHS body, and

- receive compensation if you've been harmed.

Who should I complain to?

You can complain either to the service that you're unhappy with, or you can complain to your local primary care trust (PCT) that commissioned the service.

Even though internal procedures are relatively accessible, it cannot be assumed that people will always complain or appeal when decisions are wrong (or, for that matter, that people will complain or appeal only against wrong decisions). In all probability, a significant proportion of wrong decisions are not questioned or challenged. This is why HHJ Robert Martin's report warned that statistics on the number of cases dealt with by tribunals are an unreliable guide to the quality of initial decisions.

There are many reasons why people may not complain, including that they may not have access to advice or appropriate support, that they may believe there to be no point trying to question decisions of officials, that the process may seem too arduous, or that they may be deterred by the fear that complaining may have adverse repercussions for their future relationship with the public body.[14]

---

[12] The compatibility of internal procedures with the independence requirement in Art. 6(1) ECHR has been questioned in the UK courts and in the European Court of Human Rights. In *Begum (Runa) v Tower Hamlets LBC* [2003] UKHL 5, it was held that judicial review provides a sufficient element of independence; in *Tsfayo v UK* [2006] ECHR 981, it was held that judicial review does not provide a sufficient element of independence in cases in which the internal review decision is based on the credibility of the claimant—something that cannot be tested in judicial review proceedings.

[13] http://www.nhs.uk/choiceintheNHS/Rightsandpledges/complaints/Pages/NHScomplaints.aspx.

[14] Hazel Genn, *Paths to Justice* (1999, Oxford: Hart Publishing).

Failure to use complaints procedures is very common even in cases, as in homelessness, in which there is a right to have an adverse initial decision by a local housing authority reviewed internally by the local authority.[15] Professors David Cowan and Simon Halliday[16] open their study of internal reviews in homelessness cases with an illustration.

David Cowan and Simon Halliday, *The Appeal of Internal Review,* (2003, Oxford: Hart Publishing), p. 1

Shortly before Christmas 2000, Andrew Holt applied with his girlfriend, Pamela McKenzie, to Brisford Council for somewhere to live. Andrew was 35 years old, Pamela was 29. Both had histories of drug use but had recently been through detoxification programmes. They each also suffered from other medical problems. They were unemployed and in receipt of welfare benefits. They were sleeping rough and were desperate to get off the streets as winter was setting in. Pamela was pregnant. Not long after making their housing application, however, Pamela tragically died in a fire. Andrew continued in his application for housing, but was eventually rejected as not having a 'priority need' as a homeless person. He was informed that he could have this refusal reviewed by a senior officer. There were no other housing options available to him and he was desperate for housing. During our taped interview with him he took hold of the microphone and pleaded for help from Brisford Council:

'I'll tell you what, keep this for the record, yes? Keep this one for the record and I'll tell 'em this then, I'll speak into your microphone: [Brisford] Council, will you please help me out? Will you please give me some permanent accommodation? Thank you very much. I would appreciate it. I will pay the rent. I will pay the bills and you know, I will be an absolutely model citizen. I will be an absolute model of a tenant for you, thank you very much. There you go.'

However, Andrew never pursued his grievance with the Council. He did not take up the opportunity to have his decision reviewed internally, and so lost his right to have the decision reviewed subsequently in court.

The interesting and, in our view, surprising and worrying thing about this is that Andrew's reaction to the refusal of help, despite his desperate plight, is by far the normal response. The vast majority of homeless applicants specifically, and welfare applicants in general, fail to challenge adverse decisions despite their continuing sense of need. Surprisingly little is known about why citizens do not challenge adverse decisions from government agencies. [...]

QUESTIONS

1. What lessons about administrative justice can be learnt from this account? How could government and others respond to these lessons?

2. What remedies or procedures might have been available to Andrew Holt?

---

4 TRIBUNALS

Tribunals (the term 'tribunal' is used because these bodies typically have three members, a chair and two others) adjudicate upon a wide range of disputes between individuals and

---

[15] *Begum (Runa) v Tower Hamlets LBC* [2003] UKHL 5; [2003] 2 AC 430.
[16] With Caroline Hunter, Paul Maginn, and Lisa Naylor.

public bodies involving matters as diverse as social welfare issues, questions involving the liberty of people detained under the mental health legislation, immigration and asylum cases, and disputes over the value of property for the purposes of assessing liability to local taxes. They also deal with private disputes: for example, employment tribunals handle conflicts between employers and employees.

The tribunal system was radically reformed by the enactment of the Tribunals, Courts and Enforcement Act 2007. The main features of the 'tribunals world' immediately prior to that Act are summarized in the following account from a study commissioned by the Department for Constitutional Affairs.

Hazel Genn, Ben Lever, and Lauren Grey, with Nigel Balmer and National Centre for Social Research, *Tribunal for Diverse Users* (2006, London: Department for Constitutional Affairs), p. 2

The tribunals world

Tribunals are an important part of the justice system, dealing annually with around one million cases involving, principally, disputes between the citizen and the State. Tribunals are informal court-like bodies created by statute to review decisions made by Government Departments and Agencies of the State and in a few cases to adjudicate on private disputes. The system of tribunals in England and Wales has developed and grown over the last 50 years and now comprises around 70 different tribunal jurisdictions covering a wide-range of subjects, with new tribunals established piecemeal over the years in response to a growing body of regulation. They deal with a huge range of activities, rights and entitlements with jurisdictions as diverse as rent assessment, HGV licences, school exclusion, war pensions, parking fines, social security benefits, mental health, immigration, employment, and meat hygiene. Tribunals are generally administered by their 'sponsoring Department' – which is the body whose initial decisions the tribunal has been established to review. ... [tribunals] ... have historically been regarded as flexible and relatively informal forums for adjudication with some common features that are distinct from court processes. Some of the most notable of these features are:

- Adjudication often by a mixed panel of legal, specialist and lay decision-makers
- Relatively simple processes for initiating applications
- Absence of procedural steps prior to hearing
- Absence of court dress
- Flexible hearing procedures with relaxed rules of evidence
- Interventionist decision-makers
- Variable but often low level of legal representation at hearings
- No fee for use
- Costs not normally awarded

The difference between tribunals and courts has also been commented on by Baroness Hale.

Gillies v Secretary of State for Work and Pensions (Scotland)
[2006] UKHL 2

Baroness Hale

[...] I add a few words only because, as a former member of the Council on Tribunals, I take a particular interest in the tribunal system.

[36] Tribunals were once regarded with the deepest of suspicion but they are now an essential part of our justice system. They are mostly there to secure justice between citizen and state in a wide variety of contexts, the most numerically important of which is entitlement to the financial benefits provided by the welfare state [... it is ...] recognised that tribunals can have important advantages over courts of law. These are 'cheapness, accessibility, freedom from technicality, expedition and expert knowledge of their particular subject': [see the Franks report ...] The Report of Sir Andrew Leggatt's Review of Tribunals, Tribunals for Users, One System, One Service (2001, paras 1.11 to 1.13) suggests three tests of whether tribunals rather than courts should decide cases. The first is participation; that users should be able to prepare and present their own cases effectively. The third is the need for expertise in the area of law involved: users should not have to explain to the tribunal what the law is. The second is the need for special expertise in the subject matter of the dispute [...] Expertise on the tribunal not only improves decision-making and reduces the need for outside expertise; it also thereby increases the accessibility and user-friendliness of the proceedings.

[37] Ever since the Franks Report, the watchwords by which any tribunal system has been judged are its 'openness, fairness and impartiality': [...]

[38] Impartiality is not the same as independence, although the two are closely linked. Impartiality is the tribunal's approach to deciding the cases before it. Independence is the structural or institutional framework which secures this impartiality, not only in the minds of the tribunal members but also in the perception of the public.

(a) THE GROWTH OF TRIBUNALS

Bodies resembling modern tribunals have existed since the end of the eighteenth century, when the General and Special Commissioners of Income Tax were established to deal with disputes generated by the imposition of an income tax. In their modern form, however, tribunals can be traced to the major social reforms introduced by the Liberal government in the early twentieth century—particularly the introduction of pensions for the elderly[17] and National Insurance.[18]

The courts could have been used to deal with disputes arising from these schemes, but they were considered too expensive and too formal. There was also a fear that judges would sabotage the schemes, either because they were innately conservative or because they were out of touch with the needs of ordinary people, and would be unable to approach them in a balanced and sensitive way.[19]

---

[17] Old Age Pensions Act 1908.

[18] National Insurance Act 1911.

[19] H. Street, *Justice in the Welfare State*, 2nd edn (1975, London: Stevens), p. 9; B. Abel-Smith and R. Stevens, *In Search of Justice*, (1968, London: Allen Lane), p. 111. See generally J.A.G. Griffith, *The Politics of*

Nonetheless, some argued that it was wrong to bypass the courts. Lord Hewart, a former Lord Chief Justice, for example, argued that 'administrative' tribunals (as they were referred to at the time) were, at best, a necessary evil established to save courts from being overwhelmed and, at worst, a subversion of the rule of law.[20] He considered that the use of administrative tribunals undermined the rule of law because these bodies were established, and largely controlled, by the government departments with whom individuals were in dispute.

This concern raised critical questions about how tribunals should be viewed and where they should fit: should they be part of the administrative system operated by government departments to resolve disputes internally, or should they be part of the justice system that was independent of government?

The Franks Committee report

This question was considered by the Franks Committee in its 1957 report.[21] The Committee had been established following the Crichel Down affair, which concerned land that had been compulsorily purchased by a government department and then let to a tenant in breach of promise to invite public tenders.[22] The affair had nothing specifically to do with tribunals, but allegations of corruption and departmental wrongdoing fanned public concern about the behaviour of government and its treatment of individuals, including the absence of redress against government wrongdoing.

Despite the submissions of government to the contrary, the Franks Committee was clear that tribunals should be part of the justice system and independent of government departments. It stressed that tribunals should possess three basic characteristics: openness, fairness, and impartiality.

The Franks Committee, *Report of the Committee on Administrative Tribunals and Enquiries*, Cmnd 218 (1957)

The choice between tribunals and courts of law

38. We agree [...] that tribunals have certain characteristics which often give them advantages over the courts. These are cheapness, accessibility, freedom from technicality, expedition and expert knowledge of their particular subject [...]. But as a matter of general principle we are firmly of the opinion that a decision should be entrusted to a court rather than to a tribunal in the absence of special considerations which make a tribunal more suitable.

39. [... I]f all decisions arising from new legislation were automatically vested in the ordinary courts the judiciary would by now have been grossly overburdened. [...]

Tribunals as machinery for adjudication

40. Tribunals are not ordinary courts, but neither are they appendages of Government Departments. Much of the official evidence, including that of the Joint Permanent Secretary to the Treasury, appeared to reflect the view that tribunals should properly be regarded as

---

the Judiciary, 5th edn (1997, London: Fontana Press).

[20] Lord Hewart, *The New Despotism* (1929, London: Ernest Benn).

[21] *Report of the Committee on Administrative Tribunals and Enquiries*, Cmnd 218 (1957).

[22] *Report of Sir Andrew Clark into the Disposal of Land at Crichel Down* (1954), Cmnd 9176; D.N. Chester, 'The *Crichel Down* case' 32 [1954] Public Administration 389.

part of the machinery of administration, for which the Government must retain a close and continuing responsibility. Thus, for example, tribunals in the social service field would be regarded as adjuncts to the administration of the services themselves. We do not accept this view. We consider that tribunals should properly be regarded as machinery provided by Parliament for adjudication rather than as part of the machinery of administration. The essential point is that in all these cases Parliament has deliberately provided for a decision outside and independent of the Department concerned, either at first instance (for example in the case of Rent Tribunals and the Licensing Authorities for Public Service and Goods Vehicles) or on appeal from a decision of a Minister or of an official in a special statutory position (for example a valuation officer or an insurance officer). [. . .] T]he intention of Parliament to provide for the independence of tribunal is clear and unmistakable.

To satisfy the principles of openness, fairness, and impartiality, the Franks Committee recommended that:

- those who chaired tribunals should be legally qualified;
- members of tribunals should not be chosen by departments;
- hearings should normally be in public;
- individuals should normally have the right to legal representation;
- legal aid should be available;
- tribunals should give reasons for their decisions;
- there should be a right of appeal on 'fact, law and merits' from tribunals to courts; and
- tribunals should be supervised by an independent body to be known as the 'Council on Tribunals'.

The main thrust[23] of these recommendations was subsequently implemented by the Tribunals and Inquiries Acts 1958, later amended in 1992.

Scottish Consumer Council, *Administrative Justice in Scotland: The Way Forward—The Final Report of the Administrative Justice Steering Group* (2009, Glasgow: Consumer Focus Scotland)

3.9 The significance of Franks can be summarised as follows. First, as the specific recommendations above indicate, the most important legacy of Franks has been its encouragement of the judicialisation of tribunals. Second, however, Franks also promoted the idea that tribunals were different from courts in important respects notably their informality and accessibility. The assumption that tribunals are more user-friendly than courts has had important policy consequences, including . . . limitations on the availability of legal aid for tribunals. Third, Franks did nothing to restrain the proliferation of tribunals. Although recommending that proposals for any new tribunals should be referred to the suggested Councils, Franks also said that there was little scope for amalgamation of tribunals, and proliferation has continued until very recently.

---

[23] Legal aid has never been extended to more than a handful of tribunals.

As the final comment in this extract indicates, in the decades following Franks, the number of tribunals grew phenomenally.[24] By 2006, there were seventy different tribunal jurisdictions each established at different times for different reasons. Some—such as those concerned with social security, employment, asylum, tax, land registration, and mental health—were handling over half a million cases a year, whereas others did very little, if anything. The haphazard growth and the variety of tribunals highlighted the absence of any system. Moreover, with the enactment of the Human Rights Act 1998, there was concern that, despite the post-Franks reforms, tribunals remained insufficiently independent of government to satisfy the requirements of Art. 6 of the European Convention on Human Rights (ECHR). In response to these concerns, in 2000, the government commissioned Sir Andrew Leggatt, a former Lord Justice of Appeal, to conduct a wide-ranging review of tribunals.

The Leggatt Report was published in August 2001,[25] along with a government consultation paper.[26] The report was critical of the haphazard way in which tribunals were being established to meet the needs and convenience of departments, and said that 'users' often found tribunal procedures to be daunting and intimidating. Significantly, it stressed the need to increase the independence of tribunals and to establish a more coherent system of tribunals. To achieve this, the Leggatt Report called for a new independent 'Tribunal Service', analogous to the Court Service, to take over the management of tribunals from departments. It also recommended the creation of a single two-tier tribunal structure under the leadership of a senior judge.

The main elements of the Leggatt Report were adopted by the UK government and presented in its 2004 White Paper, *Transforming Public Services: Complaints Redress and Tribunals*.[27] In some respects, the White Paper went further than Leggatt in stressing the need for a more holistic, innovative, and even radical approach to reform.

Secretary of State for Constitutional Affairs and Lord Chancellor, *Transforming Public Services: Complaints, Redress and Tribunals* (Cm 6243) July 2004

1.12 [Sir Andrew Leggatt's] report – *Tribunals for Users – One System, One Service* – was published in August 2001 and gave a picture of an incoherent and inefficient set of institutions which [...] provided a service to the public which was well short of what people are entitled to expect and what can be achieved. Sir Andrew set out a convincing case for change and this White Paper acts as a response to his report. But we do not believe that tribunal reform can or should stand alone. What matters to people is the quality and responsiveness of the system as a whole.

Unified tribunal

6.4 [... The] unified tribunals system will become a new type of organisation, not just a federation of existing tribunals. It will have a straightforward mission: **to resolve disputes in the best way possible and to stimulate improved decision-making so that disputes do not happen as a result of poor decision making**. All of its activities will be subordinated to these aims. [...] Its key features need to be independence, professionalism, accessibility and efficiency [...].

---

[24] Michael Adler, 'Tribunal reform: Proportionate dispute resolution and the pursuit of administrative justice' (2006) 69(6) Modern Law Review 958–85, 959, quoting Harlow and Rawlings.
[25] Sir Andrew Leggatt, *Tribunals for Users: One System, One Service* (2001, London: HMSO).
[26] Lord Chancellor's Department, *Tribunals for Users: A Consultation Paper* (2001, London: HMSO).
[27] Cm 6243.

A radical approach

6.20 But the bringing together of these tribunals into a new organisation with a new mission also means that the whole way in which services are provided can be reviewed. At the moment, for instance, all cases which require a decision can mean an oral hearing by the judiciary. For some tribunals, such as the Appeals Service and the Immigration Appellate Authority (IAA), the overwhelming majority of cases are disposed of in this way. Yet we know that decisions do not have to be made this way. Ombudsman services have shown that perfectly sound decisions can be made which fully respect the rights of parties without formal hearings. Telephone and video conferencing already makes it possible to have virtual hearings but we need to go further and to re-engineer processes radically so that just solutions can be found without formal hearings at all. We expect this new organisation to innovate. The leadership of the new organisation will have the responsibility to ensure that it does. [...]

The Tribunal Service was established as an executive agency under the Department for Constitutional Affairs in April 2006. The Tribunals Service has now joined the Courts Service in the HM Courts and Tribunals Service, an integrated agency of the Ministry of Justice created in April 2011. In July 2007, the Tribunals, Courts and Enforcement Act 2007 was enacted, establishing a new system for tribunals. In November 2007, Sir Robert Carnwath, a Lord Justice of Appeal, was appointed as the first senior President of Tribunals. [28]

The main elements of the tribunal system are summarized in the following account by Sir Robert Carnwath.

Sir Robert Carnwath, 'Tribunal justice: A new start' [2009] Public Law 48, 50–2 (footnotes omitted)

The Tribunals, Courts and Enforcement Act 2007 [TCEA]

Part 1 of the TCEA provided the framework for the creation of the new tribunal structure. ...

Section 1 confirms the place of the tribunal judiciary as part of the independent judicial system of the country, protected by the same statutory guarantees of independence as their court colleagues.[29] It thus confirms the place of tribunals as part of the judicial system, rather than as an appendage of the administration. Section 2 creates the new post of Senior President of Tribunals, as a free-standing statutory office. His responsibilities extend to non-devolved tribunals throughout the United Kingdom. The appointment is made by the Lord Chancellor with the concurrence of the Lord Chief Justice for England and Wales, and his counterparts in Scotland and Northern Ireland.

The statutory functions of the Senior President are modelled in many respects on those of the Lord Chief Justice under the Constitutional Reform Act 2005. They confer wide-ranging responsibility for judicial leadership, including training, welfare and guidance of the tribunal judiciary, and for representing their views to Parliament and to ministers. [...]

The Act creates two new tribunals: the First-tier Tribunal and the Upper Tribunal. They will each be divided into "Chambers", each with its own Chamber President [ss. 3–7 TCEA]. [...] The intention is that most existing tribunal jurisdictions, first-instance and appellate, will in due course be transferred into one or other of the new tribunals, so as to create a comprehensive two-tier structure.

---

[28] Sir Robert Carnwath has now been appointed to the UK Supreme Court and Lord Justice Jeremy Sullivan is the current Senior President of Tribunals.

[29] Section 1 TCEA extends the duty (in Constitutional Reform Act 2005, s. 3) upon the Lord Chancellor and other ministers to respect the continued independence of the judiciary to tribunal chair and members.

The current chambers of the First-tier and Upper-tier Tribunals are shown in Box 15.1. More chambers will be added to the system over time, but even in its present form, the breadth and scale of decision-making brought within the structure is striking: nearly 600,000 cases were dealt with by the Tribunals Service in 2008–09.[30]

BOX 15.1 AN OVERVIEW OF THE TRIBUNAL STRUCTURE

First-tier Tribunal

- **Social Entitlement Chamber:**

    – Asylum Support
    – Social Security and Child Support
    – Criminal Injuries Compensation

- **Health, Education and Social Care Chamber:**

    – Care Standards
    – Mental Health
    – Special Educational Needs & Disability
    – Primary Health Lists

- **Tax Chamber**

    – Tax
    – MPs expenses

- **War Pensions and Armed Forces Compensation Chamber**

    – War Pensions and Armed Forces Compensation

- **Regulatory Chamber**

    – Alternative Business Structures
    – Charity appeals
    – Claims Management Services
    – Consumer Credit appeals
    – Environment
    – Estate Agent appeals
    – Gambling appeals
    – Immigration services
    – Information rights
    – Local Government Standards in England
    – Transport

- **Immigration and Asylum Chamber**

Upper Tribunal

- **Administrative Appeals Chamber**

- **Tax and Chancery Chamber**

- **Lands Chamber**

- **Immigration and Asylum Chamber**

---

[30] Tribunals Service Annual Report 2008–09, HC599 (July 2009), p. 8.

Note that the new structure excludes tribunals that sit only in Scotland, Wales, or Northern Ireland. It also currently excludes a large number of English tribunals, including those dealing with local government issues such as school admission and exclusion panels, parking and traffic adjudicators, and valuation tribunals—although the AJTC has had oversight of these tribunals as well.

(b) CONSTITUTIONALISM VS PROPORTIONATE DISPUTE RESOLUTION: A CLASH OF VALUES?

Earlier, we referred to Le Sueur's argument that, in the area of administrative justice, tension exists between two sets of values: those rooted in constitutionalism and those rooted in concepts such as proportionate dispute resolution (PDR). The implication is that constitutionalism is rooted in principles such as the rule of law,[31] whereas the goals of PDR are motivated by pragmatic considerations such as the desire to save money and achieve efficiency gains. Moreover, the effects of PDR may be to diminish the quality of fairness to individuals and reduce access to, and involvement of, the courts.

There can be no doubt that the new tribunal system furthers the aims of constitutionalism in so far as it provides a statutory structure for tribunals that ensures their independence from government and enables coherence that was previously lacking. It places the tribunal judiciary on the same constitutional footing as judges in the civil and criminal justice systems.[32] Also, it should make it easier to develop standards that can be applied across the main tribunal jurisdictions, while recognizing the specialist needs of the different Chambers. 'Legal constitutionalists' are likely to see these developments as being positive.

But is there tension between these developments and the call for new radical and innovative approaches to decision-making, and will these compromise standards and the quality of justice? What does it mean, for example, to say that *'processes must be radically engineered'* (as the UK government said in its 2004 White Paper)? Should legal constitutionalists be worried by suggestions that tribunals should seek to resolve disputes by telephone, by virtual hearings, or by mediation, rather than through oral hearings before a panel of tribunal members?

Two of the leading authorities on administrative justice, Professor Dame Hazel Genn and Professor Genevra Richardson, consider such questions. They accept that the reforms have strengthened the institutional independence of tribunals from government departments. They argue, however, that certain aspects of the reform agenda, including the aim of achieving PDR, could have negative implications both for tribunal independence and the quality of justice. The following extract from a wide-ranging article focuses on the importance of oral hearings, and their advantages and disadvantages. It draws on empirical research relating to how tribunal users experience oral hearings. The article also considers situations in which oral hearings may be necessary and those in which they may be replaced without materially diminishing the quality of justice.

---

[31] On constitutionalism, see Chapter 2.
[32] On the independence of the judiciary, see Chapter 14.

Genn and Richardson note that while the '*adversarial oral hearing has been regarded by many as the gold standard of procedural fairness*',[33] the common law principles of procedural fairness do not always require an oral hearing. Much depends on the context:

> 'The closer the decision in question resembles a determination of rights between disputing parties, the more formal will be the procedures required. The more administrative the nature of the decision, the more flexible and informal the procedural requirements will be.'[34]

They also discuss the requirement for a fair and public hearing before an independent and impartial tribunal set out in Art. 6 ECHR. Assuming that Art. 6 applies to tribunals and therefore that people have a right to a public hearing, they point out that this requirement will be satisfied '*so long as access to a hearing is provided at some stage in the decision-making process*'. In other words, an internal or paper hearing at the initial stages of decision-making would not necessarily be incompatible with Art. 6, provided that there are later opportunities to take the matter to an oral hearing before a court, such as in judicial review proceedings.[35]

Genevra Richardson and Hazel Genn, 'Tribunals in transition: Resolution or adjudication?' [2007] Public Law 116, 128–32 (footnote numbering changed and some footnotes omitted)

In favour of oral hearings

According to the European Court of Human Rights (ECtHR), an oral hearing is said to protect litigants from "the administration of justice in secret with no public scrutiny" and to "maintain public confidence in the courts and the administration of justice".[36] Thus oral hearings enhance transparency and maintain public confidence. [...]

The Leggatt review of tribunals consulted on the question of oral hearings and reported that many respondents considered oral hearings more "user friendly than written procedures", and particularly suitable where cases turned on "disputed facts or complex issues where it was necessary to test the evidence rigorously".[37] Some respondents also considered that oral hearings provide a better opportunity to uncover evidence and some [...] suggested that oral hearings [...] allowed justice to be seen to be done in a more transparent way than written procedures.[38] Research both by Genn and Genn and by Raine and Dunstan confirms the apparent advantage to users provided by oral hearings. Higher success rates are recorded in personal hearings as compared with "postal hearings".[39]

---

[33] Genevra Richardson and Hazel Genn, 'Tribunals in transition: Resolution or adjudication?' [2007] Public Law 116, 126.

[34] Ibid., 127.

[35] *Begum (Runa) v Tower Hamlets LBC* [2003] UKHL 5; [2003] 2 AC 430.

[36] *Diennet v France* (1996) 21 EHRR 554.

[37] Leggatt Report, para. 8.16.

[38] Ibid.

[39] H. Genn and Y. Genn, *The Effectiveness of Representation in Tribunals* (1989, London: Lord Chancellor's Department); J. Raine and E. Dunstan, *Mindsets, Myths and Misunderstandings at the Administrative: Judicial Divide—The Case of the Parking Appeals Tribunal* (2005, Birmingham: University of Birmingham Institute of Local Government Studies).

Both the views of the ECtHR and those reported by Leggatt reflect an instrumental view of process values. Oral hearings are regarded as valuable either because they improve the accuracy of individual decisions or outcomes, or because they enhance the reputation of the system as a whole. [. . .] However, there are other possible interpretations. Oral hearings provide a transparent and structured opportunity for the parties to participate in the decision and it is in relation to the role of participation that alternative approaches can be seen. Although many commentators still analyse the value of participation in primarily instrumental terms, there are those who argue that participation has a value that is independent of the decision outcome. For some this value is seen in terms of support for the dignity of the individual, for others it is tied to the idea of democratic legitimacy. As citizens we are entitled to participate in all decisions of public authorities which affect us. The nature of that participation will depend on the subject-matter of the decision and the stage of the decision-making process. In relation to national policy formulation and the legislative process our participation might be adequately achieved through the electoral system, but in relation to a specific application of policy affecting an individual citizen an oral hearing might be the most appropriate mechanism to ensure appropriate participation.

Disadvantages of oral hearings

In 2005, following the reform proposals set out in the White Paper, the Council on Tribunals issued a consultation paper designed to canvass views on the role of the traditional oral hearing.[40] [. . .In this] the Council listed a number of the advantages and disadvantages commonly attributed to oral hearings. Included among the disadvantages were the possible stress caused to citizens by the need to appear at an oral hearing, particularly if that hearing is regarded as daunting and legalistic, and the possible additional costs imposed by oral hearings. [. . .] The Council also referred to the fear that oral hearings can cause delays and create difficulties in securing attendance and suitable venues.

What are the views of those who use tribunals?

The above arguments for and against oral hearings are taken mainly from the courts, official publications and academic literature. It is necessary, however, to move from the theoretical to the reality of tribunal users' experiences. [. . .M]ost of the evidence about users' perceptions of the fairness of redress systems comes from the United States and tends to isolate seven or eight factors which appear to be critical in users' judgments about whether they have been treated fairly. Of these, Tyler[41] has identified four primary factors: "opportunities for participation (voice), the neutrality of the forum, the trustworthiness of the authorities, and the degree to which people receive treatment with dignity and respect". Thus people value the opportunity to present their case but, according to Genn, trust in the decision-maker is the primary factor in shaping evaluations of procedural fairness: "the opportunity to present a case will not in itself lead to a perception of fairness unless the tribunal communicates that they have considered the arguments seriously and this is understood by the user".[42]

While there is no express reference to the need for an oral hearing in Tyler's four primary factors, the importance of participation, or voice, is emphasised and it might be assumed that much of the reassurance that users are seeking could be more readily provided face to face.

---

[40] *The Use and Value of Oral Hearings in the Administrative Justice System*, Consultation Paper (2005, London: Council on Tribunals).

[41] T. Tyler, 'Social justice: Outcome and procedure' (2000) 35 International Journal of Psychology 117–25.

[42] H. Genn and Y. Genn, *The Effectiveness of Representation in Tribunals* (1989, London: Lord Chancellor's Department), p. 194.

Genn's 2006 study certainly provides support for the importance of voice. The oral hearing, when well executed, gives the citizen the opportunity to be heard and to observe that they have, indeed, been heard by the tribunal. Moreover, tribunal hearings offer unrepresented claimants with poor literacy a better opportunity than in a written submission alone to explain their circumstances and the basis of their claim [...].

In this discussion, Genn and Richardson show that there are advantages and disadvantages attached to having oral hearings. Whether oral hearings are needed in order to serve the interests of justice therefore depends on how these various factors are weighed, which, in turn, will depend on the context.

They go on to distinguish between three different types of issue that are dealt with by tribunals. First, there are fundamental rights cases. Examples include decisions involving the compulsory detention of patients in hospital under mental health legislation or decisions on whether asylum should be granted. In such cases, they argue that *independent adjudication through an oral hearing was essential*.

At the other end of the spectrum, are cases in which *the claimed entitlements could not themselves satisfy the claimants and where the interests of the parties might be better served by a negotiated resolution*.[43] An example would be the right of parents to express a preference for a particular school for their child. Expressing a preference gives no right to a place and the preference can be denied if the placement would not be compatible with 'efficient education' or the 'efficient use of resources'.[44]

Between these two ends of the spectrum are situations in which people are entitled to material benefits (such as welfare benefits or criminal injuries compensation). Here, Genn and Richardson draw the following conclusion.

Genevra Richardson and Hazel Genn, 'Tribunals in transition: Resolution or adjudication?' [2007] Public Law 116, 141

[N]egotiated resolution was an inappropriate goal and that the parties must retain ultimate access to adjudication if agreement cannot be reached through early intervention. While the procedure for this adjudication must be sufficient to achieve an accurate determination of the merits [...] it might not have to follow the pattern of the traditional oral hearing.

QUESTIONS

1. Can you summarize the advantages and disadvantages of oral hearings from the perspectives of:

   (a) tribunals themselves;

   (b) people who use tribunals; and

   (c) the wider public interest?

2. What do you understand by the term 'instrumentalist' in the context of this discussion? Can you provide 'non-instrumentalist' arguments in favour and against

---

[43] Genevra Richardson and Hazel Genn, 'Tribunals in transition: Resolution or adjudication?' [2007] Public Law 116, 139.

[44] Education Act 1996, Sch. 27, para. 3.

oral hearings? (See further p. 724 in Chapter 16 Genevra Richardson, 'Existing Approaches to Process in Administrative Law: The Legal Regulation of Process'.)

3. Having read this extract, do you think that there is necessarily a clash between the values of 'constitutionalism' and 'informality' in the context of how hearings should be conducted?

4. Do you agree with Genn and Richardson that, in fundamental rights cases, an oral hearing is necessary? Explain your answer.

5 OMBUDSMEN

Whereas tribunals adjudicate between parties and reach binding decisions on the facts or law in the particular case, ombudsmen typically investigate complaints about the way in which the administration has handled a matter, and report their findings and make recommendations.

Administrative Justice Steering Group of the Scottish Consumer Council, *Administrative Justice in Scotland: The Way Forward—The Final Report* (2009, Glasgow: Consumer Focus Scotland)

3.15 Ombudsmen represented a new type of machinery for handling complaints which were not considered suitable for the courts primarily because they were complaints of deficiencies in administration rather than of illegality. Before the advent of ombudsmen, such complaints were not covered by statutory grievance machinery, but could be pursued by elected representatives using parliamentary and local government procedures. The most distinctive features of ombudsmen were, first, that they followed an investigative approach rather than the adversarial adjudicative approach employed by the courts, and, second, that they had power to recommend remedies for citizens, but no powers to enforce them.

(a) THE MAIN OMBUDSMEN

Ombudsmen are now widely used both in the public and the private sectors to investigate complaints and resolve disputes.[45] The following are the principal public sector 'ombudsmen'. Note that not all bodies referred to as being 'ombudsmen' include this term in their title.

The Parliamentary and Health Service Ombudsman

The Parliamentary and Health Service Ombudsman (PHSO) is actually two ombudsmen:

- the Parliamentary Commissioner for the Administration (the Parliamentary Ombudsman, or PO), established by the Parliamentary Commissioner Act 1967; and

- the Health Service Commissioner (the Health Service Ombudsman), which derives most of its powers from the Health Service Commissioners Act 1993.

[45] The British and Irish Ombudsman Association (http://www.ombudsman.org.uk) provides information on the many ombudsmen and complaint handlers.

The same person—currently, Dame Julie Mellor—holds both offices and, for many purposes, they can be treated as a single institution. They share the same home page, available online at http://www.ombudsman.org.uk/.

Local Government Ombudsman for England

Three 'ombudsmen' deal with complaints concerning local authorities across England. The main legislation dealing with the Local Government Ombudsman (LGO) is the Local Government Act 1974. The LGO's home page is http://www.lgo.org.uk/.

Public Services Ombudsman for Wales

The Public Services Ombudsman for Wales was established by the Public Services Ombudsman (Wales) Act 2005. It deals with complaints concerning a wide range of bodies in Wales including the Welsh Assembly government, the National Assembly for Wales Commission, local authorities, and health authorities: see http://www.ombudsman-wales.org.uk/.

The Scottish Public Services Ombudsman

The Scottish Public Services Ombudsman (SPSO) was established by the Scottish Public Services Ombudsman Act 2002. Like its Welsh counterpart, the SPSO can consider complaints against a broad range of public bodies. It can be found online at http://www.spso.org.uk/.

The Northern Ireland Ombudsman

The Northern Ireland Ombudsman was established in 1969, and deals with complaints from government departments and public bodies in Northern Ireland. Its powers are currently set out in the Ombudsman (Northern Ireland) Order 1996 (SI 1996/1298) and the Commissioner for Complaints (Northern Ireland) Order 1996 (SI 1996/1297). It can be found online at http://www.ni-ombudsman.org.uk/.

(b) THE PRINCIPAL CHARACTERISTICS OF THE PUBLIC SECTOR OMBUDSMEN

Typically, the public sector ombudsmen possess the following characteristics.

- They are independent of the bodies that they may investigate.
- They are concerned with complaints that 'maladministration' has caused 'injustice'.[46]
- They operate through investigatory powers (rather than by adjudication, as in the case of courts and tribunals).
- They cannot force public bodies to comply with their findings and recommendations.

In this chapter, we focus on the PHSO, and in particular, on the PO. Unless otherwise indicated, we use the terms 'Ombudsman', Parliamentary Ombudsman (PO), and Parliamentary and Health Service Ombudsman (PHSO) interchangeably.

---

[46] The local government ombudsmen can now also investigate complaints arising from the provision of services or a failure to provide services. The Health Service Ombudsman has a wider remit to investigate complaints about hardship or injustice caused by failures in service provision. This ombudsman can also investigate exercises of clinical judgement: Health Service Commissioner Act 1993, s. 3.

(c) THE PARLIAMENTARY OMBUDSMAN AND HEALTH SERVICE OMBUDSMAN

A short history[47]

The Parliamentary Commissioner for the Administration (PCA), established by the Parliamentary Commissioner for the Administration Act 1967 (PCAA 1967), was the first ombudsman in the United Kingdom. The concept of an ombudsman (meaning 'grievance-handler') had, however, been used in Sweden since 1809, when the Swedish Ombudsman was created to investigate allegations that the government had been improperly trying to influence civil servants. The concept was adopted into the United Kingdom to improve redress against government, especially when the courts could not be used. We noted earlier that the Crichel Down affair (1954) acted as a catalyst for the establishment of the Franks Committee; it also stimulated interest in the creation of an ombudsman.

The most influential call for an ombudsman came in a report by JUSTICE in 1961 (the Whyatt Report).[48] The proposal that a new institution be established to deal with complaints about central government was controversial. Many members of Parliament (MPs) feared that it would detract from their role as complaints-handlers for their constituents and others. It was also feared that an ombudsman able to look into the work of central government departments would undermine the doctrine of ministerial responsibility. With these concerns in mind, the Whyatt Committee proposed a Parliamentary Commissioner who would strengthen the House of Commons and support MPs vis-à-vis central government. For an initial period of five years, while the body was bedding in, citizens would have to route their complaints to MPs, who would then refer them to the Parliamentary Commissioner. The substance of the proposal was finally adopted by Wilson's Labour government with the enactment of the Parliamentary Commissioner Act 1967.

The Act, however, did not meet all of the Whyatt Committee's recommendations. In particular, while Whyatt had recommended that the MP filter should be temporary, the Act made it permanent and it has been retained despite many calls for its removal. Nor was any attempt made to link the ombudsman to the courts or to tribunals—indeed, as we shall see, the ombudsman was prevented from handling matters that could be dealt with by the courts. The fact that decisions of the ombudsman were not to be legally enforceable was also criticized, as was the range of functions that fell beyond the jurisdiction of the ombudsman. The Act, for example, prevented the ombudsman from examining complaints arising from the government's commercial transactions or involving civil service personnel matters.[49] We shall return to these matters later in the chapter, suffice to say here that because of these limitations some complained that rather than an ombudsman, the Act had created an 'ombudsmouse'.[50]

Despite these criticisms, the Act created a new type of institution that could significantly strengthen the ability of MPs and Parliament in relation to the administration, and it established a model that was widely adopted by the other public service ombudsmen, as well as by the private sector.

---

[47] R. Gregory and P. Giddings, *The Ombudsman, the Citizen and Parliament* (2002, London: Politico's Publishing).

[48] Sir J. Whyatt, *The Citizen and the Administration: Redress of Grievances* (1961, London: Justice).

[49] Schedule 3 of the PCAA 1967 (see Restrictions and exclusions, on p. 665).

[50] W. Gwyn, 'The British PCA: Ombudsman or ombudsmouse?' [1973] 35 Journal of Politics 45–69.

(d) THE OMBUDSMAN IN PRACTICE: SOME FACTS AND FIGURES

In the following extract, the previous PO Ann Abraham, provides an idea of the scale and range of the work done by the public sector ombudsmen. She also summarizes the remedies that have been secured following ombudsmen investigations. In this context, she notes that public bodies normally comply with the recommendations of ombudsmen and makes the interesting point that compliance with ombudsmen recommendations is *almost certainly far higher than compliance with judgments imposed by the civil courts*.

Given that decisions of ombudsmen are generally not legally enforceable, what explanations are there for this? Is it because there is more respect for the ombudsmen than for civil courts? Is it to do with the way in which ombudsmen work? Is it because ombudsmen have a higher level of understanding of public administration than judges? Is it because their procedures are able to secure the involvement, cooperation, and trust of public bodies? These are important questions and we will return to them later.

Ann Abraham, 'The ombudsman and "paths to justice": A just alternative or just an alternative?' [2008] Public Law 1, 2–3 (footnotes omitted)

Between them, public sector ombudsmen handle complaints about all the main public services delivered in England, Northern Ireland, Scotland and Wales. In 2006/07 the PHSO dealt with over 14,000 inquiries; and completed over 2,500 investigations. Over 1,100 of the cases reported on arose in the health sector (the Healthcare Commission, NHS Hospital Trusts, Primary Care Trusts and primary care providers accounting for the majority). The balance related to a wide range of government departments and agencies, with the biggest repeat customers being HM Revenue and Customs (especially in respect of tax credits), Jobcentre Plus, the Child Support Agency, the Pension Service, and the Immigration and Nationality Directorate (IND), as it then was. In 62 per cent of cases investigated, the Ombudsman upheld the complaint in full or in part. In every one of the cases reported on in 2006/07, the parties complied with the Ombudsman's recommendations.

These quantitative figures disclose substantial reach and scope. The remedies achieved as a result of PHSO investigation are equally diverse. In some cases, the remedy is pecuniary: a payment of £335 by the IND for a postal fee unnecessarily incurred; compensation from Jobcentre Plus for £18,000 arrears of income support, late payment of benefit, lost entitlement to free school meals and help with school uniforms; remittance by the Revenue of an overpayment of £7,500; reimbursement by the Disability and Carers Service of £9,500 to cover lost disability allowance plus interest over a four year period.

In others, it is non-pecuniary: a trust-wide audit of clinical records and the institution of training in the handling of MRSA positive patients; the review of a decision by a Primary Care Trust to refuse funding of continuing care; improvement of supervision, ward staffing levels and skill mix in the management of patients with dementia and poor communication; provision of weekend senior medical cover and better transfer procedures within a Primary Care Trust.

Levels of satisfaction with the PHSO's work are high (especially when it is remembered that many complainants walk away empty handed): in our most recent customer satisfaction survey 63 per cent of complainants were satisfied or very satisfied with the way in which their complaint was handled; and 51 per cent spoke highly and positively of the Ombudsman and the service provided, with a large majority considering the Ombudsman to be responsive, accessible, sympathetic and fair.

> [...]
> Compliance rates with the PHSO's recommendations are very high, and almost certainly far higher than compliance with judgments imposed by the civil courts. [...] There is no indication that the inability to make binding recommendations impairs the PHSO's ability to deliver substantive justice.

For up-to-date figures, you should look at the annual reports of the ombudsmen. These can be found online at the relevant ombudsman's website. There, for example, you will see from the Annual Report for 2011–2012 (July 2012), that during that year the PO received 23,846 inquiries, more than ever before, with the vast majority from people who simply needed advice on where or how to complain about public services in the first instance.

ONLINE RESOURCE CENTRE
The Online Resource Centre provides current data relating to ombudsmen.

(e) EXAMPLES OF INVESTIGATIONS

The Sachsenhausen case (1967)

The first major investigation undertaken by the Parliamentary Ombudsman was into complaints by former British servicemen who had been held within the Sachsenhausen concentration camp by the Nazis during the Second World War. They complained that they had been unfairly treated by the Foreign Office when it rejected their application for compensation. The Parliamentary Ombudsman found that the complainants had been victims of injustice caused by maladministration and persuaded the Foreign Office to pay them compensation. As Richard Kirkham says, this outcome gave Parliament and the media early notice of the potential importance of the ombudsman.[51]

A rather different investigation was used by Ann Abraham in a recent lecture to illustrate how the PO gives practical effect to human rights principles of fairness, respect, equality, dignity, and autonomy. The example concerns Mr R.

Ann Abraham, *The Parliamentary Ombudsman and Administrative Justice: Shaping the Next 50 Years*, JUSTICE, Tom Sargant Memorial Annual Lecture, October 2011

Mr R has learning disabilities and a mental health condition. He went overseas on holiday to stay with some family friends. His parents had intended to travel with him but were unable to do so because of his father's ill health. This was the first time that Mr R had travelled abroad alone. On his return he was stopped at his local airport by two trainee customs officers because he was carrying a large amount of tobacco. He was then interviewed about his trip abroad, how it had been funded, and the tobacco. Contrary to the UK Border Agency's

---

[51] Dr Richard Kirkham, *The Parliamentary Ombudsman: Withstanding the Test of Time*, Fourth Report, Session 2006–07 (HC 421, March 2007), p. 6.

own guidance, the customs officers did not check at the start of the interview whether Mr R was fit and well, or whether he had any medical condition they needed to be aware of. Nor did they ask him to read and sign the notes of the interview. If they had done, they would have discovered that Mr R could not read or write. The officers strip-searched Mr R – at one point leaving him naked. One of the reasons given for the strip-search was that Mr R appeared 'nervous' and 'evasive' when questioned. Although Mr R had referred to his disabilities and one of the officers had written 'Mental health problems, disability' in his notebook, the officers simply continued with the interview and the search. No drugs were found. Mr R was eventually allowed to leave, but the tobacco he had been carrying was seized.

My investigation found that the UK Border Agency had not had regard to Mr R's disability rights in the way that it had carried out its functions. As soon as Mr R referred to his disabilities, the customs officers should have stopped the interview and re-arranged it so that an appropriate adult could be present. Instead they had pressed on regardless, they had failed to follow the Agency's own interviewing protocols, which might have helped them to identify Mr R's disabilities and deal with him appropriately as a vulnerable adult.

An appropriate adult should have been able to explain that Mr R's difficulties in answering questions were due to his learning disabilities and not evidence of evasive behaviour. Not only was it unlikely that the encounter would have progressed so far as a strip search, but Mr R would have had the support and protection he was entitled to in what for him was a terrifying situation. Not surprisingly, he never wanted to go near an airport again.

We upheld the complaint. The UK Border Agency apologised to Mr R and paid him £5,000 compensation for the distress, humiliation and anxiety they had caused him.

In an attempt at restorative justice we asked the Agency to explore with Mr R and his mother what they might do to enable Mr R to feel comfortable using his local airport in future.

The Agency also agreed to review the disability awareness training provided to their customs officers, with a particular emphasis on identifying non-visible disabilities such as learning disabilities and mental health conditions.

So a good example of the Ombudsman providing redress for the individual—and also recommending systemic improvements for a wider public benefit.

The following summarizes some of the other important investigations undertaken by the Parliamentary Ombudsman between 1975 and 2005. Later in the chapter, we look more closely at two high-profile investigations: the occupational pensions case and the Equitable Life case.

Parliamentary and Health Service Ombudsman, 'Timeline'[52]

[...]

29 July 1975 [Court Line travel group]

The report was published of an investigation into complaints about misleading official assurances about the safety of the Court Line group of travel companies that had been made by Ministers shortly before the group collapsed, with the loss of several hundred jobs and tens of thousands of holidays. The Government of the day initially refused to accept the Ombudsman's report, but the position was eventually remedied through the enactment of the Air Travel Reserve Fund Act 1975, which made provision for compensation to be paid to

[52] Reproduced from a timeline published to mark the Parliamentary and Health Service ombudsman's 40th anniversary in 2007.

those who had lost their holidays through the collapse of Court Line and which established an industry-wide compensation scheme to deal with future holiday company failures.

[...]

25 March 1976 [Asbestosis]

A report was published of an investigation into asbestosis among workers at the Acre Mill factory at Hebden Bridge and the role of the Department of Employment Inspectors in the enforcement of health and safety legislation there. As a result of this report, the Government announced five days later that it would establish an Advisory Committee on Asbestosis which, in due course, laid down enhanced health and safety rules and whose work led to systematic checks for the presence of asbestos in industrial plants across the UK.

[...]

18 January 1995 [Child Support]

A report of investigations into complaints about the Child Support Agency was published. A further report was published on 6 March 1996 – and complaints about the CSA have ever since constituted a significant proportion of the casework of the Parliamentary Ombudsman.

[...]

15 March 2000 [SERPS]

[...] The Ombudsman found that misleading official information had been given by the Department of Social Security over many years about Inherited SERPS. As a result of this report, the Government delayed the introduction of new inheritance provisions at an estimated cost of over £13 billion. The Ombudsman's follow up report of 23 February 2001 said that these proposals for redress were reasonable.

[...]

20 February 2003 [NHS funding for long-term care]

[...] The Ombudsman found that Department of Health guidance had not enabled the operation of a fair and transparent system of eligibility for funding; that guidance had been misinterpreted and misapplied by some health authorities; and that certain some people had suffered injustice and hardship. The Ombudsman made several recommendations to the Government and to NHS bodies to remedy the position. A follow-up report on progress made was published on 16 December 2004.

[...]

22 June 2005 [Tax Credits]

A report into complaints about the administration of the Tax Credits system was published. The report identified significant problems with the system and made recommendations to improve the system covering the way in which the Inland Revenue dealt with overpayments, communication issues, and the steps to be taken to reduce the risk of citizens experiencing financial hardship.

12 July 2005 [A Debt of Honour]

'A Debt of Honour' – the third section 10(3) report [see below] in the history of the Parliamentary Ombudsman's office – was published. This report concerned complaints about the administration of an *ex-gratia* scheme for compensation for surviving members of British groups who had been interned by the Japanese during the Second World War. Following an inquiry by the Select Committee, the Government eventually accepted the Ombudsman's findings and implemented those of her recommendations that had initially been rejected.

In September 2011 the PO told the Government to 'hang its head in shame' after its report, *Defending the Indefensible*, highlighted repeated failings by the Ministry of Defence to treat fairly a family who were interned by the Japanese during the Second World War. Ann Abraham described this as: 'The worst example I have seen, in nearly nine years ... of a government department getting things wrong and then repeatedly failing to put things right or learn from its mistakes.' She said that her report should be required reading for every aspiring senior civil servant.[53]

(f) THE JURISDICTION OF THE PARLIAMENTARY OMBUDSMAN

The Parliamentary Ombudsman can deal with complaints against any of the bodies specifically listed in Sch. 2 of the PCAA 1967.[54] This extends to all of the departments of central government and most other public bodies, but the list is not exhaustive. It is updated as new bodies are created and old ones abolished, or when decisions are made to extend the ombudsman's jurisdiction. Nonetheless, it has been observed that '*this method of proceeding is hardly transparent and it may help to explain why so many complaints to the PCA fall outside his* [sic] *jurisdiction*'.[55] In her annual report for 2008–09, Ann Abraham notes that, in that year, 2,830 inquiries out of 16,317 were outside the ombudsman's remit. Many of these were about private companies, solicitors, financial institutions, and local councils.[56] During 2011–2012 there were 23,846 inquiries, of which 2,794 concerned matters that were beyond the PO's remit.[57]

BOX 15.2 THE TOP FIVE DEPARTMENTS BY COMPLAINT 2009–10

	No. of complaints
1. Department of Work and Pensions	3,000
2. HM Revenue & Customs	1,896
3. Home Office	952
4. Ministry of Justice	931
5. Department of Transport	353
Other	1,411
	8,543 (Total)

Source: PHSO Annual Report 2009–10 (HC 274), p. 20.

---

[53] See Annual Report for 2011–2012.

[54] By s. 4 (1) PCAA 1967, the Ombudsman's jurisdiction extends to the '*government departments, corporations and unincorporated bodies*' listed in Sch. 2 to the Act.

[55] C. Harlow and R. Rawlings, *Law and Administration*, 3rd edn (2009, Cambridge: Cambridge University Press), p. 532.

[56] Annual Report of the PHSO, *Every Complaint Matters*, Fourth Report, Session 2008–09 (HC 786) July 2009, p. 7.

[57] Annual Report of the PHSO, *Moving Forward*, 2011–12 (HC 251) July 2012.

(g) COMPLAINANTS MUST HAVE SUSTAINED 'INJUSTICE IN CONSEQUENCE OF MALADMINISTRATION'

The task of the ombudsman is to investigate complaints that 'injustice' has been caused by 'maladministration' on the part of the public body concerned (s. 5(1)(a) PCAA 1967). The terms 'injustice' and 'maladministration' were not defined in the Act, but were left to be interpreted and developed by the ombudsmen. 'Injustice' has been interpreted broadly. Sedley J (as he then was) said that it is not limited to types of injury that are *redressible in a court of law* and extends, for example, to *the sense of outrage aroused by unfair or incompetent administration, even where the complainant has suffered no actual loss*.[58]

'Maladministration' is a 'highly flexible concept'[59] that focuses on administrative errors that affect the *manner* in which decisions are reached and the *manner* of their implementation, rather than only the merits of decisions.[60] Richard Crossman MP—who, as the leader of the House of Commons at the time, steered the Parliamentary Commissioner Bill through the Commons—explained 'maladministration' by listing the type of wrongdoing that might be covered. His list (known as 'the Crossman catalogue') mentioned: bias; neglect; inattention; delay; incompetence; ineptitude; perversity; turpitude; and arbitrariness.[61]

In the following extract, Richard Kirkham (in an official report published by the PHSO) assesses the way in which the 'maladministration' test has been interpreted. He shows that while the test may have been intended to steer the ombudsman away from criticizing the merits of decisions, it has not prevented the ombudsman from exploring the merits of decisions or from criticizing unreasonable decisions. He also considers the overlap between 'maladministration' and legal grounds for challenging decisions.

Richard Kirkham, *The Parliamentary Ombudsman: Withstanding the Test of Time,* Fourth Report, Session 2006–07 (HC 421, March 2007), pp. 7–8 (footnotes omitted)

Although most ombudsman investigations focus on administrative procedures, this does not mean that ombudsmen cannot investigate the merits of decisions of public authorities. The 1967 Act left a degree of flexibility on the issue. Section 12(3) prevents the PO from questioning 'the merits of a decision taken *without* maladministration' (added emphasis). This implies that where a decision is taken *with* maladministration then the PO can legally consider the merits of the decision. More controversially, an administrative decision that is wholly unreasonable to most rationally minded people is a clear example of maladministration. Either way, the PO is entitled to explore the merits of a particular administrative decision during the course of an investigation. Were this not the case, it would often be impossible to come to a conclusion as to whether maladministration or an injustice had occurred.

A further key aspect of the concept of maladministration is that it can be used to resolve complaints where legal grounds could also be argued. For instance, in the *Debt of Honour* report, the PO found that the manner in which an *ex gratia* compensation scheme had been

---

[58] *R v Parliamentary Commissioner for Administration, ex parte Balchin (No. 1)* [1998] 1 PLR 1, 11.

[59] M. Seneviratne, *Ombudsmen: Public Services and Administrative Justice* (2002, London: Butterworths), pp. 40–5; also M. Seneviratne, 'Updating the Local Government Ombudsman' [2008] Public Law 627, 630–2.

[60] Section 12(3) PCAA 1967 provides '*that nothing in this Act authorises or requires the Commissioner to question the merits of a decision taken without maladministration*'.

[61] See also Carnwath LJ, *R(Equitable Members Action Group) v HM Treasury and ors* [2009] EWHC 2495 (Admin), [36]; *R v Local Commissioner, ex parte Bradford Council* [1979] 1 QB 287, 311–12.

announced by the Ministry of Defence amounted to maladministration due 'to the misleading impression that it created'. For the Ministry of Defence, this finding was not easy to accept, partly because the Court of Appeal had previously found that the same announcement lacked sufficient precision to create a legitimate expectation according to the law.[62] Such a finding demonstrates that the duties that can be inferred from the maladministration test can actually go further than equivalent doctrines in law. This principle is supported by the courts and is one to which public authorities should pay more attention.

The test of maladministration, therefore, has proved to be a powerful and adaptable tool for the task to which the PO was assigned.

The idea that the public have a right to complain in cases in which maladministration has occurred has been developed by the PHSO and given a more positive twist in the enunciation of six basic 'principles of good administration', which should be respected by public bodies in all that they do. Identification of these principles reflects the way in which the PHSO can build on the experience gained when dealing with individual complaints to improve the general quality of public administration. This proactive role is an important feature of ombudsmen, and one that tribunals and courts are less well equipped to perform. Richard Kirkham argues that this is a *'step to be encouraged'* and is evidence of the way in which the PHSO has matured: '[I]*n terms of the development of administrative law more generally, it could represent the beginning of one of the most important innovations in recent years.*'

Parliamentary and Health Service Ombudsman, *Principles of Good Administration* (February 2009)

1. Getting it right
2. Being customer focused
3. Being open and accountable
4. Acting fairly and proportionately
5. Putting things right
6. Seeking continuous improvement

[The core requirements of each of the principles are also set out. For example, getting it right involves:]

• Acting in accordance with the law and with regard to the rights of those concerned.
• Acting in accordance with the public body's policy and guidance (published or internal).
• Taking proper account of established good practice.
• Providing effective services, using appropriately trained and competent staff.
• Taking reasonable decisions, based on all relevant considerations.

[Acting fairly and proportionately involves:]

• Treating people impartially, with respect and courtesy.

---

[62] *Association of British Civilian Internees: Far East Region v Secretary of State for Defence* [2003] EWCA Civ 473; [2003] QB 1397; see also Chapter 16, section 4(h).

- Treating people without unlawful discrimination or prejudice, and ensuring no conflict of interests.
- Dealing with people and issues objectively and consistently.
- Ensuring that decisions and actions are proportionate, appropriate and fair

(h) RESTRICTIONS AND EXCLUSIONS

A major criticism of the PCAA 1967 has been that it contains too many restrictions and limitations. One leading authority said that the effect of these was to exclude most of the matters about which people complain.[63] Certainly, there is a long list of matters that cannot be investigated,[64] including:

- action taken in matters affecting relations between the UK government and any other government, or any international organization of states or governments;
- action taken by the Secretary of State relating to extradition;
- action taken for the purposes of investigating crime or of protecting the security of the state, including action so taken with respect to passports;
- the commencement or conduct of civil or criminal proceedings before any court in the United Kingdom, or of proceedings before any international court or tribunal;
- action taken by administrative staff of any court or tribunal taken at the direction of any person acting in a judicial capacity;
- any exercise of the prerogative of mercy;
- action taken in matters relating to contractual or other commercial transactions of government;
- action taken in respect of personnel matters relating to service personnel or civil -servants; and
- the grant of honours, awards, or privileges within the gift of the Crown.

The exclusion of the government's commercial transactions and civil service personnel matters have been the most controversial exclusions.

Parliamentary and Health Service Ombudsman, *The Parliamentary Ombudsman: Withstanding the Test of Time*, Fourth Report, Session 2006–07 (HC 421, March 2007), p. 11 (footnotes omitted)

The need for these exclusions has been regularly questioned by, amongst others, Parliamentary select committees. They have been justified on the basis that the core role of the PO is 'to investigate the complaints against government by the governed and not against government in its role as employer or customer'. It is also arguable that in these areas alternatives, such as the courts, are usually more appropriate. Nevertheless, in an era when private sector provision has become an increasingly important feature of governance, the exclusion of contractual and commercial arrangements needs to be monitored to ensure

---

[63] H. Street, *Justice in the Welfare State*, 2nd edn (1975, London: Stevens), p. 116.
[64] PCAA 1967, Sch. 3.

that this governance technique is not used as a means by which to prevent accountability. Another issue here is the interpretation that the PO gives to the public/private divide, as for example, where a public function is contracted out to a private supplier. Fortunately, once more this is an area where the Office does retain some discretion and appears to have used it in a positive fashion.

(i) THE RELATIONSHIP BETWEEN THE PARLIAMENTARY OMBUDSMAN AND THE COURTS

Section 5(2) of the PCAA 1967 provides that the Parliamentary Ombudsman shall not conduct an investigation when the person aggrieved has, or had, a remedy in any court of law or a tribunal.[65] This is one of the least satisfactory features of the Act. Since the 1960s, judicial review has expanded to such an extent that many complaints of maladministration could now give rise to judicial review proceedings and a strict interpretation of this restriction could add a significant obstacle to complainants who would be forced to resort to the courts. Fortunately, the Act allows the ombudsman discretion to deal with complaints if satisfied that, in the particular circumstances, it is not reasonable to expect the complainant to seek legal redress and this discretion seems to be regularly used. For example, in the *Debt of Honour* case,[66] the PO undertook an investigation, despite a previous decision of the Court of Appeal in *Association of British Civilian Internees: Far Eastern Region (ABCIFER) v Secretary of State for Defence*.[67] The importance of the discretion to investigate even in cases in which legal proceedings are possible may also be illustrated by *Anufrijeva v Secretary of State for the Home Department*.[68] In this case, the Court of Appeal recognized that maladministration in the meeting of housing and welfare needs could lead to a breach of Art. 8 ECHR and to a claim for damages. This was a positive step in the development of human rights law, but it could have had the negative effect of limiting access to the ombudsman, which is not what the court intended. In practice, as well as the need for a flexible approach to s. 5(2), the decision reinforces the value of ombudsmen in the protection of human rights.

It is clear that ombudsmen may be challenged by judicial review, and that they must conduct investigations and reach findings in accordance with the principles of judicial review. The first time that a decision of the PO was quashed, and twice sent back for reconsideration, was in the *Balchin* saga (as we saw on p. 635), in which the PO was held to have failed irrationally to take account of the powers of central government concerning *ex gratia* payments by local authorities.[69]

Another example of a successful challenge, this time to an investigation conducted by the Health Service Commissioner, is provided by *Cavanagh and ors v Health Service Commissioner*.[70] In this case, the Court of Appeal held that the Commissioner has power

---

[65] Section 5(2). In *R v Local Commissioner, ex parte Bradford Council* [1979] 1 QB 287, 310, Lord Denning MR said that Parliament was 'at pains' to ensure that the Ombudsman should not conduct an investigation that '*might trespass in any way on the jurisdiction of the courts of law or of any tribunals*'.

[66] 'A Debt of Honour': The Ex Gratia Scheme for British Groups Interned by the Japanese During the Second World War, Fourth Report, Session 2005–06, HC 324.

[67] [2003] QB 1397.

[68] [2003] EWCA Civ 1406; [2004] QB 1124.

[69] *R (Balchin and ors) v Parliamentary Commissioner for Administration* [1996] EWHC Admin 152; [1999] EWHC Admin 484.

[70] [2005] EWCA Civ 1578.

to investigate only particular complaints and may not undertake investigations 'at large' into matters about which there has been no complaint. While the ombudsman was investigating a complaint brought by a parent of a disabled child about the way in which the child was being treated, the ombudsman commissioned her own experts and, acting on the basis of their reports, rejected the complaint. The father, together with the doctors who had been criticized, successfully claimed judicial review of the way in which the ombudsman had conducted the investigation. The Court of Appeal stressed that while the Commissioner has wide investigative powers, she is unable to *'expand the ambit of a complaint beyond what it contains, nor to expand her investigation of it beyond what the complaint warrants'*.[71] Investigations must also be conducted in accordance with the common law requirements of fairness. The Court was particularly concerned that the doctors who had been criticized by the ombudsman knew only about the full nature of the criticisms when they saw her draft report, to which they did not have a full chance to respond.[72]

Ombudsman investigations may also be used to help to mount litigation against the body about which complaint has been made. *Congreve v Home Office*[73] is a well-known example. The case concerned the renewal of television licences. Anticipating an increase in the licence fee, Congreve (and 20,000 others) bought a new licence before the increase took effect and before his old licence had expired. The Home Office, hoping to prevent a loss of revenue, at first demanded an extra £6 from these 'overlappers'. It then changed its position and said that the new licences would be revoked early. Some of those affected complained to the Parliamentary Ombudsman, who, after an investigation, said that injustice had been caused by maladministration.[74] Armed with this finding, Congreve successfully challenged the Home Office in the courts.[75]

Here, we are primarily concerned with the way in which ombudsmen may be used and their powers, but we should also note in passing that there is another dimension that has to do with access to the courts. As we shall see in the next chapter, claimants for judicial review have to show that they have exhausted other available remedies, such as ombudsmen and alternative dispute resolution (ADR); they may be refused admission to the courts if they have not done so.[76]

While requirements such as these may be justified, they underscore the complexities that face ordinary people when deciding whether and how to complain against official action; they also underscore once again the problems revealed in the *Balchin* case. One response is to improve flexibility across institutions. It has, for example, been argued that it should be made easier for matters to be transferred between ombudsmen and the courts and tribunals. In the following extract, the AJTC lends its support to recommendations made by the Law Commission.

---

[71] *Per* Lord Justice Sedley at [16].

[72] For an unsuccessful judicial review challenge on the grounds of fairness, see *R v Parliamentary Commissioner for the Administration, ex parte Dyer* [1994] 1 All ER 375.

[73] [1976] QB 629.

[74] Seventh Report of the Parliamentary Commissioner for the Administration for Session 1974–75, para. 38.

[75] The decision of the Administrative Court in *Elias v Secretary of State for Defence* [2005] EWHC 1435 (Admin) was probably partly responsible for the Ministry of Defence's decision to accept the Ombudsman's recommendations in the *Debt of Honour* case (see p. 666).

[76] *R (Cowl) v Plymouth City Council* [2002] 1 WLR 803.

Administrative Justice and Tribunal Council, *The Developing Administrative Justice Landscape*, September 2009

42. [...] The Law Commission for England and Wales published in 2008 a consultation paper on *Administrative Redress: Public Bodies and the Citizen*, [...]. The paper [...] considered the relationship "between two of the central pillars of administrative redress", the public sector ombudsmen and the courts. Essentially, the Law Commission was applying the idea of trying to match the dispute, and the potential redress, to the most appropriate method of resolution. Whether a case is begun with the ombudsman or the court, it may become subsequently apparent that the other redress mechanism is more appropriate. Therefore it should be possible to transfer to the more appropriate mechanism.

43. The Law Commission's provisional recommendations proceeded on the footing that ombudsmen provide a system of justice in their own right. The Commission thought this could be strengthened by enabling the courts to stay proceedings so that a case could be referred to an ombudsman, providing the ombudsmen with a power to refer matters of law to the courts for adjudication, and modifying the statutory bar which precludes the ombudsmen from investigating a complaint if the complainant has or had recourse to legal remedy before a court or tribunal. The AJTC strongly agrees that facilitating the transfer of cases from one forum to another in this way would serve the user well. The idea could be developed further, for example by applying the same principles to the relationship between ombudsmen and tribunals.

Accessing the Parliamentary Ombudsman

People cannot complain directly to the Parliamentary Ombudsman; complaints must instead be routed through an MP.[77] As we have seen, the Whyatt Committee proposed that the 'MP filter', as it is known, should be in place for only an initial five years. Many were disappointed when the PCAA 1967 made the MP filter a permanent feature and this has continued to be one of the most criticized aspects of the Act.

Originally, two arguments were used to justify the MP filter. One was that it protects the role of MPs in relation to their work helping their constituents—but it has been said that this argument *'is barely credible today'*.[78] Only a small proportion of constituency work is associated with the use of the ombudsman and there is evidence that MPs themselves do not consider the filter to be necessary. A recent survey of MPs conducted jointly by the Parliamentary Ombudsman and the Public Administration Select Committee, for example, found that 66 per cent of MPs questioned favoured removal of the filter.[79]

The second justification for the MP filter was the expectation that it would protect the ombudsman from being inundated by complaints. While it is difficult to know whether there would have been significantly more complaints without the filter, there is no evidence that the ombudsman has been inundated. On the contrary, as the following extract indicates, there

---

[77] PCAA 1967, s. 5(1)(a).

[78] Dr Richard Kirkham, *The Parliamentary Ombudsman: Withstanding the Test of Time*, Fourth Report, Session 2006–07 (HC 421, March 2007), p. 12.

[79] Parliamentary and Health Service Ombudsman, *Summary Results of the Survey of Members of Parliament on the Work of the Ombudsman*, cited in Kirkham, op. cit., p. 24, fn. 68. See also, *Report on the Consultation on Direct Access to the Parliamentary Ombudsman*, November 2011.

has been concern that the Parliamentary Ombudsman has been underused—in part because the Parliamentary Ombudsman has had a low public profile.[80]

House of Commons Library (Oonagh Gay), *The Ombudsman: the Developing Role in the UK* (Standard Note SN/PC/04832) October 2008 (footnotes omitted)

A fundamental question about the Ombudsman's role and workload was asked by the former Ombudsman, Sir Michael Buckley, in March 2002, giving evidence to the Public Administration Committee, at which he said:

[...] if one looks at the history of the office over its 35 years of history, on average it has received about one and a half complaints per Member per year. Since, for most of its history, the only way of dealing with a complaint, taking positive action on a complaint, was to issue a statutory report—and there were lots of those—on average a Member of the House of Commons has received a report perhaps once every three years. It does seem to me that if Richard Crossman had been asked that question 'What is the workload of the office?' and had a good crystal ball with him and had said what I have just said, he would have been laughed out of the chamber.

Sir Michael had succeeded in increasing the throughput of cases during his tenure of the office, and his successor, Ann Abraham, has achieved further increases. However [...] overall numbers of cases for the parliamentary ombudsman (including health service work) remain small by international standards [...].

Both the Public Administration Select Committee and the AJTC have recommended the abolition of the MP filter.[81] The Parliamentary Ombudsman believes that while the MP filter has not significantly impeded the effectiveness of the Office,[82] its removal would help to make the ombudsman more transparent and accessible.[83]

Investigatory powers

The Parliamentary Ombudsman has very broad investigatory powers, which are contained in s. 8 of the PCAA 1967. The ombudsman has powers equivalent to those of the courts in relation to the attendance and examination of witnesses, and ministers and officials are required to furnish information and provide documents that are relevant to investigations. In some respects, the ombudsman's powers are significantly greater than those of the courts. For example, s. 8(3) in effect says that the Crown cannot prevent the ombudsman from having access to documents on grounds of public interest immunity.[84] These powers are important, but it is widely argued that, in order to be an effective investigator of complaints, the ombudsman must be able to rely on the cooperation of those being investigated.

---

[80] Also R. Gregory and J. Pearson, 'The Parliamentary Ombudsman after twenty-five years [1992] 70 Public Administration 469.

[81] Public Administration Select Committee, *Annual Report of the Parliamentary Ombudsman*, Fourth Report, Session 1999–2000 (HC 106), para. 6; The Administrative Justice and Tribunals Council Response to the Law Commission's Consultation Paper, *Administrative Redress: Public Bodies and the Citizen*.

[82] Parliamentary and Health Service Ombudsman, *The Parliamentary Ombudsman: Withstanding the Test of Time*, Fourth Report, Session 2006–07 (HC 421, March 2007), Foreword, p. 1.

[83] Ibid., p. 12.

[84] Note, however, that there are limits imposed by s. 8(4) (dealing with cabinet proceedings) and (5) (dealing with privilege other than public interest immunity).

Parliamentary and Health Service Ombudsman, *The Parliamentary Ombudsman: Withstanding the Test of Time,* Fourth Report, Session 2006–07 (HC 421, March 2007), p. 11 (footnotes omitted)

Investigatory powers

One of the key reasons why the PO has become accepted as an important redress mechanism has been the Office's ability to produce independent, well reasoned and accurate reports. It is highly doubtful that this could have been achieved without the strong investigatory powers created in the 1967 Act. In the history of the Office there have been very few occasions when the government has used its residuary powers under the 1967 Act to refuse disclosure. This level of access to information gives to the work of the PO enhanced credibility and enables the Office to take on with confidence even politically sensitive investigations. On the other hand, the PO has periodically had cause to complain to Parliament that the government has been slow to comply with requests for information. Under the 1967 Act, the PO could tackle this problem through legal proceedings, but to achieve successful outcomes the PO is reliant on maintaining good relations with the government.

Reports, findings, and recommendations

Following an investigation, the ombudsman reports its findings and may make recommendations. A report must be sent to the relevant MP, the principal officer of the department or authority concerned, and to any other person alleged in the complaint to have taken or authorized the action of which complaint has been made.[85] The ombudsman cannot force compliance with its findings, nor can it compel adoption of its recommendations—although, as we will shortly see, government can only reject ombudsman findings if there are 'cogent reasons' for doing so.[86]

If there has been a finding of injustice caused by maladministration and it appears to the ombudsman that the matter has not been, or will not be, remedied, the ombudsman's formal powers are limited to laying a special report before Parliament.[87] This places the matter in the public and political arena, and it is here that the government must explain why it has not accepted the ombudsman's findings. To date, there have only been five occasions on which a 'section 10(3) report' has been used. As we saw earlier, Ann Abraham said that despite the absence of enforcement powers, non-compliance with the findings of the Parliamentary Ombudsman is extremely rare and this, therefore, does not seriously impede the ombudsman's effectiveness.[88]

Richard Kirkham argues that, when discussing whether the absence of enforcement power is a weakness, account must be taken of three factors. The first is that the vast majority of findings are respected—although, in some cases, it seems that the ombudsman has had to make considerable efforts to persuade government departments. In the following extract, Kirkham explains the other two considerations.

[85] PCAA 1967, s. 10(1).

[86] *R (Bradley) v Department of Works and Pensions* [2007] EWHC 242, see extract, Richard Kirkham, Brian Thompson, and Trevor Buck, 'When putting things right goes wrong: Enforcing the recommendations of the Ombudsman', on p. 674.

[87] PCAA 1967, s. 10(3).

[88] Parliamentary and Health Service Ombudsman, *The Parliamentary Ombudsman: Withstanding the Test of Time,* Fourth Report, Session 2006–07 (HC 421, March 2007), Foreword, p. 1.

Richard Kirkham, *The Parliamentary Ombudsman: Withstanding the Test of Time*, Fourth Report, Session 2006–07 (HC 421, March 2007), p. 13 (footnotes omitted)

A second consideration is the principal reason why the PO lacks enforcement powers. Far from being an unusual flaw in ombudsman design, this is a common solution in ombudsman schemes and goes to the heart of the work that the institution is expected to perform. Ombudsmen are given almost total access to information and people within public bodies, and possess a very broad remit with which to investigate public sector activity. Given the potential depth of such investigations, the consequences of an ombudsman's report can have a huge impact on the design of future policy. Recognition of the potentially sensitive nature of the ombudsman's work is one of the reasons why ombudsman schemes tend to leave the power of implementation in the hands of the public authority concerned. Political accountability between the decision-maker and the electorate for the consequences of an ombudsman's report is thereby maintained. Arguably, another important benefit of this arrangement is that because public authorities know that they retain control of their decision-making, they are more likely to be encouraged to participate constructively in the investigation. It is this fear that powers of legal enforcement would radically alter the hitherto cooperative nature of the ombudsman's work that best explains why most ombudsmen are reluctant to go down this route.

Building on this understanding, a third point needs to be taken on board. As public authorities retain the final decision to provide redress, for the purposes of Article 6 of the European Convention of Human Rights, it is unlikely that the investigations and reports of the PO could be considered determinations of civil rights. Were the PO to possess powers of enforcement, this position could change. Such a development would almost certainly force the Office to reconsider its working practices. This could mean the increased use of formal hearings and more frequent legal representation. If this were the case, then the whole ethos and rationale of the ombudsman institution would be severely challenged and it is possible that many of the benefits would be lost.

Ann Abraham stressed that ombudsmen operate in ways that are different from courts and tribunals, on the one hand, and from systems based on mediation or negotiation, on the other. Unlike courts, '*ombudsman practice* [...] *has always prized its relative informality, its common sense approach to evidence, its inquisitorial process and its capacity to do justice in the individual case, unfettered by the burden of binding precedent*'.[89] She argues that an ombudsman will also have available a range of devices that are both capable of securing justice for the individual complainant and 'crucially' of facilitating systemic change.[90]

These themes are developed by Nick O'Brien when he compares the approaches of courts and ombudsmen in the context of disputes over social rights issues.

Nick O'Brien, 'Ombudsmen and social rights adjudication' [2009] Public Law 466, 468–9 (footnotes omitted)

If the court process can be characterised by its relative formality, expense, delay, complexity and rule-dominated qualities, the ombudsman process is by contrast relatively informal, free to both parties at the point of delivery, relatively quick, unfettered by complex rules of evidence or process, and normative in its application of principle rather than in the imposition

---

[89] Ann Abraham, 'The ombudsman and "paths to justice": A just alternative or just an alternative?', [2008] Public Law 1, 4.
[90] Ibid., 5.

of rules. There are, however, three specific aspects of ombudsman practice that are especially salient to the issue of their suitability for social rights adjudication. These aspects are their inquisitorial process, their functional flexibility, and their deliberative form of decision-making.

[...] In the context of human rights (and especially social rights) adjudication, [the] inquisitorial process in principle gives the ombudsman an advantage when it comes to the business of harnessing the sort of evidence needed to weigh the balance of priorities in what will frequently be disputes about indeterminate and open-ended positive obligations on a public authority. Advantage is gained too on the issue of citizen access, since in most cases it is the ombudsman who carries the burden of gathering evidence and the ombudsman too who frames argument and shapes conclusions. In the course of conducting that balancing exercise, the ombudsman effectively counters any inequality of arms that might otherwise diminish the fairness of the process. Free to both parties at the point of delivery, the public sector ombudsman is rarely as passive as a conventional court in amassing and harnessing evidence or in articulating the key points at issue.

It is also a feature of the ombudsman's inquisitorial process that it leaves room for the exercise of administrative expertise in a way that generally eludes the courts. Frequently the ombudsman [and its staff] ... will be drawn from the world of public administration, will have played a part in framing the principles that apply to the area of administration under investigation, and will have grappled in practice with similar circumstances in the course of their own organisational experience. The reticence that properly attends judicial examination of administrative practice is to that extent reduced when it is an ombudsman who is engaged in the work of adjudication.

Critical also is the functional flexibility of the ombudsman institution. The concept of maladministration is itself notoriously fluid [...] Ombudsmen have not habitually found it desirable to establish the precise boundaries of maladministration by prescribing a set of rules that will bind public authorities. Instead, they express a desire to achieve an equitable outcome, to do whatever is just and reasonable in the particular circumstances of the case. That conceptual fluidity at the heart of the ombudsman remit is matched by a significant measure of functional flexibility. [...] At the heart of ombudsman practice is the ambition of drawing upon the empirical experience of adjudication to identity patterns of maladministration and poor service, and to propose remedies that have systemic bite. [...]

It is this functional flexibility, comprising so-called 'fire-fighter', 'firewatcher', and 'fire-prevention' roles, that enables the ombudsman to address directly the key ambition of social rights: the future amelioration of large-scale violation. If the adversarial judicial process is essentially individualistic in its concerns, inherently preoccupied with the particular and the immediate, it falls to the ombudsman to take a more expansive adjudicative perspective, to look to the underlying causes of citizen grievance and, over time, and by way of a cumulative and iterative process, to make recommendations that will remedy not just the plight of the individual complainant but of others already, or yet to be, in the same or similar situation.

[O'Brien goes on to emphasize that a further important difference between ombudsmen and the courts lies in the nature of the outcome that is delivered.]

[The ombudsmen's outcome is] an authoritative but unenforceable contribution to a continuing debate about the merits of the case and of the policy and other factors that shaped it [...]. The ombudsman's word carries weight, but it is frequently far from the last word. It might be said that the ombudsman's 'style of control' is to that extent 'co-operative' rather than 'coercive', more a mandate of 'influence' than of 'sanction'.

Both the complainant and the authority can claim a sense of ownership in the outcome. This, O'Brien suggests, increases the likelihood that public bodies will find it easier to comply with recommendations of an ombudsman rather than decisions of courts.[91]

The importance of this discussion has been highlighted by two high-profile ombudsman investigations, which, following government refusals to accept the ombudsman's findings, led to judicial review proceedings. The first of these concerned the ombudsman's investigation into the handling of occupational pensions and the second concerned the investigation into the failures of the regulatory regime prior to the collapse of Equitable Life. These cases raise interesting issues for students of the constitutional system, but they need to be approached bearing in mind that they are atypical, and do not reflect normal relationships between the ombudsman and government.

(j) OMBUDSMAN CASE STUDY I: THE OCCUPATIONAL PENSIONS AFFAIR

Many people lost substantial sums of money when their private sector final-salary pension schemes were wound up. Complaints were made to the Parliamentary Ombudsman that the government and the Department of Works and Pensions (DWP) had failed to regulate the pension providers properly. Following her investigation, the ombudsman made several findings of maladministration.[92] In particular, she found that official literature provided by the government *was sometimes inaccurate, often incomplete, largely inconsistent and therefore potentially misleading*,[93] and that the method used to calculate the value of pension schemes had been changed without regard to all of the relevant considerations and without excluding irrelevant considerations. This maladministration caused injustice. It created a sense of outrage and denied the complainants information that was necessary in order for them to make informed decisions about their pensions. The House of Commons Public Administration Select Committee agreed with the PO after carrying out its own investigation.[94]

The government rejected these findings. It said that the information in the leaflet on which the complainants had relied was only introductory and clearly stated that people should take professional advice before taking out a pension. Regarding the finding in relation to the method by which the value of pensions were calculated, the government said that it had relied on its own specialist adviser, the Government's Actuary's Department, and that it would have been open to criticism had it not done so. The government also argued that even if it had been guilty of maladministration, this had not caused the injustice. It said that the real injustice, the financial losses, had been caused by decisions taken by trustees of the pension schemes.

Some of the individuals affected then took the unusual step of seeking judicial review of the government's refusal to accept the ombudsman's findings. The Administrative Court

---

[91] See further M. Hertogh, 'Coercion, cooperation and control: Understanding the policy impact of administrative courts and the ombudsman in the Netherlands' (2001) 23 Law and Policy 47.

[92] Parliamentary and Health Service Ombudsman, *Trusting the Pension Promise: Government Bodies and the Security of Final-salary Occupational Pensions*, Sixth Report, Session 2005–06 (HC 984).

[93] Ibid., para. 5.167.

[94] Public Administration Select Committee, *The Ombudsman in Question: The Ombudsman's Report on Pensions and its Constitutional Implications*, Session 2005–06 (HC 1081). For a discussion, see Richard Kirkham, Brian Thompson, and Trevor Buck, 'When putting things right goes wrong: Enforcing the recommendations of the Ombudsman' [2008] Public Law 510, 514.

partially upheld the challenge.[95] Although there was an appeal to the Court of Appeal, the government changed its mind at the last minute and decided to accept the main thrust of the ombudsman's recommendations. Nonetheless, the decision of the Court of Appeal is important. It held that the government was not free to disregard findings of the ombudsman. Findings can only be rejected if 'cogent reasons' exist for doing so,[96] and no cogent reasons existed for rejecting the finding relating to the quality of information contained in the leaflet. This was the first time that it has been held that public bodies are not free to reject, without good reason, the findings of an ombudsman.

In the following extract, Richard Kirkham, Brian Thompson, and Trevor Buck discuss the implications of the decision.

Richard Kirkham, Brian Thompson, and Trevor Buck, 'When putting things right goes wrong: Enforcing the recommendations of the Ombudsman' [2008] Public Law 510, 521–30 (footnotes omitted)

[...T]here is a risk that granting legal authority to ombudsman findings may upset the delicate balance in the working practice of the Ombudsmen. In particular, such a move could legalise the whole process, both in terms of the ombudsman's relations with the public bodies under investigation and by encouraging public bodies and complainants to expose ombudsman findings to more frequent judicial scrutiny. The extent of these concerns, however, is debatable. Very few ombudsman reports lead to conflict between the ombudsman and the public body investigated, and the general trend in the ombudsman community has been to issue fewer formal reports and concentrate efforts on arriving at agreed settlements. Nor should the prospect of judicial review intimidate the Ombudsmen. [...I]n the private sector a number of ombudsmen operate with powers that, to a greater or lesser extent, mean that their decisions are binding on the bodies ruled against. Significantly, with none of these schemes have any major drawbacks to the ombudsman's work been noted as a result of clarifying the legal status of ombudsman reports.

The central justifying argument behind granting some form of legal authority to the findings of an ombudsman is relatively simple. [...] According to standard liberal conceptions of justice, in order to maintain the fairness and legitimacy of this process, a minimum requirement is that the final proclamation as to the validity of the complaint is given by an independent body or person. To maximise the effect of the ombudsman scheme, therefore, this is the role that should be the sole prerogative of the ombudsman. By contrast, were the body complained against to have the final say on the findings of an ombudsman report then this would devalue the process; objectivity would not be secured and public confidence in the strength of the ombudsman system would be much reduced. [...]

Objections to making the ombudsman's findings binding

Contrary to this reasoning there are two standard lawyer's objections against making ombudsman findings legally enforceable. First, the ombudsman establishes her findings on the basis of informal procedures which do not allow for a fair hearing of the issues involved, or cross-examination on either side. Secondly, ombudsman schemes do not provide for an independent

---

[95] *R (Bradley) v Department of Works and Pensions* [2007] EWHC 242.
[96] [2008] EWCA Civ 36, [72], *per* Sir John Chadwick.

appeal mechanism. Assuming that the ombudsman is as capable of making mistakes as anyone else, this arrangement denies public bodies an appropriate opportunity to defend or clear their name. Therefore, because of the lack of adequate safeguards, the recognised investigative role of the ombudsman should mean that reports are kept at an investigative status only.

These objections, however, both undervalue the fairness of the procedures open to the ombudsman and overplay the importance of the adversarial approach to justice. [...] One of the strengths of the ombudsman model is that the office is not restricted by the straitjacket of judicial procedures and has the flexibility to choose the method of investigation most appropriate to the investigation concerned. [...] but [...] the [...] ombudsman legislation [...] 'provides for a substantial degree of due process', particularly with regard to the public body. By law, the public body complained against is afforded 'an opportunity to comment on any allegations contained in the complaint' and, by practice, the Ombudsmen submit their draft reports to the public body for comment on the factual accuracy of the investigation. ... [The authors go onto to argue that there are also very good reasons why an appeal mechanism should not be included in ombudsman schemes] ... [e]ven if the Bradley ruling means that a public body may be burdened by an ombudsman finding that it fundamentally disagrees with, it can choose not to implement the ombudsman's recommendations if it concludes that they are politically or economically unrealistic. Admittedly, this position may be harder for a public body to defend to its electorate, but such an inconvenience is hardly a sound argument for reducing the status of ombudsman reports to that of advisory only.

[They conclude their discussion with the following observation.]

[...] the Occupational Pensions affair has served to emphasise the role that the Ombudsmen perform within the constitution. No one argues that public bodies should not be able to dispute ombudsman reports. The issue is that when they do so they should be required to operate according to a convention that pays due respect to the ombudsman's office and the political process set up to support it.

(k) OMBUDSMAN CASE STUDY II: THE EQUITABLE LIFE SAGA

The Equitable Life Assurance Society (Equitable), founded in 1762, was the world's oldest mutual life insurance society. It specialized in providing pensions, especially 'with-profits' schemes. On 8 December 2000, Equitable closed for new business. Following this closure, the value of its with-profits policies fell and many people lost money. Complaints were made to the ombudsman by those who claimed to have suffered injustice due to maladministration on the part of the public bodies responsible for regulating Equitable.

The ombudsman undertook an extensive four-year investigation into the way in which Equitable had been regulated. This was possibly the most complex investigation yet undertaken by the ombudsman. In July 2008, Ann Abraham laid her report, *Equitable Life: A Decade of Regulatory Failure* (HC 815), before both Houses of Parliament. In this report, she made ten findings of maladministration and she found that in six of these cases people had suffered 'injustice'. She recommended that the government should establish a scheme to compensate those affected.

Parliamentary and Health Service Ombudsman, 'Equitable Life: A decade of regulatory failure', Press release, 16 July 2008

In a report published today, Ann Abraham, the Parliamentary Ombudsman, has called on the Government to apologise to Equitable Life policyholders and to establish and fund a compensation scheme for those policyholders.

In her report, the Ombudsman makes ten determinations of maladministration on the part of the former Department of Trade and Industry, the Government Actuary's Department, and the Financial Services Authority, in relation to their regulation of Equitable in the period before 1 December 2001.

In addition to upholding several specific complaints, the Ombudsman has upheld a general complaint about the period before Equitable closed to new business on 8 December 2000, namely that:

[…] the public bodies responsible for the prudential regulation of insurance companies […] and the Government Actuary's Department failed for considerably longer than a decade properly to exercise their regulatory functions in respect of Equitable Life.

Finding that injustice resulted from maladministration, the Ombudsman has recommended that a compensation scheme should be established to assess the individual cases of Equitable's current and former policyholders, with a view to paying compensation to remedy any financial losses which would not have been suffered had those people invested elsewhere than with Equitable. […]

The Ombudsman has also recommended that the Government should apologise to policyholders for what her report describes as the 'serial regulatory failure' that she has identified. The Ombudsman said:

'The failings I have identified in this case were not failures of the system of regulation that was in place at the relevant time. […] Parliament gave those operating that system robust and wide-ranging powers, which the regulators were under a duty to consider using where appropriate. The regulators at the time said that they would deliver regulation in a proactive and vigorous way. That singularly failed to happen in the case of Equitable.'

The ombudsman's recommendations were endorsed by the Public Administration Select Committee of the House of Commons in two reports.[97]

The government's response[98]

The government accepted some of the ombudsman's findings and rejected others. In particular, the government rejected the recommendation for a compensation scheme, while accepting that some *ex gratia* compensation payments should be made. The government appointed Sir John Chadwick (who happened to have sat in the Court of Appeal in *Bradley*, but who had subsequently retired) to advise on these payments.

The ombudsman's response to the government

In May 2009, the ombudsman laid a second report before Parliament under s. 10(3) of the PCAA 1967.[99] This was only the fifth time that the ombudsman had considered it necessary

---

[97] http://www.publications.parliament.uk/pa/cm/cmpubadm.htm.

[98] http://www.hm-treasury.gov.uk/equitablelife_govt_response.htm.

[99] Parliamentary and Health Service Ombudsman, *My Assessment of the Government's Response: Injustice Unremedied—The Government's Response on Equitable Life*, Third Report, Session 2008–09 (HC 435).

to use this power. In this report, she expressed deep dissatisfaction with the government's reaction to her findings.

Parliamentary and Health Service Ombudsman, *My Assessment of the Government's Response: Injustice Unremedied—The Government's Response on Equitable Life*, Third Report, Session 2008–09 (HC 435)

28. I have reviewed very carefully the Government's oral and published response to my report, the evidence given by Ministers to the Select Committee concerning that response, and the papers giving further information about its basis which are contained within the court papers. I have also seen the exchanges in the House that have occurred on this subject.

29. Nothing that I have seen when reviewing any of these sources persuades me that my findings of maladministration and injustice were mistaken or that the Government have provided a sufficient basis for rejecting many of those findings. Nor am I persuaded that their response has properly and fully addressed the basis on which I made the findings that have been rejected.

The judicial review

As in the occupational pensions case, legal proceedings followed. A claim for judicial review was brought by the Equitable Members' Action Group—a company limited by guarantee, the members of which comprised about 21,000 policyholders with the Equitable. The key argument, based on the *Bradley* decision, was that the government had failed to provide cogent reasons for rejecting the ombudsman's findings and that it had acted unlawfully in failing to accept the recommendation that a compensation scheme be established.

The decision of the Queen's Bench Divisional Court, Carnwath LJ and Gross J, was delivered on 15 October 2009. Applying *Bradley*, the Court held that no cogent reasons had been given for rejecting three of the six findings that injustice had been caused by maladministration. It did not, however, accept the challenge to the government's refusal to establish a compensation scheme, essentially because this decision involved the allocation of financial resources, with which the Court was reluctant to interfere.

Parliamentary and Health Service Ombudsman, 'Ombudsman comments on judicial review', Press release, 15 October 2009

'As I have reported to Parliament, the Government's response to my report was deeply disappointing, providing insufficient support for the rejection of many of my findings of maladministration on the part of the regulators and my conclusions that injustice resulted from those failings.

'The court has now found that the Government's response was in large part unlawful, not being supported by cogent reasons for rejecting my findings.

'How this judgment affects the Government's proposals for an ex gratia scheme is a matter for others to consider. However, while this judgment is welcome I am very aware that the injustice suffered by many people affected by the Equitable Life affair remains unremedied so many years after the relevant events.

'I therefore hope that every effort is now made to ensure a just and speedy outcome for all those people.'[100]

---

[100] For further developments see the Equitable Life Members Support Group: http://www.equitablelife-members.org.uk/

(l) A SELF-ASSESSMENT: A CONSTITUTIONAL FORCE TO BE RECKONED WITH

In the following extract, Ann Abraham gives her assessment of the success and role of the Parliamentary Ombudsman.

Parliamentary and Health Service Ombudsman, *The Parliamentary Ombudsman: Withstanding the Test of Time*, Fourth Report, Session 2006–07 (HC 421, March 2007), Foreword (footnotes omitted)

[...T]he life and times of the Parliamentary Ombudsman have not been without their challenges. Born of a political climate in the 1960s that placed the emphasis firmly on modernisation, this innovative statutory office brought to these shores an institution conceived on foreign soil, the product of a Scandinavian legal and administrative ethos unfamiliar to the common law and UK constitutional settlement. In ways somewhat reminiscent of the reception 30 years later of the Human Rights Act, detractors feared the consequential decline of nothing less than parliamentary democracy itself. Even the office's supporters lamented the tendentious legislative framework within which it would operate, its 'botched' fabric and 'limping' gait. The jibe of 'Ombudsmouse' still wounds 40 years later.

[...] From its first major investigation, *Sachsenhausen* in 1967-8 [...] right through to my recent report on occupational pensions in 2005-06, when the Department for Work and Pensions was not quite so easily persuaded to provide a remedy for the complainants' loss of pension rights, the office of Parliamentary Ombudsman has shown itself a constitutional force to be reckoned with.

[...] The original purpose of providing an aid to Parliament in its constitutional scrutiny of the Executive has evolved alongside the increasing sophistication of administrative law in the intervening period. Whilst the office would not expressly espouse a role as 'people's champion' in emulation of some overseas models, it has certainly carved for itself a distinctive niche in the judicial landscape, as a source of dispute resolution, as a guardian of good public administration, and as a systematic check upon departmental effectiveness.

These three distinctive, but inter-related, roles define much of what the office is currently about and where its future challenges lie. [...] The Ombudsman is not a court or tribunal [...] Ombudsmen and courts are like chalk and cheese: superficially similar, but of very different texture and ingredients. Liberated from the burden of imposing enforceable remedies, with wide discretion, the Ombudsman is free to establish a very different relationship between the disputing parties, based upon trust and shared understandings, not formal compliance. [...]

Before her retirement Ann Abrahams once again stressed the constitutional importance of the PO and the distinctive contribution it makes, as well as the need for some key reforms.

Ann Abraham, *The Parliamentary Ombudsman and Administrative Justice: Shaping the Next 50 Years*, JUSTICE, Tom Sargant Memorial Annual Lecture, October 2011

MAKING THE VISION A REALITY

[...] we have at times lost sight of the basic insights that shaped the Whyatt Report and indeed the Franks Report before it. In particular, we have failed to remember, that the

Parliamentary Ombudsman has a constitutional role that cannot simply be confined to the function of dispute resolution, important though that is; that the Ombudsman system of justice is distinctive yet integral to a broader administrative justice system as a whole; and that the framework of values within which the work of the Ombudsman can be located is that of the protection and promotion of citizens' rights. From that recognition we can extrapolate a number of more concrete proposals.

First, I would echo the recommendations of the Law Commission that the MP filter as sole gateway to the Ombudsman, and other barriers to access such as the need to

put complaints in writing, must go [. . .]

Secondly, I propose that the time has finally come to acknowledge the power of own initiative investigation, to accept that, in the absence of a specific individual complaint, the Ombudsman should not stand idly by. [. . .]

Thirdly, we must accept that if we are to achieve a genuine 'system' of administrative justice, with Ombudsmen as an integrated and coherent part, we must pay close attention to the currently fragmented structures of regulation, inspection and accountability throughout the UK and across the devolved administrations, protecting the Ombudsman 'brand' whenever necessary and making sense of the disparate and disjointed structures that so frustrate aggrieved citizens and at times defy all logic. [. . .]

And finally, if we are to maintain the distinctive qualities of the Ombudsman system of justice within that broader administrative justice landscape, we must resist any temptation to model the Ombudsman process on that of the courts. And resist also those changes that would reduce the Ombudsman function to just a form of dispute resolution, a mechanism of consumer redress devoid of systemic and structural bite.

What matters is that the Ombudsman is a just alternative – not just an alternative. In short, we must recognise that the origins of the Ombudsman system in the contested territory between individual and State are especially salient at a time when the boundaries of the State itself – and of the public services delivered in its name – are under daily scrutiny.

The need for a fundamental review of Ombudsmen in this country, to match Sir Andrew Leggatt's review of tribunals, is more urgent than ever. I suggest we get on with it. [. . .]

And finally then, if we are to continue the task of humanising the bureaucracy, of maintaining public relationships that bear the stamp of democratic values, and of protecting the entitlement of ordinary citizens to dignity and respect, we should acknowledge the insight of 'Whyatt' and remain protective of its legacy, not just now but in the future, and if necessary for the next 50 years.

QUESTIONS

1. Which of the following two statements in your view is the more accurate?

   - 'The Parliamentary Ombudsman is an "ombudsmouse": all squeak and no real power or influence.'

   - 'The Parliamentary Ombudsman is a constitutional force to be reckoned with.'

2. 'The Parliamentary Ombudsman is essentially part of the political process by which government is held to account. It is not necessary, and it may be undesirable, to give the Ombudsman greater legal power to enforce its findings.' Discuss.

3. In what ways do courts and ombudsmen differ? Are there any lessons to be learnt by judges from the way in which ombudsmen work? For example, should judges issue press releases if their judgments are not respected by government?

4. In the lecture, Ann Abraham says that '*What matters is that the Ombudsman is a just alternative—not just an alternative [to courts]*'. What do you think she means by this in concrete terms?

5. What, if any, reforms are needed to the PO? Why have these reforms not yet been made?

6 CONCLUDING COMMENTS

Despite recent developments, as yet, there is no single coherent system of administrative justice. The chapter has explored some of the key elements of administrative justice, including the need to get decisions right first time and the concept of proportionate dispute resolution. It has also examined two pillars of administrative justice—tribunals and ombudsmen—with particular reference to the parliamentary ombudsman. For the latest developments, visit the Online Resource Centre.

In the chapters that follow, we turn to the courts.

7 FURTHER READING

Adler, M., (ed.) *Administrative Justice in Context* (2010, Oxford and Portland, Oregon: Hart Publishing)

Cane, P., *Administrative Tribunals and Adjudication* (2009, Oxford: Hart Publishing)

Harlow, C., and Rawlings, R., *Law and Administration*, 3rd edn (2009, Cambridge: Cambridge University Press), esp. chs 10–12

Harris, M., and Partington, M., (eds) *Administrative Justice in the 21st Century* (1999, Oxford: Hart Publishing)

Buck, T., Kirkham R., and Thompson, B., *The Ombudsman Enterprise and Administrative Justice*, (2011, Farnham: Ashgate).

Purdue, M., 'Investigations by the Public Service Ombudsmen', in D. Feldman (ed.) *English Public Law*, 2nd edn (2009, Oxford: OUP), ch. 21

Richardson, G., 'Tribunals', in D. Feldman (ed.) *English Public Law*, 2nd edn (2009, Oxford: OUP), ch. 20

Thomas, R., *Administrative Justice and Asylum Appeals: A Study of Tribunal Adjudication* (2011, Oxford and Portland, Oregon: Hart Publishing)

 ONLINE RESOURCE CENTRE

Further information about the themes discussed in this chapter can be found on the Online Resource Centre at www.oxfordtextbooks.co.uk/orc/lesueur2e/

16

JUDICIAL REVIEW

CENTRAL ISSUES

1. Judicial review is one of the principal means by which the rule of law is enforced. It enables people to challenge the actions of public authorities on the grounds that authorities have misunderstood, exceeded, or abused their legal powers, or breached rights protected by the common law. It also provides a route for protecting rights under European Union law, and under the Human Rights Act 1998.

2. As well as providing redress, judicial review imposes legal accountability on public authorities that requires them to justify the legality of their actions to the courts.

3. Judicial review has grown in importance over the past few decades, both in the scale of its use, and in terms of its constitutional and political standing. In high-profile cases, judges have forced government to rethink important decisions, including in areas as sensitive as the prevention of terrorism.

4. This has led to debate about the constitutional foundations for judicial review in the UK system. From where do judges derive their authority to review the legality of government's decisions? How can unelected judges review the actions of elected ministers and local authorities?

5. Across the territorial jurisdictions of the United Kingdom, different requirements are imposed upon claimants and defendants. Differences include provisions relating to who can bring a claim ('standing') and which decisions are 'amenable' to review.

6. The grounds of judicial review are the arguments that claimants can put forward when challenging the legality of a decision. These include illegality, irrationality, proportionality, and procedural impropriety. The grounds are developed by the judges as part of the common law.

7. Acts of Parliament have sometimes attempted to prevent the courts from exercising the judicial review jurisdiction in relation to particularly sensitive decisions. Understandably, the courts have been keen to minimize the success of these 'ouster clauses'.

1 INTRODUCTION

(a) OVERVIEW

Judicial review is the process by which the legality of the exercise of public functions may be challenged in the United Kingdom. In many other constitutional systems, 'judicial review' refers to the power of a constitutional or a supreme court to strike down legislation as being contrary to the (written) constitution. As discussed earlier, the courts in the United Kingdom have more limited powers when it comes to reviewing legislation than many of their counterparts in other countries.[1] In the United Kingdom, judicial review is therefore mostly concerned with the legality of executive action (particularly taken by government ministers and their officials, and by local authorities), decisions taken by courts and tribunals with limited jurisdiction; and it may also be used to challenge delegated legislation.[2]

The three separate territorial jurisdictions in the United Kingdom each have their own judicial review court processes. In Scotland, proceedings for judicial review are dealt with by the Court of Session.[3] In England and Wales, judicial review claims are dealt with by the Administrative Court (part of the Queen's Bench Division of the High Court) in London or in regional centres, currently in Cardiff, Birmingham, Manchester, and Leeds. In Northern Ireland, applications for judicial review are heard in the High Court of Northern Ireland in Belfast. A significant proportion of the caseload of the UK Supreme Court consists of appeals in judicial review cases from the three territorial jurisdictions.

The Upper Tribunal also has a judicial review jurisdiction in relation to decisions taken by the First-tier Tribunal. In exercising this jurisdiction, it must apply the same principles as the High Court and, broadly speaking, it may grant the same forms of relief as the High Court.[4] Other courts and tribunals also exercise a jurisdiction similar to judicial review, including the county court, in relation to homelessness appeals from decisions of local housing authorities, and the Special Immigration Appeal Commission, in relation to challenges to decisions taken by the Home Secretary on grounds of national security.[5]

We look in more detail at the various grounds of review later in the chapter; these are broadly similar in each of the United Kingdom's territorial jurisdictions. For the time being, it is sufficient to know that the underlying arguments that a judicial review claimant may make fall into four broad types:

(a) that the terms of legislation have not been complied with—for example, a duty conferred on a public body has not been carried out, or a statutory procedure for making a decision has not been followed;

(b) that the requirements of the common law have not been followed—over the years, the courts have developed various principles, especially in relation to the way in which discretionary powers must be exercised and the need to adopt fair decision-making procedures;

---

[1] On the three jurisdictions of the United Kingdom, see Part IV Introduction.

[2] See Chapter 11.

[3] See SPICe Briefing Judicial Review, Sarah Harvie-Clark (The Scottish Parliament), 27 October 2009, 09/75.

[4] See Tribunals Courts and Enforcement Act 2007, ss 15–21.

[5] See Chapter 17.

(c) that there has been a breach of s. 6 of the Human Rights Act 1998, wh
compliance with the 'Convention rights' listed in the Act—judges in the
'take account of' the case law of the European Court of Human Rights;[6] and

(d) that there has been a breach of a requirement imposed by European Union (EU) le
islation or the case law of the European Court of Justice (ECJ).[7]

Note that the arguments mentioned in (a) and (b) are the bedrock common law arguments associated with judicial review, and that while the arguments mentioned in (c) and (d) can be made in judicial review cases, they can also be made in other proceedings. This chapter focuses on (a) and (b). The arguments in (c) are dealt with in Chapter 17; those in (d) are dealt with in Chapter 18.

Judicial review is one of the key ways of providing legal redress against public bodies and ensuring that they are legally accountable even when no other forms of redress are available within the domestic system. It is therefore of *constitutional* importance, giving practical effect to the rule of law.

(b) HISTORICAL DEVELOPMENT

Many of the underlying legal principles of judicial review are centuries old. For example, although not a judicial review case in the modern sense, *Entick v Carrington* (1765) enunciated the core principle that continues to underpin judicial review—namely, that government bodies and others exercising public functions must have legal authority for their actions and must act in accordance with the law.[8] While this principle is centuries old, it has been continually developed and expanded upon by the judges. During the past few decades, judicial review has been one of the most dynamic and fascinating areas of law, as judges have created new grounds of review and applied principles of review to novel situations.

Commentators have been interested in why the courts have been so active in recent years and different explanations are given. Some have contrasted the more activist approach of the judges today with the more cautious approach that dominated during the early part of the twentieth century. Professors Wade and Forsyth tell us that, during that period, the courts became reluctant to develop the principles of judicial review and *'showed signs of losing confidence in their constitutional function and they hesitated to develop new rules in step'*[9] with the growth in the scale of government. For these writers, then, whether judges take a more or less activist approach depends on judicial confidence. But what factors are likely to influence the confidence of judges to assert legal principles against government authorities?

Two factors were particularly important during the first half of the twentieth century. First, the two World Wars contributed greatly to a legal–political climate that encouraged judicial deference to the executive and discouraged judicial activism.

Perhaps the best-known example of the deferential approach is the infamous 1942 decision of the House of Lords in *Liversidge v Anderson*.[10] The date of this case is important, because it was decided at a stage of the Second World War during which the British war effort was at its most stretched and there was a widely held view that the institutions of the

---

[6] Section 2(1) HRA, see Chapter 17.

[7] See Chapter 18.

[8] See Chapter 3.

[9] H.W.R. Forsyth and C. Forsyth, *Administrative Law*, 10th edn (2009, Oxford: OUP), p. 12.

[10] [1942] AC 206. See further A.W. Brian Simpson, *In the Highest Degree Odious: Detention without Trial in Wartime Britain* (1994, Oxford: OUP).

…The Defence (General) Regulations 1939—a piece of delegated
…cutive to detain persons without trial '*if the Secretary of State*
…*e*' that the person had hostile associations. In using this word-
…itely rejected an alternative form of wording that would have
…more subjective) power to detain 'if satisfied' that the person
…onetheless, the majority of the House of Lords held that even
…d individual liberty and the legislation specifically said that the
…y act if he had 'reasonable cause', the courts could not review the
…er this power. Lord Atkin disagreed and delivered a withering
…n by the majority of his colleagues.

[1942]…

Lord Atkin (dissenting)

I view with apprehension the attitude of judges who on a mere question of construction when face to face with claims involving the liberty of the subject show themselves more executive minded than the executive [...] In this country, amid the clash of arms, the laws are not silent. They may be changed, but they speak the same language in war as in peace. It has always been one of the pillars of freedom, one of the principles of liberty for which [...] we are now fighting, that the judges are no respecters of persons and stand between the subject and any attempted encroachments on his liberty by the executive, alert to see that any coercive action is justified in law. In this case I have listened to arguments which might have been addressed acceptably to the Court of King's Bench in the time of Charles I.

QUESTIONS

1. What do you think Lord Atkin means when he says that laws may be changed, '*but they speak the same language in war as in peace*'?

2. Why does he say that, in this case, he has '*listened to arguments which might have been addressed* [...] *to the Court of King's Bench in the time of Charles I*'?

3. It is said that these days there is a 'war on terror'. As we will see in Chapter 17, the courts have ruled that central aspects of the anti-terrorist legislation (notably, detention of suspects without charge or trial) have been unlawful.[12] Is this evidence that the judges have become more confident in asserting their powers? If so, how can this be explained?

Deference to the executive during times of war was one element—but other factors also gave rise to a lack of confidence among the judges and limited their willingness to review decisions of public bodies. The early years of the twentieth century saw an extension of the franchise, and a consequential growth in the democratic legitimacy of Parliament and of government itself. Government became increasingly concerned to step in and to develop

[11] On delegated legislation, see Chapter 11.
[12] See Chapter 17, section 5, Case Study: Human Rights and Terrorism.

systems that were designed to improve people's quality of life in areas ranging from education, to health, to land use planning, to the provision of general welfare provision. This inevitably led to a reassessment of older attitudes to concepts such as the rule of law.

In Chapter 2, we saw that 'legal constitutionalists' view the rule of law as a shield that protects people from government and as a brake on government powers that will prevent the executive from interfering with rights. Harlow and Rawlings have labelled this the 'red light' approach, because it emphasizes the law's role in controlling and limiting government.[13] As we noted, some legal constitutionalists would like the rule of law to have an even greater role as *the* controlling principle of the UK constitution, with the judges having power to review judicially not only *government*, but also *Parliament*. If this change were ever to come about, it would mark a major departure from the principle of parliamentary supremacy.

During the twentieth century, an alternative approach evolved, which was much closer to that adopted by the 'political constitutionalists'. This recognized that government can make a positive contribution and that legal principles have a role in enabling government to use its powers for the common good. Harlow and Rawlings call this the 'green light' approach. The 'red light' and 'green light' metaphors are still useful in summarizing two of the main ways of understanding the relationship between law and government, and the task of the judges in judicial review, and they continue to inform debate, with some writers and judges tending to lean towards one or other of the approaches.

The main point being made for now, however, is that, during the first half of the twentieth century, some of the leading judges were acutely aware of the growing democratic legitimacy of government and its social welfare programme. They were also aware of their own weak democratic credentials and of the limitations of the adjudication process in determining complex public interest issues. During this period, in a number of important cases, the judges explained the principles that the courts could apply when reviewing decisions of public bodies and the need to balance these principles with the needs of government. One of the best-known examples is *Associated Provincial Picture Houses Ltd v Wednesbury Corporation* (discussed later in the chapter), in which Lord Greene MR stressed the limited ability of the judges to review the exercise of discretionary powers by local authorities.

The mood of the judiciary changed during the 1960s under the judicial leadership of judges such as Lord Denning and Lord Reid. Of particular importance was a series of extremely influential decisions of the House of Lords that completely rejuvenated the principles of judicial review and the constitutional standing of the courts. The three key decisions are summarized in Box 16.1.

BOX 16.1 THREE KEY JUDICIAL REVIEW DECISIONS OF THE 1960s

RIDGE V BALDWIN [1964] AC 40

This case placed the principles of natural justice on a modern footing, so that they could be applied to a wide range of government decisions, and not only to decisions of courts and administrative actions that were 'judicial' in character. (The practical result was that Chief Constable Ridge was held to have a right to notice of allegations made against him and a right to respond before the police authority removed him from office.)

---

[13] Carol Harlow and Richard Rawlings, *Law and Administration*, 3rd edn (2009, Cambridge: Cambridge University Press), ch. 1.

PADFIELD V MINISTER OF AGRICULTURE [1968] AC 997

This case reiterated that legislation never gives unfettered discretion to ministers. Whenever they are given discretion by an Act of Parliament, ministers must always use that discretion to further the 'policy and objects' of the Act. The courts and not ministers are the final arbiters of how an Act of Parliament is to be interpreted. (The result was that it was unlawful for the minister, solely for reasons of wanting to avoid political embarrassment, to refuse to set up an inquiry into the operation of a milk marketing scheme.)

ANISMINIC V FOREIGN COMPENSATION COMMISSION [1969] 2 AC 147

This case held that the jurisdiction of the courts to review decisions of public bodies cannot be ousted by Parliament without the clearest words. Legislation that said that a 'determination' of a public body could not be 'called into question in any court of law' was not sufficiently clear. It could not stop the courts reviewing the legality of the 'determination'. (The result was that the claimant was able to challenge the lawfulness of the FCC's decision to refuse to award compensation for assets that had been appropriated by the Egyptian government.)

These decisions, which are discussed later in this chapter, mark the start of the modern phase of judicial review, which, during the past fifty or so years, has seen the courts develop the availability and scope of judicial review. Judicial review has shifted from being a remedy essentially concerned with the quality of day-to-day administration and the legal limits of public bodies' powers to a process of constitutional importance in which the courts are also concerned to uphold constitutional rights.

Jeffrey Jowell, 'Beyond the rule of law: Towards constitutional judicial review'
[2000] Public Law 671, 674–5 (footnotes omitted)

The explicit recognition of constitutional rights

Rather late in the era of the development of judicial review, the courts began to base their reasoning upon an explicit recognition of individual democratic rights against the state. First, the right to life was recognised, in an asylum case *R v Secretary of State for the Home Department ex p Bugdaycay* [1987] AC 514 as meriting 'the most anxious scrutiny' of an administrative decision. In the *Leech* case [*R v Secretary of State for the Home Department, ex parte Leech (No. 2)* [1994] QB 198]...Lord Steyn held that a prisoner's right to communicate in confidence with his solicitor was a 'constitutional right'—that of access to justice—even where no specific litigation was contemplated. It could only be interfered with where there was a 'pressing need' and the intrusion even then should be the minimum necessary to ensure that the correspondence was bona fide. The Home Secretary, it was held, had not in that case discharged the onus of satisfying that test. [...]

We have therefore seen that our courts have begun to shift the boundaries of administrative law into the constitutional realm by explicitly endorsing a higher order of rights inherent in our constitutional democracy.[14]

---

[14] On the notion of 'higher order' law, see Chapter 1.

The constitutional importance of judicial review has been given additional impetus by devolution and by the Human Rights Act 1998—especially s. 6(1), which created a new ground of review and which provides that '*It is unlawful for a public authority to act in a way which is incompatible with a Convention right*'. These developments are discussed in more detail elsewhere.[15] As Aileen Kavanagh puts it: "[R]ather than starting from the premise that review of democratically elected bodies is somehow constitutionally suspect, the courts now start from the premise that they have a democratic mandate to engage in strong constitutional review".[16]

Developments in the case law have been accompanied by important reforms to the procedure for seeking judicial review and the remedies available to claimants.

BOX 16.2 SUMMARY OF MAIN RECENT DEVELOPMENTS IN JUDICIAL REVIEW

- Relaxation of rules of 'standing' (which determine who is allowed to make judicial review challenges) in England and Wales, and Northern Ireland
- Review of prerogative powers[17]
- Creation of new grounds of judicial review, including the adoption of the proportionality test to protect Convention and EU rights
- Modernization of the court procedures and remedies in judicial review cases in England and Wales

---

2 THE CONSTITUTIONAL JUSTIFICATIONS FOR JUDICIAL REVIEW

As the courts have become more interventionist and public bodies have discovered that their actions are increasingly vulnerable to legal challenge, debate surrounding the legitimacy of judicial review has grown in intensity both in the political arena and among legal theorists.

Anthony King, a political scientist, provides a feel of the growing antagonism within the UK government towards the judges during the 1980s and 1990s following a series of judicial review cases that were critical of ministerial actions. He goes so far as to liken the relationship between the UK government and the courts to a state of war. The following extract from his book *The British Constitution* picks up the story when Tony Blair's Labour government was elected in 1997.

Anthony King, *The British Constitution* (2007, Oxford: OUP), pp. 141–3 (footnotes omitted)

It might have been expected that the departure of the Major government and the election of the Blair government in 1997 would have ended the war between judges and ministers. Admittedly, Lord Irvine of Lairg, the incoming Lord Chancellor had, while Labour was still in

---

[15] See especially Chapter 17.

[16] Aileen Kavanagh, *Constitutional Review under the UK Human Rights Act*, (Cambridge University Press, 2009), p. 347.

[17] See Chapter 9, section 3(e). Prerogative and statute, on p. 347.

opposition, defended elected governments' 'administrative autonomy' and counselled judges against saying or doing anything that smacked of 'judicial supremacism'. He had insisted that 'judicial self-restraint [...] must inform decision making in public law' and sought to make it plain 'that those judges who lay claim to a judicial power to negate Parliamentary decisions, contrary to the established law and uses of our country, make an exorbitant claim. [...] Lord Irvine was being true to Labour's historic suspicion of judicial activism [...] It turned out that the war between the Major government and the judges had not been a mere spat [...] it had been a manifestation of a relatively new but by now inbuilt constitutional tension between the claims of judges to defend the rule of law, including human rights, and the claims of ministers to be the sole and legitimate custodians of the country's long-term national interests. [...] The principal combatant on the government side was David Blunkett, home secretary between 2001 and 2004 and, as it quickly emerged, Labour's own version of Michael Howard. His language often sounded remarkably like Howard's. When one judge ruled that a recent piece of legislation violated the European Convention on Human Rights, Blunkett told the BBC, 'Frankly, I'm personally fed up with having to deal with a situation where parliament debates issues and the judges then overturn them.'

David Blunkett MP was making a political point, but he was also raising a serious constitutional question: from where do judges—who are not elected or politically accountable—acquire authority to review, and strike down, decisions that have been taken by ministers who are politically accountable to Parliament?

A similar question is asked in all constitutional systems in which a judicial review jurisdiction exists. In most systems, the answer is provided by the written constitution, which either expressly provides for judicial review of governmental powers or arguably implicitly does so. The latter situation is the case in the US Constitution. Although this does not expressly give the US Supreme Court a judicial review jurisdiction, it was held in *Marbury v Madison*[18] that the US Supreme Court must be able to review the legality of the actions of the other branches of government—including the legislature—in order to ensure compliance with the written Constitution. This jurisdiction was implicit in the existence of the written Constitution, because without it, the Constitution could not be enforced.

Nonetheless, even when a written constitution exists, debate over the appropriate scope of judicial review can be intense. In the United States, for instance, there has been long-standing discussion over whether the Supreme Court should be able to review legislation enacted by Congress and if so, on what grounds[19]. Professor Mauro Cappelletti, a comparative lawyer, goes so far as to say that tension between judicial review and democratic theory poses a 'theoretically insoluble contradiction'.[20]

[18] 5 U.S. (1 Cranch) 137 (1803).

[19] See, e.g., John Hart Ely, *Democracy and Distrust: A Theory of Judicial Review* (Harvard, 1980), where Ely argues the judicial review should be limited to supporting people's rights to democratic participation; and Jeremy Waldron, 'The Core of the Case Against Judicial Review, 115 Yale L.J. 1346 (2006), where Waldron argues against judicial review of legislation in a liberal democracy.

[20] M. Cappelletti, *The Judicial Process in Comparative Perspective* (1989, Oxford/New York: Clarendon Press), p. xvii.

(a) DEBATE OVER THE CONSTITUTIONAL BASIS OF JUDICIAL REVIEW: THE INTENTION OF PARLIAMENT VS THE COMMON LAW

In the British context, debate among constitutional lawyers over the constitutional basis for judicial review has focused on the relationship between two fundamental principles of the constitutional system: the supremacy of the UK Parliament and the rule of law.[21] Some argue that judicial review is based on Parliament's supremacy—that the role of judges is to give effect to the expressed or implied intention of Parliament, as expressed in the words of Acts of Parliament. Others argue that judicial review is rooted not in parliamentary intent (whether express or implied), but in common law principles that enshrine the rule of law and in the judges' role in developing common law rules. We need not deal with these competing arguments in great detail, but it is important to be aware of the main strands of the debate.

Judicial review is founded upon the supremacy of the UK Parliament

Those advocating this position (the main advocate has been Professor Christopher Forsyth) say that the essential task for the courts when asked to review the actions of public bodies is to ensure that these bodies have not exceeded the powers conferred upon them by Parliament, using the *ultra vires* ('beyond the powers') doctrine. This approach, often referred to as the '*ultra vires* approach', assumes that public bodies derive their legal powers expressly or implicitly from Parliament, and that when public bodies are challenged in judicial review proceedings, the task of the court is to check whether the body has acted in accordance with Parliament's intentions. From this perspective, then, the judicial review jurisdiction derives its authority from the principles of parliamentary democracy. While judges are not themselves elected, they play a crucial part in the democratic process by ensuring that public bodies act within the powers conferred by Parliament.

Judicial review is founded upon the common law

Other commentators, including Professors Dawn Oliver, Paul Craig, and Jeffrey Jowell, argue that this approach does not provide a satisfactory basis for explaining the constitutional justification for judicial review.[22] Two levels of criticism are made.

The first focuses on the realities of current judicial review. At this level, the basic criticism is that since developments in judicial review have been judge-made, it is simply unrealistic to say that they have been driven by parliamentary intentions. Sir John Laws, for example, has observed that modern developments in administrative law '*are categorically, judicial creations. They owe neither their existence nor their acceptance to the will of the legislature. They have nothing to do with the intention of Parliament, save as a fig leaf to cover their true origins. We do not need the fig leaf any more*'.[23]

---

[21] On parliamentary supremacy see Chapter 2, and for the rule of law, see Chapter 3. See also the argument against judicial review from a political constitutionalist perspective in Richard Bellamy, *Political Constitutionalism: A Republican Defence of the Constitutionality of Democracy* (2007, Cambridge: Cambridge University Press).

[22] Dawn Oliver, 'Is ultra vires the basis of judicial review?' [1987] Public Law 543, 567. See also Paul Craig, 'Ultra vires and the foundations of judicial review' [1999] CLJ 63; Jeffrey Jowell, 'Beyond the rule of law: Towards constitutional judicial review' [2000] Public Law 671.

[23] Sir John Laws, 'Law and Democracy' [1995] Public Law 72, 79.

The more fundamental criticisms of the *ultra vires* approach have a political and a constitutional perspective. From the former, it may be argued that to justify judicial review on the basis that it serves Parliament, and therefore parliamentary democracy, relies on a concept of democracy that is too narrow. As we have seen, the track record of the UK Parliament in holding ministers to account, according to many commentators, is not good.[24] Moreover, there are concerns that elected politicians in Parliament and government may not respect the interests of unpopular minorities (such as asylum seekers, prisoners, gypsies, and terrorist suspects). In other words, the democratic credentials of the *ultra vires* approach are tarnished by a system that Lord Hailsham (a former Conservative Lord Chancellor) famously described as being an 'elective dictatorship'.[25]

These observations echo the arguments of those who call for a reassessment of the very theory of parliamentary supremacy. Various points are made, but the essential claim is that the UK Parliament cannot have truly unlimited powers because its legal authority derives from the unwritten constitution (Sir John Laws refers to what he calls a 'higher order law'). Parliament must act compatibly with the fundamental requirements of the unwritten constitution, because it is this unwritten constitution that provides the foundation of Parliament's own authority. On this view, judicial review is also based on the unwritten constitution. In the last resort, as in *Marbury v Madison*, courts derive their authority from the constitution and have ultimate responsibility for ensuring that the constitution is applied. This might conceivably require them to judge whether the UK Parliament has acted unconstitutionally.[26]

Jackson v Attorney General
[2005] UKHL 56

Lord Steyn

[102.] [...] In exceptional circumstances involving an attempt to abolish judicial review or the ordinary role of the courts, the [...] Supreme Court may have to consider whether this is a constitutional fundamental which even a sovereign Parliament acting at the behest of a complaisant House of Commons cannot abolish.

More recently Lord Hope has commented that '*The question whether the principle of the sovereignty of the United Kingdom Parliament is absolute or may be subject to limitation in exceptional circumstances is still under discussion.*'[27] If it is conceivable that the courts may be able to review primary legislation of the UK Parliament at Westminster, albeit in very exceptional situations, the authority of the courts must be based on something more fundamental than Parliament's own sovereignty: otherwise, the courts would have to respect Parliament's will even when Parliament is seeking to act contrary to a constitutional fundamental.

In the following extracts, Professor Forsyth responds to these criticisms. The extract deals with the 'fig-leaf argument' made by Sir John Laws (Forsyth calls this the 'weak' criticism of

---

[24] On accountability of ministers, see Chapter 7.

[25] Lord Hailsham of St Marylebone, *The Dilemma Of Democracy* (1978, London: Collins).

[26] Legislation enacted by the Scottish Parliament is subject to judicial review to ensure it complies with the Scotland Act 1998, but the courts cannot use common law grounds of judicial review in this context: see *AXA General Insurance Limited and others (Appellants) v The Lord Advocate and others (Respondents) (Scotland)* discussed in Chapter 2 and Chapter 5.

[27] *AXA General Insurance Limited and others (Appellants) v The Lord Advocate and others (Respondents) (Scotland)* [2011] UKSC 46 at para. 50.

the *ultra vires* approach) and with the argument relating to parliamentary supremacy itself (which Forsyth calls the 'strong' criticism of his approach).

Christopher Forsyth, 'Of fig leaves and fairy tales: The ultra vires doctrine, the sovereignty of Parliament and judicial review' [1996] Cambridge Law Journal 122, 134–40 (footnotes omitted)

It clearly is the case that the modern law of judicial review is a judicial creation. It is the judges that have made it; and they rightly enjoy the admiration of administrative lawyers for their achievement. And it is unarguable that judicial attitudes and insights have been predominant in determining all aspects of the developed law. It cannot be plausibly asserted that the implied intent of the legislature provides any significant guidance to the reach of the rules of natural justice or the fine distinctions to be drawn between decisions that are unreasonable but not irrational and the like. The 'weak' critics make a powerful case.

But the judicial achievement in creating the modern law did not take place in a constitutional vacuum. It took place against the background of a sovereign legislature that could have intervened at any moment (and sometimes did). This was recognised by the judiciary in many of their most creative decisions. More importantly, however, since the legislature took no steps to overturn the extension and development of judicial review by the judges, it may reasonably be taken to have accepted the creativity of the judicial role. The consequence is that the legislature may reasonably be taken to have given tacit approval to the development by the judiciary of the principles of judicial review, subject, crucially, to the recognition of legislative supremacy. [...] the legislature nor the executive can evaluate everything. It is [...] common sense; and, most importantly, implies no infraction of the principle of legislative supremacy. In these circumstances an assumption that the judges have been given the task of so developing the law, within any limits which may be set by the legislature, seems entirely reasonable. And it implies no breach of the doctrine of ultra vires; in so developing the law the judges are doing what Parliament intended, or may reasonably be taken to have intended, them to do.

[...] Sir John Laws has misunderstood the fig-leaf metaphor when he says that the intention of Parliament serves only 'as a fig-leaf to cover [the] true origins [of the grounds of review]. We do not need the fig-leaf any more.' The point about the fig-leaf metaphor (and why it is so apt) is that fig-leaves do not deceive anyone as to what lies beneath them. The fig-leaf, like the swimming costume on a crowded beach, is to preserve the decencies. It enables individuals to interact in an appropriate manner without threatening the social order. The doctrine of ultra vires plays a similar role in public law. No one is so innocent as to suppose that judicial creativity does not form the grounds of judicial review; but by adhering to the doctrine of ultra vires the judiciary shows that it adheres to its proper constitutional position and that it recognises that Parliament is free to dispense with the judicially developed principles of judicial review.

[Professor Forsyth then turns to the strong criticism of his approach and the argument that the courts do have the ultimate ability to strike down primary legislation if that legislation conflicts with fundamental principles of the constitution.]

[...T]he sovereignty of Parliament, for good or ill, remains a fundamental element of the constitutional order; and it is not for the judges acting on their own motion to try to change that.

The most fundamental reason for this is that in a democratic polity change in the constitutional order must - or at any rate should - come about through the democratic process. And the judiciary, as important as its independence is to the rule of law, is a non-elected part of the constitutional order. How can some judges suppose they are entitled to change the fundamentals of the constitution without reference to the elected elements of that constitution? It may very well be a good thing if the judges were to have the task of protecting democracy and fundamental rights against the legislature, but they should be given that task by the people; it is unseemly that they should seize it themselves.

Sir William Wade has remarked that one possible result 'from our lack of a written constitution [is] that the closer judges come to the constitutional bedrock, the more prone to disorientation they seem to be'. The attack by some judges on the doctrine of ultra vires and the sovereignty of Parliament is but the latest example of judges missing their footing on that bedrock. It is to be hoped that it is the last.

Professor Paul Craig, one of the main contenders for the common law approach to judicial review, disagrees with Forsyth's analysis on both historical and conceptual grounds. His historical case is that '*judicial review was not originally founded on the idea of effectuating legislative intent, and that this only became a central focus in the nineteenth century*'.[28] The following extract is concerned with his conceptual argument.

Paul Craig, 'Ultra vires and the foundations of judicial review' [1998] Cambridge Law Journal 63, 86–9 (footnotes omitted)

The conceptual perspective

We have already seen that proponents of the traditional ultra vires doctrine defend it on the ground, *inter alia*, that it legitimates judicial review, by making it referable to Parliamentary intent. They question whether any other conceptual justification for the courts' powers of judicial review could be found, and maintain this position even while acknowledging some of the shortcomings of the ultra vires doctrine. This is an important argument which must be directly addressed.

The most dramatic way of doing so is, of course, to attack the foundations of the argument directly, by challenging established ideas of Parliamentary supremacy. This is a possible line of argument and as indicated earlier I believe that there are indeed strong reasons for rethinking traditional ideas of Parliamentary supremacy. [...] It will however be argued that a sound conceptual foundation for judicial review can be found even if Parliamentary supremacy remains unaltered. The essence of the argument can be put quite simply.

It is common for lawyers to think in the pigeon-holes represented by their specialty. [...] This is particularly true when we consider public and private law. Important work has been done on the differences and similarities between the two fields, but a significant difference has not been noted.

In public law, the view is [...] that controls on public power must be legitimated by reference to legislative intent. In private law, there is no such assumption. It is accepted that constraints on the exercise of private power can and have been developed by the common law in and of itself, and there are numerous examples of this in contract, tort, restitution and property law. [...] The absence of any formal divide between public and private law helps us

---

[28] C. Forsyth (ed.) *Judicial Review and the Constitution*, (2000, Oxford: Hart Publishing), p. 61.

to understand why it would not have appeared at all odd to a Coke, Heath, Holt or a Mansfeld to base judicial review on the capacity of the common law to control public power. [...]

There are consequential interesting differences in the sense of legitimation which operates in the two areas. In public law, the traditional ultra vires model sees legitimation in terms of the *derivation* of judicial authority, flowing from legislative intent. The prime focus is not on the *content* of the heads of review. We are of course concerned about content, but this is not the primary focus when we are thinking about the legitimacy of judicial review itself. This is in part a consequence of the fact that, as we have seen, the ultra vires doctrine is capable of vindicating virtually any chosen heads of review. In private law, by way of contrast, we tend to think of legitimation in terms of the *content* of the common law norm which the courts have imposed, and more specifically about its *normative justification*. We ask whether certain constraints imposed on the exercise of private power in, for example, contract and tort, are sensible, warranted and justified in the light of the aims of the particular doctrinal area in question. [...]

An important consequence of conceiving of judicial review in this manner is that it better expresses the relationship between courts and legislature in a constitutional democracy. The fact that the legislature could ultimately limit review, given traditional notions of sovereignty, does not mean that the institution of review has to be legitimated by reference to legislative intent in the absence of any such limits being imposed. The constitution assigns a role to the courts as well as the legislature. [...] if we accept that [...] review powers rest on the common law we can then employ the same approach which we bring to bear in the context of private law. The focus would be where it ought to be, on the existence of a reasoned justification, which was acceptable in normative terms, for the particular head of review which was in question. Thus, for example, rather than 'justifying' a particular reading of jurisdictional error by reference to legislative intent, there should instead be a reasoned argument as to why this view of jurisdictional error was felt to be correct.

A middle way?

These extracts show that it would be an oversimplification to say that of the two claimed constitutional foundations for judicial review—the intention of Parliament and the common law—only one can be totally correct. Both sides of the argument accept that the reality is more complicated and subtle. This is not surprising. After all, judicial review has had a long history, and its roots pre-date current understandings of democracy and the modern role of Parliament. Many changes have occurred over the centuries and, as we saw when discussing the prerogative, caution must be exercised when looking at older understandings of the relationship between the courts and the other institutions of government through twenty-first-century spectacles. Craig, for example, is no doubt correct to say that seventeenth-century authorities would not have rooted judicial review in parliamentary intent—but, in those days, Parliament was a very different institution from Parliament today, the quantity of legislation was far less, and ideas of democratic legitimacy were also very different.

Another factor that adds to the complexity is that judicial review involves the courts in a very wide range of issues, from relatively routine disputes (over matters such as local authority licensing, planning, and housing) to high-profile and constitutionally important matters (such as the review of executive powers in relation to terrorism or the legal status of primary legislation). Much of the day-to-day work of the judicial review judge concerns interpreting and applying legislation, and checking to see whether public bodies have acted in accordance with the requirements set out in Acts of Parliament. In such cases, there can be no doubt that the *ultra vires* approach is dominant, both in terms of what the judges consider their role to be and in terms of what they are actually doing.

Equally, judges are now regularly called upon to make constitutional decisions that have a bearing both on legal powers of the executive and the legislature itself. In such situations, judicial review cannot be adequately justified in terms of parliamentary intention. In the following extract from the conclusion to his book, *The Constitutional Foundations of Judicial Review*, Dr Mark Elliott responds to issues such as these by arguing that it is unrealistic to seek to base judicial review on a single foundation stone.[29]

Mark Elliott, *The Constitutional Foundations of Judicial Review* (2001, Oxford: Hart Publishing), pp. 252–3

The notion that judicial review rests on a set of constitutional foundations, rather than on a single foundation, captures two central truths about the juridical underpinnings of the supervisory jurisdiction.

In the first place, it emphasises that the ethos lying at the heart of orthodox ultra vires theory—that judicial review is based solely on the intention of the legislature—is fundamentally incorrect. In truth, judicial review's legitimacy is secured, and its ambit determined, by the rich set of constitutional principles most notably the rule of law, the separation of powers and the sovereignty of Parliament—on which the constitution is founded. It is in the interaction of those constitutional fundamentals, rather than in the legislative command of the sovereign, that the justification for judicial review is to be found. Secondly, the pluralism which inheres in the notion of constitutional foundations reflects the fact that judicial review must be justified in ways which are appropriate to the diverse areas within which it now operates. The search for a single doctrine capable of furnishing a juridical rationalisation of all judicial review is futile— albeit that this conclusion emphatically does not detract from the fact that review in all its contexts rests on a common normative basis.

QUESTIONS

1. Summarize the main arguments for and against the proposition that, in exercising the judicial review jurisdiction, judges give effect to the intention of Parliament.

2. If the courts are ultimately responsible for ensuring that the executive and the legislature act in accordance with the unwritten constitution, who is to ensure that the courts interpret the constitution correctly?

3. 'The search for a single doctrine capable of furnishing a juridical rationalization of all judicial review is futile—albeit that this conclusion emphatically does not detract from the fact that review in all its contexts rests on a common normative basis.' Elliott. Discuss.

---

[29] Note also the argument that the relationship between courts and Parliament and the executive should be understood as a 'dialogue'. See Further Chapter 17 and, in particular, Aileen Kavanagh, *Constitutional Review under the UK Human Rights Act*, (Cambridge University Press, 2009), Chapter 14.

3 JUDICIAL REVIEW IN PRACTICE

Having looked at questions associated with the constitutional foundations of the judicial review, we now change gear and turn to consider some practical aspects of the process.

Judicial review is often important in practice because it is a remedy of last resort. Claimants turn to judicial review when they have exhausted other avenues of appeal (such as to the First-tier Tribunal) or when no such avenues exist (because they have not been created by any Act of Parliament). But even then, judicial review may only be a limited remedy. This is because, even if claimants are successful in their claims, a judicial review does not mean that the courts will replace the decision that has been challenged with their own decision. A court hearing a judicial review case cannot make a fresh decision as if it were standing in the shoes of the public authority that made the challenged decision.[30] Judicial review is generally about the way in which decisions are made (for example, whether people were properly consulted) and the limits of a public authority's legal powers, rather than the *merits* of the decision (for example, whether it was the best or wisest decision in the circumstances).[31] Judges often stress that, when reviewing a decision, it is irrelevant whether they agree or disagree with it.

Subject to an important qualification, even if a claimant succeeds, the matter will normally be sent back ('remitted') to the original decision-maker for a fresh decision to be made in the light of the court's judgment. When this happens, the decision-maker may reach the same decision as that which was originally challenged, but hopefully, this time, the decision maker will have acted lawfully. (This is an important limitation of which potential claimants—and students—must be aware.)

The qualification concerns situations in which the judicial review procedure is used to protect 'Convention rights' under the Human Rights Act 1998. If a court decides that a public authority has infringed Convention rights, the authority may not be able to reach the same decision after a reconsideration. This is considered in more detail in Chapter 17.

The value of judicial review is that it requires bodies to comply with the law in their decision-making. Judicial review case law also sets standards of good administration, so that public bodies and the wider community may know what the law expects. In this way, judicial review should help to improve the quality of government. To what extent it does so in practice is an important empirical question that has been examined by researchers, to which we shall return in the conclusion to this chapter.[32]

(a) THE JUDICIAL REVIEW PROCEDURE

The three territorial jurisdictions in the United Kingdom each have different court procedures for claiming judicial review, and, as we noted earlier, a range of courts and tribunals exercise a jurisdiction that involves reviewing the legality of public actions. In this section

---

[30] In England and Wales, the Civil Procedure Rules give the court power to '*take the decision itself*' if the court '*considers that there is no purpose to be served in remitting the matter back to the decision-maker*' (CPR 54.19(3)). In practice, however, this remedy is hardly ever used, because it is qualified by the requirement that '*Where a statutory power is given to a tribunal, person or other body it may be the case that the court cannot take the decision itself*'.

[31] As we shall see, judges may review the substance of decisions on *Wednesbury* grounds.

[32] See generally Marc Hertogh and Simon Halliday (eds) *Judicial Review and Bureaucratic Impact* (2004, Cambridge: Cambridge University Press).

of the chapter, we examine the procedure known as the 'claim for judicial review' procedure, which applies in England and Wales.

The claim for judicial review procedure in England and Wales is set out in Pt 54 of the Civil Procedure Rules (delegated legislation made under the Civil Procedure Act 1997).

Civil Procedure Rules (CPR), Pt 54

JUDICIAL REVIEW

Scope and interpretation

54.1

(1) This Section of this Part contains rules about judicial review.

(2) In this Section –

(a) a 'claim for judicial review' means a claim to review the lawfulness of –

(i) an enactment; or

(ii) a decision, action or failure to act in relation to the exercise of a public function.

In England and Wales, and in Northern Ireland, the judicial review procedure consists of two basic stages.

1. Claimants must first obtain the permission of a judge to bring a claim (before the modernization of terminology in 2000, this was called 'leave').
2. Only if permission is granted will the claim proceed to be dealt with by the court.

Scotland does not have a permission stage, although the Gill Committee has recommended that a permission requirement should be introduced.[33]

(b) PERMISSION

In order to obtain permission, the claimant will have to persuade the judge, usually in writing, that:

(a) the claim is made within the time limits (claims must be made promptly and in any event within three months of the decision being challenged);
(b) the claimant has a sufficient interest in the case (standing); and
(c) other potential avenues of redress have been exhausted (for example, an internal appeal) and that there is no other suitable way of challenging the decision (for example, a statutory appeal to the First-tier Tribunal).

Most importantly, claimants must also satisfy the judge that their claim is arguable.[34]

The information in Box 16.3 is based on the Official Judicial Statistics. It shows that, over the period 1996–2011, the number of claims for judicial review increased from 3,901 to 11,200 and that the percentage of claims that were granted permission fell from 58 per cent to 16 per cent. These figures must be treated with some caution. In particular because

---

[33] Report of the Scottish Civil Courts Review, September 2009, vol. 2, ch. 12.

[34] See Andrew Le Sueur and Maurice Sunkin, 'Applications for judicial review: The requirement of leave' [1992] Public Law 102–29.

they do not reveal that approximately 60 per cent of the cases concerned immigration and asylum and that there was little if any growth in other types of judicial review. These figures, nonetheless, show that many more weaker claims were being made over the period, or that the nature of cases being dealt with at the permission stage has changed, or that it became harder to persuade judges to grant permission.[35]

BOX 16.3 CLAIMS, PERMISSION DECISIONS, AND GRANT RATES IN ALL CATEGORIES OF JUDICIAL REVIEW 1996–2006

Year	Claims filed (receipts)	Permission decisions	Permission grants	Grants as % of permission decisions
1996	3,901	2,169	1,257	58
1997	3,848	2,209	1,278	58
1998	4,539	1,767	1,020	58
1999	4,959	2,798	1,373	49
2000	4,247	3,403	1,464	43
2001	4,732	4,967	1,400	28
2002	5,377	5,330	1,124	21
2003	5,949	5,232	1,440	28
2004	4,207	3,772	1,036	27
2005	5,381	3,140	744	24
2006	6,458	3,390	752	22
2007	6,690	4,116	847	21
2008	7,169	4,800	914	19
2009	9,097	4,472	862	19
2010	10,548	6,285	1,100	18
2011	11,200	7,611	1,220	16

Source: Annual Judicial and Court Statistics.

QUESTIONS

1. How would you interpret the figures in Box 16.3 if:

   (a) you were a civil servant working in the Treasury and you have been asked to find ways of cutting back on legal aid for judicial review claims?

   (b) you were a lawyer in a firm of solicitors that represents claimants in judicial review proceedings?

   (c) you were a High Court judge?

   (d) you were a student researching a project on access to judicial review?

2. Consider the three basic justifications that are given for the permission requirement:

---

[35] For a discussion of these factors see: Varda Bondy and Maurice Sunkin, 'Accessing judicial review' [2008] Public Law 647. Note that in this article, the authors draw attention to the limitations of the official statistics.

> (a) It protects the court from being inundated with weak cases.
>
> (b) It protects public authorities from having to respond to weak cases.
>
> (c) It promotes access by keeping the system open for claimants with good cases.
>
> Which of these do you consider the most important?

(c) THE LAWFULNESS OF AN ENACTMENT

You will have noticed that Pt 54.1 of the Civil Procedure Rules (CPR) says that a claim for judicial review means a claim to review the lawfulness of an enactment, or the lawfulness of decisions or actions (or non-actions) in relation to the exercise of a public function.

The term 'enactment' means an item of legislation. As we have seen at various points in the book, it is now possible to use judicial review proceedings to question whether primary legislation enacted by the UK Parliament at Westminster is compatible with EU law.[36] Judicial review is also one route by which claimants may seek a declaration that legislation is incompatible with Convention rights under s. 4 of the Human Rights Act 1998.[37] Challenges may also be made challenging legislative provisions enacted by the National Assembly for Wales and (using judicial review in Scotland) legislation enacted by the Scottish Parliament.[38] However, the most common form of legislation to be challenges is delegated legislation made by ministers or local government.[39]

(d) THE LAWFULNESS OF DECISIONS OR ACTIONS IN RELATION TO THE EXERCISE OF A PUBLIC FUNCTION: AMENABILITY

Part 54.1 of the CPR indicates that judicial review claims may challenge the way in which 'public functions' are exercised. Note that the wording of Pt 54.1 does not refer to the bodies that may be challenged in judicial review proceedings (or, as is it is often put, the bodies that are amenable to judicial review); instead, it says that judicial review claims are concerned with the exercise of public functions. This recognizes that judicial review may be used against any decision-maker that exercises 'public functions', even if that body is not a government body in the usual sense of that term (such as ministers and local authorities)— so, for example, charities and self-regulatory organizations may find themselves subject to judicial review challenge in respect of their 'public functions'. As Lord Nicholls explains in the following extract, public, or government, functions are nowadays exercised by a wide range of bodies, including some in the private sector. While the *Aston Cantlow* case concerned the application of the Human Rights Act 1998, rather than judicial review, Lord Nicholls' explanation is pertinent in the current context.[40]

---

[36] See Chapter 18.
[37] See Chapter 17, section 2(e), Declarations of incompatibility.
[38] See the *AXA* case, fn. 26 on page 690.
[39] See Chapter 11.
[40] See Chapter 17, section 2(f), The Section 6 Duty and its enforcement.

Aston Cantlow and Wilmcote with Billesley Parochial Church Council v Wallbank and anor
[2003] UKHL 37

Lord Nicholls of Birkenhead

[9.] [...] In a modern developed state governmental functions extend far beyond maintenance of law and order and defence of the realm. Further, the manner in which wide-ranging governmental functions are discharged varies considerably. In the interests of efficiency and economy, and for other reasons, functions of a governmental nature are frequently discharged by non-governmental bodies. Sometimes this will be a consequence of privatisation, sometimes not. One obvious example is the running of prisons by commercial organisations. Another is the discharge of regulatory functions by organisations in the private sector, for instance, the Law Society.

The main way in which judges determine whether a body is amenable to judicial review is to look at the source of the body's powers. If the powers in question derive from statute or the prerogative, the decision will normally be reviewable. By contrast, decisions taken under powers contained in a contract are not considered to be reviewable, because in these cases the source of the legal power is a 'private' agreement between the contracting parties rather than a grant of power by Parliament or the common law.

Council of Civil Service Unions v Minister for the Civil Service
[1985] AC 374, 409

Lord Diplock

For a decision to be susceptible to judicial review the decision-maker must be empowered by public law (and not merely, as in arbitration, by agreement between private parties) to make decisions that, if validly made, will lead to administrative action or abstention from action by an authority endowed by law with executive powers, which have one or other of the consequences mentioned in the preceding paragraph. The ultimate source of the decision-making power is nearly always nowadays a statute or subordinate legislation made under the statute; but in the absence of any statute regulating the subject matter of the decision the source of the decision-making power may still be the common law itself, ie that part of the common law that is given by lawyers the label of 'the prerogative'.

It is clear that the exercise of statutory and prerogative power is reviewable, and that the use of contractual powers are not normally reviewable—but suppose that the source of a body's powers cannot be identified. This issue arose in the *Datafin* case. Although it performed important functions, the City Panel on Takeovers and Mergers appeared to have no formal legal powers at all. Did this mean that its decisions could not be challenged in the courts? The Court of Appeal held that the Panel could be reviewed because of the importance and impact of its functions.

R v Panel on Takeovers and Mergers, ex parte Datafin
[1987] QB 815, 824–36

Sir John Donaldson MR

The Panel on Take-overs and Mergers is a truly remarkable body. Perched on the 20th floor of the Stock Exchange building in the City of London, both literally and metaphorically it oversees and regulates a very important part of the United Kingdom financial market. Yet it performs this function without visible means of legal support.

The panel is an unincorporated association without legal personality and, so far as can be seen [...] It has no statutory, prerogative or common law powers and it is not in contractual relationship with the financial market or with those who deal in that market.

[...]

The issue is thus whether the historic supervisory jurisdiction of the Queen's courts extends to such a body [...] Mr. Alexander, for the panel, submits that it does not. He says that this jurisdiction only extends to bodies whose power is derived from legislation or the exercise of the prerogative. Mr. Lever for the applicants, submits that this is too narrow a view and that regard has to be had not only to the source of the body's power, but also to whether it operates as an integral part of a system which has a public law character, is supported by public law in that public law sanctions are applied if its edicts are ignored and performs what might be described as public law functions [...] In all the reports it is possible to find enumerations of factors giving rise to the jurisdiction, but it is a fatal error to regard the presence of all those factors as essential or as being exclusive of other factors. Possibly the only essential elements are what can be described as a public element, which can take many different forms, and the exclusion from the jurisdiction of bodies whose sole source of power is a consensual submission to its jurisdiction.

This important decision showed that, in determining whether a body is amenable to judicial review, the courts would, if necessary, look not only at whether the body derives its powers from statute or prerogative, but also at whether the body performs functions that have a 'public element'. Sir John Donaldson MR says that the necessary public element can 'take many different forms'. In *Datafin*, the Court of Appeal discerned the public element from the nature and impact of the Panel's functions, and the extent to which it was linked into a statutory scheme. Here, it was clear that Parliament had enacted legislation on the assumption that the Panel existed. Had it not existed, Parliament would have needed to establish a statutory body to perform similar (public) functions.

The reference to the exercise of a public function in Pt 54.1 CPR reflects the approach taken in *Datafin*. As we shall see in Chapter 17, similar wording is used in s. 6 of the Human Rights Act 1998 in order to identify which bodies are public authorities for the purposes of that Act.

The courts have not always found it easy to decide whether public functions are being exercised or not. Difficult issues, for example, have been raised in cases in which claimants have tried to use judicial review to challenge decisions taken by private companies and charities when performing functions that were previously undertaken by local authorities.

In *R v Servite Houses and Wandsworth LBC, ex parte Goldsmith*,[41] for example, a person was placed in a private care home by a local authority acting under powers in the National

---

[41] (2000) 3 Community Care Law Reports 325.

Assistance Act 1948 (NAA). The owner of the private care home, Servite Homes, later decided to close the home. Could a resident challenge this decision in judicial review? The resident argued that although Servite Homes was a not a government body, in providing accommodation and care to people who would have been previously looked after by a local authority under the NAA, it was exercising public functions. In essence, the claimant argued that these functions were public when exercised by a local authority and that they did not cease to be public when exercised by Servite Homes. The High Court rejected this argument. It held that the relationship between the resident and the care home was governed solely by contract, and therefore that judicial review was not appropriate; if a remedy existed, it should be in contract. In other words, the Court looked not at the nature of the function—providing care to those in need under the terms of the NAA—but rather at the nature of the legal arrangements under which the functions were delivered to the individual. As we shall see, the approach in this decision was applied after the enactment of the Human Rights Act 1998 in cases in which claimants tried to argue that housing associations and charities in a similar position to Servite Homes were bound by the Human Rights Act 1998.[42]

This discussion indicates that there is no definitive list of which bodies can be judicially reviewed. This reflects the fact that in the United Kingdom there is no precise definition of the state and no definitive list of bodies that constitute the state. It also means that there is no clear statement of which bodies must comply with the principles of judicial review and which bodies need not do so.

Note that even if a body is amenable to judicial review in principle, a particular decision taken by the body may not be reviewable. If, for example, the decision is taken in pursuance of contractual powers, the courts may decide that the proper method of seeking legal redress is by way of an action for breach of contract.

(e) STANDING TO MAKE A JUDICIAL REVIEW CLAIM

In order to obtain permission to seek judicial review, claimants in England and Wales, and Northern Ireland, must show that they have a 'sufficient interest in the matter' to which the claim relates.[43] What constitutes a 'sufficient interest' is not defined in legislation and has been left to the judges to determine. In most cases, it is obvious that claimants have a sufficient interest, because they will be challenging decisions that clearly directly affect them. The situation may be more problematic when claimants say that they are representing others (for example, a trade union representing its members) or where they claim to represent more general public interests (for example, claims made by a campaigning environmental organization). While some judges have preferred to take a 'closed' approach to such cases—insisting that claimants will only have a sufficient interest if they can show that they are directly adversely affected by the decision being challenged—nowadays the legal principles governing standing favour a much more open approach and allow claimants into court if they have an arguable case on the law.[44]

---

[42] See Chapter 17, section 2(f).

[43] Senior Courts Act 1981, s. 31 (England and Wales); Judicature (Northern Ireland) Act 1978, s. 18. In Scotland, there are no special standing rules for judicial review proceedings and the ordinary principles of civil litigation apply: see Lord Hope of Craighead, 'Mike Tyson comes to Glasgow—a question of standing' [2001] Public Law 294.

[44] For an argument that the courts should take a closed approach, see Sir Konrad Shiemann, 'Locus standi' [1990] Public Law 342; also C. Harlow, 'Public law and popular justice' (2002) 65 Modern Law Review 1.

An important early decision on standing after the modernization of the judicial review procedures in the 1980s was *IRC v National Federation of the Self-employed and Small Businesses Ltd*[45] (the *IRC* case). The Federation, an interest group, wanted to challenge the legality of a decision by the tax authorities to grant a tax 'amnesty' to print workers employed on a casual basis by newspapers. The Federation was angered that the amnesty was granted when the Inland Revenue went to great lengths to collect tax from its members. The majority in the House of Lords held that, in order to determine whether the Federation had a sufficient interest in the matter, it was necessary to look at the substance of the claim. They therefore examined the legal and factual context. Having done so, the majority decided that the Federation did not have a sufficient interest in the matter: *'one taxpayer has no sufficient interest in asking the court to investigate the tax affairs of another taxpayer or to complain that the latter has been under-assessed'*. Moreover, *'an aggregate of individuals* [such as the Federation] *each of whom has no interest cannot of itself have an interest'*.[46]

Lord Diplock took a rather different approach. His view was that standing should be only a preliminary or threshold issue used to reject 'simple' cases. Once leave (now permission) was granted, the courts should concern themselves exclusively with the substance and quality of the arguments. He decided against the Federation, not on grounds of standing but because the Federation had failed to show that the Inland Revenue had acted unlawfully.

IRC v National Federation of the Self-employed and Small Businesses Ltd
[1982] AC 617, 644

Lord Diplock

The whole purpose of requiring that leave should first be obtained to make the application for judicial review would be defeated if the court were to go into the matter in any depth at that stage. If, on a quick perusal of the material then available, the court thinks that it discloses what might on further consideration turn out to be an arguable case in favour of granting to the applicant the relief claimed, it ought, in the exercise of a judicial discretion, to give him leave to apply for that relief. [...] It would, in my view, be a grave lacuna in our system of public law if a pressure group, like the federation, or even a single public-spirited taxpayer, were prevented by outdated technical rules of locus standi from bringing the matter to the attention of the court to vindicate the rule of law and get the unlawful conduct stopped.

Lord Diplock's approach has become the dominant approach. An example is provided by *R v Secretary of State for Foreign Affairs, ex parte World Development Movement Ltd*.[47] WDM is a pressure group that campaigns to improve the quality of aid to developing countries. It challenged the Foreign Secretary's decision to provide funding for the Pergau Dam project in Malaysia. WDM did not claim to represent a particular group of people in the United Kingdom who were adversely affected by the decision; rather, it claimed to represent broader public interests, including the interests of people in developing countries. Nonetheless, WDM was held to have a sufficient interest in the matter.

---

[45] [1982] AC 617.
[46] *Per* Lord Wilberforce at 644.
[47] [1995] 1 All ER 611. Also *R v HMIP, ex parte Greenpeace Ltd* [1994] 1 WLR 570; [1994] 4 All ER 329.

R v Secretary of State for Foreign Affairs, ex parte World Development Movement Ltd
[1995] 1 All ER 611, 620

Rose LJ

[...T]here seem to me to be a number of factors of significance in the present case: the importance of vindicating the rule of law, as Lord Diplock emphasised in [IRC]; the importance of the issue raised [...] the likely absence of any other responsible challenger [...] the nature of the breach of duty against which relief is sought [...] and the prominent role of these applicants in giving advice, guidance and assistance with regard to aid [...] All, in my judgment, point, in the present case, to the conclusion that the applicants here do have a sufficient interest in the matter to which the application relates [...].

Some have argued that courts should confine themselves to protecting clear legal rights and directly affected interests, and that they should not permit pressure groups to use the judicial review process as a platform for protest or to achieve political ends.[48] While this argument highlights a danger, in practice, even in cases such as the *WDM* case, the courts are very careful to ensure that claimants have an arguable case on the law. In *WDM*, for example, the WDM claimed to represent broad public interests, its argument on the law was specific and orthodox: in essence, it was that the Foreign Secretary had misused powers conferred by legislation. After interpreting the legislation and considering the evidence, the court held that he had.

In this context, compare the decision in *R (on the application of Wheeler) v Office of the Prime Minister*,[49] in which the courts rejected Wheeler's argument that the government's failure to hold a referendum on the Lisbon Treaty was unlawful because it was in breach of a legitimate expectation that a referendum would be held. The challenge failed, not because the claimant lacked standing, but because the decision to hold a referendum was held to lie deeply in the political field that the court should not enter.[50]

QUESTIONS

1. Consider the following scenario: a local authority proposes to grant a licence to a business to open a sex shop (an establishment that sells pornography). Who of the following would or should be able to bring a claim for judicial review?

   (a) The business (for example, because it disputes the legality of conditions that the local authority says it will impose on opening hours).

   (b) A local resident (for example, who says that she was not properly consulted).

   (c) A national anti-pornography campaign organization.

   (d) An individual who lives 250 miles away.

2. Would your answers have been different if, instead of granting a licence to a business to open a sex shop, the local authority decided to subsidize the provision of support for children with terminal illnesses? In this situation, who of the following would or should be able to bring a claim for judicial review?

---

[48] See, e.g., C. Harlow, 'Public law and popular justice' (2002) 65 Modern Law Review 1.
[49] [2008] EWHC 1409 (Admin).
[50] At [43].

> (a) A local resident who objects to the expenditure on the grounds that he was not properly consulted, has no children, and firmly believes that public money should not be spent on supporting those who are soon to die.
>
> (b) A national organization that campaigns for reductions in the level of taxation.
>
> (c) An individual who lives 250 miles away.

(f) REMEDIES[51]

Claimants for judicial review may seek various orders from the court. In England and Wales (following modernization of the terminology in 2000), the following main remedies may be granted.[52]

(a) A quashing order (such orders mean that the decision challenged will have no legal effect).

(b) A quashing order is often combined with an order remitting the matter to the original decision-maker '*with a direction to reconsider it and reach a decision in accordance with the findings*' of the court.

(c) A prohibiting order (prohibiting a public body from doing or continuing to do something).

(d) A mandating order (ordering the body to perform a duty).

(e) A declaration (a formal statement by the court about the legal rights of the parties).

(f) An injunction (injunctions can be temporary or permanent. They can stop something being done or force something to be done).

(g) If the claim includes arguments about Convention rights, it may be appropriate for the court to make a 'declaration of incompatibility' under HRA 1998, s. 4.[53]

(h) Damages may also be claimed. But damages will only be available if they could be obtained in non-judicial review proceedings. This means that damages cannot be sought in claims based only on the common law grounds of judicial review. They can only be obtained in claims based on contract, tort, or a breach of Convention Rights or rights under EU law.

The grant of a remedy is discretionary, so the court may decide that even though the claimant has succeeded on the legal arguments, no formal order should be made. This may happen, for example, if there has been delay in making the claim or if a remedy would serve no useful purpose.

4 THE GROUNDS OF JUDICIAL REVIEW

The grounds on which the courts review the legality of the exercise of public functions have been, and continue to be, developed by the judges. There is no codified statement of these.[54]

---

[51] See further D. Feldman (ed.) *English Public Law,* 2nd edn (2009, Oxford: OUP) ch. 18.

[52] Senior Courts Act 1981, s. 31.

[53] See Chapter 17.

[54] For a discussion of the merits and disadvantages of codification in the light of codifications in other jurisdictions see T.H. Jones, 'Judicial review and codification' (2000) 20 Legal Studies 517. Professor Jones concludes that codification would not be advantageous.

There are, however, many judicial statements of the basic grounds, the most widely cited being Lord Diplock's in the *GCHQ* case.[55]

Council of Civil Service Unions v Minister for the Civil Service
[1985] AC 374, 410–11

Lord Diplock

Judicial review has I think developed to a stage today when [...] one can conveniently classify under three heads the grounds on which administrative action is subject to control by judicial review. The first ground I would call 'illegality', the second 'irrationality' and the third 'procedural impropriety'. That is not to say that further development on a case by case basis may not in course of time add further grounds. I have in mind particularly the possible adoption in the future of the principle of 'proportionality' which is recognised in the administrative law of several of our fellow members of the European Economic Community. [...]

By 'illegality' as a ground for judicial review I mean that the decision-maker must understand correctly the law that regulates his decision-making power and must give effect to it. Whether he has or not is par excellence a justiciable question to be decided, in the event of dispute, by those persons, the judges, by whom the judicial power of the state is exercisable.

By 'irrationality' I mean what can by now be succinctly referred to as '*Wednesbury* unreasonableness' [see the *Wednesbury case* below]. It applies to a decision which is so outrageous in its defiance of logic or of accepted moral standards that no sensible person who had applied his mind to the question to be decided could have arrived at it. Whether a decision falls within this category is a question that judges by their training and experience should be well equipped to answer, or else there would be something badly wrong with our judicial system. [...] 'Irrationality' by now can stand on its own feet as an accepted ground on which a decision may be attacked by judicial review.

I have described the third head as 'procedural impropriety' rather than failure to observe basic rules of natural justice or failure to act with procedural fairness towards the person who will be affected by the decision. This is because susceptibility to judicial review under this head covers also failure by an administrative tribunal to observe procedural rules that are expressly laid down in the legislative instrument by which its jurisdiction is conferred, even where such failure does not involve any denial of natural justice.

Since this judgment, there has been rapid development in the law—notably, in the principles relating to proportionality, legitimate expectations, and abuse of powers. When *GCHQ* was decided, legitimate expectations were only protected if they related to procedural matters such as the expectation to be consulted. It is now accepted that claimants may have substantive legitimate expectations as well.[56] While Lord Diplock's three heads of review are broad enough to encompass most developments of this sort, it will not always be easy to categorize specific arguments under one or other of his heads. The heads, then, provide a useful guide, but they should not be treated as categories into which arguments must be squeezed. In the example just given, legitimate expectation arguments may be thought to be an aspect of procedural impropriety or illegality depending on the circumstances.

---

[55] For the background to the case, see Chapter 9, section 3(e), Prerogative and statute.
[56] See section 4(h), Legitimate expectations.

(a) ILLEGALITY

Lord Diplock said that: '[T]*he decision-maker must understand correctly the law that regulates his decision-making power and must give effect to it.*' One of the basic responsibilities falling upon decision-makers is therefore to ensure that what they do is permitted by law. Decision-makers must properly understand what their legal duties and powers are. They must properly perform their duties, and their powers must be used to further the aims and policies for which the powers were given. These basic requirements have been reiterated in many cases and cover a very broad range of situations, from misinterpreting statutes, to exercising discretionary powers in a manner that breaches established common law principles, such as those discussed by Lord Greene MR in the *Wednesbury* case.

The *Wednesbury* case

In the early days of the cinema, 'picture houses', as they were then often known, were licensed by local authorities. Controversially, local authorities could allow picture houses to open on Sundays, but they had freedom to impose '*such conditions as they thought fit*' (s. 1(1) of the Sunday Entertainments Act 1932). This broad power appeared to allow local authorities to impose whatever conditions they considered desirable in the circumstances. In other words, it appeared to give councils complete or unfettered discretion.

Wednesbury Corporation granted the claimants a licence to open their cinema on Sundays, but, wanting to protect the moral welfare of children in its area, the Corporation imposed a condition that '*no children under the age of 15 years shall be admitted [...] whether accompanied by an adult or not*'.

The claimants feared that the condition would prevent families from going to the cinema on Sundays, making it uneconomic to open on that day, thereby undermining the value of the licence. They challenged the legality of the condition using two main arguments. First, they argued that, despite appearances, the discretion of the local authority to impose conditions was not unfettered. In particular, it had to be used to further the purposes contemplated by the legislation by which it was conferred. The legislation concerned licensing of cinemas and not the protection of the moral welfare of children. The local authority had therefore used its power for reasons that were irrelevant in order to achieve purposes that were improper given the scope of the legislation.

Second, they argued that even if the authority could use its discretion in order to protect the welfare of children, the actual condition imposed was unlawful because it was unreasonably wide. The moral welfare of children, they said, could be protected without a total exclusion of children from cinemas on Sundays. A narrower condition, such as one that required children to be accompanied by a parent or guardian, would have been just as effective and would have been less damaging to the plaintiffs.

The claimants lost their case. The Court of Appeal held that the local authority could take the moral welfare of children into account. In relation to the second argument, the Court said that it would have intervened had the condition been so unreasonable that no reasonable authority could have imposed it. This, however, had not been established.

The decision—especially in relation to the second argument—has been cited over the years as an example of judicial restraint, and many commentators and judges have rightly said that judges should now be less cautious. Nonetheless, the following extract from Lord Greene MR's judgment contains a clear statement of principles that remain relevant and important to understand.

Associated Provincial Picture Houses Ltd v Wednesbury Corporation
[1948] 1 KB 223, 228

Lord Greene MR

[...] When [...] discretion is entrusted by Parliament to a body such as the local authority in this case, what appears to be an exercise of that discretion can only be challenged in the courts in a strictly limited class of case. As I have said, it must always be remembered that the court is not a court of appeal. When discretion of this kind is granted the law recognizes certain principles upon which that discretion must be exercised [...]. What then are those principles? They are well understood. [...] The exercise of [...] a discretion must be a real exercise of the discretion. If, in the statute conferring the discretion, there is to be found expressly or by implication matters which the authority exercising the discretion ought to have regard to, then in exercising the discretion it must have regard to those matters. Conversely, if the nature of the subject matter and the general interpretation of the Act make it clear that certain matters would not be germane to the matter in question, the authority must disregard those irrelevant collateral matters [...].

(b) ILLEGALITY: THERE MUST BE A REAL EXERCISE OF DISCRETION

Discretion

When legislation is being drafted, policymakers have a choice between imposing duties upon public authorities to act or leaving it up to authorities to decide whether and how to act to further the aims of the legislation (for example, by using words such as 'may' or 'thinks fit'). The latter approach is often described as giving the public authority 'discretion'. The scope of discretion conferred may vary. For example, when discussing *Liversidge v Anderson* earlier in this chapter,[57] we saw that decision-makers may be given discretion to act when they 'are satisfied' that a certain state of affairs exists (subjective discretion), or Parliament may indicate that decision-makers should only be able to act if a particular state of affairs does, in fact, exist, such as 'when there are grounds for believing' that someone has hostile associations (objective discretion)—although, in *Liversidge*, the majority of their Lordships were willing to treat an objectively worded power as if it were subjectively worded.

Discretion is given in order allow flexibility so that public bodies can make decisions in accordance with their perception of the public interest and in order to meet particular circumstances including the needs of individuals. K.C. Davis, the US administrative lawyer, referred to this as the 'individualization of justice'.[58] Discretion also enables decisions to be made in the light of changing circumstances. When legislation confers discretion on a body, it may be assumed that it does so because that body is considered best placed to make the relevant decisions. Local authorities, for example, might be considered better placed to make decisions affecting their localities than Parliament is when it passes legislation. These factors inform the approach taken by courts when reviewing the exercise of discretionary powers.

In principle, those given discretion cannot delegate that discretion to others, unless they are authorized to do so; nor can they prevent themselves from using their discretion by, for

---

[57] See extract on p. 684.
[58] Kenneth Culp Davis, *Discretionary Justice: A Preliminary Inquiry* (1971, Baton Rouge, LA: Louisiana State University Press).

example, adopting blanket policies that tie their hands in future situations and prevent them from making decisions in individual cases. This is often referred to as the 'obligation not to fetter discretion'.

Discretionary powers cannot be delegated

The following is a case example cited in *The Judge Over Your Shoulder*, a guide prepared by the Government Legal Service for civil servants, explaining the principles of administrative law, including judicial review.

Government Legal Service, *The Judge Over Your Shoulder*, 4th edn (2006, London: TSol), para. 2.35

[D]eportation under the Immigration Act 1971 was a two stage process: 1) the giving of a Notice of Intention to deport (which attracted a right of appeal), and 2) the signing of the Deportation Order. Under the 1971 Act, both functions were conferred on 'the Secretary of State'. The Secretary of State delegated the first of these functions to Immigration Officers. The delegation was challenged at judicial review on the grounds that, although it was accepted that the power could be exercised on the Secretary of State's behalf by members of his Department (ie the Home Office), Immigration Officers had functions under the Act separate from the Secretary of State. The House of Lords held that despite the distinct functions conferred on Immigration Officers under the Act, they were capable of exercising the power under the responsibility of the Secretary of State. But it remained his personal responsibility, after reviewing each case, to sign the Deportation Order at the end of the process: *R v Secretary of State for the Home Department ex parte Oladehinde* [1991] 1 AC 254.

Deferring to others

Bodies may also fall foul of the obligation to exercise their discretion if they consider themselves bound by the views of others. For example, in *Lavender v Ministry of Housing and Local Government*,[59] a minister was held to have acted unlawfully when he rejected an appeal against a refusal of planning permission because he considered himself bound by the view of the Minister of Agriculture that planning should be refused. While it was no doubt sensible for the Minister of Housing to take account of his colleague's view, he could not treat himself as being bound by what his colleague thought: the discretion had been given to him, not to the other minister.

Permitted delegation

The obligation not to delegate unlawfully raises important practical issues for large organizations such as local authorities or UK government departments. Legislation is drafted to

---

[59] [1970] 1 WLR 1231.

place powers and duties on 'the authority' or 'the Secretary of State', but it would not be feasible for a full meeting of all elected councillors (in the case of local authorities) or the minister personally (in the case of Secretary of State powers) to make every decision. The law therefore recognizes these realities.

In relation to local authorities, s. 101(1) of the Local Government Act 1972 provides that 'a local authority may arrange for the discharge of any of their functions—(a) by a committee, a sub-committee or an officer of the authority [...]'. Every local authority adopts a 'scheme of delegation' that specifies by whom within a local authority a statutory power may be exercised. A failure to follow a scheme of delegation is unlawful and may be challenged by judicial review.

The approach in relation to ministerial powers is rather different. The courts have simply recognized that while a minister may be formally responsible and accountable for the legal exercise of powers, in practice, the vast majority of decisions are taken by civil servants. There is, however, no need for a scheme of delegation to be adopted in each department. This is because of a principle referred to as the 'Carltona doctrine', after the decision in *Carltona Ltd v Commissioner of Works*.[60] The Commissioners for Works, a central government department, had power to requisition land (to demand that owners of land give up control of their land) 'if it appears necessary or expedient to do so'. Although the power had been given to the Commissioners, in practice, decisions to requisition were made by officials. The Court of Appeal held that this was entirely lawful.

In the following extract, Lord Greene MR provides the classic statement of the doctrine.

Carltona Ltd v Commissioner of Works
[1943] 2 All ER 560, 563

Lord Greene MR

In the administration of government in this country the functions which are given to ministers [...] are functions so multifarious that no minister could ever personally attend to them. To take the example of the present case no doubt there have been thousands of requisitions in this country by individual ministers. It cannot be supposed that this regulation meant that, in each case, the minister in person should direct his mind to the matter. The duties imposed upon ministers and the powers given to ministers are normally exercised under the authority of the ministers by responsible officials of the department. Public business could not be carried on if that were not the case. Constitutionally, the decision of such an official is, of course, the decision of the minister. The minister is responsible. It is he who must answer before Parliament for anything that his officials have done under his authority, and, if for an important matter he selected an official of such junior standing that he could not be expected competently to perform the work, the minister would have to answer for that in Parliament. The whole system of departmental organisation and administration is based on the view that ministers, being responsible to Parliament, will see that important duties are committed to experienced officials. If they do not do that, Parliament is the place where complaint must be made against them.

60 [1943] 2 All ER 560.

(c) FETTERING DISCRETION: TREATING POLICIES AS BINDING[61]

It is proper, and often necessary, for public bodies to adopt policies in order to help them to make decisions and to provide guidance as to how decisions will be reached. This provides transparency and aids the achievement of consistency. For example, if a local authority has a statutory discretion to provide financial assistance to shopkeepers to maintain their shop fronts in traditional styles, it may want to adopt policies on the proportion of repair costs that will be funded, which streets can benefit from this help, and so on.

There is nothing wrong with adopting policies, but policies must be applied with the following factors in mind. First, the policy must itself be lawful. Second the policy ought to be published, but if not published, the policy must not conflict with policy that is published.[62] Third, public bodies must always be prepared to depart from a policy if a particular case justifies doing so; on the other hand, principles of good administration make it desirable that public bodies should follow their own self-created policies and practices. In some situations, the adoption of a policy may give rise to a 'legitimate expectation' that it will be followed and so they must be careful when they decide to alter their policy. We shall deal with willingness to depart from policy here. 'Legitimate expectations' are dealt with later in the chapter (on p. 727).

R v Secretary of State for the Home Department, ex parte Venables
[1998] AC 407, 497

Lord Brown-Wilkinson

When Parliament confers a discretionary power exercisable from time to time over a period, such power must be exercised on each occasion in the light of the circumstances at that time. In consequence, the person on whom the power is conferred cannot fetter the future exercise of his discretion by committing himself now as to the way in which he will exercise his power in the future. [. . .]

These considerations do not preclude the person on whom the power is conferred from developing and applying a policy as to the approach which he will adopt in the generality of cases [. . .] But the position is different if the policy adopted is such as to preclude the person on whom the power is conferred from departing from the policy or from taking into account circumstances which are relevant to the particular case in relation to which the discretion is being exercised. If such an inflexible and invariable policy is adopted, both the policy and the decisions taken pursuant to it will be unlawful.

British Oxygen Co Ltd v Minister of Technology[63] is a leading decision on this issue. The Board of Trade had discretionary power to give grants to help firms with their capital expenditure. It adopted a policy not to pay grants in cases in which individual items cost less than £25.

---

[61] See further Chris Hilson, 'Judicial review, policies and the fettering of discretion' [2002] Public Law 111.
[62] See *Walumba Lumba v Secretary of State for the Home Department* [2011] UKSC 12.
[63] [1971] AC 610.

BOC spent £4m buying new gas cylinders and applied for a grant. Its application was turned down on the basis that, despite the overall sum involved, each cylinder cost less than £25 and it would have been contrary to the Board's policy to confer a grant. The BOC unsuccessfully challenged the decision arguing that the Board had applied its policy without considering the merits of its application. While this argument failed on the facts of the case, Lord Reid set out the key principles.

British Oxygen Co Ltd v Minister of Technology
[1971] AC 610, 625

Lord Reid

In this Act Parliament has clearly laid down the conditions for eligibility for grants and it has clearly given to the Board a discretion so that the Board is not bound to pay to every person who is eligible to receive a grant. [. . .] It was argued on the authority of *Rex v Port of London Authority, Ex parte Kynoch Ltd.* [1919] 1 K.B. 176 that the Minister is not entitled to make a rule for himself as to how he will in future exercise his discretion. [. . .] The general rule is that any- one who has to exercise a statutory discretion must not 'shut his ears to an application' [. . .] There may be cases where an officer or authority ought to listen to a substantial argument reasonably presented urging a change of policy. What the authority must not do is to refuse to listen at all. But a Ministry or large authority may have had to deal already with a multitude of similar applications and then they will almost certainly have evolved a policy so precise that it could well be called a rule. There can be no objection to that, provided the authority is always willing to listen to anyone with something new to say [. . .].

Government Legal Service, *The Judge Over Your Shoulder,* 4th edn (2006, London: TSol), para. 2.32

Applying policy flexibly: Case example

P had been convicted of a serious assault upon a child and sentenced to a term of imprison- ment. The Secretary of State had a policy that persons convicted of such serious offences, and who were judged still to be dangerous, should be detained in Category A conditions, which was reserved for 'prisoners whose escape would be highly dangerous to the public [. . .], no matter how unlikely that escape might be and for whom the aim must be to make escape impossible'.

One practical effect of the strict application of this policy to P was greatly to restrict the range of treatment available to him. In fact P had never shown any propensity to escape and was in such poor health that there was no realistic prospect of his escaping. The Court held that in itself the policy of making escape impossible for prisoners such as P was not unlaw- ful, but since the Secretary of State had failed to have regard to P's particular circumstances and to exercise any discretion in relation to his case, the application of the policy to P was unlawful. *The Queen on the application of Pate v Secretary of State for the Home Department* [2002] EWHC 1018.

(d) ILLEGALITY: RELEVANT AND IRRELEVANT CONSIDERATIONS AND IMPROPER PURPOSES

In *Wednesbury*, the legislation had not specifically set out the purposes to be achieved or the factors to be considered. These matters were determined by the judges by interpreting the legislation to work out what was Parliament's intention. A similar set of issues arose in the constitutionally more important context of judicial review of executive powers in *Padfield v Ministry of Agriculture, Fisheries and Food*,[64] one of the most important landmark decisions in modern judicial review. In this case, the House of Lords confirmed that members of the executive do not have unfettered discretion, even when their legislative powers appear unrestricted.

Padfield v Ministry of Agriculture, Fisheries and Food

The case arose out of a scheme designed to ensure that milk was available across the country at a broadly level cost. It involved farmers selling their milk to the Milk Marketing Board for a price set centrally, which could vary from region to region. The Milk Marketing Act 1958 provided for the establishment of a committee of investigation to look into disputes arising from the scheme. Section 19 of the Act provided that disputes could be referred to a committee '*if the Minister in any case so directs*'. The section also gave the minister power to amend the scheme '*if he thinks fit to do so after considering*' a report of the committee.

Milk producers in the south-east of England complained that the pricing policy treated them unfairly, because it meant that they would be paid less for their milk than producers in other parts of the country. They therefore asked the minister to refer their complaint to a committee of investigation. He refused to do so. His decision letter said that the matter was not suited for an investigation because it 'raised wide issues'. It also indicated the minister's belief that he would be required to alter the scheme if the committee were to uphold the complaint. He was not prepared to do this, in part because it would be politically embarrassing.

The producers applied for a mandamus (now a mandating order) to force the minister to refer their complaint. The minister responded by arguing that the legislation gave him complete discretion in the matter. In response to the claim that he had based his decision on irrelevant factors, he argued that since he was under no obligation to give reasons for his decision, he could not be found to have acted improperly on the basis of reasons that he had voluntarily given.

The majority of the House of Lords (Lord Morris dissenting) rejected the minister's arguments. It held that the minister had misconstrued his legal powers and acted for reasons that were irrelevant to the purposes of the legislation.

Padfield v Ministry of Agriculture, Fisheries and Food
[1968] AC 997, 1030–3

Lord Reid

The question at issue in this appeal is the nature and extent of the Minister's duty under section 19(3)(*b*) of the Act of 1958 in deciding whether to refer to the committee of investigation

---

[64] [1968] AC 997.

a complaint as to the operation of any scheme made by persons adversely affected by the scheme. The respondent contends that his only duty is to consider a complaint fairly and that he is given an unfettered discretion with regard to every complaint either to refer it or not to refer it to the committee as he may think fit. The appellants contend that it is his duty to refer every genuine and substantial complaint, or alternatively that his discretion is not unfettered and that in this case he failed to exercise his discretion according to law because his refusal was caused or influenced by his having misdirected himself in law or by his having taken into account extraneous or irrelevant considerations.

In my view, the appellants' first contention goes too far. There are a number of reasons which would justify the Minister in refusing to refer a complaint. For example, he might consider it more suitable for arbitration, or he might consider that in an earlier case the committee of investigation had already rejected a substantially similar complaint, or he might think the complaint to be frivolous or vexatious. So he must have at least some measure of discretion. But is it unfettered?

[...] Parliament must have conferred the discretion with the intention that it should be used to promote the policy and objects of the Act, the policy and objects of the Act must be determined by construing the Act as a whole and construction is always a matter of law for the court. In a matter of this kind it is not possible to draw a hard and fast line, but if the Minister, by reason of his having misconstrued the Act or for any other reason, so uses his discretion as to thwart or run counter to the policy and objects of the Act, then our law would be very defective if persons aggrieved were not entitled to the protection of the court.

[...]

I must now examine the Minister's reasons for refusing to refer the appellants' complaint to the committee. [...] The first reason [...] was that this complaint was unsuitable for investigation because it raised wide issues. Here it appears to me that the Minister has clearly misdirected himself. Section 19(6) contemplates the raising of issues so wide that it may be necessary for the Minister to amend a scheme or even to revoke it. [...] Then it is said that [...] 'the Minister owes no duty to producers in any particular region,' [...] I can find nothing in the Act to limit this responsibility or to justify the statement that the Minister owes no duty to producers in a particular region. The Minister is, I think, correct in saying that the board is an instrument for the self-government of the industry. So long as it does not act contrary to the public interest the Minister cannot interfere. But if it does act contrary to what both the committee of investigation and the Minister hold to be the public interest the Minister has a duty to act. And if a complaint relevantly alleges that the board has so acted, as this complaint does, then it appears to me that the Act does impose a duty on the Minister to have it investigated. If he does not do that he is rendering nugatory a safeguard provided by the Act and depriving complainers of a remedy which I am satisfied that Parliament intended them to have.

Paragraph 3 of the letter of May 1, 1964, refers to the possibility that, if the complaint were referred and the committee were to uphold it, the Minister 'would be expected to make a statutory Order to give effect to the committee's recommendations.' If this means that he is entitled to refuse to refer a complaint because, if he did so, he might later find himself in an embarrassing situation, that would plainly be a bad reason. [...]

It was argued that the Minister is not bound to give any reasons for refusing to refer a complaint to the committee, that if he gives no reasons his decision cannot be questioned, and that it would be very unfortunate if giving reasons were to put him in a worse position. But I do not agree that a decision cannot be questioned if no reasons are given. If it is the Minister's duty not to act so as to frustrate the policy and objects of the Act, and if it were to appear from all the circumstances of the case that that has been the effect of the Minister's refusal, then it appears to me that the court must be entitled to act.

Lord Upjohn (at 1062)

[...] If [the minister] does not give any reason for his decision it may be, if circumstances warrant it, that a court may be at liberty to come to the conclusion that he had no good reason for reaching that conclusion and order a prerogative writ to issue accordingly.

Following the decision, the minister established a committee. In due course, it upheld the complaint, as he had feared it would. The saga ended, however, when the minister told the House of Commons that he refused to accept the committee's decision and that he would not alter the pricing scheme.

QUESTIONS

1. What is the basic principle enunciated by Lord Reid in *Padfield*?

2. '*Discretionary powers conferred by Parliament can never be unfettered and purely subjective. They must always be exercised in accordance with the law.*' Explain this statement. Is the statement applicable in all circumstances? Suppose a similarly wide discretion to take '*such steps as the minister considers necessary*' were given in the (hypothetical) National Emergency Act?

3. '[I]*f a complaint relevantly alleges that the board has* [...] *acted* [contrary to the public interest], *as this complaint does, then it appears to me that the Act does impose a duty on the Minister to have it investigated. If he does not do that he is rendering nugatory a safeguard provided by the Act and depriving complainers of a remedy which I am satisfied that Parliament intended them to have.*' (Lord Reid)

   Is this statement compatible with the view that the minister had a discretion to refer matters to the investigation committee?

4. Can it be argued that, in the case, the unfettered discretion of the minister became the unfettered discretion of the judges?

5. '*The outcome of the* Padfield *case confirms that judicial review is concerned with the process of decision making and not the merits of governmental decisions. The decision delayed government, but it did not prevent it from doing what it wants. Only political accountability could do this. This is how it should be.*' Discuss.

Where legislation specifies factors to be taken into account

The *Wednesbury* and *Padfield* decisions concerned discretionary powers that were not expressly limited by the wording used in the legislation. Often, legislation makes it clear that discretion must be used for particular reasons, or that public bodies must take account of certain factors. Consider the following example.

Disability Discrimination Act 1995, s. 49A

Public authorities must have due regard to the need to eliminate disability

(1) Every public authority shall in carrying out its functions have due regard to –

   (a) the need to eliminate discrimination that is unlawful under this Act;

   (b) the need to eliminate harassment of disabled persons that is related to their disabilities;

   (c) the need to promote equality of opportunity between disabled persons and other persons;

   (d) the need to take steps to take account of disabled person's disabilities, even where that involves treating disabled persons more favourably than other persons;

   (e) the need to promote positive attitudes towards disabled persons; and

   (f) the need to encourage participation by disabled persons in public life.

What exactly does the duty to have 'due regard' in this legislation mean? The question was raised in a case supported by the Public Law Project (PLP, a national charity concerned with improving access to public law remedies) against the London Borough of Hammersmith and Fulham. The authority had previously decided to cut its council tax by 3 per cent. This inevitably meant that the council had less money to spend. As a consequence, it decided to charge disabled people for non-residential home care services. The PLP challenged this decision, arguing, *inter alia*, that the authority had failed to have due regard to the factors listed in s. 49A of the Disability Discrimination Act 1995 (DDA). The challenge failed because the authority satisfied the court that it had properly taken its responsibilities under the legislation into account when making its decision. The Court of Appeal distinguished the previous decision in *R (Chavda) v London Borough of Harrow*.[65]

R (Domb and ors) v Hammersmith and Fulham London Borough Council [2009] EWCA Civ 941

Rix LJ

52. [The cases show that . . .] the duty is to have due regard, not to achieve results or to refer in terms to the duty; that due regard does not exclude paying regard to countervailing factors, but is 'the regard that is appropriate in all the circumstances'; that the test of whether a decision maker has had due regard is a test of the substance of the matter, not of mere form or box-ticking, and that the duty must be performed with vigour and with an open mind; and that it is a non-delegable duty.

53. [. . .] In *Chavda*, where Harrow restricted home care services to people with critical needs only, there was a total failure to mention the DDA duty in any of the documents produced for Harrow's decision makers. There was no effort proactively to seek the views of the disabled or to refer to the duty in the planning stages of the consultation. There was no equality impact assessment. Harrow nevertheless submitted that it had observed its duty in substance, and

---

[65] [2007] EWHC 3064 Admin.

had engaged in consultation and other ways with the disabled. However, what Judge Mackie considered as critical was that 'There is no evidence that this legal duty and its implications were drawn to the attention of the decision-takers who should have been informed not just of the disabled as an issue but of the particular obligations which the law imposes' (at para 40). However, I cannot say that I derive any assistance from that, very different, case.

[Lord Justice Sedley commented that the appeal in the case had been conducted on the 'highly debatable premise' that the prior decision of the council to cut its council tax had to be implemented.]

Lord Justice Sedley

80. [...T]he only practical choice for social services was going to be to raise the eligibility threshold or to charge for home care. [...] The object of this exercise was the sacrifice of free home care on the altar of a council tax reduction for which there was no legal require-ment. The only real issue was how it was to be accomplished. As Rix LJ indicates, and as I respectfully agree, there is at the back of this a major question of public law: can a local authority, by tying its own fiscal hands for electoral ends, rely on the consequent budgetary deficit to modify its performance of its statutory duties? But it is not the issue before this court.

Exercising powers for improper purposes

The cases so far discussed have concerned specific statutory powers—but the courts will also apply similar principles to impose more general obligations upon public authorities. In *Magill v Porter*, for example, the House of Lords held that local authorities have a general obligation to act in the public interest and that powers cannot be used to serve the inter-ests of the ruling political group. In the case, the Conservative-controlled local authority decided to use its statutory powers to sell its housing stock in a way that was intended to help the Conservatives to win the next local election. This was held to be unlawful.

Magill v Porter; Magill v Weeks
[2001] UKHL 67

Lord Bingham

[21] [...] Elected politicians of course wish to act in a manner which will commend them and their party (when, as is now usual, they belong to one) to the electorate. Such an ambition is the life blood of democracy and a potent spur to responsible decision-taking and administra-tion. Councillors do not act improperly or unlawfully if, exercising public powers for a public purpose for which such powers were conferred, they hope that such exercise will earn the gratitude and support of the electorate and thus strengthen their electoral position. The law would indeed part company with the realities of party politics if it were to hold otherwise. But a public power is not exercised lawfully if it is exercised not for a public purpose for which the power was conferred but in order to promote the electoral advantage of a political party. The power at issue in the present case is s 32 of the Housing Act 1985, which conferred power on local authorities to dispose of land held by them subject to conditions specified in the Act. Thus a local authority could dispose of its property, subject to the provisions of

the Act, to promote any public purpose for which such power was conferred, but could not lawfully do so for the purpose of promoting the electoral advantage of any party represented on the council.

(e) 'IRRATIONALITY' OR 'WEDSNESBURY UNREASONABLENESS'

In the *Wednesbury* case, Lord Greene MR distinguished between two senses of unreasonableness. He explained that, on the one hand, the term may be used as '*a general description of the things that may not be done*'. In this sense, it would cover the grounds that we have already discussed. He went on to explain, however, that unreasonableness may also be used in a more specific way to refer to decisions that are 'absurd'.

Associated Provincial Picture Houses Ltd v Wednesbury Corporation
[1948] 1 KB 223, 229

Lord Greene MR

It is true the discretion must be exercised reasonably. Now what does that mean? [...] It has frequently been used and is frequently used as a general description of the things that must not be done. [...] Similarly, there may be something so absurd that no sensible person could ever dream that it lay within the powers of the authority. Warrington L.J. in *Short v Poole Corporation* (1) gave the example of the red-haired teacher, dismissed because she had red hair. That is unreasonable in one sense. In another sense it is taking into consideration extraneous matters. It is so unreasonable that it might almost be described as being done in bad faith; and, in fact, all these things run into one another [...]. It is true to say that, if a decision on a competent matter is so unreasonable that no reasonable authority could ever have come to it, then the courts can interfere. That, I think, is quite right; but to prove a case of that kind would require something overwhelming, and, in this case, the facts do not come anywhere near anything of that kind.

In the *GCHQ* case, Lord Diplock preferred to speak about 'irrationality', a term which he said '*applies to a decision which is so outrageous in its defiance of logic or of accepted moral standards that no sensible person who had applied his mind to the question to be decided could have arrived at it*'.

Whether we use the expression 'unreasonableness' or 'irrationality', this head of challenge recognizes that courts can review the substance of decisions and are not limited to reviewing the process by which decisions are taken—although both Lord Greene and Lord Diplock conceived of this head of review as being limited to an exceptional class of case in which it could be shown that the public authority had very obviously stepped outside the range of decisions that it could reasonably make. Over the years, significant criticisms have been made of *Wednesbury* unreasonableness, both in academic commentaries and in judgments. The attack was led by Professor Jowell and Anthony Lester QC.

Jeffrey Jowell and Anthony Lester, 'Beyond *Wednesbury*: Substantive principles of administrative law' [1987] Public Law 368, 371–2 (footnotes omitted)

Once independent substantive review is recognised then the way lies open to develop governing principles. Is the present test of (*Wednesbury*) unreasonableness a satisfactory principle on its own?

We suggest that it is unsatisfactory for three reasons. First, it is inadequate. The incantation of the word 'unreasonable' simply does not provide sufficient justification for judicial intervention. Intellectual honesty requires a further and better explanation as to why the act is unreasonable. The reluctance to articulate a principled justification naturally encourages suspicion that prejudice or policy considerations may be hiding underneath *Wednesbury's* ample cloak.

Secondly, the context of Wednesbury unreasonableness is unrealistic. Attempting as it does to avoid judicial intervention in the merits of decisions assigned to officials, it seeks to prevent review except in cases where the official has behaved absurdly or has 'taken leave of his senses.' In practice, however, the courts are willing to impugn decisions that are far from absurd and are indeed often coldly rational. Were the courts only to interfere with decisions verging on the insane, a zone of immunity would be drawn around many oppressive or improper decisions that are in reality vulnerable to judicial review. And public authorities which had taken leave of their senses could use the language of rationality to circumvent judicial review.

Thirdly, the Wednesbury test is confusing, because it is tautologous. It allows the courts to interfere with decisions that are unreasonable, and then defines an unreasonable decision as one which no reasonable authority would take. (Imagine a law allowing the demolition of unfit houses, and then defining 'unfit' not in the normal sense of that word but in the sense that no fit house could so be!) One can understand that Lord Greene's definition of unreasonableness sought to make the judges think twice about interfering with the merits of official decisions, but a test which requires the official action not to be ordinarily reasonable, but only, in effect, extremely unreasonable, is unhelpful as a practical guide.

Judges have also been critical.

R v Secretary of State for the Home Department, ex parte Daly
[2001] UKHL 26

Lord Cooke of Thorndon

[32.] [...] And I think that the day will come when it will be more widely recognised that [*Wednesbury*] was an unfortunately retrogressive decision in English administrative law, insofar as it suggested that there are degrees of unreasonableness and that only a very extreme degree can bring an administrative decision within the legitimate scope of judicial invalidation. The depth of judicial review and the deference due to administrative discretion vary with the subject matter. It may well be, however, that the law can never be satisfied in any administrative field merely by a finding that the decision under review is not capricious or absurd.

When the *Wednesbury* principle was first set out, it was intended to catch decisions that were so obviously outrageous that the decision fell outside the range of lawful decisions available to a public authority. In the ensuing years, the courts have made the *Wednesbury* test more elaborate by assuming the existence of a sliding scale of scenarios, with the court taking different approaches according to where a case falls along that scale.

At one end are cases involving decisions by public authorities that affect fundamental rights or interests. In a 1996 case in which four members of the armed forces challenged the Ministry of Defence's blanket policy of dismissing any member discovered to be gay, Sir Thomas Bingham MR held that *'the more substantial the interference with human rights, the more the court will require by justification before it is satisfied that the decision is reasonable'*.[66] Since the Human Rights Act 1998 came into force, many of these situations have been approached not as *Wednesbury* unreasonableness cases, but instead using the proportionality test required by the European Convention on Human Rights (ECHR).[67] But the 'anxious' or 'heightened' scrutiny approach remains important for rights beyond those contained in the Human Rights Act 1998. As the Court of Appeal put it, *'it is not open to the decision-maker to risk interfering where fundamental rights in the absence of compelling justification'*.[68] The burden of argument is on the public body to show to the court that what it has done is reasonably necessary.

In the middle of the scale are ordinary cases, in which a 'so unreasonable that no reasonable authority could have made it' test—the standard *Wednesbury* approach—is applied. As we noted, this creates a high threshold for a claimant to demonstrate.

At the other end of the scale are situations in which the decision under challenge involves broad political judgements—for example, about setting levels of public expenditure or taxation. In such scenarios, the courts will apply only a 'light touch' review, asking whether the minister has *'taken leave of his senses'*,[69] or they may even hold that the subject matter of the dispute is 'non-justiciable' (meaning that the courts will not even embark on the process of assessing its rationality and lawfulness).

(f) PROPORTIONALITY

In some circumstances, the courts may hold that a public body's decision is unlawful because it is disproportionate. The concept of 'proportionality' involves a balancing exercise between what is thought to be needed in the public interest and the effect that the decision has on individuals; a fair balance of interests must be struck. To use a colloquial figure of speech: public authorities should not use sledgehammers to crack nuts when nutcrackers will do.

As we noted, in the mid-1980s in the *GCHQ* case, Lord Diplock suggested that proportionality might be growing into a separate ground of review. Since, then, however, the courts have been reluctant to develop the common law in this direction. In 2007, the Law Lords held, in a judicial review challenge to the Scottish government about policies on segregating prisoners, that *'it would not be appropriate for your Lordships to reach a decision'* on whether *'want of proportionality is a relevant complaint of unlawfulness at common law'*.[70]

---

[66] [1996] QB 517. The service personnel lost their judicial review in England, but secured victory in a subsequent application to the European Court of Human Rights, which forced the Ministry of Defence to change its policy.

[67] See Chapter 17.

[68] *R v Lord Saville of Newdigate, ex parte A* [2000] 1 WLR 1855, [37].

[69] *R v Secretary of State for the Environment, ex parte Nottinghamshire County Council* [1986] AC 240, 247–8, *per* Lord Scarman.

[70] *Sommerville v Scottish Ministers* [2007] UKHL 44; [2007] 1 WLR 2734.

Although reluctant to adopt proportionality as a ground of review in the common law, the courts have however come to use it as a result of the requirements of both branches of European law. Proportionality is an aspect of EU law.[71] It is also the approach required under the ECHR for dealing with the 'qualified rights'—such as the right to respect for private and family life (Art. 8), freedom of thought, conscience, and religion (Art. 9), freedom of expression (Art. 10), and freedom of assembly and association (Art. 11).[72]

The difference between the *Wednesbury* and proportionality approaches was explained by Lord Steyn in *R v Secretary of State for the Home Department, ex parte Daly*. Daly, a long-term prisoner, challenged the legality of the Home Secretary's blanket policy that authorized cell searches in prisons, and the examination of correspondence between prisoners and their legal advisers in the absence of the prisoners. The House of Lords, reversing the Court of Appeal, held that the blanket policy infringed Daly's common law right to legal professional privilege. It also held that the infringement was disproportionate because it was greater than could be shown to be justified (it was, for example, not always necessary to exclude prisoners when searches were being conducted). In delivering his judgment, Lord Steyn 'clarified' (and effectively overruled) one of the very early judgments of the Court of Appeal under the Human Rights Act 1998. Lord Phillip of Worth Matravers MR had said, in *R v Secretary of State for the Home Department, ex parte Mahmood*,[73] that the British courts should use 'anxious scrutiny' irrationality as the test when reviewing whether one of the qualified Convention rights had been breached.

R v Secretary of State for the Home Department, ex parte Daly
[2001] UKHL 26

Lord Steyn

[26] The explanation of the Master of the Rolls [in *Mahmood*] requires clarification. It is couched in language reminiscent of the traditional *Wednesbury* ground of review [. . .] and in particular the adaptation of that test in terms of heightened scrutiny in cases involving fundamental rights as formulated in *R v Ministry of Defence, Ex p Smith*. There is a material difference between the Wednesbury and Smith grounds of review and the approach of proportionality applicable in respect of review where convention rights are at stake.

[27] The contours of the principle of proportionality are familiar. In *de Freitas v Permanent Secretary of Ministry of Agriculture, Fisheries, Lands and Housing* [1999] 1 AC 69 [. . .] the Privy Council adopted a three stage test. Lord Clyde observed, at p 80 [. . .] that in determining whether a limitation (by an act, rule or decision) is arbitrary or excessive the court should ask itself:

'whether: (i) the legislative objective is sufficiently important to justify limiting a fundamental right; (ii) the measures designed to meet the legislative objective are rationally connected to it; and (iii) the means used to impair the right or freedom are no more than is necessary to accomplish the objective.'

---

[71] See Chapter 18.
[72] For further Chapter 17.
[73] [2001] 1 WLR 840.

Clearly, these criteria are more precise and more sophisticated than the traditional grounds of review. What is the difference for the disposal of concrete cases? Academic public lawyers have in remarkably similar terms elucidated the difference between the traditional grounds of review and the proportionality approach: [he cites the work of Professors Jeffrey Jowell, Paul Craig, and David Feldman], The starting point is that there is an overlap between the traditional grounds of review and the approach of proportionality. Most cases would be decided in the same way whichever approach is adopted. But the intensity of review is somewhat greater under the proportionality approach. [. . .] I would mention three concrete differences without suggesting that my statement is exhaustive. First, the doctrine of proportionality may require the reviewing court to assess the balance which the decision maker has struck, not merely whether it is within the range of rational or reasonable decisions. Secondly, the proportionality test may go further than the traditional grounds of review inasmuch as it may require attention to be directed to the relative weight accorded to interests and considerations. Thirdly, even the heightened scrutiny test developed in *R v Ministry of Defence, Ex p Smith* [. . .] is not necessarily appropriate to the protection of human rights. It will be recalled that in *Smith* the Court of Appeal reluctantly felt compelled to reject a limitation on homosexuals in the army. The challenge based on art 8 [ECHR . . .] foundered on the threshold required even by the anxious scrutiny test. The European Court of Human Rights came to the opposite conclusion: *Smith and Grady v United Kingdom* (1999) 29 EHRR 493. The court concluded, at p 543, para 138:

'the threshold at which the High Court and the Court of Appeal could find the Ministry of Defence policy irrational was placed so high that it effectively excluded any consideration by the domestic courts of the question of whether the interference with the applicants' rights answered a pressing social need or was proportionate to the national security and public order aims pursued, principles which lie at the heart of the court's analysis of complaints under article 8 of the Convention.'

In other words, the intensity of the review, in similar cases, is guaranteed by the twin requirements that the limitation of the right was necessary in a democratic society, in the sense of meeting a pressing social need, and the question whether the interference was really proportionate to the legitimate aim being pursued.

[28] The differences in approach between the traditional grounds of review and the proportionality approach may therefore sometimes yield different results. It is therefore important that cases involving convention rights must be analysed in the correct way. This does not mean that there has been a shift to merits review. On the contrary, as Professor Jowell [2000] PL 671, 681 has pointed out the respective roles of judges and administrators are fundamentally distinct and will remain so [. . .].

The decision in *Daly* reinforced calls both among academics and among some judges that the proportionality test be extended beyond cases involving qualified Convention rights and EU law. The Court of Appeal in the *R (Association of British Civilian Internees: Far East Region) v Secretary of State for Defence* set out some strong reasons why proportionality should replace *Wednesbury* unreasonableness in cases in which a court has to consider whether the balance struck between public and individual interests was lawfully struck. But, as you will see, it did not see this as something that could be achieved by the Court of Appeal.

R (Association of British Civilian Internees: Far East Region) v Secretary of State for Defence
[2003] EWCA Civ 473, [34]–[35]

Dyson LJ

Support for the recognition of proportionality as part of English domestic law in cases which do not involve Community law or the Convention is to be found in para 51 of the speech of Lord Slynn of Hadley in *R (Alconbury Developments Ltd) v Secretary of State for the Environment, Transport and the Regions* [2003] 2 AC 295, 320-321; and in the speech of Lord Cooke of Thorndon in *R (Daly) v Secretary of State for the Home Department* [2001] 2 AC 532, 548-549, para 32. See also *de Smith, Woolf & Jowell, Judicial Review of Administrative Action*, 5th ed (1995), p 606. It seems to us that the case for this is indeed a strong one. As Lord Slynn points out, trying to keep the *Wednesbury* principle and proportionality in separate compartments is unnecessary and confusing. The criteria of proportionality are more precise and sophisticated: see Lord Steyn in the *Daly* case, [...] It is true that sometimes proportionality may require the reviewing court to assess for itself the balance that has been struck by the decision-maker, and that may produce a different result from one that would be arrived at on an application of the *Wednesbury* test. But the strictness of the *Wednesbury* test has been relaxed in recent years even in areas which have nothing to do with fundamental rights: [...] The *Wednesbury* test is moving closer to proportionality and in some cases it is not possible to see any daylight between the two tests: see Lord Hoffmann's Third John Maurice Kelly Memorial Lecture 1996 'A Sense of Proportionality', at p 13. Although we did not hear argument on the point, we have difficulty in seeing what justification there now is for retaining the *Wednesbury* test. [...] But we consider that it is not for this court to perform its burial rites.

The burial rites were not performed by the House of Lords[74] and have yet to be performed by the Supreme Court.[75]

QUESTIONS

1. What are the differences, if any, between the *Wednesbury* approach and proportionality in cases in which fundamental rights are involved?

2. Why have the courts been so reluctant to use a proportionality test when neither human rights nor EU law is involved?

(g) PROCEDURAL IMPROPRIETY

In *GCHQ*, Lord Diplock explained that procedural impropriety can involve two types of claim: a claim that the decision-maker has failed to follow the procedures required by legislation; and a claim that the decision-maker has failed to comply with the common law requirements of procedural fairness (or natural justice).

---

[74] See *Docherty and ors v Birmingham City Council* [2008] UKHL 57, [134]–[135], *per* Lord Mance.
[75] For a defence of *Wednesbury*, see James Goodwin, 'The Last Defence of Wednesbury' [2012] Public Law 445.

Statutory procedures

The following extract from *Judge Over Your Shoulder* summarizes the main principles that apply when legislation requires certain procedures to be followed, and explains the distinction between 'mandatory' and 'directory' requirements.

Government Legal Service, *The Judge Over Your Shoulder*, 4th edn (2006, London: TSol)

Does the Power Have to Be Exercised in a Particular Way? Procedure.

2.38 Legislation can impose express procedural conditions or requirements which must be satisfied before a power can be exercised. For example, 'The Secretary of State must:

- Consult with Local Authority representatives;
- Publish his decision in draft;
- Make due inquiry;
- Consider any objections before making a decision'.

These are called 'mandatory' requirements, and failure to comply with them will usually make a decision invalid. The decision-maker will need to fulfil them (and be able to show he has fulfilled them) in spirit, as well as literally.

2.39 A statutory requirement will be presumed to be 'mandatory'. Occasionally, if the requirement is trivial or technical, or breach of the required procedure does not defeat the purpose of the statute or damage the public, this presumption can be rebutted, and the requirement will be described as 'directory'. In that case, a failure to satisfy it will not necessarily be fatal to the decision.
[...]

Case Example

The Secretary of State for Social Services was empowered to make regulations setting up a housing benefit scheme. Before doing so, the Minister was required to 'consult with organisations appearing to him to be representative of the [local] authorities concerned.' The Association of Metropolitan Authorities was granted a few days to comment on various proposed amendments, the actual wording of some of which was not sent to them. The Court held that the essence of consultation was the communication of a genuine invitation to give advice, and a genuine consideration of that advice. Sufficient **information** had to be given to the consultee to enable him to give helpful advice, and enough **time** allowed to enable him to do that. *R v Secretary of State for Social Services ex parte Association of Metropolitan Authorities* [1986] 1 WLR 1 QBD.

Procedural fairness as a requirement of the common law

Today, the expressions 'procedural fairness' and 'natural justice' are often used interchangeably to refer to two main requirements:

(a) that decision-makers be neutral, independent, and unbiased; and

(b) that those adversely affected by decisions should be given a fair hearing at which they can present their side of the case.

These two requirements are clearly very important in any court or judicial hearing—but are they necessarily appropriate in other decision-making contexts, such as when local authorities allocate housing or community care, or when ministers make decisions applying their policy? The important decision of the House of Lords in *Ridge v Baldwin*[76] held that the test for deciding whether a body has to respect natural justice is not whether it must adopt a judicial procedure, but whether its decisions affect rights and important interests. This means that the obligation to respect natural justice, or to use the more flexible expression– to act fairly, is not limited to situations in which public bodies must follow procedures that are similar to those used by courts and tribunals, but potentially applies to all types of decision-making.

The requirements of natural justice or procedural fairness may overlap with the obligation to comply with Art. 6 ECHR. This provides a right to have '*civil rights and obligations, or any criminal charge*', determined '*by a fair and public hearing within a reasonable time by an independent and impartial tribunal established by law*'.

Why is procedural fairness important?

The answer to this question may appear obvious: surely fairness is important because it is just and fair for public functions to be executed fairly? There is truth in such a response, but the answer is too circular to be helpful. One of the main reasons for thinking about why procedural fairness is important is to help determine what fairness requires in concrete situations. If all that we can say is that fairness is required in order to be fair, courts and officials will be left none the wiser about what fairness requires in practical terms.

One approach to this question is to distinguish between instrumental reasons for requiring fairness and value-based reasons for doing so. The distinction is explained by Professor Genevra Richardson.[77]

Genevra Richardson, 'Existing Approaches to Process in Administrative Law: The Legal Regulation of Process', in G. Richardson and H. Genn (eds) *Administrative Law & Government Action* (1994, Oxford: Clarendon Press), ch. 5, pp. 111–14 (footnotes omitted)

Broadly speaking, there are two basic approaches within the literature. The first, which comes in a wide variety of guises, views the insistence on 'fair' process as justified primarily by reference to the beneficial effect of process on the direct outcome of the decision. Thus strict procedural requirements can be justified if they encourage accurate decisions. The second sees 'fair' processes as justified in so far as they protect values which exist independently of the direct outcome of the decision. For example, my right to be heard before a decision which affects me is taken is essential in order to protect my personal dignity and autonomy, and is thus justified irrespective of the impact of my participation on the ultimate decision.

Instrumentalism

The first approach emphasizes the link between process and direct outcome. Thus, assuming it is possible to identify the 'correct' outcome, a procedural requirement is justified to the

---

[76] [1964] AC 40.

[77] See also the discussion of proportionate dispute resolution in Chapter 15.

extent that it encourages such an outcome. So, if the sole purpose of the criminal trial is to reach an accurate finding of guilt or innocence, then any procedural requirement that encourages accuracy is justified and any which fails to do so is not. Procedures are not, however, free and if an efficiency objective is introduced the ideal level of procedural regulation will be that which minimizes both the cost of the procedure itself (direct costs) and the costs of reaching a wrong, e.g. inaccurate, decision (error costs). Any attempt to calculate this ideal level, however, is likely to encounter major difficulties.

[...]

Process values

[...] An alternative approach is to see processes as designed to protect values which are independent of the direct outcome of the decision, such as participation, fairness, and the protection of individual dignity. While such values may contribute to correct outcomes, that may not be their primary justification. For example, respect for individual dignity may be regarded as a value worthy of protection in decision-making structures irrespective of its impact on the direct decision outcome. [...] Whatever the precise foundation of the approach [...] the claim is made that the need to provide procedural fairness, particularly in the form of participation, springs from the obligation to respect a person's dignity and autonomy as a human being. To deny an individual the opportunity to participate in decisions affecting her is to deprive her of the conditions necessary for continued moral agency. The primary justification for a claim to fair process, accordingly, lies not in the ability of such processes to achieve correct outcomes, but in the respect that they afford to the dignity and autonomy of individuals. The instrumental value of fair procedures is not denied by dignitary theorists, it is merely viewed as secondary.

QUESTIONS

1. In the light of what Richardson says, should the courts take a different view of the importance of being unable to make representations in the following two situations?

   (a) X applies for a licence and is given no chance to make representations to the decision-maker. She is refused the licence for reasons that have nothing to do with the representations that she wanted to make.

   (b) Y applies for a licence and is also given no chance to make representations. She is also refused the licence, but for reasons that she could have addressed had she been able to make representations.

2. Note the following comment in the Government Legal Service's publication for civil servants, *The Judge Over Your Shoulder* (p. 21).

'IT WOULDN'T HAVE MADE ANY DIFFERENCE!'

2.46 Failures of consultation (and indeed other lapses in due process) usually occur through inadvertence on the part of the decision-maker; because he is in a hurry; and so on. When such a lapse forms the basis of a challenge to the decision, the decision-maker may be tempted to say: 'But it was an open and shut case. Consultation [or an oral hearing, or full disclosure of reasons] would have made no difference. The decision would inevitably have been the same.' That may well be true, but the Court is unlikely to be sympathetic to such a response. And for good reason: the principle is that only a fair procedure will enable the merits to be determined with confidence, and must therefore come first.

Does this comment reflect the 'instrumental' or 'process values' approach, or a combination of the two?

Fairness depends on context

The precise requirements of fairness will depend on the context, including the interests involved, the nature of the decision, and the nature of the body making the decision. What is fair in some circumstances will be unfair in others and what is fair to some participants may be unfair to others.

R v Secretary of State for the Home Department, ex parte Doody
[1994] 1 AC 531, 560

Lord Mustill

What does fairness require in the present case? My Lords, I think it unnecessary to refer by name or to quote from, any of the often-cited authorities in which the courts have explained what is essentially an intuitive judgment. They are far too well known. From them, I derive that (1) where an Act of Parliament confers an administrative power there is a presumption that it will be exercised in a manner which is fair in all the circumstances. (2) The standards of fairness are not immutable. They may change with the passage of time, both in the general and in their application to decisions of a particular type. (3) The principles of fairness are not to be applied by rote identically in every situation. What fairness demands is dependent on the context of the decision, and this is to be taken into account in all its aspects. (4) An essential feature of the context is the statute which creates the discretion, as regards both its language and the shape of the legal and administrative system within which the decision is taken. (5) Fairness will very often require that a person who may be adversely affected by the decision will have an opportunity to make representations on his own behalf either before the decision is taken with a view to producing a favourable result; or after it is taken, with a view to procuring its modification; or both. (6) Since the person affected usually cannot make worthwhile representations without knowing what factors may weigh against his interests fairness will very often require that he is informed of the gist of the case which he has to answer.

The precise requirements of fairness, then, depend on the context and may vary over time.

(a) Fairness will often require those adversely affected by a decision to be given an opportunity to make representations before the decision is made. Fairness, however, does not necessarily require an oral hearing.

(b) Fairness will often require that a person be informed of the gist of the case against him or her, or why an adverse decision has been made. This normally requires decision-makers to give reasons why decisions have been made. Reasons provide transparency and help people to decide whether to challenge or complain about decisions.

(c) Fairness may also require a level of impartiality and open-mindedness: there is no point in allowing representations to be made if decision-makers have already made up their mind, or are unable or unwilling to listen to what is said, or have conflicting interests. This is obviously important in the case of judges, who must be unbiased, independent, and neutral.[78] But it also applies to other decision-makers as well: for example, officials employed by local authorities to review initial decisions made by housing officers must be open-minded when looking again at decisions previously made.[79]

Much therefore depends on the circumstances and the issues involved. In the *GCHQ* case, for example, the House of Lords said that fairness would normally have required the government to consult before removing the right to union membership—but, in the circumstances, the interests of national security outweighed the need for fairness. A similar approach has been taken in other situations in which national security has been involved.[80]

(h) LEGITIMATE EXPECTATIONS

The ground of judicial review called 'legitimate expectations' arises where claimants argue that public bodies have said or done things that have created an expectation that they will act in accordance with past practice, policies, promises, or representations.[81] In *GCHQ*, for example, the unions claimed a legitimate expectation, based on past practice, that they would be consulted about proposed changes to the terms and conditions under which civil servants worked at that establishment. In that case, the legitimate expectation was therefore procedural in nature. Until recently, the courts were only willing to accept procedural claims of this type. The view was that public authorities cannot be prevented from making decisions in the public interest and therefore they cannot be bound to provide discretionary *substantive* benefits to individuals on the ground that they have indicated that they would do so. In one case, the idea of a legitimate expectation requiring a public body to provide a substantive benefit was said to be a 'heresy'.[82]

That view has now changed. It is now accepted that substantive legitimate expectations may be generated by public bodies and that these must be respected, unless there is some overriding public interest in allowing the public body to go back on its word or conduct. Whether or not a legitimate expectation has arisen is for the court to decide; it is not a matter of what a claimant may have subjectively expected or hoped for.

R v North and East Devon Health Authority, ex parte Coughlan

Miss Coughlan was seriously injured in a road accident and, as a result, was tetraplegic, doubly incontinent, and partially paralysed. In 1993, with her agreement, she was moved from a hospital that the health authority wished to close to Mardon House, a NHS facility for the long-term disabled. The health authority assured her, and other residents, that Mardon House would be their home for life. Despite this assurance, in 1998, following a

---

[78] See Chapter 14.

[79] See Chapter 15.

[80] For example, *R v Secretary of State for the Home Department, ex parte Hosenball* [1977] 3 All ER 452. See further Chapter 17, in which we discuss the litigation concerning the legality of control orders made under the Prevention of Terrorism Act 2005 and, in particular, the decision of the House of Lords in *Secretary of State for the Home Department v AF and anor* [2009] UKHL 28.

[81] For a recent discussion see Paul Reynolds, ' Legitimate Expectations and the Protection of Trust in Public Officials', [2011] Public Law 330.

[82] See *R v Secretary of State for the Home Dept, ex parte Hargreaves* [1997] 1 All ER 397, 412. See Sedley LJ's judgment in *Niazi v Secretary of State* [2008] EWCA 755.

public consultation, the health authority decided to close Mardon House. Miss Coughlan challenged the decision, in part, on the ground that the clear promise that she had been given created a legitimate expectation that Mardon House would be her home for life. The decision to close the home breached this legitimate expectation and was therefore unlawful. The High Court agreed with her and said that the health authority had shown no overriding public interest that entitled it to break the promise. The health authority appealed unsuccessfully to the Court of Appeal.

The following is an extract from the judgment of the Court of Appeal, to which all members of the Court contributed (Lord Woolf MR, Mummery LJ, and Sedley LJ). The principles outlined in the judgment have been followed in subsequent cases and are widely accepted as being correct.[83]

R v North and East Devon Health Authority, ex parte Coughlan (Secretary of State for Health and anor)
[2001] QB 213

The Promise of a Home for Life

50. The Health Authority appeals on the ground that the judge wrongly held that it had failed to establish that there was an overriding public interest which entitled it to break the 'home for life' promise. In particular, the judge erred in concluding that the Health Authority had applied the wrong legal test in deciding whether the promise could or should be broken and that it had wrongly diluted the promise and treated it as merely a promise to provide care. It contends that it applied the correct legal test and that the promise had, in the decision making process, been plainly and accurately expressed and given appropriate prominence.
[..]

52. It has been common ground throughout these proceedings that in public law the health authority could break its promise to Miss Coughlan that Mardon House would be her home for life if, and only if, an overriding public interest required it. [. . .]

Legitimate expectation—the court's role

55. [. . . I]t is necessary to begin by examining the court's role where what is in issue is a promise as to how it would behave in the future made by a public body when exercising a statutory function. In the past it would have been argued that the promise was to be ignored since it could not have any effect on how the public body exercised its judgment in what it thought was the public interest. Today such an argument would have no prospect of success [. . .]

56. What is still the subject of some controversy is the court's role when a member of the public, as a result of a promise or other conduct, has a legitimate expectation that he will be treated in one way and the public body wishes to treat him or her in a different way. Here the starting point has to be to ask what in the circumstances the member of the public could legitimately expect. In the words of Lord Scarman in *Findlay v Secretary of State for the Home Dept* [1985] AC 318 at 338: 'But what was their *legitimate* expectation?' Where there is a dispute as to this, the dispute has to be determined by the court, as happened in *Findlay's* case.

---

[83] *R (Reprotech (Pebsham) Ltd) v East Sussex County Council* [2002] UKHL 8, *per* Lord Hoffmann; also Lord Carswell in *R (Bancoult) v Secretary of State for Foreign and Commonwealth Affairs* [2008] UKHL 61, [133].

This can involve a detailed examination of the precise terms of the promise or representation made, the circumstances in which the promise was made and the nature of the statutory or other discretion.

57. There are at least three possible outcomes. (a) The court may decide that the public authority is only required to bear in mind its previous policy or other representation, giving it the weight it thinks right, but no more, before deciding whether to change course. Here the court is confined to reviewing the decision on *Wednesbury* grounds [...] This has been held to be the effect of changes of policy in cases involving the early release of prisoners (see *Findlay's* case; *R v Secretary of State for the Home Dept, ex p Hargreaves* [1997] 1 All ER 397, [1997] 1 WLR 906). (b) On the other hand the court may decide that the promise or practice induces a legitimate expectation of, for example, being consulted before a particular decision is taken. Here it is uncontentious that the court itself will require *the opportunity for consultation* to be given unless there is an overriding reason to resile from it (see *A-G of Hong Kong v Ng Yuen Shiu* [1983] 2 All ER 346, [1983] 2 AC 629) in which case the court will itself judge the adequacy of the reason advanced for the change of policy, taking into account what fairness requires. (c) Where the court considers that a lawful promise or practice has induced a legitimate expectation of a *benefit which is substantive*, not simply procedural, authority now establishes that here too the court will in a proper case decide whether to frustrate the expectation is so unfair that to take a new and different course will amount to an abuse of power. Here, once the legitimacy of the expectation is established, the court will have the task of weighing the requirements of fairness against any overriding interest relied upon for the change of policy.

58. The court having decided which of the categories is appropriate, the court's role in the case of the second and third categories is different from that in the first. In the case of the first, the court is restricted to reviewing the decision on conventional grounds. The test will be rationality and whether the public body has given proper weight to the implications of not fulfilling the promise. In the case of the second category the court's task is the conventional one of determining whether the decision was procedurally fair. In the case of the third, the court has when necessary to determine whether there is a sufficient overriding interest to justify a departure from what has been previously promised.

[...]

60. We consider that [counsel for the Health Authority and counsel for Miss Coughlan] are correct, as was the judge, in regarding the facts of this case as coming into the third category. [...] Our reasons are as follows. First, the importance of what was promised to Miss Coughlan [...]; second, the fact that promise was limited to a few individuals, and the fact that the consequences to the health authority of requiring it to honour its promise are likely to be financial only.

Note how the Court of Appeal in *Coughlan* explains when public bodies may act contrary to legitimate expectations. It will be unlawful to frustrate a substantive legitimate expectation if the court decides that there has been an abuse of power. 'Here...the court will have the task of weighing the requirements of fairness against any overriding interest relied upon for a change of policy' (para. [57]). In undertaking this weighing exercise the court, it appears, will apply a proportionality test.[84] Where an authority says that an overriding public interest justified it in frustrating a substantive expectation the court will expect to see evidence

[84] In *Paponette* The Privy Council approved of the approach taken by Laws LJ in *R (Nadarajah and Abdi) v Secretary of State for the Home Department* [2005] EWCA Civ 1363.

showing that its decision was required by an overriding public interest, and if evidence is not forthcoming the court may not be persuaded.[85]

Representations must not conflict with statute

Where a legitimate expectation is claimed on the basis of a representation or promise, the representation or promise must not conflict with applicable statutory provisions. In *R v Department of Education and Employment, ex parte Begbie*[86] (see extract *R (Wheeler) v Office of the Prime Minister* on p. 734), the applicant had been offered a place on the assisted places scheme, under which children were allowed places at independent schools with their fees paid from public funds. Following the general election in 1997, however, the new Labour government abolished the scheme. The applicant argued that this decision was in breach of her legitimate expectation to a place based on an offer that had been made prior to the election. The claim failed on the ground that the offer could not create a legitimate expectation in this case, because that would conflict with legislative provisions that enabled (but did not require) the minister to allow children to take advantage of the assisted places scheme in exceptional situations. This was not the type of situation envisaged by the legislation.

The representation must be clear and unequivocal

In order to generate legitimate expectations, representations must be 'clear and unequivocal'.[87] *Association of British Civilian Internees: Far Eastern Region (ABCIFER) v Secretary of State for Defence*[88] concerned a scheme set up to compensate British people who had been interned by the Japanese during the Second World War. Those eligible would receive an *ex gratia* payment of £10,000. The minister announced to Parliament that '*British civilians who were interned*' would benefit. The eligibility criteria were later changed, however, so that payments would be made only to '*British subjects whom the Japanese interned and who were born in the UK, or had a parent or grandparent born here*'. Some ex-prisoners were therefore excluded and they claimed judicial review on the grounds that earlier announcements had created a legitimate expectation that they would benefit. The Court held that the minister's announcement was not sufficiently clear and unequivocal to create a substantive legitimate expectation.

The decision of the House of Lords in *R (Bancoult) v Secretary of State for Foreign and Commonwealth Affairs*[89] illustrates that what is clear to some judges may be unclear to others. This case was brought by the Chagos Islanders, who challenged Orders in Council that, in effect, forbade them from returning to islands in the Indian Ocean (a British colony) from which they had been compulsorily removed by the Crown. The original Order under which that removal was undertaken—the Immigration Ordinance Order 1971—had been quashed in judicial review proceedings in 2000. Immediately after that decision, the then Foreign Secretary, Robin Cook, made the following statement.

---

[85] Lord Dyson, *Paponette v Att Gen of Trinidad and Tobago* [2010] UKPC 32, para. [42]

[86] [1999] All ER(D) 983.

[87] Dyson LJ, *R (Association of British Civilians: Far Eastern region) v SS for the Defence* [2003] QB 1397, [62]; *R v IRC, ex parte MFK Underwriting Agents* [1990] 1 AC, 1569; also *R (Wheeler v Office of the Prime Minister* [2008] EWHC 1409 (Admin).

[88] [2003] QB 1397.

[89] [2008] UKHL 61; see Chapter 9, section 3(e), Prerogative and statute.

Robin Cook's statement

I have decided to accept the Court's ruling and the Government will not be appealing.

The work we are doing on the feasibility of resettling the Ilois [viz the Chagossians] now takes on a new importance. We started the feasibility work a year ago and are now well underway with phase two of the study.

Furthermore, we will put in place a new Immigration Ordinance which will allow the Ilois to return to the outer islands while observing our Treaty obligations.

The Government has not defended what was done or said thirty years ago. As Lord Justice Laws recognised, we made no attempt to conceal the gravity of what happened. I am pleased that he has commended the wholly admirable conduct in disclosing material to the Court and praised the openness of today's Foreign Office.

Following this statement, a new Immigration Ordinance was made that enabled the Chargossians to return home—but the government changed its mind and, in 2004, new Orders in Council were made that forbade them doing so. It was these Orders that were challenged. The challenge succeeded in the Administrative Court and the Court of Appeal—but it failed in the House of Lords, where a majority of their Lordships ruled against the Chargossians (Lords Bingham and Mance dissenting).

One of main issues was whether Robin Cook's statement generated a legitimate expectation that was breached by the 2004 Orders in Council. Lord Hoffmann, with the majority, held that no legitimate expectation had been created. Each of the judges in the Court of Appeal was, however, clear that the Orders had breached a legitimate expectation and Lord Mance (who dissented in the House of Lords) agreed with them.

R (Bancoult) v Secretary of State for Foreign and Commonwealth Affairs
[2008] UKHL 61

Lord Hoffmann

[61.] [...] In my opinion this claim falls at the first hurdle, that is, the requirement of a clear and unambiguous promise [...] It was obvious that no one contemplated the resettlement of the Chagossians unless the government, taking into account the findings of the feasibility study, decided to support it. If they did not, a new situation would arise. The government might decide that little harm would be done by leaving the Chagossians with a theoretical right to return to the islands and for two years after the feasibility report, that seems to have been the view that was taken. But the Foreign Secretary's press statement contained no promises about what, in such a case, would happen in the long term. [...] No doubt the Chagossians saw things differently. [60–61].

Lord Mance

[183.] [...] On the facts of the present case, I have come to the conclusion that the courts below reached the right result. [...] there is no indication that the Government gave any real weight to the legitimate expectation generated by its words and conduct in 2000. [...]

[185.] [...] The present case concerns an unequivocal assurance and conduct, on a matter on which it is not suggested that there can have been any mistake. The assurance was directed at Chagossians as defined by the Ordinance of 3 November 2000. It was intended to right an historic grievance, and was understood and no doubt relied upon (in the sense that it was given credence) accordingly. The sense of grievance likely to arise from its revocation without the most careful consideration and strong reason is obvious. The Secretary of State's argument that no-one acted upon his statement and Ordinance to his or her detriment between 3 November 2000 and 10 June 2004 is in my view answered by the considerations that specific detriment is not an absolute pre-condition and that in the context of a general public statement proof of individual reliance may not be expected [...] But the dominant consideration in my opinion is that the Government's statement and conduct were intended and understood to resolve the long-standing controversy regarding the Chagossians' right to enter and be present in the outer Chagos Islands, and that it would be and in the circumstances was maladministration to go back on that resolution without any consultation and without strong cause, which has not been shown.

Promises and representations must be directed to particular individuals or groups

In *Coughlan*, one of the important considerations for the Court of Appeal was that the promise had been made to a small group of people who were directly affected by it. As Lord Mance's judgment indicates, legitimate expectations may nonetheless arise from statements about future practice or policy that affect a wider range of people.

The range of people affected was addressed in the decision of the Court of Appeal in *Niazi v Secretary of State*.[90] The government decided to abolish the discretionary (non-statutory) scheme for compensating victims of miscarriages of justice, so that, in future, compensation for miscarriages of justice would be claimed only under the statutory compensation scheme established under the Criminal Justice Act 1988. The government also reduced the costs that solicitors dealing with claims that were still being processed under the discretionary scheme could claim. Two types of challenge were brought against these decisions. The first was by three people who claimed to be victims of miscarriages of justice and who could have claimed under the discretion scheme, but who were not eligible under the statutory scheme. They argued, *inter alia*, that the withdrawal of the discretionary scheme with immediate effect breached their legitimate expectations that this scheme would be available. The second challenge was by solicitors who said that they should have been consulted before the changes were made. Both claims failed at first instance and in the Court of Appeal. Laws LJ and Sedley LJ commented on the developing law in this area.[91]

Niazi v Secretary of State
[2008] EWCA 755

Laws LJ

[29] [...] The paradigm case arises where a public authority has provided an unequivocal assurance, whether by means of an express promise or an established practice, that it will give notice or embark upon consultation before it changes an existing substantive policy:

---

[90] [2008] EWCA 755.
[91] See also the judgment of Laws LJ in *R (Nadarajah and Abdi) v Secretary of State for the Home Department* [2005] EWCA Civ 1363.

[30] In the paradigm case the court will not allow the decision-maker to effect the proposed change without notice or consultation, unless the want of notice or consultation is justified by the force of an overriding legal duty owed by the decision-maker, or other countervailing public interest such as the imperative of national security (as in CCSU). [...] There may be questions such as whether the Claimant for relief must himself have known of the promise or practice, or relied on it [...]. that there are in my view significant difficulties in the way of imposing such qualifications. My reason is that in such a procedural case the unfairness or abuse of power which the court will check is not merely to do with how harshly the decision bears upon any individual. It arises because good administration [...] generally requires that where a public authority has given a plain assurance, it should be held to it. [...]

[32] A substantive legitimate expectation arises where the court allows a claim to enforce the continued enjoyment of the content – the substance – of an existing practice or policy, in the face of the decision-maker's ambition to change or abolish it. Thus it is to be distinguished from a merely procedural right. [...]

[36] The concept of substantive legitimate expectation [...] poses a question: what are the conditions under which a prior representation, promise or practice by a public decision-maker will give rise to an enforceable expectation of a substantive benefit? [...]

[43] Authority shows that where a substantive expectation is to run the promise or practice which is its genesis is not merely a reflection of the ordinary fact [...] that a policy with no terminal date or terminating event will continue in effect until rational grounds for its cessation arise. Rather it must constitute a specific undertaking, directed at a particular individual or group, by which the relevant policy's continuance is assured. [...]

[He goes on to discuss *ex parte Khan* [1984] 1 WLR 1337 and *ex parte Coughlan*.]

[46] These cases illustrate the pressing and focused nature of the kind of assurance required if a substantive legitimate expectation is to be upheld and enforced. I should add this. Though in theory there may be no limit to the number of beneficiaries of a promise for the purpose of such an expectation, in reality it is likely to be small, if the court is to make the expectation good. There are two reasons for this, and they march together. First, it is difficult to imagine a case in which government will be held legally bound by a representation or undertaking made generally or to a diverse class. [...] The second reason is that the broader the class claiming the expectation's benefit, the more likely it is that a supervening public interest will be held to justify the change of position complained of.

Sedley LJ

67 [...] Policies have the virtue of combining consistency in unexceptional cases with flexibility in marginal or out-of-the ordinary cases, but the vice of being unenforceable in law despite the reliance that people are compelled to place on them. Public law has grown to meet the needs of justice on the one hand and of good government on the other by holding public administration to as much of its public undertakings—its policies—as is necessary and fair.

68 A duty to consult before modifying policy may arise from an explicit promise to do so. It may also arise from practice which generates a similarly legitimate expectation that, other things being equal, there will continue to be no change without prior consultation. But there is no equivalent expectation that policy itself, and with it any substantive benefits it confers, will not change. [...] the most that the beneficiary of a current policy can legitimately expect in substantive terms is, first, that the policy will be fairly applied or disapplied in his particular case, and secondly that if the policy is altered to his disadvantage, the alteration

must not be effected in a way which unfairly frustrates any reliance he has legitimately placed on it.

69 The most striking illustration of this, Coughlan...precisely the same principle was engaged in *R v MAFF, ex parte Hamble Fisheries* [1995] 2 All ER 714. There a change of policy had frustrated the shipowners' continuing accumulation of licences to enable them, pursuant to the existing policy, to undertake beam-trawling for pressure stocks; but because the new policy made reasonable transitional provisions to mitigate the impact of the change in pipeline cases, it was held that such legitimate expectation as existed of benefits under the policy had been met. The time has come, I respectfully think, to say that the description of this decision in *Ex parte Hargreaves* [1997] 1 WLR 906 as heretical is shown by a solid body of authority both before and since to have been mistaken. As can be seen from the cases cited by Lord Justice Laws, the concept of a policy — which is of course a form of public promise — giving rise to a substantive expectation which the courts will not allow to be unjustly frustrated, far from being heretical, is today entirely orthodox.

Reliance

While some judges suggest that a legitimate expectation will arise only if the claimant has relied on a promise or a representation, the better view is that reliance is not necessary, although if it can be established that the claimant has relied on a promise to their detriment the claim will be strengthened.[92] As we have seen, Lord Justice Laws explained in *Niazi* that the obligation to respect legitimate expectations is rooted in the requirements of good administration and does not depend on whether individuals have relied on, or been adversely affected by, representations made by public bodies.[93]

Legitimate expectations and political promises

In *R (Wheeler) v Office of the Prime Minister*,[94] Wheeler claimed that the government's decision not to hold a referendum on the Lisbon Treaty was unlawful because it breached a legitimate expectation that there would be a referendum. It was argued that the expectation was based on the government's undertaking that there would be a referendum before the United Kingdom ratified the Treaty establishing the Constitution for Europe. The claim failed essentially because the court said that the decision to hold a referendum was a deeply political one for which the government should be held to account by Parliament and not the courts. Richards LJ made the following observations.

R (Wheeler) v Office of the Prime Minister
[2008] EWHC 1409 (Admin)

Richards LJ

[43] [...] In our view a promise to hold a referendum lies so deep in the macro-political field that the court should not enter the relevant area at all. If the government, on election, had

---

[92] Lord Dyson, *Paponette v Att Gen of Trinidad and Tobago* [2010] UKPC 32, para. [37]. It has been held that where a representation is made to a single person the absence of detrimental reliance may be fatal: *Oxfam v H.M. Revenue and Customs* [2009] EWCA 3078.

[93] See also H. Woolf, J. Jowell, and A. Le Sueur, *De Smith's Judicial Review*, 6th edn (2007, London: Sweet and Maxwell), para. 12.040.

[94] [2008] EWHC 1409 (Admin).

promised the electorate that it would call a further general election after, say, three years in office, it is to our mind unthinkable that this would be held to give rise to a legitimate expectation enforceable in the courts: the consequences of going back on such a promise would be a matter for Parliament and, when the opportunity next arose, for the electorate to determine. The same must be true of a promise to afford the electorate the opportunity to vote in a referendum on a particular issue such as the Lisbon Treaty. Indeed, the position may be considered stronger in relation to such a referendum since, unlike the calling of an early general election, the decision lies as we have said with Parliament and not with the executive.

[44] In reaching that view we proceed on the basis that it is relevant but not decisive that the promise is made to and affects the public at large. There is authority that the doctrine of legitimate expectation cannot reasonably extend to the public at large, as opposed to particular individuals or bodies who are directly affected by the executive action under consideration: *R v Secretary of State for the Home Department, ex parte Fire Brigades Union* [1995] 2 AC 513 [...] per Lord Keith at 545H, applied in *R v Secretary of State for Wales, ex parte Emery* [1998] 1 All ER 367, 374g-375d [...] By contrast, we have already referred at para 20 above to the passage in *ex parte Begbie* in which Sedley LJ said he had no difficulty with the proposition that in cases where government has made known how it intends to exercise powers which affect the public at large it may be held to its word irrespective of whether the Applicant has been relying specifically on it. [...]

QUESTIONS

1. If a promise made by a public authority can no longer be ignored, in what circumstances can it be broken?

2. Are substantive legitimate expectations compatible with the principle that judicial review is generally concerned only with the process of decision-making?

3. How would you explain the relationship between the principles relating to fettering of discretion, on the one hand, and the need to respect legitimate expectations, on the other?

4. '*Authority shows that where a substantive expectation is to run the promise or practice which is its genesis is not merely a reflection of the [...] fact [...] that a policy with no terminal date or terminating event will continue in effect until rational grounds for its cessation arise. Rather it must constitute a specific undertaking, directed at a particular individual or group, by which the relevant policy's continuance is assured.*' (Lord Justice Laws, *Niazi*, [43].

Why does Lord Justice Laws say that there must be a specific undertaking directed at a particular individual or group?

---

5 PREVENTION OF JUDICIAL REVIEW

Can an Act of Parliament oust the court's judicial review jurisdiction? Can it, in other words, prevent the courts from ensuring that governmental bodies, including ministers, comply with the requirements of legality set out in this chapter? At the root of this contentious question lies a clash between the UK Parliament's supremacy and the rule of law. If the UK

Parliament can oust the jurisdiction of the courts, how can the rule of law be safeguarded? As we have seen, there is now mounting support for the view that Parliament's supremacy is limited and that it does not extend to abolishing judicial review, which is a fundamental aspect of the UK constitution. The words used by Lord Steyn in the *Jackson* case have been cited elsewhere in the book, but are worth repeating here.

Jackson v Her Majesty's Attorney General
[2005] UKHL 56

Lord Steyn

[102] [...] the supremacy of Parliament is still the general principle of our constitution. It is a construct of the common law. The judges created this principle. If that is so, it is not unthinkable that circumstances could arise where the courts may have to qualify a principle established on a different hypothesis of constitutionalism. In exceptional circumstances involving an attempt to abolish judicial review or the ordinary role of the courts, the [...] new Supreme Court may have to consider whether this is a constitutional fundamental which even a sovereign Parliament acting at the behest of a complaisant House of Commons cannot abolish.

In considering this issue, it is important to remember that a distinction exists between appeals and the judicial review jurisdiction. Even those who argue that the purpose of judicial review is to serve parliamentary intentions acknowledge that judicial review is a common law jurisdiction. It may exist with the acquiescence of Parliament, but its existence does not depend on whether Parliament thinks it should. Opportunities to appeal, by contrast, are created by statute, and statute determines to whom appeals may be made and on what grounds. This means that Parliament can choose whether or not to create rights of appeal.

(a) Parliament can establish appeal procedures to be used instead of judicial review. For example, the Housing Act 1996 established a new right of appeal to the county court from decisions of local housing authorities to refuse to provide accommodation to people who claim to be homeless. Previously, the only remedy was to seek judicial review. Statute often allows appeals on 'a point of law' and it is now accepted that this will enable appeals on all of the normal grounds of judicial review.[95] In cases in which an appeal exists, judicial review can be used only in exceptional circumstances, such as when the appeal would not remedy the situation.[96]

(b) Parliament can require certain types of legal claim to be dealt with by a specialized tribunal rather than by way of judicial review. For example, in *A v B (Investigatory Powers Tribunal: Jurisdiction)*,[97] the Court of Appeal held (by a majority) that the Investigatory Powers Tribunal established by the Regulation of Investigatory Powers Act 2000 was the only tribunal that could deal with a case brought under the Human Rights Act 1998 by a former member of the security service challenging the refusal to permit him to publish a book about his time in the service.

---

[95] For example, *Begum v Tower Hamlets LBC* [2003] UKHL 5, [7], [17], and [98].

[96] *R v Secretary of State for the Home Department, ex parte Swati* [1986] 1 WLR 477; cf. *R v Chief Constable of Merseyside Police, ex parte Calverley* [1986] QB 424.

[97] [2009] EWCA Civ 24.

A v B (Investigatory Powers Tribunal: Jurisdiction)
[2009] EWCA Civ 24[98]

Laws LJ

[22.] [...] It is elementary that any attempt to oust altogether the High Court's supervisory jurisdiction over public authorities is repugnant to the constitution. But statutory measures which confide the jurisdiction to a judicial body of like standing and authority to that of the High Court, but which operates subject to special procedures apt for the subject-matter in hand, may well be constitutionally inoffensive.

(c) Parliament can also impose time limits within which proceedings must be brought. In the context of land use planning, legislation frequently provides that people can appeal against a decision of a public authority within six weeks, but after this period, decisions 'cannot be questioned in any legal proceedings whatsoever'. Time limit clauses of this sort are imposed in order to provide administrative certainty, so that planning schemes and development can go ahead without the fear of later challenge.[99]

In these instances, Acts of Parliament seek to regulate access to the courts or to provide appeal systems that are considered more suitable than judicial review in the circumstances. In this section of the chapter, we are concerned with a rather different situation—namely, that in which an Act of Parliament attempts to exclude or oust judicial review altogether.

(a) *ANISMINIC V FOREIGN COMPENSATION COMMISSION*

Attempts to exclude judicial review are not new. In *Anisminic v Foreign Compensation Commission*,[100] an Act of Parliament had established the Foreign Compensation Commission (FCC) to deal with claims from those whose property had been damaged or lost in fighting abroad. The fund from which the compensation was paid had a fixed amount of money in it, which was not necessarily sufficient to meet all potential claims. The FCC therefore had discretion as to the making of compensation payments, which were purely *ex gratia*. This meant that claimants did not have a legal right to particular sums. In order to reinforce this aspect of the scheme, s. 4(4) of the Foreign Compensation Act 1950 provided that '*The determination by the commission of any application made to them under this Act shall not be called in question in any court of law*'.

Anisminic unsuccessfully claimed compensation for property that was lost or damaged in Egypt during the Suez crisis. It argued that, in determining its claim, the FCC had made an error of law, and that its decision was therefore a nullity and should be judicially reviewable. The FCC said that s. 4(4) prevented the courts from dealing with the matter. At first instance, Brown J held that the courts were not excluded. His decision was overturned by a unanimous decision of the Court of Appeal. The House of Lords, by a majority of three to two, upheld Anisminic's appeal.

---

[98] Affirmed by the UK Supreme Court in [2009] UKSC 12.

[99] *Smith v East Elloe* [1956] AC 736; for a more recent case, see e.g. *Derwent Holdings Ltd v Liverpool City Council* [2008] EWHC 3023 (Admin).

[100] [1969] 2 AC 147.

Anisminic v Foreign Compensation Commission
[1969] 2 AC 147

Lord Reid

The next argument was that, by reason of the provisions of section 4(4) of the [Foreign Compensation Act] 1950 [...], the courts are precluded from considering whether the respondent's determination was a nullity [...]

[He sets out s. 4(4) of the 1950 Act.]

The respondent maintains that these are plain words only capable of having one meaning. Here is a determination which is apparently valid: there is nothing on the face of the document to cast any doubt on its validity. If it is a nullity, that could only be established by raising some kind of proceedings in court. But that would be calling the determination in question, and that is expressly prohibited by the statute. The appellants maintain that that is not the meaning of the words of this provision. They say that 'determination' means a real determination and does not include an apparent or purported determination which in the eyes of the law has no existence because it is a nullity. Or, putting it in another way, if you seek to show that a determination is a nullity you are not questioning the purported determination - you are maintaining that it does not exist as a determination. It is one thing to question a determination which does exist: it is quite another thing to say that there is nothing to be questioned.
   [...]
Statutory provisions which seek to limit the ordinary jurisdiction of the court have a long history. No case has been cited in which any other form of words limiting the jurisdiction of the court has been held to protect a nullity. If the draftsman or Parliament had intended to introduce a new kind of ouster clause so as to prevent any [such] inquiry [...] I would have expected to find something much more specific than the bald statement that a determination shall not be called in question in any court of law. Undoubtedly such a provision protects every determination which is not a nullity. But I do not think that it is necessary or even reasonable to construe the word 'determination' as including everything which purports to be a determination but which is in fact no determination at all [...] if that were intended it would be easy to say so [...] I have come without hesitation to the conclusion that in this case we are not prevented from inquiring whether the order of the commission was a nullity.

Anisminic had not argued that Parliament could never exclude judicial review; rather, it said—and Lord Reid agreed—that judicial review could be excluded only by clear words. The 'bald statement' that '*a determination shall not be called into question*' was insufficiently clear: did it prevent the courts from declaring a purported determination to be a nullity, or did it only prevent them from questioning a valid determination? Faced with this ambiguity, the House of Lords gave the word 'determination' the meaning that was compatible with maintaining the jurisdiction of the courts rather than the meaning that removed this jurisdiction. This may seem a rather artificial way of dealing with the issue: after all, how could the courts conclude that a 'purported determination' was a nullity without it being 'called into question' in the courts? It may have been artificial, but it was also a very orthodox approach to statutory interpretation: it left Parliament free to oust judicial review if sufficiently clear language could be found.

Parliament quickly responded by enacting the Foreign Compensation Appeals Act 1969. This provided for an appeal to the Court of Appeal on points of law, by way of the case stated procedure. It also provided a new definition of the term 'determination' in s. 3(3): '*In this section "determination" includes a determination which under rules under section 4(2) of the Foreign Compensation Act 1950 (rules of procedure) is a provisional determination, and anything which purports to be a determination.'*

QUESTION

If you were a government lawyer charged with suggesting responses to Lord Reid's judgment in *Anisminic*, could you come up with an 'ouster clause' that would work?

(b) EXCLUDING JUDICIAL REVIEW IN ASYLUM CASES

Since the *Anisminic* saga, various other attempts have been made by the government to find ways in which to exclude judicial review. The most infamous was the government's attempt to prevent access to judicial review in asylum cases. For much of the past two decades, immigration and asylum decisions have generated the majority of judicial review claims. As well as burdening the court system, the use of judicial review in asylum cases has been an irritant to government. In addition, there is a widespread view that a substantial proportion of judicial review claims in this area have been weak and designed to delay removals from the United Kingdom. The government has therefore sought to shift asylum challenges out of the judicial review process, and into a specially designed and more streamlined statutory review procedure.

In the following extract, Andrew Le Sueur summarizes these attempts and the reactions that they have generated. These, he says, '*provoked something of a constitutional crisis*'.

Andrew Le Sueur, 'Three strikes and it's out? The UK Government's strategy to oust judicial review from immigration and asylum decision making' [2004] Public Law 225–33 (footnotes omitted)

Strike one: proposals to turn the IAT into a Superior Court of Record

The first tactic to reduce the incidence of judicial review in immigration and asylum decision-making did not get off the Home Office drawing board, but nonetheless demands attention. In its February 2002 White Paper, *Secure Borders, Safe Haven: Integration with Diversity in Modern Britain*, the government said it wanted 'further streamlining' of the appeal process through: Making the Immigration Appeal Tribunal a Superior Court of Record. This will reflect the fact that a high court judge heads the Tribunal and recognises the importance of its jurisdiction. As a Superior Court of Record there should be no scope for judicial review of its decisions, particularly of refusals to grant leave to appeal that are made in an attempt to frustrate removal. The Tribunal will focus entirely on the lawfulness of adjudicators' decisions rather than their factual basis. There will also still be a right of appeal from the Tribunal to the Court of Appeal on a point of law.

It appears that the proposal was opposed by senior members of the judiciary. [and was subsequently dropped] [. . .]

Strike two: statutory review replaces judicial review proper

Section 101 of the Nationality, Immigration and Asylum Act 2002 gave a legislative basis to the new statutory review procedure. The Home Office press release described it as 'a paper-based, fast and final review'. During the passage of the NIA Bill through Parliament [...] Simon Hughes M.P. (Lib Dem) [said]:

The Government [...] have a perverse and obsessive belief that going to court for a judicial review of administrative decisions is a hindrance to government. However, whether one is dealing with immigration, asylum or any other matter, it is fundamental to our constitution that the court, not Ministers, is the place of last resort. In a country with no written constitution, it is vital that the independent judiciary at all levels makes decisions on the law and the facts. [...]

Members of the government sought to reassure Parliament that the new procedure did not threaten the role of the Administrative Court in supervising the legality of IAT decisions. Baroness Scotland said:

This is not a strategy to try to get rid of judicial review. There is nothing underhand or inappropriate. We understand that we are moving to a new process, which is different from that to which we have been used over a long period of time, namely, judicial review. We are confident that this new statutory review process will succeed. If, for a reason that we cannot currently divine, it proves not to be the most successful or most just way of dealing with such applications [...] judicial review would return.

[...]

Strike three: the ouster clause

On October 27, 2003, within four months of the new statutory review procedure coming into operation, the Home Office issued a brief consultation letter on further reforms to the immigration and asylum appeals system. A month later, the government published the Asylum and Immigration (Treatment of Claimants, etc) Bill. It places further restrictions on the ability of immigrants and asylum-seekers to challenge the lawfulness of decisions made about them by the immigration authorities. It is proposed to replace the existing two-tier tribunal appeal structure (adjudicators plus the IAT) with a new, single-tier tribunal to be called the Asylum and Immigration Tribunal (AIT), with most cases being heard by a single judge. There will be the possibility of some sort of internal review of first-level appeal decisions, the details of which are as yet unclear. A minister explained:

[...] The only external supervisory oversight of the new tribunal would be through a reference procedure whereby the President of the AIT (not the parties to the appeal) may seek guidance on questions of law from the Court of Appeal (in England and Wales) and the Court of Session (in Scotland). There would be no possibility of appeal to the House of Lords from the Court of Appeal/Court of Session's decision. The *ouster* clause was to become s. 108A of the Nationality, Immigration and Asylum Act 2002:

108A Exclusivity and finality of Tribunal's jurisdiction

(1) No court shall have any supervisory or other jurisdiction (whether statutory or inherent) in relation to the Tribunal.

(2) No court may entertain proceedings for questioning (whether by way of appeal or otherwise)—

(a) any determination, decision or other action of the Tribunal (including a decision about jurisdiction and a decision under section 105A),

[...]

(3) Subsections (1) and (2)—

> (a) prevent a court, in particular, from entertaining proceedings to determine whether a purported determination, decision or action of the Tribunal was a nullity by reason of—
>
> > (i) lack of jurisdiction,
> >
> > (ii) irregularity,
> >
> > (iii) error of law,
> >
> > (iv) breach of natural justice, or
> >
> > (v) any other matter.
>
> [...]
>
> The ouster clause provoked an extraordinary amount of comment and criticism. The Bar Council of England and Wales, not noted for its extravagant use of language, said in a written briefing on the Bill:
>
> > The intended effect of that clause is to 'oust' the jurisdiction of the High Court to review the new Tribunal's decisions, even where the Tribunal has got the law wrong or acted in breach of natural justice. This is a startling proposition. It would be startling if done in a dictatorship. It is incredible that it is proposed in the United Kingdom—the so-called mother of the Common Law.
>
> > Some lawyers went further still, suggesting that enactment of the ouster clause would require the courts to call into question the foundational principle of parliamentary supremacy. [...] In the face of unprecedented opposition, on March 15, 2004 the Government withdrew the ouster clause from the Bill at its second reading in the Lords. The only thing that seems certain in this time of constitutional flux is that, sooner or later, the Home Office will have another go at getting rid of judicial review.

The Asylum and Immigration (Treatment of Claimants, etc.) Act 2004 was enacted without inclusion of an ouster clause designed to prevent judicial review of the Asylum and Immigration Tribunal (IAT), but it retained the review and reconsideration procedure by which parties to a decision made by the IAT can apply to a senior immigration judge or a High Court judge for an order that the IAT reconsider its decision.[101]

In early 2010, the immigration appeals procedure was further simplified and streamlined. Appeals are no longer made to the IAT; instead, they now go to the Immigration and Asylum Chamber of the First-tier Tribunal, with an appeal on a point of law to the Upper Tribunal (but only if permission has been given by the First-tier Tribunal or the Upper Tribunal).[102] The review and reconsideration process has therefore been replaced, and the High Court is no longer involved. This has the benefit of relieving pressure on the High Court. It highlights the importance of the Upper Tribunal and it also raises the question of whether the Upper Tribunal may be judicially reviewed.[103]

(c) THE UPPER TRIBUNAL AND JUDICIAL REVIEW

The Tribunals, Courts and Enforcement Act 2007 gives the Upper Tribunal a judicial review jurisdiction over the First-tier Tribunal, applying the same principles as the High Court.[104]

---

[101] Robert Thomas, 'After the ouster: Review and reconsideration in a single-tier tribunal' [2006] Public Law 674.

[102] See further Box 15.1 in Chapter 15 on p. 650.

[103] On the Upper Tribunal see further Chapter 15.

[104] Section 15(4) and (5).

The Act also says that the Upper Tribunal is a 'superior court of record'.[105] Does this mean that decisions of the Upper Tribunal cannot be judicially reviewed? This issue was considered in a case brought by Mr Cart.[106]

Mr Cart complained that a decision to vary his child maintenance payments was unfairly made without him being notified. He appealed unsuccessfully to the First-tier Tribunal on this and other grounds. That Tribunal refused him permission to appeal on the notification issue to the Upper Tribunal. The Upper Tribunal also refused him permission to appeal. Because legislation does not provide for an appeal against a decision of the Upper Tribunal to refuse permission to appeal, Mr Cart sought to challenge the Upper Tribunal's refusal using judicial review. He was met with the argument that decisions of the Upper Tribunal are not subject to judicial review because the Upper Tribunal is a 'superior court of record.'

This argument was roundly rejected by the Divisional Court.[107]

R (Cart) v Upper Tribunal and ors
[2009] EWHC 3052 (Admin)

Laws LJ

[31] [...] the proposition that judicial review is excluded by...[the words 'superior court of record']...is a constitutional solecism. The supervisory jurisdiction [...] can only be ousted "by the most clear and explicit words": see *per* Denning LJ in *R v Medical Appeal Tribunal ex parte Gilmore* [1957] 1 QB 574, 583, [...] The learning discloses a litany of failed attempts to exclude judicial review. [...]

[32] I need not multiply citations. A conspicuous case is the seminal authority of *Anisminic v Foreign Compensation Commission* [...] Against this background it cannot be supposed that judicial review may be ousted by an implication...But that is the sum of the Defendants' case. [...]
If judicial review were so excluded, SIAC and UT – and any other body which might be immunised against judicial review by a like formula – would (in matters not subject to statutory appeal) be the last judges of the law they have to apply. They would not be required to respect any other interpretation but their own. The sense of the rule of law with which we are concerned rests in this principle, that statute law has to be mediated by an authoritative judicial source, independent both of the legislature which made the statute, the executive government which (in the usual case) procured its making, and the public body by which the statute is administered.
[...]

[Laws LJ went on to draw a distinction between the High Court and courts of limited jurisdiction]

[68] The true contrast is between the High Court on the one hand and courts of limited jurisdiction on the other...The High Court as a court of unlimited jurisdiction cannot be subjected

---

[105] Section 3(5). Remember what Andrew Le Sueur says in the extract given, about the government's attempt to oust judicial review by designating the IAT as a superior court of record.

[106] Whether the Special Immigration Appeals Commission (SIAC), which is also designated to be a 'superior court of record', is judicially reviewable was considered in a case decided at the same time as Mr Cart's. On the SIAC, see further Chapter 17, section 5, Case Study: Human Rights and Terrorism.

[107] *R (Cart) v Upper Tribunal and ors* [2009] EWHC 3052 (Admin).

to review. On the other hand courts whose jurisdiction is limited will generally be so subject: they will be amenable to higher judicial authority – the High Court – to fix the limits of their authority.

Applying this to SIAC and to the Upper Tribunal, Laws LJ considered whether either of these bodies can be considered to be equivalent to the High Court. He concluded that the limited jurisdiction of SIAC means that it cannot be considered to be equivalent to the High Court and is therefore amenable to judicial review.

The position of the Upper Tribunal, he said, is very different. Because the Upper Tribunal is the apex of the Tribunal system and has been given a judicial review type jurisdiction by Parliament, Laws LJ said that it should be considered to be an *alter ego* of the High Court and therefore only subject to judicial review in the 'grossly improbable event' of it acting clearly beyond the four corners of its statutory remit.[108] Since his case did not fall within this wholly exceptional situation Mr Cart's claim failed. His appeal to the Court of Appeal also failed.[109]

The Court of Appeal disagreed with Law LJ in relation to his description of the Upper Tribunal as the *alter ego* of the High Court. However, it agreed that the Upper Tribunal is reviewable but only on very limited grounds: essentially if it exceeded its jurisdiction. This limited judicial review would, the Court of Appeal suggested, achieve the right balance between retaining 'the relative autonomy' of the Tribunal system and 'the constitutional role of the High Court as the guardian of standards of legality and due process from which the UT…is not exempt.'[110]

Mr Cart appealed, unsuccessfully, to the UK Supreme Court.[111] By the time the case had reached the Supreme Court it had been accepted by all parties that the Upper Tribunal was not immune from judicial review. The 'real question', said Lady Hale, 'is what level of independent scrutiny outside the tribunal system is required by the rule of law' [para. 51]. The main issues at this stage therefore concerned whether the Courts below had achieved the right balance between maintaining the independence of the Tribunal system and the need for external supervision. Should judicial review be limited to the exceptional situations referred to by the Laws LJ and the Court of Appeal, or should it be more generally available?

The Supreme Court was not in favour of the approach taken by the courts below. To limit judicial review to exceptional circumstances would lead to 'a return to some of the technicalities of the past' (Lady Hale, [40]). On the other hand, some limitation on judicial review was considered necessary, not least to avoid the courts being flooded with claims. In order to adopt an approach that was in the words of Lady Hale 'principled but proportionate' the Court held that judicial review of non-appealable decisions (such as refusals to allow an appeal) should only be possible when there is an important point of principle or practice involved, or when there's another compelling reason. This is referred to as the second-tier appeal criteria as it is the test used when considering whether appeals should be heard by the Court of Appeal.

---

[108] At [99].

[109] [2010] EWCA Civ 859.

[110] Per Sedley LJ at [35].

[111] [2011] UKSC 28. In the Supreme Court the case was joined by another: *R(MR(Pakistan)) v The Upper Tribunal* which raised the same issue but involving asylum. A case from Scotland was also dealt with by the same court: *Eba v Advocate General for Scotland* UKSC [2011] 29.

The Scottish case[112], brought by Ms Eba, was decided by the UK Supreme Court at the same time as *Cart*. Lord Hope delivered the judgment of the Court agreeing with the approach taken in *Cart*, stressing 'that there is, in principle, no difference between the law of England and Scots law as to the substantive grounds on which a decision by a tribunal which acts within its jurisdiction may be open to review.'[113]

QUESTION

You work in the Government Legal Service and have been asked to prepare a memorandum responding to the following question.

Can the UK Parliament prevent the High Court from judicially reviewing:

(a) decisions of other courts or tribunals?

(b) decisions taken by government ministers or local authorities?

What would be your conclusions and why?

---

6 CONCLUDING COMMENTS

This chapter has looked at the recent history of judicial review, the constitutional foundations for judicial review, and some key issues relating to the use of judicial review. It has also surveyed the grounds of judicial review, and examined what has happened when government and Parliament have attempted to oust judicial review. Perhaps the central question is whether judicial review matters, not only to the parties in the cases that are brought and fought in the courts, but also in a broader sense to the quality of government. Judges often refer to the link between judicial review and good administration. This implies that judges are concerned both with providing just results in individual cases, and with using judicial review as a way in which to improve the quality of public administration.

The following are some general observations based on the findings of a research study on the impact of judicial review on the quality of local government services.

Maurice Sunkin, Lucinda Platt, Todd Landman, and Kerman Calvo, *The Impact of Judicial Review on the Quality of Local Government Services in England & Wales*[114]

Local authorities do their best to implement judgments. As one respondent expressed it: '*they tend to respond ultimately to what the court orders them to do because that's how local authorities operate*'. Respondents also noted that it helps to clarify legal duties. As one interviewee put it: '*I think as the law has been clarified we've been clearer as to what our advice to the client department should be and we'll be saying 'you've got a duty to meet needs here' and the judicial review never gets off the ground*'.

---

[112] See fn 111.

[113] Lord Hope at [34]. There are, however, differences in other respects, notably that judicial review in Scotland is a matter of right rather than judicial discretion (e.g., there is no permission hurdle in Scotland). For an overall assessment of these decisions, see Emma Laurie, 'Assessing the Upper Tribunal's Potential to Deliver Administrative Justice' [2012] Public Law 288.

[114] http://www.publicservices.ac.uk/wp-content/uploads/judicial-review-summary.pdf. See further http://www.publicservices.ac.uk/index.php/library/dp0801-does-judicial-review-influence-the-quality-of-local-authority-services/.

The researchers were also told that litigation can reshape internal balances of power and give new legitimacy to the claims and interests of marginalised sectors or groups. It was found that when responding to judicial decisions, authorities are motivated by a combination of considerations extending from concern to meet financial targets to desire to pursue other service oriented goals, including furthering the needs of client groups and respecting the law.

But, the pace and extent of implementation varies according to the nature of decisions, authorities' legal competence, organisational capacity and culture, and other contextual factors, such as local and national political considerations.

What difference do the judgments make?

Judicial review judgments have the capacity to challenge local authorities and may do so from an awkward and often unpredictable angle. Respondents talked about decisions that *'came out of the blue'* and which were *'a shock to a lot of local authorities'*.

They may also create financial problems for authorities. Referring to a decision that held that a local authority had a wider range of duties than it had previously believed, a respondent said that the cost implications meant '[...] *it's sort of beyond the power of the local authority to implement the judgment'*.

Nevertheless, there was much that was regarded as positive about judgments. As well as clarification of responsibilities, certain judgments were regarded as enabling authorities to better meet clients' needs. Looking back on one decision that had been particularly critical of local authority practice, one interviewee described its initial devastating effect on officials and on the reputation of the authority. With hindsight, however, the judgment is seen to have had *'a massive effect'*, and to have contributed substantially to the improvement of services. Certainly, many respondents emphasised that judicial review does not hinder them in their work. As one put it: *'As a general point we were not sitting around worrying about judicial review and it's not making us defensive, we're much more proactive about doing things right than defensive about trying to avoid making mistakes.'*

7 FURTHER READING

Bellamy, R., *Political Constitutionalism: A Republican Defence of the Constitutionality of Democracy* (2007, Cambridge: Cambridge University Press).

Feldman, D., (ed.) *English Public Law*, 2nd edn (2009, Oxford: OUP), chs 7, 13–16, and 18

Government Legal Service, *The Judge Over Your Shoulder*, 4th edn (2006, London: TSol)

Woolf, H., Jowell, J., and Le Sueur, A., *De Smith's Judicial Review*, 6th edn (2007, London: Sweet and Maxwell)

ONLINE RESOURCE CENTRE

Further information about the themes discussed in this chapter can be found on the Online Resource Centre at www.oxfordtextbooks.co.uk/orc/lesueur2e/

17

USING HUMAN RIGHTS IN UNITED KINGDOM COURTS

CENTRAL ISSUES

1. Public authorities must act compatibly with certain 'Convention rights' in the European Convention for the Protection of Human Rights and Fundamental Freedoms (ECHR). The Human Rights Act 1998 enables proceedings to be brought to enforce these rights in UK domestic courts and tribunals.

2. The Human Rights Act 1998 (HRA) requires UK courts and tribunals to take account of the case law developed by the European Commission on Human Rights (when it existed) and the European Court of Human Rights (ECtHR). It also requires legislation to be interpreted in a manner that is compatible with Convention rights, so far as this is possible. If legislation cannot be given a human rights-compatible interpretation, the senior or higher courts may make a declaration of incompatibility.

3. While core public authorities, such as central government and its agencies, and local authorities must comply with the HRA, the Act also extends to private bodies that exercise 'functions of a public nature'. The meaning of this expression has given rise to significant debate.

4. The application of the HRA has also given rise to significant debate over the appropriate relationship between the courts and the executive and parliament, especially when government believes that infringements of human rights are necessary in order to protect public security. In such situations, to what degree, if at all, should courts defer to the executive and legislature?

5. The chapter considers two case studies that illustrate key issues in the law. The first is Shabina Begum's challenge to her school's decision not to permit her to dress in accordance with her religious belief. In this case, the House of Lords explained the difference between the approach to be taken by judges in human rights cases and that to be taken in cases in which the claimants rely on the common law grounds of judicial review.

6. The second case study deals with the most challenging issue in this area of law since the enactment of the HRA—the relationship between human rights and terrorism. The case study examines the landmark decision in the *Belmarsh* case and its aftermath, as well as challenges to control orders made under the Prevention of Terrorism Act 2005.

1 INTRODUCTION

In Chapter 6 we saw how developments in international human rights law at the global and European levels have helped to establish common law constitutional rights in the United Kingdom. We also looked at the background to the Human Rights Act 1998 (HRA), which was designed to 'bring rights home' by enabling litigants to rely on most of the rights and freedoms set out in the European Convention for the Protection of Human Rights and Fundamental Freedoms (ECHR) in domestic courts, thereby removing the need to take lengthy proceedings before the European Court of Human Rights (ECtHR) in Strasbourg. In Chapter 16, we examined the common law grounds used by courts when reviewing the legality of actions taken by public authorities. We noted that s. 6(1) of the HRA makes it unlawful for public authorities to act in a manner that is incompatible with 'Convention rights'.

We now look more specifically at the use of human rights in the domestic courts of the United Kingdom. There has been unprecedented development in domestic human rights law since the enactment of the HRA—and human rights arguments have been relevant across a very broad spectrum of cases. There have, for example, been leading decisions involving matters as diverse as residential care homes,[1] the maintenance of churches,[2] the rights of tenants and their families[3], and school admissions and uniform policies.[4]

The period since the enactment of the HRA has largely coincided with what President Bush called the 'war on terror' and the need to reconcile human rights with the fight against terrorism has been a defining aspect of the past decade or so. One consequence is that the courts have been faced with many challenges involving anti-terrorist legislation and its application. This has forced judges to reassess whether the deferential approach to the executive displayed in cases such as *Liversidge v Anderson*[5] remains appropriate, given the obligations contained in the ECHR and the HRA.

Section 2 of this chapter examines the main features of the HRA, while section 3 considers the issue of judicial deference to the executive and Parliament in human rights situations. In sections 4 and 5, the chapter considers two case studies. The first of these is the litigation brought by Shabina Begum challenging her school's decision preventing her from wearing a jilbab[6] to school.

The second case study considers the litigation that followed the enactment of Pt IV of the Anti-terrorism, Crime and Security Act 2001, and the challenges to control orders imposed under the Prevention of Terrorism Act 2005.

2 THE MAIN FEATURES OF THE HUMAN RIGHTS ACT 1998

The purpose of the HRA, as expressed in its long title, is *'to give further effect to the rights and freedoms guaranteed under the European Convention on Human Rights'*. The Act enables

---

[1] *YL (by her litigation friend the Official Solicitor) (FC) v Birmingham City Council and ors* [2007] UKHL 27.

[2] *Aston Cantlow and Wilmcote, with Billesley Parochial Church Council v Wallbank and anor* [2003] UKHL 37.

[3] *Pinnock v Manchester City Council* [2010] UKSC 45.

[4] The *Begum* case, see section 4, Case Study: The Denbigh High School Case—School uniforms and the right to manifest one's religion; *R (on the application of E) v The Governing Body of JFS and the Admissions Appeal Panel of JFS and ors* [2009] UKSC 15.

[5] [1942] AC 206.

[6] A long coat-like garment that conceals the shape of the wearer's arms and legs.

claimants to rely on most (but not all) of the rights and freedoms contained in the ECHR and its Protocols in domestic legal proceedings.[7] This was a significant breakthrough. Until the HRA, the ECHR could be used in UK courts to support arguments that public bodies had acted *Wednesbury* unreasonably, or that ambiguously worded legislation should be interpreted in a manner that favoured human rights. But the rights contained in the Convention were not part of domestic law and therefore could not be relied on directly: public authorities could not be held to have acted unlawfully solely because they had acted contrary to the Convention. Convention rights could be enforced only by lengthy proceedings in Strasbourg, once domestic avenues had been exhausted. The HRA therefore significantly improved people's ability to enforce human rights obligations—but the Act is not only about enforcing obligations in particular cases. It also has the broader aim of inculcating a general culture of respect for human rights—especially within public authorities, which must comply with human rights in all of their activities, irrespective of whether legal challenges are involved.

(a) BASIC SCHEME OF THE HUMAN RIGHTS ACT 1998

The basic scheme of the HRA was summarized in Chapter 6, but it is worth reiterating the elements here.

- All legislation (both primary and secondary) '*must be read and given effect in a way which is compatible with Convention rights in so far as it is possible to do so*' (s. 3). This interpretative obligation is imposed on everyone who has to apply legislation. It is most important for judges, who are ultimately responsible for explaining what legislation means.

- If legislation cannot be interpreted in a way that is compatible with Convention rights, the higher courts can issue '*a declaration of incompatibility*' (s. 4). If such a declaration is made, it makes it clear that the legislation conflicts with Convention rights, but this does not affect the validity of the legislation. Parliament's ability to legislate contrary to human rights is retained. Ministers in charge of a Bill must make a written statement that the Bill is compatible with Convention rights or, if not, that the government nonetheless wishes the Bill to proceed (s. 19).

- Where legislation has been declared to be incompatible with Convention rights, ministers are given powers to take steps to make delegated legislation to amend provisions in an Act of Parliament so as to remove the incompatibility (s. 10(2) and (3)).

- It is unlawful for public authorities to act in a way that is incompatible with Convention rights (s. 6).

- Public authorities may have a defence if primary legislation requires them to act in the way that they did (s. 6(2)).

- Those claiming to be 'victims' of actions (or threatened actions) of public authorities that are unlawful under s. 6 can rely on Convention rights in any legal proceedings, including (but not limited to) claims for judicial review. If successful, the court has a wide range of remedies, including the ability to award damages (ss 7 and 8).

---

[7] The Act does not apply to the right to a remedy in Art.13, nor to the right not to be discriminated against in Protocol 12 of the ECHR, to which the United Kingdom has yet to agree.

(b) THE DUTY 'TO TAKE INTO ACCOUNT' CONVENTION CASE LAW

Section 2(1) of the HRA imposes a duty on courts and tribunals to 'take into account' the case law of the European Commission of Human Rights (abolished in 1998) and the European Court of Human Rights (ECtHR). This recognizes that the HRA gives domestic effect to rights and freedoms that are established by the ECHR, which have been interpreted and explained by the Strasbourg institutions; the HRA did not establish new free-standing rights. Although UK domestic courts are not bound by decisions of the Strasbourg Court, as we shall see when we look at the decision of the House of Lords in *AF v Secretary of State for the Home Department and anor*,[8] Lord Hoffmann, while disliking a decision of the ECtHR, considered that the House was, in reality, bound to apply it.[9]

AF v Secretary of State for the Home Department and anor
[2009] UKHL 28

Lord Hoffmann

[70] [...] It is true that s 2(1)(a) of the Human Rights Act 1998 requires us only to 'take into account' decisions of the ECtHR. As a matter of our domestic law, we could take the decision in *A v United Kingdom* into account but nevertheless prefer our own view. But the United Kingdom is bound by the Convention, as a matter of international law, to accept the decisions of the ECtHR on its interpretation.[10]

Notice how Lord Hoffmann links the practical effect of the HRA to the legal obligations of the UK in international law. Others, however, stress that what matters is domestic rather than international law, arguing that in our dualist system it is legally acceptable for domestic judges to disagree with the ECtHR.

Lord Irvine of Lairg, who as the Lord Chancellor at the time, steered the Human Rights Bill through Parliament has recently argued that the approach taken by Lord Hoffmann is wrong, pointing out that Parliament, need not have used the words 'take account of' in section 2(1). It could instead have told courts that they must 'follow', or 'give effect to' or 'be bound by' by decisions of the ECtHR.[11,12]

Lord Irvine of Lairg, 'A British Interpretation of Convention Rights' [2012] Public Law 237, at 239 (emphasis in original)

Section 2 means that the domestic courts *always have a choice*. Further, not only is the domestic court *entitled* to make the choice, its statutory duty under s. 2 *obliges* it to confront the question whether or not the relevant decision of the [ECtHR] is sound in principle and should be given effect domestically. Simply put, the domestic must decide the case for itself.

---

8 [2009] UKHL 28, see p. 749.

9 Lord Rodger agreed with this.

10 Compare *R v Horncastle and ors* [2009] UKSC 14, in which the UK Supreme Court said that it would depart from Strasbourg case law where that concerned Continental trial procedures that differ from those used in the UK criminal process.

11 Lord Irvine of Lairg, 'A British Interpretation of Convention Rights' [2012] Public Law 237, at 239.

12 Ibid.

In Lord Irvine's view the proper approach is that set out by Lord Neuberger on behalf the unanimous nine justice UK Supreme Court in *Pinnock v Manchester City Council:*[13]

Lord Neuberger, *Pinnock v Manchester City Council*
[2010] UKSC 45

[48] … This court is not bound to follow every decision of the European court. Not only would it be impractical to do so: it would sometimes be inappropriate, as it would destroy the ability of the court to engage in the constructive dialogue with the European court which is of value to the development of Convention law [...] Of course, we should usually follow a clear and constant line of decisions by the European court: *R (on the application of Ullah) v Special Adjudicator* [below] [...] But we are not actually bound to do so [...] Where, however, there is a clear and constant line of decisions whose effect is not inconsistent with some fundamental substantive or procedural aspect of our law, and whose reasoning does not appear to overlook or misunderstand some argument or point of principle, we consider that it would be wrong for this court not to follow that line.

(c) CAN UK COURTS EXTEND CONVENTION RIGHTS?

Related to the obligation to take account of Strasbourg case law is the question of whether UK courts are free to take a more expansive approach to rights than that adopted by the Strasbourg Court: as commentators have expressed it, does the Strasbourg case law impose a ceiling upon rights or does it provide a floor?

When we consider the decision of the House of Lords in the *Begum* case, we shall see that Lord Bingham said that the purpose of the HRA '*was not to enlarge the rights or remedies of those in the United Kingdom whose Convention rights have been violated but to enable those rights and remedies to be asserted and enforced by the domestic courts of this country and not only by recourse to Strasbourg*'—echoing his statement in an earlier case.

R (on the application of Ullah) v Special Adjudicator
[2004] UKHL 26

Lord Bingham

[20] [...] It is course open to member states to provide for rights more generous than those guaranteed by the Convention, but such provision should not be the product of interpretation of the Convention by national courts, since the meaning of the Convention should be uniform throughout the states party to it. The duty of the courts is to keep pace with the Strasbourg jurisprudence as it evolves over time: no more, but certainly no less.

This view has generated much debate and has been challenged by those who argue that it is contrary to the intent and wording of the HRA, which was designed to provide 'a floor of

---

[13] Cf Sir Philip Sales, 'Strasbourg Jurisprudence and the Human Rights Act: A response to Lord Irvine' [2012] Public Law 253; Richard Clayton 'Smoke and Mirrors: the Human Rights Act and the impact of the Strasbourg Case Law' [2012] Public Law, 639.

rights protection', but not to impose a ceiling on the ability of the courts to interpret rights dynamically. In *Al Skeini* [14] Lord Brown said that Lord Bingham's statement could as well have ended 'no less, certainly no more', Baroness Hale agreed [15], and Lord Bingham did not take issue with it. Lord Hope has said that: 'Lord Bingham's point, with which I respectfully agree, was that Parliament never intended to give the courts of this country the power to give a more generous scope to those rights than that which was to be found in the jurisprudence of the Strasbourg Court. To do so would have the effect of changing them from Convention rights, based on the treaty obligation, into free-standing rights of the court's own creation.'[16] Lord Dyson said in this case that this and similar statements are *'not entirely apposite'* where, although Strasbourg has spoken on the issue 'there is no clear and constant line of authority'. [17] He went on to argue that in such a situation the court duty is to 'give effect to the domestically enacted Convention rights'.[18] Here then Lord Dyson indicates that under the HRA the Convention rights are to be interpreted and to be developed as part of domestic law. This approach reflects what he said in the UK Supreme Court a few months earlier in July 2011. In *Al Rawi v The Security Service and Ors* Lord Dyson stressed Lord Bingham's opening words *'[I]t is course open to member states to provide for rights more generous than those guaranteed by the Convention'.* Lord Dyson then commented that *'[I]t is therefore open to our courts to provide greater protection through the common law than that which is guaranteed by the Convention.'*[19]

As we saw in Chapter 6, the government's White Paper, *Rights Brought Home*, envisaged domestic judges being able to make a *'distinctively British contribution to the development of the jurisprudence of human rights in Europe'.*[20] The argument is that judges are unable to make such a contribution if they are limited to ensuring that domestic law keeps pace with Strasbourg jurisprudence. This is particularly important where the Strasbourg Court has made decisions that are considered in this country to be conservative and cautious, perhaps because that Court is conscious of its need to move at a pace that is acceptable to a large number of states.

An interesting example of the sort of issue that can arise is provided by the decision of the House of Lords in *Re P and ors.*[21] This was a case from Northern Ireland, in which the House held that it would be contrary to s. 6(1) of the HRA for the Family Division of the High Court to apply delegated legislation that made it impossible for unmarried couples to adopt children, whatever the circumstances. The House held that the legislation discriminates against unmarried couples on the basis of their status (being unmarried) contrary to Art. 14 in relation to Art. 8 (right to a family life). The decision was reached despite Convention jurisprudence indicating that the ECtHR could, consistently with its earlier jurisprudence, decide that the legislation was not unlawful. This, then, is an example of a case in which the House of Lords reached a decision knowing that it may well have done more than only keep pace with Strasbourg jurisprudence.

---

[14] [2007] UKHL 26 [106].

[15] Ibid [90].

[16] *Ambrose v Harris (Procurator Fiscal, Oban)* [2011] UKSC 43 at [19]. Lord Brown agreed [86].

[17] Ibid [101]-[102].

[18] Ibid [103].

[19] Lord Dyson, in *Al Rawi v The Security Service and Ors* [2011] UKSC 34, [68].

[20] Secretary of State for the Home Department, *Rights Brought Home: the Human Rights Bill* (Cm 3782, October 1997), para. 1.14; see further Jonathan Lewis, 'The European ceiling on human rights' [2007] Public Law 720; Jane Wright, 'Interpreting section 2 of the Human Rights Act 1998: Towards an indigenous jurisprudence of human rights' [2009] Public Law 595.

[21] [2008] UKHL 38.

(d) THE INTERPRETATIVE OBLIGATION

Human Rights Act 1998, s. 3

(1) So far as it is possible to do so, primary legislation and subordinate legislation must be read and given effect in a way which is compatible with the Convention rights.

(2) This section—

    (a) applies to primary legislation and subordinate legislation whenever enacted;

    (b) does not affect the validity, continuing operation or enforcement of any incompatible primary legislation; and

    (c) does not affect the validity, continuing operation or enforcement of any incompatible subordinate legislation if (disregarding any possibility of revocation) primary legislation prevents removal of the incompatibility.

As you can see, s. 3 says that primary and subordinate (that is, delegated) legislation '*must be read and given effect in a way which is compatible with Convention rights*', but only '*so far as it is possible to do so*'. It also indicates that legislation will remain valid and enforceable in operation even if a human rights-compatible interpretation is not possible.[22]

In relation to subordinate legislation, s. 3(2)(c) indicates that the validity, operation, and enforcement of subordinate legislation that is incompatible with Convention rights may be affected, unless primary legislation prevents the removal of the incompatibility. In other words, if primary legislation dictates that subordinate legislation be incompatible with Convention rights, then that subordinate legislation will continue to be operative and enforceable—but if primary legislation does not do this, the subordinate legislation may be rendered invalid.[23]

As we have seen elsewhere in this book, prior to the HRA, judges had presumed that unclear or ambiguous legislative provisions should be interpreted in a way that was compatible with the UK's international human rights obligations and common law constitutional rights. Parliament was taken to have intended that its legislation would be read to be compliant with human rights, unless it had expressly stated otherwise. This principle—widely referred to as 'the principle of legality'—was stated by Lord Hoffmann in *R v Secretary of State for the Home Department, ex parte Simms*.[24]

The White Paper, *Rights Brought Home*, explained the interpretative obligation in the following way.

Secretary of State for the Home Department, *Rights Brought Home*, Cm 3782, October 1997, para. 2.7

[The interpretative obligation] goes far beyond the present rule which enables the courts to take the Convention into account in resolving any ambiguity in a legislative provision. The courts will be required to interpret legislation so as to uphold the Convention rights unless the legislation itself is so clearly incompatible with the Convention that it is impossible to do so.

---

[22] Compare the wording of s. 2(4) of the European Communities Act 1972, which provides that '*any enactment* [...] *shall be construed and have effect subject to* [EU] *law*'.

[23] For a case concerning subordinate legislation, see *Re P and ors* [2008] UKHL 38.

[24] [2000] 2 AC 115, 131, discussed in Chapter 3.

This indicated that courts would be obliged to give human rights-compatible meanings both where legislation is ambiguous and where it is clear. Suppose, then, that provisions are not ambiguous, but are clearly incompatible with Convention rights. Section 3 says that courts must do what is possible to give legislation a human rights-compatible meaning—but what is possible? Suppose that the court considers that another form of words would render the legislation compatible with human rights: is it possible for the judge to rewrite the legislation and insert new words into the legislation as if the judge were legislating? If this is possible, how far should the courts go and at what point would judges trespass upon the legislative function? These and related questions have been widely discussed by academic commentators and by the judges.[25] They have also been considered by the House of Lords in the leading decision on the interpretative obligation, *Ghaidan v Godin-Mendoza*.[26]

Ghaidan v Godin-Mendoza

The main issue in *Ghaidan* was whether a same-sex partner who had, for many years, lived in a close and stable relationship with someone who had a statutory tenancy under the Rent Act 1977 could succeed to the statutory tenancy when the tenant died. Paragraph 2(1) of Sch. 1 to the Act granted a right of succession to the 'surviving spouse' of a tenant. The meaning of 'surviving spouse' was extended in 1988 to include '*a person who was living with the original tenant as his or her wife or husband*'. Did a same-sex partner qualify under this provision? Could a same-sex partner be said to have been living with his or her partner '*as his or her wife or husband*'?

In *Fitzpatrick v Sterling Housing Association*,[27] a case with the same facts that was decided before the HRA was applicable, the House of Lords had held that a same-sex survivor would *not* qualify under the wording of these provisions. The question in *Ghaidan* was whether that decision remained applicable following the HRA.

In *Ghaidan*, the House of Lords was unanimous in its view that it would be contrary to Art. 14, taken together with Art. 8, to deny Mr Godin-Mendoza the right to succeed to a statutory tenancy. But was it possible to read the 1977 Act, as amended, in a way that made it compatible with these provisions? The majority said that it was possible to do so, but Lord Millett disagreed. In his view, the approach taken by the majority involved rewriting the legislation and trespassing beyond permissible judicial interpretation into Parliament's legislative domain.

Ghaidan v Godin-Mendoza
[2004] UKHL 30

Lord Nicholls

[26] Section 3 is a key section in the Human Rights Act 1998. It is one of the primary means by which Convention rights are brought into the law of this country. Parliament has decreed that all legislation, existing and future, shall be interpreted in a particular way. All legislation must be read and given effect to in a way which is compatible with the Convention rights "so far as it is possible to do so". This is the intention of Parliament, expressed in s 3, and the courts must give effect to this intention.

---

[25] For example, Geoffrey Marshall, 'The lynchpin of parliamentary intention: Lost, stolen, or strained?' [2003] Public Law 236; Lord Irvine, 'The impact of the Human Rights Act: Parliament, the courts and the executive', [2003] Public Law 308; Aileen Kavanagh, *Constitutional Review under the UK Human Rights Act*, (Cambridge University Press, 2009); and see references given later in the chapter.

[26] [2004] UKHL 30.

[27] [2001] 1 AC 27.

[27] Unfortunately, in making this provision for the interpretation of legislation, s 3 itself is not free from ambiguity. Section 3 is open to more than one interpretation. The difficulty lies in the word "possible". Section 3(1), read in conjunction with s 3(2) and s 4, makes one matter clear: Parliament expressly envisaged that not all legislation would be capable of being made Convention-compliant by application of s 3. Sometimes it would be possible, sometimes not. What is not clear is the test to be applied in separating the sheep from the goats. What is the standard, or the criterion, by which "possibility" is to be judged? A comprehensive answer to this question is proving elusive. The courts, including your Lordships' House, are still cautiously feeling their way forward as experience in the application of s 3 gradually accumulates.

[28] One tenable interpretation of the word "possible" would be that s 3 is confined to requiring courts to resolve ambiguities. Where the words under consideration fairly admit of more than one meaning the Convention-compliant meaning is to prevail. Words should be given the meaning which best accords with the Convention rights.

[29] This interpretation of s 3 would give the section a comparatively narrow scope. This is not the view which has prevailed. It is now generally accepted that the application of s 3 does not depend upon the presence of ambiguity in the legislation being interpreted. Even if, construed according to the ordinary principles of interpretation, the meaning of the legislation admits of no doubt, s 3 may nonetheless require the legislation to be given a different meaning. The decision of your Lordships' House in *R v A (No 2)* [2002] 1 AC 45, [2001] 3 All ER 1 is an instance of this. The House read words into s 41 of the Youth Justice and Criminal Evidence Act 1999 so as to make that section compliant with an accused's right to a fair trial under Article 6. The House did so even though the statutory language was not ambiguous.

[30] From this it follows that the interpretative obligation decreed by s 3 is of an unusual and far-reaching character. Section 3 may require a court to depart from the unambiguous meaning the legislation would otherwise bear. In the ordinary course the interpretation of legislation involves seeking the intention reasonably to be attributed to Parliament in using the language in question. Section 3 may require the court to depart from this legislative intention, that is, depart from the intention of the Parliament which enacted the legislation. The question of difficulty is how far, and in what circumstances, s 3 requires a court to depart from the intention of the enacting Parliament. The answer to this question depends upon the intention reasonably to be attributed to Parliament in enacting s 3.

[31] On this the first point to be considered is how far, when enacting s 3, Parliament intended that the actual language of a statute, as distinct from the concept expressed in that language, should be determinative. Since s 3 relates to the "interpretation" of legislation, it is natural to focus attention initially on the language used in the legislative provision being considered. But once it is accepted that s 3 may require legislation to bear a meaning which departs from the unambiguous meaning the legislation would otherwise bear, it becomes impossible to suppose Parliament intended that the operation of s 3 should depend critically upon the particular form of words adopted by the parliamentary draftsman in the statutory provision under consideration. That would make the application of s 3 something of a semantic lottery. If the draftsman chose to express the concept being enacted in one form of words, s 3 would be available to achieve Convention-compliance. If he chose a different form of words, s 3 would be impotent.

[32] From this the conclusion which seems inescapable is that the mere fact the language under consideration is inconsistent with a Convention-compliant meaning does not of itself make a Convention-compliant interpretation under s 3 impossible. Section 3 enables language to be interpreted restrictively or expansively. But s 3 goes further than this. It is also apt

to require a court to read in words which change the meaning of the enacted legislation, so as to make it Convention-compliant. In other words, the intention of Parliament in enacting s 3 was that, to an extent bounded only by what is "possible", a court can modify the meaning, and hence the effect, of primary and secondary legislation.

[33] Parliament, however, cannot have intended that in the discharge of this extended interpretative function the courts should adopt a meaning inconsistent with a fundamental feature of legislation. That would be to cross the constitutional boundary s 3 seeks to demarcate and preserve. Parliament has retained the right to enact legislation in terms which are not Convention-compliant. The meaning imported by application of s 3 must be compatible with the underlying thrust of the legislation being construed. Words implied must, in the phrase of my noble and learned friend Lord Rodger of Earlsferry, "go with the grain of the legislation". Nor can Parliament have intended that s 3 should require courts to make decisions for which they are not equipped. There may be several ways of making a provision Convention-compliant, and the choice may involve issues calling for legislative deliberation.

[...]

[35] In some cases difficult problems may arise. No difficulty arises in the present case. Paragraph 2 of Schedule 1 to the Rent Act 1977 is unambiguous. But the social policy underlying the 1988 extension of security of tenure under para 2 to the survivor of couples living together as husband and wife is equally applicable to the survivor of homosexual couples living together in a close and stable relationship. In this circumstance I see no reason to doubt that application of s 3 to para 2 has the effect that para 2 should be read and given effect to as though the survivor of such a homosexual couple were the surviving spouse of the original tenant. Reading para 2 in this way would have the result that cohabiting heterosexual couples and cohabiting heterosexual couples would be treated alike for the purposes of succession as a statutory tenant. This would eliminate the discriminatory effect of para 2 and would do so consistently with the social policy underlying para 2. The precise form of words read in for this purpose is of no significance. It is their substantive effect which matters.

Lord Steyn

[44] It is necessary to state what s 3(1), and in particular the word "possible", does not mean. First, s 3(1) applies even if there is no ambiguity in the language in the sense of it being capable of bearing two *possible* meanings. The word "possible" in s 3(1) is used in a different and much stronger sense. Secondly, s 3(1) imposes a stronger and more radical obligation than to adopt a purposive interpretation in the light of the ECHR. Thirdly, the draftsman of the Act had before him the model of the New Zealand Bill of Rights Act which imposes a requirement that the interpretation to be adopted must be reasonable. Parliament specifically rejected the legislative model of requiring a reasonable interpretation.

[45] Instead the draftsman had resort to the analogy of the obligation under the EEC Treaty on national courts, as far as possible, to interpret national legislation in the light of the wording and purpose of directives. In *Marleasing SA v La Comercial Internacional de Alimentación SA* (Case C-106/89) [1990] ECR I-4135, 4159 the European Court of Justice defined this obligation as follows:

"It follows that, in applying national law, whether the provisions in questions were adopted before or after the directive, the national court called upon to interpret it is required to do so, as far as possible, in light of the wording and the purpose of the directive in order to achieve the result pursued by the latter and thereby comply with the third paragraph of Article 189 of the Treaty."

Given the undoubted strength of this interpretative obligation under EEC law, this is a significant signpost to the meaning of section 3(1) in the 1998 Act.

[...]

[49] [...] there has sometimes been a tendency to approach the interpretative task under s 3(1) in too literal and technical a way. In practice there has been too much emphasis on linguistic features. If the core remedial purpose of s 3(1) is not to be undermined a broader approach is required. That is, of course, not to gainsay the obvious proposition that inherent in the use of the word "possible" in s 3(1) is the idea that there is a Rubicon which courts may not cross. If it is not possible, within the meaning of s 3, to read or give effect to legislation in a way which is compatible with Convention rights, the only alternative is to exercise, where appropriate, the power to make a declaration of incompatibility. Usually, such cases should not be too difficult to identify. An obvious example is *R (Anderson) v Secretary of State for the Home Department* [2003] 1 AC 837, [2002] 4 All ER 1089. The House held that the Home Secretary was not competent under Article 6 of the ECHR to decide on the tariff to be served by mandatory life sentence prisoners. The House found a s 3(1) interpretation not "possible" and made a declaration under s 4. Interpretation could not provide a substitute scheme. *Bellinger* is another obvious example. As Lord Rodger of Earlsferry observed "[...] in relation to the validity of marriage, Parliament regards gender as fixed and immutable": [2003] 2 WLR 1174, 1195, para 83. Section 3(1) of the 1998 Act could not be used.

[50] Having had the opportunity to reconsider the matter in some depth, I am not disposed to try to formulate precise rules about where s 3 may not be used. Like the proverbial elephant such a case ought generally to be easily identifiable. What is necessary, however, is to emphasise that interpretation under s 3(1) is the prime remedial remedy and that resort to s 4 must always be an exceptional course. In practical effect there is a strong rebuttable presumption in favour of an interpretation consistent with Convention rights. Perhaps the opinions delivered in the House today will serve to ensure a balanced approach along such lines.

BOX 17.1 A SUMMARY OF THE APPROACH OF THE MAJORITY IN *GHAIDAN*

1. It is not always possible for courts to give legislation a meaning that is compatible with Convention rights, but they must do what is possible to try to achieve this. When, despite efforts, legislation is nonetheless incompatible with Convention rights, the higher courts may make a declaration of incompatibility under s. 4 of the HRA.

2. It may be 'possible' under s. 3 for courts to depart from the unambiguous meaning of legislation and thus from the intention of the Parliament that enacted it.

3. Courts should initially focus on the words of the legislation, but they should not be limited to the words used, because this *'would make the application of s 3 something of a semantic lottery'*.

4. Courts may *'read in words which change the meaning of the enacted legislation, so as to make it Convention-compliant'*.

5. But Parliament, when enacting the HRA *'cannot have intended that in the discharge of this extended interpretative function the courts should adopt a meaning inconsistent with a fundamental feature of legislation. That would be to cross the constitutional boundary s 3 seeks to demarcate and preserve'*.

> 6. There are two limitations on what is possible under s. 3:
>
>   (a) it is not possible to give words meanings that are incompatible *'with the underlying thrust of the legislation being construed'* or that *'go against the grain of the legislation'*; and
>
>   (b) it is not possible for courts to make decisions *'for which they are not equipped'*.[28]

Lord Millett disagreed with the majority. While accepting the breadth of the interpretative obligation in s. 3, he emphasized that it is concerned with the *'process of interpretation alone'*. It does not permit courts to legislate *'and does not entitle the court to supply words which are inconsistent with a fundamental feature of the legislative scheme; nor to repeal, delete, or contradict the language of the offending statute'*.[29] More particularly, he disagreed with the way in which the majority altered the meaning of the specific legislative provisions. In his view, this amounted to rewriting legislation and usurped the role of Parliament. In his view, the only solution would be to consider declaring the legislative provisions to be incompatible with Convention rights—an option that he was disinclined to take.

Ghaidan v Godin-Mendoza
[2004] UKHL 30

Lord Millet

[99] [...] By what is claimed to be a process of interpretation of an existing statute framed in gender specific terms, and enacted at a time when homosexual relationships were not recognised by law, it is proposed to treat persons of the same sex living together as if they were living together as husband and wife and then to treat such persons as if they were lawfully married. It is to be left unclear as from what date this change in the law has taken place. If we were to decide this question we would be usurping the function of Parliament; and if we were to say that it was from the time when the European Court of Human Rights decided that such discrimination was unlawful we would be transferring the legislative power from Parliament to that court. It is, in my view, consonant with the Convention for the contracting states to take time to consider its implications and to bring their laws into conformity with it. They do not demand retrospective legislation.

[100] Worse still, in support of their conclusion that the existing discrimination is incompatible with the Convention, there is a tendency in some of the speeches of the majority to refer to loving, stable and long-lasting homosexual relationships. It is left wholly unclear whether qualification for the successive tenancy is confined to couples enjoying such a relationship or, consistently with the legislative policy which Parliament has hitherto adopted, is dependent on status and not merit.

[101] In my opinion all these questions are essentially questions of social policy which should be left to Parliament. [...] it is in my view not open to the courts to foreclose them by adopting an interpretation of the existing legislation which it not only does not bear but which is manifestly inconsistent with it.

---

[28] On this second limit, see further Alison L. Young, *'Ghaidan v Godin-Mendoza*: Avoiding the deference trap' [2005] Public Law 23.

[29] *Ghaidan v Godin-Mendoza* [2004] UKHL 30, [68].

> **QUESTION**
>
> Was the approach taken by the majority an exercise of interpretation or an example of law-making?

Does the intention of Parliament still matter?

Ghaidan v Godin-Mendoza
[2004] UKHL 30

Lord Nicholls

[30] In the ordinary course the interpretation of legislation involves seeking the intention reasonably to be attributed to Parliament in using the language in question. Section 3 may require the court to depart from this legislative intention, that is, depart from the intention of the Parliament which enacted the legislation.

[...]

[32] [...] the intention of Parliament in enacting s 3 was that, to an extent bounded only by what is "possible", a court can modify the meaning, and hence the effect, of primary and secondary legislation.

Do these comments mean that the courts no longer have to heed the intention of Parliament as expressed in the words of the enactment being interpreted? Do they mean that once judges have decided that provisions are incompatible with Convention rights, they can disregard the wording used and the intention behind them? In *R(Wilkinson) v IRC*,[30] Lord Hoffmann explained that the wording of legislation still matters.

In this case, a widower claimed that he was entitled to a tax allowance that had been available only to widows. Section 262 of the Income and Corporation Taxes Act 1988 provided that '*Where a married man whose wife is living with him dies, his widow shall be entitled [...] to an income tax reduction*'. He argued, among other things, that in order to avoid unlawful discrimination (a breach of Art. 14, read in conjunction with Art. 8 and Art. 1 of the First Protocol of the ECHR), the court should apply the presumption '*that unless the contrary intention appears [...] words importing the feminine gender include the masculine*'.[31]

Lord Hoffmann delivered a judgment with which the other members of the House, including Lord Nicholls, agreed. Rejecting Wilkinson's argument, he said that the 1988 Act is 'brim-full' of indications that references to the feminine gender were not intended to include the masculine. Lord Hoffmann then made the following observations on the interpretative obligation, stressing the need to focus on the actual words used by Parliament.

R (Wilkinson) v IRC
[2005] UKHL 30

Lord Hoffmann

17. [...] The important change in the process of interpretation which was made by section 3 was to deem the Convention to form a significant part of the background against which all

---

[30] [2005] UKHL 30.
[31] Interpretation Act 1978, s. 6.

statutes, whether passed before or after the 1998 Act came into force, had to be interpreted. Just as the "principle of legality" meant that statutes were construed against the background of human rights subsisting at common law (see *R v Home Secretary, Ex p Simms* [...]), so now, section 3 requires them to be construed against the background of Convention rights. There is a strong presumption, arising from the fundamental nature of Convention rights, that Parliament did not intend a statute to mean something which would be incompatible with those rights. This of course goes far beyond the old-fashioned notion of using background to "resolve ambiguities" in a text which had notionally been read without raising one's eyes to look beyond it. [...] the question is still one of interpretation, i.e. the ascertainment of what, taking into account the presumption created by section 3, Parliament would reasonably be understood to have meant by using the actual language of the statute.

18. It is therefore sometimes possible, as my noble and learned friend Lord Nicholls of Birkenhead pointed out in *Ghaidan v Godin-Mendoza* [...] to construe a statutory provision as referring to, or qualified by, some general concept implied rather than expressly mentioned in the language used by Parliament. Thus in the Ghaidan case, the words "*as his or her wife or husband*" (my emphasis) were interpreted to refer to a relationship of social and sexual intimacy exemplified by, but not limited to, the heterosexual relationship of husband and wife. The deemed background of the Convention enabled the House to adopt this construction in preference to the more restricted construction adopted before the 1998 Act came into force. It may have come as a surprise to the members of the Parliament which in 1988 enacted the statute construed in the *Ghaidan* case that the relationship to which they were referring could include homosexual relationships. In that sense the construction may have been contrary to the "intention of Parliament". But that is not normally what one means by the intention of Parliament. One means the interpretation which the reasonable reader would give to the statute read against its background, including, now, an assumption that it was not intended to be incompatible with Convention rights.

The meaning of the expression the 'intention of Parliament' has long been debated and, in the following extract, Aileen Kavanagh summarizes her analysis of the ways in which this expression has been used since the enactment of the HRA. As you will see, her final concluding comments warn us against assuming that the HRA has had significant adverse effects on judicial approaches to statutory interpretation.

Aileen Kavanagh, 'The role of parliamentary intention in adjudication under the Human Rights Act 1998' (2006) 26 Oxford Journal of Legal Studies 179 (footnotes omitted)

[In this paper] We discovered that reference to the 'intention of Parliament' has many meanings. It may refer to Parliament's **enacted intention**, i.e. that which is manifest and expressed in the text of the statute. Alternatively, it may refer to the **legislative purposes** which Parliament may have sought to achieve by enacting the legislation. Finally, there are the **presumed intentions** which can be attributed to Parliament due to longstanding principles of the common law. We also discovered that although the HRA brings about some changes in the role of Parliamentary intention, it does not 'abolish' its relevance altogether. [...]

However, there is no denying that interpretation under s 3 brings about significant changes in the traditional role of Parliamentary intention in statutory interpretation. It shifts the interpretive focus away from what Parliament originally intended, towards fulfilling the overriding goal of achieving compatibility with the Convention. When interpreting under s 3, judges can detach legislative meaning from its original contextual setting. Moreover, within certain constraints, they can rectify the *enacted intention* of the statute, if to do so would render it Convention-compatible. Finally, if we view s 3 as introducing a new presumption of Parliamentary intention, it means that at least with reference to pre-HRA legislation, judges are applying a presumption which Parliament could not have known or foreseen when it enacted the original legislation. Even when an innovative decision is reached under s 3, the judiciary is nonetheless keen to emphasize the limits of that creativity, rather than its breadth. Judicial reference to 'the will of Parliament' is a way of expressing those limits.

The complex and multi-faceted nature of this issue reveals that there can be no formulaic answer to Lord Nicholl's question in *Ghaidan* about 'how far, and in what circumstances, s 3 requires a court to depart from the intention of the enacting Parliament'. There is no single 'test' which, if applied by the judiciary, will give them the key to the appropriate degree of departure from parliamentary intention in every case. All one can say is that judges are entitled under s 3(1) to depart from both the *enacted* and *unenacted intentions* of Parliament embodied in primary legislation, but should do so only to the extent necessary to achieve compatibility with the Convention, if this is desirable in the context of the individual case. The desirability of a s 3 interpretation will depend on many factors, such as whether it would involve far-reaching legal change which might be better for Parliament to carry out, or alternatively, whether the change can be successfully achieved by judicial law-reform and is not in tension with other provisions within the legislation, or indeed the broader legislative context. An assessment of this issue can only be made in the context of all the factors relevant in the particular case. The case-law reveals that the judges are generally concerned to fulfil their obligations under s 3(1), whilst simultaneously reconciling a novel interpretation with some version of parliamentary intent as embodied in the original legislation.

One final point: before the HRA ever came into force, judges have had at their disposal devices with which they could, in appropriate cases, rectify, improve and update statutory provisions. The familiar presumptions of statutory interpretation are just such a device. [...] Much of the alarm about the expanded judicial power under the HRA has perhaps been due to a mischaracterization of the nature of statutory interpretation which existed prior to it. The idea that the only task of the judge before 1998 was to ascertain 'the intention of Parliament' and apply the existing law, is [...] part of such a misrepresentation.[...] we should not fall into the trap of characterizing pre-HRA interpretation in terms of a fairytale, in order to cast the HRA as the big bad wolf. The Act certainly brings about changes in the judicial law-making function, but it does not create that function anew. Moreover, it does not remove the general judicial obligation to secure continuity between changes in the law and the existing body of law, including the statutory framework set out by Parliament.

QUESTIONS

1. What do you understand to be the meaning(s) of the expression 'the intention of Parliament'?

2. Did the HRA alter the obligation upon judges to interpret legislation as Parliament intended?

(e) DECLARATIONS OF INCOMPATIBILITY

Section 4 of the HRA enables senior or higher courts to make a declaration that legislative provisions are incompatible with Convention rights—but a declaration of incompatibility *'does not affect the validity, continuing operation or enforcement of the provision in respect of which it is given'*.[32] Here, then, is another reminder of Parliament's legal supremacy: its legislation remains valid and effective even when a court has declared that it conflicts with Convention rights. Another important feature is that declarations of incompatibility are not binding on the parties to the proceedings.[33] In this sense, declarations do not provide tangible remedies for claimants and do not impose legal obligations upon public authorities. For example, in the *Belmarsh* case (so-called because the claimants had been kept in Belmarsh prison—see p. 791), although the House of Lords declared legislative provisions under which the claimants were detained to be incompatible with the right to liberty in Art. 5 of the ECHR, the Home Secretary was not required to release the claimants from prison, and nor was it considered necessary to compensate them.

Nor do declarations of incompatibility compel government or Parliament to change the law. Nonetheless, in Chapter 6, we saw Professor Bradley's argument that the courts' ability under 4 of HRA to "deliver a wound to Parliament's handiwork that is likely to prove fatal" does in reality affect the sovereignty of Parliament.[34]

It is perhaps not surprising, given the potential power of a declaration of incompatibility, that the courts regard this remedy as being a last resort. As Lord Steyn emphasized in his judgment in *Ghaidan*, *'interpretation under s 3(1) is the prime remedial remedy and […] resort to s 4 must always be an exceptional course'*. Some academic commentators argue that this is as it should be.[35] Others argue, however, that the use of s 4 should be norm. We shall return to this issue in a moment.

Before doing so, let us suppose that the majority in *Ghaidan* had agreed with Lord Millett that the legislation could not be given a meaning that was compatible with Convention rights. Had this been the case, the judges would have considered making a declaration of incompatibility. As you can see from the word 'may' in s. 4(2), judges have discretion whether or not to do so. Despite his view on the meaning of the words, it seems that Lord Millett would have been inclined against making a declaration. He said that it *'may be a matter for debate whether it would be appropriate to do so at a time when not merely has the Government announced its intention to bring forward corrective legislation in due course […] but Parliament is currently engaged in enacting remedial legislation'*.[36] Lord Millett is here referring to the Civil Partnerships Bill that was then going through Parliament: the implication is that the declaration of incompatibility would serve no useful purpose in this situation.

Baroness Hale of Richmond disagreed with this. In her view, the purpose of a declaration of incompatibility would have been to *'warn Government and Parliament that, in our view, the United Kingdom is in breach of its international obligations. It is then for them to decide what, if anything, to do about it'*.[37]

In order to help to expedite responses to such declarations, the HRA enables ministers, if they consider there to be 'compelling reasons', to make 'remedial orders' that amend the legislation to

---

[32] Section 4(2)(a).

[33] Section 4(2)(b).

[34] See extract Anthony Bradley, 'The Sovereignty of Parliament: Form or Substance?' in Chapter 6, p. 193.

[35] See eg G Phillipson '(Mis)-reading section 3 of the Human Rights Act' (2003) 119 LQR 183.

[36] *Ghaidan v Godin-Mendoza* [2004] UKHL 30, [56].

[37] *R (Animal Defenders International) v Secretary of State for Culture, Media and Sport* [2008] UKHL 15, [53].

remove the incompatibility. By this process, reforms may be made without the full Parliamentary process, although a draft order must be approved by both Houses of Parliament.[38]

Declarations of incompatibility: dialogue between the courts, Parliament and government

The difference just mentioned between Lord Millet and Lady Hale raises an important question about the role of declarations of incompatibility and the relationship between the courts on the one hand and Parliament and government on the other. Lady Hale clearly sees the courts as having a positive role to play in warning Parliament and informing debate about the content of future legislation. Many writers argue that the courts are, and should be, involved in a dialogue (or even a partnership) with policy and lawmakers, and that the ability of make declarations of incompatibility is an important tool in this process. There are variations on this theme within the writing, but the general argument is that the relationship between courts and government can no longer be understood (if it ever could be) as a relationship based on conflict. On the contrary, the relationship is subtle and on-going with government and Parliament taking account of judicial decisions in their discussion about sensitive policy issues.[39]

In *Public Law after the Human Rights Act*[40], Tom Hickman cites Professor Tom Campbell's argument that '… *it would be best if declarations of incompatibility were to be seen as routine and unproblematic*', as this would recognise that human rights issues are often inherently controversial: '*courts should be regarded as having the right to make only provisional determinations*' of what the ECHR requires and '*[t]hese determinations may, with perfect propriety, be challenged and overturned by elected governments after public debate.*'[41] Hickman explains that such an approach is compatible with the view of the courts as participants in a dialogue with other branches of the system. Hickman goes on to explain that:

Tom Hickman, *Public Law after the Human Rights Act* (Hart Publishing, 2010) p. 60[42]

"[The 'dialogic' approach] …envisages courts proposing arguments of principle to the political branches …[and] in this way, the Human Rights Act provides for an effective synthesis of parliamentary democracy and human rights by forging a partnership between legislature, executive and judiciary".

Whether, and how, government or Parliament responds to declarations of incompatibility is a matter of considerable interest and importance. As the following extract shows, this has a bearing on whether declarations of compatibility could ever be considered to be an effective

---

[38] Section 10 HRA and Sch. 2, paras 1 and 2.

[39] See also, extract Mark Elliott, *The Constitutional Foundations of Judicial Review* in Chapter 16, p. 694. There is now a large literature on dialogue, including: Aileen Kavanagh, *Constitutional Review under the UK Human Rights Act*, (Cambridge, 2009); D Nicol, 'Law and Politics after the Human Rights Act [2006] Public Law 722; Alison L. Young, 'Is Dialogue Working Under the Human Rights Act 1998? [2011] Public Law 773. From the perspective of a political constitutionalist, see Richard Bellamy, 'Political Constitutionalism and the Human Rights Act' [2011] I. J.C.L. 86.

[40] Hart Publishing 2010, p. 60.

[41] T. Campbell, 'Incorporation through Interpretation' in T. Campbell, K.D. Ewing and A. Tomkins (eds) *Sceptical Essays on Human Rights* (Oxford, OUP 2001).

[42] In this work Hickman explores the broader constitutional implication of the dialogic approach.

remedy, bearing in mind that the United Kingdom has an obligation under Art. 13 of the ECHR to provide effective remedies for human rights violations and that claimants must exhaust domestic remedies before going to Strasbourg.

Ministry of Justice responding to human rights judgments, *Report to the Joint committee on the Government's response to human rights judgments* 2010–11, September 2011, Cm 8162

Declarations of Incompatibility

Between the Human Rights Act 1998 coming into force on 2 October 2000 and 8 August 2011, 27 declarations of incompatibility were made.
Of these:

19 have become final (in whole or in part) and are not   subject to further appeal;

8 have been overturned on appeal; and

Of the 19 declarations of incompatibility that have become final:

12 will have been remedied by later primary legislation44

2 will have been remedied by a remedial order under section 10 of the Human Rights Act;45

4 related to provisions that had already been remedied by primary legislation at the time of the declaration;

1 is under consideration as to how to remedy the incompatibility.

Parliamentary Joint Committee on Human Rights, *Monitoring the Government's Response to Court Judgments Finding Breaches of Human Rights*, 16th Report, Session 2006–07

Is a declaration of incompatibility an effective remedy?

110. The importance of swift and comprehensive Government responses to declarations of incompatibility under the Human Rights Act was recently highlighted by the European Court of Human Rights in its judgment in the case of *Burden v UK*. It is a requirement of the ECHR that an applicant to the Court in Strasbourg must first exhaust all their domestic remedies. Unless a domestic remedy is considered "effective", however, it need not be exhausted before pursuing an application to Strasbourg.

111. In *Burden*, the ECtHR confirmed that applicants may not be required to pursue their claim in the domestic courts if the only possible remedy is a declaration of incompatibility under the Human Rights Act [and] that the declaration of incompatibility cannot be considered an effective remedy for the purposes of the requirement that domestic remedies be exhausted. The ECtHR accepted that should evidence emerge at a "future date" of a "long-standing and established practice" of Ministers giving effect to courts' declarations of incompatibility, this might support a different conclusion. In our view this decision makes even more important Parliament's role in scrutinising the promptness and adequacy of the Government's response to declarations of incompatibility. If the Government can demonstrate to Parliament's-satisfaction that it consistently responds promptly and adequately to such declarations, the ECtHR may in time come to regard a declaration of incompatibility as an effective remedy which must first be exhausted before an individual can apply to Strasbourg.

ONLINE RESOURCE CENTRE

The Ministry of Justice reports, broadly annually, to the Joint Committee on Human Rights setting out the government's position on the implementation of adverse judgments of the ECtHR and on declarations of incompatibility. An extract of the most recent report has already been set out. You should also keep an eye on the work of the Joint Committee. See e.g. its report, *Enhancing Parliament's role in relation to human rights judgments*, Session 2009–10, Fifteenth Report.

QUESTIONS

1. *'The practical choice facing the House in* Ghaidan *was between breathing life into the legislation or making a declaration of incompatibility. The former was a far better option in the circumstances and fully justified the relatively minor legislative action that was undertaken.'* Discuss.

2. In what circumstances, if any, would a declaration of incompatibility be an effective remedy for claimants?

3. In what ways may declarations of incompatibility be said to further a dialogue between courts and politicians and government?

(f) THE SECTION 6 DUTY AND ITS ENFORCEMENT

Section 6 is the key enforcement provision in the HRA. This section says that it is unlawful for public authorities to act in a way that is incompatible with Convention rights. Several points should be noted.

(a) The s. 6(1) obligation can be enforced by proceedings in any appropriate tribunal or court (s. 7(1)). Although human rights arguments are often made in judicial review proceedings, these are not the only proceedings in which they may be made.

(b) The s. 6(1) obligation applies to all actions or inactions of public authorities. It applies, for example, even when public authorities are using their private law powers and in situations in which they may not be amenable to judicial review.

(c) Section 6(2) allows public authorities a defence when primary legislation prevents them from acting differently, or when they are enforcing provisions in primary or secondary legislation that are incompatible with Convention rights.

(d) Finally, in this context, section mentions only 'public authorities'. This is important and reflects the 'vertical' nature of human rights obligations under the Act.

Vertical and horizontal effects

Traditionally, international human rights obligations are imposed on states and it is states that are parties to the ECHR. Since the purpose of the HRA is to give better effect to rights under this Convention, the Act retains the principle that it is the United Kingdom as a state that is responsible for protecting rights—but gives it a domestic twist. Within the United Kingdom, there is no legal concept of the state as such and so the Act imposes obligations on bodies that could be brought under the umbrella of the state—namely, public authorities.

This means that unless individuals and private bodies perform functions of a public nature (see later), however powerful and influential they are, they have no direct obligation under the HRA to comply with human rights. Having said this, they may have obligations imposed upon them by the indirect effect of the Act. For example, a local authority may impose contractual obligations to observe human rights standards on those with whom it contracts. Human rights requirements have also been built into the common law as a consequence of *the courts*' obligation (as public authorities under s. 6) to respect human rights: in this situation, the common law obligations will be binding on private and public bodies alike, with the result that human rights standards can be imposed by one individual upon another individual. Where this occurs, it is said that the HRA has 'indirect horizontal effect' (between individuals), as well its 'vertical effects' (between individuals and public authorities).[43]

The situation may be illustrated by the case brought by the model Naomi Campbell against the Mirror Group in respect of articles and photographs that were published in the *Daily Mirror*. Campbell sued in tort, claiming breach of confidentiality.

Campbell v MGN Ltd
[2004] UKHL 22

Lord Nicholls of Birkenhead

17. The time has come to recognise that the values enshrined in articles 8 and 10 are now part of the cause of action for breach of confidence. [...] The values embodied in articles 8 and 10 are as much applicable in disputes between individuals or between an individual and a non-governmental body such as a newspaper as they are in disputes between individuals and a public authority.

18. [...] This approach has been adopted by the courts in several recent decisions, reported and unreported, where individuals have complained of press intrusion. A convenient summary of these cases is to be found in Gavin Phillipson's valuable article 'Transforming Breach of Confidence? Towards a Common Law Right of Privacy under the Human Rights Act' (2003) 66 MLR 726, 726–728.

The meaning of 'public authority'[44]

While of central importance, the term 'public authority' is not defined in the HRA. The Act tells us only that it includes the following.

---

[43] For discussion of the horizontal effect of the HRA, see, e.g. Murray Hunt, 'The "horizontal effect" of the Human Rights Act' [1998] Public Law 423; R. Buxton, 'The Human Rights Act and private law' (2000) 116 Law Quarterly Review 48; H.W.R. Wade 'Horizons of horizontality,' (2000) 116 Law Quarterly Review 217; A. Lester and D. Pannick, 'The impact of the Human Rights Act: The knight's move' (2000) 116 Law Quarterly Review 380; N. Bamforth, 'The true "horizontal effect" of the Human Rights Act 1998' (2001) 117 Law Quarterly Review 34; I. Hare, 'Verticality challenged: Private parties, privacy and the Human Rights Act' [2001] European Human Rights Law Review 526; J. Morgan 'Questioning the "true effect" of the Human Rights Act' (2002) 22 Legal Studies 259.

[44] See also amenability to judicial review, Chapter 16, section 3(d) The lawfulness of decisions or actions in relation to the exercise of a public function: amenability on p. 698.

Human Rights Act 1998, s. 6(3)

(3) [...]

    (a) a court or tribunal, and

    (b) any person certain of whose functions are functions of a public nature, but does not include either House of Parliament or a person exercising functions in connection with proceedings in Parliament.

(4) In subsection (3) "Parliament" does not include the House of Lords in its judicial capacity.

(5) In relation to a particular act, a person is not a public authority by virtue only of subsection (3)(b) if the nature of the act is private.

Note that neither of the Houses of Parliament are public authorities for the purpose of the Act. This means that they cannot be held to have acted unlawfully for participating in the enactment of legislation that breaches rights.

Core public authorities

Aston Cantlow and Wilmcote with Billesley Parochial Church Council v Wallbank and another
[2003] UKHL 37

Lord Nicholls of Birkenhead

[7] [...] the phrase 'a public authority' in section 6(1) is essentially a reference to a body whose nature is governmental in a broad sense of that expression. It is in respect of organisations of this nature that the government is answerable under the European Convention on Human Rights. Hence, under the Human Rights Act a body of this nature is required to act compatibly with Convention rights in everything it does. The most obvious examples are government departments, local authorities, the police and the armed forces. Behind the instinctive classification of these organisations as bodies whose nature is governmental lie factors such as the possession of special powers, democratic accountability, public funding in whole or in part, an obligation to act only in the public interest, and a statutory constitution: see the valuable article by Professor Dawn Oliver, 'The Frontiers of the State: Public Authorities and Public Functions under the Human Rights Act', [2000] PL 476.

Hybrid public authorities

The bodies to which Lord Nicholls refers in this extract are clearly public authorities—but s. 6(3)(b) of the HRA also includes within the expression 'public authority' persons or bodies that are private, but which perform functions of 'a public nature'. Such bodies are referred to as 'hybrid' public authorities.

    The problem is that the Act does not tell us what constitutes a 'function of a public nature'. This expression is capable of having very different meanings and there has been much debate.[45] On the one hand, are those such as Professor Dawn Oliver (one of whose articles was referred to by Lord Nicholls in this extract) who argue that the expression should be interpreted narrowly, so that the reach of the HRA is limited. From this perspective, public functions are those that are typically exercised by the state, rather than by private bodies, and which require special and unusual powers that individuals do not possess. For example, running prisons and keeping people in detention is normally a state activity, and is a function of a public nature. But private companies are permitted to run prisons and have special statutory powers for doing so. When a private company is running a prison, it is therefore performing a function of a public nature and must comply with the HRA.

Others have argued that the expression 'public function' should be interpreted more broadly, so that it extends beyond situations in which special powers are needed. They would argue that it is the nature and importance of the function that matters, rather than the institution or the power being used to perform it. For example, providing education or health care is sufficiently important to warrant being regarded as a 'public function', even though it can be performed by private schools or private care providers without using special governmental powers. If this approach were taken, the HRA would have a much broader reach, extending to many bodies in the private sector.

This has been more than simply an academic debate. It has been highly relevant in cases in which local authority functions, such as managing public housing stock or running care homes, have been privatized or contracted out to private companies or charities. In such situations, one of the main questions under the HRA has been whether tenants or care home residents have retained their right to rely on Convention rights after privatization has occurred. In a series of decisions culminating in *YL (by her litigation friend the Official Solicitor) v Birmingham City Council and ors*,[46] the courts have adopted the narrow approach advocated by Professor Oliver and rejected the argument that functions previously performed by local authorities under statutory powers should be considered to be 'functions of a public nature' when performed by a private body.

In *YL*, the claimant relied on the HRA when challenging a decision by a private care home, run as a business, to give notice to an elderly resident suffering from Alzheimer's disease terminating her placement in the home.[47] Interestingly, the government supported the arguments made by the claimant, because it thought that the HRA should be extended to private care homes providing residential care to those in need. The claim nonetheless failed. The majority in the House of Lords (Lord Bingham and Baroness Hale dissenting) held that a care home run as a business was not performing functions of a public nature when providing residential accommodation and care to people whose places were funded by local authorities (which had a statutory duty to arrange and subsidize placements). This was

[45] Dawn Oliver 'The frontiers of the state: Public authorities and public functions under the Human Rights Act' [2000] Public Law 476; Dawn Oliver, 'Functions of a public nature under the Human Rights Act' [2004] Public Law 328; cf. Murray Hunt 'Constitutionalism and the Contractualisation of Government', in Taggart (ed.) *The Province of Administrative Law* (1997, Oxford: Hart), ch. 2; P. Craig, 'Contracting out: The Human Rights Act and the scope of judicial review' (2002) 118 Law Quarterly Review 551; Joint Committee on Human Rights, *The Meaning of Public Authority Under the Human Rights Act*, Seventh Report, Session 2003–04, HL Paper 39, HC Paper 382; Maurice Sunkin, 'Pushing forward the frontiers of human rights protection: The meaning of public authority under the Human Rights Act' [2004] Public Law 643; Stephanie Palmer, 'Public functions and private services: A gap in human rights protection' (2008) 6 ICON 585.

[46] [2007] UKHL 27. In particular, see *Poplar Housing Association v Donoghue* [2001] EWCA Civ 595; *R (Heather) v Leonard Cheshire Foundation* [2002] EWCA Civ 366.

[47] See also the discussion of the pre-HRA decision in *R v Servite Houses and Wandsworth LBC, ex parte Goldsmith* (2000) 3 Community Care Law Reports 325 at p. 700.

essentially because the relationship between the care home and its residents was contractual in nature, and when the home was delivering a contractual obligation owed to residents, it was performing a private, rather than a public, function. The majority said that it would be wrong to characterize the situation as one in which local authorities had delegated their functions to the company running the home. Moreover, the provision of care and accommodation was not, they held, inherently a government function.

Many, including the Joint Committee on Human Rights and the government, were very disappointed by this restrictive decision.[48] Legislation was quickly introduced to change the law and make it clear that the provision of residential care to those who qualify as being in need under the provisions of the National Assistance Act 1948 is a public function, even when the provider is a private care home acting under contractual powers.[49] Section 145 of the Health and Social Care Act 2008 now provides as follows.

Health and Social Care Act 2008, s. 145

(1) A person who provides accommodation, together with nursing or personal care, in a care home for an individual under arrangements made with [that person] under [sections 21(1) (a) and 26 National Assistance Act 1948] is to be taken...to be exercising a function of a public nature [...].

[...]

The legislation is of limited scope and applies only to care homes and does not necessarily clarify the application of the HRA in situations in which other functions are performed by private sector bodies, and even within the care home sector, it does not necessarily mean that the HRA can be used in all proceedings brought by residents against private care homes. Certain disputes will still be considered contractual (and therefore private) in nature.[50]

The victim requirement

A claimant under s. 6(1) of the HRA must show that he or she is *'a victim of the unlawful act'*.[51] The Convention jurisprudence indicates that a person will only be a victim if he or she is, or will be, directly affected by the violation.[52] In *Dudgeon v UK*,[53] a gay man living in Northern Ireland was allowed to make a claim (which was successful) about the criminalization of homosexual conduct in private between consenting adults, even though he had not been prosecuted. In this case, he was clearly directly affected by the legislation. In some circumstances, family members of victims are also able to bring proceedings.[54]

---

[48] Joint Committee on Human Rights, Eighth Report, Session 2007–08, HL 46/HC 303.

[49] Joint Committee on Human Rights, 23rd Report, Session 2007–08, HL 126/HC 303, Appendix 6 and 7.

[50] *London and Quadrant Housing Trust v Weaver* [2009] EWCA Civ 587.

[51] Section 7(1)(b).

[52] In *Leigh v UK* (1984) DR74 (claimants not directly affected by the breach were not victims); cf. *Open Door and Dublin Well Women v Ireland (1992) 15 EHRR 244,* in which two abortion advice centres and two counsellors who offered advice abortion advice, and women who wished to seek the advice, were accepted as being victims in a challenge to an injunction under Art. 10.

[53] (1981) 4 EHRR 149.

[54] *Jordan v UK* (2003) 37 EHRR 2 (in which a father was able to bring a claim in respect of a son who had been shot by a police officer).

The 'victim' requirement, however, is narrower than the standing requirement for judicial review proceedings.[55] For example, public interest groups cannot claim to be victims (although they may be permitted to participate in proceedings before the ECtHR). Note also that public authorities cannot be victims and are not included among those able to take cases to the ECtHR (in Art. 34 ECHR). And one reason why the courts have taken a narrow approach when identifying hybrid public bodies has been concern that a private body will lose its ability to rely on the HRA if it is classified as a public authority.[56]

(g) REMEDIES UNDER THE HRA

When a court has decided that a public authority has, or is proposing to, act unlawfully under s. 6(1) of the HRA, it may grant *'such relief or remedy, or make such order within its powers as it considers just and appropriate'*.[57] The remedies can include any that could be obtained in judicial review,[58] or an order to pay damages or compensation.[59] As in judicial review, there is no right to obtain a remedy under the HRA. Damages may be awarded if the court considers this necessary to afford 'just satisfaction', having regard to all of the circumstances of the case and to the principles applied by the ECtHR.[60] The Court is generally considered to be cautious in its award of damages, especially in cases in which no financial losses are involved, such as in infringement of liberty cases.[61] In *Johnson v UK*,[62] the ECtHR awarded £10,000 in a case in which there had been a wrongful detention in a maximum security psychiatric hospital for three-and-a-half years. When the ECtHR upheld the claims following the *Belmarsh* case, it awarded substantially lower sums of between €3,900 and €1,700 to those who had been unlawfully detained, plus a total award of €60,000 for legal costs.[63]

3 HUMAN RIGHTS: DEFERENCE AND THE DISCRETIONARY AREA OF JUDGMENT

How intrusive should judges be when determining the legality of action taken by the executive? This is among the most important and most difficult of the issues to be determined by the judges in judicial review and human rights litigation. As we have seen elsewhere in the book, in the past,

---

[55] See Chapter 16, section 3(e), Standing to make a judicial review claim.

[56] See Lord Nicholls in *Aston Cantlow and Wilmcote with Billesley Parochial Church Council v Wallbank and anor* [2003] UKHL 37. See, Alexander Williams, 'A Fresh Approach on Hybrid Public Authorities under the Human Rights Act: Private Contractors, Rights-Stripping and "Chameleonic" Horizontal Effect' [2011] Public Law 139.

[57] Section 8(1).

[58] See Chapter 16, section 3(f) Remedies.

[59] Damages may also be awarded on tortuous principles where the situation gives raise to a tort as well as a breach of convention rights, see e.g. *Muuse v Secretary of State for the Home Department* [2010] EWCA Civ 453 where exemplary damages, of £27,000 plus £25,000 compensatory damages and £7,500 aggravated damages were awarded against the Home Office for acting unconstitutionally and arbitrarily in imprisoning Muuse. Contrast *R (on the application of Lumba) v Secretary of State for the Home Department* [2011] UKSC 12, where nominal damages of £1 were awarded.

[60] Commentators have pointed out that it is difficult to identify these principles: J. Wadham, H. Mountfield Q.C., E. Prochaska, and C. Brown (eds) *Blackstone's Guide to the Human Rights Act 1998*, 6th edn (2011, Oxford: OUP), p. 81, 4.57. See *R (Greenfield) v Secretary of State for the Home Department* [2005] UKHL 14.

[61] *Blackstone*, op. cit., p. 90.

[62] (1999) 27 EHRR 296.

[63] See p. 797.

courts tended to defer to the executive when called upon to review the legality of governmental action—especially when it had been taken on public interest or national security grounds.

Under the HRA, judges have a duty to determine whether governmental actions breach human rights. This duty substantially reduces the ability of judges to shy away from making decisions by relying on the argument that the executive or Parliament is better placed than courts to make decisions that interfere with rights. There are situations, however, in which judges must still decide whether discretion remains with public authorities. For example, in the *Belmarsh* case (see *A v Secretary of State for the Home Department* (the *Belmarsh* case) in the House of Lords, on p. 791), the House of Lords had to determine whether an order enabling the derogation from Art. 5 of the ECHR (the right to liberty) was lawful. As we shall see, a derogation order can be made if there is a '*public emergency that threatens the life of the nation*'. If a derogation order is made, the right to liberty can be infringed to an extent that is 'strictly required' by the situation. Who then decides whether there is a threat to the nation and whether infringements of Art. 5 are strictly required? Are these matters to be left to the government, or are they for the courts? If the courts are involved, how much weight should be attached to the views of government or (if legislation is involved) of Parliament?

These questions have caused much discussion among the judges and among academic commentators.[64] For the most part, the debate has been between those (such as Lord Hoffmann) who have argued that constitutional law requires courts to defer to government or Parliament in relation to matters such as national security, and those (such as Lord Steyn) who say that there is no such legal obligation. They say that whether the courts 'defer' to the executive is a matter of judicial discretion that will depend on the circumstances. There is also a less important terminological discussion about whether the term 'deference' should be used in this context.

Secretary of State for the Home Department v Rehman
[2001] UKHL 47

Lord Hoffmann

[50] [...] the question of whether something is "in the interests" of national security is not a question of law. It is a matter of judgment and policy. Under the constitution of the United Kingdom and most other countries, decisions as to whether something is or is not in the interests of national security are not a matter for judicial decision. They are entrusted to the executive.

R (ProLife Alliance) v BBC
[2003] UKHL 23

Lord Hoffmann

[75] My Lords, although the word 'deference' is now very popular in describing the relationship between the judicial and the other branches of government, I do not think that its

---

[64] As well as the work by Professor Jowell that we refer to, other examples of work on this issue includes: Richard Clayton QC, 'Judicial deference and democratic dialogue: The legitimacy of judicial intervention under the Human Rights Act 1998' [2004] Public Law 33; Aileen Kavanagh, 'Judging the judges under the Human Rights Act: Deference, disillusionment and the "war on terror"' [2009] Public Law 287; Aileeen Kavanagh, 'Defending deference in public law and constitutional theory', [2010] LQR 222; Alison L. Young, 'Deference, dialogue and the search for legitimacy' [2010] O.J.L.S. 815; . TRS Allan, 'Judicial deference and judicial review: legal doctrine and legal theory', [2011] LQR 96; Paul Daly, 'Deference on Questions of Law' (2011) MLR 694.

overtones of servility, or perhaps gracious concession, are appropriate to describe what is happening. In a society based upon the rule of law and the separation of powers, it is necessary to decide which branch of government has in any particular instance the decision-making power and what the legal limits of that power are. That is a question of law and must therefore be decided by the courts.

[76] This means that the courts themselves often have to decide the limits of their own decision-making power. That is inevitable. But it does not mean that their allocation of decision-making power to the other branches of government is a matter of courtesy or deference. The principles upon which decision-making powers are allocated are principles of law. The courts are the independent branch of government and the legislature and executive are, directly and indirectly respectively, the elected branches of government. Independence makes the courts more suited to deciding some kinds of questions and being elected makes the legislature or executive more suited to deciding others The allocation of these decision-making responsibilities is based upon recognised principles. The principle that the independence of the courts is necessary for a proper decision of disputed legal rights or claims of violation of human rights is a legal principle. It is reflected in Art.6 of the Convention. On the other hand, the principle that majority approval is necessary for a proper decision on policy or allocation of resources is also a legal principle. Likewise, when a court decides that a decision is within the proper competence of the legislature or executive, it is not showing deference. It is deciding the law.

Professor Jowell QC, 'Judicial deference, servility, civility or institutional capacity?' [2003] Public Law 592, 599[65]

In so far as the courts [...] concede competence to another branch of government, it seems to me that such a concession is not a matter of law, nor based upon any legal principle as Lord Hoffmann contends. Lord Hoffmann is right that it is for the courts to decide the scope of rights, but there is no magic legal or other formula to identify the 'discretionary area of judgment' available to the reviewed body. In deciding whether matters such as national security, or public interest, or morals should be permitted to prevail over a right, the courts must consider not only the rational exercise of discretion by the reviewed body but also the imperatives of a rights-based democracy. In the course of some of the steps in the process of this assessment the courts may properly acknowledge their own institutional limitations. In doing so, however, they should guard against a presumption that matters of public interest are outside their competence and be ever aware that they are now the ultimate arbiters (although not ultimate guarantors) of the necessary qualities of a democracy in which the popular will is no longer always expected to prevail.

[65] See also Professor Jowell QC, 'Judicial Deference and Human Rights: A Question of Competence', in P.P. Craig and R. Rawlings (eds) *Laws and Administration in Europe* (2003, Oxford: OUP); Richard Clayton QC, 'Judicial deference and democratic dialogue: The legitimacy of judicial intervention under the Human Rights Act 1998' [2004] Public Law 33; Aileen Kavanagh, 'Judging the judges under the Human Rights Act: Deference, disillusionment and the "war on terror"' [2009] Public Law 287.

Lord Steyn, 'Deference: A tangled story' [2005] Public Law 346–59 (footnotes omitted)

[...] even in the Law Lords Corridor, there are opposing philosophies on the subject of deference. The matter is of such importance that it deserves a public airing. Lord Hoffmann and I have different views on the subject [...] [He refers to Lord Hoffmann's comments in *Rehman* and *ProLife Alliance*.] [...] These observations of Lord Hoffmann were clearly carefully considered and are important. I have enormous respect for the views of Lord Hoffmann. But I disagree with him on this subject.

Let me now start with the 1998 Act. By our bill of rights, Parliament has entrusted to the courts the duty to stand guard over the irreducible and universal human rights contained in the ECHR. It is therefore the duty of the courts to define the contours of our rights-based democracy. Let me illustrate the point by reference to the cluster of Convention rights contained in Art.8 (Right to respect for private life), Art.9 (Freedom of thought, conscience and religion), Art.10 (Freedom of expression) and Art.11 (Freedom of assembly and association). The articles contain many concepts reflecting matters of general and public interest upon which the legislative and executive branches of government would have a view. Examples are "national security" (under Arts 8, 10, 11), "public safety" (under Arts 8, 9, 10, 11), "the economic wellbeing of the country" (under Art.8), "public order" (under Art.9), "the protection of health or morals" (under Arts 8, 9, 10, 11), or "the prevention of disorder or crime" (under Arts 8, 10, 11). These are all qualified escape routes from the application of Convention rights. In all these cases, however, the structure of the ECHR makes clear that an interference with the relevant Convention right is only justifiable if it is in accordance with the law and necessary in a democratic society, criteria upon which the view of the executive cannot possibly be conclusive. Indeed it is the very ethos of the ECHR that the courts will be the arbiters of these criteria.

In one sense all these concepts involve matters of policy under Lord Hoffmann's formulation in *ProLife Alliance*. But it cannot be right to say that these are issues which constitutional principle withdraws from decision by the courts. While a national court may have to accord some appropriate deference to the executive (for example, a national security issue based on intelligence assessments) it must also address the questions: Does the interference serve a legitimate objective? Is it necessary in a democratic society? [...]

So far I have examined the reasoning of Lord Hoffmann mainly in the context of national security, public safety and related concepts. I have done so first because the occasion for deference will perhaps most frequently and credibly arise in this area. But Lord Hoffmann's reasoning strikes wider. He states that "the principle that majority approval is necessary for a proper decision on policy or allocation of resources is also *a legal* principle". On this reasoning such decisions are beyond the competence of the courts. Apart from Lord Hoffmann's observation I am not aware of any authority for this view. [...] The sweep of Lord Hoffmann's legal principle is massive. Most legislation is passed to advance a policy. And frequently it involves in one way or another the allocation of resources. I am, of course, not saying that policy issues are not relevant, and that costs must be ignored. These factors will often be relevant in searching for the best interpretation. What I am saying is that there cannot be a legal principle requiring the court to desist from making a judgment on the issues in such cases. In interpreting legislation the courts must simply, with the aid of all relevant internal and external sources, try to find the contextual meaning of a given text. There is in my view no justification for a court to adopt an *a priori* view in favour of economic conservatism. [He cites M. Chamberlain, 'Democracy and deference in resource allocation cases: A riposte to Lord Hoffmann' [2003] JR 12.]

In common law adjudication it is an everyday occurrence for courts to consider, together with principled arguments, the balance sheet of policy advantages and disadvantages. It would be a matter of public disquiet if the courts did not do so. Of course, in striking the balance the courts may arrive at a result unacceptable to Parliament. In such cases Parliament can act with great speed to reverse the effect of a decision. It has done so in the past. That is in the spirit of our constitution, and is wholly in accord with the democratic ideal. But there is no need to create a legal principle requiring the courts to abstain from ruling on policy matters or allocation of resource issues. [...]

[Lord Steyn quotes the passage from Professor Jowell QC extracted above, which he commends as encapsulating 'a balanced approach', and continues.]

[...] I return to the reasoning of Lord Hoffmann in *Rehman*. His first reason for deferring was that the executive has special expertise in these matters. In the context of national security issues that seems to me uncontroversial. Lord Hoffmann's second reason was that such decisions must be made by persons whom the public have elected, and whom they can remove. [...] If this reasoning were to be extended to Convention rights, courts would be required automatically to defer, on constitutional grounds, on any occasion on which a qualified Convention right was claimed to be defeated by a particular public interest. It would diminish the role of courts under the ECHR. If such a view were generally accepted, it would seriously emasculate the ECHR, the 1998 Act and our bill of rights.

QUESTION

Why might it matter whether 'deference' is an issue of law or judicial discretion?

---

4 CASE STUDY: THE *DENBIGH HIGH SCHOOL* CASE—SCHOOL UNIFORMS AND THE RIGHT TO MANIFEST ONE'S RELIGION

Shabina Begum was nearly 14 years old and had been a pupil at the Denbigh High School in Luton for two years. The school is a mixed-sex maintained secondary school for children aged between 11 and 16 years, and is open to people of all faiths, or no faith. At the time, four of six parent governors were Muslim, the chairman of the Luton Council of Mosques was a community governor, and three of the local education authority governors were Muslim. The head teacher was from a Bengali Muslim family and had grown up in India. It had a diverse intake, with twenty-one different ethnic groups and ten religious groupings represented. Approximately 79 per cent of its pupils were Muslim.

On 3 September 2002, the first day of the new school year, Shabina Begum went to school with her older brother and another man. She was wearing a jilbab,[66] which she wanted to wear to school. In her previous years at school, she had, in accordance with the school's uniform policy, worn a shalwar kameeze.[67] Given her age, Shabina now believed that her religion dictated that she should wear a jilbab in mixed company.

---

[66] A long loose-fitting garment that includes a hijab, which covers the head and much of the face.

[67] A sleeveless, smock-like dress with a square neckline revealing the wearer's collar and tie, with loose trousers, tapering at the ankles, worn with a long-sleeved white shirt and pullover, depending on the weather.

They asked to speak to the head teacher, but she was not available, and instead they spoke to the assistant head, Mr Moore. Mr Moore said that the school's policy on school uniforms did not permit pupils to wear a jilbab. In the words of one of the Law Lords, who was eventually to deal with the case, *'the men told Mr Moore at length and in forceful terms that Shabina was entitled under human rights law to come to school wearing a jilbab and that unless she was admitted they would sue the school'.*[68] Mr Moore responded by telling Shabina to go home and get changed. She, her older brother, and the other man left.

On the same day, the head teacher, who had been informed of the incident, wrote to Shabina's mother and brother (with whom she lived), setting out an account of the incident. The head teacher said that the uniform policy had been agreed with the governing body and the local education authority, and was, in her view, reasonable in taking into account the cultural and religious concerns of the community and the school population. But the matter did not end there: neither side was prepared to alter its position.

Shabina claimed that she had been excluded from the school and did not attend during that academic year. In the meantime, as the dispute continued, the school and the local education authority obtained independent advice on whether the school's uniform policy offended Islamic dress code. They were advised that it did not. Shabina also obtained an expert opinion that the jilbab was the accepted dress for mature Muslim women.

Shabina was urged to return to the school, or to seek a place at one of the other schools in the area. One of these was a single-sex girls' school, in which the jilbab would not have been necessary; the other two schools would have permitted the jilbab. In October 2003 (after the beginning of the next school year), she applied to the single-sex school, but was told that, by this date, it did not have a place available. Eventually, she went to another school that allowed her to wear the jilbab.

(a) THE CLAIM

On 13 February 2004, Shabina Begum—advised by the Children's Legal Centre, based at the University of Essex—issued a claim for judicial review arguing that the decisions to prevent her wearing the jilbab and to exclude her until she was prepared to dress in accordance with school's uniform policy were contrary to her human rights, and therefore unlawful under s. 6 of the HRA.

(b) THE ISSUES TO BE CONSIDERED

Pausing here, let us briefly consider some of the obstacles that Shabina and her lawyers confronted on these facts. The main preliminary issue was to identify legal arguments that could be made and whether the HRA applied to the situation. In order to answer this question, the lawyers had to look in particular at ss 6 and 7 of the Act. As we have seen, it is unlawful for 'a public authority' to act incompatibly with a Convention right. In Shabina's case, it is clear that Denbigh High School, its governors, and the local education authority were public authorities. Had the school been a private school, the situation might have been more complex, because the school may then have been able to argue that its uniform policy was a matter of contract between it and those who paid fees, and therefore not within the scope of the HRA.[69]

---

[68] Lord Hoffmann, at [46].
[69] See section 3(f), discussion of hybrid public bodies on p. 766.

Likewise, in this case, it is clear that Shabina was able to claim to be a victim under s. 7 of the HRA. By contrast, had the case been brought by her brother or her friend, for example, it is unlikely that they would satisfy this requirement on these facts.[70]

The lawyers next had to identify the Convention rights that were engaged. From the list of rights set out in Sch. 1 to the HRA 1998, the lawyers identified two that appeared directly relevant to Shabina. The first was Art. 9 on freedom of thought, conscience, and religion, and the second was the right to an education contained in Art. 2 of the First Protocol to the ECHR. We shall concentrate on Shabina's claim under Art. 9.

Article 9 Freedom of thought, conscience, and religion

(1) Everyone has the right to freedom of thought, conscience and religion; this right includes freedom to change his religion or belief and [...] freedom, either alone or in community with others and in public or private, to manifest his religion or belief, in worship, teaching, practice and observance.

(2) Freedom to manifest one's religion or beliefs shall be subject only to such limitations as are prescribed by law and are necessary in a democratic society in the interests of public safety, for the protection of public order, health or morals, or for the protection of the rights and freedoms of others.

In order to establish a breach of Art. 9, the lawyers had to look very carefully at its wording. Because of the duty in s. 2 of the HRA 'to take account of' the jurisprudence developed by the ECtHR and the now-abolished European Commission of Human Rights, they also had to look carefully at this case law. They would have been aware of the following statement by the ECtHR stressing the importance of the rights contained in Art. 9 (but pointing out that the freedom to manifest one's religion, alone among the freedoms protected by Art. 9(1), may be limited on the grounds set out in Art. 9(2)).

Kokkinakis v Greece
ECtHR, 25 May 1993, Series A No 160-A, p. 17

31. As enshrined in Article 9, freedom of thought, conscience and religion is one of the foundations of a 'democratic society' within the meaning of the Convention. It is, in its religious dimension, one of the most vital elements that go to make up the identity of believers and their conception of life, but it is also a precious asset for atheists, agnostics, sceptics and the unconcerned. The pluralism indissociable from a democratic society, which has been dearly won over the centuries, depends on it.

While religious freedom is primarily a matter of individual conscience, it also implies, inter alia, freedom to 'manifest [one's] religion'. Bearing witness in words and deeds is bound up with the existence of religious convictions.

[...]

33. The fundamental nature of the rights guaranteed in Article 9 para 1 [...] is also reflected in the wording of the paragraph providing for limitations on them. Unlike the second paragraphs of Articles 8, 10 and 11 [...] which cover all the rights mentioned in the first paragraphs of

---

[70] *Leigh v UK* (1984) DR74 (claimants not directly affected by the breach were not victims).

> those Articles, that of Article 9 refers only to 'freedom to manifest one's religion or belief'. In so doing, it recognises that in democratic societies, in which several religions co-exist within one and the same population, it may be necessary to place restrictions on this freedom in order to reconcile the interests of the various groups and ensure that everyone's beliefs are respected.

They would also have been aware that the decision of the European Commission on Human Rights in *Karaduman v Turkey*[71] (holding that a Turkish university could refuse to allow women to wear headscarves when having their graduation certificate photographs taken, in order to prevent people passing themselves off as graduates) was being challenged in the ECtHR, and that the decision was about to be given.[72]

QUESTIONS

Put yourself in the position of the lawyers and look again at Art. 9 with the following questions in mind.

(a) What freedoms are protected by Art. 9(1)?

(b) Which of these freedoms are most relevant to Shabina's claim?

(c) Which of these freedoms can be limited under Art. 9(2)?

(d) In what circumstances may limitations be imposed and do any of these appear relevant in Shabina's case?

Shabina's lawyers took the view that Shabina's strongest claim under Art. 9 would be in relation to her freedom to manifest her religion: the essence of her claim would be that, by stopping her from wearing the jilbad, the school had prevented her from manifesting her religion.

QUESTION

Were Shabina also to have argued that the school had limited her freedom of religion (rather than the freedom to manifest her religion), what obstacle(s) would she have faced?

Anticipating the school's response

The lawyers will have recognized that establishing a breach of Art. 9 was unlikely to be straightforward and they will have tried to anticipate the arguments that were likely to be used by the school. Two main arguments were likely to have been anticipated.

(a) The school was likely to argue that its uniform policy did not prevent Shabina from manifesting her religion; it only prevented her from wearing a jilbab at Denbigh High School. She could have chosen to go to one of the other schools in the area at which she would have been free to manifest her religion. In other words, it was her choice of

---

[71] (1993) 74 DR 93.

[72] In fact, the decision of the ECtHR was delivered on 29 June 2004, upholding the legality of the ban on headscarves. This decision was confirmed by the Grand Chamber on 18 November 2005: *Leyla Sahin v Turkey*, Application No. 44774/98. The ban was justified in the interests of protecting the principle of secularism in Turkish society.

school that led to her being unable to manifest her religion in this situation, and not the school's policy or its decision to apply the policy in her case.

(b) As we have seen, the freedom to manifest one's religion in Art. 9(1) is a qualified right that can be limited in the circumstances set out in Art. 9(2). The school was likely to argue that, even if it had infringed Art. 9(1), the infringement was justified under Art. 9(2). This was to become a central issue in the case and led to a serious difference between the Court of Appeal and the House of Lords.

Suppose that the HRA had not been enacted or was not applicable

Before moving on to see how the case fared in the courts, it is worth briefly considering how the case might have been presented had the HRA not been applicable or enacted. In this situation, Shabina could not rely directly on Art. 9 and the claim would have been much weaker. Shabina could still challenge the school's decision, but she would have had to rely on general principles of judicial review. She could, for example, have argued that the school had not taken proper account of her rights under Art. 9, or that its policy had been applied in an overly rigid fashion without giving sufficient attention to her particular situation.[73] It is unlikely that she could have successfully argued that the school's decision was *Wednesbury* unreasonable and irrational.[74]

Irrationality aside, these traditional arguments would have focused on the school's process of decision-making, but they would not have directly confronted the substance of Shabina Begum's real complaint—that is, that her human rights had been violated because she had been prevented from doing what her religious beliefs demanded.

(c) THE ADMINISTRATIVE COURT

Shabina was unsuccessful in the Administrative Court.[75] Bennett J accepted that her claim engaged rights under Art. 9, but there was, he said, no breach of Art. 9(1): '*Although her refusal* [to respect the school uniform policy] *was motivated by religious beliefs, she was excluded for her refusal to abide by the school uniform policy rather than her religious belief as such.*'[76]

Although not necessary, given his decision, Bennett J went on to consider whether, had there been a breach of Art. 9(1), this would have been justified under Art. 9(2).

R (Begum) v The Headteacher and Governors of Denbigh High School
[2004] EWHC 1389 (Admin)

Bennett J

[91] In my judgment the school uniform policy and its enforcement has, and continues to have, a legitimate aim and is proportionate. The legitimate aim was the proper running of a multi-cultural, multi-faith, secular school. The limitation was also proportionate to the legitimate aim pursued. The limitation was specifically devised with the advice of the Muslim

---

73 See Chapter 16, section 4(c), Fettering discretion: treating policies as binding.
74 See Chapter 16, section 4(e), Irrationality' or '*Wednesbury* unreasonableness'.
75 *R (Begum) v The Headteacher and Governors of Denbigh High School* [2004] EWHC 1389 (Admin).
76 At [74].

community. Although it appears that there is a body of opinion within the Muslim faith that only the jilbab meets the requirements of its dress code, there is also a body of opinion that the shalwar kameeze does as well. In my judgment, the adoption of the shalwar kameeze by the Defendant as the school uniform for Muslim (and other faiths) female pupils was and continues to be a reasoned, balanced, proportionate policy.

Shabina Begum and her lawyers decided to appeal against this judgment. In the Court of Appeal, her legal team was led by Cherie Booth QC.

(d) THE COURT OF APPEAL

The Court of Appeal (Brooke, Mummery, and Scott Baker LLJ) was unanimous in disagreeing with Bennett J and allowed Shabina's appeal.[77] It held that Shabina had been excluded from the school because she was not willing to comply with the school's uniform policy and that the policy had infringed her freedom to manifest her religion under Art. 9(1). It also held that the infringement of her right had not been justified under Art. 9(2). The lead judgment was delivered by Brooke LJ and the core of his reasoning on Art. 9 was as follows.

Begum v Denbigh High School
[2005] EWCA Civ 199

Brooke LJ

50. [...] SB's freedom to manifest her religion or beliefs may only be subject to limitations that are prescribed by law and are necessary in a democratic society in the interests of public safety, for the protection of public morals, or for the protection of the rights and freedoms of others. There was no suggestion that the protection of public morals had any relevance, and a justification on health and safety grounds was dismissed by the judge and not resurrected on the appeal once evidence had showed that other schools (including the local school which the claimant now attends) had been able to accommodate girls wearing the jilbab without any serious concern being raised on that ground.

[...]

74. The position of the School is already distinctive in the sense that despite its policy of inclusiveness it permits girls to wear a headscarf which is likely to identify them as Muslim. The central issue is therefore the more subtle one of whether, given that Muslim girls can already be identified in this way, it is necessary in a democratic society to place a particular restriction on those Muslim girls at this school who sincerely believe that when they arrive at the age of puberty they should cover themselves more comprehensively than is permitted by the school uniform policy.

75. The decision-making structure should therefore go along the following lines:

1) Has the claimant established that she has a relevant Convention right which qualifies for protection under Article 9(1)?

2) Subject to any justification that is established under Article 9(2), has that Convention right been violated?

---

[77] [2005] EWCA Civ 199.

3) Was the interference with her Convention right prescribed by law in the Convention sense of that expression?

4) Did the interference have a legitimate aim?

5) What are the considerations that need to be balanced against each other when determining whether the interference was necessary in a democratic society for the purpose of achieving that aim?

6) Was the interference justified under Article 9(2)?

76. The School did not approach the matter in this way at all. Nobody who considered the issues on its behalf started from the premise that the claimant had a right which is recognised by English law, and that the onus lay on the School to justify its interference with that right. Instead, it started from the premise that its uniform policy was there to be obeyed: if the claimant did not like it, she could go to a different school.

[...]

78. In my judgment [...] because it approached the issues in this case from an entirely wrong direction and did not attribute to the claimant's beliefs the weight they deserved, the School is not entitled to resist the declarations she seeks [...]

Not surprisingly, the decision received widespread attention in the media and not all views were positive. In the *Daily Telegraph*, for example, a comment on the case was headed, 'The school uniform case was a victory for bigots'.[78]

But criticism of the decision was not limited to the press coverage: there was also significant academic criticism of the Court of Appeal's approach. Thomas Poole, for example, wrote an article in *Public Law* that was extremely critical of the way in which the Court of Appeal had applied the proportionality test to the Art. 9(2) question.[79] He argued that, in finding that the school had approached Shabina's case '*from an entirely wrong direction*', the Court of Appeal had focused on the procedure adopted by the school rather than on the substance of its decision. In other words, the Court of Appeal had approached the case using the traditional judicial review approach, rather than the approach required by the HRA. He said that the Court of Appeal implied that the way in which authorities decide things is more important than the impact that decisions have on people's rights—that is, that procedure is more important than substance.

Thomas Poole, 'Of headscarves and heresies: *The Denbigh High School* case and public authority decision-making under the Human Rights Act' [2005] Public Law 685, 689–91 (footnotes omitted)

There are problems [...] with the approach taken by the Court of Appeal in the *Denbigh High School* case. First and foremost, it rests on a basic mistake. Proportionality is a [test] to be applied by the court when reviewing decisions of public authorities after they have been made [...]. It is not a test which ought to mean that public authorities should themselves

---

[78] *Daily Telegraph*, 6 March 2005.

[79] Also T. Linden and T. Hetherington, 'Schools and human rights: *Denbigh High School*' [2005] Education Law Journal 229.

adopt a proportionality approach to the structuring of their decision-making [as they are being made].

There is nothing in the Human Rights Act, the European Convention or Convention jurisprudence which would seem to require public authorities to act in this way. [...] The wording of [s. 6] indicates that the obligations public authorities are required to fulfil relate to the substance of their policies, decisions and actions. As Ian Leigh observed [I. Leigh, 'Taking rights proportionately: Judicial review, the Human Rights Act and Strasbourg' [2002] Public Law 265, 283] the primary question asked by s.6 is *result-orientated—were* the claimant's rights violated by the public authority?—and, if the answer to that question is affirmative, "the *process* by which the public authority came to violate his or her Convention rights is irrelevant". [...]

QUESTION

Do you agree with this criticism of the Court of Appeal's approach, given what Brooke LJ said about the importance of protecting Shabina's rights under Art. 9?

The matter, however, did not end with the Court of Appeal. The school appealed to the House of Lords. At this stage, the Secretary of State for Education and Skills also appeared as an intervener, arguing that the approach adopted by the Court of Appeal revealed '*a fundamental misunderstanding of the 1998 Act*'.

(e) THE HOUSE OF LORDS

The House of Lords allowed the appeal and reinstated the decision of Bennett J. All five Law Lords agreed with this result. There were, however, significant differences between them. Lords Bingham, Hoffmann, and Scott agreed with Bennett J that Shabina Begum's freedom to manifest her religion had not been limited by the school, and that even if it had been, the limitation would have been proportionate and justified under Art. 9(2). Lord Nicholls and Baroness Hale were inclined to the view that Shabina Begum's freedom to manifest her religion had been interfered with, but agreed that the interference was justified.

R (on the application of Begum) v Head Teacher and Governors of Denbigh High School
[2006] UKHL 15

Lord Bingham of Cornhill

[The] case concerns a particular pupil and a particular school in a particular place at a particular time. It must be resolved on facts which are now, for purposes of the appeal, agreed. The House is not, and could not be, invited to rule whether Islamic dress, or any feature of Islamic dress, should or should not be permitted in the schools of this country. That would be a most inappropriate question for the House in its judicial capacity and it is not one which I shall seek to address.

[He reiterated the fundamental importance of Art. 9 in a pluralistic, multicultural society and continued.]

[21] It is common ground in these proceedings that [...] the respondent sincerely held the religious belief which she professed to hold. [...] it is accepted, obviously rightly, that art 9(1) is engaged or applicable. That, in itself, makes this a significant case, since any sincere religious belief must command respect, particularly when derived from an ancient and respected religion. The main questions for consideration are, accordingly, whether the respondent's freedom to manifest her belief by her dress was subject to limitation (or, as it has more often been called, interference) within the meaning of art 9(2) and, if so, whether such limitation or interference was justified under that provision.

Interference

[...]

[23] The Strasbourg institutions have not been at all ready to find an interference with the right to manifest religious belief in practice or observance where a person has voluntarily accepted an employment or role which does not accommodate that practice or observance and there are other means open to the person to practise or observe his or her religion without undue hardship or inconvenience.

[...]

[25] In the present case the respondent's family chose for her a school outside their own catchment area. It was a school which went to unusual lengths to inform parents of its uniform policy. The shalwar kameeze, and not the jilbab, was worn by the respondent's elder sister throughout her time at the school and by the respondent for her first two years without objection. It was, of course, open to the respondent, as she grew older, to modify her beliefs, but she did so against a background of free and informed consent by her and her family. It is also clear that there were three schools in the area at which the wearing of the jilbab was permitted. The respondent's application for admission to one of these was unsuccessful because the school was full and it was asserted in argument that the other two were more distant. There is, however, no evidence to show that there was any real difficulty in her attending one or other of these schools, as she has in fact done and could no doubt have done sooner had she chosen. On the facts here, and endeavouring to apply the Strasbourg jurisprudence in a reasonable way, I am of opinion that in this case [...] there was no interference with the respondent's right to manifest her belief in practice or observance. I appreciate, however, that my noble and learned friends Lord Nicholls and Lady Hale of Richmond incline to a different opinion. It follows that this is a debatable question, which gives the issue of justification under art 9(2) particular significance.

Justification

[26] To be justified under art 9(2) a limitation or interference must be (a) prescribed by law and (b) necessary in a democratic society for a permissible purpose, that is, it must be directed to a legitimate purpose and must be proportionate in scope and effect. It was faintly argued for the respondent that the school's uniform policy was not prescribed by law, but both the judge [...] and the Court of Appeal [...] held otherwise, and rightly so. The school authorities had statutory authority to lay down rules on uniform and those rules were very clearly communicated to those affected by them. It was not suggested that the rules were not made for the legitimate purpose of protecting the rights and freedoms of others. So the issue is whether the rules and the school's insistence on them were in all the circumstances proportionate. This raises an important procedural question on the court's approach to proportionality and, depending on the answer to that, a question of substance.

[27] In para [75] of his leading judgment in the Court of Appeal, Brooke LJ set out a series of questions to be asked and answered by a decision-maker resolving an issue raised under art 9. He observed (at [76]) that the school did not approach the matter in that way at all. Since, therefore, the school had approached the issues from an entirely wrong direction [...]

[29] I am persuaded that the Court of Appeal's approach to this procedural question was mistaken for three main reasons. First, the purpose of the 1998 Act was not to enlarge the rights or remedies of those in the United Kingdom whose Convention rights have been violated but to enable those rights and remedies to be asserted and enforced by the domestic courts of this country and not only by recourse to Strasbourg. This is clearly established by authorities [...] But the focus at Strasbourg is not, and has never been, on whether a challenged decision or action is the product of a defective decision-making process, but on whether, in the case under consideration, the applicant's Convention rights have been violated. [...] the House has been referred to no case in which the Strasbourg court has found a violation of Convention right on the strength of failure by a national authority to follow the sort of reasoning process laid down by the Court of Appeal. [...]

[30] Secondly, it is clear that the court's approach to an issue of proportionality under the Convention must go beyond that traditionally adopted to judicial review in a domestic setting. The inadequacy of that approach was exposed in *Smith v UK* (1999) 29 EHRR 493 at 543 (para 138) and the new approach required under the 1998 Act was described by Lord Steyn in *R v Secretary of State for the Home Dept, ex p Daly* [2001] UKHL 26 [...] in terms which have never to my knowledge been questioned. There is no shift to a merits review, but the intensity of review is greater than was previously appropriate and greater even than the heightened scrutiny test adopted by the Court of Appeal in *R v Ministry of Defence, ex p Smith* [1995] 4 LRC 300 at 307. The domestic court must now make a value judgment, an evaluation, by reference to the circumstances prevailing at the relevant time [...] Proportionality must be judged objectively by the court (see *R (on the application of Williamson) v Secretary of State for Education and Employment* [2005] 5 LRC 670 at [51]). As Davies observed, [in 'Banning the Jilbab: Reflections on Restricting Religious Clothing in the Light of the Court of Appeal in *SB v Denbigh High School*' (2005) 1.3 European Constitutional Law Review 511), 'The retreat to procedure is of course a way of avoiding difficult questions'. But it is, in my view, clear that the court must confront these questions, however difficult. The school's action cannot properly be condemned as disproportionate, with an acknowledgement that on reconsideration the same action could very well be maintained and properly so.

[31] Thirdly, and as argued by Poole [...] I consider that the Court of Appeal's approach would introduce 'a new formalism' and be 'a recipe for judicialisation on an unprecedented scale'. The Court of Appeal's decision-making prescription would be admirable guidance to a lower court or legal tribunal, but cannot be required of a head teacher and governors, even with a solicitor to help them. If, in such a case, it appears that such a body has conscientiously paid attention to all human rights considerations, no doubt a challenger's task will be the harder. But what matters in any case is the practical outcome, not the quality of the decision-making process that led to it.

[...]

[34] On the agreed facts, the school was, in my opinion, fully justified in acting as it did. It had taken immense pains to devise a uniform policy which respected Muslim beliefs but did so in an inclusive, unthreatening and uncompetitive way. The rules laid down were as far from being mindless as uniform rules could ever be. The school had enjoyed a period of harmony and success to which the uniform policy was thought to contribute. On further inquiry it still appeared that the rules were acceptable to mainstream Muslim opinion. It was feared that acceding to

the respondent's request would or might have significant adverse repercussions. It would, in my opinion, be irresponsible of any court, lacking the experience, background and detailed knowledge of the head teacher, staff and governors, to overrule their judgment on a matter as sensitive as this. The power of decision has been given to them for the compelling reason that they are best placed to exercise it and I see no reason to disturb their decision. [...]

Lord Hoffmann

[68] Quite apart from the fact that, in my opinion, the Court of Appeal would have failed the examination for giving the wrong answer to [the question whether the Art 9 (1) right has been violated] the whole approach seems to me a mistaken construction of art 9. In domestic judicial review the court is usually concerned with whether the decision-maker reached his decision in the right way rather than whether he got what the court might think to be the right answer. But art 9 is concerned with substance, not procedure. It confers no right to have a decision made in any particular way. What matters is the result: was the right to manifest a religious belief restricted in a way which is not justified under art 9(2)? The fact that the decision-maker is allowed an area of judgment in imposing requirements which may have the effect of restricting the right does not entitle a court to say that a justifiable and proportionate restriction should be struck down because the decision-maker did not approach the question in the structured way in which a judge might have done. Head teachers and governors cannot be expected to make such decisions with textbooks on human rights law at their elbows. The most that can be said is that the way in which the school approached the problem may help to persuade a judge that its answer fell within the area of judgment accorded to it by the law.

(f) THE IMPACT OF THE DECISION

As with the earlier court decisions, the decision of the House of Lords attracted massive public attention, and was both widely applauded and widely criticized across the media. Many schools will have been relieved to know that the courts had upheld the legality of the uniform policy and the way in which it had been applied.

Aspects of their Lordships' decision have proved controversial. One of these is Lord Bingham's observation that courts should not use the HRA to expand on the scope of human rights protection—in other words, that the Act imposes a ceiling to human rights protection rather than a floor. It is somewhat ironic that the House of Lords reversed a unanimous decision of the Court of Appeal upholding human rights protection, while criticizing that Court for being overly concerned with process, The most important criticisms of the judgment, however, have come from those who believe that the outcome-based approach adopted by the House of Lords is misconceived and likely to have negative effects. David Mead, for instance, points to three main disadvantages with this approach.

David Mead, 'Outcomes Aren't all: Defending Process-Based Review of Public Authority Decisions under the Human Rights Act' [2012] Public Law 61, 76-78 (footnotes omitted)

First, *Denbigh* effects a shift towards court-based enforcement and judicial protection, away from protection by those best placed to do so ... those on whom discretionary political power is conferred. [...] An internalised, prospective process-driven model of human rights protection creates – or at least has the potential to create – human rights equally for all. That is its beauty. The judicial enforcement of fair procedures, where decision-makers know they must ask the right questions in the right order for the right reasons should mean that your rights are as well protected as mine: protection is systemic and institutionalised. In contrast, a system in which outcomes are all mean that aggrieved citizens must pursue individualised one-off legal remedies to protect their rights, with the costs of enforcement and protection shifted onto them. [...]

Secondly, the House of Lords has removed any incentive for decision makers to reach decisions by a process that is Convention-sensitive. Why not just toss a coin? For a decision to survive scrutiny, a decision-maker needs only to demonstrate that the decision is what a panel of judges at some time in the future considers to be proportionate. There is a fifty-fifty chance it will. Such decisions are not hedged in shades of grey – they are either proportionate or they are not. That a decision-maker did not actually consider whether other less restrictive measures could have been employed will have no bearing on the result. In fact, [...] there is a double whammy here in favour of decision makers. They will be able to array evidence and arguments not necessarily before them or in their minds at the time. So long as they do not waver on the outcome, it matters not that wholly different arguments are paraded before the Administrative Court than were called upon by a council's planning committee. As Hickman notes, "where reliance can be placed on an ex post facto justifications, it is also much more difficult for claimants to predict in advance their chances of success" [T. Hickman, *Public Law after the Human Rights Act*, p 240]. [...]

Thirdly, [...]The aim in 1997 was to bring human rights home, pervasively at the point of delivery. [...] Changing public service culture to one where human rights discourse permeates thinking at all levels was one of the government's avowed intentions in introducing the HRA. That objective is supported by process-based review but stunted by *Denbigh*.

The following comment by David Pannick QC (now Lord Pannick) summarizes some of the broader issues raised by the case in the light of the decision of the ECtHR in *Leyla Sahin v Turkey*,[80] which had, by now, been delivered.

David Pannick QC, 'Drawing a jilbab over a schoolgirl's religious rights', *Times Online*, 14 February 2006

[...]

It would be surprising were the House of Lords to recognise that Ms Begum had a right to wear a jilbab at school. Last November, the European Court of Human Rights decided, by 16-1, that it was not a breach of the right to religious freedom for a female university student in Turkey to be refused admission to lectures if she insisted on wearing an Islamic headscarf. The court emphasised that, in a multicultural society, restrictions on the manifestation of religion might be necessary to protect the interests of others. The university authorities were entitled to require the removal of the headscarf in order to protect female students who did not wish to wear such an item and who would otherwise come under severe pressure from extremist groups to comply with religious requirements.

The evidence on behalf of the school expressed similar concerns. A secular school is entitled to refuse to allow its female pupils to wear the more conservative jilbab if there is

---

[80] See fn. 54.

a reasonable basis for concern that girls who would wish to follow a more liberal tradition would then be pressured to conform to an extreme religious conception of the female role that they want to avoid. Ms Begum's religious rights have to be balanced against the rights and interests of other pupils, especially when the school adopts a dress code that is consistent with majority Muslim tradition.

Shabina Begum v Denbigh High School is not just a case about the rights of a schoolgirl to wear a jilbab. It is also a case about whether a secular school may protect other pupils from religious pressures that seek to dictate the role of women.

(g) THE AFTERMATH

The decision in *Leyla Sahin v Turkey* no doubt influenced the decision not to take Shabina's case to the ECtHR. Since the *Begum* case, the courts have considered several other cases involving similar questions. In *R (X) v Headteachers of Y School and anor*,[81] Silber J held that a Muslim girl's rights under Art. 9 had not been infringed when she was prevented from wearing a niqab veil,[82] because she could have accepted an offer of a place at a similar school that would allow the veil and to which it was easy for her to travel. In *R (on the application of Playfoot) v Governing Body of Millais School*,[83] the High Court rejected a challenge to a school that had stopped a pupil from wearing a 'purity' ring (which was a symbol of the pupil's commitment to celibacy before marriage). The Court held that her beliefs did not oblige her to wear the ring, that she had voluntarily accepted the school's policy, and that there were other means open to her to practise her beliefs.

Perhaps the most significant recent decision is that of the High Court in *R (Watkins-Singh) v Governing Body of Aberdare Girls' High School*.[84] The claimant, a 14-year-old girl of Punjabi–Welsh heritage, was refused permission to wear a 'Kara' to school (a plain steel bangle), which she said was central to her ethnic identity as an observant member of the Sikh community. Silber J upheld her claim on the grounds that the school's decision had constituted indirect discrimination on grounds of race contrary to the Race Relations Act 1976 and on the grounds of religion under the Equality Act 2006, which the school had not been able to justify. An important aspect of this case is that it reminds us that human rights arguments are not limited to the HRA and that claimants may rely on other legislative provisions.

QUESTIONS

1. Which of the following statements is the most accurate?

    (a) In *Begum*, the House of Lords decided that the school had acted lawfully because, when making its decision, it had paid sufficient attention to Shabina Begum's

---

[81] [2007] EWHC 298.

[82] A veil that covers the entire face and head, except for the eyes.

[83] [2007] EWHC 1698.

[84] [2008] EWHC 1865. See also *SG v St Gregory's Catholic Science College* [2011] EWHC 1452 (Admin), where Collins J held that a school's ban of the cornrows hairstyle, in so far as it applied to the child in question, was unlawful. Collins J rejected the school's argument that a voluntarily decision to have cornrows did not attract the protection of the discrimination legislation, holding that family and social customs can form 'part of ethnicity'.

rights. (By contrast, the Court of Appeal had decided that insufficient attention had been paid to her rights.)

(b) In *Begum*, the House of Lords agreed with the school that pupils should not be allowed to wear the jilbab.

(c) In *Begum*, the House of Lords had no opinion as to whether the school was right or wrong, but it did accept that the school's policy was aimed at achieving a lawful objective, that its decision in this case furthered that policy, and that it did not unnecessarily limit Shabina's rights.

2. The core reason why the House disagreed with the Court of Appeal's approach in *Begum* is contained in Lord Bingham's comment that '*The school's action cannot properly be condemned as disproportionate, with an acknowledgement that on reconsideration the same action could very well be maintained and properly so*'. Discuss and explain the difference between the task of the courts in a judicial review case in which HRA issues are not involved and the approach to be taken when they are involved.

3 If you were a lawyer advising schools, what are the most important things that you would tell schools in relation to the *Begum* decision?

4. If you were advising the government, what principles of general application emerge from the decision?

5 CASE STUDY: HUMAN RIGHTS AND TERRORISM

(a) BACKGROUND

This case study examines the litigation generated in the wake of the terrorist bombing of the World Trade Centre in New York and the other related attacks on 11 September 2001. It is, however, important to remember the following.

A.T.H. Smith, 'Offences against the State', in D. Feldman (ed.) *English Public Law*, 2nd edn (2009, Oxford: OUP), ch. 27, p. 1161

It would be a mistake to suppose that the UK law devoted to the suppression of terrorism is particularly modern, let alone a reaction to the events that convulsed the world following the attacks in the United States in September 2001. Continuing problems in Northern Ireland meant that the statute books were replete with offences directed against terrorist groups and their activities.[85]

The United Kingdom's legislative reaction to what President Bush called the 'war on terror', nonetheless has raised fundamental questions about the balance between the government's legitimate need to protect the public (and the corresponding right of the public to security), on the one hand, and the rights of individuals to be protected from state action, on the other. Coming so soon after the enactment of the HRA 1998, reaction to terrorism was to test

---

[85] See also Clive Walker, *Blackstone's Guide to the Anti-terrorism Legislation* (2002, Oxford: OUP).

the effectiveness of the new Act; it would also profoundly test the relationship between the judges and the executive and Parliament. Would the judges adopt their traditional stance of deferring to the executive whenever the government justified breaching individual human rights in the interests of national security, or would the judges be more robust in their application of the HRA and the rights that it had brought home?

The responses to international terrorism have extended across a very broad range of activities, and have led to several extensive Acts of Parliament and to much debate, as well as to a very substantial literature. In this chapter, we shall focus on one aspect—namely, the litigation that has been generated in reaction to two sets of legislative regime. The first—Pt IV of the Anti-terrorism Crime and Security Act 2001—permitted detention without trial. The second—the Prevention of Terrorism Act 2005—enabled the making of control orders in relation to those suspected of being involved in terrorist activities.

The legal response to the events on 11 September 2001

On 11 November 2001, the Home Secretary made a Derogation Order under s. 14 of the HRA enabling the United Kingdom to take steps that would otherwise constitute a deprivation of liberty contrary to Art. 5 ECHR (the right to liberty).[86] The ECHR gives states limited power to derogate from (that is, act contrary to) some of the Articles in the Convention, including Art. 5, but not Art. 3 (the prohibition of torture and degrading treatment or punishment). Derogations can be made only '*in time of war or other public emergency threatening the life of the nation*' and derogations are only permissible '*to the extent strictly required by the exigencies of the situation*'.[87]

Parliament also swiftly enacted the Anti-terrorism, Crime and Security Act 2001 (ATCSA). The speed of enactment and the short time available for Parliament to consider the proposals have been summarized by the ECtHR.

A and ors v UK
Grand Chamber of the ECtHR, Application No. 3455/05 (19 February 2009)

12. On 12 November 2001 the Anti-Terrorism Crime and Security Bill, containing the clauses which were to eventually become Part 4 of the Anti- Terrorism Crime and Security Act 2001 [...] was introduced into the House of Commons. The Bill was passed by Parliament in two weeks, with three days of debate on the floor of the House of Commons set aside for its 125 clauses in a restrictive programming motion, prompting both the Joint Committee of Human Rights and the Home Affairs Select Committee to complain of the speed with which they were being asked to consider the matter.

13. The 2001 Act came into force on 4 December 2001.

In order to understand the relevant provisions of the ATCSA, we need to go back a step to the 1996 decision of the ECtHR in *Chahal v UK*.

---

[86] The Human Rights Act 1998 (Designation Derogation) Order 2001 (SI 2001/3644). The United Kingdom also derogated from Art. 9 of the International Covenant on Civil and Political Rights 1966.
[87] Article 15 ECHR.

Chahal v UK[88]

Chahal was an Indian citizen resident in the United Kingdom. The Home Secretary believed that he had been involved in terrorist activities in support of Sikh separatism and he sought to deport him, believing that Chahal's presence in the United Kingdom was not conducive to the public interest on national security grounds. Under the Immigration Act 1971, a person subject to a deportation order on these grounds had no right to appeal to a court against the decision and no right to see the evidence upon which the Home Secretary had acted.[89] Instead, he or she could make representations, without a right to legal representations, to an advisory panel of 'three wise men'.

Chahal took his case to the ECtHR, making two lines of argument. He argued that the procedure adopted was unlawful because it infringed his right to a court hearing under Art. 5(4) (which requires those who are deprived of their liberty to have access to a court), as well as his right to an effective remedy in Art. 13.

Chahal also argued that if he were deported and returned to India, there was a real risk that he would be tracked down and killed by lawless Punjab police. This claim had been accepted in a separate case by the Immigration Appeal Tribunal, and was corroborated by reports of the US Department of State and by Amnesty International.[90] He argued that, in this situation, deportation would constitute a breach of Art. 3 of the ECHR.

The ECtHR upheld each of these claims. The decision was to have a very significant effect on the United Kingdom. It had two major implications. First, it meant that a new procedure had to be introduced that would enable people to challenge decisions to deport made on grounds of national security, but which would not enable the release of confidential information. In giving its judgment, the ECtHR referred to the practice adopted in Canada whereby the confidentiality of sensitive material was maintained by holding closed sessions in the absence of the person concerned and his or her legal representatives.

The decision in *Chahal* also led to the enactment of the Special Immigration Appeals Commission Act 1997 establishing the Special Immigration Appeals Commission (SIAC), modelled on the Canadian practice referred to by the Court.

The Special Immigration Appeals Commission

The SIAC (as we saw in Chapter 16) is a superior court of record that was established to hear appeals against decisions to deport on national security grounds. It is composed of a High Court judge or some other holder of high judicial office, an expert on immigration matters, and an intelligence expert. It operates under procedural rules that allow it to hold closed hearings in the absence of the appellant or the appellant's lawyer. These procedures are exceptional and known as Closed Material Procedures or CMPs.[91] and in cases in which closed hearings take place, the Act enables the appointment of special advocates (experienced lawyers who have been security cleared) to represent the interests of appellants. The procedure is described by John Ip.

---

[88] (1996) 23 EHRR 413.

[89] Section 15 (3); see *R v Secretary of State for the Home Department, ex parte Hosenball* [1977] 1 WLR 766.

[90] See Keir Starmer, 'Setting the record straight: Human rights in an era of international terrorism' (2007) European Human Rights Law Review 2, 123–32.

[91] CMP are used when Parliament provides for them: *Al-Rawi v Security Service* [2011] UKSC 34.

John Ip, 'The rise and spread of the special advocate' [2008] Public Law 717, 721 (footnotes omitted)

The appeal hearing is conducted in open and closed sessions. The open session, in which the appellant and his representatives can participate, occurs first; the special advocate is also present. During the closed session, all parties other than the Home Secretary and the special advocate leave. The special advocate may then challenge the government's case by, adducing evidence, cross-examining witnesses, and making representations to SIAC about the closed material. Although the special advocate is able to see all the closed material, the special advocate's ability to take instructions or communicate with the appellant is restricted once the advocate has seen the closed material. If the special advocate wishes to consult with the appellant or his or her lawyer, SIAC must authorise it after notifying the Secretary of State, who may object. The appellant may also communicate in writing with the special advocate via counsel.

As we shall see, there has been much litigation concerning the compatibility of SIAC procedures with human rights.

Chahal and Art. 3

While government and Parliament could respond to the procedural aspect of *Chahal* by reforming the process, it was less easy for them to respond to the decision on the effect of Art. 3. The rights in Art. 3 are absolute and they can neither be infringed, nor derogated from. While the United Kingdom is a party to the ECHR, it is therefore bound to respect Art. 3, as interpreted by the ECtHR. The HRA also means that people in Chahal's situation can rely directly on Art. 3 before domestic courts.

The implications of the decision have been summarized by the government as follows:

'The implications of *Chahal* for the government's ability to deport or remove people whose presence in the UK threatens national security', Derogation lodged with the Secretary General of the Council of Europe on 18 December 2001

[...] where the intention remains to remove or deport a person on national security grounds, continued detention may not be consistent with Article 5(1)(f) as interpreted by the Court in the *Chahal* case. This may be the case, for example, if the person has established that removal to their own country might result in treatment contrary to Article 3 of the Convention. In such circumstances, irrespective of the gravity of the threat to national security posed by the person concerned, it is well established that Article 3 prevents removal or deportation to a place where there is a real risk that the person will suffer treatment contrary to that article. If no alternative destination is immediately available then removal or deportation may not, for the time being, be possible [...] In addition, it may not be possible to prosecute the person for a criminal offence given the strict rules on the admissibility of evidence in the criminal justice system of the United Kingdom and the high standard of proof required.

The government has never liked this aspect of *Chahal*. Indeed, on 5 August 2005, the then Prime Minister Tony Blair suggested that unless the government could persuade courts to depart from *Chahal*, the government would consider amending the HRA to force domestic courts to do so. The government has intervened in litigation before the ECtHR to argue that the Court should alter its approach. To date the court has refused to do so. [92]

Suffice to say, the restrictions imposed by *Chahal* on the ability to deport people who constitute a threat to national security have significantly influenced the design of the anti-terrorist legislation.

> ### QUESTION
>
> If you were a government lawyer asked to advise on how the HRA might be amended to remove the effect of the *Chahal* case, what advice would you give?

(b) PART 4 OF THE ANTI-TERRORISM, CRIME AND SECURITY ACT 2001 (ATCSA)

Part 4 of ATCSA allowed foreign nationals to be indefinitely detained without charge when the Home Secretary had certified them to be suspected international terrorists who could not be deported from the United Kingdom as a consequence of *Chahal*.[93] Those in this situation could choose to leave the United Kingdom, but if they chose not to do so, they would remain in detention, subject to a six-month review by the SIAC. As well as its duty to review certifications, the Act gave the SIAC exclusive jurisdiction to hear challenges to certifications and to deal with derogation matters, with further appeal on a point of law to the Court of Appeal. The government accepted that this form of detention was incompatible with Art. 5 of ECHR, which would have been contrary to the ECHR but for the 11 November 2001 Derogation Order.

Sixteen people were certified and detained under Pt IV. These detentions generated challenges to:

(a) the legality of the derogation and the legislative scheme; and
(b) individual certifications.

We shall start by considering the challenges to the legality of the Derogation Order and the legislative scheme.

(c) THE LEGALITY OF THE DEROGATION ORDER AND OF THE LEGISLATION[94]

The broadest line of challenge was to the legality of the Derogation Order. If this could be successfully challenged, the legislative provisions infringing Art. 5 would be incompatible with the ECHR and would almost certainly have to be repealed or amended. Remember that derogation from the ECHR is only possible in situations in which there is an emergency that threatens the life of the nation. The government's position was that it was solely responsible for determining whether such an emergency existed and its judgment could not be upset by the courts.

---

[92] In *Saadi v Italy*, the Grand Chamber of the ECtHR unanimously reaffirmed the absolute nature of the Art. 3 and its approach in *Chahal*. Application No. 37201/06, Judgment 28 February 2008. Also *A v Netherlands Appln* 4900/06 and *N v Sweden Appln* 23505/09. Judgment 20 July 2010.

[93] Sections 21–23 ATCSA.

[94] [2004] UKHL 56.

If the court was not prepared to hold the derogation unlawful, a second line of challenge was to the proportionality of the legislative provisions. Even if there were an emergency that justified the Derogation Order, the steps taken to meet the emergency must be 'strictly required' by the situation. Here, the claimants argued that the key provisions in Pt IV were not strictly required. Once again, the government would argue that this was not a matter for the courts, but for Parliament.

These arguments were first considered by the SIAC. After examining both open and closed material, and hearing submissions from special advocates, as well as counsel for the parties and for Liberty (which had been joined as an interested party), the SIAC held, on the basis of the open material, that it was satisfied that the threat from al-Qaeda had created a public emergency threatening the life of the nation, within the meaning of Art. 15 of the Convention. The closed material confirmed this view.

The SIAC also held that while it was possible that the public could have been protected by other methods, this did not mean that the measures adopted were not strictly necessary. Moreover, that the detainees could leave the United Kingdom if they wished to do so demonstrated that the measures were properly tailored to the state of emergency.

The SIAC held, however, that the relevant provisions of Pt IV of the 2001 Act unjustifiably discriminated against foreign nationals, in breach of Art. 14 of the ECHR. For this reason, it quashed the Derogation Order of 11 November 2001 and issued a declaration of incompatibility in respect of s. 23 of the 2001 Act, under s. 4 of the HRA. It adjourned the applicants' individual appeals against certification, pending the outcome of any appeals that there may have been against its decision on the legality of the derogation and the legislative provisions.

The government successfully appealed against this decision to the Court of Appeal, which delivered its judgment on 25 October 2002.[95] The Court of Appeal held that the SIAC had been entitled to find that there was a public emergency threatening the life of the nation. Unlike the SIAC, however, it held that the approach adopted by the Secretary of State could be objectively justified. There was a rational connection between the detention of non-nationals, who could not be deported because of fears for their safety, and the purpose that the Secretary of State wished to achieve, which was to remove non-nationals who posed a threat to national security. In its view, there was no discrimination contrary to Art. 14 of the ECHR, because British suspect terrorists were in a different situation from that of foreign suspects who could not be deported because of Art. 3: foreign nationals have no right to remain in the country, but only a right, for the time being, not to be removed for their own safety. The Court of Appeal noted that, in international law, there are situations in which states can distinguish between nationals and non-nationals, especially in times of emergency.

We may note in passing that, in May 2003, after the Court of Appeal's decision, the SIAC started to hear the individual challenges to certification under s. 21, but we shall return to the SIAC's decisions on these later.

(d) *A V SECRETARY OF STATE FOR THE HOME DEPARTMENT* (THE *BELMARSH* CASE) IN THE HOUSE OF LORDS[96]

The detainees appealed to the House of Lords. Here, they once again argued that their detention was inconsistent with the obligations of the United Kingdom under the ECHR, that the

---

[95] *A and ors v Secretary of State for the Home Department* [2002] EWCA Civ 1502.

[96] Two of the appellants had, by the time the appeal was heard, exercised their right to leave the country (one went to Morocco and the other to France); one had been transferred to Broadmoor Hospital on grounds of mental illness; another had been released on bail.

Derogation Order was unlawful, and that the statutory provisions under which they were detained were incompatible with the ECHR. In what is probably the most significant human rights case yet decided by the UK courts, the House of Lords quashed the 2001 Derogation Order and made a declaration that s. 23 of the 2001 Act was incompatible with Arts 5 and 14 of the ECHR. The judgments of the nine judges[97] ran to 240 paragraphs and should be carefully read.

Here, we summarize the main findings, as follows.

1. **In relation to the legality of the Derogation Order, was there a public emergency that threatened the life of the nation?**

While the United Kingdom had been the only party to the ECHR to derogate from Art. 5 in the wake of the attacks of the 11 September 2001, the House of Lords—by a majority of eight to one—agreed with the SIAC that there was power to derogate from Art. 5. Lords Bingham and Scott reached this view with hesitation, and Lord Hoffmann dissented. In reaching their decision, the majority took account of an early decision of the ECtHR that had accepted that Ireland could derogate from the Convention even though it was not shown that a widespread loss of life or an attack on the territorial integrity of the state was involved.[98] The majority also attached great weight to the judgment of the Home Secretary and Parliament on whether there was a threat to the life of the nation.

A v Secretary of State for the Home Department
[2004] UKHL 56

Lord Bingham

[29] [...] I would accept that great weight should be given to the judgment of the Home Secretary, his colleagues and Parliament on this question, because they were called on to exercise a pre-eminently political judgment. [...] I do not accept the full breadth of the Attorney General's argument on what is generally called the deference owed by the courts to the political authorities. It is perhaps preferable to approach this question as one of demarcation of functions or what Liberty in its written case called "relative institutional competence". The more purely political (in a broad or narrow sense) a question is, the more appropriate it will be for political resolution and the less likely it is to be an appropriate matter for judicial decision. The smaller, therefore, will be the potential role of the court. It is the function of political and not judicial bodies to resolve political questions. Conversely, the greater the legal content of any issue, the greater the potential role of the court, because under our constitution and subject to the sovereign power of Parliament it is the function of the courts and not of political bodies to resolve legal questions. The present question [whether a derogation order was necessary] seems to me to be very much at the political end of the spectrum [...]

Lord Hoffmann dissented on this point and held that the Derogation Order was unlawful because there was no threat to the life of the nation. It is worth setting out the following extract from his judgment, especially bearing in mind the way in which Lord Hoffmann had approached the issue of deference in the past.

---

[97] Lords Bingham of Cornhill, Nicholls of Birkenhead, Hoffmann, Hope of Craighead, Scott of Foscote, Rodger of Earlsferry, Walker of Gestingthorpe, and Carswell, and Baroness Hale of Richmond.
[98] *Lawless v Ireland (No. 3)* (1961) 1 EHRR 15.

A v Secretary of State for the Home Department
[2004] UKHL 56

Lord Hoffmann

[93] The Home Secretary has adduced evidence, both open and secret, to show the existence of a threat of serious terrorist outrages. [...] despite the widespread scepticism which has attached to intelligence assessments since the fiasco over Iraqi weapons of mass destruction, I am willing to accept that credible evidence of such plots exist. The events of 11 September 2001 in New York and Washington and 11 March 2003 in Madrid make it entirely likely that the threat of similar atrocities in the United Kingdom is a real one.

[94] But the question is whether such a threat is a threat to the life of the nation....Of course the government has a duty to protect the lives and property of its citizens. But that is a duty which it owes all the time and which it must discharge without destroying our constitutional freedoms. There may be some nations too fragile or fissiparous to withstand a serious act of violence. But that is not the case in the United Kingdom. [...]

[95] This is a nation which has been tested in adversity, which has survived physical destruction and catastrophic loss of life. I do not underestimate the ability of fanatical groups of terrorists to kill and destroy, but they do not threaten the life of the nation. Whether we would survive Hitler hung in the balance, but there is no doubt that we shall survive Al-Qaeda. [...]

[96] [...] The real threat to the life of the nation, in the sense of a people living in accordance with its traditional laws and political values, comes not from terrorism but from laws such as these. That is the true measure of what terrorism may achieve. It is for Parliament to decide whether to give the terrorists such a victory.

2. **The Derogation Order was lawful, but what about the provisions of the 2001 Act relating to the powers of detention proportionate? Were they 'strictly required by the exigencies of the situation'?**

The House considered that proportionality was a question of law and therefore a matter for courts. The powers of detention related only to foreign nationals who could not be deported. But the majority stressed that foreign nationals were not the only threat. Moreover, even when they were a threat, the 2001 Act left them free to leave the United Kingdom and carry on their activities from abroad. In other words, the legislative provisions infringed Art. 5 and the infringements were not rationally directed at the reasons for the emergency—that is, the prevention of terrorism. The House of Lords—by a majority of seven to one (Lord Walker of Gestingthorpe dissented and Lord Hoffmann expressed no view on this issue)—held that the proportionality requirement had not been met, essentially because s. 23 was not specifically focused on the actual threat posed. As Lady Justice Mary Arden has put it, '*in a word, s. 23 was irrational*'.[99]

A v Secretary of State for the Home Department
[2004] UKHL 56

Lord Bingham

[37] [...] the Attorney General [...] submitted that as it was for Parliament and the executive to assess the threat facing the nation, so it was for those bodies and not the courts to judge

---

[99] Mary Arden, 'Human rights in an age of terrorism' (2005) 121 Law Quarterly Review 604–27, 608.

the response necessary to protect the security of the public. These were matters of a political character calling for an exercise of political and not judicial judgment. Just as the European Court allowed a generous margin of appreciation to member states, recognising that they were better placed to understand and address local problems, so should national courts recognise, for the same reason, that matters of the kind in issue here fall within the discretionary area of judgment properly belonging to the democratic organs of the state. It was not for the courts to usurp authority properly belonging elsewhere. The Attorney General drew attention to the dangers identified by Richard Ekins in *"Judicial Supremacy and the Rule of Law"* (2003) 119 LQR 127. This is an important submission, properly made, and it calls for careful consideration.

[Lord Bingham reviewed the domestic and international authorities, and continued as follows.]

[42] [...] I do not accept the full breadth of the Attorney General's submissions. I do not in particular accept the distinction which he drew between democratic institutions and the courts. It is of course true that the judges in this country are not elected and are not answerable to Parliament. It is also of course true, as pointed out in para 29 above, that Parliament, the executive and the courts have different functions. But the function of independent judges charged to interpret and apply the law is universally recognised as a cardinal feature of the modern democratic state, a cornerstone of the rule of law itself. The Attorney General is fully entitled to insist on the proper limits of judicial authority, but he is wrong to stigmatise judicial decision-making as in some way undemocratic. It is particularly inappropriate in a case such as the present in which Parliament has expressly legislated in s 6 of the 1998 Act to render unlawful any act of a public authority, including a court, incompatible with a Convention right, has required courts (in s 2) to take account of relevant Strasbourg jurisprudence, has (in s 3) required courts, so far as possible, to give effect to Convention rights and has conferred a right of appeal on derogation issues. The effect is not, of course, to override the sovereign legislative authority of the Queen in Parliament, since if primary legislation is declared to be incompatible the validity of the legislation is unaffected (s 4(6)) and the remedy lies with the appropriate minister (s 10), who is answerable to Parliament. The 1998 Act gives the courts a very specific, wholly democratic, mandate. [...]

[43] The Appellants' proportionality challenge to the Order and s 23 is, in my opinion, sound, for all the reasons they gave and also for those given by the European Commissioner for Human Rights and the Newton Committee. The Attorney General could give no persuasive answer. [...] the choice of an immigration measure to address a security problem had the inevitable result of failing adequately to address that problem (by allowing non-UK suspected terrorists to leave the country with impunity and leaving British suspected terrorists at large) while imposing the severe penalty of indefinite detention on persons who, even if reasonably suspected of having links with Al-Qaeda, may harbour no hostile intentions towards the United Kingdom. The conclusion that the Order and s 23 are, in Convention terms, disproportionate is in my opinion irresistible.

Lord Nicholls of Birkenhead

[78] All courts are very much aware of the heavy burden, resting on the elected government and not the judiciary, to protect the security of this country and all who live here. All courts are acutely conscious that the government alone is able to evaluate and decide what counter-terrorism steps are needed and what steps will suffice. Courts are not equipped to make such decisions, nor are they charged with that responsibility.

[79] But Parliament has charged the courts with a particular responsibility. It is a responsibility as much applicable to the 2001 Act and the Human Rights Act 1998 (Designated

Derogation) Order 2001 as it is to all other legislation and ministers' decisions. The duty of the courts is to check that legislation and ministerial decisions do not overlook the human rights of persons adversely affected. [...]

[80] In the present case I see no escape from the conclusion that Parliament must be regarded as having attached insufficient weight to the human rights of non-nationals. The subject matter of the legislation is the needs of national security. This subject matter dictates that, in the ordinary course, substantial latitude should be accorded to the legislature. But the human right in question, the right to individual liberty, is one of the most fundamental of human rights. Indefinite detention without trial wholly negates that right for an indefinite period. With one exception all the individuals currently detained have been imprisoned now for three years and there is no prospect of imminent release. It is true that those detained may at any time walk away from their place of detention if they leave this country. Their prison, it is said, has only three walls. But this freedom is more theoretical than real. This is demonstrated by the continuing presence in Belmarsh of most of those detained. They prefer to stay in prison rather than face the prospect of ill treatment in any country willing to admit them.

3. **The third main issue was whether the detention powers in s. 23 violated Art. 14 of the ECHR by discriminating unjustifiably between British and foreign nationals.**

Disagreeing with the Court of Appeal, the House of Lords held that the appropriate comparators were UK nationals who were suspected terrorists, and not, as the government argued, non-UK nationals who were suspected terrorists, but who could be deported to third countries (that is, who did not fall within the *Chahal* class of case). For this reason, s. 23 was incompatible with Art. 14, read in conjunction with Art. 5. Again, Lord Walker of Gestingthorpe dissented and Lord Hoffmann expressed no view on this point, not wanting to suggest that the government could remedy the situation by extending the powers to UK citizens.

QUESTIONS

1. What do you understand by the term 'relative institutional competence' in the context of judicial review of executive and Parliamentary decision-making?

2. According to Lord Hoffmann, who in the UK constitution should decide whether there is a threat to the life of the nation? Does this view appear to be compatible with his earlier statements on deference?

3. 'The Belmarsh *decision illustrates the contentious nature of democracy in the UK constitution.*' Discuss.

(e) THE IMPACT OF THE DECISION

Mary Arden, 'Human rights in an age of terrorism' (2005) 121 Law Quarterly Review 604–27, 605

The result in this case was remarkable. [...] The *A* case may well be the first time that a court of the United Kingdom has dealt such a body blow to legislation conferring powers on the executive to meet a threat to national security.

As Lady Justice Arden has said, there was a 'startling difference' between the approach taken in the *Belmarsh* case and that taken in *Liversidge v Anderson*.[100] In *Liversidge*, the majority had held that the balancing of the interests of national security against those of the individual was the sole prerogative of the Home Secretary; here, the House held that the courts have a duty to review the way in which this balance is struck in order to ensure that both the Home Secretary and Parliament act in conformity with human rights requirements. The House took the view that there is no jurisdictional barrier to the review of national security decisions and that national security is not a 'no-go' area for the courts or the law.

Mary Arden, 'Human rights in an age of terrorism' (2005) 121 Law Quarterly Review 604, 614 (footnotes omitted)

[...] what is the significance of the decision of the House of Lords in the *A* case? Some measure of the importance of the issues can be gleaned from the fact that it is a decision of nine members of the Appellate Committee, which normally sits in constitutions of five. In my view, the significance of the decision may be expressed in these terms: the decision in the *A* case is a landmark decision that will be used as a point of reference by courts all over the world for decades to come, even when the age of terrorism has passed. It is a powerful statement by the highest court in the land of what it means to live in a society where the executive is subject to the rule of law. Even the Government, and even in times when there is a threat to national security, must act strictly in accordance with the law.

She went on to quote the following statement of President Barak in a decision of the Israeli Supreme Court.

Public Committee Against Torture v Israel (the Ticking Time Bomb case), 26 May 1999, HC 5100/94(4)PD 817, 845[101]

President Barak, President of the Israeli Supreme Court

We conclude this judgment by revisiting the harsh reality in which Israel finds itself [...] We are aware that this decision does not make it easier to deal with that reality. This is the fate of democracy, as not all means are acceptable to it, and not all methods employed by its enemies are always open before it. Sometimes, democracy must fight with one hand tied behind its back. Nonetheless, it has the upper hand. Preserving the rule of law and recognition of individual liberties constitute an important component of its understanding of security. At the end of the day, they strengthen its spirit and this strength allows it to overcome its difficulties.

From another perspective, the decision may provide further evidence of the judiciary using human rights arguments to frustrate government's attempts to protect the public from terrorism and of the way in which the HRA operates as a charter for terrorists and other undesirables.[102]

---

[100] [1942] AC 206, see Chapter 16, section 1(b), Historical development.
[101] Cited by Mary Arden at p. 623.
[102] See Chapter 6, section 7, The Human Rights Act under challenge.

Criticisms of this sort are misplaced. Far from saying that government could not take steps to protect the public, the message given by the judges was that the route chosen by the government was irrational and, as Keir Starmer QC (now the Director of Public Prosecutions) explains, likely to be ineffective.

Keir Starmer, 'Setting the record straight: Human rights in an era of international terrorism' (2007) 2 European Human Rights Law Review 123, 124

[...] the Law Lords found that the 2001 Act did not rationally address the threat posed by Al-Qa'ida terrorists and their supporters because it did not address the threat presented by UK nationals. As the events of July 7, 2005 in London underlined, that was timely advice for which the Government ought to have been grateful. Secondly, the Law Lords were concerned that the 2001 Act, grounded as it was in immigration law rather than criminal law, permitted suspected terrorists to leave the United Kingdom on a voluntary basis and carry on their activities abroad. In one case the individual in question simply got the Eurostar to France. Thirdly, the Law Lords were concerned that the 2001 Act permitted the detention of individuals who sympathised with terrorist activity abroad but posed no threat to the United Kingdom. Against that background it can hardly be suggested that their Lordships were mischievously dismantling the Government's anti-terrorism strategy. They were simply pointing out that the Government's approach was discriminatory, irrational and, worst of all, ineffective.

Impact on the individuals concerned

Despite the constitutional importance of the principles enunciated by the House of Lords, the declaration of incompatibility did not affect 'the validity, continuing operation or enforcement' of s. 23, nor did it bind the Home Secretary.[103] Immediately after the announcement of the decision, Mr Charles Clarke, then Home Secretary, told the House of Commons: 'My primary role as Home Secretary is to protect national security and to ensure the safety and security of this country. I will not be revoking the certificates or releasing the detainees, whom I have reason to believe are a significant threat to our security.' The detainees would remain in prison, he said, until Parliament decided 'whether and how we should amend the law'. He said that he would study the judgment to see whether it was possible to modify the legislation 'to address the concerns raised by the House of Lords'.[104]

On 21 January 2005, those who were still detained started proceedings in the ECtHR. These led to the decision, *A and ors v UK*, which was given by the Grand Chamber of that Court four years later, on 19 February 2009.[105] In its judgment, the Grand Chamber agreed with the House of Lords in the *Belmarsh* case on the principal issues with which it had dealt. It also addressed the compatibility of the process used by the SIAC with the obligation to provide a fair hearing in Arts 6 and 5(4). We will consider this aspect of the decision later in the chapter.

---

[103] Section 4(6) HRA 1998.

[104] Oral statement by Charles Clarke, Home Secretary, to the House of Commons, 26 January 2005. Two of the detainees elected to leave the United Kingdom and one was released on bail conditions that were equivalent to control order conditions.

[105] Application No. 3455/05.

The legislative response to the *Belmarsh* decision

On the 26 January 2005, Mr Charles Clarke made a statement to the House of Commons setting out proposals to repeal Pt 4 of the 2001 Act and to establish a new scheme. This would adopt a twin-track approach. Foreign nationals who were suspected of being involved in terrorist activities would be deported once assurances were obtained from the countries to which they would be sent that they would not be treated in a manner that contravened Art. 3. Those who could not be deported would be subject to a new system of control orders. The proposed control orders could be made irrespective of the person's nationality and would therefore also apply to British nationals suspected of terrorist activity. The control orders would impose a range of controls restricting movement, including preventing people from leaving their residence (subjecting them to a curfew), preventing association between named individuals, tagging, and restricting access to telecommunications and the Internet.[106]

(f) CONTROL ORDERS

The Prevention of Terrorism Act 2005 (PTA) came into force on 11 March 2005.[107] This enabled the Secretary of State to make derogating and non-derogating control orders. The former would breach Art. 5 of the ECHR and would be imposed only if a derogation from that Article was in place. Such orders were intended to be used only for individuals considered to pose a high risk to public safety associated with the public emergency that justified the derogation. They would be made by a court on application by the Secretary of State and they would be reviewed by the court after six months. No derogating control orders were made.

Non-derogating control orders were intended to be compatible with Art. 5 of the ECHR and were made by the Secretary of State when he had '*reasonable grounds for suspecting*' that someone is or has been '*involved in terrorism-related activity*'[108] and he considered it '*necessary, for purposes connected with protecting members of the public from the risk of terrorism, to make a control order*'.

The making of control orders was supervised by the SIAC, which had the task of determining whether these requirements were satisfied.[109] As with its other national security-related tasks, including challenges to certifications under (the repealed) Pt IV of ATSCA, SIAC is permitted by its rules of procedures to consider material in closed sessions and to use special advocates who are unable to reveal or discuss the contents of any closed material with the person concerned. The legislation was reviewed annually and the Joint Committee on Human Rights reported on the reviews.[110]

The appellants in the *Belmarsh* case who remained detained were released on 11 March 2005 and immediately made subject to non-derogating control orders. In response to this, Sangeeta Shah noted as follows.

---

[106] HC Deb, vol. 430, col. 307, 26 January 2005.
[107] And the derogation order was withdrawn.
[108] Section 2(1).
[109] Section 3(10).
[110] *Counter-terrorism Policy and Human Rights (Fourteenth Report): Annual Renewal of Control Orders Legislation 2009*, Fifth Report, Session 2008–09.

Sangeeta Shah, 'The UK's anti-terror legislation and the House of Lords: The first skirmish' (2005) Human Rights Law Review 5(2), 403–21, 419

Between 2001 and 2004, 17 individuals were certified as being a risk to national security and suspected international terrorists and as such warranted indefinite detention in prison. Yet by 2005 these individuals could be released subject to certain restrictions. Ha[d] the risk they pose diminished? Or [was] this further vindication that the measures under Part 4, ATCSA were … disproportionate?

On 11 August 2005, following negotiations, the UK government secured assurances from the Algerian and Jordanian governments that deportees would not be ill treated if they were returned to these countries. With these assurances secured, the government served notices of intention to deport on seven people who had been taken into immigration custody pending removal to Algeria and Jordan. On 9 April 2008, the Court of Appeal[111] ruled that Omar Othman (known as 'Abu Qatada') could not be lawfully extradited to Jordan, because it was likely that, in Jordan, evidence that had been obtained by torture could be used against him, in flagrant violation of his right to a fair trial. Perhaps somewhat surprisingly, given the recent record of House of Lords, this decision was overturned by the appellate committee in February 2009.[112] Abu Qatadar took his case to the ECtHR where he was successful.[113]

(g) THE LEGALITY OF CONTROL ORDERS

The control order regime led to a large number of legal challenges, including several top-court decisions. Two main lines of argument were made. One focused on whether the non-derogating control orders infringed the Art. 5(1) right to liberty, even though they purported to be compatible with this right. It would, of course, be unlawful under s. 6(1) of the HRA for the Secretary of State to make control orders that were incompatible with Art. 5 of the ECHR. It would, on normal judicial review grounds, also be beyond the powers conferred by the PTA.

(h) CONTROL ORDERS AND THE RIGHT TO LIBERTY

In *Secretary of State for the Home Department v JJ*,[114] the House of Lords agreed with the Court of Appeal[115] that a non-derogating control order that prevented a person from leaving

---

[111] [2007] EWCA Civ 808, [2008] EWCA Civ 290.

[112] *RB (Algeria) (FC) and anor (Appellants) v Secretary of State for the Home Department; OO (Jordan) (Original Respondent and Cross-appellant) v Secretary of State for the Home Department (Original Appellant and Cross-respondent)* [2009] UKHL 10. Julia Hall, for Human Rights Watch, said that '*The Law Lords have given the government a green light to send people back to places where they risk torture and ill-treatment*' (see http://www.hrw.org).

[113] *Othman v United Kingdom* (8139/09) (2012) 55 EHRR 1; 32 BHRC 62. The court held that Arts 3 and 5 did not prevent a terrorist suspect being deported from the United Kingdom to Jordan, subject to assurances given in a memorandum of understanding that he would be treated consistently with the UK's obligations under the European Convention on Human Rights. However, there remained a real risk that evidence obtained by torture would be used at a trial in Jordan and this would constitute a flagrant denial of justice. For this reason the deportation would violate art.6 ECHR. That decision was subsequently applied by the SIAC (SC/15/2005) 12 November 2012. The government is appealing to the Court of Appeal.

[114] [2007] UKHL 45; cf. *Secretary of State for the Home Department v E* [2007] UKHL 47, in which the House of Lords said that a control order imposing a curfew of twelve hours, with other less onerous restrictions, was held to be lawful.

[115] [2006] EWCA Civ 1141.

a one-bedroom flat for eighteen hours in every twenty-four (an eighteen-hour curfew) and imposed very restricted controls that effectively meant that the person's life was wholly regulated by the Home Office was contrary to Art. 5. After reviewing the jurisprudence of the ECtHR and UK law, Lord Bingham reached the conclusion that is set out in the following extract.[116]

Note that, in *Guzzardi v Italy*,[117] to which Lord Bingham refers, the ECtHR held there to be a deprivation of liberty when a person was forced to stay on a small island, in dilapidated accommodation, without social intercourse. He was under almost constant supervision, had a nine-hour overnight curfew, and was obliged to report to the authorities twice a day and to inform them of any person whom he wished to telephone; he also had to obtain consent to visit Sardinia on the mainland.

Secretary of State for the Home Department v JJ
[2007] UKHL 45

Lord Bingham

24. [...] The effect of the 18-hour curfew, coupled with the effective exclusion of social visitors, meant that the controlled persons were in practice in solitary confinement for this lengthy period every day for an indefinite duration, with very little opportunity for contact with the outside world, with means insufficient to permit provision of significant facilities for self-entertainment and with knowledge that their flats were liable to be entered and searched at any time. The area open to them during their six non-curfew hours was unobjectionable in size, much larger than that open to Mr Guzzardi. But they were (save for GG) located in an unfamiliar area where they had no family, friends or contacts, and which was no doubt chosen for that reason. The requirement to obtain prior Home Office clearance of any social meeting outside the flat in practice isolated the controlled persons during the non-curfew hours also. Their lives were wholly regulated by the Home Office, as a prisoner's would be, although breaches were much more severely punishable. The judge's analogy with detention in an open prison was apt, save that the controlled persons did not enjoy the association with others and the access to entertainment facilities which a prisoner in an open prison would expect to enjoy.

Lords Hoffmann and Carswell dissented. Lord Hoffmann said that the right to liberty was an unqualified right under the ECHR and that it was therefore essential not to give liberty an over-expansive interpretation. Article 5, he said, should apply only to literal physical restraint and not to restrictions of the type imposed.

(i) CONTROL ORDERS AND PROCEDURAL FAIRNESS

A second line of argument focused on the legality of the procedures adopted when the SIAC reviewed decisions of the Secretary of State. Two particular issues were raised: the first was

---

[116] Compare *R (on the application of Gillan) v Commissioner of Police of the Metropolis* [2006] UKHL 12, in which the House of Lords held that the exercise of stop and search powers did not involve a deprivation of liberty. This case was taken to the European Court of Human Rights, which held that the exercise of stop and search powers under the anti-terrorism legislation were unlawful: *Gillan and Quinton v United Kingdom*, Application No. 4158/05, 12 January 2010.

[117] (1980) 3 EHRR 533.

whether the SIAC could use information that may have been obtained as a consequence of torture; the second concerned the use of secret material in closed hearings.

The use of torture evidence

The House of Lords has unanimously decided that evidence obtained by torture cannot be used by the SIAC. In reaching this decision, the House overturned the Court of Appeal—but while the seven judges were agreed that torture evidence cannot be used, they disagreed about the approach to be taken when it is not certain that evidence has been obtained by torture. The majority (Lords Hope of Craighead, Rodger of Earlsferry, Carswell, and Brown of Eaton-under-Heywood) held that if the SIAC is in doubt as to whether the evidence was obtained by torture, then it should admit it, but bear its doubt in mind when evaluating the evidence. The minority (Lords Bingham, Nicholls, and Hoffmann) disagreed with this. They said that in cases in which there was doubt about the use of torture, the SIAC should refuse to admit the evidence. Given the fundamental nature of the obligation not to torture, the view of the minority must be correct in principle.

A, D and C v Secretary of State for the Home Department
[2005] UKHL 71

Lord Bingham

51 The Secretary of State is right to submit that SIAC is a body designed to enable it to receive and assess a wide range of material, including material which would not be disclosed to a body lacking its special characteristics. And it would of course be within the power of a sovereign Parliament (in breach of international law) to confer power on SIAC to receive third party torture evidence. But the English common law has regarded torture and its fruits with abhorrence for over 500 years, and that abhorrence is now shared by over 140 countries which have acceded to the Torture Convention. I am startled, even a little dismayed, at the suggestion (and the acceptance by the Court of Appeal majority) that this deeply rooted tradition and an international obligation solemnly and explicitly undertaken can be overridden by a statute and a procedural rule which make no mention of torture at all. [...] The matter is governed by the principle of legality very clearly explained by my noble and learned friend Lord Hoffmann in *R v Secretary of State for the Home Department, Ex p Simms* [2000] 2 AC 115, 131. [See Chapter 2, p. 55 and further discussion of the principle of legality in extract *R v Secretary of State for the Home Department, ex parte Pierson* in Chapter 3 on p. 95.]

[...] It trivialises the issue before the House to treat it as an argument about the law of evidence. The issue is one of constitutional principle, whether evidence obtained by torturing another human being may lawfully be admitted against a party to proceedings in a British court, irrespective of where, or by whom, or on whose authority the torture was inflicted. To that question I would give a very clear negative answer.

QUESTION
Why do you think the Law Lords differed in relation to situations in which it is uncertain whether evidence has been obtained by torture? Which approach do you think to be:

(a) the most principled?

(b) the most practical?

Closed hearings and secret evidence

The challenges brought by *AF* illustrate this aspect of the litigation. AF was born in the United Kingdom in 1980. His mother is English and divorced from his Libyan father. He has both UK and Libyan nationality. Although brought up in Libya, he has lived in England since 2004. A control order, confining him to his flat for eighteen hours a day, was first imposed on him on 24 May 2006. That order was revoked following the Court of Appeal's decision in *JJ*. A new order was imposed on 11 September 2006. This reduced the curfew period from eighteen hours to fourteen hours.

AF initially argued that this control order was an unlawful infringement of his liberty, but this ultimately failed in the House of Lords.[118] His second challenge was directed against the procedure adopted by the SIAC and, in particular, the reliance on closed material that neither he, nor his lawyers, were able to see. He argued that this was fundamentally unfair and contrary to his right to a fair hearing, as required by Arts 6 and 5(4) of the ECHR.

This aspect of the case reached the House of Lords on two occasions. On the first, Lord Bingham decided that the procedure was unfair; Lord Hoffmann disagreed with him. The three other judges delivered judgments that fell between those of Lord Bingham and Lord Hoffmann. They expressed the view that, in some cases, it would be possible for the controlee, with the assistance of the special advocate, to have a fair trial notwithstanding the admission of closed material and that, in others, it would not. The fair trial issue was fact-specific and the trial judge was best placed to resolve it.

As a result the case was remitted back to Stanley Burnton J, who held that, in the circumstances, the procedure was unfair. The Secretary of State appealed to the Court of Appeal, which, by a majority, allowed the appeal and held that there was no absolute requirement to disclose the essence of the case against AF. Lord Justice Sedley dissented, saying that a hearing could not be fair unless the case against AF were disclosed to him so that he could answer it. AF appealed once again to the House of Lords.

Re-enter *Belmarsh*

On 19 February 2009, shortly before the House of Lords was to hear AF's appeal, the Grand Chamber of the ECtHR handed down its judgment in *A and ors v UK*,[119] the case that had been taken to Strasbourg four years earlier by those who remained detained after the decision of the House of Lords in the 2004 *Belmarsh* case.

As we have mentioned, the Grand Chamber reiterated the main conclusions reached by the House of Lords—but the Court also made important pronouncements on the fairness of the closed procedure used by the SIAC when it dealt with challenges to certifications made under Pt IV of the ATCSA. Although Pt IV has been repealed, the judgment is important because it is relevant to other aspects of the SIAC's work. The judgment also has a wider significance in explaining the requirements of fairness. The core conclusions on this aspect of the Grand Chamber's unanimous decision are set out in the following extract.

---

[118] *Secretary of State for the Home Department v AF and MB* [2007] UKHL 46.
[119] Application No. 3455/05.

A and ors v UK
Grand Chamber of the ECtHR, Application No. 3455/05 (19 February 2009)

215. The Court recalls that although the judges sitting as SIAC were able to consider both the "open" and "closed" material, neither the applicants nor their legal advisers could see the closed material. Instead, the closed material was disclosed to one or more special advocates, appointed by the Solicitor General to act on behalf of each applicant. During the closed sessions before SIAC, the special advocate could make submissions on behalf of the applicant, both as regards procedural matters, such as the need for further disclosure, and as to the substance of the case. However, from the point at which the special advocate first had sight of the closed material, he was not permitted to have any further contact with the applicant and his representatives, save with the permission of SIAC. In respect of each appeal against certification, SIAC issued both an open and a closed judgment.

216. The Court takes as its starting point that, as the national courts found and it has accepted, during the period of the applicants' detention the activities and aims of the al'Qaeda network had given rise to a 'public emergency threatening the life of the nation'. [...]

217. Balanced against these important public interests, however, was the applicants' right under Article 5 (4) to procedural fairness. [...] in the circumstances of the present case, and in view of the dramatic impact of the lengthy - and what appeared at that time to be indefinite - deprivation of liberty on the applicants' fundamental rights, Article 5 (4) must import substantially the same fair trial guarantees as Article 6 (1) in its criminal aspect [...]

218. Against this background, it was essential that as much information about the allegations and evidence against each applicant was disclosed as was possible without compromising national security or the safety of others [...].

219. The Court considers that SIAC, which was a fully independent court [...] and which could examine all the relevant evidence, both closed and open, was best placed to ensure that no material was unnecessarily withheld from the detainee. In this connection, the special advocate could provide an important, additional safeguard through questioning the State's witnesses on the need for secrecy and through making submissions to the judge regarding the case for additional disclosure. On the material before it, the Court has no basis to find that excessive and unjustified secrecy was employed in respect of any of the applicants' appeals or that there were not compelling reasons for the lack of disclosure in each case.

220. The Court further considers that the special advocate could perform an important role in counterbalancing the lack of full disclosure and the lack of a full, open, adversarial hearing by testing the evidence and putting arguments on behalf of the detainee during the closed hearings. However, the special advocate could not perform this function in any useful way unless the detainee was provided with sufficient information about the allegations against him to enable him to give effective instructions to the special advocate. While this question must be decided on a case-by-case basis, the Court observes generally that, where the evidence was to a large extent disclosed and the open material played the predominant role in the determination, it could not be said that the applicant was denied an opportunity effectively to challenge the reasonableness of the Secretary of State's belief and suspicions about him. In other cases, even where all or most of the underlying evidence remained undisclosed, if the allegations contained in the open material were sufficiently specific, it should have been possible for the applicant to provide his representatives and the special advocate with information with which to refute them, if such information existed, without his having to know the detail or sources of the evidence which formed the basis of the allegations. An example would be the allegation made against several of the applicants that they

had attended a terrorist training camp at a stated location between stated dates; given the precise nature of the allegation, it would have been possible for the applicant to provide the special advocate with exonerating evidence, for example of an alibi or of an alternative explanation for his presence there, sufficient to permit the advocate effectively to challenge the allegation. Where, however, the open material consisted purely of general assertions and SIAC's decision to uphold the certification and maintain the detention was based solely or to a decisive degree on closed material, the procedural requirements of Article 5 (4) would not be satisfied.

The House of Lords immediately applied this judgment in *Secretary of State v AF and anor.*

Secretary of State for the Home Department v AF and anor
[2009] UKHL 28

Lord Phillips

[59] [The decision of the Grand Chamber] establishes that the controlee must be given sufficient information about the allegations against him to enable him to give effective instructions in relation to those allegations. Provided that this requirement is satisfied there can be a fair trial notwithstanding that the controlee is not provided with the detail or the sources of the evidence forming the basis of the allegations. Where, however, the open material consists purely of general assertions and the case against the controlee is based solely or to a decisive degree on closed materials the requirements of a fair trial will not be satisfied, however cogent the case based on the closed materials may be.

[...]

[62] [...] What is in issue in control order cases is whether there are reasonable grounds for suspecting involvement on the part of the controlee in terrorism-related activity. This is a low threshold to cross and there are, so it seems to me, bound to be cases where the closed evidence is so cogent that the judge can rightly form the conclusion that there is no possibility that the controlee would be able, if this evidence were disclosed to him, to dispel the reasonable suspicion. [...]

[63] There are, however, strong policy considerations that support a rule that a trial procedure can never be considered fair if a party to it is kept in ignorance of the case against him. The first is that there will be many cases where it is impossible for the court to be confident that disclosure will make no difference. Reasonable suspicion may be established on grounds that establish an overwhelming case of involvement in terrorism-related activity but, because the threshold is so low, reasonable suspicion may also be founded on misinterpretation of facts in respect of which the controlee is in a position to put forward an innocent explanation. A system that relies upon the judge to distinguish between the two is not satisfactory, however able and experienced the judge. Next there is the point made by Megarry J [in *John v Rees* [1970] Ch 345, in respect of the feelings of resentment that will be aroused if a party to legal proceedings is placed in a position where it is impossible for him to influence the result. The point goes further. Resentment will understandably be felt, not merely by the controlee but by his family and friends, if sanctions are imposed on him on grounds that lead to his being suspected of involvement in terrorism without any proper explanation of what those grounds are. Indeed, if the wider public are to have confidence in the justice system, they need to be able to see that justice is done rather than being asked to take it on trust.

[64] The best way of producing a fair trial is to ensure that a party to it has the fullest information of both the allegations that are made against him and the evidence relied upon in support of those allegations. [...] Both our criminal and our civil procedures set out to achieve these aims. In some circumstances, however, they run into conflict with other aspects of the public interest, and this is particularly the case where national security is involved. How that conflict is to be resolved is a matter for Parliament and for government, subject to the law laid down by Parliament. That law now includes the Convention, as applied by the HRA. That Act requires the courts to act compatibly with Convention rights, in so far as Parliament permits, and to take into account the Strasbourg jurisprudence. That is why the clear terms of the judgment in *A v United Kingdom* resolve the issue raised in these appeals.

[Once again, Lord Hoffmann dissented.]

Lord Hoffmann

[70] [...] I agree that the judgment of the European Court of Human Rights ('ECtHR') [...] requires these appeals to be allowed. I do so with very considerable regret, because I think that the decision of the ECtHR was wrong and that it may well destroy the system of control orders which is a significant part of this country's defences against terrorism. Nevertheless, I think that your Lordships have no choice but to submit. It is true that s 2(1)(a) of the Human Rights Act 1998 requires us only to 'take into account' decisions of the ECtHR. As a matter of our domestic law, we could take the decision in *A v United Kingdom* into account but nevertheless prefer our own view. But the United Kingdom is bound by the Convention, as a matter of international law, to accept the decisions of the ECtHR on its interpretation. To reject such a decision would almost certainly put this country in breach of the international obligation which it accepted when it acceded to the Convention. I can see no advantage in your Lordships doing so.

[...]

[74] [...] It is sometimes said that it is better for ten guilty men to be acquitted than for one innocent man to be convicted. Sometimes it is a hundred guilty men. The figures matter. A system of justice which allowed a thousand guilty men to go free for fear of convicting one innocent man might not adequately protect the public. Likewise, the fact in theory there is always some chance that the Applicant might have been able to contradict closed evidence is not in my opinion a sufficient reason for saying, in effect, that control orders can never be made against dangerous people if the case against them is based 'to a decisive degree' upon material which cannot in the public interest be disclosed. This, however, is what we are now obliged to declare to be the law.

QUESTIONS

1. Consider the two following perspectives.

'[...T]here are [...] bound to be cases where the closed evidence is so cogent that the judge can rightly form the conclusion that there is no possibility that the controlee would be able, if this evidence were disclosed to him, to dispel the reasonable suspicion.' '[...] There are, however, strong policy considerations that support a rule that a trial procedure can never be considered fair if a party to it is kept in ignorance of the case against him.' (Lord Phillips)

'A system of justice which allowed a thousand guilty men to go free for fear of convicting one innocent man might not adequately protect the public. Likewise, ... that in theory there is always some chance that the Applicant might have been able to contradict closed evidence is not ... a sufficient reason for saying ...that control orders can never be made against dangerous people if the case against them is based "to a decisive degree" upon material which cannot in the public interest be disclosed.' (Lord Hoffmann)

(a) Which of these two views is to be preferred?

(b) Given the importance of policy in these judgments, should fairness ultimately be determined by judges or by those who are politically accountable?

2. What do these judgments tell us about the nature of the duty upon UK judges 'to take account' (s. 2(1) HRA) of decisions of the ECtHR?

3. Is Lord Hoffmann correct to say that the consequence of the majority's decision is that dangerous people have to be turned free?

The aftermath of the decision

As Lord Hoffmann had predicted, following the decision, the Home Secretary decided to free AF after three years 'under virtual house arrest' rather than disclose the secret intelligence case against him. In the media, it was predicted that twenty other people would also be released. But this was not to be the end of the litigation. Legal proceedings were started with a view to obtaining compensation, although if successful the sums awarded are likely to be small.

Note that in the situations we have been considering the Closed Material Procedures (CMP) were used in proceedings that affected liberty. Where such procedures are used in situations that do not affect liberty or other fundamental rights the UK Supreme Court has held both that legislation permitting the use CMP is compatible with Art 6 and that no obligation exists to provide the person concerned with the 'gist' of the case against them.[120]

Finally, in this context we may note that the UK Supreme Court has held that the courts do not have the jurisdiction to permit the use of CMP to be extended to ordinary civil cases. The core reason is contained in Lord Dyson's leading judgment in *Al Rawi and ors v The Security Services*.

Lord Dyson Al Rawi and ors v The Security Services
[2011] UKSC 34,

47 Closed material procedures and the use of special advocates continue to be controversial. In my view, it is not for the courts to extend such a controversial procedure beyond the boundaries which Parliament has chosen to draw for its use thus far. It is controversial precisely because it involves an invasion of the fundamental common law principles [of openness and natural justice] ... [he cites Lord Phillips in *Secretary of State for the Home Department v AF (No 3)* [2009] UKHL 28] [...]

48 The common law principles to which I have referred are extremely important and should not be eroded unless there is a compelling case for doing so. If this is to be done at all, it is better done by Parliament after full consultation and proper consideration of the sensitive issues involved. [...]

---

[120] *Tariq v Home Office* [2011] UKSC 35.

Following that decision, the government issued a Green Paper, *Justice and Security* [121] proposing legislation to permit the use of CMP in ordinary civil proceedings. The Justice and Security Bill is in the House of Lords at the time of writing. Needless to say, the proposed extension of CMP is attracting considerable opposition. [122]

(j) THE IMPACT OF THE CONTROL ORDER LITIGATION

Different views exist on the implications of the litigation that we have described. Many commentators and human rights groups saw the legal challenges as the inevitable consequence of legislation that was hastily enacted with insufficient regard to the human rights consequences. Many will agree with Lord Hoffmann that the '*real threat to the life of the nation, in the sense of a people living in accordance with its traditional laws and political values, comes not from terrorism but from laws such as these*'.[123] From this perspective, the task of the courts has been to 'arrest the slide' from the principles enshrined in the HRA.[124] Others emphasized the potentially ameliorating influence of judgments, and the way in which the judges have drawn attention to weaknesses in legislative schemes and provided guidance for their improvement. This perspective arguably illustrates the existence of a dialogue between the courts and the other institutions of government, that we have discussed earlier in this chapter.

In terms of the effects of the judicial decisions on the way in which the control order scheme functioned, the following is an assessment by Professor Clive Walker.

Clive Walker, 'The threat of terrorism and the fate of control orders' [2010] Public Law 4–17 (footnotes omitted)

It is arguable that the principal consequence has been to minimise the use of control orders [...] There were dire predictions when the PTA 2005 was passed that control orders could affect "hundreds—thousands, who knows". Yet, just 15 orders were in force at the end of 2008. This paltry total stands in stark contrast to the apocalyptic analysis in 2007 of Jonathan Evans, the Director of the Security Service, that there were 2,000 specific people who posed a direct threat to national security, plus as many again yet to be identified. Clearly, the meagre number of control orders is not for a want of customers but relates to their relative lack of security effectiveness and legal certainty compared to criminal prosecution. The application by the courts of arts 5 and 6 and their willingness to traduce the assertions of the state are significant factors in this outcome.

The then Labour government, while clearly frustrated by some of the judgments not surprisingly, put a positive spin on its experience in the courts, arguing that the case law confirmed that the control order regime was not fundamentally flawed from a human rights perspective and stressing that the courts had adopted a nuanced approach that explained

---

[121] Cm 8194).

[122] See, e.g. JUSTICE, *Justice and Security Bill, House of Lords Second Reading Briefing* (June 2012).

[123] At [96], see p. 793 *A v Secretary of State for the Home Department*.

[124] David McKeever, 'The Human Rights Act and anti-terrorism in the UK: One great leap forward by Parliament, but are the courts able to slow the steady retreat that has followed?' [2010] Public Law 110, 139.

how individual circumstances should be handled.[125] However the overwhelming view, reflected by the Joint Committee on Human Rights, was that the control order regime was unsustainable and required reform.[126]

The Coalition Agreement of 20 May 2010 stated that the Government would 'urgently review control orders as part of a wider review of counter- terrorist legislation ...'.[127] On 13 July 2010 the Home Secretary launched a consultation on reform of anti terrorism legislation. The outcome was reported on 26 January 2011.[128] On the same day the Home Secretary, Theresa May, announced that Control Orders were to be replaced by a new regime known as Terrorism Prevention and Investigation Measures (TPIMS).[129] The Terrorism Prevention and Investigation Measures Bill was introduced to Parliament on 23 May 2011 and received the Royal Assent on 14 December 2011, after lengthy debates. The Joint Committee on Human Rights produced two reports on the Bill.[130]

The following are two extracts from the report of David Anderson QC, the Independent Reviewer of Terrorism Legislation, on the Prevention of Terrorism Act 2005. The first provides an overview of the new regime and the main differences between it and control orders. The Second extract is from his conclusion and offers some observations that are highly pertinent in the context of this case study.

David Anderson QC, Control Orders in 2011, Final Report of the Independent Reviewer on the Prevention of Terrorism Act 2005, March 2012 (footnotes omitted)

The new regime

5.6. The structure of the TPIM regime closely resembles that of the old control order regime. Thus:

- TPIM notices are made by the Secretary of State [TPIMA ss 2–3] after police and prosecutors have been consulted on whether there is evidence that could realistically be used to prosecute the intended subject. [TPIMA s. 10]

- A wide (though finite) range of measures may be imposed, including an overnight residence requirement, travel restrictions and restrictions on electronic communications and association with other persons.

- Permission to make a notice is required from the High Court, which goes on to hold a full review hearing unless the subject decides otherwise or the court decides to discontinue the review. [TPIMA ss 6–9]

- Appeals lie against any decision to vary, extend or revive a TPIM notice and any decision to refuse to vary or revoke a TPIM notice.[TPIMA s. 16]

---

[125] UK Government, *Reply to the Fifth Report from the Joint Committee on Human Rights* (Cm 7625, May 2009).

[126] Joint Committee on Human Rights, *Counter-terrorism Policy and Human Rights (Fourteenth Report): Annual Renewal of Control Orders Legislation 2009*, Fifth Report, Session 2008–09 (HL Paper 37, HC 282). See also Joint Committee on Human Rights, *Counter-terrorism Policy and Human Rights (Seventeenth Report): Bringing Human Rights Back In*, Sixteenth Report, Session 2009–10, HL Paper 86, HC 111.

[127] http://webarchive.nationalarchives.gov.uk/20100526084809/http://programmeforgovernment.hmg. gov.uk/civil-liberties/.

[128] *Review of Counter-Terrorism and Security Powers: Findings and Recommendations* 26 January 2011, Cm 8004.

[129] http://www.bbc.co.uk/news/uk-12287074.

[130] Legislative Scrutiny: Terrorist Prevention and Investigation Measures Bill (First Report) July 2011; (Second Report), 18 October 2011.

- In any court proceedings where secret evidence is involved, a system of special advocates is used. [TPIMA Sch. 4]

5.7. In addition to judicial scrutiny, two of the safeguards applicable under PTA 2005 apply also to the TPIM regime. Thus:

- The Secretary of State must produce a quarterly report on the exercise of her powers under the Act. [TPIMA s. 19]

- The Independent Reviewer must carry out an annual review of the operation of the Act, and produce an annual report which is laid before Parliament.

5.8. TPIMA 2011 however contains no equivalent to the requirement that PTA 2005 be annually renewed by Parliament. It lasts for five years, and may be further extended by the Secretary of State after consulting the Independent Reviewer, the Intelligence Services Commissioner, and the Director-General of the MI5, and after a resolution of each House of Parliament. [TPIMA S 21]

Principal differences

5.9. The absence of an annual sunset clause (5.8, above) is the one respect in which TPIMA 2011 is less liberal than the control order regime that it replaces. The annual renewal debates were described by Lord Carlile [David Anderson's predecessor] as *'a bit of a fiction, to be frank'*. The Joint Committee on Human Rights however considered the absence of annual reviews to be regrettable, since its effect is to normalise a system whose utility remains controversial. It is for consideration whether my annual reports on the operation of the TPIMA 2011 might be used to inform regular (or occasional) reviews by the Joint Committee or other Parliamentary Committees: […]

5.10. The other differences between the TPIM regime and the control order regime conform to the Coalition Government's expressed desire to remove the more intrusive elements of control orders and improve the safeguards for those subject to them. […] Those which seem to me potentially the most significant … [include]

Reasonable suspicion

5.11. The *'reasonable suspicion'* test in PTA 2005 has been replaced by a test of *reasonable belief* that a person is, or has been, involved in terrorism-related activity.[[TPIMA s. 3(1) *'Reasonable belief'* is a harder test to satisfy. […]

Two-year limit

5.16. There was no limit on the number of times a 12-month control order could be extended, so long as the necessity test continued to be met. As is evident from the table at 3.47 above, some controlled persons were subject to control orders for periods exceeding four years.

5.17. A TPIM notice, by contrast is subject to a two-year limit [TPIMA s. 5]

Range of Measures

5.21. The difference is most striking in relation to **geographical restrictions**. Thus:

- The power to **relocate** controlled persons to different towns and cities is removed. A Londoner must thus be allowed to continue to reside in London, even if his network is nearby: the option of sending him to a provincial town or city has gone. This is notwithstanding the fact that relocation was undoubtedly effective in disrupting networks, and that it had been upheld as proportionate in two cases during 2011.

- The frequently exercised power to *confine controlled persons to a particular area* is replaced by a much weaker power to exclude them from particular specified areas or places. So while a person may be prevented from visiting a particular street where an associate lives, he cannot be restricted to his own borough, or to a part of his own town [...]

5.22. *Curfews* of up to 16 hours are replaced by *"overnight residence measures"*. While no maximum length is specified, it would be surprising if these could be for more than 10 or 12 hours.

5.23. A power that potentially extended to a complete ban all *electronic communications* is replaced by a provision which requires the subject to be allowed the use of fixed line and mobile telephones and a computer with internet access.

5.24. Limits on the *freedom to associate* are relaxed [...] Association with named individuals can still be prohibited: but the previous practice of prohibiting all prearranged meetings and all visitors is to be abandoned, in favour of a policy to require new associations to be notified on the first occasion only.

5.25. *Police searches* for the purpose of determining whether there is compliance with TPIMs now require a warrant from the appropriate judicial authority

---

David Anderson QC, Control Orders in 2011, Final Report of the Independent Reviewer on the Prevention of Terrorism Act 2005, March 2012: Conclusions (footnotes omitted)

6. CONCLUSIONS

6.1. Early predictions that control orders could affect *'hundreds – thousands, who knows'* proved fortunately wide of the mark. So, less happily, did hopes that control orders might prove a useful accompaniment to the gathering of evidence for criminal prosecutions.

6.2. Instead, the control order came to occupy a small but important niche in the counter-terrorism armoury, useful and indeed necessary 'for a small number of cases where robust information is available to the effect that the individual in question presents a considerable risk to national security, and conventional prosecution is not realistic'.

6.3. Rarely has the exercise of governmental power been subject to more intense examination. I observed during the period under review that decisions on the making and review of control orders were prepared to the highest standards by officials, and taken with appropriate care and seriousness by Ministers. Expert High Court judges, attended by small armies of taxpayer-funded lawyers, scrutinised every order for compliance with statute and with ECHR rights. The appellate courts, crucially guided by Strasbourg where the vital question of disclosure was concerned, fashioned from not always promising statutory material a procedure that ensured at least the semblance of a fair trial. It is a matter for pride that in this area at least, the administrative and legal cultures of the United Kingdom addressed so conscientiously their responsibility to balance the sometimes irreconcilable requirements of national security and of individual freedom.

6.4. For all this, there remained something profoundly alien and unsettling about the control order. Individuals were placed under extraordinary and intrusive restrictions, often (in the early years of the regime) without explanation other than that they were suspected to be a threat to national security. Explanations became fuller after *AF (No. 3)*, but relocation became increasingly common. Legal review was far from immediate; and when the hearing came around, controlled persons spent crucial parts of it excluded from the court, oblivious both of the detailed accusations made against them and of the submissions made by Special Advocates who were able neither to communicate fully with them nor (in practice) to call evidence on their behalf. This could go on indefinitely. As one family member put it, '*You literally feel as though you are fighting a ghost and there never seems to be any light at the end of the tunnel.*' Only in the face of strong necessity could it ever be justifiable for the individual to be placed in such a position by the State.

6.5. Though TPIMs are in several respects a less severe version of control orders, it is to be hoped that executive orders of this kind, however expertly prepared and reviewed they may be, will never need to be used on a larger scale than has been the case to date. The ideal would be for renewal of the TPIM system beyond its initial 5-year currency to be judged unnecessary. whether or not this proves possible, it is important that efforts continue to improve the amenability of terrorist activity to trial by criminal process, including if it is feasible to do so the admission of the intercept evidence prohibited by RIPA section 17 but accepted by nearly all other common law countries.

[...]

What is to be expected of TPIMs?

6.31. TPIMs are a different animal from control orders. The raising of the threshold from reasonable suspicion to reasonable belief of involvement in terrorism-related activity is a positive development, though of limited practical significance since the higher threshold seems already to be met in practice. Of greater importance are two other changes: the ending of involuntary relocation, and the limitation of TPIMs (save in cases where fresh evidence comes to light) to two years.

6.32. It is important to understand that both these changes were voluntary political decisions. They were not a consequence of judicial disapproval of the previous system, either in the United Kingdom or in Strasbourg.

6.33. In each case, there were sound national security reasons to perpetuate the previous system. Relocation was undoubtedly effective, in some cases, as a means of disrupting and diffusing terrorist networks. Similarly, the ability to maintain restrictions for more than two years was of obvious utility in the case of persons who could still not be prosecuted or deported at the end of that period, and had not been deradicalised during it. Knowledge that the restrictions can (absent fresh evidence) last for only two years has the potential to strengthen the resolve of a terrorist who – confronted with an order of potentially indefinite length – might have proved more willing to compromise. [...]

6.35. In evaluating the package as a whole, it is also relevant that significant extra resources for covert investigative techniques, including human and technical surveillance, were allocated to police and MI5. This led Jonathan Evans, Director General of MI5, to deliver the carefully worded verdict that '*as a result of the replacement legislation and the additional funding that has been made available, there should be no substantial increase in overall risk*'. However surveillance – which begins and ends with observation – is not a complete substitute for disruptive measures such as relocation.

6.36. Ultimately, the replacement of control orders by TPIMs was a political decision, taken on civil liberties rather than national security grounds. I do not criticise the Government for its attempts to balance those two factors, for as the Justice Secretary recently wrote:

'The primary role of any government is to keep its citizens safe and free. That means both protecting them from harm and protecting their hard-won liberties.'

As so often, however, liberty has a price. The aim of the Coalition Government has been to ensure that the price of the change to TPIMs will be paid only in financial terms, rather than in a substantially increased risk of terrorism-related activity.

6.37. Unlike its predecessor, TPIMA 2011 will not be subject to annual review by Parliament. I welcome comments from those with experience of it, and look forward to monitoring its operation and to summarising it in my first report under the Act, early in 2013.

ONLINE RESOURCE CENTRE

Visit the Online Resource Centre for up-to-date information on the impact of the control order legislation.

QUESTIONS

1. '*The control order cases showed both the effectiveness of the HRA and that there is a healthy democratic dialogue between the judiciary and the government and Parliament.*' Is there evidence of this in the report by David Anderson QC?

2. 'Ultimately, the replacement of control orders by TPIMs was a political decision, taken on civil liberties rather than national security grounds', David Anderson QC. Is this is a sign that lawyers and the courts have too much power in the UK's constitutional system?

6 CONCLUDING COMMENTS

By enabling litigants to rely on the Convention rights in domestic courts, the Human Rights Act 1998 has transformed arguments about human rights. It has also obliged judges to become centrally engaged in some of the most difficult and sensitive issues—not least that of determining where responsibility lies, within the UK constitutional system, for balancing the public interest in security and the rights of individuals who threaten that security. But the chapter has also shown that human rights law is not only about terrorism: it also touches the lives of ordinary people, including schoolchildren, and those who live in care and nursing homes.

As we saw in Chapter 6, there is continuing debate about the future of the HRA and there is a strong possibility that some form of UK Bill of Rights will be enacted that could replace or supplement the HRA. Were the HRA to be repealed, what effect might this have? Of course, the answer will depend on what, if anything, replaces it. If the HRA were repealed and not replaced, litigants would lose the ability to rely on the ECHR directly in domestic courts—but it is strongly arguable that the principles and standards that are contained in its provisions have now been absorbed into the common law, and would be enforceable by means of judicial review or by other forms of action, such as in tort.

7 FURTHER READING

Amos, M., *Human Rights Law* (2006, Oxford: Hart Publishing)

Beatson, J., Grosz, S., Hickman, T., Singh, R., and Palmer, S., *Human Rights: Judicial Protection in the United Kingdom* (2008, London: Sweet & Maxwell)

Feldman, D., (ed.) *English Public Law*, 2nd edn (2009, Oxford: OUP), chs 7–12 and 19

Hickman, T., *Public Law after the Human Rights Act*: (2010, Oxford: Hart Publishing)

Kavanagh, A., *Constitutional Review under the UK Human Rights Act* (2009, Cambridge: Cambridge University Press)

Wadham, J., Mountfield, H., Prochaska, E., and Brown, C., *Blackstone's Guide to the Human Rights Act 1998*, 6th edn (2011, Oxford: OUP)

Walker, C., *Terrorism and the Law*: (2011, Oxford: OUP)

ONLINE RESOURCE CENTRE

Updates on the reform of the Human Rights Acts and further developments can be found on the Online Resource Centre at www.oxfordtextbooks. co.uk/orc/lesueur2e/

18

EUROPEAN UNION LAW IN THE UNITED KINGDOM COURTS

CENTRAL ISSUES

1. This chapter will begin by examining the key European Union (EU) principles of direct effect and supremacy. These twin principles continue to determine national judicial responses to EU law. Neither direct effect nor supremacy have a formal basis in the Treaty on the Functioning of the European Union (TFEU) but were developed by the European Court of Justice (ECJ) on its understanding that the EU constitutes 'a new legal order'. Direct effect applies in principle to all binding provisions of EU law, although its exact meaning remains contested. The doctrine of supremacy means that, in the event of conflict between a provision of European and national law, the national courts are duty-bound to apply the former.

2. In their attempts to reconcile the doctrines of direct effect and supremacy with the doctrine of parliamentary sovereignty, the UK courts have produced two responses to EU law in their case law: the 'construction' approach and the 'disapplication' approach. The requirement to 'disapply', or 'set aside', national law does not mean that national law is nullified and rendered void; rather, the offending provision of national law remains valid law and may be legitimately applied in another case not involving EU law.

3. Many national courts are uneasy with the idea of unconditional supremacy and have reserved for themselves a power of ultimate constitutional review of EU law. By way of contrast, the UK courts have traditionally not been as assertive. The most important case to date has been the House of Lords' decision in *Factortame*. This chapter will not only examine the factual background of the case, but also analyse the constitutional impact that the case has had.

4. Although the House of Lords appears to accept the ECJ's monist view of unconditional supremacy, the High Court, in the case of *Thoburn*, took a different approach.

1 INTRODUCTION

This chapter is about how membership of the European Union (EU) has affected public law cases. Most litigation involving issues of EU law takes place not in the European Court of Justice (ECJ)[1] in Luxembourg, but in the courts and tribunals of the member states. In the United Kingdom, questions of EU law arise in many different types of proceeding in diverse courts and tribunals. This chapter will examine the constitutional challenges for the national courts upon the United Kingdom's accession to the European Economic Community (EEC) on 1 January 1973, as well as the evolution of their responses since that date. Having initially accepted the incoming tide of Community law, either through consistent interpretation of national law in conformity with Community law or through disapplication of contrary national law, the tide appears to be turning and national courts in the United Kingdom, as well as in other member states, have started to argue that they will assert nationally protected fundamental rights against the supremacy of EU law.

BOX 18.1 EUROPEAN COMMUNITY LAW AND EUROPEAN UNION LAW

In the course of this chapter we will be referring to 'European Community (EC) law', as well as to 'European Union (EU) law'. Prior to the Lisbon Treaty, the distinction between European Community (Pillar I) law and European Union (Pillars II and III) law was significant and substantive: it was only in cases in which a conflict arose between EC law and the law of a member state that EC law took precedence. (EU law, by contrast, was intergovernmental in nature and did not create 'a new legal order' that produced rights and obligations for individuals.)

As we discussed in Chapter 12, the Lisbon Treaty changes not only the structure of the European Union (the 'European Community' has ceased to exist), but also the terminology. 'Community law' is now confined to history. As a result, references in this chapter to 'Community law' have to be understood in that (historical) context. As of 1 December 2009, EU law is superior to, and takes precedence over, all forms of national law. In cases in which the ECJ's decisions on EC law have continuing and general relevance, the new terminology of 'EU law' is used.

---

2 THE CREEPING CONSTITUTIONALIZATION OF EUROPEAN UNION LAW

Two legal principles have not only shaped the constitutional architecture of the EU, but (more importantly for present purposes) also underpin the way in which EU law issues are handled by the UK courts and tribunals. The first principle of *direct effect* means that individuals are able to enforce EU rights and obligations directly before their national courts. Correspondingly, national courts are under an obligation to apply EU law. The second and

---

[1] The ECJ's official name changed, following the entry into force of the Lisbon Treaty, from the 'Court of Justice of the European Communities' to the 'Court of Justice' (see further Chapter 14). For the sake of clarity and simplicity it is still customary, however, to refer to the Court as the 'European Court of Justice' (or simply as the ECJ).

related principle of the *supremacy* of EU law means that any national law in conflict with EU law is rendered inapplicable. UK courts still do not have the power of constitutional review—that is, they cannot deem a statute to be null and void because it is 'unconstitutional'. In the context of EU law, they do, however, have an obligation to 'disapply', or set aside, national law that is found to be in conflict with EU law.

These two principles cannot be found in the treaties.[2] They were developed by the ECJ in two cases, decided in the early 1960s, which are the cornerstones of the EU legal order. The two principles have been accepted by all member states as part of the *acquis communautaire* (that is, the entire body of European laws). In short, the principles of direct effect and supremacy determine the situations in which a litigant appearing in a UK court or tribunal can claim that rights or obligations are created *directly* by EU legislation itself, without the need for any national legislation to have implemented it into the legal system of the member state. This method was particularly important during the early phases of the Common Market and heralded the 'creeping constitutionalization' of Community law.

The first landmark case involves a Dutch haulage company called van Gend en Loos. The company was importing a consignment of a chemical product into the Netherlands. Confronted by an increase in the duty applicable to the product, the company objected that the change to the Dutch rules infringed the Treaty. The Dutch authorities responded that the rules in the Treaty did not create rights on which individuals or companies could rely. The Dutch court referred the case under Art. 167 TFEU to the ECJ, which set out the basic principle of *direct effect*.

Case 26/62 *NV Algemene Transporten Expeditie Onderneming van Gend & Loos v Nederlandse Administratie der Belastingen*
Netherlands Inland Revenue Administration [1963] ECR 1, 12

The European Economic Community constitutes a new legal order of international law for the benefit of which the States have limited their sovereign rights, albeit within limited fields, and the subjects of which comprise not only the Member States but also their nationals.

Independently of the legislation of Member States, Community law not only imposes obligations on individuals but is also intended to confer upon them rights which become part of their legal heritage. These rights arise not only where they are expressly granted by the Treaty but also by reason of obligations which the Treaty imposes in a clearly defined way upon individuals as well as upon the Member States and upon the institutions of the Community.

[. . .]

According to the spirit, the general scheme and the wording of the EEC Treaty, [Article 30 TFEU] must be interpreted as producing direct effects and creating individual rights which national courts must protect.

You will recall from Chapter 12 that, under Art. 288 TFEU, EU regulations are 'directly applicable' in each member state. 'Directly applicable' means that certain provisions of EU law (such as regulations and some Treaty provisions) become national law without further enactment. The concept of direct applicability stems from the original Treaty and refers to the method of incorporation. This should not be confused with direct effect, which is a tool developed by the ECJ in *van Gend* and applies in principle to all binding EU law (Treaty

---

[2] This principle of supremacy (or primacy) was made express by Art. I-6 of the Draft Constitutional Treaty, and is now moved to a footnote in Declaration No. 17 to the Lisbon Treaty.

provisions, regulations, and directives) that can be relied on by individuals in their national courts. Certain provisions of EU law are directly effective in that they create '*individual rights that the national courts have to protect*' without any implementing measure in the member state in question.[3]

When the ECJ uses the term 'direct effect', it refers to rights (not obligations); more specifically, it refers to the rights that are enforceable by legal individuals (natural persons or privately held companies) rather than by public authorities. There are two ways in which direct effect can be understood. On the one hand, direct effect may be understood as 'objective direct effect'. According to this understanding, direct effect refers to '*the capacity of a provision of EU law to be invoked before a national court*'. But on the other hand, it may also be understood as 'subjective direct effect': it refers to the '*capacity of a provision of EU law to confer rights on individuals which they may enforce before national courts*'.[4] The difference between the two understandings may only be slight, but it has important practical consequences. Under the first definition, an individual has only the *right to invoke* EU law, whereas under the second definition, an individual has the *right to rely on a substantive EU right* before the national court—for example, the right not to be discriminated against on ground of nationality.[5]

The ECJ, in *van Gend*, identified three conditions to be met before a Treaty provision could have direct effect.

1. The provision must be clear and precise (that is, the concepts contained in the provision must not leave to the member states an element of discretion in applying EU law).
2. It must be unconditional (that is, it must not depend on the control, judgement, or discretion of an EU institution or another member state).
3. Its operation must not be dependent on further action being taken by EU or national authorities (sometimes, the rights granted by EU law will come into effect when further action of a legislative or executive nature has been taken by the EU or the member states).

These initial conditions have been modified over the years, but, for now, they convey the essence of direct effect, which is that a provision of EU law has to be 'self-executing'. It is therefore possible for a directive to be directly effective (if it is clear, precise, unconditional, and creates rights), but not directly applicable (a directive requires further implementation), for a Treaty provision to be directly applicable, but not directly effective (because it does not satisfy the three conditions of direct effect), and for a regulation to be both directly applicable and directly effective.

The second landmark case, *Costa v ENEL*, established the supremacy, primacy, or precedence of Community (now EU) law over national law. Since the purpose of the EEC was the creation of a common market between different states, the ECJ argued that this aim would be undermined if Community law were to be deemed to be subordinate to the national laws of the member states. *Costa* involved a challenge to the legality of an electricity bill issued by the newly nationalized Italian state electricity authority. The Court echoed its ruling in *van Gend*, but also went one step further.

---

[3] Case 26/62 *Van Gend en Loos* [1963] ECR 1, 2.
[4] P. Craig and G. de Búrca, *EU Law*, 4th edn (2008, Oxford: OUP), p. 270.
[5] Case 57/65 *Lütticke v Hauptzollamt Saarlouis* [1966] ECR 205.

Case 6/64 *Flaminio Costa v ENEL*
[1964] ECR 585, 593–4

By contrast with ordinary international treaties, the EEC Treaty has created its own legal system which, on the entry into force of the Treaty, became an integral part of the legal systems of the member states and which their courts are bound to apply.

By creating a Community of unlimited duration, having its own institutions, its own personality, its own legal capacity and capacity of representation on an international plane and, more particularly, real powers stemming from a limitation of sovereignty or a transfer of powers from the states of the Community, the member states have limited their sovereign rights, albeit within limited fields, and have thus created a body of law which binds both their nationals and themselves.

The integration into the laws of each member state of provisions which derive from the Community, and more generally the terms and the spirit of the Treaty, make it impossible for the states, as a corollary, to accord precedence to a unilateral and subsequent measure over a legal system accepted by them on a basis of reciprocity. Such a measure cannot therefore be inconsistent with that legal system. The executive force of Community law cannot vary from one state to another in deference to subsequent domestic laws, without jeopardizing the attainment of the objectives of the Treaty set out in [Art. 4(3) TEU].

The obligations undertaken under the Treaty establishing the Community would not be unconditional, but merely contingent, if they could be called in question by subsequent legislative acts of the signatories. Wherever the Treaty grants the states the right to act unilaterally, it does this by clear and precise provisions [. . .]. Applications, by member states for authority to derogate from the Treaty are subject to a special authorization procedure [. . .] which would lose their purpose if the member states could renounce their obligations by means of an ordinary law.

The precedence of Community law is confirmed by [Art. 267 TFEU], whereby a regulation 'shall be binding' and 'directly applicable in all member states'. This provision, which is subject to no reservation, would be quite meaningless if a state could unilaterally nullify its effects by means of a legislative measure which could prevail over Community law.

It follows from all these observations that the law stemming from the Treaty, an independent source of law, could not, because of its special and original nature, be overridden by domestic legal provisions, however framed, without being deprived of its character as Community law and without the legal basis of the Community itself being called into question.

According to the ECJ, Community law (now EU law) is an autonomous system of law, the validity of which cannot be called into question by the national laws of the member states. The continuing net effect of *van Gend* and *Costa* is that national courts are required to apply directly effective EU law in the course of litigation. Any national law that could hinder the application of EU law must either be ignored or set aside. This may be acceptable when it comes to custom duties or product standards (in relation to which the need for harmonization across the member states is more obvious and less controversial)—but what if EU law collides with national constitutional law (for example, fundamental rights)?

In *Internationale Handelsgesellschaft*,[6] the ECJ held that the legal status of a conflicting national measure was not relevant to the question of whether Community (now EU) law

---

[6] Case 11/70 *Internationale Handelsgesellschaft mbH v Einfuhr- und Vorratsstelle für Getreide und Futtermittel* [1970] ECR 1125.

should take precedence. In other words, not even a fundamental rule of national constitutional law could be invoked to challenge the supremacy of directly applicable EU law. The ECJ ruled that it was the only court that was authorized to set EU measures aside and that the national courts had no power to do so.

In the *Simmenthal*,[7] the ECJ repeated and reinforced its earlier rulings. It held that all national courts must directly and immediately enforce a clear and unconditional provision of Community law, even where there is a directly conflicting national law and even if that national law was adopted *after* the enactment of the provision of Community law in question.

3 PARLIAMENTARY SOVEREIGNTY AND THE EUROPEAN UNION

The United Kingdom joined the EEC (in effect, a trade grouping of eight western European states) on 1 January 1973.[8] The United Kingdom had needed to overcome a number of political and psychological (but not legal) obstacles. Its application to join the EEC in 1961 had been twice vetoed by French President Charles de Gaulle, who thought that France's voice in world affairs would be weakened by the United Kingdom's close ties with the USA and that the British government was not sufficiently committed to European integration. The United Kingdom also had to overcome its ambivalence about the EEC, which it continued to view from the perspective of a former colonial power whose legal and political system was superior over, rather than subject to, its counterparts on the Continent.

As far as the clarity of European law was concerned, the doctrines of direct effect and supremacy were already a decade old; *Internationale Handelsgesellschaft* had also already been decided. Still, as one commentator put it, '*no country was constitutionally as ill-prepared for what was to come as the UK*'.[9] This is arguably true for several familiar reasons.

(a) EU law (especially the principles of direct effect and supremacy) contradicts the 'negative' limb of Dicey's formulation by stipulating that there is a body other than the Crown in Parliament that has the right to override or set aside the legislation of Parliament.

(b) According to Dicey[10] and Wade,[11] Parliament cannot bind its successor. As a result, the limitations imposed by the European Communities Act 1972 (namely, not to legislate contrary to EU law) are a severe limitation on the legislative freedom of later Parliaments.

(c) UK courts cannot annul an Act of Parliament on the ground that it conflicts with 'higher' norms (be they common law or EU law). In other words, a statute properly enacted by the Crown in Parliament will be interpreted by the courts as representing the will of Parliament.[12]

---

[7] Case 106/77 *Amministrazione delle Finanze dello Stato v Simmenthal SpA* [1978] ECR 629.

[8] See the Treaty of Accession (1972) Cmnd 7461.

[9] J. Cornford, 'On writing a constitution' (1991) 44 Parliamentary Affairs 558.

[10] A.V. Dicey, *Introduction to the Study of the Law of the Constitution* (1885; 10th edn 1959, London: Macmillan & Co), pp. 41–3.

[11] H.W.R. Wade, 'The basis of legal sovereignty' (1955) Cambridge Law Journal 172, 174.

[12] *Edinburgh and Dalkeith Railway Co v Wauchope* (1842) 8 Cl & Fin 710; *Lee v Bude and Torrington Junction Rly Co* (1871) LR 6 CP 576; *British Railways Board v Pickin* [1974] AC 765.

(d) Finally, Danny Nicol argues that members of Parliament (MPs) knew very little of the constitutional implications when they conducted the debate as to EEC membership. He claims that the political nature of the UK constitution made it harder for politicians to ascertain the legal implications of their actions and, regarding the EEC, to appreciate fully the legal aspects of membership.[13]

But these positions are not gospel and have been vigorously contested. In relation to the first, Neil Walker notes that Dicey's 'positive' limb (that Parliament can make or unmake any law whatsoever) remains untouched by the European Communities Act 1972. Walker points out that this limb is *'the true kernel of Parliamentary sovereignty and its logically prior element, since the terms of the positive doctrine necessarily imply the power to secure the proposition contained in the "negative" side'.*[14]

In relation to the second point, Parliament may be able to accept limitations regarding 'manner and form' by altering its composition or the procedures by which valid laws are made.[15] For example, it could require a super-majority in Parliament or a referendum by the people before a particular statute could be amended. Applied to the EU, it might be argued that the European Communities Act 1972 has amended the 'manner and form' of subsequent legislation and has *procedurally* bound future Parliaments.[16]

The third point, that a court cannot question the validity of an Act of Parliament, is challenged by an obligation under EU law to give effective protection to rights and enforce obligations created by EU law. In large part, this stems from an important provision in the Treaty.

Article 4 TEU

Member States shall take any appropriate measure, general or particular, to ensure fulfilment of the obligations arising out of the Treaties or resulting from the acts of the institutions of the Union.

The Member States shall facilitate the achievement of the Union's tasks and refrain from any measure which could jeopardise the attainment of the Union's objectives.[17]

On the final point, there is ample evidence to suggest that parliamentarians in the Commons and the Lords did know exactly what they were letting themselves in for—especially in

---

[13] D. Nicol, *EC Membership and the Judicialization of British Politics* (2001, Oxford: OUP).

[14] 'Fundamental Law', in J.D. Stair (ed.) *The Laws of Scotland: Stair Memorial Encyclopaedia—Constitutional Law* (2002, Edinburgh: Butterworths), p. 44.

[15] See generally R.F.V. Heuston, *Essays in Constitutional Law*, 2nd edn (1964, London: Stevens), ch. 1. See also the discussion of the European Union Act 2011 in Chapter 12.

[16] Voices in favour: J.D.B. Mitchell, 'British law and British membership' (1971) 2 Europarecht 97, 100–3; G. Winterton, 'The British Grundnorm: Parliamentary supremacy revisited' (1976) 92 Law Quarterly Review 591, 614–15: s. 2(1) of the European Communities Act 1972 has created a new legislature, consisting of the Crown and both Houses of Parliament, which has given its permanent consent to Community law and the legislative organs of the Community. Voices against: T.C. Hartley, *Constitutional Problems of the European Union* (1999, Oxford: Hart Publishing), p. 171, fn. 21: *'Parliament did not redefine or abolish itself when it passed the European Communities Act, nor did it redefine what constitutes an Act of Parliament or change the procedures required to enact one.'*

[17] Article 10 TEC used to provide: *'Member States shall take all appropriate measures, whether general or particular, to ensure fulfilment of the obligations arising out of this Treaty or resulting from action taken by the institutions of the Community. They shall facilitate the achievement of the Community's tasks. They shall abstain from any measure which could jeopardise the attainment of the objectives of this Treaty.'*

relation to sovereignty, which was obviously at stake.[18] In 1960, Lord Kilmuir, the Lord Chancellor, advised Edward Heath (then Lord Privy Seal) in a letter that:

> Adherence to the [1957] Treaty of Rome would, in my opinion, affect our sovereignty in three ways: Parliament would be required to surrender some of its functions to the organs of the Community; the Crown would be called on to transfer part of its treaty-making power to those organs; our courts of law would sacrifice some degree of independence by becoming subordinate in certain respects to the European Court of Justice... In the long run we shall have to decide whether economic factors require us to make some sacrifice of sovereignty...'.[19]

In spite of this advice, the government gave numerous political assurances before the United Kingdom acceded to the Treaty of Rome that 'nothing in [the European Communities Act 1972] abridges the ultimate sovereignty of Parliament'.[20] The government produced two White Papers,[21] which insisted that there was 'no question of any erosion of essential national sovereignty'.[22] Moreover, successive Lord Chancellors[23] denied that Parliament would surrender its sovereignty or that the Act by which the United Kingdom acceded to the EEC would be irreversible.

House of Lords Hansard, 8 May 1967, vol. 282, cols 1202–3

The Lord Chancellor, Lord Gardiner

This United Kingdom legislation would be an exercise of Parliamentary sovereignty and Community law, existing and future, would derive its force as law in this country from it. The Community law so applied would override our national law so far as it was inconsistent with it. Under the British constitutional doctrine of Parliamentary sovereignty no Parliament can preclude its successors from changing the law. It is, however, implicit in acceptance of the Treaties that the United Kingdom would not only accept existing Community law but would also refrain from enacting future legislation inconsistent with Community law. Such a restraint on our legislative system would not be unprecedented. Our legislation often takes account—has to take account—of treaty obligations; for example the Charter of the United Nations, NATO, GATT, the Ottawa Agreements and the Warsaw and Guadalajara Conventions, which your Lordships were considering earlier this afternoon. Further, several Acts of Parliament have reduced for all time vast territorial areas of our sovereignty—the Statute of Westminster and the various Acts of Independence granted to India and other countries. It is the continuing incidence of legislation emanating from the Community institutions that would be without precedent.

There is in theory no constitutional means available to us to make it certain that no future Parliament would enact legislation in conflict with Community law. It would, however, be

---

[18] See generally J. Forman, 'The European Communities Act 1972' (1973) 10 Common Market Law Review 39.

[19] Public Records Office (PRO), FO 371/150369.

[20] Sir G. Rippon, 831 HC Deb 278, 15 February 1972.

[21] In 1967, on *Legal and Constitutional Implications of United Kingdom Membership of the European Communities* (Cmnd 3301); in 1971, on *UK and European Communities* (Cmnd 4715).

[22] 1971 White Paper, para. 29.

[23] See also Lord Hailsham of St Marylebone, HL Deb, 27 July 1971, vol. 323, cols 195–256.

> unprofitable to speculate upon the academic possibility of a future Parliament enacting legislation expressly designed to have that effect. Some risk of inadvertent contradiction between United Kingdom legislation and Community law could not be ruled out; but, of course, we must remember that if we joined the Community we should be taking part in the preparation and enactment of all future Community law and our participation would reduce the likelihood of incompatibility.

The Treaty of Accession was also subject to a legal challenge in 1971 (that is, before it was signed) by a litigant in person called Raymond Blackburn. He argued that the government would be acting unlawfully if it were to join the EEC, because the government would be surrendering 'the sovereignty of the Crown in Parliament'. The Court of Appeal struck out his action. A closer look at Lord Denning's judgment reveals that legal and political actors in the United Kingdom were very much aware of the consequences of joining the EEC. Notice how Lord Denning adopts the language of the ECJ in *Costa* when he says that sovereignty will, in the future, be 'limited' and 'shared'.

Blackburn v Attorney General
[1971] 1 WLR 1037, 1039–40

Lord Denning

It does appear that if this country should go into the Common Market and sign the Treaty of Rome, it means that we will have taken a step which is irreversible. The sovereignty of these islands will thenceforward be limited. It will not be ours alone but will be shared with others. [. . .]

Mr. Blackburn points out that many regulations made by the European Economic Community will become automatically binding on the people of this country: and that all the courts of this country, including the House of Lords, will have to follow the decisions of the European court in certain defined respects, such as the construction of the treaty. [. . .]

Mr. Blackburn takes a second point. He says that, if Parliament should implement the treaty by passing an Act of Parliament for this purpose, it will seek to do the impossible. It will seek to bind its successors. According to the treaty, once it is signed, we are committed to it irrevocably. Once in the Common Market, we cannot withdraw from it.[24] No Parliament can commit us, says Mr. Blackburn, to that extent. He prays in aid the principle that no Parliament can bind its successors, and that any Parliament can reverse any previous enactment. He refers to what Professor Maitland said about the Act of Union between England and Scotland. Professor Maitland in his *Constitutional History of England* (1908) said, at p. 332:

> "We have no irrepealable laws; all laws may be repealed by the ordinary legislature, even the conditions under which the English and Scottish Parliaments agreed to merge themselves in the Parliament of Great Britain."

We have all been brought up to believe that, in legal theory, one Parliament cannot bind another and that no Act is irreversible. But legal theory does not always march alongside political reality. Take the Statute of Westminster 1931, which takes away the power of Parliament to legislate for the Dominions. Can any one imagine that Parliament could or would reverse

---

[24] That position changed after the Lisbon Treaty which, under Art. 59 TEU, provides for an express route to withdrawal.

that Statute? Take the Acts which have granted independence to the Dominions and territories overseas. Can anyone imagine that Parliament could or would reverse those laws and take away their independence? Most clearly not. Freedom once given cannot be taken away. Legal theory must give way to practical politics. It is as well to remember the remark of Viscount Sankey L.C. in *British Coal Corporation v The King* [1935] A.C. 500, 520:

"[. . .] the Imperial Parliament could, as matter of abstract law, repeal or disregard section 4 of the Statute of Westminster . But that is theory and has no relation to realities."

What are the realities here? If Her Majesty's Ministers sign this treaty and Parliament enacts provisions to implement it, I do not envisage that Parliament would afterwards go back on it and try to withdraw from it. But, if Parliament should do so, then I say we will consider that event when it happens. We will then say whether Parliament can lawfully do it or not.

In essence, Lord Denning is saying the following. If the sovereignty doctrine is designed to be a reflection of political life in the United Kingdom, then it must be able to explain those instances in which Parliament abandons its sovereignty over particular territories. This it does in effect by stating that future parliaments will no longer be able to legislate on their behalf without their consent.[25] A.V. Dicey, too, had acknowledged that although Parliament could not bind its successors, it was, however, able to abdicate its overall sovereignty—for example, by transfer to another body.[26] This may happen in two situations. First, Parliament can transfer its jurisdiction over British territory to another legislature (as it did by recognizing the independence of Ireland or other UK colonies, which Lord Denning discusses in the extract). Second, it can transfer legislative competence over certain matters to another body—for example, an international organization such as the EU, the North Atlantic Treaty Organization (NATO), or the United Nations (UN). So, constitutionally speaking, neither decolonization nor membership in international organizations should pose any problems. In both cases, however, Parliament survives the transfer and (since it is sovereign) can pass repealing or conflicting legislation—hence the constitutional headache.

In the context of Community membership, the doctrine of parliamentary sovereignty was both an advantage and a source of difficulty. Whereas other countries such as Germany and Ireland had to amend their constitutions, the United Kingdom needed only to pass a standard statute—the European Communities Act 1972—to give effect to Community law and to recognize its supremacy over national law—although only by alluding to the direct applicability and supremacy of Community law over UK law in the obscure language of the statute.

European Communities Act 1972, s. 2

General implementation of Treaties

(1) All such rights, powers, liabilities, obligations and restrictions from time to time created or arising by or under the Treaties [. . .] are without further enactment to be given legal effect or used in the United Kingdom [. . .].

---

[25] See, e.g., Canada Act 1982, s. 2, which provides that: '*No Act of the Parliament of the United Kingdom passed after the Constitution Act, 1982 comes into force shall extend to Canada as part of its law.*'

[26] A.V. Dicey, *Introduction to the Study of the Law of the Constitution* (1885; 10th edn 1959, London: Macmillan & Co), p. 69, fn. 1.

> (4) [...] any enactment passed or to be passed [...] shall be construed and have effect subject to the foregoing provisions of this section [...].

Section 2(1) is best understood as the 'gateway' for directly applicable provisions of Community law into the UK legal order, which are to be given legal effect 'without further enactment'. As Lord Gardiner notes, no guarantee could be given that Parliament would not, in the future, legislate (advertently or inadvertently) in a manner contrary to Community law. But s. 2(4) was specifically drafted to avoid the possibility of conflict between Community law and subsequent UK statutes.

4 THE RECEPTION OF COMMUNITY LAW BY THE UK COURTS

This chapter discusses how successful Parliament was in actually legislating against a conflict of national and Community (now EU) law. It tells the story of the attempts by the UK courts to get to grips with the European doctrines of direct effect and supremacy, on the one hand, and the domestic doctrine of parliamentary sovereignty, on the other. Between 1981 and 2008, the House of Lords gave almost a hundred judgments that dealt with substantial European law. The cases occurred at the rate of about one a year in the 1980s, four a year in the 1990s, and five a year in the 2000s. The House of Lords also referred thirty-six of those cases to the ECJ—a respectable proportion of the 434 references made by all UK courts and tribunals. Although these statistics clearly reflect the growing importance of European law,[27] '... the attitude of the Law Lords to the ECJ over the first 30 years of UK membership of the European Union has for the most part been one of loyal and uncritical compliance ...'.[28]

You should be able to see by now that the courts are in a potentially sensitive situation, guided as they are by the supremacy of EU law and the doctrine of parliamentary sovereignty. They have attempted to reconcile these competing constitutional demands in three ways:

(a) by applying the later statute and overriding Community law;
(b) by constructing the later statute in conformity with Community law; and
(c) by giving effect to Community law by 'disapplying' the later statute.

(a) NATIONAL LAW OVERRIDES COMMUNITY LAW

There is a strand of legal practice that treats customary international law as an automatic part of the common law. This goes back to William Blackstone (1723–80) who opined that *'the law of nations [...] is here adopted in its full extent by the common law, and is held to be*

---

[27] F. Jacobs and D. Anderson, 'European Influences', in L. Blom-Cooper et al. (eds) *The Judicial House of Lords 1876–2009* (2009, Oxford: OUP), pp. 486–7; A. Le Sueur, *A Report on Six Seminars About the UK Supreme Court*, Queen Mary School of Law Legal Studies Research Paper No. 1/2008, p. 48.

[28] D. Anderson, 'The Law Lords and the European Courts' in A. Le Sueur (ed.) *Building the UK's New Supreme Court* (2004, Oxford: Oxford University Press), p. 204.

part of the law of the land.[29] This so-called 'monist' view, which merges public international law with national law, is, however, heavily compromised by the rule that national law must override international law in the case of inconsistency,[30] although the courts will assume parliamentary intent to conform to its established principles.[31]

Interestingly, in the first case in which the Court of Appeal had to consider the Treaty of Rome, the Treaty was understood to have become part of domestic law *precisely as if the terms of the Treaty were contained in an enactment of the Parliament of the United Kingdom*.[32] Lord Denning MR, in particular, in a number of mid-to-late 1970s cases, defined the judiciary's approach to Community law. In a further case (decided on the same day as *Application des Gaz*), he found that the Treaty of Rome was *'part of our law. It is equal in force to any statute'*.[33] As a result, it had lost its international character, was formally no different from any other Act of Parliament, and could be overruled under the doctrine of implied repeal.

These words obviously stem from the early days of Community membership during which the true character of Community law was not yet appreciated by the judiciary. In any event, though, the UK constitution is not 'monist', but 'dualist', meaning that public international law must first be *incorporated* by an Act of Parliament into national law before it can be invoked in the courts.[34] Indeed, in an article from 1962, Keenan falsely assumed that Britain, upon joining the Communities, would have to 'incorporate' the Treaty of Rome into English law.[35]

But dualism is not the correct way to conceive EU law either. The suggestion that Community (now EU) law would become part of British law either through incorporation or delegation (like public international law) is wrong for three reasons. First, from a national constitutional perspective, EU law is not transformed into national law in the same way in which public international law is; on the contrary, the original treaties are detached from general international law and are not incorporated into national law by the European Communities Act 1972. Second, the incorporation model does not take account of the need for EU law to produce direct effect before it can be enforced by a national court. Third, the delegation model (according to which directly effective EU law is a subordinate instrument of the national legal system) cannot coexist with the supremacy of EU law. Both incorporation and delegation are products of Diceyan sovereignty theory. As such, they tend to emasculate the idea of EU law as a new and distinct legal order for the benefit of which the member states have voluntarily shifted the boundaries of their sovereign powers.

It should be clear that EU law possesses an overriding quality that international law does not have and which Diceyan constitutional theory does not support. This explains why Lord Denning had initially made the impact of Community law conditional upon statutory recognition, which, in turn, reasserted the sovereignty of Parliament. In situations in which a later statute conflicted with an earlier statute, then a proper application of the doctrine of implied repeal would only require consideration of the later statute regardless of the fact that the earlier norm is the European Communities Act 1972. This is what happened in *Felixstowe*

---

[29] W. Blackstone, *Commentaries on the Law of England Vol. IV* (1769, Oxford: Clarendon Press), p. 67.

[30] *Cheney v Conn (Inspector of Taxes)* [1968] 1 All ER 779, 782, *per* Ungoed-Thomas J.

[31] *Salomon v Customs and Excise Commissioners* [1967] 2 QB 116, 143, *per* Diplock LJ.

[32] *Application des Gaz v Falks Veritas* [1974] Ch. 381, 399 E, *per* Stamp LJ.

[33] *HP Bulmer Ltd v J. Bollinger SA* [1974] Ch 401, 418E–419C.

[34] See further Chapter 12.

[35] P.B. Keenan, 'Some legal consequences of Britain's entry into the European Common Market' [1962] Public Law 327.

Docks Railway Co v British Transport Docks Board,[36] in which an Act of Parliament was in clear conflict with Art. 86 EEC (now Art. 102 TFEU).[37] Lord Denning reiterated his earlier mantra ('*Article 86 is now part of English law*') and, having equalized Acts of Parliament with the Treaty of Rome, asserted the ultimate authority of Parliament: '*It seems to me that once the Bill is passed by Parliament and becomes a Statute, that will dispose of all this discussion about the Treaty. These Courts will then have to abide by the Statute without regard to the Treaty at all.*'[38]

This is a clear case of national law overriding Community law in the event of conflict. Lord Diplock, speaking extrajudicially and a few years before the *Felixstowe* case, had made a similar point.

Lord Diplock, 'The Common Market and the common law' (1972) 6 Law Teacher 3, 8

It is a consequence of the constitutional doctrine of the supremacy of the Queen in Parliament that if a subsequent Act of Parliament were passed that was in conflict with any provision of the Treaty which is of direct application in the member states [...] the courts of the United Kingdom would be bound to give effect to the Act of Parliament notwithstanding any conflict.

The *Felixstowe* case is a startling example of Diceyan orthodoxy in the European context. It suggests that any conflict between an earlier norm (in these cases, always the European Communities Act 1972) and a later Act of Parliament has to be resolved in favour of the latter. According to Murray Hunt, the case was '*an isolated example of outright judicial rejection of the supremacy of Community law*',[39] although—as Lord Diplock's comment suggests—not an isolated view at the time.

A mere two years after *Felixstowe*, however, Lord Denning was already revising his views in *Shields v E Coombes (Holdings) Ltd.*[40] Lord Denning recognizes for the first time that decisions and opinions of the ECJ (and, in this case, the doctrines of direct effect and supremacy) were binding on national courts by virtue of s. 3(1) of the European Communities Act 1972.

Shields v E Coombes (Holdings) Ltd
[1978] 1 WLR 1408, 1415A–B, 1416A–B

Lord Denning

[W]henever there is a conflict or inconsistency between the law contained in an article of the Treaty and the law contained in the internal law of one of the member states, whether passed before or after joining the Community, it says that in any such event the law of the Community shall prevail over that of the internal law of the member state

---

[36] [1976] 2 CMLR 655, 664.

[37] This provision in EU competition law prohibits the abuse by a company of its dominant position, e.g. by monopolising the market.

[38] At 664–5.

[39] M. Hunt, *Using Human Rights Law in English Courts* (1997, Oxford: Hart Publishing), p. 67.

[40] [1978] 1 WLR 1408.

> [He then toyed with imagery that has become a famous part of European law mythology in the UK.]
>
> All this shows that the flowing tide of Community law is coming in fast. It has not stopped at high-water mark. It has broken the dykes and the banks. It has submerged the surrounding land. So much so that we have to learn to become amphibious if we wish to keep our heads above water.

The following sections discuss how the UK courts learned to become 'amphibious'—that is, how they learned to steer a course between the safe and dry lands of national law and the deep and unknown waters of EU law.

(b) THE CONSTRUCTION APPROACH

Statutory construction based on the ECA 1972

The second approach that the courts have used to deal with conflicting Community law is that of statutory interpretation. In *Macarthy's v Smith*, Mrs Smith argued that she had been discriminated against on the grounds of gender when she took up a stockroom keeper's position at £50 per week, replacing a male equivalent who had left his job with the employer more than four months before she was appointed and who had been paid £60 per week. In proceedings before an industrial tribunal, she claimed that she was entitled to equal pay under s. 1(2) of the Equal Pay Act 1970, as amended by the Sex Discrimination Act 1975. Her employers argued that s. 1(2) applied only in cases in which a man and a woman were employed by the same employer on like work *at the same time*. Mrs Smith argued that s. 1(2) should be interpreted so as to give effect to the principle contained in Art. 157 TFEU that men and women should receive equal pay for equal work, and that this provision also covered cases in which a woman was employed on like work *in succession* to a man. Interestingly, the ECJ had already decided that Art. 157 TFEU was directly effective[41] and so could be relied on by Mrs Smith before the national court.

Macarthy's v Smith
[1979] 3 All ER 325, 331–4; 334–6

> **Lawton LJ**
>
> This case started by raising what seemed to the parties to be an issue of fact, namely whether Mrs Smith had been employed on like work of a broadly similar nature to that done by her immediate predecessor, a Mr McCullough, in the job of taking charge of the employer's stockroom. It will end as a case of historical interest as being the first to be sent by this court to the [...] European Court of Justice for an opinion on the construction and application of an article of the EEC Treaty. Further it may be of constitutional importance if the opinion when given conflicts with the clear terms of a statute. [...]
>
> I [...] start with the issues as I see them. They are these: first, is the meaning of the relevant parts of the Equal Pay Act 1970 as amended, (hereinafter referred to as 'the Act') clear? If it is, what is it? Secondly, if it is not clear, how is the Act to be construed? Thirdly, is the

---

[41] Case 43/75 *Defrenne v SABENA* [1976] ECR 455.

meaning of [Art. 157 TFEU] of the EEC Treaty clear? If it is, what is it? Fourthly, if they clear meaning conflicts with the clear meaning of the relevant parts of the Act, what should this court do? Fifthly, if the meaning of [Art. 157 TFEU] is not clear, what should this court do?

The Act envisages that women's contracts of employment shall contain an equality clause: see s 1(1). Such a clause is to contain provisions having specified effects: see s 1(2). In my judgment the grammatical construction of s 1(2) is consistent only with a comparison between a woman and a man in the same employment at the same time. The words, by the tenses used, look to the present and the future but not to the past. They are inconsistent with a comparison between a woman and a man, no longer in the same employment, who was doing her job before she got it. [...]

As the meaning of the words used in s 1(2) and (4) is clear, and no ambiguity, whether patent or latent, lurks within them, under our rules for the construction of Acts of Parliament the statutory intention must be found within those words. It is not permissible to read into the statute words which are not there or to look outside the Act, as counsel for Mrs Smith invited us to do and Phillips J did, to read the words used in a sense other than that of their ordinary meaning. Counsel for Mrs Smith submitted that the Act should be read in harmony with the Sex Discrimination Act 1975; but that Act, as s 6(6) expressly provides, 'does not apply to benefits consisting of the payment of money when the provision of those benefits is regulated by the woman's contract of employment'. It follows, so it seems to me, to be irrelevant that the Sex Discrimination Act 1975 does allow a comparison between the benefits, other than those consisting of money, which a man got when doing a job and which his successor, a woman, did not get when doing the same job, whereas under the Act relied on by Mrs Smith in this case comparison in relation to pay is outside it.

What led Phillips J to construe s 1(2) and (4) of the Act so as to allow such a comparison were the provisions of [Art. 157 TFEU] [...]. In this court counsel on both sides have submitted that the meaning of this article is clear; but they have differed as to what that meaning is. Counsel for Mrs Smith has submitted that under [Art. 157 TFEU] a woman should receive the same pay as a man she follows in a job, unless there are factors, other than sex discrimination, which justify the difference. If this be right, [Art. 157 TFEU] says something different from what I adjudge to be the plain, unambiguous meaning of s 1(2) and (4) of the Act. When an Act and an article of the EEC Treaty are in conflict, which should this court follow? Counsel for Mrs Smith says the article, because s 2 of the European Communities Act 1972 so provides, as does European Community law. Thus in *Amminstrazione delle Finanze dello Stato v Simmenthal SpA* ([1978] ECR 629 at 630) the European Court of Justice adjudged

'A national court which is called upon, within the limits of its jurisdiction, to apply provisions of Community law is under a duty to give full effect to those provisions, if necessary refusing of its own motion to apply any conflicting provision of national legislation, even if adopted subsequently, and it is not necessary for the court to request or await the prior setting aside of such provisions by legislative or other constitutional means.'

Counsel for the employers submitted that [Art. 157 TFEU] envisages that men and women working side by side for the same employer and doing like or broadly similar work should be paid the same. He further submitted that the opening words of the article, 'Each Member State shall [...] ensure and subsequently maintain [...]', envisages that the member states should enact their own legislation to ensure and maintain the application of the principle that men and women should receive equal pay for equal work. He argued that the United Kingdom had done so by amending the Equal Pay Act 1970 and that if the Commission of the European Communities [...] thought that the United Kingdom had not done enough in this respect, it was not for this court to ignore what it had done by way of legislation but for the European Court of Justice to adjudge whether the United Kingdom had discharged its Treaty obligations. [...]

In my opinion there is some doubt whether [Art. 157 TFEU] applies to the facts of this case.

We cannot, as counsel for the employers submitted, ignore [Art. 157 TFEU] and apply what I consider to be the plain meaning of the Act. The problem of the implementation of [Art. 157 TFEU] is not one for the EEC Commission to take up with the government of the United Kingdom and Northern Ireland, as counsel for the employers submitted it was. [Art. 157 TFEU] gives rise to individual rights which our courts must protect. [...]

Being in doubt as to the ambit of [Art. 157 TFEU] and being under an obligation arising both from the decisions of the European Court of Justice...and s 2 of the European Communities Act 1972 to apply that article in our courts, it seems to me that this is a situation to which [Art. 267 TFEU] applies. I consider that a decision is necessary as to the construction of [Art. 157 TFEU] and I would request the European Court of Justice to give a ruling on it.

Cumming-Bruce LJ

I agree with the reasoning and conclusion of Lawton LJ. The first question is: what does s 1(2)(a)(i) of the Equal Pay Act 1970 as amended by the Sex Discrimination Act 1975 mean? This question has to be answered by applying the ordinary rules of construction which have been established in this country. One such rule is that words in an Act of Parliament have their natural and ordinary meaning unless such a meaning is manifestly inconsistent with the context, or gives rise to such absurdity or injustice that Parliament cannot have intended such meaning. [...]

I am left so far wholly unconvinced that there is any reason for giving s 1 (2)(a)(i) a meaning other than that which at first impression I thought was the ordinary and natural meaning of the words. [...]

Like Lawton LJ I do not find it easy to discern the application of [Art. 157 TFEU] to the circumstances contemplated by s 1 (2)(a)(i) of the English statute having regard to my construction thereof. I take the view that [Art. 157 TFEU], which expresses a general principle, may be perfectly consistent with the English legislation as I construe it. But I am not sure about that, and therefore agree that the court at Luxembourg should give an authoritative answer to that question. Secondly, I do not think that it is permissible, as an aid to construction, to look at the terms of the Treaty. If the terms of the Treaty are adjudged in Luxembourg to be inconsistent with the provisions of the Equal Pay Act 1970, European law will prevail over that municipal legislation. But such a judgment in Luxembourg cannot affect the meaning of the English statute.

The majority of the Court (Lawton and Cumming-Bruce LJJ) reasoned that the plain meaning of the statutory language was of primary importance. For the first time, a UK court had found that it was under a duty to give priority to a directly effective provision of Community law that stood in conflict with an Act of Parliament. It clearly recognized that Art. 157 TFEU could not be ignored, because it gave rise to individual rights that required protection. The Court of Appeal's emphasis is on the rules of construction in the approach that it took.

- The national Court interprets national law according to the traditional rules of statutory construction.
- It considers Community law separately.
- If the meaning of Community law is unclear, the correct procedure is to refer the case to the ECJ under Art. 267 TFEU and not to second-guess the ECJ's own rules of construction.
- If there is a conflict, Community law prevails over national law.

By giving priority to Community law in case of conflict, does the Court of Appeal also endorse the view that s. 2(4) of the European Communities Act 1972 has been entrenched, and that the doctrine of parliamentary sovereignty has been compromised?

M. Hunt, *Using Human Rights Law in English Courts* (1997, Oxford: Hart Publishing), p. 71

Yet significantly, though unsurprisingly, the majority did not consider their conclusion to involve any compromise of Parliamentary sovereignty. For them, the reconciliation with sovereignty theory was straightforward. Far from subverting the sovereignty of Parliament, they believed that they were in fact applying it, because Parliament, 'by its own act in the exercise of its sovereign powers', has enacted that European Community law is to be given direct effect (s. 2(1)) and accorded supremacy (s. 2(4)). It followed that the Court was merely implementing the will of Parliament expressed in the 1972 Act, in the absence of any indication in the subsequent Act that Parliament had changed its mind.

Macarthy's is, however, not remembered for the reasoning of the majority, but for Lord Denning's dissent. His dissent was groundbreaking because of the innovative way in which his statutory interpretation started with Community law and worked its way downwards to national law. Later cases were to follow Lord Denning's approach.

Macarthy's v Smith
[1979] 3 All ER 325, 328–31

Lord Denning (dissenting)

The EEC Treaty

[Art. 157 TFEU] says:
'Each Member State shall during the first stage ensure and subsequently maintain the application of the principle that men and women should receive equal pay for equal work [...]'
That principle is part of our English law. It is directly applicable in England. So much so that, even if we had not passed any legislation on the point, our courts would have been bound to give effect to [Art. 157 TFEU]. If a woman had complained to an industrial tribunal or to the High Court and proved that she was not receiving equal pay with a man for equal work, both the industrial tribunal and the court would have been bound to give her redress: [see *Defrenne v SABENA].*

In point of fact, however, the United Kingdom has passed legislation with the intention of giving effect to the principle of equal pay [in Art. 157 TFEU]. It has done it by the Sex Discrimination Act 1975 and in particular by s 8 of that Act amending s 1 of the Equal Pay Act 1970. No doubt the Parliament of the United Kingdom thinks that it has fulfilled its obligations under the Treaty. But the European Commission take a different view. They think that our statutes do not go far enough.

What then is the position? Suppose that England passes legislation which contravenes the principle contained in the Treaty, or which is inconsistent with it, or fails properly to implement it. There is no doubt that the European Commission can report the United Kingdom to the European Court of Justice; and that court can require the United Kingdom to take the necessary measures to implement [Art. 157 TFEU]. That is shown by [Art. 258 TFEU] and [Art. 260 TFEU] [...].

It is unnecessary, however, for these courts to wait until all that procedure has been gone through. Under s 2(1) and (4) of the European Communities Act 1972 the principles laid down in the Treaty are 'without further enactment' to be given legal effect in the United Kingdom; and have priority over 'any enactment passed or to be passed' by our Parliament So we are entitled and I think bound to look at [Art. 157 TFEU] because it is directly applicable here; and also any directive which is directly applicable here: see *Van Duyn v Home Office (No. 2)*. We should, I think, look to see what those provisions require about equal pay for men and women. Then we should look at our own legislation on the point, giving it, of course, full faith and credit, assuming that it does fully comply with the obligations under the Treaty. In construing our statute, we are entitled to look to the Treaty as an aid to its construction; but not only as an aid but as an overriding force. If on close investigation it should appear that our legislation is deficient or is inconsistent with Community law by some oversight of our draftsmen then it is our bounden duty to give priority to Community law. Such is the result of s 2(1) and (4) of the European Communities Act 1972.

I pause here, however, to make one observation on a constitutional point. Thus far I have assumed that our Parliament, whenever it passes legislation, intends to fulfil its obligations under the Treaty. If the time should come when our Parliament deliberately passes an Act with the intention of repudiating the Treaty or any provision in it or intentionally of acting inconsistently with it and says so in express terms then I should have thought that it would be the duty of our courts to follow the statute of our Parliament. I do not however envisage any such situation. [...]

[Article 157 TFEU]

[Article 157 TFEU] is framed in European fashion. It enunciates a broad general principle and leaves the judges to work out the details. In contrast the Equal Pay Act is framed in English fashion. It states no general principle but lays down detailed specific rules for the courts to apply (which, so some hold, the courts must interpret according to the actual language used) without resort to considerations of policy or principle. [...]

In my opinion [...] [Art. 157 TFEU] is reasonably clear on the point; it applies not only to cases where the woman is employed on like work *at the same time* with a man in the same employment, but also when she is employed on like work in succession to a man, that is, in such close succession that it is just and reasonable to make a comparison between them.

The Equal Pay Act 1970

Now I turn to our Act to see if that principle has been carried forward into our legislation. The relevant part of this Act was passed not in 1970 but in 1975 by s 8 of the Sex Discrimination Act 1975. [...]

Now stand back and look at the statutes as a single code intended to eliminate discrimination against women. They should be a harmonious whole. To achieve this harmony s 1(2)(a)(i) of the Equal Pay Act should not be read as if it included the words 'at the same time'. It should be interpreted so as to apply to cases where a woman is employed at the same job doing the same work 'in succession' to a man.

Combining the two provisions

By so construing the Treaty and the statutes together we reach this very desirable result: it means that there is no conflict between [Art. 157 TFEU] and s 1(2) of the Equal Pay Act; and that this country will have fulfilled its obligations under the Treaty. [...]

So I would hold, in agreement with Phillips J, that both under the Treaty and under the statutes a woman should receive equal pay for equal work, not only when she is employed *at the same time* as the man, but also when she is employed at the same job *in succession* to him, that is, in such close succession that it is just and reasonable to make a comparison between them.

According to Lord Denning, a court in a case such as *Macarthy's* should construct or interpret national law by:

- examining the relevant principles in the Treaty that are directly applicable;
- taking into account any directive that may be directly applicable; and
- looking at the relevant national legislation, giving it 'full faith and credit', and assuming that it fully complies with the Treaty obligations.

Lord Denning dissented from the majority view that Community law could supersede UK law in the sense of supplanting it and rendering it void; instead, Community law was merely an aid to the construction of national law.

Given that s. 2(4) of the European Communities Act 1972 touches upon the issue of supremacy, Lord Denning's construction approach is, on the one hand, an attractive way of giving effect to EU law: it is a domestic principle of statutory interpretation rooted in domestic law (rather than an ECJ imposition in the form of direct effect and supremacy). The words '*shall be construed and have effect*' in s. 2(4) mean neither that Parliament intended statutes to override EU law, nor that the hands of future parliaments are substantively tied. Inconsistencies are resolved in favour of EU law unless Parliament spells out expressly that it wishes to legislate contrary to EU law. On the other hand, Lord Denning's reasoning is also characterized by a degree of subversiveness.

T.R.S. Allan, *Law, Liberty, and Justice: The Legal Foundations of British Constitutionalism* (1993, Oxford: Clarendon Press), p. 277

Lord Denning's position may be regarded as lying at the borderline between creative interpretation and (notional) disobedience. Directly applicable Community law would override an inconsistent Act of Parliament except where Parliament had expressly stipulated for the opposite result. He naturally assumed Parliament's continuing, underlying intention to fulfil its obligations under the Treaty: 'If the time should come when our Parliament deliberately passes an Act with the intention of repudiating the Treaty or any provision in it or [...] of acting inconsistently with it *and says so in express terms* then [...] it would be the duty of our courts to follow the statute of our Parliament.' The result is to establish a presumption of legislative intent which can be defeated only by the adoption of explicit statutory language in rebuttal. This is in effect to impose a special requirement of form—if not of 'manner and form'—for a particular purpose; and the distinction between the application of statute and its interpretation has all but disappeared.

The novelty of Lord Denning's dissent lay in the acceptance of Community law as part of the nationally valid sources of law. The Court was thus given a choice of sources with which to resolve the conflict without first having to refer the case to the ECJ. Since then, the dominant line of cases has used strong principles of construction. In *Pickstone v Freemans*[42] and in *Litster v Forth Dry Dock*,[43] the House of Lords was not prepared to approve a literal interpretation of statutory instruments and was unanimous in holding that words ought to be implied into national law in order to achieve the purpose of giving effect to the EC directive.

The employer in *Pickstone* employed both men and women as warehouse operatives, and as checker warehouse operatives. The applicants were five female 'warehouse operatives', who claimed that they were entitled to equal pay with a male 'checker warehouse operative' employed by the same mail order company, on the basis that their work was of equal value within the meaning of s. 1(2)(c) of the Equal Pay Act 1970, as amended by the Equal Pay (Amendment) Regulations 1983. The draft Regulations of 1983 were presented to Parliament as giving full effect to the ECJ's decision in *Commission v UK*.[44]

The employer argued that a woman warehouse operative was employed for like work to that of the male warehouse operatives, so that a claim under s. 1(2)(c) of the 1970 Act was barred. This was a literal interpretation of the 1970 Act. The employer succeeded before the industrial tribunal and the Employment Appeals Tribunal (EAT). The Court of Appeal allowed the appeal on the ground that, in the circumstances, the female employees were entitled to pursue equal value claims under Art. 157 TFEU, and the House of Lords dismissed the employer's appeal.

Pickstone v Freemans Plc
[1989] AC 66, 111–12, 123, 125–8

Lord Keith

The opposite result would leave a large gap in the equal work provision, enabling an employer to evade it by employing one token man on the same work as a group of potential women claimants who were deliberately paid less than a group of men employed on work of equal value with that of the women. This would mean that the United Kingdom had failed yet again fully to implement its obligations under [Art. 157 TFEU] and the Equal Pay Directive, and had not given full effect to [*Commission v UK*] It is plain that Parliament cannot possibly have intended such a failure. The draft Regulations of 1983 were presented to Parliament as giving full effect to the decision in question. The draft Regulations were not subject to the Parliamentary process of consideration and amendment in Committee, as a Bill would have been. In these circumstances and in the context of section 2 of the European Communities Act 1972 I consider it to be entirely legitimate for the purpose of ascertaining the intention of Parliament to take into account the terms in which the draft was presented by the responsible Minister and which formed the basis of its acceptance. [...] There was no suggestion that the exclusionary words in paragraph (c) were intended to apply in any other situation than where the man selected by a woman complainant for comparison was one in relation to whose work paragraph (a) or paragraph (b) applied. It may be that, in order to confine the words in question to that situation, some necessary implication falls to be made into their literal meaning. The precise terms of that implication do not seem to me to matter. It is

---

[42] [1989] AC 66.
[43] [1990] 1 AC 546.
[44] Case 61/81 [1982] ICR 578.

sufficient to say that the words must be construed purposively in order to give effect to the manifest broad intention of the maker of the Regulations and of Parliament. I would therefore reject the employers' argument.

Lord Templeman

In *Duke v Reliance Systems Ltd.* [1988] A.C. 618 this House declined to distort the construction of an Act of Parliament which was not drafted to give effect to a Directive and which was not capable of complying with the Directive as subsequently construed by the European Court of Justice. In the present case I can see no difficulty in construing the Regulations of 1983 in a way which gives effect to the declared intention of the Government of the United Kingdom responsible for drafting the Regulations and is consistent with the objects of the E.E.C. Treaty, the provisions of the Equal Pay Directive and the rulings of the European Court of Justice. I would dismiss the appeal.

Lord Oliver

A construction which permits the section to operate as a proper fulfilment of the United Kingdom's obligation under the Treaty involves not so much doing violence to the language of the section as filling a gap by an implication which arises, not from the words used, but from the manifest purpose of the Act and the mischief it was intended to remedy. The question is whether that can be justified by the necessity – indeed the obligation - to apply a purposive construction which will implement the United Kingdom's obligations under the Treaty. [...]

It must [...] be recognised that so to construe a provision which, on its face, is unambiguous involves a departure from a number of well-established rules of construction. The intention of Parliament has, it is said, to be ascertained from the words which it has used and those words are to be construed according to their plain and ordinary meaning. The fact that a statute is passed to give effect to an international treaty does not, of itself, enable the treaty to be referred to in order to construe the words used other than in their plain and unambiguous sense. Moreover, even in the case of ambiguity, what is said in Parliament in the course of the passage of the Bill, cannot ordinarily be referred to assist in construction. I think, however, that it has also to be recognised that a statute which is passed in order to give effect to the United Kingdom's obligations under the E.E.C. Treaty falls into a special category and it does so because, unlike other treaty obligations, those obligations have, in effect, been incorporated into English law by the European Communities Act 1972. [...]

[...] I am satisfied that the words of section 1(2)(c), whilst on the face of them unequivocal, are reasonably capable of bearing a meaning which will not put the United Kingdom in breach of its Treaty obligations. This conclusion is justified, in my judgment, by the manifest purpose of the legislation, by its history, and by the compulsive provision of section 2(4) of the Act of 1972. It is comforting indeed to find, from the statement made by the Minister to which my noble and learned friend has referred, that this construction does in fact conform not only with what clearly was the parliamentary intention but also with what was stated to be the parliamentary intention. I do not, however, think that it is necessary to rely upon this, since the conclusion is, in my judgment, amply justified by the other factors which I have mentioned. For these reasons and for those given by my noble and learned friend, Lord Templeman, I agree that the appeal should be dismissed.

Pickstone v Freemans shows a very assured Lord Keith fully rejecting the employer's narrow and literal interpretation, and fully embracing the purposive construction of the national law in question. In doing so, he offers little guidance as to how exactly the literal meaning of the statutory words are to be modified. According to Lord Keith, it was sufficient to construe the words purposively in order to give full effect to the 1983 Regulations and Parliament's intentions.

Lord Oliver's reasoning, in contrast, was more cautious. He acknowledged that the purposive approach was novel and that it involved a departure from traditional rules of statutory interpretation. Nevertheless, in the end, Lord Oliver came to realize that the equal pay legislation fell into a 'special category' and had to be construed in light of the United Kingdom's Community obligations.

In *Litster v Forth Dry Dock*, the Council Directive 77/187/EEC provided for the protection of employee's rights in the event of a change of employer. According to the Directive, an employer could not evade unfair dismissal or redundancy payment legislation simply by transferring the business to someone else. In other words, an employee's contractual rights could be enforced against the new employer. The UK Transfer of Undertakings (Protection of Employment) Regulations 1981[45] were designed to incorporate the Directive—but they applied only to employees who were employed 'immediately' before the transfer. The employees in *Litster* (a permanent workforce of twelve skilled ship workers of various trades) were sacked at 3.30 p.m. and the takeover took place at 4.30 p.m. of the same day. The question for the Court was whether the one-hour gap eliminated the workers' contractual rights against the new owner, which would be the case if they were not employed 'immediately' before the transfer.

The House of Lords acknowledged that a strictly literal interpretation of the Regulations supported the employer's argument (a gap of one hour was not the same as 'immediately'). But Lord Oliver referred to *Pickstone* (in particular, to Lord Templeman's speech) to justify a purposive construction of domestic law in order to give effect to the Council Directive. Lord Oliver was more confident this time in observing that a purposive construction may be applied to legislation even though it might involve some departure from the strict and literal application of the words that the legislature has elected to use.

Litster v Forth Dry Dock
[1990] 1 AC 546, 559, 576

Lord Oliver

The approach to the construction of primary and subordinate legislation enacted to give effect to the United Kingdom's obligations under the E.E.C. Treaty have been the subject matter of recent authority in this House (see *Pickstone v Freemans Plc.* [1989] A.C. 66) and is not in doubt. If the legislation can reasonably be construed so as to conform with those obligations – obligations which are to be ascertained not only from the wording of the relevant Directive but from the interpretation placed upon it by the European Court of Justice at Luxembourg – such a purposive construction will be applied even though, perhaps, it may involve some departure from the strict and literal application of the words which the legislature has elected to use.

[...] the purpose of the Directive and of the Regulations was and is to "safeguard" the rights of employees on a transfer and that there is a mandatory obligation to provide remedies which are effective and not merely symbolic to which the Regulations were intended to give effect. The remedies provided by the [Employment Protection (Consolidation) Act 1978] in

[45] SI 1981/1794.

the case of an insolvent transferor are largely illusory unless they can be exerted against the transferee as the Directive contemplates and I do not find it conceivable that, in framing Regulations intending to give effect to the Directive, the Secretary of State could have envisaged that its purpose should be capable of being avoided by the transparent device to which resort was had in the instant case. *Pickstone v Freemans Plc.* [1989] A.C. 66, has established that the greater flexibility available to the court in applying a purposive construction to legislation designed to give effect to the United Kingdom's Treaty obligations to the Community enables the court, where necessary, to supply by implication words appropriate to comply with those obligations: see particularly the speech by Lord Templeman [...]

In neither *Pickstone* nor *Litster* do the judges stipulate the basis for a 'purposive' approach. Lord Templeman, in both cases, finds the interpretative obligation in Community law (the ECJ's decision in *Von Colson*), whereas Lord Oliver appears to follow Lord Diplock's principle of construction in *Garland v British Rail Engineering* (discussed in the following section). Interestingly, not one of the judgments in either case relies on ss 2(1) and (4) of the European Communities Act 1972 to justify their purposive approach, which tends to suggest that the duty on the courts to interpret Acts of Parliament in conformity with EU law stems from a source independent of the 1972 Act. In any event, both cases recognize that there is something constitutionally special about EU law: they concern the interpretation of statutory instruments passed under s. 2(2) of the 1972 Act, and so their purpose was evidently to implement EU law obligations. But interestingly neither approach presents a direct threat to orthodox theories of sovereignty. The fact remains, however, that EU law, and since 2000 also the Human Rights Act 1998, impose new interpretative obligations upon the courts. The question is not only what meaning the words are capable of yielding, but also whether the words can be made to yield a sense consistent with EU law and Convention rights.

QUESTIONS

1. Can you explain the source of disagreement in *Macarthy's v Smith* between Lawton and Cumming-Bruce LLJ, on the one hand, and Lord Denning, on the other?

3. Why did judges in later cases follow Lord Denning's dissent rather than the majority opinion in *Macarthy's v Smith*?

Statutory construction based on the common law

Whereas, in *Macarthy's*, the duty to construe Acts of Parliament in line with Community law was derived from the European Communities Act 1972—a national statute—an alternative source of that obligation was identified in *Garland v British Rail Engineering Ltd*. Mrs Garland was employed by British Rail Engineering. The company operated a scheme under which all employees, their spouses, and dependent children were entitled to (without having a contractual right to) concessionary travel rates during the employee's employment. After retirement, all former employees (male and female) retained their entitlement to some form of concession. In the case of male employees only, concessions also continued to apply to spouses and dependent children. In other words, families of retired women were not entitled to travel concessions. Mrs Garland claimed that the scheme was discriminatory and the question before the House of Lords was whether discretionary travel facilities provided by an employer that continued for male employees after retirement came within the definition of 'pay' under Art. 157 TFEU.

The House of Lords held that, in this case, discretionary travel concessions did amount to pay.

Garland v British Rail Engineering Ltd
[1983] 2 AC 751, 771

Lord Diplock

[...] even if the obligation to observe the provisions of [Art. 157 TFEU] were an obligation assumed by the UK under an ordinary international treaty or convention and there were no question of the treaty obligation being directly applicable as part of the law to be applied by the courts in this country without need for further enactment, it is a principle of construction of UK statutes, now too well established to call for citation of authority, that the words of a statute passed after the Treaty has been signed and dealing with the subject matter of the international obligation of the UK, are to be construed, if they are reasonably capable of bearing such a meaning, as intended to carry out the obligation, and not to be inconsistent with it. A fortiori is this the case where the Treaty obligation arises under one of the Community treaties to which s. 2 ECA applies.

The instant appeal does not present an appropriate occasion to consider whether, having regard to the express direction as to the construction of enactments "to be passed" which is contained in section 2(4), anything short of an express positive statement in an Act of Parliament passed after January 1, 1973, that a particular provision is intended to be made in breach of an obligation assumed by the United Kingdom under a Community treaty, would justify an English court in construing that provision in a manner inconsistent with a Community treaty obligation of the United Kingdom, however wide a departure from the prima facie meaning of the language of the provision might be needed in order to achieve consistency.

The House of Lords stresses that Community law is relevant to the correct interpretation of the domestic statute. The basis of the construction approach, however, is not s. 2(4) of the European Communities Act 1972, as in *Macarthy's v Smith*, but a common law obligation to read statutes in light of the earlier treaty, especially if the treaty in question is the Treaty of Rome. According to Lord Diplock, this principle was so well established that he did not need to support it with the citation of authority—although he could have cited *Salomon v Customs and Excise Commissioners*.

Salomon v Customs and Excise Commissioners
[1967] 2 QB 116, 143

Diplock LJ

There is a prima facie presumption that Parliament does not intend to act in breach of international law, including therein specific treaty obligations; and if one of the meanings which can reasonably be ascribed to the legislation is consonant with the treaty obligations and another or others are not, the meaning which is consonant is to be preferred.

Lord Diplock's approach appears to reject the approach of the majority in *Macarthy's v Smith* and favour Lord Denning's alternative approach, which was to refer the questions of interpretation and direct applicability of Community law to the ECJ *before* attempting to construe the Act. The purpose of the reference was to provide the national court with material to aid it in the construction of the domestic statute.

It should be noted that Lord Diplock's alternative approach suffers from its 'parochial' legal reasoning. The common law obligation to read statutes in light of the earlier treaty is not compatible with the 'new legal order' principle in *van Gend* '*for the benefit of which the states have limited their sovereign rights*'. It is arguably also in breach of s. 3 of the European Communities Act 1972 (the meaning, validity, and effect of Community law is to be determined either by the ECJ or with reference to its case law). Moreover, Lord Diplock does not refer to the new rule of statutory interpretation in s. 2. He nonetheless manages to achieve the result required by the 1972 Act: a UK court should construe all domestic legislation in a manner respecting EEC obligations '*however wide a departure from the prima facie meaning of the provision might be needed in order to achieve consistency*'.

So, to sum up, in a case in which national legislation is found to conflict with Community law, the UK courts developed two approaches in as many cases.

(a) According to the majority opinion by the Court of Appeal in *Macarthy's v Smith*, a UK court is not allowed to stretch the words of an Act of Parliament through interpretation or construction. The Treaty cannot affect the meaning of national law, and therefore cannot be used as an aid to statutory construction. Instead, the court should refer the case to the ECJ, whereupon national legislation is adjudged either to be compatible or incompatible with the Treaty.

(b) In contrast, Lord Denning's dissent in the same case states that the courts should initially look to the Treaty as an aid to statutory construction and try to render national law compatible with EU law. If that attempt fails, then, by virtue of s. 2(1) and (4) of the European Communities Act 1972, the courts need to give priority to the 'overriding force' of EU law.

This latter approach finds favour with Lord Diplock who, however, bases the construction approach on the common law presumption of statutory interpretation regarding international treaty obligations. But statutory interpretation has linguistic limits that are reached when the statutory words cannot be reconciled with EU law. Lord Diplock's opinion offers no guidance for that scenario. Presumably, in such a case, the courts would interpret the inconsistent words in the statute as Parliament's intent to legislate contrary to EU law and directly effective EU law would be impliedly repealed.

M. Hunt, *Using Human Rights Law in English Courts* (1997, Oxford: Hart Publishing), p. 81

Lord Denning's approach in *Macarthy's* therefore achieved a greater degree of entrenchment for Community law than Lord Diplock's weaker construction approach in *Garland*. The difference, however, is one of degree rather than kind. Both are forms of entrenchment. Both focus on the interpretive role of judges in a way which is capable of transcending the inevitable conundrums which attend the traditional acceptance of the sovereignty of Parliament as the premise from which all else flows. The essential difference resides only in the degree to which each judge is prepared to recognise an evolution of judicial obligation away from the uncomplicated fealty traditionally owed to the UK Parliament.

Lord Diplock was prepared to interpret statutes flexibly and creatively in the light of Community law, so as to avoid inconsistencies wherever possible, but was not prepared to go beyond what he considered to be the legitimate bounds of interpretation. Although apparently closer to traditional ideas of sovereignty than Lord Denning, even this approach amounts to a significant modification. Implied repeal is theoretically preserved, but is likely to be a rare event as the court will strive to find an interpretation which avoids inconsistency arising. Lord Denning, on the other hand, was not only prepared to go further than Lord Diplock in attempting to arrive at an interpretation of a domestic statute which avoided conflict, but was prepared to give precedence to Community law in cases of irreconcilable conflict. Parliament was still sovereign, not only in the ultimate sense that it could repeal the ECA, but also, it would seem, in the slightly less ultimate sense that Parliament could still, in any given statute, express its intention to legislate inconsistently with Community law. For Lord Diplock, by comparison, Parliament did not need to express its intention so explicitly: it was enough if the language of the statute could not be given a meaning which was consistent with the relevant Community law without going beyond what for him were the more tightly drawn bounds of legitimate interpretation.

The construction approach can be summarized as follows.

- There is a rule of interpretation (either a common law rule concerning international treaty obligations, or s. 2(4) of the European Communities Act 1972) to the effect that Parliament is presumed not to intend statutes to override EU law.
- Inconsistencies between UK statutes and EU law are resolved in favour of the latter unless Parliament passes a future Act expressly stating that it intends to override EU law.

The realization that neither construction approach was merely a matter of orthodox statutory interpretation, but had, in fact, resulted in a degree of entrenchment, dawned on Lord Denning some years after he retired from the Bench, when he reconfigured his famous metaphor of EU law in *Shields v Coombes* as an incoming tide.

Lord Denning, 'Introduction', in Gavin Smith, *The European Court of Justice: Judges or Policy Makers?* (1990, London: Bruges Group), pp. 7–8

[O]ur sovereignty has been taken away by the European Court of Justice. It has made many decisions impinging on our statute law and says that we are to obey its decisions instead of our own statute law.

It has done this by two means. *Firstly* it has done it by its own method of interpretation. It has *not* obeyed the words of the Treaty. It has *not* interpreted those words according to their true meaning. It has put on the Treaty an interpretation according to their own views of policy [...].

Secondly, the European Court has held that all the European directives are binding within each of the European Countries; and must be enforced by the national courts; even though they are contrary to our national law. They are a supreme law overriding all our national laws. Our courts must no longer enforce our national laws. They must enforce Community law. [...]

[...] I propose to amend my 1974 dictum in this way:

No longer is European law an incoming tide owing up the estuaries of England. It is now like a tidal wave bringing down our sea walls and flowing inland over our fields and houses—to the dismay of all.

This sentiment achieved widespread public recognition in the aftermath of the legendary episode that is discussed in the next section.

QUESTIONS

1. In what way does Lord Diplock in *Garland* follow Lord Denning's dissent in *Macarthy's*? How does he differ?

2. What are the limits of the construction approach, according to Lord Denning and according to Lord Diplock?

3. EU law *'is now like a tidal wave bringing down our sea walls and flowing inland over our fields and houses—to the dismay of all'*. Do you agree?

(c) THE 'DISAPPLICATION' APPROACH

As we have seen, before 1991, the main judicial approach when faced with a statute that did not conform to Community law was to use 'strong principles of construction' to render the national statute compatible with Community law. But this option ran out of steam in the seminal *Factortame* case.[46] The background of *Factortame* is the Common Fisheries Policy (CFP), which divided up fishing quotas on national lines, and the Act of Accession of Spain to the EEC, which restricted the number of Spanish vessels allowed to fish in Community waters. In order to circumvent these restrictions, Spanish fishing companies started 'quota-hopping'—that is, registering their boats as British and then fishing under the British quota, even though they lacked any genuine link with the United Kingdom.

In 1988, the United Kingdom passed the Merchant Shipping Act 1988 and the Merchant Shipping (registration of Fishing Vessels) Regulations 1988,[47] which were intended to put an end to quota-hopping by Spanish boats. The 1988 Act created a new register for all British fishing vessels, including those already registered under the Merchant Shipping Act 1894. According to s. 14 of the 1988 Act, a fishing vessel could be registered in the new register only if:

(a) the vessel was British-owned;[48]
(b) the vessel was managed, and its operations directed and controlled, from within the United Kingdom; and
(c) any charterer, manager, or operator of the vessel was a qualified (British) person or company.[49]

Officials and ministers were aware of the obviously discriminatory and segregationist nature of their economic policy, and also of the risk that their legislation could amount to a sufficiently serious breach of EC law that, in turn, could give rise to damages for Factortame.

---

[46] *R v Secretary of State for Transport, ex parte Factortame Ltd. and ors (No. 1)* [1990] 2 AC 85.
[47] SI 1988/1926.
[48] According to s. 14(2). A fishing vessel was deemed to be British-owned if the legal title to the vessel was vested wholly in one or more qualified persons or companies and if the vessel was beneficially owned by one or more qualified companies or, in relation to not less than 75 per cent, by one or more qualified persons.
[49] According to s. 14(7), 'qualified person' meant a person who was a British citizen resident and domiciled in the United Kingdom, and 'qualified company' meant a company incorporated in the United Kingdom and having its principal place of business there, at least 75 per cent of its shares being owned by one or more qualified persons or companies, and at least 75 per cent of its directors being qualified persons.

R v Secretary of State for Transport, ex parte Factortame (No. 5)
[2000] 1 AC 524, 543

Lord Slynn

The Secretary of State for Transport wrote to the Attorney-General on 22 October 1987. "Officials have [...] concluded that we should proceed as originally intended. While this does pose a risk to our position on damages, the official view was that the applicant would have to overcome so many obstacles – not least of which would be winning his case in the European Court on the substantive issue on whether our law is compatible with the Treaty - that the risk was worth taking given the drawbacks of the alternatives."

[We are also told that, on 24 February 1987, counsel advised the government that:]

"[...a]ny discrimination that arises out of the proposed measures is a natural consequence of the [common fisheries policy] itself which divides quotas along national lines. [...] We consider that rules on nationality of fishing vessels are the most appropriate way of establishing a genuine link between the Member States and the vessel intending to fish for the Member State's quota, particularly having regard to possible alternatives."

On 28 March 1988, before the Bill received royal assent, the European Commission warned the UK government that the proposed conditions were prima facie contrary to the right of establishment. After the 1988 Act came into force, the United Kingdom was successfully challenged at Community level by the Commission, which brought infringement proceedings against the United Kingdom under Art. 258 TFEU for a declaration that s. 14 of the 1988 Act breached the right of freedom of establishment.[50]

But the United Kingdom was also challenged at national level, in judicial review proceedings brought by the owners or operators of ninety-five fishing vessels that had been registered as British under the Merchant Shipping Act 1894, but which could not satisfy one or more of the conditions laid down in the 1988 Act, and so were deprived of the right to fish from April 1989. The Divisional Court made an Art. 267 TFEU reference on the substantive issues of Community law raised in the proceedings (the case that became *Factortame II*). The Divisional Court also ordered that, by way of interim relief, the application of the 1988 Act and the 1988 Regulations had to be suspended. This was, however, overturned by a unanimous Court of Appeal, which held that, under *national* law, the courts had no power to suspend the application of Acts of Parliament because, at common law, an interim injunction could not be granted against the Crown.[51]

BOX 18.2 THE CROWN PROCEEDINGS ACT 1947

The more specific reason for not granting injunctions against ministers was the Crown Proceedings Act 1947. Introduced in the wake of the Second World War, this legislation sought to remove many, but by no means all, of the legal immunities and privileges of the Crown in litigation. In other words, it was designed to make it easier for

---

[50] Case C-246/89R *EC Commission v United Kingdom (Re Merchant Shipping Rules)* [1989] ECR 3125.

[51] [1989] 2 CMLR 353. This position is now reversed so that it is possible to grant interim relief against the Crown: see *M v Home Office* [1994] 1 AC 377.

aggrieved citizens to obtain justice against central government. Section 21 provided that (emphasis added):

(1) In any civil proceedings by or against the Crown the court shall, subject to the provisions of this Act, have power to make all such orders as it has power to make in proceedings between subjects [...] Provided that:

    (a) where in any proceedings against the Crown [...] the court *shall not grant an injunction* or make an order of specific performance, but may in lieu thereof make an order declaratory of the rights of the parties

(2) The court shall not in any civil proceedings *grant any injunction or make any order against an officer of the Crown* if the effect of granting the injunction or making the order would be to give any relief against the Crown which could not have been obtained in proceedings against the Crown.

For the purposes of the Act, ministers are 'officers of the Crown'.

The *Factortame* litigation illustrates the potential injustice that this could cause. The Spanish fishermen applied for judicial review of the Secretary of State for Transport's decision not to register their trawlers to fish in UK waters under the Merchant Shipping Act 1988. Their lawyers knew that it would take many months for the courts to hear and reach a decision on their application, which would have financially ruined the businesses and left their employees without a job. Consequently, the Spanish applicants wanted an interim injunction to prevent the minister from deregistering their vessels until the final outcome of the case was known. At first, the English courts refused to grant an interim injunction, on the ground that they had no power to do so, because this would fall foul of s. 21(2) of the 1947 Act.

The House of Lords agreed with the Court of Appeal on its interpretation of national law, but referred the case to the ECJ on Community law.

Case C-213/89 *R v Secretary of State for Transport, ex parte Factortame Ltd (Factortame I)*
[1990] ECR I-2433

13 The House of Lords, before which the matter was brought, gave its abovementioned judgment of 18 May 1989. In its judgment it found in the first place that the claims by the appellants in the main proceedings that they would suffer irreparable damage if the interim relief which they sought were not granted and they were successful in the main proceedings were well founded. However, it held that, under national law, the English courts had no power to grant interim relief in a case such as the one before it. More specifically, it held that the grant of such relief was precluded by the old common-law rule that an interim injunction may not be granted against the Crown, that is to say against the government, in conjunction with the presumption that an Act of Parliament is in conformity with Community law until such time as a decision on its compatibility with that law has been given.

14 The House of Lords then turned to the question whether, notwithstanding that rule of national law, English courts had the power, under Community law, to grant an interim injunction against the Crown. [...]

[...]

20 The [ECJ] has [...] held that any provision of a national legal system and any legislative, administrative or judicial practice which might impair the effectiveness of Community law by withholding from the national court having jurisdiction to apply such law the power to do everything necessary at the moment of its application to set aside national legislative provisions which might prevent, even temporarily, Community rules from having full force and effect are incompatible with those requirements, which are the very essence of Community law.[52]

21 It must be added that the full effectiveness of Community law would be just as much impaired if a rule of national law could prevent a court seised of a dispute governed by Community law from granting interim relief in order to ensure the full effectiveness of the judgment to be given on the existence of the rights claimed under Community law. It follows that a court which in those circumstances would grant interim relief, if it were not for a rule of national law, is obliged to set aside that rule.

According to the ECJ, it is *Community* law that requires the granting of interim relief to secure effective interim protection of directly effective rights. For this reason, s. 21 of the Crown Proceedings Act 1947 (no injunction against the Crown) had to be set aside. The ECJ's ruling was wholly in line with the earlier case of *Simmenthal* (a case that was referred to by Lawton LJ in *Macarthy's v Smith*), in which it had ruled that any conflicting provision of national law was deemed 'automatically inapplicable' by Community law. Nonetheless, its decision in *Factortame I* provoked strong reactions regarding the demise of parliamentary sovereignty. Jonathan Aitkin MP described the ruling as '*an historical surrender of some constitutional significance*';[53] Teddy Taylor MP said that the decision was '*one of the most frightening things that has happened since the time of King Charles*'.[54] In light of the constitutional difficulties that the ECJ's ruling unearthed, would the House of Lords respond by strengthening the United Kingdom's sovereignty doctrine or by accepting the ECJ's supremacy doctrine?

R v Secretary of State for Transport, ex parte Factortame Ltd (No. 2)
[1991] 1 AC 603, 658

Lord Bridge

Some public comments on the decision of the Court of Justice, affirming the jurisdiction of the courts of the member states to override national legislation if necessary to enable interim relief to be granted in protection of rights under Community law, have suggested that this was a novel and dangerous invasion by a Community institution of the sovereignty of the United Kingdom Parliament. But such comments are based on a misconception. If the supremacy within the European Community of Community law over the national law of member states was not always inherent in the EEC Treaty it was certainly well established in the jurisprudence of the Court of Justice long before the United Kingdom joined the Community. Thus, whatever limitation of its sovereignty Parliament accepted when it enacted the European Communities Act 1972 was entirely voluntary. Under the terms of the 1972 Act it has always been clear that it was the duty of a United Kingdom court, when delivering final judgement,

---

[52] Case 106/77 *Amministrazione delle finanze dello Stato v Simmenthal SpA* [1978] ECR 629, [22]–[23].

[53] Quoted in 'European Court Order Criticized', *The Times*, 27 October 1989.

[54] Quoted in R. Ford and F. Gibb, 'Law officers prepare reply to EC ruling on UK laws', *The Times*, 21 June 1990.

to override any rule of national law found to be in conflict with any directly enforceable rule of Community law. Similarly, when decisions of the Court of Justice have exposed areas of United Kingdom statute law which failed to implement Council directives, Parliament has always loyally accepted the obligation to make appropriate and prompt amendments. Thus there is nothing in any way novel in according supremacy to rules of Community law in areas to which they apply and to insist that, in the protection of rights under Community law, national courts must not be prohibited by rules of national law from granting interim relief in appropriate cases is no more than a logical recognition of that supremacy.

The construction approach reached its limits here, because it was no longer possible to construe the Merchant Shipping Act 1988 in accordance with Community law. For this reason, the ECJ requires national law, which is found to be inconsistent with directly effective Community law, to be 'set aside'—in other words, that the statute is rendered 'inoperative' in the circumstances of the particular case. It does not mean that the statute is 'null', 'void', or 'repealed'. The disapplication approach is at least formally reconcilable with sovereignty theory, because it does not involve the court in any invalidation of Acts of Parliament.

Following *Factortame*, the House of Lords went one step further in 1995 in *R v Secretary of State for Employment, ex parte Equal Opportunities Commission*.[55] The Employment Protection (Consolidation) Act 1978 distinguished between three categories of workers with respect to bringing a claim of unfair dismissal before the Industrial Tribunal, and to gain the right to redundancy pay.

- Category 1: an employee working 16 or more hours per week had to be with the same employer continuously for at least two years
- Category 2: those who worked between 8 and 16 hours per week had to show five years' continuous employment.
- Category 3: those working fewer than 8 hours per week did not acquire any rights.

In other words, the Act draws a legal distinction between part-time workers (most of whom were, in fact, women) and full-time workers (most of whom were, in fact, men) in relation to the conditions for receipt of statutory redundancy pay and compensation for unfair dismissal. We have already seen that the EU protects the principle of equal pay both as a general principle of primary legislation under Art. 157 TFEU and in more detail in secondary legislation.[56] Although the Act did not discriminate on grounds of gender (its provisions applied equally to men and to women), it clearly resulted in indirect discrimination against women. The main question for the House of Lords was whether the indirect discrimination against women could be objectively justified. It could not: *Factortame* clearly stood for the proposition that the UK courts had to give effect to directly effective Community law rights.

Another question related to the 'trickle-down effect' after *Factortame*, i.e. the extent to which the lower courts (here: the Divisional Court) were under an obligation to apply Community law and to disapply any conflicting national law.

---

[55] [1995] 1AC 1.

[56] Council Directive 75/117/EEC of 10 February 1975 ('the Equal Pay Directive'); Council Directive 76/207/EEC of 9 February 1976 ('the Equal Treatment Directive').

R v Secretary of State for Employment, ex parte Equal Opportunities Commission
[1995] 1 AC 1, 28

Lord Keith of Kinkel

The issues at stake are similar in character to those which were raised in *Factortame*. The Divisional Court is the only English forum in which the E.O.C., having the capacity and sufficient interest to do so, is in a position to secure the result which it desires. It is said that the incompatibility issue could be tested in proceedings before the European Court of Justice instituted by the European Commission against the United Kingdom under [Art. 258 TFEU]. That may be true, but it affords no reason for concluding that the Divisional Court is an inappropriate forum for the application by the E.O.C. designed towards a similar end and, indeed, there are grounds for the view that the Divisional Court is the more appropriate forum, since the European Court of Justice has said that it is for the national court to determine whether an indirectly discriminatory pay practice is founded on objectively justified economic grounds.[57]

After this decision, *The Times* opened its leading article of 7 March 1994 with the following sentence: '*Britain may now have, for the first time in its history, a constitutional court.*' It suggested that the House of Lords had 'struck down' the 1978 Act as 'unconstitutional', and had thereby upset the traditional constitutional balance between Parliament and the courts. The leader was also concerned that the Law Lords had examined the 1978 Act with reference to its social and economic impact in the manner of a constitutional court.[58] The following commentator pursues a similar argument, pointing out correctly, however, that it was not the House of Lords, but the Divisional Court (!), that had acted in the manner of a constitutional court.

Danny Nicol, 'Disapplying with relish? The Industrial Tribunals and Acts of Parliament' [1996] *Public Law* 579–589, 589.

...the dismantling of Parliamentary sovereignty has advanced step-by-step. In *Factortame* the House of Lords made it clear that it would ultimately uphold Community law rather than Acts of Parliament. *Ex parte Equal Opportunities Commission* showed that the House no longer feels the need for a reference to the ECJ before impugning an Act of Parliament; the supervisory jurisdiction of the Divisional Court now extends to declaring an Act of Parliament incompatible with Community law without recourse to Luxembourg. To that extent, the Divisional Court is now a constitutional court. The post-*Equal Opportunities Commission* case law shows that lower courts and tribunals too have joined the fray in setting primary legislation aside. A common feature of these Industrial Tribunal and Employment Appeal Tribunal decisions is the terseness with which they deal with the issue of disapplication: it appears that lower courts and tribunals now see no need to justify their actions by referring to the European Communities Act 1972; rather the subordination of Acts of Parliament to Community law is simply taken as read. To borrow a phrase from the Duke of Wellington, we are witnessing a revolution by due process of law.

---

[57] See Case 170/84 *Bilka-Kaufhaus G.m.b.H. v Weber von Hartz* [1987] ICR 110, 126.

[58] See also Patricia Maxwell, 'The House of Lords as a Constitutional Court: The Implications of *Ex Parte EOC*', in B. Dickson and P. Carmichael (eds) *The House of Lords: Its Parliamentary and Judicial Roles* (1999, Oxford: Hart Publishing), ch. 10.

After the *EOC* case, Michael Howard—the Conservative Home Secretary at the time—presented a paper to Cabinet arguing for the 'repatriation' of powers from Brussels and for the removal of the rights of British courts to enforce Community law.[59] The *EOC* case reveals both the continuing fracturing of the Conservative Party over the European Union, as well as legitimate concerns about the shift of political power away from Parliament.

We will now return to *Factortame* in order to discuss the repercussions of that shift in more detail.

(d) *FACTORTAME*: A CONSTITUTIONAL REVOLUTION?

Factortame involved tensions between different sources of law. At one level, the common law and the Crown Proceedings Act 1947—which denied interim injunctive relief in actions against the Crown—were found to be contrary to Community law by the ECJ. Thus, the earlier norms were overruled by the later norms of Community law, which had become part of UK law by virtue of s. 2(4) of the European Communities Act 1972. This was relatively uncontentious because of the doctrine of implied repeal.

At another level, however, *Factortame* involved a tension between certain provisions of the Treaty of Rome and the later Merchant Shipping Act 1988 (that is, between a treaty of international law and a statute, not between two statutes). The chronology (and possible hierarchy) of norms thus viewed is:

(a) the Treaty of Rome 1957;
(b) the European Communities Act 1972; and
(c) the Merchant Shipping Act 1988.

Why was the doctrine of implied repeal not applied in this instance? Lord Bridge argued that the United Kingdom knew—or ought to have known—what kind of legal system it was plugging into and that, in passing the 1972 Act, Parliament voluntarily accepted limitations upon its sovereignty.

Professor Wade's assessment of the 1972 Act is stronger.

H.W.R. Wade, 'Sovereignty: Revolution or evolution?' (1996) 112 Law Quarterly Review 568–75, 573

Nothing in Lord Bridge's language suggests that he regarded the issue as one of statutory construction. He takes it for granted that Parliament can "accept" a limitation of its sovereignty which will be effective both for the present and for the future. It is a statement which could hardly be clearer: Parliament can bind its successors. If that is not revolutionary, constitutional lawyers are Dutchmen. Craig seems to be putting it mildly when he says "the reasoning of Lord Bridge does not therefore fit well with that articulated by the traditional theory".

But neither does Lord Bridge's reasoning fit well with any theory based upon statutory construction, such as the theory that every post-1972 statute is to be construed as impliedly subject to Community law, subject only to express provision to the contrary. Nothing of that kind is suggested by Lord Bridge's doctrine of "voluntary acceptance" by Parliament

---

[59] 'Howard splits Cabinet on Europe', *The Independent*, 18 May 1996. Conservative leader David Cameron rehearsed the same theme after the Lisbon Treaty was finally signed by all member states in November 2009.

of Community law as a "limitation of its sovereignty". The truth is, apparently, that so far from containing "nothing in any way novel", the new doctrine makes sovereignty a freely adjustable commodity whenever Parliament chooses to accept some limitation. The effect may be similar to implying limitations into future statutes, as Lord Bridge himself explains. But "voluntary acceptance" goes much deeper into the foundations of the constitution, suggesting by its very novelty that the courts are reformulating the fundamental rules about the effectiveness of Acts of Parliament.

Wade's argument is that the Parliament of 1972 inadvertently brought about a constitutional revolution. The House of Lords invocation of the European Communities Act 1972 to 'disapply' the Merchant Shipping Act 1988 is evidence that the Parliament of 1972 (contrary to orthodox doctrine) has succeeded in binding its successors: *'While Britain remains in the Community we are in a regime in which Parliament has bound its successors successfully, and which is nothing if not revolutionary.'*[60]

H.W.R. Wade, 'Sovereignty: Revolution or evolution?' (1996) 112 Law Quarterly Review 568–75, 574

But is "revolutionary" the right word as a matter of law? Has the House of Lords adopted a new "rule of recognition" or "ultimate legal principle", as to the validity and effect of Acts of Parliament? As Craig puts it, "The entry of the United Kingdom into the EEC might therefore be regarded as a catalyst for a partial change in the rule of recognition, or ultimate legal principle, as it operates in the United Kingdom." As previously supposed, the rule was that an Act of Parliament in proper form had absolutely overriding effect, except that it could not fetter the corresponding power of future Parliaments. It is a rule of unique character, since only the judges can change it. It is for the judges, and not for Parliament, to say what is an effective Act of Parliament. If the judges recognise that there must be a change, as by allowing future Parliaments to be fettered, this is a technical revolution. That is what happens when the judges, faced with a novel situation, elect to depart from the familiar rules for the sake of political necessity. [...] in *Factortame* the House of Lords elected to allow the Parliament of 1972 to fetter the Parliament of 1988 in order that Community law might be given the primacy which practical politics obviously required. This in no way implies that the judges [...] decided otherwise than for what appeared to them to be good legal reasons. The point is simply that the rule of recognition is itself a political fact which the judges themselves are able to change when they are confronted with a new situation which so demands.

Wade's view must be contrasted with that of Professor Craig, who argues that the 1972 Act creates only a *rule of construction* for subsequent statutes. In the absence of express words to the contrary, statutes must be interpreted as compatible with rights arising under Community law.

P.P. Craig, 'Sovereignty of the United Kingdom Parliament after *Factortame*' (1991) 11 Yearbook of European Law 221, 250–1

The advocates of the traditional view would argue as follows. It has already been seen that the foundation of the Diceyan argument is a blend of the empirical and the normative. What is

[60] (1996) 112 LQR 568, 571.

important for the purposes of the present discussion is that the idea of unlimited Parliamentary power is not on Dicey's, or Wade's, species of reasoning, immutable. It is not a static concept, but one which is capable of transformation. This transformation could be effected by the empirical evidence altering, in the sense that some other institution does begin to assert control over the subject matter or form of legislation. The change in the traditional idea could also come about because of a reassessment of the normative foundations on which Dicey constructed his own view. The realization that these foundations were flawed even at the time when Dicey himself wrote, and that they have been further undermined since then, might cause some other institution, such as the courts, to consider whether they should be exercising control over parliamentary power. In either eventuality, the advocates of the traditional view would accept that the content of the ultimate legal principle can alter. [...]

The entry of the United Kingdom into the EEC might therefore be regarded as a catalyst for a partial change in the rule of recognition, or ultimate legal principle, as it operates in the United Kingdom. The fact of entry would not in and of itself bring about this change, but it could be the catalyst prompting a re-thinking of previous orthodoxy. This could occur in one of two ways. On the one hand, it would be perfectly possible in principle for the courts and Parliament to modify the prior orthodoxy so that the rule. of recognition would now read: 'Parliament can do anything by simple majority, except in the area covered by the EEC, in which area EEC law takes precedence.' The most extreme form of this type of change to the ultimate legal principle would mean that the very validity of statutes which were inconsistent with Community law would be called in question. At the very least, it would mean that the doctrine of implied repeal was no longer applicable in the context of clashes between Community law and national law. Whether this can be taken to have occurred will depend on the courts' reaction to clashes between EEC law and national law in cases such as *Factortame*; and to Parliament's response to that reaction. If the legislature acquiesces in an approach by the national judiciary which accords supremacy to the EEC in the event of a clash between national law and EEC law, then the modification to the rule of recognition will be smoother and quicker. On the other hand, the courts could, less dramatically, treat section 2(4) of the European Communities Act 1972 as a rule of interpretation to the effect that Parliament is presumed not to intend statutes to override EEC law. On this view inconsistencies between United Kingdom statutes and EEC law would be resolved in favour of the latter, unless, 'Parliament clearly and expressly states in a future Act that it is to override Community law.' This appears to be the view taken by at least some judges, although the extent to which the courts have been willing in the past to read statutes so as to conform to EEC law has differed from case to case.' The longer that we remain in the EEC the more likely it is that the courts will adopt this rule of construction, which serves to preserve the formal veneer of Diceyan orthodoxy while undermining its substance.

Craig builds on Lord Denning's construction approach in *Macarthy's*. He argues that unless and until Parliament passes a statute with the express intention of overriding Community law or leaving the European Union, the courts should start from the assumption that national law complies with EU law. In other words, the courts should bend over backwards to give effect to EU law (even if the words of the statute are not clear and may be in conflict). Craig here endorses the setting of a double standard: the duty of the courts is to construct—where possible—a later statute in conformity with EU law, or—where impossible—to disapply the later statute. The construction approach thus satisfies the ECJ's supremacy doctrine, while preserving the 'veneer' of parliamentary sovereignty: the construction approach does not view the 1972 Act as having been entrenched.

QUESTIONS

1. Do you think that the UK government acted in bad faith in passing the Merchant Shipping Act 1988?

2. Do you agree with the following statements by Lord Bridge in *Factortame*?

    (a) '[W]*hatever limitation of its sovereignty Parliament accepted when it enacted the European Communities Act 1972 was entirely voluntary.*'

    (b) ''[T]*here is nothing in any way novel in according supremacy to rules of [EU] law in areas to which they apply.*'

    (c) '*The construction approach thus satisfies the ECJ's supremacy doctrine whilst preserving the "veneer" of parliamentary sovereignty.*' What does Professor Craig mean by this statement?

3. Is it correct to say, at least in relation to directly applicable European Union law, that the UK Supreme Court acts like a constitutional court?

BOX 18.3 IMPLIED REPEAL AND ENTRENCHMENT

The revolution thesis is often supported with evidence that the European Communities Act 1972 has never been implicitly repealed by subsequent conflicting legislation and so must have been *de facto* entrenched against implied repeal. In other words, the UK courts should have held that the Sex Discrimination Act 1975 in *Macarthy's* and the Merchant Shipping Act 1988 in *Factortame* had implicitly repealed s. 2(4) of the 1972 Act. This argument is false for three reasons.

1. As a matter of judicial precedent, it is accepted that changes to the constitution cannot be accidental or ambiguous. In one case, the court required 'drastic' changes to the constitution to be made 'plainly and distinctly' by Parliament.[61] In another case, explicit statutory language was required to amend the constitution. In that case, the court held that '*it would require a convincing demonstration to satisfy me that Parliament intended to effect a constitutional change so momentous and far-reaching by so furtive a process*'.[62] So the entrenchment in *Factortame* (if any) is of a weak *procedural* (or 'manner and form') kind, as discussed at the beginning of this chapter: the only requirement is that a simple parliamentary majority expresses itself in clear and express terms.

2. As a matter of principle, implied repeal can occur only when there are two statutes (one earlier and one later) that deal with the same object of policy, and when the later one contradicts (advertently or inadvertently) the earlier one. Implied repeal works horizontally in relation to express rules with like objectives. Inconsistent norms are thus rejected. The later statute prevails over the earlier to the extent of the inconsistency. This is patently not the situation in *Macarthy's*. The conflict in that case was between EU law on sex discrimination—that is, Art. 157 TFEU—and national law on sex discrimination—s. 8 of the Sex Discrimination Act 1975. It was not between two national pieces of legislation.

---

[61] *Chorlton v Lings* (1868) LR 4 CP 374 (no statutory right by women under the Franchise Act 1867 to vote).

[62] *Nairn v University of St Andrews* [1909] AC 147 (HL), *per* Lord Loreburn LC.

3. The European Communities Act 1972 is a different legislative animal. Whereas the Equal Pay Act 1970, as amended by the Sex Discrimination Act 1975, *creates* new rights, the 1972 Act 'only' *gives effect* to existing rights. The 1972 Act does not have normative content, but is a bridging statute that refers to the EU legal order. It does not conflict with the normative content of policy statutes. It is therefore counter-intuitive to use implied repeal. The Court of Appeal in *Macarthy's* applied s. 2(4) in the manner for which it was designed: it directed the Court to prioritize as between future pieces of legislation. The 1972 Act cannot be abrogated by an implied repeal. Another Act of the same kind would be required expressly to undo the effect of the European Communities Act 1972, but certainly not an 'ordinary' Act.

The third argument mentioned relates to democracy (which was discussed in Chapter 12). A traditional UK constitutional perspective suggests that the later Act should always be applied by the courts because it reflects the most recent (democratic) will of Parliament. But Professor Loveland argues persuasively that EU law reflects a different version of democracy: it is not the result of majoritarian law-making, but of a process of consensual negotiations; it may conflict with national law, but it has received a '*cross-national seal of legislative approval*' and, in the case of the treaties, unanimous approval by every member state (with different legal cultures and political histories). Loveland is scathing of the traditional position, as well as of legal analysis that is limited to understanding *Factortame* purely in terms of the relationship between Parliament and the courts. There is a broader political and social context that must be borne in mind when discussing democracy and legitimacy.

Ian Loveland, *Constitutional Law, Administrative Law, and Human Rights: A Critical Introduction,* 6th edn (2012, Oxford: OUP), p. 405

What has rather been forgotten in respect of *Factortame* is that this particular constitutional episode was triggered by the deliberate decision of a xenophobic minoritarian government to use its Commons and Lords majorities (the one generated by the support of 34% of the electorate; the other derived from the principle of hereditary peerages) to enact a crudely segregationist economic policy which – in addition to clearly breaching the Treaty of Rome – was intended to bankrupt several business enterprises and throw many people into unemployment. It would be a very strange view of 'democracy' which nonetheless accorded primacy to such behaviour.

Returning to the relationship between Parliament and courts, Wade has repeatedly argued that:

(a) since the United Kingdom joined the European Union, Parliament has lost its unrestricted power of enacting and amending laws; and

(b) the judges have unilaterally changed the rule of recognition by following EU law, thus initiating a technical revolution.

Wade's position can also be attacked from a jurisprudential perspective. He claims that the role of the courts has been restricted to the recognition of parliamentary sovereignty as a political fact from which the legitimacy of all law emanates. So, when the UK courts prioritized Community law over national law in *Factortame*, they singlehandedly changed the political fact (and hence the meaning) of sovereignty. The courts have achieved a technical legal revolution by flouting the ultimate constitutional principle. Wade claims that '*a change in this* grundnorm *can be achieved only by a legal revolution, and only if the judges elect to abandon their deeply rooted allegiance to the ruling Parliament of the day*'.[63] He regards the court's decision to apply Community law as opposed to statute law as changing the ultimate legal principle on which the legal system rests. On this account, the outcome of *Factortame*, the issue of an interim injunction against the Crown, and the disapplication of an Act of Parliament can only be described as '*the most dramatic event in constitutional adjudication since the seventeenth century*'.[64]

Trevor Allan disputes this line of reasoning.

T.R.S. Allan, 'Parliamentary sovereignty: Law, politics, and revolution' (1997) 113 Law Quarterly Review 443, 444

The difficulty with Professor Wade's thesis is immediately apparent from his reassurance that despite the change of fundamental rule "for reasons of political necessity" – that Community law should be given the primacy which practical politics required – we should not assume that in [. . .] *Factortame* [. . .] the judges "decided otherwise than for what appeared to them to be good legal reasons". Now, it is scarcely possible to argue both that changes in the rule of recognition are made or acknowledged for "good legal reasons" and that such a rule constitutes only a "political fact", subject to alteration for reasons of "political necessity". Legal reasons are usually understood to ground a legitimate judicial decision by invoking settled doctrine or principle: they serve to justify it by explaining the sense in which it was required by the standards of the existing legal order. A revolution occurs, or is cemented, only when a new source of authority is acknowledged, or fundamental rule adopted, which is *not* justified by the existing order, from which the courts have for whatever reason withdrawn their allegiance.

If legal reasons exist, drawn from accepted legal principles or constitutional doctrine, they can be inspected and weighed. If sufficiently strong they will justify a judicial decision; if not, the judges will either have erred in law or abandoned law for politics. Which alternative does Professor Wade envisage as the appropriate explanation of *Factortame*? The preservation of a distinction between legal principle, on the one hand, and political expediency, on the other, is surely essential to any coherent understanding of the rule of law. Judges who make political decisions which violate accepted constitutional principles plainly act improperly: their conduct, when properly so described, should be condemned as illegitimate even if it is expedient or popular.

The existence of good legal reasons for the *Factortame* decisions shows that, far from any dramatic, let alone unauthorised, change in the "rule of recognition", the House of Lords merely determined what the existing constitutional order required in novel circumstances. The view that the acknowledgement of exceptions or qualifications to the rule that courts should give unconditional obedience to statutes amounts to "revolution" is simply dogmatic, and ultimately incoherent. Every other common law rule is subject to such modification and qualification in successive decisions, and there is no reason for treating the rule of obedience to statutes differently.

---

[63] H.W.R. Wade, 'Sovereignty and the European Communities' (1972) 88 Law Quarterly Review 1, 5.

[64] P. Birkinshaw, 'United Kingdom Report', in J. Schwarze (ed.) *The Birth of a European Constitutional Order: The Interaction of National and European Constitutional Law* (2001, Baden-Baden: Nomos), p. 273.

In the same way that the union of 1707 ought to be viewed as an organic outcome arising out of the 1688 reconfiguration, so the 1972 accession ought to be viewed as an evolution, rather than a revolution, of the constitution.

Even if Allan is right and *Factortame* was not 'dramatic' from a judicial perspective, the case does have far-reaching consequences regarding the acceptance not only by the judiciary, but also by Parliament, of the ECJ's decision. Parliamentary acceptance was not simply a legal formality. According to the ECJ, a breach by a member state of *any* provision of EC law may give rise to damages[65] and, in due course, the United Kingdom had to pay somewhere between £55m and £100m in compensation to the Spanish fishermen (the claims submitted by Factortame totalled £285m before interest).[66]

From a parliamentary perspective, the outcome of *Factortame* does have grave implications for the relationship between law and politics.

M. Loughlin, *Sword and Scales: An Examination of the Relationship Between Law and Politics* (2000, Oxford: Hart Publishing), pp. 40–1

The most basic point is that the structure of the European Union —constituted by law and driven by legal instruments—has ensured that issues of legal interpretation are now placed at the centre of the political process. When in 1964 the judiciary ruled that the UK government should pay compensation to a major corporation for destroying its property in wartime and the government did not like the result, it simply promoted an Act which nullified the court ruling.'[67] The contrast with the quota-hopping saga thirty years later could scarcely be more stark. In the contemporary world, the language of rights and the decisions of the judiciary are now able to penetrate to the core of power politics.

(e) *THOBURN V SUNDERLAND CITY COUNCIL*:[68] THE *METRIC MARTYRS* CASE

We have already come across the colourful High Court case of *Thoburn* in the context of distinguishing between constitutional and ordinary statutes (Chapter 2). You will recall that Laws LJ distinguished between 'ordinary' and 'constitutional' statutes, and that the European Communities Act 1972 belonged to the latter group.[69] From this distinction, it follows that '*Ordinary statutes may be impliedly repealed. Constitutional statutes may not*'.[70] A constitutional statute can only be amended, according to Laws LJ, by unambiguous and express words in the later statute. But how does Laws LJ reach this novel conclusion?

In a first step, Laws LJ had to deal with the argument adduced by legal counsel that EU law had become entrenched rather than incorporated in UK law; that '*so long as the UK remains a Member State, the pre-accession model of Parliamentary sovereignty is of historical, but not actual, significance*';[71] and that EU law was to be accorded primacy in the UK domestic legal systems simply by virtue of the claims of EU law itself. Laws LJ rejected this assertion as 'false'.[72]

---

[65] Joined Cases C-46/93 and C-48/93 *Brasserie du Pêcheur SA v Federal Republic of Germany and The Queen v Secretary of State for Transport, ex parte Factortame Ltd and ors* [1996] ECR I-1029.
[66] House of Lords Hansard, vol. 621, 8 February 2001.
[67] *Burmah Oil Co v Lord Advocate* [1964] 2 All ER 348; War Damage Act 1965, discussed in Chapter 10.
[68] [2002] EWHC 195 Admin; [2003] QB 151.
[69] *Thoburn v Sunderland City Council* [2002] EWHC 195 Admin; [2003] QB 151, [62].
[70] Ibid., [63].
[71] See the propositions put forward by Eleanor Sharpston QC in paras [53]–[57].
[72] Ibid. [58].

Thoburn v Sunderland City Council
[2002] EWHC 195 Admin; [2003] QB 151

Laws LJ

[59] Whatever may be the position elsewhere, the law of England disallows any such assumption. Parliament cannot bind its successors by stipulating against repeal, wholly or partly, of the ECA. It cannot stipulate as to the manner and form of any subsequent legislation. It cannot stipulate against implied repeal any more than it can stipulate against express repeal. Thus there is nothing in the ECA which allows the Court of Justice, or any other institutions of the EU, to touch or qualify the conditions of Parliament's legislative supremacy in the United Kingdom. Not because the legislature chose not to allow it; because by our law it could not allow it. That being so, the legislative and judicial institutions of the EU cannot intrude upon those conditions. The British Parliament has not the authority to authorise any such thing. Being sovereign, it cannot abandon its sovereignty. Accordingly there are no circumstances in which the jurisprudence of the Court of Justice can elevate Community law to a status within the corpus of English domestic law to which it could not aspire by any route of English law itself. This is, of course, the traditional doctrine of sovereignty. If is to be modified, it certainly cannot be done by the incorporation of external texts. The conditions of Parliament's legislative supremacy in the United Kingdom necessarily remain in the United Kingdom's hands. But the traditional doctrine has in my judgment been modified. It has been done by the common law, wholly consistently with constitutional principle.

Laws LJ rejects the 'Euro-centric' argument that EU law could 'bootstrap' itself into supremacy within the United Kingdom: EU law does not have supremacy simply because the ECJ has said that it is a principle of Community law that it has supremacy. This approach is, after all, incompatible with constitutional orthodoxy, which says that it is beyond the powers of Parliament to abandon or limit its sovereignty or that of its successors. So how does Laws LJ manage to give effect to EU law in this case? He does it with a clever and innovative trick: the traditional doctrine of sovereignty is still central to UK public law, but (and this is the trick) it has been *modified* by the common law, which recognizes that certain statutes (such as the European Communities Act 1972) are 'constitutional' and require express words in a later statute to effect repeal or abrogation.

An often overlooked consequence of Laws LJ's judgment is, however, that, apart from progressively developing the common law, it articulates a rival vision to the ECJ's doctrine of supremacy of EU law.

Thoburn v Sunderland City Council
[2002] EWHC 195 Admin; [2003] QB 151

Laws LJ

[69] In my judgment (as will by now be clear) the correct analysis of that relationship [between EU and UK law] involves and requires these following four propositions. (1) All the specific rights and obligations which EU law creates are by the ECA incorporated into our domestic law and rank supreme: that is, anything in our substantive law inconsistent with any of these rights and obligations is abrogated or must be modified to avoid the inconsistency. This is true even where the inconsistent municipal provision is contained in primary legislation. (2) The ECA is

a constitutional statute: that is, it cannot be impliedly repealed. (3) The truth of (2) is derived, not from EU law, but purely from the law of England: the common law recognises a category of constitutional statutes. (4) The fundamental legal basis of the United Kingdom's relationship with the EU rests with the domestic, not the European, legal powers. In the event, which no doubt would never happen in the real world, that a European measure was seen to be repugnant to a fundamental or constitutional right guaranteed by the law of England, a question would arise whether the general words of the ECA were sufficient to incorporate the measure and give it overriding effect in domestic law. But that is very far from this case.

You will remember that the ECJ had, in *Costa v ENEL*, held that '*the law stemming from the Treaty, an independent source of law, could not, because of its special original nature, be overridden by domestic legal provisions, however framed*'. And remember also that, in *Internationale Handelsgesellschaft*, it emphasized that '*the validity of a community measure or its effect within a member state cannot be affected by allegations that it runs counter to either fundamental rights as formulated by the constitution of that state or the principles of a national constitutional structure*'.[73]

The ECJ's staunch position was problematic for member states with a constitutional code and a constitutional court that acted as its guardian (initially, Germany and Italy). As we saw in Chapter 12, the 1993 Maastricht Treaty involved further transfers of sovereign powers from the member states to the European Union, as well as a fear that a more powerful EU might make decisions under the flexibility clause in Art. 308 TEC (now Art. 352 TFEU) that exceeded those conferred powers.

5 MINI CASE STUDY ON THE RELATIONSHIP BETWEEN NATIONAL CONSTITUTIONAL LAW AND THE SUPREMACY OF EUROPEAN UNION LAW

Article 308 TEC

If action by the Community should prove necessary to attain, in the course of the operation of the common market, one of the objectives of the Community and this Treaty has not provided the necessary powers, the Council shall, acting unanimously on a proposal from the Commission and after consulting the European Parliament take the appropriate measures.[74]

Brunner v European Union Treaty ('Maastricht')
[1994] 1 CMLR 57 (Federal Constitutional Court, Germany), [49]

[...] if European institutions [...] were to treat or develop the Union Treaty in a way that was no longer covered by the Treaty [...] the resultant legislative instruments would not be legally binding within the sphere of German sovereignty.

---

[73] Case 11/70 *Internationale Handelsgesellschaft mbH* [1970] ECR 1134, [3].

[74] Article 352 TFEU provides: '*If action by the Union should prove necessary, within the framework of the policies defined in the Treaties, to attain one of the objectives set out in the Treaties, and the Treaties have not provided the necessary powers, the Council, acting unanimously on a proposal from the Commission and after obtaining the consent of the European Parliament, shall adopt the appropriate measures. Where the measures in question are adopted by the Council in accordance with a special legislative procedure, it shall also act unanimously on a proposal from the Commission and after obtaining the consent of the European Parliament.*'

Opinion 2/94
[1996] ECR 1-1788, [30] (ECJ)

[Article 308] cannot serve as a basis for widening the scope of Community powers beyond the general framework created by the provisions of the Treaty as a whole and, in particular, by those that define the tasks and the activities of the Community. On any view, Article [308] cannot be used as a basis for the adoption of provisions whose effect would, in substance, be to amend the Treaty without following the procedure which it provides for that purpose.

Carlsen v Rasmussen ('Maastricht')
[1999] 3 CMLR 854 (Supreme Court, Denmark), [33]

Danish courts must rule that an E.C. act is inapplicable in Denmark if the extraordinary situation should arise that with the required certainty it can be established that an E.C. act which has been upheld by the European Court of Justice is based on an application of the Treaty which lies beyond the surrender of sovereignty according to the Act of Accession. Similar interpretations apply with regard to Community law rules and legal principles which are based on the practice of the European Court of Justice.

PI US 50/04 Sugar Quota Regulation II
(Constitutional Court, Czech Republic), Judgment of 8 March 2006[75]

[...] the delegation of a part of the powers of national organs may persist only so long as these powers are exercised in a manner that is compatible with the preservation of the foundations of state sovereignty of the Czech Republic, and in a manner which does not threaten the very essence of the substantive law-based state. In such determination the Constitutional Court is called upon to protect constitutionalism (Art. 83 of the Constitution of the Czech Republic).

Lisbon Treaty Decision
BVerfG, 2 BvE 2/08, Judgment of 30 June 2009, [240]–[241] (Federal Constitution Court, Germany)

If legal protection cannot be obtained at the Union level, the Federal Constitutional Court reviews whether legal instruments of the European institutions and bodies [...] keep within the boundaries of the sovereign powers accorded to them by way of conferred power. [...]

The *ultra vires* review [...] can result in Community law or Union law being declared inapplicable in Germany.

In other words, the German, Czech, and Danish top courts have said that they will monitor the activities of the EU institutions, and that if they go beyond the remit of the treaties (that is, if they act *ultra vires*), then the national state organs and officials would be 'prevented' on constitutional grounds from applying EU law in those member states. In *Thoburn*, Laws LJ adds the relatively weak voice of the UK High Court to the list of sceptical constitutional courts.

---

75 English version available online at http://www.legislation.gov.uk/ukpga/2011/12/section/18/enacted.

Aidan O'Neill, 'Fundamental rights and the constitutional supremacy of Community law in the United Kingdom after devolution and the Human Rights Act' [2002] Public Law 724–42, 739–40

Laws L.J.'s rejection of the "bootstrap" model as a foundation for the primacy of Community law over domestic law [...] and his attempt to reconcile the duty to uphold fundamental national constitutional rights with the duty to give effect to Community law brings the United Kingdom courts into line with the constitutional courts in many other Member States. The history of the relationship between the ECJ and the higher courts of Germany, France, Italy, Denmark, Spain and indeed Ireland show just this kind of tension between the application of national constitutional norms and the requirements of Community law. Clearly, national supreme and constitutional courts which have been established to protect the integrity of their national constitutions will have difficulty in reconciling this duty with that of applying a body of supra-national law which claims a supremacy and legitimacy over and against those national constitutions. [...] By contrast where, as in the United Kingdom, there is no written constitution, there have been no specific national norms which might be appealed to by national courts to challenge the influence and influx of Community law. The coming into force of the HRA 1998 changes that position radically. Now United Kingdom courts have fundamental rights to appeal to over and against the demands of Community law. It can perhaps be anticipated that the House of Lords' previously enthusiastically *communautaire* approach and willingness to apply European Community law principles and doctrines to national issues will undergo some degree of reassessment by the Appellate Committee [now the Supreme Court]. The approach generally taken is that, given that Parliament has committed the United Kingdom to continued full membership of the European Union, the national courts in the United Kingdom have no option but to apply the law as developed by the ECJ, even where this leads to them challenging and striking down legislation emanating from the national Parliament on the grounds of its incompatibility with Community law, or legal principles will be difficult to sustain in a case in which fundamental rights considerations point to a different result. It is suggested that a new "paradigm shift" in the United Kingdom constitution is therefore now underway, based on considerations relative to the national court's effective protection of fundamental rights against the executive, Parliament and, indeed, the institutions of the European Union.

Laws LJ's judgment is driven by, and has resulted in, increasingly vocal concerns among constitutional lawyers in relation to the judiciary. In the context of EU law, Wade's argument (see H.W.R. Wade, 'Sovereignty: Revolution or evolution?' on p. 63) is that EU membership triggered a modification of the ultimate constitutional rule (the rule of recognition or *Grundnorm*) in the UK.[76] In the context of common law constitutionalism (see Chapter 3), both academics and judges have also intimated that were Parliament to enact legislation undermining the rule of law on which the written constitution rests, the courts would not be under a duty to uphold such legislation. The most significant development since *Thoburn* has been Parliament's response to this debate in the form of the European Union Act (EUA) 2011. Section 18[77] in particular was drafted to counter the argument put forward (unsuccessfully, as we have seen) by legal counsel in *Thoburn* that EU law constitutes a new higher autonomous legal order which has become an integral part of the UK's legal system inde-

---

[76] See e.g. H.W.R. Wade, 'Sovereignty: Revolution or evolution?' (1996) 112 *Law Quarterly Review* 568–575.
[77] The other provisions are considered in more detail in Ch. 12.

pendent of statute.[78] Although initially much more ambitious and controversial, the final wording of the provision appears to be harmless at first sight.

European Union Act 2011, s.18

'Directly applicable or directly effective EU law (that is, the rights, powers, liabilities, obligations, restrictions, remedies and procedures referred to in section 2(1) of the European Communities Act 1972) falls to be recognised and available in law in the United Kingdom only by virtue of that Act or where it is required to be recognised and available in law by virtue of any other Act'.

Section 18 is not a 'sovereignty clause' (it neither mentions the word 'sovereignty', nor does it address the supremacy of EU law which stems from the acceptance by the UK judiciary), but a declaratory provision that affirms the validity of EU law as stemming from section 2(1) ECA. So what was the reason for introducing this provision in the EUA?

M. Gordon and M. Dougan, 'The United Kingdom's European Union Act 2011: "Who won the bloody war anyway?"', (2012) 37(1) *European Law Review* 3-30, 7–8

[Section 18] is intended to neuter the potential argument that a shift in the United Kingdom's constitutional paradigm has occurred, and that the supremacy of EU law throughout the Union derives from a European grundnorm, which is not susceptible to domestic alteration or renunciation. Such an argument is, however, essentially political, and most closely associated with a Eurosceptic rhetoric lacking a persuasive evidential foundation. It is well established as a matter of UK constitutional law that the domestic supremacy of EU law stems from Parliament's enactment of the ECA. [...]

It may be that, some two decades after the decision of the House of Lords in *Factortame (No.2)*, there is some virtue in s.18 reminding us that the domestic supremacy of EU law rests alone on its continuing statutory basis. It certainly seems to provide further evidence that while Laws L.J. was correct to assert in *Thoburn v Sunderland City Council* that the domestic supremacy of EU law did not stem from EU law itself, he was wrong to argue that it was achieved as a result of the common law affording the ECA a special "constitutional" status, thus rendering it immune from implied repeal. Instead, the applicability and effectiveness of EU law within the United Kingdom is exclusively traced by s.18 to the legislation itself, with no mention of an intervention by the common law. This point is, however, principally a matter of domestic interest, relating in particular to the clash between common law constitutionalism and parliamentary sovereignty, and has only an incidental impact on the relationship between domestic and European law, in so far as it might establish which constitutional agent, the courts or Parliament, is entitled to determine the extent to which these two legal orders can coexist.

Gordon and Dougan's reading of s. 18 EUA is far more charitable than Lord Hannay of Chiswick who was scathing of the effects of legal counsel's misconstruction of the correct position in *Thoburn*: 'If this Parliament legislates every time a prosecuting attorney makes

---

[78] Para 120, Explanatory Notes.

a bosh like that and it is dismissed by the judge, we would be here every day of the year for about 20 years. Surely it is not a basis for legislation. It is simply unnecessary.'[79]

Instead of asserting Parliament's ultimate legislative supremacy over EU law as planned and promised at the Bill stage, s. 18 EUA falls silent on the matter. It neither resolves the constitutional debates about the proper role of the judiciary, nor does it offer new guidance to judges operating in the post-*Factortame* era of statutory interpretation. In political terms, the provision is embarrassing (it was intended as a 'sovereignty' clause, but ultimately only allowed to repeat s. 2(1) ECA 1972), and in constitutional terms it is pointless.

QUESTIONS

1. Can you explain the difference between 'directly applicable' and 'direct effect'?

2. Have another look at the extract in *Blackburn v Attorney-General*. Lord Denning quotes Viscount Sankey, who says: '*Parliament could, as matter of abstract law, repeal or disregard section 4 of the Statute of Westminster* [or the European Communities Act 1972, for that matter]. *But that is theory and has no relation to realities.*' Do you agree that future repeal is a moot issue?

3. Do you agree with Allan's suggestion that, by dissenting from the majority opinion in *Macarthy's*, Lord Denning was disobeying constitutional doctrine?

4. Should the House of Lords in *Factortame* have used the doctrine of implied repeal to give effect to the Merchant Shipping Act 1988? Find arguments in favour and against.

5. Do you agree with the assessment by an eminent legal historian that *Factortame* marked '*the first time since the day of Sir Edward Coke that an English or British Act of Parliament was overturned by a court of law*'?

6. Professor Loveland seems to suggest that the Merchant Shipping Act 1988 was not necessarily a democratic statute. Explain and critically assess this view.

7. Can a category of common law values be identified as 'fundamental'? Are judges the proper persons to determine the rights that fall within this category?

8. Does Laws LJ in *Thoburn* successfully reconcile the ECJ's doctrine of supremacy of EU law with the United Kingdom's doctrine of parliamentary sovereignty?

9. What is the rationale for giving priority to EU law in the United Kingdom according to:

   (a) William Wade?

   (b) Paul Craig?

   (c) Trevor Allan?

   (d) Lord Bridge in *Factortame*?

   (e) Laws LJ in *Thoburn*?

   (f) Section 18 of the European Union Act 2011 (see Chapter 12)?

   (g) the European Court of Justice?

10. Do you agree that there is virtue in s. 18 EUA 'reminding us that the domestic supremacy of EU law rests alone on its continuing statutory basis'?

---

[79] *Hansard*, HL Vol.727, col.1670.

6 CONCLUDING COMMENTS

Thoburn represents the third stage in the reception of EU law by UK courts. The construction approach resulted in the 'incoming tide' of Community law. The disapplication approach reinforced the metaphor of the 'tidal wave'. One reading of *Thoburn* suggests that the UK courts may now be erecting flood defences: Laws LJ's dicta, and the presence of s. 18 EUA, suggest a retreat to fundamental national values that demand protection of the highest (constitutional) order in light of the EU law tsunami that will overwhelm national sovereignty.

But on another reading, *Thoburn* is an enlightened, up to date, and original account of the UK constitution and its legal sources. By breaking the dominant constitutional paradigm, Laws LJ effectively breaks new ground by emphasizing a national position that is open to EU law. In contrast, the House of Lords in *Factortame* gave a cautious and restrained judgment and managed to accommodate EU law through a doctrine of interpretation, thus diminishing the implied repeal arguments that were put forward.

The future trajectory of the constitutional relationship between national law and EU law remains to be seen : either it will continue to break with the traditional doctrine of parliamentary sovereignty and with the simple logic of implied repeal, and this break will be reflected in a judicial trend that progressively develops an explicit constitutional jurisprudence; or the primacy of EU law and (in another context) the common law will result in a regression towards parochial common law values. Either way, by privileging the common law, Laws LJ has manoeuvred judicial reasoning into previously unchartered waters, and all eyes are on future cases of a European and constitutional nature, and whether they will endorse, reject, or distinguish Laws LJ's innovative approach in *Thoburn* which must now be read in conjunction with s. 18 EUA.

7 FURTHER READING

Allan, T.R.S., 'Parliamentary sovereignty: Law, politics, and revolution' (1997) 113 Law Quarterly Review 443–52

Allan, T.R.S., 'Parliamentary sovereignty: Lord Denning's dexterous revolution' (1983) 3 Oxford Journal of Legal Studies 22

Craig, P., 'Britain in the European Union', in J. Jowell and D. Oliver (eds) *The Changing Constitution*, 7th edn (2011, Oxford: OUP), ch. 4

Laws, J., 'Law and democracy' [1995] Public Law 72

Marshall, G., 'Metric measures and martyrdom by Henry VIII clause' (2002) 118 Law Quarterly Review 493–502

Wade, H.W.R., 'Sovereignty and the European Communities' (1972) 88 Law Quarterly Review 1

Wade, H.W.R., 'What has happened to the sovereignty of Parliament?' (1991) 107 Law Quarterly Review 1

ONLINE RESOURCE CENTRE
Further information about the themes discussed in this chapter can be found on the Online Resource Centre at www.oxfordtextbooks.co.uk/orc/lesueur2e/

19

CONSTITUTIONAL CHANGE

CENTRAL ISSUES

1. Since 1998 there has been series of far-reaching constitutional reform initiatives led by government. Further changes are on the horizon.

2. The process of constitutional change in the United Kingdom is described as 'fluid' and 'pragmatic'.

1 THE REFORM AGENDA

Harold Wilson, Prime Minister in the 1960s and 70s, famously said *'a week is a long time in politics'*. While constitutional change does not (and should not) happen with quite that pace, nonetheless a list of the principal constitution-related reforms introduced by government since 1997 shows how much of the UK constitution has changed:

i) the Human Rights Act 1998[1]

ii) devolution to Northern Ireland, Scotland and Wales thought the 'devolution Acts' of 1998, with further developments introduced by the Government of Wales Act 2006, the Scotland Act 2012[2]

iii) the introduction of city-wide strategic local government in London (a mayor and the Greater London Authority) in 1998 (but a failure to win over voters in a referendum on regional government for England in 2004)

iv) removal of all but 92 hereditary peers from the House of Lords by the House of Lords Act 1999[3]

v) the Freedom of Information Act 2000 and the Data Protection Act 1998 provide new rights to information and personal data

vi) the Civil Contingencies Act 2004 creates a new framework for government in times of emergency

---

[1] Discussed in particular in Chapter 2, Chapter 6 and Chapter 17.
[2] Discussed in Chapter 5.
[3] See Chapter 13 and later.

vii) creation of the UK Supreme Court, reform of the office of Lord Chancellor, and new judicial appointments process by the Constitutional Reform Act 2005[4]

viii) the Inquiries Act 2005 puts in place a new (and still controversial) structure for holding public inquires[5]

ix) creation of new tribunal system by the Tribunals, Courts and Enforcement Act 2007[6]

x) reforms to the rules and processes relating to MPs and members of the House of Lords' expenses and outside interests introduced, following a scandal, by the Parliamentary Standards Act 2010

xi) reform of prerogative powers in relation to treaty making and regulation of the civil service by the Constitutional Reform and Governance Act 2010[7]

xii) removal of Prime Minister's discretion under prerogative powers to call a general election and creation of fixed-term 5-year parliaments by the Fixed-term Parliaments Act 2011

xiii) the Localism Act 2011 provides local authorities with significantly broader powers than have ever existed before[8]

xiv) proposals for an 'alternative vote' for House of Commons elections was rejected in a referendum but a reduction to the size of the House of Commons is enabled by the Parliamentary Voting System and Constituencies Act 2011

xv) the European Union Act creates a system for referendums to be held when decisions are made at EU level to amend or replace the two foundational EU treaties (the TEU and TFEU)[9]

xvi) *The Cabinet Manual* was published in October 2011 setting out for the first time a succinct account of the important rules of the constitution relating to the executive.[10]

xvii) the rules of Royal succession changed to ensure that female children of the monarch are not in future displaced by sons, and allowing members of the royal family to marry Roman Catholics without losing their place in the line of succession[11]

To this, we can add a further list of reform proposals under active consideration in mid-2012

i) further reforms to the judicial appointments system are proposed in the Crime and Courts Bill 2012[12]

ii) the Commission on a Bill of Rights is due to report by the end of 2012 with proposals for the reform of the Human Rights Act 1998[13]

iii) a referendum of the people of Scotland on independence from the United Kingdom and, possibly, also on devolution of further fiscal and economic powers, is expected in 2014.[14]

---

[4] See Chapter 14.
[5] See Chapter 14.
[6] See Chapter 15.
[7] See Chapter 9.
[8] See Chapter 5.
[9] See Chapter 12.
[10] See Chapter 1.
[11] See Chapter 6.
[12] See Chapter 14.
[13] See Chapter 6 and Chapter 17.
[14] See Chapter 5.

A final list can be suggested of constitutional issues that are *not* currently at the forefront of the political agenda:

i) the adoption of a codified constitution

ii) composition of the House of Lords—as we shall discuss on p. 863, debate on this ground to a standstill in mid-2012 when the government abandoned the House of Lords Reform Bill it had introduced in the face of backbench opposition and certain defeat

iii) a referendum on the United Kingdom's future relationship with the European Union.

(a) THE DEVOLUTION SETTLEMENT

As we have seen, the devolution process—delivering executive and legislative power to new bodies in Northern Ireland, Scotland, and Wales—has made profound changes to the traditional 'Westminster model'.[15]

In Northern Ireland, the hoped-for future is a continuation of constitutional politics and a permanent end to the paramilitary activity and sectarian violence that has blighted this part of the United Kingdom. The suspension of the devolution arrangements from 2002 to 2007, with a return of direct rule from London, is a potent reminder of the fragility of the new constitutional arrangements. A model of democracy quite different from elsewhere in the United Kingdom has enabled sharing of political power between parties of radically different standpoints. Rather than a majoritarian approach (the party with the most votes wins), a 'consociational' model is used, to guarantee that a variety of identified 'community groups' are represented in the Assembly and Executive. One recent academic assessment is that '*In sum, Northern Ireland seems to be in democratic "neutral", with little constructive politics, but also little destructive terrorism.*'[16] Perhaps that is the most that is possible?

In Scotland, the process of devolution has continued with the implementation by the Scotland Act 2012 of the Calman Commission recommendations for greater powers to be transferred to the Scottish Government and Scottish Parliament from Whitehall and Westminster. The nationally organized political parties are all unionist in outlook: they oppose independence for Scotland. The challenge for them is that the people of Scotland in 2011 voted in a landslide number of Scottish National Party Members of the Scottish Parliament, sufficient to form a single-party government. The Scottish Government is committed to a referendum of the Scottish people on the constitutional future of Scotland. This is likely to be held in 2014. In mid-2012, opinion polls suggest a 'no' vote on independence—though wrangling is likely over the precise wording of the referendum question(s). 'Do you agree that Scotland should be an independent country?' (said to be the SNP's preferred question) may elicit a different result from: 'Do you want Scotland to remain part of the United Kingdom? If independence arguments do not win the day, there will nonetheless be continued pressure for greater fiscal and economic powers to be transferred to Scotland.

In Wales, the coming into force of Pt 4 of the Government of Wales Act 2006 in 2011 will continue to bed down. Nationalist sentiment in Wales is not as strongly expressed as in Scotland. The nationalist party Plaid Cymru's agenda is to call for more powers to be transferred within the current framework: it 'believes that in time, further powers may be transferred to the National Assembly beginning with the police and criminal justice, and followed by energy and broadcasting'.[17]

---

[15] See Chapter 5.

[16] A. Aughey, 'Northern Ireland narratives of British democracy' (2012) 33 Policy Studies 145, 156.

[17] http://www.english.plaidcymru.org/our-national-future/ (accessed 8 August 2012).

For England, regional government is off the agenda completely. Instead, the focus is on 'localism' with relatively small areas of local government being empowered with unprecedented broad legal powers through the Localism Act 2011's 'general power of competence'.

(b) HOUSE OF LORDS REFORM

It matters who legislators are and from where they derive their legitimacy. For over a hundred years, the basis of membership of the second chamber of the UK Parliament has been the subject of criticism by progressive voices. Until the 1960s, it was composed entirely of hereditary peers (dukes, marquesses, earls, viscounts, and barons)—many of whom were members of the landed aristocracy and overwhelmingly conservative as well as Conservative in outlook. The Life Peerages Act 1958 brought a new class of people, appointed for life, into the chamber. The House of Lords Reform Act 1999, phase 1 of intended reforms, introduced by the Labour Government reduced the number of heredity peers to ninety-two.[18] Since then, efforts to build a consensus on a model for the future have been fruitless. The last attempt was by the Coalition government in 2012. In June 2012, the House of Lords Reform Bill proposed a second chamber of 360 elected members (80 per cent), ninety appointed (20 per cent), with twelve bishops of the Church of England plus government ministers; this was designed to reduce membership by about half. Election would take place for large multi-member regional constituencies, using a 'semi-open party list' proportional representation system for Great Britain and single transferable vote system for Northern Ireland—broadly similar, though not identical, to voting methods for electing Members of the European Parliament. Members of the House of Lords would serve a single, non-renewable, 15-year term. The Bill stated expressly that no change was to be made to the relative roles and powers of the Commons and Lords under the Parliament Acts 1911 and 1949.[19]

As the 2012 London Olympics were being held, the Prime Minister faced up to the fact that there was not sufficient support within the House of Commons for this particular set of proposals for the Bill to progress. Few commentators were expecting the Bill to reach the statute book. It was therefore withdrawn after its second reading debate. The Prime Minister's decision caused friction with the junior coalition party, the Liberal Democrats. Major House of Lords reform is now off the political agenda until at least after the 2015 House of Commons general election.

The perennial focus on the composition of the House of Lords has detracted attention from what is arguably the more important question: what does a second chamber *do*? The 2000 Royal Commission on the Reform of the House of Lords identified the following as the second chamber's major roles: '*to require the Government and the House of Commons to reconsider proposed legislation and take account of any cogent objections to it*'; it should '*act as a "constitutional long-stop", ensuring that changes are not made to the constitution without full and open debate and an awareness of the consequences*'; and the reformed second chamber should '*make a strong contribution*' to '*enhanced Parliamentary scrutiny of secondary legislation*'.[20] As Nick Barber argues, it is not self-evident that an elected chamber best performs functions such as this.

---

[18] For more details of current composition, see Part III Introduction.
[19] Discussed in Chapter 13.
[20] Royal Commission on the Reform of the House of Lords (Chair: Lord Wakeham), *A House for the Future* (2000, London: The Stationery Office) Cm 4534.

N.W. Barber, 'House of Lords Reform: A Look in the Long Grass' UK Const. L. Blog
(12 July 2012) (available at http://ukconstitutionallaw.org)

Lovers of democracy should be wary of making the second chamber elected. Forty years ago a strong argument could have been made that this was needed; that the Commons was too powerful. This argument is no longer attractive. The Commons is hemmed in on all sides. There are other democratic institutions — at the devolved and European level — that effectively check what the Commons can do. And the courts now have a limiting role, too, using European Law and the Human Rights Act to shape and, sometimes, restrict Parliament's statutes. At present there is no need for another elected body in the constitution.

(c) THE HOUSE OF COMMONS

The picture in relation to the future of the House of Commons is of modest-scale reform. Asked in a May 2011 referendum whether to change the voting system from the current first-past-the-post to a more proportional alternative vote method for electing MPs, the 42 per cent of people who voted did so decisively in favour of the status quo. Further debate on the subject is unlikely in the foreseeable future.

Two other significant reforms have, however, been put in place. The Fixed-term Parliament Act 2011 removes the Prime Minister's general discretion to ask the Queen to trigger a general election and replaces that with a pattern of elections scheduled on the first Thursday of May, every five years. The Parliamentary Voting System and Constituencies Act 2011 creates a framework for reducing the size of the House of Commons. There is a widely held view that there are too many MPs and too much variation in the numbers of constituents they each represent. A reduction from 250 to 600 is justified on the basis that devolution has transferred many areas of law-making and scrutiny roles to the new legislatures in Northern Ireland, Scotland, and Wales. What, at the time of writing, remains to be agreed is the detailed scheme for achieving this. The two-party Coalition government has fallen out over this and it remains to be seen if the recommendations of the independent Boundary Commissions will be voted through Parliament.

(d) HUMAN RIGHTS

As we discussed in Chapter 6, in 2011 the Coalition government set up an independent Commission on a Bill of Rights to '*investigate the creation of a UK Bill of Rights that incorporates and builds on all our obligations under the European Convention on Human Rights, ensures that these rights continue to be enshrined in UK law, and protects and extend our liberties*'. It must report no later than the end of 2012. At the time of writing (August 2012), the Commission's recommendations are therefore unknown.

Christine Bell has written about a plethora of human rights instruments applicable in the United Kingdom.[21] A list consists of: (i) the European Convention on Human Rights; (ii) the European Union Charter of Rights; (iii) the UK Human Rights Act; (iv) a Northern Ireland Bill of Rights, required under the Belfast Agreement 1998); (v) an all-Ireland Charter

---

[21] Christine Bell, 'Bill of Rights and Devolution: from the Universal to the Particular' UK Const. L. Blog (15 November 2012) (available at http://ukconstitutionallaw.org).

of Rights (ditto); (vi) the UK Bill of Rights being considered by the Commission; (vii) the National Human Rights Action Plan referred to by the Scottish Human Rights Commission; (viii) suggestions that there should be a Welsh human rights action plan. Alluding to Oscar Wilde, Bell argues that '*To produce one Bill of rights may be regarded as a misfortune. To produce eight, looks like carelessness*'.

QUESTIONS

1. Which reforms do you regard as of most long-term significance?
2. To what extent are these reforms a coherent package?
3. Which, if any, reforms do you disagree with?
4. Are there any other reforms that are still needed?

---

2 DOING CONSTITUTIONAL REFORM

Many (but not all) of the reforms would, had they been introduced in a country with a codified constitution, would have required a formal amendment process to be followed. The 'agreed authorization procedures' may include referendums and, in those countries subdivided into different territories, the agreement of the legislatures of each part.[22] Consider the following examples.

Constitution of Ireland, art. 46.2

Every proposal for an amendment of this Constitution shall be initiated in Dáil Éireann [that is, the House of Representatives] as a Bill, and shall upon having been passed or deemed to have been passed by both Houses of the Oireachtas, be submitted by Referendum to the decision of the people in accordance with the law for the time being in force relating to the Referendum.

Constitution of Canada (Constitution Act 1982), s. 38(1)

An amendment to the Constitution of Canada may be made by proclamation issued by the Governor General under the Great Seal of Canada where so authorized by

(a) resolutions of the Senate and House of Commons [that is, the legislature of the whole of Canada]; and

(b) resolutions of the legislative assemblies of at least two-thirds of the provinces that have, in the aggregate, according to the then latest general census, at least fifty per cent of the population of all the provinces.

[Canada consists of ten provinces.]

---

[22] See Chapter 1.

In 2011, the House of Lords Constitution Committee conducted an inquiry into the process of constitutional change in the United Kingdom. The Committee recognized that there were strengths in the current practices.

House of Lords Constitution Committee, *The Process of Constitutional Change*,
Fifteenth Report of 2010-11, HL Paper 177

20. The way in which the UK's constitutional arrangements may be changed is more flexible than in virtually any other western democracy. Our witnesses argued that the UK constitution is able to respond promptly when a need for change arises, thus avoiding the constitutional stasis sometimes seen elsewhere. The Deputy Prime Minister [Nick Clegg MP] emphasised that 'We have a suppleness, a fluidity and a pragmatism to our arrangements, which many constitutional experts around the world recognise is a strength.'

21. The participants in our seminar also stressed that the fluid definition of what is constitutional can itself be a strength. For example, the equalisation of constituency boundaries and the referendum on the voting system introduced by the Parliamentary Voting System and Constituencies Act 2011 were clearly regarded as significant constitutional measures; in countries with a codified constitution, important details such as these may not be included within the constitutional settlement.

The Committee went on to consider a variety of criticisms of the current practice. There 'is no formal system of checks and balances by which the integrity of the UK constitution can be safeguarded and protected', the Committee acknowledged, which meant that the choice of *how* to introduce and implement change 'lies essentially within the gift of the government of the day'. The Committee were critical of how governments have failed to have regard to the wider constitutional arrangements when introducing a specific reform, how changes may be rushed and that sometimes there had been a lack of consultation. The Committee went on to make a series of recommendations on '*how the good standards occasionally observed in relation to the process of constitutional change can be applied more consistently*'.

House of Lords Constitution Committee, *The Process of Constitutional Change*,
Fifteenth Report of 2010-11, HL Paper 177

Our recommended process for constitutional change

124. We believe that the best way to proceed at the present time is to seek to strengthen the role that both Houses of Parliament and the existing parliamentary committees can play in relation to the process of constitutional change. This can best be done by ensuring that the government abide by what is currently accepted as best practice. We do not, however, accept that the government should continue to pick and choose which processes to apply to which proposals. We therefore recommend that a clear and consistent process be set down in a manner which retains flexibility whilst also holding the government to account for their decisions. (Para 67)

125. We recommend that when a government bill is introduced into either House of Parliament, the minister responsible for the bill in that House make a written ministerial statement. The minister responsible for the bill when introduced into the second House should

also make a written ministerial statement. For ease of reference, a copy of each statement should be included in the relevant explanatory notes. (Para 71)

126. Both statements should set out whether, in each minister's view, the bill provides for significant constitutional change and, if so:

- what is the impact of the proposals upon the existing constitutional arrangements;
- whether and, if so, how the government engaged with the public in the initial development of the policy proposals and what was the outcome of that public engagement;
- in what way were the detailed policies contained in the bill subjected to rigorous scrutiny in the Cabinet committee system;
- whether a green paper was published, what consultation took place on the proposals, including with the devolved institutions, and the extent to which the government agree or disagree with the responses given;
- whether a white paper was published and whether pre-legislative scrutiny was undertaken and the extent to which the government agree or disagree with the outcome of that process;
- what is the justification for any referendum held, or to be held, on the proposals;

and

- when and how the legislation, if passed, will be subject to post-legislative scrutiny.

(Para 72)

127. We stress that this is intended to be a comprehensive package from which the government should depart only in exceptional circumstances and where there are clearly justifiable reasons for so doing. Where the government have not undertaken one or more specific parts of the recommended process, each minister should set out the reasons in their written statement. (Para 73)

128. We reserve our right to disagree with the government's assessment, both as to whether a bill provides for significant constitutional change and as to whether the bill has been subjected to the proper process. (Para 74)

129. We agree that public engagement during the policy-making process is a desirable element of the constitutional change process but that there is no one model which should be adopted for all proposed changes. Nor is public engagement at this stage of the process always a necessary requirement. However, if not undertaken, the government should be able to justify their decision not to conduct a public engagement exercise. If a public engagement exercise has been conducted, whether by the government or otherwise, each minister should set out in their written statement what account the government have taken of the results of that exercise in formulating their policies. (Para 80)

130. We reaffirm our belief both in the importance of Cabinet government and in the essential role that the Cabinet committee system plays as part of the system of collective ministerial responsibility. These mechanisms are particularly important in relation to proposals for significant constitutional change. The government should ensure that proposals for significant constitutional change continue to be subject to rigorous internal government scrutiny in the Cabinet and its committees. (Para 85)

131. The nature of a significant constitutional change is that its impact will outlast whichever government initiated it. Whilst internal government processes are clearly important, the process of significant constitutional change is too important to be left solely to the government. Thus, in relation to any proposal for significant constitutional change, the government should

initially set out their proposals in a green paper. The government should in each relevant case consult the devolved institutions. Ministers should consider the responses received and either change their proposals accordingly or explain in the written ministerial statement why they have chosen not to do so. (Para 90)

132. We agree with the Leader's Group and continue to believe that significant constitutional legislation should be subject to pre-legislative scrutiny. This requirement should be departed from only in exceptional circumstances; if the government do not publish a bill in draft, each minister should formally explain and justify that approach to Parliament in their written statement. (Para 95)

133. We concluded earlier in this report that it is not possible to provide a watertight definition of significant constitutional legislation. We stress the importance of proper parliamentary scrutiny of all bills, but we do not recommend that any new parliamentary procedures such as super-majorities should apply to significant constitutional bills. However, parliamentary scrutiny of such bills should not be rushed unless there are justifiable reasons for fast-tracking them, and, in particular, the government should not seek to pass significant constitutional legislation during the wash-up. (Para 99)

134. We consider that comprehensive post-legislative scrutiny should be a requirement for all significant constitutional legislation. Each minister should set out the government's plans for such scrutiny in their written statement. (Para 104)

135. We believe that abiding by the processes outlined above will do much to remedy many of the weaknesses that exist in the current practice of constitutional change in the United Kingdom. The need to set out within a written ministerial statement the processes to which a bill has been subjected and the outcomes of those processes should, we believe, focus the minds of ministers and help to bring about a cultural change in Whitehall regarding constitutional legislation. The requirement to justify and explain any decision not to subject a bill to a particular process will help to underline the importance of each of the above processes. (Para 105)

QUESTIONS

1. What are the strengths and weaknesses of a flexible constitution?

2. Do you think the House of Lords Constitution Committee's recommendations will significantly improve the process of constitutional change?

3. What does the *process* of constitutional change tell us about the nature of the British constitution?

---

3 FURTHER READING

Bogdanor, V., Khaitan, T., and Vogenauer, S., 'Should Britain Have a Written Constitution?' (2007) 78 The Political Quarterly 499

Gordon, R., *Repairing British Politics: A Blue Print for Constitutional Change* (2010, Oxford: Hart Publishing)

Hazell, R., (ed.), *Constitutional Futures Revisited: Britain's Constitution to 2020* (2008, Basingstoke: Palgrave Macmillan)

Hockman, S., Bogdanor, V., et al., 'Towards a codified constitution' (2010) 7 JUSTICE Journal 74

INDEX